CASES AND MATERIALS ON CONTRACTS

CASES AND MATERIALS ON CONTRACTS

Edited by

J. B. MILNER

Professor, Faculty of Law
University of Toronto

UNIVERSITY OF TORONTO PRESS

Printed in Canada

Reprinted 1964, 1967

Reprinted in 2018

ISBN 978-1-4875-7897-8 (paper)

TO PRATT

INTRODUCTION

This collection of "cases and materials" is one version of what is commonly called a "casebook" and is intended as a teaching aid in a process commonly called teaching by the "case method." A definition of the "case method" is better not attempted; it should be sufficient to warn any of you who may have heard talk about the case method that there is no such thing—if anything, the reference should be to "case methods," in the plural, and you should expect to find as many methods as you have teachers. With this warning in mind a few words may be said about this book, which is admittedly a casebook.

It is first of all a portable library, designed to prevent the excessive wear and tear on library books when a hundred students are sent to read the same six or seven pages in the same volume, year after year. It consists of extensively reproduced reports of law suits (about 250) usually in the higher courts, but sometimes in the trial court. There are some less extensive excerpts. And there are some excerpts that can best be described as notes of reports. The word "materials" covers these lesser excerpts, but it also covers a variety of other "legal" things, sections of statutes, clauses from contracts, text notes, and questions and problems. Some explanation of what you are expected to do with all these cases and materials is offered in this short introduction.

WHAT DOES THE CASE STAND FOR? Early in their legal education many law students pick up a virus from some unknown source that drives them to ask of each case, what does it stand for? They seem to assume that the cases are building blocks, that each has an understandable shape and will fit neatly into a little wall of law, snugly and certainly. The correct answer to the question is that the case "stands for" what it is, a little segment of human history, history of an event or of an idea, or of both. The important question is: What is to be done with this case? The answer can really only be fully appreciated by experiencing the study of law, but a few suggestions may be helpful.

The importance of the facts. If the case is regarded as the history of an event the event consists of a set of facts. Although, as we shall see, your interest will centre mainly around the ideas also included in most cases, an understanding of the facts of a case is vital to an understanding of the idea —any principle is better understood if it is thought about in the context of a specific situation. This is one of the great merits of the so-called "case method," that it tends to keep the discussion in an understandable framework of the reasonably familiar.

The facts of cases are not always fully known or available for study. The report of the case sometimes quotes from the "record." These facts are the proven facts, and under the common law system the judge is supposed to confine himself to proven facts and not to act on his own knowledge. Indeed, if he has any personal knowledge of the facts he should consider seriously whether he should disqualify himself and get some other judge to handle the case.

Our trial system is far from perfect and you need not assume that the record will necessarily show all the facts that might have been proven. Witnesses are not perfect: their powers of perception may be very limited, they may have poor memories, sometimes they are simply inarticulate and fail to communicate, and, of course, some lack veracity. The lying witness is not the most frequent cause of an inaccurate record, however. Witnesses are more often likely to tell the truth than most law students seem to believe. The other three dangers are much greater threats to an accurate record.

But even if the record is fairly complete, we do not, usually, have access to it in the reports. We have to rely on the abstract of the facts that the judges write in their decisions, and there is always a possibility, sometimes quite real, that the abstracting by the judge will, deliberately or otherwise, omit reference to facts that other judges or students might have considered of value. Clearly then we deal with an imperfect set of facts.

Sometimes we haven't even an abstraction from the trial record, because the issue of law is tried, not on proven facts, but on alleged facts which may or may not be proven in the subsequent trial. Such a trial of an issue was said in the old pleadings to be on a "demurrer." An illustration of a case where the facts alleged, which were assumed on the demurrer, apparently did not get proved at the trial, which came to an opposite decision, may be seen in *Angel* v. *Duke*, on page 526.

Sometimes the judge may not repeat the facts at all, or too briefly to be of use to us, and the reporter of the case may then summarize the facts himself, which may or may not be accurate. *Hadley* v. *Baxendale*, on page 5, illustrates this possibility, as does *Dickinson* v. *Dodds*, on page 345. The reporter may be content to reproduce at length the pleadings in the case which, of course, give a perfectly accurate account of the allegations. The difficulty with this method is that it is wasteful of space, since the older pleadings particularly were repetitious. I have, therefore, taken the liberty in some cases of writing a note about the facts myself, and I hope these shorter statements, which are designed to save you time, are sufficiently complete and accurate for their purpose. In any case, where my summary is inadequate, one citation of the case is immediately available and the full report may easily be consulted. I should like, however, to avoid this inadequacy in another edition and I hope you will bring your complaints to my attention.

Variations of the facts. The discipline of the case lies in its facts. Law students show a very human tendency to want to change the facts, ever so slightly perhaps, to make them "fit" an idea, usually a preconceived idea with which the student is familiar. The student must resist this temptation in discussion in class, and especially in answering examination questions! Intellectual honesty demands that the facts be considered as they are, not as we would like them to be. This distortion, consciously or unconsciously, of the facts on record, is sometimes observed in judges as well as law students, and it is no more admirable on the bench than in the classroom. In classroom discussion it is a commonplace to consider many variations of the facts but each variation must be dealt with honestly, especially if the "logical" result is disturbing. It is just this disturbance that may lead to a new insight or understanding of the problem being considered.

One other aspect of the facts may be mentioned. In considering variations on the original theme, students sometimes ask, "How can you prove such a fact? It's only the plaintiff's word against the defendant's." Discussion on the merits would bog down pretty quickly if one had to imagine, not only the variant of the facts, but the kind of evidence that would be necessary to prove it. Let it suffice that most facts can be proved, and many a lawsuit has been won by a plaintiff because the judge or jury believed his testimony and rejected the defendant's. The problem of proof is best left to the course on Evidence, where problems of this sort form the main core of the subject.

One qualification is, however, necessary here. There are some kinds of facts that may be considered incapable of proof, and a rule of law based on such a fact is always suspect. A typical example is the proof of "intention," a "fact" frequently considered relevant in the law of contracts. As Brian C.J. put it in 1477, "The thought of man is not triable, for the Devil himself knoweth not the thought of man." (Y.B. (1477) P. 17 E. 4. 2a, pt. 2.) He intended to imply, I think, that if the Devil, with all his satanic powers, couldn't find out, for mere man the task would be hopeless. Modern psychiatry is making headway, admittedly, but so far the psychiatrist's methods do not appear to have too much value in the trial process. Meanwhile, you may look with some scepticism on rules that purport to give effect to the "intention of the parties." You will find, however, that notions of "intent" play a useful and important part in the law of contracts.

Facts that are not on the record, but which nevertheless exist, are assuming an increasing importance in the study of law. These background facts, which are sometimes rather specific and intimate facts, sometimes rather large general facts, may be purposely kept out of the record, perhaps because of desire by one party and ignorance by the other or because they are so extensive their proof becomes too inconvenient or expensive. These facts about the facts, what really happened, sometimes point up the real problem. *Jacob and Youngs, Inc.* v. *Kent*, on page 619, is a case where one is tempted to think that the real dispute has been carefully hidden from the court. Here the background facts, undisclosed, were probably highly personal. In *Hadley* v. *Baxendale*, on page 5, the background facts that obviously influenced the thinking of the court were very general. You may even wonder whether they were "facts." Facts of this latter class are frequently invoked by students who want to settle a dispute by reference to the "custom of the trade." It is often quite difficult to convince beginning law students that the "custom" may not be very customary, and that proof may be impossible because the custom simply doesn't exist. There may be almost as many "customs" as there are "traders." Professor Fuller has a very nice account of this problem in a note on "Proving the business background of a contract" in his *Basic Contract Law*. (See pages 415–418.)

The importance of facts may be appreciated from a remark made in my presence by a distinguished member of the Supreme Court of Canada some ten years ago. He said, "I sometimes feel that when I have mastered the facts I have done seventy-five per cent of my job." He was expressing a familiar experience of lawyers, that the facts have a habit of dictating a solution. It might be said to be one of the principal tasks of the lawyer to try to explain why that solution seems to be so irresistibly indicated. The law has been described as the perfection of reason and no lawyer, or at least no judge, likes to leave his decision without the crutches of reason if only because he wants the respect of his colleagues and he thinks, quite rightly, that a reasoned decision will earn it more quickly than a hunch, no matter how acceptable.

The sources of the ideas. The principal sources of ideas in this casebook are the reports of judges' decisions in actual litigation. These reports have been appearing since shortly after the Norman conquest. Originally their reporting was the work of private individuals, sometimes the judges themselves, and much later, series of reports were started by commercial publishers who retained reporters, usually young and unemployed barristers, to report cases for them. The early reports are known by the names of the reporters. In 1865 the English profession set up the Incorporated Council of Law Reporting, which has since been responsible for what are sometimes called the "official reports," although they have no other "official" status. Both English and Canadian governments have been loath to publish law reports, although Canada does publish, through the Queen's Printer, the *Canada Law Reports*, better known as the *Exchequer Court Reports* and the *Supreme Court Reports*. The best coverage of Canadian cases is to be found in the *Dominion Law Reports*, a privately published series commenced in 1911 by the Canada Law Book Company and covering all of Canada, but with relatively less emphasis on Quebec. Not all cases are reported; the choice is made by the editor, who uses his own criteria. No accurate information is available, but one could hazard a guess that not fifty per cent of the cases are reported. Yet hundreds of thousands of cases have been reported over the centuries, and in the United States the number is over the million mark.

The reports in this casebook are not exclusively from any one jurisdiction. The largest number from any one jurisdiction are from England. This should not surprise you. Except for the province of Quebec, Canada is a "common law" country and it has its legal roots deep in the common law as it originated and developed in England. Naturally enough, the next largest number come from Canada, particularly from Ontario. There is no chauvinistic influence whatever in this selection. The English cases are chosen sometimes because they have historical importance and enable you to trace the history of an idea, sometimes because they have rather striking sets of facts, or rather well expressed statements of law, or novel notions worth reflecting about. The Canadian cases have been chosen for the same reasons. Generally speaking the earlier Canadian courts frequently tended not to discuss a problem on its merits, but merely recited English cases thought to have a bearing, or even to be binding on the Canadian courts. Such cases have little teaching value. In more recent years the tendency has started the other way, and Canada has a rather enviable position in the Commonwealth in that it has had a "new" Supreme Court since appeals to the Privy Council were abolished, and the possibilities of a renaissance in the Canadian common law, though hardly probable, are not to be ignored.

I do not apologize for any undue number of Canadian cases. Others may think there are too few. But since this book is intended for use in a Canadian law school it is only sensible, I think, to present as full a picture of Canadian contracts, in and out of courts, as it is possible to do, simply because Canadian law students are likely to understand the Canadian background of Canadian cases better than they will understand either English or American backgrounds. And there seems to be some virtue in concentrating study in one familiar area rather than spreading one's self too thinly. Nevertheless I have not hesitated to take advantage of cases from any common law country, particularly the United States, and even, in one case, from a civil law country. I hope the richness of variety of ideas presented has not suffered from the shortage of American decisions, but American casebooks and textbooks are fortunately readily available if it does.

Some references have been made to code provisions from civil law jurisdictions. These are not presented with any naive notion that Canadian common law students can learn the civil law from a half dozen excerpts, but I do hope that these few glimpses will alert you to the fact that there exists another major legal system with different ideas from those of the common law. If you are interested in the relation of law to society you may note that the people of some civil law countries seem to be both happy and prosperous.

Further ideas are to be found in the occasional excerpts from the statute law. There probably should be more of these. First year law students can too easily get the impression that life in the law is just one continuous lawsuit. Case study falsely emphasizes this impression. The cases are almost always cases in courts, and the constant reading of cases may tend to drive out of mind the other areas in which law is equally operative. Perhaps some figures about law practice may help to improve your sense of proportion. The number of lawyers in practice in Canada is something over 14,000. It would not be too far from the fact to say that not as many as 500 of these lawyers earn their living exclusively from court practice. In England, where the legal profession is divided into solicitors (office lawyers) and barristers (court lawyers), the ratio is about ten to one. There are something like 20,000 solicitors and 2,000 barristers, and in fact only about half of the barristers are actively engaged in their profession. This slight apology for so many cases is not quite abject, because first year law students are expected to learn thoroughly the judicial process, how and why it works and what its limitations are, and this can best be done by a thorough examination of the results of the process. As I shall point out later, in law practice *predicting* the outcome of possible litigation underlies most of the lawyer's general office practice. *Influencing* the outcome is his task in court.

The statute law is not only important as a second source of ideas, but also as a source of ideas of a very different kind. The statute represents, usually, an attempt to solve a problem by a general rule, rather than by the settlement of a single dispute. This approach carries with it a different set of ground rules, and you are invited to investigate the principles of legislation as you go along. The statute is a special device for solving special problems, and like contract and adjudication, it has its special limitations.

There are interspersed throughout the cases, and in special separate notes, a few clauses from contracts. These clauses are useful sources of ideas that have often been tried because the ideas worked out by the courts or legislatures are unsatisfactory. Probably there should be more of these examples, but I trust that there are enough to alert you to the possibilities of drafting better solutions for familiar and unfamiliar problems.

Among the other sources of ideas should be mentioned the few examples of private opinion, from textbooks and periodical literature, and the great American Law Institute *Restatement of the Law of Contracts*, something rather like a code of the law, compiled by a group of practising and teaching lawyers. The *Restatement* has no official status, but it has received considerable favourable notice in American courts.

Finally, but in a place of honour at the bottom of the list, comes you, the law student. It is you who will be shaping the law twenty years from now, and the ideas you have now, or that you develop as you proceed with your study of the law, are not unimportant. At the beginning you may feel that you know too little to contribute, but before you have been completely brain washed I hope you may add to the intellectual ferment that ought to characterize any lively classroom of beginning law students.

Supplementary reading. Let me give you one word of advice. You will find in the casebook relatively few references to other reading. I have not even included all the citations to the full reports of the cases in this book!

Needless to say, there is an incredible amount of material to which you might be sent. There is much too much. You may easily become overwhelmed at the prospect of it, and you may believe that somewhere in there is the answer to your problem. Don't look for it. Think it out for yourself, or in collaboration with your friends in your class. Discussion with them will be surprisingly profitable. Take some comfort from these words of Professor I. A. Richards, who says, in his *Speculative Instruments*, at pages 61–2, "Modern scholarship positively gets in the way. The critical apparatus of approach to the great things keeps them from their would be student. He is daunted incessantly by the thought that somewhere there is something which would, if he only knew it, help him to understand better. He comes to distrust the direct approach, and lives in an unhealthy terror of his ignorance—which will anyhow for all men to time's end be infinite. He forgets that we do not help ourselves or others by collecting more facts and comments, but by understanding more clearly our problems and theirs. We learn best to do this by reflecting upon such problems and by seeing them through the eyes of the best minds." Believe me, this is not just an excuse for not knowing everything.

How to read a case. May I leave this topic with an attempt to state shortly what I think you, as a beginning law student, are expected to do with these facts and ideas? I think you have to try to do two rather irreconcilable things. You have to get to know the best which has been thought and said about the law of contracts, and you must turn a stream of fresh and free thought upon our stock notions and habits. I apologize to Matthew Arnold. You have to know what judges and legislatures have said but you also have to know that there are other, and sometimes better, ideas that they might have expressed; and you have to know the legal system, how and why it works, or doesn't work, so that you, as future law reformers, may have some hope that your better ideas will be adopted.

I believe it is futile to try to tell other people how to study, and any attempt to explain how to read a case is likely to meet with little success. You must work out your own methods of study, which you will doubtless modify as you increase your understanding of the study of law. Here are some general suggestions that may help in that understanding. Remember that a case is the settlement of a dispute by a third person and if you are to understand the settlement you must know the issue. Who is suing whom for what? Before what court? What happened, what are the facts? Who won? What was the remedy? What were the reasons given? These questions represent the minimum you must know about the case, where that minimum is given in the casebook. Sometimes only the facts are given, in which case you are obviously expected only to speculate how those facts might have been treated by a court. Judgments or opinions have sometimes been omitted so that you don't come to rely wholly on what you may regard as so superior a source of ideas that it stultifies your own analysis and creative thought.

There are, of course, other matters to be noticed in a case. Are the reasons consistent with other judgments you have read? Do you agree with the judge's interpretation of earlier decisions or statutes? Are his reasons consistent within themselves? Has the judge used words ambiguously? Has he disclosed an attitude inconsistent with the ideal detachment of a judge? Sometimes I have pointed to some of these matters by inserting questions after the case. Where there are no questions you should develop the habit of asking your own. I have not put questions after every case because you may not bother to ask your own if you spend too much time wondering about mine. Your own efforts will be more rewarding in the long run. Take nothing for granted until you are forced to. Ask yourself whether you fully understand the judge's point of view before you attempt to criticise it, but do not hesitate to criticise it constructively. Reading the case is important, and it must *precede* class discussion if you are to get the most out of the discussion. But reading and thinking cannot occupy the same space at the same time, and much of the editing of these cases and materials has been directed to cutting down the reading time necessary for you to get the facts and ideas to think about. This is especially true of the first three chapters, which have been pruned to the limit, so that you could get an early start with your own thinking. The cases in the later chapters are more extensively reported because by then you should be able to read and absorb a judgment more quickly.

After you have read the case, what should you remember? Students frequently ask whether they have to memorize the names of cases, the facts, the decisions, the reasons for judgment or the names of the judges, or any of these, for "examination purposes." It seems to me that most students tend to remember the essentials as a by-product of their reading, thinking and discussion. Particular facts can usually be forgotten. The particular facts that prove to be crucial in distinguishing situations must be remembered, I suppose, but they can often be stated in more general terms, and fitted into the statement of principle that one wants to remember in any event.

The names of the cases stay in some minds without effort, in others no amount of effort seems to work. But the names are only useful as a shorthand means of referring to the case and a longer description of some highlight will usually be as good, although expensive in time during the writing of examinations. Some lawyers sometimes indulge in a kind of gamesmanship with case names, but I doubt whether the gamesmanship is very important. Canadian and English lawyers probably tend to learn more of the same cases in their law schools. The Americans have a much greater pool to draw from, and I suspect that few Americans remember many cases by names.

The names of judges are a bit of a luxury, but the position of the court in the judicial hierarchy is a very important matter in estimating the weight that will be attached to the decision. Obviously the fact that the idea you are promoting comes from a Supreme Court of Canada judge or from an inexperienced trial judge may justify no inference about its quality but the source may matter a great deal about its acceptability in some circles!

IS THIS CASE RIGHTLY DECIDED? Early in your legal education many of your teachers will have picked up a virus from some unknown source that drives them to ask you, of each case, is it rightly decided? You may be tempted to ask, if you have been bitten by the bug of semantics, "What do you mean by 'right'?" The question is a fair one, and no law teacher or law student should try to dodge it, even if you or they may occasionally feel you are poised on the brink of philosophical chaos. To ask this question is to introduce the element of ethics into the rather more precise world of legal propositions. Nevertheless by asking and trying to answer the question, you may gain a very useful insight into the legal system. In England, where all litigation points toward one final court, in the House of Lords, one can understand the tendency to judge "rightness" by reference to what the House of Lord has said, or will say. Of course the element of prediction involved in guessing what the House *will* say opens the door just a little bit to the question of "rightness," although the House may shut it in counsel's face if it has spoken on the subject before. See, however, the rather interesting view of Viscount Simonds on this subject, in *Midland Silicones Ltd.* v. *Scruttons Ltd.*, on page 447, and in *Director of Public Prosecutions* v. *Shaw*, on page 448.

In Canada there is a somewhat different attitude, although there may be a tendency for Canadians (and Americans) to overstate the conservatism of English courts and the liberality of their own. As I have already mentioned, Canada is at a rather interesting stage in the development of her national judiciary. We have, in effect, a new Supreme Court whose judges, many of them only appointed since the "new" Court came into being in 1950, may prove to be more aware of the truly creative role a supreme court can play, not only in constitutional matters, but generally in the application and development of the common law. They may yet be moved by the boast of the great English judge, Lord Mansfield, who said in 1744, "the common law . . . *works itself pure* by rules drawn from the fountains of justice." (*Omychund* v. *Barker* (1744), 1 Atk. 21 at page 33; 27 E. R. 15 at pages 22–3.)

In Canada we have ten separate provinces, and, for some purposes, each of those provinces is a separate law district, or jurisidiction. This is obviously the case in matters of legislation. The legislature of Ontario does not make law for the province of Nova Scotia or British Columbia. But when it comes to the statement of the common law, it is possible in most cases to take an important issue of law to the Supreme Court of Canada, and that Court has usually taken the view that the common law (as distinct from statute law) is common to all provinces except Quebec, and that there isn't a common law of Ontario, another of British Columbia and so on throughout the nine common law provinces. In the United States, another federal state, the system works the other way, and fifty states have fifty sovereign common law jurisdictions. When, in proper circumstances, a case from a state gets to the United States Supreme Court, that Court now takes the view that it must decide first which state law to apply and then to decide it according to its view of that state law. Earlier it had taken the view that there were individual state laws and a federal common law as well. It apparently never thought it a good idea to try to make uniform the state common law as the Supreme Court of Canada does. Hence the degree of intellectual boiling-over in the United States is higher than in Canada because the lid is constantly off. In Canada, while nine common law provincial courts of appeal may boil at their pleasure, the Supreme Court may at any time put on the lid.

What, then, is the answer to the teacher's question, "Is the case 'right'?" Can there be any less of an answer than an examination of the possible reasonable and practical alternatives? The answer to the question may be a qualified "yes, but" in some cases, because on a proper view of the problem of the case it may appear that there are other legal processes better adapted to its solution than the adjudicative. While the case as presented may be "rightly" decided, the problem of the case, which is also the law student's concern, is not satisfactorily solved. It is admittedly a dangerous question, one that opens up large and exciting vistas, and yet, in a *university*, no matter how modern, can one properly refuse to consider it?

WHAT IS THE LAW OF THIS *JURISDICTION*? Early in their legal education many law students pick up a second virus from some unknown source that drives them to ask after the discussion of cases from other jurisdictions, what is the local law? Some English critics of North American casebooks have been heard to say that they present the law of nowhere.

This criticism is more aptly applied to national casebooks in American schools, where it is quite possible that cases from every state may be included in the assigned casebook. The alternative, presumably, would be to select cases from only one state. It would be interesting to speculate about the student enrolment at Harvard (which is representative of every state in the Union and many foreign countries) if it professed to teach only the law of Massachusetts! The question I think arises from two related sources of student concern, at least at the beginning of his law studies.

What is law? The first source is the uncertainty in the law, which he probably did not anticipate. He probably expected the law to consist of a long series of settled rules which he was expected to memorize and to understand. The second source is the dilemma in which he finds himself once he discovers that law is not all that settled. He soon learns that he is expected to "know the law" and, at the same time, to have explored the "unknown," not to say the "unknowable." He has to become an *educated* as well as an *informed* student of the law. On the whole it is a perfectly natural intellectual state for any student. He must accept the discipline of his subject and yet he must try to think creatively and imaginatively. From the teacher's point of view this dilemma has only one unfortunate aspect: the chronic pressure of examinations, which the student may think, and sometimes rightly, will stress more the knowledge of the law than the creative or imaginative attack of problems. This is a weakness of the examination system, not of the conflicting objectives of legal education, and if it will comfort, encourage or scare the student, there is an ever present possibility that the examination system may be improved! On this depressing thought that the examination plays too great a role in university education let me return to the first concern.

Beginning law students come with only a vague notion about what law is. They expect to find somewhere a set of rules. If they have heard of the "case method" they probably expect to find the rules buried in the cases. Some of them become impatient with this tedious method of extracting them. They hurry off to a library to read a text book written by someone they suppose has already done the tedious work and will tell them what the law is. Text writers sometimes say, in their introduction, "The law is presented as of January 31, 1963." One is tempted to ask who is going to change it or add to it after that date? How can the law "be" at a date that is now past? Why this continuous temporal limitation? What *is* the law?

Attempts to fix a final single meaning for the word "law" have occupied the time of many scholars and filled many books, but the attempts are surprisingly barren or incomplete. If you now think of law as a series of rules laid down (by whom?) to govern human behaviour, you have some distinguished scholars on your side. But for a student who looks forward to the practice of law a collection of rules is far from a complete qualification. Recent graduates are often heard to complain that no client ever asks them anything they learned in the law school. Of course a client rarely asks a lawyer what the law is (and when he does he is often sidetracked); he asks more commonly what can he do, or not do, in particular circumstances. He wants advice on how to act in a situation that presents a variety of courses of action. He does not want an abstract statement of what the law is, or what some lawyer believes it to be. It does not follow that the lawyer can think only in terms of what Tennyson, in *Aylmer's Field*, called

"... the lawless science of our law,
That codeless myriad of precedent,
That wilderness of single instances."

To begin with, there are large areas of what might be called "accepted doctrine," with which any lawyer can quickly familiarize himself from text books, once he has gained sufficient insight into the legal system to enable him to use text books intelligently. Relatively few of a lawyer's problems, however, can be settled by reference to accepted doctrine, and it is surprising how much doctrine (accepted or unaccepted) a business man knows that his lawyer may not. The business man does not consult his lawyer about such matters. When he needs a lawyer his accepted doctrine has failed him: he is either in trouble, or, less frequently, but increasingly more commonly, he wants to avoid trouble and he is not sure what to do. He wants advice.

Law as prediction. If the trouble is far enough advanced a lawsuit may be inevitable and the lawyer may be asked to anticipate what a court will do in the circumstances. One famous definition of the law is limited to just this. Oliver Wendell Holmes, a distinguished American judge, said "The prophecies of what the courts will do in fact, and nothing more pretentious, are what I mean by the law." ("The Path of the Law" (1897), 10 *Harvard Law Review* 457.) The definition is far too limited to be useful; not even Holmes himself entirely agreed, for he said later on, in the same talk, "Still it is true that a body of law is more rational and more civilized when every rule it contains is referred articulately and definitely to an end which it subserves, and when the grounds for desiring that end are stated or are ready to be stated in words. . . . For the rational study of the law the black letter man may be the man of the present, but the man of the future is the man of statistics and the master of economics."

Even predicting what a court will do is obviously much more than merely mastering a series of rules, for if it were certain what rule the court would follow "prediction" would not result in the parties financing two or more opposing lawyers through a trial court, a court of appeal, and the Supreme Court of Canada.

So far as the law consists of prediction, it may be likened to weather predictions in the daily papers. The short, overly simplified "black letter" version usually appears on the front page in an upper corner. The Toronto *Globe and Mail* announced there, on August 30, 1954: "Sunny, Warm, High Here 80." Anyone interested in the conflicting influences which led to the summary statement could turn to page two, where an incomprehensible map showing these influences was supposed to make everything clear. As a matter of interest, and to complete the analogy with law as prediction, the forecast turned out, in this instance, to be rather misleading. On page two of the same paper, on August 31, the maximum temperature for the day before was said to be 68 and 0.65 inches of rain fell. It was explained that "the disturbance over Lake Ontario was retarded in its eastward trek by the slow northward motion of the hurricane off the North Carolina coast." The corresponding situations in law would probably be called black letter law, functional analysis, and the law-in-action. We are, I think, still lagging behind the other social sciencies in our study of the law-in-action, yet that is where the functional analysis receives its only important testing. Obviously, the analogy with weather prediction falls down when we remember that the lawyers in a case influence the court's decision, so that the prediction of law becomes a complex purposive activity of man, not an observation of inanimate elements having no known purpose.

This limited definition of law as prediction led Benjamin Cardozo, another well known American judge, to say, derisively, of it, "Law never *is*, but is always about to be." (*The Nature of the Judicial Process* (1921), page

126.) Curiously, one can give his words quite another meaning, in which I think they convey a greater insight into the common law. Compare them with Lord Mansfield's remark I quoted above, that the common law works itself pure by drawing on the fountains of justice. It is *always* about to be. That, I think, is a great idea.

Law as process. The weakness of the definition of law as prediction is that it limits our sights too restrictively. As I have already pointed out, most lawyers are not employed as barristers, and although to a very important degree they have to base all their actions on at least an educated guess at what a court might, in the long run, say about their advice and solution, they have an infinite variety of short run problems in which the ultimate judicial decision, which they may hope will not have to be sought, will play a secondary role. Their professional action will be based on their predictions, but it may take the form of, for example, drafting clauses in a contract, persuading an administrative official to vary a regulation, or a legislative committee to recommend an amendment to a statute, or organizing a new corporation. All of these activities are in a sense legislative, rather than adjudicative, and they justify, in my view, an even greater emphasis on the legislative area than our legal education presently offers.

For the student about to study the law of contract, the prediction definition is peculiarly inapt or incomplete, because it suggests that "law" is limited to the occasion when contract disputes are litigated. Yet contract is in fact the principal means whereby individuals make private arrangements to control their affairs *without* the interference of the state. If "law" is limited to judicial action, the law student would presumably have little concern with the many problems of drafting contracts in order that the parties may achieve their purposes. Yet almost every lawyer may be asked to help his clients draft contracts as well as get them out of difficulties resulting from their own insufficient planning. The "law" of contracts, therefore, it seems to me, consists about equally of understanding how, when and, above all, *why* the state may interfere in private arrangements and of understanding how private arrangements may be made more effective, and what the limits of effective action through private arrangements may be. An understanding of contract, as a legal process, can, I think, be gained by studying the results of litigation, for in this way you may acquire experience vicariously, but you must use this experience to think about the problems of planning private affairs, as well as the problems of state interference. All of this should make apparent to you the importance to the law of human purposes. These purposes are many, varied, and conflicting; the task of the law is to sort them out and promote those that should be promoted and suppress those that should be suppressed. We might call the difficult task of selection the basic problem of justice.

The legal discipline. Can it be said, in view of this combination of elements, that the law has any claim to be called an intellectual discipline, entitled to a place in the classical university? I think it has. It may be impossible to explain what that discipline is to students who haven't yet immersed themselves in it, but I am going to suggest some guides to which you may return as you gain the insights of experience.

It seems to me that the law may be regarded as consisting of three basic processes having as their objective what might be called "justice." Each process has its place in the sun, and because this is a casebook on contracts, I put the contract process, of negotiation, promise and exchange, as the first. It doesn't matter whether it is more or less important than the other two, but I think a lawyer has to know what can be done by contract, or private arrangement, and what can not. That is the first branch of his discipline.

The second basic process is adjudication, of which the judicial process is an instance, but so is arbitration. The study of cases is the study of the judicial process in itself, as well as a study of the substantive field with which the cases deal. Just as there are limitations on what you can do by way of private arrangement, so there are on what you can do by way of adjudication and the important subclass, the judicial process. The second branch of the discipline is the process of adjudication.

The third basic process is legislation, or the exercise of power by a body authorized to make rules for general application or decisions in particular cases, but without the incidents of adjudication. How, when and why a social or individual problem should be solved by the exercise of some authority by a private individual or an official of the state is the peculiar subject matter of the process of legislation. This allocation of authority should not be thought of as exclusively the function of a state legislative body because private individuals may be given a great deal of power by contract, or private arrangement. The obvious illustration of this private power is that given by contract to their employer by a group of employees, whose affairs are managed by the employer for a large part of their waking life. The obvious example is the modern collective agreement.

THE ORGANIZATION OF THESE MATERIALS. The materials presented here may be divided into two parts, although no such formal breakdown has been indicated in the table of contents. The first part deals chiefly with the interference of the state in private arrangements, and attempts to search out the purposes sought by the individual contracting parties and the purposes of the state in interfering. The second part deals chiefly with the planning of private arrangements and the drafting of contracts to serve them, but since the materials are still judicial decisions, they are also illustrative of judicial, or state interference.

Throughout all of these materials the thing being closely examined is the *promise*. The word is used in its ordinary sense, with one exception. We ordinarily think of a promise as being a personal prediction that a stated event over which the person promising has some control will come to pass. My Concise Oxford Dictionary defines a promise as an "assurance given to a person that one will do or not do something or will give or procure him something." In most contexts this is all that is meant by "promise" in these cases and materials. But in some commercial contexts it is common for a man to give an "assurance" that a particular state of affairs, or quality of a thing, exists, or is true. We may thus assure a person that a car we are about to sell him is a "good" car. If we admit this meaning, then we can say that, thus supplemented, the word "promise" is used with its ordinary meaning. The course might then be called the law about, and the social use of, promises. I shall not now attempt any definition of contract; you may do that yourself whenever you feel ready for it.

The first chapter deals with the remedies the state offers for the breach of a promise. There are two reasons for starting here. First, the essential situation is simple and familiar since everyone has experienced the disappointment of a broken promise and nearly everyone has caused such disappointment at some time or other. To keep the discussion under reasonable control, you must assume that there is a promise and that it is enforceable. In later chapters both of these assumptions are examined.

The second reason for starting with remedies is that it will give you an excellent perspective of the purposes of the law in enforcing contracts. Later, when you are asked to decide whether a court would interfere in particular negotiations or how a particular clause should be drafted, you must know what kind of interference is possible and probable before you try to answer the questions. Hence the study of remedies gets at a most fundamental aspect of the "law" of contracts: the extent of the legal protection given to private arrangements. Throughout the book emphasis is constantly laid on the fact that contract is a purposive activity and that the state in turn interferes in private arrangements only for good reason, and it is, I think, very important to get this perspective at the start of the course. I think you will find that Chapter 1 gives you an introduction to many aspects of the law that you later learn in more detail.

Chapter 2 assumes only the existence of a promise, and asks why it should be enforced. Unless there is an absolute rule that all promises be enforced, or none, there are bound to be differences between reasonable men about drawing the line. The fact that drawing the line in individual cases may be difficult is not in itself a sufficient reason for reverting to absolute rules, but you must reconcile yourself to the prospect of unsatisfactory solutions in some cases, and you must examine closely the process by which the line is drawn. Where the law does not have a rule, the *process* of drawing the line is the heart of the law.

Chapter 3 assumes neither the promise nor its quality of enforceability. It asks the most difficult of the questions in the first three chapters: when, in the intricacies of contract negotiation, should the state interfere and take sides? When has the negotiation matured to the point where one of the parties should be able to call for help? This question involves so much of life beyond the experience of most law students that the cases probably seem much simpler than they really are.

Chapter 7 begins what I called the second part, that relating primarily to the planning of private arrangement aided by a well drafted contract. At the heart of this planning is the conditional promise, not an entirely new idea to you by this time, but one having implications you probably by then haven't suspected. In parts 3 and 5 of this chapter some concession is made to a proposition we sometimes hear, that there is no general law of contracts, there is a special law for each kind of contract. Here the two classes discussed are building contracts and employment contracts. This emphasis may be detected elsewhere throughout the materials as well. The building contract cases are chosen because that kind of contract is of great importance to the Canadian economy and is one of the most frequently found in business. The employment contract is, of course, even more commonplace, and it is hoped the materials here will provide a background for a later course in Labour Law. Other kinds of contracts that might well receive more emphasis, the contract for the sale of goods, the sale of land, and insurance, all receive special attention in later years in courses on Commercial Law, Real Estate Transactions, and Insurance.

One final word. This introduction has been deliberately written in the first person because I intend it primarily for my own classes. I should warn any other reader that the objectives of legal education and the consequent arrangement of topics in a course are highly personal, and my views may very well not be shared by other law teachers.

ACKNOWLEDGEMENTS

I am glad to acknowledge the kind permission generously given by the authors and publishers to reproduce the following copyright matter: The Incorporated Council of Law Reporting for England and Wales for material from *The Law Reports* and *The Weekly Law Reports*; Butterworth & Co. (Publishers) Ltd., for material from *The All England Law Reports*, and *The Law Times*; Sweet and Maxwell, Ltd., for material from the *Law Journal Reports*; the Times Publishing Co. Ltd., for material from *The Times Law Reports* and the *Commercial Cases*; Professor Lon L. Fuller and the West Publishing Company, as copyright holder, for the material from *Basic Contract Law*, and the *Yale Law Journal* for part of "The Reliance Interest in Contract Damages" of which Mr. Perdue was co-author, and the *Columbia Law Review*, as original publisher, for part of "Consideration and Form"; the many sections from the *Restatement of the Law of Contracts*, Copyright 1932, reprinted with the permission of The American Law Institute; Ward-Price, Limited, for permission to reproduce their auction sale contract, the Canadian Construction Association and The Royal Architectural Institute of Canada for permission to use parts of the standard form Canadian construction contract. I have made every attempt to obtain necessary permission to use copyright material but if any such material has been used improperly by oversight I hope the error will be brought to my attention so that suitable acknowledgement can be made in a later revision.

I am also glad to acknowledge the invaluable assistance of my wife for her large part in the endless proof reading, of Miss Carole Harris for her patience in helping to prepare the manuscript, and of Miss Jean Houston of the University of Toronto Press for her editorial help. Mr. Roger Hunt kindly drew the two diagrams.

Some faint resemblance to Dean Wright's original casebook on contracts may still be found, and I should be most ungrateful if I did not acknowledge his contribution to all Canadians teaching this subject. My great debt to Professor Lon Fuller is frequently apparent throughout the book. Needless to say all the mistakes are mine.

J. B. Milner

Faculty of Law
University of Toronto, 1963

CONTENTS

TABLE OF CASES

Only the cases reproduced wholly or in part are listed in this table. The page numbers of the cases more fully reproduced are italicized.

CASES AND MATERIALS ON CONTRACTS

CHAPTER 1

REMEDIES FOR BREACH OF PROMISE

In discussion and reflection about the materials in this chapter the existence of an enforceable promise should be assumed. The question is, what happens when that promise is broken? The basic fact situations are essentially simple. A promise has been made and broken. The problems are concerned with the kind and extent of protection the state ought to give to the interests of the aggrieved and of the defaulting parties. These interests have been described in many ways, and one convenient classification is set out below.

How can these interests be protected? Is the payment of some amount of money enough? How do you determine the amount? Should a promise-breaker be penalized? Why is the interest being protected? Should the defaulting party be made to perform his promise? When you have brought your horse to the well, how do you make him drink? Can you ever put the parties back where they were at the start? When ought the protection of the state to become available? For how long? As you read these first cases, keep these questions in mind, and keep in mind the practical limitations on the realization of justice, which may be an idealized solution that may suffer somewhat during its conversion to the actual world of the 20th century.

1. DAMAGES AND RESTITUTION

FULLER AND PERDUE, "THE RELIANCE INTEREST IN CONTRACT DAMAGES"
1936. 46 Yale Law Journal 52, 53-4, 56-7

It is convenient to distinguish three principal purposes which may be pursued in awarding contract damages. These purposes, and the situations in which they become appropriate, may be stated briefly as follows.

First, the plaintiff has in reliance on the promise of the defendant conferred some value on the defendant. The defendant fails to perform his promise. The court may force the defendant to disgorge the value he received from the plaintiff. The object here may be termed the prevention of gain by the defaulting promisor at the expense of the promisee; more briefly, the prevention of unjust enrichment. The interest protected may be called the *restitution interest*. For our present purposes it is quite immaterial how the suit in such a case be classified, whether as contractual or quasi-contractual, whether as a suit to enforce the contract or as a suit based upon a rescission of the contract. These questions relate to the superstructure of the law, not to the basic policies with which we are concerned.

Secondly, the plaintiff has in reliance on the promise of the defendant changed his position. For example, the buyer under a contract for the sale of land has incurred expense in the investigation of the seller's title, or has neglected the opportunity to enter other contracts. We may award damages to the plaintiff for the purpose of undoing the harm which his reliance on the defendant's promise has caused him. Our object is to put him in as good a position as he was in before the promise was made. The interest protected in this case may be called the *reliance interest.*

Thirdly, without insisting on reliance by the promisee or enrichment of the promisor, we may seek to give the promise the value of the expectancy which the promise created. We may in a suit for specific performance actually compel the defendant to render the promised performance to the plaintiff or, in a suit for damages, we may make the defendant pay the money value of this performance. Here our object is to put the plaintiff in as good a position as he would have occupied had the defendant performed his promise. The interest protected in this case we may call the *expectation interest. . . .*

It is obvious that the three "interests" we have distinguished do not present equal claims to judicial intervention. It may be assumed that ordinary standards of justice would regard the need for judicial intervention as decreasing in the order in which we have listed the three interests. The "restitution interest," involving a combination of unjust impoverishment with unjust gain, presents the strongest case for relief. If, following Aristotle, we regard the purpose of justice as the maintenance of an equilibrium of goods among members of society, the restitution interest presents twice as strong a claim to judicial intervention as the reliance interest, since if A not only causes B to lose one unit but appropriates that unit to himself, the resulting discrepancy between A and B is not one unit but two.

On the other hand, the promisee who has actually relied on the promise, even though he may not thereby have enriched the promisor, certainly presents a more pressing case for relief than the promisee who merely demands satisfaction for his disappointment in not getting what was promised him. In passing from compensation for change of position to compensation for loss of expectancy we pass, to use Aristotle's terms again, from the realm of corrective justice to that of distributive justice. The law no longer seeks merely to heal a disturbed status quo, but to bring into being a new situation. It ceases to act defensively or restoratively, and assumes a more active role. With the transition, the justification for legal relief loses its self-evident quality. It is as a matter of fact no easy thing to explain why the normal rule of contract recovery should be that which measures damages by the value of the promised performance. Since this "normal rule" throws its shadow across our whole subject it will be necessary to examine the possible reasons for its existence. It may be said parenthetically that the discussion which follows, though directed primarily to the normal measure of recovery where damages are sought, also has relevance to the more general question, why should a promise which has not been relied on ever be enforced at all, whether by a decree of specific performance or by an award of damages? . . .

[The reference is to Aristotle, *Nicomachean Ethics*, 1132*a*-1132*b*.]

SALLY WERTHEIM *v.* CHICOUTIMI PULP COMPANY
Quebec. Privy Council. [1911] A.C. 301

LORD ATKINSON: . . .And it is the general intention of the law that, in giving damages for breach of contract, the party complaining should, so far as it can be done by money, be placed in the same position as he would have been in if the contract had been performed. . . . That is a ruling principle. It is a just principle.

HADLEY *v.* BAXENDALE
England. King's Bench, 1854. 9 Exch. 341; 156 E.R. 145

At the trial before Crompton J., at the last Gloucester Assizes, it appeared that the plaintiffs carried on an extensive business as millers at Gloucester; and that, on the 11th of May, their mill was stopped by a breakage of the crank shaft by which the mill was worked. The steam-engine was manufactured by Messrs. Joyce & Co., the engineers, at Greenwich, and it became necessary to send the shaft as a pattern for a new one to Greenwich. The fracture was discovered on the 12th, and on the 13th the plaintiffs sent one of their servants to the office of the defendants, who are the well-known carriers trading under the name of Pickford and Co., for the purpose of having the shaft carried to Greenwich. The plaintiffs' servant told the clerk that the mill was stopped, and that the shaft must be sent immediately; and in answer to the inquiry when the shaft would be taken, the answer was, that if it was sent up by twelve o'clock any day, it would be delivered at Greenwich on the following day. On the following day the shaft was taken by the defendants, before noon, for the purpose of being conveyed to Greenwich, and the sum of £2 4s. was paid for its carriage for the whole distance; at the same time the defendants' clerk was told that a special entry, if required, should be made to hasten its delivery. The delivery of the shaft at Greenwich was delayed by some neglect; and the consequence was, that the plaintiffs did not receive the new shaft for several days after they would otherwise have done, and the working of their mill was thereby delayed, and they thereby lost the profits they would otherwise have received.

On the part of the defendants, it was objected that these damages were too remote and that the defendants were not liable with respect to them. The learned Judge left the case generally to the jury, who found a verdict with £25 damages beyond the amount paid into Court.

Whately in last Michaelmas Term, obtained a rule nisi for a new trial, on the ground of misdirection.

ALDERSON B.: We think that there ought to be a new trial in this case; but, in so doing, we deem it to be expedient and necessary to state explicitly the rule which the Judge, at the next trial, ought, in our opinion, to direct the jury to be governed by when they estimate the damages.

It is indeed, of the last importance that we should do this; for, if the jury are left without any definite rule to guide them, it will, in such cases as these, manifestly lead to the greatest injustice. . . .

Now we think the proper rule in such a case as the present is this:- Where two parties have made a contract which one of them has broken, the damages which the other party ought to receive in respect of such breach of contract should be such as may fairly and reasonably be considered either arising naturally, i.e., according to the usual course of things, from such breach of contract itself, or such as may reasonably be supposed to have been in the contemplation of both parties, at the time they made the contract, as the probable result of the breach of it. Now, if the special circumstances under which the contract was actually made were communicated by the plaintiffs to the defendants, and thus known to both parties, the damages resulting from the breach of such a contract, which they would reasonably contemplate, would be the amount of injury which would ordinarily follow from a breach of contract under these special circumstances so known and communicated. But, on the other hand, if these special circumstances were wholly unknown to the party breaking the contract, he, at the most, could only be supposed to have had in his contemplation the amount of injury which would arise generally, and in the great multitude of cases not affected by any special circumstances, from such a breach of contract. For, had the special circumstances been known, the parties might have specially provided for the breach of contract by special terms as to damages in that case; and of this advantage it would be very unjust to deprive them. Now the above principles are those by which we think the jury ought to be guided in estimating the damages arising out of any breach of contract. It is said, that other cases, such as breaches of contract in the non-payment of money, or in the not making a good title to land, are to be treated as exceptions from this, and as governed by a conditional rule. But as, in such cases, both parties must be supposed to be cognisant of that well-known rule, these cases may, we think be more properly classed under the rule above enunciated as to cases under known special circumstances, because there both parties may reasonably be presumed to contemplate the estimation of the amount of damages according to the conventional rule.

Now, in the present case, if we are to apply the principles above laid down, we find that the only circumstances here communicated by the plaintiffs to the defendants at the time the contract was made, were, that the article to be carried was the broken shaft of a mill, and that the plaintiffs were the millers of that mill. But how do these circumstances shew reasonably that the profits of the mill must be stopped by an unreasonable delay in the delivery of the broken shaft by the carrier to the third person? Suppose the plaintiffs had another shaft in their possession put up or putting up at the time, and that they only wished to send back the broken shaft to the engineer who made it; it is clear that this would be quite consistent with the above circumstances, and yet the unreasonable delay in the delivery would have no effect upon the intermediate profits of the mill. Or again, suppose that, at the time of the delivery to the carrier, the machinery of the mill had been in other respects defective, then, also, the same results would follow. Here it is true that the shaft was actually sent back to serve as a model for a new one, and that the want of a new one was the only cause of the stoppage of the mill, and that the loss of profits really arose from not sending down the new shaft in proper time, and that this arose from the delay in delivering the broken one to serve as a model. But it is obvious that, in the great multitude of cases of millers sending off broken shafts to third persons by a carrier under ordinary circumstances, such consequences would not, in all probability, have occurred; and these special circumstances were here never communicated by the plaintiffs to the defendants. It follows, therefore, that the loss of profits here cannot reasonably be considered such a consequence of the breach of contract as could have been fairly and reasonably contemplated by both parties when they made this contract. For such loss would neither have followed naturally from the breach of this contract in the great multitude of such cases occurring under ordinary circumstances, nor were the special circumstances, which, perhaps, would have made it a reasonable and natural consequence of such breach of contract, communicated to or known by the defendants. The Judge ought, therefor, to have told the jury that, upon the facts then before them, they ought not to take the loss of profits into consideration at all in estimating the damages. There must therefore be a new trial in this case. *Rule absolute.*

QUESTIONS. On the facts as reported, did the court apply its own principle in this case? What were the "real facts" of the case? For purposes of "precedent," what were the facts? What was the issue? What did the court "decide" here? What evidence do you suppose the court had of what happens "in the great multitude of cases of millers sending off broken shafts to third persons by a carrier"?

Suppose that the plaintiffs had taken their shaft in at ten o'clock in the morning, and that at eleven o'clock the plaintiffs' servant came in again and said, "The mill is stopped; we can't make any flour until we get that shaft back. Please hurry it." Then suppose that at twelve noon Samuel Stranger came in and the defendants agreed to take a chest in the only available conveyance to Penzance in time for his daughter's wedding the next day. Suppose that he offered to pay £5, twice the usual rate. If the defendants accepted this proposal and returned the plaintiffs their £2 4s., should this deliberate breach of the promise after the work stoppage was known affect the calculation of damages? *Corbin on Contracts* (vol. 5, s. 1008) suggests that we distinguish between wilful and non-wilful breach, and in the latter case make the material time for notice of unusual loss the time the defendant chose to commit the wilful breach. The distinction has not been adopted in Canadian or English cases.

HORNE *v.* THE MIDLAND RAILWAY COMPANY. 1873. L.R. 8 C.P. 131 (England. Exchequer Chamber). The plaintiffs, shoe manufacturers in Kettering, were under contract to supply a quantity of shoes to a firm in London for the use of the French army, at the unusually high price of 4s. per pair. By the terms of the contract with the London firm, the plaintiff was bound to deliver the shoes by the 3rd of February, 1871, and to meet this provision he sent the shoes to the defendant's station at Kettering in time to be delivered in the usual course in the evening of that day, when they would have been accepted and paid for by the consignees. Notice was given to the station-master (which notice was, for the purpose of the case, deemed to be notice to the company) at the time the shoes were delivered to him that the plaintiffs were under contract to deliver the shoes by the 3rd, and that unless they were so delivered they would be thrown upon the plaintiffs' hands. The shoes were not delivered in London until the morning of the 4th of February, when the consignee refused them, and the plaintiffs were obliged to sell them at the best price obtainable, namely 2s. 9d. per pair.

In an action against the defendants for the delay in delivering the shoes, they paid into court a sum of £20 which would be sufficient to cover any ordinary loss such as expenses incidental to the re-sale, but the plaintiffs further claimed the sum of £267 as the difference between the price at which they had contracted to sell the shoes and the price which they ultimately received.

On a stated case to the Court of Common Pleas, the defendant received a judgment (L.R. 7 C.P. 583), which was affirmed in this appeal.

BLACKBURN J.: ". . . Then if there was no special contract, what was the effect of the notice? In the case of Hadley v. Baxendale it was intimated that, apart from all question of a special contract with regard to amount of damages, if there were a special notice of the circumstances the plaintiff might recover the exceptional damages. This doctrine has been adverted to in several subsequent decisions with more or less assent, but they appear to have all been cases in which it was held that the doctrine did not apply because there was no special notice. It does not appear that there has been any case in which it has been affirmatively held that in consequence of such a notice the plaintiff could recover exceptional damages. The counsel for the plaintiff could not refer to any such case, and I know of none. If it were necessary to decide the point, I should be much disposed to agree with what my Brother Martin has suggested, viz., that in order that the notice may have any effect, it must be given under such circumstances, as that an actual contract arises on the part of the defendant to bear the exceptional loss. Before, however, deciding the point, I should have wished to take time to consider . . . "

HYDRAULIC ENGINEERING CO. LTD. *v.* McHAFFIE. 1878. 4 Q.B.D. 670 (England). BRAMWELL L. J.: "It has occurred to me that the true explanation is that a person contemplates the performance and not the breach of his contract; he does not enter into a kind of second contract to pay damages, but he is liable to make good those injuries which he is aware that his default may occasion to the contractee." COTTON L.J.: "It cannot be said that damages are granted because it is part of the contract that they shall be paid; it is the law which imposes or implies the term that upon breach of a contract damages must be paid."

RIVERS *v.* GEORGE WHITE & SONS CO. [1919] 2 W.W.R. 189 (Saskatchewan Court of Appeal). HAULTAIN C.J.S.: "It may be observed that this theory 'of a kind of second contract to pay damages' has been mainly developed in actions against carriers, on the ground that a common carrier has no discretion to decline a contract."

KINGHORNE *v.* THE MONTREAL TELEGRAPH CO. 1859. 18 U.C.Q.B. 60 (Ontario. Queen's Bench). In an action for failure to deliver a telegram that cost sixty cents and might have led to a contract that might have been carried out the jury awarded £57 13s. 7d. as damages. On a motion for a non-suit, held, for the defendant. MCLEAN J.: "It is, in my opinion, extremely doubtful whether in any such case a party who avails himself of the facilities afforded in communicating by telegraph can expect that a telegraph company shall be responsible for all damages, no matter what amount, which may arise in the hurry of transmitting a message from any verbal inaccuracy of an operator, or from an omission in forwarding or delivering it when received. It ought not to be expected that so great facilities are to be afforded for so small a remuneration, and at a risk which might bring ruin upon any company if obliged to indemnify for every possible loss."

VICTORIA LAUNDRY LTD. *v.* NEWMAN INDUSTRIES LTD.
England. Court of Appeal. [1949] 1 A11 E.R. 997

ASQUITH L.J. read the following judgment of the court.: This is an appeal by the plaintiffs against a judgment of Streatfeild J., in so far as that judgment limited the damages to £110 in respect of an alleged breach of contract by the defendants which is now uncontested. The breach of contract consisted in the delivery of a boiler sold by the defendants to the plaintiffs some twenty odd weeks after the time fixed by the contract for delivery. The short point is whether, in addition to the £110 awarded, the plaintiffs were entitled to claim in respect of loss of profits which they say would have made if the boiler had been delivered punctually.

The defendants are and were at all material times a limited company which described itself on its invoices as "Electrical and Mechanical Engineers and Manufacturers." They did not manufacture the boiler in question. They just happened to own it. The plaintiffs were at all material times a limited company carrying on the business of laundrymen and dyers in the neighbourhood of Windsor. In January, 1946, the plaintiffs were minded to expand their business, and to that end required a boiler of much greater capacity than the boiler they then possessed. . . . Seeing an advertisement by the defendants on Jan. 17, 1946, of two boilers which appeared suitable . . . they negotiated for the purchase of one of them, and by Apr. 26, 1946, had concluded a contract for its purchase at a price of £2,150, loaded free on transport at Harpenden.

Seeing that the issue is as to the measure of recoverable damages and the application of the rules in *Hadley* v. *Baxendale* it is important to inquire what information the defendants possessed at the time when the contract was made as to such matters as the time at which, and the purpose for which, the plaintiffs required the boiler. The defendants knew before and at the time of the contract that the plaintiffs were laundrymen and dyers and required the boiler for purposes of their business as such. They also knew that the plaintiffs wanted the boiler for immediate use. On the latter point the correspondence is important. The contract was concluded by, and is contained in, a series of letters . . . and finally, on Apr. 26, in the concluding letter of the series by which the contract was made: "We are most anxious that this" (that is, the boiler) "should be put into use"—we call attention to this expression—"in the shortest possible space of time." Hence, up to and at the very moment when a concluded contract emerged, the plaintiffs were pressing on the defendants the need for expedition, and the last letter was a plain intimation that the boiler was wanted for immediate use. This is none the less so because when, later, the plaintiffs encountered delays in getting the necessary permits and licences, the exhortations to speed come from the other side, who wanted their money, which, in fact, they were paid in advance of delivery. The defendants knew the plaintiffs needed the boiler as soon as the delays should be overcome, and they knew by the beginning of June that such delays had by then, in fact, been overcome. The defendants did not know at the material time the precise role for which the boiler was cast in the plaintiffs' economy, *e.g.*, whether (as the fact was) it was to function in substitution for an existing boiler of inferior capacity, or in replacement of an existing boiler of equal capacity, or as an extra unit to be operated side by side with and in addition to any existing boiler. It has, indeed, been argued strenuously that, for all they knew, it might have been wanted as a "spare" or "standby," provided in advance to replace an existing boiler, when, perhaps some time hence, the latter should wear out, but such an intention to reserve it for future use seems quite inconsistent with the intention expressed in the letter of Apr. 26 to "put it into use in the shortest possible space of time." In this connection, certain admissions made in the course of the hearing are of vital importance. The defendants formally admitted what in their defence they had originally traversed, namely, the facts alleged in para. 2 of the statement of claim. That paragraph reads as follows:

"At the date of the contract herinafter mentioned the defendants well knew as the fact was that the plaintiffs were launderers and dyers carrying on business at Windsor and required the said boiler for use in their said business and the said contract was made upon the basis that the said boiler was required for the said purpose."

On June 5, the plaintiffs, having heard that the boiler was ready, sent a lorry to Harpenden to take delivery. Mr. Lennard, a director of the plaintiff company, preceded the lorry in a car. He discovered on arrival that four days earlier the contractors employed by the defendants to dismantle the boiler had allowed it to fall on its side, receiving damage. Mr. Lennard declined to take delivery of the damaged boiler in its existing condition and insisted that the damage must be made good. He was, we think, justified in this attitude, since no similar article could be bought on the market. After a long wrangle, the defendants agreed to perform the necessary repairs, and, after further delay through the difficulty of finding a contractor who was free and able to perform them, completed the repairs by Oct. 28. Delivery was taken by the plaintiffs on Nov. 8 and the boiler was erected and working by early December. The plaintiffs claim, as part —the disputed part—of the damages, loss of the profits they would have earned if the machine had been delivered in early June instead of November.

Evidence was led for the plaintiffs with the object of establishing that, if the boiler had been punctually delivered, then, during the twenty odd weeks between then and the time of actual delivery (1) they could have taken on a very large number of new customers in the course of their laundry business, the demand for laundry services at that time being insatiable—they did, in fact, take on extra staff in the expectation of its delivery—and (2) that they could and would have accepted a number of highly lucrative dyeing contracts for the Ministry of Supply. In the statement of claim, para. 10, the loss of profits under the first of these heads was qualified at £16 a week and under the second at £262 a week. The evidence, however, which promised to be voluminous, had not gone very far when counsel for the defendants submitted that in law no loss of profits was recoverable at all, and that to continue to hear evidence as to its *quantum* was mere waste of time. He suggested that the question of remoteness of damage under this head should be decided on the existing materials, including the admissions to which we have referred. The learned judge accepted counsel's submission, and on that basis awarded £110 damages under certain minor heads, but nothing in respect of loss of profits, which he held to be too remote. It is from that decision that the plaintiffs now appeal. It was a necessary consequence of the course which the case took that no evidence was given on behalf of the defendants, and only part of the evidence available to the plaintiffs. It should be observed parenthetically that the defendants had added as third party the contractors who, by dropping the boiler, so causing the injuries to it, prevented its delivery in early June and caused the defendants to break their contract. Those third party proceedings have been adjourned pending the hearing of the present appeal as between the plaintiffs and the defendants. The third party, nevertheless, was served with notice of appeal by the defendants and argument was heard for him at the hearing of the appeal.

The ground of the learned judge's decision . . . may be summarised as follows. He took the view that the loss of profit claimed was due to special circumstances, and, therefore, recoverable, if at all, only under the second rule in *Hadley* v. *Baxendale,* and not recoverable in the present case because such special circumstances were not at the time of the contract communicated to the defendants. He also attached much significance to the fact that the object supplied was not a self-sufficient profit-making article, but part of a larger profit-making whole. . . . Before commenting on the learned judge's reasoning, we must refer to some of the authorities. The authorities on recovery of loss of profits as a head of damages are not easy to reconcile. At one end of the scale stand cases where there has been non-delivery or delayed delivery of what is on the face of it obviously a profit-earning chattel, for instance, a merchant or passenger ship; . . . or some essential part of such a ship for instance, a propeller, . . . or engines. . . . In such cases loss of profit has rarely been refused. A second and intermediate class of case in which loss of profit has often been awarded is where ordinary mercantile goods have been sold to a merchant with knowledge by the vendor that the purchaser wanted them for re-sale, at all events, where there was no market in which the purchaser could buy similar goods against the contract on the seller's default. . . . At the other end of the scale are cases where the defendant is not a vendor of the goods, but a carrier. In such cases the courts have been slow to allow loss of profit as an item of damage. This was not, it would seem, because a different principle applies in such cases, but because the application of the same principle leads to different results. A carrier commonly knows less than a seller about the purposes for which the buyer or consignee needs the goods or about other "special circumstances" which may cause exceptional loss if due delivery is withheld.

Three of the authorities call for more detailed examination. First comes *Hadley* v. *Baxendale* itself. . . .

British Columbia, etc., Saw Mill Co. v. *Nettleship* (1868), L.R. 3 C.P. 499, annexes to the principle laid down in *Hadley* v. *Baxendale* a rider to the effect that, where knowledge of special circumstances is relied on as enhancing the damages recoverable, that knowledge must have been brought home to the defendant at the time of the contract and in such circumstances that the defendant impliedly undertook to bear any special loss referable to a breach in those special circumstances. The knowledge which was lacking in that case on the part of the defendant was knowledge that the particular box of machinery negligently lost by the defendant was one without which the rest of the machinery could not be put together and would, therefore, be useless.

Cory v. *Thames Ironworks Co.* (1868), L.R. 3 Q.B. 181—a case strongly relied on by the plaintiffs—presented the peculiarity that the parties contemplated respectively different profit-making uses of the chattel sold by the defendants to the plaintiff. It was the hull of a boom derrick and was delivered late. The plaintiffs were coal merchants, and the obvious use, and that to which the defendants believed it was to be put, was that of a coal store. The plaintiffs, on the other hand, the buyers, in fact intended to use it for transhipping coals from colliers to barges, a quite unprecedented use for a chattel of this kind, one quite unsuspected by the sellers, and one calculated to yield much higher profits. The case, accordingly, decides, *inter alia,* what is the measure of damages recoverable when the parties are not *ad idem* in their contemplation of the use for which the article is needed. It was decided that in such a case no loss was recoverable beyond what would have resulted if the intended use had been that reasonably within the contemplation of the defendants, which in that case was the "obvious" use. This special complicating factor, the divergence between the knowledge and contemplation of the parties respectively, has somewhat obscured the general importance of the decision, which is in effect that the facts of the case brought it within the first rule of *Hadley* v. *Baxendale* and enabled the plaintiff to recover loss of such profits as would have arisen from the normal and obvious use of the article. The "natural consequences," said Blackburn J. (L.R. 3 Q.B. 191), of not delivering the derrick was that £420 representing those normal profits was lost. Cockburn C.J., interposing during the argument (ibid., 187), made the significant observation:

"No doubt, in order to recover damage arising from a special purpose the buyer must have communicated the special purpose to the seller; but there is one thing which must always be in the knowledge of both parties, which is, that the thing is bought for the purpose of being in some way or other profitably applied."

This observation is apposite to the present case. These three cases have on many occasions been approved by the House of Lords without any material qualification.

What propositions applicable to the present case emerge from the authorities as a whole, including those analysed above? We think they include the following: (1) It is well settled that the governing purpose of damages is to put the party whose rights have been violated in the same position, so far as money can do so, as if his rights had been observed. This purpose, if relentlessly pursued, would provide him with a complete indemnity for all loss *de facto* resulting from a particular breach, however improbable, however unpredictable. This, in contract at least, is recognised as too harsh a rule. Hence, (2) In cases of breach of contract the aggrieved party is only entitled to recover such part of the loss actually resulting as was at the time of the contract reasonably foreseeable as liable to result from the breach. (3) What was at that time reasonably foreseeable depends on the knowledge then possessed by the parties, or, at all events, by the party who later commits the breach. (4) For this purpose, knowledge "possessed" is of two kinds—one imputed, the other actual. Everyone, as a reasonable person, is taken to know the "ordinary course of things" and consequently what loss is liable to result from a breach of that ordinary course. This is the subject-matter of the "first rule" in *Hadley* v. *Baxendale*, but to this knowledge, which a contract-breaker is assumed to possess whether he actually possesses it or not, there may have to be added in a particular case knowledge which he actually possesses of special circumstances outside the "ordinary course of things" of such a kind that a breach in those special circumstances would be liable to cause more loss. Such a case attracts the operation of the "second rule" so as to make additional loss also recoverable. (5) In order to make the contract-breaker liable under either rule it is not necessary that he should actually have asked himself what loss is liable to result from a breach. As has often been pointed out, parties at the time of contracting contemplate, not the breach of the contract, but its performance. It suffices that, if he had considered the question, he would as a reasonable man have concluded that the loss in question was liable to result. . . . (6) Nor, finally, to make a particular loss recoverable, need it be proved that on a given state of knowledge the defendant could, as a reasonable man, forsee that a breach must necessarily result in that loss. It is enough if he could forsee it was likely so to result. It is enough . . . if the loss (or some factor without which it would not have occurred) is a "serious possibility" or a "real danger." For short, we have used the word "liable" to result. Possibly the colloquialism "on the cards" indicates the shade of meaning with some approach to accuracy.

If these, indeed, are the principles applicable, what is the effect of their application to the facts of the present case? We have, at the beginning of this judgment, summarised the main relevant facts. The defendants were an engineering company supplying a boiler to a laundry. We reject the submission for the defendants that an engineering company knows no more than the plain man about boilers or the purposes to which they are commonly put by different classes of purchasers, including laundries. The defendant company were not, it is true, manufacturers of this boiler or dealers in boilers, but they gave a highly technical and comprehensive description of this boiler to the plaintiffs by letter of Jan. 19, 1946, and offered both to dismantle the boiler at Harpenden and to re-erect it on the plaintiffs' premises. Of the uses or purposes to which boilers are put, they would clearly know more than the uninstructed layman. Again, they knew they were supplying the boiler to a company carrying on the business of laundrymen and dyers, for use in that business. The obvious use of a boiler, in such a business, is surely to boil water for the purpose of washing or dyeing. A laundry might conceivably buy a boiler for some other purpose, for instance, to work radiators or warm bath water for the comfort of its employees or directors, or to use for research, or to exhibit in a museum. All these purposes are possible, but the first is the obvious purpose which, in the case of a laundry, leaps to the average eye. If the purpose then be to wash or dye, why does the company want to wash or dye, unless for purposes of business advantage . . . ?

Since we are differing from a carefully reasoned judgment, we think it due to the learned judge to indicate the grounds of our dissent. . . . The answer to [his] reasoning has largely been anticipated in what has been said above, but we would wish to add, first, that the learned judge appears to infer that because certain "special circumstances" were, in his view, not "drawn to the notice of" the defendants, and, therefor, in his view, the operation of the "second rule" was excluded, *ergo*, nothing in respect of loss of business can be recovered under the "first rule." This inference is, in our view, no more justified in the present case than it was in *Cory* v. *Thames Ironworks Co.*

Secondly, while it is not wholly clear what were the "special circumstances" on the non-communication of which the learned judge relied, it would seem that they were or included the following:—(a) the "circumstance" that delay in delivering the boiler was going to lead "necessarily" to loss of profits, but the true criterion is surely not what was bound "necessarily" to result, but what was likely or liable to do so, and we think that it was amply conveyed to the defendants by what was communicated to them (plus what was patent without express communication) that delay in delivery was likely to lead to "loss of business"; (b) the "circumstance" that the plaintiffs needed the boiler "to extend their business." It was surely not necessary for the defendants to be specifically informed of this as a precondition of being liable for loss of business. Reasonable persons in the shoes of the defendants must be taken to foresee, without any express intimation, that a laundry which, at a time when there was a famine of laundry facilities, was paying £2,000 odd for plant and intended at such a time to put such plant "into use" immediately, would be likely to suffer in pocket from five months' delay in delivery of the plant in question, whether they intended by means of it to extend their business, or merely to maintain it, or to reduce a loss; (c) the "circumstance" that the plaintiffs had the assured expectation of special contracts, which they could only fulfil by securing punctual delivery of the boiler. Here, no doubt the learned judge had in mind the particularly lucrative dyeing contracts to which the plaintiffs looked forward. . . . We agree that in order that the plaintiffs should recover specifically and as such the profits expected on these contracts, the defendants would have had to know, at the time of their agreement with the plaintiffs, of the prospect and terms of such contracts. We also agree that they did not, in fact, know these things. It does not, however, follow that the plaintiffs are precluded from recovering some general (and perhaps conjectural) sum for loss of business in respect of dyeing contracts to be reasonably expected any more than in respect of laundering contracts to be reasonably expected. Thirdly, the other point on which Streatfeild J., largely based his judgment was that there is a critical difference between the measure of damages applicable when the defendant defaults in supplying a self-contained profit-earning whole and when he defaults in supplying a part of that whole. In our view, there is no intrinsic magic, in this connection, in the whole as against a part. The fact that a part only is involved is only significant in so far as it bears on the capacity of the supplier to foresee the consequences of non-delivery. If it is clear from the nature of the part (or the supplier of it is informed) that its non-delivery will have the same effect as non-delivery of the whole, his liability will be the same as if he had defaulted in delivering the whole. The cases . . . so strongly relied on . . . were all cases in which, through want of a part, catastrophic results ensued, in that a whole concern was paralysed or sterilized—a mill stopped, a complex of machinery unable to be assembled, a threshing machine unable to be delivered in time for the harvest, and, therefore, useless. In all three cases the defendants were absolved from liability to compensate the plaintiffs for the resulting loss of business, not because what they had failed to deliver was a part, but because there had been nothing to convey to them that want of that part would stultify the whole business of the person for whose benefit the part was contracted for. There is no resemblance between these cases and the present, in which, while there was no question of a total stoppage resulting from non-delivery, yet there were ample means of knowledge on the part of the defendants that business loss of some sort would be likely to result to the plaintiffs from the defendants' default in performing their contract.

We are, therefore, of opinion that the appeal should be allowed and the issue referred to an official referee as to what damage, if any, is recoverable in addition to the £110 awarded by the learned trial judge. The official referee would assess those damages in consonance with the findings in this judgment as to what the defendants knew or must be taken to have known at the material time, either party to be at liberty to call evidence as to the *quantum* of the damage in dispute.

Appeal allowed with costs. Costs on the issue of profit damages to be reserved to the official referee. No order as to third party costs of appeal.

QUESTIONS. ASQUITH L.J. cited the *British Columbia Saw-Mill* case, but he did not quote Bovill C.J. who said, "It is to be observed that the defendant is a carrier, and not a manufacturer of goods supplied for a particular purpose." STUART J. drew attention to this distinction in *Canada Foundry Co. Ltd.* v. *Edmonton Portland Cement Co. Ltd.*, [1913] 1 W.W.R. 382 (Alberta), and he also said, "There are indeed numbers of cases in which loss of profits has been awarded for breach of contract. . . . In actions against carriers the Courts have perhaps hesitated more than they have in actions against manufacturers and builders." Is the distinction valid? Should a distinction be made between a carrier, a seller and a manufacturer?

MUNROE EQUIPMENT SALES LTD. *v.* CANADIAN FOREST PRODUCTS LTD. 1961. 29 D.L.R. (2d) 730 (Manitoba. Court of Appeal). The plaintiff agreed early in December, 1956, to rent a second-hand Allis Chalmers HD15 tractor to the defendant at the rate of $1,500 a month. The defendant wanted the tractor to be used along with his other equipment (including other tractors) in road clearing operations that winter, so that his pulpwood could be brought to market. When the contract was made the defendant stressed that the tractor was needed to open roads, that time was short and that frost had set in. Nevertheless the contract was made on December 13 when the defendant's superintendent "accidentally bumped into" a salesman of the plaintiff. The tractor broke down within two days and thereafter its performance was sporadic and it was not much used until January 20, 1957. During this time the defendant made no effort to get a replacement largely because the plaintiff's salesman thought the tractor could be repaired sooner than it could be replaced. Two subcontractors got additional equipment "when they became tired of waiting for the HD 15." The final breakdown occurred on February 20 and from then until the end of the season the tractor was abandoned. By agreement no rent was charged for the month ending January 17, but in this action the plaintiff claimed $6,667.99. The trial Judge allowed him $2,075.00 made up of $1,500 for one month's rent and freight charges. But he also allowed a counterclaim of $6,958.37 (the defendant asked for $14,298.12) most of which was based on lost profits because the defendant was prevented from removing 3,500 cords of pulpwood. He relied on *Hadley* v. *Baxendale* and found the defendant's loss "was a natural and probable consequence that ought to have been in plaintiff's contemplation." On appeal the Court divided three to two in modifying the verdict by reducing the plaintiff's award to $1,826.43 and dismissing the counterclaim altogether. MILLER C.J.M.: "With respect, I do not think *Victoria Laundry (Windsor) Ltd.* v. *Newman Industries Ltd.*, [1949] 1 All E.R. 997, 2 K.B. 528, quoted by the learned trial Judge, is of much help to defendant. In any event, that decision is not binding on this Court. I prefer the reasoning of the trial Judge to that of the Judges of Appeal so far as the application of the law to the facts is concerned. . . . [*Anson on Contract,* 21st ed., pp. 460–3, quoted and adopted.]

"It seems to me that in the case at bar the defendant cannot succeed on its counterclaim unless it establishes that the special circumstances in connection with the use of the tractor were communicated and made known to the plaintiff company. There was nothing discussed in the negotiations for the tractor which would indicate whether the defendant company intended to remove 100 cords or 100,000 cords of wood; nor, so far as the knowledge of, or the knowledge imparted to, the plaintiff company was concerned, how much wood was cut and ready to be moved. Nor was it in any way indicated to the plaintiff that all the wood which the defendant company had cut by itself or its subcontractors had to be moved that year. The fact that the defendant had labour trouble in the fall of 1956, as deposed by Knelman the general manager of defendant, was not disclosed to plaintiff, or that, as a result thereof, the defendant was going to attempt to remove all wood that season. As stated above, it is not uncommon in the business in question to leave a substantial portion of 1 year's cut in the bush for removal in another year. Neither was it made known to the plaintiff company that the defendant company had a sale for any specific quantity of wood. The rental contract covering the HD 15 was of indeterminate duration and presumably could have been determined by either party at virtually any time.

"It seems to me that the defendant company was seeking—and urgently seeking—a tractor, and was glad to obtain this rebuilt tractor. The defendant (not the plaintiff) was the originator of the contract in issue.

"It appears to me that if it were a matter of such urgency to the defendant company that this tractor should bear the brunt of the roadwork, the defendant company would not have left the securing of same until as late as December 1956 when hauling operations were ready to begin. It also seems logical to me that if the defendant company were going to hold the plaintiff company responsible in such large damages for any failure of a second-hand rebuilt unit, the defendant company should have made clear to the plaintiff the extent of the work to be done. I do not believe the plaintiff acted in any improper way and I do believe that any representations the salesman of the plaintiff company may have made were made innocently, in good faith, and were not intended as a guarantee: but, as above pointed out, the learned trial Judge found that the salesman had guaranteed the tractor to be in good mechanical condition—whatever that may have meant with respect to a second-hand unit. There is no warranty or guarantee in the written rental agreement ex. 3.

"In my opinion it is unreasonable to expect that such a burden of responsibility for damages as now claimed by the defendant should be assumed from the rental of a second-hand unit. Surely no reasonable person could contemplate, under the circumstances of the renting of this machine, that the lessor of one second-hand tractor was underwriting and virtually insuring the removal of all this pulpwood from the bush. . . .

"Had the plaintiff contemplated possible liability for such damage as claimed by the counterclaim, it is scarcely conceivable that it would have risked letting a second-hand tractor bear such responsibility; nor would any reasonable person do so. Such damages do not ordinarily flow from the fact that a second-hand tractor does not "stand-up", and therefore in order to fix the plaintiff with responsibility for such damages the defendant, at the time of making the contract, should have made clear its version of the extraordinary responsibility the defendant might seek to impose upon the plaintiff. At least it should have warned the plaintiff of its (defendant's) intention to remove all wood that season, the quantity involved, the sale contracts for wood that defendant had made, and such like. If this had been done it is probable the defendant would not have secured the tractor or the plaintiff would have insisted upon contracting itself out of any liability. . . ."

CANADA FOUNDRY COMPANY LTD. *v*. EDMONTON PORTLAND CEMENT COMPANY LTD. [1918] 3 W.W.R. 866 (Privy Council from Alberta). Canada Foundry agreed to supply steel for the construction of a factory in which Edmonton Cement would manufacture cement after installing equipment. The action was started by Canada Foundry to enforce a mechanic's lien imposed by Canada Foundry because Edmonton Cement defaulted in payment on the contract. Edmonton Cement counterclaimed for $76,584.15 for loss of profits of 71 cents on 110,865 barrels that could have been produced between the dates of promised delivery and actual delivery. The trial judge found Canada Foundry liable on the counterclaim but in calculating damages he took much smaller figures and arrived at only $10,000. The Court of Appeal affirmed, and STUART J. remarked, "That is not so bad a result or a start considering the contengencies of all such kinds of business. . . . The defendants must remember that it is impossible always to get exact and full reparation for a breach of contract. . . . In *Cory* v. *Thames Iron Works* . . . the purchaser was shown to have actually suffered a greatly larger loss of profits than was awarded him but was confined to an amount which was more in accordance with the anticipations of the vendors as to the use of the article in question. Here we cannot assert that the plaintiffs had any definite knowledge of the possible or actual extent of the defendants' proposed business and aspirations. . . . I am strongly inclined to think that the value of the use of such extensive buildings for such a length of time would be found to be as much as $10,000 in any case."

The Privy Council affirmed the Court of Appeal. Speaking of the exculpatory clause in the contract, LORD ATKINSON said, after quoting the clause [The Company shall not be responsible or liable for any direct or indirect damage, loss, stoppage, or delay which the purchaser may sustain, whether the said plant or machinery is specified for any particular purpose or not.]:

"It is difficult to say what this provision means.

"Literally construed it would mean that the appellants might delay the shipment, delivery, or erection of this steel frame as often and as long as it seemed good to them. That would be in itself an irrational result, and besides would be altogether irreconcilable with the earlier provision binding them to deliver the plant and machinery with due despatch. The document must be construed as a whole, effect being, as far as possible, given to each part. And the only way in which that can be done is to hold either that the second clause does not at all apply to the plant and machinery mentioned in the earlier clause of the document, or that if it does apply to them it was only intended to protect the appellants from being responsible for consequential damage. Their Lordships are, however, like the learned trial Judge and the Court of Appeal, of opinion that it does not apply to such breaches of contract as the long-delayed shipment, delivery, or erection of the steel frame contracted for. It cannot, therefore, in itself, furnish any defence to the respondents' counterclaim."

CORBIN *v*. THOMPSON. 1907. 39 S.C.R. 575 (Nova Scotia. Supreme Court of Canada). The Plaintiff sold the defendant a boiler and engine with a guarantee that it would work satisfactorily. The engine proved to be unworkable and the plaintiff agreed to take it back for repair. It was returned two months later. In the meantime, the defendant had rented a second-hand engine for $20 a month but it didn't work either. The plaintiff had expected to repair the engine within a few days and he knew the defendant wanted it so that he could return the rented engine as soon as possible. In an action for the contract price the defendant counterclaimed for damages. The trial judge allowed "$150 for the loss of the use of his mill" and $277 for wages paid by him to his men whom he retained in camp. The Supreme Court of Nova Scotia *en banc* rejected the reliance item for wages paid, but allowed the $150 for loss of the use of the mill which they distinguished from loss of profits. The Supreme Court of Canada restored the judgment for $277 but rejected the $150. If that amount was correctly calculated it should include everything recoverable. DAVIES J.: "Nor am I able to follow Russell J. [who dissented in the Court below] in allowing these damages as anticipated profits. Such profits are only recoverable when they can be held to be what are called primary profits, such as would have occurred and grown out of the contract itself as the direct and immediate result of its fulfilment. Then they are part and parcel of the contract itself and must have been in contemplation of the parties when the agreement was entered into. But if they are such as would have been realized from other independent and collateral undertakings although entered into in consequence and on the faith of the principal contract, then they are too uncertain and remote to be taken into consideration as part of the damages occasioned by the breach of the contract in suit, unless indeed the defaulting contractor has expressly contracted to be bound for such consequences or the special circumstances are such that he may be held to have impliedly contracted to be so bound." It was conceded that if the defendant could have rented another engine for $40 or $50 a month and should have done so, that would have been the full amount of damages. Since defendant reasonably expected his own engine back in a few days he was not obliged to rent another.

ADDIS *v.* GRAMOPHONE COMPANY LIMITED
England. House of Lords. [1909] A.C. 488

The plaintiff was employed by the defendants as manager of their business in Calcutta at £15 per week as salary, and a commission on the trade done. He could be dismissed by six months' notice.

In October, 1905, the defendants gave him six months' notice, but at the same time they appointed Mr. Gilpin to act as his successor, and took steps to prevent the plaintiff from acting any longer as manager. In December, 1905, the plaintiff came back to England.

The plaintiff brought this action in 1906, claiming an account and damages for breach of contract. That there was a breach of contract is quite clear. If what happened in October, 1905, did not amount to a wrongful dismissal, it was, at all events, a breach of the plaintiff's right to act as manager during the six months and to earn the best commission he could make.

When the action came to trial it was agreed to refer the matters of account to arbitration. The causes of action for breach of contract were tried by Darling J. and a jury. The jury found for the plaintiff in respect of wrongful dismissal £600, and £340 in respect of excess commission over and above what was earned by the plaintiff's successor between October, 1905, and April, 1906.

The Court of Appeal by a majority held that upon their view of the facts there was (apart from the account which must be taken) no cause of action, and they entered judgment for the defendants.

LORD ATKINSON: My Lords, I entirely concur with the judgment of my noble and learned friend on the woolsack. Much of the difficulty which has arisen in this case is due to the unscientific form in which the pleadings, as amended, have been framed, and the loose manner in which the proceedings at the trial were conducted.

The rights of the plaintiff, disembarrassed of the confusing methods by which they were sought to be enforced, are, in my opinion, clear. He had been illegally dismissed from his employment. He could have been legally dismissed by the six months' notice, which he, in fact, received, but the defendants did not wait for the expiry of that period. The damages plaintiff sustained by this illegal dismissal were (1) the wages for the period of six months during which his formal notice would have been current; (2) the profits or commission which would, in all reasonable probability, have been earned by him during the six months had he continued in the employment; and possibly (3) damages in respect of the time which might reasonably elapse before he could obtain other employment. He has been awarded a sum possibly of some hundreds of pounds, not in respect of any of these heads of damage, but in respect of the harsh and humiliating way in which he was dismissed, including, presumably, the pain he experienced by reason, it is alleged, of the imputation upon him conveyed by the manner of his dismissal. This is the only circumstance which makes the case of general importance, and this is the only point I think it necessary to deal with.

I have been unable to find any case decided in this country in which any countenance is given to the notion that a dismissed employee can recover in the shape of exemplary damages for illegal dismissal, in effect damages for defamation, for it amounts to that, except the case of *Maw* v. *Jones* (1890), 25 Q.B.D. 107.

In that case Matthew J., as he then was, during the argument, while counsel was urging . . . that the measure of damages for the improper dismissal of an ordinary domestic servant was a month's wages and nothing more, no doubt interjected in the shape of a question the remark, "Have you ever heard the principle applied to a case where a false charge of misconduct has been made?" But the decision was that the direction of the judge at the trial was right.

Now, what was the character of that direction? The defendant had power to dismiss his apprentice, the plaintiff, on a week's notice, and had also power to dismiss him summarily if he should show a want of interest in his work. He dismissed the apprentice summarily without notice, assigning as a reason that he had been guilty of frequent acts of insubordination and that he had gone out at night without leave.

The judge at the trial told the jury that they were not bound to limit the damages to the week's notice he had lost, but that they might take into consideration the time the plaintiff would require to get new employment—the difficulty he would have as a discharged apprentice in getting employment elsewhere—and it was on this precise ground the direction was upheld. I do not think that this case is any authority what ever for the general proposition that exemplary damages may be recovered for wrongful dismissal, still less, of course, for breach of contract generally; but, such as it is, it is the only authority in the shape of a decided case which can be found upon the first-mentioned point.

I have always understood that damages for breach of contract were in the nature of compensation, not punishment. . . .

There are three well-known exceptions to the general rule applicable to the measure of damages for breach of contract, namely, actions against a banker for refusing to pay a customer's cheque when he has in his hands funds of the customer's to meet it, actions for breach of promise of marriage, and actions like that in *Flureau* v. *Thornhill* (1776), 2 W.Bl. 1078, where the vendor of real estate, without any fault on his part, fails to make title. I know of none other.

The peculiar nature of the first two of these exceptions justified their existence. Ancient practice upholds the last, though it has often been adversely criticized, as in *Bain* v. *Fothergill* (1873), L.R. 7 H.L. 158. If there be a tendency to create a fourth exception it ought, in my view, to be checked rather than stimulated; inasmuch as to apply in their entirety the principles on which damages are measured in tort to cases of damages for breaches of contract would lead to confusion and uncertainty in commercial affairs, while to apply them only in part and in particular cases would create anomalies, lead occasionally to injustice, and make the law a still more "lawless science" than it is said to be.

For instance, in actions of tort, motive, if it may be taken into account to aggregate damages, as it undoubtedly may be, may also be taken into account to mitigate them, as may also the conduct of the plaintiff himself who seeks redress. Is this rule to be applied to actions of breach of contract? There are few breaches of contract more common than those which arise where men omit or refuse to repay what they have borrowed, or to pay for what they have bought. Is the creditor or vendor who sues for one of such breaches to have the sum he recovers lessened if he should be shown to be harsh, grasping, or pitiless, or even insulting, in enforcing his demand, or lessened because the debtor has struggled to pay, has failed because of misfortune, and has been suave, gracious, and apologetic in his refusal? On the other hand, is that sum to be increased if it should be shewn that the debtor could have paid readily without any embarrassment, but refused with expression of contempt and contumely, from a malicious desire to injure his creditor?

Few parties to contracts have more often to complain of ingratitude and baseness than sureties. Are they, because of this, to be entitled to recover from the principal, often a trusted friend, who has deceived and betrayed them, more than they paid on that principal's behalf? If circumstances of aggravation are rightly to be taken into account in actions of contract at all, why should they not be taken into account in the case of the surety, and the rules and principles applicable to cases of tort applied to the full extent?

In many other cases of breach of contract there may be circumstances of malice, fraud, defamation, or violence, which would sustain an action of tort as an alternative remedy to an action for breach of contract. If one should select the former mode of redress, he may, no doubt, recover exemplary damages, or what is sometimes styled vindictive damages; but if he should choose to seek redress in the form of an action for breach of contract, he lets in all the consequences of that form of action. One of these consequences is, I think, this: that he is to be paid adequate compensation in money for the loss of that which he would have received had his contract been kept, and no more.

I can conceive nothing more objectionable and embarrassing in litigation than trying in effect an action of libel or slander as a matter of aggravation in an action for illegal dismissal, the defendant being permitted, as he must in justice be permitted, to traverse the defamatory sense, rely on privilege, or raise every point which he could raise in an independent action brought for the alleged libel or slander itself.

In my opinion, exemplary damages ought not to be, and are not according to any true principle of law, recoverable in such an action as the present, and the sums awarded to the plaintiff should therefore be decreased by the amount at which they have been estimated, and credit for that item should not be allowed in his account.

LORD COLLINS: . . . when the law of damages is traced backwards, it will be found that the so-called exceptions, including that of dishonoured cheques, are merely recurrences to the old rule, which . . . has been sometimes forgotten or ignored. But, for the reason I have given, I think we are not bound to disallow such damages in this case, and I am not disposed, unless compelled by authority to do so, to curtail the power of the jury to exercise what . . . is a salutary power, which has justified itself in practical experience, to redress wrongs for which there may be, as in this case, no other remedy. Such discretion, when exercised by a jury, would be subject to the now unquestioned rights of the Courts to supervise, just as is done every day, where this form of action is tort. That a trespass carrying with it an imputation may be the subject of exemplary damages swelled by the fact of the imputation was decided by Lord Ellenborough in *Bracegirdle* v. *Orford* (1813), 2 M.&S. 77, overruling the contention that the imputation could only be brought into consideration as the subject for a separate count for slander.

In all other respects I agree in the opinion of the Lord Chancellor.

[Lord Loreburn L.C., and Lords James of Hereford, Gorrell, and Shaw of Dunfermline also gave judgments.]

D. *v*. B. 1917. 40 O.L.R. 112 (Ontario Court of Appeal). Plaintiff and defendant were engaged to be married and the defendant broke the engagement. Plaintiff sued and recovered a verdict for $5,000. She did not prove any actual damage. The $5,000 was almost entirely sentimental and in the middle of the war may have unduly reflected the defendant's Austrian background. He was an Austrian by birth but had been educated in Canada and had been admitted to the Bar two years before the action. He worked for a legal firm for $1,500 a year and had dependent relatives for whom he was morally if not legally responsible. Plaintiff was a Russian, had been in the country for only a year, and was expected to return to Russia, in which case "her prospects of future marriage will not probably be affected." On appeal a new trial was ordered. FERGUSON J.A.: "The principles of law and rules governing the trial of an action for breach of promise are considered in *Smith* v. *Woodfine* (1857), 1 C.B.N.S. 660; 140 E.R. 272. In that case Mr. Justice Willes, at p. 667, quotes with approval from the American work, Sedgwick on Damages, 2nd ed., p. 368, as follows: 'The action for breach of promise of marriage . . . though nominally an action founded on the breach of an agreement, presents a striking exception to the general rules which govern contracts. This action is given as an indemnity to the injured party for the loss she has sustained, and has always been held to embrace the injury to the feelings, affections, and wounded pride, as well as the loss of marriage. . . . From the nature of the case, it has been found impossible to fix the amount of compensation by any precise rule; and as in tort, the measure of damages is a question for the sound discretion of the jury in each particular instance . . . subject, of course, to the general restriction that a verdict influenced by *prejudice*, *passion*, or corruption, will not be allowed to stand. Beyond this the power of the Court is limited, as in cases of tort, almost exclusively to questions arising on the admissibility of evidence when offered by way of enhancing or mitigating damages. . . .' In my opinion, the verdict, is, under all the circumstances, excessive. . . ." MEREDITH C.J.O.: ". . . The prejudice to the appellant was, I think, greatly aggravated by the contrast between the parties, evidently sought to be impressed upon the jury by painting the respondent as a refugee from our ally Russia, while the appellant was of Austrian enemy origin. . . . I am always reluctant to interfere with the finding of a jury, and endeavour to be on my guard against usurping the functions of a jury in a case in which they have come to a conclusion different from that which I have formed as to the result of the evidence; but, at a time like this, when the minds of the people are rightly inflamed against the German and Austrian peoples, it is, I think, incumbent on the Court to guard against that feeling being used to the detriment of a litigant who comes or is brought into a Court of Justice, and to be astute to see that, where it has been played upon by the successful litigant, he is deprived of any advantage thus unfairly obtained; and it is not, I think, unfair to presume against such a litigant that his effort has had the desired effect."

NOTE. The exception to the rule limiting damages to compensation made in what are sometimes called "heart balm" cases has led to frequent abuse. Compare the two legislative solutions reproduced below, both as to substance and as to form and style. Can you suggest other, and perhaps better ways of dealing with excessive damage awards? What is the purpose of section 61-a in the New York Laws? Is it necessary in Ontario? Is it a Good Thing?

THE EVIDENCE ACT

Ontario. Revised Statutes. 1960. Chapter 125

13. The plaintiff in an action for breach of promise of marriage shall not recover unless his or her testimony is corroborated by some other material evidence in support of the promise.

NEW YORK LAWS

New York. Statutes. 1935. Chapter 263

61-a. *Declaration of public policy of state.* The remedies heretofore provided by law for the enforcement of actions based upon alleged alienation of affections, criminal conversation, seduction and breach of contract to marry, having been subjected to grave abuses, causing extreme annoyance, embarrassment, humiliation and pecuniary damage to many persons wholly innocent and free of any wrongdoing, who were merely the victims of circumstances, and such remedies having been exercised by unscrupulous persons for their unjust enrichment, and such remedies having furnished vehicles for the commission or attempted commission of crime and in many cases having resulted in the perpetration of frauds, it is hereby declared as the public policy of the state that the best interests of the people of the state will be served by the abolition of such remedies. Consequently, in the public interest, the necessity for the enactment of this article is hereby declared as a matter of legislative determination.

61-b. *Certain causes of action hereafter accruing abolished.* The rights of action heretofore existing to recover sums of money as damage for the alienation of affections, criminal conversation, seduction, or breach of contract to marry are hereby abolished. . . .

61-d. *Legal effect of certain acts hereafter occurring.* No act hereafter done within this state shall operate to give rise, either within or without this state, to any of the rights of action abolished by this article. No contract to marry, hereafter made or entered into in this state shall operate to give rise, either within or without this state, to any cause or right of action for the breach thereof....

HERBERT CLAYTON AND JACK WALLER LTD. *v.* OLIVER
England. House of Lords. [1930] A.C. 209

Barrie Oliver, a young actor, agreed with Messrs. Clayton and Waller, producers, "to play one of three leading comedy parts" in a musical production at the London Hippodrome for £55 a week for six weeks certain. Oliver considered that the part offered to him did not meet this test and declined to appear in it. His view was accepted by the House of Lords, Lord Buckmaster remarking, "Making all necessary allowances for the fact that the kind of humour of such a play seems melancholy in print, the part assigned to the plaintiff is so trivial that even in relation to this play the verdict is fully warranted." No other part was offered and Oliver commenced this action for damages for loss of salary and for loss of the advertisement and reputation he would have enjoyed had the contract been performed. The jury awarded £165 for loss of salary and £1,000 for loss of advertisement. The Court of Appeal learned that Oliver had obtained service at an equivalent remuneration elsewhere and refused the £165, but confirmed the £1,000.

LORD BUCKMASTER: ... The next question is what was the measure of the damage? It is true that as a general rule the measure of damage for breach of contract is unaffected by the motives or manner of its breach. What are known as vindictive or exemplary damages in tort find no place in contract nor accordingly can injury to feelings or vanity be regarded. The action of breach of promise of marriage is an exception to the general rule, for, strictly assessed, the loss to a woman as a husband of a man who declines with insult to marry her might be assumed to be nil, but that is not the way such damages are determined.

In the present case the old and well established rule applies without qualification, the damages are those that may reasonably be supposed to have been in the contemplation of the parties at the time when the contract was made, as the probable result of its breach, and if any special circumstances were unknown to one of the parties, the damages associated with and flowing from such breach cannot be included. Here both parties knew that as flowing from the contract the plaintiff would be billed and advertised as appearing at the Hippodrome, and in the theatrical profession this is a valuable right.

In assessing the damages, therefore, it was competent for the jury to consider that the plaintiff was entitled to compensation because he did not appear at the Hippodrome, as by his contract he was entitled to do, and in assessing those damages they may consider the loss he suffered (1) because the Hippodrome is an important place of public entertainment and (2) that in the ordinary course he would have been "billed" and otherwise advertised as appearing at the Hippodrome. The learned judge put the matter as a loss of reputation, which I do not think is the exact expression, but he explained that as the equivalent of loss of publicity and that summarizes what I have stated as my view of the true situation.

As to the amount, that was for the jury; the damages appear to me extravagant ... but they are not so extravagant as to vitiate the verdict....

[Lords Blanesburgh and Tomlin agreed with Lord Buckmaster. Viscount Dunedin gave a short concurring judgment. Lord Warrington of Clyffe agreed.]

TURNER *v.* SAWDON & CO. [1901] 2 K.B. 653 (Engish Court of Appeal). The Court refused damages for failure to discharge an alleged obligation on the masters that during the period over which the contract was to extend, they should find continuous, or at least some, employment for the plaintiff. STIRLING L.J., said, in part: "Throughout the argument and at the present moment I feel more doubt as to the construction of this contract than my learned brethren. It is an agreement by which the defendants agreed to engage and employ the plaintiff, and the plaintiff agreed to devote the whole of his time to their service. The question is, what is the meaning of the word 'employ' as used in this agreement? It seems to me clear, and if authority be required we find it in the case of *Emmens* v. *Elderton,* (1853) 13 C.B. 495; 138 E.R. 1292 that the word 'employ' is capable of two meanings—to retain in service, or to give actual work to be done by the person employed. . . . There was evidence given at the trial that in order that a salesman may duly perform his duties he must be in constant contact with the market. In that state of things there is some approximation to the case of an actor; but, as there are other elements pointed out by my learned brethren to which they attach weight, I am not prepared to differ from the conclusion at which they have arrived."

ONTARIO ASPHALT BLOCK CO. *v.* MONTREUIL
Ontario. Supreme Court of Canada. 1915. 52 S.C.R. 541

Ontario Asphalt Block Co. leased from Montreuil certain land and a water lot on a lake for ten years from 1903 with an option to purchase for $22,000, Montreuil promising to deliver a deed in fee simple free of incumbrances. Ontario Asphalt agreed to pay a rent of $1,000 a year and to construct a dock costing at least $6,000, which was to become Montreuil's property unless the option to purchase was exercised. In fact the Company built a dock costing about $200,000. In 1908 it discovered that Montreuil had only a life estate in the land, and that his children, all of whom were over twenty-one in 1903, were entitled to the remainder. The water lot belonged to Montreuil in fee. At this time at least $80,000 had been spent on the dock and factory. At a later trial Mr. Fleming, a lawyer and secretary of Ontario Asphalt, testified: "A. . . . we had not any idea but what when we spent the first dollar on the property that we had purchased under the option we could not afford to spend the money without doing that. . . . Q. Why did you take the lease instead of buying out-right at the first? A. Because $1,000 a year is less than 5% on the purchase price of $22,000, and in addition to that $22,000 meant a lot to us in establishing a plant of this sort. . . . His Lordship: And then you went right on after the discovery; after 1908 you went on? A. Yes, my Lord, we had to take care of the business; it was a case of necessity. Mr. Rodd: What position would your client have been in if you had not gone on? A. We would not have been able to have taken care of the increase of business; business has to grow or go back, we could not stand still." Attempts by the Company to have Montreuil persuade his children to join in a deed were ignored. An action was commenced for specific performance of the promise to convey and for damages. Lennox J. at the trial awarded specific performance of the promise to convey with an abatement or reduction in the purchase price in the proportion in which a fee simple exceeded Montreuil's life estate in value at the end of the term. He also awarded damages beyond the abatement because Montreuil "by his deliberate and continuous silence invited and encouraged the plaintiff company to continue its improvements and expenditures and to believe, as it evidently did believe, that the defendant would be able to and would in fact carry out his contract." The Court of Appeal varied the judgment by refusing the damages beyond the abatement. Meredith C.J.O. said, for the Court, ". . . It is, I think, clear, upon principle, that a purchaser who elects to take what the vendor can convey, with an abatement of the purchase-money for a deficiency in title is not entitled to anything beyond that. He is not bound to take what the vendor can give, but may rescind the contract or claim damages for the breach of it. . . . To give to the purchaser in a case such as this . . . damages for not getting that which the vendor cannot convey, would be, I think, directly contrary to what was decided in *Bain v. Fothergill*. . . ." Ontario Asphalt appealed to the Supreme Court of Canada.

FITZPATRICK C.J. (dissenting): The judgment of the appeal court proceeds on the rule established by the jurisprudence of the English courts that the contract for sale of real property is an exception to the ordinary rules of law applicable to the question of the damages recoverable upon a breach of contract.

This rule, first laid down in the case of *Flureau* v. *Thornhill* (1776), 2 W. Bl. 1078; 96 E.R. 635, is that upon a contract for the purchase of real estate if the vendor, without fraud, is incapable of making a good title the intended purchaser is not entitled to any compensation for the loss of his bargain. . . .

The rule in *Flureau* v. *Thornhill* finds little favour in the United States. In Sedgwick on Damages, 9th ed., vol. 3, at p. 2121, we read:—

"If the defendant fails to convey because he has not a good title, he is always liable in substantial damages. This is commonly called the United States Supreme Court Rule, and represents one extreme of the series of principles of which the highest English court has adopted the other extreme. It seems to be the correct one on principle."

I have thought it well to make the foregoing remarks as perhaps affording support to the appeal, but the real ground on which I rest my judgment is that in any event this case is outside the transactions to which in its widest interpretation the rule making exception to the general law of contracts has any application. . . .

Is it not obvious that the damages sustained by the apellant by reason of the failure of the respondent to implement his agreement are altogether special and by no means such loss of a bargain as alone is contemplated by the rule in *Flureau* v. *Thornhill*?

I think it is impossible to hold that such an agreement is to be governed by an admittedly anomalous rule of law in England, one based on reasons which may have little application here; presupposing entirely different conditions and intended to have application not to any damage sustained by the purchaser, but solely to the possible loss of his prospective profit on a resale of the property.

It cannot, I think, be necessary to treat this very special rule as absolutely inflexible regardless of all attendant conditions. . . .

Then as to the remarks of Chief Justice Meredith concerning the appellants' means of knowledge of the respondent's title. The latter being only tenant for life could, of course, make no demise to endure beyond his own life and, therefore, was in no position to make the lease for ten years, still less to covenant for its renewal for a further term of ten years. The lessee could not call for or dispute the lessor's title and until the option to purchase was exercised there was no contract for sale which would have entitled the appellant to call for the title.

The Chief Justice says that the appellant had the same opportunity of knowing what the nature of the respondent's title was as the respondent himself had. I think this must be going too far in any case; the respondent must surely as devisee under the will of his father be credited with better knowledge than the appellant. But in any case such knowledge would have been accidental in this particular case and cannot, I think, affect the principle involved.

That it would have been the more prudent course for the appellant when making the contract to have insisted on immediate preliminary proof of the respondent's title may be admitted and perhaps the company may have to suffer loss in any event as a consequence of not doing so, but that is no reason for relieving the respondent from the liability for failure to fulfil his contractual obligations. . . .

DAVIES J. (dissenting): The question in this case to be determined is whether the facts bring it within the rule of law laid down in *Bain* v. *Fothergill* (1873), L.R. 7 H.L. 158, that if a vendor of land without fraud is incapable of making a good title the intending purchaser is not entitled to recover compensation in damages for the loss of his bargain.

That rule has for many years been adopted as part of their jurisprudence by the Ontario courts and it is not my desire or intention to call that adoption in question.

The question arising in this appeal is not whether that rule is in force in Ontario, but whether the facts of this case bring it within the rule.

I understand a majority of the court holds that the rule applies and I desire to state very shortly my reasons for dissenting.

In the case of *Day* v. *Singleton,* [1899] 2 Ch. 320, the Court of Appeal held that:

"A purchaser of leasehold property which the vendor cannot assign without a licence from his lessor, is entitled to damages (beyond return of the deposit, with interest and expenses) for loss of his bargain by reason of the vendor's omission to do his best to procure such licence."

In delivering the judgment of the court, Lord Lindley M.R. said, p. 328:—

"Singleton never asked the lessors to accept Day as their tenant without a bar and consequently it would be for him, Singleton to show that if he had asked them they would have refused."

Now, in the present case, it is contended that when the respondent Montreuil ascertained that he could not give the Ontario Asphalt Company a good title and that he had only a life estate, the remainder being in his children, it became his duty as between him and the Asphalt Company with whom he had covenanted to give a good title to do all that lay in his power to enable him to carry out his contract and to shew that he had applied to his children to join with him in conveying to the Asphalt Company and that they had refused to do so.

There was evidence that they did join with him upon request in the conveyance of other portions of the same property, but no evidence that he had applied to them to do so with respect to the property in dispute.

I confess I was much struck with this argument. If it was Montreuil's duty "to do all that lay in his power" to give appellants a good title, then it seems reasonable that it would be part of his duty to the Asphalt Company under the peculiar facts of this case to try and obtain the signature of his children to the deed and so complete his contracts with them. . . .

I do not desire, however, to rest my judgment upon that ground, but rather upon the ground that the special facts of this case and the special terms of the lease to the company with the option of purchase at the end of the term of ten years, provided six months' notice of the lessee's intention to purchase was given, together with the covenant on the lessor, Montreuil's part to convey a good title in fee simple, and a covenant from the lessee to build a dock on the demised premises within a year from the granting of the lease at a cost of *at least* $6,000, which dock was to become the property of the lessor at the end of the demised term, unless the lessee purchased under his option, all combine to convince me that this is not a case in which the rule in *Bain* v. *Fothergill* should be applied, but rather one in which on the neglect, refusal or inability of the lessor to comply with his covenant to give a good title free from incumbrance substantial damages should be awarded.

The evidence shewed that the company had after entering upon the lands under the lease erected an expensive manufacturing plant and docks partly on the leased upland and partly on the water lot in front of it as to which latter lot Montreuil had obtained a grant from the Crown, the whole expenditure aggregating $200,000, besides yearly betterments and improvements. A part of this expenditure at least was made in pursuance of respondent's covenant in the lease to expend at least $6,000 in dock construction.

The Appellate Division, reversing the trial judge, who had decreed specific performance and an abatement in the price amounting to substantial damages the latter to be determined on a reference, directed that the abatement in the purchase money should be based upon the value of the interest in the lands which the defendant could convey, having regard to the "purchase price" of the whole and refusing other damages beyond the abatement.

I cannot accede to the principle on which the Appellate Court has directed the abatement, basing it upon the stipulated purchase price and limiting it to that while ignoring the expenditure which as part of the consideration for the granting of the lease the lessees covenanted to make in building a dock on the lands.

This expenditure, the minimum amount of which was placed at $6,000 and the maximum of which might reach $60,000 or more, was really and substantially as much a part of the purchase price as the $22,000 mentioned and has just as much right to be considered in determining what abatement should be made as the latter sum.

But over and beyond that I do not think the case is one within the principle of *Bain* v. *Fothergill,* nor that substantial damages should be denied the vendee. That principle is as Lindley M.R. says in *Day* v. *Singleton,* "an anomalous rule based upon and justified by difficulties in shewing a good title to real property in this country, *but one which ought not to be extended in cases to which the reasons on which it is based do not apply.*"

Now, I take it that one of the reasons on which the rule is based is that it is not within the contemplation of both parties in the ordinary case of a contract for sale of land, that if the vendor is incapable of making a good title the intending purchaser is to receive compensation for the loss of his bargain beyond the expenses he has incurred.

But if there are special facts in the case shewing that it was and must have been in contemplation of both parties that failure on the part of the vendor to carry out his covenant to

"execute and deliver to the purchaser a good and sufficient deed in fee simple of the land."

must inevitably cause the intending purchaser great damage, as was the case here; and if, in addition, the purchaser has bound himself on the faith of this covenant to expend very large sums of money on dock and other improvements as the purchaser did here, then I say in the event of the vendor failing to give the good title he covenanted to give, the common law rule as to damages for breach of contract applies and the "anomalous rule" laid down in *Bain* v. *Fothergill*, relating to ordinary contracts between vendor and vendee with respect to the sale of lands does not apply.

I do not contend that any damages can be recovered in respect of anything that the purchaser did or incurred after he discovered the defect in the title; I limit my observations to those incurred by him before such discovery.

For these reasons, I would allow the appeal.

IDINGTON J.: I think the judgment appealed from is right for the reasons assigned in support thereof by the learned Chief Justice for Ontario.

The case seems a hard one, but that is no reason for our adopting bad law and disturbing the minds of those who prefer that well-settled law should be upheld. . . .

ANGLIN J.: Admitting the applicability of the rule laid down in *Bain* v. *Fothergill* to the original option in this case, the appellants have sought to bring it within the qualifications upon that rule recognized in *Day* v. *Singleton.* But in the latter case the Court of Appeal, as the judgment of Lord Lindley shews (p. 328), took the view that the correspondence between Singleton's solicitors and the lessor established that if Singleton (the vendor of the leasehold) did not actually procure the refusal of the lessors' assent to the assignment to Day, he

"certainly made no effort to obtain it . . . as it was his duty to do . . . and it ought to be inferred as against Singleton that the lessors would have accepted Day if Singleton had asked them to do so."

The decision there proceeded upon the fact, held to have been sufficiently proven, that it was within the vendor's powers to carry out his contract and that he refused or neglected to take the means available. Here the plaintiffs rely upon the fact that the defendant maintained silence after his inability to make title had become known and they had asked him to obtain confirmation of the option from the remaindermen, the fact that the remaindermen had (under what circumstances, or for what consideration does not appear) confirmed the title of some other grantees of the defendant who were in like plight with the plaintiffs, and the further fact that, in answer to the plaintiff's suit for specific performance, other defences were set up in addition to that of inability to make title. I am quite unable to find in these bald facts—and the plaintiffs have nothing else—enough to warrant an inference that the defendant after discovery of the defect in his title made no effort to procure the concurrance of the remaindermen; still less do I find enough to warrant the inference that such an effort, if made would have been successful.

The appeal, in my opinion, fails and should be dismissed with costs.

[The opinion of Idington J. is drastically cut. Duff and Brodeur JJ. agreed in dismissing the appeal. The decision is thus four to two for dismissal.]

NOTE. In *Bain* v. *Fothergill*, upon which the majority relied, the defendants paid into Court a sum sufficient to cover the deposit, interest and expenses. What happened to that money is not apparent from the report, but it would appear that the Court made no decision of the question of damages based on reliance. Is there good reason for distinguishing between the expectation interest and the reliance interest here? Is there good reason for following *Bain* v. *Fothergill* in Canada, where questions of title are somewhat simpler due to the widespread use of the registry system or the Torrens system?

MONTREUIL *v.* THE ONTARIO ASPHALT BLOCK COMPANY. 1922. 63 S.C.R. 401. After getting their order for specific performance of the conveyance of the water lot, and the estate pur autre vie in the land, Ontario Asphalt remained in possession until August of 1918. Montreuil having died in January of 1918 the children brought an action for ejectment. Ontario Asphalt relied on what is now section 38(1) of *The Conveyancing and Law of Property Act,* R.S.O. 1960, c. 66, which provides:

"38. (1) Where a person makes lasting improvements on land under the belief that it is his own, he or his assigns are entitled to a lien upon it to the extent of the amount by which its value is enhanced by the improvements, or are entitled or may be required to retain the land if the court is of opinion or requires that this should be done, according as may under all circumstances of the case be most just, making compensation for the land, if retained, as the court directs."

The Court held, Idington and Duff JJ. dissenting, that a lessee with an option to purchase was not an "owner" within the meaning of the section. Anglin J. said, at p. 426, "This statute gives the court the extraordinary power of depriving a lawful owner of his property against his will, although for a compensation. . . . The condition on which a jurisdiction so much in derogation of common law right is conferred must be strictly construed and fully satisfied." But the Court went on to hold that Ontario Asphalt was entitled to equitable relief by way of compensation for its improvements prior to the discovery that Montreuil was not the owner of the fee but merely had a life estate.

THE VENDORS AND PURCHASERS ACT
Ontario. Revised Statutes. 1960. Chapter 414

5. Every contract for the sale and purchase of land shall, unless otherwise stipulated, be deemed to provide that, . . .

(c) the vendor has thirty days in which to remove any objection made to the title, but if he is unable or unwilling to remove any objection that the purchaser is not willing to waive, he may cancel the contract and return any deposit made but is not otherwise liable to the purchaser. . . .

[This section was first introduced in 1926, *The Vendors and Purcasers Act, 1926* (Ontario, c. 41). What effect, if any, would this section have had in the *Ontario Asphalt* case?]

NURSE *v.* BARNS
England. 1664. Sir T. Raymond 77; 83 E.R. 43

The plaintiff declares, that the defendent in consideration of £10 promised to let him enjoy certain iron mills for six months; and it appeared that the iron mills were worth but £20 per annum, and yet damages were given to £500 by reason of the loss of stock laid in; and *per Curiam* the jury may well find such damages, for they are not bound to give only the £10 but also all the special damages.

PAYZU LIMITED *v.* SAUNDERS
England. Court of Appeal. [1919] 2 K.B. 581

By a contract in writing dated November 9, 1917, the defendant, who was a dealer in silk agreed to sell the plaintiffs 200 pieces of crepe de chine at 4s. 6d. a yard and 200 pieces at 5s. 11d. a yard, "delivery as required January to September, 1918; conditions 2½ per cent 1 month," which meant that payment for goods delivered up to the twentieth day of the month should be made on the twentieth day of the following month, subject to 2½ per cent discount. At the request of the plaintiffs, the defendants delivered, in November 1917, a certain quantity of the goods under the contract, the price of which amounted to £76 less 2½ per cent discount. On December 21st the plaintiffs drew a cheque in favor of the defendant in payment of these goods, but the cheque was never received by the defendant. Early in January, 1918, the defendant telephoned to the plaintiffs asking why she had not received a cheque. The plaintiffs then drew another cheque, but owing to a delay in obtaining the signature of one of the plaintiffs' directors, this cheque was not sent to the defendant until January 16th. On that day the plaintiffs gave an order by telephone for further deliveries under the contract. The defendant in the belief, which was in fact erroneous, that the plaintiffs' financial position was such that they could not have met the cheque which they alleged had been drawn in December, wrote to the plaintiffs on January 16, refusing to make any further deliveries under the contract, unless the plaintiffs paid cash with each order. The plaintiffs refused to do this, and after some further correspondence brought this action claiming damages for breach of contract. The damages claimed were the difference between the market price in the middle of February 1918, and the contract price of the two classes of goods, the difference alleged being respectively 1s. 3d. and 1s. 4d. a yard.

McCardie J: . . . in my opinion, the defendant's letter of January 16 did in fact and in law amount to an unjustifiable refusal by her to carry out her contractual obligations, for she announced in clear terms that she would thenceforth deliver no further goods to the plaintiffs under the contract unless the plaintiffs paid cash to cover each invoice. The market price of these goods was rising from the beginning of January and continued to rise up to the middle of February. The plaintiffs claim to be entitled to damages based on the market price at that date. I find as a fact that the market prices in February were respectively 6d. and 7d. per yard in excess of the contract prices. The plaintiffs did not in fact purchase goods as against their contract with the defendant. They asserted that the market was so bare of goods as to render purchases impracticable.

Now a serious question of law arises on the question of damages. I find as a fact that the defendant was ready and willing to supply the goods to the plaintiffs at the times and places specified in the contract, provided the plaintiffs paid cash on delivery. Mr. Matthews [of counsel for the plaintiffs] argued with characteristic vigour and ability that the plaintiffs were entitled to ignore that offer on the ground that a person who has repudiated a contract cannot place the other party to the contract under an obligation to diminish his loss by accepting a new offer made by the party in default.

The question is one of juristic importance. What is the rule of law as to the duty to mitigate damages? I will first refer to the judgment of Cockburn C.J., in *Frost* v. *Knight,* (1872), L.R. 7 Ex. 111, 115, where he said: "In assessing the damages for breach of the performance, a jury will of course take into account whatever the plaintiff has done, or has had the means of doing and, as a prudent man, ought in reason to have done, whereby his loss has been or would have been, diminished."...

The question, therefore, is what a prudent person ought reasonably to do in order to mitigate his loss arising from a breach of contract. I feel no inclination to allow in a mercantile dispute an unhappy indulgence in far-fetched resentment or an undue sensitiveness to slights or unfortunately worded letters. Business often gives rise to certain asperities. But I agree that the plaintiffs in deciding whether to accept the defendant's offer were fully entitled to consider the terms in which the offer was made, its bona fides or otherwise, its relation to their own business methods and financial position, and all the circumstances of the case; and it must be remembered that an acceptance of the offer would not preclude an action for damages for the actual loss sustained. Many illustrations might be given of the extraordinary results which would follow if the plaintiffs were entitled to reject the defendant's offer and incur a substantial measure of loss which would have been avoided by their acceptance of the offer. The plaintiffs were in fact in a position to pay cash for the goods but instead of accepting the defendant's offer, which was made perfectly bona fide, the plaintiffs permitted themselves to sustain a large measure of loss which as prudent and reasonable people, they ought to have avoided. But the fact that the plaintiffs have claimed damages on an erroneous principle does not preclude me from awarding to them such damages as they have in fact suffered, calculated upon the correct bases. . . . They have suffered serious and substantial business inconvenience, and I conceive that I am entitled to award them damages for that. . . . Moreover, even if the plantiffs had accepted the defendant's offer, they would nevertheless have lost a very useful period of credit which the contract gave them. Taking into consideration all the circumstances of the case I have come to the conclusion that the right sum to award as damages is £50. I give judgment for the plaintiffs for that amount, and in view of the important points involved, I give costs on the High Court Scale.

[The plaintiffs appealed to the Court of Appeal on the question of damages.]

BANKS L.J.: At the trial of this case the defendant, the present respondent, raised two points: first, that she had commited no breach of the contract of sale, and secondly that, if there was a breach, yet she had offered and was always ready and willing to supply the pieces of silk, the subject of the contract, at the contract price for cash; that it was unreasonable on the part of the appellants not to accept that offer, and that therefore they cannot claim damages beyond what they would have lost by paying cash with each order instead of having a month's credit and a discount of 2½ per cent. We must take it that this was the offer made by the respondent. The case was fought and the learned judge has given judgment on that footing. It is true that the correspondence suggests that the respondent was at one time claiming an increased price. But in this court it must be taken that the offer was to supply the contract goods at the contract price except that payment was to be by cash instead of being on credit.

In these circumstances the only question is whether the appellants can establish that as a matter of law they were not bound to consider any offer made by the respondent because of the attitude she had taken up. . . .

It is plain that the question what is reasonable for a person to do in mitigation of his damages cannot be a question of law but must be one of fact in the circumstances of each particular case. There may be cases where as matter of fact it would be unreasonable to expect a plaintiff to consider any offer made in view of the treatment he had received from the defendant. If he had been rendering personal services and had been dismissed after being accused in presence of others of being a thief, and if after that his employer had offered to take him back into his service, most persons would think he was justified in refusing the offer and that it would be unreasonable to ask him in this way to mitigate the damages in action for wrongful dismissal. But that is not to state a principle of law, but a conclusion of fact to be arrived at on a consideration of all the circumstances of the case. Mr. Matthews complained that the respondents had treated his clients so badly that it would be unreasonable to expect them to listen to any proposition she might make. I do not agree. In my view each party was ready to accuse the other of conduct unworthy of a high commercial reputation and there was nothing to justify the appellants in refusing to consider the respondent's offer. I think the learned judge came to a proper conclusion on the facts, and that the appeal must be dismissed.

SCRUTTON L.J.: I am of the same opinion. Whether it be more correct to say that a plaintiff must minimize his damages, or to say that he can recover no more than he would have suffered if he had acted reasonably, because any further damages do not reasonably follow from the defendant's breach, the result is the same. . . . In certain cases of personal service it may be unreasonable to expect a plaintiff to consider an offer from the other party who has grossly injured him; but in commercial contracts it is generally reasonable to accept an offer from the party in default. However, it is always a question of fact. About the law there is no difficulty. *Appeal dismissed.*

[Parts of the opinions reproduced, as well as Eve J.'s, are omitted.]

WITHERS *v.* GENERAL THEATRE CORPORATION, LIMITED

England. Court of Appeal. [1933] 2 K.B. 536

The contract between the plaintiff and the defendant company, which was dated June 19, 1931, provided that he should appear and perform his sketch at the London Palladium for three consecutive weeks commencing July 6, 1931, at a gross salary of £300 per week, he providing the supporting actors and properties. On the margin of the printed contract was the following clause, initialled by the plaintiff: "In consideration of this agreement it is understood and agreed that notwithstanding anything in this agreement to the contrary, should the management so desire, the artiste agrees to transfer these engagements to any hall owned, controlled by, or associated with the management either in London or the provinces without charging transfer expenses." During the negotiations the plaintiff was told by the defendants: "We may give you two weeks at the Palladium and one week at another hall. This will, of course, depend on how you stand up at the Palladium during the first two weeks."

The plaintiff did not wish to start at once at the Palladium with a company which he engaged in England, as it required considerable rehearsal to get the sketch to work neatly and to time. He accordingly asked to have a preliminary trial week at Portsmouth at a considerably lower salary. He started on the week's performance at Portsmouth, and on the Monday the performance went all wrong: the properties did not work at the right time, and the supporting artistes did not work with the properties at the right time. On Wednesday, July 1, the Palladium authorities went down to Portsmouth and saw the performance, and came to the conclusion that the sketch would not be in a fit state to be performed at the Palladium on the following Monday, and they communicated their decision to the plaintiff, who protested. On July 2, 1931, the defendants gave the plaintiff written notice that they did not intend to allow him to perform at the London Palladium under the agreement.

The plaintiff thereupon brought the present action, claiming that by reason of the defendants' breach and repudiation of the contract he had sustained loss and damage, including loss of publicity and reputation as a variety artiste and performer.

SCRUTTON L.J.: . . . Therefore it is quite clear that the contract is not a contract under which Mr. Withers has an absolute right to appear at the Palladium, it is a contract under which the defendants have an option to require the plaintiff to transfer the engagement to some other hall which they control.

Now where a defendant has alternative ways of performing a contract at his option, there is a well settled rule as to how the damages for breach of such a contract are to be assessed. . . . A very common instance explaining how that works is this: A. undertakes to sell to B. 800 to 1200 tons of a certain commodity; he does not supply B. with any commodity. On what basis are the damages to be fixed? They are fixed in this way. A. would perform his contract if he supplied 800 tons, and the damages must therefore be assessed on the basis that he has not supplied 800 tons, and not on the basis that he has not supplied 1200 tons, not on the basis that he has not supplied the average, 1000 tons, and not on the basis that he might reasonably be expected, whatever the contract was, to supply more than 800 tons. The damages are assessed . . . on the basis that the defendant will perform the contract in the way most benficial to himself and not in the way that is most beneficial to the plaintiff. . . .

[Only a small part of Scrutton L.J.'s opinion is reproduced. Greer and Romer L.JJ. also gave opinions in agreement. Most of the discussion is concerned with damages for loss of publicity.]

COTTER *v.* GENERAL PETROLEUMS LTD.

Alberta. Supreme Court of Canada. [1950] 4 D.L.R. 609

A lease for 160 acres contained a covenant on the part of the lessee to commence drilling for oil within six months and to drill to a depth of 5,500 feet. He could obtain an extension of six months on payment to the lessor of $1,000. The lessee sublet 80 acres to the respondents who agreed to drill the well, the cost of drilling to be recovered as a share in the sale of the product of the well. In May and June, 1948, wells about a mile away were abandoned after being drilled to about 5,500 feet and the respondents decided at the end of June, 1948, not to commence drilling. The appellant lessee took the position that the respondents were bound to drill a well, and the respondents replied that in view of the location it would be a needless waste of money. On August 31, 1948, the appellant sued for $100,000 damages. The trial judge held that the respondents were obliged to drill by August 1, 1948 and were in breach. He assessed damages at $54,500, being $53,500, the admitted cost of the drilling, and $1,000 paid by the appellant for an extension of the lease. Geologists gave evidence on the likelihood of there being any oil, and the finding was that the chances were far from favourable but couldn't be completely ruled out. The Court of Appeal reversed on other grounds.

CARTWRIGHT J.: . . . I respectfully agree with the learned trial judge that that the respondents are liable in damages to the appellant for failure to drill a well to the prescribed depth. . . . It remains to be considered on what principle and at what amount the damages should be assessed. . . . In the case at bar if the respondents had carried out the contract the appellant would not have had to pay the $1,000 for a 6 months' extension which he did in fact pay to the head-lessor. The circumstances as to the necessity of making such payment were known to the parties and I agree with the learned trial Judge that that sum is recoverable. What further benefits would have resulted to the appellant from the performance of the contract? If the respondents had drilled the well to the prescribed depth and it had proved a producer, the appellant would have received, (a) his share of the proceeds and, (b) the benefit of having the head lease validated, by the performance of the lessee's covenant to drill, not only as to the 80 acres described in the sublease but as to the whole 160 acres described in the head lease. If on the other hand, as, from the evidence of the geologists, would seem much more probable, the well had proved a failure the appellant would not have received benefit (a) but would have received benefit (b). It must be remembered however that as a result of the respondents' breach the appellant holds the whole 160 acres free from any claim of the respondents. No part of the consideration which under the contract would have passed to the respondents has passed, except that from April 21, 1948, until some time in June, 1948, when they repudiated the agreement, the respondents had rights in the 80 acres and the appellant was not free to deal therewith. Under these circumstances, I do not think that the cost of drilling is the proper measure of damages. Suppose that instead of the consideration set out in the contract the appellant had agreed to pay the respondents $53,500 to drill the well and the respondents had repudiated the contract before the date set for the commencement of the work and before any monies had been paid to them. In such a case by analogy to the rule in the case of building contracts the measure of damages would seem to be the difference (if any) between the price of the work agreed upon and the cost to which the appellant was actually put in its completion. I think it will be found that those cases in which it has been held that the cost of drilling is the proper measure of damages are cases where the consideration to be given for the drilling had actually passed to the defendant. Examples of such cases are *Cunningham* v. *Insinger*, [1924], 2 D.L.R. 433, S.C.R. 8, and *Pell* v. *Shearman* (1855), 10 Exch. 766, 156 E.R. 650 (a contract to sink a shaft).

The appellant did not seek to put his case on the ground that by reason of the breach he stood to lose the head lease, but rather that he intended to make and was in process of making other arrangements to have a well drilled. In my view, the proper measure of his damages under the circumstances of this case is the difference between the value to him of the consideration for which the respondents agreed to drill the well and the value to him of the consideration which, acting reasonably, he should find it necessary to give to have the well drilled by others. I am unable to find in the record evidence on which the damages can be assessed on this basis. It is well settled that the mere fact that the damages are difficult to estimate and cannot be assessed with certainty does not relieve the party in default of the necessity of paying damages and is no ground for awarding only nominal damages, but the onus of proving his damages still rests upon the plaintiff. The evidence of the appellant given at the trial on December 3, 1948, was to the effect that he and his associates had been and still were in negotiation with an oil company but that they had found themselves forced to deal with the whole 160 acres instead of 80 acres. As Mr. Steer pointed out there is no evidence as to the terms offered by such company and such terms may have been more or less advantageous to the appellant than those contained in the contract sued on. It would have been open to the appellant to have delayed bringing his action until the completion of his arrangements to have the well drilled by which time the damages, if any, would have been more easily ascertained. But the appellant, as he had a right to do, brought his action to trial before that date. There is no complaint that any evidence he wished to tender in support of his claim for damages was rejected, nor was there any request made for a reference to fix the damages and the case must be decided upon the evidence in the record. In my view, there is no evidence to support an award of damages other than the $1,000 paid for the extension of the time for drilling. If the evidence showed that the appellant had suffered or must of necessity suffer substantial damages, over and above the $1,000 already mentioned, by reason of the respondents' breach, the Court should, I think, seek some means of arriving at a proper assessment, but in my view the most that the evidence can be said to indicate is a probability of some loss. It is possible that there has been no loss at all. . . .

Appeal allowed.

[Rinfret C.J.C. joined with Kerwin J. in a judgment allowing the appeal, and Fauteux J. joined with Cartwright J. Locke J. dissented on other grounds.]

CARSON *v.* WILLITTS. 1930. 65 O.L.R. 456 (Ontario. Appellate Division). A contract to bore three oil wells. The defendant bored one well and refused to carry on. MASTEN J.A.: "Then what is the basis on which this court should now direct the damages to be assessed? In my opinion, what the plaintiff lost by the refusal of the defendant to bore two more wells was a sporting or gambling chance that valuable oil or gas would be found when the two further wells were bored. If the wells had been bored and no oil or gas of value had been found, the effect would be that the plaintiff has lost nothing by the refusal of the defendant to go on boring. On the other hand, if valuable oil or gas had been discovered, by the boring of these two wells, he had lost substantially. It may not be easy to compute what that chance was worth to the plaintiff, but the difficulty in estimating the quantum is no reason for refusing to award any damages.

"In Mayne on Damages, 10th ed., p. 6, it is said:—

" 'A distinction must be drawn between cases where absence of evidence makes it impossible to assess damages, and cases where the assessment is difficult because of the nature of the damage proved. In the former case only nominal damages can be recovered. In the latter case, however, the difficulty of assessment is no ground for refusing substantial damages.' "

GROVES v. JOHN WUNDER CO.
Minnesota. Supreme Court. 1939. 286 N.W. 235

STONE J.: Action for breach of contract. Plaintiff got judgment for a little over $15,000. Sorely disappointed by that sum, he appeals.

In August, 1927, S. J. Groves & Sons Company, a corporation (hereinafter mentioned simply as Groves), owned a tract of 24 acres of Minneapolis suburban real estate. It was served or easily could be reached by railroad trackage. It is zoned as heavy industrial property. But for lack of development of the neighborhood its principal value thus far may have been in the deposit of sand and gravel which it carried. The Groves company had a plant on the premises for excavating and screening the gravel. Near by defendant owned and was operating a similar plant.

In August, 1927, Groves and defendant made the involved contract. For the most part it was a lease from Groves, as lessor, to defendant as lessee; its term seven years. Defendant agreed to remove the sand and gravel and to leave the property "at a uniform grade, substantially the same as the grade now existing at the roadway . . . on said premises, and that in stripping the overburden . . . it will use said overburden for the purpose of maintaining and establishing said grade."

Under the contract defendant got the Groves screening plant. The transfer thereof and the right to remove the sand and gravel made the consideration moving from Groves to defendant, except that defendant incidentally got rid of Groves as a competitor. On defendant's part it paid Groves $105,000. So that from the outset, on Groves' part the contract was executed except for defendant's right to continue using the property for the stated term. (Defendant had a right to renewal which it did not exercise.)

Defendant breached the contract deliberately. It removed from the premises only "the richest and best of the gravel" and wholly failed, according to the findings, "to perform and comply with the terms, conditions, and provisions of said lease . . . with respect to the condition in which the surface of the demised premises was required to be left." Defendant surrendered the premises, not substantially at the grade required by the contract "nor at any uniform grade." Instead, the ground was "broken, rugged, and uneven." Plaintiff sues as assignee and successor in right of Groves.

As the contract was construed below, the finding is that to complete its performance 288,495 cubic yards of overburden would need to be excavated, taken from the premises, and deposited elsewhere. The reasonable cost of doing that was found to be upwards of $60,000. But, if defendant had left the premises at the uniform grade required by the lease, the reasonable value of the property on the determinative date would have been only $12,160. The judgment was for that sum, including interest, thereby nullifying plaintiff's claim that cost of completing the contract rather than difference in value of the land was the measure of damages. The gauge of damage adopted by the decision was the difference between the market value of plaintiff's land in the condition it was when the contract was made and what it would have been if defendant had performed. The one question for us arises upon plaintiff's assertion that he was entitled, not to that difference in value, but to the reasonable cost to him of doing the work called for by the contract which defendant left undone.

1. Defendant's breach of contract was wilful. There was nothing of good faith about it. Hence, that the decision below handsomely rewards bad faith and deliberate breach of contract is obvious. That is not allowable. Here

the rule is well settled, ... that where the contractor wilfully and fraudulently varies from the terms of a construction contract he cannot sue thereon and have the benefit of the equitable doctrine of substantial performance. That is the rule generally....

2. In reckoning damages for breach of a building or construction contract, the law aims to give the disappointed promisee, so far as money will do it, what he was promised....

Never before, so far as our decisions show, has it even been suggested that lack of value in the land furnished to the contractor who had bound himself to improve it any escape from the ordinary consequences of a breach of the contract....

Even in case of substantial performance in good faith, the resulting defects being remediable, it is error to instruct that the measure of damage is "the difference in value between the house as it was and as it would have been if constructed according to contract." The "correct doctrine" is that the cost of remedying the defect is the "proper" measure of damages....

Value of the land (as distinguished from the value of the intended product of the contract, which ordinarily will be equivalent to its reasonable cost) is no proper part of any measure of damages for wilful breach of a building contract. The reason is plain.

The summit from which to reckon damages from trespass to real estate is its actual value at the moment. The owner's only right is to be compensated for the deterioration in value caused by the tort. That is all he has lost. But not so if a contract to improve the same land has been breached by the contractor who refuses to do the work, especially where, as here, he has been paid in advance. The summit from which to reckon damages for that wrong is the hypothetical peak of accomplishment (not value) which would have been reached had the work been done as demanded by the contract.

The owner's right to improve his property is not trammeled by its small value. It is his right to erect thereon structures which will reduce its value. If that be the result, it can be of no aid to any contractor who declines performance. As said long ago in *Chamberlain* v. *Parker,* 45 N.Y. 569, 572:

"A man may do what he will with his own, ... and if he chooses to erect a monument to his caprice or folly on his premises, and employs and pays another to do it, it does not lie with a defendant who has been so employed and paid for building it, to say that his own performance would not be beneficial to the plaintiff."

To the same effect is *Restatement, Contracts,* s. 346, p. 576, Illustrations of Subsection (1), par. 4.

Suppose a contractor were suing the owner for breach of a grading contract such as this. Would any element of value, or lack of it, in the land have any relevance in reckoning damages? Of course not. The contractor would be compensated for what he had lost, i.e., his profit. Conversely, in such a case as this, the owner is entitled to compensation for what he has lost, that is, the work or structure which he has been promised, for which he has paid, and of which he has been deprived by the contractor's breach.

To diminish damages recoverable against him in proportion as there is presently small value in the land would favor the faithless contractor. It would also ignore and so defeat plaintiff's right to contract and build for the future. To justify such a course would require more of the prophetic vision that judges possess. This factor is important when the subject matter is trackage property in the margin of such an area of population and industry as that of the Twin Cities. . . .

[Under] a construction contract, the thing lost by a breach such as we have here is a physical structure or accomplishment, a promised and paid for alteration in land. That is the "injury" for which the law gives him compensation. Its only appropriate measure is the cost of performance.

It is suggested that because of little or no value in his land the owner may be unconscionably enriched by such a reckoning. The answer is that there can be no unconscionable enrichment, no advantage upon which the law will frown, when the result is but to give one party to a contract only what the other has promised; particularly where, as here, the delinquent has had full payment for the promised performance.

3. It is said by the Restatement, Contracts, s 346, Comment b:

"Sometimes defects in a completed structure cannot be physically remedied without tearing down and rebuilding, at a cost that would be imprudent and unreasonable. The law does not require damages to be measured by a method requiring such economic waste. If no such waste is involved, the cost of remedying the defect is the amount awarded as compensation for failure to render the promised performance."

The "economic waste" declaimed against by the decisions applying that rule has nothing to do with the value in money of the real estate, or even with the product of the contract. The waste avoided is only that which would come from wrecking a physical structure completed, or nearly so, under the contract. . . . Absent such waste, as it is in this case, the rule of the Restatement, Contracts, s 346, is that "the cost of remedying the defect is the amount awarded as compensation for failure to render the promised performance." That means that defendants here are liable to plaintiff for the reasonable cost of doing what defendants promised to do and have wilfully declined to do. . . .

The judgment must be reversed with a new trial to follow.

JULIUS J. OLSON J. (dissenting): . . .

Since there is no issue of fact, we should limit our inquiry to the single legal problem presented: What amount in money will adequately compensate plaintiff for his loss caused by defendant's failure to render performance? . . .

As the rule of damages to be applied in any given case has for its purpose compensation, not punishment, we must be ever mindful that, "if the application of a particular rule for measuring damages to given facts results in more than compensation, it is at once apparent that the wrong rule has been adopted." *Crowley* v. *Burns Boiler Co.,* 110 N.W. 969, 973.

We have here then a situation where, concededly, if the contract had been performed, plaintiff would have had property worth, in round numbers, no more than $12,000. If he is to be awarded damages in an amount exceeding $60,000 he will be receiving at least 500 per cent more than his property, properly leveled to grade by actual performance, was intrinsically worth when the breach occurred. To so conclude is to give him something far beyond what the parties had in mind or contracted for. There is no showing made, nor any finding suggested, that this property was unique, specially desirable for a particular or personal use, or of special value as to location or future use different from that of other property surrounding it. Under the circumstances here appearing, it seems clear that what the parties contracted for was to put the property in shape for general sale. And the lease contemplates just that, for by the terms thereof defendant agreed "from time to time, as the sand and gravel are removed from the various lots . . . leased, it will surrender said lots to the lessor" if of no further use to defendant "in connection with the purposes for which this lease is made."

The theory upon which plaintiff relies for application of the cost of performance rule must have for its basis cases where the property or the improvement to be made is unique or personal instead of being of the kind ordinarily governed by market values. His action is one at law for damages, not for specific performance. As there was no affirmative showing of any peculiar fitness of this property to a unique or personal use, the rule to be applied is, I think, the one applied by the court. The cases bearing directly upon this phase so hold. Briefly, the rule here applicable is this: Damages recoverable for breach of a contract to construct is the difference between the market value of the property in the condition it was when delivered to and received by plaintiff and what its market value would have been if defendant had fully complied with its terms. . . .

No one doubts that a party may contract for the doing of anything he may choose to have done (assuming what is to be done is not unlawful) "although the thing to be produced had no marketable value." In *Restatement, Contracts,* s. 346, pp. 576, 577, Illustrations of Subsection (1), par. 4, the same thought is thus stated:

"A contracts to construct a monumental fountain in B's yard for $5,000, but abandons the work after the fountain has been laid and $2,800 has been paid by B. The contemplated fountain is so ugly that it would decrease the number of possible buyers of the place. The cost of completing the fountain would be $4,000. B can get judgment for $1,800, the cost of completion less the part of price unpaid."

But that is not what plaintiff's predecessor in interest contracted for. Such a provision might well have been made, but the parties did not. They could undoubtedly have provided for liquidated damages for nonperformance . . . or they might have determined in money what the value of performance was considered to be and thereby have contractually provided a measure for failure of performance.

The opinion also suggests that this property lies in an area where the owner might rightly look for future development, being in a so-called industrial zone, and that as such he should be privileged to so hold it. This he may of course do. But let us assume that on May 1, 1934, condemnation to acquire this area had so far progressed as to leave only the question of price (market value) undetermined; that the area had been graded in strict conformity with the contract but that the actual market value of the premises was only $12,160, as found by the court and acquiesced in by plaintiff, what would the measure of his damages be? Obviously, the limit of his recovery could be no more than the then market value of his property. In that sum he has been paid with interest and costs; and he still has the fee title to the premises, something he would not possess if there had been condemnation. In what manner has plaintiff been hurt beyond the damages awarded? As to him "economic waste" is not apparent. Assume the defendant abandoned the entire project without taking a single yard of gravel therefrom but left the premises as they were when the lease was made, could plaintiff recover damages upon the basis here established? The trouble with the prevailing opinion is that here plaintiff's loss is not made the basis for the amount of his recovery but rather what it would cost the defendant. No case has been decided upon that basis until now. Plaintiff asserts that he knows of no rule "giving a different measure of damages for public contracts and for private contracts in case of nonperformance." It seems to me there is a clear distinction to be drawn with respect to the application of the rule for recoverable damages in case of breach of a public works contract from that applicable to contracts between private parties. The construction of a public building, a sewer, drainage ditch, highway, or other public work, permits of no application of the market value doctrine. There simply is and can be no "market value" as to such. And for this cogent reason there can be but one rule of damages to apply, that of cost of completion of the thing contracted to be done. I think the judgment should be affirmed.

[Stone J. delivered the judgment of the Court save that Hilton and Loring JJ. took no part, and Holt J. joined in the dissenting judgment.]

NOTE. If the "reasonable value of the property on the determinative date would have been only $12,160," why is the plaintiff entitled to $15,000 representing the $12,160 plus interest? The defendant surrendered the land to the plaintiff, must it not have some value? Should this value not be deducted from the $12,160? Professors Dawson and Harvey in their casebook on *Contracts and Contract Remedies* (1959) report (p. 28) that the case was compromised and the defendant paid $55,000 in cash settlement. In 1953 three fifths of the land was sold for $45,000 after $6,000 had been spent on levelling that portion. It was left at a higher level than planned, but still suitable for a railroad siding.

CANADIAN GENERAL ELECTRIC CO. LTD. *v.* UNITED ELECTRICAL WORKERS
Ontario. Labour Arbitration Board. 1952

By an award dated January 8, 1951, this Board [Professor Bora Laskin, Miss Idele Wilson and J. C. Adams] determined by a majority decision that the union was in breach of an express obligation of its collective agreement with the Company by reason of a work stoppage that occurred in September, 1949. The stoppage began after the 9:30 a.m. rest period on Friday, September 9, 1949 and continued throughout the rest of the day. It carried over to the whole of Monday, September 12, (by way of rotating stoppages in the various departments) and through the morning of Tuesday, September 13, terminating when all employees returned to work at 1 p.m.

By the terms of the award of January 8, 1951, this Board remained seized of the case to assess damages which the Company claimed as reparation for the Union's breach of agreement. . . .

So far as this Board is aware, this is the first time that an arbitration tribunal in Canada has been called upon to assess damages claimed by a Company against a Union for breach of a collective agreement. It is of considerable importance then that the Board should be satisfied not only by proof of the items of loss put in issue by the Company but also that applicable principles of assessment make such items appropriate for consideration. . . .

Damages are not an inevitable or invariable remedy for breach of a collective agreement obligation. Some obligations of such an agreement do not lend themselves to money compensation as a consequence of non-performance. In this case the Board is concerned with a remedy for breach of a "no-strike" clause resulting in an interruption of production. Not only are damages an appropriate remedy for a breach of this kind, but their assessment and measurement appear to involve the same considerations which operate in commercial contracts. The application of these considerations is not affected by reason of the continuing nature of the collective bargaining relationship. Nor is it an offsetting factor to urge that employer loss from an unlawful strike may be so high as to be beyond union financial ability to redress. The evolution of collective bargaining under legislative encouragement and sanction, and the introduction of self-government in industry through collective agreements containing their own machinery for enforcement, have invited, and, in fact, demanded, sobering responsibility by employers and trade unions. Part of that responsibility lies in a duty to redress established breaches of their collective engagements. The very prospect of having to answer for a breach is, or should be, a factor in securing adherence to obligations voluntarily assumed. . . .

The Company indicated that it could not practically segregate Davenport production to permit an appraisal of its net profit considered alone. It asserted only that its statistics of product lines indicated that the Davenport lines were profitable. . . .

Of the $11,035 claimed by the Company only $3,652.31 was for loss of profit. The remaining sum, $7,382.25, was for continuing expenses during the period of stoppage. . . . The items of continuing expense so apportioned included: (1) depreciation on fixed assets; (2) insurance premiums, mainly for fire insurance; (3) rent of outside property used for storage; (4) salaries of office and managerial staff; (5) local taxes; (6) telephone and telegraph service; (7) travelling expenses; and (8) heat. Salaries, depreciation and heat constituted the overwhelming portion of the total amount; in fact, the first two items represented the substance of the claim for continuing expense. Evidence was given by W. I. Hetherington, a member of a firm of chartered accountants which does accounting work for insurance adjusters, that the items of continuing expense claimed here were not as extensive as those included in the usual business interruption coverage. . . . The Board appreciated, of course, that the coverage for business interruption is a matter of direct contract and is not controlling in a matter such as the one involved in this arbitration proceeding. . . .

It is axiomatic that the Company is not entitled to double recovery. However, the claim for continuing expenses made in this case in no way overlaps the claim for lost profits. The wrongful work stoppage resulted in a loss of production on which the Company would have realized a profit but it also involved the Company in an outlay for which it is likewise entitled to be recouped. A simple illustration may be put. Suppose the loss of production were fixed at $10,000 of which $1,000 was the expected profit. The remaining amount would consist of the value of labour and materials and overhead expenses. While the Company could not recover for labour and material since there was no outlay for these items, the continuing overhead expenses stand in a different position. The claim made in this case under the heading of continuing expenses is not unusual and all of the items are in the usual category of overhead expense, that is, they are the kind of expenditures made by any manufacturer in contemplation of work being performed by the production workers. This type of expenditure can not be discontinued merely because production ceases. No doubt if the interruption of production had continued for a long period, some reduction in these expenditures could be arranged, but no issue with respect to this arises in this case, and there is accordingly no reason for disallowing any of the items claimed by the company under the heading of continuing expense, and on this branch of the Company's claim it is entitled to recover $7,382.25, this being the proportion of the Company's overall expense which can properly be attributed to that section of the Davenport Works where the work stoppage took place and adjusted by the ratio between 8 hours, the extent of the work stoppage, and the total available working time during the calendar year 1949. . . .

It remains hence for the Board to determine how much of the Company's claim for $3,652.31 (representing lost profits) should be allowed. Since the Company has relied on a measuring formula which has inherent defects as already pointed out, and since there was nothing to indicate that the formula erred in favour of the Union rather than the Company, it is entirely proper to apply it against the Company and, accordingly, to diminish the allowance for lost profits. The Board cannot pretend to make perfect compensation. It is satisfied that a loss of profit occurred and that Company evidence indicated the limit of the loss while failing to measure it exactly. In the Board's view, one-half of the sum claimed for loss of profits should be allowed under this head, viz., $1,826.15.

In the result, it is the Board's award that the Union pay the Company $9,208.40 as damages for breach of the collective agreement, being the total of the sums allowed for continuing expenses and lost profits. This amount should be paid within 90 days or within such further time as may be mutually agreed upon between Company and Union.

Miss Wilson, the Union's nominee on this Board, who dissented from the Board's finding of liability, does not join in this award.

NOTES AND QUESTIONS. Would the formula in the principal case work conveniently if the Canadian General Electric Co. Ltd. happened to be operating its Davenport works at a loss at that time? Should the union be made to guarantee operating costs if the gross revenue is not sufficient to meet them? Could you suggest a simple formula? Would it be better to talk about "profit and loss," so that it would be clear that if the "profits" were a minus quantity they would be deducted from the operating costs?

Do you agree that a collective agreement should be enforced in the same way as a commercial contract? The rule of *stare decisis* is not applicable to arbitrations but it is remarkable that no other awards of damages against unions have been made since 1952. Another board, of which Professor Laskin was also chairman, recently indicated its intention to award damages against the union its and the union challenged its authority by a motion for *certiorari,* a procedure by which the Ontario High Court could review the arbitration proceedings and decide whether the collective agreement, which provided for the arbitration, authorized the board to award damages. The Court held that the arbitration board was so authorized. See *Re Polymer Corporation and Oil, Chemical and Atomic Workers International Union, Local 16-14*, (1961) 26 D.L.R. (2d) 609 (Ontario High Court). McRuer C.J.H.C.: "However, a collective agreement is different in some aspects from an ordinary commercial contract. In the first place, it is an agreement between a labour union and the employer of its members and that raises the question of the power to award damages against the Union. This I shall discuss later. In the second place, it is not that sort of contract that can be terminated by repudiation by one party merely because the other party has broken one of its terms. Under the statute 'all differences between the parties' must be settled without stoppage of work.

I think this aspect of the matter raises a stronger inference that the matter of damages for breach of the agreement should be assessed by the Board of Arbitration than in the case of a mere commercial contract. It was not argued that if the employer breached the agreement with respect to pay for overtime, for example, an arbitration board would not have power to award just compensation to the employees that had suffered by the breach. A breach of the agreement is a 'grievance' to be dealt with and disposed of by an award of the arbitrators.

"My conclusion is that unless there is force in the argument that the Board cannot award damages against the Union because it is not a legal entity, I think it must be taken that it has the same jurisdiction with respect to damages suffered by the employer as by the employees."

McRuer C.J.H.C. also concluded that the union had "the capacity to incur liability for damages."

An appeal was dismissed by the Court of Appeal, 28 D.L.R. (2d) 81, and the Supreme Court of Canada, 33 D.L.R. (2d) 124.

Are there other differences between a collective agreement and a commercial contract? The court gave little weight to the argument that because the *Industrial Relation and Disputes Investigation Act,* R.S.C. 1952, c. 152, provided a penalty for breach of the agreement the parties could not have contemplated damages as well. Do you agree? For a discussion of the problem, see Palmer, "Remedial Authority of Labour Arbitrators," *Current Law and Social Problems* (1960), 126.

COLLECTIVE AGREEMENT between Canadian Broadcasting Corporation and Association of Radio and Television Employees of Canada. 1957-59. Article 71. *"Arbitration Board—Award.* The Arbitration Board shall not have the power . . . to award costs or damages against either party, but it shall have the power to direct, if it thinks proper, that any employee who has been wrongfully suspended, discharged or otherwise disciplined shall be reinstated with pay and with any other benefit under this Agreement which may have been lost."

QUESTIONS. Do you suppose Article 71 in the Collective Agreement was introduced as the result of "reason" or "trade," or perhaps a little of both? How would you argue the Union's case for putting the Article in at the bargaining table? How much is the C.B.C giving up? How frequent in fact are wild cat strikes for which the Union can be held responsible rather than or in addition to individual strikers? How often do collective agreements contain express promises by the Union not to strike? Note that the existence of the clause has become a question of bargaining rather than litigation since the *Polymer* decision.

HUSBAND TRANSPORT CO. LTD. *v.* TEAMSTERS, CHAUFFEURS, WAREHOUSEMEN AND HELPERS UNION, LOCAL 880
Ontario. Arbitration Board. 1962.

LASKIN Q.C. wrote the opinion of the Board: By an award dated August 31, 1961, the Board [Professor Bora Laskin Q.C., M. O'Brien and R.S. Riddell Q.C.] found that the Union had violated article 9 of its collective agreement with the Company in connection with a work stoppage which occurred among the Company's employees in London on April 19, 1960. The Board determined that liability of the Union arose at 9 a.m. on that day in respect of the maintenance garage in London and at 10 a.m. in respect of the Company's London terminal. Work was resumed at the garage at 5 p.m. on April 19, 1960, and at the terminal during the hour between 5 p.m. and 6 p.m. Following the establishment of liability, and in accordance with the Board's directions, the Company served particulars of the loss or damage which it had claimed when it filed the grievance which was the subject of the award of August 31, 1961. A hearing to assess damages was convened on October 2, 1962, and what follows herein is concerned with that question.

The Company made no claim for any loss in respect of the work stoppage at the maintenance garage. What it did claim was $3,238.28 as the loss it suffered by reason of the work stoppage at the London terminal. This sum is the product of a calculation formula (which will be reviewed in detail later on) applied to or projected on an estimate of lost revenue for April 19, 1960. Two items of loss are said to be reflected by use of the formula as arising from the lost revenue: first, a loss of net operating profit of $89.94, and, second, a loss of $2,818.43 in recoverable continuing expenses which the revenue would have yielded had it not been lost by reason of the work stoppage. A third item, in itself not really challenged by the Union, was the cost of $329.91 incurred in moving empty trailers from London to various branches.

The Company's method of calculating the first two items of loss abovementioned (and here the Board is speaking of the calculation as such and not of the mode of proof offered) was as follows. It employed a system of averaging to fix the loss of revenue for April 19, 1960 by reason of the work stoppage in London. The sum yielded by the averaging was the total of average "outbound" revenue and "inbound" revenue, and from this sum was deducted the actual yield of "inbound" revenue for the day in question (there was no "outbound" revenue on that day), resulting in a sum of $4,966.23. Treating its London operations as merely a part of a composite province-wide, and, indeed, partly interprovincial, operation carried on in eleven branches in Ontario and one in Quebec (Montreal), the Company took its freight revenue for the calendar year 1960 (the calendar year is also the fiscal year), its net operating profit for that year, and its continuing expenses (as shown on a schedule in its exhibit of particulars), and from these figures related to the alleged revenue loss of $4,966.23 it projected a formula of calculation which is best explained by reproducing the exact summary which the Company filed:

HUSBAND TRANSPORT LIMITED
CALCULATION OF NET OPERATING LOSS
DUE TO STRIKE APRIL 19, 1960

FREIGHT REVENUE:	
For the year ended December 31, 1960 after deducting amount paid to other carriers	$5,190,852.64
Estimated loss of revenue due to strike	4,966.23
Estimated revenue had there been no strike	5,195,818.87
OPERATING PROFIT	
Net profit as per statement	106,551.17
Less: Sundry Income	12,465.07
Net profit from operations for the year	94,086.10

CALCULATION OF NET OPERATING PROFIT LOST

$94{,}086.10 \times \frac{4{,}966.23}{5{,}195{,}818.87} =$			$89.94
CONTINUING EXPENSES — As per Schedule	$3,600,844.59		
Add: Wages lost by dockmen and drivers while on strike	623.90		
	3,601,468.49		
Calculation of Continuing Expenses which would have been recovered from lost revenue			
$3{,}601{,}468.49 \times \frac{4{,}966.23}{5{,}195{,}818.87} =$	3,422.33		
Less: Wages lost by dockmen and drivers while on strike	623.90		2,818.43
OTHER EXPENSES INCURRED AS A RESULT OF THE STRIKE			
Cost incurred in moving empty trailers to various branches			329.91
TOTAL ESTIMATED LOSS DUE TO STRIKE:			$3,238.28

At the hearing counsel for the Union did not challenge the formula which the Company used to determine its loss but he did make objections to some of the figures to which the formula was applied. He challenged the estimated loss of revenue of $4,966.23 and he also contested some of the items included by the Company in its schedule of continuing expenses. The figures taken from the Company's annual financial statement for 1960, namely, its freight revenue and net operating profit, were not questioned.

The estimated loss of revenue is a prime factor in this case, not only in its own right but because it is integral to the formula of loss calculation. Two questions concern the Board in this connection; first, the basis on which the sum of $4,966.23 was put forward, and, second, the mode of proof by which it was sought to establish that sum as the lost revenue for the period of the strike. These two questions are not completely separate but they provide a convenient way to test proof of damage in a class of case in labour arbitration which seems to be increasing. . . .

The Company called only one witness, Mr. R. G. Woods, comptroller, who has been with the Company since 1951 and is a qualified chartered accountant. He prepared and offered in evidence the statement of particulars of loss to which reference has already been made. . . . Mr. Woods produced a figure of $1,958.82 as representing inbound London revenue in respect of goods picked up at other terminals on April 19, 1960 and billed for that day as destined to London. This sum was credited against the estimated revenue loss of $6,925.05 for the day and the resulting balance of $4,966.23 is, as already pointed out, the key figure in the overall picture.

The loss estimate of $6,925.05 was based on an averaging of outbound and inbound revenue for the ten working days immediately preceding April 19, 1960 and for the ten working days immediately succeeding the day of the strike. Mr. Woods took the figures for each of the twenty days from the Company's records at London and from the records at other terminals relating to inbound London traffic. For outbound traffic in the twenty days the daily average was $3,236.89; for inbound traffic in that span the daily average was $3,688.16. The total of the two sums makes up, of course, the claimed gross loss of revenue.

Is averaging of this kind a proper way of proving loss and, if so, was it sufficient for Mr. Woods to produce figures from Company records compiled by others? . . . As to the method of proving the daily outbound and inbound revenue, the Board has some reservations about the inbound revenue figures because their segregation and collection for attribution to London from an integrated operation such as that carried on by the Company extending over different terminals, must inevitably involve questions which should be answered by the very persons who made up the figures. The same difficulty does not apply to figures for outbound revenue because they are a matter of a single terminal's records which Mr. Woods could easily examine. Presumably the vouchers or shipping orders could be checked if necessary but the Union did not seek such a check, and the Board has no reason to doubt the accuracy of the sums listed by the Company. In the circumstances, the Board will allow the inbound as well as the outbound sums to stand, but this does not mean that they are conclusive for the purpose of showing probable loss.

Despite the absence of evidence of any calls from shippers for outbound pickups on April 19, 1960, the Board is in this case prepared to accept the averaged loss of outbound revenue as indicative of the probable loss on April 19, 1960. The Company shows this as $3,236.89, and it will do no great violence to the situation if the Board takes the round figure of $3,200.00 as representing the outbound revenue loss. Other considerations are present however, in respect of the alleged probable inbound revenue loss, and these inhibit the Board from accepting to the same degree the averaged figure of $3,688.16, even when reduced by deduction of the actual revenue intake of $1,958.82.

The inbound revenue figures for the averaging days at the time of the strike for which the Union is liable, and at the time of wildcat strike action at other terminals for which no liability attached, are lower than the figures for the other days of the period. The Company relied on these as supporting its contention that inbound revenue was as irretrievably lost as outbound revenue because shippers would have made other arrangements on being notified by branch managers of the labour trouble at London. As indicated above, there was wanting any evidence of how the branch managers handled the situation. Beyond this, however, it was admitted that wildcat strike action at Windsor between April 12 and April 20 for which no liability attached to the Union, and also at Montreal where Local 880 was not involved, would have affected inbound revenue relative to the day of the strike at London. The Board is hence of opinion that it must offset the averaged inbound revenue loss in the light of the foregoing factors.

The deduction from probable inbound revenue loss of actual inbound revenue of $1,958.82 represents the amount attributed to freight despatched to London in the evening of April 19, 1960. No evidence was presented to show the extent of the inflow of traffic to London from the various other terminal points operated by the Company; for example, the Board was not told or shown whether London's heaviest inflow was from Toronto or from Windsor or from Montreal, and so on. Moreover, the Board was not even told of the terminal sources of the earned inbound revenue of $1,958.82. It is proper, in such circumstances, to assess the situation more strongly against the Company than would otherwise be the case. The Board's best judgment on this phase of the matter is to discount the averaged loss of inbound revenue so as to leave (after deduction of the earned sum of $1,958.82) the sum of $400.00 as the probable loss. The revenue loss in respect of the strike on April 19, 1960, both outbound and inbound, is therefore fixed at $3,600.00....

The central question that now arises is how much of the gross revenue loss of $3,600,00 is chargeable to the Union by reason of its breach of the collective agreement which produced the loss....

This method of calculating compensable loss reduced itself to the following: the Company would have gained $3,600.00 in revenue had there been no strike. It would have had to lay out a certain amount for wages to gain that revenue and certain sums for overhead expenses which it saved in this particular case (e.g. cost of gasoline and servicing of vehicles). The total of the sum not paid is deductible from the total revenue not gained; the balance is the extent of the liability....

The method used by the Company is perhaps a more sophisticated way of estimating loss; more complicated in its computations but more manageable in its constituent data. Instead of working with the estimated loss of revenue as the gross loss from which certain deductions are made, the revenue loss figure is used to develop a ratio in respect of its relation to total amount revenue in order to ascertain what amount of net operating profit would be produced by that revenue had it not been lost. Again, the ratio is applied to operating expenses which went on despite the strike and were not saved by reason thereof. The Company had recovered its continuing expenses for 1960 in its revenue for that year (having shown a net profit) and it is hence proper to estimate the recoverable portion of continuing expenses which would have been reflected in the lost revenue.

Accepting therefore, as previously indicated, the frame of reference for estimating loss put forward by the Company, it remains only to make the necessary calculations on the basis of a revenue loss of $3,600.00. It will be convenient, however, before doing the arithmetic to determine the loss of net operating profit to deal with the Union's objections to certain items included by the Company in its list of continuing expenses.... Although the logic of some of the exclusions and some of the inclusions could be questioned, the Board is not persuaded of any serious error and it fixes the continuing expenses estimated by the Company at $3,600,844.59, at the round sum of $3,595,400.00.

It remains only to make the necessary ratio calculations to fix the compensable loss. The applicable ratio is found by adding $3,600.00 to the freight revenue of $5,190,852.64 and then applying the results as follows to both the net profit and the continuing expenses in the manner done by the Company in its exhibit reproduced earlier in this award:

1. Calculation of net operating profit lost:

$$\$94{,}086.10 \times \frac{3{,}600.00}{5{,}194{,}452.64} = \qquad \$\ 65.2$$

2. Recoverable continuing expenses:
   $3,595,400: lost wages of strikers
   of $623.90

$$\$3{,}596{,}023.90 \times \frac{3{,}600.00}{5{,}194{,}452.64} = \qquad \$2{,}492.21 \text{ less}$$

   wages lost by strikers of $623.90 = $1,868.31

To the sums of $65.21 and $1,868.31 there must be added the uncontested sum of $329.91 laid out to move empty trailers from London. The total loss suffered by the Company is accordingly $2,263.43, and there will be an order for payment thereof by the Union.

GILES *v.* EDWARDS. 1797. 7 T.R. 181; 101 E.R. 920 (England. King's Bench). An action for money had and received. The defendant agreed to sell to the plaintiffs certain cordwood, ready cut, at 11*s.* 6*d.* a cord. The custom was for the seller to trim the wood and cord it, and for the buyer to record it, after which it became the property of the buyer. The defendant cut sixty cords, ten of which he corded, and the plaintiffs recorded half a cord and measured the rest. The plaintiffs paid the defendant twenty guineas, but the defendant failed to cord the rest of the wood and this action was brought to recover back the twenty guineas. LORD KENYON C.J. said: ". . . this was an entire contract; and as by the defendant's default the plaintiffs could not perform what they had undertaken to do, they had a right to put an end to the whole contract and recover back the money that they had paid under it; they were not bound to take a part of the wood only."

HUNT *v.* SILK

England. King's Bench. 1804. 5 East 449; 102 E.R. 1142

The defendant promised to execute a lease of a house within ten days, and to make certain repairs, in consideration of £10 to be paid on the execution of the lease and of a yearly rent of £93. The plaintiff took immediate possession and in confidence that the repairs would be made, paid the £10 at the same time. More than ten days elapsed but despite the plaintiff's urging, the defendant failed to do the work. The plaintiff gave up possession and sued to recover his £10. Lord Ellenborough thought the plaintiff was too late to "rescind" and directed a non suit. The plaintiff appealed.

LORD ELLENBOROUGH C.J.: Without questioning the authority of the case cited [*Giles* v. *Edwards*], which I admit to have been properly decided, there is this difference between that and the present; that there by the terms of the agreement the money was to be paid antecedent to the cording and delivery of the wood, and here it was not to be paid till the repairs were done and the lease executed. The plaintiff there had no opportunity by the terms of the contract of making his stand to see whether the agreement were performed by the other party before he paid his money, which the plaintiff in this case had: but instead of making his stand, as he might have done, on the defendant's non-performance of what he had undertaken to do, he waived his right, and voluntarily paid the money; giving the defendant credit for his future performance of the contract; and afterwards continued in possession notwithstanding the defendant's default. Now where a contract is to be rescinded at all, it must be rescinded *in toto*, and the parties put *in statu quo*. But here was an intermediate occupation, a part execution of the agreement, which was incapable of being rescinded. If the plaintiff might occupy the premises two days beyond the time when the repairs were to have been done and the lease executed, and yet rescind the contract, why might he not rescind it after a twelve month on the same account. This objection cannot be gotten rid of: the parties cannot be put *in statu quo*.

[The opinions of Lawrence and LeBlanc JJ. are omitted. Grose J. concurred.]

[What does the word "rescind" mean?]

MINER *v*. BRADLEY. 1839. 22 Pick. 457 (Supreme Judicial Court of Massachusetts). An action for money had and received and money paid. The defendant, among other things, put up at auction a certain cow and 400 pounds of hay, which was then in a bay with other hay. The plaintiff bid off the cow and the hay for $17, which he paid at the time. He then received the cow, and afterwards demanded the hay which was refused by the defendant, who had used it. Plaintiff sought the price paid for the hay being some part of the $17. The defendant objected to the plaintiff's recovery on the ground that this was an entire contract that the plaintiff could not recover back the price paid, or any portion of it, without rescinding the whole contract, and that this could not be done without returning the cow. The trial court instructed the jury that the plaintiff was entitled to recover a sum equal to the value of the hay. The appeal court granted a new trial. MORTON J. speaking for the court said, in part: "And it seems to us very clearly, that the contract was entire; that it was incapable of severence: that it could not be enforced in part and rescinded in part; and that it could not be rescinded without placing the parties *in statu quo*. . . ."

ERLANGER *v*. THE NEW SOMBRERO PHOSPHATE COMPANY. 1878. 3 App. Cas. 1218. Baron Erlanger, a Paris banker, headed a syndicate (or partnership) that on August 30, 1871, acquired for £55,000 a lease of an island in the West Indies believed to contain valuable phosphate mines. He proceeded to organize a corporation with directors of his own choosing and the corporation bought the mines for £110,000 on September 20, 1871. At the first ordinary general meeting of the Company on February 2, 1872, a shareholder queried the sale, which the first directors had already confirmed, but no action was taken. At the first annual general meeting on June 19, 1872, a committee was appointed to investigate rumours about the sale. The committee reported on August 29, and on December 24 the Company filed suit against Erlanger and others asking to have the contract set aside, the £110,000 repaid to the Company, the Company to deliver up the island and to account for profits (if any) made by working it. It was so ordered. Most of the judgments are taken up with the question of the duty of promoters in equity to make full disclosure, and with the question of the separate identities of the promoters, the Company, and its handful of shareholders on September 20, 1871, and on June 19, 1872. On the question of restitution, LORD BLACKBURN said: "It is, I think, clear on principles of general justice, that as a condition to a rescission there must be a *restitutio in integrum*. The parties must be put *in statu quo*. . . . It is a doctrine which has often been acted upon both at law and in equity. But there is a considerable difference in the mode in which it is applied in Courts of Law and Equity, owing, as I think, to the difference of the machinery which the Courts have at command. I speak of these Courts as they were at the time when this suit commenced, without inquiring whether the Judicature Acts make any, or if any, what difference.

"It would be obviously unjust that a person who has been in possession of property under the contract which he seeks to repudiate should be allowed to throw that back on the other party's hands without accounting for any benefit he may have derived from the use of the property, or if the property, though not destroyed, has been in the interval deteriorated, without making compensation for that deterioration. But as a Court of Law has no machinery at its command for taking an account of such matters, the defrauded party, if he sought his remedy at law, must in such cases keep the property and sue in an action for deceit, in which the jury, if properly directed, can do complete justice by giving as damages a full indemnity for all that the party has lost. . . .

"But a Court of Equity could not give damages, and, unless it can rescind the contract, can give no relief. And, on the other hand, it can take accounts of profits, and make allowance for deterioration. And I think the practice has always been for a Court of Equity to give this relief whenever, by the exercise of its powers, it can do what is practically just, though it cannot restore the parties precisely to the state they were in before the contract. And a Court of Equity requires that those who come to it to ask its active interposition to give them relief, should use due diligence, after there has been such notice or knowledge as to make it inequitable to lie by. And any change which occurs in the position of the parties or the state of the property after such notice or knowledge should tell much more against the party *in morâ*, than a similar change before he was *in morâ* should do."

DEGLMAN *v*. GUARANTY TRUST CO. AND CONSTANTINEAU
Ontario. Supreme Court of Canada. [1954] 3 D.L.R. 785

RAND J.: In this appeal the narrow question is raised as to the nature of part performance which will enable the Court to order specific performance of a contract relating to lands unenforceable at law by reason of s. 4 of the *Statute of Frauds*, R.S.O. 1950, c. 371. The respondent Constantineau claims the benefit of such a contract and the appellant represents the next-of-kin other than the respondent of the deceased, Laura Brunet, who resist it.

The respondent was the nephew of the deceased. Both lived in Ottawa. When he was about 20 years of age, and while attending a technical school, for 6 months of the school year 1934-35 he lived with his aunt at No. 550 Besserer St. Both that and the house on the adjoining lot, No. 548, were owned by the aunt and it was during this time that she is claimed to have agreed that if the nephew would be good to her and do such services for her as she might from time to time request during her lifetime she would make adequate provision for him in her will, and in particular that she would leave to him the premises at No. 548. While staying with her the nephew did the chores around both houses which, except for an apartment used by his aunt, were occupied by tenants. When the term ended he returned to the home of his mother on another street. In the autumn of that year he worked on the national highway in the northern part of Ontario. In the spring of 1936 he took a job on a railway at a point outside of Ottawa and at the end of that year, returning to Ottawa, he obtained a position with the city police force. In 1941 he married. At no time did he live at the house No. 548 or, apart from the 6 months, at the house No. 550.

The performance consisted of taking his aunt about in her own or his automobile on trips to Montreal and elsewhere, and on pleasure drives, of doing odd jobs about the two houses, and of various accomodations such as errands and minor services for her personal needs. . . .

[RAND J. considered the argument of part performance, which he rejected, reversing the courts below, and holding the contract unenforceable under the *Statute of Frauds* and continued:]

There remains the question of recovery for the services rendered on the basis of a *quantum meruit*. On the findings of both Courts below the services were not given gratuitously but on the footing of a contractual relation: they were to be paid for. The statute in such a case does not touch the principle of restitution against what would otherwise be an unjust enrichment of the defendant at the expense of the plaintiff. This is exemplified in the simple case of part or full payment in money as the price under an oral contract; it would be inequitable to allow the promisor to keep both the land and the money and the other party to the bargain is entitled to recover what he has paid. Similarly is it in the case of services given.

This matter is elaborated exhaustively in the Restatement of the Law of Contract issued by the American Law Institute and Professor Williston's monumental work on Contracts, 1936, vol. 2, s. 536 deals with the same topic. On the principles there laid down the respondent is entitled to recover for his services and outlays what the deceased would have had to pay for them on a purely business basis to any other person in the position of the respondent. The evidence covers generally and perhaps in the only way possible the particulars, but enough is shown to enable the Court to make a fair determination of the amount called for; and since it would be to the benefit of the other beneficiaries to bring an end to this litigation, I think we should not hesitate to do that by fixing the amount to be allowed. This I place at the sum of $3,000.

The appeal will therefore be allowed and the judgment modified by declaring the respondent entitled to recover against the respondent administrator the sum of $3,000; all costs will be paid out of the estate, those of the administrator as between solicitor and client.

CARTWRIGHT J.: . . . I agree with the conclusion of my brother Rand that the respondent is entitled to recover the value of these services from the respondent administrator. This right appears to me to be based, not on the contract, but on an obligation imposed by law.

In *Fibrosa Spolka Akcyjna* v. *Fairbairn Lawson Combe Barbour Ltd.*, [1943] A.C. 32 at p. 61, Lord Wright said: "It is clear that any civilized system of law is bound to provide remedies for cases of what has been called unjust enrichment or unjust benefit, that is to prevent a man from retaining the money of or some benefit derived from another which it is against conscience that he should keep. Such remedies in English law are generically different from remedies in contract or in tort, and are now recognized to fall within a third category of the comon law which has been called quasi-contract or restitution."

And at p. 62: "Lord Mansfield does not say that the law implies a promise. The law implies a debt or obligation which is a different thing. In fact, he denies that there is a contract; the obligation is as efficacious as if it were upon a contract. The obligation is a creation of the law, just as much as an obligation in tort. The obligation belongs to a third class, distinct from either contract or tort, though it resembles contract rather than tort."

Lord Wright's judgment appears to me to be in agreement with the view stated in Williston on Contracts referred to by my brother Rand. . . .

In the case at bar all the acts for which the respondent asks to be paid under his alternative claim were clearly done in performance of the existing but unenforceable contract with the deceased that she would devise 548 Besserer St. to him, and to infer from them a fresh contract to pay the value of the services in money would be . . . to draw an inference contrary to the fact.

In my opinion when the *Statute of Frauds* was pleaded the express contract was thereby rendered unenforceable, but the deceased having received the benefits of the full performance of the contract by the respondent, the law imposed upon her, and so on her estate, the obligation to pay the fair value of the services rendered to her.

If this is, as I think, the right view of the nature of the obligation upon which the respondent's claim rests it follows that the *Limitations Act* can have no application. . . . In my opinion the obligation which the law imposes upon the respondent administrator did not arise until the deceased died intestate. It may well be that throughout her life it was her intention to make a will in fulfilment of the existing although unenforceable contract and until her death the respondent had no reason to doubt that she would do so. The statutory period of limitation does not commence to run until the plaintiff's cause of action has accrued; and on the facts of the case at bar the cause of action upon which the respondent is entitled to succeed did not accrue until the death of the deceased intestate.

For the above reasons I would dispose of the appeal as proposed by my brother Rand.

[Rinfret C.J.C. and Taschereau J. concurred with Rand J. and Estey, Locke and Fauteux JJ. concurred with Carwright J.]

BOONE *v*. COE. 1913. 154 S.W. 900 (Kentucky Court of Appeals). The plaintiffs Boone and J. T. Coe were farmers in Kentucky. The defendant J. F. Coe, a farmer in Texas, orally promised them a lease of his farm for a year, to commence on their arrival at the farm in Texas. He also promised to build them a dwelling ready for occupancy on their arrival, to provide materials for a stock and grain barn, and to share with them a portion of the crop which the plaintiffs were to sow and cultivate. The plaintiffs did move to Texas, with their families, wagons, horses, and camping outfit, taking about fifty-five days, at an expense of $1,387.80 including $8 a day for the fifty-five days, and twenty-two days while they remained in Texas, cash outlay en route $361.80, $100 for loss of time on the return trip, which took four days and $150 for losses suffered in abandoning their homes and businesses in Kentucky. They returned because the defendant J. F. Coe failed to carry out any of his promises. In an action for damages the court held the contract was unenforceable under the *Statute of Frauds*, which required a promise for a lease for more than a year to be in writing and refused relief. CLAY C. said: ". . . In the case under consideration the plaintiffs merely sustained a loss. Defendant received no benefit. Had he received a benefit, the law would imply an obligation to pay therefore. Having received no benefit, no obligation to pay is implied. The statute says that the contract of defendant made with plaintiffs is unenforceable. Defendant therefore had the legal right to decline to carry it out. To require him to pay plaintiffs for losses and expenses incurred on the faith of the contract, without any benefit accruing to him, would, in effect, uphold a contract upon which the statute expressly declares no action shall be brought. The statute was enacted for the purpose of preventing frauds and perjuries. That it is a valuable statute is shown by the fact that similar statutes are in force in practically all, if not all, of the states of the Union. Being a valuable statute, the purpose of the lawmakers in its enactment should not be defeated by permitting recoveries in cases to which its provisions were intended to apply. . . ."

[Why is the *Statute of Frauds* not intended to apply when the plaintiff confers a benefit, but is intended to apply when the plaintiff confers no benefit? The history, interpretation and effect of the *Statute of Frauds* are set out briefly in text notes in Section 10 of Chapter 2. You should read the Section now.]

MOSES *v*. MACFERLAN. 1760. 2 Burr. 1005; 97 E.R. 676. Lord Mansfield said: "If the defendant be under an obligation, from the ties of natural justice, to refund; the law implies a debt, and gives this action, founded in the equity of the plaintiff's case, as it were upon a contract (*quasi ex contractu*, as the Roman law expresses it). . . . This kind of equitable action, to recover back money, which ought not in justice to be kept, is very beneficial, and therefore much encouraged. It lies only for money which, *ex aequo et bono*, the defendant ought to refund . . . it lies for money paid by mistake; or upon a consideration which happens to fail; or for money got through imposition, (express or implied); or extortion; or oppression; or an undue advantage taken of the plaintiff's situation, contrary to laws made for the protection of persons under those circumstances.

"In one word, the gist of this kind of action is that the defendant, upon the circumstances of the case, is obliged by the ties of natural justice and equity to refund the money."

MATHESON *v*. SMILEY
Manitoba. Court of Appeal. [1932] 2 D.L.R. 787

ROBSON J. A. delivered the judgment of the Court: . . . Plaintiff is a surgeon and brought this action to recover $150 from defendant as executrix of the last will and testament of John J. Smiley, deceased. The claim alleges that the professional services were rendered "by the plaintiff to the said deceased at the defendant's request.". . .

There was no allegation by plaintiff of any status to sue, or as I read the claim, of any request by Smiley, now deceased, upon which to base a contract creating an obligation against the estate. The parties contested the case on the evidence without formal objection and as the issues appear clearly from the evidence there is no reason why this Court should not deal with the appeal in the same way.

The fact is that Smiley was found lying on the floor in an upstairs room in his home in Brandon having received in his body evidently by his own hand the discharge from a shotgun. He was no doubt in a very serious condition. The defendant was not there but two friends named Wright and Cousins were downstairs and on being alarmed and making the discovery one of them immediately send for Dr. A. T. Condell. Dr. Condell, considering it to be a case for a surgeon, brought in the plaintiff who has specialized in that branch. Smiley was taken to the hospital. Plaintiff did what he could to reduce the effects of the injury but Smiley succumbed.

It is almost needless to say that all that was done by the two friends and Dr. Condell and plaintiff was done in good judgment in the emergency. Plaintiff's present claim is for his remuneration for his professional service on the occasion. I think it may safely be said that it is really the thought that the fee charged is too large that actuates the defendant in contesting the claim. Be that as it may, the defendant is entitled to raise the questions she has raised here. . . .

I think it is not within reason that even in such circumstances as are revealed here a person in such a plight should simply be allowed to die without an effort being made by those in contact with him and without resort to all reasonable means to secure his recovery that may be at hand to them. And surely the person to pay should be the person for whose benefit the service is rendered. I hardly think it an answer to say in any case there was no hope. In such circumstances no one gives up while a spark remains. . . .

I think the friends of deceased present, Wright and Cousins, only acted within their duty in calling in Dr. Condell and that his calling the plaintiff was merely a natural sequence in the nature of the case. . . .

I look upon the surgeon's service as a necessary for Smiley even though the effort was unavailing. I therefore think a right to recover from defendant's estate exists in favour of the plaintiff. . . .

As to the reasonableness of the fee charged, the plaintiff being questioned on the subject said:—"Well, I think for an operation of that kind it was a very, very reasonable fee." The learned trial Judge thought the fee charged proper, saying:—"In an emergency such as this one the services of a surgeon are not to be measured by the length of time required to perform the operation but by the skill and services rendered."

There were two cases cited to us as to the amount to be allowed. In *Wood* v. *McMartin* (1917), 54 Que. S.C. 391, it was held by Guerin, J., that where a court has to determine the fee it must take into account not only the standing of the physician but also the position, the earning power and the responsibilities of the patient. In *Gibson* v. *MacKay* (1907), 10 O.W.R. 1081, Anglin, J., had before him a case where a well-to-do person had employed a physician and surgeon to look after shipwrecked mariners who had suffered grievously from freezing. In that case the learned Judge seems to have been concerned as to whether there should be a rich man's rate of remuneration or a poor man's It was a question in the circumstances of what the surgeon would reasonably expect to receive as remuneration and what the defendant would reasonably expect to pay, considering the status of the patient rather than the financial capacity of the defendant.

In the present case the standing of the plaintiff was proved, but nothing was said as to the position in life of the deceased. The cross-examination of plaintiff was on the point as to the short period of time taken in the operation. That seems to have been the ground of attack on the reasonableness of the charge and it evidently led to the words of the trial judge above-quoted. The trial Judge had the plaintiff and Dr. Condell and Smiley's friend Cousins before him and heard the whole matter. He learned the plaintiff's status and heard the evidence as to the deceased's position to minimize the fee within the test of *Gibson* v. *MacKay*. He, sitting as a Judge of fact, concluded that $150 was not unreasonable. It seems to me that he had evidence on which he could come to that conclusion. Possibly the defendant found difficulty in securing any professional evidence questioning the fee as was available in *Gibson* v. *MacKay*, but that is defendant's misfortune. Its absence renders it impossible, in my view, for an Appellate Court to say the trial Judge was wrong in finding for $150 on the evidence before him being that only on which he could act.

For these reasons I think the appeal should be dismissed, with costs.

Appeal dismissed.

[For comment, see 46 *Harv. L. Rev.* 528.]

2. Penalty Clauses: A Drafting Problem

The cases in this short section present a problem for the draftsman who, despite the views of Bramwell L.J. in the *Hydraulic Engineering* case noted in section 1, contemplates the breach of the contract and wants to avoid the uncertainties of litigation over damages by stating an agreed amount in his contract. Clauses of this sort are sometimes prompted by the practical difficulties of calculating damages by any accepted test, sometimes by the overbearing of a contractor in a stronger bargaining position, and sometimes by a desire to limit liability to a sum less than that a court might be expected to award.

An example of the last case has been seen in the *Canada Foundry* case, noted in Section 1. This kind of clause is not uncommon. See, for example, the exculpatory clause on a box of photographic film. It will probably read something like this: "X Film Company will replace this film with unexposed film of the same kind if this film is defective in manufacture, labeling, or packaging, or if it is damaged or lost by the Company or a subsidiary Company. Except for such replacement, the sale or subsequent handling of this film is without warranty, guarantee, or other liability of any kind." Suppose an amateur photographer takes a picture of a sensational disaster he happens to witness and his film, which could be sold for $1,000, is destroyed in the process of development by the X Company. What damages would he be awarded? Would the clause help to reduce liability?

The cases below do not deal with this kind of limited liability, which is involved in other problems discussed later. The cases here are concerned with the fixing of an amount that is neither too high nor too low.

SHATILLA *v.* FEINSTEIN
Saskatchewan. Court of Appeal. [1923] 3 D.L.R. 1035

Feinstein carried on business as a wholesale drygoods merchant in Saskatoon and on April 16, 1920, sold his business to Shatilla on the express understanding that Feinstein and his brother, who were most active in the business, would not compete within the corporate limits of Saskatoon for five years. They agreed to pay $10,000 on breach of the covenant recoverable on each and every such breach as liquidated damages and not as a penalty. During 1921 Feinstein became a shareholder and director of Harley Henry Ltd. who engaged in the wholesale drygoods business. Shatilla sued to recover on the covenant. The trial judge held the covenant to be a penalty and unenforceable, but he also held that there had been a breach and directed a reference to ascertain actual damages. The plaintiff appealed on the ground, among others not here material, that the covenant was valid as a genuine pre-estimate of liquidated damages.

MARTIN J.A. delivered the judgment of the Court: . . . The main question to be determined is, whether or not the sum fixed by the covenant is a penalty, or whether it is recoverable by way of liquidated damages. When the damages which may arise out of the breach of a contract are in their nature uncertain, the law permits the parties to agree beforehand as to the amount to be paid in case of breach. Whether such an agreement has been made by the parties or not, or whether the sum agreed upon is a penalty, must depend upon the circumstances of each case. If the sum fixed is in excess of any actual damage which can possibly arise from the breach of the contract, the sum fixed as damage is not considered to be a *bonâ fide* pre-estimate of the damage. The same principle is applied when the payment of a larger sum is stipulated in the event of the breach of a covenant to pay a smaller sum. In the case of a contract containing a single stipulation which, if broken at all, can be broken once only—such as a covenant not to reveal a trade secret—when the parties have agreed to the amount which shall be paid in case of breach and referred to such sum as liquidated damages, there would appear to be no reason, on the authorities, why the Court should not treat such sum as liquidated damages. If, however, the covenant is one which is capable of being broken more than once, such as an agreement not to solicit the customers of a firm, or an agreement not to sell certain specified articles below a certain price, the question is a more difficult one. In such a case, however, the damage in the case of each breach is of the same kind, and the fact that such damage may vary in amount for each breach has not been held by the Courts to raise a presumption that the sum agreed upon is a penalty, particularly where the parties have agreed to the sum as liquidated damages. This, I think, is a fair deduction from the decision in the House of Lords in *Dunlop Pneumatic Tyre Co. Ltd.* v. *New Garage and Motor Co.*, [1915] A.C. 79.

In cases, however, where it is agreed to pay a fixed sum on the breach of a number of stipulations of various degrees of importance, a presumption is said to be raised against the sum so fixed being treated as liquidated damages, even though the parties have referred to it as such; that is, there is a presumption against the parties having pre-estimated the damages. The damage likely to accrue from breaches of various kinds in such a case is different in kind and amount, and a separate estimate in the case of each breach would be necessary. Such a presumption may, however, be rebutted if it is shown on the face of the agreement, or on the evidence, that the parties have taken into consideration the different amounts of damages that might occur, and had actually arrived at an amount which was considered proper under all the circumstances. Even then, however, the amount fixed must not be extravagant or unreasonable.

In *Elphinstone* v. *Monkland Iron & Coal Co.* (1886), 11 App. Cas. 332, the facts were that the lessees of land had been granted the privilege of placing slag from blast furnaces on land let to them, and covenanted to restore the land at a certain date. Provision was made that failing performance the lessees should pay the lessors "at the rate of £100 per Imperial acre for all ground not so restored, together with legal interest thereon, from and after the date when the operations should have been completed until paid." It was held that the sum, although it was described in one part of the agreement as "the penalty therein stipulated," was not a penalty but estimated or stipulated damages. Lord Watson, at pp. 342-3, said:—

"When a single lump sum is made payable by way of compensation, on the occurence of one or more or all of several events, some of which may occasion serious and others but trifling damage, the presumption is that the parties intended the sum to be penal, and subject to modification. The payments stipulated in article 12 are not of that character; they are made proportionate to the extent to which the respondent company may fail to implement their obligations, and they are to bear interest from the date of the failure. I can find neither principle nor authority for holding that payments so adjusted by the contracting parties with reference to the actual amount of damage ought to be regarded as penalties."...

In *Clydebank Engineering & Shipbuilding Co.*, v. *Don Jose Castaneda*, [1904] A.C. 6, the shipbuilding company contracted for the construction of four vessels of war for the Spanish Government, each of which was to be completed at a certain date. In the event of non-completion they were to pay £500 for each ship for every week's delay. The contract entered into contained the following clause:—"The contractors undertake that the said vessel shall be finished, complete and ready for sea, the first vessels in six and three-quarter months, and the second in seven and three-quarter months from signing of this contract and accompanying specifications and plans." And also:—"The penalty for later delivery shall be at the rate of £500 per week for each vessel not delivered by the contractors in contract time."

It appeared from the evidence that the sum to be paid on breach of delivery was suggested by the contracting company itself, and this fact must have had some influence on the decision of the Court. It was held that the sum stipulated was liquidated damage, and not a penalty. . . .

In *Webster* v. *Bosanquet*, [1912] A.C. 394, the plaintiff and defendant carried on business as partners in exporting and selling Ceylon tea. The partnership was dissolved, and an agreement was entered into which contained the following provisions at p. 396:—

"And the said Bosanquet shall not be at liberty to sell during the period aforesaid [10 years] the whole or any part of the tea crops of the Marawilla and or Palamcotta estates to any person other than the said Webster without first offering to the said Webster the option of buying the same, so long as Webster shall pay to Bosanquet the yearly payment of 75*l*; and if the said Bosanquet shall fail, neglect, or refuse to sell the whole or any part of the crop of the Marawilla and or Palamcotta estates as hereinbefore provided to the said Webster, he shall pay to Webster the sum of 500*l* as liquidated damages and not as a penalty."

It was held by Privy Council that the claim was recoverable by way of liquidated damages. Lord Mersey, at pp. 397-8, said:

"The cases in which the Courts have had to consider whether a stipulated payment in respect of the breach of a contract should be regarded as liquidated damages fixing once for all the sum to be paid, or merely as a penalty covering the damages though not assessing them, are innumerable and perhaps difficult to reconcile. But it is unnecessary to examine them, for their effect is sufficiently and very clearly stated in the *Clydebank* case. From that case it appears that, whatever be the expression used in the contract in describing the payment, the question must always be whether the construction contended for renders the agreement unconscionable and extravagant and one which no court ought to allow to be enforced."

And again at pp. 398-9:—"It was suggested in the course of the argument that to treat the £500 as liquidated damages might involve such extravagant consequences as to render the agreement absurd, for the sum might be claimed in respect of every pound of tea sold in breach of the stipulation. Their Lordships, however, are of the opinion that the stipulation is not capable of such an interpretation. The parties to the agreement were merchants using language in the sense which it is used in their trade. When they speak of 'a part of a crop' they are not contemplating packets which might be sold over a grocer's counter, but parcels such as were in fact sold in the present case."

In *Dunlop Pneumatic Tyre Co.* v. *New Garage*, [1915] A.C. 79, the defendants had agreed not to sell the plaintiffs' goods at prices less than those set out in the price list of the plaintiffs and not to sell to certain persons whom the plaintiffs did not desire to supply, and to pay £5 for each and every article sold in breach of the agreement "as and by way of liquidated damages and not as a penalty." It was held that the stipulation was to be construed as one for liquidated damages. . . .

The covenant in the present case covers a number of matters which would constitute breach of it. It provides that the defendant shall not "carry on or be engaged in or take part in or be in any way interested in the business of wholesale drygoods, etc." This, the main portion of the covenant, is further described by words preceding it: "directly or indirectly, either as principal or agent or as director or manager of a company, or as a servant in any capacity." There could be many breaches of this covenant, some of which would be very important, others of a less important and even trivial character. For instance, if the defendant had engaged as a clerk with some one carrying on a similar business, or if he purchased a small amount of stock in a similar business, it could scarcely be said that such action would cause serious damage to the plaintiffs, not that it would constitute an important breach of the agreement; certainly it would seem "extravagant and unconscionable" that for either one of such breaches he should pay damages amounting to $10,000. On the other hand, if he actually went into business in partnership with some one or carried on a competing business on his own account, or became manager of a company carrying on a similar business, or purchased a large interest in a similar concern carrying on business as a company and became a director of such company, such breach as would be of an important character and might conceivably cause serious damage to the plaintiffs. I think the law as laid down by Lord Watson in the *Elphinstone case, supra* is applicable to the facts of this case, and that it must be held that covenant provides a penalty which the Court will not enforce. The covenant provides for the payment of a lump sum upon the occurrence of any one of a number of things differing in importance, and some of them trivial in character, and where a sum is stipulated to be paid as liquidated damages, and is payable not on the happening of a single event but of one or more of a number of events, some of which might result in inconsiderable damage, the Court may decline to construe the words "liquidated damages" according to their ordinary meaning and may treat such a sum as a penalty. Lord Dunedin, in the *Dunlop* case, [1915] A.C. at p. 89, considers that if there are various breaches to which an indiscriminate sum is applied, "then the strength of the chain must be taken to be its weakest link," and if it can be seen clearly that the loss in one particular breach could never amount to the sum stated then the conclusion that the sum is a penalty may be reached. I think this statement of the law is peculiarly applicable to the facts of the present case. . . .

HOWE *v.* SMITH

England. Court of Appeal. 1884. 27 Ch.D. 89

FRY L.J.: . . . On the 24th of March, 1881, the Defendant and Plaintiff entered into an agreement in writing, by which the Defendant agreed to sell and the purchaser agreed to buy certain real estate for £12,500, of which £500 was in the contract stated to have been paid on the signing of the agreement as a deposit and in part payment of the purchase-money. The contract provided for the payment of the balance on the 24th of April, 1881, and it further provided by the 8th condition that if the purchaser should fail to comply with the agreement the vendor should be at liberty to resell the premises, and the deficiency on such second sale thereof, with all expenses attending the same, should be made good by the defaulter and be recoverable as liquidated damages.

The Plaintiff, the purchaser, did not pay the balance of his purchase-money on the day stipulated, and he has been guilty of such delay and neglect in completing that, according to our judgment already expressed, he has lost all right to the specific performance of the contract in equity.

The question then arises which has been argued before us, . . . whether or not the Plaintiff is entitled to recover the £500 paid on the signing of the contract.

The £500 was paid, in the words of the contract, as "a deposit and in part payment of the purchase-money." What is the meaning of this expression? The authorities seem to leave the matter in some doubt. . . .

These authorities appear to afford no certain light to answer the inquiry whether, in the absence of express stipulation, money paid as a deposit on the signing of a contract can be recovered by the payer if he has made such default in performance of his part as to have lost all right to performance by the other party to the contract or damages for his own non-performance.

Money paid as a deposit must, I conceive, be paid on some terms implied or expressed. In this case no terms are expressed, and we must therefore inquire what terms are to be implied. The terms most naturally to be implied appear to me in the case of money paid on the signing of a contract to be that in the event of the contract being performed it shall be brought into account, but if the contract is not performed by the payer it shall remain the property of the payee. It is not merely a part payment, but is then also an earnest to bind the bargain so entered into, and creates by the fear of its forfeiture a motive in the payer to perform the rest of the contract.

The practice of giving something to signify the conclusion of the contract, sometimes a sum of money, sometimes a ring or other object, to be repaid or redelivered on the completion of the contract, appears to be one of the great antiquity and very general prevalence. It may not be unimportant to observe as evidence of this antiquity that our own word "earnest" has been supposed to flow from a Phoenician source. . . .

Taking these early authorities into consideration, I think we may conclude that the deposit in the present case is the earnest or *arrha* of our earlier writers; that the expression used in the present contract that the money is paid "as a deposit and in part payment of the purchase-money," relates to the two alternatives, and declares that in the event of the purchaser making default the money is to be forfeited, and that in the event of the purchase being completed the sum is to be taken in part payment.

Such being my view of the nature of the deposit, it appears to me to be clear that the purchaser lost all right to recover it if he has lost both his right to specific performance in equity and his right to sue for damages for its non-performance at law. . . .

In a word, the purchaser has, in my opinion, been guilty of such delay, whether measured by the rules of law or equity, as deprives him of his right to specific performance, and of his right to maintain an action for damages—and under these circumstances I hold that the purchaser has no right to recover his deposit. . . .

[The opinions of Cotton and Bowen L.JJ. are omitted and that of Fry L.J. has been severely cut.]

DePALMA *v.* RUNNYMEDE IRON & STEEL CO.
Ontario. Court of Appeal. [1950] 1 D.L.R. 557

Runnymede was a fabricator of steel and agreed to supply and erect the structural steel for an office building to be built by DePalma. The agreement was confirmed in a letter dated September 9, 1946, in which the price, based on 125 tons, was set out at $17,500. In the lower left hand corner the letter was endorsed "Received cheque 2500/Balance 'J.T.' 15000.00/Accepted this 9th day/of September 1946,/'A. E. DePalma' " (J.T. stood for J. Tanenbaum, one of the Runnymede partners). The steel was procured and cut to specifications but before any was erected DePalma announced that he was not going ahead. Runnymede treated the contract as terminated and sold the steel. DePalma claimed a return of his $2500 which Runnymede refused and DePalma commenced this action. LeBel J. at the trial found that the contract was repudiated but that Runnymede suffered no damages as a result. He held that DePalma's claim for recovery of the $2500 failed. Both the statement of claim and the defence described the $2500 as "a deposit." DePalma appealed.

LAIDLAW J.A.: . . . It was next argued that: "The defendants may retain the money only if it is clearly a deposit to guarantee performance, and not if it is part payment under the contract." In support of his argument that a cheque for the amount of $2,500, received by the respondent, was a part payment only under the contract and not a deposit to guarantee performance of it, counsel for the appellant referred to and relied upon the evidence of Mr. Joseph Tanenbaum as to what took place at the time the contract was signed. I quote that part of the evidence as follows:

"Q. You met together, at all events, you and Mr. DePalma? A. Yes, and I told him what we are basing it on, that we are basing it on 125 tons according to them drawings. He said, 'Well, what do you want? Do you want a cheque for it in full?' I said, 'No, I don't think that is necessary. If you just give us a deposit and give us the balance when the job is completed, that is our customary way of doing it.' So he gave me a cheque for $2500 and I marked on there that I received it."

It is to be observed at once that the appellant was a man of much business experience, and I think he would fully understand and appreciate the meaning and consequences which attach to the use of the word "deposit.". . .

Mr. Tanenbaum made it plain that he was accepting the deposit from the appellant and would look for the balance when the job was completed, in accordance with their "customary way of doing it." The appellant would know that the deposit made by him in the transaction was by way of guarantee that he would perform his part of the contract. Apart altogether from the evidence quoted and relied upon by counsel for the appellant, there is an inference that the deposit was paid as a guarantee for the performance of the contract.

I quote the words of Pollock B. in *Collins* v. *Stimson* (1883), 11 Q.B.D. 142 at pp. 143-4, quoted also by Cotton L.J. and Fry L.J. in *Howe* v. *Smith*, as follows: "According to the law of vendor and purchaser the inference is that such a deposit is paid as a guarantee for the performance of the contract, and where the contract goes off by default of the purchaser, the vendor is entitled to retain the deposit."

That inference has not been overcome by evidence in the case presently under consideration. I, therefore, hold that the payment of $2,500 by the appellant was a deposit paid as a guarantee for the performance of the contract. . . .

It was argued finally that: "The money paid could be retained only if the defendant suffered loss in excess of that amount." I think there is nothing in the decision in *Howe* v. *Smith* or in the cases that followed it, which supports that argument when it appears that the money paid was a deposit to guarantee the performance of the contract.

The appellant did not suggest at any time before the contract was made that the payment of $2,500 should be regarded in any other way than as the usual guarantee that he would perform his part of the contract. He did not suggest that the payment should be returned to him if the contract fell through for any reason. He did not ask that any such provision be included in the written document showing the bargain made by the parties. The appellant has no expressed right to the return of the money, and I am quite unable to find any implied right in his favour. It is to be observed, too, that in the statement of claim, in the statement of defence, and in the proceedings in the Court below, the payment made by the appellant to the respondent was described and treated as a deposit and not as part payment on account of the total contract price.

I conclude that the appellant receded from his contract and abandoned it. He cannot now take advantage of his own wrong and cannot recover the deposit of $2,500 paid by him to the respondent at the time the contract was made between the parties.

I would dismiss the appeal with costs.

[Hogg and Aylesworth JJ.A. also gave reasons for dismissing the appeal.]

QUESTIONS. If Runnymede sold the iron elsewhere at the same or a better price, did they not lose the expenses of one of the sales? How does a deposit differ from a penalty? See *Re Karrys Investments Limited* (1959), 19 D.L.R. (2d) 760 for a case where a deposit was $9400 and the purchase price $9500! In the principal case, would a promise to pay $2500 as liquidated damages and not as a penalty have been enforced? In recent years few Canadian courts have held a penalty clause invalid. Why?

GISVOLD *v*. HILL. 1963. 37 D.L.R. (2d) 606 (British Columbia. Supreme Court). The plaintiffs agreed to sell a house to the defendants and in a *standard form* of real estate contract acknowledged receipt of one dollar "being deposit on account of proposed purchase price" of $17,500. The balance of the purchase price was to be paid on closing. At that time the defendants failed to pay. Three months later the plaintiffs sold the house for $17,900 but the higher price actually netted a lower return to the plaintiffs since they had to pay a salesman's commission of $700 which meant that they received only $17,200, a loss of $300. The court would have allowed the $300 as damages but for a clause in the agreement which provided, "It is understood that time shall be of the essence hereof, and unless the balance of the cash payment is paid and a formal agreement entered into within the time mentioned to pay the balance, the owner may (at his option) cancel this agreement, and in such event the amount paid by the purchaser shall be absolutely forfeited to the owner as liquidated damages." Held, the one dollar deposit was liquidated damages fixed "in advance of the breach and the plaintiffs are bound thereby regardless of the actual damage." AIKINS J.: ". . . Regardless of whether or not in appropriate circumstances a sum of money stated to be liquidated damages and which is disproportionately small in relation to the probable loss may be regarded as a penalty, and relief given to the party to whom the sum is to be paid by allowing him to recover his actual loss, and I do not purport to decide this question, the circumstances of the present case are not in my opinion such as to justify any such relief being given. In the present case the parties entered into a binding agreement to sell and purchase. The parties agreed to a deposit of one dollar. It was stipulated that time should be of the essence. The plaintiffs and the defendants agreed that if the defendants did not make the payment they agreed to make on the agreed date then the plaintiffs would have the right to cancel the agreement and in such event that the deposit would be forfeited as liquidated damages. The Interim Agreement was dated the 16th of March and the cash payment of the balance was to be made on the 25th day of the same month. This is a comparatively short period, nine days only, and I cannot conceive that the parties, if they had directed their minds consciously to the question of what loss the plaintiffs might suffer if the purchase price was not paid at the end of the nine day period, would have come to the conclusions that the value of the house would fluctuate in any substantial amount over such a short time, and that there might be substantial damages. In these circumstances, on the plaintiffs exercising their right, given to them by the agreement, of electing to cancel and retain the house and forfeit the deposit, I do not think it can be said that the forfeiture of the deposit of $1.00 as liquidated damages is unreasonable. It is also an important circumstance of this case that the plaintiffs on default by the defendants were not left in the position that the only thing they could do was forfeit the one dollar deposit. The plaintiffs had an election, they did not have to accept the one dollar, they could, if they had seen fit to do so, have sued to enforce the agreement. In these circumstances the plaintiffs must be held to their bargain. The plaintiffs' action is accordingly dismissed with costs."

[The full report indicates that the plaintiffs signed the standard form in the space for the signature of the vendor's agent and they may not have fully understood the nature of the document they were signing.]

3. Specific Performance And Injunctions

In the preceding sections the remedy awarded by the courts ultimately resulted in the payment of money damages except in the *Ontario Asphalt* case. It was not an "order" to pay a particular sum promised in a contract, although in some cases of course the award may have been calculated by direct reference to such a sum. The successful litigant "recovered" damages. If the defendant failed to pay the damages the state's long arm could reach out and seize his property (if any) to be sold to raise the amount. Generally speaking this was the extent of the remedy and its sanction in the common law courts.

However, along with the development of the "law" in the common law courts, there also developed a supplementary system commonly called "equity," to which reference was made in the *New Sombrero Phosphate* case. If an aggrieved party wanted to have his expectation interest more specifically satisfied, if he wanted to have the promise actually performed, he could turn to equity. This "law" was administered by the Court of Chancery. Generally speaking its remedies were available when it considered the remedies of the common law inadequate. The Chancery Court commonly ordered specific performance of contracts for the sale of the land on the theory that any land, including a jerry-built house on a subdivision lot indistinguishable from its next fifty neighbours on either side, is unique, and no amount of damages could compensate for its loss! If the defendant refused to execute the conveyance when so ordered, he might be sent to prison for contempt.

Today in most jurisdictions the two systems have been merged by merging the courts and providing that where the rules of law and equity conflict, the rules of equity prevail. But just as the rules of law developed through analysis of fact situations, from case to case, so did the rules of equity, and the equitable remedies in our modern legal system are not applied generally, but only to the kinds of fact situation to which the Court of Chancery had applied them. (This broad statement is of course subject to considerable reservation but the reservations can wait until you are ready to deal with them.) To understand the equitable remedies, therefore, you must know the historical processes (accidents?) that took some kinds of disputes into the Chancery Courts but not others.

By far the most common application of the remedy of specific performance is in the sale of land, but the many problems arising from these cases are best left to a course on real estate transactions. The cases that follow raise problems concerning the administration of specific performance in other kinds of contracts where special difficulties and considerations of one sort or another have severely limited it. The emphasis here on building and employment contracts merely anticipates the same emphasis throughout this casebook.

STEWART *v*. KENNEDY. 1890. 15 App. Cas. 75 (Scotland. House of Lords). LORD WATSON: "... I do not think that upon this matter any assistance can be derived from English decisions; because the laws of the two countries regard the right to specific performance from different standpoints. In England the only legal right arising from a breach of contract is a claim of damages; specific performance is not a matter of legal right, but a purely equitable remedy, which the Court can withhold when there are sufficient reasons of conscience or expediency against it. But in Scotland the breach of a contract for the sale of a specific subject such as landed estate, gives the party aggrieved the legal right to sue for implement, and, although he may elect to do so, he cannot be compelled to resort to the alternative of an action of damages unless implement is shewn to be impossible, in which case, *loco facti imprestabilis subit damnum et interesse*. Even where implement is possible, I do not doubt that the Court of Session has inherent power to refuse the legal remedy upon equitable grounds, although I know of no instance in which it has done so. It is quite conceivable that circumstances might occur, which would make it inconvenient and unjust to enforce specific performance of a contract of sale; but I do not think that any such case is presented in this appeal. The fact that the construction of a term in the contract is attended with doubt and difficulty, evidenced it may be by the different meanings attributed to it by Courts or individual judges, ought not, in my opinion, to prevent its receiving its full legal effect, according to the interpretation finally put upon it by a competent tribunal. The argument that, in this case, a decree for specific performance would necessarily impose upon the appellant the duty of performing a long series of personal acts under the supervision of the Court does not appear to me to have a solid basis in fact. The acts which such a decree enjoins would be entirely within his power, and practically might be performed *uno flatu, viz.*, by his signing a conveyance in favour of the respondent, and at the same time giving instructions to his agents to take the necessary steps for obtaining its approval by the Court."

FALCKE *v.* GRAY
England. Chancery. 1859. 29 L.J. Ch. 28

In a suit for specific performance of a contract giving Mr. Falcke the option of purchasing two valuable china jars it appeared that Mr. Falcke had rented a house from Mrs. Gray and had accepted an option to buy some furniture including what Mr. Falcke's counsel described as "a couple of large Oriental jars, with great ugly Chinese pictures upon them." The jars were valued by agreement at £40. Later Mrs. Gray was offered £200 by Messrs. Watson, to whom she promptly sold them. Mrs. Gray stated the jars were left her by a lady who had been offered £100 for them by King George IV. Mr. Falcke was a dealer in the same trade as Messrs. Watson and should have known the actual value of the jars.

KINDERSLEY V.C.: The defendants insist, in the first place, that this bill cannot be maintained on the ground that the plaintiff can have no right to the specific performance of a contract relating solely to chattels. On this question, my opinion is entirely in favour of the plaintiff, that the Court will not refuse such relief. In the eye of this Court, there is no difference between real and personal estate in the performance of a contract; and a contract for one stands in no position different from a contract for the other. The principle upon which this Court decrees specific performance, as enunciated by Lord Redesdale, in *Harnett* v. *Yielding*, 2 Sch. & Lef. 549, is, that a Court of laws deals with the contract, and gives such a decree as it is competent to give in consequence of non-performance—that is, by giving compensation in the shape of damages for the non-performance. But a Court of equity says that it is not enough; and in many cases the mere remuneration and compensation in damages is not sufficient satisfaction. Apply that principle to chattels—and why is it less applicable to them than to real estate? In ordinary contracts, as for the purchase of ordinary articles of use and consumption, such as coals, corn or consols, this Court will not decree specific performance. And why? Because you have only to go into the market and buy another equally good article, and so you can get your compensation. It is not because it is a chattel, but because you can get adequate compensation for it. Now, here these articles are of unusual distinction and curiosity, if not unique; and it is altogether doubtful what price they will fetch. I am of opinion, therefore, that this is a contract which this Court can enforce; and if the case stood alone upon that ground I would decree specific performance. . . .

[The bill was dismissed on another ground, and part of the judgment of the Vice-Chancellor is omitted.]

COSTER *v.* LONG AND BISBY. 1896. 26 S.C.R. 430. STRONG C.J.: "Although not ordinarily interfering in the case of chattels, courts of equity would always take jurisdiction in two cases viz., where the chattel was of particular value so that damages would be no adequate compensation. . . . The other ground was where a fiduciary relationship existed between the parties; there, irrespective altogether of the nature and value of the property, the jurisdiction of equity could always be invoked for the protection of the *cestui que trust.*"

COHEN *v.* ROCHE
England. King's Bench Division. [1927] 1 K.B. 169

At an auction sale Hepplewhite chairs (lot 145) which belonged to the auctioneer, the defendant, himself were knocked down to the plaintiff. After the sale the auctioneer refused to hand over the chairs to the plaintiff. Thereupon the plaintiff brought an action against the defendant in which he claimed for the delivery up of the chairs and alternatively damages for alleged breach of contract.

McCARDIE J.: . . . I now take the final point in the case. The plaintiff sued in detinue only. The writ and statement of claim contain no alternative demand for damages for breach of contract. They ask (a) for delivery up of the chairs or payment of their value, and (b) damages for detention. I have however allowed an amendment whereby the statement of claim asks damages for breach of contract. The plaintiff vigorously contends that he is entitled as of right, once a binding contract is established, to an order for the actual delivery of the chairs, and that he is not limited to damages for breach of bargain. This point raises a question of principle and practice. Here I may again state one or two of the facts. The Hepplewhite chairs in lot 145 possessed no special feature at all. They were ordinary Hepplewhite furniture. The plaintiff bought them in the ordinary way of his trade for the purpose of ordinary resale at a profit. He had no special customer in view. The lot was to become a part of his usual trade stock.

The form of order in detinue cases for the delivery of goods is, in substance, this: "It is this day adjudged that the plaintiff do have a return of the chattels in the statement of claim mentioned and described (here set out description) or recover against the defendant their value (here set out value). . . . and damages for their detention.". . . By order XLVIII., r. 1, however, the Court has power to direct that execution shall issue for the delivery of the goods without giving to the defendant the option to retain the property upon payment of the assessed value. Now in the case before me, the plaintiff desires to secure a warrant for the compulsory and specific delivery of the chairs to him. . . .

But at this point there arise other considerations. In *Chinery* v. *Viall* (1860), 5 H. & N. 288, it was laid down that as between buyer and seller the buyer cannot recover larger damages by suing in tort instead of contract. . . . Bearing *Chinery* v. *Viall* in mind, it is necessary to mention next s. 52 of the *Sale of Goods Act, 1893*, which provides that in any action for breach of contract to deliver specific or ascertained goods the Court may, if it thinks fit, on the application of the plaintiff, direct by its judgment that the contracts shall be performed specifically without giving the defendant the option of retaining the goods on payment of damages. It has been held that s. 52 applies to all cases where the goods are ascertained, whether the property therein has passed to the buyer or not: see Parker J. in *Jones* v. *Earl of Tankerville*, [1909] 2 Ch. 440, 445. It seems clear that the discretionary provisions of s. 52 cannot be consistent with an absolute right of a plaintiff to an order for compulsory delivery under a detinue judgment in such a case as the present. How, then, does the law stand as to detinue? In my view the power of the Court in an action of detinue rests upon a footing which fully accords with s. 52 of the Sale of Goods Act, 1893. In *Whitely, Ld.* v. *Hilt*, [1919] 2 K.B. 808, 819, (an action of detinue) Swinfen Eady, M.R. said: "The power vested in the Court to order the delivery up of a particular chattel is discretionary, and ought not to be exercised when the chattel is an ordinary article of commerce and of no special value or interest, and not alleged to be of any special value to the plaintiff, and where damages would fully compensate." In equity, where a plaintiff alleged and proved the money value of the chattel, it was not the practice of the Court to order its specific delivery: see *Dowling* v. *Betjemann* (1862), 2 J. & H. 544. The law is thus, I am glad to find, consistent in its several parts. In the present case the goods in question were ordinary articles of commerce and of no special value or interest and no grounds exist for any special order for delivery. The judgment should be limited to damages for breach of contract. The plaintiff in his evidence said that the chairs were worth from £70 to £80. With this I agree. I assess the damages at the sum of £15.

For the reasons given I therefore enter judgment for the plaintiff for £15 damages for breach of contract. . . .

[The statement of facts is abridged, and part of the judgment of McCardie J. dealing with the *Statute of Frauds* is omitted. Section 50 of *The Sale of Goods Act*, R.S.O. 1960, c. 358, is substantially the same as s. 52 of the English Act, which has been adopted in all the common law provinces of Canada.]

QUESTION. Suppose the plaintiff buyer in *Cohen* v. *Roche* had agreed to sell the chairs to someone else at a specially lucrative price, which, naturally enough, he had not mentioned to the defendant seller. Should specific performance be granted to enable the plaintiff to take advantage of the contract at no extra expense to the defendant where the advantage might not be accounted for in calculating damages?

BEHNKE *v*. BEDE SHIPPING CO., LTD. [1927] 1 K.B. 649. An action for specific performance of a contract for the sale of a ship. WRIGHT J.: "In the present case there is evidence that the *City* was of peculiar and practically unique value to the plaintiff. She was a cheap vessel, being old, having been built in 1892, but her engines and boilers were practically new and such as to satisfy the German regulations, and hence the plaintiff could, as a German shipowner, have her at once put on the German register. A very experienced ship valuer has said that he knew of only one other comparable ship, but that may now have been sold. The plaintiff wants the ship for immediate use, and I do not think damages would be an adequate compensation. I think he is entitled to the ship and a decree of specific performance in order that justice may be done." It had been contended that the plaintiff had the option of inspecting the vessel and of requiring the sellers to repair any damages found and since the Court would not order performance of a contract to do work the option constituted a bar to specific relief. Wright J. rejected the contention. The sellers were not dry dock owners nor ship-repairers and anyway the plaintiff might not require the inspection.

GILBERT *v*. BARRON

Ontario. High Court. 1958. 13 D.L.R. (2d) 262

WILSON J.: . . . The company, Amerwood (Eastern) Canada Ltd., is incorporated as a public company under the Ontario *Companies Act* by letters patent of this Province dated October 26, 1948. Under agreement with an American company it manufactures and sells a plywood product known as Amerwood, and since 1954 it also manufactures and distributes another product known as Cellotex. The dispute in this action arises out of a struggle for control of the ownership of the shares of the Ontario company, hereinafter called Amerwood.

The plaintiff MacDonald, a successful salesman who resides in the City of Toronto, is responsible for the organization of Amerwood. He sold much treasury stock at Owen Sound, where the company, when organized, carried on its manufacturing operations. As was natural, he became one of the principal shareholders. The other two principal shareholders were one Parkes and the plaintiff Gilbert, an investment broker of many years' standing, who resides in Toronto. Gilbert became a shareholder in 1948, and at the annual meeting in February 1950 he was elected a director. In June 1954 he was elected president, an office he held until he was succeeded by Barron in 1956 in the circumstances hereinafter related. Shortly after his election as a director in 1948, he and Parkes, who was the general manager of the company from its inception until his resignation and retirement on account of ill-health on January 2, 1954, and MacDonald, who was a director and vice-president from the organization of the company until the annual meeting in 1957, entered into an agreement with the object of holding and preserving among the three of them stock control of the company. The terms of this agreement were that if any one of the three should purchase shares in the company, he would offer one-third to each of the other two at cost price. The agreement did not necessarily require the two shareholders to take up the offer but at least they had this right to purchase. This agreement was acted upon when Parkes' son sold his shares to his father. Gilbert and MacDonald agreed that they should be sold to Parkes Sr. because the quantity of shares made no real difference as to the balance of control.

Early in 1953 Parkes became ill, and subsequent to his resignation in January 1954, he died. In January 1954, before his resignation, he sold most of his shares to the defendant Barron, with the approval of Gilbert and MacDonald, after Barron agreed to the same arrangement with respect to the acquisition of future shares as had existed among Parkes, Gilbert and MacDonald. This agreement was made before Barron acquired his shares. The exact date of the agreement is not of great importance. I am satisfied it was made before Barron acquired Parkes' shares. Moreover, as appears later, the agreement was acted upon, and, later again, acknowledged on a Sunday in February 1955 at a meeting, at which Barron, MacDonald and Gilbert were present in Barron's office at Port Credit. I find that Barron acted upon the agreement when he purchased in December 1954 the shares which were known as the 500 Russell shares. This number did not lend itself to an even division, and after negotiation among the three they were divided 150 shares to each of Gilbert, MacDonald and Barron and 50 shares to a member of the staff, Miss Dorothy Gilbank.

By February 1956, without the knowledge of his two fellow shareholders Gilbert and MacDonald, Barron had decided to secure control of the company. He purchased options to buy enough shares to give him voting control of the company and at the annual meeting he had enough proxies and shares in his name to give him voting control of it. After the meeting he took up the options thus acquiring stock control.

Gilbert and MacDonald learned of this control just before the annual meeting and in due course made demands upon Barron for their shares in accordance with the agreement among them. These demands were not replied to, and on February 8, 1957, this action was commenced. In the interval between this annual meeting and the commencement of the action the plaintiffs were acting upon legal advice. . . .

[After considering and rejecting three defences: (1) a denial of the agreement, (2) no consideration, and (3) the *Statute of Frauds*, Wilson J. continued:

The plaintiffs are entitled to specific performance of the agreement in respect of all shares claimed by them. He must tender one-third—that is to say, 816 common and 816 preferred—to each of the plaintiffs who will, upon such tender, pay for them in accordance with the agreement....

The plaintiffs also ask an injunction restraining the defendants from voting the shares to which they are entitled, and from selling, pledging or transferring them. They will have judgment for this relief (directly and indirectly) in respect of Barron. He has apparently placed the shares in the name of Port Credit Lumber Co., of which he has voting share control. However, it is quite apparent that Barron was only using this company as well as his co-defendants as his agent to break the agreement with the plaintiffs. In any event, Barron has not pleaded that it is impossible for him to comply with the contract.

The plaintiffs also ask damages. To this they are entitled as against Barron. No evidence was adduced to prove the amount of damages suffered. I should think there would be some at least loss of salary as directors, but I am unable to conclude there was more. I think the sum of $200 to each of the plaintiffs as nominal damages would suffice. These are the directors' fees they appear to have lost. In other circumstances, even though the task seems an impossible one from the practical point of view, the damages could be assessed at a much higher figure.

In addition to the costs already dealt with, the plaintiffs will have their costs of the action against the defendant Barron which includes the costs they have incurred against the other defendants.

TANENBAUM *v.* W. J. BELL PAPER CO. LTD.
Ontario. High Court. 1956. 4 D.L.R. (2d) 177

The W. J. Bell Paper Co. Ltd., in October, 1951, purchased a parcel of land, marked A on the sketch, from one Tanenbaum, as a site for its new head office and plant. Tanenbaum retained the parcel C on the sketch, and the contract of sale contained a promise by the Bell Co. that it would construct "a roadway not less than twenty-eight feet in width, similar to that at present constructed on Wicksteed Avenue" along the western boundary of parcel A, and that Tanenbaum should have a right of way over it. The Bell Co. also agreed to install sewer and water pipes of unspecified size along the new road to provide service for parcel C which was to be used for "industrial operations." Wicksteed Avenue, a street built by the Town of Leaside, is twenty-eight feet wide, without sidewalks. It had an eight inch Portland cement base with two and one half inches of asphalt "hot-mix" top. The surface was twenty-six feet wide and on each side were twelve inch brick gutters and concrete curbs. After some delay the Bell Co. actually constructed a road with an eight inch crushed stone base and with one and one half to three inches of asphalt, hot or cold mix, on top, with no gutters or curbing. The road was finished in May, 1953, at a cost of about $25,000. The Bell Co. also installed a two inch water main from its own plant to the northern limits of parcel C. The road proved troublesome and in this action for specific performance and damages the court interpreted the contract as calling for a road like Wicksteed Avenue, with a concrete base and gutters and curbs, and a water main at least six inches in diameter.

GALE J.: . . . The defendant must, therefore, be held accountable for the for the breach of contract. The plaintiff asks for specific performance of

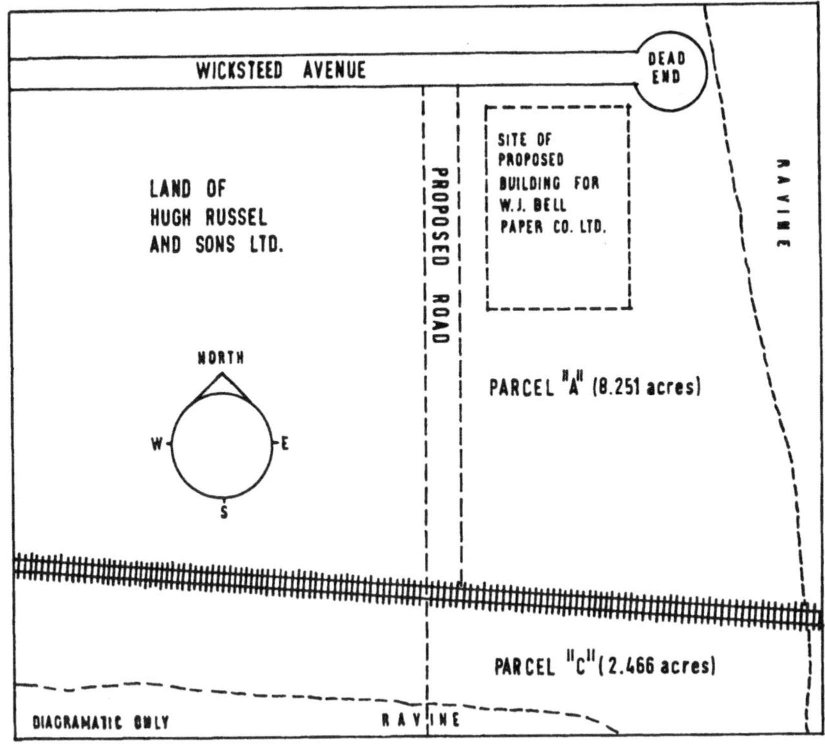

the covenants but the defendant urges that such relief would be inappropriate and too drastic in the circumstances of this case.

Generally the Court will not order a contract to build or to repair to be specifically performed. But an exception to that rule is now recognized and it is my understanding of the authorities that specific performance ought to be decreed where a person undertakes accommodation works on lands possessed by him in consideration for obtaining those lands or in consideration of the purchase-price of other lands sold by him, if the particulars of the work are sufficiently clear and defined and the Court comes to the conclusion that damages will not provide an adequate remedy for the breach of the contract. . . .

That the Court will enforce building contracts in certain circumstances was firmly established in *Wolverhampton Corp.* v. *Emmons*, [1901] 1 K.B. 515. That was a decision of the English Court of Appeal and may well be regarded as the leading modern authority on the subject. In pursuance of a scheme of improvement the plaintiffs, an urban sanitary authority, conveyed to the defendant some lands abutting on a street. The defendant covenanted that he would erect buildings thereon within a certain time. Subsequently the nature and particulars of the houses to be erected were agreed upon, but the defendant failed to fulfil his covenant to build. The plaintiffs thereupon brought the action and were held entitled to a decree of specific performance. That was not a case involving a railway company. Romer L.J. at pp. 524-5 describes the exception to which I have alluded as follows: "There is no doubt that as a general rule the Court will not enforce specific performance of a building contract, but an exception from the rule has been recognised. It has, I think, for some time been held that, in order to bring himself within that exception, a plaintiff must establish three things. The first is that the building work, of which he seeks to enforce the performance, is defined by the contract; that is to say, that the particulars of the work are so far definitely ascertained that the Court can sufficiently see what is the exact nature of the work of which it is asked to order the performance. The second is that the plaintiff has a substantial interest in having the contract performed, which is of such a nature that he cannot adequately be compensated for breach of the contract by damages. The third is that the defendant has by the contract obtained possession of land on which the work is contracted to be done."

The exception so defined by Romer L.J. was considered and expanded somewhat by Farwell J., as he then was, in *Carpenters Estates Ltd.* v. *Davies*, [1940] Ch. 160. In that case the defendant sold certain land to the plaintiffs for building development and agreed to install roads, mains, sewers and drains on other lands retained by her. The covenant having been broken, the plaintiffs succeeded in an action for specific performance. After setting out, *inter alia*, the passage in the *Emmons* case which I have quoted above, Farwell J. seemed to express himself as being of the view that if the conditions as to clarity and inadequacy of damages were present, the plaintiff would be entitled to succeed on his quest for a decree by showing merely that the defendant was in possession of the lands upon which the work was to have been done, and the exception may now perhaps be regarded as being as broad as that. I do not have to settle that question here.

It may be that the learned Judge did not intend to carry the extension of the exception so far because later in his judgment he said at p. 165: "The defendant has contracted to do the work on her own land in consideration of the purchase price of other land belonging to her, and if the other two conditions are fulfilled, I am unable to see why the Court should be debarred from granting relief by way of specific performance." He was not, however, prepared to accept as being completely exhaustive the statement of Romer L.J. and for the moment, therefore, I prefer to express the exception to the general rule as I have done.

Perhaps it is scarcely necessary to add that the exception which I have outlined has been worked into the fabric of the law of Canada. It was acknowledged and applied by two of the three Judges in *Colton* v. *Rookledge* (1872), 19 Gr. 121, and was reasserted by Idington J. in one of the judgments of the Supreme Court of Canada in *Gross* v. *Wright,* [1923], 2 D.L.R. 171, S.C.R. 214. In the latter case the litigants entered into a party-wall agreement under which the defendant was to build a wall 2 ft. or more in thickness with its middle line to coincide with the boundary-line. The wall erected by the defendant complied with the agreement to the level of the second storey but was narrowed from there up on the defendant's side, while remaining perpendicular on the plaintiff's side. The latter discovered this situation some years after the wall formed part of the defendant's building and sued for a mandatory injunction to compel the latter to pull down that which had been erected and for specific performance of the agreement. The majority of the Court granted a mandatory injunction on the theory that having obtained a licence to enter on the land for a particular purpose and having breached that licence, the defendant was committing a trespass. However, Idington J. expressly awarded the decree which was sought on the ground that the Court had jurisdiction to grant specific performance of the agreement itself. Indeed at p. 176 D.L.R., p.

219 S.C.R., he stated that in his opinion specific performance was the only appropriate remedy in the circumstances and certainly the other members of the Court did not take the position that the relief being ordered could not have been based on the claim for specific performance of the contract between the parties.

Here the defendant argues that specific performance is not available to the plaintiff, firstly because the terms of the agreement, ex. 1, as to the road and watermain are not sufficiently explicit, secondly, because the plaintiff can be appropriately compensated in damages if those works do not comply with the provisions of the agreement; and lastly, because the plaintiff has had some performance from the defendant.

As already indicated, I am of the opinion that the road and watermain which were to have been installed by the defendant were sufficiently described by the contract and that the defendant failed to fulfil its obligations in that respect. It is very difficult, if not impossible, to set down a general formula as to what degree of certainty is required in a contract before the Court will enforce its performance, so much depends upon the facts of each case. But I think it may be said with confidence that the certainty which is essential must be a reasonable one, having regard to the nature and subject-matter of the undertaking and the attendant conditions under which and with regard to which it was entered into. The authorities on this point substantiate such a conclusion....

All the defendant had to do here was to have copied the essential elements of a named street and to have installed a main which, in view of what must have been in the minds of the parties, would be at least 6 ins. in diameter. There was no room for doubt as to what was to be done and accordingly I hold that the plaintiff is not to be denied his decree by reason of any suggestion of uncertainty or ambiguity as to the nature of the work.

Probably the most serious objection to the granting of specific performance comes from the submission that if the road and watermain do not meet the terms of the agreement, the plaintiff can be properly and sufficiently compensated in damages. Let me say at once, however, that it is my view that such relief, even if capable of being calculated, would be quite inadequate to atone for the inadequacy of the watermain. As long as that pipe remains its sole source of water, parcel "C" cannot be put to its full use and certainly its potential sale value cannot be realized. I suspect that counsel for the defendant was aware of the hopelessness of his arguments that a pecuniary award could counterbalance the lack of a suitable main, because, while stoutly resisting all efforts to have the road replaced, he conceded that the installation of a new watermain would not be a very serious matter.

The question whether damages ought to be substituted for performance with respect to the road has not been easy to decide but here again I do not subscribe to the idea that an award of damages would give the proper relief. It would be futile to attempt to lay down a general rule as to when damages will be ordered in lieu of enforcing performance. . . .

The best statement on the subject that I have been able to find appears in Williston on Contracts, rev. ed., vol. 5, s. 1423, pp. 3976-7, where this appears: "In contracts other than those ordinarily designated as contracts of service, it is generally true so far as affirmative relief is concerned, that 'Equity will not award specific performance where the duty to be enforced is continuous and reaches over a long period of time, requiring constant supervision by the court.' Therefore, 'There is no doubt that as a general rule the Court will not enforce specific performance of a building contract.' The basis of equity's disinclination to enforce building contracts specifically is the difficulty of enforcing a decree without an expenditure of effort disproportionate to the value of the result. But where the inadequacy of damages is great, and the difficulties not extreme, specific performance will be granted and the tendency in modern times has been increasingly towards granting relief, where under the particular circumstances of the case damages are not an adequate remedy."

In this instance certainly the difficulties which would follow a decree of specific performance would not be extreme. The present roadway would have to be taken up and replaced with what should have been installed there in the first place and that would, of course, be an expensive undertaking. Indeed, the defendant protests strenuously that the cost of having to supplant the present road would not only be substantial but would also be out of all proportion to the advantages to be achieved by doing so. However, in many judgments upon the subject it has frequently been declared that mere hardship on the party in default should not be allowed to overcome the exercise of the Court's discretion in favour of ordering performance. Needless to say, if damages could be easily ascertained and were relatively insignificant in amount, I would pause long before making an order which might seriously prejudice the defendant's existence. Obviously that is not the situation here. As I shall point out in a moment, any attempt to assess damages is likely to prove abortive and the cost of building a proper road, while heavy by some standards, will by no means cripple the defendant company. And it must never be forgotten that if the decree were withheld the Court would, in one sense, be permitting the defendant to take advantage of its own wrong. . . .

If for no other reason . . . the conduct of the defendant and its contractor would probably induce me to grant that relief, for, as I have already mentioned, the reckless and almost wilful manner in which the plaintiff's rights were put aside would cause any Court to deal with the defendant quite dispassionately.

It strikes me too that the inadequacy of damages would be of significance here for the added reason that the full enjoyment of worth of the plaintiff's land is permanently impaired while the road is allowed to remain as it is.

However, perhaps the most formidable obstacle to the granting of damages comes from the fact that to try to calculate those damages would be an almost insuperable task. They arise in several ways. The plaintiff should have an amount equivalent to the difference between the estimated cost of repairing the private roadway and that of repairing one like Wicksteed Ave. during the life span of the latter. Counsel for the defendant urged that a monetary allowance for that difference would represent the full loss sustained by its adversary, but I do not agree, for clearly the enjoyment of parcel "C" and its disposal-value will continue to be adversely affected so long as the present road is there. I propose to examine those two sources of damages to determine whether either can be properly ascertained.

In the first place, it is questionable who will be making any future repairs. Certainly the defendant has the right to rebuild or repair the road but it is not obliged to do since the agreement contains no covenant to that effect. Conversely, the plaintiff has no right to alter or rebuild that which is there. But can he repair the road? On behalf of the defendant it was said that Mr. Tanenbaum could enter upon it to make minor repairs at his own expense and counsel for the plaintiff concurred in that suggestion. It is extremely difficult to say, however, to what extent that privilege can be exercised. For example, the plaintiff could not close off the road at any time for that purpose without obtaining permission, for the defendant has already granted further rights of way over it to the Russell company and perhaps to others. It occurs to me, therefore, that it would not be easy to define in advance the scope of the repairs which the plaintiff might make; asuredly he could not make material alterations to that which is there.

Even assuming that the plaintiff is at liberty to mend the surface of the road as it deteriorates, how could the present value of the cost of doing so be reckoned? The evidence proved beyond doubt that Wicksteed Ave. would not require as much in the way of maintenance as the private road but that on occasions when repairs will have to be made the cost of doing so will exceed that which will have to be expended for individual repairs to the private road. That being so, anyone fastened with the unenviable duty of assessing damages would be required to determine the life-expectancy of a cement-based road and then try to estimate what the repairs to this road over that period of time would amount to. I am completely convinced that it would be quite impossible to do that with any degree of accuracy because the extent of future repairs and their frequency will depend on the volume and weight of the traffic the road will be called upon to carry and the speeds at which the vehicles will pass over it. Even if the magnitude and volume of repairs could be predicted, how could anyone come to a conclusion as to what those repairs would cost, bearing in mind that no one can know when they will be needed? Prices ten years hence may bear no relation to to-day's prices. And if all of these data could in some miraculous way be calculated, they would still have to be compared with similar data concerning an imaginary cement-based road.

If the damages relating to the comparative cost of repairs could be determined the struggle would not be over, for there would still have to be a decision as to the amount of damages accruing to the plaintiff because the present road causes and will continue to cause some reduction in the disposal-value of parcel "C". . . .

The defendant finally contended that specific performance ought not to be granted because the plaintiff has been provided with a hard-surfaced road which can be used. In other words, counsel suggested that since the plaintiff has had some measure of performance, he is precluded from obtaining anything but damages. Once again I do not agree and I am substantiated by the authorities. In *Lane* v. *Newdigate* (1804), 10 Ves. 192, 32 E.R. 818, the decree was made and again in *Gross* v. *Wright*, [1923], 2 D.L.R. 171, S.C.R. 214, the Court, and particularly Idington J., did not hesitate to order the demolition of a substantial part of an existing building and the reconstruction of a wall which had been built but did not comply with the agreement between the parties. If it were otherwise, it would mean that a person who has determined upon non-observance of a contract could arbitrate on what was to be done. I concede, of course that specific performance would probably be refused if the disparity of execution were slight, but that is not the situation here. The differences between the two roads are notable and the fact that the plaintiff will always be out of possession of the lands on which the road is laid and that he has no certain or clear right to effect even minor repairs to it is one which should never be overlooked.

For those reasons I order the defendant to cause to be installed along westerly boundary of its lands a roadway similar to Wicksteed Ave. and by that I have in mind that there should be laid a road at least 28 ft. wide, having an 8-in. Portland cement base, a 2½-in. asphaltic standard highway hot-mix top, two brick gutters 12 ins. in width and consisting of 3 courses of brick and cement curbs. That roadway should extend, of course, from the southerly limit of Wicksteed Ave. to the north rail of the present railway siding. In addition, the defendant must also cause to be installed a 6-in. watermain leading from or close to the defendant's hydrant which is approximately 363 ft. south of the Town main to parcel "C". If the plaintiff desires to have an 8-in. main he will have to pay the difference between the installation of one of that dimension and the 6-in. main I have ordered. I see no reason why both of these works cannot be completed within 4 months from the date of this judgment. . . .

[A large part of the judgment dealing with damages arising from the delay in performance and the resulting inaccessibility of steel stored on Tanenbaum's land is omitted.]

RYAN *v*. MUTUAL TONTINE WESTMINSTER CHAMBERS ASSOCIATION

England. Chancery Division. [1893] 1 Ch. 116

KAY L.J.: . . . This remedy by specific performance was invented, and has been cautiously applied, in order to meet cases where the ordinary remedy by an action for damages is not adequate compensation for breach of contract. The jurisdiction to compel specific performance has always been treated as discretionary, and confined within well-known rules. In this case the Plaintiff is the lessee of a flat, which forms portion of a large building. In the lease is a covenant to the effect that the premises are taken by the lessee subject to certain regulations made by the lessors with respect to the duties of the resident porter and other matters, which are set out in a schedule. By the schedule it is stated that the building is divided into blocks, and the rooms in each block are, together with the entrance and staircase belonging to it, in charge of a resident porter, appointed and removeable by the lessors, but who shall be and act as the servant of the tenants of the several rooms in the block. The tenants are to have the right to the general services of the porter resident in their block within the scope of his general duties, as defined by rule 6. They are also to have the right to the special services of such porter, as defined by rules 8, 9 and 10. The Plaintiff's right under this covenant appears to me to be to have the advantage of the performance of the specified duties by the resident porter. In this case a man was appointed as porter, and held office; the complaint really was that he was not a proper porter, and the tenant did not get the advantage of the services stipulated for in the schedule; that he was not constantly in attendance; but, being engaged elsewhere, was not on the premises as much as he should be; and that, when he was there, he did not perform his duties himself. When one looks at that which was the real gravamen of the action, the contention seems rather odd that we ought to divide the contract into two parts—one that a porter should be appointed, the other that he should perform the duties specified. The lessor's covenant being in substance that the lessee should have the advantage of the performance of certain services by the porter, a covenant which I cannot conceive to be divisible, as was ingeniously suggested, the Plaintiff's claim is shaped thus. It is alleged that the lessee took possession under the lease, but that a porter was not appointed, and the lessee does not get the advantage of the performance of the porter's duties. He therefore asks for some remedy by means of which he may have these duties performed. That is really the nature of the action. But now it is sought to overlook that, and to say that, though a contract that the lessee shall have the benefit of the performance by the porter of his duties is not the sort of contract of which the Plaintiff can have specific performance, yet he can claim to have the contract performed specifically to this extent; he can ask the Court to compel the appointment of a proper porter, though, when he is appointed, the Court is not asked to compel performance of his duties. As I have said, the contract is really a single contract—viz., that the Plaintiff shall have the advantage of performance by the porter of his duties; and I dissent entirely from the notion that this contract can be divided in to two parts in the way suggested, and the Court asked to grant specific performance of one part, but not of the other.

There are, no doubt, certain cases where a contract may be treated as divisible for the purpose of specific performance. The common case is where there is a contract like that in *Lumley* v. *Wagner* (1852), 1 De G.M. & G. 604; 42 E.R. 687, in which case the contract was to sing for the plaintiff, and not to sing for others. The Court says in such cases, though we cannot enforce performance of the contract to sing for a particular person, and so cannot enforce the whole contract; nevertheless, there being the independent negative stipulation against singing for others, we can enforce that by injunction. In the case of *Lumley* v. *Wagner,* the Lord Chancellor . . . expressly said that if he had to deal with the affirmative covenant only that the defendant would sing for the plaintiff, he would not have granted an injunction. That is one exception to the rule.

There is another exception to the general rule as to the specific performance. Ordinarily the Court will not enforce specific performance of works, such as building works, the prosecution of which the Court cannot superintend; not only on the ground that damages are generally in such cases an adequate remedy, but also on the ground of the inability of the Court to see that the work is carried out. . . . An exception to this rule has been established in cases where a railway company has taken lands from a landowner on the terms that it will carry out certain works. In those cases, because damages are not adequate remedy, the Court has gone to great lengths, and has granted specific performance of the definite works—they must be defininte works—which the company that has taken the lands has contracted to do. This case does no come within either of the exceptions to which I have alluded. Therefore, for the reasons stated by the Master of the Rolls, this case is not one in which the Court could compel specific performance.

There appears to me to be also another reason for our decision which is quite sufficient. At the time when the action was brought there had been a breach of covenant. The learned Judge found no difficulty in assessing damages for breach of the contract down to that time. Why should there be any difficulty with regard to future breaches of contract? I have heard no sufficient reason adduced in the argument. If for the breach of contract down to action brought adequate compensation may be given by damages, that appears to me to be a reason for the Court not exercising its extraordinary jurisdiction. A sufficient reply to this argument is not afforded by the mere fact that these damages are not compensation for future breaches of contract. If that were sufficient, I cannot conceive of any case of a continuing contract where specific performance might not be granted. For these reasons I differ respectfully from the learned Judge, and think that nothing but a judgment for the damages found by him should be given.

[The opinions of Lord Esher M.R. and Lopes L.J. are omitted. The trial judge awarded specific performance but in case he was wrong he also assessed damages at £25.]

WARNER BROS. PICTURES INCORPORATED *v*. NELSON
England. King's Bench. [1937] 1 K.B. 209

BRANSON J.: The facts of this case are few and simple. The plaintiffs are a firm of film producers in the United States of America. In 1931 the defendant then not well known as a film actress [Miss Bette Davis], entered into a contract with the plaintiffs. Before the expiration of that contract the present contract was entered into between the parties. Under it the defendant received a considerably enhanced salary, the other conditions being substantially the same. This contract was for fifty-two weeks and contains options to the plaintiffs to extend it for further periods of fifty-two weeks at ever-increasing amounts of salary to the defendant. No question of construction arises upon the contract, and it is not necessary to refer to it in any great detail; but in view of some of the contentions raised it is desirable to call attention quite generally to some of the provisions contained in it. It is a stringent contract, under which the defendant agrees "to render her exclusive services as a motion picture and/or legitimate stage actress" to the plaintiffs, and agrees to perform solely and exclusively for them. She also agrees, by way of negative stipulation, that "she will not, during such time"—that is to say, during the term of the contract—"render any services for or in any other phonographic, stage or motion picture production or productions or business of any other person . . . or engage in any other occupation without the written consent of the producer being first had and obtained."

With regard to the term of the contract there is further clause, clause 23, under which, if the defendant fails, refuses or neglects to perform her services under the contract, the plaintiffs "have the right to extend the term of this agreement and all of its provisions for a period equivalent to the period during which such failure, refusal or neglect shall be continued."

In June of this year the defendant, for no discoverable reason except that she wanted more money, declined to be further bound by the agreement, left the United States and, in September, entered into an agreement in this country with a third person. This was a breach of contract on her part, and the plaintiffs on September 9 commenced this action claiming a declaration that the contract was valid and binding, an injunction to restrain the defendant from acting in breach of it, and damages. The defence alleged that the plaintiffs had committed breaches of the contract which entitled the defendant to treat it as at an end; but at the trial this contention was abandoned and the defendant admitted that the plaintiffs had not broken the contract and that she had; but it was contended on her behalf that no injunction could as a matter of law be granted in the circumstances of the case.

At the outset of the considerations of law which arise stands the question, not raised by the pleadings but urged for the defendant in argument, that this contract is unlawful as being in restraint of trade. The ground for this contention was that the contract compelled he defendant to serve the plaintiffs exclusively, and might in certain circumstances endure for the whole of her natural life. No authority was cited to me in support of the proposition that such a contract is illegal, and I see no reason for so holding. Where, as in the present contract, the covenants are all concerned with what is to happen whilst the defendant is employed by the plaintiffs and not thereafter, there is no room for the application of the doctrine of restraint of trade. . . .

I turn then to the consideration of the law applicable to this case on the basis that the contract is a valid and enforceable one. It is conceded that our Courts will not enforce a positive covenant of personal service; and specific performance of the positive covenants by the defendant to serve the plaintiffs is not asked in the present case. The practice of the Court of Chancery in relation to the enforcement of negative covenants is stated on the highest authority by Lord Cairns in the House of Lords in *Doherty* v. *Allman* (3 App. Cas. 709). His Lordship says: "My Lords, if there had been a negative covenant, I apprehend, according to well-settled practice, a Court of equity would have had no discretion to exercise. If parties, for valuable consideration, with their eyes open, contract that a particular thing shall not be done, all that a Court of Equity has to do is to say, by way of injunction, that which the parties have already said by way of covenant, that the thing shall not be done; and in such case the injunction does nothing more than give the sanction of the process of the Court to that which already is the contract between the parties. It is not then a question of the balance of convenience or inconvenience, or of the amount of damage or of injury—it is the specific performance, by the Court, of that negative bargain which the parties have made, with their eyes open, between themselves."

That was not a case of a contract of personal service; but the same principle had already been applied to such a contract by Lord St. Leonards in *Lumley* v. *Wagner* (1852), 1 De G.M. & G. 604; 42 E.R. 687. The Lord Chancellor used the following language: "Wherever this Court has no proper jurisdiction to enforce specific performance, it operates to bind men's consciences, as far as they can be bound, to a true and literal performance of their agreements; and it will not suffer them to depart from their contract at their pleasure, leaving the party with whom they have contracted to the mere chance of any damages which a jury may give. The exercise of this jurisdiction has, I believe, had a wholesome tendency towards the maintenance of that good faith which exists in this country to a much greater degree perhaps than in any other; and although the jurisdiction is not to be extended, yet a judge would desert his duty who did not act up to what his predecessors have handed down as the rule for his guidance in the administration of such an equity." . . .

The defendant, having broken her positive undertakings in the contract without any cause or excuse which she was prepared to support in the witness-box, contends that she cannot be enjoined from breaking the negative covenants also. The mere fact that a covenant which the Court would not enforce, if expressed in positive form, is expressed in the negative instead, will not induce the Court to enforce it. . . . The Court will attend to the substance and not to the form of the covenant. Nor will the Court, true to the principle that specific performance of a contract of personal service will never be ordered, grant an injunction in the case of such a contract to enforce negative covenants if the effect of so doing would be to drive the defendant either to starvation or to specific performance of the positive covenants. . . .

Rely-a-Bell Burglar and Fire Alarm Co., Ltd. v. *Eisler,* [1926] Ch. 609 which was strongly relied upon by the defendant, . . . Russell, J., as he then was, said, . . ."It was said that the covenants . . . were so framed that the servant, if the covenants were enforced, could make his living neither by serving nor by carrying on business independently; whereas in the present case the covenant only prohibited serving. Therefore, it was said, he was still free to start in business on his own account, and it could not be said, if an injunction were granted in the terms of the covenant, that he would be forced to remain idle and starve. That distinction seems to me somewhat of a mockery. It would be idle to tell this defendant, a servant employed at a wage, that he must not serve anybody else in that capacity, but that the world was still open to him to start business as an indepedent man. It seems to me that if I were to restrain this man according to the terms of the covenant, he would be forced to remain idle and starve." Had it not been for that view of the facts, I think that the learned Judge would have granted an injunction in that case.

The conclusion to be drawn from the authorities is that, where a contract of personal service contains negative covenants the enforcement of which will not amount either to a decree of specific performance of the positive covenants of the contract or to the giving of a decree under which the defendant must either remain idle or perform those positive covenants, the Court will enforce those negative covenants; but this is subject to a further consideration. An injunction is a discretionary remedy, and the Court in granting it may limit it to what the Court considers reasonable in all the circumstances of the case.

This appears from the judgment of the Court of Appeal in *William Robinson & Co., Ltd.* v. *Heuer,* [1898] 2 Ch. 451. The particular covenant in that case is set out at p. 452 and provides that "Heuer shall not during this engagement, without the previous consent in writing of the said W. Robinson & Co., Ltd.," and so forth, "carry on or be engaged either directly or indirectly, as principal agent, servant, or otherwise, in any trade, business or calling, either relating to goods of any description sold or manufactured by the said W. Robinson & Co., Ltd. . . . or in any other business whatsoever.". . .

Before parting with that case, I should say that the Court there proeeded to sever the covenants and to grant an injunction, not to restrain the defendant from carying on any other business whatsoever, but framed so as to give what was felt to be a reasonable protection to the plaintiffs and no more. The plaintiffs waived an option which they possessed to extend the period of service for an extra five years, and the injunction then was granted for the remaining period of unextended time. . . .

The case before me is, therefore, one in which it would be proper to grant an injunction unless to do so would in the circumstances be tantamount to ordering the defendant to perform her contract or remain idle or unless damages would be the more appropriate remedy.

With regard to the first of these considerations, it would, of course, be impossible to grant an injunction covering all the negative covenants in the contract. That would, indeed, force the defendant to perform her contract or remain idle; but this objection is removed by the restricted form in which the injunction is sought. It is confined to forbidding the defendant, without the consent of the plaintiffs, to render any services for or in any motion picture or stage production for any other than the plaintiffs.

It was also urged that the difference between what the defendant can earn as a film artiste and what she might expect to earn by any other form of activity is so great that she will in effect be driven to perform her contract. That is not the criterion adopted in any of the decided cases. The defendant is stated to be a person of intelligence, capacity and means, and no evidence was adduced to show that, if enjoined from doing the specified acts otherwise than for the plaintiffs, she will not be able to employ herself both usefully and remuneratively in other spheres of activity, though not as remuneratively as in her special line. She will not be driven, although she may be tempted to perform the contract, and the fact that she may be so tempted is no objection to the grant of an injunction. This appears from the judgment of Lord St. Leonards in *Lumley* v. *Wagner*, where he used the following language: "It was objected that the operation of the injunction in the present case was mischievous, excluding the defendant J. Wagner from performing at any other theatre while this Court had no power to compel her to perform at Her Majesty's Theatre. It is true, that I have not the means of compelling her to sing, but she has no cause of complaint, if I compel her to abstain from the commission of an act which she has bound herself not to do, and thus possibly cause her to fulfil her engagement. The jurisdiction which I now exercise is wholly within the power of the Court and being of the opinion that it is a proper case for interfering, I shall leave nothing unsatisfied by the judgment I pronounce. The effect, too, of the injunction, in restraining J. Wagner from singing elsewhere may, in the event"—that is a different matter—"of an action being brought against her by the plaintiff, prevent any such amount of vindictive damages being given against her as a jury might probably be inclined to give if she had carried her talents and exercised them at the rival theatre: the injunction may also, as I have said, tend to the fulfilment of her engagement; though, in continuing the injunction, I disclaim doing indirectly what I cannot do directly."

With regard to the question whether damages is not the more appropriate remedy, I have the uncontradicted evidence of the plaintiffs as to the difficulty of estimating the damages which they may suffer from the breach by the defendant of her contract. I think it is not inappropriate to refer to the fact that, in the contract between the parties, in clause 22, there is a formal admission by the defendant that her services, being "of a special, unique, extraordinary and intellectual character" gives them a particular value "the loss of which cannot be reasonably or adequately compensated in damages" and that the breach may "cost the producer great and irreparable injury and damage," and the artist expressly agrees that the producer shall be entitled to the remedy of injunction. Of course, parties cannot contract themselves out of the law; but it assists, at all events, on the question of evidence as to the applicability of an injunction in the present case, to find the parties formally recognizing that in cases of this kind injunction is a more appropriate remedy than damages.

Furthermore, in the case of *Grimston* v. *Cuningham*, [1894] 1 Q.B. 125, which was also a case in which a theatrical manager was attempting to enforce against an actor a negative stipulation against going elsewhere, Wills, J., granted an injunction and used the following language: "This is an engagement of a kind which is pre-eminently subject to the interference of the Court by injunction, for in cases of this nature it very often happens that the injury suffered in consequence of the breach of the agreement would be out of all proportion to any pecuniary damages which could be proved or assessed by a jury. This circumstance affords a strong reason in favour of exercising the discretion of the Court by granting an injunction."

I think that that applies to the present case also, and that an injunction should be granted in regard to the specified services.

Then comes the question as to the period for which the injunction should operate. The period of the contract, now that the plaintiffs have undertaken not as from October 16, 1936, to exercise the rights of suspension conferred upon them by clause 23 thereof, will, if they exercise their options to prolong it, extend to about May, 1942. As I read the judgment of the Court of Appeal in *Robinson* v. *Heuer* the Court should make the period such as to give reasonable protection and no more to the plaintiffs against the ill effects to them of the defendant's breach of contract. The evidence as to that was perhaps necessarily somewhat vague. The main difficulty that the plaintiffs apprehend is that the defendant might appear in other films whilst the films already made by them and not yet shown are in the market for sale or hire and thus depreciate their value. I think that if the injunction is in force during the continuance of the contract or for three years from now, whichever period is the shorter, that will substantially meet the case.

The other matter is as to the area within which the injunction is to operate. The contract is not an English contract and the parties are not British subjects. In my opinion all that properly concerns this Court is to prevent the defendant from committing the prohibited acts within the jurisdiction of this Court, and the injunction will be limited accordingly.

BETTE DAVIS, THE LONELY LIFE. 1962. Chapter eleven and the first of chapter twelve of this autobiography tell in some detail the story of *Warner Brothers* v. *Nelson* from Mrs. Nelson's point of view. When she left the United States she had already won an Academy Award, and felt confined by her contract and convinced that Warner Brothers had no serious intention of letting her choose her own parts or find parts she would approve. A few other actors and actresses were also battling the restrictive terms of the standard form of actor's contract. Mrs. Nelson mentions familiar names, James Cagney, Margaret Sullavan, Carole Lombard and Eddie Cantor. In a comparatively new industry, the "stars" were beginning to realize their contribution and were rebelling against the "slavery" of the contract designed to serve the convenience of a more experienced business management. Apparently Mrs. Nelson thought she could not be stopped from working abroad. The litigation cost Mrs. Nelson over $30,000. Sir William Jowitt, retained for the defence, had "recommended" that Mrs. Nelson immediately give him a $10,000 retainer. At this time Mrs. Nelson was, of course, under suspension and receiving no salary. Her decision not to appeal was largely influenced by the actor George Arliss, who had said, "I admire your courage in this affair but now—go back and face them proudly." In fact, Warner Brothers welcomed Mrs. Nelson with open arms and graciously assumed their share of the costs and part of hers. Their standard form had received a shot in the arm that gave assurance to the management side of the whole film industry. In recent years several Hollywood actors have assumed the added role of producer in order to overcome the restraints of the older standard forms.

DETROIT FOOTBALL CO. *v*. DUBLINSKI. 1957. 7 D.L.R. (2d) 9 (Ontario Court of Appeal). The Detroit Football Club applied on June 16, 1955, for an injunction restraining Dublinski from playing football with the

Toronto Argonauts and alleging irreparable damage if Dublinski's breach of his contract with the Club were not restrained. Dublinski deposed that his livelihood was solely dependent on his playing professional football and if restrained he would be unable to earn a livelihood. This "evidence, however strange it may seem, stands unimpeached and uncontradicted." An interlocutory injunction was refused by WELLS J. ([1955] 4 D.L.R. 176). By the time the action came on for trial before MCRUER C.J.H.C. on July 26, 1956 (4 D.L.R. (2d) 688) the contract and the renewal had expired. The action was for damages and a declaration that the Club was entitled to have Dublinski restrained. MCRUER C.J.H.C. said, referring to the *Warner Brothers* case: "This is a decision of a single Judge and I do not think it applies to this case. If it purports to hold that a Court of equity will enforce a negative convenant attached to a contract of employment by granting an injunction where the injunction will protect no interest by enforcing the negative covenant apart from the interest flowing from the positive covenant, I decline to follow it. But a careful examination of the argument in that case shows that what the plaintiff wished to be protected against was the exploitation of the defendant's services by a company competing with it that had a world market. . . . All through the cases runs the thread of the principle that a Court of equity will only protect a plaintiff for a period against *likely damage* by reason of the breach of a negative covenant, express or implied. . . ." Since the Detroit Club and the Toronto Argonauts played in separate and distinct leagues, for different audiences, and the Detroit Club had broken off its relationship with Dublinski, the fact that "the defendant played football or was likely to play football for the Argonaut Club during the playing season of 1955 did the plaintiff no more harm than if he had remained idle." The plaintiff Club appealed. The Court of Appeal did not deal with the question of the injunction, but awarded damages in the amount of $6,950. ROACH J. A. said, "It requires only a mathematical calculation to demonstrate that, leaving out of consideration the value of the players traded to the Washington Red Skins [there was no evidence on this point], it cost the plaintiff $6,950 to fill the gap caused by the defendant breaking his contract. That calculation is as follows:

'To paid in acquiring the substitute	$10,000.00	
'To paid salary of substitute	11,200.00	
'By credit—Salary of defendant		$ 7,750.00
'By credit—Salary of one traded player		6,500.00
	$21,200.00	$14,250.00
	14,250.00	
'Net cost to plaintiff	$ 6,950.00' "	

ROACH J.A. accepted the submission that this calculation did not adequately account for the heavy investment of the plaintiff Club in training Dublinski. "It is very much like the case of the owner of a thoroughbred colt. . . . If the animal should break its legs the day before the race, all the money spent on it is a dead loss. Here, the defendant broke his contract, and it seems reasonable to me that the plaintiff, like the owner of the colt, has suffered some loss." However there was no evidence on this point to enable the court to assess the amount. "It is possible that [the Club] suffered a greater loss. The Court however, cannot fix a sum that would amount to perfect compensation and I have concluded that on all evidence, justice would probably be done by fixing the damages at $6,950."

4. When the Remedies May Be Sought

FROST *v.* KNIGHT
England. Exchequer Chamber. 1872. L.R. 7 Exch. 111

Cockburn C.J.: This case comes before us on error, brought in a judgment of the Court of Exchequer arresting the judgment in the action on a verdict given for the plaintiff.

The action was for breach of promise of marriage. The promise, as proved, was to marry the plaintiff on the death of the defendant's father. The father still living, the defendant announced his intention of not fulfilling his promise on his father's death, and broke off the engagement, whereupon the plaintiff, without waiting for the father's death, at once brought the present action. The plaintiff having obtained a verdict, a rule nisi was applied for to arrest the judgment, on the ground that a breach of the contract could only arise on the father's death, till which event no claim for performance could be made, and, consequently, till its occurrence, no action for breach of the contract be maintained. A rule nisi having been granted, a majority of the Court of Exchequer concurred in making it absolute, Martin B., dissenting; and the question for us is, whether the judgment of the majority was right. . . .

The law with reference to a contract to be performed at a future time, where the party bound to performance announces prior to the time his intention not to perform it, as established by the cases . . . may be thus stated: The promisee, if he pleases, may treat the notice of intention as inoperative, and await the time when the contract is to be executed, and then hold the other party responsible for all the consequences of non-performance; but in that case he keeps the contract alive for the benefit of the other party as well as his own; he remains subject to all his own obligations and liabilities under it, and enables the other party not only to complete the contract, if so advised, notwithstanding his previous repudiation of it, but also to take advantage of any supervening circumstance which would justify him in declining to complete it.

On the other hand, the promisee may, if he thinks proper, treat the repudiation of the other party as a wrongful putting an end to the contract, and may at once bring his action as on a breach of it; and in such action he will be entitled to such damages as would have arisen from the non-performance of the contract at the appointed time, subject, however, to abatement in respect of any circumstances which may have afforded him the means of mitigating his loss.

Considering this to be now settled law, . . . we should have no difficulty in applying the principle of the decision in *Hochster* v. *De La Tour* (1853), 2 E.&B. 678; 118 E.R. 922, to the present case, were it not for the difference which undoubtedly exists between that case and the present, viz., that, whereas there the performance of the contract was to take place at a fixed time, here no time is fixed, but the performance is made to depend on a contingency, namely, the death of the defendant's father during the lifetime of the contracting parties. It is true that in every case of a personal obligation to be fulfilled at a future time, there is involved the possible contingency of the death of the party binding himself, before the time of performance arrives; but here we have a further contingency depending on the life of a third person, during which neither party can claim performance of the promise. This being so, we thought it right to take the time to consider whether an action would lie before the death of the defendant's father had placed the plaintiff in a position to claim the fulfilment of the defendant's promise.

After full consideration we are of opinion that, notwithstanding the distinguishing circumstance to which I have referred, this case falls within the principle of *Hochster* v. *De La Tour*, and that consequently, the present action is well brought.

The considerations on which the decision in *Hochster* v. *De La Tour* is founded are that the announcement of the contracting party of his intention not to fulfil the contract amounts to a breach, and that it is for the common benefit of both parties that the contract shall be taken to be broken as to all its incidents, including non-performance at the appointed time; as by an action being brought at once, and the damages consequent on non-performance being assessed at the earliest moment, many of the injurious effects of such non-performance may possibly be averted or mitigated.

It is true, as is pointed out by the Lord Chief Baron in his judgment in this case, that there can be no actual breach of contract by reason of non-performance so long as the time for performance has not yet arrived. But, on the other hand, there is—and the decision in *Hochster* v. *De La Tour* proceeds on that assumption—a breach of the contract when the promisor repudiates it and declares he will no longer be bound by it. The promisee has an inchoate right to the performance of the bargain, which becomes complete when the time for performance has arrived. In the meantime he has a right to have the contract kept open as a subsisting and effective contract. Its unimpaired and unimpeached efficacy may be essential to his interest. His rights acquired under it may be dealt with by him in various ways for his benefit and advantage. Of all such advantage the repudiation of the contract by the other party, and the announcement that it never will be fulfilled, must of course deprive him. It is therefore quite right to hold that such an announcement amounts to a violation of the contract *in omnibus*, and that upon it the promisee, if so minded, may at once treat it as a breach of the entire contract, and bring this action accordingly.

The contract having been thus broken by the promisor, and treated as broken by the promisee, performance at the appointed time becomes excluded, and the breach by reason of the future non-performance becomes virtually involved in the action as one of the consequences of the repudiation of the contract; and the eventual non-performance may therefore, by anticipation, be treated as a cause of action, and damages be assessed and recovered in respect of it, though the time for performance may yet be remote.

It is obvious that such a course must lead to the convenience of both parties; and though we should be unwilling to found our opinion on grounds of convenience alone, yet the latter tend strongly to support the view that such an action ought to be admitted and upheld. By acting on such a notice of the intention of the promisor, and taking timely measures, the promisee may in many cases avert, or at all events materially lessen, the injurious effects which would otherwise flow from the non-fulfilment of the contract; and in assessing the damages for breach of performance, a jury will of course take into account whatever the plaintiff has done, or has had the means of doing, and, as a prudent man, ought in reason to have done, whereby his loss has been, or would have been, diminished.

It appears to us that the foregoing considerations apply to the case of a contract the performance of which is made to depend on a contingency, as much as one in which the performance is to take place at a future time; and we are therefor of the opinion that the principle of the decision of *Hochster* v. *De La Tour* is equally applicable to such a case as the present.

It is next to be observed that the law as settled by *Hochster* v. *De La Tour* . . . is obviously quite as applicable to a contract in which personal status or personal rights are involved as to one relating to commercial or pecuniary interests. Indeed, the contract of marriage appears to afford a striking illustration of the expediency of holding that an action may be maintained on the repudiation of a contract to be performed *in futuro*. On such a contract being entered into, not only does a right to its completion arise with reference to domestic relations and possibly pecuniary advantages, as also to the social status accruing on marriage, but a new status, that of betrothment, at once arises between the parties. This relation, it is true, has not, by the law of England, the same important consequences which attached to it by the canon law and the law of many other countries. Nevertheless it carries with it consequences of the utmost importance to the parties. Each becomes bound to the other; neither can, consistently with such a relation, enter into a similar engagement with another person; each has an implied right to have this relation continued till the contract is finally accomplished by marriage. To the woman, more especially, it is all-important that the relation shall not be put an end to. Independently of the mental pain occasioned by the abrupt termination of such an engagement, the fact of its existence, if followed by such a termination, must necessarily operate to her serious disadvantage. During its continuance others will naturally be deterred from approaching her with matrimonial intentions; nor could she admit of such approaches, if made; while the breaking off of the engagement is too apt to cast a slur upon one who has been thus treated.

We see therefore, every reason for applying the principle of *Hochster* v. *De La Tour* to such a case, and for holding the contract, if repudiated, to be broken, not only in its present, but also in its ultimate obligations and consequences. To hold that the aggrieved party must wait till the time fixed for marrying shall have arrived, or the event on which it is to depend shall have happened, would have the effect of aggavating the injury, by preventing the party from forming any other union, and by reason of advancing age rendering the probability of such a union constantly less.

It has been suggested, indeed, that the desire of marrying and the happiness to be expected from it diminish with advancing years, and therefore that, when by terms of the contract marriage is only to take place at a remote time, the value of the marriage and the damages to be recovered for a breach of the promise would be less if the refusal were made when the time for marrying was accomplished; and that, consequently an action ought not to be allowed till the time when the fulfilment of the contract could have been claimed. We cannot concur in this view. We think that, in estimating the amount of injury done and of the compensation to be made for it, if the contract were broken when the time for marrying had arrived, the wasted years and the impossibility of forming any other engagement during the intermediate time should be taken into account, and not merely the age of the parties and the then existing value of the marriage. It is, therefore, manifest that it is better for both parties—for the party intending to break the contract, as well as for the party wronged by the breach of it—that an express repudiation of the contract should be treated as a violation of it in all its incidents, and should give the right to the party wronged to bring an action at once, and have the damages assessed at the earliest moment. No one can doubt that, morally speaking, a party who determines to break off a matrimonial engagement acts far more commendably if he at once gives notice of his intention than if he keeps that intention secret till the time for fulfilling the promise has come. The reason is that the giving such notice at the earliest moment tends to mitigate, while the delay in giving it necessarily aggravates, the injury to the party wronged. It has been urged that there must be a great difficulty in thus assessing damages prospectively. But this must always be more or less the case whenever the principle of *Hochster* v. *De La Tour* comes to be applied. . . .

[Keating and Lush JJ. concurred. The judgment of Byles J. is omitted.]

QUESTION ON LEGAL METHOD. Why should a judge be "unwilling to found his opinion on grounds of convenience alone"? What place should "convenience" play in reaching a decision?

WHITE & CARTER (COUNCILS), LTD. *v.* McGREGOR
Scotland. House of Lords. [1961] 3 All E.R. 1178

LORD REID: My Lords, the pursuers supply to local authorities litter bins which are placed in the streets. They are allowed to attach to these receptacles plates carrying advertisements and they make their profit from payments made to them by the advertisers. The defender carried on a garage in Clydebank and in 1954 he made an agreement with the pursuers under which they displayed advertisements of his business on a number of these bins. In June, 1957, his sales manager made a further contract with the pursuers for the display of these advertisements for a further period of three years. The sales manager had been given no specific authority to make this contract and when the defender heard of it later on the same day he at once wrote to the pursuers to cancel the contract. The pursuers refused to accept this cancellation. [The contract, itself, stated that it could not be cancelled by the advertiser.] They prepared the necessary plates for attachment to the bins and exhibited them on the bins from Nov. 2, 1957, onwards. [It was found by the Court of Session and the Sheriff Court that the appellants made no effort to minimise their loss by procuring another advertiser to take up the advertising space included in the contract.]

The defender refused to pay any sums due under the contract and the pursuers raised the present action in the Sheriff Court craving payment of £196 4s. the full sum due under the contract for the period of three years. After sundry procedure the sheriff-substitute on Mar. 15, 1960, dismissed the action. He held that the sales manager's action in renewing the contract was within his apparent or ostensible authority and that is not now disputed. The ground on which he dismissed the action was that in the circumstances an action for implement of the contract was inappropriate. He relied on the decision in *Langford & Co., Ltd.* v. *Dutch*, [1952] S.C. 15, and cannot be criticised for having done so.

The pursuers appealed to the Court of Session and on Nov. 29, 1960, the Second Division refused the appeal. The present appeal is taken against their interlocutor of that date. That interlocutor sets out detailed findings of fact and, as this case began in the Sheriff Court, we cannot look beyond those findings. The pursuers must show that on those findings they are entitled to the remedy which they seek.

The case for the defender (now the respondent) is that, as he repudiated the contract before anything had been done under it, the appellants were not entitled to go on and carry out the contract and sue for the contract price: he maintains that in the circumstances the appellants' only remedy was damages, and that, as they do not sue for damages, this action was rightly dismissed.

The contract was for the display of advertisements for a period of 156 weeks from the date when the display began. This date was not specified but admittedly the display began on Nov. 2, 1957, which seems to have been the date when the former contract came to an end. The payment stipulated was 2s. per week per plate together with 5s. per annum per plate both payable annually in advance, the first payment being due seven days after the first display. The reason why the appellants sued for the whole sum due for the three years is to be found in cl. 8 of the conditions:

"8. In the event of an instalment or part thereof being due for payment, and remaining unpaid for a period of four weeks or in the event of the advertiser being in any way in breach of this contract then the whole amount due for the 156 weeks or such part of the said 156 weeks as the advertiser shall not yet have paid shall immediately become due and payable."

A question was debated whether this clause provides a penalty or liquidated damages but on the view which I take of the case it need not be pursued. The clause merely provides for acceleration of payment of the stipulated price if the advertiser fails to pay an instalment timeously. As the respondent maintained that he was not bound by the contract he did not pay the first instalment within the time allowed. Accordingly, if the appellants were entitled to carry out their part of the contract notwithstanding the respondent's repudiation, it was hardly disputed that this clause entitled them to sue immediately for the whole price and not merely for the first instalment.

The general rule cannot be in doubt. It was settled in Scotland at least as early as 1848 and it has been authoritatively stated time and again in both Scotland and England. If one party to a contract repudiates it in the sense of making it clear to the other party that he refuses or will refuse to carry out his part of the contract, the other party, the innocent party, has an option. He may accept that repudiation and sue for damages for breach of contract whether or not the time for performance has come; or he may if he chooses disregard or refuse to accept it and then the contract remains in full effect. . . .

I need not refer to the numerous authorities. They are not disputed by the respondent but he points out that in all of them the party who refused to accept the repudiation had no active duties under the contract. The innocent party's option is generally said to be to wait until the date of performance and then to claim damages estimated as at that date. There is no case in which it is said that he may, in face of the repudiation, go on and incur useless expense in performing the contract and then claim the contract price. The option, it is argued, is merely as to the date as at which damages are to be assessed. Developing this argument, the respondent points out that in most cases the innocent party cannot complete the contract himself without the other party doing, allowing or accepting something, and that it is purely fortuitous that the appellants can do so in this case. In most cases by refusing co-operation the party in breach can compel the innocent party to restrict his claim to damages. Then it was said that even where the innocent party can complete the contract without such co-operation it is against the public interest that he should be allowed to do so. An example was developed in argument. A company might engage an expert to go abroad and prepare an elaborate report and then repudiate the contract before anything was done. To allow such an expert then to waste thousands of pounds in preparing the report cannot be right if a much smaller sum of damages would give him full compensation for his loss. It would merely enable the expert to extort a settlement giving him far more than reasonable compensation.

The respondent founds on the decision of the First Division in *Langford & Co., Ltd.* v. *Dutch*. There an advertising contractor agreed to exhibit a film for a year. Four days after this agreement was made the advertiser repudiated it but, as in the present case, the contractor refused to accept the repudiation and proceeded to exhibit the film and sue for the contract price. The sheriff-substitute dismissed the action as irrelevant and his decision was affirmed on appeal. In the course of a short opinion the Lord President (LORD COOPER) said:

"It appears to me that, apart from wholly exceptional circumstances of which there is no trace in the averments on this record, the law of Scotland does not afford to a person in the position of the pursuers the remedy which is here sought. The pursuers could not force the defender to accept a year's advertisement which she did not want, though they could of course claim damages for her breach of contract. On the averments the only reasonable and proper course, which the pursuers should have adopted, would have been to treat the defender as having repudiated the contract and as being on that account liable in damages, the measure of which we are, of course, not in a position to discuss."

The Lord President cited no authority and I am in doubt what principle he had in mind. In the earlier part of the passage which I have quoted he speaks of forcing the defender to accept the advertisement. Of course, if it had been necessary for the defender to do or accept anything before the contract could be completed by the pursuers, the pursuers could not and the court would not have compelled the defender to act, the contract would not have been completed, and the pursuers' only remedy would have been damages. But the peculiarity in that case, as in the present case, was that the pursuers could completely fulfil the contract without any co-operation of the defender. The Lord President cannot have meant that because of non-acceptance the contract had not been completely carried out, because that in itself would have been a complete answer to an action for the contract price. He went on to say that the only reasonable and proper course which the pursuers should have adopted would have been to treat the defender as having repudiated the contract, which must, I think, mean to have accepted the repudiation. It is this reference to "the only reasonable and proper course" which I find difficult to explain. It might be, but it never has been, the law that a person is only entitled to enforce his contractual rights in a reasonable way and that a court will not support an attempt to enforce them in an unreasonable way. One reason why that is not the law is no doubt because it was thought that it would create too much uncertainty to require the court to decide whether it is reasonable or equitable to allow a party to enforce his full rights under a contract. The Lord President cannot have meant that. . . .

Langford & Co., Ltd. v. *Dutch* is indistinguishable from the present case. Quite properly the Second Division followed it in this case as a binding authority and did not develop LORD COOPER's reasoning: they were not asked to send this case to a larger court. We must now decide whether that case was rightly decided. In my judgment it was not. It could only be supported on one or other of two grounds. It might be said that, because in most cases the circumstances are such that an innocent party is unable to complete the contract and earn the contract price without the assent or co-operation of the other party, therefore in cases where he can do so he should not be allowed to do so. I can see no justification for that.

The other ground would be that there is some general equitable principle or element of public policy which requires this limitation of the contractual rights of the innocent party. It may well be that, if it can be shown that a person has no legitimate interest, financial or otherwise, in performing the contract rather than claiming damages, he ought not to be allowed to saddle the other party with an additional burden with no benefit to himself. If a party has no interest to enforce a stipulation he cannot in general enforce it: so it might be said that if a party has no interest to insist on a particular remedy he ought not to be allowed to insist on it. And, just as a party is not allowed to enforce a penalty, so he ought not to be allowed to penalise the other party by taking one course when another is equally advantageous to him. If I may revert to the example which I gave of a company engaging an expert to prepare an elaborate report and then repudiating before anything was done, it might be that the company could show that the expert had no substantial or legitimate interest in carrying out the work rather than accepting damages. I would think that the de minimis principle would apply in determining whether his interest was substantial and that he might have a legitimate interest other than an immediate financial interest. But if the expert had no such interest then that might be regarded as a proper case for the exercise of the general equitable jurisdiction of the court. But that is not this case. Here the respondent did not set out to prove that the appellants had no legitimate interest in completing the contract and claiming the contract price rather than claiming damages, there is nothing in the findings of fact to support such a case, and it seems improbable that any such case could have been proved. It is, in my judgment, impossible to say that the appellants should be deprived of their right to claim the contract price merely because the benefit to them as against claiming damages and reletting their advertising space might be small in comparison with the loss to the respondent: that is the most that could be said in favour of the respondent. Parliament has on many occasions relieved parties from certain kinds of improvident or oppressive contracts, but the common law can only do that in very limited circumstances. Accordingly, I am unable to avoid the conclusion that this appeal must be allowed and the case remitted so that decree can be pronounced as craved in the initial writ.

LORD MORTON OF HENRYTON (dissenting): My Lords, the facts of this case have already been fully stated. It is plain that the respondent (defender in the action) repudiated the contract of June 26, 1957, immediately after his sales manager had entered into it and some months before the time for performance of it by the appellants, and persisted in his repudiation throughout. Nothwithstanding this, the appellants proceeded with the preparation of plates advertising the respondent's garage business and, as the sheriff-substitute held, they

"made no effort to procure another advertiser to take up the advertising space included in said contract and thus minimise their loss."

The plates were first exhibited on the litter bins on Nov. 2, 1957, and they remained on display during the whole of the contract period of 156 weeks. The respondent throughout made it clear that he did not want the advertisements and refused to pay for them. The present action is brought to recover £196 4s., the full sum payable under the contract. Alternatively, the appellants claim the same sum as liquidated damages. The respondent contends that in the circumstances of the present case the only remedy of the appellants was damages, to be assessed according to ordinary principles.

My Lords, I think that this is a case of great importance, although the claim is for a comparatively small sum. If the appellants are right, strange consequences follow in any case in which, under a repudiated contract, services are to be performed by the party who has not repudiated it, so long as he is able to perform these services without the co-operation of the repudiating party. Many examples of such contracts could be given. One, given in the course of the argument and already mentioned by my noble and learned friend, Lord Reid, is the engagement of an expert to go abroad and write a report on some subject for a substantial fee plus his expenses. If the appellants succeed in the present case, it must follow that the expert is entitled to incur the expense of going abroad, to write his unwanted report, and then to recover the fee and expenses, even if the other party has plainly repudiated the contract before any expense has been incurred.

It is well established that repudiation by one party does not put an end to a contract. The other party can say "I hold you to your contract, which still remains in force". What, then, is his remedy if the repudiating party persists in his repudiation and refuses to carry out his part of the contract? The contract has been broken. The innocent party is entitled to be compensated by damages for any loss which he has suffered by reason of the breach, and in a limited class of cases the court will decree specific implement. The law of Scotland provides no other remedy for a breach of contract, and there is no reported case which decides that the innocent party may act as the appellants have acted. The present case is one in which specific implement could not be decreed, since the only obligation of the respondent under the contract was to pay a sum of money for services to be rendered by the appellants. Yet the appellants are claiming a kind of inverted specific implement of the contract. They first insist on performing their part of the contract, against the will of the other party, and then claim that he must perform his part and pay the contract price for unwanted services. In my opinion, my Lords, the appellants' only remedy was damages, and they were bound to take steps to minimise their loss, according to a well-established rule of law. Far from doing this, having incurred no expense at the date of the repudiation, they made no attempt to procure another advertiser, but deliberately went on to incur expense and perform unwanted services with the intention of creating a money debt which did not exist at the date of the repudiation.

The only cases cited in which a claim of the kind now put forward has been considered are *Langford & Co., Ltd.* v. *Dutch* when it was rejected by the Court of Session, and *White & Carter (Councils), Ltd.* (that is, the present appellants) v. *A. R. Harding* (May 21, 1958; unreported). The latter case is, I think, distinguishable from the present case but if it cannot be distinguished it was, in my opinion, wrongly decided by the Court of Appeal. The former case is directly in point, and was, in my opinion, rightly decided, and rightly followed by the Court of Session in the present case.

The facts in Langford's case have been stated by my noble and learned friend, LORD REID. The Court of Session held that the law of Scotland did not "afford to a person in the position of the pursuers the remedy which is here sought." These words are quoted from the short opinion of the Lord President (LORD COOPER), and he continued:

"the pursuers could not force the defender to accept a year's advertisement which she did not want, though they could of course claim damages for her breach of contract."

These two sentences embodied, I think, the basis of the learned Lord President's opinion, but he added:

"On the averments the only reasonable and proper course, which the pursuers should have adopted, would have been to treat the defender as having repudiated the contract and as being on that account liable in damages, the measure of which we are, of course, not in a position to discuss."

My Lords, I think that this last sentence was merely a comment on the behaviour of the pursuers, which applies with equal force to the appellants in the present case. The course of action followed by the appellants seems to me unreasonable and oppressive, but it is not on that ground that I would reject their claim. I would reject it for the reasons which I have already given. . . .

I would dismiss the appeal.

LORD KEITH OF AVONHOLM (dissenting): . . . The contract was to come into operation on Nov. 2, 1957, when the previous contract expired. But it involved, in the absence of other advertising matter supplied by the defender, the display by the appellants of at least the name, business and address of the advertiser. I should hesitate to say that any contractor was entitled to display these particulars of the defender against his wish, even if the withholding of his assent be in breach of contract.

Some play was made by counsel for the appellants with an expression used by ASQUITH, L. J., in *Howard* v. *Pickford Tool Co., Ltd.*, [1951] 1 K.B. 417 at p. 421 that "An unaccepted repudiation is a thing writ in water . . ." A graphic phrase, or expression, has its uses even in a law report and can give force to a legal principle, but it must be related to the circumstances in which it is used. Howard was a managing director with a six years contract of service. He thought that the company with which he was serving had shown by the conduct of its chairman that it no longer intended to be bound by its agreement. He brought an action which, as amended, sought a declaration that the company by so acting had repudiated the contract and excused the plaintiff from further performance of his obligations under it. EVERSHED, M.R., said at p. 420:

"It is quite plain . . . that if the conduct of one party to a contract amounts to a repudiation, and the other party does not accept it as such but goes on performing his part of the contract and affirms the contract, the alleged act of repudiation is wholly nugatory and ineffective in law."

ASQUITH, L. J., said:

"An unaccepted repudiation is a thing writ in water and of no value to anybody: it confers no legal rights of any sort or kind."

The declaration was held to be academic and the claim struck out. These observations must be read in the light of the facts which they relate. They were directed to an alleged repudiation unaccepted by the man who said there was a repudiation before any cause of action had arisen. At best the case was no more than one of an intended repudiation, for performance was going on. The servant was still serving and the employer was continuing to employ him. What the court was saying was that the plaintiff had at that time no cause of action. But in the case of repudiation of a contract when performance is tendered, or due to be given by the other party, the repudiation cannot be said to be writ in water. It gives rise immediately to a cause of action. This does not involve acceptance of the repudiation. There has been a breach of contract which the complaining party denies the other had any right to commit. I know of no authority for saying that the offended party can go quietly on as if the contract still continued to be fully operative between both parties. He is put to his remedy at the date of the breach. It has been said that when an anticipatory repudiation is not treated as a cause of action the contract remains alive. It does until the contract would become operative, when the repudiation, if still maintained, then becomes a cause of action and all pleas and defences then existing are available to the respective parties.

The party complaining of the breach also has a duty to minimise the damage he has suffered, which is a further reason for saying that after the date of breach he cannot continue to carry on his part of an executory contract. A breach of a contract of employment will serve to illustrate the nature of this duty. A person is engaged to serve for a certain period, say three months, to commence at a future date. When that date arrives the prospective employer wrongfully refuses to honour the engagement. The servant is not entitled to see out the three months and then sue the recalcitrant employer for three months' wages. He must take steps by seeking other employment to minimise his loss. It is true, of course, that a servant cannot invoke a contract to force himself on an unwilling master, any more than a master can enforce the service of an unwilling servant. But if the appellants' contention is sound, it is difficult to see why, by parity of reasoning, it should not apply to a person who keeps himself free to perform the duties of his contract of service during the whole period of the contract and is prevented from doing so by the refusal of the other contracting party. Yet in *Hochster* v. *De La Tour* (26) from which the whole law about anticipatory repudiation stems, LORD CAMPBELL, C.J., plainly indicated that if the courier in that case, instead of accepting as he did the repudiation of his engagement as a cause of action, before it was due to commence, had waited till the lapse of the three months of the engagement he could not have sued as for a debt. The jury, he said (27), would be entitled to look at all that might "increase or mitigate the loss of the plaintiff down to the day of trial." There is no difference in this matter between the law of England and the law of Scotland. . . .

This brings me to *Langford & Co., Ltd.* v. *Dutch*. I took part in the judgment in that case, though the only opinion delivered in the case was given by the Lord President (Lord Cooper), with whom I and the other judges of the division concurred. The judgment was not a reserved judgment and the case was not, I think, so fully argued as the case now before your Lordships. It is, if rightly decided, determinative of the present appeal and is, so far as I am aware, the only other case in which the question raised on this appeal has ever been considered. . . . I have reconsidered the decision in *Langford & Co., Ltd.* v. *Dutch* in the light of the further argument on this appeal. I have come to the conclusion that it was rightly decided and that the Second Division in the present case was bound to follow it. . . .

[Lord Tucker agreed with Lord Hodson, whose decision is omitted, in allowing the appeal. The opinion of Lord Keith is considerably cut.]

KLOEPFER WHOLESALE HARDWARE & AUTOMOTIVE CO. *v*. ROY

Ontario. Supreme Court of Canada. [1952] 3 D.L.R. 705

KERWIN J.: By a written agreement dated November 29, 1949, the appellant agreed to sell and the respondent agreed to purchase certain lands and premises, and the sale was to be completed on or before January 29, 1950. On December 5, 1949, the appellant telegraphed to the respondent that it repudiated the contract, and on December 14th, the respondent's solicitors wrote the solicitors for the appellant denying the latter's right to repudiate. On January 10, 1950, the writ of summons in this action was issued and the statement of claim delivered on January 17th. It was argued that, admitting the respondent could immediately take advantage of the appellant's anticipatory breach and sue before the time fixed for completion, he could do so only on the basis that the contract was at an end, and he would, therefore, be confined to an action for damages for breach of contract. It was said that on the date of the writ, January 10th, the respondent had no cause of action in the sense of being able to ask (as he did) for a declaration that the agreement of November 29th was a binding contract and that it ought to be specifically performed and carried into effect. That, of course, it may be observed is one of the usual claims in an action for specific performance and the judgment follows the claim.

No authority has been cited for the proposition advanced on behalf of the appellant and we find it untenable. It is settled that an action may be brought upon an anticipatory repudiation of a contract (Fry on Specific Performance, 6th ed., para. 1062), and in para. 1311, p. 3708, of Williston on Contracts, 1937, vol. 5, it is said:

"But would a court, it may be asked, grant specific performance on January 1, of a contract to convey Blackacre the following July, on the ground that the defendant had been guilty of an anticipatory repudiation on the earlier day? If such repudiation is an actual breach justifying an action at law, there seems no reason why a suit in equity should not be maintainable. Certainly no decree would require performance before July 1, and it would at least be made clear that repudiation does not accelerate the obligations of a contract."

With that statement we agree.

The argument of the appellant overlooks the power of the Court to make a declaratory judgment: *Judicature Act*, R.S.O. 1950 c. 190, s. 15(*b*). Although it was submitted that the point had not been advanced in *Roberto* v. *Bumb*, [1943], 2 D.L.R. 613, O.R. 299, in the same manner as here, Laidlaw J.A. in that case did say, at p. 620 D.L.R., p. 310 O.R.: "The cause of action was not complete when the proceedings were commenced in the Court" and "I think that a Court of Equity would not permit an appellant to avoid the contract merely because the action was started prematurely, nor would the respondent be thus deprived of his equitable right to a decree of specific performance, if he were entitled to it." If these extracts mean merely that at the time of the issue of the writ the Court could not have ordered that specific performance be carried out immediately, no objection may be found with them; but it they mean that the plaintiff did not have a complete cause of action for a declaration that the agreement was a binding contract and that it ought to be specifically enforced, we are unable to agree. Having that right the agreement would be carried out when the time for completion had expired.

The last sentence in para. 468 of 31 Hals., 2nd ed., p. 401, "in such cases neither party can claim specific performance" can only refer to the earlier part of the paragraph where it is stated that if one party has evinced an intention no longer to be bound by a contract, the other party is entitled to treat that as a repudiation and to accept it as such. If it means more, it cannot be supported.

The respondent was not put to any election upon the receipt of the telegram of December 5, 1949, and he has consistently taken the position that the appellant could not repudiate while the appellant has continued to aver that it was entitled to do so. The respondent's right to ask the Court for a declaration of validity and to specifically perform the contract arose immediately and nothing intervened before the date fixed for completion of the contract to change the position of the parties. The respondent was a party to a contract with the appellant which the latter had definitely stated it would not carry out and, therefore, it is not a case of a plaintiff not being able to show an actual existing interest in the subject-matter at the date of the issue of the writ. It is of some significance and assistance that a vendor may bring an action for specific performance, and the inquiry as to title is whether he can make a good title and not whether he could do so at the date of the contract and, therefore, when once the inquiry has been directed, he may make out his title at any time before the certificate (Fry, para. 1366).

The contract between the parties was complete and without uncertainty. Performance of the whole contract could be enforced, and it must not be forgotten that by the time of the trial, the appellant had been in possession during the period for which it was to have a lease under the terms of the contract. Both Courts below have found that there was no mistake, and nothing was shown on the argument to cause us to think that that conclusion is not the right one on the evidence. A tender was not required when as was apparent from the actions of the appellant and from the proceedings and evidence at the trial, the appellant never intended to perform the contract. It is not necessary in connection with any of these points to refer to the clause in the contract: "It is agreed that there is no representation, warranty, collateral agreement or condition affecting this agreement or the real property or supported there by other than is expressed herein in writing."

Finally, as to the suggestion that damages would be sufficient because it is contended that the plaintiff desired to use the property as an investment, it is sufficient to say that generally speaking, specific performance applies to agreements for the sale of lands as a matter of course.

The appeal must be dismissed with costs.

[Estey and Fauteux JJ. joined in Kerwin J.'s judgment. The joint judgment of Locke and Cartwright JJ. dismissing the appeal is omitted.]

POLLARD *v.* CLAYTON

England. Chancery. 1855. 1 K. & J. 462; 69 E.R. 540

The Plaintiff company operated an iron and steel mining and smelting business in Yorkshire. They agreed to purchase from the Defendants all the coal in specified mines owned by the Defendants estimated to contain about 150,000 tons, very conveniently situated with reference to the Plaintiff company's collieries and ironworks, and of a kind for which the Plaintiff company had great need. The Defendant agreed to mine and deliver the coal at the rate of 500 tons per week. The Defendants delivered coal until October, 1853, when deliveries were curtailed, temporarily, it was said. Earlier in 1853 an agreement had been reached whereby the Plaintiff company agreed thereafter to drain the Defendant's coal beds. In February, 1854 the Plaintiff's agent wrote asking why the Defendants refused to fulfil their agreement, he having just learned that the Defendants had mined coal, sold some of it to others and kept some of it for himself. (There was no "negative clause" in the principal agreement.) On March 20, 1854, the matter was referred to the parties' solicitors. Thereafter the Plaintiff company repeatedly requested the Defendants to deliver coal and offered to drain the beds. The Plaintiff's bill, filed February 20, 1855, prayed for specific performance of the contract to mine and sell the coal to the Plaintiffs. The Defendants demurred to the bill for want of equity.

VICE CHANCELLOR WOOD: This demurrer must be allowed. . . .

Independently of the difficulty arising from the nature of the contract itself, there is in this case, on the ground of delay alone, so serious an objection that it would be impossible for the Court to perform the contract. Before noticing, however, the effect of that delay, I must first make some observations upon the nature of the contract itself. . . .

I should therefore have to make a decree, on the one hand, that the Defendants continue the working of their colliery, involving the employment of their capital and men, and all the other operations necessary in order to raise 500 tons per week; and, on the other hand, that the Plaintiff continue the draining of the work, so as to enable these 500 tons per week to be raised. I can scarcely conceive a contract more difficult to be executed through the medium of a Court of Equity, or one in which more incessant applications must necessarily be made, to know whether, on the one hand, the Defendants are putting their best strength forward in order to raise, with a given number of workmen, at a given rate of wages, the stipulated quantity of 500 tons per week; and whether, on the other hand, the Plaintiff is performing his contract with full effect, in draining sufficiently and adequately the works which are in operation. . . .

The question of instalments could not be so easily estimated by damages; and upon that question, looking into the authorities to which I have already adverted I might have paused; although I should still have felt the extraordinary and enormous inconvenience of this Court having to superintend the performance of such a contract as the present. But, here, I have the further circumstance of the delay on the part of the Plaintiff in seeking the relief prayed by his bill. Surely, even if this contract were one which this Court ought specifically to perform, still, being a contract for the purchase of a commodity, which, as I may take judicial cognizance, varies in price from week to week, the delay which has occurred since the Plaintiff became aware of the failure of the Defendants to perform their part of the contract is at once an answer to a bill for specific performance. Eleven months ago the Defendants tell the company they must take their own course. The company are aware of the breach of contract as early as the 4th of March 1854. This is clear, for in their letter of that date they complain that the Defendants are laying up coal, and refusing to send it in to the company. Besides, the bill expressly avers that on the 4th of March the Plaintiff was "informed (as the fact was) that the Defendants had not delivered any coal to the company since February 1854, but that they were nevertheless laying up and stacking what they had sold and ought to have delivered to the company." There is also an averment that the Defendants had, in fact, between February and March, raised and got a large quantity of coal, and instead of delivering it were selling part of it to other persons, using other part of it, and laying up and stacking and the remainder. Then follows the correspondence of the 20th and 21st of March 1854. [His Honour read the letters of these dates, and proceeded.] It is said, and it is truly said, that the latter of these letters, in which the Defendants say they have no wish to repudiate and name their solicitors, is not a distinct and positive throwing up of the contract. But, although that may be so, thus much is clear: the company, after writing to complain that coal had been stacked up, and other coal supplied to other parties in breach of the agreement, are told in reply, as long since as March 1854, the names of the Defendants' solicitors, although, the Defendants say they do not want to repudiate their contract; and the next averment is that the company have repeatedly applied to and requested the Defendants to perform their contract, and the Defendants have as often refused. Under the state of circumstances, although it is true, the Defendants cannot be heard to say, "You were only entitled to have this coal delivered at the rate of 500 tons a week, in consecutive weeks, and therefore cannot have it at any longer intervals of time," if they, by their own wrong, have prevented the Plaintiff's having it weekly, in breach of the agreement, yet they are entitled to say, "If you allow a gap where the contract says that 500 tons weekly are to be delivered, it is, at least incumbent upon you, the commodity being one so variable in price as coals, the moment you find any neglect, or delay, or hesitation on our part to perform the agreement still more when we refer you to our solicitors (which is the usual way of bringing these matters to an issue) to file your bill at once, if you mean to file one at all, to have the benefit of that agreement." Instead of that, the Plaintiff waits eleven months, and then, at last, the bill is filed. I do not look out of the bill, as the case made has not done so; but it is enough for me to say that coal, like all other articles of constant use and constant sale, is a commodity fluctuating from day to day in its market price; and during the interval which has elapsed there may have been every possible variety of price, of rise or decline, and the parties are not now in the same position. Those who seek specific performance of contracts relating to such commodities must be unusually vigilant and active in asserting their rights. It is not equitable, and in this Court especially it would be improper, to give relief of that description, after such a period of delay as in this case has been allowed to occur between the time when the Plaintiff was first in a position to file a bill, and the time when he took upon himself to file it.

Having regard to the circumstance of delay alone, the Court ought not to give relief after *laches* of this description. I must, therefore, allow the demurrer.

QUESTION. In *Warner Brothers* v. *Nelson* would the court have ordered Bette Davis to stop playing in a stage production in London if the action had been commenced three months after the play opened and there was still "standing room only"?

LINDSAY PETROLEUM COMPANY *v*. HURD. 1874. L.R. 5 P.C. 221 (Ontario. Privy Council). LORD SELBORNE L.C. said: "Now the doctrine of laches in Courts of Equity is not an arbitrary or a technical doctrine. Where it would be practically unjust to give a remedy, either because the party has, by his conduct, done that which might fairly be regarded as equivalent to a waiver of it, or where by his conduct and neglect he has, though perhaps not waiving that remedy, yet put the other party in a situation in which it would not be reasonable to place him if the remedy were afterwards to be asserted, in either of these cases, lapse of time and delay are most material. But in every case, if an argument against relief, which otherwise would be just, is founded upon mere delay, that delay of course not amounting to a bar by any statute of limitations, the validity of that defence must be tried upon principles substantially equitable. Two circumstances, always important in such cases, are, the length of the delay and the nature of the acts done during the interval, which might affect either party and cause a balance of justice or injustice in taking the one course or the other, so far as relates to the remedy."

THE LIMITATIONS ACT

Ontario. Revised Statutes. 1960. Chapter 214

45. (1) The following actions shall be commenced within and not after the times respectively hereinafter mentioned: . . .

(b) an action upon a bond, or other specialty . . . within twenty years after the cause of action arose; . . .

(d) an action upon an award where the submission is not by specialty; . . .

(g) an action for trespass to goods or land, simple contract or debt grounded upon any lending or contract without specialty, debt for arrears of rent, detinue, replevin or upon the case other than for slander, within six years after the cause of action arose;

47. Where a person entitled to bring any action mentioned in either sections 45 or 46 is at the time the cause of action accrues an infant, mental defective, mental incompetent or of unsound mind, the period within the action should be brought shall be reckoned from the date when such person became of full age or of sound mind.

48. If a person against whom any cause of action mentioned in sections 45 or 46 accrues is at such time out of Ontario, the person entitled to the cause of action may bring the action within such times as are before limited after the return of the absent person to Ontario.

5. Protection from Interference by Strangers

LUMLEY *v.* GYE

England. Queen's Bench. 1853. 2 El. & Bl. 216; 118 E.R. 749

Plaintiff was lessee and manager of the Queen's Theatre, for performing operas for gain to him; and he contracted with Johanna Wagner to perform in the theatre for a certain time, with a condition, amongst others, that she would not sing nor use her talents elsewhere during the term without his consent in writing. Yet defendant, knowing the premises, and maliciously intending to injure plaintiff as lessee and manager of the theatre, whilst the agreement with Wagner was in force, and before the expiration of the term, enticed and procured Wagner to refuse to perform: by means of which enticement and procurement of defendant, Wagner wrongfully refused to perform, and did not perform during the term.

Crompton J.: . . . It was said, in support of the demurrer, that it did not appear in the declaration that the relation of master and servant ever subsisted between the plaintiff and Miss Wagner; that Miss Wagner was not averred, especially in the first two counts, to have entered upon the service of the plaintiff; and that the engagement of a theatrical performer, even if the performer has entered upon the duties, is not of such a nature as to make the performer a servant, within the rule of law which gives an action to the master for the wrongful enticing away of his servant. And it was laid down broadly, as a general proposition of law, that no action will lie for procuring a person to break a contract, although such procuring is with a malicious intention and causes great and immediate injury. And the law as to enticing servants was said to be contrary to the general rule and principle of law, and to be anomalous, and probably to have had its origin from the state of society when serfdom existed, and to be founded upon, or upon the equity of, the Statute of Labourers. It was said that it would be dangerous to hold that an action was maintainable for persuading a third party to break a contract, unless some boundary or limits could be pointed out; and that the remedy for enticing away servants was confined to cases where the relation of master and servant, in a strict sense, subsisted between the parties; and that, in all other cases of contract, the only remedy was against the party breaking the contract.

Whatever may have been the origin or foundation of the law as to enticing of servants, and whether it be, as contended by the plaintiff, an instance and branch of a wider rule, or whether it be, as contended by the defendant, an anomaly and an exception from the general rule of law on such subjects, it must now be considered clear law that a person who wrongfully and maliciously, or, which is the same thing, with notice, interrupts the relation subsisting between master and servant by procuring the servant to depart from the master's service, or by harbouring and keeping him as servant after he has quitted it and during the time stipulated for as the period of service, whereby the master is injured, commits a wrongful act for which he is responsible at law. I think that the rule applies wherever the wrongful interruption operates to prevent the service during the time for which the parties have contracted that the service shall continue: and I think that the relation of master and servant subsists, sufficiently for the purpose of such action, during the time for which there is in existence a binding contract of hiring and service between the parties; and I think that it is a fanciful and technical and unjust distinction to say that the not having actually entered into the service, or that the service not actually continuing, can make any difference. The wrong and injury are surely the same, whether the wrong doer entices away the gardener, who has hired himself for a year, the night before he is to go to his work, or after he has planted the first cabbage on the first morning of his service; and I should be sorry to support a distinction so unjust, and so repugnant to common sense, unless bound to do so by some rule or authority of law plainly shewing that such distinction exists. The proposition of the defendant, that there must be a service actually subsisting, seems to be inconsistent with the authorities that shew these action to be maintainable for receiving or harbouring servants after they have left the actual service of the master. . . .

The objection as to the actual employment not having commenced would not apply in the present case to the third count, which states that Miss Wagner had become the artiste of the plaintiff, and that the defendant had induced her to depart from the employment. But it was further said that the engagement, employment or service, in the present case, was not of such a nature as to constitute the relation of master and servant, so as to warrant the application of the usual rule of law giving a remedy in the case of enticing away servants. The nature of the injury and of the damage being the same, and the supposed right of action being in strict analogy to the ordinary case of master and servant, I see no reason for confining the case to services or engagements under contracts for services of any particular description; and I think that the remedy, in the absence of any legal reason to the contrary, may well apply to all cases where there is an unlawful and malicious enticing away of any person employed to give his personal labour or service for a given time under the direction of a master or employer who is injured by the wrongful act; more especially when the party is bound to give such personal services exclusively to the master or employer; though I by no means say that the service need be exclusive. . . . The action for maliciously interfering with persons in the employment of another is not confined to menial servants. . . . It appears to me that Miss Wagner had contracted to do work for the plaintiff within the meaning of this rule; and I think that, where a party has contracted to give his personal services for a certain time to another, the parties are in the relation of employer and employed, or master and servant, within the meaning of this rule. And I see no reason for narrowing such a rule; but I should rather, if necessary, apply such a remedy to a case "new in its instance, but" "not new in the reason and principle of it" (per Holt C.J., in *Keeble* v. *Hickeringill,* 11 East, 573, 575) that is, to a case where the wrong and damage are strictly analogous to the wrong and damage in a well recognized class of cases. In deciding this case on the narrower ground, I wish by no means to be considered as deciding that the larger ground taken by Mr. Cowling is not tenable, or as saying that in no case except that of master and servant is an action maintainable for maliciously inducing another to break a contract to the injury of the person with whom such a contract has been made. It does not appear to me to be a sound answer, to say that the act in such cases is the act of the party who breaks the contract; for that reason would apply in the acknowledged case of master and servant. Nor is it an answer, to say that there is a remedy against the contractor, and that the party relies on the contract; for, besides that reason also applying to the case of master and servant, the action on the contract and the action against the malicious wrong-doer may be for a different matter; and the damages occasioned by such malicious injury might be calculated on a very different principle from the amount of the debt which might be the only sum recoverable on the contract. . . . The servant or contractor may be utterly unable to pay anything like the amount of the damage sustained entirely from the wrongful act of the defendant: and it would seem unjust, and contrary to the general principles of law, if such wrongdoer were not responsible for the damage caused by his wrongful and malicious act. . . .

Without however deciding any such more general question, I think that we are justified in applying the principle of the action for enticing away servants to a case where the defendant maliciously procures a party, who is under a valid contract to give her exclusive personal services to the plaintiff for a specified period, to refuse to give such services during the period for which she had so contracted, whereby the plaintiff was injured.

I think, therefore, that our judgment should be for the plaintiff.

[The opinions of Erle and Wightman JJ., who agreed with Crompton J., as well as that of Coleridge J., who dissented, are omitted. The case is more fully reproduced in Wright's *Cases on the Law of Torts* where the tort element is developed to its current position. For purposes of understanding the scope of protection given by the state to a contract, an introduction to the principle is sufficient here.]

QUESTIONS. If Gye broke his contract with Miss Wagner, and she sued him, would a court allow him to argue that the contract ought not to be enforced, since it was made as the result of his wrong doing? If Miss Wagner broke her contract with Gye, and he sued, could she set up the defence? Would it matter whether she broke it in order to fulfil her engagement with Lumley, or to take a holiday in Cornwall? Whose interests are being protected here, and why?

NOTE ON LEGAL METHOD. Lumley v. *Gye* is sometimes relied upon today to justify state interference with picketing, in labour cases, on the theory that the picketers are trying to induce the workers to break their contract with their employer, although it is open to grave doubt whether so-called "hourly paid" employees have any contract. If you are troubled by this extension of a legal concept into a controversial modern social problem without much social analysis by the judges, you might reflect on the following excerpt from Professor Herman Oliphant's presidential address on "A Return to Stare Decisis" to the Association of American Law Schools, in 1927. The whole article is worth reading at a later date when you have had more experience with reading cases yourself. It will be found in the Handbook of the Association for 1927, beginning at p. 61. The excerpt begins at p. 64:

"*What Does a Case Decide?* In the first place, a court, in deciding a case, may throw out a statement as to how it would decide some other case. Now if that statement is a statement of another case which is as narrow and specific as the actual case before the court, it is easily recognized as dictum and given its proper weight as such. In the second place, the court may throw out a broader statement, covering a whole group of cases. But, so long as that statement does not cover the case before the court, it is readily recognized as being not a decision, much less the decision of the case. It is dictum, so labeled and appraised. But, in the third place, a court may make a statement broad enough to dispose of the case in hand as well as to cover also a few or many other states of fact. Statements of this third sort may cover a number of fact situations ranging from one other to legion. Such a statement is sometimes called the *decision* of the case. Thereby the whole ambiguity of that word is introduced and the whole difficulty presented.

"If a more careful usage limits the word *decision* to the *action* taken by the court in the specific case before it—i.e., to the naked judgment or order entered—the difficulty is not met; it is merely shifted. *Stare decisis* thus understood becomes useless for no decision in that limited sense can ever be followed. No identical case can arise. All other cases will differ in some circumstance, in time if no other, and most of them will have differences which are not trivial. *Decision* in the sense meant in *stare decisis* must therefore refer to a proposition of law covering a group of fact situations, a group including as a minimum the fact situation of the instant case and at least one other.

"To bring together into one class even this minimum of two fact situations, however similar they may be, always has required and always will require an abstraction. If Paul and Peter are to be thought of together at all, they must both be apostles or be thought of as having some other attribute in common. Classification is abstraction. An element or elements common to the two fact situations put into one class must be drawn out from each to become the content of the category and the subject of the proposition of law which is thus applied to the two cases.

"But such a grouping may include multitudes of fact situations so long as a single attribute common to them all can be found. Between these two extremes lies a gradation of groups of fact situations, each with its corresponding proposition of law, ranging from a grouping subtending but two situations to those covering hosts of them. This series of groupings of fact situations gives us a parallel series of corresponding propositions of law, each more and more generalized as we recede farther and farther from the instant state of facts and include more and more fact situations in the successive groupings. It is a mounting and widening structure, each proposition including all that has gone before and becoming more general by embracing new states of fact. For example, A's father induces her not to marry B as she promised to do. On a holding that the father is not liable to B for so doing, a gradation of widening propositions can be built, a very few of which are:

"1. Fathers are privileged to induce daughters to break promises to marry.
"2. Parents are so privileged.
"3. Parents are so privileged as to both daughters and sons.
"4. All persons are so privileged as to promises to marry.
"5. Parents are so privileged as to all promises made by their children.
"6. All persons are so privileged as to all promises made by any one.

"There can be erected upon the action taken by a court in any case such a gradation of generalizations, and this is commonly done in the opinion. Sometimes it is built up to dizzy heights by the court itself, and, at times, by law teachers and writers, it is reared to those lofty summits of the absolute and the infinite.

"Where on that gradation of propositions are we to take our stand and say, 'This proposition is the decision of this case within the meaning of the doctrine of *stare decisis*'? Can a proposition of law of this third type ever become so broad that, as to any of the cases it would cover, it is mere dictum?"

CRIMINAL CODE

Canada. Statutes. 1953–54. Chapter 51

365. (1) Every one who willfully breaks a contract, knowing or having reasonable cause to believe that the probable consequences of doing so, whether alone or in combination with others, will be

(a) to endanger human life,
(b) to cause serious bodily injury,
(c) to expose valuable property, real or personal, to destruction or serious injury,
(d) to deprive the inhabitants of a city or place, or part thereof, wholly or to a great extent, of their supply of light, power, gas or water, or
(e) to delay or prevent the running of a locomotive engine, tender, freight or passenger train or car, on a railway that is a common carrier,

is guilty of

(f) an indictable offence and is liable to imprisonment for five years, or
(g) an offence punishable on summary conviction.

[Subsection (2) excuses lawful union activity.]

(3) No proceedings shall be instituted under this section without the consent of the Attorney General.

CHAPTER 2

THE KINDS OF PROMISES LEGALLY ENFORCED

In Chapter 1 the existence of an enforceable promise was assumed and the problems were concerned with what should be done for the aggrieved party and to the defaulting party. In this Chapter the existence of a promise is assumed, but the questions are, Why should it be enforced? Why enforce any promise? Why not enforce all promises? And if the answer favours enforcing some promises, but not all, then an even more difficult question follows. How do you select the promises that are to be enforced? In our society we *expect* promises to be kept. We speak of someone who is "a man of his word," by which we mean that we respect him because he keeps his promises. But it is generally agreed by philosophers and practical men alike that it would be wrong to hold a man to all of his promises, regardless of the circumstances under which they were made. The debate begins when you try to prescribe the kind of promises to be enforced. The method of the common law has been to follow certain historical rules and to engage in what may appear to you as rather unreal and technical argument in applying the old rules to modern conditions. The rules fall into two classes, those that depend upon *form*, and those that depend upon the notion of *exchange*, which has come to be called "consideration" through accidents of history. Underlying both classes is the element of *intention*, either the intention of the promisor or the "intent of the transaction" as Lord Mansfield once put it. And underlying both classes is the element of *reliance*, which today may be emerging as a development or refinement of the old rules.

The materials that follow are intended to enable you to understand what has been accomplished by these rules and to turn what Matthew Arnold called a "stream of fresh and free thought upon our stock notions and habits, which we follow staunchly but mechanically, vainly imagining that there is a virtue in following them staunchly which makes up for the mischief of following them mechanically."

1. FORM

The oldest of the rules followed by the courts is the rule that an action may be brought on a promise in writing ending with a *testimonium*, or witnessing clause, that said, in substance: "In witness whereof I (or, "the parties hereto") have hereunto set my (or, "their") hand and seal." Below the *testimonium* the promisor (or promisors) signed the deed and opposite his signature he placed his seal. In addition to the *testimonium*, there was also an attestation clause, which said, "Signed, sealed, and delivered, in the presence of" and was followed by the signature of a witness to the execution of the deed.

The seal, in the early days, consisted of a blob of wax, usually red, upon which the promisor impressed his seal, if he had one. *Corbin on Contracts* (p. 797) reports Edward III as reciting, "In witness that this is sooth, I bite this wax with my tooth, in the presence of Magge, Maud and Margery, and my third son Henry." Henry III is reported to have used William Marshall's seal because "We have no seal." The Chinese used a thumb print, although it is doubtful whether they appreciated its distinctive characteristic. Before the seal, a religious symbol, the mark of the Cross, was used. Sir Edward Coke, 1552-1633 (3 Inst. 169) said, "*Sigillum est cera impressa quia cera sine impressione non est sigillum.*" *Corbin* comments (pp. 798-9), "The fact that this is an excellent example of begging the question, pompously concealed by putting it into a dead language, should not cause us to overlook the fact that Coke's statement may have been true. Indeed, Coke had so great an influence over English law that by merely stating it in Latin he could make it true for a century or more."

Of these three elements of form, signing, sealing, and delivering, little remains.

As to signing, it was never considered that the signature was as important as the sealing. See *Martin v. Barnes* (1863), 5 N.S.R. (1 Oldright) 291, esp. at pp. 304, 307. Plucknett, *A Concise History of the Common Law* (5th ed., 196), comments: "We do not commonly find signatures on deeds before the sixteenth century, and they did not become generally necessary until the Statute of Frauds." In medieval and renaissance England very few people could read or write.

As to sealing, Boyd C. said, in *Re Bell and Black* (1882), 1 O.R. 125 at p. 126,". . . the current of modern decisions has worn away every distinctive feature of this ancient definition. Neither wax, wafer, nor other adhesive substance is now required." The modern practice (1963) includes the use of the printed word "seal" inside a circle, opposite the space for the signature. More ambiguous is the use of the two letters "L.S." inside the circle. If these letters are taken to stand for "legal seal," as some suppose, it could properly be regarded as a sealed instrument. If the letters are taken to stand for the Latin *locus sigilli*, the place of the seal, and no seal has been put in the place, it could properly be regarded as not a sealed instrument.

As to delivering, it is clear that delivery is as much a symbol as a fact.

The use of the *testimonium* itself is not essential. See *Whittier* v. *McLennan* (1856), 13 U.C.Q.B. 638. Robinson C.J. said, ". . . we cannot say that it is indispensable to the creation of a specialty, that besides sealing the party should expressly affirm that he seals it." See, for interesting sets of facts, *Clauda* v. *Lodge*, [1952] 4 D.L.R. 570 (British Columbia), and *Ray v. Gillmore* (1957), 11 D.L.R. (2d) 443 (British Columbia).

The practical significance of a formal promise lies in the fact that no exchange of any sort is required. The court enforces what is sometimes called "a barren promise" or a "voluntary promise," or, putting it in Latin, a *nudum pactum*. Almost as practical is the extension of liability for breach of the promise from six to twenty years under the *Limitations Acts*.

EZRA AND EDWARD ZWICKER *v*. ERI ZWICKER

Canada. Supreme Court. 1899. 29 S.C.R. 527

This was an action brought by Eri Zwicker, as administrator of his father, Joseph Zwicker, intestate, seeking, among other things, the delivery up of certain personal property and a deed dated April 5, 1877, from Joseph Zwicker to Eri, Ezra, and Edward Zwicker. Ezra and Edward Zwicker, the defendants (appellants), denied having any personal property, or a deed, that belonged to Eri *as administrator*. Evidence was produced of the signing and sealing of the deed, but its delivery was disputed.

STRONG C.J.: . . . At the trial before a judge without a jury, the facts appeared to be that the deed of the 5th of April, 1877, was an indenture made between Joseph Zwicker, the intestate, of the one part, and his three sons the respondent and the appellants of the other part, whereby the grantor purported to convey certain lands to his sons in fee. It also contained a disposition of chattel property in the following words:

"I also give unto my two sons, Ezra and Edward, all my stock of cattle, household furniture, farming implements, all personal property but the notes of hand and mortgages, and the house shall be jointly owned by my three sons.". . .

It is however urged, and the court below have given effect to the objection, that there is no proof of the delivery of the deed. It is assumed, and it is I think the proper conclusion from the evidence, that the deed was retained in the possession of the grantor until his death, and this fact has been considered sufficient to show that the deed never was so delivered as to take effect as a duly executed instrument. It is in the face of decided cases of the highest authority out of the question to say that a deed must be presumed to have been inoperative for want of delivery merely because the grantor has retained it in his possesion for many years and up to the time of his death. . . .

In all these cases it was held that the retention of the deed after its signing and sealing by the grantor did not show that the execution was defective for want of delivery even in the case where the fact of its existence had never up to the grantor's death been communicated to the parties claiming under it. In *Fletcher* v. *Fletcher* (1844), 4 Hare 67; 67 E.R. 564, Wigram V.C. says:

"The case of *Doe* v. *Knight* (1826), 5 B. & C. 671; 108 E.R. 250, shows that if an instrument is sealed and delivered the retainer of it by the party in his possession does not prevent it from taking effect. No doubt the intention of the parties is often dissappointed by holding them to be bound by deeds which they have kept back but such is unquestionably the law."

In *Xenos* v. *Wickham* (1866), L.R. 2 H.L. 296, Mr. Justice Blackburn in delivering his opinion to the House of Lords thus states the law:

"No particular technical form of words or acts is necessary to render an instrument the deed of the party sealing it. . . . It is clear on the authorities as well as on the reason of the thing that the deed is binding on the obligor before it comes into the custody of the obligee, nay before he even knows of it."

In the same case Lord Cranworth says:

"In the first place the efficacy of a deed depends on it being sealed and delivered by the maker of it, not on his ceasing to retain possession of it. This as a general proposition of law cannot be controverted."

In *Moore* v. *Hazelton* (1864), 9 Allen (Mass.) 102, the court says: "Execution of the deed in the presence of an attesting witness is sufficient evidence from which to infer a delivery."

Although these authorities are not referred to in the judgment under appeal I assume they were cited in the court below, and that their decision holding the deed inoperative proceeded on the ground that the facts in evidence rebutted the presumption in favour of the due execution of the instrument. These facts are said to consist not only in the retention of the deed by the grantor, but also in the fact that it comprised all the property which he possessed, and that it professed to dispose of this property immediately and that inconsistently with its tenor the grantor retained the possession and enjoyment of his property until his death. No case is referred to as warranting the proposition that this is sufficient to control the effect of the deed, and in the absence of authority I see nothing to authorise it. The circumstance of non-communication to those taking benefits under the deed (if we are to assume such to have been the fact), is shown by the cases referred to to be immaterial, and it may well be that the intestate thought fit to trust to the good feeling and affection of his sons not to disturb him in his enjoyment. At all events we could not disregard a rule of law sanctioned by such high authority and in so many reported decisions without making a precedent which we should be compelled to follow in other cases.

When Joseph Zwicker died in 1894 this deed came into the possession of his sons, and they, including the respondent, agreed to act upon it, and did act upon it by placing it upon the county registry deeds in order to do which they had of course to treat it as a valid and subsisting instrument by proving it in the manner required by the law. The respondent, moreover, contributed his share of the expense of registration.

Further, it is out of the question to say that there was no communication of the deed to the sons during the grantor's lifetime. One of the documents sought to be recovered is the bond already mentioned dated the 2nd of October, 1884. By this instrument the three sons became bound to pay certain sums to three grandsons of the intestate named Ernst, sons of two of his daughters, both of whom were dead. These sums were duly paid on the testator's decease. To this bond there is appended a memorandum also under seal of the intestate himself.... The division referred to in this memorandum must be taken to have reference to the division effected by the deed as no other division is suggested....

[How does this "deed" differ from a "will"?]

SHARINGTON *v.* STROTTON. 1566. 1 Plowden 298; 75 E.R. 454. BROMLEY, in argument: ". . . where the agreement is by deed, there is more time for deliberation. For when a man passes a thing by deed, first there is the determination of the mind to do it, and upon that he causes it to be written, which is one part of deliberation, and afterwards he puts his seal to it, which is another part of deliberation, and lastly he delivers the writing as his deed, which is the consummation of his resolution. . . . So that there is great deliberation used in the making of deeds, for which reason they are received as a *lien* final to the party, and are adjudged to bind the party without examining upon what cause or consideration they were made."

FULLER, "CONSIDERATION AND FORM"
1941. 41 Columbia Law Review 799, 800-1. (1941)

. . . *The Evidentiary Function.*—The most obvious function of a legal formality is, to use Austin's words, that of providing "evidence of the existence and purport of the contract, in case of controversy." The need for evidentiary security may be satisfied in a variety of ways: by requiring a writing, or attestation, or the certification of a notary. It may even be satisfied, to some extent, by such a device as the Roman *stipulatio*, which compelled an oral spelling out of the promise in a manner sufficiently ceremonious to impress its terms on participants and possible bystanders.

The Cautionary Function.—A formality may also perform a cautionary warrant the application of the useful rule of law giving a remedy in case of or deterrent function by acting as a check against inconsiderate action. The seal in its original form fulfilled this purpose remarkably well. The affixing and impressing of a wax wafer—symbol in the popular mind of legalism and weightiness—was an excellent device for inducing the circumspective frame of mind appropriate in one pledging his future. To a less extent any requirement of a writing, of course, serves the same purpose, as do requirements of attestation, notarization, etc.

The Channeling Function.—Though most discussions of the purposes served by formalities go no further than the analysis just presented, this analysis stops short of recognizing one of the most important functions of form. That a legal formality may perform a function not yet described can be shown by the seal. The seal not only insures a satisfactory memorial of the promise and induces deliberation in the making of it. It serves also to mark or signalize the enforceable promise; it furnishes a simple and external test of enforceability. This function of form Ihering described as "the facilitation of judicial diagnosis" and he employed the analogy of coinage in explaining it.

"Form is for a legal transaction what the stamp is for a coin. Just as the stamp of the coin relieves us from the necessity of testing the metallic content and weight—in short, the value of the coin (a test which we could not avoid if uncoined metal were offered to us in payment), in the same way legal formalities relieve the judge of an inquiry *whether* a legal transaction was intended, and—in case different forms are fixed for different legal transactions—*which* was intended."

In this passage it is apparent that Ihering has placed an undue emphasis on the utility of form for the judge, to the neglect of its significance for those transacting business out of court. If we look at the matter purely from the standpoint of the convenience of the judge, there is nothing to distinguish the forms used in legal transaction from the "formal" element which to some degree permeates all thinking. Even in the field of criminal law "judicial diagnosis" is "facilitated" by formal definitions, presumptions, and artificial construction of fact. The thing which characterizes the law of contracts and conveyances is that in this field forms are deliberately used, and are intended to be so used, by the parties whose acts are to be judged by the law. To the business man who wishes to make his own or another's promise binding, the seal was at common law available as a device for the accomplishment of his objective. In this aspect form offers a legal framework into which the party may fit his actions, or, to change the figure, it offers channels for the legally effective expression of intention. It is with this aspect of form in mind that I have described the third function of legal formalities as "the channeling function."...

CHILLIBACK *v.* PAWLIUK
Alberta. 1956. 1 D.L.R. (2d) 611

EGBERT J.: The plaintiff, who was a gratuitous passenger in the defendant's car, sues for damages arising out of injuries sustained in an accident allegedly caused by the gross negligence of the defendant.

The defence is twofold—that the defendant was not grossly negligent, and secondly, that if he did become liable to compensate the plaintiff, the latter subsequently released the defendant by signing a written release under seal.

At the conclusion of the trial I found on the evidence that the accident, and the plaintiff's consequent injuries had been caused by the gross negligence of the defendant. Counsel for the defendant then asked for leave to file a written argument on the second line of defence, relating to the alleged release. This leave was granted and both counsel have now filed written arguments on this point.

The accident occurred on June 10, 1953. This action was commenced on June 8, 1954. In the interval, on October 30, 1953, the plaintiff signed the alleged release.

The parties were on friendly terms before the accident and remained on similar terms after the accident, until at least some time after the execution of the alleged release at the end of October, 1953, although after the accident they did not see one another so frequently, since the plaintiff, because of his injuries, was unable to continue his work in Big Valley, where the defendant was also located, and where the parties frequently saw one another.

On October 30, 1953, the plaintiff went into the beer parlour of an hotel in Edmonton. According to his evidence he had some six glasses of beer with a friend who cannot now be located, when another friend, Mercer, came along. Each of the three men had another four or six beers. At this point, when the plaintiff had been in the beer parlour about three hours, the defendant entered, found the group, and said to the plaintiff, "I have a paper here I'd like you to sign, because I'd like to get my driver's licence back" (or very similar words). The plaintiff had once had his own driver's licence taken away for "impaired driving", and knew what the defendant was talking about. The plaintiff then signed a paper which the defendant handed to him. He received no money or other consideration for signing, and says that he signed to help the defendant get his licence back. He had consulted Mr. Dubensky, a solicitor in Edmonton, before this about the possibility of taking action against the defendant, but says that he did not know this paper had anything to do with the lawsuit. He admits that the defendant used no force, or threat or promise to induce him to sign the paper. He denies that he was drunk when he signed the document. The defendant made any insertions or alterations in the document that appear in hand-writing. (These consist of the insertion of the date, and the insertion of the word "nil" in two places.) The plaintiff signed the document and Mercer signed it as witness to the plaintiff's signature. The document itself is contained on one sheet of paper, and reads as follows:

"RELEASE AND DISCHARGE

"IN CONSIDERATION of the payment or settlement of the sum of ($) Nil Dollars, the receipt whereof is hereby acknowledged), I Fred Chilliback do hereby release and forever discharge William Pawliuk from all and any actions, cause of actions, claims and demands for, upon or by reason of any damage, loss or injury which heretofore have been or which hereafter may be sustained by in in consequence of the accident of June 10th, 1953

IT BEING FURTHER AGREED AND UNDERSTOOD that the payment of the said ($) nil Dollars is not to be construed as an admission on the part of the said William Pawliuk of any liability whatever in consequence of said accident. I further state that I have carefully read the foregoing release, and know the contents thereof, and I sign the same of my own free will.

IN WITNESS WHEREOF, I have hereunto set my hand and seal this 30 day of October 1953.

SIGNED, SEALED AND DELIVERED)
IN THE PRESENCE OF)
(Name) 'J. F. Mercer') (SIGNATURE) 'F. Chillibäck'
(Address) 10860—73 St.) (Seal)
) To bear the signature of
) Fred Chillibäck.
Witness"

In the space in the right lower corner marked "Seal" is affixed a red wafer seal.

It appears to be common ground that this document was prepared by the Motor Vehicle Branch of the Highways Department, but it is not common ground that that Branch affixed the seal before the document was sent out, or, in fact, that the seal had actually been placed on the document before the plaintiff signed it. The evidence of both parties and of the witness Mercer, appears to be silent on this point. In the absence of evidence, and in the light of a statement made to me by counsel for the defendant, I think I must assume that the seal had been affixed to the document by the Motor Vehicle Branch, and was affixed to it at the time the plaintiff signed it, despite the suggestion of counsel for the plaintiff that it was affixed at some later time.

The defendant states in his evidence that the plaintiff read over the release before he signed it, and had no difficulty in understanding it, and himself suggested that the defendant write in the word "nothing" in the space relating to the consideration. This is not denied by the plaintiff. The defendant admits that he gave the plaintiff no consideration for the release.

The plaintiff's skull injuries affected his mental processes to some extent. His demeanour in the witness-box indicated a mental slowness, which other evidence substantiated, but there was no evidence on which a conclusion could be based that the plaintiff was unable to understand either the nature or the contents of the release.

Counsel for the plaintiff argues in the first place that the execution of the release was a case of *non est factum*. . . . It is not a case where the principle of *non est factum* is applicable. There is nothing to indicate that the minds of the parties did not meet. It may be that the plaintiff did not appreciate the full legal effect of the release, but that is not an unusual circumstance. How many men fully understand the complete legal effect of the contracts they sign?

The defence resolves itself into the sole question of whether the complete lack of consideration is offset by the presence of the red seal opposite the plaintiff's signature. I am left with no doubt that if there had been no seal the release would have been inoperative because of the absence of consideration. Does the presence of the small, red wafer seal make it operative?

I have no doubt on the evidence, or possibly I should say on the lack of evidence touching the matter of the seal, that both the plaintiff and the defendant were, at the time of the execution of the release, entirely oblivious to its existence, and to the effect of its presence. Indeed, counsel for the defendant states in his argument "neither the plaintiff nor the defendant were at all concerned, nor probably even cognizant of the fact that a seal was on the document or required to be on the document". With this statement I entirely agree. There is no evidence that the plaintiff said any word or did any act which in any way amounted to an adoption by him of the seal as *his* seal. So far as the plaintiff was concerned, he was *signing* a document submitted to him by the defendant—that was the transaction and the whole transaction insofar as he understood it. Nevertheless the document he signed did have affixed to it, opposite the space for his signature, the seal now in question, and the defendant now produces a release purporting to be signed and sealed by the plaintiff.

As is stated in most textbooks and in many ancient authorities, a seal was said to "import" consideration, so that a document under seal might be enforced even though no consideration appeared on the face of the instrument. In other words, the seal itself constituted *prima facie* proof that consideration had passed. . . . But how can it be said that a seal "imports" consideration when the document itself expressly states that there is no consideration? In this case we not only have an express negation of consideration in the instrument, but all the available evidence proves conclusively that no consideration passed from the defendant to the plaintiff, and that the plaintiff himself recorded that fact in the instrument.

In my view, the evidence discloses that the parties did not intend that this document should be executed as a sealed document.

Somewhat similar circumstances were discussed by Stuart J. in *Sawyer & Massey Ltd.* v. *Bouchard* (1910), 13 W.L.R. 394, when he arrived at the same conclusion. As Stuart J. said, after reviewing a number of authorities [p. 398]: "It will be seen, I think, from an examination of these cases, that the whole question is one of fact, and that the question is, not whether there is a seal on the instrument, but whether the person executing it affixed his seal thereto, either by doing so in fact or by doing something which the law will hold as equivalent thereto. The sealing must be either directly or indirectly the act of the party executing the instrument."

As Stuart J. points out, when a person signs his name to an instrument already sealed, he is presumed to have adopted the seal affixed—this is one of the equivalents above referred to accepted by the law. But it is only a presumption which is raised, and this presumption may be rebutted by evidence by which a contrary intention is proved or from which it may be inferred. In this case, as I have said, the evidence is, in my view, clear that both parties were quite oblivious to the presence of the seal, and that there was no intention on the part of either of them that the document should be sealed. It is true that in *Sawyer & Massey Ltd.* v. *Bouchard* there was no *testimonium* clause as there is here, and that Stuart J. refers to its absence, and says that had there been such a clause, it "would probably, though I refrain from expressing any decided opinion, have been enough to have shewn an intention to adopt the printed seal as his own" [p. 399]. It will be observed, however, that Stuart J. does refrain from expressing a decided opinion, and since, as he had previously observed, the question is one of intention, I think I am justified in holding that the mere presence of the *testimonium* clause is not sufficient if the evidence otherwise leads to a conclusion that the intention to execute the document under seal did not exist.

I accordingly hold, in the first place, that the release is not an instrument under seal, and therefore since no consideration passed to the plaintiff, it is not enforceable by the defendant.

In the second place, I hold that even if the document is under seal, it is, under the circumstances, not enforceable for want of consideration. As I have said, the document itself, as well as the surrounding evidence, negatives consideration, so that the mere presence of a seal cannot "import" consideration, or raise an irrebuttable presumption of a consideration which did not, in fact, exist. The Court, in the exercise of its equitable jurisdiction may look at the true bargain between the parties, and refuse to enforce an otherwise unenforceable agreement, merely because it is under seal. . . .

Having found that the release relied on by the defendant is unenforceable, it only remains to assess the plaintiff's damages. . . .

NOTE. Apart from Egbert J.'s point that Chilliback didn't intend to *seal*, but merely to *sign*, the instrument, the basis of his decision that the seal is merely presumptive evidence of consideration is quite without historical foundation. The formal promise was enforced long before the doctrine of consideration became current. But the earliest cases were cases where, even if there had been no seal, the facts disclosed sufficient consideration to enable a modern court to enforce the promise without the formality. Pollock and Maitland, in *The History of English Law* (2d ed., 1898, Vol. 2, 213-14) "doubt whether in the thirteenth century a purely gratuitous promise, though made in a sealed instrument, would have been enforced if its gratuitous character had stood openly revealed." For a comment on the principal case, see Weston, "Contracts under Seal—Enforceability—Necessity of Consideration" (1956), 34 *Can. Bar Rev.* 453. See also Milner, "The Common Law of Contract" in *Canadian Jurisprudence* (ed. McWhinney), 90-117.

As to Chilliback's intention, or lack of it, if the seal is there, should his intention be called into account? How might Ihering have dealt with this case?

MARTIN *v.* BARNES. 1863. 5 N.S.R. (1 Oldright) 291. YOUNG C.J.: "[U]nless our legislature interferes, as they have done in Connecticut, (which I would not be understood, however, as approving,) and enact that conveyances and bonds shall be valid without seals, we must adhere to the common law rule . . . we ought to require evidence of some positive and serious public inconvenience, before we at one stroke annihilate so well established and venerable a practice as the use of seals in the authentication of deeds. Of the use of seals in the authentication of writs, we had a memorable instance in this Court in the recent case of *The Queen* v. *Burdell and Lane*, when the want of a bit of wafer reduced the crime of homicide from murder to manslaughter."

THE LAND TITLES ACT

Ontario. Revised Statutes. 1960. Chapter 204

81. Notwithstanding any statute or rule of law, a charge or transfer of registered land may be duly made by an instrument not under seal and, if so made, the instrument and every agreement, stipulation and condition therein has the same effect for all purposes as if made under seal.

NOTE ON THE ABOLITION OF SEALS. Canadian legislatures have not hastened to "abolish the seal," whatever that expression may mean, but legislatures in the United States have been quite active. For example, California, Idaho, Montana, North Dakota and Oklahoma have language like California's *Civil Code*, section 1629, "All distinctions between sealed and unsealed instruments are abolished." As a result of this section, are unsealed promises as enforceable as sealed ones used to be? Or are sealed instruments no longer enforceable unless consideration is proven?

The California *Code* also provided, in section 1614, "A written instrument is presumptive evidence of consideration."

Compare the *Uniform Written Obligations Act* approved by the Commissioners on Uniform State Laws in 1925. It is in force only in Pennsylvania:

"A written release or promise hereafter made and signed by the person releasing or promising shall not be invalid or unenforceable for lack of consideration, if the writing also contains an additional express statement, in any form of language, that the signer intends to be legally bound."

Williston, who advocated the model Act, says (*Williston on Contracts*, 3d ed., sec. 219, p. 794) "efforts to fill the gap created by statutory abolition of the seal have proved largely unsuccessful." See *Corbin on Contracts*, sec. 257, for a short criticism. Critics have also suggested that the form of words can become as sterile as the seal through mass reproduction in fine print on ready made forms of contracts and the further suggestion has been made that the model Act be modified to require that the words be in the handwriting of the promisor after the principle of holograph wills. See also Steele, "The Uniform Written Obligations Act—A Criticism" (1920), 21 *Illinois Law Review* 185.

No attempt has been made to reproduce the wide variety of American legislative attempts to "abolish the seal," but merely to indicate the kind of legislative drafting and interpretative problems involved in this apparently simple exercise.

QUEBEC CIVIL CODE

1208. A notarial instrument received before one notary is authentic if signed by all the parties. . . .

1210. An authentic writing makes complete proof between the parties to it and their heirs and legal representatives:
   1. Of the obligation expressed in it;
   2. Of what is expressed in it by way of recital, if the recital have a direct reference to the obligation or to the object of the parties in executing the instrument. . . .

COMPARATIVE LAW NOTE. A notary has no counterpart in the common law system. Although a private practitioner, with substantially the same training as a lawyer, his function in authenticating "notarial instruments" is a "public" one. Attention is drawn to this provision merely because it represents an alternative formal method of authenticating contracts. Its use in Quebec is limited and it is more cumbersome than the common law seal.

2. Consideration: The Bargain Theory

CURRIE *v.* MISA. 1875. L.R. 10 Ex. 153, 162, affirmed, 1 App. Cas. 554. Lush J.: "A valuable consideration, in the sense of the law, may consist either in some right, interest, profit, or benefit accruing to the one party, or some forbearance, detriment, loss, or responsibility, given, suffered, or undertaken by the other." [This definition has frequently been cited with approval in Canadian courts.]

DUNLOP PNEUMATIC TYRE CO. *v.* SELFRIDGE & CO. [1915] A.C. 847, 855. Lord Dunedin: "My Lords, I am content to adopt from a work of Sir Frederick Pollock, to which I have often been under obligation, the following words as to consideration: 'An act or forbearance of one party, or the promise thereof, is the price for which the promise of the other is bought, and the promise thus given for value is enforceable.' (Pollock on Contracts, 8th ed., p. 175)." [This definition seems not to have been cited in any Canadian court.]

WESTLAKE *v*. ADAMS. 1858. 5 C.B.N.S. 248; 141 E.R. 99, 106. BYLES J.: "It is an elementary principle, that the law will not enter into an enquiry as to the adequacy of the consideration. . . ."

HOBBES, LEVIATHAN. 1651. "The value of all things contracted for is measured by the appetite of the contractors, and therefore the just value is that which they be contented to give."

VERNON *v*. BETHELL. 1762. 2 Eden 110; 28 E.R. 838, 839 (England, Chancery), NORTHINGTON L.C.: ". . . necessitous men are not, truly speaking, free men, but, to answer a present exigency, will submit to any terms that the crafty may impose upon them." [This attitude is representative of a court of equity, in this case deciding that a mortgagee had made "an undue use of the influence of a mortgage."]

NOTE ON LEGAL METHOD. Obviously numerous difficulties will arise in the application of these definitions: What is an exchange? Must it be equal in value to the promise? If so, who is to decide the relative values? Must it be contemporaneous with the promise? And so on. These difficulties are raised by the cases in this chapter. On thinking about them, it is important to remember that many people feel (as a matter of intuition) that a man who makes a serious promise ought to keep it, whether he exacted anything in exchange or not. The result is that courts are usually under some pressure to enforce a "barren" promise by "implying" a requested exchange, or "interpreting" the facts to show that there was one in circumstances where it is quite easy to reach the opposite conclusion.

A short tale from *Huckleberry Finn* may throw some light on this judicial peculiarity. The account is taken from Pound, "Law in Books and Law in Action" (1910) 44 American Law Review 12.

"When Tom Sawyer and Huck Finn had determined to rescue Jim by digging under the cabin where he was confined, it seemed to the uninformed lay mind of Huck Finn that some old picks the boys had found were the proper implements to use. But Tom knew better. From reading he knew what was the right course in such cases, and he called for case-knives. 'It don't make no difference,' said Tom, 'how foolish it is, it's the *right way*—and it's the regular way. And there ain't no other way that ever I heard of, and I've read all the books that gives any information about these things. They always dig out with a case-knife.' So, in deference to the books and the proprieties, the boys set to work with case-knives. But after they had dug till nearly midnight and they were tired and their hands were blistered, and they had made little progress, a light came to Tom's legal mind. He dropped his knife and, turning to Huck, said firmly, 'Gimme a case-knife.' Let Huck tell the rest:

" 'He had his own by him, but I handed him mine. He flung it down and says, "Gimme a *case-knife*."

" 'I didn't know just what to do—but then I thought. I scratched around amongst the old tools and got a pickaxe and give it to him, and he took it and went to work and never said a word.

" 'He was always just that particular. *Full of principle*.'

"Tom had made over again one of the earliest discoveries of the law.

When tradition prescribed case-knives for tasks for which pickaxes were better adapted, it seemed better to our forefathers, after a little vain struggle with case-knives, to adhere to principle—but use the pickaxes. They granted that law ought not to change. Changes in law were full of danger. But, on the other hand, it was highly inconvenient to use case-knives. And so the law has always managed to get a pickaxe in its hands, though it steadfastly demanded a case-knife, and to wield it in the virtuous belief that it was using the approved instrument."

NOTE ON THE HISTORY OF CONSIDERATION. The neat formulas defining consideration hide their mixed ancestry rather well, but some general understanding of the early development of the idea of consideration may help in grappling with modern problems. One word of warning may not be out of place. Legal history is frequently based on rather slim evidence, often there is only a sketchy report of a case separated from the next report by a number of years. What happened between these reports is largely a matter of guesswork.

In the late nineteenth century a major simplification of procedure in law suits was attempted, but before that, each action was commenced by the appropriate one of a number of writs each of which instituted a particular form of action having its own peculiarities. If a lawyer selected the wrong one, he might end up in failure and have to start from the beginning after making a red faced explanation to his client, whose money he had just wasted.

One of the earliest forms of action was *debt*, which lay for the recovery of a "sum certain" promised, as we would say today, but perhaps "granted" (but not yet handed over) might be closer to the ancient idea, in return for services rendered or goods supplied. If the promise was to deliver a specific chattel, the form of action was *detinue*. In each case the promise was enforceable only after the goods had been delivered or the services rendered. And there had to be an express promise of a stated amount of money. The remedy was therefore limited—it was of no use if the plaintiff's act still remained to be performed or if the amount of money was not agreed upon. This exchange of goods for a sum certain came to be called a *qui pro quo*, a sort of exchange of "grants," rarely thought of as a promise.

Another limitation lay in the fact that the defendant could "wage" his law, a curious defence in which the merits of the case could be avoided, and the defendant merely had to swear that he was not indebted. He then had to produce some number, usually a dozen, "compurgators" or "oath-helpers," men who were prepared to swear that the defendant's oath was trustworthy. They were a kind of character witness. They did not testify to facts. (See Plucknett, *A Concise History of the Common Law*, 5th ed., p. 115.) This strange defence was not so easy as it sounds, nor so unequal to a trial on the merits. In those days the oath was a fearsome thing, and on the other hand, methods of fact-finding were primitive—parties could not testify, few people could read or write, and juries were not limited to the evidence produced before them. Wager of law was theoretically permissible in England until abolished in 1833.

One of the peculiarities of English legal development lay in the competition between courts. Supreme judicial tribunals are a relatively modern phenomenon, and they appear to be open to attack now by rival administrative tribunals, e.g. the Workmen's Compensation Board. In early days the action of debt with its defence of wager of law lay only in the Court of

Common Pleas. Hence, if you could find a form of action that would let you into the Court of King's Bench, you could avoid wagers of law and be sure your case would be tried on its merits. And the Court was not unwilling to strain a point of practice to acquire the new business.

In the King's Bench, which had no great interest in contract, apart from formal covenants, the first appearance of contract was in a form of action that evolved very slowly from the favourite tort action of trespass, trespass on the case, in which it was alleged that something was undertaken (in Latin *Assumpsit*—the name by which the writ came to be known) and performed in such a way as to injure the plaintiff. Injury to the plaintiff of the kind familiar in trespass actions was originally very important. Injury to an expectation interest came slowly, although in covenant it was quite familiar. This gradually developed in *assumpsit* for non-feasance, where the promise was not performed at all. In the development of the action of assumpsit the expression "in consideration of" which appears in early forms, seems to have led to the use of the word "consideration" to denote something done by the plaintiff in exchange for the undertaking. We would call this an "executed consideration" because the requested act had been performed before the action was brought. This, of course, was familiar to minds accustomed to the *quid pro quo* of debt. The next development lay in the recognition of a promise by the plaintiff as a sufficient "consideration."

The attractiveness of the growing *assumpsit* brought lawyers from the Court of Common Pleas into the King's Bench. The attempt was made to fit *assumpsit* to facts to which *debt* clearly applied. The original "grant" (or promise) to pay a sum certain seems not to have been acceptable as an *assumpsit* (undertaking) but if the debtor made a second promise later, this could be taken as the assumpsit, and thus, in effect, debt moved into the King's Bench. The action was called *indebitatus assumpsit*, "being indebted, he undertook." (Curiously enough, at this stage, it seems not to have troubled the Court that any consideration for the second promise must have been executed before that promise was made. This later, in 1615, did cause some trouble. See *Lampleigh* v. *Brathwait*, reproduced in section 4 of this chapter.) Of course, the second promise would not always be made, and any debtor who hoped to wage his law would presumably be careful to avoid a second commitment. In a momentous decision in the Exchequer Chamber (a Court hearing appeals from the King's Bench, normally consisting of the judges of Common Pleas(!) and the Barons of the Exchequer) it was held, in effect, that the second promise need not be proved, it might be presumed. See *Slade's Case* (1602) 4 Co. Rep. 91a; 76 E.R. 1072.

On this whole subject, very sketchily presented here as a basis for discussion of the cases in class, see Plucknett, *A Concise History of The Common Law*, 5th ed., pp. 637-656. A short discussion of the basis of contractual liability is to be found in Fuller, *Basic Contract Law*, pp. 289-313. On mutual promises see pp. 391-5 of the same book.

WHITE (EXECUTOR) *v*. WILLIAM BLUETT
England. Court of Exchequer. 1853. 23 L.J. Ex. (N.S.) 36

Action upon a promissory note made payable to John Bluett; the testator: Plea that Bluett was the father of the defendant, and that in his lifetime, the defendant William Bluett complained to his father that he had not received at his hands so much money or so many advantages as the other children and controversies arose between them. Bluett afterward admitted the defendant's complaints were well founded, and it was agreed that the defendant should forever cease to make such complaints, and that in consideration thereof, and in order to do justice to the defendant, and also out of Bluett's natural love and affection toward the defendant, he, Bluett, would discharge the defendant of and from all liability in respect of the promissory note.

Demurrer and joinder.

[Parke B., during the argument, asked: "Is an agreement by a father in consideration that his son will not bore him, a binding contract?"]

POLLOCK C.B.: The plea is clearly bad. By the argument a principle is pressed to an absurdity, as a bubble blown until it bursts. Looking at the words merely, there is some foundation for the argument, and, following the words only, the conclusion may be arrived at. It is said the son had a right to an equal distribution of his father's property, and did complain to his father because he had not an equal share, and said to him, "I will cease to complain if you will not sue upon this note." Whereupon the father said, "If you will promise me not to complain I will give up the note." If such a plea as this could be supported, the following would be a binding promise: A man might complain that another person used the public highway more than he ought to do, and that the other might say, "Do not complain, and I will give you £5." It is ridiculous to suppose that such promises could be binding. So, if the holder of a bill of exchange were suing the acceptor, and the acceptor were to complain that the holder had treated him hardly, or that the bill ought never to have been circulated, and the holder were to say, "Now if you will not make any more complaints I will not sue you." Such a promise would be like that now set up. In reality, there was no consideration whatever. The son had no right to complain, for the father might make what distribution of his property he liked; and the son's abstaining from doing what he had no right to do can be no consideration. *Judgment for the plaintiff.*

QUESTIONS ON LEGAL METHOD. In the sentence beginning "The son had no *right* to complain . . . ," what does the word *right* mean? Is Pollock C.B. saying that the son could not succeed in an action against his father, or his father's estate, for a share of that estate; or is he saying that the son was not entitled to annoy his father with his complaints? If the word *right* involves this ambiguity, would it not be better to find two words instead of the one? Try *claim* for the first and *privilege* for the second. Could giving up a privilege at the request of the promisor constitute consideration?

SHARON *v.* SHARON. 1885. 8 P. 614 (California). An action based on the following writing. "Palace Hotel. San Francisco, Nov. 7, 1880. I hereby agree to pay Miss S. A. Hill 250 dollars for each and every month of the year A. D. 1883 [*sic*]. Wm. Sharon." Although the defendant denied any consideration for his note, he averred that "to induce the plaintiff to desist from making unwelcome visits and annoying and disturbing him in his rooms, and on the consideration that she would cease to disturb him, he executed the document in question. *Judgment for the plaintiff.*

DUNTON *v.* DUNTON. 1892. 18 Vict. L.R. 114 (Australia). The marriage of John and Louisa Dunton was dissolved on March 12, 1890. John

Dunton, in a written agreement dated August 30, promised to pay Louisa £6 a month from September 1, 1890, during the continuance of the agreement. The agreement would be ended if Louisa committed any act to bring personal hate, contempt or ridicule on either of them, or if she did not conduct herself with sobriety, and in a respectable, orderly, and virtuous manner. The agreement recited John Dunton's desire, notwithstanding the dissolution, to make provision for his former wife. In an action to recover payment of £6 under the agreement, the question of consideration was raised. Held, for the plaintiff. HIGINBOTHAM J.: ". . . But it was said this was only a promise to do that which the plaintiff was already bound to do, and that such a promise does not constitute a good consideration. . . . [A] promise not to do, or to do something which the promisor may lawfully and without wrong to the promisee do or abstain from doing, is a good consideration. . . . She was legally at liberty, so far as the defendant was concerned, to conduct herself in these respects as she might think fit, and her promise to surrender liberty and to conduct herself in the manner desired by the defendant constituted, in my opinion, a good consideration. . . ." WILLIAMS J.: ". . . She was under no legal obligation to the defendant, or to anyone, not to get drunk in her own or any friend's house. . . ." HOOD J., who dissented, said: "It was, however, contended that the real consideration is an implied promise by her that she will conduct herself with sobriety. . . . I cannot imply such a promise from the document but even if it were expressed therein it would not, in my opinion, constitute a consideration. . . . A promise in order to be good consideration must be such as may be enforced. It must, therefore, be not only lawful, and in itself possible, but it must also be reasonably definite. Now [this] promise . . . seems to me to be about as vague a promise as can well be imagined."

QUESTIONS. Is an agreement to get drunk enforceable? See the cases on illegal and immoral consideration in section 9, below. B, a married man, has been seen by A in public with a notorious prostitute, and promises A, "If you promise not to tell anyone you have seen us together, I will give you $1,000." A promises. B refuses to pay the money. Will A recover in an action for breach of the promise? See, on this question, Goodhart, "Blackmail and Consideration in Contracts" (1928), 44 *Law Quarterly Review* 436.

SCHNELL *v.* NELL. 1861. 17 Ind. 29 (Supreme Court of Indiana). Theresa Schnell made a will leaving $200 each to Nell and others. After her death it appeared that all of her property was jointly held with her husband Zacharias Schnell, and reverted to him on her death. In consideration of the love and respect he bore for his wife, etc., Zach promised to pay Nell and others $200 each, and in consideration Nell and the others "agree to pay the above-named sum of money (one cent), and to deliver up to said Schnell, and abstain from collecting any real or supposed claims upon him or his estate, arising from the said last will and testament of the said Theresa Schnell, deceased." Held, for Schnell. PERKINS J.: "The consideration of one cent will not support the promise of Schnell. It is true, that as a general proposition, inadequacy of consideration will not vitiate an agreement. . . . But this doctrine does not apply to a mere exchange of sums of money, of coin, whose value is exactly fixed, but to the exchange of something of, in itself, indeterminate value, for money, or perhaps for other thing of indeterminate value. In this case had the one cent mentioned been some particular one cent, a family piece, or ancient, remarkable coin, possessing an indeterminate value, extrinsic from its simple money value, a different view might be taken. As it is, the mere promise to pay six hundred dollars for one cent, even had the portion of that cent due from the plaintiff been tendered, is an unconscionable contract, void, at first blush upon its face, if it be regarded as an earnest one. . . . The consideration of one cent is, plainly, in this case, merely nominal, and intended to be so."

NOTE. Professor Fuller, in his *Basic Contract Law*, at p. 347 comments on the argument of counsel for the defendant in *Schnell* v. *Nell* and points out that he did not advance the argument about the inadequacy of the one cent consideration in the form adopted by the court. He referred to a text proposition that where an agreement is unconscionable a court of equity will not give specific performance and a court of common law will give only reasonable damages. As Schnell had apparently already paid Nell $98.67 that should be sufficient. Counsel relied chiefly on *James* v. *Morgan* (below).

JAMES *v.* MORGAN
England. King's Bench. 1664. 1 Lev. 111; 83 E.R. 323

Assumpsit to pay for a horse a barley-corn a nail, doubling it every nail; and avers that there were thirty-two nails in the shoes of the horse, which being doubled every nail, came to five hundred quarters of barley: and on *non assumpsit* pleaded, the cause being tried before Hyde at Hereford, he directed the jury to give the value of the horse in damages, being £8 and so they did: and it was afterwards moved in arrest of judgment for a small fault in the declaration, which was over-ruled, and judgment given for the plaintiff.

THORNBOROUGH *v.* WHITACRE
England. King's Bench. 1705. 6 Mod. 305; 87 E.R. 1044

Assumpsit, that in consideration of half a crown by the plaintiff in hand paid to the defendant, he promised to pay two grains of rye upon Monday the twenty-ninth of March in such a year, four grains the next Monday after, and so on by progressional arithmetick every Monday for a year; and *non assumpsit* pleaded.

Per Curiam, upon motion: let them go to trial; and though this would amount to a vast quantity, yet the jury will consider of the folly of the defendant, and give but reasonable damages against him.

VANBERGEN *v.* ST. EDMUNDS PROPERTIES, LTD.
England. Court of Appeal. [1933] 2 K.B. 233

The plaintiff, being indebted to the defendants in London, and threatened by them with bankruptcy, promised to pay the amount owing into a bank in Eastbourne for the credit of the defendants in London, if the defendants would withhold service of the bankruptcy notice. The defendants served the notice to the knowledge of business associates of the plaintiff in an alleged breach of their promise. Macnaghten J. allowed general damages of £500 by analogy to the cases where a banker refuses to honour a customer's cheque. On the question of consideration he said, [1933] 1 K.B. 345, at p. 348: "The plaintiff, by going to Eastbourne, obtaining the money, and remitting it in the manner suggested, made it a binding contract on the part of Mr. Kennard that he would not serve the bankruptcy notice. . . . according to the terms proposed, the plaintiff was not to pay his debt to his creditors, but was to secure the payment of the money to the account of Stanley Evans & Co. at the Law Courts branch of the Bank of England. He was under no obligation to do that, and there was, therefore, sufficient consideration to prevent the alleged contract being nudum pactum."

The defendants appealed.

ROMER L.J.: . . . The jury, having returned a verdict in favour of the plaintiff for £500, must be taken to have arrived at the conclusion that the agreement, sued upon by the plaintiff and alleged by him in para. 2 of the statement of claim, was in fact made. The agreement so stated in para. 2 is in these terms: "On the 6th day of July, 1932, the defendants, by their solicitor, Mr. Kennard, verbally agreed with the plaintiff that if the plaintiff would on the 7th day of July, 1932, pay into any bank at Eastbourne the sum of £208 6s. 3d. in cash for the credit of Messrs. Stanley Evans & Co., the defendants' solicitors, at the Law Courts branch of the Bank of England such payment would satisfy all sums which the plaintiff owed to the defendants and the bankruptcy notice which they had issued on June 24, 1932, for £140 8s. 5d. would not be served on him." That being the agreement alleged, and found by the jury to have been arrived at, the question is whether there was any good consideration for such an agreement. It was suggested by Mr. Comyns Carr [one of counsel] that the consideration is to be found in, and indeed consisted of, the obligation undertaken by the plaintiff to proceed to Eastbourne and there endeavour to borrow money from somebody—from whom was not stated, but from somebody—of a sufficient amount to enable him to pay this debt of £208 odd, which the plaintiff at that time was owing. In the first place, that is not the agreement alleged, and if it had been the agreement alleged there is no evidence to support such an agreement, that is to say, an agreement that the plaintiff at the request of the defendants should proceed to Eastbourne on any such errand. The evidence, to my mind, makes it perfectly clear what the arrangement come to on July 6 was. It must be remembered that the plaintiff had been given until July 7 to pay this £208 odd, and on July 6 he rang up the defendants' solicitor and explained that he was not able to find the money on the 7th. Mr. Kennard, the defendants' solicitor, was naturally annoyed, but on being pressed by the plaintiff he agreed to give him still further time—namely, up to 12 o'clock noon on the following day, Friday, July 8. He was induced to do that because the plaintiff said he had to go down to Eastbourne on the following day and he hoped when he got there he would be able to raise the money from some other source. Then he explained to Mr. Kennard, who had been insisting on being paid cash in London by 12 o'clock on the Friday, that there would be some difficulty in his getting back from Eastbourne on that day, and thereupon Mr. Kennard pointed out to the plaintiff that there was a very easy way of providing for payment in cash in London by 12 o'clock on Friday—namely, by paying the money into the bank at Eastbourne to the account of Mr. Kennard at the Bank of England. That was the suggestion made by Mr. Kennard to help the plaintiff out of the difficulty. In point of fact, what was done on July 6 was, as pointed out by Lawrence L.J., that Mr. Kennard made two concessions to the plaintiff: one was that he should have up to 12 o'clock to pay cash, and the other concession, if concession indeed it was, was that he should pay in this particular way instead of having to come and pay it personally. In my opinion, there is no consideration for the agreement to give time until 12 o'clock on the Friday, nor for the agreement which the jury find was concluded that if it was paid by 12 o'clock the bankruptcy notice should not be served.

For these reasons I agree that this appeal must be allowed with the consequences that have been indicated by the Master of the Rolls.

[The judgments of Lord Hanworth M.R. and Lawrence L.J. to the same effect, are omitted. Lawrence L.J. observed "Speaking for myself, I have had the greatest difficulty in this case in ascertaining the terms of the agreement."]

3. Mutual Promises

THORP *v.* THORP. 1702. 12 Mod. 455; 88 E.R. 1448, 1450. Holt C.J.: ". . . where the doing of a thing will be a good consideration, a promise to do that thing will be so too. . . ."

HARRISON *v.* CAGE. 1698. 5 Mod. 411; 87 E.R. 736. A case of mutual promises to marry, breach by the woman. Action on the case. Holt C.J.: "Why should not a woman be bound by her promise as well as a man is bound by his? Either all is *nudum pactum*, or else the one promise is as good as the other. You agree a woman shall have an action; now what is the consideration of a man's promise? Why, it is the woman's. Then why should not his promise be a good consideration for her promise, as well as her promise is a good consideration for his? There is the same parity of reason in the one case as there is in the other, and the consideration is mutual." Turton J.: "This action is grounded on mutual promises."

NOTE ON LEGAL METHOD. The ease with which an eighteenth century judge could hold the exchange of a promise good consideration for a promise has not been characteristic of later centuries, notably the latter half of the nineteenth and the first half of the twentieth. Pollock, for example, in his *Contracts* (13th ed., p.144), inclines to the view that an exchange of promises cannot be logically explained in terms of benefit and detriment. This rule, "the most important for the business of life" has "no conclusive reason other than the convenience of so holding." Unless the promise given in exchange is binding, how has the promisee suffered a legal detriment, or changed his position at the request of the promisor? It seems rather unconvincing to argue that the promisee is privileged to utter words or not, as he pleases, and that he gives up this privilege, because there is no reason to think that the promisor requests such an utterance. He requests a binding promise, that is, a legal thing, not a mere physical noise. On the other hand, if the promise is considered binding because of the exchanged promise, and the exchanged promise is binding because it, in turn, is given in consideration of the first promise, the circular argument is objectionable. There is an obvious way out of this dilemma, but it apparently didn't attract those rationalizers of the law who put internal symmetry above all else. The answer, of course, is to inquire into the purpose to be served by consideration, and explain the fact that the common law has treated mutual promises as good consideration, which it has, consistently since *Harrison* v. *Cage* in 1698 (Pollock traces it back to 1555), by accepting an exchange of promises as a sufficient indication of deliberateness, and proof, and letting it go at that. Such a solution was unacceptable to legal rationalizers who seemed to regard the purpose of legal rules as irrelevant to their analysis and synthesis.

THE GREAT NORTHERN RAILWAY COMPANY *v.* WITHAM
England. Common Pleas. 1873. L.R. 9 C.P. 16

In October, 1871, the plaintiffs advertised for tenders for the supply of goods (amongst other things iron) to be delivered at their station at Doncaster, according to a certain specification. The Defendant sent in a tender as follows:-

I, the undersigned, hereby undertake to supply the Great Northern Railway Company, for twelve months from the 1st of November, 1871, to 31st of October, 1872, with such quantities of each or any of the several articles named in the attached specification as the company's storekeeper may order from time to time, at the price set opposite each article respectively, and agree to abide by the conditions stated on the other side.

(Signed) SAMUEL WITHAM.

The tender was accepted and several orders for iron were given by the company, which were from time to time duly executed by the defendant; but ultimately the defendant refused to supply any more, whereupon this action was brought.

A verdict having been found for the plaintiffs, Digby Seymour, Q.C., moved to enter a nonsuit, on the ground that the contract was void for want of mutuality. He contended that, as the company did not bind themselves to take any iron whatever from the defendant, his promise to supply them with iron was a promise without consideration. . . .

BRETT J.: The company advertised for tenders for the supply of stores, such as they might think fit to order, for one year. The defendant made a tender offering to supply them for that period at certain fixed prices; and the company accepted his tender. If there were no other objection, the contract between the parties would be found in the tender and the letter accepting it. This action is brought for the defendant's refusal to deliver goods ordered by the company; and the objection to the plaintiff's right to recover is, that the contract is unilateral. I do not, however, understand what objection that is to a contract. Many contracts are obnoxious to the same complaint. If I say to another, "If you will go to York, I will give you £100" that is in a certain sense a unilateral contract. He has not promised to go to York; but if he goes it cannot be doubted that he will be entitled to receive the £100. His going to York at my request is a sufficient consideration for my promise. So, if one says to another, "If you will give me an order for iron, or other goods, I will supply it at a given price:" if the order is given, there is a complete contract which the seller is bound to perform. There is in such a case ample consideration for the promise. So, here, the company having given the defendant an order at his request, his acceptance of the order would bind them. If any authority could have been found to sustain Mr. Seymour's contention, I should have considered that a rule ought to be granted. But none has been cited. *Burton* v. *Great Northern Railway Company*, 9 Ex. 507, is not all to the purpose. This is matter of every day's practice; and I think it would be wrong to countenance the notion that a man who tenders for the supply of goods in this way is not bound to deliver them when an order is given. I agree that this judgment does not decide the question whether the defendant might have absolved himself from the further performance of the contract by giving notice. *Rule refused.*

[The concurring opinions of Keating and Grove JJ. are omitted.]

QUESTIONS. Does Brett J. refer by "unilateral contract" to the same situation as Digby Seymour, Q.C., does with his expression "want of mutuality"? Did the court find a contract in this case? Was it unilateral or bilateral? What do these expressions mean? How do you "absolve yourself" from performance of a contract by giving notice unless the contract itself provides for notice, or notice can be reasonably implied? Under the contract found by the court, does the railway have to buy any iron? Is it free to buy iron from anybody else if it chooses?

Speaking of this case, Professor Corbin, in "The Effect of Options on Consideration" (1925), 34 *Yale Law Journal* 571, said: "In cases like this it may be reasonably argued that there was no contract because of lack of acceptance in accordance with the offer rather than for lack of consideration; orders were asked of the offeree and not illusory promises. Often however, the offeror does not so understand his own offer and makes no such contention; lack of consideration is a good defense. If an order is given before the offer is withdrawn, a contract is made." Do you agree? What are the terms of the "contract" that is so made?

By "illusory promise" Professor Corbin means a "promise that is not a promise. . . . the chief feature of contract law is that by an expression of his will today the promisor limits his freedom of voluntary choice in the future. . . . To fall within this field, therefore, a promise must in its terms express a willingness to effect this limitation on freedom of choice. . . . [An] illusory promise is neither enforceable against the one making it, nor is it operative as a consideration for a return promise."

Should a promise to sell the *entire output* of the promisor's plant be regarded as equally illusory? What about a promise to buy all the promisor's *needs* in a certain line from the promisee? Will the analysis differ if there are promises not to sell the *output* to third persons, or to buy *needs* from third persons?

PERCIVAL *v.* LONDON ETC. COMMITTEE. 1918. 87 L.J.K.B. 677. ATKIN J.: "One knows that these tenders are very often in a form under which the purchasing body is not bound to give the tenderer any order at all; in other words, the contractor offers to supply goods at a price, and if the purchasing body chooses to give him an order for goods during the stipulated time, then he is under an obligation to supply the goods in accordance with the order; but apart from that nobody is bound."

IN RE THE GLOUCESTER MUNICIPAL ELECTION PETITION. [1901] 1 K.B. 683. A tender to supply goods which the council might want in a certain period, when accepted was held to result in a contract. DARLING J.: "There is a good obligation to order from the respondent such of the goods included in his tender as the council might require . . . for I do not think that the council would have been justified in treating the respondent's tender as a mere price list, and ordering the goods which they required from any one whom they might choose. . . . There was a contract, because there was an obligation on both sides."

REGINA *v.* DEMERS. [1900] A.C. 103 (Quebec). On March 18, 1897, a contract was signed by Her Majesty represented by the Provincial Secretary of Quebec and Demers under which Demers covenanted to execute for Her Majesty for a term of eight years from January 1, 1897, at price Demers had received for the same work since 1892, the printing and binding of the public documents specified in the contract. The Government was defeated in the election shortly after and on May 28, 1897, their successors came into office. On June 30, the contract was cancelled. Demers sued to recover $85,000 for lost profits. Held, for the defendant province. LORD MACNAGHTEN: "The contract . . . does not purport to contain any covenant or obligation of any sort on the part of the Crown. The respondent undertakes to print certain public documents at certain specified rates. For all work given to him on the footing of the contract the Government was undoubtedly bound to pay according to the agreed tariff. But the contract imposes no obligation on the Crown to pay the respondent for work not given to him for execution. There is nothing in the contract binding the Government to give to the respondent all or any of the printing work referred to in the contract, nor is there anything in it to prevent the Government from giving the whole of the work, or such part as they think fit, to any other printer." [The Superior Court had held that the contract could not bind the Crown for payments extending over future years without legislative sanction. The Court of Queen's Bench held that because the printing was not unusual and the habit being to make such contracts for a term of years, the making of the contract was a matter of administration although, of course, the legislature might interfere if it chose. Damages granted in the Superior Court for the fiscal year were confirmed with future rights reserved.]

BERLIN MACHINE WORKS, LIMITED *v.* RANDOLPH & BAKER, LIMITED. 1917. 45 N.B.R. 201 (New Brunswick. Appeal Division). In an action for the purchase price of machinery sold to the defendant for his lumber mill the defendant counterclaimed for damages because the machinery proved unsatisfactory. One item of damage was the loss sustained by the defendant in performing his contract to deliver the output of his mill to a purchaser. The plaintiff was aware of the contract. To meet his supposed obligation the defendant went out and purchased 1,000,000 feet of lumber which he delivered to the purchaser for fifty cents a thousand less than he paid for it. This item of $500 was not allowed because the defendant was not "bound to deliver any specific quantity of logs" or "any other logs than those cut in his own mill." WHITE J.: "I think it quite clear that the allowance of the $500 could only be sustained by proof that the defendants were legally bound to make delivery to MacKay of this million feet which they purchased . . . there is no such proof."

GREENBERG *v.* LAKE SIMCOE ICE SUPPLY CO. 1917. 39 O.L.R. 32 (Ontario High Court). The Lake Simcoe Company, a dealer in coal, confirmed an arrangement with Greenberg, a retailer of coal, in these words: "We beg to confirm our quotation on coal taken by you at our Dupont or Florence street yards, namely, . . . $6.75 per ton for all coal taken from September 1st to April 30, 1917." No quantity of coal was agreed to be supplied and there was no undertaking to purchase any coal. In fact about forty tons were supplied before the Company sought to put aside the arrangement because of suspected dishonest dealings. Greenberg sued for damages. Held, no contract. LATCHFORD J.: "The plaintiff was not under the slightest obligation to purchase a single ton of coal from the defendants. There was no consideration from him to the defendants, and no acceptance . . . except in so far as the plaintiff from time to time prior to the revelation of his fraud, applied for and was supplied with coal. Until each such transaction was completed, there was no mutuality of obligation."

TOBIAS *v.* DICK AND T. EATON CO.
Manitoba. King's Bench. [1937] 4 D.L.R. 546

DYSART J.: The plaintiff sues John Dick and the T. Eaton Co. Ltd.,—the one for a breach of an alleged contract, and the other for interfering with his rights under that contract. He also charges both defendants with conspiracy, and asks for an injunction and damages.

The "contract" in question was originally drawn up by the plaintiff Tobias himself, who, by trickery, induced the defendant to sign it in its present changed form; but this defendant has by conduct since confirmed it, and cannot repudiate it. It reads thus—

"Morden, Manitoba., April th., 1935.

"AGREEMENT

"This is to confirm that A. M. Tobias of Morden, Manitoba has the exclusive selling agency, to sell and organize territory and appoint his own agents for the John Dick Crushers, from the above date, April th., 1935 to December 31st., 1937, for all Manitoba, Saskatchewan and Alberta.

"John Dick reserves the right to sell in the district and tributary of Emerson, Manitoba, and for a radius of 30 miles East, West, North and South of the Town of Emerson, Manitoba.

"The cost of the grain grinders to A. M. Tobias is $43.00 F.O.B. Emerson. . . .

"At no time must there be more than five machines unpaid for, and all machines must be paid for in cash, unless with the consent of John Dick.

"Witness H. Dueck A. M. Tobias
"Jno. E. Dick."

The parties to this litigation assumed to the very last day of the trial that this document constituted a contract binding on both parties thereto. In my opinion, it is not a contract at all. It has no mutuality—it is entirely a one-sided arrangement. By it, Tobias gets the exclusive right "to sell" Dick's machines within a stated territory for a stated time, but does not promise to sell any of the machines. The term "to sell" by implication gives Tobias the right first to *buy*, in order that he may then sell. In essence therefore, the document gives him the exclusive right to *buy* Dick's entire output of machines. This construction finds confirmation in the later provisions of the document fixing the price and terms upon which Tobias may buy the machines from Dick.

These provisions taken together clearly indicate that there is no control left in Dick over the machines, nor over Tobias' dealings in respect of the machines after Tobias has bought them; nor over the appointment of agents or the organization of a selling staff. Tobias' profits are not based on commission, but he is free to resell the machines at his own price and terms, and through his own appointed agents. Clearly, therefore, the agreement, notwithstanding an express declaration to that effect, does not create an agency.

The indirect promise by Dick "to sell" to Tobias is not supported by any consideration moving from Tobias, and so is not binding upon Dick. There is therefore no contract. The document evidences nothing more than an offer from Dick open for a given time. This offer of course remains open for acceptance until withdrawn, and has never been formally withdrawn. It is of such a nature, having regard to Dick's method of manufacturing, that it could be accepted in part, from time to time. And so far as it was accepted, it was accepted by instalments.

Tobias ordered a number of machines on two separate occasions, took delivery of them and paid for them. Some of these he is unable to sell, but he does not pretend that he can return them to Dick and have the price refunded, as he might do if he were an agent.

Apart from these two partial acceptances, Tobias has not requested any more machines, and there has therefore been no refusal by Dick to live up to his offer. Dick was only too anxious to sell more machines to Tobias, and repeatedly urged Tobias to take those that were already completed. Only after Dick had lost all hope of disposing of his machines to Tobias did he decide to ignore his "agreement" altogether and sell his machines elsewhere.

To sum up, there was no contract between these two parties, and therefore no breach. The plaintiff's action against Dick must be dismissed with costs. . . .

The plaintiff's action against the T. Eaton Co. will also be dismissed with costs. . . . *Action dismissed.*

WOOD *v.* LUCY, LADY DUFF-GORDON. 1917. 222 N.Y. 88, 118 N.E. 214 (New York Court of Appeals). Wood was given the exclusive right for one year, renewable, subject to Lady Duff-Gordon's approval, to place her endorsement on dresses, hats and the like, and in return she was to have one-half of all profits and revenues from any contracts Wood might make. The agreement recited that "The said Otis F. Wood possesses a business organization adapted to the placing of such endorsements as the said Lucy, Lady Duff-Gordon, has approved." Lady Duff-Gordon broke the agreement, placed her endorsement without Wood's knowledge, and withheld profits. Wood sued and Lady Duff-Gordon denied consideration. Held, for plaintiff. CARDOZO J.: "It is true that he does not promise in so many words that he will use reasonable efforts to place the defendant's endorsements and market her designs. We think, however, that such a promise is fairly to be implied. The law has outgrown its primitive stage of formalism when the precise word was the sovereign talisman, and every slip was fatal. It takes a broader view today. A promise may be lacking, and yet the whole writing may be 'instinct with an obligation', imperfectly expressed. . . . If that is so, there is a contract. . . . His promise to pay the defendant one-half of the profits and revenues resulting from the exclusive agency and to render accounts monthly was a promise to use reasonable efforts to bring profits and revenues into existence."

QUESTIONS. If Lady Duff-Gordon were suing Wood because he failed to bring any profits and revenues into existence what standard of effort on Wood's part would she have to prove? How would the damages be measured? If Wood were also under the same "contract" with another equally prominent person, how would he have to divide his efforts? Is the business incentive on Wood's part enough to justify holding Lady Duff-Gordon to her promise? Could we say that Lady Duff-Gordon exchanged her promise for the chance, given her by Wood, that he would likely bring into existence profits and revenues?

PROBLEM. In his *Basic Contract Law* Professor Fuller poses the following problem (p. 424) to show what a draftsman is up against where want of mutuality may be raised as a defence. Elsewhere Professor Fuller has conceded that there is "no ready solution."

"Fish refuse is a by-product of the operations of a fish filleting company. This refuse cannot profitably be transported, but can find a market for the manufacture of glue if a glue factory is adjacent to the filleting plant. Negotiations begin between the fish filleting company and the glue manufacturing company looking toward the establishment of a glue factory on premises of the filleting company. The filleting company is willing to bind itself to sell its entire output of fish refuse for ten years to the glue company, and to give the glue company a ten year lease, at a satisfactory rental, of a portion of its premises. The glue company is willing to pay a satisfactory price for the refuse, and to bind itself to absorb the entire output in fish refuse of the filleting company for ten years. Negotiations finally break down, however, on the following point. The glue company does not wish to expend money for a factory on this site, and to forego the opportunity of locating elsewhere, unless it has some assurance that the filleting company will continue to have a substantial output of fish refuse during the next ten years. The filleting company, on the other hand, points out that the value of the fish refuse is only one tenth of the value of its total production, and that its business is subject to many contingencies of an operational, financial, and even of a biological and climatic nature, and that it is therefore impossible for it to enter into a commitment to maintain its present output of fish refuse, or any particular output, for a period of ten years in the future. It suggests that its own self interest is sufficient to keep it in business as long as possible, and that this self-interest offers the glue company a sufficient basis for entering the contract. It assures the glue company that it intends to deal fairly in any future contingencies that may arise. Representatives of the glue company say, however, that they would be remiss in their duty to stockholders if they did not insist on a contractual provision covering the basic raw material of the company's operations before building a plant. They point out that the filleting company might find various measures advantageous to it which would be ruinous to the glue company, such as a discontinuance of this plant and a removal to a locality where it would be impossible to operate a glue factory. Is there any procedure, contract clause, or legal or economic device which will break up this log jam in negotiation?"

BUSHWICK-DECATUR MOTORS, INC. *v.* FORD MOTOR CO.

New York. United States Circuit Court of Appeals. 1940. 116 F. 2d. 675

CLARK, Circuit Judge: This is a controversy between a former Ford automobile dealer and the Ford Motor Company, arising out of the allegedly unjustifiable termination of that relation by the latter. To show its right to relief herein the plaintiff dealer sets forth three causes of action: one founded on a written agreement between the parties, purporting to govern their relations as "Dealer" and "Company"; another founded on oral promises alleged to have been made by Ford regional officials, that the "dealership" contract would not be terminated without cause; and the third, on further oral promises to allocate to the plaintiff more profitable territory as soon as available. . . . The appeal concerns the dismissal of the three causes of action first stated, upon defendant's motion for summary judgment, and upon extensive affidavits of both parties. We shall consider each of these three causes, in order.

I. The written agreement between the parties is in the standard form of Ford dealership contracts. Its major provisions are stated at some length in the opinion of the court below, D.C.E.D.N.Y., 30 F.Supp. 917, 919, 920; and many provisions are also quoted in *Buggs* v. *Ford Motor Co.*, 7 Cir., 113 F.2d 618, 620. It provides that the "Company agrees to sell and Dealer agrees to purchase Ford automobiles" and other products, "subject to the right reserved to Company to sell to other Dealers and direct to retail purchasers in any part of the United States without obligations for any commission to Dealer on any such sale." The Company's sales to dealer are "at such net list price, or at such discounts from published list prices as are from time to time fixed by Company," and "List Prices" are subject to change even as to the price of products "shipped, or paid for but not in transit." There are also several terms relating to the methods of shipment and payment, and many relating to the manner in which the dealership business should be conducted. It is agreed that the law of Michigan should govern construction of the contract. No formula is stated for determining a minimum or maximum amount of products which the Company is obligated to sell, or the dealer to buy, nor is a period fixed for the duration of the agreement; but a paragraph entitled "Termination" states: "This agreement may be terminated at any time at the will of either party by written notice to the other party given either by registered mail or by personal delivery, and such termination shall also operate to cancel all orders theretofore received by Company and not delivered."

It is not disputed that four and a half years after the inception of this dealership, notice of termination was duly given by the Company. Plaintiff contends, however, that such termination was malicious, in bad faith, and contrary to the custom of the trade, and therefore wrongful; in its complaint and affidavits it makes a showing of substantial loss. Defendant stands firmly on its unqualified power to terminate, irrespective of its reasons for doing so, though its affidavits do challenge the charges of malice and bad faith.

Exactly the same termination clause in the same form of contract has been construed to give Ford an unqualified power to terminate the relationship in *Buggs* v. *Ford Motor Co.*, supra; *Ford Motor Co.* v. *Kirkmyer Motor Co.*, 4 Cir., 65 F.2d 1001; . . . and *Terre Haute Brewing Co.* v. *Dugan,* 8 Cir., 102 F. 2d 425. Other cases are cited and discussed in the Buggs case and in the opinion below. These precedents vary slightly in the legal doctrine they apply. In the *Buggs* case the contract was held valid and binding throughout, with the power of termination effective and applicable; while in the *Kirkmeyer* and *Dugan* cases the contract was said to be void for want of mutuality, except as to sales already made. See also *Willard, Sutherland & Co.* v. *United States*, 262 U.S. 489, 43 S.Ct. 592, 67 L.Ed. 1086. For our present purposes these theories lead to identical results, though the first would appear appropriate. The *Dugan* case makes reference to, though it does not apply, a special Missouri doctrine that an "agent" who has incurred expense induced by his appointment may recover it if he has not had sufficient opportunity to recoup it from the business—a doctrine seemingly not applicable where the relationship has already endured for some time.

With this weight of precedent, in the light of the clear intent of the parties, we feel constrained to hold that defendant had ended its obligations under the contract. But plaintiff contends that the law of Michigan is otherwise and cites therefore *J. R. Watkins Co.* v. *Rich*, 254 Mich. 82, 235 N.W. 845, 846, holding that a power of termination, extended to "either of the parties" "at any time by giving the other party notice thereof," of a contract with a definite and stated duration did not authorize termination in the absence of "good faith." We do not find that this contention has been considered in the cited cases, though at least in the *Buggs* case the contract contained the provision before us here that the law of Michigan should govern its construction.

In the *Rich* case, a sales agent, substantially indebted to his principal, obtained the latter's assent to an extension of the agency and the debts for another year on condition that the former would procure several sureties on his written obligation to pay both the past debts and those arising in the course of the extended agency. After the agent had done so, but before he had had opportunity to make sales by the profit from which he could retire part of the old debts, the principal took advantage of the termination clause and sued the sureties for the entire amount due. Recovery was denied for lack of "good faith" in the termination. But in spite of the citing of "satisfaction" cases, such as *Holton* v. *Monarch Motor Car Co.*, 202 Mich. 271, 168 N.W. 539, "good faith" here seems to have meant an original intention to offer the agent a fair opportunity, without which the contract would obviously have been void for fraud in its inception. Compare 45 *Harv.L.Rev.* 378 and 17 *Corn.L.Q.* 479. Only such an interpretation will prevent a conflict with the earlier decisions it did not overrule, which held a sales agency terminable entirely at the discretion of the parties merely for lack of any expressly fixed duration. . . . In the *Rich* case the contract was for a definite period from its execution May 8, 1928, until March 1, 1929. Here the agreement was without stated duration except for the provision making it terminable at any time "at the will of either party." The difference in language alone might not be a sufficient basis for distinguishing the case; but that difference, coupled with the rather clear indication of fraud and its inconsistency otherwise with Michigan precedents, leads us to view it as not a binding authority upon us here.

With a power of termination at will here so unmistakably expressed, we certainly cannot assert that a limitation of good faith was anything the parties had in mind. Such a limitation can be read into the agreement only as an overriding requirement of public policy. This seems an extreme step for judges to take. The onerous nature of the contract for the successful dealer and the hardship which cancellation may bring him have caused some writers to advocate it, however; and an occasional case has seized upon elements of overreaching to come to such a result on particular facts. See, for example, *Philadelphia Storage Battery Co.* v. *Mutual Tire Stores*, 161 S.C. 487, 159 S.E. 825; the criticism of this case in 45 *Harv.L.Rev.* 378 and the answering arguments in 17 *Corn.L.Q.* 479 (and see also 31 *Col.L.Rev.* 830, 840, 842) well indicate the opposing views. But, generally speaking, the situation arises from the strong bargaining position which economic factors give the great automobile manufacturing companies: the dealers are not misled or imposed upon, but accept as nonetheless advantageous an agreement in form bilateral, in fact one-sided. To attempt to redress this balance by judicial action without legislative authority appears to us a doubtful policy. We have not proper facilities to weigh economic factors, nor have we before us a showing of the supposed needs which may lead the manufacturers to require these seemingly harsh bargains. In the *Buggs* case the court had before it a recent Wisconsin statute, St.1937, § 218.01(3) (a) 17, providing for suspension or revocation of a license of a manufacturer who had "unfairly without due regard to the equities of said dealer and without just provocation," canceled the dealer's franchise. There the statute was held not applicable, at least to an existing valid contract. But it suggests the proper source of remedy, if one is needed.

II. The second of the causes of action relied on is an alleged oral promise of defendant, "in consideration of plaintiff's agreement to invest further sums of money in the promotion of the sale and distribution of Ford products," not to cancel the dealership contract "except for a just and proper cause and upon adequate hearing first being given" to plaintiff. The court below held that there was not adequate showing of such a contract with duly authorized agents of defendant and also that it was "void and unenforceable as too uncertain, vague and indefinite." [30 F. Supp. 917, 923.] We are agreed in affirming this judgment on one or the other of these grounds, though we differ somewhat as to our reasons....

My brothers feel that under Michigan law, therefore, the alleged contract is unenforceable [for uncertainty]. They prefer this ground to any dealing with insufficiency of its proof, for they think the latter cannot be determined on summary judgment. I agree that no enforceable new contract, differently terminable than the first one, was set forth, but I prefer to place that conclusion upon matter presented in the record beyond the simple allegations of the complaint; for as to those alone, I think the law as it is developing is at least not clear. . . . It should be noticed that here we have the question of total invalidity of the contract, not that of exercise of a power to cancel under a valid contract, as we viewed the first question above. Though defendant claimed good cause existed here, that could not be established from the affidavits; moreover, as alleged, there was the important additional requirement of a hearing which was not claimed to have been held.

But the other documents of record show conclusively, I think, how vague and uncertain was this supposed oral agreement. A bill of particulars ordered by the court (which becomes a part of the complaint, Federal Rule 12(e), 28 U.S.C.A. following section 723c) states that the oral contract "in substance" provided that the dealership contract was not to be canceled by defendant "without cause and fair opportunity being given to the plaintiff to be heard thereon"; that defendant's settled policy was "Once a Ford dealer, always a Ford dealer"; that by the dealership contract "the plaintiff had become a member of the great Ford family; that the plaintiff would remain a Ford dealer as long as it wanted to"; that the Ford policy, settled for many years, "was a guarantee of this; and that the plaintiff need have no hesitation whatever in investing all available funds in the promotion of the sale and servicing of Ford products as such investments would be perfectly safe." Then, after giving the names of the Ford officials who were supposed to have made the agreement, it is asserted that the agreement was reaffirmed "at various times during the years 1935, 1936 and 1937, the exact dates of which plaintiff is unable at present to state," and that "at all such occasions, plaintiff was encouraged to enlarge its facilities, increase its sales force and expand its business, in reliance on the assurances given by the defendant that plaintiff was 'in' as a Ford dealer as long as it wanted and should have no concern over the wisdom of making long term commitments and long term plans."

These, therefore, are the formal allegations of the contract. It should be noted that nowhere do they come to a clear-cut promise for a definite consideration, but the asserted statements are quite contradictory. Thus, if plaintiff could remain a Ford dealer as long as it wanted to, the other provisions for termination were improper. I think it clear that these were at most only "puffing" arguments to induce plaintiff to continue its activities, that no later definite substitutionary agreement was shown, and that in any event the power of termination of the original contract was not cancelled or superseded. That provided that it could be amended only "by an instrument in writing" executed by named officials of the Ford company. Perhaps an earlier contract may be employed to limit the contracting powers of the parties; at least it can show that the parties agreed not to be bound by indefinite oral asseverations. . . .

If we turn from the formal allegations to the supporting affidavits, no different conclusion seems possible. Plaintiff's two active officers, Mr. and Mrs. Charles J. Burke, presented lengthy and argumentative affidavits, containing much material of an irrelevant and hearsay nature, but nevertheless valuable as showing that they were setting forth their entire case in its most favorable light—perhaps more favorable than would have been possible at a trial subject to legal rules of evidence. They make oath to a number of these inducing statements by Ford regional officials, but all in the indefinite and contradictory form noted above and each obviously made without intent on the part of the speaker that what he said should supersede the formal dealership contract. . . .

III. The promise alleged in the third cause, to "allocate to the plaintiff a more profitable territory" as soon as such "would become available," even if it could stand against the same objections of lack of showing of its legal execution, is nevertheless as much subject to the written power of termination as are the original provisions of that contract. It must therefore be considered to be abrogated for the same reasons. . . .

[Chase, Circuit Judge, concurred in the result.]

BUGGS *v.* FORD MOTOR CO. 1940. 113 F. 2d. 618 (Circuit Court of Appeals, Seventh Circuit. Wisconsin). EVANS, Circuit Judge: "Plaintiff alleges that he has held a Ford dealer franchise in Janesville, Wisconsin, since October, 1913; that the franchise has been renewed from time to time; the last renewal bears date of May 26, 1932; that he has equipped his garage to handle efficiently this agency and has expended $7600 in building a warehouse necessary for the assembling of Ford cars. He has purchased Ford parts, expended money and efforts in building up Ford trade believing that he would have the agency permanently; that he has put in over twelve hours a day in the work and has expended over $100,000, in building up the business. The contract of May 26, 1932, was a Ford standard dealer agency contract and contained a provision for termination as above stated. The defendant notified plaintiff, by registered mail, on September 25, 1937, that the agency was cancelled.

"The defendant in its answer, in addition to claiming the absolute right to terminate, alleges that the plaintiff did not devote adequate time or attention to the agency, and alleges that it did not violate the subsections of the Wisconsin Statute—which statute it contends is not applicable, first, because it is not retroactive and second, because it grants plaintiff no cause of action for money damages. . . .

"Most sharply controverted is the question of the validity of the contract. Plaintiff contends that it lacks mutuality. In short, it is unilateral.

"An examination of its terms, which are many, indicates that it was dictated by the manufacturer at Detroit, and drawn by its counsel with the avowed purpose of protecting the manufacturer to the utmost and granting, if any, few rights to, and the smallest possible protection of, the agent.

"It is one which affords some support for the wisdom and the necessity of legislation which protects the weak against a strong party in situations like the instant one. The terms of this and other similar agreements had, no doubt, a causal bearing upon the passage of the legislation which the State of Wisconsin enacted in 1937. It cannot be ignored in considering the validity of such legislation.

"Similar contracts have been before the courts on many occasions, and there are numerous decisions, entitled to weight and respect, which hold these contracts to be void for lack of mutuality. . . .

"Such disagreement as seemingly exists in the decisions may be partly attributed to the differences in the terms of the agreements under attack.

"We are convinced that the agreement before us is not unilateral and is valid. . . .

"For appellant it is contended that the agreement to sell does not definitely specify the prices at which the product would be sold. Moreover, he argues that the contract was terminable at any time.

"Vital and determinative are paragraphs 1 and 2. The first obligates defendant to sell, but upon "terms, conditions and provisions hereinafter specifically set forth." These conditions and terms are set forth in paragraph 2, which provides defendant "will sell its products to plaintiff f.o.b. Detroit, Michigan at such net list price, or at such discount from published list prices as are from time to time fixed by Company." This seems, under the authorities and on reason, sufficiently definite. . . .

"Having reached the conclusion that the agreement was valid and binding and therefore subject to cancellation by either party upon the giving of written notice, the only remaining question is the effect of the Wisconsin statute upon such an existing contract.

"We are convinced that the legislature did not intend to make its legislation, nor did the legislation, by its own terms, apply to and include existing contracts. . . ." [The Court said nothing about the argument that the contract was terminable at any time.]

NOTE. The Wisconsin statute referred to in the *Buggs* case is 218.01 (3) (a) 17, enacted July 14, 1937, and it provided in part for the suspension or revocation of a license of a manufacturer "who has unfairly, without due regard to the equities of said dealer and without just provocation, canceled the franchise of any motor vehicle dealer."

AUTOMOBILE DEALER SUITS AGAINST MANUFACTURERS

United States. Statutes. 1956. U.S.C.A. Title 15. Chapter 27

1221. As used in this chapter—

(a) The term "automobile manufacturer" shall mean any person, partnership, corporation, association, or other form of business enterprise engaged in the manufacturing or assembling of passenger cars, trucks, or station wagons, including any person, partnership, or corporation which acts for and is under the control of such manufacturer or assembler in connection with the distribution of said automotive vehicles.

(b) The term "franchise" shall mean the written agreement or contract between any automobile manufacturer engaged in commerce and any automobile dealer which purports to fix the legal rights and liabilities of the parties to such agreement or contract.

(c) The term "automobile dealer" shall mean any person, partnership, corporation, association, or other form of business enterprise, resident in the United States or in any Territory thereof or in the District of Columbia operating under the terms of a franchise and engaged in the sale or distribution of passenger cars, trucks, or station wagons.

(d) The term "commerce" shall mean commerce among the several States of the United States or with foreign nations, or in any Territory of the United States or in the District of Columbia, or among the Territories or between any Territory and any State or foreign nation, or between the District of Columbia and any State or Territory or foreign nation.

(e) The term "good faith" shall mean the duty of each party to any franchise, and all officers, employees, or agents thereof to act in a fair and equitable manner toward each other so as to guarantee the one party freedom from coercion, intimidation, or threats of coercion or intimidation from the other party: *Provided*, That recommendation, endorsement, exposition, persuasion, urging or argument shall not be deemed to constitute a lack of good faith.

1222. An automobile dealer may bring suit against any automobile manufacturer engaged in commerce, in any district court of the United States in the district in which said manufacturer resides, or is found, or has an agent, without respect to the amount in controversy, and shall recover the damages by him sustained and the cost of suit by reason of the failure of said automobile manufacturer from and after August 8, 1956 to act in good faith in performing or complying with any of the terms or provisions of the franchise, or in terminating, canceling, or not renewing the franchise with said dealer: *Provided*, That in any such suit the manufacturer shall not be barred from asserting in defense of any such action the failure of the dealer to act in good faith.

NOTE. The above statute, of which only the material sections have been reproduced, is popularly known as the *Automobile Dealer's Day in Court Act*. For an account of its legislative history, see 1956 U.S. Code Congressional and Administrative News at p. 4596. For an instance of its operation, see *Leach* v. *Ford Motor Co.* (1960), 189 F. Supp. 349 (Cal.). On the whole subject, see Kessler and Brenner, "Automobile Dealer Franchises: Vertical Integration by Contract," (1957), 66 *Yale Law Journal* 1135.

HOLT *v*. WARD CLARENCIEUX. 1732. 2 Strange 937; 93 E.R. 954 (England, King's Bench). The plaintiff and defendant agreed to marry, the female plaintiff being fifteen years old. The defendant did not marry her but did marry someone else. In an action for £4,000 plaintiff obtained a verdict for £2,000 and demurred to the plea of infancy. LORD RAYMOND L.C.J.: "The objection in this case is, that, the plaintiff not being bound equally with the defendant, this is *nudum pactum*, and the defendant cannot be charged in this action. . . . [The] single question is, whether this contract, as against the plaintiff, was absolutely void. And we are all of opinion that this contract is not void, but only voidable at the election of the infant; and as to the person of full age it absolutely binds.

"The contract of an infant is considered in law as different from the contracts of all other persons. In some cases his contract shall bind him; such is the contract of an infant for necessaries, and the law allows him to make this contract as necessary for his preservation; and therefore in such case a single bill shall bind him, though a bond with a penalty shall not. . . .

"Where the contract may be for the benefit of the infant or to his prejudice, the law so far protects him as to give him an opportunity to consider it when he comes of age; and it is good or voidable at his election. . . . But though the infant has this privilege, yet the party with whom he contracts has not; he is bound in all events. And as marriage is now looked upon to be an advantageous contract, and no distinction holds whether the party suing be man or woman, but the true distinction is whether it may be for the benefit of the infant, we think that though no express case upon a marriage contract can be cited, yet it falls within the general reason of the law with regard to infants' contracts. And no dangerous consequence can follow from this determination, because our opinion protects the infant even more than if we rule the contract to be absolutely void. And as to persons of full age, it leaves them where the law leaves them, which grants them no such protection against being drawn into inconvenient contracts.

"For these reasons we are all of opinion that the plaintiff ought to have her judgment upon the demurrer."

ELEANOR THOMAS *v*. BENJAMIN THOMAS
England. Queen's Bench. 1842. 2 Q.B. 851; 114 E.R. 330

The defendant was executor with Samuel Thomas (since deceased) of the will of John Thomas who had intended that his widow, the plaintiff, should have some further protection and orally expressed a wish that she should have the house he lived in, with all its contents, or £100 instead. Shortly after his death his executors attempted to put his wish into effect. A written agreement was executed by the parties reciting this desire and the desire of the executors to fulfil it, and the executors promised "in consideration of such desire and of the premises" to convey the house to the widow for life or as long as she continued unmarried, "provided nevertheless, and it is hereby further agreed and declared, that the said Eleanor Thomas . . . shall . . . at all times during which she shall have possession of the said dwelling house . . . pay to the . . . executors . . . the sum of £1 yearly towards the ground rent . . . and shall . . . keep the said . . . house . . . in good . . . repair." The plaintiff was left in possession for some time, but the defendant, after the death of the co-executor, refused to execute a conveyance and ejected the plaintiff. The plaintiff sued on the agreement. Verdict for plaintiff. A rule nisi was obtained to enter a non suit.

LORD DENMAN, C.J.: There is nothing in this case but a great deal of ingenuity, and a little wilful blindness to the actual terms of the instrument itself. There was nothing whatever to show that the ground-rent was payable to a superior landlord; and the stipulation for the payment of it is not a mere proviso, but an express agreement. (His Lordship here read the proviso.) This is in terms an express agreement, and shows a sufficient legal consideration quite independent of the moral feeling which disposed the executors to enter into such a contract. Mr. Williams' definition of consideration is too large: the word *causa* in the passage referred to means one which confers what the law considers a benefit to the party. Then the obligation to repair is one which might impose charges heavier than the value of the life estate.

PATTESON J.: It would be giving *cause* too large a construction if we were to adopt the view urged for the defendant; it would be confounding consideration with motive. Motive is not the same thing with consideration. Consideration means something which is of some value in the eye of the law, moving from the plaintiff: it may be some detriment to the plaintiff, or some benefit to the defendant; but at all events it must be moving from the plaintiff. Now that which is suggested as the consideration here—a pious respect for the wishes of the testator—does not in any way move from the plaintiff: it moves from the testator; therefore, legally speaking, it forms no part of the consideration. Then it is said that, if that be so, there is no consideration at all, it is a mere voluntary gift: but when we look at the agreement we find that this is not a mere proviso that the donee shall take the gift with the burthens; but it is an express agreement to pay what seems to be a fresh apportionment of a ground-rent, and which is made payable not to a superior landlord but to the executors. So that this rent is clearly not something incident to the assignment of the house; for in that case, instead of being payable to the executors, it would be payable to the landlord. Then as to the repairs: these houses may very possibly be held under a lease containing covenants to repair, but we know nothing about it: for anything that appears, the liability to repair is first created by this instrument. The proviso certainly struck me at first as Mr. Williams [one of counsel] put it, that the rent and repairs were merely attached to the gift of the donors; and, had the instrument been executed by the donors only, there might have been some ground for that construction; but the fact is not so. Then it is suggested that this would be held to be a mere voluntary conveyance as against a subsequent purchaser for value: possibly that might be so: but suppose it would: the plaintiff contracts to take it, and does take it, whatever it is, for better for worse: perhaps a bona fide purchase for a valuable consideration might override it; but that cannot be helped. *Rule discharged.*

[The opinion of Coleridge J. is omitted.]

QUESTIONS. Has Eleanor Thomas expressly or impliedly promised to take possession or keep possession? Is there mutuality of obligation here? If Eleanor had no right to possession, did she, by remaining in possession, incur a detriment such that might be good consideration?

4. PAST CONSIDERATION

LAMPLEIGH *v.* BRATHWAIT

England. Common Pleas. 1615. Hobart 105; 80 E.R. 255

Anthony Lampleigh brought an assumpsit against Thomas Brathwait, and declared that, whereas the defendant had feloniously slain one Patrick

Mahume, the defendant, after said felony done, instantly required the plaintiff to labor and do his endeavor to obtain his pardon from the king; whereupon the plaintiff upon the same request did, by all the means he could and many days' labor, do his endeavor to obtain the king's pardon for the said felony; viz., in riding and journeying at his own charges from London to Reiston, when the king was there, and to London back, and so to and from Newmarket, to obtain pardon for the defendant for the said felony. Afterwards in consideration of the premises, the said defendant did promise the said plaintiff to give him £100 and that he had not, to his damage £120.

To this, the defendant pleaded *non assumpsit*, and found for the plaintiff, damage £100. It was said in arrest of judgment that the consideration was past.

It was agreed that a mere voluntary courtesy will not have a consideration to uphold an assumpsit. But if that courtesy were moved by a suit or request of the party that gives the assumpsit, it will bind; for the promise, though it follows, yet it is not naked, but couples itself with the suit before, and the merits of the party procured by that suit, which is the difference. . . .

KENNEDY *v*. BROUN. 1863. 13 C.B.N.S. 677; 143 E.R. 268, 292. ERLE C.J.: "In *Lampleigh* v. *Brathwait*, it was assumed that the journeys which the plaintiff performed at the request of the defendant, and the other services he rendered, would have been sufficient to make any promise binding if it had been connected therewith in one contract; the peculiarity of the decision lies in connecting a subsequent promise with a prior consideration after it had been executed. Probably at the present day, such service or such request would have raised a promise by implication to pay what it was worth; and the subsequent promise of a sum certain would have been evidence for the jury to fix the amount."

STEWART *v*. CASEY. [1892] 1 Ch. 104 at 115. BOWEN L.J.: "That raises the old question—or might raise it, if there was not an answer to it—of *Lampleigh* v. *Brathwait*, a subject of great interest to every scientific lawyer, as to whether a past service will support a promise. . . . Even if it were true, as some scientific students of law believe, that a past service cannot support a future promise, you must look at the document and see if the promise cannot receive a proper effect in some other way. Now, the fact of a past service raises an implication that at the time it was rendered it was to be paid for, and, if it was a service which was to be paid for, when you get in the subsequent document a promise to pay, that promise may be treated either as an admission which evidences or as a positive bargain which fixes the amount of that reasonable remuneration on the faith of which the service was originally rendered."

QUESTION ON LEGAL METHOD. What is a "scientific lawyer"?

EASTWOOD *v*. KENYON

England. Queen's Bench. 1840. 11 A. & E. 438; 113 E.R. 482

The plaintiff was executor of the will of John Sutcliffe who died leaving an infant daughter Sarah Sutcliffe (now married to the defendant). During Sarah's infancy the plaintiff acted as her guardian and agent and expended

£140 of his own money in looking after her and her property. Plaintiff borrowed the money from one Blackburn, to whom he gave a promissory note. When Sarah reached full age she then assented to the loan. She also asked the plaintiff to turn the management of her affairs over to one Stanfield, as her agent, which he did, and Sarah promised the plaintiff to pay and discharge the amount of the note and did pay Blackburn one year's interest on the £140. After Sarah's marriage to the defendant, he, having full knowledge of these events, promised the plaintiff that he would pay and discharge the note. The defendant failed to pay and this action was brought. At the trial there was a verdict for the plaintiff, subject to a motion to enter a verdict for the defendant on the defence of the Statute of Frauds. A rule nisi was obtained according to the leave reserved and also for arresting judgment on the ground of lack of consideration.

LORD DENMAN delivered the judgment of the court: [The portion of the opinion dealing with the Statute of Frauds is omitted.]

The second point arose in arrest of judgment, namely; whether the declaration shewed a sufficient consideration for the promise. . . .

Upon motion in arrest of judgment, this promise must be taken to have been proved, and to have been an express promise, as indeed it must of necessity have been, for no such implied promise in law was ever heard of. It was then argued for the plaintiff that the declaration disclosed a sufficient moral consideration to support the promise.

Most of the older cases on this subject are collected in a learned note to the case of *Wennall* v. *Adney* (1802), 3 B. & P. 247; 127 E.R. 137, and the conclusion there arrived at seems to be correct in general, "that an express promise can only revive a precedent good consideration, which might have been enforced at law through the medium of an implied promise, had it not been suspended by some positive rule of law; but can give no original cause of action, if the obligation, on which it is founded, never could have been enforced at law, though not barred by any legal or statute provision." Instances are given of voidable contracts, as those of infants ratified by an express promise after age, and distinguished from void contracts, as of married women, not capable of ratification by them when widows; *Lloyd* v. *Lee* (1718), 1 Str. 94; 93 E.R. 406; debts of bankrupts revived by subsequent promise after certificate; and similar cases. Since that time some cases have occurred upon this subject which require to be more particularly examined. *Barnes* v. *Hedley* (1809), 2 Taunt. 184; 127 E.R. 1047, decided that a promise to repay a sum of money, with legal interest, which sum had originally been lent on usurious terms, but, in taking the account of which, all usurious items had been by agreement struck out, was binding. *Lee* v. *Muggeridge* (1813), 5 Taunt. 36; 128 E.R. 599, upheld an assumpsit by a widow that her executors should pay a bond given by her while a feme covert to secure money then advanced to a third person at her request. On the latter occasion the language of Mansfield C.J. and of the whole Court of Common Pleas, is very large, and hardly susceptible of any limitation. It is conformable to the expressions used by the Judges of this Court in *Cooper* v. *Martin* (1803), 4 East, 76; 102 E.R. 759, where a stepfather was permitted to recover from the son of his wife, after he had attained his full age, upon a declaration for necessaries furnished to him while an infant, for which, after his full age, he promised to pay. It is remarkable that in none of these there was any allusion made to the learned note in 3 Bosanquet and Puller above referred to, and which has been very generally thought to contain a correct statement of the law. The case of *Barnes* v. *Hadley* is fully consistent with the doctrine in that note laid down. *Cooper* v. *Martin*, also, when fully examined, will be found not to be inconsistent with it. This last case appears to have occupied the attention of the Court much more in respect of the supposed statutable liability of a stepfather, which was denied by the Court, and in respect of what a Court of Equity would hold as to a stepfather's liability, and rather to have assumed the point before us. It should, however, be observed that Lord Ellenborough in giving his judgment says, "The plaintiff having done an act beneficial for the defendant in his infancy, it is a good consideration for the defendant's promise after he came of age. In such a case the law will imply a request; and the fact of the promise has been found by the jury;" and undoubtedly the action would have lain against the defendant whilst an infant, inasmuch as it was for necessaries furnished at his request in regard to which the law raises an implied promise. The case of *Lee* v. *Muggeridge* must however be allowed to be decidedly at variance with the doctrine in the note alluded to, and is a decision of great authority. It should however be observed that in that case there was an actual request of the defendant during coverture, though not one binding at law; but the ground of decision there taken was also equally applicable to *Littlefield* v. *Shee* (1831), 2 B. & Ad. 811; 109 E.R. 1343, tried by Gaselee J. at N.P., when that learned Judge held, notwithstanding, that "the defendant having been a married woman when the goods were supplied, her husband was originally liable, and there was no consideration for the promises declared upon." After time taken for deliberation this Court refused even a rule to shew cause why the nonsuit should not be set aside. *Lee* v. *Muggeridge* was cited on the motion, and was sought to be distinguished by Lord Tenterden, because the circumstances raising the consideration were set out truly upon the record, but in *Littlefield* v. *Shee* the declaration stated the consideration to be that the plaintiff had supplied the defendant with goods at her request, which the plaintiff failed in proving, inasmuch as it appeared that the goods were in point of law supplied to the defendant's husband, and not to her. But Lord Tenterden added, that the doctrine that a moral obligation is a sufficient consideration for a subsequent promise is one which should be received with some limitation. This sentence, in truth, amounts to a dissent from the authority of *Lee* v. *Muggeridge*, where the doctrine is wholly unqualified.

The eminent counsel who argued for the plaintiff in *Lee* v. *Muggeridge*, spoke of Lord Mansfield as having considered the rule of nudum pactum as too narrow, and maintained that all promises deliberately made ought to be held binding. I do not find this language ascribed to him by any reporter, and do not know whether we are to receive it as a traditional report, or as a deduction from what he does appear to have laid down. If the latter, the note to *Wennall* v. *Adney*, shews the deduction to be erroneous. If the former, Lord Tenterden and this Court declared that they could not adopt it in *Littlefield* v. *Shee*. Indeed the doctrine would annihilate the necessity for any consideration at all, inasmuch as the mere fact of giving a promise creates a moral obligation to perform it.

The enforcement of such promises by law, however plausibly reconciled by the desire to effect all conscientious engagements, might be attended with mischievous consequences to society; one of which would be the frequent preference of voluntary undertakings to claims for just debts. Suits would thereby be multiplied, and voluntary undertakings would also be multiplied, to the prejudice of real creditors. The temptations of executors would be much increased by the prevalence of such a doctrine, and the faithful discharge of their duty be rendered more difficult.

Taking then the promise of the defendant, as stated on this record, to have been an express promise, we find that the consideration for it was past and executed long before, and yet it is not said to have been at the request of the defendant, nor even of his wife while sold (though if it had, the case of *Mitchinson* v. *Hewson* (1797), 7 T.R. 348; 101 E.R. 1013, shews that it would not have been sufficient), and the declaration really discloses nothing but a benefit voluntarily conferred by the plaintiff and received by the defendant, with an express promise by the defendant to pay money.

If the subsequent assent of the defendant could have amounted to a *ratihabitio*, the declaration should have stated the money to have been expended at his request, and the ratification should have been relied on as matter of evidence; but this was obviously impossible, because the defendant was in no way connected with the property or with the plaintiff, when the money was expended. If the ratification of the wife while sole were relied on, then a debt from her would have been shewn, and the defendant could not have been charged in his own right without some further consideration, as a forbearance after marriage, or something of that sort; and then another point would have arisen upon the Statute of Frauds which did not arise as it was, but which might in that case have been available under the plea of non assumpsit.

In holding this declaration bad because it states no consideration but a past benefit not conferred at the request of the defendant, we conceive that we are justified by the old common law of England . . . while the principle of moral obligation does not make its appearance till the days of Lord Mansfield, and then under circumstances not inconsistent with this ancient doctrine when properly explained.

Upon the whole, we are of opinion that the rule must be made absolute to arrest the judgment.

ROSCORLA *v.* THOMAS

England. Queen's Bench. 1842. 3 Q.B. 234; 114 E.R. 496

The plaintiff bought a horse from the defendant for £30. There was apparently no promise made at the time about the horse's qualities. Later the defendant did promise the plaintiff that the horse was not over five years old and was sound and free from vice. It then appeared that the horse was "very vicious, restive, ungovernable, and ferocious." In an action based on the later promise (assumpsit) there was a verdict for the plaintiff but the defendant obtained a rule nisi to arrest the judgment on the ground that there was no consideration.

LORD DENMAN C.J. delivered the judgment of the Court: . . . It may be taken as a general rule, subject to exception not applicable to this case, that the promise must be co-extensive with the consideration. In the present case, the only promise that would result from the consideration as stated, and be co-extensive with it, would be to deliver the horse upon request. The precedent sale without a warranty, though at the request of the defendant, imposes no other duty or obligation upon him. It is clear therefore that the consideration stated would not raise an implied promise by the defendant that the horse was sound or free from vice.

But the promise in the present case must be taken to be, as in fact it was, express and the question is, whether that fact will warrant the extension of the promise beyond that which would be implied by law; and whether the consideration, though insufficient to raise an implied promise, will nevertheless support an express one. And we think that it will not.

The cases in which it has been held that, under certain circumstances, a consideration insufficient to raise an implied promise will nevertheless support an express one, will be found collected and reviewed in the note (a) to *Wennal* v. *Adney,* (1802), 3 B. & P. 247; 127 E.R. 137, and in the case of *Eastwood* v. *Kenyon* [above]. They are cases of voidable contracts subsequently ratified, of debts barred by operation of law subsequently revived, and of equitable and moral obligations which, but for some rule of law, would of themselves have been sufficient to raise an implied promise. All these cases are distinguishable from, and indeed inapplicable to the present, which appears to us to fall within the general rule, that a consideration past and executed will support no other promise than such as would be implied by law.

The rule for arresting the judgment upon the first count must therefore be made absolute.

QUESTIONS. A, seeing B's house on fire, hires men to assist him in putting out the fire. B, who was absent at the time, hears of A's actions and promises to pay him $1,000. May A recover?

B is taken ill at his club. A, a doctor, attends him. On recovering B promises to give A Blackacre, worth $10,000, for his services. Can A claim Blackacre? Suppose B's promise were to pay $100. Would it make any difference as to enforceablity whether B were unconscious at the time A attended him?

REX *v.* RASH
Ontario. Court of Appeal. 1923. 53 O.L.R. 245

ROSE J.: The question as put in the stated case is, whether the magistrate was right as a matter of law in holding that a person under the age of 21 years can be convicted of the offence of removing, concealing, or disposing of any of his property, with intent to defraud his creditors (the *Criminal Code*, sec. 417(*a*)). To that question, put in that broad way, the answer is: "Yes: an infant, in some circumstances, can incur debts of certain kinds, and can have creditors; and if he disposes of his property with intent to defraud those creditors he can be convicted." But upon the whole case it is apparent that the question intended to be submitted for the opinion of the Court is a much narrower question than the one formally put. It is, in effect: "Are persons who have supplied goods to an infant trader for the purposes of his trade, and who have not been paid, 'creditors' within the meaning of sec. 417?" That is the question which was argued and which must be answered.

If a similar question arose in England, where the *Infants' Relief Act, 1874*, is in force, the answer would have to be in the negative, for the Act makes void all contracts entered into by infants, after the passing of the Act, for goods supplied (other than contracts for necessaries): and, as was admitted in *Regina* v. *Wilson* (1879), 5 Q.B.D. 28, by counsel for the prosecution, it cannot be contended that, since the passing of the Act, the contracts of an infant for goods supplied in the way of trade are valid or result in debts, or that the persons who supply such goods are creditors capable of being defrauded. But in Ontario there is no statute corresponding to the *Infants' Relief Act*, and what has to be ascertained is the relationship created, at common law, by a contract made between an infant trader and those who supply him with the goods in which he deals.

At common law, certain contracts made by infants are void, in the strict sense, and incapable of ratification: see *Beam* v. *Beatty* (1902), 3 O.L.R. 345; 4 O.L.R. 554; *Phillips* v. *Greater Ottawa Development Co.* (1916), 38 O.L.R. 315.

Others are usually described as valid. Such are contracts for necessaries, although, considering the fact that the person who supplies necessaries recovers, not the agreed price, but the value, probably confusion would have been avoided if it had been recognised that, as pointed out by Fletcher Moulton L.J., in *Nash* v. *Inman*, [1908] 2 K.B. 1, an infant, like a lunatic, is incapable of making a contract of purchase in the strict sense of the words; that, if a man satisfies the needs of an infant or lunatic by supplying to him necessaries, the law will imply an obligation to repay him for the services so rendered, and will enforce that obligation against the estate of the infant or lunatic; that consequently the basis of the action is hardly contract—the obligation arises *re* and not *consensu*.

Contracts of a third (and this the largest) class may be avoided or enforced at the option of the infant: *Bruce* v. *Warwick* (1815), 6 Taunt. 118; 128 E.R. 978, "The law so far protects him, as to give him an opportunity to consider it when he comes of age: and it is good or voidable at his election:" *Holt* v. *Ward Clarencieux* (1732), 2 Str. 937; 93 E.R. 954. These contracts are usually described as voidable. Contracts, such as are here in question, by which the infant undertakes to pay for goods supplied to him for use in trade are of this class, and what has to be determined is the precise meaning of the word "voidable" as applied to them—is it correct to say quite generally, as in Halsbury's *Laws of England*, vol. 17, p. 64, note (1), that "voidable means valid until repudiated, not invalid until confirmed;" or ought to be said, as in *Anson on Contracts*, 15th ed., p. 186, that an infant's "voidable" contracts must be divided under two heads, (a) those which are valid and binding on the infant until disaffirmed, and (b) those which are not binding until ratified after majority? If such a division as is suggested by Anson is justified, there is no doubt that contracts such as we have to deal with in this case will fall into the author's class (b); and that it is justified, will, I think, appear when there are considered, first, some of the cases which have arisen out of contracts by an infant for the purchase of goods (other than necessaries) or out of other contracts which would clearly be in class (b), if there is such a class, and secondly, some of the cases that are usually cited in support of the broad general proposition that voidable means valid until repudiated. . . . [A long discussion of cases is omitted.]

My conclusion accords with that reached, in a civil case, by the Supreme Court of Mississippi in *Edmunds* v. *Mister* (1881), 58 Miss. 765 (cited in 27 Corpus. Juris, p. 476). There, soon after attaining his majority, a man who, while an infant, had contracted debts (I use the expression in the popular sense) conveyed his property to his daughter for life with reversion to himself, the conveyance being without consideration, and with the avowed intention of defeating "creditors"—although, as the grantor said, he was unwilling to plead infancy and intended to pay his debts. The Court held that the conveyance was valid, because the holders of the demands for goods furnished during the grantor's minority were not creditors. The statement of Chalmers, C.J., upon this point is succinct, and I venture to reproduce it; he says:

"The executory contracts of infants for the payment of money, not for necessaries, impose no legal liability upon them. They furnish a sufficient consideration to support contracts thereafter made, so that if ratified in any way after majority they will be enforced; but they derive their vitality not from the original consideration, but from the new promise or ratification. They can be ratified at common law only by an act or agreement which possesses all the ingredients necessary to a new contract, save only a new consideration. The contract made during minority will furnish the consideration, but it will furnish nothing more. All else must be supplied by the new agreement. A mere acknowledgment of the debt is not sufficient, but there must be an express promise to pay, voluntarily made; and this is true under the common law authorities, without reference to the provisions of statute, which declares that the new promise or ratification must be in writing.

"There cannot be said to be any contract in any legitimate sense of the term until after the act of ratification, or until after the written promise under our statute. Before ratification, it is wholly unilateral in its bearing; that is to say, the consideration has been advanced by the adult, but there is no corresponding legal liability upon the minor. It stands, not upon the footing of a debt barred by the Statute of Limitations and afterwards revived by a new promise, because in such a case there has always been an existing, unextinguished right, since limitation affects only the remedy, and not the right; but it is rather like a debt wiped out by a discharge in bankruptcy. In such case there is no existing debt, but there is an outstanding consideration which will support a new contract. . . . It is an anomaly in pleading that the plaintiff declares upon the original contract, and to a plea of infancy replies the new promise, while all authorities declare that the recovery is not upon the original contract, but upon the new promise; and yet undoubtedly the anomaly exists. While this is true, it is clear that if the declaration should set out the whole facts,—that is, if it shewed that the articles were furnished to a minor, that they were not necessaries, and that there had been no new promise,—it would be demurrable; or if judgment by default was taken upon it, it would be reversed upon appeal. The reason is that it would show no cause of action, and it would shew no cause of action because of the absence of a new promise. It is the new promise, therefore, that makes the debt, and without it there is none."

For these reasons, my answer to the question submitted is in the negative.

[The concurring opinions of Mulock C.J.Ex., and Kelly, Masten and Orde JJ. are omitted. See MASTEN J. at p. 253: "If an adult contracts with an infant, the infant can enforce the contract though the adult cannot. This was decided by the Court of King's Bench in 1813 . . . and has ever since been accepted as the law. Such a right of action by the infant predicates and necessitates as its foundation, an existing valid contract."]

NOTE. Compare the following statements: Middleton J. in *Re Sovereign Bank* (1915), 35 O.L.R. 448 at 453: "No doubt in ordinary cases, an infant is called upon to repudiate within a reasonable time after attaining majority." Garrow J.A. at p. 456: "An infant may by contract become the holder of shares in a bank. The legal effect of such a contract is the same as that of other voidable contracts of an infant, namely, that it is valid until repudiated. See *Edwards* v. *Carter,* [1893] A.C. . . . And, the repudiation must, to be effective, take place within a reasonable time after full age is reached." It will be noticed however that the Court is here dealing with a situation of the kind described by Anson as one "when an infant acquired an interest in permanent property to which obligations attach, etc."

For a criticism of this twofold division see *Williston on Contracts,* rev. ed., secs. 231-9.

STATUTE OF FRAUDS

Ontario. Revised Statutes. 1960. Chapter 381

7. No action shall be maintained whereby to charge a person upon a promise made after full age to pay a debt contracted during infancy or upon a ratification after full age of a promise or simple contract made during infancy, unless the promise or ratification is made by a writing signed by the party to be charged therewith or by his agent duly authorized to make the promise or ratification.

MACCORD *v.* OSBORNE. 1876. 1 C.P.D. 568. After attaining his majority the debtor had written, "I promise to pay the above as a debt of honor. . . ." Held not to be an acknowledgment of a debt for which he was legally liable. GROVE J., in the course of the argument, "To satisfy the statute [similar to the Ontario Statute above] it must be an enforceable promise, not a mere recognition of the debt."

THRUPP *v.* FIELDER. 1798. 2 Esp. 628; 170 E.R. 477. LORD KENYON: "The case of infancy differs from the Statute of Limitations: in the latter case a bare acknowledgment has been held sufficient. In the case of an infant, I shall hold an acknowledgment not to be sufficient, and require proof of an express promise to pay. . . . Payment of money is no such promise."

SPENCER *v.* HEMMERDE

England. House of Lords. [1922] 2 A.C. 507

VISCOUNT CAVE: In the year 1910 Mr. Joseph Benson (through whom the appellant claims) lent to the respondent, Mr. Hemmerde, a sum of £1000; and in a letter acknowledging the loan which was dated the 2nd of March, 1910, the respondent undertook to repay it in two months and to pay interest at 7 per cent. per annum, and added: "It is extremely kind of you to assist me at this juncture by a transaction which is quite outside the ordinary rules of business security, and which I recognize to be merely a generous and timely effort to help me over a very unpleasant financial crisis."

Certain securities were deposited with Mr. Benson as security for the loan, but these were subsequently given up at the respondent's request. No part of the principal or interest was in fact paid. Mr. Benson, to whom this advance appears to have caused some financial embarrassment, from time to time pressed for payment; and ultimately on the 4th November, 1915, he wrote to the respondent a letter in which he made formal application for payment of the £1000 and interest and stated that he would not stay his hand any further and the matter would have to be settled without further delay. The writer added: "I confess I am greatly surprised that you have treated the matter so coolly, no letter or personal word. You will remember your coming to me in your time of great need, and at great personal inconvenience I helped you because I believed you would honourably fulfil your promise and repay me on an early date."

In answer to this urgent application the respondent wrote to Mr. Benson a letter dated the 4th November in the following terms:

"I think it is a pity you write me in such a tone. Have you the slightest idea what these times mean to professional men? I have not been to see you because I had absolutely nothing to tell you but what you must know already. I will look in and see you some day next week, but I cannot at present hold out the slightest hope of paying you the capital. I will tell you exactly how things stand when I see you."

This did not satisfy Mr. Benson, who on the 5th November wrote a further letter stating that a call would be useless and that unless he had some definite proposal from the respondent he should ask his solicitor to take the matter in hand and to act promptly. The respondent thereupon wrote the following letter, upon which this case appears to me to turn:—

"1, Hare Court,
Temple, E.C.
November 7th.

My dear Mr. Benson,

It is not that I won't pay you, but that I can't do so. It is important that I should see you and explain the situation, and I shall therefore ring you up tomorrow to make an appointment.

What I wrote was not that I saw no prospect at present of being able to repay the capital, but that I saw no prospect of being able to repay the capital at present. The condition of things at the Bar is such that the vast majority of us will be getting into debt rather than out of it.

I have a good deal to talk to you about, and nothing can be gained by flying to solicitors.

Yours truly,
EDWARD G. HEMMERDE."

Mr. Benson accordingly stayed his hand, and it was not until the 22nd June 1920, that the appellant (the trustee under a deed of arrangement with creditors executed by Mr. Benson) issued his writ in this action, claiming payment of the principal and interest. The respondent pleaded the *Statute of Limitations* and the appellent in his reply relied on the abovementioned two letters of the 4th and 7th November, 1915, and on other letters which are not now material, as containing a sufficient acknowledgment to take the case out of the statute. Bailhache J. held the letters to be sufficient for that purpose, and gave judgment for the appellant; but on appeal the Court of Appeal (Bankes and Atkin L.JJ.; Scrutton L.J. dissenting), . . . reversed his decision and dismissed the action. Hence the present appeal.

My Lords, the law relating to matters of this kind is not in doubt. The statute enacted that ". . . all actions of debt grounded upon any lending or contract without specialty . . . shall be commenced and sued . . . within six years next after the cause of such actions . . . and not after," and made no reference to any acknowledgment; but it was held in a series of cases that a promise by the debtor to pay the debt, if given within six years before action brought, was sufficient to create a new contract and so to take the case out of the operation of the statute, the existing debt being a sufficient consideration to support the promise. It was also held that a simple acknowledgment of the debt, without any express promise was sufficient for the purpose, an acknowledgment implying a promise to pay. Some of the earlier cases went so far as to decide that an acknowledgment was sufficient, though coupled with a promise to pay at some future which had not arrived or upon some condition that had not been performed, or even with an absolute refusal to pay; but this was set right by the decision of the Court of King's Bench in *Tanner* v. *Smart* (1827), 6 B.&C. 603; 108 E.R. 573, where Lord Tenterden, in giving the judgment of the Court, said: "Upon a general acknowledgment, where nothing is said to prevent it, a general promise to pay may, and ought to be, implied; but where the party guards his acknowledgment, and accompanies it with an express declaration to prevent any such implication, why shall not the rule *expressum facit cessare tacitum* apply?"

No doubt the doctrine so established was originally judge-made law; but it has stood unchallenged for nearly a century, and indeed it has received statutory recognition. For the statute commonly called Lord Tenterden's Act, 9 Geo. 4, c. 14, after referring to the Statute of Limitation, provided that: "In actions of debt or upon the case grounded upon any simple contract no acknowledgment or promise by words only shall be deemed sufficient evidence of a new or continuing contract, whereby to take any case out of the operation of the said enactments or either of them, or to deprive any party of the benefit thereof, unless such acknowledgment or promise shall be made or contained by or in some writing to be signed by the party chargeable thereby." This enactment refers to an "acknowledgment or promise" as if either would be sufficient to take a case out of the statute. But the words of the Act are negative only, and I think it clear that the acknowledgment there referred to must be an acknowledgment which but for this Act would have been sufficient to take the case out of the statute of James, that is to say, an acknowledgment implying a promise to pay; and it has always been so held.

Since the case of *Tanner* v. *Smart* the law as there laid down has been uniformly accepted, and it must be held to be settled law (1.) that a written promise to pay a debt given within six years before action is sufficient to take the case out of the operation of the statute of James I; (2.) that such a promise is implied in a simple acknowledgment of the debt; but (3.) that where an acknowlegment is coupled with other expressions, such as a promise to pay at a future time or on a condition or an absolute refusal to pay, it is for the Court to say whether those other expressions are sufficient to qualify or negative the implied promise to pay. The decisions upon the Act are very numerous; but in every one of them the law has been assumed to be as above stated and the decision has turned upon the meaning of the particular words used in the case. It is therefore unnecessary to refer to the authorities in detail. . . .

This being the law, I turn to the letters written in this case with a view to determining whether, according to the fair and natural meaning of those letters, they contain an express promise to pay or a clear acknowledgment of the debt, and in the latter case whether the acknowledgment is coupled with words which prevent the implication of an unconditional promise. The respondent's letter of November 4 contains neither promise nor clear acknowledgment; and its principal value to the appellant is that it serves to connect the later letters with Mr. Benson's letter of November 4, and so to identify the debt referred to in those letters as being the principal and interest payment of which was required by Mr. Benson's letter of November 4. It is on the interpretation of the respondent's letter of November 7 that the decision must turn.

What, then, does that letter mean? And, first, does it contain an acknowledgment of the debt? I think it does. The expression, "It is not that I won't pay you," appears to me to mean that the writer does not refuse to pay his debt, but on the contrary admits the debt and holds himself bound to pay it; and this interpretation is supported by the subsequent repudiation of any suggestion that he had professed to see no prospect of paying the capital, and by reference to getting out of debt. The words may not amount to an express promise to pay the principal and interest due, but at least they contain an admission of liability and a profession of the writer's willingness to discharge it, which, unless qualified by other expressions in the letters, carries with it a promise to pay.

Then, are the words, "I can't do so," and the statement that the writer sees no prospect of being able to pay the capital at present, so inconsistent with a promise to pay that they negative the implication of such a promise? I do not think they are. There is no promise to pay on a future date, or on the fulfilment of a condition, and still less is there a refusal to pay at all. There is only a profession of present inability to carry out the promise which is implied. It is urged that, when a man couples his acknowledgment of a debt with a statement that he cannot pay, it is difficult to read into his acknowledgment a promise that he will pay; and no doubt there is force in this observation, which appears to have commended itself to the Court of Appeal. . . . But it does not appear to me that the two things are really inconsistent. A debtor may well say at one and the same time: "I admit my obligation and promise to discharge it," and "I do not discharge it now, because I have not the money to do so." The important thing is that the present obligation to pay is admitted and the original promise to pay is renewed and affirmed without condition or qualification; and if that be done, there is a new promise to pay upon which an action may be founded. I do not doubt that in the present case the respondent intended his letter to be read in this sense, nor that Mr. Benson so understood it and upon the faith of the letter, so understood, delayed his proceedings; and if so, the respondent must be held to his promise. In my opinion there is a sufficient acknowledgment to prevent the statute from having effect.

My Lords, I have thought it right to deal with the letters relied upon according to their terms, and without reference to the countless decisions upon the meaning of other documents couched in different terms. . . .

Upon the whole I think that the appeal should be allowed and that the judgment of Bailhache J. should be restored with costs here and below, and I move your Lordships accordingly.

LORD SUMNER: My Lords, as Scrutton L.J. truly says, the practical question here is to decide whether the respondent's words, which it is conceded acknowledge that a debt has been contracted but has not been paid, are so coupled with words which prevent the possibility of the implication of a promise to pay it, as to destroy the effect of that acknowledgment, or whether, on the other hand, they are only accompanied by other words, which, though they are in themselves less than a promise to pay, do not necessarily put an end to such an implication. I do not propose to read the words used here in the light of words judicially interpreted elsewhere, for everybody agrees that comparison with the words of other debtors is of little use. Still less do I imagine it to be possible to extract anything that deserves to be called a principle from the decisions of three centuries, which have been directed to what is after all the task of decorously disregarding an Act of Parliament. Some "acknowledgments" save the statute and some do not. The whole doctrine is purely artificial. Acknowledgments under other Statutes of Limitations dealing with other subject matters than simple debts know nothing of these niceties about fresh promises. The only thing to be done is to ascertain what really are the tests, which have been applied by authority, for determining the class to which any given words belong. . . .

It is quite impossible that so many judges should have spoken of the old debt being the consideration for the new promise without their being fully aware that if a new cause of action is meant this is contrary to long settled rules of law as to consideration. They must have spoken of the new promise as something different from a new contract, binding in law as such. Sir William Anson does, it is true, say (*Contracts*, 14th ed., p. 128) that the case is an exception to the general rule as to past executed consideration, and, while expressly disclaiming reliance on any moral obligation to pay, suggests that in consideration of the creditor's having given everything that the debtor could get out of the contract and being unable, owing to the statute, to get anything which the contract was to have given to him, a promise by the debtor to remove the bar and pay is legally binding. I confess I do not follow this. It is not a consideration that moves to the debtor; it is a matter of honour, if it is anything, as to which one may say that the creditor has only his own good nature to thank for his loss, and in any case it is a consideration inapplicable when the debt is not yet barred, though the doctrine which it purports to explain applies equally to acknowledgments given before six years have run as to those given afterwards. I find that the great preponderance of the cases is against regarding the new promise as a new cause of action, and it seems to me that reason also is against it. Surely the real view is, that the promise, which is inferred from the acknowledgment and "continues" or "renews" or "establishes" the original promise laid in the declaration, is one which corresponds with and is not a variance from or in contradiction of that promise. This alone seems to accord with the language used in *Tanner* v. *Smart*, as reproduced in *Hart* v. *Prendergast* (1845), 14 M. & W. 741, 743; 153 E.R. 674, where after Mr. Lush had said in argument, "the questions are, first, does this letter taken altogether, amount to a promise to pay. Secondly, does it support the promise laid in the declaration, to pay on request?" the judges, Parke, Alderson and Rolfe BB., said, respectively, that the promise must "fit" or must "maintain" or must "support" the promise declared upon. If so, there is no question of any fresh cause of action. . . .

Order of the Court of Appeal reversed, and judgment of Bailhache J. restored.

[Lords Atkinson, Wrenbury and Carson also delivered opinions.]

THE LIMITATIONS ACT

Ontario. Revised Statutes. 1960. Chapter 214

50. (1) Where an acknowledgment in writing, signed by the principal party or his agent, is made by a person liable upon an indenture, specialty, judgment or recognizance, or where an acknowledgment is made by such person by part payment, or part satisfaction, on account of any principal

or interest due on the indenture, specialty, judgment or recognizance, the person entitled may bring an action for the money remaining unpaid and so acknowledged to be due, within twenty years . . . after such acknowledgment in writing, or part payment, or part satisfaction, or where the person entitled is, at the time of the acknowledgment, under disability as aforesaid, or the person making the acknowledgment is, at the time of making the same, out of Ontario, then within twenty years . . . after the disability has ceased, or the person has returned, as the case may be.

51. (1) No acknowledgment or promise by words only shall be deemed sufficient evidence of a new or continuing contract whereby to take out of the operation of this Part, any case falling within its provisions respecting actions, . . .

(b) on simple contract or of debt grounded upon any lending or contract without specialty . . .

or to deprive any party of the benefit thereof, unless the acknowledgment or promise is made or contained by or in some writing signed by the party chargeable thereby, or by his agent duly authorized to make the acknowledgment or promise.

(2) Nothing in this section alters, takes away or lessens the effect of any payment of any principal or interest by any person.

NOTE ON LEGISLATIVE DRAFTING. When Viscount Cave said he doubted "whether the Act meant two different things when it said 'promise or acknowledgment' " whose "meaning" did he refer to? Parliament's? The draftsman of the Act? Why did the draftsman use both words if they mean the same thing? Is it ever a good idea for a draftsman to use two words when one will do? Does the word "acknowledgment" in s. 50 (1) above have a different meaning from the "same word" in s. 51 (1) where it is coupled with "or promise"?

NOTES. Part payment of a debt has always been regarded as equivalent to an acknowledgment when made voluntarily by a debtor and without words or other circumstances negativing the ordinary implication of acknowledgment and promise to pay farther, and such payment may take the form of balancing accounts between debtor and creditor or otherwise applying on the debt any amount due by the creditor to the debtor, always providing the debtor assents to the amount being so applied. See *Evans* v. *Davies* (1836), 4 A. & E. 840; 11 E.R. 1000 (payment of interest proved the obligation to pay the principal); *Turney* v. *Dodwell* (1845), 3 E. & B. 136; 118 E.R. 1091 (part payment by bill or note); *Guilbert* v. *Cummings*, [1929] 4 D.L.R. 705 (Man.) (part payment by an agreed set-off.).

Where there are several debts owed by a debtor to a creditor, and the debtor makes a payment without specifying on which debt the money is to be applied the creditor may appropriate such payment to any or all statute-barred debts, provided that the debtor has not expressly or impliedly appropriated the payment to any later or other debt. See *Wood* v. *Richmond*, [1929] 2 D.L.R. 552 (Sask.); *Kaulbach* v. *Eichel*, [1930] 1 D.L.R. 983 (N.S.).

Such appropriation by the creditor will revive the balance of the debt, the assent of the debtor to such appropriation being required to raise the implication of promise. *Ball* v. *Parker* (1877), 1 O.A.R. 593 at 604. It is impossible to have a payment made with the intention of being applied to all the separate debts. In such case the statutory defence will be removed as to all. See *Wood* v. *Richmond, supra.*

If a debtor makes a promise to pay a statute barred debt in part or in instalments on what is the creditor suing? See *Earle* v. *Oliver* (1848), 2 Exch. 71; 154 E.R. 410 at 418.

What is the reason for refusing to allow a promise to pay a statute barred tort liability, the same effect as a debt? See *Williston on Contracts*, students' revised edition, secs. 186 and 188.

Suppose X makes a promisory note payable to A or order. A endorses the note to B. After the statute has run, X writes A saying, I have not forgotten my note in your favour. I will pay it at once: May B sue X? See *Watson* v. *Sample* (1899), 12 Man. L.R. 373 at 379; *Stamford, etc. Banking Co.* v. *Smith*, [1892] 1 Q.B. 765. Would your answer be different according to whether you viewed the promise, (1) as evidence negativing a presumption of payment within six years; (2) as "reviving" the original cause of action; (3) as constituting a new cause of action?

A owes B $500 but the statute has run against the debt. After the limitation period has expired A gives B a bill of exchange for $500. Has B a cause of action? On what? See *La Touche* v. *La Touche* (1865), 3 H. & C. 576; 159 E.R. 657; *Wright* v. *Wright* (1876), 6 O.P.R. 295. Compare a bill of exchange given to discharge an obligation unenforceable by reason of Statute of Frauds. *Kenzie* v. *Harper* (1908), 15 O.L.R. 582 and compare *Black* v. *Gesnet* (1847), 3 N.J.R. 157.

5. Performance of Duty

HARRIS *v.* WATSON

England. Nisi Prius, 1791. Peake 102; 170 E.R. 94

In this case the declaration stated, that the plaintiff being a seaman on board the ship "Alexander," of which the defendant was master and commander, and which was bound on a voyage to Lisbon: whilst the ship was on her voyage, the defendant, in consideration that the plaintiff would perform some extra work, in navigating the ship, promised to pay him five guineas over and above his common wages. There were other counts for work and labour, &c.

The plaintiff proved that the ship being in danger, the defendant, to induce the seamen to exert themselves, made the promise stated in the first count.

Lord Kenyon: If this action was to be supported, it would materially affect the navigation of this kingdom. It has been long since determined, that when the freight is lost, the wages are also lost. This rule was founded on a principle of policy, for if sailors were in all events to have their wages, and in times of danger entitled to insist on an extra charge on such a promise as this, they would in many cases suffer a ship to sink, unless the captain would pay an extravagant demand they might think proper to make. The plaintiff was nonsuited.

STILK *v.* MYRICK

England. Nisi Prius. 1809. 2 Camp. 317; 170 E.R. 1168

This was an action for a seaman's wages, on a voyage from London to the Baltic and back.

By the ship's articles, executed before the commencement of the voyage, the plaintiff was to be paid at the rate of £5 a month; and the principal question in the cause was, whether he was entitled to a higher rate of wages. In the course of the voyage two of the seamen deserted; and the captain having in vain attempted to supply their places at Cronstadt, there entered into an agreement with the rest of the crew, that they should have the wages of the two who had deserted equally divided among them, if he could not procure two other hands at Gottenburgh. This was found impossible; and the ship was worked back to London by the plaintiff and eight more of the original crew, with whom the agreement had been made at Cronstadt.

LORD ELLENBOROUGH: I think *Harris* v. *Watson* [the preceding case] was rightly decided; but I doubt whether the ground of public policy, upon which Lord Kenyon is stated to have proceeded, be the true principle on which the decision is to be supported. Here, I say the agreement is void for want of consideration. There was no consideration for the ulterior pay promised to the mariners who remained with the ship. Before they sailed from London they had undertaken to do all they could under all the emergencies of the voyage. They had sold all their services till the voyage should be completed. If they had been at liberty to quit the vessel at Cronstadt, the case would have been quite different; or if the captain had capriciously discharged the two men who were wanting, the others might not have been compellable to take the whole duty upon themselves, and their agreeing to do so might have been a sufficient consideration for the promise of an advance of wages. But the desertion of a part of the crew is to be considered an emergency of the voyage as much as their death; and these who remain are bound by the terms of their original contract to exert themselves to the utmost to bring the ship in safety to her destined port. Therefore, without looking to the policy of this agreement, I think it is void for want of consideration, and that the plaintiff can only recover at the rate of £5 a month.

Verdict accordingly.

HARTLEY *v*. PONSONBY. 1857. 7 E. & B. 872; 119 E.R. 1471. The crew of a ship was so reduced in number that "for the ship to go to sea with so few hands was dangerous to life. If so, it was not incumbent on the plaintiff to perform the work; and he was in the condition of a free man." It was held there was consideration for the contract to pay him an additional sum to work the ship home.

QUESTIONS. Suppose the captain in *Stilk* v. *Myrick* had requested the seamen to give him a peppercorn (if they had one with them). Suppose he had put his promise in writing and under seal?

HOLMES, THE COMMON LAW (1881)

. . . The only universal consequence of a legally binding promise is, that the law makes the promisor pay damages if the promised event does not come to pass. In every case it leaves him free from interference until the time for fulfilment has gone by, and therefore free to break his contract if he chooses. . . .

If, when a man promised to labour for another, the law made him do it, his relation to his promise might be called a servitude *ad hoc* with some truth. But that is what the law never does. It never interferes until a promise has been broken, and therefore cannot possibly be performed according to its tenor. It is true that in some instances equity does what is called compelling specific performance. But, in the first place, I am speaking of the common law, and, in the next, this only means that equity compels the performance of certain elements of the total promise which are still capable of performance. . . .

NOTE. Holmes is suggesting that the duty of the promisor under a contract is *either* to perform his contract *or* to pay damages. It is then arguable that since the promisor has his choice, that is, this privilege of performing one duty or the other, by giving up this privilege and agreeing to perform the contract rather than pay damages he has given up a valuable legal right, called in technical terms a *privilege.* And that, of course, is a valid exchange constituting a legal detriment. On this basis *Stilk* v. *Myrick* must be wrongly decided, but *Harris* v. *Watson* may be right.

Does Holmes' theory not settle the whole legal character of a promise (or contract) by what happens in one type of case? He concedes that the equitable remedy of specific performance does not fit into his theory. Does *Stilk* v. *Myrick?* Has the common law not succeeded in denying the alternative here? Would it be true to say that the "law" requires a promisor to perform his promise, but administrative necessity sometimes (usually) permits him to escape by paying damages, but sometimes (rarely) obtains actual performance, and sometimes (more rarely, as in the principal cases) indirectly obtains actual performance by refusing to recognize the "right" to break a contract as the alternative to performance? In the last situation administrative necessity, which usually filters out specific performance, places no obstacle in the path of complete legal recognition of the duty to perform. In other words, the duty to perform is on what the semanticists might call a different level of abstraction from the duty to pay damages, and the two ought not to be considered as alternatives. Damages are supplementary to performance.

SMITH *v.* DAWSON

Ontario. Court of Appeal 1923. 53 O.L.R. 615

The plaintiffs agreed with the defendant to build her a house for $6,464. When the house was nearly finished, a fire took place in it doing considerable damage.

The defendant effected insurance on the house as it was being built. The plaintiffs effected no insurance. After the fire the defendant asked the plaintiffs to go ahead and complete the house. The plaintiffs said they would if the defendant promised to pay them the insurance monies.

RIDDELL J.: . . . The situation then seems quite clear—the plaintiffs, learning that the defendant had received some insurance money on the house, objected to go on without some kind of assurance that they were to get the insurance money—the defendant demurred, as she had lost considerably by the destruction of her furniture, but finally said, "All right, go ahead and do the work." If this constituted a contract at all, it was that she would give them the insurance money which she had received, if they would go ahead and do the work they were already under a legal obligation to do.

In some of the United States a doctrine has been laid down that (at least in building contracts) the contractor has the option either to complete his contract or to abandon it and pay damages. These Courts have accordingly held that the abandonment by the contractor of his option to abandon is sufficient consideration for a promise to pay an extra amount.

The Courts of Illinois, Indiana, and Massachusetts seem to have adopted this rule. . . . But such a course is to allow a contractor to take advantage of his own wrong, and other American Courts reprobate it: 9 *Corpus Juris,* 720; 13 *Corpus Juris,* 354, sec. 210, and cases cited in notes.

This is not and never was law in Ontario, as it is not and never was law in England. It has long been text-book law that "not the promise or the actual performance of something which the promisee is legally bound to perform" is a consideration for a promise:

Halsbury's *Laws of England,* 385, para. 798; "the performance of an existing contract by one of the parties is no consideration for a new promise by the other party": Leake on Contracts, 7th ed., p. 455, and cases cited.

I am of the opinion that the promise (if there was one) to pay for the work to be done was not binding for want of consideration, and would allow the appeal with costs here and below. If there be any difficulty in moulding the judgment, one of us may be spoken to.

[The judgments of Latchford and Middleton JJ. are omitted. Logie J. agreed with Riddell J.]

SHADWELL *v.* SHADWELL

England. Common Pleas. 1860. 30 L.J.C.P. 145

Charles Shadwell wrote from Gray's Inn, to his nephew, then unmarried, on August 11, 1838 as follows: "My dear Lancey, I am glad to hear of your intended marriage with Ellen Nicholl; and as I promised to assist you at starting, I am happy to tell you that I will pay to you £150 yearly during my life, and until your annual income derived from your profession of a Chancery barrister shall amount to 600 guineas, of which your own admission will be the only evidence that I shall receive or require." Lancey Shadwell married Ellen Nicholl and claimed to have earned eighteen yearly sums of £150 in his uncle's lifetime and that he never earned as much as 600 guineas. He had received twelve such sums and £12 on account of the thirteenth, but his uncle defaulted in paying the rest. On his uncle's death Lancey Shadwell commenced this action against his uncle's executor. On a demurrer it was contended that there was no consideration for the promise: Lancey was already engaged to be married when Charles Shadwell promised and had not been requested by him to marry, and, moreover, he had abandoned the practice of a Chancery barrister in 1858.

ERLE C. J.: . . . Then, do these facts show that the promise was in consideration, either of the loss to be sustained by the plaintiff, or the benefit to be derived from the plaintiff to the uncle at his, the uncle's request? My answer is in the affirmative. First, do these facts show a loss sustained by the plaintiff at the uncle's request? When I answer this in the affirmative, I am aware that a man's marriage with the woman of his choice is in one sense a boon, and in that sense the reverse of a loss; yet, as between the plaintiff and the party promising an income to support the marriage, it may be a loss. The plaintiff may have made the most material changes in his position, and have induced the object of his affections to do the same, and have incurred pecuniary liabilities resulting in embarrassments, which would be in every sense a loss if the income which had been promised should be withheld; and if the promise was made in order to induce the parties to marry, the promise so made would be, in legal effect, a request to marry. Secondly, do these facts show a benefit derived from the plaintiff to the uncle at his requests? In answering again in the affirmative, I am at liberty to consider the relation in which the parties stood, and the interest in the status of the nephew which the uncle declares. The marriage primarily affects the parties thereto; but in the second degree it may be an object of interest with a near relative, and in that sense a benefit to him. This benefit is also derived from the plaintiff at the uncle's request, if the promise of the annuity was intended as an inducement to the marriage; and the averment that the plaintiff, relying on the promise, married, is an averment that the promise was one inducement to the marriage. This is a consideration averred in the declaration, and it appears to me to be expressed in the letter, construed with the surrounding circumstances. No case bearing a strong analogy to the present was cited, but the importance of enforcing promises which have been made to induce parties to marry has been often recognized. . . . I do not feel it necessary to add anything about the numerous authorities referred to in the learned arguments addressed to us, because the decision turns on a question of fact, whether the consideration for the promise is proved as pleaded. I think it is, and therefore my judgment on the first demurrer is for the plaintiff. The second demurrer raises the question, whether the plaintiff's continuing at the bar was made a condition precedent to the right to the annuity. I think not. The uncle promises to continue the annuity until the professional income exceeds the sum mentioned, and I find no stipulation that the annuity shall cease if the professional diligence ceases. My judgment on this demurrer is also for the plaintiff, and I should state that this is the judgment of my Brother Keating and myself, my Brother Byles differing with us.

BYLES J.: I am of opinion that the defendant is entitled to the judgment of the court. . . . The inquiry . . . narrows itself to this question. Does the letter itself disclose any consideration for the promise? The consideration relied on by the plaintiff's counsel being the subsequent marriage of the plaintiff, I think the letter discloses no consideration. . . . It is by no means clear that the words "at starting" mean "on marriage with Ellen Nicholl," or with any one else. The more natural meaning seems to me to be "at starting in the profession," for it will be observed that these words are used by the testator in reciting a prior promise, made when the testator had not heard of the proposed marriage with Ellen Nicholl, or, so far as appears, heard of any proposed marriage. This construction is fortified by the consideration that the annuity is not, in terms, made to begin from the marriage, but, as it should seem, from the date of the letter. Neither is it in terms made defeasible if Ellen Nicholl should die before marriage.

But even on the assumption that the words "at starting" mean "on marriage," I still think that no consideration appears sufficient to sustain the promise. The promise is one which, by law, must be in writing; and the fourth plea shows that no consideration or request, dehors the letter, existed, and, therefore, that no such consideration or request can be alluded to by the letter. Marriage of the plaintiff at the testator's express request would be, no doubt, an ample consideration, but marriage of the plaintiff without the testator's request is no consideration to the testator. It is true that marriage is, or may be a detriment to the plaintiff; but detriment to the plaintiff is not enough, unless it either be a benefit to the testator or be treated by the testator as such, by having been suffered at his request. Suppose a defendant to promise a plaintiff, "I will give you £500 if you break your leg," would that detriment to the plaintiff, should it happen, be any consideration? If it be said that such an accident is an involuntary mischief, would it have been a binding promise if the testator had said, "I will give you £100 a year while you continue in your present chambers"? I conceive that the promise would not be binding for want of a previous request by the testator.

Now, the testator in the case before the court derived, so far as appears, no personal benefit from the marriage. The question, therefore, is still further narrowed to this point, Was the marriage at the testator's request? Express request there was none. Can any request be implied? The only words from which it can be contended that it is to be implied are the words, "I am glad to hear of your intended marriage with Ellen Nicholl." But it appears from the fourth plea that that marriage had already been agreed on, and that the testator knew it. These words, therefore, seem to me to import no more than the satisfaction of the testator at the engagement as an accomplished fact. No request, can as it seems to me, be inferred from them.

And, further, how does it appear that the testator's implied request, if it could be implied, or his promise, if that promise alone would suffice or both together, were intended to cause the marriage, or did cause it, so that the marriage can be said to have taken place at the testator's request, or, in other words, in consequence of that request? It seems to me, not only that this does not appear, but that the contrary appears; for the plaintiff before the letter had already bound himself to marry by placing himself not only under a moral, but under a legal obligation to marry, and the testator knew it. The well known cases which have been cited at the bar in support of the position that a promise, based on the consideration of doing that which a man is already bound to do, is invalid, apply to this case; and it is not necessary, in order to invalidate the consideration, that the plaintiff's prior obligation to afford that consideration should have been an obligation to the defendant. It may have been an obligation to a third person. . . . The reason why the doing what a man is already bound to do is no consideration, is not only because such a consideration is in judgment of law of no value, but because a man can hardly be allowed to say that the prior legal obligation was not his determining motive.

But whether he can be allowed to say so or not, the plaintiff does not say so here. He does, indeed, make an attempt to meet this difficulty by alleging, in the replication to the fourth plea, that he married relying on the testator's promise; but he shrinks from alleging that though he had promised to marry before the testator's promise to him, nevertheless, he would have broken his engagement, and would not have married without the testator's promise. A man may rely on encouragements to the performance to his duty who yet is prepared to do his duty without those encouragements. At the utmost, the allegation that he relied on the testator's promise seems to me to import no more than that he believed the testator would be as good as his word. It appears to me, for these reasons, that this letter is no more than a letter of kindness, creating no legal obligation. In their judgment on the other portions of the record I agree with the rest of the Court.

Judgment for the plaintiff.

DE CICCO *v.* SCHWEIZER. 1917. 221 N.Y. 431; 117 N.E. 807 (New York, Court of Appeals). Joseph Schweizer promised Count Oberto Gulinelli in writing to pay to Schweizer's daughter Blanche, who was about to marry the Count, the sum of $2500 annually during her lifetime. The agreement recited the intended marriage as consideration for the promise. The first payment was made on the day of the marriage, January 20, 1902. Payments were continued until 1912. About then the Count and Blanche assigned the agreement to Attilio De Cicco, who brought this action to recover the installment due in 1912. Consideration was denied on the ground that the Count and Blanche were already engaged when Schweizer gave his promise. CARDOZO J.: "The courts of this state are committed to the view that a promise by A to B to induce him not to break his contract with C is void. . . . If that is the true nature of this promise, there was no consideration. We have never held, however, that a like infirmity attaches to a promise by A, not merely to B, but to B and C jointly, to induce them not to rescind or modify a contract which they are free to abandon. . . . It would not have been enough that the Count remained willing to marry. The plain import of the contract is that his bride also should be willing, and that marriage should follow. The promise was intended to affect the conduct, not of one only, but of both. This becomes the more evident when we recall that though the promise ran to the Count, it was intended for the benefit of the daughter. . . . The situation, therefore, is the same in substance as if the promise had run to husband and wife alike, and had been intended to induce performance by both. They were free by common consent to terminate their engagement or to postpone the marriage. If they forebore from exercising that right and assumed the responsibilities of marriage in reliance on the defendant's promise, he may not now retract it." Judgment for the plaintiff affirmed.

SCOTSON AND OTHERS *v.* PEGG
England. Exchequer. 1861 6 H. & N. 295; 158 E.R. 121

Plaintiffs, who were under contract with other persons to deliver a cargo of coal to the defendant, were promised by the defendant that if they would deliver the coal he, the defendant, would unload it at the rate of forty-nine tons a day. Plaintiffs delivered the coal but the defendant failed to unload it at the agreed rate, and in fact took five days longer. Plaintiffs claimed damages for having to maintain the ship and its crew for the extra time. Defendant pleaded that because the plaintiffs were already obliged to other persons (from whom the defendant had bought the coal) to deliver it to the defendant, there was no consideration in their promising the defendant to do what they were already obliged to do.

[In the argument the following comments were made. . . . WILDE B.: . . . A man may be bound by his contract to do a particular thing, but while it is doubtful whether or no he will do it, if a third person steps in and says, "I will pay you if you will do it," the performance is a valid consideration for the payment. Martin B. If a builder was under contract to finish a house on a particular day, and the owner promised to pay him a sum of money if he would do it, what is to prevent the builder from recovering the money?]

MARTIN B.: I am of opinion that the plea is bad, both on principle and in law. It is bad in law because the ordinary rule is, that any act done whereby the contracting party receives a benefit is a good consideration for a promise by him. Here the benefit is the delivery of the coals to the defendant. It is consistent with the declaration that there may have been some dispute as to the defendant's right to have the coals, or it may be that the plaintiffs detained them for demurrage; in either case there would be good consideration that the plaintiffs, who were in possession of the coals, would allow the defendant to take them out of the ship. Then is it any answer that the plaintiffs had entered into a prior contract with other persons to deliver the coals to their order upon the same terms, and that the defendant was a stranger to that contract? In my opinion it is not. We must deal with this case as if no prior contract had been entered into. Suppose the plaintiffs had no chance of getting their money from the other person, who might perhaps have become bankrupt. The defendant gets a benefit by the delivery of the coals to him, and it is immaterial that the plaintiffs had previously contracted with third parties to deliver to their order.

WILDE B.: I am also of opnion that the plaintiffs are entitled to judgment. The plaintiffs say, that in consideration that they would deliver to the defendant a cargo of coals from their ship, the defendant promised to discharge the cargo in a certain way. The defendant, in answer, says, "You made a previous contract with other persons that they should discharge the cargo in the same way, and therefore there is no consideration for my promise." But why is there no consideration? It is said, because the plaintiffs, in delivering the coals, are only performing that which they were already bound to do. But to say that there is no consideration is to say that it is not possible for one man to have an interest in the performance of a contract made by another. But if a person chooses to promise to pay a sum of money in order to induce another to perform that which he has already contracted with a third person to do, I confess I cannot see why such a promise should not be binding. Here the defendant, who was a stranger to the original contract, induced the plaintiffs to part with the cargo, which they might not otherwise have been willing to do, and the delivery of it to the defendant was a benefit to him. I accede to the proposition that, if a person contracts with another to do a certain thing, he cannot make the performance of it a consideration for a new promise to the same individual. But there is no authority for the proposition that where there has been a promise to one person to do a certain thing, it is not possible to make a valid promise to another to do the same thing. Therefore, deciding this matter on principle, it is plain to my mind that the delivery of the coals to the defendant was a good consideration for his promise, although the plaintiffs had made a previous contract to deliver them to the order of other persons.

Judgment for the plaintiffs.

McDEVITT *v.* STOKES. 1917. 174 Ky. 515; 192 S.W. 681 (Kentucky. Court of Appeals). Mike McDevitt, a jockey, was hired by one Shaw, the owner of the mare Grace, to drive her in the Kentucky Futurity race. Stokes, who ran a stock farm and owned Peter the Great and Orianna, the sire and dam of Grace, afterwards promised McDevitt $1000 if he would drive in the race and win. He drove and won. Stokes paid $200 but failed to pay the balance. In this action to recover $800, Stokes denied any fresh consideration for his promise. McDevitt showed that the value of Peter the Great had increased by $10,000, of Orianna, by $5000, and of other horses in Stokes' farm by $5000 each. Held, "the petition fails to state a cause of action against appellee. The latter was, it is true, benefited by the winning of the Kentucky Futurity purse by the mare Grace, driven by appellant, but the benefit was purely incidental and one to which he was entitled regardless of appellant's undertaking. . . ." [In this context, what does the word "entitled" mean? Does it refer to a legal relationship?]

ENGLAND *v*. DAVIDSON. 1840. 11 Ad. & E. 856; 113 E.R. 640 (England. Queen's Bench). The defendant offered a reward of £50 to anyone giving information leading to the conviction of persons who broke into his house. The plaintiff, a police constable on duty in the area in which the defendant's house was located, did give such information and claimed the reward. The defendant paid him five guineas but failed to pay the balance. In an action to recover the balance it was objected that the plaintiff had given no consideration since as a police constable he was bound to give such information anyway. Judgment for the plaintiff. LORD DENMAN C.J.: "I think there may be services which the constable is not bound to render and which he may therefore make the ground of a contract. We should not hold a contract to be against the policy of the law, unless the grounds for so deciding were very clear."

NOTE. Martin, counsel for the defendant in the case just noted, had argued that the contract was against public policy. To what policy is it obnoxious? Do rewards operate to deflect a policeman's attention from his regular duties? Should this fact, if it is a fact, justify the promisor's failure to carry out his promise? Some police forces have a rule that any rewards earned by a member of the force must be pooled for the benefit of all members. Some forces do not allow members to accept awards. Should a court concern itself with such a question, or should it be left to the chief of police?

REIF *v*. PAGE. 1882. 55 Wisc. 496. A husband offered a reward to anyone who would rescue his wife, dead or alive, from a burning building. A fireman who took out the dead body was held entitled to recover. The court said that a fireman was not legally bound to risk his life in effecting a rescue.

LAW REVISION COMMITTEE, SIXTH INTERIM REPORT
England. 1937. Cmnd. 5449; 15 *Can. Bar Rev*. 585

In 1934 the Lord Chancellor appointed a committee "to consider how far, having regard to the Statute Law and to judicial decisions, such legal maxims and doctrines as the Lord Chancellor may from time to time refer to the Committee require revision in modern conditions." These excerpts are from the report on the *Statute of Frauds* and the Doctrine of Consideration. The Committee's general attitude toward reform is a realistic, if pessimistic one, and may be seen from the first of the following paragraphs:

27. Many of us would like to see the doctrine abolished root and branch. But a recommendation to this effect would probably be unwise. It is so deeply embedded in our law that any measure which proposed to do away with it altogether would almost certainly arouse suspicion and hostility. An opportunity should, however, be taken to prune away from the doctrine those aspects of it which can create hardship or cause unnecessary inconvenience. If the proposals which follow are accepted, the doctrine will survive, though deprived of most of its mischievous features. . . .

36. Three cases must be discussed:

(a) Where A makes a promise to B in consideration of B doing or promising to do something which he is already bound to do by reason of a duty imposed upon him by the law, whether by a Statute or otherwise: for instance, the duty of a local police authority to afford adequate protection to A and his property;

(b) Where A makes a promise to B in consideration of B doing or promising to do something which he is already bound to do under a contract with A;

(c) Where A makes a promise to B in consideration of B doing or promising to do something which he is already bound to do under a contract with C.

In cases (a) and (b) where the thing promised or performed is precisely the thing which the promisor is already bound to do, and no more, and there is no dispute that he is bound to do it, there is said to be no consideration or only illusory consideration for the new promise, and it is not enforceable. In case (c) the law is not so clear and frequently other factors are present out of which a consideration for the promise can be manufactured.

In our opinion, in all three cases, a promise made by A to B in consideration of B doing or promising to do something which he is already bound to do should be enforced by the law, provided that in other respects such as legality and compatibility with public policy it is free from objection; thus a promise in return for an agreement by a police authority to give precisely the amount of protection it was by law bound to give and no more should be unenforceable as being against public policy.

The dominant factor is that A thought it worth his while to make the promise to B in order that he should feel more certain that B would do the thing bargained for, and we can see no reason in general why A, having got what he wanted, should be allowed to evade his promise. Moreover, why did the promisor make a new promise if it was to have no legal effect? The connection between the general rule under discussion and the dictum in *Pinnel's Case,* which is a particular application of it, will not have escaped notice, and the observations by Lord Blackburn already quoted are equally relevant to the cases now under discussion.

6. Changing the Duty

RAGGOW *v.* SCOUGALL AND CO.

England. Divisional Court. 1915. 31 T. L. R. 564

This was an appeal by the defendants, Messrs. Scougall and Co., who were a firm of mantle-makers, from a decision of Judge Rentoul in the City of London Court, by which plaintiff, a mantle designer, recovered judgment for £58.

In August, 1913, the plaintiff by an agreement in writing agreed to become the defendants' designer for two years at a certain salary. It was provided that if the business should be discontinued during the period the agreement should cease to be of any effect. When the war broke out many customers cancelled orders which they had given to the firm, and the defendants had to consider whether they should close the business altogether. They called their employees together, and most of them agreed to a reduction of wages during the war if the defendants would continue the business. The plaintiff entered into a new agreement in writing, in which he, like other employees of the firm, agreed to accept a smaller salary for the duration of the war, provided that when the war was over the terms of the old agreement should be revived. He went on with his work and accepted the new salary until February last, when the defendants received a solicitor's letter claiming payment in full at the rate fixed in the old agreement; and as they refused to pay the excess this action was brought.

In the Court below judgment was given for the plaintiff on the ground that no consideration had been shown for the new agreement to accept a reduced payment. . . .

MR. JUSTICE DARLING said that the appeal must be allowed. It was clear from the provision in the new agreement that the terms of the old one should be revived when the war came to an end and that until the war ended the old agreement was dead. The parties had in fact torn up the old agreement and made a new one by mutual consent. They could have done it by recitals setting out the existence and rescission of the old agreement, but they had adopted a shorter course. The new agreement was an agreement contemplating employment on certain terms while the war lasted, and on certain other terms, which could be ascertained by reference to the older document, after the war had ended. The point, therefore, as to want of consideration failed and the appeal succeeded. He was the more glad to be able to arrive at this conclusion on the law, for it was evident that the plaintiff was trying to do a very dishonest thing.

[Coleridge J. agreed.]

QUESTIONS. Could the defendant company at any time have terminated the employment of the plaintiff at all? Suppose an employer promised an employee in September a Christmas bonus, in reliance on which the employee refrained from taking another job. Could he recover on the promise? If so, how does he differ from the sailors in *Stilk* v. *Myrick*? On the question of bonus payments see the note on *Sloan* v. *Union Oil Company of Canada Limited* in section 7, below, pp. 196–7.

COOK *v.* WRIGHT

England. Queen's Bench. 1861. 1 B. & S. 559; 121 E.R. 822

BLACKBURN J.: In this case it appeared on the trial that the defendant was agent for a Mrs. Bennett, who was non-resident owner of houses in a district subject to a local act. Work had been done in the adjoining street by the commissioners for executing the act, the expenses of which, under the provisions of their act, they charged on the owners of the adjoining houses. Notice had been given to the defendant, as if he had himself been owner of the houses, calling on him to pay the proportion chargeable in respect of them. He attended at a board meeting of the commissioners, and objected both to the amount and nature of the charges, and also stated that he was not the owner of the houses, and that Mrs. Bennett was. He was told that if he did not pay he would be treated as one Goble had been. It appeared that Goble had refused to pay a sum charged against him as owner of some houses, and the commissioners had taken legal proceedings against him, and he had then submitted and paid with costs. In the result it was agreed between the commissioners and the defendant that the amount charged upon him should be reduced, and that time should be given to pay it in three instalments; he gave three promissory notes for the three instalments; the first was duly honored, the others were not, and were the subject of the present action. At the trial it appeared that the defendant was not in fact owner of the houses. As agent for the owner he was not personally liable under the act. In point of law, therefore, the commissioners were not entitled to claim the money from him; but no case of deceit was alleged against them. It must be taken that the commissioners honestly believed that the defendant was personally liable, and really intended to take legal proceedings against him, as they had done against Goble. The defendant, according to his own evidence, never believed that he was liable in law, but signed the notes in order to avoid being sued as Goble was. Under these circumstances the substantial question reserved (irrespective of the form of the plea) was whether there was any consideration for the notes. We are of opinion that there was.

There is no doubt that a bill or note given in consideration of what is supposed to be a debt is without consideration if it appears that there was a mistake in fact as to the existence of the debt, *Bell* v. *Gardiner* (1842), 4 M. & Gr. 11; 134 E.R. 5; and, according to the cases of *Southall* v. *Rigg* and *Forman* v. *Wright* (1851), 11 C.B. 481; 138 E.R. 560, the law is the same if the bill or note is given in consequence of a mistake of law as to the existence of the debt. But here there was no mistake on the part of the defendant either of law or fact. What he did was not merely the making an erroneous account stated, or promising to pay a debt for which he mistakenly believed himself liable. It appeared on the evidence that he believed himself not to be liable; but he knew that the plaintiffs thought him liable, and would sue him if he did not pay, and in order to avoid the expense and trouble of legal proceedings against himself he agreed to compromise; and the question is, whether a person who has given a note as a compromise of a claim honestly made on him, and which but for that compromise would have been at once brought to a legal decision, can resist the payment of the note on the ground that the original claim thus compromised might have been successfully resisted.

If the suit had been actually commenced, the point would have been concluded by authority. In *Longridge* v. *Dorville* (1821), 5 B. & A. 117; 106 E.R. 1136, it was held that the compromise of a suit instituted to try a doubtful question of law was a sufficient consideration for a promise. In *Atlee* v. *Blackhouse* (1838), 3 M. & W. 633; 150 E.R. 1298 where the plaintiff's goods had been seized by the excise, and he had afterwards entered into an agreement with the commissioners of excise that all proceedings should be terminated, the goods delivered up to the plaintiff, and a sum of money paid by him to the commissioners, Parke B., rests his judgment, p. 650, on the ground that this agreement of compromise honestly made was for consideration, and binding. In *Cooper* v. *Parker* (1855), 15 C. B. 822; 139 E.R. 650 the Court of Exchequer Chamber held that the withdrawal of an untrue defense of infancy in a suit, with payment of costs, was a sufficient consideration for a promise to accept a smaller sum in satisfaction of a larger.

In these cases, however, litigation had been actually commenced; and it was argued before us that this made a difference in point of law, and that though, where a plaintiff has actually issued a writ against a defendant, a compromise honestly made is binding, yet the same compromise, if made before the writ actually issues, though the litigation is impending, is void. *Edwards* v. *Baugh* (1843), 11 M. & W. 641; 152 E.R. 962, was relied upon as an authority for this proposition. But in that case Lord Abinger expressly bases his judgment (pp. 645, 646) on the assumption that the declaration did not, either expressly or impliedly, show that a reasonable doubt existed between the parties. It may be doubtful whether the declaration in that case ought not to have been construed as disclosing a compromise of a real bona fide claim, but it does not appear to have been so construed by the court. We agree that unless there was a reasonable claim on the one side, which it was bona fide intended to pursue, there would be no ground for a compromise; but we cannot agree that (except as a test of the reality of the claim in fact) the issuing of a writ is essential to the validity of the compromise. The position of the parties must necessarily be altered in every case of compromise, so that, if the question is afterward opened up they cannot be replaced as they were before the compromise. The plaintiff may be in a less favorable position for renewing his litigation, he must be at an additional trouble and expense in again getting up his case, and he may no longer be able to produce the evidence which would have proved it originally. Besides, though he may not in point of law be bound to refrain from enforcing his rights against third persons during the continuance of the compromise to which they are not parties, yet practically the effect of the compromise must be to prevent his doing so. For instance, in the present case, there can be no doubt that the practical effect of the compromise must have been to induce the commissioners to refrain from taking proceedings against Mrs. Bennett, the real owner of the houses, while the notes given by the defendant, her agent, were running; though the compromise might have afforded no ground of defense had such proceedings been resorted to. It is this detriment to the party consenting to a compromise arising from the necessary alteration in his position which, in our opinion forms the real consideration for the promise, and not the technical and almost illusory consideration arising from the extra cost of litigation. The real consideration therefore depends, not on the actual commencement of a suit, but on the reality of the claim made and the bona fides of the compromise.

In the present case we think that there was sufficient consideration for the notes in the compromise made as it was.

The rule to enter a verdict for the plaintiff must be made absolute.

CALLISHER *v.* BISCHOFFSHEIM. 1870. L.R. 5 Q.B. 449 (England). COCKBURN C.J.: "If the defendant's contention were adopted, it would result that in no case of a doubtful claim could a compromise be enforced. Every day a compromise is effected on the ground that the party making it has a chance of succeeding in it; and if he bona fide believes he has a fair chance of success, he has a reasonable ground for suing, and his forbearance to sue will constitute a good consideration. When such a person forbears to sue he gives up what he believes to be a right of action, and the other party gives an advantage; and, instead of being annoyed with an action, he escapes from the vexation incident to it."

MILES *v.* NEW ZEALAND ALFORD ESTATE CO. 1886. 32 Ch. D. 266 (England. Court of Appeal). COTTON L.J.: "Now, what I understand to be the law is this, that if there is in fact a serious claim honestly made, the abandonment of the claim is a good 'consideration' for a contract. . . . Now, by 'honest claim', I think is meant this, that a claim is honest if the claimant does not know that his claim is unsubstantial, or if he does not know facts, to his knowledge unknown to the other party, which show that his claim is a bad one. Of course, if both parties know all the facts, and with the knowledge of those facts obtain a compromise, it cannot be said that that is dishonest. . . . The doubt of the Master of the Rolls [expressed in *Ex parte Banner* (1881), 17 Ch.D. 480] seems to have been whether a compromise would not be bad, or a promise to abandon a claim would be a good consideration if, on the facts being elicited and brought out, and on the decision of the Court being obtained, it was found that the claim which was considered the consideration for the compromise was a bad one. But if the validity of a compromise is to depend upon whether the claim was a good one or not, no compromise would be effectual, because if it was afterward disputed, it would be necessary to go into the question whether the claim was in fact a good one or not; and I consider, notwithstanding the doubt expressed by the Master of the Rolls, that the doctrine laid down in *Cook* v. *Wright* and *Callisher* v. *Bischoffsheim* . . . is the law of this Court."

ALLIANCE BANK *v*. BROOM. 1864. 2 Dr. & Sm. 289; 62 E.R. 631. The plaintiffs, having lent £22,000 to the defendants, wrote the latter asking for security. The defendants, stating they were entitled to certain goods, wrote the plaintiffs' manager promising to hypothecate the goods to the bank. Subsequently, the defendant having refused to hypothecate the goods, the bank sued, asking for an order to the defendant to deliver the goods. The defendant pleaded that his promise was without consideration. The court overruled this objection stating that although forbearance was not promised, it was in effect given, and the defendant received the benefit of it. Moreover, the court stated that if the promise had not been given the creditor would have sued for the debt, therefore the fact that he did not "necessarily involved the benefit to the debtor of a certain amount of forbearance, which he would not have derived, if he had not made the agreement." [Did the defendant ask for forbearance as the price of his promise? Did the plaintiff offer forbearance in return for the promise? See the discussion of *Alliance Bank* v. *Broom,* in *Glegg* v. *Bromley,* [1912] 3 K.B. 474 at 481]

FAIRGRIEF *v*. ELLIS

British Columbia. Supreme Court. 1935. 49 B.C.R. 413

McDONALD J.: Defendant is a retired gentleman, 72 years of age, owning and residing upon a small parcel of land on Lulu Island, worth approximately $2,500. For some years his relations with his wife have been strained; she refused to live with him in British Columbia and maintained her residence in California.

Plaintiffs are sisters, cultured maiden ladies about 50 years of age, who until the year 1933 lived in Winnipeg where they had been employed in clerical work though in recent times they were for considerable periods out of employment. They had been close friends of the defendant over a period of some 25 years and their relations may be judged from the fact that they called him "Dad." In the spring of 1933 the plaintiff Cornelia Fairgrief came to British Columbia on an excursion and visited with the defendant for some three days. Following that occasion some letters passed between the defendant and the plaintiff Anne Fairgrief wherein the plaintiff Anne Fairgrief was invited to visit the defendant. This invitation she declined. In August of that year defendant's son, who had for some months been residing with him, departed for the United States whereupon defendant wrote the plaintiff Anne Fairgrief stating that he was alone and that he required a housekeeper and that he wished the plaintiffs to come and keep house for him, final arrangements to be made after their arrival. Plaintiffs thereupon came to the defendant's home and took up their residence with him upon a verbal agreement that if they would become his housekeepers and take charge of his home during his lifetime the home would become theirs upon his death.

Pursuant to the above agreement plaintiffs entered upon their duties, took full charge of the home, performed all the household duties and did a good deal of work outside including painting, cleaning up the ground and other works of a more or less permanent nature. In addition to being his housekeepers they were his congenial companions and the three lived comfortably and happily until August, 1934, when the defendant's wife (much to his surprise for he had expected nothing of the sort) suddenly arrived in Vancouver. Defendant requested the plaintiffs to remain and be kind to his wife while she should reside with them, he feeling quite assured that her stay would not be a lengthy one. At the end of about a month defendant told the plaintiffs that he was grieved to be obliged to tell them that his wife insisted that they should depart the premises as she intended to remain and take charge. Defendant, knowing of his obligation to the plaintiffs, promised them if they would give up their rights under the agreement already entered into, and would depart from his home he would on or about the 1st of October, 1934, pay them $1,000. That offer was accepted and plaintiffs removed themselves from the premises. The plaintiffs now bring action to recover that sum of $1,000. I have no doubt at all that the defendant's repudiation of his agreement resulted from the interference of his wife. Having persistently refused to live with him and assist him in making a happy and comfortable home, she was determined that the plaintiffs should not be allowed to render that assistance which she herself declined to render. Incidentally it may be said that her further actions justify to some extent this assumption for she again left her husband on November 2nd, 1934, and has not returned to him. Although there is a conflict of evidence I find the facts to be as above stated.

On the above facts, can the plaintiffs succeed? It is contended in the first instance that the agreement first made cannot be enforced by reason of the 4th section of the Statute of Frauds, the agreement being one relating to an interest in land. With that contention I agree and I also agree that the plaintiffs cannot rely upon the fact that they have partly performed their contract for the reason that the acts which they performed are not necessarily referable to the contract alleged by them but might equally be referable to the contract set out by the defendant, *viz*:

"That the agreement under which the plaintiffs came to reside with the defendant . . . was that in return for their board and lodging the plaintiffs were to keep house for the defendant until the defendant's wife came up from California."

See *Haddock* v. *Norgan* (1923), 33 B.C. 237; (1924), 34 B.C. 74.

Notwithstanding the above, however, I cannot understand why the plaintiffs cannot succeed on their claim for $1,000. When the agreement was made in September to pay the plaintiffs $1,000 the defendant thought that he was under an obligation to the plaintiffs and in order to be released from that obligation and so that the plaintiffs might agree to peacefully vacate his premises, he made the second agreement. Even although he was not in law bound to perform the first agreement nevertheless I think there was good consideration to support the promise to pay $1,000. . . .

There will be judgment for the plaintiffs for $1,000. . . .

FOAKES *v.* BEER

England. House of Lords. 1884. L.R. 9 App. Cas. 605

In 1875 Mrs. Beer recovered judgment against Dr. Foakes for £2090 19s. including costs. In an agreement dated December 21, 1876, Dr. Foakes promised to pay "the whole sum", £500 down and the balance in fixed payments over some five years; and Mrs. Beer promised not to take any proceedings on the judgment. This in effect meant that Mrs. Beer would not claim any interest on the unpaid part of the judgment. In 1882 Mrs. Beer commenced this action on the judgment for the interest, the principal amount having been paid as agreed. Cave J. held Mrs. Beer was not entitled to judgment because of the agreement. The Queen's Bench Division discharged an order for a new trial on the ground of misdirection. The Court of Appeal reversed that decision and entered judgment for the respondent for the interest due, with costs. Dr. Foakes appealed to the House of Lords.

HOLL Q.C. for the appellant: Apart from the doctrine of *Cumber* v. *Wane* (1721), 1 St. 425; 93 E.R. 613, there is no reason in sense or law why the agreement should not be valid, and the creditor prevented from enforcing his judgment if the agreement be performed. It may often be much more advantageous to the creditor to obtain immediate payment of part of his debt than to wait to enforce payment, or perhaps by pressing his debtor to force him into bankruptcy with the result of only a small dividend. Moreover if a composition is accepted friends, who would not otherwise do so, may be willing to come forward to assist the debtor. And if the creditor thinks that the acceptance of part is for his benefit who is to say it is not? The doctrine of *Cumber* v. *Wane* has been continually assailed, as in *Couldery* v. *Bartrum* (1880), 19 Ch. D. 394, 399, by Jessel M.R. In the note to *Cumber* v. *Wane* (1 Smith L.C. 4th ed. p. 253, 8th ed. p. 367) which was written by J. W. Smith and never disapproved by any of the editors, including Willes and Keating JJ., it is said "that its doctrine is founded upon vicious reasoning and false views of the office of a Court of law, which should rather strive to give effect to the engagements which persons have thought proper to enter into, than cast about for subtle reasons to defeat them upon the ground of being unreasonable. Carried to its full extent the doctrine of *Cumber* v. *Wane* embraces the exploded notion that in order to render valid a contract not under seal, the adequacy as well as the existence of the consideration must be established. Accordingly in modern times it has been, as appears by the preceding part of the note, subjected to modification in several instances," *Cumber* v. *Wane* was decided on a ground now admitted to be erroneous, viz. that the satisfaction must be found by the Court to be reasonable. The Court cannot inquire into the adequacy of the consideration. *Reynolds* v. *Pinhowe* (1595), Cro. Eliz. 429; 78 E.R. 669, which was not cited in *Cumber* v. *Wane* . . . decided that the saving of trouble was a sufficient consideration; "for it is a benefit unto him to have his debt without suit or charge." . . . *Pinnel's Case* (1602), 5 Coke's Rep. 117a; 77 E.R. 237, was decided on a point of pleading; the dictum that payment of a smaller sum was no satisfaction of a larger, was extra-judicial, and overlooked all considerations of mercantile convenience, such as mentioned in *Reynolds* v. *Pinhowe*; and it is also noticeable that it was a case of a bond debt sought to be set aside by a parol agreement. It is every day practice for tradesmen to take less in satisfaction of a larger sum, and give discount, where there is neither custom nor right to take credit. . . . The result of the cases is that if *Cumber* v. *Wane* be right, payment of a less sum than the debt due, by a bill, promissory note or cheque is a good discharge; but payment of such less sum by sovereigns or Bank of England notes is not. Here the agreement is not to take less than the debt, but to give time for payment of the whole without interest. Mankind have never acted on the doctrine of *Cumber* v. *Wane*, but the contrary; nay few are aware of it. By overruling it the House will only declare the universal practice to be good law as well as good sense.

[EARL OF SELBORNE L.C.: Whatever may be the ultimate decision of this appeal the House is much indebted to Mr. Holl for his exceedingly able argument.]

EARL OF SELBORNE L.C.: . . . The question, therefore, is nakedly raised by this appeal, whether your Lordships are now prepared, not only to overrule, as contrary to law, the doctrine stated by Sir Edward Coke to have been laid down by all the judges of the Common Pleas in *Pinnel's Case* in 1602, and repeated in his note to Littleton, sect. 344, but to treat a prospective agreement, not under seal, for satisfaction of a debt, by a series of payments on account to a total amount less than the whole debt, as binding in law, provided those payments are regularly made; the case not being one of a composition with a common debtor, agreed to, *inter se*, by several creditors. I prefer so to state the question instead of treating it (as it was put at the Bar) as depending on the authority of the case of *Cumber* v. *Wane*, decided in 1718. It may well be that distinctions, which in later cases have been held sufficient to exclude the application of that doctrine, existed and were improperly disregarded in *Cumber* v. *Wane*; and yet that the doctrine itself may be law, rightly recognized in *Cumber* v. *Wane*, and not really contradicted by any later authorities. And this appears to me to be the true state of the case. The doctrine itself, as laid down by Sir Edward Coke, may have been criticised, as questionable in principle, by some persons whose opinions are entitled to respect, but it has never been judicially overruled; on the contrary I think it has always since the sixteenth century, been accepted as law. If so, I cannot think that your Lordships would do right, if you were now to reverse, as erroneous, a judgment of the Court of Appeal, proceeding upon a doctrine which has been accepted as part of the law of England for 280 years.

The distinction between the effect of a deed under seal, and that of an agreement by parol, or by writing not under seal, may seem arbitrary but it is established in our law; nor is it really unreasonable or practically inconvenient that the law should require particular solemnities to give to a gratuitous contract the force of a binding obligation. If the question be (as, in the actual state of the law, I think it is), whether the consideration is, or is not, given in a case of this kind, by the debtor who pays down part of the debt presently due from him, for a promise by the creditor to relinquish, after certain further payments on account, the residue of the debt, I cannot say that I think consideration is given, in the sense in which I have always understood that word as used in our law. It might be (and indeed I think it would be) an improvement in our law, if a release or acquittance of the whole debt, or payment of any sum which the creditor might be content to receive by way of accord and satisfaction (though less than the whole), were held to be, generally, binding, though not under seal; nor should I be unwilling to see equal force given to a prospective agreement, like the present, in writing though not under seal; but I think it impossible, without refinements which partially alter the sense of the word, to treat such a release or acquittance as supported by any new consideration proceeding from the debtor. . . .

My conclusion is, that the order appealed from should be affirmed, and the appeal dismissed, with costs, and I so move your Lordships.

[The opinions of Lords Blackburn, Fitzgerald and Watson to the same effect are omitted.]

GODDARD *v.* O'BRIEN 1882. 9 Q.B.D. 37. Held, that the giving of a cheque by the debtor for a less sum and received as settlement "on the cheque being honoured" operated as a good accord and satisfaction. [But see Fletcher Moulton L.J. in *Hirachand* v. *Temple*, [1911] 2 K.B. 330 at 340: "I have grave doubts whether *Goddard* v. *O'Brien* was rightly decided, because, when the facts are looked at it appears that the cheque was there given, not in substitution for the debt, but only as conditional payment of the amount, so that the case really stood on the same footing as payment of a less sum in discharge of a greater."]

NOTE. Payment of a debt, or part of a debt, by a third person has been held to operate as a discharge of the original debtor. "The effect of such an agreement between a creditor and a third party with regard to the debt is to render it impossible for the creditor afterwards to sue the debtor for it. The way in which this is worked out in law may be that it would be an abuse of the process of the Court to allow the creditor under such circumstances to sue, or it may be, and I prefer that view, that there is an extinction of the debt; but whichever way it is put, it comes to the same thing, namely that, after acceptance by a creditor of a sum offered by a third party in settlement of the claim against the debtor, the creditor cannot maintain an action for the balance." Fletcher Moulton L.J. in *Hirachand* v. *Temple*.

Where several creditors agree with the debtor to accept a proportion of their claim in satisfaction, such composition agreements are held good. See *Good* v. *Cheesman* (1831), 2 B. & Ad. 328; 109 E.R. 1165. It is usually stated that the promise of each creditor is consideration for the promise of every other creditor. If the creditors promise not to sue the debtor, how can this avail the debtor? That it does operate in his favour is undoubted.]

HISTORY AND SUBSEQUENT FATE OF FOAKES *v.* BEER. The House of Lords in the principal case relied on *Pinnel's Case*, which was decided in the Court of Common Pleas in 1602. The report is very brief:

"Pinnel brought an action of debt on a bond against Cole of £16 for payment of £8 10s. the 11th day of Nov. 1600. The defendant pleaded, that he at the instance of the plaintiff, before the said day, *scil.* 1 Octob. *anno* 44, *apud W. solvit querenti £5 2s. 2d. quas quidem £5 2s. 2d.* the plaintiff accepted in full satisfaction of the £8 10s. And it was resolved by the whole court, that payment of a lesser sum on the day in satisfaction of a greater, cannot be any satisfaction for the whole, because it appears to the Judges that by no possibility, a lesser sum can be a satisfaction to the plaintiff for a greater sum. But the gift of a horse, hawk, or robe, &c. in satisfaction is good. For it shall be intended that a horse, hawk, or robe, &c., might be more beneficial to the plaintiff than the money, in respect of some circumstances, or otherwise the plaintiff would not have accepted of it in satisfaction. But when the whole sum is due, by no intendment the acceptance of parcel can be a satisfaction to the plaintiff; but in the case at bar it was resolved, that the payment and acceptance of parcel before the day in satisfaction of the whole would be a good satisfaction in regard of circumstance of time; for peradventure parcel of it before the day, would be more beneficial to him than the whole at the day, and the value of the satisfaction is not material.

So if I am bound in £20 to pay you £10 at Westminster, and you request me to pay you £5 at the day at York, and you will accept it in full satisfaction of the whole £10 it is a good satisfaction for the whole: for the expences to pay it at York is sufficient satisfaction: but in this case the plaintiff had judgment for the insufficient pleading; for he did not plead that he had paid the £5 2s. 2d. in full satisfaction (as by the law he ought) but pleaded the payment of part generally; and that the plaintiff accepted it in full satisfaction. And always the manner of the tender and of the payment shall be directed by him who made the tender on payment, and not by him who accepts it. And for this cause judgment was given for the plaintiff."

The House evidently took the view that this case was decided on its merits, although it seems that it might have been decided on deficiencies in the pleadings. It is to be noted that *Pinnel's Case* is an action in debt and the defence of accord and satisfaction is peculiar to this form of action. Is there any reason why the "law" of debt and accord and satisfaction should apply to *assumpsit* or to modern contract?

The House also relied on *Cumber* v. *Wane*, decided in the King's Bench, in 1721. It was an action *indebitatus assumpsit* for £15. The defendant pleaded that he gave the plaintiff a promissory note for £5 in satisfaction and that the plaintiff received it in satisfaction. Pratt C.J. said, in part,

"We are all of the opinion that the plea is not good, and therefore the judgment must be affirmed: as the plaintiff had a good cause of action, it can only be extinguished by a satisfaction he agrees to accept and it is not his agreement alone that is sufficient, but it must appear to the court to be a reasonable satisfaction; or at least the contrary must not appear, as it does in this case. If £5 be (as is admitted) no satisfaction for £15 why is a simple contract to pay £5 a satisfaction for another simple contract of three times the value? In the case of a bond, another has never been allowed to be pleaded in satisfaction, without a bettering of the plaintiff's case, as by shortening the time of payment. . . ."

But the House did not mention the case of *Reynolds* v. *Pinhowe* decided in the Court of King's Bench in 1595 and obviously relied on heavily by Holl Q.C. That too, was an action in assumpsit. The available report is sketchy, but very much to the point:

"Whereas the defendant had recovered five pounds against the plaintiff; in consideration of four pounds given him by the plaintiff, that the defendant assumed to acknowledge satisfaction of that judgment before such a day; and that he had not done it. And it was thereupon demurred; for it was moved, that there was not any consideration; for it is no more than to give him part of the money which he owed him, which is not any consideration. But all the court held it to be well enough; for it is a benefit unto him to have it without suit or charge; and it may be there was error in the record; so as the party might have avoided it. Wherefore it was adjudged for the plaintiff."

Neither counsel nor the House mentioned *Bagge* v. *Slade*, another decision in the King's Bench, in 1616, 3 Bulst. 162; 81 E.R. 137, decided by

Sir Edward Coke himself, and, of course, long before *Cumber* v. *Wane*. In that case Coke C.J. is reported to have said,

". . . if a man be bound to another by a bill in £1000 and he pays unto him £500 in discharge of this bill, the which he accepts of accordingly, and doth upon this assume and promise to deliver up unto him his said bill of £1000, this £500 is no satisfaction of the £1000 but yet this is good and sufficient to make a good promise, and upon a good consideration, because he had paid money, £500, and he had no remedy for this again. . . ."

Can *Pinnel's Case* and *Cumber* v. *Wane* be distinguished? If not, ought their 280 years of respectability be left intact despite the admitted inconsistency with modern business practice?

THE ADMINISTRATION OF JUSTICE ACT, 1885

Ontario. Statutes. 1885. Chapter 13

6. Part performance of an obligation, either before or after a breach thereof, when expressly accepted by the creditor in satisfaction, or rendered in pursuance of an agreement for that purpose, though without any new consideration, shall be held to extinguish the obligation.

NOTE. This section is now section 16 of *The Mercantile Law Amendment Act*, R.S.O. 1960, c. 238. Like any statute, it is better understood when applied to specific facts. Would it have produced a different result in *Foakes* v. *Beer*? Suppose Mrs. Beer had commenced her action before Dr. Foakes had made the £500 down payment, could the statute have been invoked? Suppose after Dr. Foakes had completed all but the last payment Mrs. Beer had made her claim?

Some American states have adopted similar legislation. See, for example, *California Civil Code*, s. 1524. In some states an executory agreement is made binding if it is in writing. See, for example, *Michigan Compiled Laws of 1948*, s. 566.1.

ROMMERILL *v*. GARDENER

British Columbia. Court of Appeal. 1962. 35 D.L.R. (2d) 717

DAVEY, J.A.: By an oral judgment that was not recorded the learned County Court Judge found that the defendant (respondent) agreed to pay and the plaintiff (appellant) to accept $599.19 in full of his claim for commissions amounting to $1,187.23. There is ample evidence to support that finding.

From the learned Judge's notes of the evidence of the respondent and her husband it would appear that the respondent either told the appellant that she would pay the amount by Easter, 1960, or agreed that it was to be paid by that date. Appellant's evidence is no help on this point because he denied the agreement. The learned County Court Judge must have thought that the agreement to accept the $599.19 in full was not terminated by the failure to pay that amount by Easter. We are quite unable to say from the fragmentary notes of the evidence that the learned Judge was wrong in not regarding the promise to pay by Easter as a condition of the settlement.

The appellant wrote in October of that year demanding payment of $1,187.23. The respondent then sent him a cheque for $599.19, which he retained but did not cash; thereupon he commenced action for $1,187.23. Two days before trial the respondent paid appellant $599.19, which he accepted on account and proceeded to trial. The learned County Court Judge held, so counsel tell us, that the payment was as good as if made at Easter and dismissed the action. Appellant appeals.

Unless respondent can bring the payment of $599.19 within the terms of s. 2(33) of the *Laws Declaratory Act*, R.S.B.C. 1960, c. 213, it is obvious that the payment of the lesser amount without new consideration will not satisfy the greater sum of $1,187.23 otherwise due.

The clause, which is substantially the same as enactments in Ontario, Saskatchewan and Alberta, and similar to one in Manitoba, reads as follows:

> (33) Part performance of an obligation either before or after a breach thereof, when expressly accepted by the creditor in satisfaction or rendered in pursuance of an agreement for that purpose, though without any new consideration, shall be held to extinguish the obligation.

The first branch of the subsection may be dismissed at once for both counsel agree that the $599.19 was not accepted by the appellant in satisfaction of the greater amount. If the payment of $599.19 extinguished the obligation it must be because it was rendered in pursuance of the agreement that it be paid and accepted in full of the obligation.

To that appellant's counsel makes two submissions:

First: He says that the agreement mentioned in the clause means a contract under seal or supported by consideration, and that there was no consideration for the parol agreement in question.

Secondly: He contends that the appellant in October, 1960, had before payment demanded the whole amount of $1,187.23, and consequently effectively terminated any agreement to take the lesser amount in full.

In support of his first submission counsel relies upon the judgment of Gregory, J., in *Bell* v. *Quagliotti et al.* (1918), 25 B.C.R. 460 in which he held that the agreement mentioned in the clause means a binding agreement, supported by consideration when not under seal, *i.e.*, a contract, and consequently that a lesser sum paid in pursuance of an agreement not constituting a contract would not operate to extinguish an obligation to pay a greater sum. But this part of the judgment was *obiter*. The judgment of the Court of Appeal (1919), 26 B.C.R. 482, affirming his decision, cannot be taken to support that particular proposition.

Also, this dictum is contrary to several judgments of single Judges in the other Provinces. The Ontario section was discussed by Rose, J., in Bank of *Commerce* v. *Jenkins* (1888), 16 O.R. 215, but the reasons do not indicate whether Rose, J., regarded the agreement in that case as having been made without consideration. MacMahon, J., who sat with Rose, J., had some reservations about his construction of the section.

It is somewhat difficult to follow the reasoning of Beck, J., in *Goodchild* v. *Bethel* (1914), 19 D.L.R. 161, 8 A.L.R. 98, Scott and Simmons, JJ., agreeing, in holding that an immediate payment of part of arrears that otherwise would not have been paid at all, was valuable consideration for the agreement to take that part and certain other sums in full satisfaction of the debtor's obligations. It is not clear from the report what that learned Judge's opinion would have been if he had concluded there was no consideration for the agreement.

In *MacKiw* v. *Rutherford*, [1921] 2 W.W.R. 329, the agreement in question, although in writing, seems to have been made without legal consideration, but $100 was paid at once on account of the lesser sum to be ultimately paid in discharge of the full amount. Curran, J., without discussing the question of consideration, held that the payment of the $100 and a tender of the balance due under the agreement extinguished the original obligation.

In *A. R. Williams Machinery Co.* v. *Winnipeg Storage Ltd.* [1928] 1 D.L.R. 12 at p. 24, 37 Man. R. 187, Fullerton, J.A., in allowing an appeal upon the Manitoba section said that it required no consideration for the agreement Perdue, C.J.M., allowed the appeal on another ground, and Dennistoun, Prendergast and Trueman, JJ.A., merely concurred in the result, so it cannot be said from the report that they concurred in the reasoning of Fullerton, J.A.

In *Hoolahan* v. *Hivon*, [1944] 4 D.L.R. 405 at p. 409, Ewing, J.A., sitting as a trial Judge, said that in his opinion the payment of $100 as the first payment due under an agreement made without consideration brought the case within the second branch of the statute so as to prevent the agreement being revoked while in the course of being performed.

The weight of subsequent authority seems to be against the view expressed by Gregory, J., in *Bell* v. *Quagliotti*, *supra*. As a matter of pure construction, I should think that for the purposes of the clause the agreement need not by itself be a binding contract, and consequently need not be supported by consideration. The words "though without any new consideration," while relating grammatically to the verbs "accepted" and "rendered," in my opinion point significantly to the purpose of the clause. Moreover a part performance rendered pursuant to a binding contract based upon a new consideration to accept that part performance in full would by that very fact constitute an accord and satisfaction at common law. When the clause says rendered without any new consideration, it must mean that there need not be consideration for the agreement upon which the part performance is rendered.

Appellant cannot succeed on that branch of his argument.

Turning to the second ground of appeal, the respondent admits that about October, 1960, the appellant demanded payment of the full sum of $1,187.23, in response to which she sent him the cheque for $599.19, which was never cashed. But the letter making that demand is not before us, and so far as the notes of evidence go there was no secondary evidence of its contents, consequently we do not know the tenor of the demand. It is unlikely that it was a demand terminating the unperformed agreement because of default, because the appellant denied at the trial that there was such an agreement. I suppose that under some circumstances a bare demand of the greater sum might terminate an unperformed agreement made without consideration to take a lesser sum in full satisfaction of the indebtedness, but it is by no means evident to me at the moment that such a bare demand would by itself necessarily terminate an agreement that the creditor denied. Without the letter I am unable to come to any conclusion upon this ground of appeal. This makes it unnecessary to consider whether under cl. (33) such a creditor can terminate at will a voluntary agreement before it has been partly performed; see *Bank of Commerce* v. *Jenkins*, 16 O.R. 215 at p. 225; *Mason* v. *Johnston* (1893), 20 O.A.R. 412 at p. 415; *MacKiw* v. *Rutherford*, [1921] 2 W.W.R. 329 at p. 333, and *Hoolahan* v. *Hivon*, [1944] 4 D.L.R. 405.

The learned County Court Judge dismissed the action without costs.

Appellant contends that because tender was not made or pleaded he should have had the costs of the trial up to the time of the payment two days before the trial opened; but in that event he would have had to pay the costs of the trial.

The respondent's failure to make and plead tender were circumstances requiring a special direction as to costs within the meaning of s. 161 of the *County Courts Act*, R.S.B.C. 1960, c. 81, and I am quite unable to see anything wrong with the way the learned Judge exercised his discretion in those circumstances.

I would dismiss the appeal.

McMANUS *v*. BARK. 1870. L.R. 5 Exch. 65 (England, Exchequer). An action by the executor of John McManus, against John Bark, on Bark's promissory note for £520 with interest at 5 per cent. Bark relied on an agreement which provided: ". . . The said John Bark owing the said John McManus the sum of £520 for which the said John McManus has already a promissory note, it has been mutually agreed this day that the principal shall be repaid at £25 each quarter, with interest after the rate of £5 per cent, per annum. . . ." KELLY C.B.: . . . We are all of opinion that the agreement constitutes no bar to the present action, inasmuch as it was made for no consideration whatever. It was argued that there was a consideration for it in one of two ways. The mode of payment of interest was varied, it was said, and a quarterly instalment secured to the deceased. But that circumstance cannot be relied on; for the note was payable with interest on demand, and at any moment the payment of the whole, with interest, could have been insisted on. Then, again, the counsel for the defendant contended that the agreement gave the deceased a secure investment for the amount of the note for a fixed time at a sufficient rate of interest. This, however, depends on whether the defendant was left at liberty to come at any time and tender the whole amount. We think he was at liberty to do so. There was no obligation upon him to remain indebted, unless he pleased. Nor, on the other hand, was the deceased under any obligation not to sue on the note after demand. There was, therefore, no consideration for the agreement relied on by the defendant, and the rule must be refused.

QUESTION. How might the agreement have been drafted to prove effective as a bar to this action?

COULDERY *v*. BARTRUM. 1880. 19 Ch. D.394. JESSEL M. R.: "According to English Common Law a creditor might accept anything in satisfaction of his debt except a less amount of money. He might take a horse, or a canary, or a tomtit if he chose, and that was accord and satisfaction; but, by a most extraordinary peculiarity of the English Common Law, he could not take 19s. 6d. in the pound; that was *nudum pactum*. Therefore, although the creditor might take a canary, yet, if the debtor did not give him a canary together with his 19s. 6d., there was no accord and satisfaction; if he did, there was accord and satisfaction. That was one of the mysteries of English Common Law."

KAULBACH *v*. EICHEL. [1930] 1 D.L.R. 983 (Supreme Court of Nova Scotia *en banc*). On March 13, 1897, one Kaulbach agreed to sell his farm near Bridgewater to Eichel for $700, payment to be made by a promissory note bearing interest annually. In 1901 Eichel paid $25 represented by a pair of yearling steers and in 1903 he paid $30, the price of a cow. No further payments were made until after May 2, 1910. Kaulbach died in 1907 and in 1910 the plaintiff, Kaulbach's executor, orally agreed to a new arrangement under which $500 would be accepted in full payment. As to the objection that there was no consideration for the promise to accept a lesser sum, Ross J., referring to *Foakes* v. *Beer* and *Pinnel's Case,* said: "However, it must be remembered that part of the payment to be made by Eichel consisted of a pair of oxen, a pair of steers, a cow and a heifer. It seems reasonable to infer from the evidence that the defendant, at the time the 1910 negotiations were commenced, had about decided to abandon the place. When these negotiations commenced, however, he told plaintiff that he had six head of cattle on his place which he would hand over as part of the consideration, which he afterwards did. . . . Eichel was reluctant to part with those cattle until he made sure of the arrangement with the plaintiff and went to the telephone and communicated with him before giving up the cattle. On the other hand, it was, no doubt, under all the circumstances, to the advantage of the plaintiff to get the cattle." Plaintiff's claim was dismissed and he was ordered to reconvey the farm to the defendant, it having been bought by the plaintiff after he got judgment at the trial.

LAW REVISION COMMITTEE, SIXTH INTERIM REPORT

England. 1937. Cmnd. 5449; 15 *Can. Bar Rev.* 585

34. In *Foakes* v. *Beer* Lord Blackburn was evidently disposed to hold that it was still open to the House of Lords to reconsider the rule based on the dictum [in *Pinnel's Case*], but in deference to his colleagues who were of a different opinion he did not press his views. In a few words (at p. 622) he summed up what appears to us to be a powerful argument for the abolition of the rule. He said:

"What principally weighs with me in thinking that Lord Coke made a mistake of fact is my conviction that all men of business, whether merchants or tradesmen, do every day recognize and act on the ground that prompt payment of a part of their demand may be more beneficial to them than it would be to insist on their rights and enforce payment of the whole. Even where the debtor is perfectly solvent, and sure to pay at last, this often is so. Where the credit of the debtor is doubtful it must be more so."

35. In our opinion this view is as valid as it was fifty years ago, and we have no hesitation in recommending that legislation should be passed to give effect to it. This legislation would have the additional value of removing the logical difficulty involved in finding a consideration for the creditor's promises in a composition with creditors when not under seal. It would be possible to enact only that actual payment of the lesser sum should discharge the obligation to pay the greater, but we consider that it is more logical and more convenient to recommend that the greater obligation can be discharged either by a promise to pay a lesser sum or by actual payment of it, but that if the new agreement is not performed then the original obligation shall revive.

CENTRAL LONDON PROPERTY TRUST LIMITED *v.* HIGH TREES HOUSE LIMITED

England. High Court. [1947] K.B. 130

The plaintiffs leased a block of flats to the defendants, a wholly owned subsidiary, for 99 years from September 29, 1937, at a rent of £2500 a year. Only about one-third of the flats had been let by the outbreak of war in 1939 and on January 3, 1940, the plaintiffs agreed with the defendants to accept a reduced rent of £1250 a year "as from the commencement of the lease." In March of 1941 the affairs of the plaintiffs were handed over to a receiver, who after that managed the company. Only the reduced rent was paid until the receiver looked at the lease in September of 1945, when he claimed the whole amount for the quarter ending September 29, 1945, and arrears of £7916. The defendants did not pay and these "friendly proceedings" were commenced to recover £625 rent for each of the quarters ending September 29, 1945, and December 25, 1945. By early 1945 the flats were fully let.

DENNING J.: . . . If I were to consider this matter without regard to recent developments in the law, there is no doubt that had the plaintiffs claimed it, they would have been entitled to recover ground rent at the rate of £2,500 a year from the beginning of the term, since the lease under which it was payable was a lease under seal which, according to the old common law, could not be varied by an agreement by parol (whether in writing or not), but only by deed. Equity, however stepped in, and said that if there has been a variation of a deed by a simple contract (which in the case of a lease required to be in writing would have to be evidenced by writing), the courts may give effect to it as is shown in *Berry* v. *Berry*, [1929] 2 K.B. 316. That equitable doctrine, however, could hardly apply in the present case because the variation here might be said to have been made without consideration. With regard to estoppel, the representation made in relation to reducing the rent, was not a representation of an existing fact. It was a representation, in effect, as to the future, namely, that payment of the rent would not be enforced at the full rate but only at the reduced rate. Such a representation would not give rise to an estoppel, because, as was said in *Jorden* v. *Money* (1854), 5 H.L.C. 185; 10 E.R. 868, a representation as to the future must be embodied as a contract or be nothing.

But what is the position in view of developments in the law in recent years? The law has not been standing still since *Jorden* v. *Money*. There has been a series of decisions over the last fifty years which, although they are said to be cases of estoppel are not really such. They are cases in which a promise was made which was intended to create legal relations and which, to the knowledge of the person making the promise, was going to be acted on by the person to whom it was made, and which was in fact so acted on. In such cases the courts have said that the promise must be honoured. The cases to which I particularly desire to refer are: *Fenner* v. *Blake,* [1900] 1 Q.B. 426, *In re Wickham* (1917), 34 T.L.R. 158 *Re William Porter & Co., Ld.*, [1937] 2 All E.R. 361 and *Buttery* v. *Pickard*, [1946] W.N. 25. As I have said they are not cases of estoppel in the strict sense. They are really promises—promises intended to be binding, intended to be acted on, and in fact acted on. *Jorden* v. *Money* can be distinguished, because there the promisor made it clear that she did not intend to be legally bound, whereas in the cases to which I refer the proper inference was that the promisor did intend to be bound. In each case the court held the promise to be binding on the party making it, even though under the old common law it might be difficult to find any consideration for it. The courts have not gone so far as to give a cause of action in damages for the breach of such a promise, but they have refused to allow the party making it to act inconsistently with it. It is in that sense, and that sense only, that such a promise gives rise to an estoppel. The decisions are a natural result of the fusion of law and equity: for the cases of *Hughes* v. *Metropolitan Ry. Co.* (1877), 2 App. Cas. 439, *Birmingham and District Land Co.* v. *London & North Western Ry. Co.* (1888), 40 Ch. D. 268 and *Salisbury* (*Marquess*) v. Gilmore, [1942] 2 K.B. 38, afford a sufficient basis for saying that a party would not be allowed in equity to go back on such a promise. In my opinion, the time has now come for the validity of such a promise to be recognized. The logical consequence, no doubt is that a promise to accept a smaller sum in discharge of a larger sum, if acted upon, is binding notwithstanding the absence of consideration: and if the fusion of law and equity leads to this result, so much the better. That aspect was not considered in *Foakes* v. *Beer* (1884), 9 App. Cas. 605. At this time of day however, when law and equity have been joined together for over seventy years, principles must be reconsidered in the light of their combined effect. It is to be noticed that in the Sixth Interim Report of the Law Revision Committee, pars. 35, 40, it is recommended that such a promise as that to which I have referred, should be enforceable in law even though no consideration for it has been given by the promisee. It seems to me that, to the extent I have mentioned, that reult has now been achieved by the decisions of the courts.

I am satisfied that a promise such as that to which I have referred is binding and the only question remaining for my consideration is the scope of the promise in the present case. I am satisfied on all the evidence that the promise here was that the ground rent should be reduced to £1,250 a year as a temporary expedient while the block of flats was not fully, or substantially fully let, owing to the conditions prevailing. That means that the reduction in the rent applied throughout the years down to the end of 1944, but early in 1945 it is plain that the flats were fully let, and, indeed the rents received from them (many of them not being affected by the Rent Restrictions Acts), were increased beyond the figure at which it was originally contemplated that they would be let. At all events the rent from them must have been very considerable. I find that the conditions prevailing at the time when the reduction in rent was made, had completely passed away by the early months of 1945. I am satisfied that the promise was understood by all parties only to apply under the conditions prevailing at the time when it was made, namely, when the flats were only partially let, and that it did not extend any further than that. When the flats became fully let, early in 1945, the reduction ceased to apply.

In those circumstances, under the law as I hold it, it seems to me that rent is payable at the full rate for the quarters ending September 29 and December 25, 1945.

If the case had been one of estoppel, it might be said that in any event the estoppel would cease when the conditions to which the representation applied came to an end, or it also might be said that it would only come to an end on notice. In either case it is only a way of ascertaining what is the scope of the representation. I prefer to apply the principle that a promise intended to be binding, intended to be acted on and in fact acted on, is binding so far as its terms properly apply. Here it was binding as covering the period down to the early part of 1945, and as from that time full rent is payable.

I therefore give judgment for the plaintiff company for the amount claimed.

IMPERATOR REALTY CO., INC. *v*. TULL
New York. Court of Appeals. 1920. 127 N.E. 263

The parties to this action agreed in writing and under seal to exchange two parcels of land. The agreement was subject to the Statute of Frauds in force in the state of New York. On the day fixed for completion the defendant deliberately defaulted. In his defence he relied on a clause in the agreement to the effect that all requirements of the municipality of the city of New York be complied with by the seller. The plaintiff gave evidence which proved that after the making of the contract, the parties orally agreed that each would accept a deposit in a named Title Insurance Company to satisfy and discharge any municipal requirements of the other's parcel. The evidence showed that the plaintiff was, on the day for completion, ready and willing to convey, and although he could not convey free of municipal requirements, he was able and willing to deposit a sufficient amount of cash to free the property according to the oral agreement.

CARDOZO J.: . . . I think it is the law that, where contracts are subject to the statute, changes are governed by the same requirements of form as original provisions. . . . A recent decision of the House of Lords reviews the English precedents, and declares the rule anew: *Morris* v. *Baron & Co.*, [1918] A.C. 1. Oral promises are ineffective to make the contract, or any part of it, in the beginning. . . . Oral promises must also be ineffective to vary it thereafter. . . . Grant and consideration alike must find expression in a writing. . . .

A contract is the sum of its component terms. Any variation of the parts is a variation of the whole. The requirement that there shall be a writing extends to one term as to another. There can therefore be no contractual obligation when the requirement is not followed. This is not equivalent to saying that what is ineffective to create an obligation must be ineffective to discharge one. Duties imposed by law irrespective of contract may regulate the relations of parties after they have entered into a contract. There may be procurement or encouragement of a departure from literal performance which will forbid the assertion that the departure was a wrong. That principle will be found the solvent of many cases of apparent hardship. There may be an election which will preclude a forfeiture. There may be an acceptance of substituted performance, or an accord and satisfaction. . . . What there may not be, when the subject-matter is the sale of land, is an executory agreement, partly written and partly oral, to which, by force of the agreement and nothing else, the law will attach the attribute of contractual obligation.

The contract, therefore, stood unchanged. The defendant might have retracted his oral promise an hour after making it, and the plaintiff would have been helpless. He might have retracted a week before the closing, and, if a reasonable time remained within which to remove the violations, the plaintiff would still have been helpless. Retraction even at the very hour of closing might not have been too late if coupled with the offer of an extension which would neutralize the consequences of persuasion and reliance. . . .

The difficulty with the defendant's position is that he did none of these things. He had notified the plaintiff in substance that there was no need of haste in removing the violations, and that title would be accepted on deposit of adequate security for their removal in the future. He never revoked that notice. He gave no warning of a change of mind. He did not even attend the closing. He abandoned the contract, treated it as at an end, held himself absolved from all liability thereunder, because the plaintiff had acted in reliance on a consent which, even in the act of abandonment, he made no effort to recall.

I do not think we are driven by any requirement of the Statute of Frauds to sustain as lawful and effective this precipitate rescission, this attempt by an *ex post facto* revocation, after closing day had come and gone to put the plaintiff in the wrong. "He who prevents a thing from being done may not avail himself of the nonperformance, which he has, himself, occasioned, for the law says to him, in effect: 'This is your own act, and, therefore, you are not damnified.' " *Dolan* v. *Rodgers*, 149 N.Y. 489, 491, 44 N.E. 167, quoting *West* v. *Blakeway*, 2 M. & Gr. 751. The principle is fundamental and unquestioned . . . *Mackay* v. *Dick*, 6 App. Cas. 251; *New Zealand Shipping Co.* v. *Societe des Ateliers, etc.*, 1919 A.C. 1, 5. Sometimes the resulting disability has been characterized as an estoppel, sometimes as a waiver. . . . We need not go into the question of the accuracy of the description. *Ewart on Estoppel*, pp. 15, 70; *Ewart on Waiver Distributed*, pp. 23, 143, 264. The truth is that we are facing a principle more nearly ultimate than either waiver or estoppel, one with roots in the yet larger principle that no one shall be permitted to found any claim upon his own inequity or take advantage of his own wrong. . . . The Statute of Frauds was not intended to offer an asylum of escape from that fundamental principle of justice. An opposite precedent is found in *Thomson* v. *Poor*, 147 N.Y. 402, 42 N.E. 13. In deciding that case, we put aside the question whether a contract within the Statute of Frauds could be changed by spoken words. We held that there was disability, or, as we styled it, estoppel, to take advantage of an omission induced by an unrevoked consent. A like principle is recognized even in the English courts, which have gone as far as those of any jurisdiction in the strict enforcement of the statute. They hold in effect that, until consent is acted on, either party may change his mind. After it has been acted on, it stands as an excuse for nonperformance. *Hickman* v. *Haynes*, L.R. 10 C.P. 598, 605; *Ogle* v. *Lord Vane*, 2 Q.B. 275; 2 I.B. 272, *Cuff* v. *Penn*, 1 Maule & S. 21; *Morris* v. *Baron & Co.* The defendant by his conduct has brought himself within the ambit of this principle. His words did not create a new bilateral contract. They lacked the written form prescribed by statute. They did not create a unilateral contract. Aside from the same defect in form, they did not purport to offer a promise for an act. They did, however, constitute the continuing expression of a state of mind, a readiness, a desire, persisting until revoked. A seller who agrees to change the wall paper of a room ought not to lose his contract if he fails to make the change through reliance on the statement of the buyer that new paper is unnecessary and that the old is satisfactory. The buyer may change his mind again and revert to his agreement. He may not summarily rescind because of the breach which he encouraged. That is what the defendant tried to do. When he stayed away from the closing and acted upon an election to treat the contract as rescinded, he put himself in the wrong.

[The opinion of Chase J. with whom Cardozo J. concurred is omitted. Hiscock C.J., Pound and Andrews JJ. also concurred. Collin and Crane JJ. dissented.]

7. Alternatives to Consideration

Although the courts rarely discuss the purposes behind the doctrine of consideration they are usually conceded to be some proof of the deliberateness of the promisor and perhaps some evidence of the terms of the promise, both of which are strongly suggested by proof of a bargain as distinct from a bare promise. In hard cases, however, the courts have sometimes yielded, or appeared to yield, to the pressure of an interest not normally protected: an expectation interest for which no exchange has been made and no formality has been observed.

One obvious alternative that the courts might readily seize upon, is proof of the promise by writing. The only requirement of writing in the early law was that implicit in the covenant, but in 1677 the *Statute of Frauds* (see Section 10 below) was passed and it required at least some note or memorandum in writing before certain limited types of action could be brought.

PILLANS *v*. VAN MIEROP. 1765. 3 Burr. 1663; 97 E.R. 1035. Lord Mansfield: "I take it, that the ancient notion about want of consideration was for the sake of evidence only: for when it is reduced into writing, as in covenants, specialties, bonds, &c., there was no objection to the want of consideration. And the Statute of Frauds proceeded upon the same principle. In commercial cases amongst merchants, the want of consideration is not an objection." Wilmot J.: "[Consideration] was made requisite, in order to put people upon attention and reflection, and to prevent obscurity and uncertainty: and in that view, either writing or certain formalities were required. . . . Therefore it was intended to guard against rash inconsiderate declarations: but if an undertaking was entered into upon deliberation and reflection, it had activity; and such promises were binding."

RANN *v*. HUGHES. 1778. 7 T.R. 350, note (*a*); 101 E.R. 1014 (House of Lords). Skynner L.C.B.: "It is undoubtedly true that every man is by the law of nature bound to fulfil his engagements. It is equally true that the law of this country supplies no means, nor affords any remedy to compel the performance of an agreement made without sufficient consideration. Such agreement is *nudum pactum ex quo non oritur actio*; and whatsoever may be the sense of this maxim in the civil law it is in the last mentioned sense only that it is to be understood in our law . . . All contracts are by the law of England distinguished into agreement by specialty, and agreements by parol; nor is there any such third class as some of the counsel have endeavoured to maintain, as contracts in writing."

LAW REVISION COMMITTEE, SIXTH INTERIM REPORT
England. 1937. Cmnd. 5449; 15 *Can. Bar Rev*. 585

29. Basing themselves on the views of Lord Mansfield stated in *Pillans* v. *Van Mierop*, which we have quoted above, many judges and writers of textbooks (see, in particular, Professor Holdsworth, *History of English Law*, Vol. VIII, p. 48) have advocated that a promise in writing, though not under seal and not supported by consideration, should be enforceable. The only justification for the doctrine of consideration at the present day, it is said, is that it furnishes persuasive evidence of the intention of the par-

ties concerned to create a binding obligation, but it does not follow from this that consideration should be accepted as the *sole* test of such intention. This intention ought to be provable by other and equally persuasive evidence such as, e.g., the fact that the promisor has put his promise in writing. We agree with this view, and we therefore recommend that consideration should not be required in those cases in which the promise is in writing.

We must make it clear when we speak of the promise being in writing we mean the promise which is being sued upon, and we do not mean that, in the case of a contract consisting of mutual promises both the promises must be in writing.

30. On the other hand we are of the opinion that the entire promise should be in writing to bring it within the rule and that no other evidence of the promise, whether in writing or partly in writing and partly oral, should be considered sufficient. Nor do we recommend that the written promise must be signed: all that is necessary is that the Court should be satisfied that the writing (which includes typescript and print) is that of the promisor or his agent. This can be proved in the same way as any other question of fact is proved. Thus the requirement of writing which we are now recommending has nothing to do with the old "memorandum or note" of the Statute of Frauds. It differs both in purpose and in content.

This recommendation does not mean that a promise in writing will be binding in every case. It will still be necessary for the Court to find that the parties intended to create a binding obligation. Just as the presence of consideration today does not convert a social engagement into a legal contract, so the presence of writing will not convert a gratuitous promise into a legally binding one unless the Court determines that the parties intended it to be legally binding.

31. It would be possible to leave the doctrine of consideration otherwise untouched if these proposals are accepted and to defend this course on the ground that parties to an agreement can, by resorting to writing, escape any inconvenience or hardship consequent on the present state of the doctrine. But there will still continue to be promises not in writing in dealing with which the Courts might find themselves obliged to give effect to the absurdities of certain aspects of consideration. Moreover, the policy of leaving untouched rules which are admittedly inconvenient or unjust is one we should only adopt with the greatest reluctance.

NOTE. Although the early attempts to substitute writing for, or in an addition to, consideration have not yet succeeded, despite contemporary renewal of interest, the courts have not entirely ignored the hard cases caused by literal insistence on consideration. Because of the fiction upon which common law courts usually proceed, that they do not make law, but merely declare it, as if it were, in Holmes' famous words, "some brooding omnipresence in the sky," the treatment of hard cases is too often complicated by the pretence that the alternative to consideration is "really" consideration, Tom Sawyer's case knife, no less. The next cases should be examined closely to see upon what facts, actual or implied (or, supplied) by the courts, consideration is established. In the next cases consideration is somehow related to *bailment.*

WHEATLEY *v.* LOW. 1623. Cro. Jac. 668; 79 E.R. 578 (King's Bench). In an action on the case, it appeared that the plaintiff owed one J.S. £40 on a bond securing the payment of £20, and he gave the defendant £10 to be paid to J.S. for him in part payment of the debt. The defendant failed to pay and J.S. sued the plaintiff on the debt. In this action the defendant objected that there was no consideration because the defendant had not requested the plaintiff to give him the £10, and the defendant's acceptance of it to deliver to J.S. was no benefit to the defendant. The court held that "he accepted this money to deliver, and promised to deliver it, it is a good consideration to charge him."

COGGS *v.* BERNARD. 1703. 2 Ld. Raym. 909; 92 E.R. 107. The surrender of a chattel by the bailor is sufficient consideration to support a contract form of action against a gratuitous bailee for damage caused by "gross negligence."

ELSEE *v.* GATWARD. 1793. 5 T.R. 143; 101 E.R. 82. An action on the case (not *assumpsit*). A count in the declaration, that the defendant, who was a carpenter, did not perform work undertaken by him before a given day, could not be supported; but a count that the defendant used new materials instead of the old supplied by the plaintiff, thus increasing the cost, could be. ASHURST J. said in part: "The second count may be maintained, inasmuch as it appears that the defendant was retained by the plaintiffs, that he entered upon the work in consequence of that retainer, and that he did not perform it according to the terms of the retainer, by using new materials instead of old, which subjected the plaintiffs to a considerable expense. . . . The distinction is this: if a party undertake to perform work, and proceed on the employment, he makes himself liable for any misfeasance in the course of that work: but if he undertake, and do not proceed on the work, no action will lie against him for the nonfeasance. In this case, the defendant's undertaking was merely voluntary, no consideration for it being stated."

AMES, "THE HISTORY OF ASSUMPSIT." 1888. 2 *Harv. Law Rev.* 1: "The action against a bailee for negligent custody was looked upon . . . as a tort, and not as a contract. The immediate cause of the injury in the case of the bailee was, it is true, a nonfeasance, and not, as in the case of the surgeon or carpenter, a misfeasance. . . . The action against the bailee sounding in tort, consideration was no more an essential part of the count than it was in action against a surgeon . . . Oddly enough, the earliest attempts to charge bailees in assumpsit were made when the bailment was gratuitous. These attempts, just before and after 1600, were unsuccessful, because the plaintiff could not make out any consideration. The gratuitous bailment was of course not a benefit, but a burden to the defendant; and, on the other hand, it was not regarded as a detriment, but an advantage to the plaintiff. But in 1623 it was finally decided, not without a great straining, it must be conceded, of the doctrine of consideration, that a bailee might be charged in assumpsit on a gratuitous bailment." [See also Seavey, "Reliance on Gratuitous Promises" (1951), 64 *Harv.L.R.* 913.]

BAXTER *v.* JONES. 1903. 6 O.L.R. 360 (Ontario. Court of Appeal). The plaintiff asked the defendant, his fire insurance agent, through whom he was placing extra insurance on his mills and machinery, to notify the other companies who held his insurance. The defendant gratuitously agreed to do this but failed to carry out his promise. On a fire damage claim the other companies, not having been notified of the extra insurance, denied liability, but settled for $1000 less than they would have had to pay under the increased policies. This action was to recover the $1000. Held, for the plaintiff. MACLENNAN J.A.: ". . . Mr. Baxter says he went to [Mr. Jones] for this additional insurance just because his other risks were in his office, and, it is not contended that there was any consideration between the plaintiffs and the defendant in connection with the business. The only consideration in the matter was the premium which was paid to the company. As between the plaintiffs and defendant, therefore, the whole business was voluntary. It was contended that the procurement of the policy and the promise to notify the companies were one single transaction, and that having undertaken the business and performed it negligently, the defendant was responsible although there was no consideration for the contract: *Coggs* v. *Bernard* and *Elsee* v. *Gatward*." [Why should an action on the supposedly gratuitous promise of the defendant to notify the other companies be justified by the ancient law? Is it not reasonable interpretation of the facts that the plaintiff agreed to buy insurance through the defendant agent at his request so that he would earn a commission on the premium? Then could not the one act be consideration for two promises, to procure and to notify?]

DE LA BERE *v*. PEARSON, LIMITED. [1908] 1 K.B. 280 (England. Court of Appeal). The defendants published a newspaper in which "readers . . . desiring financial advice in these columns" were invited to address their queries to the City Editor. The plaintiff, a regular reader (it is not reported that he was a purchaser or subscriber), wrote asking how best he could invest £800, and specifically requesting the name of a "good stock broker." The City Editor turned the letter over to an "outside stock broker" who persuaded the plaintiff to invest £1400 with him. No shares were bought, the money instead was appropriated to the stock broker's private affairs. He was an undischarged bankrupt. The City Editor knew that the broker was not on the Stock Exchange, but did not know of his bankruptcy although he could have found out. The publishers had done what they could to help several of their readers who had lost money to the broker. The plaintiff sued the defendant publishers for damages for breach of contract to exercise due care in giving financial advice to the plaintiff. The Lord Chief Justice held that the plaintiff was entitled to recover the £1400 sent by him to the broker for investment. The defendant appealed but the appeal was dismissed. On the question of consideration, nothing appears in the report of the argument. VAUGHAN WILLIAMS L.J.: "In the first place, I think there was a contract as between the plaintiff and the defendants. The defendants advertised, offering to give advice with reference to investments. The plaintiff, accepting that offer, asked for advice, and asked for the name of a good stock broker. The questions and answers were, if the defendants chose, to be inserted in their paper as published; such publication might obviously have a tendency to increase the sale of the defendants' paper. I think that this offer, when accepted, resulted in a contract for good consideration." [What was the bargained-for exchange?]

KIRKSEY *v*. KIRKSEY
Alabama. Supreme Court. 1845. 8 Ala. 131

Assumpsit by the defendant, against the plaintiff in error. The question is present in this Court, upon a case agreed, which shows the following facts:

The plaintiff was the wife of defendant's brother, but had for some time been a widow, and had several children. In 1840, the plaintiff resided on public land, under a contract of lease, she had held over, and was comfortably settled, and would have attempted to secure the land she lived on. The defendant resided in Talladega County, some sixty, or seventy miles off. On the 10th October, 1840, he wrote to her the following letter:

"Dear sister Antillico—Much to my mortification, I heard, that brother Henry was dead, and one of his children. I know that your situation is one of grief, and difficulty. You had a bad chance before, but a great deal worse now. I should like to come and see you, but cannot with convenience at present. . . . I do not know whether you have a preference on the place you live on, or not. If you had, I would advise you to obtain your preference, and sell the land and quit the country, as I understand it is very unhealthy, and I know society is very bad. If you will come down and see me, I will let you have a place to raise your family, and I have more open land than I can tend; and on the account of your situation, and that of your family, I feel like I want you and the children to do well."

Within a month or two after the receipt of this letter, the plaintiff abandoned her possession, without disposing of it, and removed with her family, to the residence of the defendant, who put her in comfortable houses, and gave her land to cultivate for two years, at the end of which time he notified her to remove, and put her in a house, not comfortable, in the woods, which he afterwards required her to leave.

A verdict being found for the plaintiff, for two hundred dollars, the above facts were agreed, and if they will sustain the action, the judgment is to be affirmed, otherwise it is to be reversed.

ORMOND J.: The inclination of my mind, is, that the loss and inconvenience, which the plaintiff sustained in breaking up, and moving to the defendant's, a distance of sixty miles, is a sufficient consideration to support the promise, to furnish her with a house, and land to cultivate, until she could raise her family. My brothers, however, think, that the promise on the part of the defendant, was a mere gratuity, and that an action will not lie for its breach. The judgment of the Court below must therefore be reversed, pursuant to the agreement of the parties.

SKIDMORE *v.* BRADFORD 1869. L.R. 8 Eq. 134. STUART V.C.: "If Edward Bradford were a mere volunteer there is no principle on which he would be entitled to come to this Court to have the testator's intended act of bounty completed. . . . But if on the faith of the testator's representation he has involved himself in any liability, or has incurred any obligation, he cannot be regarded as a volunteer, and if so, the testator's assets are liable to make good the representation on the faith of which the nephew has entered into this contract."

RE HUDSON 1885. 54 L.J.Ch. 811. COOKSON Q.C. in the argument: ". . . the testator signed a document by which he represented that the committee of the Jubilee Fund had £20,000 coming from him at their disposal, and relying on that document they have collected and expended money and incurred liabilities, and have in fact come under an obligation to provide £3,500 more than has come to their hands. The consideration for a contract need not consist of money; if a person suffers any detriment or inconvenience, that is sufficient consideration moving from him to support a contract by which another person comes under an obligation to him."

DAVEY Q.C.: "The argument is, that that which is a mere *nudum pactum* can be converted into a contract by something subsequently done by one of the parties. But that is not so. *Hammersly* v. *De Beil*, 12 Cl.&F. 45, was for a time supposed to have established the rule that a man who changes his position in reliance on an expression of intention can insist upon effect being given to that expression of intention. But that idea is now exploded. If A represents to B that something is an existing fact, and B acts on the faith of that representation, A is bound; but that is not so where the representation is of an intention and not of a fact."

MADDISON *v.* ALDERSON 1883. 8 App.Cas. 467, 473. LORD SELBORNE: "I have always understood it to have been decided . . . that the doctrine of estoppel by representation is applicable only to representations as to some state of facts alleged to be at the time actually in existence, and not to promise *de futuro*, which, if binding at all, must be binding as contracts."

HUBBS *v.* BLACK. 1918. 44 O.L.R. 545 (Ontario. Appellate Division). One Babcock purchased a cemetery plot for $10 and when his sister, Sarah Black, the defendant, expressed her intention to buy another for herself and her husband, Babcock said to her, "You need not buy a plot; I will give you and your man a burial in the plot." She replied: "If you give me a plot, I will put a tombstone there." Sarah Black bought a tombstone with her and her husband's names cut on it, and erected it on the plot. Babcock died and the plaintiff, William Hubbs, his nephew, brought this action to compel Sarah Black to refrain from further trespassing on the plot and to remove the body of her late husband from it. He had died six months before the action was commenced. Held, for the defendant. RIDDELL J.: "Refraining from buying another plot is in itself sufficient consideration. . . . The tombstone bargain and purchase make the consideration perfect even if otherwise defective. . . . The second claim, the ghoulish demand that the corpse of the defendant's husband should be dug up and carried off the plot, of course falls with the first—not that the cold clay of the dead man has any rights, but that the defendant has the right to keep the body there until the end of time. It is reasonably certain that the plaintiff's ashes, if and when they are laid in the same plot, will not receive any pollution or injury from those of his dead uncle." [Query whether Babcock ever requested Sarah Black not to buy a plot, or to erect a tombstone. If he did not, what is the consideration for his promise? Sarah Black had been in "possession" of her part of the plot for fifteen years and Clute J. thought her possessory title was therefore valid.]

LORANGER *v.* HAINES. 1921. 50 O.L.R. 268 (Ontario. Appellate Division). Action by the purchaser for specific performance. At the trial MIDDLETON J. described the facts as follows: Loranger was a Detroit attorney; Haines was associated with him in promoting a patent. Haines bought a large parcel of land in Sandwich, Ontario. He intended to build a house on part and sell the rest. "While things were going well in the patent scheme, and millions seemed to be in sight, love and affection sprang up between these men, and Haines thought all that was necessary to secure him perfect happiness was that his friend Loranger should be ever near him, so he suggested that he would present him with a building site upon which a house might be built next his own. Loranger accepted, with some pretext of coy reluctance, and drafted an agreement in which, for 'consideration hereinafter mentioned', Haines and his wife agreed to convey . . . a parcel 84 feet in width by 182 feet in depth, to him." The agreement called for Loranger to build a "residence" on this parcel, to share in the cost of sewers, watermains and a roadway which would benefit Haines as well, and to give Haines first refusal if he should decide to sell. Loranger built, without any conveyance, a house costing $12,500, and spent $1,500 improving the land. "Things did not progress any too well in the patent paint company, and this hasty alliance has resulted in leisurely repentance. Haines now finds little pleasure in contemplating the coming and going of Loranger in his motor car from the mansion along the common drive. Loranger naturally wants his land. . . . Haines takes the position that the real consideration for his contemplated gift was the pleasure to be derived from proximity to his friend, and, this now turning out of an apple of Sodom, he ought not to be compelled to conserve it." Held, for the plaintiff. On appeal, affirmed. The things that Loranger undertook to do were a sufficient consideration. MEREDITH C.J.C.P.: "And quite apart from any question of contract, the defendant should assuredly be estopped from claiming title to and taking possession of the land upon which, not only with his knowledge, but at his request, the plaintiff has expended so much money—with the defendant's knowledge and before his eyes—on the faith of his promise to convey it to the plaintiff."

SARGENT *v.* NICHOLSON
Manitoba. Court of Appeal. 1915. 25 D.L.R. 638

CAMERON J.A.: This action is brought in the County Court of Winnipeg by the plaintiff, as assignee of the Y.M.C.A. of Winnipeg, and of the treasurer of the building fund of the association, against the defendant, to recover the sum of $200, claimed to be due on an agreement in writing, which is as follows:—

"$200. Winnipeg, November 22, 1910.

For the purpose of purchasing sites and erecting and equipping buildings for the Young Men's Christian Association, of the City of Winnipeg, and in consideration of the subscriptions of others, I promise to pay to the treasurer two hundred dollars, payable as follows: One-fourth, February 1, 1911: one-fourth, August 1, 1911: one-fourth, February 1, 1912: one-fourth, August 1, 1912. Signed: Geo. Nicholson,

Address: Clarendon Hotel."

The County Court Judge entered judgment for the plaintiff for the amount claimed and costs, and from his judgment the defendant appeals. No question is raised as to the validity of the assignment.

The evidence shews that the defendant and others were canvassed for their signatures to agreements such as that set forth, in pursuance of a plan to raise a large sum of money for the erection and equipment of a building for the purpose of the association. The above agreement, with others, came into the hands of the secretary, who notified the defendant and other subscribers accordingly. The secretary states, in his evidence, that the association, on the strength of these subscriptions, proceeded with the erection of the building and purchased materials and let contracts therefore, necessarily incurring indebtedness. The secretary says he called on the defendant about his subscription and that he admitted the same.

The main contention for the appellant is that the agreement in question is merely a voluntary promise, a promise without consideration, and therefore revocable at any time by the promisor. In support of this *Re Hudson* (1885), 54 L.J.Ch. 811, was referred to, where an attempt was made to hold executors liable in the circumstances set forth in the report. The testator verbally promised to give £20,000 to the jubilee fund of the Congregational Union of England and Wales, and also signed a form, not addressed to anyone, but headed "Congregational Union of England and Wales—jubilee fund" in these words:—

"I promise to give the amount entered above (£20,000) in equal annual instalments, and to make the first payment on the 1st October, 1881."

The testator died leaving the amount of £8,000 unpaid in his contribution. The object of the committee having the matter in charge was to raise a special fund to pay off Congregation Church debts, and to this the testator specifically confined his gift. Pearson, J., held that all there was was an intention on the part of the testator to contribute to the fund, and an intention on the part of the committee in charge to distribute it according to the purposes for which it was given and that there was no consideration that could form a contract between the parties. This case is cited in *Pollock on Contracts*, p. 177, where it is stated in a footnote that:—

"A contract may arise, however, if the subscriber authorizes a definite expenditure which is incurred in reliance upon his making it good."

It was further argued that there was no previous request on the part of the defendant that the association should proceed with the erection of the building, and therefore no consideration. But it is not difficult to hold, in this case, that, while there may not have been any express request on the part of the defendant, that the association should proceed with its programme of construction, nevertheless, that request must be taken as implied in the very nature of the transaction. The defendant practically said: "Proceed with your project and I will help you to the extent of $200."

The questions involved are discussed in *Cyc*. IX, at p. 330. It is pointed out that three views have been taken on the subject of subscriptions for charitable and similar purposes. 1. That the promises of the subscribers mutually support each other, and being for the benefit of a common beneficiary, the latter may sue thereon as one made for his benefit; 2. That the person to whom the subscription is made impliedly promises to appropriate the funds subscribed in conformity with the terms of subscription, and this implied promise forms a sufficient consideration; 3. That a subscription, like any other promise, requires a consideration, either of profit to the party making it or detriment to the party to whom made, and that it is only where some obligation is incurred, or labour or money is expended on the faith of it, that the subscriber is bound, up to which time the promise is revocable; but the subscription is binding so soon as consideration is furnished by incurring obligations or expending money. This last statement of the law is spoken of as "the prevailing view."

In *Parsons on Contracts*, p. 491, the law is thus stated:—

"Where advances have been made, or expenses or liabilities incurred by others in consequence of such subscriptions, before any notice of withdrawal, this should, on general principles, be deemed sufficient to make them obligatory, provided the advances were authorized by a fair and reasonable dependance on the subscriptions; and this rule seems to be well established."

Parsons regards the argument that one promise forms a good consideration for another as reasoning in a vicious circle. In a long footnote, commencing at p. 489, Mr. Parsons states no less than seven different ways in which courts of various States have stated the nature of the consideration upon which the promise of one who subscribes for a charitable or religious purpose has been supported. The commonest theory, he states, is that set out above. His opinion is that the promise of each subscriber cannot be held a consideration for the other, because the subscribers do not promise each other but the common beneficiary, who is usually the one that brings the action. Nor is he inclined to accept the theory of a counter promise on the part of the beneficiary as supporting the consideration inasmuch as the beneficiary only undertakes to deal with the money when it is received—an obligation binding in no greater or different degree from what the law imposes. But this theory was upheld by the Massachusetts Court in *Ladies Collegiate* v. *French*, 82 Mass. 201. I refer also to the numerous authorities on the subject generally, mentioned by Parsons in his notes to pp. 492, 493.

In *Cottage St. H. E. Church* v. *Kendall*, 121 Mass, 528, an action to enforce a subscription, Grey, C.J. says:

"Where one promises to pay another a certain sum of money for doing a particular thing, which is to be done before the money is paid, and the promisee does the thing, upon the faith of the promise, the promise, which was before a mere revocable offer, thereby becomes a complete contract, upon a consideration moving from the promisee to the promisor."

The suggestion made in *Hanson Trustees* v. *Stetson*, 22 Mass. 508, that others being led to subscribe makes a sufficient consideration, he holds is inconsistent with elementary principles.

In *Martin* v. *Meles*, 179 Mass. 114, 60 N.E.R. 397, the defendants and others agreed to contribute a certain sum to defray expenses of litigation to be incurred by a committee in defending suits arising out of certain letters patent. It was held that the defendants' promise was not void as being without consideration, since either plaintiffs' promise to conduct the litigation, or their subsequent acts, were sufficient to support the defendants' promise. In his opinion Holmes C.J., refers to the judgment in *Ladies Institute* v. *French*, as holding that the committee's promise forms the consideration, and goes on to say: "In the later Massachusetts cases more weight has been laid on the incurring of other liabilities and making expenditures, than on the counter promise of the plaintiff." referring to *Cottage St.* v. *Kendall*, and *Sherwin* v. *Fletcher*, 168 Mass. 413. In his view, the defendants' promise could be supported on either of the grounds, as above stated. He apparently inclines to the view of the counter promise as the basis, but does not deem a "more definite decision" necessary as one way or the other the defendants must pay.

In a New Zealand case, *Williams* v. *Hales*, 8 N.Z.L.R. 100, *Re Hudson*, is referred to as a case where there was nothing beyond the announcement by the testator of a present intention on his part to make an annual contribution. In the New Zealand case the action was brought by the members of the church who accepted the proposal of the defendant and another who offered to contribute £1 for every £1 subscribed by others, and it was held the proposal being accepted, the proposers were bound by their contract, a case similar to an offer by advertisement.

I refer to *Hammond* v. *Small* (1858), 16 U.C.Q.B. 371, and to *Thomas* v. *Grace* (1865), 15 U.C.C.P. 462. In this last case it was averred that [in consideration that] Watson and others would promise to pay the plaintiff certain specified sums for certain purposes, and that the plaintiff would pay $100 for the same purpose, the defendant promised to pay the plaintiff $100 therefor. The plaintiff's promise was not proved. It was argued that the underlying consideration for each signing was that the others would sign and pay. This view was apparently not accepted, but it was held that the establishment in evidence of the plaintiff's promise to pay would have been sufficient.

In *Anderson* v. *Kilborn* (1875), 22 Gr. 385, a testator told the building committee of a church to collect all they could from other sources and members, and that he would see the building paid for. Proudfoot, V. C., sustained the payment of a considerable sum by the executors, as in discharge of a debt of the testator. He discusses the question of consideration at p. 396, and says:—

"In the case before me, the testator was interested in having the chapel completed, and tells the committee to collect all they can from the other members of the church, and he would see the meeting-house paid for. The committee accordingly, relying on this promise, complete the building, incur liability for the expense, collect all they can from the other members of the church, and are out of pocket a large sum. It seems to me to bring the case within the principle contained in the cases cited, and entitled the executors to discharge the debt out of the estate."

In Berkeley St. Church v. *Stevens* (1875), 37 U.C.Q.B., 9, an action to recover on a promise to pay a contribution for rebuilding a church edifice, Richards C.J., holds, at p. 24:

"If the trustees, on the faith of the promise, and before it is withdrawn, enter into obligations on the faith of it, incur the expense of plans, and accept proposals to do the work that they were induced to undertake by promised subscriptions, then, it seems to me, that the person making the promise cannot withdraw from it; and when the work is completed, as in this case, if he does not pay he may be sued for the money so promised."

The subject is by no means free from difficulty. That is clearly indicated in the observations of the text writers, and in the judgments of the various Courts where the questions involved have come up for discussion. It must be admitted that some of the *dicta* in *Re Hudson* are of a comprehensive character. But, after all, that case involved nothing more than an announcement of the testator of an intention to make a contribution, as it is put by Richmond J., in *Williams* v. *Hales*, and by Pearson J. himself. The decision, therefore, held nothing further than the expression of such an intention was a purely voluntary announcement, and that such a declaration was revocable at any stage.

The weight of opinion seems to be, as I read the authorities, that in the case of a subscription such as this before us, when, in consequence and on the faith of it, advances have been made and liabilities incurred, before revocation, then the promise becomes binding on the subscriber. Other views have been taken of the nature of the underlying consideration in such cases, but, in my judgment, the one I have stated seems to commend itself most strongly.

Here there is no trace, indeed no allegation, of any misrepresentation or mistake. The defendant could not have been surprised that the association proceeded with the construction of the building on his assurance that he would make his promise good for that is the only reason why his subscription and the subscriptions of others were procured. He cannot now have any genuine ground of complaint, if in the circumstances, he be not now allowed to repudiate his promise.

I would dismiss the appeal with costs.

HAGGART J.A.: I agree with the reasoning of Cameron J., and with the conclusion at which he has arrived.

In addition to the grounds relied upon by him, namely, that, on the faith of the subscription in question and other promised subscriptions, the Y.M.C.A. had erected buildings and incurred obligations which formed a sufficient consideration, I would observe that, in express terms, the document provides that, "in consideration of the subscriptions of others," the defendant promises, etc.

Now, supposing there are 100 subscribers all signing similar documents, then I think the 99 other promises and subsequent payments for the accomplishment of a common object would be a sufficient consideration for each of the individual promises.

The person who drafted the subscription card intended to bind the subscriber with a legal obligation, and I think he has accomplished his object.

I would observe that, by the common consent of all the subscribers, the Y.M.C.A. was made the payee of all the subscriptions. I would dismiss the appeal.

DALHOUSIE COLLEGE *v.* BOUTILIER ESTATE

Nova Scotia. Supreme Court of Canada. [1934] S.C.R. 642

CROCKET J. delivered the judgment of the court: This appeal concerns a claim which was filed in the Probate Court for the County of Halifax, Nova Scotia, in the year 1931, by the appellant College against the respondent Estate for $5,000, stated as having been "subscribed to Dalhousie Campaign Fund (1920)," and attested by an affidavit of the College Bursar, in which it was alleged that the stated amount was justly and truly owing to the College Corporation.

The subscription, upon which the claim was founded, was obtained from the deceased on June 4, 1920, in the course of a canvass which was being conducted by a committee, known as the Dalhousie College Campaign Committee, for the raising of a fund to increase the general resources and usefulness of the institution and was in the following terms:

"For the purpose of enabling Dalhousie College to maintain and improve the efficiency of its teaching, to construct new buildings and otherwise to keep pace with the growing need of its constituency and in consideration of the subscription of others, I promise to pay to the Treasurer of Dalhousie College the sum of Five Thousand Dollars, payment as follows:

Terms of payment as per letter from Mr. Boutilier.

A. 399. Name Arthur Boutilier.

Date June 4th, 1920.

Make all cheques payable to the Treasurer of Dalhousie College."

So far as the record disclosed, the subscription was not accompanied or followed by any letter from the deceased as to the terms of payment. He died on October 29, 1928, without making any payment on account. It appears that some time after he signed the subscription form he met with severe financial reverses which prevented him from honouring his pledge. That he desired and hoped to be able to do so is evidenced by a brief letter addressed by him to the President of the University on April 12, 1926, in reply to a communication from the latter, calling his attention to the subscription and the fact that no payments had been made upon it. The deceased's letter, acknowledging receipt of the President's communication, states:

"In reply I desire to advise you that I have kept my promise to you in mind. As you are probably aware, since making my promise I suffered some rather severe reverses, but I expect before too long to be able to redeem my pledge."

The claim was contested in the Probate Court by the Estate on two grounds, viz.: that in the absence of any letter from the deceased as to terms of payment, the claimant could not recover; and that the claim was barred by the Statute of Limitations. Dr. A. Stanley MacKenzie, who had retired from the Presidency of the University after 20 years' service shortly before the trial, and others gave evidence before the Registrar of Probate. Basing himself apparently upon Dr. MacKenzie's statement that in consideration of the moneys subscribed in the campaign referred to, large sums of money were expended by the College on the objects mentioned in the subscription card, between the years 1920 and 1931, the Registrar decided that there was a good consideration for the deceased's subscription, citing *Sargent* v. *Nicholson* (1915), 25 D.L.R. 638, a decision of the Appeal Court of Manitoba, and *Y.M.C.A.* v. *Rankin* (1916), 27 D.L.R. 417, a decision of the Appeal Court of British Columbia, and that no supplementary letter was necessary to complete the agreement. He further held that the deceased's letter of April 12, 1926, constituted a sufficient acknowledgment to take the case out of the Statute of Limitations.

An appeal to the Judge of the County Court sitting as Judge of the Probate Court was dismissed, but on a further appeal to the Supreme Court of Nova Scotia *en banc*, this decision was reversed by the unanimous judgment of Chisholm, C.J., and Mellish, Graham, Caroll and Ross, JJ., on the ground that the subscription was a mere *nudum pactum*, and that nothing was shewn either by the document itself or by the evidence which imposed any binding contractual obligation upon the deceased in connection therewith. This, I take it, to be the gist of the reasons for the judgment of the Appeal Court as delivered by the learned Chief Justice, and embodies the whole problem with which we have now to deal.

There is, of course, no doubt that the deceased's subscription can be sustained as a binding promise only upon one basis, viz.: as a contract, supported by a good and sufficient consideration. The whole controversy between the parties is as to whether such a consideration is to be found, either in the subscription paper itself or in the circumstances as disclosed by the evidence.

So far as the signed subscription itself is concerned, it is contended in behalf of the appellant that it shews upon its face a good and sufficient consideration for the deceased's promise in its statement that it was given in consideration of the subscription of others. As to this, it is first to be observed that the statement of such a consideration in the subscription paper is insufficient to support the promise if, in point of law, the subscriptions of others could not provide a valid consideration therefor. I concur in the opinion of Chisholm, C.J., that the fact that others had signed separate subscription papers for the same common object or were expected so to do does not of itself constitute a legal consideration. Although there have been some cases in the United States in which a contrary opinion has been expressed, these decisions have been rejected as unsound in principle both by the Supreme Court of Massachusetts and the Court of Appeals of the State of New York. See *Cottage Street M. E. Church* v. *Kendall*, 121 Mass. 528; *Hamilton College* v. *Stewart*, (1848), 1 N.Y. Rep. 581; and *Albany Presbyterian Church* v. *Cooper*, (1889), 112 N.Y. Rep. 517. In the last mentioned case the defendant's intestate subscribed a paper with a number of others, by the terms of which they "in consideration of one dollar" to each of them paid "and of the agreements of each other" severally promised and agreed to and with the plaintiff's trustees to pay to said trustees the sums severally subscribed for the purpose of paying off a mortgage debt on the church edifice on the condition that the sum of $45,000 in the aggregate should be subscribed and paid in for such purpose within one year. The Court of Appeals held that it must reject the consideration recited in the subscription paper, the money consideration, because it had no basis in fact, and the mutual promise between the subscribers, because there was no privity of contract between the plaintiff church and the various subscribers.

A perusal of the reasons for judgment of the Appeal Court of Manitoba, as delivered by Cameron, J.A., in *Sargent* v. *Nicholson* already referred to, shews that the court also rejected the contention that it was a sufficient consideration that others were led to subscribe by the subscription of the defendant. In fact Cameron, J.A.'s opinion quotes with approval a passage from the opinion of Gray, C.J.., in *Cottage Street M. E. Church* v. *Kendall*, that such a proposition appeared to the Massachusetts Supreme Court to be "inconsistent with elementary principles." The decision of the Appeal Court of British Columbia in *Y.M.C.A.* v. *Rankin* fully adopted the opinion of Cameron, J.A., in *Sargent* v. *Nicholson*, and is certainly no authority for the acceptance of other subscriptions as a binding consideration in such a case as the present one.

The doctrine of mutual promises was also put forward on the argument as a ground upon which the deceased's promise might be held to be binding. It was suggested that the statement in the subscription of the purpose for which it was made, viz.: "of enabling Dalhousie College to maintain and improve the efficiency of its teaching, to construct new buildings and otherwise to keep pace with the growing need of its constituency," constituted an implied request on the part of the deceased to apply the promised subscription to this object and that the acceptance by the College of his promise created a contract between them, the consideration for the promise of the deceased to pay the money being the promise of the College to apply it to the purpose stated.

I cannot think that any such construction can fairly be placed upon the subscription paper and its acceptance by the College. It certainly contains no express request to the College either "to maintain and improve the efficiency of its teaching" or "to construct new buildings and otherwise to keep pace with the growing need of its constituency," but simply states that the promise to pay the $5,000 is made for the purpose of enabling the College to do so, leaving it perfectly free to pursue what had always been its aims in whatever manner its Governors should choose. No statement is made as to the amount intended to be raised for all or any of the purposes stated. No buildings of any kind are described. The construction of new buildings is merely indicated as a means of the College keeping pace with the growing need of its constituency and apparently to be undertaken as and when the Governors should in their unfettered discretion decide the erection of any one or more buildings for any purpose was necessary or desirable.

It seems to me difficult to conceive that, had the deceased actually paid the promised money, he could have safely relied upon the mere acceptance of his own promise, couched in such vague and uncertain terms regarding its purpose, as the foundation of any action against the College Corporation.

So far as I can discover, there is no English or Canadian case in which it has been authoritatively decided that a reciprocal promise on the part of the promisee may be implied from the mere fact of the acceptance by the promisee of such a subscription paper from the hands of the promisor to do the thing for which the subscription is promised. There is no doubt, of course, that an express agreement by the promisee to do certain acts in return for a subscription is a sufficient consideration for the promise of the subscriber. There may, too, be circumstances proved by evidence, outside the subscription paper itself, from which such a reciprocal promise on the part of the promisee may well be implied, but I have not been able to find any English or Canadian case where it has actually been so decided in the absense of proof that the subscriber has himself either expressly requested the promisee to undertake some definite project or personally taken such a part in connection with the projected enterprise that such a request might be inferred therefrom.

It is true that there are expressions in the judgments of the Manitoba Court of Appeal in *Sargent* v. *Nicholson* (1915), 25 D.L.R. 638, and of Wright, J., of the Supreme Court of Ontario, in *Re Loblaw*, [1933] 4 D.L.R. 264; which seems to support the proposition that a request from the promisor to the promisee may be implied from the mere statement in the subscription paper of the object for which the subscription is promised and a reciprocal promise from the promisee to the promisor to carry out that purpose from the mere fact of the acceptance of the subscription, but an examination of both these judgments makes it clear that these expressions of opinion do not touch the real ground upon which either of the decisions proceeds.

There is no doubt either that some American courts have held that by acceptance of the subscription paper itself the promisee impliedly undertakes to carry out the purpose for which the subscription is made and treated this implied promise of the promisee as the consideration for the promise to pay. This view, however, has been rejected, as pointed out in 60 Corpus Juris, 959, on the ground that the promise implied in the acceptance involves no act advantageous to the subscriber or detrimental to the beneficiary, and hence does not involve a case of mutual promises and that the duty of the payee would arise from trusteeship rather than a contractual promise, citing *Albany Presbyterian Church* v. *Cooper*, above referred to. No suggestion of mutual promises was made in the last named case, notwithstanding that the subscription there involved was expressly stated to be for the single purpose of erecting a designated church building; neither was it made in the leading New York case of *Barnes* v. *Perine*, (1854), 2 Kernan's Rep. (12 N.Y. Appeals) 18, where the subscription was also stated to be for the erection of a specific church edifice.

As to finding the consideration for the subscription outside the subscription itself, the only evidence relied upon is that of Dr. MacKenzie that increased expenditures were made by the College for the purposes stated between the years 1920 and 1931 on the strength of the subscriptions obtained in the canvass of 1920. It is contended that this fact alone constituted a consideration for the subscription and made it binding. The decisions in *Sargent* v. *Nicholson*; *Y.M.C.A.* v. *Rankin*; and the judgment of Wright, J., of the Supreme Court of Ontario, in *Re Loblaw*, adopting the two former decisions, are relied upon to sustain this proposition as well as some earlier Ontario cases and several American decisions.

There seems to be no doubt that the first three cases above mentioned unqualifiedly support the proposition relied upon, as regards at least a subscription for a single distinct and definite object, such as the erection of a designated building, whether or not the expenditure would not have been made nor any liability incurred by the promisee *but for the promise* or not. The earlier Ontario cases relied upon, however, do not appear to me to go that far. They all shew that there was either a direct personal interest on the part of the subscriber in the particular project undertaken or some personal participation in the action of the promisee as a result of which the expenditure or liability was incurred.

Regarding the American decisions, upon which *Sargent* v. *Nicholson* appears to have entirely proceeded—more particularly perhaps on the dictum of Gray, C.J., in *Cottage Street M. E. Church* v. *Kendall* than any other—it may be pointed out that there are other American cases which shew that there must be something more than the mere expenditure of money or the incurring of liability by the promisee on the faith of the promise. *Hull* v. *Pearson* (1899), 56 N.Y. Sup. 518, a decision of the Appellate Division of the Supreme Court of New York, in which many of the American cases are reviewed, should perhaps be mentioned in this regard. One W. subscribed a certain sum for the work of the German department of a theological seminary. There was no consideration expressed in the memorandum, and there was no evidence of a request on the part of W. that the work should be continued, or of any expenditures on the part of the theological seminary in reliance on such request. Such department had been continued, but there was no evidence that it would not have been continued as it had been for a series of years but for the subscription. It was held that the subscription was without consideration and could not be enforced. Woodward J., in the course of his reasons, in which the full court concurred, said:

"It is true that there is evidence that the German department has been continued, but this does not meet the requirement. There is no evidence that it would not have been continued as it had been for a series of years if the subscription of Mr. Wild had not been made."

And further:

"He undoubtedly made the subscription for the purpose of aiding in promoting the work of the German department; but, in the absence of some act or word which clearly indicated that he accompanied his subscription by a request to do something which the corporation would not have done except for his subscription, there is no such request as would justify a constructive consideration in support of this promise."

These latter dicta seem to accord more with the English decisions, which give no countenance to the principle applied in *Sargent* v. *Nicholson* and *Y.M.C.A.* v. *Rankin* and in the earlier American cases, as is so pointedly illustrated by the judgments of Pearson, J., in *In Re Hudson*, and Eve, J., in *In Re Cory*, (1912), 29 T.L.R. 18. The head note in *In Re Hudson* states:

"A. verbally promised to give £20,000 to the Jubilee Fund of the Congregational Union, and also filled up and signed a blank form of promise not addressed to anyone, but headed 'Congregational Union of England and Wales Jubilee Fund,' whereby he promised to give £20,000 in five equal annual instalments of £4,000 each, for the liquidation of chapel debts. A. paid three instalments of £4,000 to the fund within three years from the date of his promise, and then died, leaving the remaining two instalments unpaid and unprovided for.

"The Congregational Union claimed £8,000 from A.'s executors, on the ground that they had been led by A.'s promise to contribute larger sums to churches than they would otherwise have done; that money had been given and promised by other persons in consequence of A.'s promise; that grants from the Jubilee Fund had been promised to cases recommended by A.; and that churches to which promises had been made by the committee, and the committee themselves, had incurred liabilities in consequence of A.'s promise."

His Lordship held there was no consideration for the promise. "There really was," he said, "in this matter, nothing whatever in the shape of a consideration which could form a contract between the parties."

And he added:

"I am bound to say that this is an attempt to turn a charity into something very different from a charity. I think it ought to fail, and I think it does fail. I do not know to what extent a contrary decision might open a new form of posthumous charity. Posthumous charity is already bad enough, and it is quite sufficiently protected by law without establishing a new principle which would extend the doctrine in its favour far more than it has been extended or ought to be extended."

In the *Cory* case a gift of 1,000 guineas was promised to a Y.M.C.A. Association for the purpose of building a memorial hall. The sum required was £150,000, of which £85,000 had been promised or was available. The committee in charge decided not to commit themselves until they saw that their efforts to raise the whole fund were likely to prove successful. The testator, whose estate it was sought to charge, promised the 1,000 guineas and subsequently the committee felt justified in entering into a building contract, which they alleged they were largely induced to enter into by the testator's promise. Eve, J., held there was no contractual obligation between the parties and therefore no legal debt due from the estate.

Chisholm, C.J., in the case at bar, said that without any want of deference to eminent judges who have held otherwise he felt impelled to follow the decisions in the English cases. I am of opinion that he was fully justified in so doing, rather than apply the principle contended for by the appellant in reliance upon the decision in *Sargent* v. *Nicholson* based, as the latter case is, upon the decisions of United States courts, which are not only in conflict with the English cases, but with decisions of the Court of Appeals of the State of New York, as I have, I think, shewn, and which have been subjected to very strong criticism by American legal authors, notably by Prof. Williston, as the learned Chief Justice of Nova Scotia has shewn in his exhaustive and, to my mind, very convincing judgment.

To hold otherwise would be to hold that a naked, voluntary promise may be converted into a binding legal contract by the subsequent action of the promisee alone without the consent, express or implied, of the promisor. There is no evidence here which in any way involves the deceased in the carrying out of the work for which the promised subscription was made other than the signing of the subscription paper itself.

I may add that, had I come to the opposite conclusion upon the legal question involved, I should have felt impelled, as Chisholm, C.J., did, to seriously question the accuracy of the statement relied upon by the appellant that "this work was done and the increased expenditures were made on the strength of the subscriptions promised," if that statement was meant to refer to all the increased expenditures listed in the comparative statements produced by Dr. MacKenzie. The statement relied on does not profess to set out verbatim the language of the witness. The record of the evidence is apparently but a brief summary taken down by the Registrar. That the summary is inaccurate was shewn by the admission made on the argument before us that it was not $220,000 which was subscribed in all in 1920, but $2,200,000. The statement produced of expenditures on buildings, grounds and equipment since 1920 shews a grand total for the more than ten years of but $1,491,687—over $700,000 less than the aggregate of the 1920 campaign subscriptions—and this grand total includes over $400,000 for Shirriff Hall, which it is well known was the object of a special donation contributed by a wealthy lady, now deceased, as a memorial to her father. In the light of this correction it becomes quite as difficult to believe that the College Corporation, in doing "this work" and making "the increased expenditures" did so in reliance upon the deceased's subscription, as if the aggregate of the subscriptions had been but $220,000, as the Registrar took the figures down, and the Nova Scotia Supreme Court supposed, and the total expenditures $1,491,687. This evidence would assuredly seem to shut out all possibility of establishing a claim against the deceased's estate on any such ground as estoppel.

The appeal, I think, should be dismissed with costs.

QUESTION. Do you think the beneficiaries of the estate have a greater or lesser claim on the Boutilier money than the Dalhousie College?

C. A. WRIGHT, CASE COMMENT. 1935. 13 *Can Bar. Rev*. 108. [Comment on *Dalhousie College* decision.] ". . . While charity seems quite inconsistent with the bargain-theory of contracts, various attempts have been made to impose liability on a subscriber, either by the form in which the subscription card is drafted, or by a forced construction placed on such card viewed in the light of subsequent events. Courts who have done the latter, have evidently felt that the social desirability of enforcing such promises might compensate for any resulting strain on the accepted doctrines of consideration. . . .

"The Supreme Court of Canada in rejecting the argument not only brings Canadian doctrine back to the principle of the English cases, but overrules many decisions in Ontario and the Western Provinces which had proceeded on this line. In so doing, the Court was much influenced by Professor Williston's trenchant criticism of the 'promissory estoppel' doctrine as it had developed in the American Courts. It is not without interest that the American Law Institute Restatement of Contracts (for which Professor Williston was Reporter) has recently adopted as a statement of existing law, a section which supports the doctrine rejected in the present case. In so doing, however, the Restatement classifies the situations in which it applies as promises binding without consideration. Strange as this may sound to the common-law lawyer, it seems clear that there are such cases in our law. We usually cover such cases by some other form of words, however, and so do not always appreciate their inconsistency with the doctrine of consideration. In addition to the charitable subscription cases, there are other situations where, although no specific act is requested by a promisor, our courts have in effect followed the doctrine in question, and have found consideration merely because some detrimental action was taken in reliance upon a promise. The present case should draw attention to the fact that consideration exists only when certain definite acts are requested as the price of the promise. It would seem that if it is deemed desirable to enforce charitable subscriptions on the faith of which many public undertakings are begun, it would be comparatively simple to pass legislation on the subject. Particularly on the death of a promisor before payment such legislation would seem desirable, since the promisor would undoubtedly have fulfilled his promise had he lived, and in competition with other beneficiaries of the deceased's bounty, there seems no reason to reject the charity.

"Another method by which charitable subscriptions have been held binding is to imply a counter-promise to apply the money subscribed for the objects set out in the subscription card. The present decision would seem to deny the validity of such an approach on the ground that this 'duty of the payee would arise from trusteeship rather than a contractual promise.' On this view, even assuming such a promise, it would not furnish consideration as it would be merely a promise to perform an existing legal duty, and as such would furnish no detriment sufficient to support the subscription promise.

"If it is desired to turn promised 'charity' into a legal obligation, the magic device of a seal is always open to the collector. The fact that seals are practically never used would seem to support the opinion that it is not believed wise to let the subscriber think he is entering any binding obligation. If that is the impression sought to be created, there is no reason for courts to be astute in transmuting charity into a commercial transaction."

PUBLIC SUBSCRIPTIONS ACT

Nova Scotia. Revised Statutes. 1954. Chapter 242

1. Where any subscription list is opened and any subscription is made in aid of the erection of any road, bridge, place of worship, schoolhouse, or in aid of any other undertaking of public utility, or which is designated in the subscription list as, or appears therefrom to be, a public undertaking, and such undertaking is commenced, every person who has engaged by written subscription to contribute money, labour or other aid towards the undertaking, shall be held liable to perform such engagement, notwithstanding any apparent want of consideration in the agreement for the same.

2. (1) The following persons may require every person who has so subscribed to perform his engagement, that is to say

(a) where a public grant is made in aid of such undertaking, the commissioner or other person appointed to expend such grant;

(b) where no public grant is made, the person to whom the performance or superintendence of such undertaking has been entrusted, and

(c) the person who has engaged in, and is then carrying on, such undertaking.

(2) If any subscriber, after a written notice of at least one month, refuses or neglects to perform his engagement, he may be sued by such commissioner or other person in this section mentioned, or by the person to whom such subscription is payable.

(3) Nothing in this section shall be construed to bind or make liable the executors or administrators of, or the estate of, any subscriber, unless it expressly appears from the instrument subscribed by him that he intended that his estate should be liable by binding his executors or administrators.

3. All moneys or other aid so subscribed and recovered shall be applied and expended for the purpose for which the same would have been so subscribed, and for no other purpose whatever.

NOTE. The above statute was referred to by Chisholm C.J. in the *Dalhousie College* case, in the Nova Scotia Supreme Court. He said, "When the Legislature of Nova Scotia first passed—several years before confederation—the statute which is now R.S.N.S. 1923, c. 209, it is fair inference that then the opinion of this Province was that gratuitous promises could not be enforced. That is why the statute was passed." Do you agree? May the statute not have been merely declaratory of the common law?

Chisholm C.J. also said, "The statute . . . has clearly no application to a case like the present. It applies by its plain terms to public undertakings." Do you agree? Would a "school house" for which no public grant is made be included? Is a "place of worship" more or less a "public undertaking" than Dalhousie College? Does the word "public," which is used once in the title, twice in section 1 and once in section 2, have the same meaning each time it is used?

Compare section 2(3) with Dr. Wright's view about the desirability of legislation in the case of the death of a promisor since in competition with other beneficiaries there would seem to be no reason to reject the charity.

Would it be fair to infer that the Nova Scotia legislature declared the public policy of the province that charitable pledges should be enforceable? Should the Supreme Court of Canada then give effect to that policy? Prince Edward Island has an Act similar to the Nova Scotia Act. Was the Supreme Court of Canada justified in rejecting the American judicial views, the principle of two provincial statutes, and four Court of Appeal decisions?

Is it fair to argue that by using the expression "in consideration of the subscriptions of others" both the draftsman and the subscriber thought they were stating a binding promise just as much as if they had used a seal? Does the subscriber "understand" the seal better than he does the words about "consideration"? What does he intend?

How would you set up a pledge card that you wanted to be binding?

PROVINCIAL SANATORIUM *v.* McARTHUR. [1935] 4 D.L.R. 255. On September 13, 1929, defendant promised the plaintiff $200 "for the purpose of raising a fund to build and equip a Provincial Tuberculosis Sanatorium," to be paid in three equal instalments on October 13, and December 31, 1929, and March 31, 1930. The Sanatorium was built but the defendant did not pay his subscription. Apparently the defendant, a Senator, was upset by an editorial in the local paper, and told the fund committee he was through. Nevertheless the plaintiff sent a ten-day draft for $200 for the defendant's acceptance on March 1, 1931, over a year after the Sanatorium opened and was receiving patients. In the record there is mention of other letters but as they were not put in evidence the court refused to consider them. Arsenault J. gave judgment for the plaintiff. The defendant appealed to a court of two judges. Mathieson C.J.

would have dismissed the appeal, Saunders J. would have allowed it. Arsenault J. was therefore affirmed on the equal division. SAUNDERS J. found the notice required by 35 & 36 Vict. c. 28 (an Act similar to the Nova Scotia Act reproduced above) was not given by the letter and draft of March 1, and held that the case had to be decided at common law. The *Dalhousie College* case (above) "now settles this matter beyond question. . . . While I accept without reservation the judgment of the Supreme Court of Canada on this point, I consider . . . the judgment of . . . Cameron J.A. in *Sargent* v. *Nicholson* . . . more in harmony with my understanding of what constitutes a good consideration in support of a promise to make a binding contract." The defendant's offer was also to be regarded as withdrawn on September 14, 1929, before the fund campaign got well underway beginning September 16, 1929, and long before the building was started about April 1, 1930. [Query, was the consideration (in the sense of *Sargent* v. *Nicholson*) the raising of the fund or the building and equipping of the sanatorium?]

CENTRAL LONDON PROPERTY TRUST LIMITED *v.* HIGH TREES HOUSE LIMITED

England. High Court. [1947] K.B. 130

[See page 169, for the report of this case.]

COMBE *v.* COMBE

England. Court of Appeal. [1951] 1 All E.R. 767

ASQUITH L.J.: I will ask Denning, L.J., to deliver the first judgment.

DENNING L.J.: In this case a wife who has divorced her husband claims maintenance from him—not in the Divorce Court, but in the King's Bench on an agreement which is said to be embodied in letters. The parties were married in 1915. They separated in 1939. On Feb. 1, 1943, on the wife's petition, a decree *nisi* of divorce was pronounced. Shortly afterwards letters passed between the solicitors with regard to maintenance. On Feb. 9, 1943 (eight days after the decree *nisi*), the solicitor for the wife wrote to the solicitor for the husband:

"With regard to permanent maintenance, we understand that your client is prepared to make [the wife] an allowance of £100 per year free of income tax."

In answer, on Feb. 19, 1943, the husband's solicitors wrote:

"The respondent has agreed to allow your client £100 per annum free of tax."

On Aug. 11, 1943, the decree was made absolute. On Aug. 26, 1943, the wife's solicitors wrote to the husband's solicitors, saying:

"Referring to your letter of Feb. 19 last, our client would like the £100 per annum agreed to be paid to her by your client to be remitted to us on her behalf quarterly. We shall be glad if you will kindly let us have a cheque for £25 for the first quarterly instalment and make arrangements for a similar remittance to us on Nov. 11, Feb. 11, May 11, and Aug. 11 in the future."

A reply did not come for nearly two months because the husband was away, and then he himself, on Oct. 18, 1943, wrote a letter which was passed on to the wife's solicitors:

". . . regarding the sum of £25 claimed on behalf of Mrs. Combe . . . I would point out that whilst this is paid quarterly as from Aug. 11, 1943, the sum is not due till Nov. 11, 1943, as I can hardly be expected to pay this allowance in advance."

He never paid anything. The wife pressed him for payment, but she did not follow it up by an application to the divorce court. It is to be observed that she herself has an income of her own of between £700 and £800 a year, whereas her husband has only £650 a year. Eventually, after nearly seven years had passed since the decree absolute, she brought this action in the King's Bench Division on July 28, 1950, claiming £675 being arrears for six years and three quarters at £100 a year. Byrne, J., held that the first three quarterly instalments of £25 were barred by the Limitation Act, 1939, but he gave judgment for £600 in respect of the instalments which accrued within the six years before the action was brought. He held, on the authority of *Gaisberg* v. *Storr*, [1949] 2 All E.R. 411, that there was no consideration for the husband's promise to pay his wife £100 but, nevertheless, he held that the promise was enforceable on the principle stated in *Central London Property Trust, Ltd.* v. *Hightrees House, Ltd.* and *Robertson* v. *Minister of Pensions*, [1949] 2 All E.R. 767, because it was an unequivocal acceptance of liability, intended to be binding, intended to be acted on, and, in fact, acted on.

Much as I am inclined to favour the principle of the *Hightrees* case, it is important that it should not be stretched too far lest it should be endangered. It does not create new causes of action where none existed before. It only prevents a party from insisting on his strict legal rights when it would be unjust to allow him to do so, having regard to the dealings which have taken place between the parties. That is the way it was put in the case in the House of Lords which first stated the principle. . . . It is also implicit in all the modern cases in which the principle has been developed. Sometimes it is a plaintiff who is not allowed to insist on his strict legal rights. Thus, a creditor is not allowed to enforce a debt which he has deliberately agreed to waive if the debtor has carried on business or in some other way changed his position in reliance on the waiver. A landlord who has told his tenant that he can live in his cottage rent free for the rest of his life is not allowed to go back on it if the tenant stays in the house on that footing. Sometimes it is a defendant who is not allowed to insist on his strict legal rights. His conduct may be such as to debar him from relying on some condition, denying some allegation, or taking some other point in answer to the claim. Thus, a government department, who had accepted a disease as due to war service, were not allowed afterwards to say it was not, when the soldier, in reliance on the assurance, had abstained from getting further evidence about it: *Robertson* v. *Minister of Pensions*. A buyer who had waived the contract date for delivery was not allowed afterwards to set up the stipulated time as an answer to the seller. A tenant who had encroached on an adjoining building, asserting that it was comprised in the lease, was not allowed afterwards to say that it was not included in the lease. A tenant who had lived in a house rent free by permission of his landlord, thereby asserting that his original tenancy had ended, was not afterwards allowed to say that his original tenancy continued. In none of these cases was the defendant sued on the promise, assurance, or assertion as a cause of action in itself. He was sued for some other cause, for example, a pension or a breach of contract, or possession, and the promise, assurance, or assertion only played a supplementary role, though, no doubt, an important one. That is, I think, its true function. It may be part of a cause of action, but not a cause of action in itself. The principle, as I understand it, is that where one party has, by his words or conduct, made to the other a promise or assurance which was intended to affect the legal relations between them and to be acted on accordingly, then, once the other party has taken him at his word and acted on it, the one who gave the promise or assurance cannot afterwards be allowed to revert to the previous legal relations as if no such promise or assurance had been made by him, but he must accept their legal relations subject to the qualification which he himself has so introduced, even though it is not supported in point of law by any consideration, but only by his word.

Seeing that the principle never stands alone as giving a cause of action in itself, it can never do away with the necessity of consideration when that is an essential part of the cause of action. The doctrine of consideration is too firmly fixed to be overthrown by a side-wind. Its ill effects have been largely mitigated of late, but it still remains a cardinal necessity of the formation of a contract, although not of its modification or discharge. I fear that it was my failure to make this clear in *Central London Property Trust, Ltd.* v. *Hightrees House, Ltd.,* which misled Byrne, J., in the present case. He held that his wife could sue on the husband's promise as a separate and independent cause of action by itself, although, as he held, there was no consideration for it. That is not correct. The wife can only enforce the promise if there was consideration for it. That is, therefore, the real question in the case: Was there sufficient consideration to support the promise?

If it were suggested that, in return for the husband's promise, the wife expressly or impliedly promised to forbear from applying to the court for maintenance—that is, a promise in return for a promise—there would clearly be no consideration because the wife's promise would not be binding on her and, therefore, would be worth nothing. Notwithstanding her promise, she could always apply to the divorce court for maintenance—perhaps, only with leave—but nevertheless she could apply. No agreement by her could take away that right. There was, however, clearly no promise by the wife, express or implied, to forbear from applying to the court. All that happened was that she did, in fact, forbear—that is, she did an act in return for a promise. Is that sufficient consideration? Unilateral promises of this kind have long been enforced so long as the act or forbearance is done on the faith of the promise and at the request of the promisor, express or implied. The act done is then in itself sufficient consideration for the promise, even though it arises *ex post facto*, as Parker, J., pointed out in *Wigan* v. *English and Scottish Law Life Assurance Assocn.*, [1909] 1 Ch. 291 at p. 298. If the findings of Byrne, J., are accepted, they are sufficient to bring this principle into play. His finding that the husband's promise was intended to be binding, intended to be acted on, and was, in fact, acted on—although expressed to be a finding on the principle of the *Hightrees House* case—is equivalent to a finding that there was consideration within this long-settled rule, because it comes to the same thing expressed in different words: see *Oliver* v. *Davis*. My difficulty, however, is to accept the findings of Byrne, J., that the promise was "intended to be acted on." I cannot find any evidence of any intention by the husband that the wife should forbear from applying to the court for maintenance, or, in other words, any request by the husband, express or implied, that the wife should so forbear. He left her to apply, if she wished to do so. She did not do so, and I am not surprised, because it is very unlikely that the divorce court would have made any order in her favour, since she had a bigger income than her husband. Her forbearance was not intended by him, nor was it done at his request. It was, therefore, no consideration.

It may be that the wife has suffered some detriment because, after forbearing to apply to the court for seven years, she might not now get leave to apply. The court, however, is nowadays much more ready to give leave than it used to be; and I should have thought that, if the wife fell on hard times, she would still get leave. Assuming, however, that she has suffered some detriment by her forbearance, nevertheless, as the forbearance was not at the husband's request, it is no consideration.

The doctrine of consideration is sometimes said to work an injustice, but I see none in this case, nor was there any in . . . *Gaisberg* v. *Storr*. I do not think it would be right for this wife, who is better off than her husband, to take no action for six or seven years and then demand from him the whole £600. The truth is that in these maintenance cases the real remedy of the wife is, not by action in the King's Bench Division, but by application in the Divorce Court. I have always understood that no agreement for maintenance, which is made in the course of divorce proceedings prior to decree absolute, is valid unless it is sanctioned by the court—indeed, I said so in *Emanuel* v. *Emanuel*, [1945] 2 All E.R. 494. I know that such agreements are often made, but their only valid purpose is to serve as a basis for a consent application to the court. The reason why such agreements are invalid, unless approved, is because they are so apt to be collusive. Some wives are tempted to stipulate for extortionate maintenance as the price of giving their husbands their freedom. It is to remove this temptation that the sanction of the court is required. It would be a great pity if this salutory requirement could be evaded by taking action in the King's Bench Division. The Divorce Court can order the husband to pay whatever maintenance is just. Moreover, if justice so requires, it can make the order retrospective to decree absolute. That is the proper remedy of the wife here, and I do not think she has a right to any other. For these reasons I think the appeal should be allowed.

[The opinions of Asquith and Birkett L.JJ. are omitted.]

SLOAN *v*. UNION OIL COMPANY OF CANADA LTD. [1955] 4 D.L.R. 664 (British Columbia Supreme Court). Sloan was employed as credit manager of Union Oil when that Company was taken over by the British American Oil Company Limited. While he was working with Union Oil the Company announced a plan for "termination allowances." The announcement of the plan ended with the words, "The Company reserves the right to terminate or modify this Plan at any time." The plan had been modified at least in 1945, 1944, and 1943, after the first announcement put in evidence, in 1941. Sloan had been working for Union Oil for about nineteen years when he began working for B.A. Oil in September, 1945, after the takeover, and he later discovered that B.A. Oil had no termination allowance. He was told that B.A. Oil would regard unfavourably any employee of theirs who tried to collect his termination allowance from Union Oil. Sloan's lawyer advised him that he was entitled to so collect, but he took no steps until after he had left the service of B.A. Oil in 1950. He issued his writ at the last moment after very little negotiation, but so as to come within the limitation period. Held, for the plaintiff. WILSON J. found the announcements about termination allowances in 1945, just before the takeover, constituted "a promise that [the Union Oil] would, if he continued in its employment until such time, short of retirement age, as it should, without cause, dismiss him from its service, pay him certain stated sums. The offer is clear. It is equally clear that there was no verbal or written acceptance of the offer; no consideration by way of a promise that he would so continue to serve. Therefore, if a consideration moved from the plaintiff to the defendant, that consideration was not a promise but a performance, the doing of an act. For undoubtedly he did fulfil the terms of the defendant's offer, he did serve them until dismissed, and it is this, and this only, that must be relied on as consideration.

"Now he was, of course, already bound to serve them during his period of employment and the consideration for that service was his salary. But he was not bound to continue to serve them until he was dismissed. He could, at any time, have quit his employment. By staying until he was discharged he did something that was not required by his contract of employment and he says that his knowledge of the provision for a termination allowance was one of the factors which induced him to continue his employment." WILSON J. referred to the *High Trees* and *Combe* cases and remarked: "The promise or assurance here was not used, as in the *High Trees* case, *supra*, to resist a claim but to enforce one. . . . I think . . . that a majority of the Court [in the *Combe* case] would have enforced the promise to pay £100 per year if it had been coupled with a condition that the wife abstain from taking proceedings to collect alimony and if the wife had so abstained. This, of course, apart from the other point [that her agreement would have been unenforceable] which might have defeated her claim. The interesting thing here is that Denning L.J., if I read him correctly, would have enforced the husband's promise on a basis entirely unrelated to his judgment in the *High Trees House* case, and on what he calls a long settled rule that a finding that there was a promise intended to be binding, intended to be acted upon and in fact acted upon is equivalent to a finding that there was consideration. . . . I think that I must not rely on but distinguish the line of cases stemming from the *High Trees House* judgment. . . . the doctrine stated [in that case] is to be used as a shield but not as a sword. Where a sword is required there must be consideration.

"But I think it is equally clear from *Combe* v. *Combe* . . . that, as stated by Denning L.J. the sword exists if the promise was in the nature of an offer, intended to be acted upon, and in fact acted upon. . . .

"It appears to me that *Combe* v. *Combe* brings latter day English law regarding consideration into a very near relationship with American law on the same subject. I propose to quote at some length from American authorities which seem to have anticipated the reasoning in *Combe* v. *Combe*, and have the added advantage of applying that reasoning to the relation of master and servant. I first cite this general statement from *Corbin on Contracts*, vol. 1, p. 221:

" 'There are cases in which an employer has promised a "bonus", some form of benefit in addition to agreed wages or salary, on condition that the employee or employees remain in service for a stated period. In such cases the offered promise is almost always so made as to make it unnecessary for the employee to give any notice of his assent. It is sufficient that he continues in the employment as requested. It is certain that after so continuing in performance, the employer cannot withdraw or repudiate his promise without liability either in damages or for a proportionate part of the bonus promised. A unilateral contract exists.' "

RESTATEMENT OF CONTRACTS
Washington. 1932. American Law Institute

90. A promise which the promisor should reasonably expect to induce action or forbearance of a definite and substantial character on the part of the promisee and which does induce such action or forbearance is binding if injustice can be avoided only by enforcement of the promise.

[What is meant by "injustice"?]

HAWKES *v*. SAUNDERS. 1782. 1 Cowper 289; 98 E.R. 1091. LORD MANSFIELD: "[The] rule laid down at the Bar, as to what is or is not a good consideration in law, goes upon a very narrow ground indeed; namely that to make a consideration to support an assumpsit, there must be either an immediate benefit to the party promising, or a loss to the person to whom the promise was made. I cannot agree to that being the only ground of consideration sufficient to raise an assumpsit.

"Where a man is under a legal or equitable obligation to pay, the law implies a promise, though none was ever actually made. A fortiori, a legal or equitable duty is a sufficient consideration for an actual promise. Where a man is under a moral obligation, which no Court of Law or Equity can inforce, and promises, the honesty and rectitude of the thing is a consideration."

COMPARATIVE LAW NOTE. The views expressed by Lord Mansfield did not, of course, prevail. See *Eastwood* v. *Kenyon* and *Thomas* v. *Thomas*, above. But coincidental with the growth of the common law, modern systems of the civil law, having a close relation with the ancient Roman law, were developing on the Continent. It is interesting that these systems, to which reference is made in the following materials, have succeeded apparently just as well as the common law, despite the absence of any requirement of an exchange in the enforcement of promises. WARNING. It is not to be supposed that these brief glimpses of another contemporary system of law are complete enough to provide a full understanding. The glimpses are, as it were, merely an opening of the door. For a full account see Arthur von Mehren, "The French Civil Code and Contract: A Comparative Analysis of Formation and Form" (1955), 15 *Louisiana Law Review* 687.

CONRADIE *v*. ROSSOUW
South Africa. Court of Appeal. [1919] S.A.L.R. (A.D.) 279

SOLOMON A.C.J.: This is an appeal from a judgment of the Cape of Good Hope Provincial Division allowing an exception to the plaintiff's declaration in an action claiming damages for breach of contract. In his declaration the plaintiff alleges that on the 19th May, 1893, he verbally hired from the defendant a certain farm known as "Plaisance," at a rental of £30, which was subsequently raised to £100: that he has made certain improvements to the property: that subsequently on the 10th July, 1904, the defendant gave him a written option, which is annexed to the declaration, to buy the farm after the death of his wife and himself for a sum not exceeding £4,000: and that on the 4th December, 1916, the defendant by letter repudiated the aforesaid document and now refuses to recognise the said option. For this alleged breach of contract the plaintiff claims damages to the amount of £2,000.

To this declaration the defendant excepted on four grounds. On the appeal, however, the first and fourth grounds were not relied upon, so that we are now concerned with only the remaining two.

The first of these is that "the annexure A is not an option as alleged in the declaration, but at most a testamentary disposition of defendant and his said wife, which might be revoked at any time, and that the testator did thereafter execute a new will revoking the provisions contained in the said document, and that the declaration, therefore, shows no cause of action.". . . .

The exception that this document is a testamentary disposition by the defendant and his wife cannot possibly be allowed. . . .

The second ground is "that even if annexure A to the declaration is held to be an option in favour of the plaintiff, no consideration is alleged to have been given therefor, and such option could in law be revoked or cancelled at any time, and was in fact revoked or cancelled on December 4th, 1916, as appears from annexure B to the declaration."

This exception, it will be seen, raises the vexed question upon which there have been conflicting decisions in South African Courts whether consideration is necessary to support a contract. The Judges below, following a series of cases in the Cape Courts from 1874 downwards, by which they considered that they were bound, held that the absence of consideration was fatal to the plaintiff's claim, and accordingly allowed the exception.

We have, therefore, now to determine whether we should adopt the decisions of the Cape or of the Transvaal Courts, in the latter of which it was held in the case of *Rood v. Wallach* (1904), T.S. 187, that consideration is not essential to a binding contract under Roman-Dutch law, but that it is sufficient that the undertaking sued upon should have been given by the defendant seriously and deliberately and with the intention of being bound thereby.

This same question had been previously raised in this Court in the case of *Fitzgerald* v. *Green* (1914), A.D. 88, but unfortunately before judgment upon this point had been delivered, the Chief Justice (Lord De Villiers) died, and it was held that it was not competent for the remaining members to dispose of the appeal. So far, therefore, as this Court is concerned, the question is still an open one. My own views on the subject were fully expressed in the case of *Rood* v. *Wallach*, in which the Cape decisions were considered and dissented from. In the same year, however, the question was again raised in the Cape Supreme Court in the case of *Mtembu* v. *Webster*, 21 S.C. 323, when the late Lord De Villiers delivered an elaborate judgment going more fully into the authorities than he had done in any of the previous decisions. In the result he felt himself unable to concur in the views expressed by the Transvaal Court in *Rood* v. *Wallach*, and re-affirmed his opinion that valuable consideration is essential to the binding obligation of a contract. I can find nothing, however, in that judgment not in the arguments which were addressed to us in this appeal, as well as in the earlier appeal of *Fitzgerald* v. *Green*, which in any way affects the conclusion at which I arrived in the case of *Rood* v. *Wallach*. Nor do I think it necessary to repeat the reasons which I gave for coming to that conclusion, more particularly in view of the fact that the law there laid down has been practically accepted by the Privy Council in the latest case of *Jayawickreme and Another* v. *Amarasuriya* (0000), 119 L.T. 499, which was an appeal from the Supreme Court of Ceylon, a colony in which the Roman-Dutch law prevails. . . . It will be seen that this judgment does not cover the whole ground which was covered by the Transvaal Court in the case of *Rood* v. *Wallach*, but in their reasons the Privy Council seem to have fully adopted the law as there laid down. It is true that *Rood* v. *Wallach* is not expressly mentioned in the judgment, nor indeed is there the slightest reference to any of the cases in the South African Courts in which this subject has been considered. It would be impossible indeed for anyone reading the Privy Council judgment to realise what a vexed question this had been in the South African Courts for many years, and how much time and attention had been devoted to its investigation. And what is perhaps still more unsatisfactory is that in deciding a question of purely Roman-Dutch law not a single one of the many purely Roman-Dutch authorities which deal with the subject is referred to. For its judgment the Privy Council relies entirely upon the case of *Lipton* v. *Buchanan* (8 Ceylon N.L. Rep. 49) and upon a text-book, Pereira's *Laws of Ceylon*, in which is quoted with approval a passage from Morice's *English and Dutch Law* . . . : "Under Dutch law a consideration in the English sense of the word is not an essential of a contract. The nearest approach to anything of the nature is a *causa*, the presence of which is essential to a contract. The *causa* was taken from the Roman law and is perhaps the germ of the English doctrine of consideration. The meaning appears clear from Grotius' expression *reasonable cause.* There must be a reason for a contract, a rational motive for it, whether that motive is benevolence, friendship, or other proper feeling, or, on the other hand, is of a commercial or business nature. In other words, the agreement must be a deliberate serious act, not one that is irrational or motiveless. This point of view would appear very similar to that of English law in recognising the validity of a contract under seal without consideration. The solemn forms of the deed under seal are assumed to involve deliberation.". . . .

The important thing, however, is that we are agreed upon the general rule that agreements seriously and deliberately made are enforceable at law. And if the rule is correctly stated above it follows as of course that consideration in the sense of the English law is wholly foreign to the conception of a contract under Roman-Dutch law, and is quite unnecessary for the purpose of creating a binding obligation. In the case of *Rood* v. *Wallach* the Chief Justice, who was unfortunately unable to sit in this case owing to his absence in Europe, said: "The contract sued on in this case affords an excellent example of an undertaking which, though given without consideration, was deliberately entered into and was undoubtedly meant to be binding." These words are equally applicable to the present case. For we find that the document of the 10th July contains an implied promise or undertaking by the defendant that after the death of himself and his wife the plaintiff should have the right to purchase the farm "Plaisance" from his executor for a sum not exceeding £4,000: that promise was given seriously and deliberately by the defendant, who manifestly intended to be bound by it; and it is not suggested that it can be impeached on any legal ground. It follows, therefore, that the document in question is binding upon the defendant, and could not be revoked by the letter of the 4th December, 1916. The appeal must therefore be allowed, with costs, and the judgment in the court below must be altered into one dismissing the exception, with costs.

MAASDORP J.A.: . . . If we accept the nude pact as a valid contract, apart from any question of consideration, we arrive at very much the same result as was the case in the Scotch law, which there is no doubt travelled the same road as the Roman-Dutch law to reach the same end. In Bell's *Principles of the Law of Scotland* (secs. 8, 9 and 10) it is laid down that a promise is an engagement, to which no preceding consideration is by law of Scotland essential, to give, deliver or pay or do or abstain; and to a perfect engagement it is necessary that there shall be a deliberate and voluntary consent. This promise in Scotland stands in somewhat the same position as our *nudum pactum* where no consideration is given. Lord Mackenzie in his work on *Roman Law* (3.3.2) says: "In Scotland it is not essential to the validity of an obligation that it should be granted for a valuable consideration, or indeed for any consideration whatever, the rule of the civil law, that no action arises from a naked paction being rejected and an obligation undertaken deliberately, though gratuitously, being binding. This is in conformity with the canon law, by which every paction produceth action. Here we find that the Scotch law followed the same course as the Roman-Dutch law. . . .

De Villiers A.J.A.: . . . The question we have to consider goes to the root of the Law of Contract. It is one which has given rise to a good deal of confusion owing mainly to the many uses to which the one word *causa* or *oorzaak* has been put. It is, therefore, not free from difficulty. At the same time I venture to think there is not much room for doubt on the question before the Court.

In every system of law there is one question of great importance: what element or elements is it in an agreement between two or more persons which makes the law put its approval upon it as a contract? . . .

Upon the reception of the Roman law in the various States of Europe, in the law of contracts as in most other departments of law a struggle for mastery went on between it and local law and custom. It was inevitable that in the struggle between the two the Roman law of contract, the main principles of which had been developed to an extraordinary degree, should triumph. In the Netherlands the Schepenen, who were acquainted with their own laws and customs and were as a rule uneducated men, were gradually but surely replaced by *doctores juris*, learned in the laws of Justinian but who as a rule had little knowledge of the laws and customs of their native land. Among these the tendency was to regard the civil law in its entirety as law. On one point however this law suffered a signal defeat. Its maxim *ex nudo pacto non oritur actio* was not incorporated into the law of Holland, nor into that of the other leading nations of the Continent.

Before its final defeat however the rule of the civil law had weighty advocates amongst the western nations. . . .

There is force in the criticism of the late Lord de Villiers (*M'tembu* v. *Webster*, at p. 338) that the difficulty in connection with the different definitions of "reasonable cause" now approved of by the Privy Council is "that besides being somewhat inconsistent with each other, they afford so little practical assistance for the decision of concrete cases as they arise." Our authorities show it is sufficient to refer to the transaction, as is indeed our practice under the Rules of Court. The transaction will show whether the defendant entered into the agreement with the intention of binding himself, whether there is any taint of illegality or immorality, and in how far a plaintiff may on that ground be debarred from recovery. . . .

As will have been observed, I have ventured to express an opinion different from that which has been recently expressed by the Privy Council in the case of *Jayawickreme*. The decisions of that tribunal are binding upon this Court and are always, it need not be said, loyally followed. And even where they do not bind us they are often so weighty that they are of the greatest value. But I may point out that the opinion expressed was not strictly necessary for the decision of the case, and I venture to hope it is not yet too late to return to the simplicity of our law.

It was a serious mistake in English law when what was merely required as proof of a serious mind was converted into an essential of every contract. It would equally be a mistake with us to introduce for a valid contract the necessity for a *causa,* whether in the shape of a valuable consideration or any other ground of obligation.

I may perhaps be permitted to add that if those who framed the Code Civile had appreciated the fundamental principles of the law of contract as clearly as did *Grotius, Vinnius* and *Voet*, and indeed their own *Molinaeus,* they would have saved the world a nightmare of confusion from which it has not yet recovered. It is satisfactory, however, to note that the German Code (*Burgerliches Gesetzbuch fur das Deutsche Reich,* secs. 134, 138) has returned to the pristine simplicity of the law as it obtained among the foremost nations of the Continent of Europe until the Code Napoleon, under the influence of Domat and of Pothier, who unfortunately was himself influenced by Domat, led them astray. . . .

RE ROSS. [1931] 4 D.L.R. 689 (Quebec. Supreme Court of Canada). Ross promised McGill University $100,000 during its campaign for funds in 1925, and signed a promissory note for three years for that amount. In 1914 Ross had promised $150,000 to McGill for the erection and equipment of a building to be known as the Ross Memorial Gymnasium on condition that McGill apply $250,000 to the costs from Ross's late father's gift to the University in his will. When World War I intervened the building was postponed, but not abandoned. In 1920 Ross pledged $200,000 to the University, on condition that the original $150,000 be included in the larger amount, and the University was released from its obligation (if any) to apply the money to a memorial gymnasium. Ross paid $100,000 of the promised amount and then ran into financial difficulties. In 1925 he asked the University for an extension of time, which was granted, and he gave McGill the promissory note. This is a claim by the University against Ross's trustee in bankruptcy. The trustee disallowed the claim for want of consideration. Panneton J. in the Superior Court of Quebec allowed McGill's appeal. The Court of King's Bench, on the trustee's appeal, affirmed Panneton J., one judge dissenting. The trustee appealed to the Supreme Court of Canada, which unanimously agreed to dismiss the appeal. NEWCOMBE J. [speaking of the 1914 promise]: "These two paragraphs (of the admissions in the pleadings) are apt to describe an arrangement whereby Ross and the University intended to be bound, it is in terms an accepted offer, and it is not denied that he incurred an obligation to pay $150,000 upon performance of the University of stipulated conditions." Speaking of the 1920 arrangement, he said: "There was, as Sir Arthur Currie [Principal of McGill] truly stated, 'a mutual release and discharge'." Apart from the liability in the promissory note, which was governed by the *Bills of Exchange Act* and English law, the promise to the University was enforceable under Quebec law whether there was consideration or not. "It is essential therefore that an obligation shall have 'a cause from which it arises', and that a contract shall have 'a lawful cause or consideration'; but it is not meant that a contract which has a lawful cause within the meaning of Article 984 [of the Quebec *Civil Code*] shall be void or defective for lack of that which, under the English authorities, would constitute valuable consideration. . . . My interpretation of the authorities, as applicable to the facts of this case, leads me to the view that there were both lawful cause and consideration for Mr. Ross's subscription, within the meaning of the Civil Code of Quebec; and that, as to the note, by the giving of which Mr. Ross, at his urgent request, secured an extension of time limited for the payment of the balance of his subscription, the consideration was valuable and satisfied the requirements of the common law and of the Bills of Exchange Act." [Has the University a good justification for its claim to rank equally with creditors who may have restitution interests as well as the reliance interest established by the University?]

QUEBEC CIVIL CODE

984. There are four requisites to the validity of a contract:
Parties legally capable of contracting;
Their consent legally given;
Something which forms the object of the contract;
A lawful cause or consideration.

[The French *Civil Code* (Article 1108) speaks only of "a licit cause."]

989. A contract without a consideration, or with an unlawful consideration has no effect; but it is not the less valid though the consideration be not expressed or be incorrectly expressed in the writing which is evidence of the contract.

990. The consideration is unlawful when it is prohibited by law, or is contrary to good morals or public order.

[The French *Civil Code* (Articles 1131-3) speaks only of "cause."]

COMMENT ON THE ALTERNATIVES. Something of the confusion of the interests sought to be protected by the law of contract and of tort is apparent in the materials just presented. A simple problem will illustrate: A promises B $10,000 as a gift, knowing B is hard pressed for money, and needs the cash for business purposes at once. B, relying on A's promise, spends $2,000 on a car for his business. A then announces his intention not to make the gift. If reasonably forseeable detrimental reliance were a substitute for consideration and B could sue A, what should be the measure of damages? What are the policy reasons that justify protecting the expectation interest? The reliance interest? Which way should the law develop?

8. INTENTION

Several of the cases in the preceding materials carry references to the intention of the parties, or one of them, to bind himself legally, and in the civil law system *cause* may perhaps, as is suggested in *Conradie* v. *Rossouw*, be little more than a requirement that the promisor be acting seriously and deliberately. If seriousness and deliberation may be equated with intention to be bound legally, there still remains the practical problem, passed over rather lightly by De Villiers A.J.A. in that case, that the "definitions of 'reasonable cause'. . . afford so little practical assistance for the decision of concrete cases as they arise." Intention is an ambiguous word, and care must be taken that the intended meaning is understood when the word appears, as it does in this casebook, and indeed throughout the law, in a variety of different contexts where the purposes served by the word may be materially different.

If intention is to be relied upon as a test of the enforcement of promises, we should decide what kind of intention we mean. When the judges speak of a promisor who intends to be bound, are they speaking only of a promisor who, in his own mind, when he spoke, thought about the matter and consciously chose to be bound? Is it likely that a promisor thinks any more about the binding character of his promise than he does about the consequences in damages if he breaks it?

If the promisor does not have to have a conscious intention to be bound, is it sufficient that he appears to have such an intention? If so, what appearances will determine the question?

The extent to which the common law has openly acknowledged the relevance of intention is explored in the next cases. The question of "intention" will appear again in the next chapter, and later again, under other headings.

WEEKS *v*. TYBALD. 1605. Noy 11; 74 E.R. 982. In this case it would appear that the plaintiff or his father was told by the defendant, whose daughter the plaintiff later married, that "he would give £100 to him that should marry his daughter with his consent." Held, for defendant. "It is not averred nor declared to whom the words were spoken, and it is not reason that the defendant should be bound by such general words spoken to excite suitors."

STAMPER *v*. TEMPLE. 1845. 6 Humph. 113 (Tennessee). TURLEY J.: "We are constrained to believe that what is called an offered reward of $200, was nothing but a strong expression of his feelings of anxiety for the arrest of those who had so severely injured him, and this greatly increased by the distracted state of his own mind, and that of his family; as we frequently hear persons exclaim, 'Oh, I would give a thousand dollars if such an event were to happen or vice versa'. No contract can be made out of such expressions; they are evidence of strong excitement, but not of a contracting intention."

BALFOUR *v*. BALFOUR

England. Court of Appeal. [1919] 2 K.B. 571

Appeal from a decision of Sargent J., sitting as an additional judge of the King's Bench Division.

The plaintiff sued the defendant (her husband) for money which she claimed to be due in respect of an agreed allowance of £30 a month. The alleged agreement was entered into under the following circumstances. The parties were married in August, 1900. The husband, a civil engineer, had a post under the Government of Ceylon as Director of Irrigation, and after the marriage he and his wife went to Ceylon, and lived there together until the year 1915, except that in 1906 they paid a short visit to this country, and in 1908 the wife came to England in order to undergo an operation, after which she returned to Ceylon. In November, 1915, she came to this country with her husband, who was on leave. They remained in England until August, 1916, when the husband's leave was up and he had to return. The wife however on the doctor's advice remained in England. On August 8, 1916, the husband being about to sail, the alleged parol agreement sued upon was made. The plaintiff, as appeared from the judge's note, gave the following evidence of what took place: "In August, 1916, defendant's leave was up. I was suffering from rheumatic arthritis. The doctor advised my staying in England for some months, not to go out till November 4. On August 8 my husband sailed. He gave me a cheque from 8th to 31st for £24, and promised to give me £30 per month till I returned." Later on she said: "My husband and I wrote the figures together on August 8; £34 shown. Afterwards he said £30." In cross-examination she said that they had not agreed to live apart until subsequent differences arose between them, and that the agreement of August, 1916, was one which might be made by a couple in amity. Her husband in consultation with her assessed her needs, and said he would send £30 per month for her maintenance. She further said that she then understood that the defendant would be returning to England in a few months, but that he afterwards wrote to her suggesting that they had better remain apart. In March, 1918, she commenced proceedings for restitution of conjugal rights, and on July 30 she obtained a decree nisi. On December 16, 1918, she obtained an order for alimony.

SARGENT J. held that the husband was under an obligation to support his wife, and the parties had contracted that the extent of that obligation should be defined in terms of so much a month. The consent of the wife to that agreement was a sufficient consideration to constitute a contract which could be sued upon. He accordingly gave judgment for the plaintiff. The husband appealed.

ATKIN L.J.: The defence to this action on the alleged contract is that the defendant, the husband, entered into no contract with his wife, and for the determination of that it is necessary to remember that there are agreements between parties which do not result in contracts within the meaning of that term in our law. The ordinary example is where two parties agree to take a walk together, or where there is an offer and an acceptance of hospitality. Nobody would suggest in ordinary circumstances that those agreements result in what we know as a contract, and one of the most usual forms of agreement which does not constitute a contract appears to me to be the arrangements which are made between husband and wife. It is quite common, and it is the natural and inevitable result of the relationship of husband and wife, that the two spouses should make arrangements between themselves—agreements such as are in dispute in this action—agreements for allowances, by which the husband agrees that he will pay to his wife a certain sum of money, per week, or per month, or per year, to cover either her own expenses or the necessary expenses of the household and of the children of the marriage, and in which the wife promises either expressly or impliedly to apply the allowance for the purpose for which it is given. To my mind those agreements, or many of them, do not result in contracts at all, and they do not result in contracts even though there may be what as between other parties would constitute consideration for the agreement. . . . Nevertheless they are not contracts, and they are not contracts because the parties did not intend that they should be attended by legal consequences. To my mind it would be of the worst possible example to hold that agreements such as this resulted in legal obligations could be enforced in the Courts. It would mean this, that when the husband makes his wife a promise to give her an allowance of 30*s*. or £2 a week, whatever he can afford to give her, for the maintenance of the household and children, and she promises to apply it, not only could she sue him for his failure in any week to supply the allowance, but he could sue her for non-performance of the obligation, express or implied, which she had undertaken upon her part. All I can say is that the small Courts of this country would have to be multiplied one-hundredfold if these arrangements were held to result in legal obligations. They are not sued upon, not because the parties are reluctant to enforce their legal rights when the agreement is broken, but because the parties, in the inception of the arrangements, never intended that they should be sued upon. Agreements such as these are outside the realm of contracts altogether. The common law does not regulate the form of agreements between spouses. Their promises are not sealed with seals and sealing wax. The consideration that really obtains for them is that natural love and affection which counts for so little in these cold Courts. The terms may be repudiated, varied or renewed as performance proceeds or as disagreements develop, and the principles of the common law as to exoneration and discharge and accord and satisfaction are such as find no place in the domestic code. The parties themselves are advocates, judges, Courts, sheriff's officer and reporter. In respect of these promises each house is a domain into which the King's writ does not seek to run, and to which his officers do not seek to be admitted. The only question in this case is whether or not this promise was of such a class or not. For the reasons given by my brethren it appears to me to be plainly established that the promise here was not intended by either party to be attended by legal consequences. I think the onus was upon the plaintiff, and the plaintiff has not established any contract. The parties were living together, the wife intending to return. The suggestion is that the husband bound himself to pay £30 a month under all circumstances, and she bound herself to be satisfied with that sum under all circumstances, and, although she was in ill-health and alone in this country, that out of that sum she undertook to defray the whole of her medical expenses that might fall upon her, whatever might be the development of her illness, and in whatever expenses it might involve her. To my mind neither party contemplated such a result. I think that the parol evidence upon which the case turns does not establish a contract. I think that the letters do not evidence such a contract, or amplify the oral evidence which was given by the wife, which is not in dispute. For these reasons I think the judgment of the Court below was wrong and that this appeal should be allowed. Appeal allowed.

WARRINGTON L.J.: . . . These two people never intended to make a bargain which could be enforced in law. The husband expressed his intention to make this payment, and he promised to make it, and was bound in honour to continue it so long as he was in a position to do so. The wife on the other hand, so far as I can see, made no bargain at all. That is in my opinion sufficient to dispose of the case. . . .

DUKE L.J.: . . . I am satisfied that there was no consideration moving from the wife to the husband or promise by the husband to the wife which was sufficient to sustain this action founded on contract.

[Is this case decided on the basis of "consideration" or "intent to contract"?]

McGREGOR v. McGREGOR, 1888, 21 Q.B.D. 424. An action on an agreement for separation. The plaintiff and defendant, who were wife and husband, took out cross-summonses against each other for assault, but, before the hearing, an oral agreement was entered into by them by which the summonses were to be withdrawn and the plaintiff and defendant were to live separate, the defendant, the husband, agreeing to pay the plaintiff, the wife, £1 a week for maintenance, and the plaintiff agreeing to maintain herself and her children and to indemnify the defendant against any debts contracted by her. The summonses were accordingly withdrawn, and the parties thenceforward lived separate. The defendant having failed to pay the weekly allowance, the plaintiff sued him for six weeks' arrears. Held, plaintiff may recover.

SIMPKINS *v*. PAYS. [1955] 3 All E.R. 10 (England. High Court). The defendant, a lady of eighty-three, had living with her her grand-daughter and the plaintiff, who had been a boarder since 1950, in circumstances that had "some element of a family circle" about it, although the plaintiff was not related to the defendant. The three ladies competed regularly in a newspaper competition under a not very formal arrangement that if they won, they would "go shares." The defendant and her grand-daughter would put their guesses on a slip of paper and the plaintiff would fill in the coupon, putting her own guess first, then the grand-daughter's and the defendant's last. Whoever happened to have stamps handy seems to have supplied the trifling amount involved each week. When the weekly entry finally won £750 on the grand-daughter's entry, the defendant claimed the whole amount. The plaintiff sued to recover £250. Held, for the plaintiff. SELLERS J.: "It may well be there are many family associations where some sort of rough and ready statement is made which would not, in a proper estimate of the circumstances, establish a contract which was contemplated to have legal consequences, but I do not so find here. I think that in the present case there was a mutuality in the arrangement between the parties. . . . This was in the nature of a very informal syndicate so that they should all get the benefit of success."

ROSE AND FRANK COMPANY *v*. J. R. CROMPTON & BROTHERS, LIMITED

England. Court of Appeal. [1923] 2 K.B. 261

J. R. Crompton and Brothers Ltd., were English manufacturers of carbonizing tissue papers. Rose and Frank Co. were merchants in the United States handling the product of the former firm. A series of contracts had been entered into by both parties dating from 1905 which contracts having been performed, the two companies in 1913 entered into negotiations for an arrangement which was to govern future dealings.

A lengthy document was drawn up and signed by both parties in July and August, 1913. This document provided *inter alia* for the duration of the arrangement, the method of determining it, the territory covered the fixation of prices. In the body of the document there was inscribed the following paragraph:—

"This arrangement is not entered into, nor is this memorandum written, as a formal or legal agreement, and shall not be subjected to legal jurisdiction in the Law Courts either of the United States or England, but it is only a definite expression and record of the purpose and intention of the three parties concerned to which they each honourably pledge themselves with the fullest confidence, based on past business with each other, that it will be carried through by each of the . . . parties with mutual loyalty and friendly co-operation."

J. R. Crompton and Bros. Ltd., becoming dissatisfied with the manner in which the plaintiffs were conducting the business in America, refused to continue the arrangement. The plaintiffs then brought this action. At the trial Bailhache J. found for the plaintiffs, adjudging the agreement of 1913 to be a legally binding contract. The defendants appealed.

SCRUTTON L.J.: . . . Now it is quite possible for parties to come to an agreement by accepting a proposal with the result that the agreement concluded does not give rise to legal relations. The reason of this is that the parties do not intend that their agreement shall give rise to legal relations. This intention may be implied from the subject-matter of the agreement, but it may also be expressed by the parties. In social and family relations such an intention is readily implied, while in business matters the opposite result would ordinarily follow. But I can see no reason why, even in business matters, the parties should not intend to rely on each other's good faith and honour, and to exclude all idea of settling disputes by any outside intervention, with the accompanying necessity of expressing themselves so precisely that outsiders may have no difficulty in understanding what they mean. If they clearly express such an intention I can see no reason in public policy why effect should not be given to their intention.

Both legal decisions and the opinions of standard text writers support this view. . . . In the early years of the war, when a member of a club brought an action against the committee to enforce his supposed rights in a golf club competition, I nonsuited him for the same reason, that from the nature of the domestic and social relations I drew the inference that the parties did not intend legal consequences to follow from them: *Lens* v. *Devonshire Club*, (Unreported. See *The Times*, Dec. 4, 1914.) . . .

Judged by this test, I come to the same conclusion as the learned judge, that the particular clause in question shows a clear intention by the parties that the rest of their arrangement or agreement shall not affect their legal relations, or to be enforceable in a Court of Law, but in the words of the clause, shall be "only a definite expression and record of the purpose and intention of the three parties concerned to which they each honourably pledge themselves," "and shall not be subject to legal jurisdiction." If the clause stood first in the document, the intention of the parties would be exceedingly plain.

The cases cited to us to the contrary were cases in which the form of the other part of the document, as a covenant in a deed, or a grant of a right in property in legal terms, clearly showed an intention to create a legal right, and where subsequent words, purporting not to define but to negative the creation of such a right, were rejected as repugnant. In *Ellison* v. *Bignold*, (1821), 2 Jac. & W. 503; 37 E.R. 720, where the parties under seal "resolved and agreed and did by way of declaration and not of covenant spontaneously and fully consent and agree," Lord Eldon laid aside "the nonsense about agreeing and declaring without covenanting." An agreement under seal is quite inconsistent with no legal relations arising therefrom. And in the present case I think the parties, in expressing their vague and loosely worded agreement or arrangement, having expressly stated their intention that it shall not give rise to legal relations but shall depend only on mutual honourable trust. This destroys the decision of

Bailhache J. so far as it is based on the view that the document of 1913 gives rise to legal rights which can be enforced.

[The opinions of Bankes and Atkin L.JJ. are omitted and only the facts and the opinion as they relate to the validity of the written agreement as a contract are given. Insofar as the Court of Appeal declared the written agreement invalid as a contract their judgment was affirmed by the House of Lords in [1925] A.C. 445.]

JONES *v.* VERNON'S POOLS, LTD. [1938] 2 All E.R. 626 (England. King's Bench Division). The plaintiff claimed that he had accurately completed a coupon which he entered in the defendant's weekly pool on football matches, a lottery which paid large sums to the successful applicants. The defendant denied that it had received the plaintiff's coupon, and relied on a statement printed on the back of all its coupons, that "the sending in and acceptance of the coupon" should not "give rise to any legal relationship . . . but [he] binding in honour only." Held, for the defendant. ATKINSON J.: ". . . I am told that there are a million coupons received every weekend. Just imagine what it would mean if half the people in the country could come forward and suddenly claim that they had posted and sent in a coupon which they never had, bring actions against the pool alleging that, and calling evidence to prove that they had sent in a coupon containing the list of winning teams, and if Vernon's had to fight case after case to decide whether or not those coupons had been sent in and received. The business could not be carried on for a day on terms of that kind. . . . There is to be no legal liability to pay. He has got to trust to them, and, if something goes wrong, as I say, it is his funeral, and not theirs."

UPTON-ON-SEVERN RURAL DISTRICT COUNCIL *v.* POWELL
England. Court of Appeal. [1942] 1 All E.R. 220

LORD GREENE M.R.: The appellant lives at Strensham, and in November 1939 a fire broke out in his Dutch barn; he thereupon telephoned to the police inspector at the Upton police office and told him that there was a fire and asked for a fire brigade to be sent. The police inspector telephoned a garage near to the fire station at Upton, which itself had no telephone, the Upton brigade was informed and immediately went to the fire, where it remained for a long time engaged in putting it out. It so happens that, although the appellant's farm is in the Upton police district it is not in the Upton fire district. It is in the Pershore fire district, and the appellant was entitled to have the services of the Pershore fire brigade without payment. The Upton fire brigade, on the other hand, was entitled to go to a fire outside its area and, if it did so, quite apart from its statutory rights, it could make a contract that it would be entitled to repayment of its expenses.

The sole question here is whether or not any contract was made by which the Upton fire brigade rendered services on an implied promise to pay for them made by or on behalf of the appellant. It appears that some six hours after the arrival of the Upton fire brigade, the officer of the Pershore brigade arrived on the scene, but without his brigade; he pointed out to the Upton officer that it was a Pershore fire, and not an Upton fire, but the Upton fire brigade continued rendering services until the next day when the Pershore fire brigade arrived and took over. In the view that I take in this case, what happened in relation to the arrival of the Pershore officer and his conversation with the Upton officer and the subsequent arrival of the Pershore fire brigade has nothing what ever to do with the issue which we have to decide. The county court judge held that the appellant when he rang up the police inspector, asked for "the fire brigade" to be sent. He also held that the inspector summoned the local Upton fire brigade, which was perfectly natural, and that he took the order as being one for the fire brigade with which he was connected. It appears that neither the appellant, nor the police officer, nor the Upton fire brigade, until it was so informed by the Pershore officer, knew that the appellant's farm was, in fact, not in Upton area, but was in the Pershore area. The county court judge then goes on to find that the inspector passed on the order and sent his fire brigade, and that was the fire brigade, I have no doubt, which the appellant expected. The county court judge said:

"The defendant did not know that if he sent for the Pershore fire brigade what advantage he would have obtained. In my view, there is no escape from the legal liability the defendant has incurred. I think he gave the order for the fire brigade he wanted, and he got it."

Now those findings are attacked, because it is said that, as the defendant did not know what fire brigade area he was in, what he really wanted was to get the fire brigade of his area, whatever it might be. It does not seem to me that there is any justification for attacking the finding of the judge on that basis. What the defendant wanted was somebody to put out his fire, and put it out as quickly as possible, and in ringing up the Upton police he must have intended that the inspector at Upton would get the Upton fire brigade; that is the brigade which he would naturally ask for when he rang up Upton. Even apart from that, it seems to me quite sufficient if the Upton inspector reasonably so construed the request made to him, and, indeed, I do not see what other construction the inspector could have put upon that request. It follows, therefore, that on any view the appellant must be treated as having asked for the Upton fire brigade. That request having been made to the Upton fire brigade by a person who was asking for its services, does it prevent there being a contractual relationship merely because the Upton fire brigade, which responds to that request and renders the services, thinks, at the time it starts out and for a considerable time afterwards, that the farm in question is in its area, as the officer in charge appears to have thought? In my opinion, that can make no difference. The real truth of the matter is that the appellant wanted the services of Upton; he asked for the services of Upton—that is the request that he made—and Upton, in response to that request, provided those services. He cannot afterwards turn round and say: "Although I wanted Upton, although I did not concern myself when I asked for Upton as to whether I was entitled to get free services, or whether I would have to pay for them, nevertheless, when it turns out that Upton can demand payment, I am not going to pay them, because Upton were under the erroneous impression that they were rendering gratuitous services in their own area." That, it seems to me, would be quite wrong on principle. In my opinion, the county court judge's finding cannot be assailed and the appeal must be dismissed with costs.

LUXMOORE L.J.: I agree.

GODDARD L.J.: I agree.

QUESTIONS. Did Powell intend to enter into a legally binding contract here? Did the Upton brigade? Suppose Powell had merely pulled a handle on a Pershore fire brigade call box and as a result of defective wiring called the Upton instead of the Pershore brigade? Who received the unpaid-for benefit in this case, Powell or the Pershore fire brigade? Could the Upton council recover from the Pershore council in the circumstances of this case? Should the case have been decided on the basis of contract at all? For a comment, see (1942) 20 *Canadian Bar Review* 557.

POLLOCK ON CONTRACTS. 13th ed., p. 3, n. 5. "An appointment between two friends to go out for a walk or to read a book together is not an agreement in the legal sense: for it is not meant to produce, nor does it produce, any new legal duty or right or any change in existing ones. Nothing but the absence of intention seems to prevent a contract from arising in many cases of this kind. A asks B for dinner. Here is proposal of something to be done by B at A's request, namely, coming to A's house at the appointed time. If B accepts, there is in form a contract by mutual promises. . . . Why is A not legally bound to have meat and drink ready for B, so that if A had forgotten his invitation and gone elsewhere B should have a right for action? Only because no legal bond was intended by the parties."

WILLISTON ON CONTRACTS Students' ed. rev. sec. 21. "The further statement of Savigny, which has been popularized for English and American lawyers by Sir Frederick Pollock and others, that not only mental assent to a promise in fact, but an intent to form a legal relation is a requisite for the formation of contracts, . . . cannot be accepted. . . . In a system of law . . . which does not enforce promises unless some benefit to the promisor or detriment to the promisee has been asked and given, there is no propriety in such a limitation. The only proof of its existence will be the production of cases holding that, although consideration was asked and given for a promise, it is, nevertheless, not enforceable because a legal relation was not contemplated."

QUESTIONS. Do you see any point to this dispute? Would you prefer to say, with Atkin L.J., "In respect of these promises each house is a domain into which the King's writ does not seek to run"? Is it desirable to enforce "domestic arrangements"? Although Scrutton L.J. appears to agree with *Balfour* v. *Balfour*, see his observation in *Czarnikow* v. *Roth, Schmidt & Co.* (reproduced in the next section), "There must be no Alsatia in England where the King's writ does not run." Despite the *Upton-on-Severn* case, can it be said that in Anglo-Canadian law intention is still an element of a contract? See the next cases for some Canadian views.

MOONEY *v.* GROUT

Ontario. High Court of Justice. Divisional Court. 1903. 6 O.L.R. 521

The action was brought to recover for services rendered by the plaintiff to her sister Frances Mooney, deceased, the defendant being the executor of her will.

The plaintiff was a married woman living with her husband at East Hawkesbury; the deceased sister was a widow without children living by herself at Vankleek Hill, five miles from the plaintiff's residence. On the 2nd of November, 1901, the deceased having been taken ill, sent for the plaintiff to come to her to nurse her. The plaintiff went and found her in bed, and remained with her at her request, nursing her at the house of the deceased until the 12th of May following, with some short intermissions. On the 12th of May the plaintiff being unable to remain away from her own home any longer, the deceased was moved to the plaintiff's house, where she remained until she died on the 31st of July, 1902. During all this time the plaintiff nursed her and cared for her in every way. The work she was obliged to do was of a most disagreeable, dangerous, and trying character owing to the nature of the malady—cancer of the womb—from which the deceased was suffering.

The deceased was, at the time of her death, the owner of a small house and lot worth about $1,800, of some household furniture of small value, and of about $1,250 in cash and mortgages.

She had made a will in February, 1901, and another in February, 1902, in each of which she had given to the plaintiff the house and lot for her life, and the income of the money also for her life. She had told the plaintiff some months before her illness that she had made a will, and the plaintiff swore that she understood that she was to have the house and lot for her life, but that the money was to be hers absolutely. The plaintiff swore that, believing this to be the case, she had not intended to make any charge for her services to the deceased, to whom she was much attached, but that, after the death of the deceased, upon hearing the will read, she was very greatly surprised, and determined to claim to be paid.

MEREDITH C.J.: The law applicable to such cases as this is well settled. Where services are performed between strangers without any agreement as to compensation, the law implies that a reasonable compensation is to be paid, from the fact of the services having been rendered at the request of the person to whom they have been rendered. But where the parties are in such relationship to one another as were these two sisters, the law is that no such presumption arises, and the duty rests upon the person who seeks pay for services rendered under those circumstances to prove a contract express or implied.

Now, here it is perfectly clear that there never was any idea on the part of the plaintiff that she was to be paid for her services. We have her own repudiation of that repeated from time to time. She says very frankly that she became very indignant when she found that the terms of the will were, as she thought, most unjust to her, and not what her sister had told her were its terms, and that she then for the first time made up her mind to make a claim for her services. That indicates to me that there was no such relationship as that of master and servant, and nothing from which there could be inferred a promise to pay. I think it was plainly a case where the one sister was moved, largely by affection, but probably also, for even the best of us are not unaffected by material considerations, the fact being that the other sister had no other relatives to whom to leave her property, by the expectation that the property would come to her, or the greater part of it. But there was no promise on the part of the sister of the plaintiff to make the will. The plaintiff had every confidence in her sister, and was content to rely on whatever she would do; believing, as she says, that she would give her the house for her life, and the personal property absolutely. . . .

On the finding I make, therefore, I dismiss the action without costs.

[An appeal was argued before the Divisional Court, Street and Britton JJ.]

STREET J. delivered the judgment of the Court: After a great deal of consideration, I find myself unable to come to the conclusion that the result arrived at by the Chief Justice can be interfered with.

It is true that the plaintiff and her sister, the deceased, each had her separate household at the time the plaintiff was requested by the deceased to take care of her in her illness. Under these circumstances the presumption, which arises in the case of services rendered by members of a family living together to one another, that such services are not to be paid for does not, I think, arise. But the presumption that services rendered by one sister to another when they are not living together as members of the same family are to be paid for is much more easily rebutted than it would be if the services had been rendered to a stranger. In the present case the plaintiff says that until after the death of her sister, and until she heard the contents of her will, she had no intention of making a charge for her services. Nor is there any reason to suppose that the deceased ever thought that the plaintiff expected to be paid. If either of them had supposed that the plaintiff was working for hire, it is but reasonable to think that the matter would have been mentioned during her nine months' attendance on the deceased. In the absence of any offer of, or request for payment during all that time, I think we may properly assume under the circumstances an understanding on the part of both that the provision in the will of the deceased in favour of the plaintiff was to be her remuneration for her trouble, and that no charge would be made. This being the case, there was no contract while the services were being rendered, and the plaintiff had no right to claim pay for them upon finding that the income of the money only, and not the principal, had been bequeathed to her.

In my opinion, the appeal should be dismissed with costs.

QUESTIONS. What is the purpose of the *category* of husband and wife, sisters living together, mother and daughter, etc. Suppose the plaintiff had been an adopted daughter by then married? An intimate friend? Suppose the plaintiff's assistance were shown to be of no real value? Suppose the plaintiff missed an opportunity to marry while she was nursing her sister? Suppose plaintiff was already married to a wealthy man? See generally, Havighurst, "Services in the Home" (1932), 41 *Yale Law Journal* 386.

Do Street and Britton JJ. agree with Meredith C.J. in their reasoning? What is the effect of the difference between them? What is a "presumption"?

THE EVIDENCE ACT

Ontario. Revised Statutes. 1960. Chapter 125

14. In an action by or against the heirs, next of kin, executors, administrators or assigns of a deceased person, an opposite or interested party shall not obtain a verdict, judgment or decision on his own evidence in respect of any matter occurring before the death of the deceased person, unless such evidence is corroborated by some other material evidence.

In some American jurisdictions the plaintiff is denied the right to testify at all, on the theory that as the deceased cannot answer it would be unfair to let plaintiff be heard. However his claim may be proved by other evidence, of course.

SOLDIERS MEMORIAL HOSPITAL *v*. SANFORD

Nova Scotia. Supreme Court *en banc*. [1934] 2 D.L.R. 334

DOULL J.: The defendant interfered in a fight between his father and some preventive officers in the County of Annapolis in the year 1928 and got badly used up in consequence. He was bruised about the head and was shot in the groin. In the end the officers were the victors and the defendant was being taken to gaol when some one suggested that the hospital was a more suitable place for him than the gaol, and he was taken to the hospital at Middleton, owned and operated by the plaintiff.

There is some doubt as to whether he was conscious or unconscious at the time he entered the hospital. In the evidence he was asked: "Q. Were you conscious when you were injured? A. Yes to a certain extent. Q. Did you know that you were being taken to the Soldiers Memorial Hospital? A. Yes sir."

On the other hand, his own counsel indicates that he was unconscious: "Q. And by the time you got to the Middleton Hospital you were unconscious? A. Yes."

Conscious or unconscious, in the view I take of the matter, the plaintiff can only recover on the ground of a contract, express or implied. There is no express contract proven although the defendant does not expressly deny that he may have promised to pay.

The plaintiff must therefore succeed if at all by virtue of an implied contract.

Contracts to pay in favour of physicians and surgeons are implied as against the patient in cases where in an emergency the services become necessary and it is unreasonable or impossible to wait to make a bargain. There are numerous American authorities which on this point we would doubtless follow; for example, *Edson* v. *Hammond* (1911), 142 N.Y. App. Div. 693, where a physician rendered service to a person injured by an accident which made him unconscious or otherwise incapable of making a request for or expressing consent to the services, the law will imply a promise from him who received the benefit of the services, to pay for them.

There are, however, limits to this doctrine; thus if a family physician is provided, another who happens to be called by one of the children would not be able to collect from the head of the family who already had provided for necessary attendance. Nor if there were any other means of attendance at hand, would the emergency be held to exist.

The liability depends in these cases on a contract implied by the law for one who is not capable for the time being of contracting for himself and implies for the benefit of the attending physician a promise to pay.

If the police had found the defendant on the road and had taken him to the hospital to save his life, I would have had no hesitation about the matter: I would have held that a contract was implied which would fix upon the defendant the same liability that is fixed on a patient in favour of a doctor in a similar case.

The doubt about the matter arises from the fact that the defendant was in the custody of the preventive officers or of some officers of the law. They were controlling his actions and were taking him either to gaol or to hospital not only without his consent but doubtless in active opposition to his wishes.

The sole question for decision is whether the law will imply a contract as against an injured man in a case where he has no freedom of physical action and is in the custody of the law. The cases cited throw no light upon that proposition. It does not help us to find that some other party is liable; for several may be liable. The only question is whether the injured prisoner is liable.

Probably we may decide this best if we try to ascertain the basis of the liability of persons who are treated in an emergency. The doctor knows very well that the bystander who calls him does not intend to make himself liable, he knows that he has not time to make a bargain with the man, or even to ask him if he wishes his services, therefore the law implies a contract in favour of the doctor as against the man.

The liability implied in these cases has a twofold significance. It fixes with liability the man who cannot act for himself and it protects from liability the good samaritan who calls the physician, or the hospital ambulance, but does not wish to be liable for the expense involved. The hospital knows very well that the bystander is only the voluntary messenger of the injured man and that it can not charge such messenger unless he definitely assumes liability.

Do the same principles apply when a man bound with handcuffs and under arrest is brought in? The police officers are not the ordinary bystander; they are in charge of the man, themselves charged with the duty of keeping him safely until he is delivered in due course of law. Under these circumstances is the hospital justified in assuming that when the police officer calls up and makes arrangement for taking care of a wounded prisoner that he is acting as a voluntary agent and that the liability is implied as being the prisoner's?

I think that the circumstances of this case where the prisoner was taken handcuffed and in custody and where he continued as a prisoner during his term in the hospital and thereafter are sufficient to rebut the presumption which arises in the case of a stranger picking a man up on the road and that the implication is that the officers were looking after the defendant in the course of their duty to safely keep and deliver him or bring him before a Magistrate in accordance with law.

The appeal therefore in my opinion fails and should be dismissed with costs.

Ross J., who dissented, said in part: It seems to me that we cannot accurately discuss the liability as arising only on an implied contract with a man in an unconscious state. Cotton, L.J., in *Re Rhodes, Rhodes* v. *Rhodes* (1890), 44 Ch. D. 94, puts the liability on the proper basis, when he says that it is not founded on an implied contract but on an obligation imposed by law, on the person served. True, he was dealing with the case of a lunatic, but the same rule should apply to a person in the condition in which defendant was on his arrival at the hospital.

It is urged however that the defendant was under arrest. I do not think it affects the case. It may well be that the obligation imposed by law is founded on some broad principle of public policy. If two things combine then the liability attaches. First, the emergency or immediate necessity, and secondly, the services rendered.

Here we have the emergency, and the prompt, and no doubt effective treatment by the hospital. I entirely agree with the Court of Appeal in Manitoba (*Matheson* v. *Smiley,* [1932] 2 D.L.R. 787) that the attitude of the person in extremity cannot be considered. The defendant was shot in the groin, and bleeding freely, besides having other minor injuries, and his protests, even if made, should not prevent sensible officers from doing the obviously sensible and prudent thing under the circumstances.

Again, even if the liability is founded on contract I do not care to subscribe to the proposition that a man is incapable of contracting, merely because his freedom of physical action is restricted. It may limit his opportunity, but not his capacity.

No good purpose can be served by further discussing the matter, because this is a dissenting judgment and cannot possibly have any effect, but with the greatest respect for the opinion of my brethren, I wish to expressly dissent from a judgment of this Court that would relieve the defendant from the primary obligation of paying for necessary services rendered to him by the hospital in an emergency case, simply because he was under arrest; especially when such emergency and arrest were both the result of his own misconduct. As I have already pointed out, the money claim is insignificant, but the decision of the Court may have far reaching results.

I think the appeal should be allowed with costs and the judgment of the Municipal Court restored.

[The judgment of Graham J., who agreed with Doull J., is omitted. Carroll J. agreed with Doull J. in dismissing the appeal from Grierson Co.Ct.J. whose decision is also reported.]

ATTORNEY GENERAL OF BRITISH COLUMBIA *v.* ESQUIMALT & NANAIMO RAILWAY COMPANY

British Columbia. Privy Council. [1950] 1 D.L.R. 305

In August, 1883, arrangements were made by Canada, British Columbia and the Dunsmuir group of contractors respecting the building of a railway on Vancouver Island to run between Nanaimo and Esquimalt. British Columbia agreed to convey the "Island Railway Belt" through which the railway was to run, to Canada. A company was to be incorporated to succeed the Dunsmuir group to build and run the railway and the Belt was to be transferred to the company by Canada as soon as the railway was satisfactorily completed. The Company was to be incorporated by the *Settlement Act,* 1884 (B.C.) c. 14, a draft of which was approved by representatives of Canada, British Columbia and the Dunsmuir group in August. Canada agreed directly with the Dunsmuir group to so convey the Belt. The *Settlement Act* was passed in December of 1883 and incorporated the Company. Section 22 provided: "The lands to be acquired by the company from the Dominion Government for the construction of the Railway shall not be subject to taxation, unless and until the same are used by the Company for other than railroad purposes, or leased, occupied, sold, or alienated." In April, 1887, the Belt was conveyed, subject to the Act, to the Company.

In 1945 the Hon. Mr. Justice Sloan of British Columbia issued a report made under the *Public Inquiries Act* on "Forest Finance and Revenue to the Crown from Forest Reserves," and he recommended that a "severance tax" be charged upon timber cut from the Belt and sold by the Company. He found that "there never was any contractual relationship between the Provincial Government and the contractors or the Railway Company in relation to the transfer of the Railway Belt to the Railway Company." This case arose on a reference to the British Columbia Court of Appeal under the *Constitutional Questions Determination Act* to determine, among other things, whether there was such a contract.

LORD GREENE: . . . The nature and object of the contention that a contractual relationship came into existence between the Province (*i.e.*, the Crown in right of the Province) and the contractors and the Railway Company (either as successors to the contractors or independently in their own right) whereby the Railway Company became contractually entitled to have and keep the benefit of the tax exemption contained in s. 22 is clearly explained in the following extract from the judgment of O'Halloran J.A. in the Court of Appeal: "We are not concerned with s. 22 in its purely statutory status. It stands as a statutory provision in the same way as any other statutory provision, *viz.*, until it is amended or repealed. But the contract argument aims to give it more lasting virtue, *viz.*, that it reflects a contract between the Province and the contractors that it would not be amended or repealed except as a breach of contract with consequential remedies to the contractors."

In the Court of Appeal O'Halloran J.A. came to the conclusion that there was no contractual relationship between the Province and the contractors or the Railway Company. Their Lordships agree with this conclusion and with the reasoning upon which it is based. Bird J.A. was of the same opinion as O'Halloran J.A. Sidney Smith J.A. dissented. In the Supreme Court all members agreed that there was no contract between the Province and the contractors. But they all took the view that a contract (or its practical equivalent) between the Province and the Railway Company had been established.

Having regard to the concurrent decisions in the Canadian Courts that there was no contractual relationship between the Province and the contractors their Lordships do not propose to do more than make some general observations on that topic. Some of them are not without relevance, in their Lordships' view, to the matter of the alleged contract between the Province and the Railway Company.

Their Lordships think it right to state clearly that they must not be understood as expressing an opinion as to any moral right to complain of the proposed taxation which the Railway Company may conceive itself to have. No such matter is raised or indeed could be raised by any of the questions referred which are concerned solely with the legal position. Not only must moral and political considerations be rigidly excluded but the dividing line between rights and liabilities created by legislation and those created by contract must not be blurred.

Besides involving an offer and an acceptance (either of which may in appropriate cases be expressed in words or by conduct) and the presence of consideration a contract can only come into existence if an intention to contract is present. That negotiations took place, that there were three parties who took part in them, *viz.*, the Dominion Government, the Provincial Government and the contractors, that the negotiations resulted in a definite arrangement under which each party was to play and did play its appointed part—all these matters are beyond dispute. Agreements were entered into in contractual form between the Province and the Dominion and between the Dominion and the contractors. But there was no such agreement between the Province and the contractors and the whole case under this head rests on the contention that such an agreement ought to be inferred from the documents and the acts of the parties. That the enactment of the *Settlement Act* and in particular of s. 22 thereof was an essential part of the arrangement is again obvious. The whole arrangement would have broken down if the Provincial Legislature had refused to enact that section. But much more than this would be needed before the existence of a contractual obligation to procure its enactment could be inferred. Even more difficult to infer in their Lordships' opinion would be any intention of a contractual nature that the section when enacted should remain for all time upon the statute book. If a promise that it should be put upon the statute book be assumed it was a promise by the Crown that there should be enacted something which in its very nature as legislation was susceptible of repeal or amendment by the Legislature. The difficulties in the way of extending such a promise so as to include an undertaking by the executive which would be broken if it were thought desirable in the public interest to introduce amending legislation on some subsequent occasion appear to their Lordships to be, for constitutional reasons alone, insurmountable.

But, it is asked, would businessmen have been content with an arrangement which on a vital matter gave them security of so precarious a nature? It appears to their Lordships that one answer to this criticism would be that if businessmen had desired to have a binding contractual promise of the kind suggested—a promise indeed of a character which (to say the least) no Government would be likely to give with alacrity—they would have obtained a written contract to that effect and not left it to be merely inferred. Moreover the lack of security must not in their Lordships' view be exaggerated. To have on the statute book a section in the terms of s. 22 was in itself an important practical safeguard. What the contractors wanted and what from the business point of view they were entitled to ask for was the enactment of the *Settlement Act* containing s. 22. This they obtained. But they obtained it not by virtue of any contractual right binding on the Province but as a mere business matter of fact. Their Lordships find no reason for inferring in addition any contractual right to call for what they in fact obtained, still less a contractual right of such a nature as would give them in law a right to complain of breach of contract if legislation diminishing or taking away the tax exemption conferred by s. 22 were to be passed at a later date.

This view is confirmed by the fact that in the case of the Dominion a written contract (the construction contract of August 20, 1883) was entered into with the contractors. This alone makes it impossible in their Lordships' opinion to imply a contract between the contractors and the Province, a contract not contained in any writing and of which there is no affirmative evidence. This written contract with the Dominion is one on which alone the contractors might be expected to have relied without requiring it to be supplemented by a further contract with the Province.

As in their Lordships' opinion no such contractual relationship as is suggested ever came into existence as between the Province and the contractors it follows that no such relationship could be claimed by the Railway Company to exist for its benefit by reason of its succession to the rights of the contractors.

The Supreme Court however thought that a contract (or what in practice was its equivalent) between the Province and the Railway Company in its own right and not as successor to the contractors ought to be inferred. Kerwin and Locke JJ. with whom Rand J. was in substantial agreement thought that the Province, by holding out the promised tax exemption as an inducement to the Railway Company, must be taken to have agreed that it should enjoy the exemption as a matter of contractual right once the railway was constructed. On this view s. 22 is to be regarded as an offer. In the words of Rand J. [p. 375 D.L.R., p. 78 C.R.T.C.] "A statutory benefit arising through the performance of conditions laid down in the statute as the *quid pro quo* of the benefit, is a contractual right: and upon performance by the company here, the engagement became binding upon the Crown." Their Lordships are unable to accept the conclusions of these learned Judges. They cannot agree that a section of an Act of Parliament is to be regarded as an offer by the executive; and there can be no question of an offer by the Legislature which no one suggests could become a party to the supposed contract. Legislation and contract are entirely different methods of creating rights and liabilities and is it essential to keep them distinct. Parliament could no doubt enact that a section of a statute should have the force of an offer by the Crown capable of being accepted by a subject. But here it has not done so and it is impossible to place such a construction on the simple language of s. 22. The Railway Company no doubt did rely on s. 22: but the only inference which in their Lordships' opinion can be drawn is that it relied on the section as an existing and valuable piece of legislation and not as an offer capable of being accepted so as to bring into existence a contract binding on the Crown. . . .

[That part of the decision relating to the validity of the tax is omitted. The appeal was allowed in part.]

QUESTIONS ON LEGAL METHOD. Why must not only moral and political considerations be rigidly excluded but the dividing line between rights and liabilities created by legislation and those created by contract not be blurred? Why the exclusion? What is the dividing line?

9. Illegal or Immoral Contracts

This section exposes part of the "inarticulate major premise" said to underlie every judicial decision. Here is an illustration of the rare cases where the common law courts conceive of their task as the weighing of conflicting social policies. The cases reported bristle with problems and they hardly need any introduction in a preliminary note. It is sufficient to remind you that by no means all the classes of case where an otherwise sufficient contract has been held to be illegal because it is against "public policy" are illustrated. A few cases have been selected, instead, to bring out the difficulty of applying social concepts to complex economic and commercial situations in a law court; to show how some contracts abuse the administration of justice; and above all, to enquire into the difficult problem of logic, justice and experience: what effect ought to be given to an illegal contract?

Obviously the traditional English attitude toward public policy in the law is most unsympathetic, as the following judicial observations make clear. Yet can a legal system ignore both consciously and unconsciously the policy problems in the law? If it cannot, is it more desirable that these questions remain undiscussed in open court or is it, as Thorson P. said in another connection in *The Queen* v. *Supertest Petroleum Corp. Ltd.*, [1954] 3 D.L.R. 245, 250, quoting Joseph H. Choate, "only on the anvil of discussion that the spark of truth can be struck out"?

The "paramount public policy," that is, the policy that the courts usually assume without discussion, is well expressed by Jessel M.R., in *Printing & Numerical Registering Co.* v. *Sampson* (1875), L.R. 19 Eq. 462, 465: ". . . if there is one thing which more than another public policy requires it is that men of full age and competent understanding shall have the utmost liberty of contracting and that their contracts when entered into freely and voluntarily shall be held sacred and shall be enforced by Courts of justice." It is against this background that the following cases should be studied.

EGERTON *v.* BROWNLOW. 1853. 4 H.L.C. 1; 10 E.R. 359. PARKE B.: "It is the province of the judge to expound the law only; the written from the statutes, the unwritten or common law from the decisions of our predecessors and of our existing Courts, from text writers of acknowledged authority, and upon the principles to be clearly deduced from them by sound reason and just inference; not to speculate upon what is best, in his opinion, for the advantage of the community. Some of these decisions may have no doubt been founded upon the prevailing and just opinions of the public good; for instance, the illegality of covenants in restraint of marriage or trade. They have become part of the recognized law, and we are therefore bound by them, but we think we are not thereby authorised to establish as law everything which we may think for the public good, and prohibit everything which we think otherwise." (E.R. p. 409.) POLLOCK L.C.B.: "My Lords, it may be that Judges are no better able to discern what is for the public good than other experienced and enlightened members of the community; but that is no reason for their refusing to entertain the question, and declining to decide upon it." (E.R. p. 419.)

NOTE. Lord Wright, in *Fender* v. *St. John-Mildmay,* [1938] A.C. 1, at p. 42, said, "[It] is, I think, clear that this dictum of Pollock C.B. and certain observations in *Egerton* v. *Brownlow* to a similar effect cannot be regarded as fixing the modern law, which in my opinion is as stated by Parke B." Why is it that two centuries ago judges could develop ideas of "public policy" but today the subject is closed? Compare *Williston on Contracts,* 1937, rev. ed., sec. 1629, who "respectfully doubts," as inconsistent with the history of our law, the dictum of Lord Halsbury in *Janson* v. *Driefontein Consolidated Mines, Ltd.,* [1902] A.C. 484, 491, "I deny that any court can 'invent a new public policy'." Williston cites in support the following cases, as instances where the courts have made new applications of the doctrines: *Wilson* v. *Carnley,* [1908] 1 K.B. 729; *Neville* v. *Dominion of Canada News Company Ltd.,* [1915] 3 K.B. 556; *Horwood* v. *Millar's Timber and Trading Co.,* [1917] 1 K.B. 305. Although *Fender* v. *Mildmay* is cited in *Williston* he does not refer to the general observations. quoted above. Is the assumption that the heads of policy are closed an assumption that the court is not concerned with public policy; that it is a matter that must be left to the legislatures? Despite the dicta in *Fender* v. *Mildmay* is there any possibility of conflict within a judge's mind as he struggles with twentieth century problems using nineteenth century and earlier tools?

See also *Corbin on Contracts,* sec. 1375, footnote 10, where he describes Baron Parke's statement as "conservative."

GORDON *v.* FERGUSON

Nova Scotia. Supreme Court *en banc.* 1961. 30 D.L.R. (2d) 420

Dr. Gordon employed Dr. Ferguson in his practice as a physician and surgeon in the town of Dartmouth which is located across the harbour from the city of Halifax and connected by the MacDonald Bridge. Over ninety per cent of Dr. Gordon's patients resided in Dartmouth and a "negligible number" resided in Halifax although Dr. Gordon and his staff used Halifax hospitals. One of the terms of the employment provided: "8 The Employee shall not, on the termination for any cause whatever of his employment herein, engage in the practice of medicine and/or surgery similar to that now carried on by the Employer, or engage to work for any person, firm or association of medical practitioners in the vicinity within the Town of Dartmouth . . . and a radius of twenty miles from the boundaries thereof, for a period of five years from the time the employment under this agreement ceases." Dr. Gordon lawfully terminated the agreement and gave the required one month's notice on December 5, 1960 and Dr. Ferguson worked with Dr. Gordon until January 5, 1961 when he opened a practice on his own in Dartmouth. Dr. Gordon then took action for an injunction to restrain the breach of Clause 8 of the agreement. Parker J. dismissed the action. Dr. Gordon appealed.

MacDonald J.: . . . The appellant contended before us that the trial Judge was in error: 1. in refusing to uphold the validity of the restrictive covenant in cl. 8 or to sever therefrom, and to enforce, such part thereof as was valid. . . .

I come now to the first contention which briefly engaged the time of the Court. The topic of cl. 8 of the Agreement set out above is the restriction of the activities of the employer subsequent to the termination of the Agreement, and it is clear that such a covenant—as between master and servant—must be kept distinct from authorities which have reference to the sale of a business or goodwill.

The clause prohibits certain types of activity in a local area for a specified period of time. The clause involves a restraint of trade and is presumed to be void as contrary to public policy but will be upheld if found to be reasonable having regard to the legitimate interests of the parties and also of the public. It can only be viewed as reasonable in the first sense if it is directed to the protection of the covenantee's proprietary interest in his business—and is no wider than is reasonably necessary for that purpose. (*See Herbert Morris Ltd.* v. *Saxelby,* [1916] 1 A.C. 688 at p. 710). The employer is entitled to covenant against misuse of trade secrets of which knowledge will be acquired in his service and against the unfair invasion of his trade connection, *i.e.,* to prevent customers, clients or patients from being enticed away from him by a servant who has acquired knowledge of them or influence over them in the course of his service. (See *Cheshire & Fifoot on Contracts,* 5th ed., p. 316.)

Accordingly it is always essential to consider the nature and extent of the business of the employer and the character of the work done for the employer during the service (*Mason* v. *Provident Clothing & Supply Co.,* [1913] A.C. 724 at p. 742; *British Reinforced Concrete Engineering Co.* v. *Schelff,* [1921] 2 Ch. 563; *Pellow* v. *Ivey* (1933), 49 T.L.R. 422) The importance of this consideration is that: "A restraint is not valid unless the nature of the employment is such that customers will either learn to rely upon the skill or judgment of the servant or will deal with him directly and personally to the virtual exclusion of the master, with the result that he will probably gain their custom if he sets up business on his own account": *Cheshire & Fifoot,* p. 317; *Routh* v. *Jones,* [1947] 1 All E.R. 179 at p. 181 (affirmed [1947] 1 All E.R. 758.

It cannot be denied that the mutual relationship herein involved was such as to give the employer a great practical interest in seeking to curtail the future activities of his professional employee. The only question is whether the restriction he imposed thereon was reasonably necessary in kind (*i.e.*, the professional activities sought to be curtailed), in area and in duration or whether it went beyond the legitimate bounds of self-protection.

The genus of prohibited activity was limited "to the practice of medicine and/or surgery similar to that carried on by the employer," which in fact embraced the general practice of medicine and minor surgery.

The trial Judge inferentially held that the covenant was reasonable as regards the parties and the public in respect of the kind of practice and the kind of work done by the employee as he invalidated the covenant on the express grounds that the restriction was unreasonable in point of area, and he could not substitute a more limited area. It is to be noted, however, that the matter of reasonableness of a restraint in this class of case is a question of law for the Court. The appellant in his notice of appeal purports to exclude from this appeal various "findings" of the trial Judge stated therein. In my view this does not preclude review of any ground otherwise relevant to the determination of the question of law as to whether the covenant was valid or invalid.

One of such grounds in my opinion is that the restriction (in so far as it prohibits the practice of medicine of the kind specified) has the effect of preventing the employee from professional dealings with prospective patients in the area in question without any limitation as to whether they had or had not any previous connection with the practice of the employer or had or had not been brought into contact with the employee in the course of his services. In this sense I think that the prohibition against the practice of medicine, etc. was excessive in that it precludes the employee from dealing with persons unconnected with the practice of the employer before or during the currency of the Agreement, including persons who have moved into the area in question since the termination of the Agreement. This is a clear ground of invalidity. (See *New Method Cleaners & Launderers Ltd.* v. *Hartley*, [1939], 1 D.L.R. 711, 46 Man. R. 414, and cases cited therein; *cf. M. & S. Drapers* v. *Reynolds*, [1957] 1 W.L.R. 9, where a covenant was held unreasonable for the converse reason that it extended to many activities connected with the servant prior to his employment.) The root idea which permits restriction of the future activities of an employee as reasonable between the parties has been well illustrated by Evershed, J.:

"Where the circumstances are such that the servant has, by virtue of his engagement, been put in the position . . . of acquiring a special or intimate knowledge of the affairs of the customers, clients or patients of his master's business or of means of influence over them, there exists a subject-matter of contract, a proprietary interest or goodwill in the matter which is entitled to protection, since otherwise the master would be exposed to *unfair competition* on the part of his former servant—*competition flowing* not so much from the personal skill of the assistant as *from the intimacies and knowledge of the master's business acquired by the servant from the circumstances of his employment*": (*Routh* v. *Jones*, [1947] 1 All E.R. 179 at p. 181 (affirmed, *ibid.*, p. 758)).

But that idea does not extend to protection against competition *per se* or to protection against matters unrelated to the service.

This inclusiveness of the ban on subsequent practice is of particular significance in this case when taken in conjunction with the width of the area (and its growing population) and the length of time to which the ban relates. Moreover, it is a factor which cannot be cured under the doctrine of severance; for its limitation would require the addition of a comprehensive proviso to the covenant.

In this Court the appellant contended (1) that the covenant was reasonable, particularly in terms of geographical area (as well as time), and (2) that if too wide in area, the provisions relating thereto could be severed.

Construed, as it must be, by reference to the ordinary rules of contractual construction (*Gare's Covenants in Restraint of Trade*, 1935, pp. 120-5; *Batt on Master & Servant*, 4th ed., pp. 114-5) the covenant related to the area formed by the then Town of Dartmouth and 20 miles from the boundaries thereof, a description which clearly embraces the City of Halifax and some of its environs. It was said that Halifax was not intended to be included; but this is by no means clear, for though the bulk of the employer's practice related to persons in and about the town, it did involve tending to patients hospitalized in Halifax. In any event, I know of no way of excluding Halifax from the area of the covenant by way of construction as distinguished from severance.

It has been suggested that the same excision can be accomplished by the admission of counsel for the plaintiff, at the trial and on the appeal, that he abandoned any claim to an injunction in respect of Halifax. It is my view, however, that once the question of the legality of cl. 8 was put in issue, the question fell to be considered on the basis of the clause as written; and that no voluntary contraction of its physical coverage can avail to save it if the clause is invalid, *cf. Mills et al.* v. *Gill*, [1952], D.L.R. 27 at pp. 41-2, O.R. 257 at pp. 271-2, 16 C.P.R. 46 at pp. 61-2, for a similar gesture; and *Allen Mfg. Co.* v. *Murphy* (1911), 23 O.L.R. 467 at p. 475, in which the Court rejected the submission—where the stated area was the Dominion of Canada—that as the injunction was limited to the City of Toronto, the agreement should be upheld to that extent—and answered that "to do so would, in effect, be making a new covenant, not that to which the parties agreed".

As to the first contention, it is clear in my view that the covenant, properly construed, is invalid for the reason indicated above and because it purports to apply to an area excessive in extent.

Upon the modern authorities there appears to me to be adequate reason for holding that the area in question is also unreasonable in extent, even if its application to the area 20 miles to the west of Dartmouth (*i.e.*, in and about Halifax) could be excluded.

The appellant placed such reliance on *Mills et al.* v. *Gill, supra,* wherein McLennan, J., upheld a covenant between a Medical Clinic and a staff physician restricting the latter from practising medicine *within the corporate limits of Oshawa and 5 miles thereof* for 5 years. The evidence established, however, that the practice of the Clinic was drawn from an area comprising Oshawa and *a radius of 25 miles therefrom*—so there could be no objection to the more restricted area prohibited by the contract. In *Lock* v. *Nelson & Harvey Ltd.* (1959), 22 D.L.R. (2d) 298, 33 C.P.R. 138, the area of exclusion was wider in appearance than in fact. There the trial Judge upheld a covenant between a customs-brokerage firm and its branch manager at Huntingdon, a port of entry, restricting the latter from engaging in a similar business *within a radius of 30 miles from Huntingdon* for 2 years; but it appears that the reference to 30 miles was designed to exclude him merely from transacting business at two nearby ports of entry where the company had branches—so that in effect the restriction was simply as to doing business at Huntingdon.

The second has reference to the so-called doctrine of severance and resolves itself into the question whether the excess of geographical area can be carved out of the area indicated so as to limit the operation of the covenant to the Town of Dartmouth (as it stood on May 1, 1959) and surrounding territory marked out by a radius of less than 20 miles.

In pursing this topic regard must be had to the fact that though area and duration are factors in the total view, each must also be considered in ıelation to the other (*Fitch* v. *Dowes*, [1921] 2 A.C. 158 at p. 163).

The topic of the Severability of Covenants in restraint of trade is one of great confusion, a study of which yields only a few conclusions:

1. That in appropriate instances where a covenant (between master and servant) taken as a whole is unreasonable, it may be made enforceable or a matter of construction by severing from it that part of it which is bad (*cf. Pauge* v. *Gauvin*, [1954] S.C.R. 15). Whether this can be done or not depends upon very technical considerations, such as whether it constitutes one entire or indivisible covenant or a series of several and independant covenants, or whether it is in such a form as to admit the excision of a word or phrase without other alteration, and so as not to change the substance of the remainder. (See generally Gare, *supra*, c. 5; Cheshire & Fifoot, *supra*, pp. 326-9; Batt, *supra*, pp. 110-14). There is, indeed, no sure test for the proper determination of such questions; but there is a general caution against carrying out of void covenants the maximum which the employer validly could have inserted, and some clue to the exercise of Severance afforded by the authoritative opinion of Younger, L.J., in *Attwood* v. *Lamont*, [1920] 3 K.B. 571 at pp. 592-6.

2. That it is seldom that any previous case is a controlling guide to decision of an instant case because of the inevitable differences in the covenants concerned.

3. (In my view) that such guidance as there may be—in a matter so largely one of public policy—is to be sought in the Canadian rather than in the English decisions as more likely to reflect what is adapted to our conditions.

Reference has been had in argument to various Canadian cases involving the questions of severance, particularly in relation to the area of restraint in contracts of service; but it is enough to discuss a few of the more significant ones:

Hall v. *More*, [1928] 1 D.L.R. 1028, 39 B.C.R. 346—a decision of the British Columbia Court of Appeal—concerned the validity of a term in an agreement between physicians engaged to render services to miners and providing that upon its termination the defendant would not for 5 years practise medicine in *the City of Nanaimo or within the radius of 20 miles therefrom.* It was held that the restriction as to space was unreasonable, particularly as restricting the exercise of the healing art in sparsely settled areas outside the city; but that as it was reasonable as to one of the areas embraced in the contract (the city) and so described as to be severable, the restriction should be confined *to the City of Nanaimo.* This is a clear case of severance as to area.

New Method Cleaners & Launderers Ltd. v. *Hartley,* [1939] 1 D.L.R. 711, 46 Man. R. 414, was a decision of the Manitoba Court of Appeal holding that a covenant by a laundry delivery man, whose route was confined to the City of Winnipeg, wherein he agreed not to solicit business from any of the employer's customers *within the Province* for 1 year, was invalid, *inter alia*, as being excessive as to area. An interim injunction having been granted restraining the laundry man from soliciting *within the City of Winnipeg*, the Court held that this was not a permissable severance of the covenant "but the substitution for it of a new covenant in which an area limited to the City of Winnipeg . . . took the place of the geographical limits of the Province". (p. 715) *Hall v. More, supra*, was distinguished on the ground that the severability present in that case was absent from the covenant in question. (*Cf. Can. Fur Auction Sales* v. *Nealy*, (1954) 62 Man. R. 148.)

In *George Weston Ltd.* v. *Baird* (1916), 31 D.L.R. 730, 37 O.L.R. 514, the Appellate Division of Ontario held invalid, as unreasonable as to space, a covenant by a cake salesman (or pedlar) not to solicit orders etc. in the City of Toronto. In holding that the covenant was not such as enabled severance to be made, reference was made to the judicial reluctance to exercise the power of severance and refusal to do so where the valid are not clearly severable from the invalid restrictions; Lennox, J., saying "The Court should not be asked to devise or frame an *ex post facto contract*". (p. 738 D.L.R., p. 527 O.L.R.)

R. C. Young Ins. Ltd. v. *Bricknell*, [1955], 5 D.L.R. 487, O.W.N. 638, 23 C.P.R. 73, is a recent decision of the Court of Appeal of Ontario. The immediate question was as to the validity of a covenant whereby an employee of the company covenanted not to carry on or be interested *in the business of an insurance agent* within the City of Niagara Falls and four other named localities for 3 years. The company was acting as a general insurance agent but there was no evidence that it engaged in every kind of insurance. The Court of Appeal unanimously held the covenant invalid on the ground that it prohibited the employee from carrying on the business of insurance agent without any limitation as to the kinds of business, and therefore extended to the carrying on of types of business which the company did not carry on. Though it is uncertain whether any question of severance arose, the judgment went on to say (p. 491 D.L.R., p. 639 O.W.N., pp. 74-5 C.P.R.):

"We think that it is improper in construing an agreement of the kind in question, to add or subtract from the plain language used by the parties in defining their rights. Either the clause is good or it is bad in law. If the effect of it goes beyond what is reasonably necessary for the protection of the employer, it is bad . . . the question is not whether the covenantee could make a valid agreement but whether the agreement actually made is valid, and *if the covenant is invalid in part, the entire covenant fails.*"

It is not necessary here to espouse the view that severance is not permissible in appropriate cases; but I can find nothing in the decisions to sanction its application to the present case so as to limit the territorial area of prohibition stated. However described, the plain intention was to enjoin the employee from competing with the employer in a defined area and it is equally plain that the employer's patients, though mainly resident in the Town of Dartmouth, were also drawn from a region of uncertain extent lying to the north, south and east of the town. The radius of 20 miles from the boundaries of the town may be an inexact description of the area of the employer's practice. Nonetheless, it was so described in plain words; and words which in my view require that cl. 8 be viewed as an indivisible covenant, and not merely an agglomeration of independent and several covenants, and therefore one admitting of no curtailment of the area of the prohibited activity by way of severance. The first contention therefore fails.

PATTERSON J.: . . . Fifty years ago when travel was largely by horse and buggy the restriction of 20 miles would undoubtedly have been excessive; in fact unreasonable from the standpoint of the public. Perhaps the same could be said of 25 years ago. I think that whether 20 miles is now reasonable or not there must be taken into consideration the rapid and convenient communications of today. I am trying to think what would have happened had the defendant carried out his contract and set up his office just outside the 20 miles limit. It seems to me that his former patients in Dartmouth, their families and those who had heard of his good reputation and thus had confidence in him would prefer him. Would this distance of 20 miles present such an inconvenience to them that they would prefer going to a strange doctor? The inconvenience was slight, a motor drive of 20 miles with a time consuming element both ways of less than an hour. And this when we know that hundreds every day are on our highways on much longer journeys with not even an idle excuse. The convenience of modern travel is in no way better illustrated than by the well-known fact that thousands of employees in Nova Scotia drive daily to their work at a distance of more than 20 miles. . . .

[The part of the opinion dealing with the second and third contentions is omitted. MacQuarrie and Currie JJ. concurred with MacDonald J. The dissenting opinion of Patterson J with whom Bissett J. concurred, is largely omitted. The judgment was affirmed by the Supreme Court of Canada, [1962] S.C.R. vii: appeal dismissed with costs.]

PEARCE *v.* BROOKS

England. Exchequer Chamber. 1866. L.R. 1 Ex. 213

The plaintiffs sold on a hire purchase agreement to the defendant a new miniature brougham, the defendant to pay £50 down and in case the brougham was returned before a second instalment was paid, fifteen guineas was to be forfeited as well as the £50, and any damage to the vehicle was to be paid for. The defendant returned the brougham before the second instalment was paid, and it was damaged. This action was brought to recover either the fifteen guineas or the amount of the damage. It was objected that to the knowledge of the plaintiffs the defendant was a prostitute and wanted the brougham "to assist her in carrying on her immoral vocation." The jury found the carriage was used by the defendant as part of her display, to attract men, and that the plaintiffs knew it was supplied to be used for that purpose. Bramwell B. at the trial directed a verdict for the defendant and the plaintiffs, pursuant to leave, obtained a rule nisi for a verdict for the fifteen guineas. It was argued that there was no evidence that the plaintiffs knew the purpose for which the brougham was to be used and that it had not been proved that the plaintiffs expected to be paid out of the receipts of the defendant's prostitution. On the first point, Bramwell B. said, in the course of the argument: "At the trial I was first disposed to think that there was no evidence on this point, and I put it to the jury, that, in some sense, everything which is supplied to a prostitute is supplied to her to enable her to carry on her trade, as, for instance, shoes sold to a street-walker; and that the things supplied must be not merely such as would be necessary or useful for ordinary purposes, and might be also applied to an immoral one; but they must be such as would under the circumstances not be required, except with that view. The jury, by the mode in which they answered the question showed that they appreciated the distinction; and on reflection I think they were entitled to draw the inference which they did. They were entitled to bring their knowledge of the world to bear upon the facts proved. The inference that a prostitute (who swore that she could not read writing) required an ornamental brougham for the purposes of her calling, was as natural a one as that a medical man would want a brougham for the purpose of visiting his patients; and the knowledge of the defendant's condition being brought home to the plaintiffs, the jury were entitled to ascribe to them also the knowledge of her purpose."

POLLOCK C.B.: We are all of the opinion that this rule must be discharged. I do not think it is necessary to enter into the subject at large after what has fallen from the bench in the course of the argument, further than to say that . . . I have always considered it as settled by law that any person who contributes to the performance of an illegal act by supplying a thing with the knowledge that it is going to be used for that purpose, cannot recover the price of the thing so supplied. If, to create that incapacity, it was ever considered necessary that the price should be bargained or expected to be paid out of the fruits of the illegal act (which I do not stop to examine), that proposition has been overruled . . . and has now ceased to be the law. Nor can any distinction be made between an illegal and an immoral purpose; the rule which is applicable to the matter is, *ex turpi causa non oritor actio*, and whether it is an immoral or an illegal purpose in which the plaintiff has participated, it comes equally within the terms of the maxim, and the effect is the same; no cause of action can arise out of either the one or the other. The rule of the law was well settled in *Cannan* v. *Bryce*, (1819), 3 B. & A. 179; 106 E.R. 628, that was a case which at time it was decided, I, in common with many other lawyers in Westminster Hall, was at first disposed to regard with surprise. But the learned judge (then Sir Charles Abbott) who decided it, though not distinguished as an advocate, nor at first eminent as a judge, was one than whom few have adorned the bench with clearer views, or more accurate minds, or have produced more beneficial results in the law. The judgment in that case was, I believe, emphatically *his* judgment; it was assented to by all the members of the Court of King's Bench, and is now the law of the land. If, therefore, this article was furnished to the defendant for the purpose of enabling her to make a display favourable to her immoral purposes, the plaintiffs can derive no cause of action from the bargain. I cannot go with Mr. Chambers in thinking that everything must be found by a jury in such a case with that accuracy from which ordinary decency would recoil. For criminal law it is sometimes necessary that details of a revolting character should be found distinctly, and minutely, but for civil purposes it is not necessary. If evidence is given which is sufficient to satisfy the jury of the fact of the immoral purpose, and of the plaintiff's knowledge of it, and that the article was required and furnished to facilitate that object, it is sufficient, although the facts are not expressed with such plainness as would offend the sense of decency. I agree with my brother Bramwell that the verdict was right and that the rule must be discharged. Rule discharged.

[The concurring opinions of Martin, Pigott, and Bramwell, BB., are omitted.]

CLARK *v.* HAGAR. 1893, 22 S.C.R. 510. The plaintiff had sold a house to one J. who was to the knowledge of the plaintiff a prostitute. J. had given a mortgage for part of the purchase and had later conveyed her equity of redemption to the defendant. This action was brought for foreclosure and the defendant alleged that the consideration for the execution of the mortgage was illegal and immoral and that therefore the mortgage was of no effect. GWYNNE J.: "All contracts entered into between a plaintiff and defendant and all instruments executed for the purpose of passing property from the former to the latter, with the intent and for the purpose, operating in the mind of the transferor, that the property transferred shall be applied by the transferee in the accomplishment of a purpose which is in contravention of the principles of the common law or the provisions of a statute, are void and incapable of being enforced by either of the parties against the other upon the illegality being made to appear in due form of law in an action upon the contract or instrument, and that an instrument executed by the transferee for the purpose of securing to the transferor payment of the consideration money for the property so transferred is in like manner void and incapable of being enforced by the transferor against the transferee upon the illegality being made to appear in like manner.

"Knowledge in the mind of the transferor that the transferee intended to apply the property when transferred to him to an illegal purpose will not avoid a contract between the parties or an instrument which transfers the property from the one to the other unless, having regard to the particular nature of the property transferred, and to the condition in life and occupation of the person to whom it is transferred, a just inference can be drawn from the facts in evidence that the property was so transferred with the intent and for the purpose, operating in the mind of the transferor, that the property when transferred should be applied by the transferee to the illegal purpose alleged in the plea.

"Applying these principles to the present case I am of opinion, for all the reasons above stated, that the appellant has wholly failed in establishing that the deed executed by the plaintiff to the appellant's grantor, and which constitutes the consideration for the execution of the mortgage sued upon and the root of the appellant's title to the premises mortgaged, is void. If the contention of the appellant should prevail I cannot see that it would be possible for any of these unfortunate creatures who lead a life similar to that led by the appellant's grantor to enter into any contract with any person knowing her character for the purchase in fee of a house to shelter her or for the purchase of any of the necessaries of life, and the golden rule laid down in *Pearce* v. *Brooks* upon which case the appellant so much relied would be utterly ignored and set at naught namely—that it is necessary in cases like the present to distinguish between such things as, while being necessary or useful for the ordinary purpose of life, may also be applied to an immoral purpose, and those which are such as under the circumstances in evidence would appear not to be required except for an immoral purpose. No such principle has yet been laid down, or is sanctioned, by any of the decided cases, and there is not in my opinion any principle of law or of public morals or of Christian morality which could sanction the affiirmation of such a principle."

HOLMAN *v*. JOHNSON

England. King's Bench. 1775. 1 Cowp. 341; 98 E.R. 1120

Assumpsit for goods sold and delivered: Plea *non assumpsit*, and verdict for the plaintiff. Upon a rule to show cause why a new trial should not be granted, Lord Mansfield reported the case, which was shortly this: The plaintiff, who was resident at and inhabitant of Dunkirk, together with his partner, a native of that place, sold and delivered a quantity of tea, for the price of which the action was brought, to the order of the defendant, knowing it was intended to be smuggled by him into England; they had, however, no concern in the smuggling scheme itself, but merely sold this tea to him, as they would have done to any other person in the common and ordinary course of their trade.

LORD MANSFIELD: There can be no doubt that every action tried here must be tried by the law of England; but the law of England says that in a variety of circumstances, with regard to contracts legally made abroad, the laws of the country where the cause of action arose shall govern. There are a great many cases which every country says shall be determined by the laws of foreign countries where they arise. But I do not see how the principles on which that doctrine obtains are applicable to the present case. For no country ever takes notice of the revenue laws of another.

The objection that a contract is immoral or illegal as between plaintiff and defendant, sounds at all times very ill in the mouth of the defendant. It is not for his sake, however, that the objection is ever allowed; but it is founded in general principles of policy, which the defendant has the advantage of, contrary to the real justice as between him and the plaintiff, by accident, if I may so say. The principle of public policy is this: *Ex dolo malo non oritur actio*. No court will lend its aid to a man who founds his cause upon an immoral or illegal act. If from the plaintiff's own stating or otherwise, the cause of action appears to arise *ex turpi causa*, or the transgression of a positive law in this country, there the court says he has no right to be assisted. It is upon that ground the court goes; not for the sake of the defendant, but because they will not lend their aid to such a plaintiff. So if the plaintiff and defendant were to change sides, and the defendant was to bring his action against the plaintiff, the latter would then have the advantage of it; for where both are *equally* in fault, *potior est conditio defenditis*.

The question therefore is, whether in this case the plaintiff's demand is founded upon the ground of any immoral act or contract, or upon the ground of his being guilty of anything which is prohibited by a positive law of this country. An immoral contract it certainly is not; for the revenue laws themselves, as well as the offences against them, are all *positivi juris*. What, then, is the contract of the plaintiff? It is this: being a resident and inhabitant of Dunkirk, together with his partner, who was born there, he sells a quantity of tea to the defendant, and delivers it at Dunkirk to the defendant's order, to be paid for in ready money there, or by bills drawn personally upon him in England. This is an action brought merely for the goods sold and delivered at Dunkirk. Where, then, or in what respect is the plaintiff guilty of any crime? Is there any law of England transgressed by a person making a complete sale of a parcel of goods at Dunkirk, and giving credit for them? The contract is complete, and nothing is left to be done. The seller, indeed, knows what the buyer is going to do with the goods, but he has no concern in the transaction itself. It is not a bargain to be paid in case the vendee should succeed in landing the goods; but the interest of the vendor is totally at an end, and his contract complete by the delivery of the goods at Dunkirk.

To what a dangerous extent would this go if it were to be held a crime. If contraband clothes are bought in France, and brought home hither, or if glass bought abroad, which ought to pay a great duty, is run into England, shall the French tailor or the glass manufacturer stand to the risk or loss attending their being run into England? Clearly not. Debt follows the person, and may be recovered in England, let the contract of debt be made where it will; and the law allows a fiction for the sake of expediting the remedy. Therefore, I am clearly of the opinion that the vendors of these goods are not guilty of any offence, nor have they transgressed against the provisions of any act of Parliament. . . .

The gist of the whole turns upon this, that the conclusive delivery was at Dunkirk. If the defendant had bespoke the tea at Dunkirk to be sent to England at a certain price; and the plaintiff had undertaken to send it into England, or had any concern in the running it into England, he would have been an offender against the laws of this country. But upon the facts of the case, from the first to the last, he clearly had offended against no law of England. Therefore, let the rule for a new trial be discharged.

The three other judges concurred.

NOTE. The dictum that the revenue laws of another country are not noticed cannot now be deemed consistent with the general policy of the law. By virtue of international comity any contract having for its object the violation of the laws of another state would undoubtedly not be enforced. See *Pollock on Contracts*, 13th ed., pp. 302-4.

COMPARATIVE LAW NOTE. The following Reuters' dispatch appeared in the Toronto *Globe and Mail* on August 25, 1962, from Chikwawa, Nyasaland:

"A 'crocodile man' who agreed to murder a girl for 90 shillings and was not paid the full amount took legal action in a native authority court—and was awarded 50 shillings.

"An African named Ellard told the court here that in 1959 another African named Odrick asked him to kill the girl, apparently because he suspected her of witchcraft. Odrick told the court he chose Ellard because he could 'appear as a crocodile at any time.'

"Ellard said he donned the head and skin of a crocodile, swam down the Shire River to where the girl was getting water, and pulled her in.

"He said he stabbed her and broke her arms, then dragged her to the bank and left her body mutilated as if by a crocodile. Her death subsequently was attributed to misadventure.

"Ellard said Odrick paid him only 10 shillings and promised to pay the balance later. The court ordered Odrick to pay 50 shillings into court in settlement and gave him a receipt.

"Police now are holding both men for questioning in the death and a spokesman said charges are being drawn up.

"A legal authority said that a native authority court deals with cases involving African native law and customs, minor criminal cases and civil cases affecting natives. It has no power over major offenses, such as murder, and was within its right to decide what was a civil matter—in this case non-payment of debt."

ALEXANDER *v.* RAYSON
England. Court of Appeal. [1936] 1 K.B. 169

Mrs. Rayson leased a flat in Piccadilly from Mr. Alexander in 1929, at a rent of £1200 a year. The arrangement was set out in two documents, one a lease which also provided for certain services, the other an agreement which provided for practically the same services and in addition for the supply and maintenance of a frigidaire. Both documents were dated October 29, 1929, and the lease provided for an annual rent of £450 payable quarterly, and the agreement for £750 also payable quarterly. Mrs. Rayson, thinking Mr. Alexander had failed to supply some of the services, on September 29, 1934, refused to pay the quarterly instalment, although she tendered the £112 10*s*. due under the lease, which Mr. Alexander refused. He then brought this action. In her defence Mrs. Rayson alleged that there was no consideration for the £750 and in any case Mr. Alexander had not performed his obligations and had thereby repudiated the lease and agreement. Later, she amended her pleadings to add the defence of illegality, alleging that the enforcement of the *agreement* would be contrary to public policy "in that its execution was obtained by the plaintiff for the purposes of defrauding the Wesminster City Council by deceiving them as to the true rateable value of the said premises and by inducing them to believe that the true rent received by the plaintiff in respect of the said premises was £450 and by concealing from them the terms of the said agreement." Testimony was offered that the flat had been assessed at £720 gross and £597 net, but Mr. Alexander had represented to the Assessment Committee that the rent of £450 was his only income from the property and the assessment was reduced to £270, until later, the Committee having itself discovered the existence of the agreement from Mrs. Rayson, the £720 gross and £579 net assessments were restored. The trial was interrupted to contest whether, if the testimony were accepted, it afforded a defence. Du Parcq J. held that it did not, and Mrs. Rayson appealed. On the question of consideration the Court of Appeal in a judgment prepared by Romer L.J. held for the plaintiff. On the question of illegality:

ROMER L.J.: . . . The second issue raises a question of much greater difficulty.

It is settled law that an agreement to do an act that is illegal or immoral or contrary to public policy, or to do any act for a consideration that is illegal, immoral, or contrary to public policy, is unlawful, and, therefore, void. But it often happens that an agreement which, in itself, is not unlawful is made with the intention of both or one of the parties to make use of the subject-matter for an unlawful purpose—that is to say, a purpose that is illegal, immoral, or contrary to public policy. The most common instance of this is an agreement for the sale or letting of an object where the agreement is unobjectionable on the face of it, but where the intention of both or one of the parties is that the object shall be used by the purchaser or hirer for an unlawful purpose. In such a case any party to the agreement who had the unlawful intention is precluded from suing on it. *Ex turpi causa non oritur actio*. The action does not lie because the Court will not lend its help to such a plaintiff. Many instances of this are to be found in the books. . . .

[In] all these cases the plaintiff was endeavouring to enforce by action an agreement, or a cause in an agreement, which was tainted by the unlawful intention of the plaintiff, or the unlawful intention of the defendant known to the plaintiff, with regard to the purposes for which the subject-matter of the agreement was to be used. To such an action the maxim *ex turpi causa non oritur actio* applies.

But the maxim does not require, nor does the language of it suggest, that a completely executed transfer of property, or of an interest in property, made in pursuance of such an agreement must be regarded as being invalid. This is laid down in clear terms in the well-known case of *Feret* v. *Hill* (1854), 15 C.B. 207; 139 E.R. 400. In that case A procured B to grant him a lease of premises by means of a false representation that he intended to carry on a certain lawful trade therein. Having obtained possession, A converted the place into a brothel, whereupon B forcibly expelled him. It was held that A might maintain ejectment, the fraudulent misrepresentation and the subsequent illegal use of the premises not being sufficient at law to avoid the lease. As the lease had been obtained by fraudulent misrepresentation it could have been set aside in equity and, since the Judicature Act, in any division of the High Court. With that aspect of the matter we are not now concerned. The importance of the case lies in the fact that the lease was held to be a valid one notwithstanding the intention of A to use the demised premises for an unlawful purpose. On this question Mr. Justice Maule expressed himself as follows, at 224: "The plaintiff is not calling upon the Court to enforce any agreement at all. The agreement was an agreement on the part of the defendant to demise certain premises to the plaintiff for a given term. When the instrument was executed, and possession was given under it, it received its full effect; no aid of a Court of Justice was required to enforce it. This action of ejectment is brought, not for the purpose of enforcing the agreement, but the plaintiff asks the Court to afford him a remedy against one who has extruded him from a lawful possession. . . ."

This distinction between an action brought to enforce an unlawful agreement and one brought to assert a right of property already acquired under such an agreement is further illustrated by the case of *Taylor* v. *Chester* (1869), L.R. 4 Q.B. 309. The defendant in that case was the keeper of a brothel and as such had supplied wine and supper to the plaintiff "for the purpose of being consumed there by the plaintiff and divers prostitutes in a debauch there to incite them to riotous, disorderly, and immoral conduct." When the debauch was over there followed, in due course, the reckoning. Being unable or unwilling to pay it at once, the plaintiff deposited with the defendant the half of a £50 note as security. He subsequently repented of his action and instituted proceedings against the defendant for the purpose of obtaining the return of the half banknote. It was held that he was not entitled to recover. The property in the half note had passed to the defendant and, in spite of the illegality of the agreement under which it had passed, the defendant was entitled to keep it. . . .

Much to the same effect is the case of *Gordon* v. *Chief Commissioner of Metropolitan Police*, [1910] 2 K.B. 1080. The money which the plaintiff was claiming in that action had been earned by him in carrying on an illegal business. But the money had become his property and he was held entitled to recover it. He was not asking the Court to enforce any illegal contract or to grant relief dependent in any way on any illegal transaction on his part, but solely on the unjustifiable detention of his money by the defendant.

In view of these various authorities it seems plain that if the plaintiff had let the flat to the defendant to be used by her for an illegal purpose he could not have successfully sued her for the rent, but the leasehold interest in the flat purporting to be granted by the lease would nevertheless have been legally vested in her. The result would have been that the defendant would be entitled to remain in possession of the flat without payment of rent until and unless the plaintiff could eject her without having to rely on the lease or agreement. . . .

In the present case the defendant does not, as a matter of fact, desire to remain in possession of the flat. She is, and has for some time been, anxious to leave it. But, if the plaintiff has by his conduct placed himself in the same position in law as though he had let the flat with the intention of its being used for an illegal purpose, he has no one but himself to thank for any loss which he may suffer in consequence.

That brings us to the real crux of this case. Has the plaintiff placed himself in that position? In the cases to which we have referred there was an intention to use the subject-matter of the agreement for an unlawful purpose. In the present case, on the other hand, the plaintiff's intention was merely to make use of the lease and agreement—that is, the documents themselves—for an unlawful purpose. Does that make any difference? In our opinion, it does not. It seems to us, and it is here that we respectfully disagree with Mr. Justice du Parcq, that the principles applicable to the two cases are identical. That this is so seems to be established by the decision of this Court in *Scott* v. *Brown, Doering, McNab and Co.*, [1892] 2 Q.B. 724. In that case the plaintiff brought an action against some stockbrokers, through whom he had purchased shares in a projected company, to obtain rescission of the purchase contract and repayment of the purchase money on the ground that the defendants, while acting as the plaintiff's brokers, had delivered their own shares to him instead of purchasing them on the Stock Exchange. At the trial it appeared from the plaintiff's own evidence that the money sought to be recovered had been paid by the plaintiff in pursuance of an agreement between him and one of the defendants by which such defendant was, with the money, to purchase on the Stock Exchange a number of shares in the company at a premium with the sole object of inducing the public to believe that there was a real market for the shares and that they were at a real premium. The object, in other words, was "to rig the market." It was held by this Court applying the principle of *ex turpi causa non oritur actio*, that the action was based on an illegal contract and that the money could not be recovered. It will be observed that there was no intention on the part of the plaintiff in that case to use the shares in an unlawful way. The intention was merely to make use of the existence of the share contract in order to defraud the public by inducing them to believe that it recorded a genuine transaction. In delivering judgment Lord Justice Lindley, as he then was, said (at p. 729): "The plaintiff's purchase was an actual purchase, not a sham purchase; that is true, but it is also true that the sole object of the purchase was to cheat and mislead the public. Under these circumstances the plaintiff must look elsewhere than to a Court of justice for such assistance as he may require against the persons he employed to assist him in his fraud, if the claim to such assistance is based on his illegal contract. Any rights which he may have irrespective of his illegal contract will, of course, be recognized and enforced. But his illegal contract confers no rights on him: see *Pearce* v. *Brooks*." It was the transaction of purchase on the market at a particular price, and not the thing purchased, of which an illegal use was to be made. So in the present case it was the formulation of the transaction in a particular way by means of the lease and agreement, and not the subject-matter of the transaction, of which an illegal use was to be made. In one sense, no doubt, it may be said that the plaintiff intended to use only the lease for an unlawful purpose, and not to use, but to conceal the agreement. In reality there was only one transaction between the parties. The splitting of it up into two documents was a device essential for the success of the plaintiff's fraud and both documents must be regarded as equally fraudulent in purpose.

For these reasons we are of opinion that the plaintiff is not entitled to seek the assistance of a Court of justice in enforcing either the lease or the agreement. Mr. Justice du Parcq (who came to a different conclusion) considered that the present case was much the same as one in which a party to an agreement enters into it with the intention of altering it at a later date and using the document so altered for his own fraudulent purposes. "I cannot think," said the learned Judge, "that if a man says 'when I have got this agreement I am going by forgery to alter it,' he is thereby precluded from getting his rights against the other party to the agreement under the agreement in fact made." He thought that in such a case it was something altogether too remote from the contract itself to say that the contract was illegal. In that we respectfully agree with him. But, with all deference, it seems to us that the case he supposed is fundamentally different from the case now before us. In the former case the document is a harmless one, and can only be rendered dangerous by a subsequent act. We see no reason why, before the commission of that act, the document should not be used for an innocent purpose. The intention was mental only and no overt step in carrying out the fraudulent intention was taken in the transaction itself. In the present case, however, the documents themselves were dangerous in the sense that they could be and were intended to be used for a fraudulent purpose, without alteration; and the splitting of the transaction into two documents was an overt step in carrying out the fraud. We cannot think that the plaintiff is entitled to bring these documents into a Court of justice and ask the Court to assist him in carrying them into effect.

The plaintiff's counsel contended that this view is inconsistent with the decision in *In re Thomas, Jaquess* v. *Thomas*, [1894] 1 Q.B. 747. But there is no such inconsistency. In that case one Jaquess had handed over money to Thomas, who was a solicitor, to be used by Thomas in conducting certain litigation. Jaquess subsequently sought to obtain from Thomas an account of the money so handed over to him and a taxation of his bill of costs. Thomas sought to resist the claim on the ground that the money in question had been subscribed by various persons under a champertous, and therefore illegal, agreement. It is not surprising that he failed in his defence, for apart altogether from the fact that Thomas was an officer of the Court—a fact on which the Court commented with some vigour—Thomas could not justify misappropriating the money of Jaquess merely because it had come to Jaquess from a tainted source. Nor, of course, was Jaquess in any way asking the Court to enforce the champertous agreement. In these respects the case is not unlike that of *Gordon* v. *Chief Commissioner of Metropolitan Police*.

Counsel for the plaintiff further contended that inasmuch as the plaintiff had failed in his attempted fraud, and therefore could no longer use the documents for an illegal purpose, he was now entitled to sue on them. The law, it was said, would allow to the plaintiff a *locus poenitentiae*. So perhaps, it would have done, had the plaintiff repented before attempting to carry his fraud into effect: see *Taylor* v. *Bowers* (1876, 1 Q.B.D. 291. But, as it is, the plaintiff's repentance came too late—namely, after he had been found out. Where the illegal purpose has been wholly or partly performed the law allows no *locus poenitentiae*. . . . It will not be any the readier to do so when the repentance, as in the present case, is merely due to the frustration by others of the plaintiff's fraudulent purpose.

In our opinion, the appeal with regard to the second issue must be allowed and the order directing payment by the defendant of the costs of that issue should be discharged. It is true that this issue (being the issue raised in paragraph 2a of the defence) goes only to the validity of the agreement. But this, in our opinion, is immaterial. The moment that the attention of the Court is drawn to the illegality attending the execution of the lease it is bound to take notice of it, whether such illegality be pleaded or not. It had not been pleaded in the case of *Scott* v. *Brown, Doering, McNab and Co.* See, too, the observations of Lord Justice Vaughan Williams in *Gordon* v. *Chief Commissioner of Metropolitan police.*

If, therefore, when the trial is resumed before Mr. Justice du Parcq the plaintiff should fail to disprove the charge of fraud made against him, his action, so far as it is based on the lease and the agreement, should be dismissed. It will, however, apparently still be open to the plaintiff to ask for leave to amend his statement of claim by alleging an oral agreement and claiming relief based on it. His application for this purpose was ordered by Mr. Justice du Parcq to stand over until after the hearing of this appeal. But we do not intend to suggest that if and when the application is made it should be granted. It should be added that the defendant seems not unwilling to pay the rent accrued due under the lease. Should she do so the plaintiff is, of course, entitled to retain it. But if he seeks the assistance of the Court to recover it such assistance must be refused. . . . *Appeal allowed; action to be further heard.*

HARSE *v.* PEARL LIFE ASSURANCE COMPANY. 1904. 20 Times L.R. 264 (England. Court of Appeal). The plaintiff had paid ten years' premiums on two policies on his mother's life and in this action sought to recover the full amount of his payments on the ground that he had no insurable interest in his mother's life and the policies were therefore illegal. He had been told by the agent that they were valid policies but the jury found this statement to be the agent's innocent opinion of the law. Held, for the defendant. THE MASTER OF THE ROLLS: "Unless there is some fraud, or duress, or oppression, or some fiduciary relationship between the parties, a party to an illegal contract who has sustained a loss in consequence of a mistake in law must submit to that loss."

MORGAN *v.* McFEE. 1908. 18 O.L.R. 30 (Ontario. Divisional Court). One Oliver, as a member of a syndicate, was organizing a company to acquire certain patents and he induced the plaintiff to invest $50, of which $10 was paid to Oliver. It later appeared that Oliver had obtained the money by false pretences and the plaintiff instituted criminal proceedings. At Oliver's request the proceedings were adjourned, and the plaintiff was persuaded to enter into agreement with the defendant that the defendants would indemnify the plaintiff against all liabilities of the syndicate, in consideration for which the plaintiff would drop out of the syndicate and forfeit his $10, and the charges against Oliver would be dropped. On the resumption of the proceedings the county Crown attorney reported all this to the police magistrate, on whose direction the proceedings were then dropped. The plaintiff was sued in respect of a liability of the syndicate, and he brought this action for a declaration that he has ceased to be a member of the syndicate and that the defendants are bound to indemnify him against the liabilities of the syndicate. Held, for the defendants. BRITTON J.: "In general any contract or security made in consideration of dropping a criminal prosecution, suppressing evidence, soliciting a pardon, or compounding any public offence, is invalid. . . . False pretences . . . is a serious offence against the public, and although a person who has parted with his money or property by means of a false pretence to him or other fraud practised upon him, or by reason of theft, is entitled to take his own property if offered to him, he is not permitted to screen the offender by an agreement not to prosecute or to drop a prosecution already entered upon. . . . Lord Denman C.J. said, in the case of *Keir* v. *Leeman* (18), 6 Q.B. 308, at p. 321 (cited by Mr. Tilley): 'We shall probably be safe in laying down that the law will permit a compromise of all offences, though made the subject of a criminal prosecution, for which offences the injured party might sue and recover damages in an action.' Then follows: 'But if the offence is of a public nature, no agreement can be valid that is founded on the consideration of stifling a prosecution for it.'. . . The distinction may be a fine in some cases between prosecutions which may be abandoned under an agreement and those where any agreement to abandon would be illegal; but it must, I think, be conceded that a charge of obtaining money under false pretences is so like theft as to be a matter in which the public interest is to be considered."

QUESTIONS. What likely injury to the public interest is involved here? Would the procedure here not be a sensible way of getting an enforceable promise not to prosecute to conviction? The magistrate, fully aware of the facts, agreed to the withdrawal. Is this imposing a duty on a magistrate that he shouldn't have? Is this case one that would probably never happen again? Is not avoidance of publicity one object of an agreement to stifle a prosecution? What is the measure of damages when an enforceable promise not to prosecute is broken and the prosecution results in a conviction? An acquittal?

HUTLEY *v.* HUTLEY
England. Queen's Bench. 1873. 8 Q.B. 112

BLACKBURN J.: The question is whether the contract disclosed on this declaration is such as can be enforced in a court of law. Putting out of the question, for the moment, the position of the plaintiff, it alleges that the defendant is heir-at-law and one of the next of kin of a deceased person who made a will by which the personal and real estate were left away from the defendant, and in consideration that the plaintiff would take the necessary steps to contest the validity of the will, and would advance certain moneys, and obtain evidence, and instruct an attorney, the defendant promised to pay to the plaintiff one half of the personal estate, and convey to him a moiety of the real estate which the defendant should recover. If that stood without more, it is clear that it is champerty by English law, which says that a bargain, whereby the one party is to assist the other in recovering property, and is to share in the proceeds of the action, is illegal. *Sprye* v. *Porter* (1856), 7 E. & B. 58; 119 E.R. 1169, 1178, was one of the cases cited, and I entirely agree with what is there said. Lord Campbell, delivering the judgment of the court, says:

"Here we have maintenance in its worst aspect. The plaintiff and Rosaz, entire strangers to the property which they say the defendant has a title to, but which is in the possession of another claiming title to it, agree with him that legal proceedings shall be instituted in his name for the recovery of it, and that they will supply him, not with any specified or definite documents or information, but with evidence that should be sufficient to enable him to recover the property. Each of them is to have one fifth of the property when so recovered; and unless the evidence with which they supply him is sufficient for this purpose, they are to receive nothing. They are not to employ the attorney, or to advance money to carry on the litigation; but they are to supply that upon which the event of the suit must depend, *evidence*; and they are to supply it of such a nature and in such quantity as to secure success. The plaintiff purchases an interest in the property in dispute, bargains for litigation to recover it, and undertakes to maintain the defendant in the suit in a manner of all others the most likely to lead to perjury and to a perversion of justice. Upon principle such an agreement is clearly illegal; and *Stanley* v. *Jones* (1831), 7 Bing. 369; 131 E.R. 143 is an express authority to that effect."

Putting aside that the plaintiff there was an absolute stranger, the present agreement goes further than that, for the present plaintiff agrees to instruct an attorney and advance money, and falls short of it so far that the present plaintiff only agrees to obtain evidence, whereas in *Sprye* v. *Porter* the plaintiff undertakes to supply evidence sufficient to ensure success. But the mischief is as great in the one case as in the other, and both agreements are void as amounting to maintenance and champerty.

But then it is argued that the position of the plaintiff with relation to the defendant and the property in question takes it out of the rule against champerty and maintenance. The declaration alleges that the plaintiff was a cousin of the deceased, and so a relation of the defendant, who was the deceased's brother; and the plaintiff's counsel cited cases which he said showed that such relationship prevented an agreement like the present from being illegal. But he produced no authority that blood relationship between the parties made any difference as to champerty. Then the further allegation was relied on, that the plaintiff believed that the will which was to be contested revoked a former will by which the testator had bequeathed certain property to the plaintiff; and it was argued that because the plaintiff thought he had an interest in the litigation by which the one will was to be upset and the other revived, the agreement was not illegal. But the litigation was to be maintained by the plaintiff, not solely, as far as he was concerned, for any benefit he might directly or indirectly derive himself from upsetting the will, but the bargain was that he would maintain the action in consideration of the defendant transferring to him half the property which the defendant might become possessed of as the fruits of the litigation. While, therefore, I incline to agree with every word that is said by Lord Abinger and Lord Cranworth in *Findon* v. *Parker*, 11 M. & W. 675, 679, that an agreement to assist in bringing an action is not made maintenance by the fact that the party turns out to be mistaken in supposing that he had a common interest with the litigant parties in the result of the suit, I cannot see that that case is any authority for the present plaintiff. If every word that is said in the declaration about the plantiff's belief in his interest in the subject-matter of the suit were true, that would not justify or make legal the agreement to share in the property to be recovered by the defendant. There must, therefore, be judgment for the defendant.

[Concurring opinions of Lush and Archibald JJ. are omitted.]

NOTE. See *Harris* v. *Brisco* (1886), 17 Q.B.D. 504, for a discussion of charity as a defence to the accusation of maintenance. See also *The Solicitors Act*, R.S.O. 1960, c. 368, which invalidates the purchase by a solicitor of the interest or any part of the interest of his client in any action, and any agreement by which a solicitor retained or employed to prosecute any action stipulates for payment only in the event of success in such action, or where the amount to be paid to him is a percentage of the amount or value of the property recovered.

THE LAW SOCIETY ACT

Manitoba. Revised Statutes. 1954. Chapter 139

74. (1) Notwithstanding any law or usage to the contrary, any attorney, solicitor or barrister in the province may contract, either under seal or otherwise, with any person or corporation as to the remuneration to be paid him for services rendered or to be rendered to the person, or corporation, in lieu of any costs that, by any tariff in force, are allowed to the attorney or solicitor; and the contract entered into may provide that the attorney or solicitor is to receive a portion of the proceeds of the subject matter of the action or suit in which the attorney or solicitor is or is to be employed, or a portion of the moneys or property for which the attorney or solicitor may be retained, whether an action or suit has been brought therefor or a defence has been entered, and the remuneration may also be in the way of commission or percentage on the amount recovered or defended or on the value of the property, about which any action, suit or transaction is concerned.

(2) In any case where any such contract has been entered into, an order may be obtained by the client on praecipe from the proper officer of the Court of Queen's Bench, in the judicial district where the solicitor resides, to refer the contract to a taxing officer of the Court of Queen's Bench, to enquire and decide whether the contract is fair and reasonable to the client, and thereupon the taxing officer shall enquire into all the facts and, if it appears to the taxing officer that the contract is not fair and reasonable to the client, the taxing officer may cancel the contract or reduce the amount payable thereunder to an amount not less than the solicitor and client costs, or order the costs, fees, charges and disbursements in respect of the business done to be taxed in the same manner as if no such contract had been made, and to give all such directions necessary or proper for the purpose of carrying the order into effect or otherwise consequential thereon as to the taxing officer seems meet.

[Subsections dealing with procedural details have been ommitted.]

SCOTT *v.* AVERY. 1856. 5 H.L.C. 811; 10 E.R. 1121. An action on three insurance policies on the ship "Alexander." It was agreed that the rules and regulations of the Newcastle A 1 Insurance Association should be binding on the assurers and the assured. Rule 25 provided that the sum to be paid on a policy should in the first instance be ascertained by the Committee and the suffering member could sue for that amount as soon as the Committee ascertained it and not before. Differences were to be settled by arbitration and a member could then sue only for the amount decided by the arbitrators. The plaintiff had refused to refer his difference to arbitration and defendant raised Rule 25 in his defence in this action. It was attacked on the ground that parties cannot by contract oust the ordinary courts of their jurisdiction. Held, for the defendant. THE LORD CHANCELLOR: "If I covenant with A to do particular acts, and it is also covenanted between us that any question that may arise as to the breach of the covenants shall be referred to arbitration that latter covenant does not prevent the covenantee from bringing an action. A right of action has accrued, and it would be against the policy of the law to give effect to an agreement that such a right should not be enforced through the medium of the ordinary tribunals. But if I covenant with A.B. that if I do or omit to do a certain act then I will pay him such a sum as J.S. shall award as the amount of damages sustained by him, then, until J.S. has made his award, and I have omitted to pay the sum awarded, my covenant has not been broken, and no right of action has arisen. The policy of the law does not prevent parties from so contracting. . . . It was argued that here the arbitrators were to decide not the mere amount, but other matters, as, for instance, what average was to be allowed, whether there had been a loss, and a variety of other matters which were to be ingeniously suggested at your Lordship's bar. . . . I am quite prepared to say that, in my view of the case, that makes no difference at all. If, in consideration of a sum of money paid to me by A.B., I agree with him that in case J.S. should decide that A.B. had fulfilled certain conditions, and had sustained certain damage, and J.S. should make his award accordingly, I would pay to A.B. the sum so ascertained and awarded, no right of action would exist until J.S. had made his award. . . . In other words, that the right of action should be, not for what a jury should say was the amount of the loss, but for what the persons designated in that particular form of agreement should so say."

THE ARBITRATIONS ACT

Ontario. Revised Statutes. 1960. Chapter 18

7. If any party to a submission [by sec. 1 "submission" means a written agreement to submit present or future differences to arbitration], or any person claiming through or under him, commences any legal proceeding in any court against any other party to the submission, or any person claiming through or under him, in respect of any matter agreed to be referred, any party to such legal proceeding may at any time after appearance and before delivering any pleading or taking any other step in the proceeding apply to that court to stay the proceeding and a judge of that court, if satisfied that there is no sufficient reason why the matter should not be referred in accordance with the submission and that the applicant was at the time when the proceeding was commenced and still remains ready and willing to do all things necessary to the proper conduct of the arbitration, may make an order staying the proceeding.

9. An arbitrator or umpire acting under a submission has, unless the submission expresses a contrary intention, power . . .

(b) to state an award as to the whole or part thereof in the form of a special case for the opinion of the court. . . .

26. An arbitrator or an umpire may at any stage of the proceedings and shall, if so directed by the court, state in the form of a special case for the opinion of the court any question of law arising in the course of the reference. . . .

[Apparently no appeal may be taken from an award save where so agreed upon in the submission (sec. 16). When an appeal is taken, subsections (8) and (9) apply.]

16. (8) Where the arbitrators proceed wholly or partly on a view or any knowledge or skill possessed by themselves or any of them, they shall also put in writing a statement thereof sufficiently full to enable a judgment to be formed of the weight that should be attached thereto.

(9) The court may require explanations or reasons from the arbitrator and may remit the matter or any part thereof to him for further consideration.

WOODALL *v.* PEARL ASSURANCE CO. [1919] 1 K.B. 593 at 607

WARRINGTON L.J.: "Arbitration clauses, speaking generally, fall into two classes. One class is where the provision for arbitration is a mere matter of procedure for ascertaining the rights of the parties with nothing in it to exclude a right of action on the contract itself, but leaving it to the party against whom an action may be brought to apply to the discretionary power of the Court to stay proceedings in the action in order that the parties may resort to that procedure to which they have agreed. The other class is where arbitration followed by an award is a condition precedent to any proceedings being taken, any further proceedings then being, strictly speaking, not upon the original contract but upon the award made under the arbitration clause."

CZARNIKOW *v.* ROTH, SCHMIDT & COMPANY
England. Court of Appeal. [1922] 2 K.B. 478

Appeal from an order of the Divisional Court setting aside an award of arbitrators.

SCRUTTON L.J.: The Refined Sugar Association require all their members to incorporate in their contracts the rules of the Association. Rule 17 provides that all disputes on such contracts shall be referred to the arbitration of the Council. Rule 19 provides that the obtaining of an award from the tribunal shall be a condition precedent to the right of either contracting party to sue the other, and the rule continues: "Neither buyer, seller, trustee in bankruptcy, nor any other person as aforesaid shall require, nor shall they apply to the Court to require, any arbitrators to state in the form of a special case for the opinion of the Court, any question of law arising in the course of the reference, but such question of law shall be determined by arbitration in manner herein directed." An arbitration took place before the Council between C. Czarnikow, Ld., and Roth, Schmidt & Co. It is not necessary to say more of the merits than that some views as to the meaning of an f.o.b. contract which were distinctly unusual were put forward by the parties. During the arbitration the buyers asked the arbitrators to state a special case for the opinion of the Court, or to adjourn to allow the buyers to apply for such a case. The tribunal declined to take either course and at once made their award. The tribunal acted thus because in their view the rules of the Association embodied in the contract in question prevented the parties from making such a request. The buyers therefore applied to the Court to set aside the award on the ground of the misconduct of the arbitrators in not affording an opportunity for an application to the Court: *In re Palmer & Co. and Hosken & Co.*, [1898] 1 Q.B. 131. The sellers replied that in view of r. 19 there was no misconduct of the arbitrators; to which the buyers rejoined that the rule was contrary to public policy as ousting the jurisdiction of the Courts. The Divisional Court did not decide this question, but did decide that under *In re Palmer & Co. and Hosken & Co.* it was misconduct of the tribunal not to give an opportunity of application to the Court for a special case. They therefore set the award aside. As however under the rules an award must be obtained before an action can be brought, this merely postpones the day when it must be decided whether the rules of the Refined Sugar Association purporting to prevent the parties from applying for a special case on matters of law are rules to which the King's Courts will pay any attention. I am of opinion that r. 19 of the rules of the Refined Sugar Association in so far as it purports to prevent a party to an arbitration before the Association from exercising his right under the Arbitration Act to ask for a special case for the opinion of the Court on a question of law is contrary to public policy and so unenforceable. In countless cases parties agree to submit their disputes to arbitrators whose decision shall be final and conclusive. But the Courts, if one of these parties brings an action, never treats this agreement as conclusively preventing the Courts from hearing the dispute. They consider the merits of the case, including the fact of the agreement of the parties, and either stay the action or allow it to proceed according to the view they form of the best method of procedure; and they have always in my experience declined to fetter their discretion by laying down any fixed rules on which they will exercise it. If they allow the action to proceed they pay no further attention, and give no legal effect, to any further proceedings in the arbitration: *Doleman Sons* v. *Ossett Corporation*, [1912] 3 K.B. 257, 269. They do not allow the agreement of private parties to oust the jurisdiction of the King's Courts. Arbitrators, unless expressly otherwise authorized, have to apply the laws of England. When they are persons untrained in law, and especially when as in this case they allow persons trained in law to address them on legal points, there is every probability of their going wrong, and for that reason Parliament has provided in the Arbitration Act, that, not only may they ask the Courts for guidance and the solution of their legal problems in special cases stated at their own instance, but that the Courts may require them, even if unwilling, to state cases for the opinion of the Court on the application of a party to the arbitration if the Courts think it proper. This is done in order that the Courts may insure the proper administration of the law by inferior tribunals. In my view to allow English citizens to agree to exclude this safeguard for the administration of the law is contrary to public policy. There must be no Alsatia in England where the King's writ does not run. It seems quite clear that no British Court would recognize or enforce an agreement of British citizens not to raise a defence of illegality by British law. . . . Without attempting precisely to define the limits within which an agreement not to take proceedings in the King's Courts is unenforceable, I think an agreement to shut out the power of the King's Courts to guide the proceedings of inferior tribunals without legal training in matters of law before them is calculated to lead to erroneous administration of law, and therefore injustice, and should therefore not be recognized by the Courts. I am ready to go very far in ignoring technicalities and irregularities on the part of arbitrators unless there is some real substance of error behind them, but I think commercial men will be making a great mistake if they ignore the importance of administering settled principles of law in commercial disputes, and trust to the judgment of business men, however experienced in business, based only on the facts of each particular case, and with no knowledge of or guidance in the principles of law which must control the facts and which arbitrators must administer.

I think it is necessary to add a word about the effect of *Scott* v. *Avery*. I have always understood it to be a decision that while parties cannot agree to oust the jurisdiction of the King's Courts, they can agree that no action shall be brought in those Courts till the amount of liability has been settled by arbitration. Alderson B. states this as agreed by all parties, and Lord Cranworth begins his judgment in the same way. I do not think the language of Lord Dunedin in commencing his judgment in *Atlantic Shipping Co.* v. *Dreyfus*, 38 Times L.R. 534, can have been meant to impugn the first part of this proposition. The Courts always decline to recognize an agreement to refer all disputes to arbitration as compelling them to stay an action, and do so because such an agreement would oust the jurisdiction of the King's Courts. I prefer the language of Lord Sumner, concurred in by Lords Buckmaster and Atkinson, to the effect that as long as a clause does not exclude the claimant from such recourse to the Courts as is always open by virtue of the provisions of the Arbitration Act, 1889, but only requires certain conditions as precedent to a valid claim, it does not oust the jurisdiction. I think that Lord Sumner would have regarded a clause depriving the claimant of the protection of the Arbitration Act as an ousting of the jurisdiction and unenforceable. And I can conceive some conditions precedent to enforcing a claim which English Courts would decline to enforce.

I am of opinion that the view of the Divisional Court was correct in regarding the action of the tribunal as wrong in refusing an opportunity to apply for a special case. Arbitrators must understand that parties before them have a right to take the opinion of the Court as to whether the arbitrators should be given the guidance of the Court in matters of law, and that they must not attempt to stop the action of the Courts by interfering with or hindering such a right of parties. For that reason I think the decision must be affirmed setting aside the award. I am also of opinion that the latter part of n. 19 is unenforceable, and that parties are entitled in spite of it to apply to the Court, and in a proper case obtain from it a special case on matters of law. I do not decide that the present is a proper case; the matter has not been argued before us. The parties however should consider their position. They must obtain an award as a condition precedent to recovering anything, and therefore must go to some arbitrators. I see no reason to assume that the present tribunal will not, if ordered to do so, state a proper special case and it may be that the best course to take is to remit the matters to the arbitrators in the existing arbitration, when an application to order them to state the appeal case can be in the usual way. The appeal however must be dismissed with costs.

[Opinions to the same effect were given by Bankes and Atkin L.JJ.]

NOTE. The following clause is taken, with permission, from the standard form of Construction Contract prepared in 1930 and revised in 1950 for use by the Royal Architecural Institute of Canada and the Canadian Construction Association. References to this standard form throughout the case book will be simply to Canadian Standard Form Construction Contract.

Article 42. Arbitration.—In the case of any dispute between the Owner or the Architect on his behalf, and the Contractor during the progress of the work, or after the determination or breach of the Contract as to any matter arising thereunder, either party hereto shall give to the other notice of such dispute.

Thereupon each party shall appoint an arbitrator and these shall jointly select a third and the decision of any two shall be final and binding upon the parties. Procedure shall conform to the laws of the province in which the work is situated. In case of failure of the two arbitrators appointed by the parties hereto to agree upon a third arbitrator such third arbitrator shall be appointed in accordance with the provisions of The Arbitration Act or Acts in force in the province in which the building is located, and if no such Act is in force, then by reference to a judge of the supreme or superior court of such province.

When the Owner or the Contractor applies for an arbitration, the application shall not be entertained until security to the amount of $250.00 has been deposited by the applicant with the Architect to apply to the cost of the arbitration. In case of a balance remaining to the credit of the Contractor, according to the certificates of the Architect, the same may be received on account of the said security to apply to the cost of arbitration.

Arbitration proceedings shall not take place until after the completion or alleged completion of the work except (a) on a question of certificate for payment, or (b) in a case where either party claims that the matter in dispute is of such a nature as to make immediate arbitration proceedings necessary while the evidence is available.

The cost of arbitration shall be apportioned against the parties hereto or against any one of them as the arbitrators may decide.

GRIFFITHS *v.* THE EARL OF DUDLEY

England. Queen's Bench Division. 1882. 9 Q.B.D. 357

Griffiths worked in the defendant's collieries and was killed in a fall resulting from a defect in certain machinery for which a fellow employee, an inspector of machinery, was found to be responsible. Griffiths' widow brought this action under the *Employers' Liability Act, 1880* to recover a sum of £150 as compensation for Griffiths' death. The defendant's defence was that Griffiths, in common with all the workmen, had agreed that he would look to the colliery benefit society alone for compensation in case of injury or death and that "neither the employer, nor any other person in his employment, whether a fellow servant or not, should be liable in respect of any defect, negligence, act or omission under the *Employers' Liability Act, 1880*, or otherwise, or in respect of any negligence occasioning such injury" and "that the contract should remain in force and operate as a contract between the workman and the owner for the time being of the colliery, so long as the workman continued to be employed at the colliery." When the Act was passed there was already in existence a "benefit society" called the "field box", to which each employee contributed weekly by a deduction from his wages, and the defendant contributed an equal sum. The payments out of the "field box" were made in the discretion of the defendant's manager, and were intended to cover, among other things, an allowance to the widow of a workman killed in the course of his employment. When the Act came into force the defendant circulated throughout the collieries, and posted in the "workmen's hovels" a notice headed "conditions of employment" which set out the clauses quoted and required every workman who continued to work in the collieries to accept the fund instead of the benefit of the Act. Griffiths read the notice and continued to work as usual and his contributions were deducted as usual. The Dudley County Court Judge held the contract to be void as against public policy and gave judgment for the widow. The Earl appealed.

FIELD J.: This case is an important one, as it is of course very desirable that there should be no uncertainty with regard to the construction of the Employers' Liability Act. The plaintiff is suing, not as administratrix of her husband, but as his widow, to recover under Lord Campbell's Act pecuniary loss sustained by her through her husband's death. The Employers' Liability Act was passed to obviate the injustice to workmen that employers should escape liability where persons having superintendence and control in the employment were guilty of negligence causing injury to the workmen. The employer was, before the passing of the Act, clearly liable where he himself was guilty of negligence. It is also clear now that for the negligence of a fellow workman not coming within any of the classes of persons specified in the Act the employer is not liable. But before the passing of the Act *Wilson* v. *Merry* (1868), L.R. 1 H.L.Sc. 326, had decided that where the injury was caused through the negligence of a superior person in the employment, the workman could recover no damages from their common employer. The object of the Act was to get rid of the inference arising from the fact of common employment with respect to injuries caused by any persons belonging to the specified classes. If therefore the person injured in the present case had not made the contract which is relied on to exempt the defendant from liability, he would himself, during his lifetime, clearly have been entitled to recover. It is also clear that the terms of the contract do expressly stipulate that the workmen shall not look to the defendant for compensation for any injury received in the employment, and that the deceased accepted the employment and was willing to continue working on those terms. There is no suggestion that the contract was induced by fraud, or by force, or made under duress, and it was not a naked bargain made without consideration for the defendant contributed an amount to the club equal to the whole amount of contributions from the workmen. I am unable to concur in the view taken by the learned county court judge of these facts and of the statute. He held that the contract was against public policy. It is at least doubtful whether, where a contract is said to be void as against public policy, some public which affects all society is not meant. Here the interest of the employed only would be affected. It is said that the intention of the legislature to protect workmen against imprudent bargains will be frustrated if contracts like this one are allowed to stand. I should say that workmen as a rule were perfectly competent to make reasonable bargains for themselves. At all events, I think the present one is quite consistent with public policy. . . .

The last point raised for the plaintiff was one suggested by myself. But I think the Court would be construing the Employers' Liability Act too narrowly if the construction which I suggested as a possible one were placed upon s. 1. At the time of the passing of the Act the law stood thus: It was an implied term of the contract between employer and workman that the latter should not recover damages if he was injured by the negligence of a person in the common employment. Then the effect of s. 1 was to do away with that implied term. The workman is obliged to rely upon the contract of service; but for that contract he would have no right of action at all; he is only entitled to be upon the employer's premises by virtue of it. I think the Court should take a broad view of the construction of the Act, having regard to the intention of the legislature. I do not think the words of the Act go far enough to compel the construction that the express contract by the workman against the operation of the Act should not take effect. In all the cases referred to in argument, in which the legislature has intended to enact that a person shall not be allowed to contract himself out of an Act of Parliament, very express words have been used. As a general rule entire freedom of contract has been preserved; it has only been interfered with in order to obviate great public injustice. It is legitimate to see what would be the consequences if the construction contended for by the plaintiff's counsel prevailed, because, if injustice would result, it is unlikely the legislature intended that construction. I think great injustice would result, because the workman might obtain the benefit of the contract for years in the form of higher wages to cover the risk of injury, and then claim full additional compensation when he was injured.

The strongest argument suggested in favour of the contention for the plaintiff is the desire of the legislature to protect workmen. Protection has been afforded them against late hours of work, unfenced machinery, the employment of children in manufactories, and in other instances. If it could be shewn in the present case that large classes of workmen would be deprived of the protection which the legislature intended to give them by a decision that they could contract themselves out of the provisions of the Employers' Liability Act, a strong argument against that construction would be afforded. But that cannot be shewn. I am of opinion, therefore, that this rule should be made absolute to enter judgment for the defendant.

EDLER v. AUERBACH. [1950] 1 K. B. 539 (England. King's Bench Division). An action for, among other things, payment to the plaintiff of a sum paid under an agreement for the illegal use of premises under the Defence (General) Regulations, 1939, Reg. 68 CA (1). The plaintiff was a solicitor and was induced by the defendant, an accountant, to rent two rooms on the second floor of premises at 9 Mansfield Street, London, for use only for professional purposes. The defendant told the plaintiff the premises had not been used residentially after December 31, 1938, although the defendant had himself been shown a letter stating that the whole premises had been used for residential purposes until the outbreak of war in 1939. This meant that 9 Mansfield Street could not be used wholly for professional purposes. The defendant himself had intended to use the second and third floors for residential purposes, and the mixed use would have been lawful. The plaintiff accepted the defendant's word and made no further inquiries. He signed a lease for the two rooms for six months from March 31, 1947, and thereafter until terminated by six months notice. The rent was £525, payable quarterly in advance and the plaintiff paid £111 1*s*. 2*d*. on April 11, 1947. He then decided to sublet one of his rooms and when he made application for a permit to have some electrical work done his illegal use was disclosed. The upshot was that the local authority agreed to let the defendant use the ground and first floors for professional purposes, and to take no action against the existing tenants on the second and third floors on an undertaking being given by the defendant that he would re-allocate the space on the ground and first floors so as to release the second and third floors for residential use. The plaintiff then gave notice terminating his lease on March 31, 1948, and brought this action to recover the rent he had paid. The defendant counterclaimed for the balance of the unpaid rent. On this point Devlin J. applied *Alexander* v. *Rayson* and held that the plaintiff could not recover the rent he had paid, but the defendant could not recover the balance owing. DEVLIN J.: "The statement of claim pleads *ex facie* illegality only. It contains no allegation about the object of the agreement or about the state of mind of either party.... Counsel for the plaintiff rightly concedes that [the agreement] cannot be construed as imposing any obligation on the tenant to use the premises at all. The plaintiff can legally perform all his obligations under the agreement. He can get no benefit from it, because he could not, assuming the prohibition in the regulation to be absolute, enter into occupation, but that is immaterial.

... "The agreement would be *ex facie* illegal only if expressly or impliedly it required the tenant to enter into occupation without first obtaining consent to professional user....

"... what has to be considered in the application of this principle is not whether the premises can legally be used for the purpose contemplated, but whether the defendant's conduct has been such as to disentitle him from obtaining the aid of the court to enforce the agreement to his own advantage. The agreement was part of the illegal scheme conceived by the defendant. It succeeded to this extent, as is clear from the minute of the meeting of the appropriate committee of the council on May 22, that, if the committee had not considered the plaintiff as being in actual occupation by reason of a *bona fide* error, they would not have given him any relief. To allow the defendant to take advantage of a consent obtained in those circumstances would give him a profit from his own wrong, but, in truth, neither success nor failure of the scheme matters. Neither would atone for the fact that it was conceived in wrongdoing. That is what matters and what debars the defendant from invoking the aid of the court.

"I turn now to the objection that I ought not to be considering any illegality except that which is pleaded. I accept the submission of counsel for the defendant that the illegality which I have found depends on the knowledge or intention of the defendant, that this is not pleaded, and that it ought to have been pleaded if it was to be relied on. Counsel then cites *North-Western Salt Co., Ltd.* v. *Electrolytic Alkali Co., Ltd.* [1914] A C. 461. That case authorises, I think, four propositions: first, that where a contract is *ex facie* illegal, the court will not enforce it, whether the illegality is pleaded or not; secondly, that where, as here, the contract is not *ex facie* illegal, evidence of extraneous circumstances tending to show that it has an illegal object should not be admitted unless the circumstances relied on are pleaded; thirdly, that where unpleaded facts, which, taken by themselves, show an illegal object have got in evidence (because, perhaps, no objection was raised or because they were adduced for some other purpose), the court should not act on them unless it is satisfied that the whole of the relevant circumstances are before it; fourthly, that where the court is satisfied that all the relevant facts are before it and it can see clearly from them that the contract had an illegal object, it may not enforce the contract, whether the facts were pleaded or not.

"... When the court comes to know of an illegality, public policy requires that it should refuse any help to the wrongdoer, and public policy cannot be circumvented by the court fictitiously deeming itself not to have heard that which in truth it has heard.

"... I am satisfied that I have all the relevant material before me. Indeed, it was not suggested that I had not or that there was any aspect of the point insufficiently exposed...."

[*Anson on Contracts* (1959), 21st ed., p. 554, n. 7, describes this as "a most inequitable decision." Do you agree?]

GRAY AND OTHERS *v.* SOUTHOUSE AND ANOTHER
England. King's Bench Division. [1949] 2 All E.R. 1019

Action for the recovery of money paid under a contract, the consideration for which, it was alleged, had wholly failed.

The plaintiffs sought to recover sums amounting to £169 8s. 6d., which they had paid to one Hunt, the second defendant, as the agent of the first defendant in negotiations for a sub-lease of a flat at 71, Perham Road, London, W. 14, as a premium to the first defendant, the tenant. During the negotiations it appeared that the first defendant was a statutory tenant and, therefore, was unable to grant a sub-tenancy, and the present claim was made, but the question arose whether it was not contrary to public policy for the court to assist the plaintiffs to recover money the payment of which they had been aware was forbidden by the law.

DEVLIN J. reviewed the evidence, found as a fact that the second defendant was the agent of the first defendant, and that the first defendant was liable to repay the premium subject to the question of public policy, and continued: With regard to this question, it was made plain that the plaintiffs knew that, in paying a premium of £150, they were doing something which the law forbade. The ordinary rule is that the court will not assist any party who comes before it to recover money if it is necessary for the party presenting the cause of action to rely on the commission by him of an illegal act. The *Increase of Rent and Mortgage Interest (Restrictions) Act, 1920*, s. 8, as amended by the *Rent and Mortgage Interest Restrictions Act, 1939*, sched. I, provides:

"(1) A person shall not, as a condition of the grant, renewal, or continuance of a tenancy or sub-tenancy of any dwelling-house to which this Act applies, require the payment of any fine, premium, or other like sum, or the giving of any pecuniary consideration, in addition to the rent, and, where any such payment or consideration has been made or given in respect of any such dwelling-house under an agreement made after September 1, 1939, the amount or value thereof shall be recoverable by the person by whom it was made or given. . . . (2) A person requiring any payment or the giving of any consideration in contravention of this section, shall be liable on summary conviction to a fine not exceeding £100. . . ."

The Act, therefore, prohibits the requiring of a payment to be made to the landlord, and it is possible that, if a tenant pays a premium, he is guilty of aiding and abetting the criminal offence for which the section provides, and since the plaintiffs appear to have lent themselves to a scheme for disguising the matter by representing their payment as one made for the cost of re-decoration I shall assume for the purposes of this case that the plaintiffs are so guilty. The main point on which counsel for the plaintiffs has relied is the provision in the section under which the premium shall be recoverable by the person by whom it was made or given. If that is given its full effect, it would mean, if this were a case under the Act, which it is not, that the plaintiffs would be able to recover the premium which they had paid.

At first sight it seems curious, when the rule is so clearly defined that a court will not assist a plaintiff to recover money which is paid as part of an illegal scheme connived at by him, that Parliament should provide that, although the tenant is *particeps criminis*, he be entitled to get his money back. I have, therefore, felt it necessary to consider whether that provision ought not to be restricted to tenants who were not *participes criminis*, and was merely intended as a procedural means provided by the statute whereby they might get their money back. On the whole, however, I think that that is not the right meaning of the provision. It is necessary to remember that when matters of this sort come before the courts the criminal offence is over. There could be no question of anything that the court does furthering the commission of a crime. The question that the court has to consider in this type of case is what is to happen to property which has been disposed of in one way or another in the course of the crime. The broad rule is that the court will assist neither side, and that the loss lies where it falls. Like all broad rules it produces hard cases. It often happens that the less guilty of the two parties is the loser, and, therefore there is nothing inherently immoral in the idea of Parliament considering that in a particular class of case it is desirable that the money should go to one side rather than to the other.

The Rent Acts are Acts for the protection of tenants, and Parliament might very well have had it in mind that, unless it altered the common law rule, the result would be that the landlord, who would generally be far the more guilty party of the two, would be left in possession of the fruits of his illegality. That is the proper view of the statute, and it is reinforced by *Browning* v. *Morris* (1778), 2 Cowp. 790; 98 E.R.1364, where Lord Mansfield, C.J., in his judgment says:

"But, where contracts or transactions are prohibited by positive statutes, for the sake of protecting one set of men from another set of men; the one, from their situation and condition, being liable to be oppressed or imposed upon by the other; *there*, the parties are *not in pari delicto*; and in furtherance of these statutes, the person injured, after the transaction is finished and completed, may bring his action and defeat the contract."

Accordingly I hold that there is no need to restrict the full meaning of the provision on which counsel for the plaintiffs relies. On the contrary, if Parliament had intended the benefit of the provision to be limited to innocent persons, it would be surprising that it used such unqualified language. After all, by 1939, when the section I am considering was before Parliament, it was widely known to all classes of the community that the giving of "key money" or premiums for tenancies of controlled dwelling-houses was illegal. The cases of innocent tenants must be very rare, and I can hardly believe that Parliament intended the wide words of the statute to be restricted to those exceptional cases. This is not a claim made under the Act, and the Act is not pleaded in support of it. All I have to do, therefore, is to satisfy myself that it is not contrary to public policy in this particular class of case that the plaintiffs should recover the sums for which they sue. I am satisfied that public policy puts no impediment in the way of their obtaining judgment.

Judgment for the plaintiffs with costs.

KINGSHOT *v.* BRUNSKILL

Ontario. Court of Appeal. [1953] O.W.N. 133

ROACH J.A. delivered the judgment of the Court: The facts of this case are simple but it raises an important question under *The Farm Products and Sales Act*, R.S.O. 1950, c. 130, and the regulations passed thereunder.

The plaintiff operates a fruit and market garden on 34 acres of land in the county of Peel. On that land he has a small apple orchard. He is not a large producer of apples and his main income is derived from the operation of greenhouses. In the fall of 1950 he had harvested his apple crop and the apples were stored on his premises. Among these apples were 846 bushels of Spy and Delicious apples. They were in bushel baskets. No effort had been made by him to grade or sort them, although there was no mixture of the two varieties in any basket. In harvesting the apples the plaintiff had taken the empty baskets and marked some of them "Fancy Delicious" and the others of them "Fancy Grade Spies." It was stated in evidence that the usual practice is to mark the baskets or hampers with name and quality of the variety which the producer intends, after grading, that those hampers shall contain. The hampers were then sent out to the orchard and the apples were picked from the tree and placed in the appropriate hampers. The plaintiff had no intention of offering those apples for sale to the public until they were first graded in compliance with the regulations passed under the Act.

The defendant resides on land about one mile distant from the plaintiff's premises. His main business is the growing and marketing of apples and purchasing apples form other apple growers, grading them and marketing them.

On 14th December the defendant came to the plaintiff's premises and inquired whether or not the plaintiff would sell his Spy apples. The plaintiff replied that he would not sell the Delicious and Spies separately and that if he sold them he wanted to sell the whole lot. It was apparent to the defendant that the apples had not been graded. After some preliminary discussion, the defendant entered into a contract with the plaintiff to purchase the apples at $1.10 per bushel and paid the plaintiff a deposit of $25. As the learned trial judge said in his reasons there was no warranty, express or implied. The defendant inspected the apples and simply bought what he saw in the premises where they were stored. Under the terms of the contract it was the defendant's obligation to remove the apples. From time to time he removed quantities of them to his own premises, graded them and sold them. By April, 1951 there were still some hampers of apples which the defendant had not yet removed. The plaintiff requested the defendant to remove them because he needed the space, and when the defendant delayed removing them the plaintiff sent them over to the defendant's premises. During the course of the removal by the defendant he paid the plaintiff on account the further sum of $200. When the last of the apples had been delivered by the plaintiff to the defendant, the defendant called an inspector appointed under the regulations and the inspector marked the last consignment of delivery with a detention order, as he was permitted to do under the regulations. Notice of that detention order was given to the plaintiff. The defendant, alleging that of the total quantity of apples received by him there were certain defective apples, computed the balance that he owed to the plaintiff and sent him a cheque for $619.80, being the amount which the defendant considered represented the balance owing by him. This cheque was marked "in full payment for apples." This cheque was not accepted by the plaintiff but was returned to the defendant. The plaintiff thereupon sued the defendant for the sum of $719.60, which sum was made up of $705.60, being the balance owing for the apples, plus $14.00 being the value of hampers which the defendant had not returned to the plaintiff.

The defendant pleaded that the apples had not been graded, packed or marked in accordance with *The Farm Products Grades and Sales Act* and the regulations passed thereunder and in particular, regulation 3(a), (c), (d), (f) and (g), and that the sale of the apples was thereby prohibited by statute and illegal. The learned trial judge gave effect to that plea and it is with some regret that I feel myself constrained to agree with that decision.

Section 2(1) of the statute authorizes the Minister of Agriculture, subject to the approval of the Lieutenant-Governor in Council, to make certain regulations respecting farm products as defined in the statute. Farm products as there defined include fruit. The regulations that the Minister may make as aforesaid include regulations,

"(a) establishing grades and classes for any farm product;

"(b) providing for the inspection, grading, packages and packing, marketing, handling, shipping, transporting, advertising, purchasing and selling of farm products within Ontario."

Pursuant to the authority contained in the statute, regulations were made and they are known as Regulations 87 (1 C.R.O. 1950, p. 431). Regulation 3 thereof provides in part as follows:

"No person shall pack, transport, ship, advertise, sell, offer for sale or have in possession for sale any produce

"(a) unless the produce has been graded, packed and marked in accordance with the provisions of the Act and these regulations;

"(b) which is below the minimum grade for the produce but this provision shall not apply to produce for an establishment [establishment is defined in Regulation 1 as including any plant, factory or premises where produce is canned, preserved or otherwise processed];

"(c) where the faced or shown surface falsely represents the contents;

"(d) in a package unless the package is properly filled and packed;

"(f) in a package which has been previously marked unless the marks are completely removed;

"(g) which is so immature or so diseased or otherwise affected as to be unfit for human consumption."

By s. 8 of the statute every person who contravenes any of the provisions of the Act or the regulations is guilty of an offence and liable on summary conviction to the penalties therein set out.

It must be concluded that the main object of the statute and the regulations passed thereunder is the protection of the public. The penalty authorized by the statute is imposed wholly for the protection of the public. Therefore, if the sale here in question was forbidden by the regulations, then it was illegal and notwithstanding that the defendant resold the apples after having graded them and made a profit thereby, the plaintiff cannot recover in an action for the price of those apples. Reference may be made to *Anderson, Limited* v. *Daniel*, [1924] 1 K.B. 138, and *Little* v. *Poole* (1829), 9 B. & C. 192.

I have looked in vain for any provision in the regulations that would exempt the plaintiff in the circumstances of this case from their application. It is not difficult to conceive a case in which a farmer who has a small orchard on his farm may have neither the manpower nor the equipment necessary to grade and pack the product of his orchard, in accordance with the regulations. His neighbour, with a much larger orchard and specializing in the growing of fruit, has the necessary help and equipment for the grading and packing of the produce not only of his own orchard but of others in the neighbourhood. It would seem not unreasonable that the first of those two farmers should be permitted to sell his whole crop of fruit to the second of those two farmers, who, having the necessary help and equipment, could grade it and pack it in accordance with the regulations before offering it for sale to the public. The regulations, however, do not appear to provide for such a case. There is no provision in the regulations that would exempt the first of those two farmers in that hypothetical case from compliance with the regulations. The Court cannot read into the regulations exemptions which might appear to the Court to be justifiable in a given set of circumstances.

For these reasons the appeal must be dismissed with costs.

QUESTION ON LEGAL METHOD. The Court's interpretation of the Act and regulations is obviously possible. Is it a necessary one?

PICBELL LTD. *v.* PICKFORD & BLACK LTD.
Nova Scotia. Supreme Court *en banc.* [1951] 2 D.L.R. 119

ILSLEY C.J.: The plaintiff's action is for a declaration that a certain agreement between the plaintiff and the defendant dated March 30, 1946, is a valid and subsisting agreement, for specific performance by the defendant of the agreement, for payment of the sum of $7,500 alleged to be due and payable by the defendant to the plaintiff for hire or use of the steamship "Dufferin Bell" for the period April 10, 1950, to May 10, 1950, under the terms of the said agreement and for such further and other relief as to the Court shall seem meet.

The agreement is set out in full in para. 4 of the statement of claim. It provided that the plaintiff would purchase one 4,700-ton Park Steamship, probably the "Dufferin Park" (also or later called the "Dufferin Bell") from the Park steamships Ltd., that on acquisition of this steamship the plaintiff would charter it to the defendant for the period of 84 months (subject to an abbreviation of this period in circumstances which have not developed) and that the defendant would pay the plaintiff $12,500 per month during the term of the charter, the first of such payments to be made one month after the date of delivery of the steamship. Provision was however made in the agreement for downward adjustments in the rate of hire and the statement of claim alleges that the rate of hire was so adjusted downward to $7,500 a month, apparently after this action was brought but before delivery of the statement of claim.

The ship came alongside her loading berth for the following voyage on April 10, 1946, and was operated by the defendant Company until April 15, 1950, when the defendant for the first time notified the plaintiff that the agreement of March 30, 1946, was a nullity. The defendant paid the plaintiff $12,500 a month during the 4 years it operated the ship.

On these facts and the others set out in the agreement and supplementary agreement "re setting down for hearing," this Court is asked to answer the following question:

"Whether or not by reason of the matters and things set out in paragraph 11 of the Defence herein, or otherwise, the charter by the Plaintiff to the Defendant of the steamship 'Dufferin Bell' purporting to be evidenced by and purporting to be made pursuant to the paper writing set out in paragraph 4 of the Statement of Claim herein is or was illegal, null and void and of no effect either in whole or in part."

The ground on which the defendant argues that the charter was illegal, null and void is that it was made in contravention of s. 9 of Order in Council P.C. 6785 [76 Can. Gaz. 718], being sch. A of the agreement re setting down for hearing. This section is as follows:

"9. All persons or parties, agencies, organizations or associations proposing to charter any vessel exceeding 150 tons gross register, not being classified by the Department of Fisheries as a fishing vessel, shall submit in advance full particulars, including rates and conditions of charter hire, to the Director for approval on behalf of the Board; and no such charter as aforesaid shall be made without such approval."

It may not be irrelevant to recall that during March and April of 1946, price control and the control of charges for services were still prevalent throughout the whole or nearly whole of the Canadian economy. . . .

If, then, there was no approval, what becomes of the charter? P.C. 6785 had the same effect as a statute. . . .

The result is clear: the making of the charter was prohibited—and prohibited for public purposes and in the public interest. Must the Court then refuse to render assistance in enforcing it? Is it null and void as an illegal contract? Many cases were cited in support of the proposition that if a contract may be performed either in a lawful or in an unlawful way and if a party in the performance of his part of the contract without the knowledge of the other party elects to perform it in an unlawful way, he cannot be heard to allege his own wrong. It was contended on behalf of the plaintiff that the contract made on March 30th for a charter which was made on April 10th could have been performed in a lawful way, that it was the charterer's duty to submit the particulars to the Director of Shipping and obtain approval thereof and that it cannot be heard to allege its own wrong in not doing so. However, the question submitted to this Court is not as to the illegality of the agreement of March 30th; it is as to the illegality of the charter. The class of cases applicable to the determination of this question is that relating not to unlawful performance, but to prohibited contracts. This was a prohibited contract. It is unnecessary to decide whose obligation it was under s. 9 to submit the particulars in advance. The concluding words of the section prohibited both parties and each party from making the charter unless the particulars had been submitted and approval obtained.

I am therefore of opinion that there was an illegal act on the plaintiff's part as well as on the defendant's part in making this charter without prior approval. However excusable it may have been in the popular sense, I think it was illegal for the plaintiff to make itself a party to this charter, whether it had *mens rea* or not. The prohibition contained in s. 9 was for public purposes and for the benefit of the public. Section 9 prohibited both parties from entering into a charter unless one of them had submitted particulars in advance and obtained approval. If neither had, both violated the section when they made the charter and became subject to the penalties set out in s. 10. . . .

If, then, the charter was illegal, was it also void? I am of opinion that it was. In *Cope* v. *Rowlands* (1836), 2 M. & W. 149 at p. 157, 150 E.R. 707, Parke B. said the following: "It is perfectly settled, that where the contract which the plaintiff seeks to enforce, be it express or implied, is expressly or by implication forbidden by the common or statute law, no court will lend its assistance to give it effect. It is equally clear that a contract is void if prohibited by a statute, though the statute inflicts a penalty only, because such a penalty implies a prohibition." Many other cases are to the like effect.

It is argued on behalf of the plaintiff, however, that the defendant having continued to hold and operate the ship after P.C. 6785 was repealed on December 31, 1946, cannot now repudiate the agreement on the ground of illegality, that having approbated the agreement in this way, the defendant is precluded from raising the question of illegality. As the Court may of its own motion raise this question, if the defendant does not do so, any such preclusion of the defendant would not help the plaintiff. And it is hardly germane to the question before the Court to consider whether the defendant is not precluded from disputing his status as a charterer under a charter of some kind. Some cases use the word "preclude" as applicable to a situation where a person disputes his status as a shareholder after a winding-up; *Re Acme Products Ltd.*, [1932] 4 D.L.R. 330 at p. 332, 40 Man. R. 444. But the real basis for deciding that persons who acquired their shares under void contracts of purchase are in some circumstances nevertheless shareholders is that they have agreed to become such by subsequent independent binding agreements resulting from their conduct: *Re Home Ass'ce Co.*, [1950] 4 D.L.R. 145 . . . The question whether the defendant is precluded from disputing his status as charterer under the charter in question is merely another way of stating the question as to whether there was a binding agreement by conduct made after December 31, 1946, reaffirming the charter. And that question is not before the Court. Whether an independent agreement from the defendant's conduct in keeping and operating the ship after December 31, 1946, and paying the agreed rate of charter hire to the plaintiff for over 3 years, can be spelled out is not for this Court to determine on the question submitted. Nor of course are the terms of that agreement, if any. It may very well be that the passage cited by Estey J. in the *Home Ass'ce Case* [p. 154] from *Re London & Northern Ins. Corp.* (1869), L.R. 4 Ch. 682 at p. 688 would apply: " 'All those acts were, however, done in conformity with, and in pursuance of, this void transaction; and there was no evidence of any separate agreement on the part of Colonel Stace and Mr. Worth.' "

Whether a new agreement arose after December 31, 1946, or not—a question on which I am not called upon to express an opinion—I am quite clear that if a contract is void at its inception because it is prohibited by statute, the repeal of the prohibitory statute will not validate that contract. *Pollock on Contracts*, 13th ed., p. 361 seems to suggest the contrary by the following language: "Perhaps the parties might be entitled to the benefit of a subsequent change in the law if their actual intention in making the contract was not unlawful." This tentative suggestion has no clear case support that I can find and in my opinion is inconsistent with the nature of a contract which is illegal and void by reason of statutory prohibition. . . .

The answer to the question is therefore as follows: The charter by the plaintiff to the defendant of the steamship "Dufferin Bell" purporting to be evidenced by and purporting to be made pursuant to the paper writing set out in para. 4 of the statement of claim herein is and was illegal, null and void and of no effect either in whole or in part.

MacDonald J.: . . . There can be little doubt that the combined effect of the prohibition in s. 9 against making an unapproved charter and the penalty provided in s. 10 for doing so was to render utterly void a charter made in contravention thereof; notwithstanding the absence of a declaration in the Order in Council that a charter so made would be void. . . .

It may be necessary to stress the fact that in law the contract was not merely unlawful or unenforceable but void; for it has been argued that as the Order in Council which it contravened was revoked as of December 31, 1946, it became valid thereupon and therefrom. . . .

If the decisions had not made it so abundantly clear that the making of such a charter in contravention of such a prohibition as that contained in s. 9 is an act devoid of legal effect, I should have sought some ground for holding that upon its repeal a Court should not refrain from giving due present-effect to it. Some precedents for such an attitude could indeed be found in recent United States decisions in relation to the repeal of usury laws and of prohibitory liquor legislation: cf. *Williston on Contracts*, ss. 1683 and 1758; and note in 50 Harv. L. Rev., p. 834.

Such an attempt might well have been based on the desirability of maintaining the effectiveness of private bargaining so far as possible, and a conclusion of present-validity reached if the contract were merely unlawful or unenforceable. The state of the law is such, however, that the charter herein cannot be regarded merely as having passed through a limbo of suspended animation or eclipse into the broad uplands of awakening validity; for it was void on its making and therefore never was in law a charter. The very fact of making the charter having been forbidden, the legal result is that no such charter was made, in the sense that it had any status as a legal fact at the time, or could gain such status as an enforceable contract upon the repeal of the prohibition which its making contravened. There is accordingly nothing in existence which may be revived by such repeal; and in any case there is no applicable doctrine providing for the revival of *void* contracts: *Williston on Contracts*, s. 1758; 31 Hals., 2nd ed., p. 557; *Dever* v. *Corcoran* (1856), 8 N.B.R. 338; and compare the *Interpretation Act*, s. 19 (1) (a) and (b).

Whether or not there has sprung from the ashes of illegality a new and enforceable contract like unto the invalid charter in its terms is a question which, fortunately, I do not have to answer.

Judgment accordingly.

[Hall, Parker and Currie JJ., concur with Ilsley C.J.]

QUESTIONS ON LEGAL METHOD. Is the argument that the contract is void on its making not begging the question? How does a "contract" become "void"? Is it not open to a court to decide that certain objective conduct should not be recognized by the state for a certain period or for certain purposes, and yet to decide that later it should be recognized for a different period and for different purposes? Is it possible to distinguish completely between the conduct of the parties and the "legal" effects to be attributed to the conduct?

If, as the Court intends, the charter is illegal and void from the beginning, what is the offence for which the penalty is provided? Did the Governor in Council intend to make it an offence to enter into a "void charter"? It was not, apparently, an offence to carry out the terms of the "void charter."

Compare section 26(1) of *The Planning Act*, R.S.O. 1960, c. 296, which authorizes a council of a municipality to designate an area as an area of subdivisional control, "and thereafter no person shall convey land in the area by way of a deed or transfer on any sale, or enter into an agreement of sale and purchase of land in the area. . . ." Is an agreement entered into in contravention of this provision "void"? See *Queensway Construction Limited and Frances Truman* v. *Trusteel Corporation (Canada)*

Limited (1961), 28 D.L.R. (2d) 480, holding that for certain purposes and in certain conditions legal effect would be given to the agreement. See also section 26(8), which provides a penalty of $500 for contravention of subdivision control. Is a deed contravening the section "void"? Can the question of illegality be properly answered without a full understanding of the purpose of the Act?

See *The Planning Act Amendment Act*, S.O., 1960-61, c. 76, which repeals section 26 and enacts a new section 26 expressly providing that "an agreement, conveyance . . . made in contravention of this section . . . does not create or convey any interest in land, but this section does not affect an agreement entered into, subject to the express condition contained therein that such agreement is to be effective only if the provisions of this section are complied with." The subsection providing for a penalty was not re-enacted. See notes, (1959), 37 *Canadian Bar Review* 636 and (1961), 39 *ibid.* 461.

10. The Statute of Frauds

The Statute of Frauds was originally passed in 1677 as 29 Car. II, c. 3. Its long title was "An Act for prevention of Frauds and Perjuries" and its preamble indicated that it was aimed at the "prevention of many fraudulent practices which are commonly endeavoured to be upheld by perjury, and subordination of perjury." It has since been adopted in virtually all commonwealth and American common law jurisdictions, with or without some modification. In a sense it can be thought of as part of the common law, and in this sense it is not a typical statute. Nevertheless it is a statute and its interpretation over nearly three hundred years has produced some surprising results. An adequate account of the Statute of Frauds would "fill a book": *Corbin on Contracts* devotes 793 pages (a whole volume) to it, and *Williston on Contracts* (3rd ed.), 599 pages. The original version contained some twenty-five sections but only sections 4 and 17 which latter section is now in the Sale of Goods Act, are of chief concern to the student of contract law. These sections are set out in modern form below. In 1677 contract law was regarded as a minor branch of the law of property and most of the sections dealt with what is now covered in law school courses in real property or land law. In this short account an attempt has been made to present a general, but, it is hoped, an accurate picture of the present status of the Statute. Because it appears rather indiscriminately throughout the law of contracts, and if examined case by case might take up too much time, the highlights are set out in the form of text notes. All that has been attempted is an introduction to some very difficult problems of statutory interpretation.

THE STATUTE OF FRAUDS
Ontario. Revised Statutes. 1960. Chapter 381

4. No action shall be brought
   [1] whereby to charge any executor or administrator upon any special promise to answer damages out of his own estate, or
   [2] whereby to charge any person upon any special promise to answer for the debt, default or miscarriage of any other person, or

[3] to charge any person upon any agreement made upon consideration of marriage, or

[4] upon any contract or sale of lands, tenements or hereditaments, or any interest in or concerning them, or

[5] upon any agreement that is not to be performed within the space of one year from the making thereof,

unless the agreement upon which the action is brought, or some memorandum or note thereof is in writing and signed by the party to be charged therewith or some person thereunto by him lawfully authorized.

[The paragraphing and numbering have been introduced for convenience in reading and for reference.]

6. No special promise made by a person to answer for the debt, default or miscarriage of another person, being in writing and signed by the party to be charged therewith, or by some other person by him thereunto lawfully authorized, shall be deemed invalid to support an action or other proceeding to charge the person by whom the promise was made by reason only that the consideration for the promise does not appear in writing, or by necessary inference from a written document.

8. No action shall be brought whereby to charge a person upon or by reason of a representation or assurance made or given concerning or relating to the character, conduct, credit, ability, trade or dealings of any other person, to the intent or purpose that such other person may obtain money, goods or credit thereupon, unless the representation or assurance is made by a writing signed by the party to be charged therewith.

THE SALE OF GOODS ACT

Ontario. Revised Statutes. 1960. Chapter 358

5. (1) A contract for the sale of any goods of the value of $40 or upwards shall not be enforceable by action unless the buyer shall accept part of the goods so sold, and actually receive the same, or give something in earnest to bind the contract or in part payment, or unless some note or memorandum in writing of the contract is made and signed by the party to be charged or his agent in that behalf.

(2) This section shall apply to every such contract, notwithstanding that the goods may be intended to be delivered at some future time, or may not at the time of such contract be actually made, procured, or provided, or fit or ready for delivery, or some act may be requisite for the making or completing thereof, or rendering the same fit for delivery.

(3) There is an acceptance of goods within the meaning of this section when the buyer does any act in relation to the goods which recognizes a pre-existing contract of sale, whether there be an acceptance in performance of the contract or not.

HISTORICAL NOTE. To appreciate the Statute it is necessary to understand something of its historical background, which is briefly set out in Plucknett, *A Concise History of the Common Law* (5th ed., 1956) 55–6. Shortly stated, there were two principal conditions commonplace then that are now completely changed. In 1677 a party to a contract was an incompetent witness. It was not until the latter half of the 19th century that we conceded that despite his interest in the outcome of a case a party might, under oath, and subject to cross-examination, tell the truth, or something like the truth. Moreover, the jury was then free to act on its own knowledge, or supposed knowledge, and it was not subject to judicial review. (See Bushel's Case (1670), Vaughan 135; 124 E.R. 1006, and Plucknett, *op. cit.* p. 131.) Rather the jury was subject to a form of penal correction known as "attainder." Now, however, parties may and almost always do testify, the judge directs the jury and may non-suit the plaintiff, and a court of appeal may upset a verdict as being against the weight of evidence and order a new trial. These procedural reforms have to a large extent removed the necessity for the Statute of Frauds, but except in two jurisdictions, it seems to be still with us. (On the whole subject of the Statute of Frauds, see Fuller, *Basic Contract Law*, Ch. 9, pp. 940-81. This short treatment is one of the most helpful available.)

THE CONTRACTS LISTED IN THE STATUTE. The odd collection of contracts included in the statute could only be understood with a full knowledge of the social conditions and economic thought of the 17th century, if then. (For a full discussion, see 6 Holdsworth, *History of English Law*, pp. 379–97, and an illustrated article: Hening, "The Original Drafts of the Statute of Frauds (29 Car. II c. 3) and Their Authors" (1913), 61 *U. of Pa. L. Rev.* 283.) It is not clear whether the purpose of the Statute was or is to prevent frauds and perjuries by guaranteeing the certainty of evidence, or to secure evidence of the deliberation of the parties, or both, and there seems today to be little reason for the selection that has persisted through almost 300 years. Consider the curious results illustrated in the following cases:

M orally hired S to work for him for fourteen months as proofreader at a monthly salary. Two weeks after the contract was made S was fired. Although both parties doubtless still retained clear recollections of the agreement, writing was just as necessary as if the contract had been broken during the thirteenth month.

B orally promised O on May 1, 1962, to erect a three storey country house according to plans and specifications, the work to be completed by October 31, 1962. O orally promised B to pay him in monthly installments as the work progressed. On June 1 B defaulted. The contract is not within the statute.

Clause [1] needs no separate consideration from clause [2]. It would appear to qualify under clause [2] as a case of a promise to answer for the debt or default of another person, the other person being the deceased. There are very few cases under clause [1] and it can be disregarded in this short exposition of the general principles of the Statute and the surprising interpretation placed on it by the courts.

Clause [2] is usually called the "guarantee" or "suretyship" section. It has generated a very considerable body of litigation and it can hardly be regarded as an example of clear drafting. The first word suggests that not every promise to answer for the debt, default or miscarriage of another person comes within the statute and must therefore be in writing. Only "special" promises are referred to in both clauses [1] and [2]. No one seems to attach any significance to the word, and its presence may now be ignored. This and other peculiarities in the Statute lead us to believe that it may have been drafted by persons who were not as careful of their words as they might have been. Hence it may very well be that the words "debt, default or miscarriage" all refer to the same thing. Just as even today draftsmen will use unnecessary pairs of words where one will do, as, for instance, "null and void", so the draftsman of 1677 may have had but one idea and a plethora of words. It is, however, easy to imagine different meanings here. "Debt" was, of course, in 1677 a term of art. But "default" was not, nor was "miscarriage." If default, however, could be limited to a failure to perform a contract duty that was not a debt, there would remain the whole range of tort liabilities of "another person" that one might promise to answer for. In *Kirkham* v. *Martin* (1819), 2 B. & Ald. 613; 106 E.R. 490, the defendant had promised orally to answer for the tortious conduct of his son, who had killed the plaintiff's horse. The defendant pleaded the Statute of Frauds (most jurisdictions require that the Statute be pleaded if it is to be relied on, unlike most "law", which is not pleaded). The plaintiff argued that the Statute of Frauds only applied to debt, but the Court, with a sympathy for the Statute that was unusual even in 1819, held that the word "miscarriage" comprehended "that species of wrongful act for the consequences of which the law would make the party civilly responsible."

A more significant interpretation of clause [2], this time, more as one might expect, narrowing the meaning of the words "answer for," is to be found in *Lakeman* v. *Mountstephen* (1874), L.R. 7 H.L. 17.

Mountstephen was a conductor who had been putting in a sewer for the town Brixham, and the Board of Health asked him to purchase pipes to connect the sewer to certain houses, whose inhabitants seemed unwilling to spend the money for the connection. The Board had power to connect the pipes itself and charge the inhabitants, but Mountstephen hesitated to take on the contract. Lakeman was Chairman of the Board, and asked Mountstephen what his objection was. Mountstephen replied, "None if you or the board will order the work, or become responsible for the payment." Lakeman then said, "Go on, Mountstephen, and do the work, and I will see you paid." Mountstephen did the work, but the Board refused to pay him because, as they said, they had not ordered it. Mountstephen then sued Lakeman on his "promise." Lakeman took the position that the Board was primarily liable, he had orally "specially promised" to answer for the Board's default, and the Statute protected him. It was held, for the plaintiff, that Lakeman had, by his words, made himself primarily liable. The Statute didn't apply because there wasn't any "other person" involved, Lakeman had promised to pay in any event. Query whether Lakeman in fact intended to be liable except in the unlikely case, as he probably thought, that the Board would not order and pay for the work. If so, he only intended to be a guarantor, or surety; that is, he only intended to pay if the Board, the real primary debtor, did not. This kind of case is sometimes labelled an "indemnity" case, but like most labels, it is dangerous to apply loosely. The intent of the transaction should be clearly exposed before the transaction is labelled anything. Since the intent has to be determined with imperfect hindsight, the Court may have a good deal of choice in determining the outcome.

In *Eastwood* v. *Kenyon* (reproduced in part on page 133, on another point) Sarah Sutcliffe's husband, the defendant, had promised the plaintiff, who owed Blackburn money advanced to help pay Sarah's expenses, that he would pay Blackburn. Apart from the consideration question, the Court held that the defendant's promise to the plaintiff to pay the plaintiff's debt to Blackburn was not within the Statute. Lord Denman said, "If the promise had been made to Blackburn, doubtless the Statute would have applied: it would then have been strictly a promise to answer for the debt of another; . . . we are of opinion that the Statute applies only to promises made to the person to whom another is answerable." (113 E.R. 482, at p. 485.) One interpretation of clause [2] has produced what might be called the primary purpose rule. The purpose referred to is that of the contracting parties, not of the Statute. Where one purpose of the contract may be that one party should become a surety for the debt of another, but it is clear that the same party has another, supposedly more important purpose that is not within the Statute, the Statute has been held not to apply. Two cases will show the basis of the rule.

(1) An importer of linseed sold some to a first buyer, who in turn sold it to a second buyer. The first buyer had not paid for his purchase and the importer could claim a lien on the linseed, but the second buyer wanted the linseed immediately and promised to pay what was owing to the importer if he would release the linseed at once. This promise was made with the object of freeing the linseed from the importer's lien which he held until he was paid by the buyer. If the first buyer paid the importer no doubt the second buyer would be discharged of his promise. The second buyer's promise was held not to be within the Statute and therefore was enforceable although oral. See *Fitzgerald* v. *Dressler* (1859), 7 C.B.N.S. 374; 141 E.R. 861. In fact the second buyer escaped liability on another ground, the promise was made on his behalf by a sixteen year old clerk who had not told the second buyer about it. Williams J. said, "At the time the promise was made the defendant was substantially the owner of the linseed in question, which was subject to the lien of the original vendors for the contract price. The effect of the promise was neither more nor less than this, to get rid of the encumbrance, or, in other words, to buy off the plaintiff's lien.

"These exceptions, where an object of the contract is to free property in which the promisor has an interest, are sometimes called the "property cases."

(2) A stock broker orally agreed with a person who was not in the Stock Exchange that the outsider would introduce customers to the stock broker and the stock broker would share half of his profits from business introduced, and the outsider would contribute one half of any losses suffered by the stock broker as a result of such business. The two were not partners. If the stock broker sued the outsider for his contribution toward a loss suffered, and the outsider pleaded the Statute, it is likely that he would not be protected. *See Sutton & Co.* v. *Grey*, [1894] 1 Q.B. 285. Relying on *Couturier* v. *Hastie* (1852), 8 Ex. 40; 155 E.R. 1250, the Court of Appeal held in a very similar situation that the outsider is like a "del credere" agent, who not only procures purchasers, but who guarantees the purchasers' credit for an extra commission. "The contract is not a guarantee with regard to a matter in which the defendant has no interest except by virtue of the guarantee, it is an indemnity with regard to a transaction in which the defendant has an interest equally with the plaintiffs." These exceptions, where the promisor has an interest beyond the guarantee, where he selects purchasers with greater care, or, as in *Grey's* case, he is almost a partner, have been called the "del credere" cases.

These propositions were reviewed in *Harburg India Rubber Comb Co.* v. *Martin*, [1902] 1 K.B. 778. In that case the plaintiffs were judgment creditors of an English company called the Crowdus Accumulator Syndicate Limited of which the defendant was a director and large shareholder. The plaintiffs were proceeding on their judgment when the defendant orally promised the plaintiff's agent that he would endorse two bills of exchange if the agent would discontinue the proceedings. On the faith of this promise the proceedings were stopped. The defendant failed to endorse the bills, and the plaintiffs commenced this action on the oral promise. The defendant pleaded the Statute and the plaintiffs argued that the transaction came within the exceptions. Mathew J. at the trial agreed and gave judgment for the plaintiffs. The Court of Appeal reversed Mathew J. and regarded the transaction as one of guarantee only. Vaughan Williams L.J. said, in part:

". . . Our attention has been called to a great number of cases in which the Court has treated various transactions, as being outside s. 4. Most of the earlier cases were what I may call 'property cases'. They were cases in which either the person who made the promise had property which he wished to relieve from liability, or there was property which he wished to acquire. It is not necessary for me to go through those cases, but I cannot agree that the present case comes within any of that class. The defendant's promise was not, as it seems to me, either a new contract of purchase, or a new contract for the release of any property which either was his or in which he had an interest.

"Our attention was next called to the exception which has been established by what I may call the 'del credere cases', beginning with *Couturier* v. *Hastie*, and coming down to *Sutton & Co.* v. *Grey*. It has been said, and I think truly, that these cases are of a different species from property cases. I say of a different species, not of a different genus, because I think there is a wider genus, which can be plainly and simply defined, within which both of these species fall. So far as I can see, the authorities have left us with a general rule, which I will attempt to define presently, and each of these two classes of cases falls within that general rule. In each of them I think, the form of the promise given by the promisor has never been held to be conclusive of the matter. He may, or he may not, promise in terms to answer for the debt of another; but, whether he does so or not, it is the substance, not the form, which is regarded.

"Before leaving these instances I wish to mention one other class, which I do not treat as an exception from s. 4, but which, I think, does not come within the section at all. I mean the cases which have been spoken of as 'indemnity cases'. Of course in one sense all guarantees, whether they come within s. 4 or not, are contracts of indemnity. But the difference between those indemnities which come within the section and those which do not is very shortly thus expressed in the notes to *Forth* v. *Stanton*, 1 Williams' *Notes to Saunders*, ed. 1871, p. 234; 'These cases establish that the statute applies only to promises made to the person to whom another is already or is to become answerable.' . . .

"In my judgment, the circumstances of the present case shew plainly that there was a guarantee of the payment of a debt for which the syndicate was primarily liable, and not an original promise by the defendant to keep the plaintiffs indemnified. In my judgment, a contract of indemnity does not come within s. 4, but I think there is nothing to justify us in holding that in the present case the contract is a contract of indemnity. In my opinion, it is a contract of guarantee—'a promise to answer for the debt of another.'

"I will now go back to those cases which, so far as the words of the contract are concerned, might come within s. 4, but which have been held not to come within it because of the object of the contract. Whether you look at the 'property cases' or at the 'del credere cases', it seems to me that in each of them the conclusion arrived at really was that the contract in question did not fall within the section because of the object of the contract. In each of those cases there was in truth a main contract—a larger contract—and the obligation to pay the debt of another was merely an incident of the larger contract. As I understand those cases, it is not a question of motive—it is a question of object. You must find what it was that the parties were in fact dealing about. What was the subject-matter of the contract? If the subject-matter of the contract was the purchase of property—the relief of property from a liability, the getting rid of incumbrances, the securing greater diligence in the performance of the duty of a factor, or the introduction of business into a stockbroker's office—in all those cases there was a larger matter which was the object of the contract. That being the object of the contract, the mere fact that as an incident to it—not as the immediate object, but indirectly—the debt of another to a third person will be paid, does not bring the case within the section. This definition or rule for ascertaining the kind of cases outside the section covers both 'property cases' and 'del credere cases'.

"Can we then in the present case find any larger contract? I cannot. It seems to me plain upon the evidence that the only matter which was present to the mind of the defendant, and was presented by him to Mr. Winter, was this: "Will you forbear for a time? Will you give the syndicate, which I believe has a future before it, an opportunity of turning round? I believe that if it has that opportunity, it will do well and will be able to pay you. And to induce you thus to forbear I will give you bills which shall secure the payment at specified periods of the judgment debt, in case the syndicate does not pay you itself.' That, I think is the true effect of the conversation, and it seems to me that was the whole of the contract, and there was neither a purchase nor a del credere arrangement, nor anything else beyond that bargain. And the mere fact that the defendant had, as he seems to have done, financed the syndicate to a large extent, and that that was his motive for thus coming forward and bargaining for forbearance, cannot make any difference in the object of the contract. That might have been the motive which induced him to make himself answerable for the debt of the syndicate, but it was not the object of the contract. The object was simply to obtain the forbearance of the creditors in respect of the debt.

"It was suggested that the true definition of cases which do not come within s. 4 should be, not those in which the obligation to pay the debt of another is an incident of a larger contract, but those in which the main object is to secure the promisor's own personal interest. But, I think, if such a definition were adopted, there would be nothing left to come within s. 4, because in every case there must be a consideration for which the promisor bargains to come to him from the promisee. That is as true of mere forbearance as of anything else. If the contract is that the promisor will be answerable for the debt due to the promisee if he will forbear, if the main object is to obtain that forbearance, and the promisor wishes to obtain it, that would be sufficient to take the case out of the statute. In my opinion so to hold would be simply to repeal s. 4. . . ."

For a collection of the cases dealing generally with guarantees see Falconbridge, "Annotation on Guarantees and the Statute of Frauds," 55 D.L.R. 1.

Clause [3]. This clause, which brings within the Statute "any agreement made upon consideration of marriage", calls for only a brief comment. It might, on a hasty reading, appear to make every engagement to marry a matter requiring writing. In such cases, however, the consideration is not *marriage*, but the mutual *promise to marry*. The common cases are those where one lover promises the other to convey property in consideration of the marriage, or where a parent promises to convey property to a son or daughter on his or her forthcoming marriage. Oddly enough, an agreement between parents of a loving couple that each will convey property to his respective child on marriage is not within the Statute because, again, the consideration is the mutual promise. See *Philpott* v. *Wallett* (1682), 3 Levinz 65; 83 E.R. 579, *Harrison* v. *Cage* (1698), 1 Ld. Raymond 386; 91 E.R. 1156, and *Tweddle* v. *Atkinson* (1861), 1 B. & S. 393; 121 E.R. 762.

Clause [4]. This clause, which is rather oddly, and probably accidentally, worded, brings within the Statute practically every land transaction. It speaks of "any contract *or* sale of lands . . . ," but there seems to be common agreement that the draftsman intended to say "any contract *for* the sale of lands. . . ." The expression "contract of lands" is not usual English, and "sale of lands" is quite a different thing from a contract, with which section 4 is mostly concerned, and other parts of the Statute deal in some detail with the "sale" of land.

In one area the contract for the sale of land may be of particular interest to students of contract law, rather than conveyancing, or real estate transactions, by whatever name the course on contracts for the sale of land may be called . When trees are cut from land and sold, there may be conversion of the "realty" into "personalty," and similarly, when gas or oil is sold after being extracted from land, it may be "personalty." Depending on where the transformation takes place, a contract for newly cut timber, or timber to be cut, may come within the Statute or not. See *Tilbury Town Gas Co. Ltd.* v. *Maple City Oil & Gas Co. Ltd.* (1915), 35 D.L.R. 4 (P.C.) 186 at p. 204, and *King* v. *Freeman*, [1942] O.R. 561 (neither case involved the Statute).

Clause [5]: "any agreement that is not to be performed within the space of one year from the making thereof." Presumably the purpose of clause [5] is to bring into the protection of the Statute contracts which from their terms may be the subject of litigation long after the parties (who couldn't testify anyway) and witnesses might have forgotten the terms. But if that was its purpose it seems to have been much broader than need be, and like so many statutory reforms, to have caught cases probably never intended by the reformers. The critical time, usually, is not how long a period there was between the making and the performing of the contract, but between its making or breaking, and the time it comes up for trial, for that is when the witnesses' memories will be tested.

The first problem case is the one where the contract itself is silent about its duration. (It will be convenient here to deal with illustrations drawn from employment contracts, and many cases are to be found in this area, but the language is broad enough to catch any kind of contract that runs over a year in performance, so do not be misled by the limits of the illustrations.) If M hires S for an indeterminate time, is the contract within the Statute? If S is a healthy young man, it may be that the parties contemplated years of service. Is the test of contemplation, or "intention" of the parties, sufficient? Suppose S in fact quits two months later? Is the test of what in fact happened sufficient? Does it leave the parties themselves with sufficient guide? Should the parties have to wait, in all such cases, to see what happens?

The test usually applied is a simpler one. The court asks what could have happened. Is performance within a year possible? If so, the oral contract is enforceable. If not, the oral contract is unenforceable. *Adams* v. *Union Cinemas, Ltd.*, [1939] 3 All E.R. 136 is a case of this type. Adams was employed as a controller of theatres by the defendant, who had suggested that he might be employed for a two year period in this post, and Adams so claimed in his reaction for wrongful dismissal. The evidence established, however, that no final agreement had been reached on this point, and that the contract was one for general hiring with no time specified. If the oral contract for two years had been proved Adams would have been caught by the Statute. Lord Justice MacKinnon commented on the odd result: "... the plaintiff and his advisers, perhaps by inadvertance or by too sanguine an expectation, thought the defendants would not be so ungentlemanly as to plead the Statute." And Du Parcq L.J. said, "I must confess that I should be very sorry to have to explain the facts of this case and the importance of the legal issues in this case to an intelligent foreigner, because I can imagine his asking; 'Why is it that counsel for the defendants was apparently much more anxious even than counsel for the plaintiff to show that his client had entered into an agreement to employ the plaintiff for a longer time and at a larger salary? Is it because of undue generosity on their part, or how is it to be explained?' I can imagine that, when one had to tell him that the reason was that, if only the defendants could satisfy the court that they had given their word to the plaintiff that they would employ him for two years, then the court would at once decide that, in the circumstances, they need not pay him a penny and they were not bound to employ him, the intelligent foreigner would find a little difficulty in understanding the explanation."

Once it was established that Adams had only a contract of indefinite duration, despite the fact that both parties had obviously contemplated a two year period although it was understood that Adams would not go on working as a controller without clear written agreement, the court applied the test of what "might be."

If the test then is, what could have happened, does death, which can always happen, mean that every oral contract not to be performed within the space of one year is enforceable notwithstanding the Statute because it could be so performed by one party dying? Perhaps the easiest answer is that a contract for a fixed period is not performed if the party dies before the fixed period is up. The party is excused for his non-performance, but legally speaking, he is not regarded as having performed. Nor is it necessary to regard a contract for an indefinite term as "performed" by death. On the other hand, a contract to perform for the rest of a party's life; for example, an appointment for life, even of a healthy young man, is fully performed if he works for six months and then is killed in a highway accident. He has done all he promised to do. The oral promises are enforceable. But see *Ste. Marie* v. *Ste. Marie*, [1929] 4 D.L.R. 1076, to the contrary, citing *Davey* v. *Shannon* (1879), 4 Ex.D. 81, which was, however, disapproved of by the Court of Appeal in *McGregor* v. *McGregor* (1888), 21 Q.B.D. 424.

If the test is, what could have happened, the case of a two year oral contract with an express provision that either party could terminate the contract by giving the other six months notice, would clearly be one where the contract could be performed in six months, certainly in less than twelve months. *Hanau* v. *Ehrlich*, [1912] A.C. 39, is such a case. You may find the Court of Appeal decisions, reported in [1911] 2 K.B. 1056, more interesting than those in the House of Lords. A. T. Lawrence L.J., said, "As in this case the employment of the plaintiff was for a period of two years, it could not be performed by either within one year. I do not think the existence of the power to give notice affects the contractual period for performance. Its exercise terminates the obligation further to perform but the exercise of this power, though contained in the contract, is not the same thing as the performance of the contract. The words 'not to be performed' in the statute apply to the obligations undertaken by each party towards the other. Giving notice is the exercise of a right; performance is the fulfilment of a duty. This view is certainly more in accordance with the express object of the Statute of Frauds than the construction contended for by the plaintiff." The plaintiff had contended that the agreement amounted to an agreement for an indefinite period within a maximum of two years, that the Statute did not apply, and that the contract was enforceable.

Do you agree with the literal analysis of A. T. Lawrence L.J. and his view that the object of the Statute was to prevent enforcement of this well proven contract? Is there a difference between the "object of the Statute" and a literal reading of some of its words?

Fletcher Moulton L.J. was less satisfied with the result. He remarked: "If I were free . . . I should say that beyond all question it might possibly be performed within the year . . . It is impossible to predicate the period of the performance of this contract is more than a year. Moreover, supposing the notice to be given, then six months after that date the contract is wholly performed. There is no ghostly survival of the contract for the remainder of the two years; the contract is wholly performed when the notice has expired. I have, therefore, no hesitation in saying that, if I were free to use my own intellect . . . I should certainly allow this appeal. . . . But I am bound by the authorities, and agree that this appeal must be dismissed." Buckley L.J. said on this question of the authorities, "It is now two centuries too late to ascertain the meaning of s. 4 by applying one's own mind independently to the interpretation of its language. Our task is a much more humble one; it is to see how that section has been expounded in decisions and how the decisions apply to the present case." This reluctant obeisance to authority by two members of the Court of Appeal probably encouraged the appeal to the House of Lords, who, however, affirmed the lower court. Lord Atkinson said, "Where the language of a statute is ambiguous and one finds that a particular construction has been put upon it by a number of authorities, extending over a very great length of time, it would be unwise and wrong to adopt a different construction."

Why should Lord Atkinson think it would be "unwise"? Is he supposing that someone relies on the "number of authorities"? Who relies on them? The courts? Lawyers? Business men? The general public, that is, contracting parties?

Another surprising interpretation is to be found in *Donellan* v. *Read* (1832), 3 B. &. Ad. 899; 110 E.R. 330, which held that where the duty of one party to a contract is to be performed within a year, the fact that the duty of the other party clearly cannot be performed within the year does not bring the contract within the protection of the Statute. In *Donellan* v. *Read* an oral promise was given to pay an increased rent of £5 a year for the remaining years of a lease, in exchange for £50 worth of improvements in the house. The improvements were carried out between

August and November in 1827 at an expense of £55. The defendant paid the increased rent for one quarter, at Christmas time 1827, but refused to pay it thereafter. Littledale J. thought it wrong that one party, having enjoyed the whole of the other party's performance, could ignore his own promise. *Donellan* v. *Read* has been much criticised. See *Williston on Contracts*, 3rd ed., sec. 504, where the various authorities are collected. In *Boydell* v. *Drummond*, (1809), 11 East 142; 103 E.R. 958, Bayley J. said "I cannot say that a contract is *performed* when a great part of it remains *un*-performed within the year, or in other words, that *part performance is performance*. The mischief meant to be prevented by the statute was the leaving to memory the terms of a contract for longer than a year. The persons might die who were to prove it, or they might lose their faithful recollection of the terms of it." The exception is sometimes justified on the distinction between an action brought or "any special promise" in clauses [1] and [2], and an action brought on "any agreement" in clause [5], the idea being that the bilateral character of the "agreement" is gone once one party has completely performed and only a unilateral "promise" remains as the subject of an action.

One final permutation remains to be considered. Suppose that an oral contract calls for a performance by one party for a specific period of three years, and the other party's performance is for an indefinite time. One might expect a combination of *Adams* v. *Union Cinemas, Ltd.*, *supra*, and *Donellan* v. *Read* to result in a holding that the Statute does not apply. This situation is essentially what confronted the Court in *Reeve* v. *Jennings*, [1910] 2 K.B. 522. Reeve employed Jennings in his dairy business on an indefinite hiring, so that Reeve's obligations to pay Jennings and to keep him in his employ could be performed within a year. Jennings, on the other hand, agreed that he would not compete in the dairy business for three years after quitting or being discharged. The original agreement was in writing, but its extension was oral. Jennings left about two years after the oral extension of the agreement and immediately entered into business on his own. The Court was faced with a nice choice of policies, since it presumably didn't wholly like either restraint of trade clauses or the Statute. The county court judge who tried the case held that the oral extension did not come within the Statute and enforced the contract. The appeal was allowed. Bray J. said, ". . . I must hold that this contract was within the statute. As regards one side it was clearly not to be performed within the year, as regards the other side it could be, *but it was not the intention of the parties that it should be performed within the year*. I think that this case does not come within the exception laid down in *Donellan* v. *Read* and the appeal must, therefore, be allowed." (Italics added.)

A commonly recurring question is raised where a contract is entered into on Monday, to start on Tuesday, and run for a year. In *Smith* v. *Gold Coast and Ashanti Explorers, Ltd.*, [1903] 1 K.B. 285, 838, Lord Alverstone, C.J., said, "I think that these cases shew that a contract for a year's service to commence on the day after the day on which the contract was made is not an agreement which is not to be preformed within the space of one year from the making thereof, within the meaning of section 4." Compare *Dollar* v. *Parkington* (1901), 84 L.J. 470 (*contra*). In *Britain* v. *Rossiter* (1899), 11 Q.B.D. 123, an oral contract made on Saturday, April 21, for a year's employment to begin on Monday, April 23, was held to come within the Statute and so be unenforceable.

The Sale of Goods Act. In the original section, which appeared as section 17 of the Statute, the words "shall not be enforceable" were "no contract . . . shall be allowed to the good."

The peculiarities of this section may be left to the more specialized courses of Commercial Law or Sales, but two features are worth noting briefly. The first is the fact that the limit of money has not changed in nominal amount since 1677, when the original section set the limit at £10. Today's value would be closer, probably, to $1000, but only in some American jurisdictions has there been any recognition of the changing value of currency. The most common limit in the United States is $500. In all likelihood the $500 limit is much closer in principle to the original £10 than $40, or $30, which is the lowest figure in any Statute of Frauds in Canada. It is obvious that the original section 17 was aimed at very substantial sales only.

The other remarkable feature about the sale of goods section is the presence of alternatives to the note or memorandum, in the form of part payment, the handing over of some earnest, or delivery, acceptance and actual receipt of the goods. No such alternative is given in section 4 clause [4], dealing with contracts for sale of land, but the Chancery Courts have, in this area, taken certain liberties with the Statute and have developed a somewhat similar rule. See below in the Note on Part Performance and *Deglman* v. *Guaranty Trust Company of Canada and Constantinean*, p. 273. See also p. 50.

THE MEMORANDUM OR NOTE. One of the most interesting interpretation problems arises from the words "some memorandum or note." It was clear that a formal contract, or even a simple contract wholly reduced to writing but not under seal, was not required although quite acceptable. What was a "note"? In *Bailey* v. *Sweeting* (1861), 9 C.B.N.S. 843; 142 E.R. 332, the dispute was over a sale of "chimney glasses" and the "note" which was held sufficient read as follows:

"Cheltenham, December 3, 1859.

Gentlemen,—In reply to your letter of the 1st instant, I beg to say that the only parcel of goods selected for ready money was the chimney-glasses, amounting to £38 10*s*. 6*d*., which goods I have never received, and have long since declined to have for reasons made known to you at the time; with regard to the other items, viz., £11 4*s*. 9*d*., £14 13*s*., and £13 13*s*., for goods had subsequently (less cases returned), those goods are, I believe, subject to the usual discount of £5 per cent, and I am quite ready to remit you cash for these parcels at once, and on receipt of your reply to this letter will instruct a friend to call on you and settle accordingly.

I am yours,

Geo. Sweeting."

In effect the "note" was a repudiation of the contract! In a modern English case, *Farr, Smith & Co.* v. *Messers, Ltd.* [1928] 1 K.B. 397, a statement of defence setting out the terms of a contract and signed by the defendant's counsel was accepted as sufficient when the action by the original plaintiff was dropped and recommenced by a corporate plaintiff.

The "note" apparently need not even be a communication between the plaintiff and defendant. A letter to the defendant's agent, setting out or referring to the written terms and signed by the defendant has been held sufficient. See *Gibson* v. *Holland* (1865), L.R. 1 C.P. 1. In that case Erle C.J. went so far as to prefer such a "note." He said: "Indeed one would incline to think that a statement made by the party to his own agent would be the more satisfactory evidence of the two."

The note need not be a contemporaneous record of the agreement. In rather unusual circumstances, in *Farr, Smith & Co.* v. *Messers Ltd.*, [1928] 1 K.B. 397, a statement of defence in an earlier action on the same contract was successfully used as the note. Counsel for the defence as agent of the defendant, had signed the defence, which contained the terms of the agreement!

Since many contracts are "unilateral" in form, and the offer is likely to be the only writing of the terms, it is not surprising that the written offer, when accepted by performance of the requested act, is regarded as a sufficient note. See *Reuss* v. *Picksley* (1866), L.R. 1 Ex. 342. Willes J. said: "Now all that was signed here was not a formal agreement but a proposal on one side, and there was an assent to that proposal on the other. All difficulty as to the terms of the proposal is out of the case. It contained the names of the parties and all the terms by reference to the letter of the 8th September, which must be taken to be recited in the letter of the 9th. The only question is, whether it is sufficient to satisfy the statute that the party charged should sign what he proposes as an agreement, and that the other party should afterwards assent without writing to the proposal? As to this it is clear, both on reasoning and authority, that the proposal so signed and assented to, does become a memorandum or note of an agreement within the 4th section of the statute.

"It has been urged upon that this conclusion will lead to fraud and perjury, and to the very mischiefs the statute was passed to prevent. We do not concur in that view, because no one will be able to enforce an agreement of the sort we are now discussing, without proving that he did or was ready to do his part to entitle him to performance on the part of the other contracting party."

Apart from the form the document takes, one might suppose that at least the parties must be reasonably identified. In *Vandenbergh* v. *Spooner* (1866), L.R. 1 Ex. 316, although Martin B. was "not well satisfied" about the meaning of the "note," Bramwell B. said for the whole court: "The document was signed by the defendant, and was in the following terms: 'D. Spooner agrees to buy the whole of the lots of marble purchased by Mr. Vandenbergh, now lying at the Lyme Cobb, at 1*s*. per foot.' Can the essentials of the contract be collected from this document by means of a fair construction or reasonable intendment? We have come to the conclusion that they cannot, inasmuch as the seller's name as seller is not mentioned in it, but occurs only as part of the description of the goods."

Evidence was also given to the effect that, after the defendant had signed this document, he wrote out what he alleged to be a copy of it, which at his request the plaintiff, supposing it to be a genuine copy, signed. This was in the following words: "Mr. J. Vandenbergh agrees to sell to W. D. Spooner the several lots of marble purchased by him, now lying at Lyme, at 1*s*. the cubic foot, and a bill at one month. (Signed) Julius Vandenbergh." The jury however were of the opinion that the first document stated the contract actually made.

Compare *Newell* v. *Radford* (1867), L.R. 3 C.P. 52, where the defendant's agent solicited an order from the plaintiff and entered in the plaintiff's book: "Mr. Newell, 32 sacks culasses at 39*s*., 280 lbs., to wait orders. June 8. John Williams." Bovill C.J. said: "In this case it is not disputed that the signature of the agent Williams would be sufficient to bind the defendant, but it is contended that the written memorandum does not sufficiently show which of the parties was the buyer. At first sight this indeed might not appear quite clear, except to a man in the trade; but it has always been held that you may prove what the parties would have understood to be the meaning of the words used in the memorandum, and that for this purpose parol evidence of the surrounding circumstances is admissible: . . . In this case it was shown that the plaintiff was a baker, and that the defendant was a dealer in flour which the plaintiff would require for his trade; and looking at the nature of the entry in relation to those facts, I think there can be no reasonable doubt that it was a sale from the defendant to the plaintiff. If however there were any doubt, looking at the entry alone, it is set at rest by the two letters which passed between the plaintiff and defendant, which sufficiently identify the contract, and in which the relative positions of the parties as buyer and seller is distinctly stated."

Although it is essential that the memorandum disclose both the contracting parties with sufficient certainty of identification it may be possible that the parties are described, rather than named, and if the description is sufficiently definite viewed in the light of surrounding circumstances the memorandum will be good. For example "if the vendor is described in the contract as 'proprietor,' 'owner.' 'mortgagee,' or the like, the description is sufficient although he is not named; but if he is described as 'vendor' or as 'client' or 'friend' of a named agent, that is not sufficient; the reasons given being, in the language of Lord Cairns, that the former description 'is a statement of matter of fact as to which there can be perfect certainty, and none of the dangers struck at by the Statute of Frauds can arise;' the reason against the latter description being that in order to find out who is vendor, client, or friend you must go into evidence on which there might possibly be a conflict." (Kay J. in *Jarrett* v. *Hunter* (1886), 4 Ch.D. 182, 184.) Hence, if a memorandum is signed by an agent "on behalf of the vendor" it will be held insufficient. *Potter* v. *Duffield* (1874), L.R. 18 Eq. 4. But if A signs "on behalf of the proprietors" the memorandum is good. *Rossiter* v. *Miller* (1878), 3 App.Cas. 1124. As to situations in which an agent signs as one of the contracting parties, though acting for an undisclosed principal, see Jessel M.R. in *Commins* v. *Scott*, (1875), L.R. 20 Eq. 11 at p. 15: "There can be no doubt that if a written contract is made in this form, A.B. agrees to sell Blackacre to C.D. for £1000, then E.F., the principal of A.B., can sue G.H., the principal of C.D., on that contract." See also *Filby* v. *Hounsell*, [1896] 2 Ch. 737.

A "note" or "memorandum" would obviously be of little help if the terms were not set out, and Grose J. said as much in *Wain* v. *Warlter* (1803), 5 East 10; 102 E.R. 972. "What is required to be in writing, therefore, is the 'agreement' (not the promise, as mentioned in the first part of the clause), or some note or memorandum of the agreement. Now the 'agreement' is that which is to show what each party is to do or perform, and by which both parties are to be bound; and this is required to be in writing. If it were only necessary to show what one of them was to do, it would be sufficient to state the promise made by the defendant who was to be charged upon it. But if we were to adopt this construction it would be the means of letting in those very frauds and perjuries which it was the object of the statute to prevent. For without the parol evidence the defendant cannot be charged upon the written contract for want of a consideration in law to support it. The effect of the parol evidence then is to make him liable: and thus he would be charged with the debt of another by parol testimony, when the statute was passed with the very intent of avoiding such a charge, by requiring that the 'agreement,' by which must be understood the 'whole agreement,' should be in writing."

Wain v. *Warlters* was an action on a promise to pay the debt of another in the "note" of which no consideration is mentioned. The case must now be considered in the light of section 6 of the Statute of Frauds. What effect has the statutory change upon the "principle" upon which *Wain* v. *Warlters* was decided? How do you determine the *ratio decidendi* of a case of interpretation?

Some rather interesting doubts can be raised by speculating on the reason the draftsman referred to a "special promise" in Clauses [1] and [2], an "agreement" in Clauses [3] and [5] and a "contract" in Clause [4] and yet requires the "agreement" to be in writing.

A nice distinction is taken in *Hoadly* v. *McLaine* (1834), 10 Bing. 482; 131 E.R. 982, where a rather common type of situation was dealt with. The plaintiff agreed in writing to build a "new, fashionable, and handsome landaulet with the following appointments" (which were set out in detail). No price was specified, but the plaintiff claimed £480 which the defendant refused to pay and to which he pleaded the statute. A "great number of coachmakers . . . proved that the landaulet was of such exquisite workmanship, and so highly ornamented, as to be cheap at the price demanded." The jury awarded £200 damages. In reply to the defence of the statute, i.e., that the price or consideration was not in writing, it was argued that the undertaking was only to pay on a "quantum meruit," and no price could be stated in the note because none had been argued. The "note" was held sufficient. Tindal C.J. said:

"What is implied by law is as strong to bind the parties as if it were under their hand. This is a contract in which the parties are silent as to price, and therefore leave it to the law to ascertain what the commodity contracted for is reasonably worth.

"It has been contended, that this would open a door for perjury, and let in the mischief which the statute of frauds proposes to exclude. But I cannot agree in that proposition; for it does not appear that any specific price was agreed on; and if it had appeared that such was the case, this note would not have been evidence of such a bargain, as the case of *Elmore* v. *Kingscote*, (1826), 5 B. & C. 583; 108 E.R. 217, expressly decides.

"Thus the law stands on the note or memorandum of May, 1832. But we may look at all the writings to see what the contract was; and here, from the defendant's letter of April, 1833, it appears that, after he had seen the carriage, he desired the plaintiff to send in his *bill*. He must have known whether he had contracted for a stipulated price or not; and it may therefore be inferred, from this letter, that he knew he was to pay the reasonable charge when the article was made up."

The "note" must be "signed by the party to be charged," that is, by the defendant (or his agent). If he signs but the plaintiff does not, only one of them would be bound, notwithstanding the "logic" of the mutuality doctrine. Of course, once the plaintiff is in court, he would presumably be required to perform his side of the bargain so far at least as it was a condition precedent to the defendant's liability. But what constitutes a signature? Apparently now a sales slip from a department store would be regarded as signed, if the slip has the name of the business printed on it. See *Evans* v. *Hoare* [1892] 1 Q.B. 593, where Denman J. said:

"This was an action for wrongful dismissal. The plaintiff entered the defendants' services as a ledger clerk at £80 a year; the salary was twice raised £10 a year until it reached £100. On February 19, 1890, the plaintiff signed an agreement as follows:

"5, Campbell Terrace, Cannhill Road,
Leytonstone, Feb. 19, 1890.

Messrs. Hoare, Marr & Co., 26, 29 Budge Row,
London, E.C.

Gentlemen,—In consideration of your advancing my salary to the sum of £130 per annum, I hereby agree to continue my engagement in your office for three years, from and commencing January 1, 1890, at a salary at the rate of £130 per annum aforesaid, payable monthly as hitherto.

Yours obediently,
George E. Evans."

"If this agreement was within s. 4 of the Statute of Frauds, the judgment was justified. The learned judge gave judgment for the defendants on the ground that the document was not signed within that section. This decision would be right unless the words 'Messrs. Hoare, Marr & Co., at the commencement, can, under the circumstances, be held to be 'a signature by a person authorized thereunto by the defendants.' In fact, the document was drawn up by one Harding, who was authorized by the defendants to draw it up and take it, in its present shape in all other respects, for the plaintiff's signature. It appears to me that the case falls within the principle of the decisions cited in favour of the plaintiff, especially *Schneider* v. *Norris* (1814), 2 M. & S. 286; 105 E.R. 388. In the preseint case it is impossible to doubt that the word 'your,' twice used in the written document, refers to the defendants, whose name and address is given in full at the head of the document. Nor can I doubt that both Harding and the defendants intended that this document, when signed by Evans, should be the final memorandum of the contract binding upon the defendants as well as the plaintiff."

In *Cohen* v. *Roche* [1927] 1 K.B. 169 a printed page from the catalogue of an auction sale was allowed as a signature when pasted into the auctioneer's book.

Perhaps the most indefensible of the interpretative glosses on the Statute is the notion that it is permissible to link up two separate documents, neither of which is sufficient in itself, by parol evidence. The extreme case is *Pearce* v. *Gardner* [1897] 1 Q.B. 688. There the only memorandum or note tendered in evidence by the plaintiff was a letter addressed to "Dear Sir" and containing the terms signed by the defendant. The plaintiff testified that the letter had been received in an envelope addressed to him, but he did not produce the envelope. In allowing the letter as a "note," Lord Esher M.R. said,

"The great struggle was as to whether in that state of things the letter and the envelope can be taken together to constitute the memorandum required. No case has been cited deciding this point either way so that we have now to determine the matter. I adopt the suggestion made in Dart on Vendors and Purchasers, at p. 253 of the 6th edition, which is as follows: 'In the case of a letter, if the name of the party to whom it is addressed appear in an indorsed direction, or be written at the foot of the letter, no difficulty on the above point can arise: if an envelope be used the name may often not appear in the letter; but the Court, it is conceived would receive evidence connecting the envelope with the enclosure." The common sense of the matter seems to me to be that the envelope and the letter within it were sent together and may be taken together; so that the effect is the same as if the name of the plaintiff had been written at the foot or indorsed on the letter."

See also *Oliver* v. *Hunting* (1890), 44 Ch.D. 205. Kekewich J.: "The elementary proposition about which there is no doubt is this,—the memorandum to be signed by the party sought to be charged, so as to bring a particular case within the Statute of Frauds, need not be on one piece of paper, nor need it be a complete document, signed by the party at one and the same time. It may be contained in two or more pieces of paper, but they must be so connected that you can read them together, so as to form one memorandum of the contract between the parties. Directly you get beyond that, you get into difficulty. One can illustrate that in a simple manner. An intending purchaser accepts an offer made by a proposing vendor thus: 'In reply to your letter of the 14th instant." Can one annex to that reply the letter of the 14th instant? Surely one cannot, without inquiring what letter it is; unless the purchaser has, with unusual prudence, completed the reference by saying, 'In reply to your letter of the 14th instant, a copy of which is on the other side.' In the absence of any such complete evidence as that, one must inquire what the letter of the 14th instant was, because *non constat,* it may have been a reference to any one of half a dozen different letters; and so, from that very simple illustration, one can go through a large variety of more complex ones. It is not for me to say that the old rule was better or worse than the present rule. . . . I take the old rule from the original edition of Lord Blackburn, *On the Contract of Sale*; . . . 'If the contents of the signed paper themselves make reference to the others so as to show by internal evidence that the papers refer to each other, they may all be taken together as one memorandum in writing [as in the case which I have mentioned of a letter referring to a previous letter, of which the copy is annexed]: but if it is necessary, in order to connect them, to give evidence of the intention of the parties that they should be connected, shown by circumstances not apparent on the face of the writings, the memorandum is not all in writing, for it consists partly of the contents of the writings and partly of the expression of an intention to unite them, and that expression is not in writing.'

"The old case of *Boydell* v. *Drummond* (1809), 11 East, 142; 103 E.R. 958 . . . might be consistent with that rule; but certainly of late a different rule has been introduced, and it is a rule, to say the least, consistent with the convenience of mankind, because if you were to exclude parol evidence to explain such a doubtful reference as 'the letter of the 14th instant,' or it might be simply 'your letter,' the result might in a large number of cases be gross injustice. Now I take it to be quite settled that in a case of that kind you may give parol evidence to show what the document referred to was. I take it that you may go further than that, and that if you find a reference to something, which may be a conversation, or may be a written document, you may give evidence to show whether it was a conversation or a written document; and, having proved that it was a written document, you may put that written document in evidence, and so connect it with the one already admitted or proved. . . . The illustration [Bramwell L.J. in *Long* v. *Millar* (1878), 4 C.P.D. 450] gives is this (at p. 454). Suppose that A writes to B, saying that he will give £1000 for B's estate, and at the same time states the terms in detail, and suppose that B simply writes back in return, "I accept your offer." In that case there may be an identification of the documents by parol evidence, and it may be shown that the offer alluded to by B is that made by A, without infringing the Statute of Frauds, sec. 4, which requires a note or memorandum in writing.' If that is sound, which I take it to be, according to other cases, and according to the convictions of Judges in older cases which are introduced into the old law, it is difficult, perhaps, to say where parol evidence is to stop; but substantially it never stops short of this, that whenever parol evidence is required to connect two written documents together, then that parol evidence is admissable. You are entitled to rely upon a written document, which requires explanation. Perhaps the real principle upon which that is based is, that you are always entitled in regarding the construction and meaning of a written document to inquire into the circumstances under which it was written, not in order to find an interpretation by the writer of the language, but to ascertain from the surrounding facts and circumstances, with reference to what, and with what intent, it must have been written. I think myself that must be the principle on which parol evidence of this kind is admitted. Turning to the case before me, I find a letter of the 12th of September, 1888, written by the defendant to Mrs. Oliver, and in that he says: 'I beg to acknowledge receipt of check, value £375 on account of the purchase-money for the Fletton Manor House estate, for which I thank you.' I have two things here perfectly clear, that there is a property called Fletton Manor House estate, which constitutes the subject of a purchase, and, therefore, the subject of a sale. I have also that £375 is part of the purchase-money for that house: but, beyond that I have no terms of a contract. I am entitled to consider the circumstances under which the letter was written, in order to give any meaning that I properly can to it—not to add terms to it, but to find out what the meaning necessarily must be, having regard to the facts and circumstances—and, having got the evidence which I have in this case, the conclusion is inevitable that it refers to a previous memorandum of terms of agreement under which Mrs. Oliver becomes the purchaser of this particular property for the price of £2,375, on account of which the check for £375 was sent. Having got that evidence in, having got the connection between the two documents, I have then enough to enable me to read the two documents together, and, reading them together, I have a distinct memorandum of contract, specifying all the terms, the second one supplying what the first one omitted to give, namely, singularly enough, the property which was intended to be purchased and sold. That being so, the objection that there is no memorandum within the Statute of Frauds fails."

Compare *Thomson* v. *McInnes* (1911), 12 Comm. L.R. 563, where the High Court of Australia held that the use of the word "purchase-money" in a receipt signed by the vendor could not refer to another document. Griffith C.J. said: "It is sufficient if the note signed by the party to be charged refers to some other document in such a manner as to incorporate it with the document signed, so that they can be read together. That has been settled for a long time. But the whole contract must be shown by the writing. The reference, therefore, in the document signed must be to some other document as such, and not merely to some transaction or event in the course of which another document may or may not have been written. . . . Whether there is a reference or not depends, first of all upon the construction of the document which is signed. You must, first of all, find some words in that document which are capable of being construed as referring to a document and not to a transaction or event. If there are words capable of such a construction, then, and not before, the question arises as to their meaning . . . in *Long* v. *Millar* the words "the purchase" used in a receipt were held to mean a written document. . . . In all the cases it was held that the word in question meant a written document. Kekewich J. in *Oliver* v. *Hunting* suggested that this was the old rule, and that there was now a new rule. With the greatest respect for that learned judge I do not agree with him. The rule has always been the same. Some judges may have been more liberal in their application of the rule than others, or may have taken a more liberal view of the words to be construed. The rule is thus stated by Baggallay L.J. in *Long* v. *Millar*: 'The true principle is that there must exist a writing to which the document signed by the party to be charged can refer, but that this document may be identified by verbal evidence! I think it unfortunate that any doubt should be entertained as to that doctrine. It is as well settled as any doctrine relating to contracts.' "

THE DOCTRINE OF PART PERFORMANCE. Not only did the Common Law Courts liberate many cases from the confines of the Statute by rather extraordinary interpretations of the words "memorandum or note," the Chancery Courts did away with the requirement of writing altogether in cases where they had other evidence from which they could infer the existence of the contract sued on. The kind of evidence required was fairly particular, and the alternative of acceptance and actual receipt expressly provided for in section 17 has been the most common ground used by the Chancery Courts in getting out of section 4. When an oral contract for the sale of land was followed by the purchaser taking possession, the act was regarded as "part performance" of the contract and was accepted as evidence from which the existence of the contract could be inferred, independently of oral evidence of its terms. Of course a contract for sale hardly ever obliges the purchaser to take possession, and his doing so is not properly called "part performance" of the contract, but the use of the label has become too settled to dislodge it now. In fact what appears to be meant is evidence of conduct by a party from which the existence of the contract on which he sues may be inferred and nothing more. The sale of goods section also excepts cases where there has been part payment on the giving of an earnest, but part payment of the purchase price of land is rarely accepted as an act of "part performance." There are some views that as long as some contract may be inferred from the conduct, the particular contract sued on need not be a necessary inference, but this view is not widely accepted in Canada. Because this rule was applied only in the Chancery Courts, it is effectively limited to clause [4] cases, which may be the subject of the equitable remedy of specific performance.

DEGLMAN *v.* GUARANTY TRUST CO. OF CANADA AND CONSTANTINEAU

Ontario. Supreme Court of Canada. [1954] 3 D.L.R. 785

RAND J.: In this appeal the narrow question is raised as to the nature of part performance which will enable the Court to order specific performance of a contract relating to lands unenforceable at law by reason of s. 4 of the *Statute of Frauds*, R.S.O. 1950, c. 371. The respondent Constantineau claims the benefit of such a contract and the appellant represents the next-of-kin other than the respondent of the deceased, Laura Brunet, who resist it.

The respondent was the nephew of the deceased. Both lived in Ottawa.

When he was about 20 years of age, and while attending a technical school, for 6 months of the school year 1934–35 he lived with his aunt at No. 550 Besserer St. Both that and the house on the adjoining lot, No. 548, were owned by the aunt and it was during this time that she claimed to have agreed that if the nephew would be good to her and do such services for her as she might from time to time request during her lifetime she would make adequate provision for him in her will, and in particular that she would leave to him the premises at No. 548. While staying with her the nephew did the chores around both houses which, except for an apartment used by his aunt, were occupied by tenants. When the term ended he returned to the home of his mother on another street. In the autumn of that year he worked on the national highway in the northern part of Ontario. In the spring of 1936 he took a job on a railway at a point outside of Ottawa and at the end of that year, returning to Ottawa, he obtained a position with the city police force. In 1941 he married. At no time did he live at the house No. 548 or, apart from the 6 months, at the house No. 550.

The performance consisted of taking his aunt about in her own or his automobile on trips to Montreal and elsewhere, and on pleasure drives, of doing odd jobs about the two houses, and of various accommodations such as errands and minor services for her personal needs. . . . These circumstances, Spence J. at trial and the Court of Appeal [[1953] O.W.N. 665], finding a contract, have held to be sufficient grounds for disregarding the prohibition of the statute.

The leading case on this question is *Maddison* v. *Alderson* (1883), 8 App. Cas. 467. The facts there were much stronger than those before us. The plaintiff, giving up all prospects of any other course of life, had spent over 20 years as housekeeper of the intestate until his death without wages on the strength of his promise to leave her the manor on which they lived. A defectively executed will made her a beneficiary to the extent of a life interest in all his property, real and personal. The House of Lords held that, assuming a contract, there had been no such part performance as would answer s. 4.

The Lord Chancellor, Earl of Selborne, states the principle in these words [p. 475]: "All the acts done must be referred to the actual contract, which is the measure and test of their legal and equitable character and consequences."

At p. 479, referring to the rule that payment of the purchase-price is not sufficient, he says: "The best explanation of it seems to be, that the payment of money is an equivocal act, not (in itself) until the connection is established by parol testimony, indicative of a contract concerning land. . . . All the authorities shew that the acts relied upon as part performance must be unequivocally, and in their own nature, referable to some such agreement as that alleged."

Lord O'Hagan, at p. 485, uses this language: "It must be unequivocal. It must have relation to the one agreement relied upon, and to no other. It must be such, in Lord Hardwicke's words, Amb. 587, 'as could be done with no other view or design than to perform that agreement.' "

At p. 489 Lord Blackburn, speaking of the delivery of possession as removing the bar of the statute, says: "This is, I think in effect to construe the 4th section of the Statute of Frauds as if it contained these words, 'or unless possession of the land shall be given and accepted.' Notwithstanding the very high authority of those who have decided those cases, I should not hesitate if it was res integra in refusing to interpolate such words, or put such a construction on the statute."

I am quite unable to distinguish that authority from the matter before us. Here, as there, the acts of performance by themselves are wholly neutral and have no more relation to a contract connected with premises No. 548 than with those of No. 550 or than to mere expectation that his aunt would requite his solicitude in her will, or that they were given gratuitously or on terms that the time and outlays would be compensated in money. In relation to specific performance, strict pleading would seem to require a demonstrated connection between the acts of performance and a dealing with the land before evidence of the terms of any agreement is admissible. This exception of part performance is an anomaly; it is based on equities resulting from the acts done; but unless we are to say that, after performance by one party, any refusal to perform by the other gives rise to them, which would in large measure write off the section, we must draw the line where those acts are referable and referable only on the contract alleged. The facts here are almost the classical case against which the statute was aimed: they have been found to be truly stated and I accept that; but it is the nature of the proof that is condemned, not the facts, and their truth at law is irrelevant. Against this, equity intervenes only in circumstances that are not present here. . . .

[The remainder of Rand J.'s judgment is reproduced on page 50. Rinfret C.J.C. and Taschereau J. concurred with Rand J. The judgment of Cartwright J., who agreed with Rand J., and with whom Estey and Locke JJ. concurred, is omitted.]

[The judgment of the Court of Appeal included this paragraph from [1953] O.W.N. at p. 666: "A more serious argument presented by the appellant was that this agreement being an agreement whereby the aunt would leave to him at her death a particular piece of property, the acts of part performance must be such as in their own nature were referable to and affected the land in question, and he relied upon the decision and judicial views expressed in the case of *Maddison* v. *Alderson* (1883), 8 App. Cas. 467. We have, however, been referred to the decision of this Court in *Fox* v. *White*, [1935] O.W.N. 316, where this Court distinguished the decision in *Maddison* v. *Alderson* and the principles there laid down from a case such as the case at bar, and in that case this Court held that if the acts relied upon as being acts of part performance were referable to some contract, and consistent with the contract alleged, then evidence was admissable as to the precise terms of the particular contract alleged. We are of the opinion that the acts in this case which are alleged to be acts of part performance are plainly referable to the existence of a contract and are consistent with the particular contract alleged, and that when the evidence is admitted as to the precise terms of the particular contract the plaintiff's case is made out and the acts of part performance take the case out of the statute."]

THE EFFECT OF THE STATUTE. The early view of the Statute was that a contract within its terms was void. As recently as 1837 Lord Abinger was able to say, in *Carrington* v. *Roots*, 2 M. & W. 248; 150 E.R. 748, "The meaning of the statute is . . . that the contract shall be altogether void." What exactly will be the meaning of the word "void," with or without adjectives like "altogether," in any given case it is difficult to anticipate, but as it happened this early view was soon repudiated. See

Leroux v. *Brown* (1852), 12 C.B. 801; 138 E.R. 1119. In *Britain* v. *Rossiter* (1899), Q.B.D. 123, Brett L.J. said, "The contract is not void under the 4th section; the contract exists, but no one is liable upon it". While no action could be brought on the oral contract barred by the statute, there was nothing to stop the defendant from raising the oral contract as a defence, since he was not thereby "bringing an action." The contract could be used as a shield but not as a sword. See *Thomas* v. *Brown* (1876), I Q.B.D. 714 and Williams, "Availability by Way of Defence of Contracts not complying with the Statute of Frauds" (1934), 50 L.Q.R. 532.

In *Britain* v. *Rossiter* there was a contract made on Saturday for a year's employment to commence the following Monday. The employee worked for some months and then was dismissed without notice. He brought an action for wrongful dismissal. Presumably he had been paid up to the time of his dismissal but if he hadn't been, he might have claimed on a quantum meruit for what he had earned separately from his claim for wrongful dismissal, which, if established, would have entitled him to be put in the position he would have been in if the contract had been carried out. That is, he would have been awarded the amount of his salary for the remainder of the year less what he could have earned elsewhere by way of mitigation of his losses. The plaintiff argued that the contract was void and that a new contract should be implied from his conduct in working for some months. Brett L.J. said:

"The contract is not void under the 4th section; the contract exists, but no one is liable upon it. It seems to me impossible that a new contract can be implied from the doing of acts which were clearly done in performance of the first contract only, and to infer from them a fresh contract would be to draw an inference contrary to fact. It is a proposition which cannot be disputed that no new contract can be implied from acts done under an express contract which is still subsisting; all that can be said is that no one can be charged upon the original contract because it is not in writing."

The plaintiff also argued that the equity doctrine of part performance should apply here. The Court agreed that that doctrine was confined to land cases. Thesiger L.J. was obviously sympathetic. He said:

"I confess that on principle I do not see why a similar doctrine should not be applied to a case of a contract of service. . . . At the same time I feel that doctrines of this nature are not to be unwarrantably extended, and that we ought not to go further than the decisions of Courts of Equity as to the principles of relief, and as to the instances to which the doctrine of part performance is to be applied. . . ."

The fate of Brett L.J.'s view may be gathered from a brief glance at some typical later reactions. In reflecting about these cases it is helpful to keep in mind the difference between the expectation interest and the restitution interest. In *Scott* v. *Pattison*, [1923] 2 K.B. 723, the plaintiff was hired for a year as a farm labourer on May 7, 1921, to start on May 12. He was ill from June 29 until September 11. He was paid his weekly wage until July 2, and he received a slightly smaller sum on July 16 and 23, but after that, during his illness he received nothing. He worked and was paid for the period from September 12 to November 20, when he again became ill and did no work and received no pay until he returned on January 24. He then worked and was paid until May 12, when his year ended. He claimed wages for the time he was ill and called a witness who testified that it was the local custom to pay full wages during sickness. The defendant relied on the Statute of Frauds. The plaintiff's solicitor contended that he did not sue on the contract proved by him but on a contract implied from the fact of his actual employment, or implied from his receipt of weekly wages. The county court judge dismissed the action on the ground of the Statute. On appeal in the Divisional Court, Darling J. said, "What the plaintiff's solicitor should have said was that the plaintiff sued on an implied contract to pay for the services already rendered, and the amount claimed could be put as the equivalent of the weekly wages although it could not be claimed as the weekly wage, because the wage arose not from the executed contract but from the terms agreed, which were unenforceable by reason of the Statute of Frauds. . . . In my opinion this case should go back to the county court judge for him to consider it upon the basis that the claim is one in assumpsit for services already rendered. It does not follow, even if he thinks that the plaintiff is entitled to succeed, that he should assess the sum to be received by the plaintiff at the same rate as the weekly wages. I also think that he should consider the question as to the existence of the alleged custom and satisfy himself whether or not there is such a custom. If there is, it may be that the custom is not to pay the full wage but something less. I do not know. There was only evidence called on one side."

In *James* v. *Kent & Co. Ltd.*, [1950] 2 All E.R. 1099, the plaintiff claimed damages for wrongful dismissal, measured by the amount of his salary due to him for the unexpired part of his three year contract. He was not claiming for work done, for which he had evidently already been paid, but for his expectation interest only. On this point the Court held against him, although it did allow damages on another ground. Denning L.J. said, "If the plaintiff had fully performed his part of the contract by serving his full time, or, what is the same thing, by serving his full time save when excused by sickness, he could sue for his stipulated wages. So, also, if he had served up to the time when any instalment fell due, he could sue for that instalment. In those cases his action would be in debt on an executed consideration to which the Statute of Frauds has no application. That was expressly laid down by Tindal C.J., in *Souch* v. *Strawbridge* (1846), 2 C.B. 808; 135 E.R. 1161 at page 1164, and is, I think, still good law today. I know that a Divisional Court in *Scott* v. *Pattison* decided the contrary, but I do not think they were right for reasons which I elaborated some time ago in an article which I wrote in the Law Quarterly Review (41 L.Q.R. 79) and to which I still adhere. Even if the servant has not served his full time, or the time necessary to earn the next instalment, but is dismissed beforehand without good cause, he can recover payment for any work he has done as on a quantum meruit. It used to be said in the old days that in that case his action was on an implied contract, but that is not a correct way of approach because, in this case, as in the other, you cannot have an implied contract covering the same ground as an existing special contract. The proper ground of the claim is not in contract at all, but in restitution. It is money which, in justice, ought to be paid for services rendered. The present claim for wrongful dismissal cannot be put on any such footing because restitution is confined to cases where the defendant has received money which he ought to restore, or benefits for which he ought to pay. A claim for damages for wrongful dismissal can only rest in contract, and, if that contract is unenforceable by reason of the Statute of Frauds, the claim must fail."

Denning L.J.'s ready acceptance of a remedy for unjust enrichment has not been so readily accepted by the House of Lords. See *Reading* v. *Attorney General*, [1951] A.C. 507, at pp. 513–14, where Lord Porter said, "It was suggested in argument that the learned judge [Denning J. as he then was] founded his decision solely upon the doctrine of unjust enrichment and that that doctrine was now recognized by the law of England. My Lords, the exact status of the law of unjust enrichment is not yet assured. It holds a predominant place in the law of Scotland and, I think, of the United States, but I am content for the purpose of this case to accept the view that it forms no part of the law of England and that a right to restitution so described would be too widely stated."

The Canadian position is now clear. After a few false starts the Supreme Court of Canada accepted unjust enrichment in the *Deglman* case reproduced on page 50. Earlier, in *Re Meston, Meston* v. *Gray*, [1925] 4 D.L.R. 887 the Court of Appeal in Saskatchewan granted relief to a son who had worked for ten years on his father's farm on the strength of an oral promise by his father that he should have all his father's property after his father's death. Both the trial Judge and the Court of Appeal held the son "entitled . . . to compensation on a *quantum meruit* basis." The trial Judge allowed wages for the full ten years, but the Court of Appeal thought the wages must be deemed to have run from year to year and that the Statute of Limitations therefore applied. The Court of Appeal only allowed six years' wages. The reasoning is not extensively set out, but apparently Turgeon J. A. thought there was to be implied a contract for yearly hiring. If a contract is implied at all, the reasoning in *Britain* v. *Rossiter* must be disregarded. On this point the *Deglman* case is more authoritative and more rational. See above, page 50. There is no need to imply a contract, and the time the obligation is imposed by law is at death, because until then there is always the possibility that the contract obligation might be fulfilled.

The limits of the doctrine of unjust enrichment in Canada remain to be determined.

NOBLE *v.* WARD

England. Exchequer. 1866. L.R. 1 Ex. 117

BRAMWELL B. delivered the judgment of the Court: This was tried before me at Manchester, and the plaintiff was nonsuited. The case comes before us on a rule to set aside that nonsuit. I think it was wrong, at least on the ground on which it proceeded. The action was for not accepting goods on a sale by the plaintiff to the defendants. The defendants pleaded, among other things, that the contract had been rescinded, and that the plaintiffs were not ready and willing to deliver. The facts were, that a contract for the sale and delivery of goods from the plaintiff to the defendants, at a future day, was entered into on the 12th of August, which may be called contract A; that another contract for sale and delivery by the plaintiff to the defendants also at a future day was entered into on the 18th of August, say contract B; that before any of the days of delivery had arrived the plaintiff and defendants agreed, verbally, to rescind, or do away with, contract A and to extend for a fortnight the time for the performance of contract B; that is to say, the plaintiff had a fortnight longer to deliver, and the defendants a fortnight longer to take and pay for these goods. This, on principle and authority, was a third contract, call it C. It was a contract in which all that was to be done and permitted on the one side was the consideration for all that was to be done and permitted on the other.... It remains to add that the declaration would fit either contract B or contract C, and that goods were tendered by the plaintiff to the defendants in time for either of these contracts. My notes, and my recollection of my ruling, are that contract B was rescinded, and contract C not enforceable, not being in writing. I think that was wrong. Either contract C was within the Statute of Frauds, or not. If not, there was no need for a writing; if yes, it was because it was a contract for the sale of goods, and so within the seventeenth section of the statute. That says that no contract for the sale of goods for the price of £10 or upwards shall be allowed to be good, except there is an acceptance, payment or writing. The expression "allowed to be good" is not a very happy one, but whatever its meaning may be, it includes this at least, that it shall not be held valid or enforced. But this is what the defendant was attempting to do. He was setting up this contract C as a valid contract. He was asking that it should be allowed to be good to rescind contract B.

It is attempted to say that what took place when contract C was made was twofold. First, that the old contracts were given up; secondly, a new one was made. But that is not so. What was done was all done at once—was all one transaction, one bargain; and had the plaintiff asked for a writing at the time, and the defendants refused it, it would all have been undone, and the parties remitted to their original contracts.

I think, therefore, that on principle it was wrong to hold that the old contract was gone. *Moore* v. *Campbell* (1854), 10 Ex. 323; 156 E.R. 467; 23 L.J. (Ex.) 310, is an authority to the same effect. It is true that that case may be distinguished on the facts, namely, that there what was to be done under the new arrangement in lieu of the old was to be done at the same time, so that it might well be the parties meant, not that the new thing should be done, but if done it should be in lieu of the old. Such an argument could not be used in this case. But it was not the ground of the judgment there, which is that the new agreement was void. The cases of *Goss* v. *Lord Nugent* (1833), 5 B. & Ad. 58; 110 E.R. 713, *Stead* v. *Dawber* (1839), 10 Ad. & E. 57; 113 E.R. 22, and others, only shew that the new contract C cannot be enforced, not that the old contract B is gone. I think it was not. Inconvenience and absurdity may arise from this. For instance, if the defendants signed the new contract, and not the plaintiff, the plaintiff would be bound to the old and the defendants to the new. Or, if in the course of the cause a writing turned up signed by the plaintiff, then they could first rely on the old, and afterwards on the new contract. But this is no more than may happen in any case within the 17th section, where there has been one contract only.

But then, it was said before us that the plaintiff was not ready and willing to deliver under contract B. Probably not, and he supposed contract C was in force. In answer to this the plaintiff contended before us that this point was not made at the trial, to which the defendants replied—neither was the point that the old contract was in force. My recollection is so—that the case was opened and maintained as on the new contract—but I agree with Mr. Mellish that a nonsuit ought to be maintained on a point not taken at the trial only when it is beyond all doubt. I cannot say this is. Consequently, I think the rule should be absolute, but under the circumstances the costs of both parties of the first trial ought to abide the event of the second.

[On appeal to the Court of Exchequer Chamber, the judgment was affirmed. (1867), L.R. 2 Ex. 135.]

MORRIS *v.* BARON
England. House of Lords. [1918] A.C. 1

The appellant was a woollen manufacturer, and the respondents were merchants of worsted goods carrying on business at Brook Street, Bradford. On September 24, 1914, the appellant contracted to sell to the respondents 500 pieces of moss blue serge at the prices fixed and on the conditions stated in the memorandum in writing signed by both parties. On March 19, 1915, the appellant commenced an action against the respondents to recover the sum of £888 4s., the value of goods supplied to that date. The respondents counter-claimed for £934 17s. 3d. for the non-delivery of goods in breach of the terms of the contract. When this action was coming on for trial the appellant and respondents made an oral arrangement and for the purpose of this appeal the terms of such arrangement may be taken to be expressed in the following letter of April 22nd, 1915:

"Dear Sirs, —As personally arranged between Mr. Morris and Mr. Baron, we herewith confirm the terms agreed upon.

Both to withdraw the legal proceedings and instruct the solicitors accordingly, and each to pay his own costs, you to allow £30 (thirty pounds) to us to meet expenses incurred through not fulfilling the orders.

The account to be left over for three months so as to give us the opportunity of selling the goods, and the goods not delivered to be kept for us if we ask for them.

We have the option of taking up the balance of pieces to complete the order, giving time to make.

Yours faithfully,
Baron & Co."

The three months' extension of credit having expired, the appellant wrote asking for payment according to agreement. The respondents wrote back saying that they would be pleased to pay the account if the appellant delivered the balance of the pieces to complete the order, and in the subsequent correspondence the respondents insisted on their right to receive delivery of the further goods before paying for the goods already delivered.

On February 15, 1916, the appellant commenced a second action against the respondents to recover the sum of £888 4s. still due to him. The respondents admitted this claim, subject to their counter-claim for damages for non-delivery of goods. This counter-claim was founded on the April contract of 1915, and alternatively on the September contract of 1914. The trial judge, Bailache J., gave judgment for the appellant on the counter-claim, but the Court of Appeal reversed this decision, and it was against this order that the appeal was brought.

Bailhache J., dealing with the case under the contract of April, dismissed the counter-claim on the ground that the respondents could not validly exercise their option while repudiating their obligation to pay. The objection that the counter-claim was not enforceable by the respondents by reason of s. 4 of the Sale of Goods Act, 1893, was raised but not argued; but it was fully argued in the Court of Appeal.

The Court of Appeal held (1) that the contract of April was an agreement for the sale of goods and was not enforceable; (2) that the contract of April being wholly inoperative, the parties must be relegated to their rights under the original contract, on the ground that a written agreement, which was required by the Sale of Goods Act to be in writing, could not be rescinded except by an agreement in writing; and the Court gave judgment for the respondents on the counter-claim.

LORD DUNEDIN: . . . For the sake of clearness and brevity I shall call the contract of September 24, 1914, contract A and the agreement of April 20, 1915, contract B. As to contract B, there is no memorandum in writing sufficient to satisfy s. 4 of the Sale of Goods Act, if that section applies to it; and its terms have been held to be for the purpose of this case set out in the letter of April 22, 1915. It is admitted that (1) the legal proceedings which had been instituted in respect of breaches of contract A, which consisted of claim and counter-claim, were withdrawn; (2) the account for goods delivered under contract A was left over for three months; (3) £30 was allowed in credit by the plaintiff to the defendants. Upon these facts the case falls to be decided.

My Lords, the case raises points of law of great nicety, chiefly for the reason that there is a mass of authority, not always consistent, dealing with questions akin to the questions here raised; and that there is a great responsibility on any one in your Lordships' House who attempts to lay down general rules, and in so doing may seem to run counter to the dicta of learned judges in the past. Nor has the case been made easier by the somewhat peculiar manner in which it was treated by the parties, and, in consequence of their attitude, by the Courts below.

The action is for the value of goods sold and delivered to the amount of £888 4s. It is not expressly founded on any contract, although the goods were doubtless delivered under contract A. The defence admits the claim as for goods sold and delivered, then sets out contract B, and averring breach counter-claims under the contract. It is true that in the pleading there is made an alternative claim as for breach of contract A, but before the trial judge the whole case for the counter-claim was put and urged on the assumption that contract B was the ruling contract and that the breach had taken place under it. The trial judge found in fact that in terms of contract B the defendants were bound to pay £888 at the end of July, being the date of the expiry of the three months; that they positively refused to do so; and on these facts he held that the counter-claim failed. It is a little difficult to say whether the learned judge held the counter-claim to fail because this maintained attitude of the defendants amounted to a repudiation of the contract; or upon the ground that as the defendants never asked for delivery, except coupled with the assertion that they refused to pay the £888 until delivery was made, that was tantamount to the defendants never really asking for delivery at all. On the learned judge's announcing his decision counsel for the plaintiff said that he had a point which he had not been able to bring forward, namely, that contract B was unenforceable under the 4th section of the Sale of Goods Act, and therefore could not be the foundation of a counter-claim. To this counsel for the defendants retorted that if that were so he might go back to the original contract, to which counsel for the plaintiff replied that he was prepared to deal with that argument. The matter then dropped.

In the Court of Appeal, the learned judges having seemingly indicated that they were not prepared to agree with the view of the learned trial judge as to the application of the facts to contract B, the plaintiff brought forward his argument that s. 4 of the Sale of Goods Act applied to contract B. This was resisted by the defendant's counsel, as appears from the judgment of Swinfen Eady L.J., who says: "The question is, was the contract of April 22 an agreement which is within the section and ought to be in writing? Was it an agreement for the sale of goods? It is contended by the defendants that it was not." The defendants however, found salvation in the defeat of their argument, for the Court of Appeal, deciding against them that contract B did fall within the section, proceeded to say that the case was ruled by the case of *Noble* v. *Ward*, and gave judgment for the counter-claim upon the alternative plea for breach of the original contract A, a view which seems to have been unpressed by the defendants themselves. Acordingly as the appeal now stands before your Lordships' House, the question to be first decided is whether, assuming that contract B is within the section, the present case really falls within the decision in *Noble* v. *Ward*.

My Lords, let me say that I unhesitatingly accept *Noble* v. *Ward* as well decided and laying down correct law. The judgment in the Exchequer was the judgment of Pollock C.B. and Bramwell, Channell, and Piggott BB. In the Exchequer Chamber the judgment was given by Willes J., and was concurred in by Blackburn, Mellor, Montague Smith and Lush JJ. He would be a bolder iconoclast than I am who should say that a judgment resting on the authority of such names did not correctly set forth the law of England. But now comes the question of what exactly it was that *Noble* v. *Ward* decided, and that is not so easy to determine as might be expected. For in truth there are three possible views of the true effect of *Noble* v. *Ward*. I shall examine each one of them. First, there is the view, strongly contended for by the appellant at your Lordships' Bar, that, inasmuch as the transaction in that case fell within the 17th section of the Statute of Frauds, which uses the expression "No contract . . . shall be allowed to be good except," &c., it was entirely void, and as such could effect nothing either by way of rescission or variation of the anterior contracts: and that as the 4th section of the Sale of Goods Act, like the 4th section of the Statute of Frauds, does not make void a contract, but only prevents enforcing it, contract B in this case, though not enforceable, might yet serve as a defence to get rid of contract A.

My Lords, it is quite true that in the Exchequer Chamber Willes J. uses the expressions "invalid" and "void," and I confess if I could have read the case as reported in the Exchequer Chamber apart from all other authority, I should have come to the conclusion that that was the ground of judgment, and that, to say the least of it, the question was still open when you had something to which s. 4 applied and s. 17 did not. But, on the best consideration I can give, I do not think that would be a safe view. For Lord Blackburn, who was a party to the judgment, distinctly said in the case of *Maddison* v. *Alderson* (1883), 8 App. Cas. 467, 488, in this House: 'I think it is now finally settled that the true construction of the Statute of Frauds, both the 4th and the 17th sections, is not to render the contracts within them void, still less illegal, but is to render the kind of evidence required indispensable when it is sought to enforce the contract. And Brett L.J. in *Britain* v. *Rossiter* (1899), 11 Q.B.D. 123, 127, says: "In my opinion no distinction exists between the 4th and the 17th sections of the statute."

In view of these opinions I am inclined to think that although, doubtless,

Noble v. *Ward* proceeded on the 17th section, yet the judgment would have been the same had there only been the 4th in question.

The second interpretation is that which the Court of Appeal have here given, adopting and relying on the views of Shearman and Sankey JJ. in the case of *Williams* v. *Moss' Empires, Ltd.*, [1915] 3 K. B. 242, 248. It is most succinctly put by Sankey J. in that case: "A contract which in compliance with the Statute of Frauds is in writing may be rescinded by a new agreement. The new agreement may be one which in order to be enforceable is required to be in writing, or it may be one which is valid though it is not in writing. If it is one which is required to be in writing and is not in writing, it is unenforceable and cannot be treated as evidence that the original contract has been rescinded, and the original contract, therefore, remains in force. But if the new agreement is in writing, or, if verbal, is one which need not be in writing, the new agreement is valid, and the original contract is rescinded." It will be noticed at once that the learned judge ignores the distinction between variation and rescission. The contract with which he was dealing was obviously a case of variation. There had been an engagement for three years at a certain salary. A verbal arrangement was made whereby the amount of salary was altered; all other terms of the original contract remained. Indeed, the learned judge says in so many words that no such distinction exists where the alteration is a material one. He says: "I think some confusion has arisen from the use of the words "variation of a contract." The result of varying the terms of an existing contract is to produce, not the original contract with a variation, but a new and different contract."

My Lords, I find myself unable to subscribe to this view. The difference between variation and rescission is a real one, and is tested, to my thinking, by this: In the first case there are no such executory clauses in the second arrangement as would enable you to sue upon that alone if the first did not exist; in the second you could sue on the second arrangement alone, and the first contract is got rid of either express words to that effect, or because the second dealing with the same subject-matter as the first but in a different way, it is impossible that the two should be both performed. When I say you could sue on the second alone, that does not exclude cases where the first is used for mere reference, in the same way as you may fix a price by a price list, but where the contractual force is to be found in the second by itself.

Now each and every of the cases cited (leaving aside for the moment *Noble* v. *Ward*) were attempts to vary; in not one of them was it a case of rescission. *Noble* v. *Ward,* though also a case of attempted variation and decided as such, yet had in it the distinction which Shearman J. ignores. In that case there were what Lord Bramwell called contracts A, B, and C. A and B were in writing, C. was a parol contract. It was entered into when A and B were both extant and partially performed. Now it was held that C could not vary B, but there was no difficulty made as to its rescinding A. I do not mean that this was decided upon adverse contentions, for neither party maintained that A was to go on. But still the only thing that rescinded or abrogated A was C, and had the plaintiffs in that case claimed damages under A as well as under B I do not doubt that the plea that A was abrogated would have been sustained. This brings me to the third view of *Noble* v. *Ward*, which I humbly think is the correct one. The criterion does not lie in the question of whether the later contract is itself a contract which needs to be in writing. The criterion is in the question whether what is intended to be effected by the second contract is rescission or variation. *Noble* v. *Ward* decided that if the second contract fell within the statute then it could not be appealed to to vary the former; but it did not decide that it could not be appealed to to rescind.

Willes J., in giving judgment and speaking of the later contract, and of the fact that a verbal contract to rescind *simpliciter* was quite good, says: "But it would be at least a question for the jury, whether the parties did intend to rescind." That contract B, if it falls within s.4 is not gone altogether although not enforceable is clear from the passage already cited from Lord Blackburn, and the like is said in the same case by Lord Selborne, 8 App. Cas. 474: "It has been determined at law, (and, in this respect, there can be no difference between law and equity) that the 4th section of the Statute of Frauds does not avoid parol contracts, but only bars the legal remedies by which they might otherwise have been enforced." If, then, the contract exists its existence must be treated as a fact, and it must be looked at to see if apart from enforceability it did or did not put an end to the former contract. For it would be an extraordinary result that although a parol contract to rescind a written contract is good, as to which there is no doubt (*Gorman* v. *Salisbury,* (1684), 1 Vern, 240; 23 E.R. 440, and Willes J. in *Noble v. Ward*), yet the same thing cannot happen if after rescinding the first contract the parties go on to make another contract which may or may not be enforceable. Accordingly, if express words to that effect are used there can be no doubt. It seems to follow that implication may do as well as express words. But here there must be a note of warning. If the implication be no more than this, that the second contract if valid would displace the first, that by itself is not enough, for, as Willes J. says in *Noble* v. *Ward* "It is quite in accordance with the cases of *Doe d. Egremont* v. *Courtney*, (1848), 11 Q.B. 702; 116 E.R. 636, and *Doe d. Biddulph* v. *Poole* (1848), 11 Q.B. 713; 116 E.R. 641 overruling the previous decision of *Doe d. Egremont* v. *Forwood*, (1842), 3 Q.B. 627; 114 E.R. 647, to hold that, where parties enter into a contract which would have the effect of rescinding a previous one, but which cannot operate according to their intention, the new contract shall not operate to affect the previously existing rights. This is good sense and sound reasoning, on which a jury might at least hold that there was no such intention." The cases there cited are all cases of surrenders of leases upon new leases granted upon which it was held that the surrender, whether express or implied, was conditional upon the new lease being good.

I now turn to the facts in this case. There had been alleged breach of contract A on both sides, and action raised with counter-claim. Now the first term of the new contract B is to put each party to withdraw legal proceedings; then to give three months' credit to the defendants in the payment of a sum admittedly due for goods already delivered; then to allow them £30 in satisfaction of the expenses they had incurred by reason of non-delivery under contract A; and lastly to substitute for the right of the plaintiff to supply and the duty of the defendants to take 277 pieces of cloth, an option on the defendants' part to take them if they pleased.

My Lords, it seems to me impossible to come to any conclusion on this but that the parties agreed that the old contract should be abrogated. I use the word "abrogate," because I think it is a better word than "rescind" when you deal with a contract which has been partly implemented, but as regards the authorities I might as well say "rescind." Further, as regards this arrangement there cannot be a restitution in integrum. The defendants have had the extended credit, have had the £30 placed to their credit, and have enjoyed an option not to take, which, if the market had been a falling one instead of a rising one, they would probably have prevailed themselves of; and these advantages have been enjoyed and cannot be taken away. In respect of these things the old contract was to be held abrogated. But the judgment of the Court of Appeal leaves the defendants with all these advantages and yet holds the old contract binding still.

I am fortified in my view by a passage in *Fry on Specific Performance* (3rd ed.). Sect. 1039 is as follows: "But where the new contract is relied on only as an extinguishment of the old one, the mere fact that it is not in writing, and so could not be put in suit, seems to be no ground for denying its effect in rescinding the original contract. The Statute of Frauds does not make the parol contract void, but only prevents an action upon it; and it does not seem to be necessary to the extinction of one contract by another that the second contract could be actively enforced. The point has never, it is believed, been matter of decision. But in point of principle it seems to stand on the same footing as a simple agreement to rescind."

I am therefore of opinion that the present case is not ruled by *Noble* v. *Ward,* because the question here is not whether contract A was varied by contract B, but whether it was rescinded by contract B, and on the facts I hold that it was.

There remains the question whether the defendants can sue for breach of contract B in so far as that contract is a contract for sale of the 277 pieces of cloth. I think they cannot for several reasons. In the first place, I think, though with some hesitation, that it falls within the 4th section of the Sale of Goods Act, and cannot therefore, being a parol contract, be actively enforced. I say "with some hesitation," because, looking at the 4th section, I cannot help feeling that the section was meant to deal with what I may call pure contracts of sale, and not contracts dealing with other arrangements as well; and I have felt doubts as to whether when, as here, you have a composite arrangement, dealing with the getting rid of competing claims under an old contract as well as providing for the supply of goods in the future by way of sale, the section ought to apply. But on the whole I have come to the conclusion that in so far as implement of that portion which is sale is asked the section must apply. But further and apart from that, and taking the case as it was taken by Bailhache J., I agree with the conclusion he reached. I think that the maintained attitude of the defendants under no circumstances to pay the £888 unless delivery were first made was equivalent to repudiation, but I do not find such an unqualified acceptance on the plaintiff's part of that repudiation as to amount to rescision. But I think also that the payment of the £888 at the end of the three months was a consideration going to the root of the contract because it was the counterpart of the plaintiff's forbearance to sue and the grant to the defendants of an option to take instead of the old duty to take, and that it was not in the position of an ordinary payment of instalment which would make the case fall within the lines of *Mersey Steel and Iron Co.* v. *Naylor, Benzon & Co.* (1884), 9 App. Cas. 434. Accordingly being a stipulation going to the root of the contract, the defendants have all along been in breach, and cannot call on the plaintiff to implement his part; and thus there can be no damages.

Order of the Court of Appeal reversed and judgment of Bailhache J. restored.

[Lord Finlay L.C., Viscount Haldane, Lord Atkinson and Lord Parmoor also gave reasons for allowing the appeal. In the course of his judgment, Lord Finlay said: ". . . *Noble* v. *Ward* does not lay down as a matter of law that the parties cannot agree to rescind a written agreement which the law requires to be in writing by the substitution for it of another agreement not in writing, and therefore unenforceable. On the contrary, Willes J. in the Exchequer Chamber says that the question would be for the jury. If the law were as the Court of Appeal in the present case has laid it down, he would have said that the judge must rule that such a rescission could not take place."]

DANFORTH HEIGHTS LIMITED *v.* McDERMID BROTHERS. 1922. 52 O.L.R. (Ontario Court of Appeal). An action by the vendors of land for specific performance of a contract for sale and purchase where time was expressed to be of the essence. The question arose whether when the vendor could not convey on time, the purchasers, by continued recognition of the agreement as still in force, had "waived" their right to insist on performance on time. It was argued that the Statute of Frauds prevented effect being given to the "oral variance" of the original contract. Completion was to be on February 5, 1920. The vendors could not remove a certificate of *lis pendens* until early in March, and this accomplishment was not communicated to the purchasers until the middle of April. Meanwhile the purchasers had written on March 20, asserting their rights under the time clause and informing the vendors that they were "unable and unwilling to carry out the deal". After a careful analysis of the facts, the Court concluded on the facts that the vendors failed to establish that the purchasers had elected not to insist upon their rights as to time. Nevertheless ROSE J. said, in part, ". . . For this ignoring of the statute and of the cases mentioned there must be some reason, and the reason which suggests itself to me, after an examination of Mr. Ewart's book on *Waiver Distributed*, is that the Judges have thought that the question whether the purchaser had precluded himself from insisting that time continued to be of the essence of the agreement did not involve any question as to the variation of the contract. The way the matter appears to me, in the light of Mr. Ewart's argument, is this: The stipulation that time shall be of the essence of the agreement does not mean that, if either party fails to complete within the time specified, the agreement shall be at an end; if it had that meaning, either party could escape his obligations by making default. What it does mean is that, if either party fails to do his part within the time specified, the other party may declare the agreement to be at an end, if he so desires. The party not in default has an option: he may elect to keep the agreement in force or he may elect to terminate it. If he elects to keep it in force he cannot afterwards say that it terminated on the expiration of the specified time; but that is not because he has effected any variation of it, or because he has 'waived' any right to terminate it; it is because he has exercised the right which he had under it. If this is so, the Statute of Frauds has no possible application; the question is not a question of enforcing a written contract with a variation; it is merely a question of finding upon the evidence whether there has or has not been an election. See this view of the law suggested, but not passed upon, by Anglin J. in *Simpson* v. *Young* (1918), 56 Can. S.C.R. 388, 406-7.

"It is true that the matter is not put in this way in any of the cases, but it is also true, I think that there is nothing in any of the equity cases or in any case since the Judicature Act, except *Plevins* v. *Downing* (1876), 1 C.P.D. 270, that is inconsistent with this way of stating it. . . .

"I am not sure that *Plevins* v. *Downing*, is necessarily inconsistent with the view which I have put forward as the correct one. . . ."

THE MOVEMENT FOR REFORM. The beginning of the movement for reform by repeal of the Statute probably dates from 1678, but it culminated in The Law Revision Committee's Sixth Interim Report (partly produced elsewhere), which recommended repeal of all the clauses except clause [4] which had by then been transferred to the *Law of Property Act, 1925* (section 40) and was outside the terms of reference of the Committee. As is often the fate of Royal Commission Reports and the like, this one languished for some fifteen years, until a new Law Reform Committee established in 1952 reported in March 1953 (Cmd. 8809), confirming the views of the earlier Committee that the sections be repealed on the grounds they had outlived the conditions which generated and, in some degree, justified them; that they operate in an illogical and often one-sided and haphazard fashion over a field arbitrarily chosen; and that on the whole they promote rather than restrain dishonesty. The Law Reform Committee agreed with the minority view of the Law Revision Committee that guarantees should be excepted, but disagreed with the notion that they should be void rather than unenforceable. This report was followed by the Law Reform (Enforcement of Contracts) Act, effective in the United Kingdom from June 4, 1954, retroactively repealing the Statute as set out above and the Sale of Goods provision except for clauses [2] and [4]. It is interesting that the movement for reform gained its momentum in the jurisdiction that first introduced this presently anachronistic anomaly into the world. The only Canadian province to follow suit is British Columbia. Both the United Kingdom and British Columbia have retained the same clauses and, of course, all the complexity of a "note or memorandum," although the wording in British Columbia merely requires that the agreement or guarantee (or indemnity!) be "evidenced in writing." Why either clause should be retained is far from clear. The observations of the minority of the Law Revision Committee in this respect are set out below, but since clause [4] was not considered, we have no way of knowing what the brain trust on the Committee would have recommended.

LAW REVISION COMMITTEE, SIXTH INTERIM REPORT
England. 1937. Cmd. 5449; 15 *Can Bas Rec.* 585

RECOMMENDATION BY A MINORITY AS TO GUARANTEES.

While we agree with the recommendation that Section 4 of the Statute of Frauds should be repealed, we are of opinion that it should be provided that a guarantee is to be invalid unless the terms thereof (other than the consideration, if any) have been embodied in a written document and signed by the guarantor. We realise that most guarantees, such for instance as those given to a Bank, will, whether the section is repealed or not, always be contained in a written document; but, if oral contracts of guarantee are allowed, we feel that there is a real danger of inexperienced people being led into undertaking obligations that they do not fully understand, and that opportunities will be given to the unscrupulous to assert that credit was given on the faith of a guarantee which in fact the alleged surety had no intention of giving. A guarantee is in any case a special class of contract;

it is generally one-sided and disinterested as far as the surety is concerned, and the necessity of writing would at least give the proposed surety an opportunity of pausing and considering, not only the nature of the obligation he is undertaking, but also its terms. The contract often gives rise to many questions, e.g., whether it is to apply to the whole of the debt or to a portion only, and, if the former, whether it is to be limited in amount or to a certain period. We think these questions ought to be definitely settled and recorded before the contract becomes binding on the surety. Parliament has in the Law of Property Act, 1925, re-enacted the requirement of a signed note or memorandum in writing in the case of contracts for the sale of land, and has quite recently enacted that a money-lending contract is invalid unless the exact terms are embodied in a document which must be given to the proposing borrower so that he may see exactly to what he is agreeing, and, while it may be doubted if a needy borrower has ever been deterred from taking a loan by this provision, at least he cannot say that he did not know to what he was consenting. We see nothing unreasonable in putting sureties in a like position and giving them the same opportunity. No doubt it may be said that there is no greater difficulty for a Court to decide between a creditor and a surety than between any other contracting parties. But neither Judges nor juries are infallible on questions of fact, and in the vast majority of cases the surety is getting nothing out of the bargain; hence the greater reason for securing, if possible, that no mistake shall occcur. It is the "small man" we desire to protect, the father or father-in-law of the small tradesman who may be pressed to guarantee the account for goods supplied to stock the shop of his son or son-in-law. Moreover, we believe that guarantees are in a class of contract that at present most people know quite definintely must be in writing. The lay public know nothing about the Statute of Frauds: but they do, we believe, appreciate that writing is necessary for a guarantee; so our proposal only perpetuates that to which they are accustomed.

The last thing we desire is to see a new body of case law grow up around guarantees. Questions as to whether the contract can be embodied in one or in a series of documents, or as to whether the whole agreement must appear in the written document, and other questions that have given rise to a mass of decisions on the fourth section, could, we think, be avoided by providing that a contract of guarantee must be embodied in a document signed by the guarantor or his authorised agent, and that otherwise the contract, or any term thereof not included in the written document, should be void.

(Signed) RAYNER GODDARD.
S. L. PORTER.
WM. EGERTON MORTIMER.
ALFRED F. TOPHAM.

STATUTE OF FRAUDS

British Columbia. Revised Statutes. 1960. Chapter 369

2. (1) No agreement concerning an interest in land is enforceable by action unless evidenced in writing, signed by the party to be charged or by his agent.

5. (1) No guarantee or indemnity is enforceable by action unless evidenced in writing, signed by the party to be charged or by his agent, but

any consideration given for the guarantee or indemnity need not appear in the writing.

(2) This section does not apply to a guarantee or indemnity arising by operation of law.

6. No action shall be brought whereby to charge any person upon or by reason of any representation or assurance made or given concerning or relating to the character, conduct, credit, ability, trade, or dealings of any other person, to the intent or purpose that such other person may obtain credit, money, or goods thereupon, unless such representation or assurance be made in writing, signed by the party to be charged therewith.

CHAPTER 3

MAKING THE PROMISE

In the preceding chapters certain assumptions were made in order to focus attention on the problems of remedies and the selection of promises to be enforced. In the first chapter the existence of an enforceable promise was assumed and in the second chapter, the existence of a promise. In this chapter it is the existence of the promise itself that is examined. The chapter has, of course, more than one objective. This topic lends itself to some of the closest legal analysis to be found in the casebook. At the same time you should not lose sight of the more functional aspect: the analysis of the process of negotiation, which lies at the heart of the institution of contract. In modern times negotiation has taken a curious turn and much of the pulling and hauling of two bargaining individuals—the horse traders of earlier days—has been replaced by the use of the "standard form" contract, where the bargaining is reduced to the take it or leave it attitude of much of modern business. There is a kind of mass production of contracts, perhaps inherent in densely populated societies. As an example: $25,000 worth of insurance can be "purchased" for half a dollar by dropping a coin into a slot machine at an airport. There is obviously no negotiation in the sense that two bargaining persons may work out the conflicts in their interests, discover the common ground and saw off their irreconcilable conflicting wants. Of course, the draftsman of the standard form makes a serious effort to anticipate what he thinks the other party wants, or perhaps ought to want, but the whole function is fundamentally different from the personally negotiated contract. It is not surprising therefore that the legal problems of the negotiated contract differ from those of the standard form, and to keep the functional distinction clear some of the problems more peculiar to the standard form contract have been put in Chapter 6, Contracts in Writing. The importance of an insight into the process of negotiation is most apparent in the interpretation of a contract, where an understanding of the preceding negotiation may be indispensable. Problems of interpretation arise constantly in contracts and no separate chapter is devoted to the subject in this casebook. You should direct your mind to interpretation wherever the opportunity appears and reflect upon the approach taken by courts in this vital process.

The question raised by this chapter may be stated in another way. When should a court interfere in the negotiation of individuals and lend its authority to one or both? It is clear that the interference will be withheld generally until a promise has been made, but since the courts have themselves invented the terms "promise" and "contract," it has been left to them to work out the appropriate times. Their determination of this time is usually obscured by the insistence that they are applying a verbal formula over which they have no control. Whether they have or not, and whether they exercise any "discretion" in applying formulae to situations, is one of the problems implicit in virtually every case in this chapter.

The traditional formula that the courts purport to follow is that a promise is formed by the acceptance of an offer. When a person makes what the court would call an "offer" to the "offeree" (the fashion in the law of adding "ee" to an otherwise unoffending verb long preceded the wartime practice of calling an escaper an "escapee," and usually results in more precise terminology), the "offeror" is said to confer a "power" of acceptance on the offeree. In this sense a "power" is an ability to alter the legal position of another, and the offeree can, by his acceptance of the offer, bind the offeror and of course himself, by a contract. The offeror is under a "liability" that the power may be exercised, which would then give the offeree a "claim" or "right" against the offeror, who is said to have a "duty" to perform his promise. On the other hand, the offeree is under no obligation to accept the offer, and his superior position is apparent. He is said to have a "privilege," that is, he is at liberty to accept or reject the offer. Fairness demands some further protection to the offeror, and some power to withdraw his offer somehow to terminate the power of acceptance has to be recognised. For a short account of the legal terminology adopted in this note, see Corbin, "Legal Analysis and Terminology" (1919), 29 *Yale L.J.* 163.

1. Preliminary Negotiations

DENTON *v*. GREAT NORTHERN RAILWAY COMPANY
England. Queen's Bench. 1856. 5 E. & B. 860; 119 E.R. 701

The plaintiff being in London in March, 1855, and having business at Peterborough on the 25th March, 1855, and at Hull on the 26th March, 1855, consulted the printed time tables issued in the usual way by the defendants for that month. In these time tables a train was advertised to leave London at 5 p.m. and reach Peterborough about 7 p.m. and thence to proceed, amongst other towns, to Hull, to arrive there about midnight. At the bottom of the time tables was the following notice:

"The Companies make every exertion that the trains shall be punctual, but their arrival or departure at the times stated will not be guaranteed, nor will the companies hold themselves responsible for delay or any consequences arising therefrom."

The time tables advertising this train were, till after 26th March, exhibited by the defendants at their stations, where the plaintiff had seen them, and were printed and circulated; and on the 25th March the plaintiff had one in his possession.

The plaintiff, having made his arrangements on the faith of these time tables, went down to Peterborough by an early train of the defendants, transacted his business at Peterborough, and went to the defendants' station at Peterborough in due time to take a ticket to Hull by the evening train so advertised: but there was no such train to Hull; nor had there been one during any part of the month of March. The explanation of this was that the whole line of railway from Peterborough to Hull was not the property of the defendants, their line ending at Askerne on the route from Peterborough to Hull. They had running power over the line of the Lancashire and Yorkshire Railway Company from Askerne to Milford Junction, where the line of the North Eastern Railway Company joins that of The Lancashire and Yorkshire Railway Company. There had been, in February, an arrangement between the three companies by which passengers booked at the stations on the line of The Great Northern Railway Company were carried in the carriages of that company to Milford Junction, and thence were conveyed by The North Eastern Railway Company to Hull by a train departing a few minutes after the arrival of the train leaving Peterborough about 7 p.m. Toward the end of February, prior to the publication by the defendants of their time tables, but after they had been prepared and printed, The North Eastern Railway Company gave notice to the defendants that, after the 1st day of March, the train from Milford Junction to Hull would be discontinued. The defendants nevertheless made no alteration in their time tables, which were published and issued for March. The plaintiff consulted them and was misled as above stated. In consequence of the absence of this train the plaintiff could not get to Hull in time for an appointment which he had made for the morning of the 26th March, and sustained damage to the amount of £5 10s. It did not appear in or by the time tables whether the train from Peterborough to Hull was or was not entirely under the control of the defendants. . . .

LORD CAMPBELL C.J.: This is a case of some importance, both as regards the public and the railway companies. It seems to me that the representations made by railway companies in their time tables cannot be treated as mere waste paper; and in the present case I think the plaintiff is entitled to recover, on the ground that there was a contract with him, and also on the ground that there was a false representation by the Company.

It seems to me that, if the Company promised to give tickets for a train, running at a particular hour to a particular place, to any one who would come to the station and tender the price of the ticket, it is a good contract with any one who so comes. I take it to be clear that the issuing of the time tables in this way amounts in fact to such a promise; any one who read them would so understand them. Then, is it a good contract in law? The consideration is one which is a prejudice to the person who makes his arrangements with a view to the fulfilment of the contract, and comes to the station on the faith of it. Is it not then within the principle of those cases in which it has been held that an action lies on a contract to pay a reward? There the promise is to the public at large, exactly as it is here; it is in effect the same as if made to each individual conditionally; and, on an individual fulfilling the condition, it is an absolute contract with him, and he may sue. That being so, there is, I think, a contract: and there is no excuse shown for breaking it. It is immaterial that the defendants are not owners of the line the whole way to Hull. It is admitted to have been often rightly held that, where there is a ticket taken out to go to a station, the contract binds the company issuing the ticket, though it is not specified how much of the line over which the journey is to be belongs to that company. Then reliance is placed on the class of cases which decide that an absolute contract must be fulfilled whatever happens, which, it is said, shows that there cannot be a contract here. But from the nature of the contract I think that there might be implied exceptions. A carrier by sea excepts the perils of the sea. It may be from the nature of this contract that the perils of the railroad are excepted. I see no inconvenience likely to arise from holding this a contract. It is put, as an example of inconvenience, that a shipowner who has advertised that his ship is bound for Calcutta as a general ship, and that he will take on board goods brought to her, would be liable to an action if when goods were brought on the faith of the advertisement he said he had got a better freight, and was now bound for Jamaica; but I see no reason why he should not be liable. It seems to me, therefore, that this is a contract, and that the plaintiff who has acted on it has his remedy on that ground. But on the other ground there is no doubt. The statement in the time tables was untrue, and was made so as to be what the law calls a fraudulent representation. It was not the original printing that was blameable; but, after notice that the train was withdrawn, the defendants continue, down to the 25th March, to issue these tables. Was not that a representation that there was such a train? And, as they knew it had been discontinued for some time, was it not a false representation? It is all one as if a person, duly authorized by the company, had, knowing it was not true, said to the plaintiff: "There is a train from Milford Junction to Hull at that hour." The plaintiff believes this, acts upon it, and sustains loss. It is well established law that, where a person makes an untrue statement, knowing it to be untrue, to another who is induced to act upon it, an action lies. The facts bring the present case within that rule.

WIGHTMAN J. It seems to me that the publication of these time tables amounted to a promise to any one of the public who would come to the station and pay for a ticket, that he shall have one by the train at seven. It is said that this will make the Company liable though there be inevitable accidents. But the provision at the foot of the time tables protects the Company in cases of delay by accident, though the proviso does not apply to the present case where the train is altogether taken off.

But, whether there be a contract or not, the defendants are liable as having induced the plaintiff by a continued knowingly false representation to believe that there was a train at seven to Hull, which he, believing, acted upon to his prejudice. All the essentials for an action for a false representation are here. The representation is untrue; it is known by the persons making it to be untrue; it is calculated to induce the plaintiff to act; and he, believing it, is induced to act accordingly.

CROMPTON J. I think also that the plaintiff is entitled to judgment.

I entirely agree in what has been said by my Lord and my brother Wightman, that an action in the nature of an action for deceit lies here. The Company make a fresh statement at every moment whilst they continue to hold out these time tables as theirs. I am besides much inclined to think that they are liable also on the ground that they have committed a breach of their duty as public carriers. A public carrier of goods must carry according to his public profession; I think, however, that there has been no decision that carriers of passengers are under the same obligation: though in *Story on Bailments*, s. 591, it is said they are. I cannot doubt that the defendants publicly professed to be carriers of passengers by this train; and therefore I am inclined to think an action would lie on that ground.

But I am not prepared to say that there is a contract. As I agree that the defendants are liable, there is no occasion to decide this; and it is true that the cases as to the recovery of rewards have an analogy to this case. But there is a difference; where a reward is offered, it is generally offered to procure a service which is entirely performed by the party claiming the reward. I never was able to see any good reason why in such cases he might not sue for work and labour done at the request of the defendant. But in the present case, or in that which might be put of a shopkeeper advertising that he had cheap goods in his shop, I doubt if the labour of coming to the station, or of crossing the threshold of the shop, really is part of the consideration at all. If it be, it is a very small one. I agree, however, that any consideration, however small, will support a promise; and perhaps the difference between me and my Lord and my brother Wightman is rather as to the fact than the law. I doubt whether the promise here in fact was in consideration of coming to the station. If it was, I see difficulty in saying that the shopkeeper does not promise to have his wares for those who will take the trouble to leave the street and come into his shop. But it is quite unnecessary for the decision of this case to come to a determination on that. I am clearly of opinion that the action lies as for a false representation. I think, though less decidedly, that it lies on the ground of their duty as public carriers of passengers to act up to their public profession. But I doubt whether they are answerable on a contract to do all that may be found in the time tables, if there be anything there beyond what would be implied as part of their duty as carriers.

Judgment for the plaintiff.

QUESTIONS ON LEGAL METHOD. What is the *ratio decidendi* of this case? Can there be two *rationes*?

ANDERSON *v.* WISCONSIN CENTRAL RAILWAY CO.
Minnesota. Supreme Court. 1909. 120 N.W. 39

ELLIOTT J.: The Wisconsin Central Railway Company, having acquired certain real property in the city of Duluth through condemnation proceedings, advertised that at a time and place stated the buildings thereon would be sold at public auction. Bids for a certain house had been made until the amount offered amounted to $675. Anderson then increased his bid $5, making his offer $680. The auctioneer refused to consider this bid, because, as he stated, the amount of the raise was too insignificant. After waiting for a time to give Anderson an opportunity to increase it, the auctioneer announced that the house was sold to the last previous bidder for $675. An entry of this sale was made by the auctioneer in his entry book, as required by section 2815, Rev. Laws 1905. Anderson demanded to know why the auctioneer had not accepted his bid, and on the same day he tendered the $680, and it was refused. Before this tender was made a bill of sale of the building had been executed and delivered to the party to whom the building had been knocked down. Anderson then brought this action for damages, and recovered a verdict for $1,500. The defendant appealed from an order denying its motion for judgment notwithstanding the verdict or for a new trial.

The conflicting contentions of the parties arise out of fundamentally different conceptions of the nature of an auction. The appellant contends that the advertisement of a sale at auction is a mere declaration of intention which does not bind the owner to sell, or to sell to any particular bidder, and that the contract is not made until the bid is accepted. The complaint charges the defendant with liability for damages resulting to the plaintiffs from its unlawful refusal to sell the building to them and to carry out the terms and conditions of the auction sale. It proceeds upon the theory that, notwithstanding the bid, no sale was in fact made to them, because the defendant refused to recognize their right to purchase. The claim, as stated in the brief, is that "the advertisement constitutes a complete memorandum of contract, not of sale, but to sell, to the person who shall comply with its conditions, i.e., become the highest bidder at the auction provided for in the writing. The proposal became a binding contract to sell to that person the building at his bid." While the action was thus brought for the breach of an agreement to sell to the highest bidder, the argument proceeds upon the theory that under such conditions a contract has its inception in the announcement or advertisement of the owner's intention to sell the designated property at public auction to the highest bidder; that, unless the contrary is expressly stated in the announcement, the sale is to be without reserve; that the bid of the highest bidder is the acceptance of the offer; that the fall of the hammer is an announcement by the agent of the owner that he will wait no longer for the higher bid; and that the one whose bid was highest when the hammer fell is the purchaser without reference to the action of the auctioneer in announcing that some other bidder is the purchaser. Reduced to its lowest terms, this means that the offer to sell is made in the advertisement of intention to sell at auction, and that the contract is completed by the acceptance of that offer by the bidder. There is some ground for this theory, but the decided weight of authority sustains the view that the announcement is a mere statement of intention to hold an auction, and that no contract of any character is made until the offer to purchase is accepted by the auctioneer.

The jury, under proper instructions, found that the property was offered without express reservations as to the amount of the bids, that the bid of $5 was made in good faith, and that under the circumstances the amount was not so small as to justify the auctioneer in declining to consider it on that ground. No exceptions were taken to the instructions which submitted these questions to the jury, and on this appeal we accept the conclusions of the jury as final. The issue is also simplified by the fact that the case involves no question of puffing or by-bidding by the owner, or of fraud or misrepresentation in the announcement of the sale. For the purpose of the argument, we assume the correctness of the respondent's claim that an advertisement or announcement of an auction sale which does not state limitations and conditions is equivalent to the announcement that the sale will be without reserve. The issue of law is thus clearly defined. . . .

In view of the general prevalence of the custom of selling by auction, it is remarkable that no very early cases are found in the English reports. The parent case of *Payne* v. *Cave* (1789), 3 Term R. 148; 100 E.R. 502, was decided by Lord Kenyon C.J., sitting at Guildhall in 1788. The plaintiff offered a distilling apparatus for sale including a pewter worm, at public auction, on the usual conditions that the highest bidder should be the purchaser. There were several bidders for the worm, of whom Cave, who bid £40, was the last. The auctioneer dwelt on this bid for some time, until Cave said: "Why do you dwell? You will not get more." The auctioneer stated that he was informed that the worm weighed at least 1,300 hundredweight, and was worth more than £40. The bidder then asked him if he would warrant it to weigh so much, and receiving an answer in the negative, he declared that he would not take it. The worm was then resold on a subsequent day for £30 and an action was brought against Cave for the difference. Lord Kenyon ruled that the bidder was at liberty to withdraw his bid at any time before the hammer fell, and nonsuited the plaintiff. On motion to set aside the nonsuit, it was contended that a bidder is bound by the conditions of the sale to abide by his bid, and could not retract; that the hammer is suspended, not for the benefit of the bidder, or to give him an opportunity for repenting, but for the benefit of the seller; and that in the meantime the person who bid last is a purchaser, conditional upon no one bidding higher. But the court thought otherwise, and held that the auctioneer was the agent of the vendor, and that the assent of both parties was necessary to make the contract binding, and "That is signified on the part of the seller, by knocking down the hammer, which was not done here until the plaintiff retracted." "An auction," said the court, "is not inaptly called a *locus poenitentiae*. Every bidding is nothing more than an offer on one side, which is not binding on the other side until assented to."

The idea that an action will lie for the breach of an implied undertaking to sell to the highest bidder was advanced in *Warlow* v. *Harrison* (1859), 1 El. & El. 309; 120 E.R. 925 and dicta supporting it will be found in *Harris* v. *Nickerson* (1873), L.R. 8 Q.B. 288, *Spencer* v. *Harding* (1870), L.R. 5 C.P. 563, *Re Agra & Masterman Bank* (1867), 2 Ch. App. 391, 397, and *Johnson* v. *Boyes*, [1899] 2 Ch. 73. These cases assume that an offer to sell property at auction is indistinguishable from the case of an offer to the general public, such as a reward for the return of lost property, where it is held that contract rights are created in favour of one who complies with the conditions of the offer. *Carlill* v. *Carbolic Smoke Ball Co.*, [1893] 1 Q.B. 256. Langdell seems to be the only text-writer who takes this view of what the law should be. In his *Summary of the Law of Contracts* (page 24) it is stated that the correct view is "that the seller makes the offer when the article is put up, namely, to sell it to the highest bidder, and when a bid is made there is an actual sale, subject to the condition that no one else shall bid higher."...

Warlow v. *Harrison*, the source of all the uncertainty, was an action against an auctioneer who had advertised that he would sell certain horses, "the property of a gentleman, without reserve," at auction. Warlow bid 60 guineas for one of the horses, whereupon the owner bid 61 guineas. Warlow refused to increase his bid, and the horse was announced as sold for 61 guineas to the owner. Warlow, claiming to be the highest goodfaith bidder, tendered the amount of his bid to the auctioneer and demanded the horse, and, on this being refused, brought an action against the auctioneer, alleging that the defendant was his agent to complete the contract, that he had refused to do so, and that he had thereby lost certain money in attending the auction and had been deprived of the benefit of his contract. The defendant pleaded (1) not guilty; (2) that the plaintiff was not the highest bidder; and (3) that the auctioneer did not become the bidder's agent to complete the sale. The plaintiff recovered a verdict, but the Common Pleas (Lord Campbell C.J., Wightman J., and Erle J.) ordered a nonsuit on the ground that the plaintiff's allegation as to the agency of the defendants and the duty of the defendant to complete the contract on behalf of the plaintiff was not sustained. It was urged in argument that an auctioneer is the agent of the bidder to receive the bid; that the bidder is a conditional purchaser; that, when the sale by the conditions is without reserve, the bidder is absolutely the purchaser, unless, there be a bona fide higher bidding; and that the auctioneer, in consideration of the bidding by which a commission will come to him, promises the highest bidder to knock down the article to him and to do all that is necessary to complete the sale. "But this reasoning," said Lord Campbell, "is wholly at variance with the case of *Payne* v. *Cave*, which has been considered good law for nearly 70 years. That case decided that a bidding at an auction, instead of being a conditional purchase, is a mere offer, that the auctioneer is the agent of the vendor, that the assent of both parties is necessary to the contract, that his assent is signified by knocking down the hammer, and that until then either party may retract. This is quite inconsistent with the notion of a conditional purchase by a bidding, and with the notion of there being any personal promise by the auctioneer to the bidder that the bidding of an intending purchaser shall absolutely be accepted by the vendor. The vendor himself and the bidder being respectively free till the hammer is knocked down, the auctioneer cannot possibly be previously bound." Holding, thus, that no action would lie against the auctioneer, the court found it unnecessary to consider whether there was any remedy against a vendor who had violated a condition that the property would be sold to the highest bona fide bidder without reserve. In the Exchequer Chamber the decision was affirmed; but, as the plaintiff might amend his declaration, the court discussed the merits of the case which might be made. Barons Martin, Byles, and Watson were of the opinion that the plaintiff was entitled to recover from the auctioneer, because the auction was announced to be "without reserve," which meant that neither the owner nor any one in his behalf should bid at the auction, and that the property would be sold to the highest bidder, whether the sum bid was equivalent to the real value or not. On the principle which creates a contract between the loser of property who offers a reward for its return and the finder, or a railway company which advertises a time-table and one who purchases a ticket, it was said that an auctioneer who put the property up for sale upon such conditions pledges himself that the sale shall be without reserve, and that the contract is made with the highest bidder, who, in case of a breach thereof, has a right of action against the auctioneer. "We think," said Baron Martin, "that the auctioneer has contracted that the sale shall be without reserve, and that the contract is broken upon a bid being made by or on behalf of the owner, whether it be during the time the property is under the hammer or it be the last bid upon which the article is knocked down. In either case the sale is not 'without reserve' and the contract of the auctioneer is broken. We entertain no doubt that the owner may, at any time before the contract is legally complete, interfere and revoke the auctioneer's authority; but he does so at his peril, and if the auctioneer has contracted any liability in consequence of his employment and the subsequent revocation or conduct of the owner he is entitled to be indemnified." Baron Bramwell and Willes J. preferred to rest the judgment upon the ground that the auctioneer had undertaken to have, and yet there was evidence that he had not, authority to sell without reserve. . . .

In *Harris* v. *Nickerson*, the nature of the advertisement was considered, and it was held that it should be construed as a mere declaration of intention, which did not amount to a contract with any one who might act upon it, or constitute a warranty that the articles advertised would be offered for sale. Certain articles were not offered, and a party who attended for the purpose of bidding brought an action to recover for his loss of time and expense. Blackburn J. said: "This is certainly a startling proposition, and would be excessively inconvenient if carried out. It amounts to any one who advertises a sale by publishing an advertisement becomes responsible to every one who attends the sale for his cab hire and travelling expenses." Referring to *Warlow* v. *Harrison*, the learned judge remarked that "there the majority of the judges hold that an action would lie for not knocking down the property to the highest bidder when the sale was advertised as without reserve; that in such a case there is a contract to sell to the highest bidder, and if the owner bids there is a breach of the contract." Quinn J. was also of the opinion that the particular action could not be maintained without going to the extent of saying that where an auctioneer issued an advertisement of the sale of goods, if he withdraws any part of them without notice, the persons attending may all maintain actions against him. He was of the opinion, however, that when a sale is advertised without reserve, and a lot is put up and bid for, there is a ground for saying, as was said in *Warlow* v. *Harrison*, that a contract is entered into between the auctioneer and the highest bona fide bidder. But that rule was not applicable to the case under consideration, as the property was never put up for sale, and it was to say that there was a contract with every one attending the sale. The real point in the case was brought out by Justice Archibald, who said: "This is an attempt on the part of the plaintiff to make a mere declaration of intention a binding contract. He has utterly failed to show authority or reason for the proposition. If a false and fraudulent representation had been made, it would have been quite another matter. But to say that a mere advertisement that certain articles are to be sold at auction amounts to a contract to indemnify all who attend, if the sale of any part of the articles does not take place, is a proposition without authority or ground for supporting it."...

In *Johnson* v. *Boyes* it appeared that Boyes had advertised the freehold of a public house for sale at auction under conditions providing that the highest bidder should be the purchaser. The plaintiff, a married woman of financial standing, sent her husband to bid for her, but did not supply him with the necessary funds. The property was knocked down to him; but the auctioneer, who knew that he was financially irresponsible, refused to accept his check for the amount of the required deposit and sold the property to another person. The husband assured the auctioneer that his wife would furnish the money to make the check good, and the court found that his statement was true. The plaintiffs sued the vendors for breach of the contract that the highest bidder should be the purchaser. It was held that the bidder had not complied with the conditions of sale, which required that the deposit should be in cash. This disposed of the case; but the court stated the action could have been maintained, had the deposit been tendered in cash and the highest bidder been refused the property. "A vendor," said Cozens-Hardy J., "who offers property for sale by auction on the terms of the printed conditions can be made liable to a member of the public who accepts the offer, if those conditions be violated"—citing *Warlow* v. *Harrison*, and *Carlill* v. *Carbolic Smoke Ball Co.*

But the doctrine of *Warlow* v. *Harrison* was never generally acquiesced in, and in Lord Halsbury's *Laws of England*, vol. 1, p. 511(n), doubt is expressed as to its correctness. In a recent English edition of *Benjamin on Sale* (1906), the learned editors say that "two points were involved in *Warlow* v. *Harrison*: (1) Is an announcement that a sale will be without reserve, or will be made to the highest bidder, an offer of the contract with the highest bona fide bidder, and accepted by his bid? (2) When an auctioneer, acting for an undisclosed principal, makes such an announcement, does he thereby offer to contract personally? Although technically *Warlow* v. *Harrison* may not have been an actual decision upon these points, yet there was the strongest intimation of opinion in the affirmative on both points on the part of three judges, from which the other two did not dissent, and the case has been subsequently treated as actually deciding them. On the second point, however, of the personal liability of the auctioneer acting for an undisclosed principal, the case was doubted by Cockburn C.J. and Shee J., in *Mainprice* v. *Westley* (1865), 6 Best & S. 420; 122 E.R. 1250 because the employment of an autioneer necessarily involves the character of agent only, and therefore, prima facie, he does not contract personally. . . . As pointed out by a learned writer (*Pollock on Contracts*, pp. 17, 19), *Warlow* v. *Harrison* involves the theory that bidding at an auction advertised to be without reserve is not, as in other cases, a mere offer, but a conditional acceptance; the condition being that no higher bidder presents himself. But this theory cannot hold good under section 58(2) of the Code, as the sale is not complete until the fall of the hammer, so that, until then, neither party is bound. Yet, when once the goods are put up, there may, perhaps, be an implied contract not to withdraw them"—citing *Johnson* v. *Boyes*.

In commenting on *Warlow* v. *Harrison* Sir Frederick Pollock says that "opinions expressed by the judges, therefore, are not equivalent to the actual judgment of a court of error, and have, in fact, been regarded with some doubt in a later case, where the Court of Queen's Bench decided that, at all events, an auctioneer whose principal is disclosed by the conditions of sale does not contract personally that the sale shall be without reserve." Pollock, Contracts (Williston Ed.) p. 18, citing *Mainprice* v. *Westley*. It is now settled that the fact of disclosure or nondisclosure of the principal is immaterial. *Wolfe* v. *Thorne,* (1877), 2 Q.B.Div. 355; *Rainbow* v. *Hawkins*, [1904] 2 K.B. 322.

Sale of Goods Act, 1893 (56 & 57 Vict. c. 71) s. 58(2), provides that ". . . (2) a sale by auction is complete when the auctioneer announces its completion by the fall of the hammer or in other customary manner. Until such announcement is made, any bidder may retract his bid." It was held in the Scotch case of *Fenwick* v. *MacDonald*, [1904] 6F. (Ct. of Sess.) 850, that, whatever may have been the law formerly, this statute entitles a bidder to withdraw his bid at any time before the fall of the hammer, and the vendor must be equally free to withdraw his offer to sell, because one party cannot be bound while the other is free. But in the recent case of *McManus* v. *Fortescue*, [1907] 2 K.B. 1, some support was again given to *Warlow* v. *Harrison*. . . .

The Canadian cases of *McAlpine* v. *Young*, 2 Ch. Chamb. Rep. (Ont.) 85, and *O'Connor* v. *Woodward*, 6 Ont. Rep. [P.R.?] 223, seem to approve the doctrine of *Warlow* v. *Harrison*; but *Hilder* v. *Jackson*, 11 U. C.C.P. 543, is to the contrary. The plaintiff there rested his claim on the theory that an auctioneer at a public auction must receive the bid of any person and does a wrong to any person whose bid he refuses to receive. After conceding, on the authority of *Warlow* v. *Harrison*, that, when the sale is advertised to be without reserve, the auctioneer cannot receive a higher bid on the behalf of the owner to the prejudice of the preceding bidder, the court said; "But in such a sale as is stated in this count I do not understand on what ground any person can claim as a right to be allowed to bid—to offer to become the purchaser. It will be going beyond any authority I have seen to hold that by holding an auction under such circumstances there is an implied duty or contract to deal with any person who presents himself, and that the auctioneer, with due regard to his responsibilities to his principal, has not a right to refuse to deal with any particular person. The principal might refuse from mere caprice to sell to A, B, or C, and might direct the auctioneer to refuse to sell to certain parties; and I can see no reason why the auctioneer (his agent) is bound by law to accept offers or bids, any more than his principal would be." See *Cull* v. *Wakefield*, 6 U.C.Q.B. (O.S.) 178. . . .

On principle and authority the correct rule is that an announcement that a person will sell his property at public auction to the highest bidder is a mere declaration of intention to hold an auction at which bids will be received: that a bid is an offer which is accepted when the hammer falls, and until the acceptance of the bid is signified in some manner neither party assumes any legal obligation to the other. At any time before the highest bid is accepted, the bidder may withdraw his offer to purchase, or the auctioneer his offer to sell. The owner's offer to sell is made at the time through the auctioneer, and not when he advertises the auction sale. A merchant advertises that on a certain day he will sell his goods at bargain prices; but no one imagines that the prospective purchaser, who visits the store and is denied the right to purchase, has an action for damages against the merchant. He merely offers to purchase, and if his offer is refused, he has no remedy, although he may have lost a bargain, and have incurred expense and lost time in visiting the store. The analogy between such a transaction and an auction is at least close. As the advertisement in this case was a mere statement of intention to offer the property for sale at public auction to the highest bidder, the respondent's bid did not complete either a contract of sale or a contract to make a sale. . . .

The order is therefore reversed, with directions to enter judgment for the defendant.

[Section 58(2) of the English Sale of Goods Act is reproduced as s. 56, R.S.O. 1960, c. 358.]

CONDITIONS OF SALE

Ontario. Ward-Price, Limited. Auctioneers. 1963

1. Any bid which is merely a nominal or fractional advance may be rejected by the Auctioneer.

2. The records kept by the clerk of the sale together with the sales record book of the Auctioneer shall, in all cases, be accepted by the buyers as final in any question that may arise as to the prices for which lots have been sold.

3. The highest bidder shall be the buyer, and if any dispute arises between two or more bidders, the Auctioneer shall either decide the same or put up for re-sale the lot so in dispute.

4. Payment shall be made of the full purchase price immediately after the sale of the lot, or such part of the purchase price as may be required, and the names and addresses of the purchasers shall be given immediately on the sale of every lot, in default of which the lot so purchased may be immediately put up again and resold. The purchaser shall write his name and address on a form provided for that purpose, at the request of an attendant.

Payment of that part of the purchase money not required to be made at the time of sale shall be made within twenty-four hours thereafter, in default of which the undersigned may either continue to hold lots at the risk of the purchaser and take such action as the undersigned deems advisable for the enforcement of the sale, or may at public or private sale, and without other than this notice, re-sell the lots for the benefit of such purchaser, and deficiency (if any) arising from such re-sale, together with all expenses, shall be a charge against such purchaser.

Accounts which are not paid within thirty days of sale shall bear interest at 8% from date of sale plus costs of collection.

5. Release of any purchase will be made only upon payment of the total amount due for all purchases at the sale.

Release of any purchase will be made only on presenting bill of purchase.

6. All goods to be removed at the expense and risk of the purchaser within 48 hours of the date of the sale thereof, but arrangements for delivery of the same, at reasonable rates may be made upon application to a member of the staff of the undersigned.

7. Storage of any purchase shall be at the sole risk of the purchaser. Title passes upon the conclusion of the bidding on each lot, and thereafter the undersigned will not be held responsible if such purchase be lost, stolen, damaged, destroyed, resold or any other occurrence.

Storage charges will be made upon all purchases not removed within forty-eight hours from the date of the sale thereof.

8. In the case of lots upon which there is a reserve, the Auctioneer shall have the right to bid on behalf of the vendor.

9. All goods advertised, displayed for preview and catalogued herein are subject to prior sale, withdrawal, subdivision or consolidation at the discretion of the Auctioneers.

10. All paintings and fine art are sold as "by or attributed to" the artists as catalogued.

11. Electrical and other goods sold as "in working condition", and upon testing found to be imperfect, must be returned for inspection within one week of the closing date of the sale, otherwise adjustments will not be made.

Release of purchases will be made on sales days only before the hours of 12 noon and for 30 minutes after the close of each sale session. Other days—holidays and Saturdays excepted—between the hours of 9 a.m. and 5 p.m. Goods will not be released during a sale session.

12. Guarantee is not made either by the owners or by the undersigned of the correctness of the description, genuineness or authenticity of any lot, and no sale will be set aside on account of any incorrectness, error of cataloguing, or imperfection. Every lot is on public exhibition one or more days prior to its sale, after which it is sold "as is" and without recourse.

SPENCER and ANOTHER *v*. HARDING and OTHERS
England. Common Pleas. 1870. L.R. 5 C.P. 561

The second count of the declaration stated that the defendants by their agents issued to the plaintiffs and other persons engaged in the wholesale trade a circular in the words and figures following, that is to say:

"28 King Street, Cheapside, May 17th 1869.

We are instructed to offer to the wholesale trade for sale by tender the stock in trade of Messrs. G. Eilbeck & Co. of No. 1 Milk Street, amounting as per stock-book to £2,503 13s. 1d., and which will be sold at a discount in one lot. Payments to be made in cash. The stock may be viewed on the premises, No. 1 Milk Street, up to Thursday, the 20th instant, on which day, at 12 o'clock at noon precisely, the tenders will be received and opened at our offices. Should you tender and not attend the sale, please address to us, sealed and enclosed, "Tender for Eilbeck's stock.' Stock-books may be had at our office on Tuesday morning.

Honey, Humphreys & Co."

And the defendants offered and undertook to sell the *said* stock to the highest bidder for cash, and to receive and open the tenders delivered to them or their agents in that behalf, according to the true intent and meaning of the *said* circular. And the plaintiffs thereupon sent to the *said* agents of the defendants a tender for the *said* goods, in accordance with the *said* circular, and also attended the *said* sale at the time and place named in the *said* circular. And the *said* tender of the plaintiffs was the highest tender received by the defendants or their agents in that behalf. And the plaintiffs were ready and willing to pay for the *said* goods according to the true intent and meaning of the *said* circular. And all conditions were performed, etc., to entitle the plaintiffs to have their *said* tender accepted by the defendants, and to be declared the purchasers of the *said* goods according to the true intent and meaning of the *said* circular; yet the defendants refused to accept the *said* tender of the plaintiffs, and refused to sell the *said* goods to the plaintiffs, and refused to open the *said* tender or proceed with the sale of the *said* goods, in accordance with their *said* offer and taking in that behalf, whereby the plaintiffs had been of profit.

Demurrer, on the ground that the count showed no promise to accept the plaintiffs' tender or sell them the goods. Joinder.

WILLES J.: I am of the opinion that the defendants are entitled to judgment. The action is brought against persons who issued a circular offering a stock for sale by tender, to be sold at a discount in one lot. The plaintiffs sent in a tender which turned out to be the highest, but which was not accepted. They now insist that the circular amounts to a contract or promise to sell the goods to the highest bidder, —that is, in this case, to the person who should tender for them at the smallest rate of discount; and reliance is placed on the cases as to rewards offered for the discovery of an offender. In those cases, however, there never was any doubt that the advertisement amounted to a promise to pay the money to the person who first gave information. The difficulty suggested was that it was a contract with all the world. But that, of course, was soon overruled. It was an offer to become liable to any person who, before the offer should be retracted, should happen to be the person to fulfil the contract of which the advertisement was an offer or tender. That is not the sort of difficulty which presents itself here. If the circular had gone on "and we undertake to sell to the highest bidder," the reward cases would have applied, and there would have been a good contract in respect of the persons. But the question is, whether there is here any offer to enter into a contract at all, or whether the circular amounts to anything more than a mere proclamation that the defendants are ready to chaffer for the sale of the goods, and to receive offers for the purchase of them. In advertisements for tenders for buildings it is not usual to say that the contract will be given to the lowest bidder, and is not always that the contract is made with the lowest bidder. Here there is a total absence of any words to intimate that the highest bidder is to be the purchaser. It is a mere attempt to ascertain whether an offer can be obtained within such a margin as the sellers are willing to adopt.

[Keating and Montague Smith JJ. concurred.]

QUESTION ABOUT DRAFTING STYLE. Does the draftsman's frequent use of the word "said" in the declaration add anything to clarity or style? The italics have, of course, been added to draw your attention to the words.

JOHNSTON BROTHERS *v.* ROGERS BROTHERS

Ontario. Divisional Court. 1899. 30 O.R. 150

An appeal by the defendants from the judgment of William Elliott, senior Judge of the County Court of Middlesex, in favour of the plaintiffs in an action in that Court, the facts of which are fully set out in the following [portion of the] opinion delivered by that Judge:

The plaintiffs are bakers, and seek to recover damages from the defendants for breach of a contract for the sale and delivery of a quantity of flour.

The following letter is the basis of the plaintiff's claim:

"Toronto, April 26, 1898.

Dear Sir,—We wish to secure your patronage, and, as we have found the only proper way to get a customer is to save him money, we therefore are going to endeavour to save you money.

It is hardly prudent for us to push the sale of flour just now, as prices are sure to advance at least 50 cents per barrel within a very few days, and to give you the advantage of a cut from 20 to 25 cents per barrel seems a very foolish thing, but nevertheless we are going to do it, just to save you money and secure your patronage.

We quote you (R.O.B. or F.O.B.) your station, Hungarian $5.40, and strong Bakers $5.00, car lots only, and subject to sight draft with bill of lading.

We would suggest your using the wire to order, as prices are so rapidly advancing that they might be beyond reach before a letter would reach us.

Yours respectfully,
Rogers Bros."

This communication was received by the plaintiffs on the 27th April. The plaintiffs telegraphed the defendants the same morning as follows:

"London, April 27, 1898.

To Rogers Bros., Confederation Life Building, Toronto.

We will take two cars Hungarian at your offer of yesterday.

Johnston Bros."

On the same day, namely, the 27th April, the plaintiffs received the following communication by telegraph:

"Toronto, Ont., April 27, 1898.

Flour advanced sixty. Will accept advance of thirty on yesterday's quotations. Further advance certain.

Rogers Bros."

Then followed a letter, dated the 28th April, from Messrs. Hellmuth & Ivey, solicitors for the plaintiffs, calling upon the defendants to fulfil the order "according to the offer contained in your letter of the 26th and duly accepted by them by wire on April 27th; and upon your refusal damages will be demanded."

FALCONBRIDGE J. delivered the judgment of the Court.: . . . The real crux of the case is whether there is a contract.

Leaving out the matters of inducement (in both the legal and the ordinary sense) in the letter of the 26th, the contract, if there is one, is contained in the following words:

Letter, Defendants to Plaintiffs

"27th April, 1898.

We quote you, F.O.B. your station, Hungarian $5.40, and strong Bakers $5.00, car lots only, and subject to sight drafts with bills of lading."

Telegram, Plaintiffs to Defendants

"27th April, 1898.

We will take 2 cars Hungarian at your offer of yesterday."

I should expect to find American authority as to the phrase "we quote you" which must be in very common use among brokers, manufacturers, and dealers in the United States; but we were referred to no decided case, and I have found none where that phrase was used.

In the *American and English Encyclopedia of Law*, 2nd ed., vol. 7, p. 138, the law is stated to be: "A quotation of prices is not an offer to sell, in the sense that a complete contract will arise out of the mere acceptance of the rate offered or the giving of an order for merchandise in accordance with the proposed terms. It requires the acceptance by the one naming the price, of the order so made, to complete the transaction. Until thus completed there is no mutuality of obligation."

Of the cases cited in support of this proposition, *Moulton* v. *Kershaw* (1884), 59 Wis. 316, 48 Am. Rep. 516, is the nearest to the present one, but in none is the word "Quote" used.

The meaning of "quote" is given in modern dictionaries as follows:

Standard (Com.)—To give the current or market price of, as bonds, stocks, commodities, etc.

Imperial, ed. 1884—In com., to name as the price of an article; to name the current price of; as, what can you quote sugar at?

Century (Com.)—To name as the price of stocks, produce, etc.; name the current price of.

Webster (Com.)—To name the current price of.

Worcester—To state the price as the price of merchandise.

See also Black's *Law Dictionary, sub tit.* "Quotation."

There is little or no difference between any of these definitions. Now if we write the equivalent phrase into the letter—"We give you the current or market price, F.O.B. your station, of Hungarian Patent $5.40—" can it be for a moment contended that it is an offer which needs only an acceptance in terms to constitute a contract?

The case of *Harty* v. *Gooderham* (1871), 31 U.C.R. 18, is principally relied on by the plaintiffs. But that case presents more than one point of distinction. There the first inquiry was from the plaintiff, which, I think, is an element in the case. He writes the defendants to let him "know your lowest prices for 50 O.P. spirits," etc. To which defendants answered, mentioning prices and particulars: "Shall be happy to have an order from you, to which we will give prompt attention," which the court held to be equivalent to saying "We will sell it at those prices. Will you purchase from us and let us know how much?" And so the contract was held to be complete on the plaintiff's acceptance.

But there is no such offer to sell in the present defendant's letter. *Harvey* v. *Facey*, [1893] A.C. 552, is strong authority against the plaintiffs.

I have not overlooked the concluding paragraph of the letter, viz., "We would suggest your using the wire to order, as prices are so rapidly advancing that they might be beyond reach before a letter would reach us." The learned Judge considers this to be one of the matters foreign to a mere quotation of prices. I venture, on the contrary, to think that this suggestion is more consistent with a mere quotation of prices, which might vary from day to day or from hour to hour. There could be no question of the prices becoming "beyond reach" in a simple offer to sell at a certain price.

In my opinion, the plaintiffs have failed to establish a contract, and this appeal must be allowed with costs, and the action dismissed with costs. . . .

QUESTIONS. Suppose the Plaintiff in *Harty* v. *Gooderham* had ordered more "spirits, etc." than the Defendant could reasonably have possessed or acquired? is *Harvey* v. *Facey* such a strong authority against the plaintiffs? What is *Harvey* v. *Facey* authority for? See (1923), 1 *Can. Bar Rev.* at pp. 398ff., and 694, 713.

HARVEY *v.* FACEY
Jamaica. Privy Council [1893] A.C. 552

LORD MORRIS: The appellants are solicitors carrying on business in partnership at Kingston, [Jamaica], and it appears that in the beginning of October, 1891, negotiations took place between the respondent L. M. Facey and the Mayor and Council of Kingston for the sale of the property in question; that Facey had offered to sell it to them for the sum of £900; that the offer was discussed by the Council at their meeting on the 6th of October, 1891, and the consideration of its acceptance deferred; that on the 7th of October, 1891, L. M. Facey was travelling in the train from Kingston to Porus, and that the appellants caused a telegram to be sent after him from Kingston addressed to him "on the train for Porus," in the following words: "Will you sell us Bumper Hall Pen? Telegraph lowest cash price—answer paid"; that on the same day L. M. Facey replied by telegram to the appellants in the following words: "Lowest price for Bumper Hall Pen £900"; that on the same day the appellants replied to the last-mentioned telegram by a telegram addressed to L. M. Facey "on train at Porus" in the words following: "We agree to buy Bumper Hall Pen for the sum of nine hundred pounds asked by you. Please send us your title deed in order that we may get early possession." The above telegrams were duly received by the appellants and by L. M. Facey. . . . Their Lordships concur in the judgment of Mr. Justice Curran that there was no concluded contract between the appellants and L. M. Facey to be collected from the aforesaid telegrams. The first telegram asks two questions. The first question is as to the willingness of L. M. Facey to sell to the appellants; the second question asks the lowest price, and the word "Telegraph" is in its collocation addressed to that second question only. L. M. Facey replied to the second question only, and gives his lowest price. The third telegram from the appellants treats the answer of L. M. Facey stating his lowest price as an unconditional offer to sell to them at the price named. Their Lordships cannot treat the telegram from L. M. Facey as binding him in any respect, except to the extent it does by its terms, viz., the lowest price. Everything else is left open, and the reply telegram from the appellants cannot be treated as an acceptance of an offer to sell to them; it is an offer that required to be accepted by L. M. Facey. The contract could only be completed if L. M. Facey had accepted the appellant's last telegram. It has been contended for the appellants that L. M. Facey's telegram should be read as saying "yes" to the first question put in the appellants' telegram, but there is nothing to support that contention. L. M. Facey's telegram gives a precise answer to a precise question, viz., the price. The contract must appear by the telegrams, whereas the appellants are obliged to contend that an acceptance of the first question is to be implied. Their Lordships are of the opinion that the mere statement of the lowest price at which the vendor would sell contains no implied contract to sell at that price to the persons making the inquiry. . . .

GRAINGER & SON *v.* GOUGH. [1896] A.C. 325 (House of Lords). LORD HERSCHELL: "The transmission of such a price list does not amount to an offer to supply an unlimited quantity of the wine described at the price named, so that so soon as an order is given there is a binding contract to supply that quantity. If it were so, the merchant might find himself involved in any number of contractual obligations to supply wine of a particular description which he would be quite unable to carry out, his stock of that wine being necessarily limited."

BOYER AND CO. *v.* D. & R. DUKE. [1905] 2 Ir.R. 617. MADDEN J.: "It is a matter of common knowledge that quotations of prices are scattered broadcast among possible customers. Business could not be carried on if each such recipient of a priced catalogue offering a desirable article—say a rare book—at an attractive price, were in a position to create a contract of sale by writing that he would buy at the price mentioned. The catalogue had probably reached many collectors. The order of one only can be honoured. Has each of the others who write for the book the right of action? Wholesale dealers have not in stock an unlimited supply of the articles the price of which they quote to the public at large. This stock usually bears some proportion to the orders which they may reasonably expect to receive. Transactions of the kind under consideration are intelligible and business-like, if we bear in mind the distinction between a quotation, submitted as a basis of a possible order, and an offer to sell which, if accepted, creates a contract for the breach of which damages may be recovered.

"These observations seem to apply with special force to a quotation furnished by a manufacturer, in the position of the defendants, stating the terms on which he is prepared to work, as to price and time for completion. He may receive and comply with many applications for quotations on the same day. If his reply in each case can be turned into a contract by acceptance, his looms might be burdened with an amount of work which would render it impossible for him to meet his engagements. In my opinion, a merchant, dealer, or manufacturer, by furnishing a quotation invites an offer which will be honoured or not according to the exigencies of the business. A quotation based on current prices usually holds good for a limited time. But it remains a quotation on the basis of which an offer will not be entertained after a certain date."

ROOKE *v.* DAWSON. [1895] Ch.D. 480 (England). The defendants announced an examination for a scholarship which they administered. The plaintiff and one other candidate competed and the plaintiff wrote the better paper. He claimed the scholarship, which the defendants refused to him. Held, for the defendants. CHITTY J.: "It is plain the plaintiff could not state that the announcement included the term that the scholarship would be awarded, in all events, to the boy who got the highest number of marks. That would be a most improbable announcement to be made by trustees in the position of these defendants." [Why?]

PHARMACEUTICAL SOCIETY OF GREAT BRITAIN *v.* BOOTS CASH CHEMISTS (SOUTHERN) LTD.

England. Court of Appeal. [1953] 1 Q.B. 401

The Pharmaceutical Society is charged with the enforcement of the *Pharmacy and Poisons Act, 1933*, section 18 of which provides in part that no person shall "sell any poison included in Part I of the Poisons List, unless . . . the sale is effected by, or under the supervision of, a registered pharmacist." "Boots," well known chain store druggists (chemist's shops) in England, operated a shop in Edgware where substances included in Part I of the Poisons List were displayed in a self service area. A customer taking one of these substances could only escape from the area by passing a cashier's desk which was near and under the supervision of the pharmacist. The cashier and the pharmacist were instructed to prevent any customers from removing any drug from the shop if the pharmacist thought fit. The Pharmaceutical Society brought this action on an agreed statement of facts to determine whether, as the Society contended, the sale took place when the customer helped himself from the shelf, or as "Boots" maintained, the sale took place when the cashier decided whether she would accept the payment. The society supposed that if the sale had already taken place it had not taken place under the supervision of a registered pharmacist and that Boots could not, therefore, refuse to accept payment or stop the customer from leaving with the prescribed drugs. Lord Goddard C.J. decided that the sale took place when the cashier accepted payment and under proper supervision. The Society appealed.

Somervell L.J.: It is not disputed that in a chemist's shop where this self-service system does not prevail a customer may go in and ask a young woman assistant, who will not herself be a registered pharmacist, for one of these articles on the list, and the transaction may be completed and the article paid for, although the registered pharmacist, who will no doubt be on the premises, will not know anything himself of the transaction, unless the assistant serving the customer, or the customer, requires to put a question to him. It is right that I should emphasize, as did the Lord Chief Justice, that these are not dangerous drugs. They are substances which contain very small portions of poison, and I imagine that many of them are the type of drug which has a warning as to what doses are to be taken. They are drugs which can be obtained, under the law, without a doctor's prescription.

The point taken by the plaintiffs is this: it is said that the purchase is complete if and when a customer going round the shelves takes an article and puts it in the receptacle which he or she is carrying, and that therefore, if that is right, when the customer comes to the pay desk, having completed the tour of the premises, the registered pharmacist, if so minded, has no power to say: "This drug ought not to be sold to this customer." Whether and in what circumstances he would have that power we need not inquire, but one can, of course, see that there is a difference if supervision can only be exercised at a time when the contract is completed.

I agree with the Lord Chief Justice in everything that he said, but I will put the matter shortly in my own words. Whether the view contended for by the plaintiffs is a right view depends on what are legal implications of this layout—the invitation to the customer. Is a contract to be regarded as being completed when the article is put into the receptacle, or is this to be regarded as a more organized way of doing what is done already in many types of shops—and a bookseller is perhaps the best example—namely, enabling customers to have free access to what is in the shop, to look at the different articles, and then, ultimately, having got the ones which they wish to buy, to come up to the assistant saying "I want this"? The assistant in 999 times out of 1,000 says "That is all right," and the money passes and the transaction is completed. I agree with what the Lord Chief Justice has said, and with the reasons which he has given for his conclusion, that in the case of an ordinary shop, although goods are displayed and it is intended that customers should go and choose what they want, the contract is not completed until, the customer having indicated the articles which he needs, the shop-keeper, or someone on his behalf, accepts that offer. Then the contract is completed. I can see no reason at all, that being clearly the normal position, for drawing any different implication as a result of this layout.

The Lord Chief Justice, I think, expressed one of the most formidable difficulties in the way of the plaintiffs' contention when he pointed out that, if the plaintiffs are right, once an article has been placed in the receptacle the customer himself is bound and would have no right, without paying for the first article, to substitute an article which he saw later of a similar kind and which he perhaps preferred. I can see no reason for implying from this self-service arrangement any implication other than that which the Lord Chief Justice found in it, namely, that it is a convenient method of enabling customers to see what there is and choose, and possibly put back and substitute, articles which they wish to have, and then go up to the cashier and offer to buy what they have so far chosen. On that conclusion the case fails, because it is admitted that there was supervision in the sense required by the Act and at the appropriate moment of time. For these reasons, in my opinion, the appeal should be dismissed.

[The judgments of Birkett and Romer L.JJ., who agreed are omitted.]

QUESTIONS. If the decision had gone the other way, would it follow, as Lord Goddard seems to have thought, that once a customer had handled a product he would have to pay for it, even if he saw another product he preferred? Is not one of the purposes of a self service system to permit customers to make more informed choices of products after comparison, without involving the time of a clerk? If this is a purpose, is there any real difficulty in interpreting the situation as one of an offer to sell acceptable only by taking the finally selected product to the cashier?

Does the *Boots* case offer any help in solving the vexing case of the window lure? During World War II shopkeepers sometimes placed scarce articles, such as nylon stockings, in their windows, hoping to induce customers to come into the shop. Of course this end would be defeated if this sole remaining pair of nylons were sold to the first customer. Has the first, or any customer who wants to buy at the stated price, and produces the money, a contractual right? If so, and the shopkeeper refuses to sell, what damages will the customer be awarded? Will the practical result that more customers will be annoyed than will be pleased by this practice be a sufficient discouragement to shopkeepers? Has the customer any "moral right" not to be lured into a shop?

FISHER *v.* BELL [1960] 3 All E.R. 731 (England. Queen's Bench Division). A 1959 statute made it an offence for anyone to "manufacture, sell or hire or offer for sale or hire, or lend or give to any other person" a spring blade knife, commonly known as a "flick knife". Respondent had such a knife displayed in his shop window, with a price tag "Ejector knife — 4s." attached. A police constable gave the respondent his opinion that it was a flick knife to which the respondent said ,"Why do the manufacturers still bring them round for us to sell?" The constable told the respondent he would be reported for offering for sale a flick knife, to which he said, "Fair enough." On a prosecution, held, for the respondent. The display of the knife was a mere invitation to treat, not an "offer for sale." LORD PARKER C.J.: "... I think that most lay people would be inclined to the view (as, indeed, I was myself when I first read these papers), that if a knife were displayed in a window like that with a price attached to it, it was nonsense to say that that was not offering it for sale. The knife is there inviting people to buy it, and in ordinary language it is for sale; but any statute must be looked at in the light of the general law of the country, for Parliament must be taken to know the general law. It is clear that, according to the ordinary law of contract, the display of an article with a price on it in a shop window is merely an invitation to treat .... [In] many statutes and orders which prohibit selling and offering for sale of goods, it is very common, when it is so desired, to insert the words, 'offering or exposing for sale', 'exposing for sale' being clearly words which would cover the display of goods in a shop window.... I, for my part, though I confess reluctantly, am driven to the conclusion that no offence was here committed."

SWISS FEDERAL CODE OF OBLIGATIONS

7. . . . The display of merchandise with a price tag is considered as a rule as an offer.

BRISTOL, CARDIFF, AND SWANSEA AERATED BREAD COMPANY *v.* MAGGS

England Chancery Division. 1890. 44 Ch.D. 616

This was an action by the Plaintiffs, the Bristol, Cardiff, and Swansea Aërated Bread Company (Limited), against the Defendant, a baker and confectioner carrying on business at 15, Duke Street, Cardiff, for the specific performance of a contract alleged to be constituted by two letters. The first was written by the Defendant to Colonel Guthrie, a director of the Plaintiff company, and was as follows:

"Cardiff, 29th of May, 1889

Dear Sir,—I beg to submit to you the following conditions for disposal of my business carried on at 15, Duke Street, Cardiff. Lease and goodwill, £450 (lease from the 29th of September, 1888, for fourteen years). All fixtures, fittings, utensils, &c., stock-in-trade connected with the premises to be taken at valuation.

Yours truly,
R. Maggs.

This offer to hold good for ten days."

The letter did not on the face of it shew to whom it was written. Colonel Guthrie, writing with the authority of the board of directors of the company, replied as follows:

"Cardiff, 1st of June, 1889.

Dear Sir,—On behalf of the Bristol, Cardiff, and Swansea Aërated Bread Company (Limited), I accept your offer for shop and lease, &c., 15, Duke Street, Cardiff.

Yours truly,
John Guthrie.
For B., C., and S. Aërated Bread Company.

Mr. R. Maggs,
15, Duke Street, Cardiff."

On the 2nd of June, 1889, the Defendant's solicitor sent Colonel Guthrie a formal memorandum of agreement for approval, with an accompanying letter. This memorandum was altered by the plaintiff's solicitors, mainly by the insertion of a clause preventing the vendor for five years from carrying on a like business within the borough of Cardiff or within a distance of five miles from the Townhall. The memorandum so altered was returned on the 4th of June, with a letter of the Plaintiff's solicitors. On the 5th of June the Defendant's solicitor wrote sending the draft again to the Plaintiffs' solicitors, with a modification of the proposed additional clause. On the 6th of June the Plaintiffs' solicitors wrote that they could not themselves agree to the proposed modification, but that they had asked Colonel Guthrie to call about it.

On the 7th the Defendant's solicitor wrote that he regretted the Plaintiffs' solicitors had not agreed to the terms of the draft contract, and continued: "Colonel Guthrie has not been near me, and by my client's instructions I beg to inform you that he declines to proceed further in the matter."

On the 8th Colonel Guthrie saw the Defendant's solicitor and said he had come to settle the agreement which had been returned to him. The answer was that he was too late; the Defendant had made other arrangements. Colonel Guthrie replied he was prepared to sign the agreement leaving out the disputed clause. The solicitor declined; and Colonel Guthrie went immediately to the Defendant, who told him that he wished to have the agreement cancelled, because his son was very much against his parting with the shop. The Defendant, it appeared, did not suggest that there was no agreement, but asked Colonel Guthrie to use his influence with his co-directors to get the sale cancelled. The memorandum of agreement contained several terms not expressed in the letters; for example, it provided for the book debts and books of account being reserved to the vendor and for the payment of a deposit of £45; it fixed the 24th of June as the day for completion of the purchase and delivery of possession; it provided for delivery of abstract of title and the date from which it was to commence, and for other matters, all of which were more or less of a formal nature.

KAY J. (after stating the facts, continued): The contested stipulation in the memorandum of agreement as to restricting the vendor from carrying on a business to that which he had sold was not by any means a matter of form. After some conflict of opinion, it has been decided by the Court of Appeal, in *Pearson* v. *Pearson* (1884), 27 Ch.D. 145, that a man who sells the goodwill of a business may not only set up a similar business next door and say that he is the person who carried on the old business, but that he may also solicit the customers of the old business to continue to deal with him, although by these proceedings he might not only destroy all benefit to the purchaser of the thing which he had bought, but might recover to himself the actual possession of it. Such a fraudulent proceeding, according to the decision, cannot be prevented by any Court of Law or Equity. It follows that the stipulation which the company's solicitors introduced into the draft was one which they were not entitled to insert if the two letters which I have read were a complete contract. In other words, they were trying to obtain an additional and most important concession from the vendor. Now . . . suppose this to pass in conversation: A. offers to B. his business, lease, and goodwill for £450 B. says, "I accept." A day or two afterwards B. asks A. to engage not to carry on a similar business within a distance of five miles. A. answers, "I cannot agree to that, but I will if you say three miles." B. takes time to consider, saying he will send an agent next day to settle the terms. The agent does not go next day, and A. accordingly says to B., "I put an end to the matter." No one could doubt that would be a continuous negotiation, and that B. could not say, "I will disregard all that followed the acceptance of the first offer, and insist on there being a complete contract by that acceptance." Well, then, still leaving out of sight the statute and authorities suppose all this to take place by letters between A. and B. instead of conversation; it is obvious the result must be the same. Some of the letters being by the principals and some by the solicitors could not make any difference. . . .

It was suggested that the ten days during which the offer was to remain open had not expired when it was withdrawn. But this can make no difference. The offer was not a contract, and the term that it should remain open for ten days was therefore not binding. It has often been held that such an offer may, notwithstanding, be withdrawn within the time limited. . . .

I decide this case against the Plaintiffs upon the ground, that although the two letters relied on would, if nothing else had taken place, have been sufficient evidence of a complete agreement, yet the Plaintiffs have themselves shewn that the agreement was not complete by stipulating afterwards for an important additional term, which kept the whole matter of purchase and sale in a state of negotiation only, and that the Defendant was therefore at liberty to put an end to the negotiations, as he did, by withdrawing his offer. . . .

[Part of the opinion dealing with the Statute of Frauds has been omitted.]

BELLAMY *v.* DEBENHAM. 1890. 45 Ch.D. 481. NORTH J.: . . ."Some of the phrases used by Mr. Justice Kay, in *Bristol, Cardiff, and Swansea Aërated Bread Co.* v. *Maggs* seem to me to go further than that. By way of illustration he put a case of a definite offer to sell a business, lease, and goodwill, and a definite acceptance, and after that negotiations between the parties as to whether a new term, limiting the area within which the vendor of the business was to carry on a similar business, should be introduced, and said that in such a case he thought that the purchaser could not disregard all that followed the acceptance of the prior offer, and insist on there being a complete contract by that acceptance. . .

"In my opinion, subsequent negotiations, first commenced on new points after a contract complete in itself has been signed, cannot be regarded as constituting a part of the negotiations going on at the time when it was signed, because, *ex hypothesi*, the Court has arrived at the conclusion that they were not going on then—that they were not thought of at that time, but related to matters first thought of subsequently.

"I do not in any way dissent from the view which Mr. Justice Kay took of the case then before him; but those remarks of his, if they meant as much as they might possibly mean, seem to me to go too far, and I should not be prepared to follow them. . . ."

HARVEY *v.* PERRY. [1953] 2 D.L.R. 465 (Alberta. Supreme Court of Canada). Negotiations were spread over several months leading to an alleged contract for the sale of eight oil leases in Alberta. Correspondence starting in January, 1950, included a letter from Perry dated May 2, rejecting terms so high "we cannot handle it at all" and continuing, "However, you might consider the following and if you feel that you could accept these terms, I am sure we could put a deal over for you. . . ." On May 8, Harvey wrote, "I will accept your proposition. . . ." On May 15, Perry wrote, "We will proceed immediately to try and consummate a deal for you at the earliest possible moment. There will, in all probability, be a counter proposal or two from our clients, and if such is the case, we will submit them to you at once." On August 24, Perry's solicitor wrote that "Mr. A. C. Perry . . . advises that he is in a position to take these leases under the terms and conditions contained in his letter to you of the 2nd May and your letter to his firm dated May 8th, 1950. Mr. Perry has asked us to prepare the Assignment . . . it will be necessary that we have access to the above leases now in our possession." In due course Harvey forwarded the leases. On August 26, the solicitor again wrote, "some discussion between you will be necessary before adequate instructions can be given to draw such an Agreement." On the same day Perry himself wrote that, "Mr. Howatt of Howatt and Howatt, my solicitor, is sending through a copy of the proposed agreement. However you and I will get together and complete the terms." The "get together" took place on September 1, when, Perry contended, "we had made a deal . . . and we shook hands on that deal right there and then in front of the Hotel." On September 2 Perry's solicitor sent a letter and draft agreement with some variations from the oral agreement, which Harvey's solicitors objected to on September 7, and to the correction of which Perry's solicitor agreed, on September 9, saying, "the terms are acceptable." On September 13 Perry forwarded a second agreement in identical terms with the first, and containing another variation from the oral agreement of September 1. Neither Harvey nor his solicitors made any further communication and Perry's letters remained unanswered. About September 15 Harvey announced that he would drill his own wells, which concluded the negotiations. The trial judge found a contract in the letters of May 2, 8, 15 and August 24 and in Harvey's sending the leases. The Alberta Court of Appeal agreed. The Supreme Court of Canada, following the *Maggs* case, reversed, ESTEY J. saying, "The letter of September 2nd, the proposed agreement enclosed therewith and respondent's solicitors' letter of September 9th, might support a conclusion that the parties had agreed, but, when read, as they must be, with respondent's solicitors' letter of September 13th and the proposed agreement enclosed therewith, it is clear that the respondent had not agreed. . . . There was no concensus ad idem because the respondent was still negotiating for better terms."

ROSSDALE *v.* DENNY
England. King's Bench. [1921] 1 Ch. 57

The plaintiff sued the defendants as vendors for specific performance of an agreement by which, as he alleged, the defendants agreed to sell him and he agreed to purchase for the sum of £75,000 certain leasehold premises in London together with certain chattels.

The alleged agreement was contained in two letters each dated August 20, 1919. The question was whether those two letters constituted a binding contract between the parties, or whether the offer which was made by the plaintiff and accepted by the defendants was conditional upon a formal contract being executed by the parties.

The plaintiff's letter, written to the defendants' agents for the sale of the property, was in the following terms:

"Dear Sirs, I understand that the premises known as the Connaught Club, Marble Arch, are held by your clients Major Denny and Mr. Denny for a term of years expiring about 1998 at a ground rent of £1400, with the benefit of the letting of the shops underneath. I hereby beg to offer £75,000 for the property, the price to include fixtures, fittings, furniture, linen, etc., and utensils in the premises and in store rooms, also goods removed to Messrs. Maples' Depository, of all of which effects you will furnish inventories to me. I am prepared to pay £7,500 deposit on signing of formal contract, completion to take place 14 days after you are in a position to give vacant possession. This offer is subject to a formal contract to embody such reasonable provisions as my solicitors may approve, and to the lease containing no unusual provisions or covenants. Kindly let me know that this offer is accepted, and please instruct your clients to send draft contracts to Messrs. Collyer-Bristow & Co., 4 Bedford Row, as soon as possible."

That letter was answered on the same day by a member of the firm of Yates & Yates, the defendants' agents: "Dear Sir, Connaught Club, Marble Arch. In reply to your letter of even date I am instructed to accept on behalf of my clients, Major Denny and Mr. Denny, the offer therein contained, and I will communicate with Major Denny at once so that he may instruct his solicitors to prepare formal contract."

The letters were the outcome of negotiations which had taken place between the parties during a period of about three weeks preceding August 20, 1919.

After that date a correspondence ensued between the respective solicitors of the plaintiff and the defendants relating to the preparation of a draft formal contract. It appeared that the plaintiff's object in acquiring the property was to turn it into an hotel. In the course of the correspondence the plaintiff's solicitors pointed this out to the defendants' solicitors and drew attention to the fact that the lease prohibited it, and requested that before contracts were actually exchanged a licence should be obtained authorizing the lessee to use the premises as an hotel.

On September 23 the defendants' solicitors wrote to the plaintiff's solicitors: "Dear Sirs, We have seen Major Denny today on the subject of the alteration in the draft contract. He cannot agree to the stipulations made by and on behalf of your client and wishes the matter to be considered at an end." This position being insisted upon by the defendants, notwithstanding that the plaintiff was prepared to approve the agreement as submitted by the defendants' solicitors without any alteration the plaintiff issued the writ in this action.

RUSSELL J.: Numerous authorities exist upon this question, and a careful selection of them has been produced to me by both sides. The result of them may, I think, be fairly stated in this way: they are unanimous in this, that the question is one entirely depending upon the true construction of the documents. If upon the true construction of the documents the reference to a formal contract amounts to an expression of a desire on the part of one or other of the parties, or both, that their already complete contract should be reduced into a more formal shape, then the fact that no such contract has been executed is no defence to the action, but the original and complete contract survives and may be enforced. If, on the other hand, the true construction of the documents is this, that either the offer or the acceptance was conditional only, then the non-execution of a formal contract affords a defence to the action upon the ground that the parties really did not intend to be bound until a formal document had in fact been executed.

I will now refer to some of the authorities and first to *Winn* v. *Bull* (1877), 7 Ch.D. 29, a decision of Sir George Jessel M.R. [His Lordship stated the facts of that case and continued:] Sir George Jessel in his judgment, says this: "I am of the opinion there is no contract. I take it the principle is clear. If in the case of a proposed sale or lease of an estate two persons agree to all the terms and say, 'We will have the terms put into form,' then all the terms being put into writing and agreed to, there is a contract. If two persons agree in writing that up to a certain point the terms shall be the terms of the contract, but that the minor terms shall be submitted to a solicitor, and shall be such as are approved of by him, then there is no contract, because all the terms have not been settled." There, it is to be observed, he was dealing with the case of a proposed sale or lease of an estate; he is covering the whole ground. Then he deals more specifically with the case of buying an estate, and then he says when you come to a contract for a lease the case is still stronger, and then, after referring to *Chinnock* v. *Marchioness of Ely* (1865), 4 D.J.&S. 638, and *Rossiter* v. *Miller* (1877), 5 Ch.D. 648 (then only in the Court of Appeal) he concludes his judgment in these terms: "it comes, therefore, to this, that where you have a proposal or agreement made in writing expressed to be subject to a formal contract being prepared, it means what it says; it is subject to and is dependant upon a formal contract being prepared. When it is not expressly stated to be subject to a formal contract it becomes a question of construction, whether the parties intended that the terms agreed on should merely be put into form, or whether they should be subject to a new agreement the terms of which are not expressed in detail." Be it observed that in that case Sir George Jessel came to the conclusion on the construction of that document that it really was a condition precedent to a liability that there should be a formal contract in writing. *Bonnewell* v. *Jenkins* (1878), 8 Ch.D. 70, illustrates the other line of view. [His Lordship read the headnote of that case and continued:] Fry J. puts it in this way: "Now if the matter were not covered by decision, it is very probable that I should feel myself drawn to the conclusion that wherever there is a reference to a future contract the letters themselves do not constitute a contract, and for this very obvious reason, that a reference to a contract as a future thing seems to negative the notion of the existence of a contract as a present thing. But it is too late for that argument to be used before me successfully, when a long series of cases has established this proposition, that the mere references to a future contract is not enough to negative the existence of a present one: and that principle has been very clearly expressed by the present Master of the Rolls in the case of *Crossley* v. *Maycock*, (1874), L.R. 18 Eq. 180. . . . I am, therefore, bound to inquire to which of these two categories the present acceptance belongs, and I come to the conclusion that it is a simple acceptance of the offer made by the plaintiff, accompanied by a mere statement of an intention that that arrangement shall be reduced into a formal contract." Fry J.'s decision was [affirmed in] the Court of Appeal. . . .

After those two authorities each of which is a sample of one of the different lines of decisions, *Rossiter* v. *Miller* went to the House of Lords.

The facts of that case have no real relation to those of the case before me, but the principle is well stated there. Lord Hatherley puts it in this way: "It has been established for far too long a time, and by some precedents in your Lordships' House, that if you can find the true and important ingredients of an agreement in that which has taken place between two parties in the course of a correspondence, then, although the correspondence may not set forth, in a form which a solicitor would adopt if he were instructed to draw an agreement in writing, that which is the agreement between the parties, yet, if the parties to the agreement, the thing to be sold, the price to be paid, and all those matters to be clearly and distinctly stated, although only by letter, an acceptance clearly by letter will not the less constitute an agreement in the full sense between the parties merely because that letter may say, We will have this agreement put into due form by a solicitor. If it is stated in so many plain and express terms (and in *Chinnock* v. *Marchioness of Ely*, that was the ground on which that case proceeded) that one of the very terms of the agreement itself was that it should not be concluded by the agent employed in the first place to enter into the negotiation, and that it should not be a concluded agreement until a solicitor intervened and drew a formal agreement; if you find that to be a term of the agreement itself, well and good, if not, the agreement stands." There is nothing in *Rossiter* v. *Miller* that throws a doubt upon the decision and the views expressed by Sir George Jessel in *Winn* v. *Bull*, and just to carry the matter down to date I will refer for this purpose to one of the latest decisions, a case before Parker J. as he then was—namely, *Von Hatzfeldt-Wildenburg* v. *Alexander*, [1912] 1 Ch.D. 284, 288. There the learned judge sums up the result of the authorities in these words: "It appears to be well settled by the authorities that if the documents or letters relied on as constituting a contract contemplate the execution of a further contract between the parties, it is a question of construction whether the execution of the further contract is a condition or term of the bargain, or whether it is a mere expression of the desire of the parties as to the manner in which the transaction already agreed to will in fact go through. In the former case there is no enforceable contract either because the condition is unfulfilled or because the law does not recognise a contract to enter into a contract."

[His Lordship then considered the construction of the letters and came to the conclusion that the effect of them was to place the parties in the position of not being bound unless and until a formal contract had been executed between them, and continued:] That of course is enough to dispose of the case and before parting with it I ought to say this, that after considering all authorities which have been brought to my attention it would appear that in every case, with two exceptions, where the words "subject to" appear, the documents in those cases have been held to amount only to a conditional offer, or a conditional acceptance, as the case might be, but not such as to constitute a binding contract apart from the execution of a formal document. I will not refer to the cases in detail. . . . The two exceptions are these. On is *Fibley* v. *Hounsell*, [1896] 2 Ch. 737, 742, before Romer J., and the reason for the decision is quite plain when the facts are looked at. The learned judge there said: "When the offer is carefully looked at it appears to me that the acceptance was absolute and not conditional." So that case, although the words 'subject to" appear therein, is not really an exception to the consistent line of authorities which have all decided in cases where those words appear that the offer is conditional. The other case is *North* v. *Percival*, [1898] 2 Ch. 128, a decision of Kekewich J. . . . As regards *North* v. *Percival* I will only say this: that it has been doubted by Parker J. in *Von Hatzfeldt-Wildenburg* v. *Alexander*, and by Neville J. in *Santa Fe Land Co.* v. *Forestal Land, Timber, and Railways Co.* (1910), 26 T.L.R. 534 where he says: "Before parting with the case I wish to add with respect to the decision of Kekewich J. in *North* v. *Percival* that if that case had come before me I should myself have come to a different conclusion." So that the only remaining exception to the line of authorities to which I have referred is *Lloyd* v. *Nowell*, [1895] 2 Ch. 744, which did not commend itself either to Parker J. or Neville J., and I will only add that it does not commend itself to me.

For these reasons I think the plaintiff's action fails and must be dismissed.

[Russel J. was affirmed on appeal, same citation.]

CHILLINGWORTH *v.* ESCHE. [1924] 1 Ch. 97 (English Court of Appeal). SARGANT L.J.: "To my mind the words 'subject to contract' or 'subject to formal contract' have by this time acquired a definite ascertained legal meaning."

PINSONNEAULT *v.* LESPERANCE. 1925. 58 O.L.R. 375 (Ontario Appellate Division). A document (in French) relating to the sale of land by Lesperance to Pinsonneault stated: "I acknowledge having received one hundred dollars ($100.00) on account of my house No. 812 Assumption, which I sell to L. P. Pinsonneault for the price of five thousand dollars ($5,000.00) on the following condition—$900 on execution of contract; $500 or more a year on principal with interest at 7%." A few days later Lesperance sold the property to his nephew for $5,500 and Pinsonneault brought this action for $1,000 damages. Held, for Pinsonneault. WRIGHT J.: ". . . I think the document itself contains all the essentials necessary for a concluded agreement, and that the contract referred to was intended merely to put in more formal language the agreement between the parties. . . ." Wright J. was affirmed on appeal, Mulock C.J.O. dissenting (same citation). The deposit of $100 was ordered returned and damages were fixed at $500, the difference between the two selling prices.

SPOTTISWOODE, BALLANTYNE & CO. LTD. *v.* DOREEN APPLIANCES LTD. and G. BARCLAY (LONDON), LTD.

England. Court of Appeal. [1942] 2 A 11 E.R. 65

Appeal by the plaintiffs from the judgment of Atkinson J., who dismissed the action for recovery of possession of certain premises and allowed the defendants' counterclaim for specific performance of an agreement to grant the defendants a lease of the premises.

LORD GREENE M.R.: The question involved is a very short one and one which, to my mind, with all respect to the judge, has a clear answer. Some time before the end of July, 1941. the parties had been in negotiation with regard to the granting of a lease. On August 1, 1941, the first defendants wrote making an offer, and on the same day Messrs. Farebrother, Ellis & Co., who were agents for the plaintiffs, wrote a letter upon the true construction of which the whole question turns. It was as follows:

"We are obliged by your letter of to-day's date, making an offer to take the first and second floors as inspected. We have submitted this to our clients who are prepared to proceed with the letting, subject in the usual way to your references being satisfactory and to the terms of a formal agreement to be prepared by their solicitors. We have today applied for the references and as soon as these are approved by our clients we will ask you to let us have your cheque for one quarter's rent in advance, viz., £68 15s. 0d., when our client will give instructions for the necessary work to be put in hand, and will be willing for you to enter into possession, provided the rent is paid from the date you take it over and you give an undertaking to vacate when called upon, if no agreement is entered into."

The last paragraph of the letter I need not read. The defendants went in; they paid the rent in advance. The necessary alterations, I think, were not done, but the premises were whitewashed or distempered by the plaintiffs, and on August 13 the plaintiffs' solicitors sent to the defendants a draft of the agreement. On August 20 there was a meeting between Mr. Woolf of Farebrother, Ellis & Co. and Mr. Blockheart of the first defendant company, at which certain discussion took place, and eventually, on August 28, the plaintiffs wrote a letter saying that they were not willing to proceed with the agreement. It was the contention of the defendants that a binding agreement was in existence and that accordingly they were entitled to have that agreement specifically performed.

The whole question turns on the meaning of the letter of August 1, 1941, which I have read. The crucial words are those which refer to the formal agreement. It is said that those words mean nothing more than this, that as soon as the solicitors for the plaintiffs had put into formal shape the matters on which the parties were in agreement a binding unconditional contract would come into existence, notwithstanding that the formal document in which those terms were to be set out was never signed and exchanged by the parties. On the other hand, it is said by the plaintiffs that this language means, on its true construction, that unless and until a formal agreement has been entered into, no contract was to exist between the parties. The problem is one which is familiar to all of us. In my opinion, the second construction is unquestionably the right one. I am quite unable to construe the words "subject to the terms of a formal agreement to be prepared by their solicitors" as meaning that "a formal agreement" there referred to is not one which is to be executed by the parties in the usual way. An unexecuted document would not be a formal agreement. Even if any doubt could remain as to the true construction of that phrase, the matter is entirety settled, in my judgment, by the words referring to the undertaking to vacate when called upon if no agreement is entered into. It is manifest that the agreement there referred to is the same thing as the formal agreement referred to in the earlier passage; and how a formal agreement is to be entered into unless it is executed and exchanged in the usual way, I for one am unable to discover. The real fact of the matter is that the language used here is equivalent to the common and more concise phrase "subject to contract," and, if anything is settled, it is that that phrase is one which makes it clear that the intention of the parties is that neither of them is to be contractually bound until a contract is signed in the usual way.

That really disposes of the whole case, but I must say a word or two with regard to the manner in which the judge dealt with a large number of authorities which he reviewed at length. It is with no disrespect to him that I venture to suggest that the examination has prevented him from seeing clearly the true nature of the question before him. Inspired, no doubt, by a desire to protect the defendants from treatment which he may have thought was high-handed, he endeavoured to draw fine distinctions between the language used in this case and that used in other cases. I do not propose to follow him by examining those authorities at length, but I am going to make a very short reference to three of them. The first is *Lockett* v. *Norman-Wright*, [1925] 1 Ch. 56. The relevant words there were: "Subject to suitable agreements being arranged between your solicitors and mine." The solicitors had come to an agreement between themselves; the draft was settled; they were ready to complete; and then the plaintiff refused to go on. Tomlin J., said this, at p. 61:

"The question is one primarily of construction. Is there any real distinction between the language used here and such phrases as "subject to a formal contract," "subject to contract," "subject to a proper contract to be prepared by the vendor's solicitor." The plaintiff urges that the phrase here means: "I agree to take a lease at the rent and for the term mentioned in the letter and upon such other terms as the solicitors of the parties may settle between themselves"; and that when once the draft lease had been approved by the solicitors and the condition was fulfilled and there was an absolute contract. I do not think I can place any such construction upon the language. I think the natural meaning of the language is that the execution of a suitable agreement or suitable agreements in a form approved by the solicitors on both sides is a condition of any concluded bargain. The construction suggested on behalf of the plaintiff is artificial, and I do not think that the court should place an artificial meaning on the language employed in order to make a contract of that which would otherwise be no contract."

The next case is *Raingold* v. *Bromley*, [1931] 2 Ch. 307. There the phrase was "subject to the terms of a lease" and an exactly similar argument was put forward. Lawrence L.J., said this, at p. 316:

"The matter, however, does not rest there, for in my opinion the true construction of the expression 'subject to the terms of a lease' is that contended for on behalf of the defendant. The expression, I think, means 'subject to the terms to be contained in a lease executed by the lessor,' and, therefore, implies that a lease has to come into existence and has to be executed by the lessor before any binding agreement is reached. The expression 'subject to the terms of a lease' is in my opinion at least as strong as 'subject to contract,' and was inserted in the letter of December 9, in order to keep the matter open until a lease had actually been executed by the defendant."

The last case is *Berry, Ltd.* v. *Brighton and Sussex Building Society*, [1939] 3 A11 E.R. 217. There the words were "subject to a lease to be drawn up by our clients' solicitors." Farwell J., said this, at p. 219:

"Counsel for the plaintiffs says that that means, as a matter of construction, that, the moment the solicitors have agreed as to the form of the lease the condition is fulfilled, and the contract is a binding contract, which his clients are entitled to enforce. On the other hand, it is said that this in effect is nothing more than a contract to enter into a contract, which, the authorities have established now quite plainly, is not a binding contract at all."

He then refers to the decision of Lawrence L.J., in *Raingold* v. *Bromley*, with the reasoning of which he says he entirely agrees, and, after quoting the passage which I have read, he proceeds as follows at p. 220:

"In my judgment, the reasoning of that passage in the judgment is conclusive in this case. It is said on behalf of the plaintiffs, however, that in that case the condition was 'subject to the terms of a lease,' and that those words differ from the words which I have before me—'subject to . . . a lease to be drawn up by our client's solicitors'—and that that is different, in that it imports into this letter a term that this is to be a binding contract, subject to a condition, which condition is fulfilled as soon as the solicitors on each side agree as to the terms of the lease."

It seems to be that the judges who decided those cases were putting a manifestly correct construction on the language before them. I am quite unable to draw between that language and the language which we have here any such fine distinctions as the judge found it possible to draw, and, as I have said, we have in this case the additional phrase "if no agreement is entered into." The appeal must be allowed and judgment entered for the plaintiff for possession and for mesne profits; and the counterclaim must be dismissed. The plaintiffs will have their costs here and below.

[Mackinnon and Goddard L.JJ. agree. A short opinion by Goddard L.J. is omitted.]

NICOLENE, LIMITED *v.* SIMMONDS. [1953] 1 Q.B. 543 (England. Court of Appeal). In a contract for the sale of 3,000 tons of steel reinforcing bars one clause stated: "We are in agreement that the usual conditions of acceptance apply." DENNING L.J.: "There were no usual conditions of acceptance at all, so the words are meaningless. There is nothing to which they can apply. On that account it is said that there was never a contract at all between the parties. In my opinion a distinction must be drawn between a clause which is meaningless and a clause which is yet to be agreed. A clause which is meaningless can often be ignored, whilst still leaving the contract good; whereas a clause which has yet to be agreed may mean that there is no contract at all, because the parties have not agreed on all the essential terms.

"I take it to be clear law that if one of the parties to a contract inserts into it an exempting condition in his own favour, which the other side agrees, and it afterwards turns out that that condition is meaningless, or what comes to the same thing, that it is so ambiguous that no ascertainable meaning can be given to it, that does not mean that the whole contract is nullity. It only means that the exempting condition is a nullity and must be rejected. It would be strange indeed if a party could escape from every one of his obligations by inserting a meaningless exception from some of them."

GREEN *v.* AINSMORE CONSOLIDATED MINES LTD. [1951] 3 D.L.R. 632 (British Columbia. Supreme Court). A letter outlining in some detail clauses for an agreement was approved by the plaintiff and signed by the appropriate officers of the defendant company. It requested that the plaintiff "submit to us a draft form of agreement" and concluded with the words: "This memorandum shall be subject to a formal agreement of sale and undertaking being prepared, satisfactory in form to the solicitors of both parties. . . ." WILSON J. found that the agreement submitted by the plaintiff, prepared by overzealous attorneys, did not conform to the meaning of the letter but that this difficulty might have been overcome by further honest discussion, and that the refusal of the defendant company to execute a written agreement was entirely due to advice given it by its solicitor that the chief disadvantage to the company arose out of resulting income tax liability. He held that the letter was not an enforceable contract, following *Chillingworth* v. *Esche*, [1924] 1 Ch. 97. "It is [not] open to me to review the reasonableness or *bona fides* of the refusal to execute a formal contract."

MAY and BUTCHER, LIMITED *v.* THE KING
England. House of Lords. 1929. [1934] 2 K.B. 17

The suppliants, May & Butcher, Ltd., who were general contractors, alleged in a Petition of Right that it was mutually agreed between them and the Controller of the Disposals Board for the purchase by the suppliants of the whole of the tentage which might become available in the United Kingdom for disposal up to March 31, 1923. The material letters for the purposes of the case were dated June 29, 1921, and January 7, 1922. By the earlier of these letters written by the Controller to the suppliants it was stated that "in consideration of your agreeing to deposit with the [Disposals & Liquidation] Commission the sum of £1000 as security for the carrying out of this extended contract, the Commission hereby confirm the sale to you of the whole of the old tentage which may become available . . . up to and including December 31, 1921, upon the following terms:

"(1) The Commission agrees to sell and [the suppliants] agree to purchase the total stock of old tentage. . . .

"(3) The price or prices to be paid, and the date or dates on which payment is to be made by the purchasers to the Commission for such old tentage shall be agreed upon from time to time between the Commission and the purchasers as the quantities of the said old tentage become available for disposal, and are offered to the purchasers by the Commission.

"(4) Delivery . . . shall be taken by the purchasers in such period or periods as may be agreed upon between the commission and the purchasers when such quantities of old tentage are offered to the purchasers by the Commission. . . .

"(10) It is understood that all disputes with reference to or arising out of this agreement will be submitted to arbitration in accordance with the provisions of the Arbitration Act, 1889."

By the second letter dated January 7, 1922, the Disposals Controller, referring to verbal negotiations that had taken place for an extension of the agreement between the Commission and the suppliants, confirmed the sale to the latter of the tentage which might become available for disposal up to March 31, 1923. This letter, which varied in certain respects the earlier terms, stated that "the prices to be agreed upon between the Commission and the purchasers in accordance with the terms of clause 3 of the said earlier contract shall include delivery free on rail . . . nearest to the depots at which the said tentage may be lying. . . ."

Some time later the proposals made by the suppliants for purchase were not acceptable to the Controller, and in August, 1922, the Disposals Board said they considered themselves no longer bound by the agreement, whereupon the suppliants filed their petition of right claiming an injunction restraining the Commission from disposing elsewhere than to the suppliants of the remainder of the tentage; an account of the tentage that had become available; and compensation for the damage done to them.

By the demurrer, answer and plea the Attorney-General said that the petition of right disclosed no sufficient and binding contract for the sale to the suppliants of any tentage, and further that it was a term of the contract (if any) that the suppliants should pay a reasonable price for the tentage and that the suppliants were not at the material time ready and willing to pay a reasonable price.

Rowlatt J. held that the letters of June 29, 1921, and January 7 and 18, 1922, constituted no contract but contained merely a series of clauses for adoption if and when contracts were made, because the price, date of payment and period of delivery had still to be agreed: and that the arbitration clause did not apply to differences of opinion upon these questions. The Court of Appeal (Scrutton L.J. dissenting) affirmed Rowlatt J.'s decision. The suppliants appealed.

LORD BUCKMASTER: . . . In my opinion there never was a concluded contract between the parties. It has long been a well recognized principle of contract law that an agreement between two parties to enter into an agreement in which some critical part of the contract matter is left undetermined is no contract at all. It is of course perfectly possible for two people to contract that they will sign a document which contains all the relevant terms, but it is not open to them to agree that they will in the future agree upon a matter which is vital to the arrangement between them and has not yet been determined. It has been argued that as the fixing of the price has broken down, a reasonable price must be assumed. That depends in part upon the terms of the Sale of Goods Act, which no doubt reproduces, and is known to have reproduced, the old law upon the matter. That provides in s. 8 that

"the price in a contract of sale may be fixed by the contract, or may be left to be fixed in manner thereby agreed, or may be determined by the course of dealing between the parties. Where the price is not determined in accordance with the foregoing provisions the buyer must pay a reasonable price";

while, if the agreement is to sell goods on the terms that the price is to be fixed by the valuation of a third party, and such third party cannot or does not make such valuation, s. 9 says that the agreement is avoided. I find myself quite unable to understand the distinction between an agreement to permit the price to be fixed by a third party and an agreement to permit the price to be fixed in the future by the two parties to the contract themselves. In principle it appears to me that they are one and the same thing. . . .

The next question is about the arbitration clause, and there I entirely agree with the majority of the Court of Appeal and also with Rowlatt J. The clause refers "disputes with reference to or arising out of this agreement" to arbitration, but until the price has been fixed, the agreement is not there. The arbitration clause relates to the settlement of whatever may happen when the agreement has been completed and the parties are regularly bound. There is nothing in the arbitration clause to enable a contract to be made which in fact the original bargain has left quite open. . . .

VISCOUNT DUNEDIN: . . . In the system of law in which I was brought up, that was expressed by one of those brocards of which perhaps we have been too fond, but which often express very neatly what is wanted: "Certum est quod certum reddi potest." Therefore, you may very well agree that a certain part of the contract of sale, such as price, may be settled by some one else. As a matter of the general law of contracts all the essentials have to be settled. What are the essentials may vary according to the particular contract under consideration. We are here dealing with sale, and undoubtedly price is one of the essentials of sale, and if it is left still to be agreed between the parties, then there is no contract. It may be left to the determination of a certain person, and if it was so left and that person either would not or could not act, there would be no contract because the price was to be settled in a certain way and it has become impossible to settle it in that way, and therefore there is no settlement. No doubt as to goods, the Sale of Goods Act, 1893, says that if the price is not mentioned and settled in the contract it is to be a reasonable price. The simple answer in this case is that the Sale of Goods Act provides for silence on the point and here there is no silence, because there is a provision that the two parties are to agree. As long as you have something certain it does not matter. For instance, with regard to price it is a perfectly good contract to say that the price is to be settled by the buyer. I have not had time, or perhaps I have not been industrious enough, to look through all the books in England to see if there is such a case; but there was such a case in Scotland in 1760, where it was decided that a sale of a landed estate was perfectly good, the price being left to be settled by the buyer himself. . . .

[Lord Warrington of Clyffe also delivered reasons for dismissing the appeal.]

W. N. HILLAS AND CO., LIMITED *v.* ARCOS, LIMITED

England. House of Lords. 1932. 38 Com. Cas. 23

On May 21, 1930, Hillas and Company agreed "to buy 22,000 standards softwood goods of fair specification" from Arcos, Limited "over the season 1930 under the following conditions. . . ." The conditions provided that "Buyers shall also have the option of entering into a contract with sellers for the purchase of 100,000 standards for delivery during 1931. Such contract to stipulate that whatever the conditions are the buyers shall obtain the goods on conditions and at prices which show to them a reduction of 5 per cent on the f.o.b. value of the official price list at any time ruling during 1931. Such option to be declared before the 1st January 1931." On December 22, 1930, Hillas and Company took up the option to purchase "100,000 standards of softwood of fair specification." Arcos, Limited replied pointing out that the May agreement had been cancelled, and refused to deliver the goods. In the ensuing action Mackinnon J. found that the agreement had not been cancelled. He interpreted the agreement as a contract to sell, first, 22,000 standards of a "*reasonable and* fair specification": and then, 100,000 standards of the same *reasonable* specification. He conceded that "the task of ascertaining what specification answers the description of a fair specification may be one of extra-ordinary difficulty. . . ." Arcos, Limited appealed, successfully. In the Court of Appeal, Scrutton L.J. said, in part: ". . . In my view, apart from authority, considering the number of things left undetermined, kinds, sizes and quantities of goods, times and ports and manner of shipment, as will be seen from the detailed terms in contracts which were agreed, but which had in this case to be determined by agreement after negotiation, the option clause was not an agreement, but what Lord Parker called in *Van Hatsfeldt's* case, 'an agreement to make an agreement,' which is not an enforceable agreement. I should have arrived at this view in the present case without further authority, but in my opinion the decision of the House of Lords in *May and Butcher* v. *The King* (not reported; decided February 22, 1929) to which the attention of the Courts below was unfortunately not drawn, binds me to take this view.

We have been furnished with the Lords' record and judgment in this case, which I thought, and still think, showed very unsatisfactory behaviour on the part of a Government Department. . . . I took the view, for the reasons stated in my judgment, that there was a contract; that if no price was agreed, the price under the Sale of Goods Act would be a reasonable price, or there would be a dispute arising out of the agreement which should be settled under the arbitration clause. My brothers Sargant and Eve took Lord Parker's view that there could not be a contract to make a contract, and that, in spite of the language of absolute sale used in the document, there was no enforceable contract. The three members of the House of Lords who heard the appeal thought there was no need to call on the respondents. They said the price should be agreed and was not agreed, and when the arbitration clause spoke of disputes arising out of the contract, its framers forgot that there was no contract. I refer to the judgment for its terms. I am afraid I remain quite impenitent. I think I was right and that nine out of ten business men would agree with me. But of course I recognize that I am bound as a Judge to follow the principles laid down by the House of Lords. But I regret that in many commercial matters the English law and the practice of commercial men are getting wider apart, with the result that commercial business is leaving the Courts and being decided by commercial arbitrators with infrequent reference to the Courts. Commercial men carry on an enormous mass of business under the system of 'string contracts,' under which A, who has made a contract with B, goes to arbitration with Z, of whom he never before heard and with whom he has in the eyes of the law no contractual relations. Their view of damages as a sufficient remedy for breach of contract entirely differs from the law's remedy of rejection. The commercial man does not think there can be no contract to make a contract when every day he finds a policy 'premium to be agreed' treated by law as a contract.

"I have great sympathy with Mackinnon J.'s judgment on that point, which I think proceeds on the lines of my dissentient judgment in the 'tentage' case, but I think if he had had cited to him the decision of the House of Lords he must have held that in the present case there was no contract enforceable in the King's Courts. . . ."

Hillas and Company then appealed to the House of Lords.

LORD WRIGHT: . . . The document of May 21st, 1930 cannot be regarded as other than inartistic, and may appear repellant to the trained sense of an equity draftsman. But it is clear that the parties both intended to make a contract and thought they had done so. Business men often record the most important agreements in crude and summary fashion; modes of expression sufficient and clear to them in the course of their business may appear to those unfamiliar with the business far from complete or precise. It is accordingly the duty of the Court to construe such documents fairly and broadly, without being too astute or subtle in finding defects; but, on the contrary, the Court should seek to apply the old maxim of English law, *Verba ita sunt intelligenda ut res magis valeat quam pereat*. That maxim, however, does not mean that the Court is to make a contract for the parties, or to go outside the words they have used, except in so far as there are appropriate implications of law, as for instance, the implication of what is just and reasonable to be ascertained by the Court as matter of machinery where the contractual intention is clear but the contract is silent on some detail. Thus in contracts for future performances over a period, the parties may neither be able to nor desire to specify many matters of detail, but leave them to be adjusted in the working out of the contract. Save for the legal implication I have mentioned, such contracts might well be incomplete or uncertain: with that implication in reserve they are neither incomplete nor uncertain. As obvious illustrations I may refer to such matters as prices or times of delivery in contracts for the sale of goods, or times for loading or discharging in a contract of sea carriage. Furthermore, even if the construction of the words used may be difficult, that is not a reason for holding them too ambiguous or uncertain to be enforced if the fair meaning of the parties can be extracted. . . .

[Clause 9] must not be construed as if it stood by itself; it is an integral part of the whole agreement; the option under it is given as one of the conditions under which the appellants agree to buy the 22,000 standards, and is part of the consideration for their agreeing to do so. It is accordingly a binding offer, which the appellants are entitled by accepting before January 1, 1931, to turn into a contract if other objections do not prevail. Some confusion has been imported, as I think, into the question by dwelling on the exact words—"The option of entering into contract," and it is said that this is merely a contract to enter into a contract. The phrase is epigrammatic, but may be either meaningless or misleading. A contract *de praesenti* to enter into what, in law, is an enforceable contract, is simply that enforceable contract, and no more or no less; and if what may not very accurately be called the second contract is not to take effect till some future date but is otherwise an enforceable contract, the position is as in the preceding illustration, save that the operation of the contract is postponed. But in each case there is *eo instanti* a complete obligation. If, however, what is meant is that the parties agree to negotiate in the hope of effecting a valid contract, the position is different. There is then no bargain except to negotiate, and negotiations may be fruitless and end without any contract ensuing yet even then, in strict theory, there is a contract (if there is good consideration) to negotiate, though in the event of repudiation by one party the damages may be nominal, unless a jury think that the opportunity to negotiate was of some appreciable value to the injured party. However, I think the words of clause 9 in this case simply mean that the appellants had the option of accepting an offer in the terms of clause 9, so that when it was exercised a contract at once came into existence, unless indeed the terms of the option embodied in the clause were not sufficiently certain and complete: before considering this matter I ought to deal with a further contention based on a construction of the second paragraph of clause 9, which is in these terms: "such contract to stipulate that, whatever the conditions are, buyers shall obtain the goods on conditions and at prices which show to them a reduction of 5 per cent on the f.o.b. value of the official price list at any time ruling during 1931."

It is argued that these words read with the preceding paragraph confirm the view that the option was merely for the preparation and agreeing of a formal contract, because the words "whatever the conditions are" mean "whatever the conditions of the contract are." Such an argument involves adding the words "of the contract," which are not expressed, and on the other grounds I do not think that it is correct. I think the word "conditions" refers to conditions affecting other people in the trade, primarily as regards price, and such analogous advantages as are dealt with in clause 8 in connection with the 1930 season. What the appellants are stipulating is that they are to have, throughout the year 1931, such conditions of this character and such prices as will secure to them in any event a clear 5 per cent advantage over other buyers who might compete. On a fair reading of the words, I think the contract is clear and complete in its stipulations as to price. It was contended that no official price list might be issued in 1931, so that the contract price was in that way uncertain and contingent. But in past years in the conduct of this business it had been an invariable practice of the respondents to issue such a list: the evidence and finding in the present case are that an official price list was issued in 1931; indeed it is difficult to see how the respondents could carry on the business unless it was issued. I think that as regards the definition of the machinery for fixing the price there is sufficient certainty here for a business transaction; the issue in 1931 of the official price list is not a mere contingency but a practical certainty: it is unnecessary to consider what would have been the legal position if the respondents had ceased to carry on business or had been dispossessed by war or revolution. Such considerations are not relevant to determining whether there is a good contract or not, but relate to such questions as frustrations or breach of the contract.

The description of the goods offered to be sold in 1931, in clause 9, is also in my judgment sufficient in law . . . In practice, under such a description, the parties will work out the necessary adjustments by a process of give and take in order to arrive at an equitable or reasonable apportionment on the basis of the respondents' actual available output, according to kinds, qualities, sizes and scantlings: but, if they fail to do so, the law can be invoked to determine what is reasonable in the way of specification, and thus the machinery is always available to give the necessary certainty. As a matter of strict procedure, the sellers would make a tender as being of fair specification, the buyers would reject it, and the Court or an arbitrator decide whether it was or was not a good tender. It is, however, said that in the present case the contract quantity is too large, and the range of variety in description, qualities, and sizes is too complicated to admit of this being done. But I see no reason in principle to think that such an operation is beyond the powers of an expert tribunal, or of a judge of fact assisted by expert witnesses. . . .

. . . Accordingly I see no reason to think that, as regards the quality and description of the goods, the contract is neither uncertain or incomplete. Nor can it justly be objected that the ascertainment of a reasonable specification is impossible. The law, in determining what is reasonable, is not concerned with ideal truth, but with something much less ambitious, though more practical. . . .

In the result I arrive at the same conclusion as Mackinnon J., viz., that the contract is valid and enforceable and that the appellants are entitled to recover damages from the respondents for its repudiation. The judgment of the Court of Appeal was otherwise. Apart from their conclusion that clause 9 was no more than an arrangement to negotiate in the future terms of a new contract for 1931, they held that in any view clause 9 was uncertain and incomplete. Scrutton L.J. held that, "Considering the number of things left undetermined, kinds, sizes, and quantities of goods, times and ports and manner of shipment . . . which had in this case to be determined by agreement after negotiation," the option clause was not an enforceable agreement. With respect to the learned Lord Justice, and for the reasons I have already explained, I cannot agree with that conclusion. He seems to base his confusion in part at least on the evidence of Mr. Hillas as to how in working out the contract in practice there would be mutual concessions and arrangements. I do not question that, as I have already explained, this would be so, but I prefer the statement of the learned Lord Justice at another part of his judgment that witnesses "were not entitled to construe the agreement or give their opinion as to how it could or ought to be worked." The conclusion of Scrutton L.J., would, in very many cases, exclude in law the possibility of business men making big forward contracts for future goods over a period, because in general in such contracts it must be impossible, as I have already indicated, to specify in advance all the details of a complicated performance. Indeed, Greer, L.J. expressly states the view that such contracts are impossible in law, though he regrets the conclusion. He holds that "if there are any essential terms of a contract of sale undetermined and therefore to be determined by a subsequent contract, there is no enforceable contract"; he adds that the Courts have not power to make for parties a contract which in its view it is probable they would have made if there had been further negotiation to deal with matters not already decided. This latter proposition stated in general terms may be correct, but I have already explained why, in my judgment, this contract was complete and enforceable without further negotiation. It must always be a matter of construction of the particular contract whether any essential terms are left to be determined by a subsequent contract.

When the learned Lord Justice speaks of essential terms not being precisely determined, i.e.—by express terms of the contract—he is, I venture with respect to think, wrong in deducing as a matter of law that they must therefore be determined by a subsequent contract; he is ignoring, as it seems to me, the legal implication in contracts of what is reasonable, which runs throughout the whole of modern English law in relation to business contracts. To take only one instance, in *Hoadly* v. *M'Laine* (1834), 10 Bing. 482; 131 E.R. 982, Tindal C.J. (after quoting older authority) said: "What is implied by law is as strong to bind the parties as if it were under their hand. This is a contract in which the parties are silent as to price and therefore leave it to the law to ascertain what the commodity contracted for is reasonably worth." It is unnecessary, in my judgment, to multiply illustrations of this principle, which goes far beyond matters of price. After all, the parties being business men ought to be left to decide what degree of precision it is essential to express in their contracts, if no legal principle is violated. The learned Lord Justices (for Romer L.J. took the same view) relied, I think mainly in regard to this aspect of the case on *May and Butcher Limited*, v. *The King* which Scrutton L.J. thought compelled him to decide as he did. There was there a contract for the sale of certain goods, somewhat inelegantly called "tentage," with an option to buy further quantities at prices to be agreed upon between the parties when the material was ready for sale. Scrutton L.J. had taken the view in the Court of Appeal that there was an effective intention to contract to sell and buy, on the terms that if the parties did not agree the price it was by implication to be a reasonable price; but he was in a minority in the Court of Appeal, and this House held that there was no binding contract there till prices had been agreed. A somewhat similar decision on another contract was given in the Court of Appeal in the case of *Loftus* v. *Roberts*, where the rule was summed up as being "Promissory expressions reserving an option as to performance do not create a contract." No one would dispute such a rule, and its application to the instrument before the House in *May and Butcher, Limited* v. *The King* has been finally determined in that case; but, in my judgment, the Court of Appeal were not justified in thinking that this

House intended to lay down universal principles of construction or to negative the rule that it must be in each case a question of the true construction of the particular instrument. In my judgment, the parties here did intend to enter into, and did enter into, a complete and binding agreement, not dependent on any future agreement for its validity. But in any event the cases cited by the Court of Appeal do not, in my judgment, apply here, because this contract contains no such terms as were considered in those cases; it is not stipulated in the contract now in question that such matters as prices or times or quantities were to be agreed. I should certainly share the regret of the Lords Justices if I were compelled to think such important forward contracts as the present could have no legal effect and were mere "gentlemen's agreements" or honourable obligations. But for the reasons given I feel constrained to dissent from their conclusions—I have only with great diffidence arrived at this conclusion—but I am supported by reflecting that I am in agreement with a learned Judge very experienced in these questions.

Appeal allowed.

[Lord Tomlin also gave a judgment for the plaintiffs, in which Lords Warrington and Macmillan concurred. Lord Thankerton's judgment is also omitted.]

FOLEY *v.* CLASSIQUE COACHES, LIMITED
England. Court of Appeal. [1934] 2 K.B. 1

The plaintiff was a retail dealer in petrol and the defendants were the owners of motor coaches who carried on business at premises adjoining those of the plaintiff at 481 Lea Bridge Road, Leyton.

By an agreement in writing dated April 11, 1930, it was agreed that the plaintiff should sell and the defendants should purchase for £1,100 the freehold property which immediately adjoined that retained by the plaintiff The sale was made subject to certain conditions, among others that the defendants would enter into an agreement with the plaintiff as to the sale of petrol and/or oil, the terms of which had been agreed between them. On the same date the agreement as to the sale of petrol and/or oil was signed. It recited that it was "supplemental to an agreement bearing even date herewith and made between the same parties as are parties thereto and whereby the vendor has agreed to sell and the company to purchase" the property in the already mentioned agreement, and "whereas the vendor and his present wife are the proprietors of a petrol and oil filling station at his said address and the company are proposing to carry on the business of a char-à-banc and garage proprietors on the said adjoining land and it has been agreed that the vendor shall supply to the company and the company will take from the vendor all petrol as shall be required by the company as hereinafter mentioned. Now it is hereby agreed as follows:—

"1. The vendor shall sell to the company and the company shall purchase from the vendor all petrol which shall be required by the company for the running of their said business at a price to be agreed by the parties in writing and from time to time.

"2. The vendor shall deliver the said petrol to the company from the vendor's pumps now or hereafter on his said land.

"3. This agreement shall remain in force during the life of the vendor and his present wife if she survives him."

Clause 4 dealt with the contingency of a strike or lock-out.

"5. In the event of the company being wound up . . . the vendor may determine this agreement at any time after the commencement of such winding-up by giving one week's notice in writing of his intention so to do . . . and upon the expiration of such notice this agreement shall cease . . . but without prejudice to the right of action of the vendor in respect of any breach of the company's agreements herein contained.

"6. The company shall not purchase any petrol from any other person or corporation so long as the vendor is able to supply them with sufficient petrol to satisfy their daily requirements but nothing herein contained shall prevent the vendor from selling petrol and/or oil to any other person or corporation to be used for any purposes whatever provided that the company and their servants shall be at liberty to purchase such petrol as may be found necessary to complete the particular journey when engaged on journeys over a distance necessitating the re-fueling of their vehicles.

"7. The vendor shall supply the said petrol of a standard and quality at present supplied by the vendor or of such other standard and quality as the company may reasonably approve.

"8. If any dispute or difference shall arise on the subject matter or construction of this agreement the same shall be submitted to arbitration in the usual way in accordance with the provisions of the Arbitration Act, 1889."

The land, the subject of the first agreement, was duly conveyed to the company, and from April 26, 1930, till October 7, 1933, the defendants bought petrol from the plaintiff in pursuance of the agreement at prices charged by the plaintiff in accounts delivered by him to the defendants each week.

Disputes then arose between the parties as to the price and quality of the petrol, and eventually the defendants' solicitor wrote this letter to the plaintiff dated September 29, 1933:

"It appears that although you have supplied petrol to my clients as and when they have required it no agreement in writing as to price has ever been made, nor any agreement of any sort thereunder. My clients have from time to time sent you their cheque in payment of statements of account rendered by you. Having considered this alleged agreement and the aforesaid facts, I have advised my clients that this document is of no force or effect, and therefore, acting on their behalf, I hereby give you notice that my clients do not intend to be bound by any of the provisions contained in this alleged agreement. As from October 8, 1933, my clients will be purchasing their petrol supplies elsewhere."

The plaintiff thereupon issued a writ claiming (1) a declaration that the petrol agreement was valid and binding upon the parties; (2) an injunction to restrain the defendants from purchasing any petrol required by them for the carrying on of their said business from any persons other than the plaintiff; (3) an account of all petrol bought by the defendants in breach of the said petrol agreement from any person other than the plaintiff; and (4) damages for breach of contract.

The defendants pleaded that no price at which petrol should be sold to them by the plaintiff had been agreed; that the provision relating to the supply of petrol did not constitute a binding and/or complete agreement; that clause 6 of the agreement was an unreasonable and unnecessary restraint of the defendants' trade and was contrary to public policy and illegal; and further, or in the alternative, that that provision was applicable when, and only so long as, the parties agreed the price at which petrol was to be supplied. . . .

Lord Hewart C.J. granted an injunction restraining the defendants, their agents and servants from any breach of clause 6 and awarded an amount of damages to be ascertained. The defendants appealed.

SCRUTTON L.J.: In this appeal I think that the Lord Chief Justice's decision was right, and I am glad to come to that conclusion, because I do not regard the appellant's contention as an honest one.

The nature of the case is this: the respondent, the plaintiff in the action, had some land, part of which was occupied by petrol pumps. Adjoining that land was some vacant land belonging to him which the appellants wanted to use as the headquarters for their char-à-bancs, and they approached the respondent, who was willing to sell on the terms that the appellants obtained all their petrol from him. It is quite clear that unless the appellants had agreed to this they would never have got the land. There was a discussion whether this term about the petrol and the agreement to purchase the land should be put in one document or in two, but ultimately it was decided to put them in two documents of even date. One relates specifically to the sale and purchase of the land, and that was to go through on condition that the appellants undertook to enter into the petrol agreement, the terms of which had been already agreed. On the same day the second agreement was signed reciting that it was supplemental to the agreement of even date, that is the agreement for the sale of the land. The petrol agreement included a clause that if any dispute or difference should arise on the subject-matter or construction "the same shall be submitted to arbitration in the usual way." It is quite clear that the parties intended to make an agreement, and for the space of three years no doubt entered the mind of the appellants that they had a business agreement, for they acted on it during that time. The petrol supplied by the respondent was non-combine petrol, but he had also combine petrol pumps. The non-combine petrol was supplied to the appellants at a price lower than that paid by the public, and an account was rendered periodically in writing and paid. In the third year some one acting for the appellants thought he could get better petrol elsewhere, and on September 29, 1933, their solicitor, thinking he saw a way out of the agreement, wrote on behalf of the appellants the letter of September 29, 1933, repudiating the agreement. Possibly the solicitor had heard something about the decision of the House of Lords in *May and Butcher* v. *The King* but probably had not heard of *Braithwaite* v. *Foreign Hardwood Co.* [1905] 2 K.B. 543, in which the Court of Appeal decided that the wrongful repudiation of a contract by one party relieves the other party from the performance of any conditions precedent. If the solicitor had known of that decision he would not have written the letter in the terms he did. Thereafter the respondent brought his action claiming damages for breach of the agreement, a declaration that the agreement is binding, and an injunction to restrain the appellants from purchasing petrol from any other person. The Lord Chief Justice decided that the respondent was entitled to judgment, as there was a binding agreement by which the appellants got the land on condition that they should buy their petrol from the respondent. I observe that the appellants' solicitor in his letter made no suggestion that the land would be returned, and I suppose the appellants would have been extremely annoyed if they had been asked to return it when they repudiated the condition.

A good deal of the case turns upon the effect of two decisions of the House of Lords which are not easy to fit in with each other. The first of these cases is *May and Butcher* v. *The King* which related to a claim in respect of a purchase of surplus stores from a Government department. In the Court of Appeal two members of the Court took the view that inasmuch as there was a provision that the price of the stores which were to be offered from time to time was to be agreed there was no binding contract because an agreement to make an agreement does not constitute a contract, and that the language of clause 10 that any dispute as to the construction of the agreement was to be submitted to arbitration was irrelevant, because there was not an agreement, although the parties thought there was. In the second case, *Hillas & Co.* v. *Arcos*, there was an agreement between Hillas & Co. and the Russian authorities under which Hillas & Co. were to take in one year 22,000 standards of Russian timber, and in the same agreement they had an option to take in the next year 100,000 standards, with no particulars as to the kind of timber or as to the terms of shipment or any of the other matters one expects to find dealt with on a sale of a large quantity of Russian timber over a period. The Court of Appeal, which included Greer L.J. and myself, both having a very large experience in these timber cases, came to the conclusion that as the House of Lords in *May and Butcher* v. *The King* considered that where a detail had to be agreed upon there was no agreement until that detail was agreed, we were bound to follow the decision in *May and Butcher* v. *The King* and hold that there was no effective agreement in respect of the option, because the terms had not been agreed. It was, however, held by the House of Lords in *Hillas & Co.* v. *Arcos* that we were wrong in so deciding and that we had misunderstood the decision in *May and Butcher* v. *The King*. The House took this line: it is quite true that there seems to be considerable vagueness about the agreement but the parties contrived to get through it on the contract for 22,000 standards, and so the House thought there was an agreement as to the option which the parties would be able to get through also despite the absence of details. It is true that in the first year the parties got through quite satisfactorily; that was because during that year the great bulk of English buyers were boycotting the Russian sellers. In the second year the position was different. The English buyers had changed their view and were buying large quantities of Russian timber, so that different conditions were then prevailing. In *Hillas & Co.* v. *Arcos* the House of Lords said that they had not laid down universal principles of construction in *May and Butcher* v. *The King*, and that each case must be decided on the construction of the particular document, while in *Hillas & Co.* v. *Arcos* they found that the parties believed they had a contract. In the present case the parties obviously believed they had a contract and they acted for three years as if they had; they had an arbitration clause which relates to the subject-matter of the agreement as to the supply of petrol, and it seems to me that this arbitration clause applies to any failure to agree as to the price. By analogy to the case of a tied house there is to be implied in this contract a term that the petrol shall be supplied at a reasonable price and shall be of reasonable quality. For these reasons I think the Lord Chief Justice was right in holding that there was an effective and enforceable contract, although as to the future no definite price had been agreed with regard to the petrol.

It was said, secondly, on behalf of the appellants that the contract was bad, as para. 6 was in restraint of trade. In my view that contention is clearly untenable. The contract is an ordinary one to purchase petrol from a particular person, and as long as petrol of a reasonable price and quality is supplied—and there is an implied term that it shall be so supplied—there is no undue restraint of trade. It is suggested, however, that the injunction granted to restrain a breach of clause 6 might have this result, that if the appellants moved their coaching business, say to Edinburgh, they would still be required to purchase their petrol in London from the respondent. That, no doubt, would be a ridiculous agreement if it had been made, but it is quite clear that the appellants' obligation to take their supplies of petrol from the respondent applies only to the business carried on by them on the land adjoining the respondent's petrol pumps, and has no application to a business carried on in Edinburgh or Aberdeen or any other place remote from London.

The appeal therefore fails, and no alteration is required in the form of the injunction that has been granted.

[The judgments of Greer and Maugham L.JJ. have been omitted.]

SCAMMELL (G.) AND NEPHEW, LIMITED *v*. OUSTON
England. House of Lords. [1941] A.C. 251

On December 8, 1937, Ouston agreed to purchase a Commer van from Scammell and Nephew, Limited for £268 in exchange for a 1935 Bedford van and "the balance of purchase price . . . on hire-purchase terms over a period of two years." Later Scammell wrote to Ouston, ". . . we have now received advice from the United Dominion Trust Co. Ltd. of their acceptance of the hire-purchase in connection with the vehicle we are supplying, and we will, in due course, forward the documents to you." A few days later on February 10, 1938 Scammell reported that the van would be ready for collection in a few days "subject to mutual acceptance of the hire-purchase agreement." He added, "We make it a condition of the supply of vehicles on hire-purchase terms that we approve terms of agreement before supply." Before the hire-purchase agreement was entered into, Scammell refused to go ahead on the ground that the Bedford van was a 1934 model and not in satisfactory condition. This ground was abandoned at the subsequent trial. Tucker J. awarded damages, the Court of Appeal dismissed the appeal, and Scammell accordingly appealed to the House of Lords.

LORD WRIGHT [after a careful review of the conflicting views of Tucker J. and Slesser, MacKinnon and Goddard L.JJ., as well as of both counsel for the Oustons in the House, as to the "true meaning" of the words "on hire-purchase terms"]: . . . There are in my opinion two grounds on which the court ought to hold that there was never a contract. The first is that the language used was so obscure and so incapable of any definite or precise meaning that the court is unable to attribute to the parties any particular contractual intention. The object of the court is to do justice between the parties, and the court will do its best, if satisfied that there was an ascertainable and determinate intention to contract, to give effect to that intention, looking at the substance and not mere form. It will not be deterred by mere difficulties of interpretation. Difficulty is not synonymous with ambiguity so long as any definite meaning can be extracted. But the test of intention is to be found in the words used. If these words, considered however broadly and untechnically and with due regard to all just implications, fail to evince any definite meaning on which the court can safely act, the court has no choice but to say that there is no contract. Such a position is not often found. But I think that it is found in this case. My reason for so thinking is not only based on the actual vagueness and unintelligibility of the words used, but is confirmed by the startling diversity of explanations, tendered by those who think there was a bargain, of what the bargain was. I do not think it would be right to hold the appellants to any particular version. It was all left too vague. There are many cases in the books of what are called illusory contracts, that is, where the parties may have thought they were making a contract but failed to arrive at a definite bargain. It is a necessary requirement that an agreement in order to be binding must be sufficiently definite to enable the court to give it a practical meaning. Its terms must be so definite, or capable of being made definite without further agreement of the parties, that the promises and performances to be rendered by each party are reasonably certain. In my opinion that requirement was not satisfied in this case.

But I think the other reason, which is that the parties never in intention nor even in appearance reached an agreement, is a still sounder reason against enforcing the claim. In truth, in my opinion, their agreement was inchoate and never got beyond negotiations. They did, indeed, accept the position that there should be some form of hire-purchase agreement, but they never went on to complete their agreement by settling between them what the terms of the hire-purchase agreement were to be. The furthest point they reached was an understanding or agreement to agree upon hire-purchase terms. But as Lord Dunedin said in *May & Butcher* v. *The King,* [1934] 2 K.B. 17, reported in a note to *Foley* v. *Classique Coaches, Ld.* [1934] 2 K.B. 1, "To be a good contract there must be a concluded bargain and a concluded contract is one which settles everything that is necessary to be settled and leaves nothing to be settled by agreement between the parties. Of course it may leave something which has still to be determined but then that determination must be a determination which does not depend upon the agreement between the parties." MacKinnon L.J. thought that in this case the agreement of the parties was complete and nothing was left for them to agree. Whatever was lacking in their agreement could and should, he thought, be supplied by the court by invoking the standard of reasonableness, on the principles laid down by this House in *Hillas & Co.* v. *Arcos*, a decision which has not found a place in the Law Reports, even in a Note, but is reported in 147 L.T. 503, and in 36 Com. Cas. 353 and 38 Com. Cas. 23. The Lord Justice's view, as I have already indicated, was, if I have understood correctly, that there was a contract for a hire-purchase agreement and that no further agreement of the parties was necessary because the court could determine for the parties what was a reasonable hire-purchase agreement and thus the contract would be complete. I am unable to concur in this conclusion. In the first place the appellants at least in their letter of February 10, 1938, expressly stated that the transaction was subject to mutual acceptance of the hire-purchase agreement. This was not demurred to by the respondents. The letter was written before any difficulty had arisen about the condition or description of the Bedford van. It seems to me that this attitude was sensible both from the point of view of business and of law. It is here necessary to remember what a hire-purchase agreement is. It is not a contract of sale, but of bailment. The owner of the chattel lets it out on hire on a periodic rent on the terms that on completion of the agreed number of payments, and on due compliance with the various terms of the agreement, the hirer is to have the option to buy the chattel on payment of one shilling or some nominal sum. . . . While the bailment continues the property remains in the letter. Such a transaction, though not a contract of sale, is used in practice to carry out a sale transaction, with the advantage to the buyer of credit facilities. Though the property in the chattel does not pass while the agreement is current, the hirer gets the use of it. What would be the price if it were a contract of sale has to be increased by whatever sum is necessary for interest and bank charges until the periodic instalments have been discharged. Terms must accordingly be arranged in respect of the period of the bailment as to user, repairs, insurance, rights of retaking possession on the hirer's default and various other matters. A hire-purchase agreement is therefore in practice a complex arrangement. Thus when in the letter of December 8, 1937, the condition of hire-purchase was introduced into what had seemed on the letters to be proceeding as a contract of sale, there was a complete change in the character of the transaction and a complex arrangement had necessarily to be substituted for a simple agreement to sell. It was not even clear who were to be parties to the hire-purchase agreement or what their respective roles were to be. The respondents it is clear were necessary parties. The appellants also were necessary parties because it was their chattel which was being dealt with. The finance company was also a necessary party. But there were at least two possible ways of carrying out the deal. The hire-purchase agreement might be in such terms that the appellants were the letters and the respondents the hirers, and the purchase price was to be discharged by periodic instalments in the form of negotiable instruments, payable to the appellants, thus enabling the appellants to discount the bills with the finance company, who on the security of the bills drawn by the respondents and endorsed by the appellants, would pay the appellants the purchase price at once, keeping as their eventual profit the extra amount which was added to the price for interest and bank charges. Such an arrangement must obviously involve the making of a special tripartite agreement. Another possible method would be for the appellants to agree with the respondents to sell the van to the finance company on the stipulation that the latter should agree to let the van to the respondents under a hire-purchase agreement. Clearly in that case also a special tripartite agreement would be necessary. There was, perhaps, a third possible mode under which the appellants sold the van for cash (at least as regards the balance, for the transaction was, in part, barter) to the respondents, who, having become purchasers, then transferred the van to the finance company on a hire-purchase agreement in consideration of the company advancing the price. Even in such a case the appellants would, I think, in practice be a necessary party because the finance company would require the undertaking of the appellants to transfer the van direct to them and the respondents' concurrence in that undertaking. Otherwise the finance company would be paying cash without at once obtaining their security in the form of the van. Thus a tripartite agreement would be necessary. But I need not consider that case because it was clearly not contemplated by the parties. The correspondence shows that the terms of the hire-purchase agreement were to be matters of joint concern to the three parties who were to agree upon them. What is clear is that while a hire-purchase agreement was being demanded, its exact form and its exact terms were left for future agreement. The true view may be that the letter of December 8, 1937, amounts to nothing more than an announcement that the deal is only to proceed upon a hire-purchase basis, the parties anticipating that the terms of such an agreement would be settled between them in due course.

What I have said will sufficiently explain why I do not feel able to agree with MacKinnon L.J. that there was a complete and enforceable agreement concluded between the parties. He cited *Hillas & Co.* v. *Arcos*, (1932), 38 Com. Cas. 23, in support of his view, but that was a quite different case. There was in that case a contract for the supply of Russian timber in 1930, which also gave an option to the buyers to purchase a further supply of 100,000 standards in the ensuing year. The option clause was extremely bare and meagre, but it was held as a matter of construction that the 100,000 standards were to be soft wood goods of fair specification for delivery during 1931. It was decided by this House, reversing the judgment of the Court of Appeal and restoring the judgment of MacKinnon J., as he then was, that no further agreement was necessary or contemplated. The court could not, indeed, make a contract for the parties or go outside the words they had used except in so far as there were appropriate implications of law, as, for instance, the implication of what was just and reasonable where the contractual intention was clear but the contract was silent in some detail which the court could thus fill in. Thus the condition of "fair specification over the season" 1931 enabled the court with the help of expert evidence to identify what was a fair and reasonable specification and a fair and reasonable distribution by way of instalment deliveries of the contract quantity. Certain other matters were similarly dealt with In the same way the court has in proper circumstances found itself able to determine what is a reasonable price when the price is not specified in the contract as was done in *Foley's* case, rightly, as I think, distinguishing *May & Butcher's* case, or to determine what is a reasonable time, or what are reasonable instalments. Many other examples of this principle might be given. And in addition the court may import terms on the proof of custom or by implication. But it is in my opinion a very different matter to make an entire contract for the parties as the court would be doing if the course suggested by MacKinnon L.J. was adopted. That is simply making a contract for the parties. The analogy he cited of a c.i.f. contract is in my opinion no true analogy. These initial letters have a definite and complete meaning under the law merchant, just as much as the meaning of a bill of exchange, or the general effect of a marine contract, it determined by the law merchant. The law has not defined and cannot of itself define what are the normal and reasonable terms of a hire-purchase agreement. Though the general character of such an agreement is familiar, it is necessary for the parties in each case to agree upon the particular terms. It may, perhaps, be that this might be done in particular circumstances by general words of reference. For instance if it were stipulated that there should be "a usual" hire-purchase agreement, the court might be able if supplied with appropriate evidence to define what are the terms of such an agreement. But there was nothing of the sort in this case.

I think this appeal should be allowed because I am of opinion upon either of the main grounds which I have explained, or on both of them, that there was no concluded contract between the appellants and respondents.

[The judgments of Viscount Simon L.C., Viscount Maugham, and Lord Russell of Killowen, who concurred in allowing the appeal, are omitted.]

CALVAN CONSOLIDATED OIL & GAS LTD. *v.* MANNING. 1959. 17 D.L.R. (2d) 1 (Alberta. Supreme Court of Canada). An agreement for the disposition of two British Columbia petroleum and natural gas permits by co-owners concluded with the words, "It is also agreed that a formal agreement will be drawn up as soon as possible." A few days later a clause was added: "It is agreed that the terms of the formal agreement are to be subject to our mutual agreement, and if we are unable to agree, the terms of such agreement are to be settled for us by arbitration by a single arbitrator, pursuant to The Arbitration Act of the Province of Alberta." The agreement was held to be sufficiently certain and settled, in view of the arbitration clause. JUDSON J. for the Supreme Court, said, on this point, "The learned trial Judge was of the opinion that the provision for arbitration in relation to a possible operating agreement was meaningless and unenforceable. If this were so, the consequence would be that contracting parties in the position of Calvan and Manning who do not know what their ultimate intentions may be if they retain the property must provide in detail for a contingency that may never arise unless they wish to run the risk of having the rest of their contractual efforts invalidated and declared unenforceable. I agree with the opinion of the Court of Appeal that such a situation may be dealt with by an agreement to arbitrate and I can see no legal or practical difficulty in the way. No more could the learned author of Russell on Arbitration, 16th ed., p. 10, when he said: 'Since an arbitrator can be given such powers as the parties wish, he can be authorised to make a new contract between the parties. The parties to a commercial contract often provide that in certain events their contract shall be added to or modified to fit the circumstances then existing, intending thereby to create a binding obligation although they are unwilling or unable to determine just what the terms of the new or modified agreement shall be. To a court such a provision is ineffective as being at most a mere "agreement to agree"; but a provision that the new or modified terms shall be settled by an arbitrator can without difficulty be made enforceable. . . .'

"Only two questions remain to be considered and these arise from the provision in the amending agreement for arbitration on the terms of the formal agreement. The questions are, first, whether this indicates an intention not to be bound until the formal agreement is executed, and, second, what terms may be incorporated in the formal agreement by the arbitrator. My opinion is that the parties were bound immediately on the execution of the informal agreement, that the acceptance was unconditional and that all that was necessary to be done by the parties or possibly by the arbitrator was to embody the precise terms, and no more, of the informal agreement in a formal agreement. This is not a case of acceptance qualified by such expressed conditions as 'subject to the preparation and approval of a formal contract', 'subject to contract' or 'subject to the preparation of a formal contract, its execution by the parties and approval by their solicitors'. Here we have an unqualified acceptance with a formal contract to follow. Whether the parties intend to hold themselves bound until the execution of a formal agreement is a question of construction and I have no doubt in this case."

DELAVAL *v.* BLOOMFIELD. [1938] 3 D.L.R. 405 (Ontario Court of Appeal). An agreement for the sale of electric milking equipment for $400 concluded with the statement, "Terms: $200 on Nov. 1st, 1937/bal. to be arranged" and was signed by Bloomfield the intending purchaser. Bloomfield failed to make the initial payment and did not "arrange" the balance. In an action by DeLaval for $200, held, for the plaintiff. An appeal was dismissed. MASTEN J.A. said, "In the present case it is not the price but the mode of payment only that is held over . . . the purchaser . . . now refuses to make any arrangement and repudiates the whole transaction. His breach of his agreement to arrange the mode of payment gives to the plaintiff a right of action." The majority relied on *Hall* v. *Conder*, below. FISHER J.A. dissented but thought no object would be served by writing reasons.

HALL *v*. CONDER. 1857. 2 C.B. (N.S.) 22; 140 E.R. 318 (England). The plaintiff sold his interest in a patent to the defendant who agreed to pay £2,500 "in such manner as shall be ultimately agreed upon" but failed to pay or to agree on a manner of payment. Held, for the plaintiff. WILLIAMS J. said on a demurrer: "The question stands thus: £2,500 was to be paid on an event that has happened (viz., the sale of a moiety of the patent) in such manner as might be agreed on. The money was due; if any particular mode of payment was agreed on, payment in that mode would fulfil the contract; but, if no mode was agreed on, there is much ground for contending that the money then due must be paid as the law directs where there is no stipulation for agreement. . . . If the agreement as to the mode of payment is a condition, the defendants, by refusing to render any agreement, have rendered the performance of it impossible, and have either placed the plaintiff in the same position as if there had been no condition, or have become liable to a claim of the same amount, as damages for wrongfully refusing to agree." At the trial the plaintiffs were successful.

JACKSON *v*. MACAULAY NICHOLLS MAITLAND & CO. LTD.

British Columbia. Court of Appeal. [1942] 2 D.L.R. 609

MCDONALD C.J.B.C.: I am forced to the conclusion that this appeal must be allowed.

The action is brought by an intending purchaser of land against the owner for return of deposit paid to her agents under an interim agreement for sale. The interim agreement set out the price as $7,500 payable on the following terms, namely: $4,000 cash on completion of agreement, of which the deposit shall form a part, the balance as follows: By assuming 1st mortgage of $3,500.00 at 6%." Actually there was no mortgage on the property; the wording was apparently the result of the salesman's mistake, he having forgotten the state of the title. The vendor did not have a complete title at the time; she had a right to purchase, on which a balance of $3,500 with interest at 6% was due.

The plaintiff purchaser called on the agents six days after the interim agreement was made, in order to complete the deal, and instead of being offered a deed subject to a mortgage, was offered an assignment of the vendor's rights under her right to purchase. Plaintiff raised no specific objection then, and asked leave to submit the document to his solicitor, which was granted. Next day his solicitor wrote to the vendor's agents repudiating the deal because "the variance between the documents and the interim receipt is so great." The same day the vendor's solicitors wrote to the plaintiff threatening to forfeit his deposit unless he completed his purchase within 48 hours. The two solicitors had an interview on that on the next day, in which both expressed hopes of a settlement, and the next day the vendor's solicitors wrote to the plaintiff's solicitors, stating that if the plaintiff preferred a mortgage this could be arranged, and offering to meet any reasonable demands. However, next day the plaintiff's solicitor wrote finally repudiating the deal and demanding return of the deposit. The owner's solicitors answered that the deposit would be forfeited unless the plaintiff gave notice by the next day that he would complete. Action followed, first against the vendor's agents only; then she was added as defendant. At the trial the claim against the agents was abandoned.

The trial, to my mind, was largely taken up with irrelevant matters. The plaintiff did a good deal of quibbling about the identity of the vendor, claiming that he thought her brother, who had represented her, was the vendor. Nothing really turned on the vendor's identity, and I am satisfied that this was mere subterfuge. Another objection stressed was that a good title was not shown, and undoubtedly up to the time of repudiation, the vendor never had anything more than a right to purchase. The vendor's agents and solicitors insisted that she could give title, and would, if the purchaser would show willingness to go on. This ability was not really shown except by inference; but I am not basing my decision on that. The real strength of the plaintiff's position, though apparently it was not grasped until he reached this Court, is that there never was a complete agreement, but only an agreement incomplete in an essential term, in that the only description of the mortgage was that it should be for $3,500 at 6%. This would probably have sufficed if there had been an existent mortgage. Actually there was none. This leaves complete uncertainty as to, *inter alia*, the identity of the proposed mortgagee (for the materiality of identity see *Gordon* v. *Street*, [1899] 2 Q.B. 641) and the duration of the proposed mortgage. Such uncertainty, in my view, precludes the existence of any complete contract: *Scammel & Nephew Ltd.* v. *Ouston*, [1941] A.C. 251, and *Murphy* v. *McSorley*, [1929] 4 D.L.R. 247.

I do not think the respondent succeeded in distinguishing these cases. The respondent's strongest authorities are those handed in since the hearing, and they show considerable difference of opinion in Ontario, most of the decisions being summarized in Boyd C.'s judgment in *Martin* v. *Jarvis* (1916), 31 D.L.R. 740. The main decisions in conflict are *McDonald* v. *Murray* (1883), 2 O.R. 573; (1885), 11 O.A.R. 101, and *Reynolds* v. *Foster* (1912), 3 D.L.R. 506; (1913), 9 D.L.R. 836, 23 O.W.R. 933. Both these decisions dealt with the question whether an agreement for sale that provides for leaving part of the purchase price simply "on mortgage" at a given rate, but fixing no other terms, such as duration, is a complete agreement.

Reynolds v. *Foster* was a direct decision of the Court of Appeal that such an agreement is incomplete and unenforceable. In *Martin* v. *Jarvis*, Boyd C. considered that *McDonald* v. *Murray* was a directly contrary decision of the Court of Appeal, and he declared his preference for *McDonald* v. *Murray*, which was prior in time. I cannot accept Boyd C.'s view. The Divisional Court certainly decided as he said, but it was reversed by the Court of Appeal on other grounds. It is true that the Justices of Appeal seem to have assumed that the agreement was binding, and Patterson J.A. in terms accepted the Divisional Court's view on the mortgage. But this was *obiter* and it was unnecessary for the Court to pass on that question. Moreover, in all the Courts, the whole question of the mortgage was treated as a minor point, and very little of the attention of Counsel or Courts seems to have been directed to it. *Reynolds* v. *Foster*, on the other hand, is a clear-cut and unanimous decision of five Justices of Appeal directly in point and a far stronger authority in my view than *McDonald* v. *Murray*. *Lightbound* v. *Warnock* (1882), 4 O.R. 187, also relied on by Boyd C., was only a decision of a single Judge following *McDonald* v. *Murray* before it was appealed.

The solution proposed in *McDonald* v. *Murray*, for settling the terms of a mortgage left unsettled by an agreement for sale, is that the mortgagor should fix his own terms, not only as to duration, but presumably as to interest dates, etc. To me this solution seems to border on the absurd, and I entirely agree with what was said against it in *Reynolds* v. *Foster* on appeal. The same solution was open in *Scammel & Nephew Ltd.* v. *Ouston* but not accepted, and must, I think, be treated as discredited.

In the present case, too, we have the added uncertainty of the mortgagee's identity. Obviously the mortgagor cannot pick his own mortgagee, nor in view of *Gordon* v. *Street*, does it seem arguable that the vendor can force any mortgagee she chooses on the purchaser. In *Peterson* v. *Bitzer* (1920), 57 D.L.R. 325, 48 O.L.R. 386; (1921), 63 D.L.R. 182, 62 S.C.R. 384, one of the documents evidencing a contract held not to be too uncertain, stated that a mortgage was to be "assumed," though it did not then exist. However, as shown in the judgment of Meredith C.J.O., which the Supreme Court of Canada adopted, the actual agreement was that the purchaser was not to assume any mortgage, but to give a mortgage to the vendor, so that there was no uncertainty as to the mortgagee. Here no one suggests that this was to be done; both parties contracted in the mistaken belief that there was an existing mortgage to be assumed. In *Peterson* v. *Bitzer*, the contract fixed the duration of the mortgage.

The appellate decision in *DeLaval* v. *Bloomfield*, goes a long way, though the facts do not much resemble those here. In my view it goes too far, and I cannot see how it is to be reconciled with the decision in *Scammel & Nephew Ltd.* v. *Ouston*. At all events, the House of Lords' decision is more closely in point here.

The vendor's solicitors state in their letter of July 23rd that the plaintiff had originally proposed to pay all cash, and if he was still of the same mind, the deal could be closed at once. Actually however this proposal was not proved, and evidence of it would have been inadmissible, either because it would vary the written contract, or would merely show intentions that had been superseded.

It has been suggested that the purchaser was bound to tender a conveyance to the vendor before he sued. This principle can however have no application where there never was a completed contract. Here obviously, the conveyance would have had to be drawn subject to a mortgage, but no such mortgage existed, and hence it could not be described.

We have still to decide whether the plaintiff can recover back his deposit which was paid as earnest-money. It is clear that the vendor could not have sued to enforce an agreement; but should the Court actively assist the plaintiff? The only ground on which assistance could be refused would be that the plaintiff must seek equity. Actually however the plaintiff could sue at law by action for money had and received: 7 Halsbury's *Laws of England* (2nd ed.), p. 287. And even in equity I do not see how he could be refused relief. He was induced to pay the deposit by misrepresentation (though innocent) as to the state of the title, and even in equity he was entitled, on discovering this, to refuse further negotiations to complete an incomplete contract. . . .

[Short concurring opinions by O'Halloran and Fisher JJ.A. are omitted.]

THOMSON GROCERIES LTD. *v.* SCOTT [1943] 3 D.L.R. 25 (Ontario Court of Appeal). An action was brought for specific performance of an agreement for the purchase of premises described in a lease between the parties. The lease contained the following clause:

"It is understood that Thomson Groceries Limited are given the option to purchase these premises for the sum of seven thousand three hundred and seventy-five dollars during the life of this lease. Terms Four thousand dollars cash, balance 1st mortgage. Interest at five per cent. per annum."

The plaintiff exercised the option by letter to which the defendant did not reply. The defendant contended that as the terms and duration of the mortgage were not provided for, the agreement was too indefinite to be considered in law a completed agreement. Held, for the plaintiff. KELLOCK J.A. said, ". . . The case is not one of an agreement incomplete in fact because of something left to be the subject-matter of future discussion, or future arrangement, nor is it one where there is a dispute as to what had in fact been agreed upon . . . With regard to the form of the mortgage, apart from the time for payment . . . [it] should be according to the Short *Forms of Mortgages Act*, R.S.O. 1937, c. 160. . . . The mortgage will be payable on demand. Where an implied liability arises from the existence of the debt in cases where there is no covenant for payment in the mortgage, such liability is enforceable on demand. . . . There is no evidence as to what the parties had in mind, apart from what they put in writing. The question then is merely as to what follows in law from that. The act of the appellant's solicitor in drawing a five year mortgage does not affect the matter."

BUYERS *v.* BEGG [1952] 1 D.L.R. 313 (British Columbia. Court of Appeal). The appellant signed an interim receipt in which he agreed to purchase a piece of property from the respondent for $7,000, having paid a deposit of $500. The receipt provided for payment of $2,000 cash, and the balance "$50 per month including interest at 6%. Vendor has the privilege of mortgaging his interest giving precedence over agreement for sale; purchaser to assume cost of mortgage. Purchaser to have the privilege of paying off the difference between cash payment and mortgage at any time without notice or bonus."

The agreement also provided: "An agreement for sale containing the usual covenants in agreements of sale of land within the Province of British Columbia to be entered into on the terms hereof."

Appellant became dissatisfied with his bargain, repudiated it, and sued to recover his deposit on the ground that there was no contract or that there was a contract to make a contract, which is unenforceable. The trial judge dismissed the action. O'Halloran and Robertson JJ.A. allowed the appeal, Sidney Smith J.A. dissenting in agreement with the trial judge. The *Jackson* case was applicable. O'HALLORAN J.A. said, ". . . In this province there is no form of agreement for sale that can properly be described as 'usual'; if there is asserted to be such a thing, evidence ought to have been adduced to that effect. Furthermore even if there were a 'usual' form of agreement for sale the unusual stipulation that the vendor should be allowed to mortgage the land in priority to his purchaser's interest (and the agreement being silent regarding mortgage terms and conditions, its assumption by purchaser, remedies upon default, and protection of purchaser in respect to his instalments paid the vendor mortgagor), in itself made it legally impossible to adopt any 'usual' form of agreement for sale." ROB-

ERTSON J.A. distinguished between cases where the mortgage is to be given by the purchaser: legal rate of interest would apply, the form of the *Short Forms of Mortgages Act*, R.S.B.C. 1948, c. 308 would apply and if no time is fixed payment would be on demand and *Thomson Groceries* is cited with approval. "It seems to me that all the appellant has agreed to is that if a mortgage is given by the respondent, it shall have precedence over the agreement for sale, but he has not agreed as to the terms of the mortgage."

BRITISH BANK FOR FOREIGN TRADE *v.* NOVINEX, LIMITED. [1949] 1 K.B. 623 (England. Court of Appeal). The defendants agreed to buy from the plaintiff's clients 20,000 oilskin suits. Their letter stated: "We confirm that we have agreed to cover you on this transaction with a commission of 4d. per oilskin suit. . . . We also undertake to cover you with an agreed commission on any other business transacted with your friends. In return for this you are to put us in direct contact with your friends." The plaintiffs did all that was necessary to earn a commission but the defendants refused to pay it because, among other defences, the "agreed commission" was never agreed. Denning J. found for the defendants as the agreement was too vague to be enforced, but an appeal was allowed and the Court of Appeal fixed the commission at a farthing an oilskin on follow-up purchases.

NOTE ON COMPULSORY BARGAINING. In recent years legislature have attempted to compel management and trade unions to bargain, something that the common law in its infinite wisdom saw fit to avoid. Even when, as in the *British Bank* case, for example, the court enforces an agreement to agree, it does not attempt specific performance, but merely substitutes its own or a jury's notion for what the parties might have agreed. Compare *The Labour Relations Act*, R.S.O. 1960, c. 202, sections 11 to 31. Certified trade unions and employers are obliged to meet and "they shall bargain in good faith and make every reasonable effort to make a collective agreement." A refusal to bargain in good faith, while it may be difficult to define, is an offence under the Act. If good faith bargaining does not result in agreement, procedures are set up for "conciliation services," provided by the Department of Labour, and a "conciliation officer . . . shall confer with the parties and endeavour to effect a collective agreement." If these services are ineffective a "conciliation board" may be appointed to make more formal attempts "to effect agreement between the parties." It is to be noticed, however, that neither the conciliation officer nor the board can impose an "agreement" on the parties. These provisions are given some force by denying an employee a right to strike until his trade union has taken advantage of conciliation procedures. Only in exceptional circumstances have negotiations toward collective agreements been compulsorily concluded by arbitration. Some of the Canadian statutes provide that the conciliation board's award may be made binding with the written consent of the parties.

"THE ECONOMIC EFFECT OF 'SLIDING SCALE' PRICES"

Fuller, *Basic Contract Law* (1947)

The period since World War I has seen an enormous increase in the use of pricing arrangements like that involved in *Foley* v. *Classique Coaches, Ltd.* Business men speak of "flexible pricing," "escalator clauses" and contracts with "open ends."

Sometimes, as in the Classique Case, the price in a supply contract is left to be set by agreement from time to time, normally with a provision for arbitration in the event of a failure of the parties to agree. Frequently no standard is established for the arbitrator other than the implied one of general fairness and prevailing price levels. At other times, the agreement will include a formula that interlocks the price to be paid by the buyer with the price of the same product, or a related product, on some designated market. At other times, particularly in agreements between corporations affiliated in ownership or management, price will be determined by actual cost to the seller plus a percentage for profit. In such "cost-plus" contracts an elaborate definition of "cost" will usually be required, as well as considerable faith in the processes by which cost accountants purport to allocate costs where more than one product is being manufactured or sold.

In long-term leases of real estate it has become increasingly common, wherever practicable, to leave the rent to be determined by some flexible standard that will reflect future changes in the general level of prices. In a few leases provisions of doubtful wisdom have been inserted making the rental depend upon some published cost-of-living index, like that issued monthly by the Bureau of Labor Statistics. The most successful device for making rent flexible has been that which determines the rental for retail premises by a percentage of gross sales. Leases containing such provisions often provide a minimum rental, and may provide a maximum. They have become very common. (See "Basing Your Rents on Your Sales," Business Week, June 31, 1936, p. 42; "Percentage Leases," Id., Jan. 8, 1938, p. 41.)

Collective bargaining agreements have sometimes made wages depend on a cost-of-living index, though there was a general abandonment of these arrangements during World War II.

Throughout the world of commerce and industry lawyers and executives are searching for formulas and devices that will safely impart a needed flexibility to the relations of supplier and customer, landlord and tenant, employer and employee. In Llewellyn's words, this quest is "symptomatic of an economy stabilizing itself along new lines." ("What Price Contract?" 1931, 40 Yale L.J. 683, 727.)

In one aspect, the chief purpose of a contract calling for a future performance may be viewed as that of severing the relation of the parties from the influence of the market. When a man contracts for the delivery of ten tons of beans three months hence, his chief object will be to shift to the seller the risk of a rise in the market. If the buyer were certain no rise would occur, he would be content to rely on the market as his source of supply. Conversely, in the case supposed the primary object of the seller is to shift to the buyer the risk that the price of beans may decline. Since the motives of these parties are fairly typical of those involved in contracts, it may seem odd that the primary quest today is for some means of importing into contracts the influence of the market. It will be noted, however, that the contracts involved in this development are long-term arrangements, and the object of the agreement is not much protection against rising or falling prices, as an avoidance of the disruption and economic waste involved in shifting from one source or outlet to another. Where such contracts are made unduly rigid, their purpose of stabilizing an economic relationship is defeated, since they are too brittle to stand up against market pressures. The depression between the two World Wars offered a gigantic object lesson in the unwisdom of projecting inflexible legal arrangements too far into the future. At that time, many leases running as long as twenty years stipulated a fixed rental. If such a lease was entered in 1926, by 1932 its rental had usually become completely out of line with prevailing levels. Since times were hard for landlords as well as tenants, landlords tended to hold as long as they could to the old rental. The result was that tenants were thrown into bankruptcy on a wholesale scale and a veritable flood of litigation occurred. It is likely that with the flexible rental provisions that have now become general in leases of business premises the disruptive effect of another decline in prices will be mitigated. Generally, sliding scale pricing in long-term contracts keeps the joints of business flexible, and gives it the strength of La Fontaine's rosebush: "Je plie et ne romps pas."

It is fairly obvious that the development of flexible pricing procedures in long-term contracts and leases is an economic revolution of profound significance for the nation's economy. Had such a change been worked by legislation, economists would have devoted volumes to an analysis of its effects. Because the change in this case has occurred gradually, and has found its chief outward expression in legal forms generally read in their entirety only by the lawyers who draft them, its significance has largely been overlooked.

Do sliding scale prices and rents aggravate, or restrain, fluctuations in price levels? Do they make the upward and downward swings of business activity more or less violent? Apparently little thought has been given to this question. One might argue that these arrangements will tend to accentuate whatever trend of prices, upward or downward, exists at the moment. If a contract contains a fixed price, it can serve as a center of inertia that will hold back the current movement of prices. On the other hand, if contracts are generally so drafted that their price terms are geared to the market, every change in price levels is immediately reflected throughout the nation's economy.

Against the view that flexible pricing aggravates and magnifies price trends, at least two counter-arguments can be made. In the first place, as has already been pointed out, flexible pricing avoids the disruptions involved in breach of contract, law suits, and lengthy negotiations between parties whose interests have become sharply opposed. In other words, flexible pricing tends to keep the wheels turning, and may thus mitigate the severity of a downward swing. In the second place, where prices are fixed by some automatic but flexible standard, the periodic renegotiation of price is avoided. This in turn reduces the "psychological factor" that plays so important a rôle in the business cycle. Where a lease expires during a period of rising prices, in negotiating a new lease the parties are apt to assume that prices will continue to rise, and fix the rent somewhat above the amount current conditions would make appropriate. This act, repeated throughout the economy, tends to make a reality of the prediction on which it is based, and accelerates the upward swing. Where rent moves up and down automatically with current business conditions, the influence of this factor is eliminated.

The planning and drafting of contracts that will strike a workable line of compromise between a too great isolation from market forces, and a too great submergence of the parties' relations in those forces, is a task that demands of the lawyer, not only great legal ingenuity and acumen but broad economic statesmanship. He must, to discharge his full duty to his client and society, concern himself with questions of the type briefly outlined above. If he does not, he can be reasonably certain that no one will.

2. The Power Of Acceptance

SHATFORD *v.* B.C. WINE GROWERS LTD.
British Columbia. Supreme Court. [1927] 2 D.L.R. 759

MURPHY J.: Plaintiff's case, on his pleadings, is, that the letter of April 21, 1926 (ex. 3) with enclosure is an offer from the defendants to plaintiff for the purchase of loganberries. . . . I think plaintiff's action must fail because he did not accept this offer within a reasonable time. The causes of this delay are immaterial. The facts are that ex. 3 was mailed on April 22, and was received probably on the 23rd, or, at latest, on the 24th. Plaintiff did not sign the contract enclosed with ex. 3 until April 30—a delay of at least some six days. He mailed the signed document to defendant on the evening of April 30. Ordinarily a proposal sent by mail calls for an acceptance, if not by return of post, at least during business hours of the day on which such offer is received (*Dunlop* v. *Higgins* (1848), 1 H.L. Cas. 381, 9 E.R. 805). In all cases the offer must be accepted within a reasonable time. Here, having regard to the commodity being bargained for, the time of year of the offer, and the necessity, under the circumstances, as shown by the evidence of prompt decision, as to whether an offer would be accepted or not, I hold the plaintiff did not accept defendants' offer within a reasonable time. Action dismissed with costs.

DOMINION BUILDING CORPORATION, LTD. *v.* THE KING. [1933] 3 D.L.R. 577 (Canada. Privy Council). One Forgie on July 27, 1925, offered in writing to purchase from His Majesty property at the corner of King and Yonge Streets in Toronto. The offer concluded with these words: "This offer of purchase, if accepted by Order of His Excellency the Governor General in Council, shall constitute a binding contract of purchase and sale, subject to all the terms and provisions thereof and which contract shall enure to the benefit of the undersigned [Forgie], his heirs, etc. and to the benefit of His Majesty, etc." An Order in Council was duly passed and a certified copy sent to Forgie, who could not remember when he received it or whether he had received a covering letter with it. The Exchequer Court held there was a binding contract, which decision the Supreme Court unanimously reversed on the ground that there was no written acceptance. LORD TOMLIN: "Their Lordships think that if any notification of acceptance of the offer was necessary, the only possible inference upon the evidence is that there was a notification of acceptance by the sending to the appellant Forgie of a certified copy of the Order in Council.

"But in fact, in their Lordships' opinion, there was not upon the true construction of the contract any need for a notification of acceptance. The language of the offer is . . . not the language of precision, but the meaning which can most naturally be and ought, in their Lordships' opinion, to be attributed to it, is that the offer shall be deemed to have been accepted when the necessary Order in Council has been made."

LARKIN *v.* GARDINER
Ontario. High Court. 1895. 27 O.R. 125

This was an action for the specific performance of a contract for the sale of land, brought by Jane Larkin, alleging herself to be the vendor, against the defendant, who had, as she alleged, entered into a contract with her.

The defendant denied the making of any contract, and alleged a want of title in the vendor and a cancellation of the contract if any existed.

The property had been placed in the hands of one Nesbitt, a land agent, by the plaintiff for sale on her behalf. The defendant went to Nesbitt and offered $1,900 for the property, Nesbitt stated, as the fact was, that he was not authorized to sell at that price, but that if the defendant would sign an agreement to purchase at that price, he would submit the matter to the plaintiff. Thereupon Nesbitt prepared a form of agreement, beginning "I, Jane Larkin of Toronto, married woman, agree to sell, through John A. Nesbitt as my agent, and I, David Gardiner of the city of Toronto, baker, agree to buy, all that certain parcel." etc.

This was signed by the defendant at about seven p.m. on the 22nd April, 1895, and left by him with Nesbitt. Early next morning Nesbitt went to the plaintiff's house and she signed the agreement. At about one o'clock on the same day, the defendant gave written notice to Nesbitt withdrawing from the offer he had made. At the time he received this notice, Nesbitt had taken no step to communicate to the defendant the fact that the plaintiff had accepted his offer or had signed the agreement. The agreement with the two signatures attached to it, had simply remained in his possession as agent for the plaintiff without communication to any one of the fact that the plaintiff had completed it by her signature. Subsequently the defendant, while always repudiating the existence of any agreement on his part to purchase, and expressly without prejudice to that position, upon being served with an abstract of title, made objections to it, and upon these not being satisfactorily answered, refused to do anything further, whereupon the present action was brought.

STREET J.: The instrument signed by the defendant, although drawn in the form of an agreement, must, in my opinion, be treated as a mere offer to purchase which might be withdrawn before it had been accepted by the plaintiff; and the only question to be determined is, whether the mere signature of the defendant without anything more was a sufficient acceptance.

In *Brogden* v. *Metropolitan R. W. Co.* (1877), 2 App. Cas. 666, Lord Blackburn, at p. 691, says: "I have always believed the law to be this, that whenever an offer is made to another party, and in that offer there is a request express or implied that he must signify his acceptance by doing some particular thing, then as soon as he does that thing, he is bound." And he goes on to say, at p. 692, "But when you come to the general proposition which Mr. Justice Brett seems to have laid down, that a simple acceptance in your own mind, without any intimation to the other party, and expressed by a mere private act, such as putting a letter into a drawer, completes a contract, I must say I differ from that."

Now, I think it would be unreasonable to hold in the present case that the defendant having made his offer to purchase, did not impliedly stipulate that in some form or other he should be made aware of the plaintiff's decision with regard to it—either by a letter informing him of the fact, or by the delivery to him of the contract signed by the plaintiff. I do not think it would be consistent with what we must assume the intention of the parties to have been that the mere signature of the plaintiff not communicated to him, should convert his offer into a binding contract. If I am right in so viewing the matter, then it follows that until the plaintiff had done something irrevocable towards communicating to him her acceptance of his offer, he was at liberty to withdraw it. The posting of a letter to him, or the verbal communication to him, of the fact that shé had signed the contract, would have been sufficient. But the delivery to her own agent of the contract with her signature to it, was a revocable act until it had been communicated to the defendant, and was of no more force than if she had kept the instrument in her own drawer after signing it. If it had been possible to hold that Nesbitt was agent for the defendant to receive notice of the completion of the contract, his knowledge that the plaintiff had signed, would of course have bound the defendant, but there is not the slightest ground for any such finding.

In my opinion, therefore, the defendant was within his rights when he withdrew the offer he had made, and no contract binding upon either party ever existed. . . .

[The judgment of Armour C.J. is omitted. Falconbridge J. concurred.]

POWELL *v*. LEE 1908. 99 L.T. 284; 24 T.L.R. 606. The plaintiff applied for the position of head master of a school conducted by the defendants, who were members of the board of country school managers. The board passed a resolution appointing the plaintiff. One of the members of the board without any authority wrote the plaintiff telling him he had been appointed. At a subsequent meeting of the board, the earlier resolution was rescinded and another person appointed. The plaintiff sued for breach of contract. Held, no contract.

COOKE *v*. OXLEY. 1790. 3 T.R. 653; 100 E.R. 785 (King's Bench). The defendant offeror gave the plaintiff offeree until four o'clock in the afternoon to make up his mind whether to purchase 286 hogsheads of tobacco at a certain price. The plaintiff claimed to have accepted the offer before four o'clock, but the defendant refused to deliver the tobacco. Held, for the defendant. BULLER J.: "In order to sustain a promise, there must be either a damage to the plaintiff, or an advantage to the defendant; but here was neither when the contract was first made. Then, as to the subsequent time, the promise can only be supported on the ground of a new contract made at four o'clock; but there is no pretence for that. It has been argued that this must be taken to be a complete sale from the time when the condition was complied with; but it was not complied with, for it is not stated that the defendant did agree at four o'clock to the terms of the sale; or even that the goods were kept till that time." [*Cooke* v. *Oxley* is today regarded as obsolete. It can be best understood if it is supposed that the Court had no notion of a "power of acceptance" but had a notion that an *actual* meeting of minds at some instant of time was required before a contract could come into being. Suppose that when the offeree returned before four o'clock, the offeror had said before the offeree could accept, "I know I promised to wait until four o'clock, but you gave me nothing in exchange. I am not bound by that promise, and I revoke my offer"?]

DICKINSON *v*. DODDS

England. Court of Appeal. 1876. 2 Ch. D. 463

On Wednesday, the 10th of June, 1874, the defendant John Dodds signed and delivered to the plaintiff, George Dickinson, a memorandum, of which the material part was as follows:

"I herby agree to sell to Mr. George Dickinson the whole of the dwelling houses, garden ground, stabling, and outbuildings thereto belonging, situ-

ated at Croft, belonging to me, for the sum of £800. As witness my hand this tenth day of June, 1874. John Dodds."
"P.S.—This offer to be left over until Friday, 9 o'clock, a.m. J.D. (the twelfth), 12th June, 1874. (signed) J. Dodds."

The bill alleged that Dodds understood and intended that the plaintiff should have until Friday, 9 a.m., within which to determine whether he would or would not purchase, and that he should absolutely have, until that time, the refusal of the property at the price of £800, and that the plaintiff in fact determined to accept the offer on the morning of Thursday, the 11th of June, but did not at once signify his acceptance to Dodds, believing that he had the power to accept it until 9 a.m. on the Friday.

In the afternoon of Thursday the plaintiff was informed by a Mr. Berry that Dodds had been offering or agreeing to sell the property to Thomas Allan the other defendant. Thereupon the plaintiff, at about half-past seven in the evening, went to the house of Mrs. Burgess, the mother-in-law of Dodds, where he was then staying, and left with her a formal acceptance, in writing, of the offer to sell the property. According to the evidence of Mrs. Burgess, this document never in fact reached Dodds, she having forgotten to give it to him.

On the following (Friday) morning, at about seven o'clock, Berry, who was acting as agent for Dickinson, found Dodds at the Darlington railway station, and handed to him a duplicate of the acceptance by Dickinson, and explained to Dodds its purport. He replied that it was too late, as he had sold the property. A few minutes later Dickinson himself found Dodds entering a railway carriage, and handed him another duplicate of the notice of acceptance, but Dodds declined to receive it, saying, "You are too late. I have sold the property."

It appeared that on the day before, Thursday, the 11th of June, Dodds had signed a formal contract for the sale of the property to the defendant Allan for £800, and had received from him a deposit of £40.

Bacon V.C., decreed specific performance in favor of the plaintiff, on the ground that by the original offer or agreement with the plaintiff, and by relation back of the acceptance to the date of the offer, Dodds had lost the power to make a sale to Allan. From this decision the defendants appealed.

JAMES L.J.: . . . That shows it was only an offer. There was no consideration given for the undertaking or promise, to whatever extent it may be considered binding, to keep the property unsold until 9 o'clock on Friday morning; but apparently Dickinson was of opinion, and probably Dodds was of the same opinion, that he (Dodds) was bound by that promise, and could not in any way withdraw from it, or retract it, until 9 o'clock on Friday morning, and this probably explains a good deal of what afterwards took place. But it is clear settled law, on one of the clearest principles of law, that this promise, being a mere *nudum pactum*, was not binding, and that at any moment before a complete acceptance by Dickinson of the offer, Dodds was as free as Dickinson himself. Well, that being the state of things, it is said that the only mode in which Dodds could assert that freedom was by actually and distinctly saying to Dickinson, "Now I withdraw my offer." It appears to me that there is neither principle nor authority for the proposition that there must be an express and actual withdrawal of the offer, or what is called a retraction. It must, to constitute a contract, appear that the two minds were at one at the same moment of time; that is, that there was an offer continuing up to the time of the acceptance. If there was not such a continuing offer, then the acceptance comes to nothing. Of course it may well be that the one man is bound in some way to let the other know that his mind with regard to the offer has been changed; but in this case, beyond all question, the plaintiff knew that Dodds was no longer minded to sell the property to him as plainly and clearly as if Dodds had told him in so many words, "I withdraw the offer." This is evident from the plaintiff's own statements in the bill.

The plaintiff says, in effect that, having heard and knowing that Dodds was no longer minded to sell to him, and that he was selling or had sold to someone else, thinking that he could not, in point of law, withdraw his offer, meaning to fix him to it, and endeavoring to bind him, "I went to the house where he was lodging, and saw his mother-in-law, and left with her an acceptance of the offer, knowing all the while that he had entirely changed his mind. I got an agent to watch for him at 7 o'clock the next morning, and I went to the train just before 9 o'clock, in order that I might catch him and give him my notice of acceptance just before 9 o'clock, and when that occurred he told my agent, and he told me, you are too late, and he then threw back the paper." It is to my mind quite clear that, before there was any attempt at acceptance by the plaintiff, he was perfectly well aware that Dodds had changed his mind, and that he had in fact agreed to sell the property to Allan. It is impossible, therefore, to say there was ever that existence of the same mind between the two parties which is essential in point of law to the making of an agreement. I am of opinion, therefore, that the plaintiff has failed to prove that there was any binding contract between Dodds and himself.

[The decision of Mellish L.J. is omitted. Baggalley J.A. concurred.]

QUESTIONS. What are the facts of this case? Mellish L.J. remarked that "Berry does not tell us from whom he heard it, but he says that he did hear it, that he knew it, and that he informed Dickinson of it." Later he referred to the offeree receiving notice "in some way" that the property has been sold. Suppose that Mrs. Dodds, if there were one, told Mrs. Dickinson, if any, at a cocktail party, that Mr. Dodds had sold the Croft place to Smith for £900; and that that was Dickinson's only "knowledge" of the sale, would you say there was an effective revocation?

GERMAN CIVIL CODE

Section 145. An offer to contract is binding upon the offeror unless he has provided for the contrary.

QUESTIONS. If the business world knows of this provision, and customarily provides for the contrary, as is said to be the case, is this evidence that the section is misconceived? Why is an offer revocable? Is the business world more likely to know the terms of the Civil Code than of the Common Law?

SAVEREUX *v.* TOURANGEAU

Ontario. Divisional Court. 1908. 16 O.L.R. 600

BRITTON J.: Appeal by defendant from judgment of Teetzel J. Action tried at Sandwich.

On the 2nd January, 1907, one Alphonse Meloche and his wife were the owners of a parcel of land . . . containing 22 15/100 acres.

On that day they entered into an agreement, in writing and under seal, with the plaintiff, by which they agreed: (1) if they were desirous of selling and intended to sell this land, they would give the plaintiff notice in writing of such intention; and (2) give the plaintiff 30 days' time within which the plaintiff could purchase; (3) and if the plaintiff wished to purchase, they would sell this land to him for $40 an acre, equal to $886 for the parcel. . . .

The defendant wanted this same parcel of land, and entered into negotiations with Meloche for its purchase.

On the 14th January the defendant obtained an offer to sell from Meloche. It is called an agreement of sale, and the expressed consideration is one dollar, but it does not appear that any money was paid. It is not under seal; there is not a full description of the land—it is called 22 1/5 acres—and it states that "this offer is binding for three months."

The defendant lost no time in coming to a conclusion to accept, so he procured a proper description of the land, and on the following day —viz., the 15th January—entered into a formal agreement with Meloche for the purchase of this land. While this agreement in writing was in course of preparation on the 15th, the defendant had express notice of the option or agreement given by Meloche to the plaintiff. Notwithstanding this, the defendant continued the negotiations with Meloche, and completed the agreement.

Both agreements were registered on the 15th January, 1907; both at 4 o'clock—the plaintiff's as no. 8812, and the defendant's as No. 8813.

As a matter of fact, the plaintiff's agreement has priority of registration, but nothing turns on that, for, as I have said, the defendant had express notice of the agreement with the plaintiff. The defendant made great haste in doing all that was possible to clinch this purchase, for, on the following day, the 16th January, he obtained the impeached conveyance of this land from Meloche, and that instrument was made "in pursuance of the Act respecting short forms of conveyances," and this conveyance was duly registered in the proper registry office on the 17th day of January, 1907.

Notwithstanding the fact of the defendant having obtained the completed conveyance, the plaintiff, on the 22nd April, 1907, obtained from Meloche what purports to be a similar conveyance of the same land.

There is no evidence of the possession of the land, or anything other than what pertains to the agreements, conveyances, payments of money, etc.

Both plaintiff and defendant wanted the property from Meloche, a weak man, of no business ability, but knowing enough to try to get money from both the plaintiff and defendant.

It is not a question of improvidence of the man Meloche or of fraud upon him.

The plaintiff says he did not, when he accepted the conveyance of 22nd April know of the actual conveyance by Meloche to the defendant—viz., the conveyance of 16th January, 1907—but he did know that the defendant was asserting a claim under the writing of 15th January or some other document.

I agree with the findings of fact as to notice and knowledge on the part of the defendant, and as to the facts and circumstances attending the execution of the documents, but all this does not warrant the conclusion that the defendant acquired nothing by the deed to him, and that this deed is fraudulent and void against the plaintiff.

The result is that, instead of the defendant acquiring nothing, he acquires all the interest of Meloche in the property in reference to which Meloche had given to the plaintiff the option to purchase.

The defendant then stood in the place of Meloche. The plaintiff had, as against the defendant, the same right as he would have had against Meloche had Meloche not conveyed, but had simply, after determining to sell, and after the plaintiff had exercised his option in favour of buying, refused to sell.

The counsel for defendant, at the trial, took the view and presented his argument, that this case was, practically, an action for specific performance and, at most, the defendant could only be held liable to the same extent as Meloche; and it was argued that the agreement could not be enforced against Meloche, because, although under seal, it was not in fact, as sufficiently appears, for valuable consideration.

The agreement after acceptance of it by the plaintiff, can no longer be treated as voluntary. When accepted, within the time and terms of Meloche's offer, then it is no longer to be treated as a voluntary agreement. . . .

At the trial the plaintiff's counsel declared with emphasis that this was not an action for specific performance; that the plaintiff already had the title; and that the action was to remove the conveyance to the defendant—as a cloud on the plaintiff's title. In my opinion, the plaintiff's rights were misconceived. I would allow the appeal, and order a new trial.

RIDDELL J.: . . . Had the agreement of the 2nd January been a mere option not under seal, I agree with the defendant that Meloche would have been at liberty to disregard it as not binding upon him, and that he might retract it before acceptance, and probably the act of negotiating a sale to the defendant would be in itself a retraction without notice to the plaintiff: *Dickinson* v. *Dodds* (1876), 2 Ch.D. 463. But I do not read this document as an option. I think it is a contract with the plaintiff to give him a binding option for thirty days after notice has been given him of the desire to sell. Being under seal, there is no need for consideration to give this contract full effect in law. . . .

It may be well to state, for the guidance of the parties, how the case appears on further analysis. As at present advised, I am of opinion that what was done by the plaintiff was, in effect, a declaration by him to the defendant and Meloche that he intended to accept the option which Meloche had agreed to give him, and I shall assume that he had a right, that the defendant was "bound to do the same acts" as Meloche. The "option," though under seal, was admittedly without consideration, and "a voluntary bond or covenant, that is, one made without a consideration, is binding in law; but in equity, though allowed full legal effect, it is not assisted with the auxiliary equitable remedies of specific performance or injunction": *Leake on Contracts*, 5th ed., pp. 429, 430.

"The Court will never lend its assistance to enforce the specific execution of contracts which are voluntary, or where no consideration emanates from the party seeking performance, even though they may have the legal consideration of a seal; and this principle applies whether the contract insisted on be in the form of an executory agreement, a covenant, or a settlement": *Fry on Specific Performance, sec.* 116.

Whether an action for damages would lie at the instance of the plaintiff against Meloche upon the deed being made to the defendant, we need not consider. Such an action would not lie against the defendant. An action for specific performance would not have lain before the execution of the deed; and it can scarcely be argued that the execution of the deed added to or increased the plaintiff's rights. . . . I cannot see that we can now, and in this action, make an order that the defendant convey to the plaintiff . . . It is possible that if all the facts were certainly before the Court, we might mould the present pleadings, and give relief of the kind, if we thought such relief was the right of the plaintiff. For reasons which I have indicated, I do not, as at present advised, think that the plaintiff is entitled to such relief at all. . . .

[Falconbridge C.J. agreed to a new trial.]

RICHES *v.* BURNS. 1924. 27 O.W.N. 203 (Ontario High Court). An option under seal stated to be in consideration of one dollar which was not in fact paid or intended to be paid, was to continue "until the said Burns commences to build upon the said land or sells the said land or part of it." Burns refused to sell when Riches took up the option, and this action for specific performance was instituted. RIDDELL J.: "The option was without consideration in fact. A seal imports consideration; but that does not assist the plaintiff in his action for specific performance," citing *Savereux* v. *Tourangeau*. The claim for specific performance failed.

GAAR SCOTT CO. *v.* OTTOSON. 1911. 21 Man.R. 462 (Manitoba Court of Appeal). PERDUE J.A.: "The order [offer to buy goods] having been executed under seal, it was not revocable before acceptance as an ordinary order might be."

DAVIDSON *v.* NORSTRANT. 1921. 61 S.C.R. 493 (Alberta. Supreme Court of Canada). Norstrant was planning to purchase five sections of land in Alberta for $86,400, with a $10,000 cash deposit, and offered Davidson the opportunity to share half the cost and profits. Davidson felt he needed the assent of his employers, as he was their agent in charge of the sale. Accordingly an option agreement was drawn up under seal, expressed to be "in consideration of the sum of $100 . . . now paid" but in fact not paid. Norstrant went ahead with the purchase and Davidson's employers approved his participation. Davidson thereupon sent his cheque for his $5,000 share, plus interest, but Norstrant returned it with the comment that "I don't need the money now as I have to pay interest on the money which I borrowed when the deal was made anyway, and this money would only be idle here." Davidson heard no more and wrote again, enclosing a second cheque. This too was returned. Davidson wrote once again, sending the second cheque to Norstrant a second time. Getting no results, he commenced this action. IDINGTON J.: "I agree that a unilateral offer of an option without consideration can be revoked at any time, unless under seal as this contract was. . . . And when the contract for an option, as here, is under seal and purports to bind for a specific time, assented to by the covenantee, it binds without the payment of any consideration. And the binding effect thereof cannot be affected by any mere omission to pay what is named as the consideration which has been declared to have been received, unless and until the offerer has demanded from him bound to pay such consideration, and been refused. None of the said several propositions of law for the most part need, I respectfully submit, any citation of authority to support them or any of them."

QUESTIONS. Is the effect of "revoking" an offer in a sealed option to terminate the "power of acceptance"? Does it matter that there may have been consideration? If an "option" is substantially an "offer" coupled with an enforceable promise, either under seal or for consideration, to keep the "offer" open, and the promise is broken, but the offeree purports to accept, does he sue on the broken promise to keep the offer open? Or on the broken promise created by his purported acceptance of the "revoked" offer? Does it matter in computing damages? Does it matter in an action for specific performance? If an option under seal is enforceable, can it not simply be enforced specifically by holding the offer in the option irrevocable? Should it be?

DICKINSON *v.* DODDS. 1876. 2 Ch.D. 463 (reproduced above). MELLISH L.J.: "It is admitted law that, if a man who makes an offer dies, the offer cannot be accepted after he is dead, and parting with the property has very much the same effect as the death of the owner, for it makes the performance of the offer impossible."

BRADBURY *v.* MORGAN

England. Exchequer. 1862. 1 H. & C. 249; 158 E.R. 877

Leigh, the deceased, wrote Bradbury, Greatorex & Co. as follows: "I request that you will give credit in the usual way of your business to Henry Jones Leigh, of Leather Lane, Holborn; and in consideration of your doing so, I hereby engage to guarantee the regular payment of the running balance of this account with you, until I give you notice to the contrary, to the extent of one hundred pounds sterling. Limit £100." Bradbury gave credit from time to time to H. J. Leigh, whose account with Bradbury, before and after Leigh's death, and before Bradbury had notice of his death, reached £100, and remained unpaid. Morgan, Leigh's executor, refused to pay the guarantee, and in this action, on a demurrer argued that since all the goods sold to H. J. Leigh were sold after Leigh's death, Leigh's estate was under no obligation.

POLLOCK C.B.: We are all of the opinion that the plaintiff is entitled to judgment. No doubt, if this were merely an implied contract which arose from a request, it would be revoked by the death of either party. *Blades* v. *Free* (1829), 9 B. & C. 167; 109 E.R. 63, is an authority that a request is revoked, but a contract is not put an end to, by death. The language here used, "I request you will give credit," is a mere mode of civil expression, and the party using it never meant to request in that sense which Mr. Brown has suggested. Instead of saying "I will thank you to give credit;" or "you will oblige me by giving credit" he says, "I request you will give credit." Whether his death was contemplated, I do not know. The probability is, that if it had been suggested the plaintiffs would have required some notice before the guarantee was determined; but this is a contract and the question is whether it is put an end to by the death of the guarantor. There is no direct authority to that effect; and I think that all reason and authority, such as there is, are against that proposition, and that the plaintiffs are therefore entitled to judgment.

BRAMWELL B.: I am of the same opinion. The general rule is thus stated in *Williams on Executors*, p. 1559, 5th ed.: "The executors or administrators so completely represent their testator or intestate, with respect to the liabilities above mentioned, that every bond, or covenant, or contract of the deceased includes them, although they are not named in the terms of it; for the executors or administrators of every person are implied in himself." The only exception is where the contract is in respect of the personal qualification of the testator or intestate, and that does not apply to the present case.... [The opinion of Channell B. is omitted.]

QUESTIONS. Does *Bradbury* v. *Morgan* deal with the effect of death upon an offer? What is meant by a "request"?

OFFORD *v.* DAVIES. 1862. 12 C.B. (N.S.) 748; 142 E.R. 1336 (England. Common Pleas). The defendants wrote the plaintiff guaranteeing "*for the space of twelve calendar months* the due payment of . . . bills of exchange [discounted by the plaintiff at their request for Davies] to the extent of £600" and undertaking to "make good any loss . . . you may sustain or incur in consequence of advancing Messrs. Davies & Co. . . . moneys." The plaintiff discounted some bills which were duly paid, others were not, during the twelve month period. In an action to recover on the guarantee, it was pleaded that the bills discounted and sums advanced were discounted as advanced after the defendants had countermanded their guarantee. The plaintiff demurred that a party giving a guarantee for a definite period has no power to countermand it without assent. ERLE C.J. delivered the judgment of the Court for the defendants: ". . . This promise by itself creates no obligation. It is in effect conditioned to be binding if the plaintiff acts upon it, either to the benefit of the defendants or to the detriment of himself. But, until the condition has been at least in part fulfilled, the defendants have the power of revoking it. In the case of a simple guaranty for a proposed loan, the right of revocation before the proposal has been acted on did not appear to be disputed. Then are the rights of the parties affected either by the promise being expressed to be for twelve months, or by the fact that the same discounts had been made before that now in question, and repaid? We think not.

"The promise to repay for twelve months creates no additional liability on the guarantor, but, on the contrary, fixes a limit in time beyond which his liability cannot extend. And, with respect to other discounts, which had been repaid, we consider each discount as a separate transaction, creating a liability on the defendant till it is repaid, and after repayment leaving the promise to have the same operation that it had before any discount was made, and no more."

LLOYD'S *v.* HARPER. 1880. 16 Ch.D. 290. LUSH L.J.: "It will be found, I think, that guarantees may . . . be divided into two classes, the one in which the consideration is entire, and the other in which the consideration is fragmentary, supplied from time to time, and therefore divisible. An instance of the first is where a person enters into a guarantee that in consideration of the lessor granting a lease to a third person he will be answerable for the performance of the covenants. . . . Instances of the second class . . . are where a guarantee is given to secure the balance of a running account at a bankers, or a balance of a running account for goods supplied."

KENNEDY *v.* THOMASSEN. 1928. 45 T.L.R. 122 (England. Chancery Division). A Mrs. Webster was entitled to an annuity of £200 under the terms of a separation agreement with Mr. Webster. Webster died and left a further annuity of £200 to his widow. Mrs. Webster later married Mr. Vyzelaar, who died a few years later. The plaintiffs, trustees of Mr. Webster's will, offered to redeem the two annuities totalling £400 from Mrs.

Vyzelaar for £5,378. Her solicitors recommended that she accept the offer if it were increased to £6,000 and a release was prepared on this basis. It was sent to Mrs. Vyzelaar who executed it and returned it to her solicitors on January 12, 1928 with instructions that they were not to part with it until they got the £6,000. On January 24 the solicitors informed the trustees that the release had been executed and they were paid on January 30. On January 31 the solicitors were first informed by the defendant that Mrs. Vyzelaar had died on January 17, and that he had been named executor under her will. The £6,000 was paid into court. Held, for the plaintiffs. The effect of Mrs. Vyzelaar's death was to determine her solicitors' agency. The release had to be "delivered," even if it were executed under seal.

FELTHOUSE *v.* BINDLEY

England. Common Pleas. 1862. 11 C.B. (N.S.) 869; 142 E.R. 1037

Action for the conversion of a horse. A verdict was found for the plaintiff, damages £33, leave being reserved to the defendant to move to enter a nonsuit. A rule nisi was obtained.

WILLES J.: I am of opinion that the rule to enter a nonsuit should be made absolute. The horse in question had belonged to the plaintiff's nephew, John Felthouse. In December, 1860, a conversation took place between the plaintiff and his nephew relative to the purchase of the horse by the former. The uncle seems to have thought that he had on that occasion bought the horse for £30, the nephew that he had sold it for 30 guineas: but there was clearly no complete bargain at that time. On the 1st of January, 1861, the nephew writes, "I saw my father on Saturday. He told me that you considered you had bought the horse for £30. If so, you are labouring under a mistake, for, 30 guineas was the price I put upon him, and you never heard me say less. When you said you would have him, I considered you were aware of the price." To this the uncle replies on the following day, "Your price, I admit, was 30 guineas. I offered £30; never offered more: and you said the horse was mine. However, as there may be a mistake about him, I will split the difference. If I hear no more about him, I consider the horse mine at £30 15s." It is clear that there was no complete bargain on the 2nd of January: and it is also clear that the uncle had no right to impose upon the nephew a sale of his horse for £30 15s. unless he chose to comply with the condition of writing to repudiate the offer. The nephew might, no doubt, also have retracted his offer at any time before acceptance. It stood an open offer: and so things remained until the 25th of February, when the nephew was about to sell his farming stock by auction. The horse in question being catalogued with the rest of the stock, the auctioneer (the defendant) was told that it was already sold. It is clear, therefore, that the nephew in his own mind intended his uncle to have the horse at the price which he (the uncle) had named, £30 15s.: but he had not communicated such his intention to his uncle, or done anything to bind himself. Nothing, therefore, had been done to vest the property in the horse in the plaintiff down to the 25th of February, when the horse was sold by the defendant. It appears to me, that, independently of the subsequent letters, there had been no bargain to pass the property in the horse to the plaintiff, and therefore that he had no right to complain of the sale. Then, what is the effect of the subsequent correspondence? The letter of the auctioneer amounts to nothing. The more important letter is that of the nephew, of the 27th of February, which is relied on as shewing that he intended to accept and did accept the terms offered by his uncle's letter of the 2nd of January. That letter, however, may be treated either as an acceptance then for the first time made by him, or as a memorandum of a bargain complete before the 25th of February, sufficient within the statute of frauds. It seems to me that the former is the more likely construction: and if so, it is clear that the plaintiff cannot recover. But, assuming that there had been a complete parol bargain before the 25th of February, and that the letter of the 27th was a mere expression of the terms of that prior bargain, and not a bargain then for the first time concluded, it would be directly contrary to the decision of the Court of Exchequer in *Stockdale* v. *Dunlop* (1840), 6 M. & W. 224; 151 E.R. 391, to hold that that acceptance had relation back to the previous offer so as to bind third persons in respect of a dealing with the property by them in the interim. . . .

[Byles J. agreed, as did Keating J., who said, "Had the question arisen as between uncle and nephew, there would probably have been some difficulty." The record shows that Bindley simply forgot the horse had been sold. The decision was affirmed by the Court of Exchequer Chamber in (1863) 7 L.T. 835.]

LUCY *v*. MOUFLET. 1860. 5 H. & N. 229; 157 E.R. 1168. POLLOCK C.B.: "Now though it is true that if a stranger were to write and say to a person, 'If I do not hear I will send goods,' the omission to reply would be no evidence of a contract, yet it is different where two persons are actually engaged in dealing or under contract with each other. Then, if a proposal is made to which assent might be reasonably expected amongst men of business, and no answer is sent to it, acquiescence may be presumed."

WHEELER *v*. KLAHOLT

Massachusetts. Supreme Court. 1901. 59 N.E. 756

HOLMES C.J.: This is an action for the price of one hundred and seventy-four pairs of shoes, and the question raised by the defendants' exception is whether there was any evidence, at the trial, of a purchase by the defendants. . . .

The evidence of the sale was this. The shoes had been sent to the defendants on the understanding that a bargain had been made. It turned out that the parties disagreed, and if any contract had been made it was repudiated by them both. Then, on September 11, 1899, the plaintiffs wrote to the defendants that they had written to their agent, Young, to inform the defendants that the latter might keep the goods "at the price you offer if you send us net spot cash at once. If you cannot send us cash draft by mail, please return the goods to us immediately via Wabash & Fitchburg Railroad, otherwise they will go through New York City and it would take three or four weeks to get them." On September 15, the defendants enclosed a draft for the price less four per cent, which they said was the proposition made by Young. On September 18 the plaintiffs replied, returning the draft, saying that there was no deduction of four per cent, and adding, "if not satisfactory please return the goods at once by freight via Wabash & Fitchburg Railroad." This letter was received by the defendants on or before September 20, but the plaintiffs heard nothing more until October 25, when they were notified by the railroad company that the goods were in Boston.

It should be added that when the goods were sent to the defendants they were in good condition, new, fresh, and well packed, and that when the plaintiffs opened the returned cases their contents were more or less defaced and some pairs of shoes were gone. It fairly might be inferred that the cases had been opened and the contents tumbled about by the defendants, although whether before or after the plaintiff's final offer perhaps would be little more than a guess.

Both parties invoke *Hobbs* v. *Massasoit Whip Co.* (1893), 33 N.E. 495, the defendants for the suggestion on page 495, that a stranger by sending goods to another cannot impose a duty of notification upon him at the risk of finding himself a purchaser against his own will. We are of opinion that this proposition gives the defendants no help. The parties were not strangers to each other. The goods had not been foisted upon the defendants, but were in their custody presumably by their previous assent, at all events by their assent implied by their later conduct. The relations between the parties were so similar to those in the case cited, that if the plaintiffs' offer had been simply to let the defendants have the shoes at the price named, with an alternative request to send them back at once, as in their letters, the decision would have applied, and a silent retention of the shoes for an unreasonable time would have been an acceptance of the plaintiffs' terms, or, at least would have warranted a finding that it was. . . .

The defendants seek to escape the effect of the foregoing principle, if held applicable, on the ground of the terms offered by the plaintiffs. They say that those terms made it impossible to accept the plaintiffs' offer, or to give the plaintiffs any reasonable ground for understanding that their offer was accepted, otherwise than by promptly forwarding the cash. They say that whatever other liabilities they may have incurred they could not have purported to accept an offer to sell for cash on the spot by simply keeping the goods. But this argument appears to us to take one half of the plaintiffs' proposition with excessive nicety, and to ignore the alternative. Probably the offer could have been accepted and the bargain have been made complete before sending on the cash. At all events we must not forget the alternative, which was the immediate return of the goods.

The evidence warranted a finding that the defendants did not return the goods immediately or within a reasonable time, although subject to a duty in regard to them. The case does not stand as a simple offer to sell for cash received in silence, but as an alternative offer and demand to and upon one who was subject to a duty to return the goods, allowing him either to buy for cash or to return the shoes at once, followed by a failure on his part to do anything. Under such circumstances a jury would be warranted in finding that a neglect of the duty to return imported an acceptance of the alternative offer to sell, although coupled with a failure to show that promptness on which the plaintiffs had a right to insist if they saw fit, but which they also were at liberty to waive. *Exceptions overruled.*

DAY *v.* McLEA

England. Court of Appeal. 1899. 22 Q.B.D. 610

LORD ESHER M.R.: This was an action to recover damages for breach of contract. The plaintiffs were claiming a considerable sum as damages, and, before action brought, the defendants sent them a cheque for £102 18s. 6d., being less than the amount claimed, with a form of receipt, to be signed by the plaintiffs, that this sum was accepted in full satisfaction of the claim. The plaintiffs kept the cheque but refused to accept it in satisfaction.

and sent a receipt on account. It was contended that the keeping of the cheque so sent was, as a matter of law, an accord and satisfaction of the claim, and that the plaintiffs were bound either to take it in full satisfaction or to return it. The contention, therefore, was that the plaintiffs having kept the cheque must be taken in law to have accepted it in satisfaction. Upon the other side it was contended that the keeping of the cheque could only be evidence of accord and satisfaction, and that whether or not it was taken in satisfaction was a question of fact to be determined according to the circumstances of the case. That argument raises the question whether the fact of keeping a cheque sent in satisfaction of a claim for a larger amount is in law conclusive that there has been an accord and satisfaction. It is said that that inference of law must be drawn even though the person receiving the cheque never intends to take it in satisfaction and says so at the time he receives it. All I can say is that if that is a conclusive inference it would be one contrary to the truth. I object to all such inferences of law. This very question, however, came before this Court in *Miller* v. *Davies*. (Not reported.) In that case the action was upon a solicitor's bill of costs for £50, and there was a plea of accord and satisfaction. Before action the defendant sent the plaintiff a cheque for £25, with a letter stating that, in order to put an end to the matter, he sent the cheque for £25, on the terms that the plaintiff would receive it in settlement. The plaintiff kept the cheque and cashed it, and wrote to the defendant that he declined to accept it in settlement and that he required a cheque for the balance. The defendant thereupon wrote in reply requesting the plaintiff to return the cheque if he would not accept it in satisfaction. The jury found that there was no accord and satisfaction. It was contended there as in the present case that the fact of the plaintiff keeping the cheque was conclusive in law that he had taken it in accord and satisfaction of the claim, inasmuch as it had been sent in satisfaction and the plaintiff was bound either to keep it upon the terms on which it had been sent or to return it. This Court, however, held that the fact of keeping the cheque was not conclusive in law, that the question was one of fact, and that the jury having found that there was no accord and satisfaction the Court would not interfere. That case is clearly in point. The question, therefore, whether there has been an accord and satisfaction is one of fact. It was for the judge to decide whether the plaintiffs agreed to take £102 18s. 6d. in satisfaction of their claim. The learned judge has found that fact in favour of the plaintiffs and consequently this appeal must be dismissed.

[The concurring opinions of Bowen and Fry L.JJ. are omitted.]

RESTATEMENT OF THE LAW OF CONTRACTS
American Law Institute 1932

72. (1) Where an offeree fails to reply to an offer, his silence and inaction operate as an acceptance in the following cases and in no others:

(a) Where the offeree with reasonable opportunity to reject offered services takes the benefit of them under circumstances which would indicate to a reasonable man that they were offered with the expectation of compensation.

(b) Where the offeror has stated or given the offeree reason to understand that assent may be manifested by silence or inaction, and the offeree in remaining silent and inactive intends to accept the offer.

(c) Where because of previous dealings or otherwise, the offeree has given the offeror reason to understand that the silence or inaction is intended by the offeree as a manifestation of assent, and the offeror does so understand.

(2) Where the offeree exercises dominion over things which are offered to him, such exercise of dominion in the absence of other circumstances showing a contrary intention is an acceptance. If circumstances indicate that the exercise of dominion is tortious the offeror may at his option treat it as an acceptance, though the offeree manifests an intention not to accept.

NEWSPAPERS AND PERIODICALS SUBSCRIPTION ACT
Nova Scotia. Revised Statutes. 1954. Chapter 199

1. No person shall be liable to pay for any newspaper, or other periodical sent by post to such person, by reason of the fact that such person has taken such newspaper or other periodical so sent by post, from any post office or way office and kept the same.

2. (1) No person shall be liable to pay for any newspaper, or other periodical for which such person has subscribed after the expiration of the year for which such person is a subscriber; or after the expiration of any current year, if such person before the end of such year notifies the publisher of the newspaper, or other periodical, to discontinue sending the newspaper or other periodical.

(2) Notice of discontinuance may be given by mailing a registered letter or by notice otherwise given, to the publisher of the newspaper, or other periodical.

3. Unilateral Contracts

A "unilateral contract" is made by accepting an offer, not by a counter promise (which would create a "bilateral contract" of mutual promises) but by performing a requested overt act. The negotiation of a unilateral contract presents a number of problems, many arising in what are sometimes called the "reward cases." To whom is a reward offered? Must the offeree, whoever he may be, notify the offeror? If so, when? Does it matter that the offeror has or has not requested notice in his offer? Must the offeree know of the offer? Suppose that while A is out for a walk he is apprehended by a tired and lonesome dog whose collar identifies him as Fido, property of B, at a given address. A returns Fido to his owner's address and leaves him with an excited small son. Later A discovers that B had offered $50 for the return of the lost dog. Should A be heard to say he has a contractual right to the $50?

Perhaps the most tantalizing problem in unilateral contracts arises when the offeror wants to revoke. The classic situation is something like *Mooney* v. *Groat*: Oldster asks Youngster to look after him for the rest of his life and promises to leave Youngster $5,000 on his death. When he has enjoyed ten years of faithful service by Youngster and is on his death bed, Oldster announces that he revokes his offer. Note that the essential characteristic of the situation is that it is not bilateral. Oldster has not asked Youngster to commit himself with a promise to serve him for any length of time. Frequently in these cases the offeree is unwilling to commit himself. When should the state interfere to protect the interests of the parties, or of one of them? What interests ought to be protected?

WILLIAMS *v.* CARWARDINE

England. King's Bench. 1833. 4 B. & Ad. 621; 110 E.R. 590

At the trial before Park J., at the last Spring Assizes for the county of Hereford, the following appeared to be the facts of the case: One Walter Carwardine, the brother of the defendant, was seen on the evening of the 24th of March, 1831, at a public house at Hereford, and was not heard of again till his body was found on the 12th of April in the river Wye, about two miles from the city. An inquest was held on the body on the 13th of April and the following days till the 19th; and it appearing that the plaintiff was at a house with the deceased on the night he was supposed to have been murdered, she was examined before the magistrates but did not give them any information which led to the apprehension of the real offender. On the 25th of April the defendant caused a handbill to be published, stating that whoever would give such information as would lead to a discovery of the murderer of Walter Carwardine, should, on conviction receive a reward of £20; and any person concerned therein, or privy thereto (except the party who actually committed the offence), should be entitled to such reward, and every exertion used to procure a pardon; and it then added, that information was to be given, and application for the above reward was to be made, to William Carwardine, Holmer, near Hereford. Two persons were tried for the murder at the Summer Assizes, 1831, but acquitted. Soon after this the plaintiff was severely beaten and bruised by one Williams; and on the 23rd of August, 1831, believing she had not long to live, and to ease her conscience, she made a voluntary statement, containing information which led to the subsequent conviction of Williams. Upon this evidence it was contended, that as the plaintiff was not induced by the reward promised by the defendant to give evidence, the law would not imply a contract by the defendant to pay her the £20. The learned Judge was of opinion that the plaintiff, having given the information which led to the conviction of the murderer, had performed the condition on which the £20 was to become payable, and was therefore entitled to recover it; and he directed the jury to find a verdict for the plaintiff, but desired them to find specially whether she was induced to give the information by the offer of the promised reward. The jury found that she was not induced by the offer of the reward, but by other motives.

Curwood now moved for a new trial. There was no promise to pay the plaintiff the sum of £20. That promise could only be enforced in favor of persons who should have been induced to make disclosures by the promise of the reward. Here the jury found that the plaintiff was induced by other motives to give the information. They have, therefore, negatived any contract on the part of the defendant with the plaintiff.

DENMAN C.J.: The plaintiff, by having given information which led to the conviction of the murderer of Walter Carwardine, has brought herself within the terms of the advertisement, and therefore is entitled to recover.

LITTLEDALE J.: The advertisement amounts to a general promise to give a sum of money to any person who shall give information which might lead to the discovery of the offender. The plaintiff gave that information.

PARKE J.: There was a contract with any person who performed the condition mentioned in the advertisement.

PATTESON J.: I am of the same opinion. We cannot go into the plaintiff's motives.

[Rule refused. From the report of the trial in 5 C. & P. 574, it might appear from an admission of the defendant's counsel that the plaintiff knew of the offer at the time she gave the information. If she did not, could she be treated as a party to a contract? Could she have given the information in fulfilment of its condition?]

LOCKHART *v.* BARNARD. 1845. 14 M. & W. 674, 153 E.R. 646. The offer of a reward stated: ". . . Whoever will give such information as will lead to the immediate recovery of the above parcel, with its contents safe, if lost, or the early apprehension of the guilty parties if stolen, shall receive the above reward." POLLOCK C.B.: "Here the plaintiff communicates certain information to Cheshire, who, in return makes a communication to him; and then, deeming their joint knowledge sufficiently important to call for further inquiry, they jointly communicate it to Robinson and others, and he, as the agent of both, communicates it to a constable. I therefore think, that the finding of the jury, that the information which led to the detection of the felon was given, not by Lockhart alone, but by him jointly with Cheshire, and the entry of the verdict upon that finding, were perfectly right, and that no rule ought to be granted."

GIBBONS *v.* PROCTOR

England. Queen's Bench Division. 1891. 64 L.T. 594

DAY J.: This action is brought to recover a reward, which the defendant advertised as payable to the person who should prosecute to conviction the perpetrator of a certain crime. The facts are simple. The defendant published on the 29th May a handbill, in which he stated that he would give £25 to any person who should give information leading to the conviction of the offender in question, such information to be given to a superintendent of police of the name of Penn. The plaintiff is a police officer, and, in the early morning of the 29th May, the day of the afternoon of which the bill was published, communicated important information which led to the conviction of the offender to a comrade and fellow policeman called Coffin, telling Coffin, as his agent, to carry the information to the proper authority. Coffin, in accordance with the rules of the force, first informed his superior officer, Inspector Lennan, and Lennan sent on the information to Superintendent Penn. Both Coffin and Lennan were the agents of the plaintiff to carry on a message set going by him, and it reached Penn at a time when he had notice that the person sending him such information was entitled to the reward of £25. The condition was fulfilled after the publication of the handbill and the announcement therein contained of the defendant's offer of the reward to the informant.

[Lawrence J. agreed, and the non-suit was set aside and a verdict entered for £25.]

FITCH *v.* SNEDAKER. 1868. 38 N.Y. 248 (New York. Court of Appeals). The defendant offered a reward of $200 to any person or persons who would give such information as should lead to the apprehension and conviction of the person or persons guilty of the murder of a certain unknown female. The plaintiff gave information resulting in the arrest of the murderer before the plaintiff heard of the reward and in fact (as it appeared in the evidence at an earlier trial) before the reward was published. After he heard, he gave further information and testified at the trial at which the murderer was convicted. The plaintiff claimed the reward, which was refused, and he brought this action. His evidence to show that his information led to the arrest was rejected because it was given before he knew of the reward. His evidence to show that his information and testimony led to a conviction was rejected because in order to claim the reward he had to show that he had brought about both the arrest and the conviction. Without his first evidence his second evidence was irrelevant. WOODRUFF J.: " . . . the first question is, Was there a contract between the parties?

"To the existence of a contract there must be mutual assent, or, in another form, offer and consent to the offer. The motive inducing consent may be immaterial, but the consent is vital. Without that there is no contract. How then can there be consent or assent to that of which the party has never heard? On the fifteenth day of October, 1859, the murderer, Fee, had, in consequence of information given by the plaintiffs, been apprehended and lodged in jail. But the plaintiffs did not, in giving that information, manifest any assent to the defendant's offer, nor act in any sense in reliance thereon; they did not know of its existence. The information was voluntary, and in every sense (material to this case) gratuitous. The offer could only operate upon the plaintiffs after they heard of it. It was prospective to those who will in the future give information."

THE CROWN *v.* CLARKE

West Australia. High Court of Australia. 1927. 40 C.L.R. 227

ISAACS A.C.J.: This is an appeal from the judgment of the Full Court of Western Australia. Evan Clarke proceeded, by petition of right under the *Crown Suits Act* 1898, to sue the Crown for £1,000 promised by proclamation for such information as should lead to the arrest and conviction of the person or persons who committed the murders of two police officers, Walsh and Pitman. . . . At the trial the Chief Justice gave judgment for the Crown. In the Full Court, by a majority, the judgment of McMillan C.J., the trial Judge, was reversed. In the result, two learned Judges thought the Crown should succeed while two others thought Clarke should succeed. . . .

The facts of this case, including inferences, are not, as I understand, in dispute. They amount to this: The information for which Clarke claims the reward was given by him when he was under arrest with Treffene on a charge of murder, and was given by him in circumstances which show that in giving the information he was not acting on or in pursuance of or in reliance upon or in return for the consideration contained in the proclamation, but exclusively in order to clear himself from a false charge of murder. In other words, he was acting with reference to a specific criminal charge against himself, and not with reference to a general request by the community for information against other persons. It is true that without his information and evidence no conviction was probable, but it is also abundantly clear that he was not acting for the sake of justice or from any impulse of conscience or because he was asked to do so, but simply and solely on his own initiative, to secure his own safety from the hand of the law and altogether irrespective of the proclamation. He has, in my opinion, neither a legal nor a moral claim to the reward. The learned Chief Justice held that Clarke never accepted or intended to accept the offer in the proclamation, and, unless the mere giving of the information without such intention amounted in law to an acceptance of the offer or to performance of the condition, there was neither "acceptance" nor "performance," and therefore there was no contract. I do not understand either of the learned Judges who formed the majority to controvert this. But they held that *Williams* v. *Carwardine* (1833), 110 E.R. 590, has stood so long that it should be regarded as accurate, and that, so regarded, it entitled the respondent to judgment. . . .

The controlling principle, then, is that to establish the *consensus* without which no true contract can exist, acceptance is as essential as offer, even in a case of the present class where the same act is at once sufficient for both acceptance and performance. But acceptance and performance of condition, as shown by the judicial reasoning quoted, involve that the person accepting and performing must act on the offer. . . .

Instances easily suggest themselves where precisely the same act done with reference to an offer would be performance of the condition, but done with reference to a totally distinct object would not be such a performance. An offer of £100 to any person who should swim a hundred yards in the harbour on the first day of the year, would be met by voluntarily performing the feat with reference to the offer, but would not in my opinion be satisfied by a person who was accidentally or maliciously thrown overboard on that date and swam the distance simply to save his life, without any thought of the offer. The offeror might or might not feel morally impelled to give the sum in such a case, but would be under no contractual obligation to do so. . . .

The appeal, however, should, in my opinion, for the reasons stated, be allowed, and the judgment of McMillan C.J. restored.

[The opinion is considerably abbreviated. The opinions of Higgins and Starke JJ. are omitted.]

CARLILL *v.* CARBOLIC SMOKE BALL COMPANY
England. Court of Appeal. [1893] 1 Q.B. 256

The defendants, who were the proprietors and vendors of a medical preparation called "The Carbolic Smoke Ball", inserted in the Pall Mall Gazette of November 13th, 1891, and in other newspapers, the following advertisement:

"£100 reward will be paid by the Carbolic Smoke Ball Company to any person who contracts the increasing epidemic of influenza, colds, or any disease caused by taking cold, after having used the ball three times daily for two weeks according to the printed directions supplied with each ball. £1000 is deposited with the Alliance Bank, Regent Street, shewing our sincerity in the matter.

"During the last epidemic of influenza many thousand carbolic smoke balls were sold as preventives against this disease, and in no ascertained case was the disease contracted by those using carbolic smoke ball.

"One carbolic smoke ball will last a family several months, making it the cheapest remedy in the world at the price, 10s. post free. The ball can refilled at a cost of 5s. Address, Carbolic Smoke Ball Company, 27, Princes Street, Hanover Square London."

The plaintiff, a lady, on the faith of this advertisement, bought one of the balls at a chemist's, and used it as directed three times a day, from November 20, 1891, to January 17, 1892, when she was attacked by influenza. Hawkins J. held that she was entitled to recover the £100. The defendants appealed.

LINDLEY L.J.: I will begin by referring to two points which were raised in the court below. I refer to them simply for the purpose of dismissing them. First, it is said no action will lie upon this contract because it is a policy. You have only to look at the advertisement to dismiss that suggestion. Then it is said that it is a bet. Hawkins J. came to the conclusion that nobody ever dreamt of a bet, and that the transaction had nothing whatever in common with a bet. I so entirely agree with him that I pass over this contention also as not worth serious attention.

Then, what is left? The first observation I will make is that we are not dealing with any inference of fact. We are dealing with an express promise to pay £100 in certain events. Read the advertisement how you will, and twist it about as you will, here is a distinct promise expressed in language which is perfectly unmistakable—"£100 reward will be paid by the Carbolic Smoke Ball Company to any person who contracts the influenza after having used the ball three times daily for two weeks according to the printed directions supplied with each ball."

We must first consider whether this was intended to be a promise at all, or whether it was a mere puff which meant nothing. Was it a mere puff? My answer to that question is No, and I base my answer upon this passage: "£1000 is deposited with the Alliance Bank, shewing our sincerity in the matter." Now, for what was that money deposited or that statement made expect to negative the suggestion that this was a mere puff and meant nothing at all? The deposit is called in aid by the advertiser as proof of his sincerity in the matter—that is, the sincerity of his promise to pay this £100 in the event which he has specified. I say this for the purpose of giving point to the observation that we are not inferring a promise; there is the promise, as plain as words can make it.

Then it is contended that it is not binding. In the first place, it is said that it is not made with anybody in particular. Now that point is common to the words of this advertisement and to the words of all other advertisements offering rewards. They are offers to anybody who performs the conditions named in the advertisement, and anybody who does perform the conditions accepts the offer. In point of law this advertisement is an offer to pay £100 to anybody who will perform these conditions, and the performance of the conditions is the acceptance of the offer. That rests upon a string of authorities, the earliest of which is *Williams* v. *Carwardine* (1833), 110 E.R. 590, which has been followed by many other decisions upon advertisements offering rewards.

But then it is said, "Supposing that the performance of the conditions is an acceptance of the offer, that acceptance ought to have been notified." Unquestionably, as a general proposition, when an offer is made, it is necessary in order to make a binding contract, not only that it should be accepted, but that the acceptance should be notified. But is that so in cases of this kind? I apprehend that they are an exception to that rule, or, if not an exception, they are open to the observation that the notification of the acceptance need not precede the performance. This offer is a continuing offer. It was never revoked, and if notice of acceptance is required—which I doubt very much, for I rather think the true view is that which was expressed and explained by Lord Blackburn in the case of *Brogden* v. *Metropolitan Ry. Co.* (1877), 2 App. Cas. 666, 691—if notice of acceptance is required, the person who makes the offer gets the notice of acceptance contemporaneously with his notice of the performance of the condition. If he gets notice of the acceptance before his offer is revoked, that in principle is all you want. I, however, think that the true view, in a case of this kind, is that the person who makes the offer shews by his language and from the nature of the transaction that he does not expect and does not require notice of the acceptance apart from notice of the performance. . . .

It appears to me, therefore, that the defendants must perform their promise, if they have been so unwary as to expose themselves to a great many actions, so much the worse for them.

BOWEN L.J.: I am of the same opinion. . . .

It was said that there was no notification of the acceptance of the contract. One cannot doubt that, as an ordinary rule of law, an acceptance of an offer made ought to be notified to the person who makes the offer, in order that the two minds may come together. Unless this is done the two minds may be apart, and there is not that consensus which is necessary according to the English law—I say nothing about the laws of other countries—to make a contract. But there is this clear gloss to be made upon that doctrine, that as notification of acceptance is required for the benefit of the person who makes the offer, the person who makes the offer may dispense with notice to himself if he thinks it desirable to do so, and I suppose there can be no doubt that where a person in an offer made by him to another person, expressly or impliedly intimates a particular mode of acceptance as sufficient to make the bargain binding, it is only necessary for the other person to whom such offer is made to follow the indicated method of acceptance; and if the person making the offer, expressly or impliedly intimates in his offer that it will be sufficient to act on the proposal without communicating acceptance of it to himself, performance of the condition is a sufficient acceptance without notification.

That seems to me to be the principle which lies at the bottom of the acceptance cases, of which two instances are the well-known judgment of Mellish L.J. in *Harris' Case* (1872), 7 Ch.App. 587, and the very instructive judgment of Lord Blackburn in *Brogden* v. *Metropolitan Ry. Co.*, in which he appears to me to take exactly the line I have indicated.

Now, if that is the law how are we to find out whether the person who makes the offer does intimate that notification of acceptance will not be necessary in order to constitute a binding bargain? In many cases you look to the offer itself. In many cases you extract from the character of the transaction that notification is not required, and in the advertisement cases it seems to me to follow as an inference to be drawn from the transaction itself that a person is not to notify his acceptance of the offer before he performs the condition, but that if he performs the condition notification is dispensed with. It seems to me that from the point of view of common sense no other idea could be entertained. If I advertise to the world that my dog is lost, and that anybody who brings the dog to a particular place will be paid some money, are all the police or other persons whose business it is to find lost dogs to be expected to sit down and write me a note saying they have accepted my proposal? Why, of course, they at once look after the dog, and as soon as they have found the dog they have performed the condition. The essence of the transaction is that the dog should be found, and it is not necessary under such circumstances, as it seems to me, that in order to make the contract binding there should be any notification of acceptance. It follows from the nature of the thing that the performance of the condition is sufficient acceptance without notification of it, and a person who makes an offer in an advertisement of that kind makes an offer which must be read by the light of that common sense reflection. He does, therefore, in his offer impliedly indicate that he does not require notification of the acceptance of the offer.

[Appeal dismissed. Part of the opinions only are given and the concurring opinion of A.L. Smith L.J. is omitted.]

WOOD *v.* LETRIK, LIMITED, The Times, January 13, 1932. The defendants in an advertisement of their electric comb, stated: "What is your trouble? Is it grey hair? In 10 days not a grey hair left. £500 guarantee." The plaintiff claimed he had bought a comb and used it as directed, the only result being that the comb scratched his head and made him feel uncomfortable. He sued for and recovered the £500. Rowlatt J. followed the *Carlill case*. Suppose that in either the *smoke-ball* or *comb case* the plaintiff had borrowed the smoke-ball or comb from a friend and had used it with disappointing results. Would you allow a recovery?

BISHOP *v.* EATON. 1894. 37 N.E. 665 (Massachusetts. Supreme Court). The defendant wrote the plaintiff, "If Harry needs more money, let him have it, or assist him to get it, and I will see that it is paid." The plaintiff endorsed a note for Harry for $200, and shortly after wrote to the defendant to this effect. The defendant denied receipt of the letter. The note was extended for one year, but the trial judge did not decide whether the defendant had agreed to the extension. If he hadn't he would be discharged. The plaintiff paid the note and the trial judge found for the plaintiff. The defendant appealed and a new trial was granted to establish whether he had consented to the extension. KNOWLTON J.: "We are of opinion that the plaintiff, after assisting Harry to get the money, did all that he was required to do when he reasonably sent the defendant the letter by mail informing him of what had been done. . . . Ordinarily there is no occasion to notify the offeror of the acceptance of such an offer, for the doing of the act is a sufficient acceptance, and the promisor knows that he is bound when he sees that action has been taken on the faith of his offer. But if the act is of such a kind that knowledge of it will not quickly come to the promisor, the promisee is bound to give him notice of his acceptance within a reasonable time after doing that which constitutes the acceptance. In such a case it is implied in the offer that, to complete the contract, notice shall be given with due diligence, so that the promisor may know that a contract has been made. But where the promise is in consideration of an act to be done, it becomes binding upon the doing of the act so far that the promisee cannot be affected by a subsequent withdrawal of it, if within a reasonable time afterward he notifies the promisor. In accordance with these principles it has been held in cases like the present, where the guarantor would not know of himself, from the nature of the transaction, whether the offer has been accepted or not, that he is not bound without notice of the acceptance, reasonably given after the performance which constitutes the consideration."

SUTHERLAND *v.* PATTERSON. 1884. 4 O.R. 565 (Ontario High Court). The defendant wrote to the plaintiff: "If you will give John a letter of credit up to $7,000 I will become responsible to you." Credit was given John for $5,000 but the guarantee was not honoured. BURTON J.: "The letter was not binding at first, and was revokable until acted upon by the plaintiff; but the question is, did it become binding even if acted upon, without some notice to the defendant of his willingness to become liable, or was some further act necessary. I am unable to distinguish this case from *McIver* v. *Richardson* (1813), 1 M. & S. 557; 105 E.R. 208 and must, I think, regard this not as a perfect and conclusive guarantee, but only as a proposition tending to a guarantee. . . ." [On appeal this judgment was upheld.]

VYSE *v.* WAKEFIELD. 1840. 6 M. &. W. 442; 151 E.R. 485, 489. LORD ABINGER: ". . . where a party stipulates to do a certain thing in a certain specific event which may become known to him, or with which he can make himself acquainted, he is not entitled to any notice unless he stipulates for it; but when it is to do a thing which lies within the peculiar knowledge of the opposite party, then notice ought to be given him."

GOLDTHORPE *v.* LOGAN

Ontario. Court of Appeal. [1943] 2 D.L.R. 519

LAIDLAW J.A. delivered the judgment of the Court: This is an appeal by the plaintiffs from a judgment of Hope J., dated April 10, 1942. The female appellant had some hairs on her face and wanted to have them removed. She saw advertisements published in a newspaper by the defendant Anne Graham Logan. She went to the place of business stated in the advertisement and consulted the defendant Kathleen Fitzpatrick, a registered nurse, who was an employee of the defendant Logan. She was told that her face could be definitely "cleared," that the hair could be removed permanently, and the result was guaranteed. She then submitted to a number of "treatments" by electrolysis for the purpose of removing the hairs but the result was not satisfactory. Hairs continued to grow on her face in the same way as before, and in spite of the efforts of the defendants to remedy the condition. . . .

There are three questions to be determined: (1) Was there any negligence on the part of the defendants which caused loss or damages to the plaintiffs? (2) Was there a contract between the defendant Logan and the plaintiff Pearl Elizabeth Goldthorpe? (3) If so, what is the result in law of a breach thereof on the part of that defendant? . . .

The plaintiffs, therefore, fail to establish liability of the defendants on the ground of negligence. But the alternative allegation to the effect that the defendant Logan is responsible in law by reason of a breach of contract made by or on her behalf with the female plaintiff requires careful consideration. The elements of a valid contract are well known, and it is only necessary to analyze the evidence to determine whether or not they exist in this case. I at once examined the advertisement published by the defendant Logan. It appears in two forms, but the portions relevant to the question now studied are the same. I excerpt the contents as follows: "Hairs . . . removed safely and permanently by Electrolysis. . . . No marks, No scars, Results Guaranteed. Anne Graham Logan . . . 140 Carlton St." What is the true nature and construction of this advertisement? It is a distinct communication by the defendant Logan to each and every member of the public. What intention did she possess and convey to such persons by the words she used? To ascertain that intention we may in this instance look at the surrounding circumstances. She was carrying on a business in which she appealed for public support and patronage. She required customers to buy services she desired to sell. She was a vendor seeking a purchaser. What she meant to say, and the sensible interpretation of her words is this: "If you will submit yourself to my treatment and pay me (certain charges) I undertake to remove hairs safely and permanently by electrolysis and I promise to obtain a satisfactory result." The effect in law of such a statement is to create an offer from the person by whom it is made to every person who is willing to accept the terms and conditions of it. It may perhaps, be suggested that this meaning and effect of the advertisement is strained and unfair. I think it is not. On the contrary, I read it in its plain meaning as the public would understand it. Moreover, after Mrs. Goldthorpe was persuaded by this public offer to attend at the defendant's place of business she was given further assurance that the hairs on her face could be successfully and permanently removed without stimulation, without risk, and without pain. The defendants again "guaranteed results." They did not ask for nor suggest any exemption, exception, or qualification of any kind, but on the contrary they made promises which were absolute and unlimited. They were reckless and rash without any regard whatever to the particular circumstances of the case. No physical examination of Mrs. Goldthorpe was required nor suggested. No inquiry was made for the purpose of disclosing any organic trouble or cause of the excessive hair. The defendants simply were content to take the risk of failure irrespective of any underlying causes of the unfortunate ailment, and they exposed themselves to just such an action as this. If the vendor's self-confidence had persuaded her into an excessive, extravagant promise, she cannot now escape a complaint from a credulous and distressed person to whom she gave assurance of future excellence and relief from her burden. The strong cannot disregard any undertaking binding in law, however lightly given, and the weak unfortunate person, however gullible, can be sure that the Courts of this country will not permit anyone to escape the responsibility arising from an enforceable promise. The words of Hawkins J., are fitting and applicable. He says: "Such advertisements do not appeal so much to the wise and thoughtful as to the credulous and weak portions of the community; and if the vendor of an article, whether it be medicine smoke or anything else, with a view to increase its sale and use, thinks fit publicly to promise to all who buy or use it that, to those who shall not find it as surely efficacious as it is represented by him to be he will pay a substantial sum of money, he must not be surprised if occasionally he is held to his promise:" *Carlill* v. *Carbolic Smoke Ball Co.*, [1893] 1 Q.B. 256.

I now consider whether there was acceptance in law of the offer made by the defendant. The offer was made to the public. Any member was free to lend oneself to the terms and conditions and assent thereto.

The female plaintiff accordingly accepted the offer, and her acceptance was communicated to the defendant Logan by her conduct. These parties had a common intention, and there was good consideration present. It was constituted by the detriment or inconvenience sustained by the female plaintiff. Her submission to the treatments, in accordance with advertisement, was a benefit sought by the advertiser. . . . I hold that there was an agreement made between the plaintiff, Pearl Elizabeth Goldthorpe and the defendant, Anne Graham Logan, and that such agreement is enforceable at law by the female plaintiff. . . .

Appeal allowed in part.

QUESTIONS. Was it necessary for the Court to bring in the *Carlill* argument at all? Was there not a concluded contract in the conversations between plaintiff and defendant's nurse before the treatments were commenced?

SHUEY, EXECUTOR *v*. UNITED STATES. 1875. 92 U.S. 73 (United States. Supreme Court). In April, 1865, the United States Secretary of War announced through the press a reward of $25,000 "for the apprehension of John H. Surratt, one of Booth's accomplices" and "liberal rewards will be paid for any information that shall conduce to the arrest of either of the above-named criminals or their accomplices." In November, 1865, the President published through the same medium his orders revoking the offered rewards. In April, 1866, Henry B. Ste. Marie, who was in the military service of the Papal government, discovered Surratt in the same service and identified him to the American Minister at Rome. Surratt had confessed to Ste. Marie his part in the plot to assassinate Lincoln and at the Minister's request Ste. Marie kept an eye on Surratt, but his arrest was arranged by the Minister. Before he was finally brought to the United States, Surratt escaped to Alexandria, where he was again arrested and identified by Ste. Marie. Ste. Marie himself had no part in Surratt's arrest on either occasion. The United States Government paid Ste. Marie $10,000, presumably as one of the "liberal rewards." This action was brought claiming $15,000 as the balance of the reward. Both Ste. Marie and the American Minster at Rome were ignorant of the revocation. Ste. Marie died and the action was continued by his executor. Held, no contract. STRONG J.: ". . . The offer of a reward for the apprehension of Surratt was revoked on the twenty-fourth day of November, 1865; and notice of the revocation was published. It is not to be doubted that the offer was revocable at any time before it was accepted, and before anything had been done in reliance upon it. There was no contract until its terms were complied with. Like any other offer of a contract, it might, therefore, be withdrawn before rights had accrued under it; and it was withdrawn through the same channel in which it was made. The same notoriety was given to the revocation that was given to the offer; and the findings of fact do not show that any information was given by the claimant, or that he did anything to entitle him to the reward offered, until five months after the offer had been withdrawn. True, it is found that then, and at all times until the arrest was actually made, he was ignorant of the withdrawal; but that is an immaterial fact. The offer of the reward not having been made to him directly, but by means of a published proclamation he should have known that it could be revoked in the manner in which it was made."

PETTERSON *v*. PATTBERG
New York. Court of Appeals. 1928. 161 N.E. 428

KELLOG J.: The evidence given upon the trial sanctions the following statement of facts: John Petterson, of whose last will and testament the plaintiff is the executrix, was the owner of a parcel of real estate in Brooklyn, known as 5301 Sixth Avenue. The defendant was the owner of a bond executed by Petterson, which was secured by a third mortgage upon the parcel. On April 4, 1924, there remained unpaid upon the principal the sum of $5,450. This amount was payable in instalments of $250 on April 25, 1924, and upon a like monthly date every three months thereafter. Thus the bond and mortgage had more than five years to run before the entire sum became due. Under date of the 4th of April, 1924, the defendant wrote Petterson as follows:

"I hereby agree to accept cash for the mortgage which I hold against premises 5301 6th Ave., Brooklyn, N.Y. It is understood and agreed as a consideration I will allow you $780 provided said mortgage is paid on or before May 31, 1924, and the regular quarterly payment due April 25, 1924, is paid when due."

On April 25, 1924, Petterson paid the defendant the instalment of principal due on that date. Subsequently, on a day in the latter part of May, 1924, Petterson presented himself at the defendant's home, and knocked at the door. The defendant demanded the name of his caller. Petterson. replied: "It is Mr. Petterson. I have come to pay off the mortgage." The defendant answered that he had sold the mortgage. Petterson stated that he would like to talk with the defendant, so the defendant partly opened the door. Thereupon Petterson exhibited the cash, and said he was ready to pay off the mortgage according to the agreement. The defendant refused to take the money. Prior to this conversation, Petterson had made a contract to sell the land to a third person free and clear of the mortgage to the defendant. Meanwhile, also, the defendant had sold the bond and mortgage to a third party. It therefore became necessary for Petterson to pay to such person the full amount of the bond and mortgage. It is claimed that he thereby sustained a loss of $780, the sum which the defendant agreed to allow upon the bond and mortgage, if payment in full of principal, less that sum, was made on or before May 31, 1924. The plaintiff has had a recovery for the sum thus claimed, with interest.

Clearly the defendant's letter proposed to Petterson the making of a unilateral contract, the gift of a promise in exchange for the performance of an act. The thing conditionally promised by the defendant was the reduction of the mortgage debt. The act requested to be done, in consideration of the offered promise, was payment in full of the reduced principal of the debt prior to the due date thereof. "If an act is requested, that very act, and no other, must be given." *Williston on Contracts*, sec. 73. . . .

An interesting question arises when, as here, the offeree approaches the offeror with the intention of proffering performance and, before actual tender is made, the offer is withdrawn. Of such a case Williston says:

"The offeror may see the approach of the offeree and know that an acceptance is contemplated. If the offeror can say 'I revoke' before the offeree accepts, however brief the interval of time between the two acts, there is no escape from the conclusion that the offer is terminated." *Williston on Contracts*, sec. 60b.

In this instance Petterson, standing at the door of the defendant's house, stated to the defendant that he had come to pay off the mortgage. Before a tender of the necessary moneys had been made, the defendant informed Petterson that he had sold the mortgage. That was a definite notice to Petterson that the defendant could not perform his offered promise, and that a tender to the defendant, who was no longer the creditor, would be ineffective to satisfy the debt. An offer to sell property may be withdrawn before acceptance without any formal notice to the person to whom the offer is made. It is sufficient if that person has actual knowledge that the person who made the offer has done some act inconsistent with the continuance of the offer, such as selling the property to a third person. *Dickinson* v. *Dodds* (1876), 2 Ch.D. 463. . . . Thus it clearly appears that the defendant's offer was withdrawn before its acceptance had been tendered.

It is unnecessary to determine, therefore, what the legal situation might have been had tender been made before withdrawal. It is the individual view of the writer that the same result would follow. This would be so, for the act requested to be performed was the completed act of payment, a thing incapable of performance, unless assented to by the person to be paid. *Williston on Contracts*, sec. 60b.

Clearly an offering party has the right to name the precise act performance of which would convert his offer into a binding promise. Whatever the act may be until it is performed, the offer must be revocable. However, the supposed case is not before us for decision. We think that in this particular instance the offer of the defendant was withdrawn before it became a binding promise, and therefore that no contract was ever made for the breach of which the plaintiff may claim damages.

The judgment of the Appellant Division and that of the Trial Term should be reversed, and the complaint dismissed, with costs in all courts.

LEHMAN J. (dissenting): The defendant's letter to Petterson constituted a promise on his part to accept payment at a discount of the mortgage he held, provided the mortgage is paid on or before May 31, 1924. Doubtless, by the terms of the promise itself, the defendant made payment of the mortgage by the plaintiff, before the stipulated time, a condition precedent to performance by the defendant of his promise to accept payment at a discount. If the condition precedent has not been performed, it is because the defendant made performance impossible by refusing to accept payment, when the plaintiff came with an offer of immediate performance. It is a principle of fundamental justice that if a promisor is himself the cause of the failure of performance either of an obligation due him or of a condition upon which his own liability depends, he cannot take advantage of the failure. *Williston on Contracts*, sec. 677. The question in this case is not whether payment of the mortgage is a condition precedent to the performance of a promise made by the defendant, but, rather, whether, at the time the defendant refused the offer of payment, he had assumed any binding obligation, even though subject to condition.

The promise made by the defendant lacked consideration at the time it was made. Nevertheless, the promise was not made as a gift or mere gratuity to the plaintiff. It was made for the purpose of obtaining from the defendant something which the plaintiff desired. It constituted an offer which was to become binding whenever the plaintiff should give, in return for the defendant's promise, exactly the consideration which the defendant requested.

Here the defendant requested no counter promise from the plaintiff. The consideration requested by the defendant for his promise to accept payment was, I agree, some act to be performed by the plaintiff. Until the act requested was performed, the defendant might undoubtedly revoke his offer. Our problem is to determine from the words of the letter, read in the light of surrounding circumstances, what act the defendant requested as consideration for his promise.

The defendant undoubtedly made his offer as an inducement to the plaintiff to "pay" the mortgage before it was due. Therefore, it is said, that "the act requested to be performed was the completed act of payment, a thing incapable of performance, unless assented to by the person to be paid." In unmistakeable terms the defendant agreed to accept payment, yet we are told that the defendant intended, and the plaintiff should have understood, that the act requested by the defendant, as consideration for his promise to accept payment, included performance by the defendant himself of the very promise for which the act was to be consideration. The defendant's promise was to become binding only when fully performed; and part of the consideration to be furnished by the plaintiff for the defendant's promise was to be the performance of that promise by the defendant. So construed, the defendant's promise or offer, though intended to induce action by the plaintiff, is but a snare and delusion. The plaintiff could not reasonably suppose that the defendant was asking him to procure the performance by the defendant of the very act which the defendant promised to do, yet we are told that, even after the plaintiff had done all else which the defendant requested, the defendant's promise was still not binding because the defendant chose not to perform.

I cannot believe that a result so extraordinary could have been intended when the defendant wrote the letter. "The thought behind the phrase proclaims itself misread when the outcome of the reading is injustice or absurdity." See opinion of Cardozo C.J., in *Surace* v. *Danna*, 161 N.E. 315. If the defendant intended to induce payment by the plaintiff and yet reserve the right to refuse payment when offered he should have used a phrase better calculated to express his meaning than the words: "I agree to accept." A promise to accept payment, by its very terms, must necessarily become binding, if at all, not later than when a present offer to pay is made.

I recognise that in this case only an offer of payment, and not a formal tender of payment, was made before the defendant withdrew his offer to accept payment. Even the plaintiff's part in the act of payment was then not technically complete. Even so, under a fair construction of the words of the letter, I think the plaintiff had done the act which the defendant requested, as consideration for his promise. The plaintiff offered to pay, with present intention and ability to make that payment. A formal tender is seldom made in business transactions, except to lay the foundation for subsequent assertion in a court of justice of rights which spring from the refusal of the tender. If the defendant acted in good faith in making his offer to accept payment, he could not well have intended to draw a distinction in the act requested of the plaintiff in return, between an offer which, unless refused, would ripen into completed payment, and a formal tender. Certainly the defendant could not have expected or intended that the plaintiff would make a formal tender of payment without first stating that he had come to make payment. We should not read into the language of the defendant's offer a meaning which would prevent enforcement of the defendant's promise after it had been accepted by the plaintiff in the very way which the defendant must have intended it should be accepted, if he acted in good faith.

The judgment should be affirmed.

[Cardozo C.J. and Pound, Crane and O'Brien JJ. concur with Kellogg J. Andrews J. concurred with Lehman J.]

BLINKOFF, COMMENT. 1928. 14 *Cornell L.Q.* 81. "Other facts in the case, not appearing in the opinion, may have influenced the court. The record of the trial (folios 95-97) reveals that the defendant was prevented from testifying as to a letter, sent to the plaintiff's testator, revoking the offer because such testimony was inadmissable under section 347 of the Civil Practice Act, which excludes the testimony of one of the interested parties, to a transaction, where the other is dead and so unable to contradict the evidence. The record (folio 59) also seems to suggest that the mortgagor knew of the previous sale of the mortgage, since he brought $4,000 in cash with him, and was accompanied by his wife and a notary public as witnesses; anticipation of the defendant's refusal by seeking to get evidence on which to base this action seems to be a plausible explanation. There was no actual proof of knowledge of the defendant's inability to carry out his offer but the situation was suspicious."

BEER *v.* LEA. 1912. 4 O.W.N. 342 (Ontario. High Court). Lea gave a thirty day option to Doolittle to buy his land for a stipulated sum. The option was without consideration and called for payment of the sum within the thirty days. Doolittle interested Beer in the deal. On the last day of the option Doolittle arranged with Lea to meet him and Beer at a certain place and take up the option. Doolittle and Beer attended at the place and the court found Beer was prepared to make the cash payment. Lea, however, deliberately refrained from attending at the arranged meeting. Doolittle later telephoned Lea for an explanation and Lea thinking the time had expired, said he would have nothing further to do with it. MIDDLETON J.: "I think the plaintiff fails. I do not think there was any acceptance of the offer before it was withdrawn. . . . I think that the offer could only be accepted by a cash payment . . . and that this was a condition precedent to the existence of any contractual relationship. . . . Mr. Johnston very forcibly contends that Lea ought to be precluded from denying that there was an acceptance of the offer, because of his failure to attend at the place arranged. . . . I cannot follow this. There can be no contract unless there is an offer and an acceptance of that offer. If there is a contract, then either party may . . . by his conduct dispense with the fulfilment of the contract, according to its terms by the other, but so far as I can find, it has nowhere been suggested that one who has made an offer can dispense with an acceptance so as to create a contractual relationship."

ERRINGTON *v.* ERRINGTON
England. Court of Appeal. [1952] 1 All E.R. 149

DENNING L.J.: The facts are reasonably clear. In 1936 the father bought the house for his son and daughter-in-law to live in. The father put down £250 in cash and borrowed £500 from a building society on the security of the house, repayable with interest by instalments of 15s. a week. He took the house in his own name and made himself responsible for the instalments. The father told the daughter-in-law that the £250 was a present for them, but he left them to pay the building society instalments of 15s. a week themselves. He handed the building society book to the daughter-in-law and said to her: "Don't part with this book. The house will be your property when the mortgage is paid." He said that when he retired he would transfer it into their names. She has, in fact, paid the building society instalments regularly from that day to this with the result that much of the mortgage has been repaid, but there is a good deal yet to be paid. The rates on the house came to 10s. a week. The couple found that they could not pay those as well as the building society instalments so the father said he would pay them and he did so.

It is to be noted that the couple never bound themselves to pay the instalments to the building society, and I see no reason why any such obligation should be implied. It is clear law that the court is not to imply a term unless it is necessary, and I do not see that it is necessary here. Ample content is given to the whole agreement by holding that the father promised that the house should belong to the couple as soon as they had paid off the mortgage. The parties did not discuss what was to happen if the couple failed to pay the instalments to the building society, but I should have thought it clear that, if they did fail to pay the instalments, the father would not be bound to transfer the house to them. The father's promise was a unilateral contract—a promise of the house in return for their act of paying the instalments. It could not be revoked by him once the couple entered on performance of the act, but it would cease to bind him if they left it incomplete and unperformed, which they have done. If that was the position during the father's lifetime, so it must be after his death. If the daughter-in-law continues to pay all the building society instalments, the couple will be entitled to have the property transferred to them as soon as the mortgage is paid off, but if she does not do so, then the building society will claim the instalments from the father's estate and the estate will have to pay them. I cannot think that in those circumstances the estate would be bound to transfer the house to them, any more than the father himself would have been. . . .

In the present case it is clear that the father expressly promised the couple that the property should belong to them as soon as the mortgage was paid, and impliedly promised that, so long as they paid the instalments to the building society, they should be allowed to remain in possession. They were not purchasers because they never bound themselves to pay the instalments, but nevertheless they were in a position analogous to purchasers. They have acted on the promise and neither the father nor his widow, his successor in title, can eject them in disregard of it. The result is that, in my opinion, the appeal should be dismissed and no order for possession should be made. I come to this conclusion on a different ground from that reached by the learned judge, but it is always open to a respondent to support the judgment on any ground. If there is a dispute between the son and the daughter-in-law as to their respective rights in the house, that must be decided under s. 17 of the Married Women's Property Act, 1882. If the father's widow should cease to pay the rates, the actual occupier must pay them, because the father did not bind himself to pay them. He only did so out of paternal affection.

[The concurring opinions of Somervell and Hodson L.JJ. are omitted.]

DAWSON *v*. HELICOPTER EXPLORATION CO. LTD.

British Columbia. Supreme Court of Canada. [1955] 5 D.L.R. 404

Dawson, an American citizen, had been negotiating by mail with Kidd and Springer, in Vancouver, an arrangement to get at some mineral deposits at the head of Leduc River in British Columbia, in very rough country, which Dawson had discovered twenty years earlier. On January 13, 1951, Dawson wrote "A large mining company in Salt Lake is showing a definite interest. To protect my interest, it will be necessary for me to arrive at some definite arrangement soon." Springer replied on January 17, "I would be interested in making some arrangement next summer to finance you in staking claims for which we would give you an interest. I would suggest that we should pay for your time and expenses and carry you for a ten per cent non-assessable interest in the claims." Dawson replied on January 22. "Your proposition . . . appeals to me as being a fair one. . . ."

Thereafter Dawson was recalled to active duty in the United States Naval Reserve Engineering Corps, and sent to the Marshall Islands. Correspondence continued under rather difficult conditions, and on February 28 Dawson wrote, "As I informed you in a previous letter, your offer of a 10% non-assessable interest for relocating and finding these properties is acceptable to me, provided there is a definite arrangement to this effect in the near future." On March 5, Springer wrote, "I hereby agree that, if you take us in to the showings and we think they warrant staking, that we will stake the claims and give you a 10% non-assessable interest. The claims would be recorded in our name and we will have full discretion in dealing with them—you to get 10% of the vendor interest." Dawson replied on April 12, "If you will inform me, if and when you obtain a pilot for your copter, I will immediately take steps for a temporary release in order to be on hand." Dawson wrote again, on May 27, "Would like to know if your plans for further exploration work in the Unuk River area have become definite. . . . For me to get away from my present duties on a furlough it may be necessary for me to have several weeks notice."

On June 7, Springer wrote:

"Up to a little over a week ago it did not look as though we would be able to secure a pilot for our helicopter. However, we have a man now who we hope will be satisfactory.

"I was talking to Tom McQuillan, who is prospecting for us this year; he said he had been over your showings at the head of the Leduc River, and in his opinion it would be practically impossible to operate there, as the showings were in behind ice fields, which along with the extreme snow falls made it very doubtful if an economic operation could be carried on.

"We have also been delayed in getting away this year, due to pilot trouble, and have so much work lined up that I am doubtful whether we will have time to visit your showings, also I do not think we would be warranted in making the effort to get in there due to the unfavorable conditions. I must advise you therefore, not to depend on our making this trip, and suggest if you are still determined to go in, to make other arrangements."

Dawson did not reply. In 1952 he discovered that the Helicopter Company had made investigations and in 1953 arrangements were made for development by the company to which Springer had sold the claims in exchange for paid up stock. Dawson commenced this action in November, 1953, and his claim was dismissed by the trial Judge, who was affirmed by the British Columbia Court of Appeal.

RAND J.: . . . The substantial contention of the respondent is that any offer contained in the correspondence and in particular the letter of March 5th called for an acceptance not by promise but by performance of an act, the location of the claims by Dawson for the respondent. It is based upon the well-known conception which in its simplest form is illustrated by the case of a reward offered for some act to be done. To put it in other words, no intention was conveyed by Springer when he said "I hereby agree" that Dawson, if agreeable, should have replied "I hereby accept" or words to that effect: the offer called for and awaited only the act to be done and would remain revocable at any time until every element of that act had been completed.

The error in this reasoning is that such an offer contemplates acts to be performed by the person only to whom it is made and in respect of which the offeror remains passive, and that is not so here. What Dawson was to do was to proceed to the area with Springer or persons acting for him by means of the respondent's helicopter and to locate the showings. It was necessarily implied by Springer that he would participate in his own proposal. This involved his promise that he would do so, and that the answer to the proposal would be either a refusal or a promise on the part of Dawson to a like participation. The offer was unconditional but contemplated a performance subject to the condition that a pilot could be obtained by the respondent.

Dawson's answer of April 12th was, as I construe it, similarly an unqualified promissory acceptance, subject as to performance to his being able to obtain the necessary leave. It was the clear implication that Springer, controlling the means of making the trip, should fix the time and should notify Dawson accordingly. As the earlier letters show, Dawson was anxious to conclude some arrangement and if he could not make it with Springer he would seek it in other quarters.

Although in the circumstances, because the terms proposed involve such complementary action on the part of both parties as to put the implication beyond doubt, the precept is not required, this interpretation of the correspondence follows the tendency of Courts to treat offers as calling for bilateral rather than unilateral action when the language can be fairly so construed, in order that the transaction shall have such "business efficacy as both parties must have intended that at all events it should have": Bowen L.J. in *The "Moorcock"* (1889), 14 P.D. 64 at p. 68. In theory and as conceded by Mr. Guild, an offer in the unilateral sense can be revoked up to the last moment before complete performance. At such a consequence many Courts have balked; and it is in part that fact that has led to a promissory construction where that can be reasonably given. What is effectual is the real intention of both parties to close a business bargain on the strength of which they may, thereafter, plan their courses. . . .

ESTEY J.: . . . It is contended that the appellant's silence, after his receipt of the letter of June 7, 1951, until his interview in December, 1952, constitutes an abandonment of the contract. . . .

The letter of repudiation is dated June 7, 1951, and during the next month Kvale and McQuillan were taken into the area by helicopter. They were again taken into the area where, on August 2nd of that year, they staked a number of claims which were duly recorded. The record does not indicate when respondent changed its mind as indicated by Springer's remark to appellant at its office in December, 1952, but it is apparent that many of the difficulties emphasized in the letter of June 7th had either disappeared or been overcome by the following month. Upon this record it rather appears that the respondent concluded it could continue without assistance from the appellant and, therefore, wrote the letter of repudiation.

The respondent, in this letter of repudiation, set forth its reasons therefor which it would be difficult for the appellant, stationed as he was in the Marshall Islands, to effectively appraise. I do not think that under such circumstances as a conclusion adverse to the appellant can be drawn from his failure to further press the respondent at that time. Immediately upon his return in December, 1950, he "wrote to the Mining Recorder at Prince Rupert" and apparently continued his examination to ascertain what had, in fact, taken place. He visited the premises in June and July, 1950, and relocated the three claims which he had found in 1931. When he had ascertained, at least in part, what had taken place, he made his position known to the respondent in December of 1952. Moreover, while silence may be evidence of repudiation, its weight must depend upon the circumstances and here I do not think his silence, coupled with the steps he took immediately upon his return from the Marshall Islands, sufficiently supports a conclusion that he, at any time, intended to abandon his rights under the contract.

Upon receipt of the letter of repudiation dated June 7, 1951, the appellant might have accepted it and forthwith claimed damages. Since, however, he did not accept it, the contract remained in force and binding upon both parties. It, therefore, remained the duty of the respondent, having obtained a pilot, to take the appellant into the area in August or September. Not only did the respondent not do so, but, notwithstanding the terms of its letter of repudiation, it, in fact, took Kvale and McQuillan into the area where they staked claims on behalf of the respondent. This conduct constituted a breach of its contract.

The appeal should be allowed with costs throughout and the matter referred back to the Supreme Court of British Columbia to determine the damages.

[Kerwin C.J. dissented. Cartwright J. concurred with Estey J. and Fauteux J. concurred with Rand J.]

RESTATEMENT OF THE LAW OF CONTRACTS
American Law Institute. 1932

45. If an offer for a unilateral contract is made and part of the consideration requested in the offer is given or tendered by the offeree in response thereto, the offeror is bound by a contract, the duty of immediate performance of which is conditional on the full consideration being given or tendered within the time stated in the offer, or, if no time is stated therein, within a reasonable time.

4. Contracts Negotiated By Correspondence

Legal systems pretty well have to develop special rules for the negotiation of contracts where the parties are not dealing face to face. Two kinds of difficulties arise. One kind results from the time factors: while the letters or telegrams are being delivered the offeror or the offeree may wish to revoke. Should he be permitted to do so and if so under what conditions? This is obviously a question of vital concern to commerce. The other kind of difficulty arises from the fact that the terms of the offer are in writing and the meaning taken from the writing may not be what the writer intended.

It may be necessary to decide when a letter takes effect, that is, when it is regarded as beyond revocation, in a variety of situations. If the offeror wishes to revoke, should his revocation take effect on dispatch or receipt? This necessarily involves deciding when the offeree's acceptance is effective, on dispatch or receipt? Another problem arises when a letter of acceptance is materially delayed or fails altogether to arrive. Is the offeror to be bound when he just cannot know the fact? During this crucial period he may have to reject other deals more advantageous to him. When does liability attach? Suppose an offer to insure property against fire is accepted and the property is destroyed by fire after the letter of acceptance is posted and before it is received? Should the decision in one of these types of case govern all of them? Are the purposes sought always the same? What interests are worthy of protection here?

A rather special type of problem arises when the offeree wants to revoke his acceptance. Conceptually it might be argued that if the posting of the acceptance created a contract, telegraphing a revocation could only be regarded as an anticipatory breach of the contract. Yet if the revocation arrived before the acceptance, functional analysis might produce quite a different result. Similar difficulties can arise where the offeree rejects the offer, and later decides to accept. Again conceptual and functional analyses may produce different results.

An entirely different type of problem arises when the contracting parties live in different provinces or countries. In legal matters the law of Ontario is not the law of British Columbia or of any other province or state. Each provincial jurisdiction is as foreign to the other as, say, a state of the United States is to France. If Offeror lives in Toronto and Offeree lives in Montreal, and their contract is entered into by letters through the post, in case of dispute what law is to be applied, that of Ontario or Quebec? The courts usually apply the law of the province where the contract was made, if the parties have not themselves indicated otherwise. Where is a contract made? The courts usually answer this by asking where the letter of acceptance was dispatched or received, on the theory that the contract was made where the last act necessary for its creation took place. Whether this is a sound test need not concern us now, but it is important to know that the court is deciding not when a contract comes into existence, but where, and for a very special purpose.

See, on the problems of this section generally, Fuller, *Basic Contract Law*. pp. 181-6.

TINN *v*. HOFFMAN AND COMPANY

England. Exchequer Chamber. 1873. 29 L.T.R. 271

Tinn, a manufacturer of iron products, carried on an extended correspondence with Hoffman and Company, iron merchants, about the purchase of 800 tons of iron for which Hoffman wanted 69s. a ton. Tinn proposed to increase his order to 1200 tons if Hoffman would lower his price. On November 28, 1871, Hoffman wrote offering a "further 400 tons . . . at the same price we quoted you by ours of the 24th inst. . . . Kindly let us have your reply by return of post as to whether you accept our offers of together 1,200 tons. . . ." On the same day Tinn wrote, "You can enter me 800 tons on the terms and conditions named in your favour of the 24th inst., but I trust you will enter the other 400, making in all, 1,200 tons, referred to in my last, at 68s. per ton." The next day Hoffman wrote rejecting "your esteemed order for 1,200 tons . . . at a lower price than 69s., and even that offer we can only leave you on hand for reply by tomorrow before twelve o'clock." On December 1, Tinn wired, "Book other 400 tons pig iron for me, same terms and conditions as before." The views of two judges (only on the issue whether the letters of November 28 constituted a contract) are reproduced:

HONYMAN J. (dissenting): I am of opinion that the judgment of the court below was wrong, and that judgment ought to be entered for the plaintiff in respect of 800 tons. . . . On November 28th, the defendants wrote the following letter, on the construction of which I believe the difference of opinion among the members of the court mainly arises. [Reads letter of that date.] What is the meaning of that letter? It amounts to this: On November 24 we offered you 800 tons for delivery at 69s.: we now repeat to you that offer, and in addition to that we make a further offer of 400 tons more—that is, we renew the offer of November 24th, and we make you a further offer of 400 tons, provided you accept those offers, "by return of post." That does not mean exclusively a reply by letter by return of post, but you may reply by telegram or by verbal message, or by any means not later than a letter written and sent by return by post would reach us. If that is so, then comes the plaintiff's letter, written on the same day, November 28th, which crosses the defendant's letter of the same date, in which the plaintiffs said, "You can enter me 800 tons on the terms and conditions in your favor of the 24th inst., but I trust you will enter the other 400, making in all 1200 tons, referred to in my last, at 68s. per ton, ex ship Portishead." I cannot agree in the opinion said to have been expressed by my Brothers Piggott and Channell in the court below. As I understand, my Brother Piggott certainly says this is not a clean offer, or a clean acceptance, of 800 tons, but that it is 800 tons on the condition or hope that they would lower the price of the other 400 tons. I cannot accede to that view of the case. I assume that it plainly amounts to this, "I will take your 800 tons on the terms and conditions mentioned in the letter of the 24th inst., but I hope you will let me have the other lot at 68s. per ton; if you choose to do that, well and good." I cannot understand how it can be said that that is not an absolute acceptance of the 800 tons, supposing it was competent to the plaintiff to accept that quantity. In the court below it seems to have been treated as if the offer of November 28th was one offer of 1200. I do not think so. I think it is a repetition of the offer of 800 tons coupled with a further offer of 400 tons, and that it was competent to the plaintiff to accept one and not accept the other. My Brother Bramwell appears to have thought that it was not material to consider whether it was two separate offers of 400 tons and 800 tons, or an offer of 1200 tons, because in either view of the case, the plaintiff could not accept the one and reject the other. If it is to be construed as strictly one offer of 1200 tons, I can understand it, and then of course he could not accept the one and reject the other. But I do not think it is one offer of 1200 tons, nor two offers, one of 400, and the other of 800 tons, but that it is a repetition of the offer of 800 tons, with a further offer of further 400 tons. To say that he could not accept the 400 tons without the 800 tons seems, in my view of the matter, to throw no light on the question whether he might accept the 800 tons without the 400 tons. That being so, it being in my judgment a separate offer of 800 tons in addition, I should have thought, had the plaintiff's letter of the 28th been written on November 29th that nobody, but for the opinions which have been expressed here today, could have entertained a doubt that it would have been an acceptance. What, then is the effect when the two letters are written on the same day and crossed each other in the post? Does it make any difference? . . . I cannot see why the fact of the letters crossing each other should prevent their making a good contract. If I say I am willing to buy a man's house on certain terms, and he at the same moment says that he is willing to sell it, and these two letters are posted so that they are irrevocable with respect to the writers, why should that not constitute a good contract? The parties are *ad idem* at one and the same moment. On these grounds it appears to me that the judgment of the court below was wrong, and ought to be reversed. I speak with some hesitation in this case when I find that the opinion of the majority of my brothers is against me, and also when the question turns entirely on the construction of a somewhat ambiguously written letter.

BRETT J.: . . . If [the defendant's letter of November 28th] were a separate offer, which I should think it was not, it then would be a new offer with regard to 800 tons, and a separate offer with regard to 400 tons, but, even if it were so, I should think that the new offer with regard to the 800 tons had never been accepted, so as to make a binding contract. The new offer would not, in my opinion, be accepted, by the fact of the plaintiff's letter of November 28th crossing it. If the defendants' letter of November 28th is a new offer of the 800 tons, that could not be accepted by the plaintiff until it came to his knowledge, and his letter of November 28th could only be considered as a cross offer. Put it thus: If I write to a person and say, "If you can give me £6000 for my house, I will sell it to you," and on the same day, and before the letter reaches him, he writes to me saying, "If you will sell me your house for £6000 I will buy it," that would be two offers crossing each other, and cross offers are not an acceptance of each other, therefore there will be no offer of either party accepted by the other. That is the case where the contract is to be made by the letters, and by the letters only. I think it would be different if there were already a contract in fact made in words, and then the parties were to write letters to each other, which crossed in the post, those might make a very good memorandum of the contract already made, unless the Statute of Frauds intervened. But where the contract is to be made by the letters themselves, you cannot make it by cross offers, and say that the contract was made by one party accepting the offer which was made to him. It seems to me, therefore, in both views, that the judgment of the court below was right.

[The judgments of eight judges favoured the defendants, not always for the same reasons. Three judges dissented.]

NOTE. Is the debate over "cross offers" merely conceptual or is there a matter of substance involved? If, as it is sometimes said, especially in the older cases, the offeror is regarded as making his offer continually, then surely cross offers result in a "meeting of minds." Equally, the cross offer cannot be said to be an answer to the other offer. What then, is the issue of substance? Is there a good reason for holding no contract? If one offeror, expecting that he has twenty-four hours before delivery of his offer, receives a better proposal, should he not be free to revoke his offer by telegraph or telephone? Reconsider why offers are revokable.

ADAMS and Others *v.* LINDSELL and Another
England. King's Bench. 1818. 1 B. & Ald. 681; 106 E.R. 250

Action for non-delivery of wool according to agreement. At the trial at the last Lent Assizes for the county of Worcester, before Burrough J., it appeared that the defendants, who were dealers in wool at St. Ives, in the county of Huntingdon, had on Tuesday, the 2nd of September, 1817, written the following letter to the plaintiffs who were woollen manufacturers residing in Bromsgrove, Worcestershire: "We now offer you eight hundred tods of wether fleeces, of a good fair quality of our country wool, at 35s. 6d. per tod, to be delivered at Leicester, and to be paid for by two months' bill in two months, and to be weighed up by your agent within fourteen days, receiving your answer in course of post."

This letter was misdirected by the defendants to Bromsgrove, Leicestershire, in consequence of which it was not received by the plaintiffs in Worcestershire till 7 p.m. on Friday, September 5th. On that evening the plaintiffs wrote an answer, agreeing to accept the wool on the terms proposed. The course of the post between St. Ives and Bromsgrove is through London, and consequently this answer was not received by the defendants till Tuesday, September 9th. On the Monday, September 8th, the defendants not having, as they expected, received an answer on Sunday, September 7th (which, in case their letter had not been misdirected would have been in the usual course of the post), sold the wool in question to another person. Under these circumstances the learned Judge held that the delay having been occasioned by the neglect of the defendants, the jury must take it that the answer did come back in due course of post; and that then the defendants were liable for the loss that had been sustained: and the plaintiffs accordingly recovered a verdict.

Jervis having in Easter Term obtained a rule nisi for a new trial, on the ground that there was no binding contract between the parties.

Dauncy, Puller, and Richardson showed cause. They contended that, at the moment of the acceptance of the offer of the defendants by the plaintiffs, the former became bound. And that was on Friday evening, when there had been no change of circumstances. They were then stopped by the Court, who called upon Jervis and Campbell in support of the rule. They relied on *Payne* v. *Cave* (1789), 100 E.R. 502, and more particularly on *Cooke* v. *Oxley* (1790), 700 E.R. 785. So here the defendants who have proposed by letter to sell this wool, are not to be held liable, even though it be now admitted that the answer did come back in due course of post. Till the plaintiffs' answer was actually received, there could be no binding contract between the parties; and before then the defendants had retracted their offer by selling the wool to other persons.

But the Court said, that if that were so, no contract could ever be completed by the post. For if the defendants were not bound by their offer when accepted by the plaintiffs till the answer was received, then the plaintiffs ought not to be bound till after they had received the notification that the defendants had received their answer and assented to it. And so it might go on *ad infinitum*. The defendants must be considered in law as making, during every instant of the time their letter was travelling, the same identical offer to the plaintiffs; and then the contract is completed by the acceptance of it by the latter. Then as to the delay in notifying the acceptance, that arises entirely from the mistake of the defendants, and it therefore must be taken as against them that the plaintiffs' answer was received in the course of post.

Rule discharged.

QUESTIONS. Do you agree with the Court's "ad infinitum" argument? Because a sequence of events may appear to go on forever is that a sufficient reason for cutting off the sequence after the first event? Why not the second? Is there good reason for preferring the offeree's convenience to the offeror's?

HOUSEHOLD INSURANCE CO. *v.* GRANT

England. Court of Appeal. 1879. 4 Ex.D. 216

THESIGER L.J.: In this case the defendant made an application for shares in the plaintiffs' company under circumstances from which we must imply that he authorized the company, in the event of their allotting to him the shares applied for, to send the notice of allotment by post. The company did allot him the shares, and duly addressed to him and posted a letter containing the notice of allotment, but upon the finding of the jury it must be taken that the letter never reached its destination. In this state of circumstances Lopes J. has decided that the defendant is liable as a shareholder. He based his decision mainly upon the ground that the point for his consideration was covered by authority binding upon him, and I am of opinion that he did so rightly, and that it is covered by authority equally binding upon this Court.

The leading case upon the subject is *Dunlop* v. *Higgins* (1848), 9 E.R. 805. It is true that Lord Cottenham might have decided that case without deciding the point raised in this. But it appears to me equally true that he did not do so, and that he preferred to rest and did rest his judgment as to one of the matters of exception before him upon a principle which embraces and governs the present case. If so the Court is as much bound to apply that principle, constituting as it did a *ratio decidendi*, as it is to follow the exact decision itself. The exception was that the Lord Justice General directed the jury in point of law that, if the pursuers posted their acceptance of the offer in due time according to the usage of trade they were not responsible for any casualties in the post office establishment. This direction was wide enough in its terms to include the case of the acceptance never being delivered at all; and Lord Cottenham, in expressing his opinion that it was not open to objection, did so after putting the case of a letter containing a notice of dishonour posted by the holder of a bill of exchange in proper time, in which case he said, "Whether that letter be delivered or not is a matter quite immaterial, because for accidents happening at the post office he is not responsible." In short, Lord Cottenham appears to me to have held that, as a rule, a contract formed by correspondence through the post is complete as soon as the letter accepting an offer is put into the post, and is not put an end to in the event of the letter never being delivered. My view of the effect of *Dunlop* v. *Higgins* is that taken by James L.J., in *Harris' Case* (1872), 7 Ch. App. 587, where he speaks of the former case as "a case which is binding upon us, and in which every principle argued before us was discussed at length by the Lord Chancellor in giving judgment." He adds, the Lord Chancellor "arrived at the conclusion that the posting of the letter of acceptance is the completion of the contract; that is to say, the moment one man has made an offer, and the other has done something binding himself to that offer, then the contract is complete and neither party can afterwards escape from it."... Now, whatever in abstract discussion may be said as to the legal notion of its being necessary, in order to the effecting of a valid and binding contract, that the minds of the parties should be brought together at one and the same moment, that notion is practically the foundation of English law upon the subject of the formation of contract. Unless therefore a contract constituted by correspondence is absolutely concluded at the moment that the continuing offer is accepted by the person to whom the offer is addressed, it is difficult to see how the two minds are ever to be brought together at one and the same moment. This was pointed out by Lord Ellenborough in the case of *Adams* v. *Lindsell* (1818), 106 E.R. 250 which is recognized authority upon this branch of the law. But on the other hand it is a principle of law, as well established as the legal notion to which I have referred, that the minds of the two parties must be brought together by mutual communication. An acceptance, which only remains in the breast of the acceptor without being actually and by legal implication communicated to the offeror, is no binding acceptance.... How then are these elements of law to be harmonized in the case of contracts formed by correspondence through the post? I see no better mode than that of treating the post office as the agent of both parties. . . . But if the post office be such common agent, then it seems to me to follow that, as soon as the letter of acceptance is delivered to the post office, the contract is made as complete and as final and absolutely binding as if the acceptor had put his letter into the hands of a messenger sent by the offeror himself as his agent to deliver the offer and receive the acceptance. What other principle can be adopted short of holding that the contract is not complete by acceptance until and except from the time that the letter containing the acceptance is delivered to the offeror, a principle which has been distinctly negatived.... The acceptor, in posting the letter, has, to use the language of Lord Blackburn, in *Brogden* v. *Directors of Metropolitan Ry. Co.* (1877), 2 App. Cas. 666, 691, "put it out of his control and done an extraneous act which clenches the matter, and shows beyond all doubt that each side is bound." How then can a casualty in the post, whether resulting in delay, which in commercial transactions is often as bad as no delivery, or in non-delivery, unbind the parties or unmake the contract? To me it appears that in practice a contract complete upon the acceptance of an offer being posted, but liable to be put an end to by an accident in the post, would be more mischievous than a contract only binding upon the parties to it upon the acceptance actually reaching the offeror, and I can see no principle of law from which such an anomalous contract can be deduced.

There is no doubt that the implication of a complete, final, and absolutely binding contract being formed, as soon as the acceptance of an offer is posted, may in some cases lead to inconvenience and hardship. But such there must be at times in every view of the law. It is impossible in transactions which pass between parties at a distance, and have to be carried on through the medium of correspondence, to adjust conflicting rights between innocent parties, so as to make the consequences of mistake on the part of a mutual agent fall equally upon the shoulders of both. At the same time I am not prepared to admit that the implication in question will lead to any great or general inconvenience or hardship. An offeror, if he chooses, may always make the formation of the contract which he proposes dependent upon the actual communication to himself of the acceptance. If he trusts to the post he trusts to a means of communication which, as a rule, does not fail, and if no answer to his offer is received by him, and the matter is of importance to him he can make inquiries of the person to whom his offer was addressed. On the other hand, if the contract is not finally concluded, except in the event of acceptance actually reaching the offeror, the door would be opened to the perpetration of much fraud, and, putting aside this consideration, considerable delay in commercial transactions, in which despatch is, as a rule, of the greatest consequence, would be occasioned; for the acceptor would never be entirely safe in acting upon his acceptance until he had received notice that his letter of acceptance had reached its destination.

Upon balance of conveniences and inconveniences it seems to me, applying with slight alterations the language of the Supreme Court of the United States in *Tayloe* v. *Merchants Fire Insurance Co.* (1850), 9 Howard S. Ct. Rep. 390, more consistent with the acts and declarations of the parties in this case to consider the contract complete and absolutely binding on the transmission of the notice of allotment through the post, as the medium of communication that the parties themselves contemplated, instead of postponing its completion until the notice had been received by the defendant. Upon principle, therefore, as well as authority, I think that the judgment of Lopes J. was right and should be affirmed, and that this appeal should therefore be dismissed.

BRAMWELL L.J. (dissenting): The question in this case is not whether the post office was a proper medium of communication from the plaintiffs to the defendant. There is no doubt that it is so in all cases where personal service is not required. It is an ordinary mode of communication, and every person who gives any one the right to communicate with him, gives the right to communicate in an ordinary manner and so in this way and to this extent, that if an offer were made by letter in the morning to a person at a place within half-an-hour's railway journey of the offeror, I should say that an acceptance by post, though it did not reach the offeror till the next morning, would be in time. Nor is the question whether, when the letter reaches an offeror, the latter is bound and the bargain made from the time the letter is posted or despatched, whether by post or otherwise. The question in this case is different. I will presently state what in my judgment it is. Meanwhile I wish to mention some elementary propositions which, if carefully borne in mind, will assist in the determination of this case.

First. Where a proposition to enter into a contract is made and accepted, it is necessary, as a rule, to constitute the contract that there should be a communication of that acceptance to the proposer, per Brian C.J., and Lord Blackburn: *Brogden* v. *Metropolitan Ry. Co.*, 2 App. Cas. at p. 692.

Secondly. That the present case is one of proposal and acceptance.

Thirdly. That as a consequence of or involved in the first proposition, if the acceptance is written or verbal, i.e., is by letter or message, as a rule, it must reach the proposer or there is no communication, and so no acceptance of the offer.

Fourthly. That if there is a difference where the acceptance is by a letter sent through the post which does not reach the offeror, it must be by virtue of some general rule or some particular agreement of the parties. As for instance, there might be an agreement that the acceptance of the proposal may be sending the article offered by the proposer to be bought, or hanging out a flag or sign to be seen by the offeror as he goes by, or leaving a letter at a certain place, or any other agreed mode, and in the same way there might be an agreement that dropping a letter in a post pillar box or other place of reception should suffice.

Fifthly. That as there is no such special agreeement in this case, the defendant, if bound, must be bound by some general rule which makes a difference when the post office is employed as the means of communication.

Sixthly. That if there is any such general rule applicable to the communication of the acceptance of offers, it is equally applicable to all communications that may be made by post. Because, as I have said, the question is not whether this communication may be made by post. If, therefore, posting a letter which does not reach is a sufficient communication of acceptance of an offer, it is equally a communication of everything else which may be communicated by post, e.g., notice to quit. It is impossible to hold, if I offer my landlord to sell him some hay and he writes accepting my offer, and in the same letter gives me notice to quit, and posts his letter which, however, does not reach me, that he has communicated to me his acceptance of my offer, but not his notice to quit. Suppose a man has paid his tailor by cheque or banknote, and posts a letter containing a cheque or banknote to his tailor, which never reaches, is the tailor paid? If he is, would he be if he had never been paid before in that way? Suppose a man is in the habit of sending cheques and banknotes to his banker by post, and posts a letter containing cheques and banknotes, which never reaches. Is the banker liable? Would he be if this was the first instance of a remittance of the sort? In the cases I have supposed, the tailor and banker may have recognised this mode of remittance by sending back receipts and putting the money to the credit of the remitter. Are they liable with that? Are they liable without it? The question then is, is posting a letter which is never received a communication to the person addressed, or an equivalent, or something which dispenses with it? It is for those who say it is to make good their contention. I ask why is it? My answer beforehand to any argument that may be urged is, that it is not a communication, and that there is no agreement to take it as an equivalent for or to dispense with a communication. That those who affirm the contrary say the thing which is not. That if Brian C.J. had had to adjudicate on the case, he would deliver the same judgment as that reported. That because a man, who may send a communication by post or otherwise, sends it by post, he should bind the person addressed, though the communication never reaches him, while he would not so bind him if he had sent it by hand, it is impossible. There is no reason in it; it is simply arbitrary. I ask whether anyone who thinks so is prepared to follow that opinion to its consequence; suppose the offer is to sell a particular chattel, and the letter accepting it never arrives, is the property in the chattel transferred? Suppose it is to sell an estate or grant a lease, is the bargain completed? The lease might be such as not to require a deed, could a subsequent lessee be rejected by the would-be acceptor because he had posted a letter? Suppose an article is advertised at so much, and that it would be sent on receipt of a post office order. Is it enough to post the letter? If the word "receipt" is relied on, is it really meant that that makes a difference? If it should be said let the offeror wait, the answer is, maybe he may lose his market meanwhile. Besides, his offer may be advertisement to all mankind. Suppose a reward for information, information posted does not reach, somone else gives it and is paid, is the offeror liable to the first man?

It is said that a contrary rule would be hard on the would-be acceptor, who may have made his arrangements on the footing that the bargain was concluded. But to hold as contended would be equally hard on the offeror, who may have made his arrangements on the footing that his offer was not accepted; his non-receipt of any communication may be attributable to the person to whom it was made being absent. What is he to do but to act on the negative, that no communication has been made to him? Further, the use of the post office is no more authorized by the offeror than the sending an answer by hand, and all these hardships would befall the person posting the letter if he sent it by hand. Doubtless in that case he would be the person to suffer if the letter did not reach its destination. Why should his sending it by post relieve him of the loss and cast it on the other party? It was said, if he sends it by hand it is revocable, but not if he sends it by post, which makes the difference. But it is revocable when sent by post, not that the letter can be got back, but its arrival might be anticipated by a letter by hand or telegram, and there is no case to shew that such anticipation would not prevent the letter from binding. It would be a most alarming thing to say that it would. That a letter honestly but mistakenly written and posted must bind the writer if hours before its arrival he informed the person addressed that it was coming, but was wrong and recalled; suppose a false but honest character given, and the mistake found out after the letter posted, and notice that it was wrong given to the person addressed.

Then, as was asked, is the principle to be applied to telegrams? Further, it seems admitted that if the proposer said, "unless I hear from you by return of post the offer is withdrawn," that the letter accepting it must reach him to bind him. There is indeed a case recently reported in the Times before the Master of the Rolls, where the offer was to be accepted within fourteen days, and it is said to have been held that it was enough to post the letter on the 14th, though it would and did not reach the offeror till the 15th. Of course there may have been something in that case not mentioned in the report. But as it stands it comes to this, that if an offer is to be accepted in June, and there is a month's post between the places, posting the letter on the 30th of June will suffice, though it does not reach till the 31st of July; but that case does not affect this. There the letter reached, here it has not. If it is not admitted that "unless I hear by return the offer is withdrawn" makes the receipt of the letter a condition, It is to say an express condition goes for nought. If it is admitted, is it not what every letter says? Are there to be fine distinctions, such as, if the words are "unless I hear from you by return of post, &c., "it is necessary the letter should reach him, but "let me know by return of post," it is not; or if in that case it is, yet it is not where there is an offer without those words. Lord Blackburn says that Mellish L.J. accurately stated that where it is expressly or impliedly stated in the offer, "you may accept the offer by posting a letter," the moment you post this letter the offer is accepted. I agree; and the same thing is true of any other mode of acceptance offered with the offer and acted on—as firing a cannon, sending off a rocket, give your answer to my servant the bearer. Lord Blackburn was not dealing with the question before us; there was no doubt in the case before him that the letter had reached. . . .

I am of opinion that this judgment should be reversed. I am of opinion that there was no bargain between these parties to allot and take shares, that to make such bargain there should have been an acceptance of the defendant's offer and a communication to him of that acceptance. That there was no such communication. That posting a letter does not differ from other attempts at communication in any of its consequences, save that it is irrevocable as between the poster and post office. The difficulty has arisen from a mistake as to what was decided in *Dunlop* v. *Higgins*, and from supposing that because there is a right to have recourse to the post as a means of communication, that right is attended by some peculiar consequences, and also from supposing that because if the letter reaches it binds from the time of posting, it also binds though it never reaches. Mischief may arise if my opinion prevails. It probably will not, as so much has been said on the matter that principle is lost sight of. I believe equal if not greater, will, if it does not prevail. I believe the latter will be obviated only by the rule being made nugatory by every prudent man saying, "your answer by post is only to bind if it reaches me." But the question is not to be decided on these considerations. What is the law? What is the principle? If Brian C.J. had had to decide this a public post being instituted in his time, he would have said the law is the same, now there is a post, as it was before, viz., a communication to affect a man must be a communication, i.e., must reach him.

Judgment affirmed.

[The opinion of Baggallay L.J. who agreed with Thesiger L.J. is omitted.]

NOTE. The only "circumstances" from which Thesiger L.J. thought he must imply that the defendant had authorized the plaintiff Company to use the post would appear to be that the defendant *handed* to one Kendrick, the plaintiff Company's local agent, a written application for shares, which Kendrick duly forwarded, presumably by post, to his principals in London.

REIDPATH'S CASE. 1870. L.R. 11 Eq. 86. LORD ROMILLY M.R. held that "evidence of a letter being posted is not enough to fix" the offeror. The facts are materially similar to *Grant's* case.

HENTHORN *v.* FRASER

England. Court of Appeal. [1892] 2 Ch. 27

After two futile attempts by Henthorn to purchase property in Birkenhead from Fraser, the secretary of the Huskisson Benefit Building Society in Liverpool (the two cities are across the mouth of the Mersey River from each other), Fraser, on July 7th orally offered to sell it for £750 and handed Henthorn a written note stating "I hereby give you the refusal of the Flamank Street property at £750 for fourteen days." On July 8 Fraser agreed to sell the same property to someone else, subject to his being able to cancel if he could not cancel his offer to Henthorn. Fraser posted a letter to Henthorn about noon that day, but it was not delivered to Henthorn's address until five o'clock and Henthorn did not in fact have it until he returned home about eight o'clock. Meanwhile Henthorn's solicitor had posted a letter in Birkenhead at ten to four that afternoon accepting the offer. The letter of acceptance was delivered at eight thirty that evening and was received by Fraser the next morning. Fraser denied the contract and Henthorn sued for specific performance in the Court of the County Palatine. His action was dismissed and he appealed.

LORD HERSCHELL: . . . If the acceptance by the plaintiff of the defendant's offer is to be treated as complete at the time the letter containing it was posted, I can entertain no doubt that the society's attempted revocation of the offer was wholly ineffectual. I think that a person who has made an offer must be considered as continuously making it until he has brought to the knowledge of the person to whom it was made that it is withdrawn. . . . The grounds upon which it has been held that the acceptance of an offer is complete when it is posted have, I think, no application to the revocation or modification of an offer. These can be no more effectual than the offer itself, unless brought to the mind of the person to whom the offer is made. But it is contended on behalf of the defendants that the acceptance was complete only when received by them, and not on the letter being posted. It cannot, of course, be denied, after the decision in *Dunlop* v. *Higgins* (1848), 9 E.R. 805, in the House of Lords, that where an offer has been made through the medium of the post, the contract is complete as soon as the acceptance of the offer is posted, but that decision is said to be inapplicable here, inasmuch as the letter containing the offer was not sent by post to Birkenhead, but handed to the plaintiff in the defendant's office at Liverpool. The question therefore arises in what circumstances the acceptance of an offer is to be regarded as complete as soon as it is posted. In the case of the *Household Insurance Company* v. *Grant* (1879), 4 Ex.D. 216, Lord Justice Baggallay said: "I think that the principle established in *Dunlop* v. *Higgins* is limited in its application to cases in which by reason of general usage, or of relations between the parties to any particular transactions, or of the terms in which the offer is made, the acceptance of such offer by a letter through the post is expressly or impliedly authorized.". . . Applying the law [there] laid down by the Court of Appeal I think in the present case an authority to accept by post must be implied. Although the plaintiff received the offer at the defendant's office in Liverpool, he resided in another town, and it must have been in contemplation that he would take the offer, which by its terms was to remain open for some days with him to his place of residence, and those who made the offer must have known that it would be according to the ordinary usages of mankind that if he accepted it he should communicate his acceptance by means of the post. I am not sure that I should myself have regarded the doctrine that an acceptance is complete as soon as the letter containing it is posted as resting upon an implied authority by the person making the offer to the person receiving it to accept by those means. It strikes me as somewhat artificial to speak of the person to whom the offer is made as having the implied authority of the other party to send his acceptance by post. He needs no authority to transmit the acceptance through any particular channel; he may select what means he pleases, the post-office no less than any other. The only effect of the supposed authority is to make the acceptance complete so soon as it is posted, and authority will obviously be implied only when the tribunal considers that it is a case in which this result ought to be reached.

I should prefer to state the rule thus: Where the circumstances are such that it must have been within the contemplation of the parties that, according to the ordinary usages of mankind, the post might be used as a means of communicating the acceptance of an offer, the acceptance is complete as soon as it is posted. It matters not in which way the propositions be stated, the present case is in either view within it. The learned Vice-Chancellor appears to have based his decision to some extent on the fact that before the acceptance was posted the defendants had sold the property to another person. The case of *Dickinson* v. *Dodds* (1876), 2 Ch.D. 463, was relied upon in support of that defence. In that case, however, the plaintiff knew of the subsequent sale before he accepted the offer, which, in my judgment, distinguishes it entirely from the present case. For the reasons I have given I think the judgment must be reversed, and the usual decree for specific performance made. The respondents must pay the costs of the appeal and of the action.

[The judgments of Lindley and Kay L.JJ. to the same effect are omitted.]

DUNLOP *v*. HIGGINS. 1848. 1 H.L.C. 381; 9 E.R. 805 (Scotland. House of Lords). Dunlop, in Glasgow, wrote to Higgins in Liverpool, offering to sell 2,000 tons of pig iron. Higgins mailed an acceptance on January 30th but not by the first post of that day. The letter was erroneously dated January 31st, and did not reach Glasgow until February 1st due to a delay in the mails. If the acceptance had been mailed 31st January the court indicated it would have been too late, but under the circumstances held a valid contract was completed. Higgins was not answerable for casualties in the Post Office.

[Suppose that Dunlop on receiving the letter and observing the date "January 31st" had sold the goods to a third party? (Lord Cottenham stated it was impossible to hold an erroneous date precluded the making of a contract "whether it produces mischief to the other party or not.") What difference if on the morning of February 1st Dunlop, not having received a reply when he was entitled to expect it, i.e. January 31st, had sold the goods to a third party?]

BYRNE & CO. *v.* LEON VAN TIENHOVEN & CO.
England. Common Pleas Division. 1880. 5 C.P.D. 344

LINDLEY J.: This was an action for the recovery of damages for the non-delivery by the defendants to the plaintiffs of 1000 boxes of tin plates, pursuant to an alleged contract, which I will refer to presently. The action was tried at Cardiff before myself without a jury; and it was agreed at the trial that in the event of the plaintiffs being entitled to damages they should be £375.

The defendants carried on business at Cardiff and the plaintiffs at New York, and it takes ten or eleven days for a letter posted at either place to reach the other. The alleged contract consists of a letter written by the defendants to the plaintiffs on the 1st of October, 1879, and received by them on the 11th, and accepted by telegram and letter sent to the defendants on the 11th and 15th of October respectively. These letters and telegram were as follows: [On the 1st of October, 1879, the defendants wrote the plaintiffs offering them 1000 boxes of tin plates at 15s. 6d. per box. The plaintiffs on the 11th of October, 1879 cabled the defendants accepting this offer, and on the 15th of October wrote the defendants confirming their previous cable of acceptance. On the 8th of October however the defendants wrote a letter to the plaintiffs informing them that as there had been a big run on the tinplate market in the last few days causing prices to rise considerably, they withdrew their offer and considered it cancelled from this date.]

... There is no doubt that an offer can be withdrawn before it is accepted, and it is immaterial whether the offer is expressed to be open for acceptance for a given time or not. ... For the decision of the present case, however, it is necessary to consider two other questions, viz: 1. Whether a withdrawal of an offer has any effect until it is communicated to the person to whom the offer has been sent? 2. Whether posting a letter of withdrawal is a communication to the person to whom the letter is sent?

It is curious that neither of these questions appears to have been actually decided in this country. As regards the first question, I am aware that Pothier and some other writers of celebrity are of opinion that there can be no contract if an offer is withdrawn before it is accepted, although the withdrawal is not communicated to the person to whom the offer has been made. The reason for this opinion is that there is not in fact any such consent by both parties as is essential to constitute a contract between them. Against this view, however, it has been urged that a state of mind not notified cannot be regarded in dealings between man and man; and that an uncommunicated revocation is for all practical purposes and in point of law no revocation at all. This is the view taken in the United States: see *Tayloe*

v. *Merchants Fire Insurance Co.* (1850), 9 How. Sup. Ct. Rep. 390, cited in *Benjamin on Sales*, pp. 56–58, and it was adopted by Mr. Benjamin. The same view is taken by Mr. Pollock in his excellent work on *Principles of Contract*, 2nd ed., p. 10, and by Mr. Leake in his *Digest of the Law of Contracts*, p. 43. This view, moreover, appears to me much more in accordance with the general principles of English law than the view maintained by Pothier.

I pass, therefore, to the next question, viz., whether posting the letter of revocation was a sufficient communication of it to the plaintiff. The offer was posted on the 1st of October, the withdrawal was posted on the 8th, and did not reach the plaintiff until after he had posted his letter of the 11th, accepting the offer. It may be taken as now settled that where an offer is made and accepted by letters sent through the post, the contract is completed the moment the letter accepting the offer is posted: *Harris' Case* (1872), 7 Ch. App. 587; *Dunlop* v. *Higgins* (1848), 1 H.L.C. 381; 9 E.R. 805, even although it never reaches its destination. When, however, these authorities are looked at, it will be seen that they are based upon the principle that the writer of the offer has expressly or impliedly assented to treat an answer to him by a letter duly posted as a sufficient acceptance and notification to himself, or, in other words, he has made the post office his agent to receive the acceptance and notification of it. But this principle appears to me to be inapplicable to the case of the withdrawal of an offer. In this particular case I can find no evidence of any authority in fact given by the plaintiffs to the defendants to notify a withdrawal of their offer by merely posting a letter; and there is no legal principle or decision which compels me to hold, contrary to the fact, that the letter of the 8th of October is to be treated as communicated to the plaintiff on that day or any day before the 20th, when the letter reached them. But before that letter had reached the plaintiffs they had accepted the offer, both by telegram and by post; and they had themselves resold the tinplates at a profit. In my opinion the withdrawal of the defendants on the 8th of October of their offer of the 1st was inoperative and a complete contract binding on both parties was entered into on the 11th of October, when the plaintiff accepted the offer of the 1st, which they had no reason to suppose had been withdrawn. Before leaving this part of the case it may be as well to point out the extreme injustice and inconvenience which any other conclusion would produce. If the defendants' contention were to prevail no person who had received an offer by post and had accepted it would know his position until he had waited such a time as to be quite sure that a letter withdrawing the offer had not been posted before his acceptance of it. It appears to me that both legal principles, and practical convenience require that a person who has accepted an offer not known to him to have been revoked, shall be in a position safely to act upon the footing that the offer and acceptance constitute a contract binding on both parties.

[The facts have been considerably abbreviated, and only that part of the case is given which deals with revocation of the offer.]

QUESTION. Is this case authority for the proposition that an acceptance by telegram takes effect upon dispatch?

CHARLEBOIS *v.* BARIL

Quebec. Supreme Court of Canada. [1928] S.C.R. 88

On August 14, 1924, the defendant handed a written offer to purchase certain property to the plaintiff's representative for delivery. On August

25 the plaintiff wrote a letter of acceptance addressed to the defendant and gave it to his son to post. It was posted the same day. The defendant denied receipt of the letter. The Courts below, doubtless relying on *Magann* v. *Auger* (1901), 31 S.C.R. 186, made no finding on the question of receipt by the defendant. He denied liability and the action was commenced to compel performance.

ANGLIN C.J.C. delivered the judgment of the Court: . . . The Courts below . . . regarded the judgment of this Court in *Magann* v. *Auger* as determining that the mailing of the plaintiff's letter of acceptance to the defendant constituted communication of it to him. With great respect this is an erroneous view of the scope and effect of the decision of this court. That case was one of contract by correspondence, i.e., the offer was sent by mail and that was held to constitute a nomination by the sender of the post office as his agent to receive the acceptance for carriage to him. The civil law of Quebec was held to be the same in this regard as the law of England. But this decision has no application to a case where the offer is communicated, as here, not by mail, but by another means. To make a contract the law requires communication of offer and acceptance alike either to the person for whom each is respectively intended, or to his authorized agent.

Here there was nothing to constitute the post office the defendant's agent and a finding of actual receipt by him of the plaintiff's acceptance was, therefore, essential. The burden of procuring such a finding was upon the plaintiff. Without it he cannot succeed. . . .

[A new trial was ordered because the Supreme Court of Canada was not in a position to pass on the now relevant issue of fact.]

NOTES AND QUESTIONS. Magann v. *Auger* was a case of a contract wholly negotiated by post, the offer having been mailed at Quebec, the letter of acceptance at Toronto, and the court talked about negotiations carried on by correspondence. Apparently the court in *Charlebois* v. *Baril* felt it should distinguish between "correspondence" consisting of letters posted and "correspondence" consisting of a letter handed over to the offeree's agent and a letter posted in reply. Is this distinction true in English law? Is *Charlebois* v. *Baril* a decision on the common law of Canada? If so, can it be assumed that the Supreme Court intended to "overrule" *Henthorn* v. *Fraser*? Is it open to the "new" Supreme Court to reconsider the matter?

UNDERWOOD & SON, LTD. *v.* MAGUIRE. 1895. Q.R. 6 Q.B. 237 (Quebec. Queen's Bench on appeal from the Superior Court). Underwood represented the plaintiff company in Canada and negotiated with Maguire in Quebec for 200 tons of hay for delivery in England. An agreement was reached and Maguire wrote Underwood in Kingston, Ontario confirming it. Underwood replied questioning the mode of payment and Maguire wrote again, this time to Toronto, repeating his original view of the transaction. Underwood posted a letter in Toronto accepting this arrangement. On the same day Maguire wrote to Underwood withdrawing his offer because his hay had been sold in Liverpool by his agents by mistake. Held, for Maguire. WURTELE J.: ". . . when parties carry on their negotiations by correspondence, it is only when the letter containing the acceptance has reached the party who made the offer and that such party has had communication of it that the contract is formed, and that the power to retract the offer has ceased to exist." French authors cited. The argument that once a letter of acceptance was posted it belonged to the addressee was rejected because "the acceptance contained in it remains nevertheless unknown to the proposer until it really comes into his hands." Two judges dissented. [It is not clear from the report whether Maguire or Underwood received the other's letter first. If Maguire had received Underwood's acceptance first would he have lost his power to revoke? In *Magann* v. *Auger* (1901), 31 S.C.R. 186, this case was effectively overruled by the Supreme Court of Canada. That Court rejected the French authors cited by Wurtele J. which they conceded to be in the majority, and preferred others who "completely refute the reasoning upon which the contrary doctrine is based." What is the effect of *Charlebois* v. *Baril* on *Magann* v. *Auger* and *Underwood* v. *Maguire*? Does it restore in part the French civil law Wurtele J. considered that he was applying?]

POST OFFICE ACT

Canada. Revised Statutes. 1952. Chapter 212

39. Subject to the provisions of this Act and the regulations respecting undeliverable mail, mailable matter becomes the property of the person to whom it is addressed when it is deposited in a post office.

[By section 2(1) (i) "post office" includes a "post box".]

NOTE. The unsuccessful argument of the *Post Office Act* in *Underwood* v. *Maguire* was repeated in *Magann* v. *Auger*, but Taschereau J. speaking for the Court does not mention it.

MILINKOVICH *v.* CANADIAN MERCANTILE INSURANCE CO. 1960. 25 D.L.R. (2d) 481 (Quebec. Supreme Court of Canada). Milinkovich had insured his house and furniture in Arntfield, Quebec, with Canadian Mercantile for $8,000 and $2,000 respectively. In February, 1952, the house and furniture were totally destroyed by fire, the loss being estimated at $43,220.45. One Callaghan, an adjuster, visited the premises and confirmed the loss a few days later. Milinkovich signed a declaration for the adjuster and asked what he had to do next. He was told, "Just wait, the company will let you know." Milinkovich then moved to Niagara Falls, Ontario, where in March he was interviewed by another adjuster, who also had him sign a declaration. In April Milinkovich consulted Mr. LaMarsh, a lawyer in Niagara Falls, who wrote the company and in reply received a letter from Callaghan dated April 14 enclosing a Proof of Loss form and saying, "Kindly have Mr. Milinkovich complete and sign this form and return to us and we will forward it to his insurers for their consideration." Mr. LaMarsh personally mailed the letter containing the completed form correctly addressed to Callaghan. Nothing further was heard from Canadian Mercantile or Callaghan, and in December a Montreal lawyer "charged with looking after the insured's interest" commenced this action for $10,000. The sole defence was that action was premature in that the insurer had not received the Proof of Loss form. Held, for Milinkovich. The Supreme Court of Canada discussed *Magann* v. *Auger* and *Charlebois* v. *Baril* and quoted Lord Hershell in *Henthorn* v. *Fraser*. FAUTEUX J.: "In accordance with the law regulating the contract of insurance between the parties, the insurer had the right to require *delivery* of the proofs of loss. This position it could modify, or authorize an agent named by it to do so. And this is what, in my opinion, actually occurred. Mr. LaMarsh did not have to question the authority and the sole discretion which in his letter of 14th April, Callaghan informed him he had received from the company. In the execution of this authority and the exercise of this discretion, Callaghan virtually invited Mr. LaMarsh by his letter to return the forms to him by post, a service of which he himself made use to send them to him. Mr. LaMarsh's obligation ceased there, and he fulfilled this obligation. . . .

"Undoubtedly the point here is not the making of a contract, but of a modification, suggested and accepted, in the conditions of its execution. Evaluated against the background of all the circumstances peculiar to this case, Callaghan's letter to Mr. LaMarsh made it only reasonable for the latter to assume that the insurer was satisfied the proofs of loss would be entrusted to the postal service on which he had relied completely to obtain delivery of them. The silence and inaction of the respondent company and of its employee, both clearly notified by the lawyer of the insured's intention to ask for the execution of the contract, as also the nature of the sole argument pleaded in defence to the action, are, in the case with which we are concerned, incompatible with the good faith which should be present in the execution of this contract of insurance. . . ."

SMITH & OSBERG LTD. *v*. HOLLENBECK
British Columbia. Supreme Court. 1938. 53 B.C.R. 296

On July 13, 1938, Hollenbeck handed Smith & Osberg Ltd. in Vancouver an option for thirty days to purchase shares in a company. On August 12 Smith & Osberg Ltd. wired Hollenbeck in Seaside, Oregon, from Vancouver, accepting the offer. There was no evidence that Hollenbeck ever received the telegram. McDonald J. gave leave to issue a writ out of the jurisdiction and Hollenbeck applied to have the order discharged.

MANSON J.: . . . In *Charlebois* v. *Baril*, [1928] S.C.R. 88, it was held in the Supreme Court of Canada that where an acceptance of a contract is made by mail, the post office only becomes the agent of the offeror where the offer was originally sent by mail but not where the offer was communicated in some other way. In the latter case an acceptor by mail who desires to enforce the contract must prove actual receipt of the letter of acceptance by the offeror.

I have not been referred to any authority which lays down that the telegraph office becomes the agent of the offeror unless the offer has been made by telegram and an acceptance by telegram thereby impliedly authorized or unless the circumstances are such as to warrant the conclusion that an acceptance by telegram was impliedly authorized as in [*Bruner* v. *Moore*, [1904] 1 Ch. 305]. It is quite true that it is common practice in business to use the telegraph service for the purpose of carrying on business negotiations, but I am not prepared to hold that the practice has been so thoroughly established as to warrant me in finding that the offeror in the circumstances of the case at Bar had constituted the telegraph office his agent for the purpose of receiving an acceptance. *Cowan* v. *O'Connor* (1888), 20 Q.B.D. 640, to which counsel for the plaintiff refers is not inconsistent with the conclusion at which I have arrived.

Had it been established that the defendant received the plaintiff's telegram, the acceptance would have been effective on its receipt and the contract would have been one concluded out of the jurisdiction. . . .

[The order was discharged and the writ set aside.]

CAROW TOWING CO. *v*. The "ED McWILLIAMS"
Canada. Exchequer Court. 1919. 46 D.L.R. 506

Action for towage. The plaintiffs carry on business at Cheboygan, Mich., U.S.A. Negotiations were begun by wire from the ship owners at Sault Ste. Marie, Ont., to Cheboygan, Mich., and a return wire to Sault Ste. Marie. No contract was formed by the telegrams. Subsequently the plaintiff telephoned from Cheboygan to Captain Climie at Sault Ste. Marie, and the parties concluded the contract over the telephone.

A question of jurisdiction arose, in which it became necessary to determine the place where the contract was made.

HODGINS L.J.A.: . . . I think the contract was one made in Ontario, for, when Captain Climie went to his telephone, he then and there received an offer, or discussed terms, which, when accepted, formed the contract. In other words, the plaintiffs at Cheboygan, Mich., by using the long distance telephone, were able to reach Captain Climie in Ontario, just as if they telegraphed to him and he had received the telegram at the Soo. His reply at the telephone is of the same effect as if he had posted a letter or sent off a telegram from an office in Ontario. . . .

MELADY *v*. JENKINS STEAMSHIP CO. 1909. 18 O.L.R. 251 (Ontario. MAGEE: ". . . in *Cowan* v. *O'Connor* (1888), 20 Q.B.D. 640, it was held that the telegraph was a mere means of communication, as if one were speaking to the other, and that a telegram sent from within the city of London accepting an order by telegraph from outside the city completed the contract within the city and gave jurisdiction to the mayor's court. On the same principle this contract, if any, was made in Toronto. . . ." [Can this be based on any "common agency" theory? Must the offeree use the same telegraph company the offeror used? In England the Post Office Department operates the telegraph service. Note that in the principal case and in *Melady* and *Cowan* the question was, *where* was the contract made? Should the questions *when* and *where* be answered by the same tests?]

ENTORES, LTD. *v*. MILES FAR EAST CORPORATION. [1955] 2 All E.R. 493 (England. Court of Appeal). An offer by a London company was accepted by agents of an American corporation in Amsterdam, by means of "Telex," a service set up by the Post Office by which the typewritten message in Holland could be read in London a minute or so later. To establish jurisdiction, it had to be shown that the contract was made in England. DENNING L.J.: "The problem can only be solved by going in stages. Let me first consider a case where two people make a contract by word of mouth in the presence of one another. Suppose, for instance, that I shout an offer to a man across a river or a courtyard but I do not hear his reply because it is drowned by an aircraft flying overhead. There is no contract at that moment. If he wishes to make a contract, he must wait till the aircraft is gone and then shout back his acceptance so that I can hear what he says. Not until I have his answer am I bound. . . .

Now take a case where two people make a contract by telephone. Suppose, for instance, that I make an offer to a man by telephone and, in the middle of his reply, the line goes "dead" so that I do not hear his words of acceptance. There is no contract at that moment. The other man may not know the precise moment when the line failed. But he will know that the telephone conversation was abruptly broken off, because people usually say something to signify the end of the conversation. If he wishes to make a contract, he must therefore get through again so as to make sure that I heard. Supose next that the line does not go dead, but it is nevertheless so indistinct that I do not catch what he says and I ask him to repeat it. He then repeats it and I hear his acceptance. The contract is made, not on the first time when I do not hear, but only the second time when I do hear. If he does not repeat it, there is no contract. The contract is only complete when I have his answer accepting the offer.

Lastly take the Telex. Suppose a clerk in a London office taps out on the teleprinter an offer which is immediately recorded on a teleprinter in a Manchester office, and a clerk at that end taps out an acceptance. If the line goes dead in the middle of the sentence of acceptance, the teleprinter motor will stop. There is then obviously no contract. The clerk at Manchester must get through again and send his complete sentence. But it may happen that the line does not go dead, yet the message does not get through to London. Thus the clerk at Manchester may tap out his message of acceptance and it will not be recorded in London because the ink at the London end fails or something of that kind. In that case the Manchester clerk will not know of the failure but the London clerk will know of it and will immediately send back a message "not receiving". Then, when the fault is rectified, the Manchester clerk will repeat his message. Only then is there a contract. If he does not repeat it, there is no contract. It is not until his message is received that the contract is complete.

In all the instances I have taken so far, the man who sends the message of acceptance knows that it has not been received or he has reason to know it. So he must repeat it. But suppose that he does not know that his message did not get home. He thinks it has. This may happen if the listener on the telephone does not catch the words of acceptance, but neverheless does not trouble to ask for them to be repeated: or if the ink on the teleprinter fails at the receiving end, but the clerk does not ask for the message to be repeated: so that the man who sends an acceptance reasonably believes that his message has been received. The offeror in such circumstances is clearly bound, because he will be estopped from saying that he did not receive the message of acceptance. It is his own fault that he did not get it. But if there should be a case where the offeror without any fault on his part does not receive the message of acceptance—yet the sender of it reasonably believes it has got home when it has not—then I think there is no contract.

My conclusion is that the rule about instantaneous communications between the parties is different from the rule about the post. The contract is only complete when the acceptance is received by the offeror: and the contract is made at the place where the acceptance is received."

RESTATEMENT OF THE LAW OF CONTRACTS
American Law Institute. 1932

64. An acceptance may be transmitted by any means which the offeror has authorized the offeree to use and, if so transmitted, is operative and completes the contract as soon as put out of the offeree's possession, without regard to whether it ever reaches the offeror, unless the offer otherwise provides.

65. Acceptance given by telephone is governed by the principles applicable to oral acceptances where the parties are in the presence of each other.

66. An acceptance is authorized to be sent by the means used by the

offeror or customary similar transactions at the time when and the place where the offer is received, unless the terms of the offer or surroundings circumstances known to the offeree otherwise indicate.

Comment: A method of acceptance may be customary, although it differs from the method adopted by the offeror. Thus, under some circumstances acceptance by telegraph may be customary, although the offer is by mail. Under other circumstances the contrary may be true.

[Is section 65 intended to deal with the problem *where* the contract is entered into?]

QUESTIONS. Wally Waffle carried on a lumber business in Halifax, Nova Scotia, and received an offer from Peter Pratt in Vancouver, British Columbia on Monday for the sale of Douglas Fir at a bargain price. Pratt's offer concluded, "Please reply by return mail." Waffle wrote Pratt Monday afternoon by surface mail accepting the offer. The course of post is four days. Tuesday morning Waffle wrote to Pratt by air mail saying, "Disregard letter of yesterday, your price is too high." Air mail from Halifax to Vancouver is, say, twenty-four hours. Tuesday afternoon Waffle, having found that his buyer had repudiated his promise just after he had sent his wire, telephoned Pratt to disregard all communications, he, Waffle, was rejecting the offer. Is there a contract? See a note in 8 *Can. Bar Rev.* 615 (1930) reviewing the authorities and concluding, "If a letter of acceptance has once been posted, a telegram revoking such acceptance is inoperative though it reaches the offer long before the letter arrives. . . . It is settled law that the contract is complete in cases of contracts by correspondence, at the moment of posting the acceptance. There is no reason for creating an exception to this rule. What really matters in commercial transactions is to have a definite settled rule (whatever it may be) and not to render it obscure by engrafting upon it a multiplicity of ultra-refined exceptions." Do you agree? How many exceptions would be necessary to put both Waffle and Pratt in an equally protected position?

SWISS FEDERAL CODE OF OBLIGATIONS

3. Where a person offers to another to enter into a contract and fixes a time limit for acceptance of the offer, the person is bound by his offer until the expiration of the time limit.

He is only released if he does not, before the expiration of the time limit, receive from the other party notice of acceptance.

7. The offeror is not bound where he adds to the offer a declaration declining liability, or where such a reservation results from the nature of the transaction or the circumstances. . . .

10. A contract entered into by absent parties takes effect at the time of the despatch of the acceptance.

ELIASON *v.* HENSHAW

United States. Supreme Court. 1819. 4 Wheaton 225

WASHINGTON J. delivered the opinion of the Court: . . . It is an undeniable principle of the law of contracts, that an offer of a bargain by one person to another imposes no obligation upon the former, until it is accepted by the latter according to the terms in which the offer was made. Any qualification of or departure from those terms invalidates the offer, unless the same be agreed to by the person who made it. Until the terms of the agreement have received the assent of both parties, the negotiation is open, and imposes no obligation upon either.

In this case, the plaintiffs in error offered to purchase from the defendant two or three hundred barrels of flour, to be delivered at Georgetown by the first water, and to pay for the same $9.50 per barrel. To the letter containing this offer they required an answer by the return of the wagon by which the letter was despatched. This wagon was at that time in the service of the defendant, and employed by him in hauling flour from his mill to Harper's Ferry, near to which place the plaintiffs then were. The meaning of the writers was obvious. They could easily calculate, by the usual length of time which was employed by this wagon in travelling from Harper's Ferry to Mill Creek, and back again with a load of flour, about what time they should receive the desired answer; and, therefore, it was entirely unimportant whether it was sent by that or another wagon, or in any other manner, provided it was sent to Harper's Ferry, and was not delayed beyond the time which was ordinarily employed by wagons engaged in hauling flour from the defendant's mill to Harper's Ferry. Whatever uncertainty there might have been as to the time when the answer would be received, there was none as to the place to which it was to be sent; this was distinctly indicated by the mode pointed out for the conveyance of the answer. The place, therefore, to which the answer was to be sent constituted an essential part of the plaintiff's offer.

It appears, however, from the bill of exceptions, that no answer to this letter was at any time sent to the plaintiffs at Harper's Ferry. Their offer, it is true, was accepted by the terms of a letter addressed Georgetown, and received by the plaintiffs at that place; but an acceptance communicated at a place different from that pointed out by the plaintiffs, and forming a part of their proposal, imposed no obligation binding upon them, unless they had acquiesced in it, which they declined doing.

It is no argument that an answer was received at Georgetown; the plaintiffs in error had a right to dictate the terms upon which they would purchase the flour; and, unless they were complied with, they were not bound by them. All their arrangements may have been made with a view to the circumstances of place, and they were the only judges of its importance. There was, therefore, no contract concluded between these parties; and the Court ought, therefore, to have given the instruction to the jury which was asked for. [Judgment reversed.]

NOTES AND QUESTIONS. If the offeree had personally met the offeror at Georgetown the day after receiving the offer and had handed him an acceptance, would there have been an acceptance? The defendant's letter was written on the 14th and dispatched on the first mail thereafter, on the 19th. The plaintiff acknowledged receipt on the 25th, all in the same month. Why does the Court practically disregard the delay?

If an acceptance is late, or does not comply with some stipulated condition, how can it be "acquiesced" in?

A writes to B making him an offer, calling for a reply "by return mail." B mails a letter of acceptance three days after receipt of the offer. When A receives B's letter he commences getting the goods together. B then wires "I will not take the goods." Result?

HYDE *v.* WRENCH

England. Chancery. 1840. 3 Beav. 334; 49 E.R. 132

LORD LANGDALE M.R.: Under the circumstances stated in this bill, I think there exists no valid binding contract between the parties for the purchase of the property. The defendant offered to sell it for £1,000, and if that had been at once unconditionally accepted, there would undoubtedly have been a perfect binding contract; instead of that, the plaintiff made an offer of his own to purchase the property for £950, and he thereby rejected the offer previously made by the defendant. I think that it was not afterwards competent for him to revive the proposal of the defendant, by tendering an acceptance of it; and that therefore there exists no obligation of any sort between the parties; the demurrer must be allowed.

NOTE. Must a counter-offer of necessity reject a previous offer? Compare the following suggested by Oliphant, "The Duration and Termination of an Offer" (1920), 18 *Mich. L. Rev.* 201: "Suppose, in reply to an offer by A, B writes, 'I shall want to consider your offer for more of the time which you have allowed me for that purpose because I am so situated now that I cannot return an immediate answer. However, the situation is such that if you want to settle the matter at once, I will close with you now at 5% less than the price you name.' "

See also the following suggested in the same article: "Suppose the offerer says when making the offer, 'I expect you to reject this offer upon first consideration, but I want you to consider it further because I think you will accept when you have thought about it a while.' The offeree immediately sends a rejection which this offerer ignores. On further thought, the offeree sends an acceptance." Is the offeror bound?

Does a letter rejecting the offer, or a letter containing a counter offer take effect on the mailing or on receipt?

Suppose A in answer to an offer mails an outright rejection. An hour later he mails an acceptance. What is the result?

If rejection is valid when mailed, suppose it were lost or delayed, but the letter of acceptance arrived first?

If rejection were valid only when received, suppose the offeror on receipt of the rejection re-sold the goods offered?

Would the fact that the rejection was contained in a counter-offer only, affect your argument?

RESTATEMENT OF THE LAW OF CONTRACTS

American Law Institute. 1932

39. Rejection by mail or telegram does not destroy the power of acceptance until received by the offeror, but limits the power so that a letter or telegram of acceptance started after the sending of the rejection is only a counter-offer unless the acceptance is received by the offeror before he receives the rejection.

STEVENSON, JACQUES & CO. *v.* McLEAN

England. Queen's Bench Division. 1880. 5 Q.B.D. 346

Action for non-delivery of a quantity of iron which it was alleged the defendant contracted to sell to the plaintiffs at 40s. per ton, net cash.

The plaintiff and defendant had been negotiating some time, and on the

27th September, the defendant wrote the plaintiff the following letter: "Mr. Fossick's clerk showed me a telegram from him yesterday mentioning 39s. for No. 3 as present price, 40s. for forward delivery. I instructed the clerk to wire you that I would now sell for 40s., net cash, open till Monday."

The plaintiff thus had on the 28th (Sunday) this letter. It was admitted that "open till Monday," meant that the defendant would hold it open all Monday.

On the Monday morning, at 9.42, the plaintiffs telegraphed to the defendant: "Please wire whether you would accept forty for delivery over two months, or if not, longest limit you would give."

This telegram was received at the office at Moorgate at 10 a.m., and was delivered at the defendant's office in the Old Jewry shortly afterwards.

No answer to this telegram was sent by the defendant, but after its receipt he sold the warrants, through Fossick, for 40s., net cash, and at 1.25 sent off a telegram to the plaintiffs: "Have sold all my warrants here for forty net to-day,"

This telegram reached Middlesborough at 1.46, and was delivered in due course.

Before its arrival at Middlesborough, however, and at 1.34, the plaintiffs telegraphed to defendant: "Have secured your price for payment next Monday—write you fully by post."

By the usage of the iron market at Middlesborough, contracts made on Monday for cash are payable on the following Monday.

At 2.06 on the same day after receipt of the defendant's telegram announcing the sale through Fossick, the plaintiffs telegraphed: "Have your telegram following our advice to you of sale, per your instructions, which we cannot revoke, but rely upon your carrying out."

The defendant replied: "Your two telegrams received, but your sale was too late; your sale was not per my instructions."

And to this the plaintiffs rejoined: "Have sold your warrants on terms stated in your letter of twenty-seventh."

The iron was sold by plaintiffs to one Walker at 41s. 6d., and the contract note was signed before 1 o'clock on Monday. The price of iron rapidly rose and the plaintiffs had to buy in fulfilment of their contract at a considerable advance on 40s.

LUSH J.: . . . The only question of fact raised at the trial was, whether the relation between the parties was that of principal and agent, or that of buyer and seller. The jury found it was that of buyer and seller, and no objection has been taken to this finding.

Two objections were relied on by the defendant: first, it was contended that the telegram sent by the plaintiffs on the Monday morning was a rejection of the defendant's offer and a new proposal on the plaintiffs' part, and that the defendant had therefore a right to regard it as putting an end to the original negotiation.

Looking at the form of the telegram, the time when it was sent, and the state of the iron market, I cannot think this is its fair meaning. The plaintiff Stevenson said he meant it only as an inquiry, expecting an answer for his guidance, and this, I think is the sense in which the defendant ought to have regarded it.

It is apparent throughout the correspondence, that the plaintiffs did not contemplate buying the iron on speculation, but that the acceptance of the defendant's offer depended on their finding some one to take the warrants off their hands. All parties knew that the market was in an unsettled state, and that no one could predict at the early hour when the telegram was sent how the prices would range during the day. It was reasonable that, under these circumstances, they should desire to know before business began whether they were to be at liberty in case of need to make any and what concession as to the time or times of delivery, which would be the time or times of payment, or whether the defendant was determined to adhere to the terms of his letter; and it was highly unreasonable that the plaintiffs should have intended to close the negotiation while it was uncertain whether they could find a buyer or not, having the whole of the business hours of the day to look for one. Then again, the form of the telegram is one of inquiry. It is not "offer forty for delivery over two months," which would have likened the case to *Hyde* v. *Wrench* (1840), 49 E.R. 132. . . . Here there is no counter proposal. The words are,"Please wire whether you would accept forty for delivery over two months, or, if not, the longest limit you would give." There is nothing specific by way of offer or rejection, but a mere inquiry, which should have been answered and not treated as a rejection of the offer. This ground of objection therefore fails.

The remaining objection was one founded on a well-known passage in Pothier, which has been supposed to have been sanctioned by the Court of Queen's Bench in *Cooke* v. *Oxley* (1790), 100 E.R. 785, that in order to constitute a contract there must be the assent or concurrence of the two minds at the moment when the offer is accepted; and that if, when an offer is made, and time is given to the other party to determine whether he will accept or reject it, the proposer changes his mind before the time arrives, although no notice of the withdrawal has been given to the other party, the option of accepting it is gone. The case of *Cooke* v. *Oxley*, does not appear to me to warrant the inference which has been drawn from it, or the supposition that the judges ever intended to lay down such a doctrine. . . .

All that the judgment affirms is, that a party who gives time to another to accept or reject a proposal is not bound to wait till the time expires. And this is perfectly consistent with legal principles and with subsequent authorities, which have been supposed to conflict with *Cooke* v. *Oxley*. It is clear that a unilateral promise is not binding, and that if the person who makes an offer revokes it before it has been accepted, which he is at liberty to do, the negotiation is at an end; see *Routledge* v. *Grant*, 4 Bing. 653. But in the absence of an intermediate revocation, a party who makes a proposal by letter to another is considered as repeating the offer every instant of time till the letter has reached its destination and the correspondent has had a reasonable time to answer it: . . . "Common sense tell us," said Lord Cottenham, in *Dunlop* v. *Higgins* (1848), 9 E.R. 805, "that transactions cannot go on without such a rule." It cannot make any difference whether the negotiation is carried on by post, or by telegraph, or by oral message. If the offer is not retracted, it is in force as a continuing offer till the time for accepting or rejecting it has arrived. But if it is retracted, there is an end of the proposal. *Cooke* v. *Oxley*, if decided the other way, would have negatived the right of the proposing party to revoke his offer.

Taking this to be the effect of the decision in *Cooke* v. *Oxley*, the doctrine of Pothier before adverted to, which is undoubtedly contrary to the spirit of English law, has never been affirmed in our Courts. Singularly enough, the very reasonable proposition that a revocation is nothing till it has been communicated to the other party, has not, until recently, been laid down, no case having apparently arisen to call for a decision upon the point. In America it was decided some years ago that "an offer cannot be withdrawn unless the withdrawal reaches the party to whom it is addressed before his letter of reply announcing the acceptance has been transmitted." *Tayloe* v. *Merchants Fire Insurance Co.* (1850), 9 How. 390, and in *Byrne & Company* v. *Leon Van Tienhoven* (1880), 5 C.P.D. 344, my brother, in an elaborate judgment, adopted this view, and held that an uncommunicated revocation is, for all practical purposes and in point of law, no revocation at all.

It follows, that as no notice of withdrawal of his offer to sell the 40s., net cash, was given by the defendant before the plaintiffs sold to Walker, they had a right to regard it as a continuing offer, and their acceptance of it made the contract, which was initiated by the proposal, complete and binding on both parties.

My judgment must, therefore, be for the plaintiffs for £1,900 but this amount is liable to be reduced by an arbitrator to be agreed on by the parties, or, if they cannot agree within a week, to be nominated by me. If no arbitrator is appointed, or if the amount be not reduced, the judgment will stand for £1,900. The costs of the arbitration to be in the arbiter's direction.

Judgment for the plaintiffs.

RE COWAN AND BOYD. 1921. 49 O.L.R. 335 (Ontario. Appellate Division). A's lease being about to expire, he wrote his landlord B on March 17th about a renewal. B replied on March 24th offering a renewal at an advanced rent of $75. A replied on March 31st saying that he was paying as high a rent as he felt he should pay, "so if you do not see your way clear to renew at the present rental we would appreciate an early reply." On April 5th B wrote that he would call and see A at the end of the month. On April 19th A wrote B, saying, "I have decided to accept your terms of $75. per month." Held, the letter of April 5th left the offer open.

ANGLO-NEWFOUNDLAND FISH CO. *v.* SMITH & CO. LTD. 1902. 35 N.S.R. 267 (Nova Scotia Supreme Court *en banc*). The plaintiffs agreed to buy 2,000 to 3,000 quintals of cod "cleaned on the face, free from black skin and liver and blood marks" at twenty-five cents above the Halifax price for ordinary bank cod not cleaned free of black skin. The defendants couldn't "see that if the fish is cured, washed, and made clean in every respect, that the dark skin on napes would make any difference to any market." The plaintiffs answered, "It is done on all the codfish . . . that is caught and cured in Ireland, Shetland, and Faroe Island, and, for that one reason, codfish of these countries will sell at a fair price, when ours can't be sold at all." The defendants replied promising to furnish the fish at the price offered and concluded, "I will do my best in regard to removing the black skin." The plaintiffs then promised to take 2,500 quintals "according to previous arrangement as to quality and price." Defendants delivered no fish and in this action denied any contract. Townshend J. held for the plaintiffs and the Court *en banc* divided two to two in dismissing the appeal. WEATHERBE J.: ". . . Commerce could not be carried on, and no contract could ever be concluded if merchants were required to use the precision of solicitors in contracts with each other. All that is required is to find out what, in reading a letter, is the main idea intended to be conveyed. . . . after using words agreeing to supply the fish asked for, defendants merely expressed a determination not to be outdone by those of other countries. . . ." GRAHAM E.J.: ". . . There is, in my opinion, a material difference between the plaintiff's proposal and that of the defendants. The plaintiffs proposed that the defendants should enter into an unconditional contract. . . . The defendants . . . would only undertake to do their best in regard to removing the black skin, etc. The removal of all black skin may have been physically possible, but it was, in their business, an untried thing; it was a question of degree in view of securing an entry into a new market, and might require such an amount of labour and care as to render it commercially impossible. And the defendants protected themselves. . . ."

5. AMBIGUITY OF TERMS

The cases in this and the next section raise some aspects of the problem of mistake on the part of one or both of the parties which one party asserts as evidence that they are not in true agreement, that a valid bargain has not been struck, that a promise has not been made. You will have already discovered that the complexities of actual negotiation are more subtle than the "offer/acceptance" analysis sometimes seems to recognize. In this section, these complexities are increased by the addition of an element of direct ambiguity in the dealings: mistake as to the terms agreed upon.

HOBBS *v*. ESQUIMALT & NANAIMO RAILWAY COMPANY
British Columbia. Supreme Court of Canada. 1899. 29 S.C.R. 450

Hobbs paid the Railway Company $120 on account of the purchase of a quarter section of land at three dollars an acre, payment to be made over three years. The receipt described the land without reservation and was signed by John Trutch, Land Commissioner for the Railway. The Company claimed that Mr. Trutch had no authority to convey the minerals and three years later offered a conveyance with minerals reserved. Hobbs asked for specific performance. The trial Judge refused it but declared that Hobbs was entitled to a conveyance with the reservation or to repayment of the purchase money with interest and compensation for improvements. The Court of Appeal denied him the option of repayment.

TASCHEREAU J. (dissenting): I would dismiss this appeal. The reason given in the courts below against the appellant's right to specific performance are, in my opinion, unanswerable. There has been no contract between this company and Hobbs. The company thought they were selling the land without the minerals. Hobbs thought he was buying the land with the minerals. So that the company did not sell what Hobbs thought he was buying, and Hobbs did not buy what the company thought they were selling. Therefore, there was no contract between them. Hobbs would not have bought if he had known that the company were selling only surface rights, and the company would not have sold if they had thought that Hobbs intended to buy the land with the minerals. The ratification by the company stands upon no better ground. It was nothing but ratification of a sale without the minerals.

The rule that any one dealing with another has the right to believe that this other one means what he says, or says what he means, is one that cannot be gainsaid. But it has no application here. Assuming that the agent sold the land with the minerals, he did what he had not the power to do. However, he did not do it.

I would dismiss the appeal with costs.

KING J.: The facts are stated in the judgment of the late Chief Justice Davie before whom the case was tried.

It is found by him that Mr. Trutch acted beyond the scope of his authority in agreeing to a sale of the land without reservation of the minerals, but that the contract so made was rectified [ratified] by the company. He, however, was of opinion that, in so ratifying it, the company were under a mistake as to its legal effect, and upon this ground he declined to compel performance but left the plaintiff to his common law remedy for breach of contract.

A first question is as to whether there was, by reason of the alleged mistake, a contract at all. . . .

Here the parties were *ad idem* as to the terms of the contract. It was expressed in perfectly unambiguous language in the offer of the plaintiff and in the acceptance of defendants; and the alleged difference is in a wholly esoteric meaning which one of them gives to the plain words.

Then the legal right existing (as held by the Court below) is it a case (as also held by it) where a court will leave the party aggrieved by a breach to his common law remedy? As already mentioned *Stewart* v. *Kennedy* (1895), 15 App. Cas. 75, is not a case relating to the effect of mistake upon the exercise of the equitable jurisdiction of English Courts of Equity, but English authorities having been referred to, the jurisprudence is thus summarized by Lord Macnaghton (p. 105):

"It cannot be disputed that the Court of Chancery had refused specific performance in cases of mistake when the mistake has been on one side only, and even when the mistake on the part of the defendant resisting specific performance, has not been induced or contributed to by any act or omission on the part of the plaintiff. But I do not think it is going too far to say that in all those cases—certainly in all that have occurred in recent times—the court has thought rightly or wrongly that the circumstances of the particular case under consideration were such that (to use a well known phrase) it would be 'highly unreasonable' to enforce the agreement specifically."

In *Tamplin* v. *James* (1880), 15 Ch. D. 215, James L.J. says:

"If a man will not take reasonable care to ascertain what he is buying he must take the consequences. It is not enough for a purchaser to swear: 'I thought the farm sold contained twelve fields which I knew, and I find it does not include them all,' or 'I thought it contained 100 acres and it only contains 80.' It would open the door to fraud if such a defence was to be allowed. Perhaps some of the cases on this subject go too far (i.e. in the direction of allowing such defence) but for the most part the cases where a defendant has escaped on the ground of a mistake not contributed to by the plaintiff have been cases where a hardship amounting to injustice would have been inflicted upon him by holding him to his bargain and it was unreasonable to hold him to it."

Hence it may be, as stated in *Fry on Specific Performance*, that the court considers with more favour as a defence the allegation of mistake in an agent than in a principal.

The alleged mistake is given in the evidence of Mr. Dunsmuir, the vice-president of the company. Speaking of the contract entered into by Mr. Trutch, he says:

"It only sold the surface. That is, we term it land in our office. We do not say surface right, we say land, land minus the minerals."

It is evident, then, that we may put Mr. Trutch aside, and treat the case on this point as if the company, upon an application by plaintiff for purchase of 160 acres of land, had entered into an agreement to sell the land in the identical words used by Mr. Trutch. In effect they say:

"We agreed to sell the land, but this means land reserving the minerals."

It may well be that in the administration of their varied business a loose but convenient form of speech may have been used in the office, but it is not stated that it was supposed to be a correct one, and it appears incredible that a company, a large part of whose business is that of a land company could reasonably suppose that in dealings with third persons for the sale of land, the word "land" means land with reservation of minerals. Mr. Trutch does not say that he misconceived the meaning of the word. His impression was that he had verbally notified the plaintiff that the minerals were to be reserved, and if he had done so the plaintiff would be precluded from obtaining the specific performance he seeks; but it has been found that notice was not given. The form of the company conveyances expressly reserving the minerals show that they were aware how to effect such object. The alleged mistake was therefore an unreasonable and careless one, and in view of the fact that the plaintiff went into possession under the contract, I do not think that it can be said to be unconscionable or highly unreasonable to enforce the specific performance of the contract.

Appeal allowed with costs.

[Gwynne, Sedgewick and Girouard JJ. concurred, Gwynne J. with written reasons. In the Appendix of Privy Council Appeals in 31 S.C.R. a note indicates that the appeal was dismissed upon settlement between the parties.]

RAFFLES *v.* WICHELHAUS

England. Exchequer. 1864. 2 H. & C. 906; 159 E.R. 375

It was agreed at Liverpool that the plaintiff should sell to the defendants 125 bales of Surat cotton, guaranteed middling fair merchant's Dhollerah, to arrive ex "Peerless" from Bombay; and that the cotton should be taken from the quay, and that the defendants would pay the plaintiff at the rate of 17s. ¼d. per pound after the arrival of the goods in England. The goods did arrive by the "Peerless" but the defendants refused to accept the goods or pay the plaintiff for them. It was pleaded that the ship mentioned in the agreement was meant by the defendants to be the ship called the "Peerless" that sailed from Bombay in October; and that the plaintiff was only ready and willing and offered to deliver to the defendants cotton which arrived by another and different ship, which was also called the "Peerless," and which sailed from Bombay in December. Demurrer, and joinder therein.

Milward, in support of the demurrer. The contract was for the sale of a number of bales of cotton of a particular description, which the plaintiff was ready to deliver. It is immaterial by what ship the cotton was to arrive, so that it was a ship called the "Peerless." The words "to arrive ex 'Peerless'" only meant that, if the vessel is lost on the voyage, the contract is to be at an end. [Pollock C.B. It would be a question for the jury whether both parties meant the same ship called the "Peerless."] That would be so if the contract was for the sale of a ship called the "Peerless," but it is for the sale of cotton on board a ship of that name. [Pollock C.B. The defendant only bought that cotton which was to arrive by a particular ship. It may as well be said, that, if there is a contract for the purchase of certain goods in warehouse A., that is satisfied by the delivery of goods of the same description in warehouse B.] In that case there would be goods in both warehouses; here it does not appear that the plaintiff had any goods on board the other "Peerless." [Martin B. It is imposing on the defendant a contract different from that which he entered into. Pollock C.B. It is like a contract for the purchase of wine coming from a particular estate in France or Spain, where there are two estates of that name.] The defendant has no right to contradict by parol evidence a written contract good upon the face of it. He does not impute misrepresentation or fraud, but only says that he fancied the ship was a different one. Intention is of no avail, unless stated at the time of the contract. [Pollock C.B. One vessel sailed in October and the other in December.] The time of sailings is no part of the contract.

Mellish (Cohen with him), in support of the plea. There is nothing on the face of the contract to show that any particular ship called the "Peerless" was meant; but the moment it appears that two ships called the "Peerless" were about to sail from Bombay, there is a latent ambiguity, and parol evidence may be given for the purpose of showing that the defendant meant one "Peerless" and the plaintiff another. That being so, there was no *concensus ad idem*, and therefore no binding contract. [He was then stopped by the Court.]

PER CURIAM: There must be judgment for the defendants.

QUESTIONS. A offers to sell goods to B ex "Peerless" from Bombay. B accepts. There are two ships "Peerless." What is the situation if

(1) A knows or has reason to know this fact, but B does not know, or have reason to know;

(2) B knows or has reason to know of it, but A does not;

(3) Both know or have reason to know of it;

(4) Neither of them knows or has reason to know it at the time of communication?

FALCK *v*. WILLIAMS. [1900] A.C. 176 (New South Wales. Privy Council). After a protracted negotiation dealing with three different proposals: a Barcelona charter for the ship "Semiramis," an offer of a Liverpool charter, and a Fiji charter the appellant telegraphed a code message, "Shale Copyright Semiramis Begloom Escorte Sultana Brilliant Argentina Bronchil." Decoded this meant, "Shale. Your rate is too low, impossible to work business at your figures. Semiramis. Have closed in accordance with your order. Confirm. Two Ports Fiji Islands, Sultana, Brilliant, Argentina. Keep a good look-out for business for this vessel and wire us when anything good offers." The appellant said the first two words dealt with both the Barcelona charter and the Liverpool proposal, and the next three words dealt with the "Semiramis." The respondent said that the first two words referred to the Liverpool proposal, the second two to the Barcelona charter, and that Escorte was to be read with what followed. Held, for the respondent. LORD MACNAGHTEN: "Indeed, the whole controversy when the matter is thrashed out seems to be narrowed down to this question—'Is the word "estcorte" to be read with what has gone before or with what follows?' In their Lordship's opinion there is no conclusive reason pointing one way or the other. The fault lay with the appellant's agent. If he had spent a few more shillings on his message, if he had even arranged the words he used more carefully, if he had only put the word 'estcorte' before the word 'begloom' instead of after it, there would have been no difficulty. It is not for their Lordships to determine what is the true construction of Buch's telegram. It was the duty of the appellant as plaintiff to make out that the construction which he put upon it was the true one. In that he must fail if the message was ambiguous, as their Lordships hold it to be. If the respondent had been maintaining his construction as plaintiff he would equally have failed."

HENKEL *v.* PAPE

England. Exchequer. 1870. L.R. 6 Ex. 7

Declaration for goods bargained and sold, and for goods sold and delivered.

Pleas, first, except as to £7 never indebted; and, secondly, as to £7, payment into Court. The plaintiffs accepted the money paid into Court, and joined issue on the first plea.

The plaintiffs are gun manufacturers in London and Birmingham, and the defendant is a gun-maker at Newcastle-upon-Tyne. On the 4th of June, 1870, the plaintiffs received from the defendant the following letter: "Send sample Snider, with sword-bayonet, forward immediately. I can fix an order for fifty, I think, and it may lead to many large orders. Can you do them at 34s. net cash on delivery, so as to secure the order? I shall have to cut very fine, and several will be in for it." In reply the plaintiffs wrote: "We have forwarded you this day sample Snider, with sword-bayonet. We cannot possibly do them for less than 35s. net cash." With this letter the sample was sent. On the 7th of June the plaintiffs received the following telegram purporting to come from the defendant: "Send by mail immediately *the* Snider rifles same as pattern. Must be here in the morning. Ship sails then." The plaintiffs on receipt of this communication sent fifty rifles to the defendant. On the 9th of June they received the following letter from him. "I am surprised that you sent fifty instead of three rifles. The telegram was to send three." In fact, the clerk who sent the telegraph message had by mistake telegraphed the word "the" instead of "three." The defendant had written "three," and not "the," on message paper. Under these circumstances the plaintiffs insisted on the defendant accepting the fifty rifles sent, but the defendant declined to take more than three. This action was then brought. The defendant paid a sum into court sufficient to cover the price of three rifles and their carriage. He denied his liability as to the residue of the plaintiffs' claim, contending that he could not be made responsible for the mistake of the telegraph clerk.

The cause was tried before Blackburn J., at the Surrey Summer Assizes, 1870, when a verdict was directed for the defendant, with leave to move to enter a verdict for the plaintiffs for the invoice price of the remaining forty-seven rifles.

H. Thompson Chitty moved accordingly: The telegraph clerk was the defendant's agent to transmit the message, and the defendant is responsible for the mistake in the transmission. *Chitty on Contracts*, 6th ed., p. 197. There is no privity between the plaintiffs and the telegraph clerk, nor can they proceed against the Post-office, his employers: *Playford* v. *United*

Kingdom Telegraph Company, L.P.4 Q.B. 706. Their right remedy is against the defendant. Suppose in a letter written by himself he had made the mistake, he would clearly have been liable; and in the transmission of each particular message the telegraph clerk is the agent of the sender. Upon the sender therefore must rest the responsibility of any error committed by the agent in the course of his employment.

KELLY C.B.: We are of opinion that in this case there should be no rule. The question is whether the defendant has entered into a contract to purchase fifty rifles, and there is no doubt he might have bound himself either by letter or a telegraphic message. But the Post-office authorities are ony agents to transmit messages in the terms in which the senders deliver them. They have no authority to do more. Now in this case the evidence is that the defendant agreed to take three rifles, and three only, and he authorized the telegraph clerk to send a message to that and to no other effect. That being so, there was no contract between the plaintiffs and defendant for the purchase of fifty rifles. The defendant cannot be made responsible because the telegraph clerk made a mistake in the transmission of the message. There was no contract between the parties such as the plaintiffs rely on. The verdict therefore ought to stand.

[Bramwell, Piggott, and Cleasby, BB. concurred. Rule refused.]

DICKSON *v.* REUTER'S TELEGRAM CO., LTD. 1877. 2 C.P.D. 62 (England. Common Pleas). In this case the plaintiff received a telegram not intended for him, and claimed damages from the defendant Company amounting to £2600 representing losses on barley shipped by mistake in reliance on the message. Held, for the defendant. There was no contractual relationship between the plaintiff recipient of the telegram and the telegraph company, and a telegraph company is not to be supposed to have guaranteed towards all mankind the accuracy and care of all their servants in all parts of the globe wherever they deliver a message. Nor is a telegraph company liable for innocent misrepresentations. [As to liability of a telegraph company to the sender, both for negligence and in contract, see *Kinghorne* v. *The Montreal Telegraph Co.* noted on p. 8.]

QUESTIONS. Suppose A writes an offer to buy sixty rifles which B accepts. A intended to write six. Is there a contract? A dictates a letter to his stenographer offering to buy six rifles. The stenographer takes it down as sixty. A signs the letter without reading it over. B accepts. Is there a contract? A, after dictating, tells his stenographer to sign the letter and mail it, and B accepts. Is there a contract? In *Henkel* v. *Pape* was there a contract for three rifles? Suppose the plaintiff were unwilling to sell three at the price quoted. Was any offer for three communicated to him?]

SMITH *v.* HUGHES

England. Queen's Bench. 1871. L.R. 6 Q.B. 597

The plaintiff, a farmer, took a sample of some oats to Hughes, the manager of the defendant, who was an owner and trainer of horses. The plaintiff claimed to have said "I have some good oats for sale" and when Hughes replied "I am always a buyer of good oats," offered forty to fifty quarters at 35s. a quarter. Hughes took away a sample, and later wrote to say that he would take the oats at 34s. and the plaintiff sent him sixteen quarters, which Hughes complained were *new* oats. The plaintiff admitted they were and denied that he had any old oats. Hughes claimed that he had replied to the plaintiff, "I am always a buyer of good *old* oats," and that the plaintiff had replied, "I have some good old oats for sale." Hughes insisted that the plaintiff take the oats back. At the trial the Judge put two questions to the jury for their consideration: Was the word "old" used by the plaintiff or the defendant? If so, they must find for the defendant. If the word "old" was not used, were they of the opinion that the plaintiff believed that Hughes believed, or was under the impression, that he was contracting for the purchase of old oats? If so, they must find for the defendant. Otherwise, for the plaintiff. The jury did not answer the questions specifically, but found a verdict for the defendant. On appeal the question was whether the direction was correct.

COCKBURN C.J.: . . . It is to be regretted that the jury were not required to give specific answers to the questions so left to them. For, it is quite possible that their verdict may have been given for the defendant on the first ground; in which case there could, I think, be no doubt as to the propriety of the judge's direction; whereas now, as it is possible that the verdict of the jury—or at all events of some of them—may have proceeded on the second ground, we are called upon to consider and decide whether the ruling of the learned judge with reference to the second question was right.

For this purpose we must assume that nothing was said on the subject of the defendant's manager desiring to buy old oats, nor of the oats having been said to be old; while on the other hand, we must assume that the defendant's manager believed the oats to be old oats, and that the plaintiff was conscious of the existence of such belief, but did nothing, directly or indirectly, to bring it about, simply offering his oats and exhibiting his sample, remaining perfectly passive as to what was passing in the mind of the other party. The question is whether, under such circumstances, the passive acquiescence of the seller in the self-deception of the buyer will entitle the latter to avoid the contract. I am of opinion that it will not. . . .

I take the true rule to be, that where a specific article is offered for sale, without express warranty, or without circumstances from which the law will imply a warranty—as where, for instance, an article is ordered for a specific purpose—and the buyer has full opportunity of inspecting and forming his own judgment, if he chooses to act on his own judgment, the rule *caveat emptor* applies. If he gets the article he contracted to buy, and that article corresponds with what it was sold as, he gets all he is entitled to, and is bound by the contract. Here the defendant agreed to buy a specific parcel of oats. The oats were what they were sold as, namely, good oats according to the sample. The buyer persuaded himself they were old oats, when they were not so; but the seller neither said nor did anything to contribute to his deception. He has himself to blame. The question is not what a man of scrupulous morality or nice honour would do under such circumstances. The case put of the purchase of an estate, in which there is a mine under the surface, but the fact is unknown to the seller, is one in which a man of tender conscience or high honour would be unwilling to take advantage of the ignorance of the seller; but there can be no doubt that the contract for the sale of the estate would be binding. . . .

Now, in this case, there was plainly no legal obligation in the plaintiff in the first instance to state whether the oats were new or old. He offered them for sale according to the sample, as he had a perfect right to do, and gave the buyer the fullest opportunity of inspecting the sample, which, practically, was equivalent to an inspection of the oats themselves. What, then, was there to create any trust or confidence between the parties, so as to make it incumbent on the plaintiff to communicate the fact that the oats were not, as the defendant assumed them to be, old oats? If, indeed, the buyer, instead of acting on his own opinion, had asked the question whether the oats were old or new or had said anything which intimated his understanding that the seller was selling the oats as old oats, the case would have been wholly different; or even if he had said anything which shewed that he was not acting on his own inspection and judgment, but assumed as the foundation of the contract that the oats were old, the silence of the seller, as a means of misleading him, might have amounted to a fraudulent concealment, such as would have entitled the buyer to avoid the contract. Here, however, nothing of the sort occurs. The buyer in no way refers to the seller, but acts entirely on his own judgment. . . .

In the case before us it must be taken that, as the defendant, on a portion of the oats being delivered, was able by inspection to ascertain that they were new oats, his manager might, by due inspection of the sample, have arrived at the same result. The case is, therefore, one of the sale and purchase of a specific article after inspection by the buyer. Under these circumstances the rule *caveat emptor* clearly applies; more especially as this cannot be put as a case of latent defect, but simply one in which the seller did not make known to the buyer a circumstance affecting the quality of the thing sold. The oats in question were in no sense defective, on the contrary they were good oats, and all that can be said is that they had not acquired the quality which greater age would have given them. There is not, so far as I am aware, any authority for the position that a vendor who submits the subject-matter of sale to the inspection of the vendee, is bound to state circumstances which may tend to detract from the estimate which the buyer may injudiciously have formed of its value. Even the civil law, and the foreign law, founded upon it, which require that the seller shall answer for latent defects, have never gone the length of saying that, so long as the thing sold answers to the description under which it is sold, the seller is bound to disabuse the buyer as to any exaggerated estimate of its value.

It only remains to deal with an argument which was pressed upon us, that the defendant in the present case intended to buy old oats, and the plaintiff to sell new, so that the two minds were not *ad idem*; and that consequently there was no contract. This argument proceeds on the fallacy of confounding what was merely a motive operating on the buyer to induce him to buy with one of the essential conditions of the contract. Both parties were agreed as to the sale and purchase of this particular parcel of oats. The defendant believed the oats to be old, and was thus induced to agree to buy them, but he omitted to make their age a condition of the contract. All that can be said is, that the two minds were not *ad idem* as to the age of the oats; they certainly were *ad idem* as to the sale and purchase of them. Suppose a person to buy a horse without a warranty, believing him to be sound, and the horse turns out unsound could it be contended that it would be open to him to say that, as he had intended to buy a sound horse, and the seller to sell an unsound one, the contract was void, because the seller must have known from the price the buyer was willing to give, or from his general habits as a buyer of horses, that he thought the horse was sound? The cases are exactly parallel.

The result is that, in my opinion, the learned judge of the county court was wrong in leaving the second question to the jury, and that, consequently, the case must go down to a new trial.

BLACKBURN J.: . . . The jury were directed that, if they believed the word "old" was used, they should find for the defendant—and this was right; for if that was the case it is obvious that neither did the defendant intend to enter into a contract on the plaintiff's terms, that is, to buy this parcel of oats without any stipulation as to their quality; nor could the plaintiff have been led to believe he was intending to do so.

But the second direction raises the difficulty. I think that, if from that direction the jury would understand that they were first to consider whether they were satisfied that the defendant intended to buy this parcel of oats on the terms that it was part of his contract with the plaintiff that they were old oats, so as to have the warranty of the plaintiff to that effect, they were properly told that, if that was so, the defendant could not be bound to a contract without any warrant unless the plaintiff was misled. But I doubt whether the direction would bring to the minds of the jury the distinction between agreeing to take the oats under the belief that they were old, and agreeing to take the oats under the belief that the plaintiff contracted that they were old.

The difference is the same as that between buying a horse believed to be sound, and buying one believed to be warranted sound; but I doubt if it was made obvious to the jury, and I doubt this the more because I do not see much evidence to justify a finding for the defendant on this latter ground if the word "old" was not used. There may have been more evidence than is stated in the case; and the demeanor of the witnesses may have strengthened the impression produced by the evidence there was; but it does not seem a very satisfactory verdict if it proceeded on this latter ground. I agree, therefore, in the result that there should be a new trial.

HANNEN J.: . . . If, therefore, in the present case, the plaintiff knew that the defendant, in dealing with him for oats, did so on the assumption that the plaintiff was contracting to sell him old oats, he was aware that the defendant apprehended the contract in a different sense to that in which he meant it, and he is thereby deprived of the right to insist that the defendant shall be bound by that which was only the apparent, and not the real bargain.

This was the question which the learned judge intended to leave to the jury; and, as I have already said, I do not think it was incorrect in its terms, but I think that it was likely to be misunderstood by the jury. The jury was asked, "whether they were of opinion, on the whole of the evidence, that the plaintiff believed the defendant to believe, or to be under the impression that he was contracting for the purchase of old oats? If so, there would be a verdict for the defendant." The jury may have understood this to mean that, if the plaintiff believed the defendant to believe that he was buying old oats, the defendant would be entitled to the verdict, but a belief on the part of the plaintiff that the defendant was making a contract to buy the oats, of which he offered him a sample, under a mistaken belief that they were old, would not relieve the defendant from liability unless his mistaken belief were induced by some misrepresentation of the plaintiff, or concealment by him of a fact which it became his duty to communicate. In order to relieve the defendant it was necessary that the jury should find not merely that the plaintiff believed the defendant to believe that he was buying old oats, but that he believed the defendant to believe that he, the plaintiff, was contracting to sell old oats.

I am the more disposed to think that the jury did not understand the question in this last sense because I can find very little, if any, evidence to support a finding upon it in favour of the defendant. It may be assumed that the defendant believed the oats were old, and it may be suspected that the plaintiff thought he so believed, but the only evidence from which it can be inferred that the plaintiff believed that the defendant thought that the plaintiff was making it a term of the contract that the oats were old is that the defendant was a trainer, and that trainers, as a rule, use old oats and that the price given was high for new oats, and more than a prudent man would have given.

Having regard to the admitted fact that the defendant bought the oats after two days' detention of the sample, I think that the evidence was not sufficient to justify the jury in answering the question put to them in the defendant's favour, if they rightly understood it; and I therefore think there should be a new trial.

BELL *v.* LEVER BROTHERS, LTD. [1932] A.C. 161 (England. House of Lords). LORD ATKIN: "The Court [in *Smith* v. *Hughes*] ordered a new trial. It is not quite clear whether they considered that if the defendant's contention was correct, the parties were not *ad idem* or there was a contractual condition that the oats were old oats. In either case the defendant would succeed in defaulting the claim.

"In these cases I am inclined to think that the true analysis is that there is a contract, but that the one party is not able to supply the very thing whether goods or services that the other party contracted to take; and therefore the contract is unenforceable by the one if executory, while if executed the other can recover money paid on the ground of failure of consideration."

QUESTIONS. Suppose that A writes B, "I offer to sell you my horse for $100." B, knowing that A intends to offer to sell his cow, and not his horse, and knowing that "horse" is an error, replies, "I accept." Is there any contract for a horse or a cow? Suppose that A, on learning of his error, now wants to hold B to take the horse, has he the right?

6. MISTAKE IN THE IDENTITY OF PARTIES

In the next cases the mistake is made in the identity of one of the parties. When A thinks he is dealing with B, a wealthy man, and it turns out that B is really C masquerading as B, or that B is really a very poor man, is there consent? The frequently arising case is one where C, having acquired goods as a result of his dealing with A, sells the goods to D, from whom A seeks to recover them. Must a court decide this question between two "innocent" parties by resorting to the same conceptual framework that it would use if the action were between the "innocent" party and the "fraud"? Are the "innocent" parties equally innocent? Could a court apportion their "carelessness"?

BOULTON *v.* JONES

England. Exchequer. 1857. 2 H. & N. 564; 157 E.R. 232

At the trial before the Assessor of the Court of Passage at Liverpool, it appeared that the plaintiff had been foreman and manager to one Brocklehurst, a pipe hose manufacturer, with whom the defendants had been in the habit of dealing, and with whom they had a running account. On the morning of the 13th of January, 1857, the plaintiff bought Brocklehurst's stock, fixtures, and business, and paid for them. In the afternoon of the same day, the defendant's servant brought a written order, addressed to Brocklehurst, for some leather hose. The goods were supplied by the plaintiff. The plaintiff's bookkeeper struck out the name of Brocklehurst and inserted the name of the plaintiff in the order. An invoice was afterwards sent in by the plaintiff to the defendants, who said they knew nothing of him. Upon these facts, the jury, under direction of the Assessor, found a verdict for the plaintiff, and leave was reserved to the defendants to move to enter a verdict for them.

POLLOCK C.B.: The point raised is, whether the facts proved did not show an intention on the part of the defendants to deal with Brocklehurst. The plaintiff, who succeeded Brocklehurst in business, executed the order without any intimation of the change that had taken place, and brought this action to recover the price of the goods supplied. It is a rule of law, that if a person intends to contract with A, B cannot give himself any right under it. Here the order in writing was given to Brocklehurst. Possibly Brocklehurst might have adopted the act of the plaintiff in supplying the goods, and maintained an action for their price. But since the plaintiff has chosen to sue, the only course the defendants could take was to plead that there was no contract with him.

MARTIN B.: I am of the same opinion. This is not a case of principal and agent. If there was any contract at all, it was not with the plaintiff. If a man goes to a shop and makes a contract, intending it to be with one particular person, no other person can convert that into a contract with him.

BRAMWELL B.: The admitted facts are, that the defendants sent to a shop an order for goods, supposing they were dealing with Brocklehurst. The plaintiff, who supplied the goods, did not undeceive them. If the plaintiff were now at liberty to sue the defendants, they would be deprived of their right of set-off as against Brocklehurst. When a contract is made in which the personality of the contracting party is or may be of importance, as a contract with a man to write a book, or the like, or where there might be a set-off, no other person can interpose and adopt the contract. As to the difficulty that the defendants need not pay anybody, I do not see why they should, unless they have made a contract either express or implied. I decide the case on the ground that the defendants did not know that the plaintiff was the person who supplied the goods, and that allowing the plaintiff to treat the contract as made with him would be a prejudice to the defendants.

CHANNELL B.: In order to entitle the plaintiff to recover he must show that there was a contract with himself. The order was given to the plaintiff's predecessor in business. The plaintiff executes it without notifying to the defendants who it was who executed the order. When the invoice was delivered in the name of the plaintiff, it may be that the defendants were not in a situation to return the goods.

Rule absolute.

[From the Law Journal report (27 L.J. Ex. 117) it appears that the defendant had a set-off against Brocklehurst, and that the case was argued on that basis.]

CUNDY *v.* LINDSAY

England. House of Lords. 1878. 3 App. Cas. 459

In 1873, one Alfred Blenkarn hired a room at a corner house in Wood Street, Cheapside; it had two side windows opening into Wood Street, but though the entrance was from Little Love Lane it was by him constantly described as 37, Wood Street, Cheapside. His agreement for this room was signed "Alfred Blenkarn." The now respondents, Messrs. Lindsay & Co., were linen manufacturers carrying on their business at Belfast. In the latter part of 1873, Blenkarn wrote to the plaintiffs on the subject of a purchase from them of goods of their manufacture,—chiefly cambric handkerchiefs. His letters were written as from "37, Wood Street, Cheapside," where he pretended to have a warehouse, but in fact occupied only a room on the top floor, and that room, though looking into Wood Street on one side, could only be reached from the entrance in 5, Little Love Lane. The name signed to these letters was always signed without any initial as representing a Christian name, and was, besides, so written as to appear "Blenkiron & Co." There was a highly respectable firm of W. Blenkiron & Son, carrying on business in Wood Street,—but at number 123, Wood Street, and not at 37. Messrs. Lindsay, who knew the respectability of Blenkiron & Son, though not the number of the house where they carried on business, answered the letters, and sent the goods addressed to "Messrs. Blenkiron & Co., 37, Wood Street, Cheapside," where they were taken in at once. The invoices sent with the goods were always addressed in the same way. Blenkarn sold the goods, thus fraudulently obtained from Messrs. Lindsay, to different persons, and among the rest he sold 250 dozen of cambric handkerchiefs to the Messrs. Cundy, who were bona fide purchasers, and who resold them in the ordinary way of their trade. Payment not being made, an action was commenced in the Mayor's Court of London by Messrs. Lindsay, the junior partner of which firm, Mr. Thompson, made the ordinary affidavit of debt, as against Alfred Blenkarn, and therein named Alfred Blenkarn as the debtor. Blenkarn's fraud was soon discovered, and he was prosecuted at the Central Criminal Court, and convicted and sentenced. Messrs. Lindsay then brought an action against Messrs. Cundy for unlawful conversion of the handkerchiefs. The cause was tried before Mr. Justice Blackburn, who left it to the jury to consider whether Alfred Blenkarn with a fraudulent intent to induce the plaintiffs to give him the credit belonging to the good character of Blenkiron & Son, wrote the letters, and by fraud induced the plaintiffs to send the goods to 37, Wood Street,—were they the same goods as those bought by the defendants, and did the plaintiffs by the affidavit of debt intend, as a matter of fact, to adopt Alfred Blenkarn as their debtor. The first and second questions were answered in the affirmative, and the third in the negative. A verdict was taken for the defendants, with leave reserved to move to enter the verdict for the plaintiffs. On motion accordingly, the court, after argument, ordered the rule for entering judgment for the plaintiffs to be discharged, and directed judgment to be entered for the defendants. On appeal, this decision was reversed and judgment ordered to be entered for the plaintiffs, Messrs. Lindsay. This appeal was then brought.

Lord Cairns L.C.: My Lords, you have in this case to discharge a duty which is always a disagreeable one for any court, namely, to determine as between two parties, both of whom are perfectly innocent, upon which of the two consequences of a fraud practised upon both of them must fall. My Lords, in discharging that duty your Lordships can do no more than apply, rigorously, the settled and well-known rules of law. Now, with regard to the title to personal property, the settled and well-known rules of law may, I take it, be thus expressed: by the law of our country the purchaser of a chattel takes the chattel, as a general rule, subject to what may turn out to be certain infirmities in the title. If he purchases the chattel in market overt, he obtains a title which is good against all the world; but if he does not purchase the chattel in market overt, and if it turns out that the chattel has been found by the person who professed to sell it, the purchaser will not obtain a title good as against the real owner. If it turns out that the chattel has been stolen by the person who has professed to sell it, the purchaser will not obtain a title. If it turns out that the chattel has come into the hands of the person who professed to sell it, by a *de facto* contract, that is to say, a contract which has purported to pass the property to him from the owner of the property, there the purchaser will obtain a good title, even although afterwards it should appear that there were circumstances connected with that contract, which would enable the original owner of the goods to reduce it, and to set it aside because these circumstances so enabling the original owner of the goods, or of the chattel, to reduce the contract and to set it aside, will not be allowed to interfere with a title for valuable consideration obtained by some third party during the interval while the contract remained unreduced.

My Lords, the question, therefore, in the present case, as your Lordships will observe, really becomes the very short and simple one which I am about to state. Was there any contract which, with regard to the goods in question in this case, had passed the property in the goods from Messrs. Lindsay to Alfred Blenkarn? If there was any contract passing that property, even although, as I have said, that contract might afterwards be open to a process of reduction upon the ground of fraud, still, in the meantime, Blenkarn might have conveyed a good title for valuable consideration to the present appellants.

Now, my Lords, there are two observations bearing upon the solution of that question which I desire to make. In the first place, if the property in the goods in question passed, it could only pass by way of contract; there is nothing else which could have passed the property. The second observation is this, your Lordships are not here embarrassed by any conflict of evidence, or any evidence whatever as to conversations or as to acts done; the whole history of the whole transaction lies upon paper. The principal parties concerned, the respondents and Blenkarn, never came in contact personally—everything that was done was done by writing. What has to be judged of, and what the jury in the present case had to judge of, was merely the conclusion to be derived from that writing, as applied to the admitted facts of the case.

Now, my Lords, discharging that duty and answering that inquiry, what the jurors have found is in substance this: it is not necessary to spell out the words, because the substance of it is beyond all doubt. They have found that by the form of the signatures to the letters which were written by Blenkarn, by the mode in which his letters and his applications to the respondents were made out, and by the way in which he left uncorrected the mode and form in which, in turn, he was addressed by the respondent; that by all those means he led, and intended to lead, the respondents to believe, and they did believe that the person with whom they were communicating was not Blenkarn, the dishonest and irresponsible man, but was a well known and solvent house of Blenkiron & Co., doing business in the same street. My Lords, those things are found as matters of fact, and they are placed beyond the range of dispute and controversy in the case.

If that is so, what is the consequence? It is that Blenkarn—the dishonest man, as I call him—was acting here just in the same way as if he had forged the signature of Blenkiron & Co., the respectable firm, to the application for goods, and as if, when, in return, the goods were forwarded and letters were sent, accompanying them, he had intercepted the goods and intercepted the letters, and had taken possession of the goods, and of the letters which were addressed to, and intended for, not himself, but the firm of Blenkiron & Co. Now, my Lords, stating the matter shortly in that way, I ask the question, how is it possible to imagine that in the state of things any contract could have arisen between the respondents and Blenkarn, the dishonest man? Of him they knew nothing, and of him they never thought. With him they never intended to deal. Their minds never, even for an instant of time, rested upon him, and as between him and them there was no consensus of mind which could lead to any agreement or any contract whatever. As between him and them there was merely the one side to a contract, where, in order to produce a contract, two sides would be required. With the firm of Blenkiron & Co. of course there was no contract, for as to them the matter was entirely unknown, and therefore the pretence of a contract was a failure.

The result, therefore, my Lords, is this, that your Lordships have not here to deal with one of those cases in which there is *de facto* a contract made which may afterwards be impeached and set aside, on the ground of fraud; but you have to deal with a case which ranges itself under a completely different chapter of law, the case namely in which the contract never comes into existence. My Lords, that being so, it is idle to talk of the property passing. The property remained, as it originally had been, the property of the respondents, and the title which was intended to be given to the appellants was a title which could not be given to them.

My Lords, I therefore move your Lordships, that this appeal be dismissed with costs, and the judgment of the Court of Appeal affirmed.

[Lords Hatherly and Penzance also gave reasons for dismissing the appeal. Lord Gordon concurred.]

KING'S NORTON METAL CO. LTD. *v*. EDRIDGE, MERRETT, & CO. LTD.

England. Court of Appeal. 1897. 14 T.L.R. 98

The action was brought to recover damages for the conversion of one ton of brass rivet wire. The plaintiffs were metal manufacturers at King's Norton, Worcestershire, and the defendants were metal merchants at Birmingham. It appeared that in 1896 the plaintiffs received a letter purporting to come from Hallam & Co., Soho Hackle Pin and Wire Works,

Sheffield, at the head of which was a representation of a large factory with a number of chimneys, and in one corner was a printed statement that Hallam & Co. had depots and agencies at Belfast, Lille, and Ghent. The letter contained a request by Hallam & Co. for a quotation of prices for brass rivet wire. In reply, the plaintiffs quoted prices, and Hallam and Co. then by letter ordered some goods, which were sent off to them. These goods were never paid for. It turned out that a man named Wallis had adopted the name of Hallam & Co., and fraudulently obtained goods by the above means, and that Wallis sold the goods to the defendants, who bought them bona fide, and with no notice of any defect of title in Wallis. It appeared that the plaintiffs had been paid for some goods previously ordered by Hallam & Co., by a cheque drawn by "Hallam and Co." The plaintiffs brought this action to recover damages for the conversion of these goods. At the trial, the learned judge non-suited the plaintiffs upon the ground that the property in the goods had passed to Wallis, who sold them to the defendants before the plaintiffs had disaffirmed the contract.

A. L. Smith L. J. said the case was a plain one. The question was whether the plaintiffs, who had been cheated out of their goods by a rogue called Wallis, or the defendants were to bear the loss. The law seemed to him to be well settled. If a person induced by false pretences contracted with a rogue to sell goods to him and the goods were delivered the rogue could until the contract was disaffirmed give a good title to the goods to a bona fide purchaser for value. The facts here were that Wallis, for the purpose of cheating, set up in business as Hallam and Co., and got note-paper prepared for the purpose, and wrote to the plaintiffs representing that he was carrying on business as Hallam and Co. He got the goods in question and sold them to the defendants, who bought them bona fide for value. The question was, With whom, upon this evidence, which was all one way, did the plaintiffs contract to sell goods? Clearly with the writer of the letters. If it could have been shown that there was a separate entity called Hallam and Co. and another entity called Wallis then the case might have come within the decision in *Cundy* v. *Lindsay* (1878), 3 App. Cas. 459. In his opinion there was a contract by the plaintiffs with the person who wrote the letters, by which the property passed to him. There was only one entity, trading it might be under an *alias*, and there was a contract by which the property passed to him. Mr. Justice Cave said that this was nothing more than a long firm fraud. Did any one ever hear of an attempt being made by a person who had delivered his goods to a long firm to get his goods back on the ground that he had made no contract with the long firm? The indictment against a long firm was always for obtaining the goods by false pretences, which presupposed the passing of the property. For these reasons there was no question to go to the jury, and the nonsuit was right.

[Rigby and Collins L.JJ. delivered judgments to the same effect.]

PHILLIPS *v.* BROOKS. [1910] 2 K.B. 243 (England. High Court). On April 15, 1918, a man entered the plaintiff's shop and asked to see some pearls and some rings. He selected pearls at the price of £2550 and a ring at the price of £450. He produced a cheque book and wrote out a cheque for £3000. In signing it, he said: "You see who I am, I am Sir George Bullough," and he gave an address in St. James' Square. The plaintiff knew there was such a person as Sir George Bullough, and finding on reference to a directory that Sir George lived at the address mentioned, he said, "Would you like to take the articles with you?", to which the man replied: "You had better have the cheque cleared first, but I should like to take the ring, as it is my wife's birthday tomorrow," whereupon the plaintiff let him have the ring. The cheque was dishonoured, the person who gave it being in fact a fraudulent person named North, who was subsequently convicted of obtaining the ring by false pretences. In the meantime, namely on April 16, 1918, North, in the name of Firth, had pledged the ring with the defendants, pawnbrokers, who, bona fide and without notice, advanced £350 upon it. Held, for the defendants. HORRIDGE J.: ". . . I think the seller intended to contract with the person present, and there was no error as to the person with whom he contracted, although the plaintiff would not have made the contract if there had not been a fradulent misrepresentation. . . ."

INGRAM *v*. LITTLE
England. Court of Appeal. [1961] 1 Q.B. 31

The Misses Ingram advertised their car for sale for £725. A stranger calling himself Hutchinson came to the house on August 3, 1957, and after an examination of the car offered Miss Elsie Ingram £700 for it. The offer was refused. After some discussion he offered £717, which was accepted. Hutchinson then took out his cheque book, but at this Miss Elsie immediately told him that she was only willing to sell for cash, that she was not prepared to accept a cheque, and started to leave the room. Hutchinson then described himself as Mr. P. G. M. Hutchinson, with business interests at Guilford and as living at Stanstead House, Stanstead Road, Caterham. Miss Hilda Ingram, who was present, slipped out and checked in the area telephone directory at the local post office. Finding an entry for "Hutchinson, P. G. M., Stanstead House, Stanstead Road, Caterham 4665" Miss Hilda returned, reported this fact, and the Misses Ingram decided to take Hutchinson's cheque and the deal was concluded. Hutchinson disappeared with the car and has not been heard of since under that name. On August 6, 1957 a man calling himself Hardy sold the Ingram car to Reginald Little in Blackpool. Hardy, or Hutchinson, disappeared and has not been heard of since under either name. In December, 1957 Little sold the car to another dealer. The plaintiffs sued Little for the return of the car or damages for its conversion. Slade J. held that Hutchinson and Hardy were the same person, and that Little had bought in good faith, but he held that the plaintiffs' mistake as to the identity of the person with whom they were dealing prevented the formation of a contract. He gave judgment for the plaintiffs for £720, the agreed value of the car. The defendant appealed.

SELLERS L.J.: . . . The decision in the present case turns solely on whether "Hutchinson" entered into a contract which gave him a title to the car which would subsist until it was avoided on the undoubted fraud being discovered. . . .

It does not seem to me to matter whether the right view of the facts is, as the judge has held and as I would agree, that there was no concluded contract before the cheque was produced and before the vital fraudulent statements were made or that there was a concluded contract which "Hutchinson" at once repudiated by refusing to pay cash and that this repudiation was accepted by the plaintiffs and the transaction was then and there at an end. The property would not have passed until cash had been paid and it never was paid or intended to be paid.

Was there a contract of sale subsequently made which led to the plaintiffs taking "Hutchinson's" cheque and in exchange for it handing over the car and its log book?

The judgment held that there never was a concluded contract, applying, as I understand it, the elementary factors required by law to establish a contract.

The judge, treating the plaintiffs as the offerors and the rogue "Hutchinson" as the offeree, found that the plaintiffs in making their offer to sell the car not for cash but for a cheque (which in the circumstances of the Bank Holiday week-end could not be banked before the following Tuesday, August 6, 1957) were under the belief that they were dealing with, and therefore making their offer to, the honest P. G. M. Hutchinson of Caterham, whom they had reason to believe was a man of substance and standing.

"Hutchinson," the offeree, knew precisely what was in the minds of the two ladies for he had put it there and he knew that their offer was intended for P. G. M. Hutchinson of Caterham and that they were making no offer to and had no intention to contract with him, as he was. There was no offer which he "Hutchinson" could accept and, therefore, there was no contract.

The judge pointed out that the offer which the plaintiffs made was one which was capable of being accepted only by the honest P. G. M. Hutchinson of Caterham and was incapable of acceptance by "Hutchinson."

In all the circumstances of the present case I would accept the judge's findings. Indeed the conclusion so reached seems self-evident.

Is the conclusion to be held wrong in law? If it is, then, as I see it, it must be on the sole ground that as "Hutchinson" was present, albeit making fraudulent statements to induce the plaintiffs to part with their car to him in exchange for his worthless cheque and was successful in so doing, then a bargain must have been struck with him personally, however much he deceived the plaintiffs into thinking they were dealing with someone else.

Where two parties are negotiating together and there is no question of one or the other purporting to act as agent for another, and an agreement is reached, the normal and obvious conclusion would no doubt be that they are the contracting parties. A contrary finding would not be justified unless very clear evidence demanded it. The unfortunate position of the defendant in this case illustrates how third parties who deal in good faith with the fraudulent person may be prejudiced.

The mere presence of an individual cannot, however, be conclusive that an apparent bargain he may make is made with him. If he were disguised in appearance and in dress to represent someone else and the other party, deceived by the disguise, dealt with him on the basis that he was that person and would not have contracted had he known the truth then, it seems clear, there would be no contract established. If words are substituted for outward disguise so as to depict a different person from the one physically present, in what circumstances would the result be different?

Whether the person portrayed, by disguise or words, is known to the other party or not is important in considering whether the identity of the person is of any moment or whether it is a matter of indifference. If a man said his name was Brown when it was in fact Smith, and both were unknown to the other party, it would be difficult to say that there was any evidence that the contract was not made and intended to be made with the person present. In *King's Norton Metal Co. Ltd.* v. *Edridge, Merrett & Co. Ltd.* (1897), 14 T.L.R. 98, one Wallis fraudulently described himself as Hallam & Co., making it appear a substantial firm with a large factory. The court held that the use of an assumed name by the buyer did not prevent a finding that the plaintiffs, the sellers of some brass rivet wire, had contracted with him.

But personal knowledge of the person fraudulently represented cannot, I think, be an essential feature. It might be a very strong factor but the qualities of a person not personally known might be no less strong. If a man misrepresented himself to be a Minister of the Crown or a stockbroker, confidence in the person so identified might arise although the individual so described was wholly unknown personally or by sight to the other party.

It would seem that there is an area of fact in cases of the type under consideration where a fraudulent person is present purporting to make a bargain with another and that the circumstances may justify a finding that, notwithstanding some fraud and deceit, the correct view may be that a bargain was struck with the person present, or on the other hand they may equally justify, as here, a finding the other way.

Some of the difficulties and perhaps confusion which have arisen in some of the cases do not, in my view, arise here.

If less had been said by the rogue, and if nothing had been done to confirm his statements by Miss Hilda Ingram, who communicated what she had learnt to Miss Elsie who was doing the main negotiation, the result might have been different, for the sellers' concern about the stability and standing of the buyer might not have been revealed and it might have been held that an offer in such circumstances was to the party present, whatever his true identity would be.

In *Phillips* v. *Brooks Ltd.* [1919] 2 K.B. 243, the rogue had apparently been in the shop some time inspecting the goods which were brought and displayed for sale to him without any regard to his identity—he was a "customer" only. The judgment of Horridge J. is, as I read it, based on a finding of fact that Phillips intended to deal with North as a customer. Viscount Haldane, in *Lake* v. *Simmons*, [1927] A.C. 487, has taken the view that the case could be explained on the ground that the fraudulent misrepresentation was not made until after the parties had agreed upon a sale.

That opinion has been criticised, mainly, I think, by academic writers, but if, as must be conceded, it is a possible view, and as *Phillips* v. *Brooks Ltd.* has stood for so long and is, as I think, a decision within an area of fact, I would not feel justified in saying it was wrong.

It is not an authority to establish that where an offer or acceptance is addressed to a person (although under a mistake as to his identity) who is present in person, then it must in all circumstances be treated as if actually addressed to him. I would regard the issue as a question of fact in each case depending on what was said and done and applying the elementary principles of offer and acceptance in the manner in which Slade J. directed himself.

The judgment quotes extensively from the article by Dr. Goodhart, the editor of the Law Quarterly Review, called "Mistake as to identity in the Law of Contract" (1941) 57 L.Q.R. 228, and I would join the judge in his expression of indebtedness to the author. Referring to *Phillips* v. *Brooks Ltd.* Dr. Goodhart asked "Did the shopkeeper believe that he was entering into a contract with Sir George Bullough and did North know this? If both answers are in the affirmative, then it is submitted that there was no contract."

I think there may be a doubt in that case whether both the answers should have been in the affirmative, but on the facts of the present case I feel no doubt and I would uphold the judge's view of no contract.

Dr. Goodhart might well be right when he said that "There is no branch of the law of contract which is more uncertain and difficult" than that involved in the present case, and I am conscious that our decision here will not have served to dispel the uncertainty. . . .

I am in agreement with the judge when he quotes, accepts and applies the following passage from Dr. Goodhart's article—"It is the interpretation of the promise which is the essential thing. This is usually based on the interpretation which a reasonable man, in the promisee's position, would place on it, but in those cases where the promisor knows that the promisee has placed a peculiar interpretation on his words, then this is the binding one. The English law is not concerned with the motives of the parties nor with the reasons which influenced their actions. For practical reasons it has limited itself to the simple questions: what did the promisor promise, and how should this be interpreted?"

Phillips v. *Brooks Ltd.* is the closest authority on which the defendant relies. Once that is distinguished on its facts, without going so far as to say it is wrong, authority leans strongly in favour of the judgment appealed from. . . .

DEVLIN L.J. (dissenting): . . . Before, therefore, I consider mistake, I shall inquire whether there is offer and acceptance in form. There is no doubt that H.'s offer was addressed to Miss Ingram and her acceptance apparently, addressed to him. But, it is argued, the acceptance was in reality addressed to P. G. M. Hutchinson, who was not the offeror, and, therefore, no contract was made. There can be no doubt upon the authorities that this argument must be settled by inquiring with whom Miss Ingram intended to contract: was it with the person to whom she was speaking or was it with the person whom he represented himself to be? . . . All that Miss Ingram or any other witness in her position can say is that she did in fact accept the offer made to her; and that, if she had not been tricked or deceived, she would not have accepted it.

Courts of law are not inexperienced in dealing with this sort of situation. They do so by means of presumptions. . . . Whether the court, when it acts in this way, is really ascertaining the intentions of the parties or whether it is simply providing a just solution of their difficulties is a theoretical question which I need not explore. . . .

In my judgment, the court cannot arrive at a satisfactory solution in the present case except by formulating a presumption and taking it at least as a starting point. The presumption that a person is intending to contract with the person to whom he is actually addressing the words of contract seems to me to be a simple and sensible one and supported by some good authority. . . .

I do not think that it can be said that the presumption is conclusive, since there is at least one class of case in which it can be rebutted. If the person addressed is posing only as an agent it is plain that the party deceived has no thought of contracting with him but only with his supposed principal; if then there is no actual or ostensible authority, there can be no contract. *Hardman* v. *Booth* (1863), 1 H. & C. 803; is I think, an example of this. Are there any other circumstances in which the presumption can be rebutted? It is not necessary to strain to find them, for we are here dealing only with offer and acceptance; contracts in which identity really matters may still be avoided on the ground of mistake. I am content to leave the question open, and do not propose to speculate on what other exceptions there may be to the general rule. What seems plain to me is that the presumption cannot in the present case be rebutted by piling up the evidence to show that Miss Ingram would never have contracted with H. unless she had thought him to be P. G. M. Hutchinson. That fact is conceded and, whether it is proved simpliciter or proved to the hilt, it does not go any further than to show that she was the victim of fraud. With great respect to the judge, the question that he propounded as the test is not calculated to show any more than that. He said: "Is is to be seriously suggested that they "were willing to accept the cheque of the rogue other than in "the belief, created by the rogue himself, that he, the rogue, was "in fact the honest P. G. M. Hutchinson of the address in Caterham with the telephone number which they had verified?" In my judgment, there is everything to show that Miss Ingram would never have accepted H.'s offer if she had known the truth, but nothing to rebut the ordinary presumption that she was addressing her acceptance, in law as well as in fact, to the person to whom she was speaking. I think, therefore, that there was offer and acceptance in form.

On my view of the law, it, therefore, becomes necessary to consider next whether there has been a mistake that vitiates the contract. As both my brethren are of opinion that there has been no offer and acceptance, the result of this further inquiry cannot affect the decision in the present case or its ratio, and I shall, therefore, state my conclusions and my reasons for it as briefly as may be.

In my judgment, there has been no such mistake. I shall assume without arguments what I take to be the widest view of mistake that is to be found in the authorities, and that is that a mistake avoids the contract if at the time it is made there exists some state of fact which, as assumed, is the basis of the contract and as it is in truth, frustrates its object. . . .

The fact that Miss Ingram refused to contract with H. until his supposed name and address had been "verified" goes to show that she regarded his identity as fundamental. In this she was misguided. She should have concerned herself with creditworthiness rather than with identity. The fact that H. gave P. G. M. Hutchinson's address in the directory was no proof that he was P. G. M. Hutchinson; and if he had been, that fact alone was no proof that his cheque would be met. Identity, therefore, did not really matter. Nevertheless, it may truly be said that to Miss Ingram, as she looked at it, it did. In my judgment, Miss Ingram's state of mind is immaterial to this question. When the law avoids a contract ab initio, it does so irrespective of the intentions or opinions or wishes of the parties themselves. . . . This rule applies in the case of mistake because the reason for the avoidance is the same, namely, that the consent is vitiated by non-agreement about essentials. It is for the court to determine what in the light of all the circumstances is to be deemed essential. In my judgment, in the present case H.'s identity was immaterial. His creditworthiness was not, but creditworthiness in relation to contract is not a basic fact; it is only a way of expressing the belief that each party normally holds that the other will honour his promise. . . .

There can be no doubt, as all this difference of opinion shows, that the dividing line between voidness and voidability, between fundamental mistake and incidental deceit, is a very fine one. That a fine and difficult distinction has to be drawn is not necessarily any reproach to the law. But need the rights of the parties in a case like this depend on such a distinction? The great virtue of the common law is that it sets out to solve legal problems by the application to them of principles which the ordinary man is expected to recognise as sensible and just; their application in any particular case may produce what seems to him a hard result, but as principles they should be within his understanding and merit his approval. But here, contrary to its habit, the common law, instead of looking for a principle that is simple and just, rests on theoretical distinctions. Why should the question whether the defendant should or should not pay the plaintiff damages for conversion depend upon voidness or voidability, and upon inferences to be drawn from a conversation in which the defendant took no part? The true spirit of the common law is to override theoretical distinctions when they stand in the way of doing practical justice. For the doing of justice, the relevant question in this sort of case is not whether the contract was void or voidable, but which of two innocent parties shall suffer for the fraud of a third. The plain answer is that the loss should be divided between them in such proportion as is just in all the circumstances. If it be pure misfortune, the loss should be borne equally; if the fault or imprudence of either party has caused or contributed to the loss, it should be borne by that party in the whole or in the greater part. In saying this, I am suggesting nothing novel, for this sort of observation has often been made. But it is only in comparatively recent times that the idea of giving to a court power to apportion loss has found a place in our law. I have in mind particularly the Law Reform Acts of 1935, 1943 and 1945, that dealt respectively with joint tortfeasors, frustrated contracts and contributory negligence. These statutes, which I believe to have worked satisfactorily, show a modern inclination towards a decision based on a just apportionment rather than one given in black or in white according to the logic of the law. I believe it would be useful if Parliament were now to consider whether or not it is practicable by means of a similar act of law reform to provide for the victims of a fraud a better way of adjusting their mutual loss than that which has grown out of the common law.

[The judgment of Pearce L.J. is omitted. The appeal was dismissed but leave was granted to appeal to the House of Lords.]

CHAPTER 4

THIRD PARTY BENEFICIARIES

TWEDDLE *v.* ATKINSON

England. Queen's Bench. 1861. 1 B. & S. 393; 121 E.R. 762

The declaration stated that the plaintiff was the son of John Tweddle, deceased and before the making of the agreement hereafter mentioned, married the daughter of William Guy, deceased; and before the marriage the parents of the parties to the marriage orally promised to give the plaintiff a marriage portion; and after the marriage in order to give effect to their promises the parents entered into the following written agreement for the plaintiff's benefit:

"High Coniscliffe, July 11, 1855.

Memorandum of agreement made this day between William Guy, of, &c., of the one part, and John Tweddle, of, &c., of the other part. Whereas it is mutually agreed that the said William Guy shall and will pay the sum of £200 to William Tweddle, his son-in-law; and the said John Tweddle, father to the aforesaid William Tweddle, shall and will pay the sum of £100 to the said William Tweddle, each and severally the said sums on or before the 21st day of August, 1855. And it is hereby further agreed by the aforesaid William Guy and the said John Tweddle that the said William Tweddle has full power to sue the said parties in any court of law or equity for the aforesaid sum, hereby promised and specified."

The declaration further alleged that afterwards and before this suit, the plaintiff and his said wife, who is still living, ratified and assented to the said agreement, yet neither the said William Guy nor his executor has paid the promised sum of £200. Demurrer and joinder therein.

CROMPTON J.: It is admitted that the plaintiff cannot succeed unless this case is an exception to the modern and well-established doctrine of the action of assumpsit. At the time when the cases which have been cited were decided the action of assumpsit was treated as an action of trespass upon the case, and therefore in the nature of a tort; and the law was not settled, as it now is, that natural love and affection is not a sufficient consideration for a promise upon which an action may be maintained; nor was it settled that the promisee cannot bring an action unless the consideration for the promise moved from him. The modern cases have, in effect, overruled the old decisions; they show that the consideration must move from the party entitled to sue upon the contract. It would be a monstrous proposition to say that a person was a party to the contract for the purpose of suing upon it for his own advantage and not a party to it for the purpose of being sued. It is said that the father in the present case was agent for the son in making the contract, but that argument ought also to make the son liable upon it. I am prepared to overrule the old decisions, and to hold that, by reason of the principles which now govern the action of assumpsit, the present action is not maintainable.

[Judgment was given for the defendant. The concurring opinions of Wightman and Blackburn JJ. are omitted.]

LAWRENCE *v*. FOX

New York. Court of Appeals. 1859. 20 N.Y. 268

Appeal from the Superior Court of the city of Buffalo. On the trial before Mr. Justice Masten, it appeared by the evidence of a bystander, that one Holly, in November, 1857, at the request of the defendant, loaned and advanced to him $300, stating at the time that he owed that sum to the plaintiff for money borrowed of him, and had agreed to pay it to him the then next day; that the defendant in consideration thereof, at the time of receiving the money, promised to pay it to the plaintiff the then next day. Upon this state of facts the defendant moved for a nonsuit, upon three several grounds, viz.: That there was no proof tending to show that Holly was indebted to the plaintiff; that the agreement by the defendant with Holly to pay the plaintiff was void for want of consideration, and that there was no privity between the plaintiff and defendant. The court overruled the motion, and the counsel for the defendant excepted. The cause was then submitted to the jury, and they found a verdict for the plaintiff for the amount of the loan and interest, $344.66, upon which judgment was entered; from which the defendant appealed to the Superior Court, at general term, where the judgment was affirmed, and the defendant appealed to this court. The cause was submitted on printed arguments.

H. GRAY J.: The first objection raised on the trial amounts to this: That the evidence of the person present, who heard the declarations of Holly giving directions as to the payment of the money he was then advancing to the defendant, was mere hearsay and therefore not competent. Had the plaintiff sued Holly for this sum of money no objection to the competency of this evidence would have been thought of; and if the defendant had performed his promise by paying the sum loaned to him to the plaintiff, and Holly had afterwards sued him for its recovery, and this evidence had been offered by the defendant, it would doubtless have been received without an objection from any source. All the defendant had the right to demand in this case was evidence which, as between Holly and the plaintiff, was competent to establish the relation between them of debtor and creditor. For that purpose the evidence was clearly competent; it covered the whole ground and warranted the verdict of the jury.

But it is claimed that notwithstanding this promise was established by competent evidence, it was void for the want of consideration. It is now more than a quarter of a century since it was settled by the Supreme Court of this State—in an able and painstaking opinion by the late Chief Justice Savage, in which the authorities were fully examined and carefully analysed —that a promise in all material respects like the one under consideration was valid; and the judgment of that court was unanimously affirmed by the Court for the Correction of Errors. *Farley* v. *Cleaveland*, 4 Cow., 432; same case in error, 9 id. 639. In that case one Moon owed Farley and sold to Cleaveland a quantity of hay, in consideration of which Cleaveland promised to pay Moon's debt to Farley; and the decision in favor of Farley's right to recover was placed upon the ground that the hay received by Cleaveland from Moon was a valid consideration for Cleaveland's promise to pay Farley, and that the subsisting liability of Moon to pay Farley was no objection to the recovery.

The fact that the money advanced by Holly to the defendant was a loan to him for a day, and that it thereby became the property of the defendant, seemed to impress the defendant's counsel with the idea that because the defendant's promise was not a trust fund placed by the plaintiff in the defendant's hands, out of which he was to realize money as from the sale of a chattel or the collection of a debt, the promise although made for the benefit of the plaintiff could not enure to his benefit. The hay which Cleaveland [Moon?] delivered to Moon [Cleaveland?] was not to be paid to Farley, but the debt incurred by Cleaveland for the purchase of the hay, like the debt incurred by the defendant for money borrowed, was what was to be paid. That case has been often referred to by the courts of this State, and has never been doubted as sound authority for the principle upheld by it, *Barker* v. *Buklin*, 2 Denio, 45; *Hudson Canal Company* v. *The Westchester Bank*, 4 id. 97. It puts to rest the objection that the defendant's promise was void for want of consideration. The report of that case shows that the promise was not only made to Moon but to the plaintiff Farley.

In this case the promise was made to Holly and not expressly to the plaintiff; and this difference between the two cases presents the question, raised by the defendant's objection, as to the want of privity between the plaintiff and defendant. As early as 1806 it was announced by the Supreme Court of this State, upon what was then regarded as the settled law of England, "That where one person makes a promise to another for the benefit of a third person, that third person may maintain an action upon it." *Schermerhorn* v. *Vanderheyden*, 1 John.R., 140, has often been re-asserted by our courts and never departed from. . . .

But it is urged that because the defendant was not in any sense a trustee of the property of Holly for the benefit of the plaintiff, the law will not imply a promise. I agree that many of the cases where a promise was implied were cases of trusts, created for the benefit of the promiser. The case of *Felton* v. *Dickinson*, 10 Mass. 189, 190, and others that might be cited are of that class; but concede them all to have been cases of trusts, and it proves nothing against the application of the rule to this case. The duty of the trustee to pay the *cestius que trust*, according to the terms of the trust, implies his promise to the latter to do so. In this case the defendant, upon ample consideration received from Holly, promised Holly to pay his debt to the plaintiff; the consideration received and the promise to Holly made it as plainly his duty to pay the plaintiff as if the money had been remitted to him for that purpose, and as well implied a promise to do so as if he had been made a trustee of property to be converted into cash with which to pay. The fact that a breach of the duty imposed in the one case may be visited, and justly, with more serious consequences than in the other, by no means disproves the payment to be a duty in both. The principle illustrated by the example so frequently quoted (which concisely states the case in hand) "that a promise made to one for the benefit of another, he for whose benefit it is made may bring an action for its breach," has been applied to trust cases, not because it was exclusively applicable to those cases, but because it was a principle of law, and as such applicable to those cases.

It was also insisted that Holly could have discharged the defendant from his promise, though it was intended by both parties for the benefit of the plaintiff, and therefore the plaintiff was not entitled to maintain this suit for the recovery of a demand over which he had no control. It is enough that the plaintiff did not release the defendant from his promise, and whether he could or not is a question not now necessarily involved; but if it was, I think it would be found difficult to maintain the right of Holly to discharge a judgment recovered by the plaintiff upon confession or otherwise, for the breach of the defendant's promise; and if he could not, how could he discharge the suit before judgment, or the promise before suit, made as it was for the plaintiff's benefit and in accordance with legal presumption accepted by him, *Berly* v. *Taylor*, 5 Hill 577–584, et seq., until his dissent was shown.

The cases cited, and especially that of *Farley* v. *Cleaveland*, establish the validity of a parol promise; it stands then upon the footing of a written one. Suppose the defendant had given his note in which, for value received of Holly, he had promised to pay the plaintiff and the plaintiff had accepted the promise, retaining Holly's liability. Very clearly Holly could not have discharged that promise, be the right to release the defendant as it may. No one can doubt that he owes the sum of money demanded of him, or that in accordance with his promise it was his duty to have paid it to the plaintiff; nor can it be doubted that whatever may be the diversity of opinion elsewhere, the adjudications in this State, from a very early period, approved by experience, have established the defendant's liability; if, therefore, it could be shown that a more strict and technically accurate application of the rules applied, would lead to a different result (which I by no means concede), the effort should not be made in the face of manifest justice.

COMSTOCK J. (dissenting): The plaintiff had nothing to do with the promise on which he brought this action. It was not made to him, nor did the consideration proceed from him. If he can maintain the suit, it is because an anomaly has found its way into the law on this subject. In general, there must be privity of contract. The party who sues upon a promise must be the promisee, or he must have some legal interest in the undertaking. In this case, it is plain that Holly, who loaned the money to the defendant, and to whom the promise in question was made, could at any time have claimed that it should be performed to himself personally. He had lent the money to the defendant, and at the same time directed the latter to pay the sum to the plaintiff. This direction he could countermand, and if he had done so manifestly the defendant's promise to pay according to the direction would have ceased to exist. The plaintiff would receive a benefit by a complete execution of the arrangement, but the arrangement itself was between other parties, and was under their exclusive control. If the defendant had paid the money to Holly, his debt would have been discharged thereby. So Holly might have released the demand or assigned it to another person, or the parties might have annulled the promise now in question, and designated some other creditor of Holly as the party to whom the money should be paid. It has never been claimed, that in a case thus situated, the right of a third person to sue upon the promise rested on any sound principle of law. We are to inquire whether the rule has been so established by positive authority. . . .

The cases in which some trust was involved are also frequently referred to as authority for the doctrine now in question, but they do not sustain it. If A delivers money or property to B, which the latter accepts upon trust for the benefit of C, the latter can enforce the trust by an appropriate action for that purpose. *Berly* v. *Taylor*, 5 Hill 577. If the trust be of money, I think the beneficiary may assent to it and bring the action for money had and received to his use. If it be of something else than money, the trustee must account for it according to the terms of the trust, and upon principles of equity. There is some authority even for saying that an express promise founded on the possession of a trust fund may be enforced by an action at law in the name of the beneficiary, although it was made to the creator of the trust. Thus, in Comyn's Digest (Action on the case upon Assumpsit, B.15), it is laid down that if a man promise a pig of lead to A, and his executor give lead to make a pig to B, who assumes to deliver it to A, an assumpsit lies by A against him. The case of *The Delaware and Hudson Canal Company* v. *The Westchester County Bank*, 4 Denio 97, involved a trust because the defendants had received from a third party a bill of exchange under an agreement that they would endeavour to collect it, and would pay over the proceeds when collected to the plaintiffs. A fund receives it. He must account for it specifically; and perhaps there is no gross violation of principle in permitting the equitable owner of it to sue upon an express promise to pay it over. Having a specific interest in the thing, the undertaking to account for it may be regarded as in some sense made with him through the author of the trust. But further than this we cannot go without violating plain rules of law. In the case before us there was nothing in the nature of a trust or agency. The defendant borrowed the money of Holly and received it as his own. The plaintiff had no right in the fund, legal or equitable. The promise to repay the money created an obligation in favor of the lender to whom it was made and not in favor of any one else. . . .

The judgment of the court below should therefore be reversed, and a new trial granted.

[Johnson C.J., Denio, Selden, Allen and Strong JJ. concurred. Grover J. also dissented. Johnson C.J. and Denio J. were of opinion that the promise was to be regarded as made to the plaintiff through the medium of his agent, whose action he could ratify when it came to his knowledge, though taken without his being privy thereto.]

QUEBEC CIVIL CODE

1029. A party in like manner may stipulate for the benefit of a third person, when such is the condition of a contract which he makes for himself, or of a gift which he makes to another; and he who makes the stipulation cannot revoke it, if the third person have signified his assent to it.

NOTE. Something of the nature of the civil law system may be learned from an attempt to see how this clause works. Does this clause convert the "contract" into a "trust"? Must the third person be named in the contract, or can he be described by reference to a class? If Father insures against accident himself and every person driving with his consent, is Son, who drives with his consent and has an accident, protected? Has Son "signified his assent"? See *Hallé v. Canadian Indemnity Co.*, [1937] S.C.R. 368, and compare the *Vandepitte* case below. To whom must the "assent" be given, to the promisor, the promisee, or both of them? How must the assent be manifest? Must it be communicated? Will it "take effect" on despatch or on receipt? What if the "third person" dies without doing anything, can his personal representative "assent" for him?

DUNLOP PNEUMATIC TYRE CO. LTD *v* SELFRIDGE & CO. LTD.

England. House of Lords. [1915] A.C. 847

The facts of this case are shortly stated by Lord Sumner. There are two instances of sale and delivery complained of by Dunlop in this case. The steps in the Jameson transaction are as follows. Those in the other, the

Strauss transaction are similar, and need not be analysed. On October 12, 1911, Messrs, Dew & Co., motor accessory factors, contracted with the appellants, the Dunlop Company, in terms of the latter's price maintenance agreement then current. By this contract Dew became bound, inter alia, to buy from the Dunlop Company motor tyres, covers, tubes, and sundries to the net value of £2000 before the expiration of September, 1912, and the appellants became bound, if the contract continued to subsist, as it did, to sell and deliver such goods up to that value, whenever reasonably required to do so.

On December 21, 1911, a Captain Jameson thought fit to ask the respondents, Selfridge's, who are described as wholesale and retail merchants, for their lowest price for a Dunlop motor tyre, grooved and non-skid, 815 by 105. Their answer was that, on receipt of his order, such a tyre would be procured and the price would be £5 18s. 2d., which was the appellants' list price, less 7½ per cent.

On January 1, 1912, Captain Jameson sent to the respondents an order for the tyre, and also the money for it, and on the same day the order was accepted, and delivery of the tyre was promised for the following day. In fact, on January 2 the respondents ordered this tyre from Dew by telephone. Dew, in turn, ordered it by telephone from the appellants; it was delivered by them to Dew, and they sent it to the respondents. These were the events of January 2. On the next day the respondents delivered it to Captain Jameson. Of course the respondents did not mention Captain Jameson to Dew, nor did Dew mention the respondents to the appellants.

So far the respondents had signed no price maintenance agreement. They had been pressed to do so, and no doubt knew that the reason why they were being pressed by Dew was because the appellants, in turn, strictly required them to obtain these agreements from those of their customers to whom they sold. Within two or three days of January 3 they did sign such an agreement, dating it January 2, and delivering it to Dew, to whom it was addressed, a week or so afterwards. It is for breach of this agreement that the appellants sued.

The parties have been desirous of knowing their reciprocal rights and duties, if any, arising out of this agreement, and have accordingly raised two broad questions: (1.) Is there any agreement between these parties at all? (2.) If so, is there any consideration moving from the appellants to support it and make it bind the respondents to them? But for this there would have been a good deal to be said for the proposition that a bargain and sale, clearly complete before this agreement was signed or dated, could be no breach of it, and that the performance of that bargain by delivery of the goods after the price maintenance agreement was made could hardly be a ground for the grant of an injunction.

Phillimore J. gave judgment for the appellants for £10, the liquidated damages in respect of the two breaches, and granted an injunction restraining the respondents from selling Dunlop motor tyres, etc., below the appellants' current list prices.

The Court of Appeal reversed this decision and gave judgment for the respondents, They held that the contract of January 2 was not a contract between the appellants and the respondents at all, but was a contract between Dew and the respondents only, and that Dew were not legally competent at one and the same time to make a contract with the respondents by themselves as principals and as agents of the appellants. They therefore held that the action was not sustainable.

VISCOUNT HALDANE L.C.: My Lords, in my opinion this appeal ought to fail. . . .

My Lords, in the law of England certain principles are fundamental. One is that only a person who is a party to a contract can sue on it. Our law knows nothing of a jus quaesitum tertio arising by way of contract. Such a right may be conferred by way of property, as, for example, under a trust, but it cannot be conferred on a stranger to a contract as a right to enforce the contract in personam. A second principle is that if a person with whom a contract not under seal has been made is to be able to enforce it consideration must have been given by him to the promisor or to some other person at the promisor's request. These two principles are not recognized in the same fashion by the jurisprudence of certain continental countries or of Scotland, but here they are well established. A third proposition is that a principal not named in the contract may sue upon it if the promisee really contracted as his agent. But again, in order to entitle him so to sue, he must have given consideration either personally or through the promisee, acting as his agent in giving it.

My Lords, in the case before us, I am of opinion that the consideration, the allowance of what was in reality part of the discount to which Messrs. Dew, the promisees, were entitled as between themselves and the appellants, was to be given by Messrs. Dew on their own account, and was not in substance, any more than in form, an allowance made by the appellants. The case for the appellants is that they permitted and enabled Messrs. Dew, with the knowledge and by the desire of the respondents, to sell to the latter on the terms of the contract of January 2, 1912. But it appears to me that even if this is so the answer is conclusive. Messrs. Dew sold to the respondents goods which they had a title to obtain from the appellants independently of this contract. The consideration by way of discount under the contract of January 2 was to come wholly out of Messrs. Dew's pocket, and neither directly nor indirectly out of that of the appellants. If the appellants enabled them to sell to the respondents on the terms they did, this was not done as any part of the terms of the contract sued on.

No doubt it was provided as part of these terms that the appellants should acquire certain rights, but these rights appear on the face of the contract as jura quaesita tertio which the appellants could not enforce. Moreover, even if this difficulty can be got over by regarding the appellants as the principals of Messrs. Dew in stipulating for the rights in question, the only consideration disclosed by the contract is one given by Messrs. Dew, not as their agents, but as principals acting on their own account.

The conclusion to which I have come on the point as to consideration renders it unnecessary to decide the further question as to whether the appellants can claim that a bargain was made in this contract by Messrs. Dew as their agents; a bargain which, apart from the point as to consideration, they could therefore enforce. If it were necessary to express an opinion on this further question, a difficulty as to the position of Messrs. Dew would have to be considered. Two contracts—one by a man on his own account as principal, and another by the same man as agent—may be validly comprised in the same piece of paper. But they must be two contracts, and not one as here. I do not think that a man can treat one and the same contract as made by him in two capacities. He cannot be regarded as contracting for himself and for another uno flatu.

My Lords, the form of the contract which we have to interpret leaves the appellants in this dilemma, that, if they say that Messrs. Dew contracted on their behalf, they gave no consideration, and if they say they gave consideration in the shape of a permission to the respondents to buy, they must set up further stipulations, which are neither to be found in the contract sued upon nor are germane to it, but are really inconsistent with its structure. That contract has been reduced to writing, and it is in the writing that we must look for the whole of the terms made between the parties. These terms cannot, in my opinion, consistently with the settled principles of English law, be construed as giving to the appellants any enforceable rights as against the respondents.

I think that the judgment of the Court of Appeal was right, and I move that the appeal be dismissed with costs.

LORD DUNEDIN.: My Lords, I confess that this case is to my mind apt to nip any budding affection which one might have had for the doctrine of consideration. For the effect of that doctrine in the present case is to make it possible for a person to snap his fingers at a bargain deliberately made, a bargain not in itself unfair, and which the person seeking to enforce it has a legitimate interest to enforce. Notwithstanding these considerations I cannot say that I have ever had any doubt that the judgment of the Court of Appeal was right....

That there are methods of framing a contract which will cause persons in the position of Selfridge to become bound, I do not doubt. But that has not been done in this instance; and as Dunlop's advisers must have known of the law of consideration, it is their affair that they have not so drawn the contract....

[Opinions to the like effect were given by Lords Atkinson, Parker of Waddington, Sumner and Parmoor.]

THE SATANITA

England. Court of Appeal. [1895] P. 248

On July 5, 1894, the Valkyria and the Satanita were manoeuvring to get into position for starting for the fifty mile race at the Mudhook Yacht Club Regatta, when the Satanita ran into and sank the Valkyria.

The entry for the Satanita for the regatta was signed by the defendant, and contained the following clause: "I undertake that, while sailing under this entry, I will obey and be bound by the sailing rules of the Yacht Racing Association and the by-laws of the club."

The rules of the Yacht Racing Association, adopted by the club, provided among other things as follows:

Rule 24: ". . . If a yacht, in consequence of her neglect of any of these rules, shall foul another yacht . . . she shall forfeit all claim to the prize, and shall pay all damages."

The plaintiffs, in an action in personam in the Admiralty Division . . . alleged that by the terms of the entry and in consideration that the owner of the Valkyrie would race with the defendant under these rules, the defendant agreed that if the Satanita fouled the Valkyrie in consequence of her neglect of any of the rules, the Satanita would pay all damages. . . . The defendant denied that he had entered into such agreement as alleged. . . .

LORD ESHER M.R.: This is an action by the owner of a yacht against the owner of another yacht, and, although brought in the Admiralty Division, the contention really is that the yacht which is sued has broken the rules which by her consent governed her sailing in a regatta in which she was contesting for a prize.

The first question raised is whether, supposing her to have broken a rule, she can be sued for that breach of the rules by the owner of the competing yacht which has been damaged; in other words, was there any contract between the owners of those two yachts? Or it may be put thus: Did the owner of the yacht which is sued enter into obligation to the owner of the other yacht, that if his yacht broke the rules, and thereby injured the other yacht, he would pay damages? It seems to me clear that he did; and the way that he has undertaken that obligation is this. A certain number of gentlemen formed themselves into a committee and proposed to give prizes for matches sailed between yachts at a certain place on a certain day, and they promulgated certain rules, and said: "If you want to sail in any of our matches for our prizes, you cannot do so unless you submit yourselves to the conditions which we have thus laid down. And one of the conditions is, that if you do sail for one of such prizes you must enter into an obligation with the owners of the yachts who are competing, which they at the same time enter into similarly with you, that if by a breach of any of our rules you do damage or injury to the owner of a competing yacht, you shall be liable to make good the damage which you have so done." If that is so, then when they do sail, and not till then, that relation is immediately formed between the yacht owners. There are other conditions with regard to these matches which constitute a relation between each of the yacht owners who enters his yacht and sails it and the committee; but that does not in the least do away with what the yacht owner has undertaken, namely, to enter into a relation with the other yacht owners, that relation containing an obligation.

Here the defendant, the owner of the Satanita, entered into a relation with the plaintiff Lord Dunraven, when he sailed his yacht against Lord Dunraven's yacht, and that relation contained an obligation that if, by any breach of any of these rules, he did damage to the yacht of Lord Dunraven, he would have to pay the damages. . . .

[Only that part of the opinion is given that deals with the formation of the contract. Rigby and Lopes L.JJ. gave judgments to the same effect. Rigby L.J. said, "To whom is the owner of that yacht to pay those damages? He cannot pay them to the club, nor do I think the club could recover them. The true and sensible construction is that he must pay the owner of the yacht fouled." The judgments were affirmed in the House of Lords *sub nomine Clarke* v. *Dunraven*, [1897] A.C. 59.]

MULHOLLAND *v*. MERRIAM
Ontario. Chancery. 1872. 19 Grant 288

STRONG V.C.: About the 6th of November, 1868, John Mulholland being possessed of a considerable amount in money and securities, the proceeds of the sale of his farm and also of some other property, executed an instrument in a very peculiar form. This document, which was prepared by Philip Green, a schoolmaster, residing in the neighbourhood of the defendant, may be thus described. The first part of it purports to be a bond by the defendant to John Mulholland in the penal sum of $400. What is declared to be the condition is as follows: John Mulholland purports thereby to assign to the defendant "all his estate real and personal, with notes and accounts, to the said William Merriam on condition that he pay his heirs in the manner following, namely," and then follows a direction to pay to each of the living children of John Mulholland except the defendant's wife $400, and the like sum to the children of two deceased daughters. It then contains the following clause: "The said William Merriam hereby becomes bound to pay the above mentioned sums to the parties herein named at the time of the decease of the said John Mulholland, or as soon after as can conveniently be done." A covenant on the part of Merriam to provide a maintenance for John Mulholland during the remainder of his life, completes the document.

This bond or agreement was executed by sealing by both John Mulholland and his son-in-law, the defendant, William Merriam.

The bill is filed by George B. Mulholland one of the sons of John Mulholland, to enforce payment of the $400, which by the instrument set forth was to be paid to him on his father's death, which took place in April, 1870. The defendant by his answer to the original bill alleges in paragraph 7 that he has "in all things fully performed the trusts and covenants in the said bond and agreement on his part to be performed."

At the hearing it was contended for the defendant, in the first place, that there was no jurisdiction; that no trust was created by the agreement, and that there was an absence of any privity, either at law or in equity, between the plaintiff and the defendant, the proper remedy on the instrument being an action at law, to be brought by the personal representative of John Mulholland. . . .

As to the first point raised by the defendant. I have had much doubt and difficulty, for it seemed to me at first that the bond could be considered in legal effect as nothing more than a personal covenant by Merriam the defendant with John Mulholland, and that consequently the only remedy on it could have been action at law by the personal representative of the latter. More mature consideration has led me to think I was wrong in my first impression both as to the proper construction of the instrument, and also as to the consequence which I thought would have attached, if that construction had been correct. . . .

I think there could be no doubt but that a personal representative of the testator recovering this money in an action at law would be considered as a trustee for the plaintiff, and, if so, it would, I think, follow that the plaintiff can maintain this suit. I quite agree that, in the naked case, where there is a covenant by one person with another to pay a sum of money to a stranger, or do any act for the benefit of a stranger who is not a party to the instrument or agreement, the person to whom the money is to be paid, or who is to be benefited, cannot sue either at law or in equity, inasmuch as there is no privity of contract. . . . There appears, it is true, to be an exception to this general rule recognized in some of the older cases, where it is laid down that the person to receive the benefit of the contract, though a stranger to it, may maintain an action upon it if he stand in such a relationship to the contracting party that it may be considered that the contract was made for his benefit, and in the very case of a contract made with a father to pay money to his son or daughter, it has been held upon this principle that the son or daughter might sue on the contract. . . . *Dutton* v. *Poole* (1678), 83 E.R. 523. . . .

This doctrine is not, however, now approved as regards courts of law, as appears from the late case of *Tweddle* v. *Atkinson* (1861), 121 E.R. 762. This, however, in my opinion, only goes to shew the applicability to a case like the present of a remedy in this Court proceeding on a doctrine which I will endeavour to point out. There can be no doubt, as I have already said, that this $400, if recovered in an action at law by a personal representative of John Mulholland, would not be assets in his hands to be distributed by him according to the *Statute* of *Distributions,* but would be impressed with a trust in equity in favor of the plaintiff. This *must* be so, for the only other alternative is, that it was in the power of the defendant entirely to defeat any or all of the gifts which the settlor made to his children, by compelling the personal representative to bring an action, the fruits of which would be free from any trust and liable to be distributed amongst the next of kin; which would of course, be absurd.

Then if the money, when recovered by the administrator, would be effected by a trust, it must also be, that the right of action which the personal representative has is also bound by a like trust; and, if this is so, there is the highest authority for saying that, even though the obligation of Merriam rests (as I have already determined it does not) merely on contract, and he should not be bound by any trust, yet, as the personal representative would be a trustee for the plaintiff, he and the plaintiff conjointly might maintain this bill. The authority which I refer to is the case of *Gregory* v. *Williams* (1817), 36 E.R. 224, decided by a very great Judge (Sir William Grant, M.R.), and it is approved by Mr. Spence, who, in his treatise, 2 *Equitable Jurisdiction,* 286, thus states both the case and the principle which it establishes: he says:

"There are instances where a third person has been expressly allowed to treat the party exacting the stipulation as his trustee, though such third person was a mere stranger to the parties. In the case of *Gregory* v. *Williams,* one Parker, who was in the possession of a farm belonging to the defendant Williams, was considerably indebted to Williams; he also owed a large debt to one Gregory. Parker, as Williams knew, was under apprehension that Gregory would arrest him; Williams, the landlord, and Parker, the tenant, entered into an agreement in writing, to which Gregory, the creditor, was neither party nor privy, to the following effect, namely: that, if Parker would make over to Williams all his stock and effects of every kind, he would pay the debt due to Gregory. Gregory subsequently was informed on this arrangement, and he and Parker filed their bill against Williams to enforce it. The stock and effects assigned to Williams by Parker had been sold at a loss; it was insisted by Williams that, if Gregory had any remedy, it was at law. Sir W. Grant considered it was at least doubtful whether Gregory could recover at law, for the engagement of Williams was not made directly to Gregory, but to Parker only, and the consideration was furnished by Parker only, for he alone did the act which constituted the consideration; Gregory was not a party to the contract; however, that learned Judge supported Gregory's right to sue in equity, saying 'Parker acts as his trustee, and Gregory may derive an equitable right through the medium of Parker's agreement, though it was at least questionable whether he could have maintained an action at law; it was like the case where a man promised the widow that, if she would allow his name to be joined with hers in the administration, he would make up the deficiency of the assets for the payment of the testator's debts; which promise was held to be binding in favour of the creditors, though they could not sue at law, as the promise was not made to them; so here, Gregory had a right to insist upon the benefit of the promise made to Parker to the extent of £900, which Parker represented to be the amount of the debt.' "

This case which never appears to have been overruled or even doubted, lays down a reasonable and convenient doctrine applying directly to the present case, and shewing that the plaintiff has an equitable right to enforce the contract (if it is nothing more than a contract) which the defendant entered into with John Mulholland. It is true that in the case of *Gregory* v. *Williams* the *quasi* trustee, Parker, was a co-plaintiff, and it may be said that a personal representative of the settlor John Mulholland ought to be a party here. But there is no such representative in existence, and if one was constituted it would only be for the express purpose of this suit since all the property of the intestate was made over by this assignment to the defendant, and there are now no assets to administer or debts to pay; and such an administrator would be a mere formal party as a trustee having not the slightest interest. I am therefore perfectly justified in directing as I do under the Consolidated Order 56, that the suit may proceed in the absence of any person representing the estate of John Mulholland.

Therefore in my judgment the suit is maintainable, *first* because the defendant is a trustee under the instrument of the 6th November, 1868, and the plaintiff is one of the *cestius que* trusts; *second*, even though the defendant be not a trustee, and is liable on contract only, the plaintiff has nevertheless an equitable right of suit on the authority of the case referred to. . . .

LES AFFRETEURS REUNIS SOCIETE ANONYME *v.* LEOPOLD WALFORD (LONDON) LIMITED. [1919] A.C. 801 (England. House of Lords). LORD WRENBURY: ". . . We have here to do with a contract between two parties reserving a benefit to a third. The two parties are the shipowners and the charterers, the third party is the broker of one of them, who is to be remunerated in respect of a contract which is being made for the hire of a ship. The particular form of contract in question is of course prepared by, or is under the eyes of the broker who is negotiating the matter. It is sent to the principals for signature, and they sign it, and there is contained in it a clause which reserves a benefit to the broker. Under those circumstances an action is brought by the broker against the shipowner for the commission which is expressed to be payable to him under the contract between the shipowner and the charterer—a contract to which he himself, I agree, was not a party. By agreement between the parties the record is to be treated as if the charterer were joined as a plaintiff in the action. The case is one in which an action can be brought on behalf of a person to whom a benefit is reserved, although he is not a party to it. That is the subject of the decision in *Robertson* v. *Wait.* Under those circumstances the shipowners, the defendants in the action, defend the action and in effect are here saying: 'It is perfectly true that we attached our signature to this document; it is perfectly true that it contains in Article 29 this stipulation in favour of a third party; but that means nothing at all—that is not the bargain at all to which we were parties. The matter is governed by a certain custom.'

"My Lords, I feel myself in great difficulty in understanding a contention of that sort. It is said that in this particular business there exists a custom (and I will take it for the moment that the custom is proved) that in time charterparties broker's commission is payable out of hire earned and is not payable unless hire is earned. In this contract, however, there is a stipulation that the commission shall be on the estimated gross amount of hire on signing the charter ship lost or not lost. I find myself quite unable to understand how it can be set up that into a contract expressed in those terms there can be introduced a custom to an exactly contrary effect. Directly it is conceded that the broker, although not a party to the contract, can sue on the contract, inasmuch as he can sue by the charterer as trustee for him, it appears to me that the case really is over. I have only to read Article 29 and I find there an express stipulation—a stipulation which is accepted by the signature of the defendants, that this payment shall be made, and for that payment it appears to me that the defendants are liable. . . ."

NOTE ON THE TRUST CONCEPT. The courts, as the last cases show, sometimes invoke the notion of a "trust" to justify a remedy for the third party beneficiary excluded by *Tweddle* v. *Atkinson*. In order to understand fully what is meant by a trust you will have to study it as a separate subject, probably in your third year. Meanwhile this short explanation may make the contract cases more intelligible. The explanation is so short, however, and so over-simplified, as to be positively dangerous, and you may prefer to read Chapter 1 of Austin Scott, *The Law of Trusts* (2d ed., 1956), which is generally acknowledged to be the modern classic.

You have already seen that, especially in conveyancing contracts, the equity courts will sometimes grant specific performance. The remedy is so available, in fact, that we speak of the purchaser having an equitable interest in the land. The vendor may have the legal title to the land, but since the court will compel him to convey it to the purchaser, that conveyance is anticipated, as it were, and the purchaser's existing interest is recognised. Thus, although the holder of the fee simple is said, sometimes, to have the largest bundle of rights in respect of the land that the law recognises, it may be that he holds very few, especially if, under a registry system, the agreement to convey can be registered so that the whole world will be deemed to know of its existence. In such circumstances it might be said that the vendor holds the fee subject to the equity of the purchaser, who can, by action, compel him to hand over the title.

A somewhat similar relationship is recognised in the case of mortgages in most jurisdictions of Canada. The mortgagor, who owns real property in fee, pledges the title with the mortgagee to secure the repayment of money within some specified time, in which event the mortgagee, to whom the mortgagor has conveyed the title, promises to reconvey. Again, equity would compel specific performance of the promise to reconvey. And again, the mortgagor has an equitable interest although the mortgagee has the legal title. Equity goes much further, in the mortgage cases, because the conveyance to the mortgagee may be subject only to a condition, rather than a promise to reconvey, and in either case, the equity courts would enforce the promise or the condition even after the time for its enforcement within the terms of the "mortgage contract" had passed. The mortgagor may redeem his title and has an "equity of redemption," not unlike the purchaser's "equity of specific performance," although the latter term is not used.

So in the case of a trust, the trustor, or settlor, the author of the trust, conveys the subject, or corpus, of the trust, usually land, to the trustee, who holds the legal title, but for the benefit of the *cestui que trust,* or beneficiary, who has an interest in the land that a court of equity would enforce against the trustee. Equity has long recognised this relationship, and elaborate rules have been built up, defining the duties of the trustee and the rights of the beneficiary. Some appreciation of the difficulty of safely attempting a short explanation of the trust concept can be had from this passage from Maitland's famous lectures on *Equity*, first published in 1910. After commenting on the difficulties of defining a "trust," he says, at p. 44:

"Where judges and text-writers fear to tread professors of law have to rush in. I should define a trust in some such way as the following—When a person has rights which he is bound to exercise on behalf of another or for the accomplishment of some particular purpose he is said to have those rights in trust for that other or for that purpose and he is called a trustee."

Maitland concedes that it is a "wide vague definition, but the best that I can make." He then proceeds to distinguish trusts from other devices of the law, including bailment. It may be helpful as well to look at Scott's attempt to distinguish trusts from contracts, which he presents at page 135 (Vol. 1) of the classic already mentioned.

Usually the subject matter of the trust is a piece of land, but this need not be so, and there is clearly no doubt that it can be a promise, and the promisee can be regarded as holding the right to enforce the promise in trust for the beneficiary of the promisee. If the trust is irrevocable, which it would be taken to be if it were not expressly made revocable, then one striking difference from contract is the absence of that freedom with which the parties to contract can agree to alter their positions, or terminate their claims and duties altogether. This difference is perhaps one good reason for hesitating, as the English courts seem prone to do, to "imply" a trust in what is rather obviously more like a contract relationship. In most cases neither party will have any such sophisticated and selfconscious intention about how his conduct should be classified, and any decision turning on "intention" is, at best, a judicial view of the "intent of the transaction," rather than of the intent of the parties.

YOUNG *v*. CANADIAN NORTHERN RAILWAY CO. [1931] A.C. 83 (Manitoba. Privy Council). Young was employed by the C.N.R. Company in 1920. He had no written agreement and, after signing an application for employment form, asked what wages he would receive. He was told he would receive the "going rate." There was then in existence a document describing itself as "Wage Agreement 4" the parties to which were, among others, the Company and "Division 4, Railway Employees' Department, American Federation of Labour." On June 13, 1927, Young was laid off although men junior to him were kept on. He contended that the Company was bound to him by the terms of "Wage Agreement 4," certain terms of which secured to him his seniority rights. He was not a member of the union, but it was admitted that as a general rule the Company applied the terms of the Agreement to all employees, irrespective of their membership in the union. Held, for the Company. LORD RUSSELL OF KILLOWEN: "[Wage Agreement No. 4] appears to their Lordships to be intended merely to operate as an agreement between a body of employers and a labour organization by which the employers undertake that as regards their workmen, certain rules beneficial to the workmen shall be observed. By itself it constitutes no contract between any individual employee and the company which employs him. If an employee refused to observe the rules, the effective sequel would be, not an action by any employee, not even an action by Division 4, against the employer for specific performance or damages, but the calling of a strike until the grievance was remedied."

THE LABOUR RELATIONS ACT
Ontario. Revised Statutes. 1960. Chapter 202

37. A collective agreement is, subject to and for the purposes of this Act, binding upon the employer and upon the trade union that is a party to the agreement whether or not the trade union is certified and upon the employees in the bargaining unit defined in the agreement.

34. (1) Every collective agreement shall provide for the final and binding settlement by arbitration, without stoppage of work, of all differences between the parties arising from the interpretation, application, administration or alleged violation of the agreement, including any question as to whether a matter is arbitrable.

VANDEPITTE *v*. PREFERRED ACCIDENT INSURANCE CORP. OF NEW YORK. [1933] A.C. 70 (British Columbia. Privy Council). Mrs. Vandepitte was injured in a motor accident as the result of Jean Berry's negligence. She recovered judgment, but Jean, who was a minor living with her father, Berry, was unable to pay. Accordingly Vandepitte claimed against the Insurance Company by virtue of section 24 of the *Insurance Act* of British Columbia. Berry carried an insurance policy with the Company, which provided protection "to any person or persons while riding in or legally operating the automobile for private or pleasure purposes, with the permission of the insured." It was contended that Jean Berry was directly and in law a party to the contract, being within the description of the persons other than Berry to whom indemnity was available, or, if not in law a party to the contract, she was a *cestui que trust* of the promise contained in the contract to extend the indemnity to such a person as herself, Berry having so stipulated as trustee. Held, for the Insurance Company, partly on the interpretation placed on the *Insurance Act*. LORD WRIGHT: ". . . In the present case there is no evidence that R. E. Berry had any intention to insure any one but himself; even if in some cases the words of the policy taken with the surrounding circumstances might be held to found the necessary inference of intention that inference would fail here by reason of the statutory application. But even if he had so intended, he had no authority from Jean Berry to insure on her behalf and at no time did she purport to adopt or ratify any insurance even if made on her behalf. In these circumstances it is impossible to say that a contract existed between Jean Berry and the respondents, that is, it cannot be held that she was in law 'insured' under the policy. . . . Furthermore there was no consideration proceeding from Jean Berry. . . . [A] party to a contract can constitute himself a trustee for a third party of a right under the contract and thus confer such rights enforceable in equity on the third party. The trustee then can take steps to enforce performance to the beneficiary by the other contracting party as in the case of other equitable rights. The action should be in the name of the trustee; if, however, he refuses to sue, the beneficiary can sue, joining the trustee as a defendant. But, though the general rule is clear, the present question is whether R. E. Berry can be held in this case to have constituted such a trust. But here again the intention to constitute the trust must be affirmatively proved: the intention cannot necessarily be inferred from the mere general words of the policy. . . . In the present case, . . . there is no evidence that R. E. Berry had any intention to create a beneficial interest for Jean Berry, either specifically or as member of a described class. Indeed, at no time either when the policy was effected or before or after the accident is there any suggestion that R. E. Berry had any such idea. . . ."

RE SCHEBSMAN. [1943] 2 All E.R. 387 (England. High Court). UTHWATT J.: "I was referred to Professor Corbin's interesting article in The Law Quarterly Review, Vol. 46, on 'Contracts for the benefit of third persons' and have considered the cases to which he refers, but I am unable to see that they justify the conclusion at which he arrived that, in some cases of the class now under consideration, a fiction has been resorted to in order to raise a trust. The cases no doubt are hard to reconcile, but, to my mind, the explanation of them is that different minds may reach differing conclusions on the question whether the circumstances sufficiently show an intention to create a trust—and inferences as to intent may vary, as the cases on general charitable intent well show."

INSURANCE ACT

British Columbia. Revised Statutes. 1960. Chapter 197

232(1) Every owner's policy shall insure the person named therein and every other person who, with his consent, personally drives any automobile specifically described in the policy, against liability imposed by law upon the insured named therein or upon any such person for loss or damage. . . . [See S.B.C., 1932, c. 30, s. 5; S.B.C., 1935, c. 38, s. 44. Similar legislation is generally in effect in the common law provinces. See R.S.O. 1960, s. 190, s. 213(1).]

McEVOY *v.* THE BELFAST BANKING COMPANY, LIMITED. [1935] A.C. 24 (Northern Ireland. House of Lords). LORD ATKIN: ". . . I am compelled to notice an elaborate argument addressed to this House on behalf of the bank to the effect that the legal title never was in the son. It is said that the effect of the contract created by the deposit of £10,000 by the father in the names of himself and his son, the opening of the joint deposit account and the giving and acceptance of the deposit receipt was the formation of a contract between the father alone and the bank. Neither the father nor the bank, it is said, purported to contract for or with the son; the son was a third party who could acquire no rights against the bank. It was as though the father had opened an account in his own name making the sums payable to himself or his son, in which case it was said the son would clearly have to prove an independent contract between himself and the bank before he could use the bank. My Lords, this contention seems to me to raise the one question of general importance in the case. It involves the whole question of the legal relations created by a bank deposit in this form. The argument, if correct, appears to me inconsistent with well established banking practice and likely to impair the confidence in deposits made in joint names. I consider it to be quite unfounded. It is, I think, significant that there appears no trace of such an argument having been put forward in the courts below. It would not have been attractive hearing for customers or potential customers of the bank in Belfast. It seems to have been reserved for the rarer atmosphere of your Lordships' House.

"The suggestion is that where A deposits a sum of money with his bank in the names of A and B, payable to A or B, if B comes to the bank with the deposit receipt he has no right to demand the money from the bank or to sue them if his demand is refused. The bank is entitled to demand proof that the money was in fact partly B's, or possibly that A had acted with

B's actual authority. For the contract, it is said is between the bank and A alone. My Lords, to say this is to ignore the vital difference between a contract purporting to be made by A with the bank to pay A or B and a contract purporting to be made by A and B with the bank to pay A or B. In both cases of course payment to B would discharge the bank whether the bank contracted with A alone or with A and B. But the question is whether in the case put B has any rights against the bank if payment to him is refused. I have myself no doubt that in such a case B can sue the bank. The contract purporting to be made by A and B with the bank to pay A or B. with them jointly and severally. A purports to make the contract on behalf of B as well as himself and the consideration supports such a contract. If A has actual authority from B to make such a contract, B is a party to the contract ab initio. If he has not actual authority then subject to the ordinary principles of ratification B can ratify the contract purporting to have been made on his behalf and his ratification relates back to the original formation of the contract. If no events had happened to preclude B from ratifying, then on compliance with the contract conditions, including notice and production of the deposit receipt, B would have the right to demand from the bank, so much of the money as was due on the deposit account.

"In my view, therefore, if nothing had happened to prevent the son from ratifying the contract, he could sue the bank on the original deposit account. . . ."

WILLIS, "THE NATURE OF A JOINT ACCOUNT"
1936. 14 *Canadian Bar Review* 457, 461–3

. . . Is the ordinary case of deposit to joint account capable of being treated as an assignment by A to A and B under the Judicature Act? Can we say that when A deposits $1000 in the X Bank in the joint names of A and B "repayable to either or the survivor," (i) A acquires, by reason of the contract between himself and the X bank, the legal title to a chose in action, value $1000, and (ii) A simultaneously transfers the legal title to his newly created piece of property, the chose in action, to A and B jointly. Assignment to A and B jointly is precisely what A intends: for he intends to make a direct gift of his right, which is in fact a contract right, and "assignment" is no more than the technical term which lawyers reserve for the transfer of that intangible piece of property which they call a chose in action. But since it is probable that a gratuitous assignment of a legal chose in action cannot be made otherwise than under the Judicature Act, it becomes necessary to determine whether the circumstances of a typical deposit to joint account are such as to satisfy the requirements of that Act.

The written contract purporting to be made between A and B and the X Bank, and signed by A, that is invariably taken on these occasions satisfies the requirements of the Act (a) that the assignment be by writing under the hand of the assignor, and (b) that express notice in writing be given to the debtor. It is immaterial that as far as B is concerned the transfer is gratuitous, for it has been decided that the Act has improved the position of a donee of a legal chose in action so as to enable him to sue at law in his own name as assignee without regard to whether or not the assignment was for value. But the Act only applies to an "absolute assignment . . . not purporting to be by way of charge only": is this assignment "absolute"? The deposit by A to the joint account of A and B is certainly not an assignment "by way of charge only": B gets, not "a mere right to payment out of the particular fund," but the whole title jointly with A to the whole fund. Nor does the fact that A retains a beneficial interest in the fund prevent the assignment being absolute: where A assigns his claim against X to B for collection, the assignment to B is "absolute" within the meaning of the Act. Here may be made a serious objection that the Act applies only to cases where A makes an out-and-out transfer to B, puts himself out of control and B wholly in control of the fund: that when A deposits $1000 to the joint account of A and B, the essence of the transaction is that A may to-morrow if he so wishes draw out every cent without rendering himself liable to B, his donee: that consequently a deposit to joint account cannot be an "absolute" assignment. The objection may, however, be answered in either of two ways. First, the Act says nothing about an out-and-out transfer. The purpose of requiring an assignment under the Act to be "absolute," as opposed for instance to conditional, is to prevent a creditor embarassing his debtor by "splitting" the claim against him so as to render it difficult for him to decide to whom he is legally bound to pay it; but A's transfer of his claim to A and B jointly cannot embarrass the bank in this manner, for neither A nor B can sue the bank for anything except the whole of the fund, and payment by the bank to either discharges the bank from its liability to both. Second, even if the Act does require an out-and-out transfer, the deposit by A to the joint account of A and B effects just that. It is quite true that A can draw out every cent from the account; but that is only natural for A never transferred anything to B except joint creditorship with A. But A has irrevocably transferred his title to A and B jointly: surely the bank would not retransfer the money back again to A's own private account without the consent of B, for by the act of transfer A has destroyed his old sole title to the claim and created instead a joint title in himself and B.

Doubt has recently been thrown upon the right of B to claim money deposited by A in the X Bank to the joint account of A and B by way of gift. Every one will agree with Lord Atkin that an argument which casts such a doubt is "inconsistent with well-established banking practice and likely to impair the confidence in deposits made in joint names," and "not attractive hearing for customers or potential customers of the bank". Unfortunately the judgments of the three concurring Law Lords and the separate judgment of Lord Atkin in the *McEvoy Case* have only increased that doubt. The writer has therefore examined four legal theories upon which B might acquire the right that common sense and inconvenience alike demand that he should have. Three of them have been dismissed as unsound: (i) the orthodox theory which extends to a joint account the principles applicable to a transfer of stock into the joint names of A and B: (ii) the theory of Lord Atkin that A, the depositor-donor, enters into a contract with the X Bank as agent for B the donee, which contract B may subsequently ratify: (iii) the theory that A in depositing the money declares himself trustee of his claim against the bank for himself and B as joint cestuis que trust. The fourth theory, that in depositing the money A simultaneously makes a contract with the bank and assigns his claim against the bank by writing under the Judicature Act to himself and B jointly, is no less fictional than the others, but it is preferable to them in that, so far as the writer can see, it does not run counter either to the intention of A or to any positive rule of law. Its novelty and complexity, however, render it a little suspect, and the writer submits it, and then with some diffidence, only because of a conviction that no long time can elapse before a court will be faced with the problem of how to give, not good, but any legal grounds at all for upholding a transaction which is every day entered into without question. When are we going to have third party beneficiary contracts?

RE SCHEBSMAN
England. Court of Appeal. [1943] 2 All E.R. 768

Schebsman had been employed for some years by La Société Générale de Surveillance S.A., a Swiss company, and its subsidiary, Cargo Superintendents (London), Ltd., an English company. Schebsman was a spendthrift with a short expectation of life. He was separated from his wife and daughter who were both dependent on him. The companies wanted to make an amicable separation with Schebsman and to that end the English company proposed to pay certain sums to him and after his death to his widow and daughter. Neither Mrs. Schebsman nor her daughter was connected with either company and neither was consulted in the negotiation. Provision was made for the wife and daughter as a "trump card" to get Schebsman to accept the arrangement. Schebsman quit his job on March 31, 1940, and executed the tripartite agreement with the two companies on September 20. He was adjudicated a bankrupt on March 5, 1942 and died on May 12, the same year. According to the agreement the sum now became payable to Mrs. Schebsman and if she died before a certain date, to her daughter.

Schebsman's trustee in bankruptcy claimed a declaration that all sums payable under the agreement formed part of the bankrupt estate. The widow, the daughter and the two companies were made parties to the action. The English company wanted to make payments in accordance with the contract. Uthwatt J. dismissed the motion.

LORD GREENE M.R.: . . . The first question which arises is whether or not Schebsman was a trustee for his wife and daughter of the benefit of the undertaking given by the English company in their favour. An examination of the decided cases does, it is true, show that the courts have on occasions adopted what may be called a liberal view on questions of this character. But in the present case, I cannot find in the contract anything to justify the conclusion that a trust was intended. It is not legitimate to import into the contract the idea of a trust when the parties have given no indication that such was their intention. To interpret this contract as creating a trust would, in my judgment, be to disregard the dividing line between the case of a trust and the simple case of a contract made between two persons for the benefit of a third. That dividing line exists, although it may not always be easy to determine where it is to be drawn. In the present case I find no difficulty. I will now turn to the other questions which arise.

At the outset of his address, counsel for the appellant suggested that the trustee in bankruptcy as claiming through Schebsman could claim all sums paid by the English company to Mrs. Schebsman or her daughter as money had and received to his use. As the discussion proceeded, this argument was abandoned by counsel for the appellant and rightly so. The transaction gave rise to no such privity between these ladies and Schebsman as would support a claim against them for money had and received. It was also conceded that at common law the English company is bound, as between itself and the trustee, to make payments to Mrs. Schebsman or her daughter in accordance with the contract: and that the trustee as claiming through

Schebsman has no right at common law to require the company to pay these sums to himself. The contract was tripartite and its terms could only be varied by the consent of all three parties. Mrs. Schebsman and her daughter have, of course, no right to demand payment from the English company since they are not parties to the contract. When the company makes a payment to one of them it is, as between the company and the payee, a gratuitous payment made with the intention of passing the property in the money paid and this is sufficient to give to the payee at common law a good title to the money against the whole world. The question, what damages could be recovered by the representatives of Schebsman if the company were to break its contract has no bearing on anything that we have to decide.

The argument of counsel for the appellant, as he developed it, rested entirely on equitable principles. It may be summarised as follows. Schebsman provided the whole of the consideration for the English company's undertaking to make the payments to his widow and daughter. These payments must, therefore, be regarded in the same light as voluntary gifts. In the case of a completed transfer of property by a man to his wife or daughter a presumption of advancement arises. But in the present case the transfer was not completed since Mrs. Schebsman and her daughter have no title to demand payment to themselves. It was, therefore, possible for Schebsman in his lifetime and for the trustee as his representative to intervene at any time and to assert as against Mrs. Schebsman and her daughter that any payments thereafter made to either of them would be held by the payee on behalf of the estate of Schebsman. The effect of such intervention, it was said, makes it impossible to treat any money in fact received thereafter by Mrs. Schebsman or her daughter as an advancement. If, notwithstanding the intervention, the company makes a payment to either of them, there will be a resulting trust for the trustee as representing Schebsman. As a corollary to this it was said that, in properly constituted proceedings, the English company can be compelled to make the covenanted payments direct to the trustee. The case, it was said, is analogous to that of an uncompleted gift or that of an imperfectly constituted trust. Mrs. Schebsman and her daughter are mere volunteers and equity will do nothing to assist them.

This argument is attractive, but, in my opinion, fallacious. It is important to bear in mind at the outset that, as between himself and the English company, Schebsman had no right to intervene and direct the company to make the payments to someone other than Mrs. Schebsman or her daughter. As between the three parties to the contract, its terms were that the payments should be made to Mrs. Schebsman and her daughter and made to them, clearly, for their own benefit. If, therefore, Schebsman in his lifetime had directed the company to make these payments to his executors, the company would have been entitled to ignore the direction. The proposition that, in properly constituted proceedings, the trustee could obtain direct payment to himself, depends for its validity upon the truth of the proposition that, as between himself and Mrs. Schebsman and her daughter, the trustee is entitled to claim the money as his own. The former proposition cannot, therefore, be relied on in order to establish the latter proposition which must be made good, if at all, on its own merits. Indeed, the former proposition relates to procedure only and means nothing more than that, if A is proposing to pay money to B which as between B and C belongs in equity to C, C can join A as a defendant in his action against B and thus procure payment by A direct to himself. It throws no light on the question which, for our purposes, is the relevant one, namely, as between B and C, does the money belong in equity to C?

We must, therefore, consider the position as between Schebsman and his wife and daughter. I do not think that any help is obtained by considering the cases of uncompleted gifts or imperfectly constituted trusts. Indeed, these analogies seem to me to be misleading. If A instructs an agent to carry a present to B, the agent's authority is in its nature revocable and A can revoke his instructions at any time before the present is delivered. Similarly, if A is minded to create a trust in favour of B, a volunteer, and fails properly to constitute the trust, B has no remedy. But the present case is quite different. When he made the contract Schebsman did not constitute the English company his mandatory to transfer property of his own to his wife and daughter. Not only was the money in question never his property, but, once having made the contract, he had, as I have already pointed out, no right to call on the company to make the payment to his estate. In making the contract, he set in motion a piece of machinery which he had no power to stop by his own unilateral action save by releasing the company from the contract. Its operation would inevitably result in money reaching the hands of his widow and daughter assuming, as we must assume, that the English company would perform its contract. This, therefore, was no revocable mandate, nor was there any lack of completeness in the constitution of the machinery devised for securing these benefits for the widow and daughter. When he made the contract, Schebsman intended that his widow should receive those benefits for herself: it was part of the bargain between himself and the two companies that she should receive them: and he reserved to himself no right to call for payment to himself. The trustee could, presumably, release the company from its undertaking, but this would do no more than deprive the trustee of the right to sue for damages for its breach. The fact that such a release can be effected is no argument for saying that the trustee can claim the moneys as his own.

The question, therefore, is not will equity help the widow and daughter to retain the sums which will inevitably be paid to them, but will equity help the trustee in bankruptcy to recover them from the payees? I can find no principle which calls for an affirmative answer to this question. If it were otherwise, the result would be a curious one. Schebsman makes a contract intended to secure benefits to his wife and daughter after his death. It is true that they obtain no right to call for those benefits, but Schebsman with good reason trusts the company to make them. The company cannot avoid making them unless it is prepared to break its contract. In this confidence, let me assume, Schebsman makes his testamentary dispositions and dies with the satisfaction of knowing that the contract makes provision for his widow and daughter. It is said that his representative can abrogate his intention and call on his widow and daughter to pay over to his estate any sums they may receive and that equity will compel them to do so. In my opinion, no principle of equity requires this to be done.

It is, of course, true that Schebsman provided part of the consideration for which the English company gave its undertaking to make the payments. But he did so with the intention that the money paid should belong to the recipients beneficially, and in this sense the provision secured by the contract for the widow and daughter may perhaps be regarded as being an advancement to them. This was clearly his intention at the date of the contract. It is true that at that date and down to the date of his death all that Mrs. Schebsman and her daughter had was an expectancy, they had no legal rights whatever. But it was an expectancy that would necessarily mature into actual payment, subject always to the possibility that the three parties to the contract or their representatives might put an end to the contract by mutual consent and the possibility that Schebsman or his successors in title might release the company from its obligation. This being so, the advancement must, in my opinion, be regarded as completed when the contract was made since it was not in the power of Schebsman to change his mind and prevent it from becoming effective unless he could secure the agreement of both the other two parties to the contract or was prepared to release the company. I do not see how there can arise a resulting trust for Schebsman of money that was never his, the receipt of which by the payees he had no power by himself to prevent save by a release.

To say that there can be no effective advancement unless and until either the subject-matter reaches the hands of the person to be advanced or that person acquires a legal title to claim it, appears to me to be too narrow a proposition. I see no reason why in principle an advancement should not be regarded as complete and effective where the person desiring to make it sets in train for that purpose a process which it is out of his power to control by his own action. If the process is one which he can by his own action control as, for example, where he uses a mandatory to deliver the subject-matter of the advancement to the person whom he desires to benefit, the case is, of course, different. But where a person has done everything which the nature of the subject-matter permits to ensure that it will reach the object of his bounty and the nature of the transaction precludes the possibility of any subsequent intervention or change of mind on his part, the advancement must, in my opinion, be regarded as complete. In the present case the special nature of the transaction satisfies these tests. The circumstances that the three parties to the contract could put an end to it by mutual consent and that the company could be released are immaterial. They mean no more than that limited powers of revocation are provided. If, and only if, one or other of those powers is exercised can the intended advancement be prevented from taking effect. Cases of advancement made by such methods as these may be rare. But that is no reason for refusing to give effect to them when they occur.

There appears to me to be an additional reason why equity should not interfere. It is a fair interference from the form and substance of the contract that the two companies had themselves an interest in seeing that the widow and daughter of their employee should be provided for. The manner in which compensation should be provided for the loss by Schebsman of his employment was agreed between the three parties to the contract. The contract on its face could only mean that the sums payable to Mrs. Schebsman and her daughter are to be paid to them for their own benefit. How can Schebsman claim them for himself without breaking his contract? I do not see how he can, and, if this view be correct, it cannot be that, as between himself and the payees Schebsman can be heard to assert in a court of equity a claim the enforcement of which involves a breach of contract even when that contract is one to which Mrs. Schebsman and her daughter were not parties. . . .

[The appeal was dismissed with costs. The opinions of Luxmore and Du Parcq L.JJ. are omitted.]

THE CONVEYANCING AND LAW OF PROPERTY ACT
Ontario. Revised Statutes. 1960. c. 66

63. (1) In this section,

(a) "employee" means an employee or former employee who is participating in a plan;

(b) "employer" includes the trustee under a plan;

(c) "plan" means an employee pension, retirement, welfare or profit-sharing fund or plan.

(2) Where in accordance with the terms of a plan an employee has designated a person or persons to receive a benefit payable under the plan in the event of the employee's death,

(a) the employer is discharged upon paying to such person or persons the amount of the benefit;

(b) such person or persons may upon the death of the employee enforce payment of the benefit, but the employer is entitled to set up any defence that he could have set up against the employee or his personal representatives.

(3) An employee may from time to time alter or revoke a designation made under a plan, but any such alteration or revocation may be made only in the manner set forth in the plan.

(4) This section does not apply to a designation of a beneficiary to which *The Insurance Act* applies.

THE INSURANCE ACT
Ontario. Revised Statutes. 1960. Chapter 190

167. (2) Subject to subsection 1, a beneficiary . . . may, at the maturity of the contract, enforce for his own benefit . . . the payment of insurance money appointed, appropriated or apportioned to him by the contract or a declaration and in accordance with the terms thereof, but the insurer shall be entitled to set up any defence which it could have set up against the insured or his personal representatives; and payment made to the beneficiary . . . shall discharge the insurer.

164. (1) Where the insured, in pursuance of the provisions of section 167, designates as beneficiary or beneficiaries, a member or members of the class of preferred beneficiaries, a trust is created in favour of the designated beneficiary or beneficiaries, and the insurance money, or such part thereof as is or has been apportioned to a preferred beneficiary, is not, except as otherwise provided in this Act, subject to the control of the insured or of his creditors and does not form part of the estate of the insured.

THE INSURANCE AMENDMENT ACT, 1961–62
Ontario. Statutes. 1961–62. Chapter 63

4. Part V of *The Insurance Act* is repealed and the following substituted therefor: . . .

156. (1) An insured may in a contract or by a declaration designate his personal representative or a beneficiary to receive insurance money.

(2) Subject to section 157, the insured may from time to time alter or revoke the designation by a declaration.

(3) A designation in favour of the "heirs", "next of kin" or "estate" of the insured, or the use of words of like import in a designation, shall be

deemed to be a designation of the personal representative of the insured.

157. (1) An insured may in a contract, or by a declaration, other than a declaration that is part of a will, filed with the insurer at its head or principal office in Canada during the lifetime of the person whose life is insured, designate a beneficiary irrevocably, and in that event the insured, while the beneficiary is living, may not alter or revoke the designation without the consent of the beneficiary and the insurance money is not subject to the control of the insured or of his creditors and does not form part of his estate.

(2) Where the insured purports to designate a beneficiary irrevocably in a will or in a declaration that is not filed as provided in subsection 1, the designation has the same effect as if the insured had not purported to make it irrevocable.

159. (1) An insured may in a contract or by a declaration appoint a trustee for a beneficiary and may alter or revoke the appointment by a declaration.

(2) A payment made by an insurer to a trustee for a beneficiary discharges the insurer to the extent of the payment.

161. A beneficiary may enforce for his own benefit, and a trustee appointed pursuant to section 159 may enforce as trustee, the payment of insurance money made payable to him in the contract or by a declaration and in accordance with the provisions thereof, but the insurer may set up any defence that it could have set up against the insured or his personal representative.

163. Where a beneficiary,

(a) is not designated irrevocably; or

(b) is designated irrevocably but has attained the age of twenty-one years and consents,

the insured may assign, exercise rights under or in respect of, surrender or otherwise deal with the contract as provided therein or in this Part or as may be agreed upon with the insurer.

164. (1) Notwithstanding the designation of a beneficiary irrevocably, the insured is entitled while living to the dividends or bonuses declared on a contract, unless the contract otherwise provides.

(2) Unless the insured otherwise directs, the insurer may apply the dividends or bonuses declared on the contract for the purpose of keeping the contract in force. . . .

KEOUGHAN *v.* HOLLAND. [1948] 1 D.L.R. 605 (Prince Edward Island. Supreme Court in Chancery). Katherine White, Agatha Heron, Laura Holland and Matthias Keoughan conveyed all their interest in 100 acres of land at Tarantum to their brother Francis Keoughan and in return Francis Keoughan promised to support and maintain his mother Margaret Keoughan for the rest of her life in the manner to which she had become accustomed and at her death to give her a "decent Christian burial." As long as she lived at Tarantum she was to have $15 a year. If she decided to live elsewhere Francis promised to pay her $100 a year instead of the $15. The support and maintenance were to be a lien and charge on the land. Maragret Keoughan resided at Tarantum until May 1939, and was looked after. Since then she had lived elsewhere and in this action claimed $800. Katherine White and Agatha Heron were dead. Laura Holland and Matthias Keoughan were named as defendants, but did not appear. Her claim was dismissed. MACGUIGAN J.: ". . . there is no trust in favour of the defendant [Margaret Keoughan] and consequently she is not able to recover under the covenant at common law. . . . However, there is another aspect of this matter to be considered. The two defendants Laura Holland and Matthias Keoughan are entitled to enforce the covenant and collect the money due thereunder, but there is nothing before the Court to show what these defendants wish in this regard. . . . I think they should be given an opportunity to appear and inform the Court whether or not they desire to collect this amount. . . . If no appearance is entered within twenty days after service of a copy of this judgment . . . the claim of Margaret Keoughan for the amount due under the covenant will be disallowed."

SMITH *v.* RIVER DOUGLAS CATCHMENT BOARD
England. Court of Appeal. [1949] 2 All E.R. 179

By an agreement under seal dated April 25, 1938, and made between a Mrs. Smith and ten other owners of land adjoining the Eller Brook in the area of the defendant catchment board, the board covenanted to "widen and deepen and make good the banks of the Eller Brook . . . take over the control of the brook and maintain for all time the work when completed." In 1940 Mrs. Smith conveyed her land to the first plaintiff purporting to transfer therewith the benefit of the agreement of 1938. In 1944 the first plaintiff let the land to the second plaintiff, Snipes Hall Farm, Ltd. In 1946, owing to faulty work by the board, the banks burst flooding the plaintiffs' land. The plaintiffs claim damages in contract and for negligence.

Morris J. held that the contractual obligations of the board were not to be regarded as running with the land, and, therefore, the plaintiffs had no right of action in contract, and, further, following the decision in *East Suffolk Rivers Catchment Board* v. *Kent*, [1940] 4 All E.R. 527. the board were not liable in tort.

DENNING L.J.: . . . Counsel for the board says that the plaintiffs cannot sue. He says that there is no privity of contract between them and the board, and that it is a fundamental principle that no one can sue on a contract to which he is not a party. That argument can be met either by admitting the principle and saying that it does not apply to this case, or by disputing the principle itself. I make so bold as to dispute it. The principle is not nearly so fundamental as it is sometimes supposed to be. It did not become rooted in our law until the year 1861 (*Tweddle* v. *Atkinson*) and reached its full growth in 1915 (*Dunlop Pneumatic Tyre Co., Ltd.* v. *Selfridge & Co., Ltd.*). It has never been able entirely to supplant another principle whose roots go much deeper. I mean the principle that a man who makes a deliberate promise which is intended to be binding, that is to say, under seal or for good consideration, must keep his promise; and the court will hold him to it, not only at the suit of the party who gave the consideration, but also at the suit of one who was not a party to the contract, provided that it was made for his benefit and that he has a sufficient interest to entitle him to enforce it, subject always, of course, to any defences that may be open on the merits. It is on this principle, implicit if not expressed, (i) that the courts ever since 1368 have held that a covenant made with the owner of land for its benefit can be enforced against the covenantor, not only by the original party, but also by his successors in title . . . (ii) that the courts of common law in the 17th and 18th centuries repeatedly enforced promises expressly made in favour of an interested person . . . (iii) that Lord Mansfield held that an undisclosed principal is entitled to sue on a contract made by his agent for his benefit, even though nothing was said about agency in the contract . . . and (iv) that Lord Hardwicke L.C. decided that a third person is entitled to sue if there can be spelt out of the contract an intention by one of the parties to contract as trustee for him, even though nothing was said about any trust in the contract, and there was no trust fund to be administered. . . . Throughout the history of the principle the difficulty has been, of course, to say what is sufficient interest to entitle the third person to recover. It has sometimes been supposed that there must always be something in the nature of a "trust" for his benefit . . . see *Vandepitte* v. *Preferred Accident Insurance Corporation of New York*, [1933] A.C. 70, but this is an elusive test which does not explain all the cases, and it involves the trustee being made a nominal party to the action either as plaintiff or defendant, unless that formality is dispensed with, as it was in *Les Affreteurs Réunis Société Anonyme* v. *Leopold Walford (London), Ltd.* [1918] A.C. 801. The truth is that the principle is not so limited. It may be difficult to define what is a sufficient interest. While it does not include the maintenance of prices to the public disadvantage, it does cover the protection of the legitimate property, rights and interests of the third person, although no agency or trust for him can be inferred. It covers, therefore, rights such as the following which cannot justly be denied—the right of a seller to enforce a commercial credit issued in his favour by a bank under contract with the buyer; the right of a widow to sue for a pension which her husband's employers promised to pay her under contract with him . . . or the right of a man's servants and guests to claim on an insurance policy, taken out by him against loss by burglary, which is expressed to cover them. . . . In some cases the legislature itself has intervened, as, for instance, to give the driver of a motor the right to sue on an insurance policy taken out by the owner which is expressed to cover the driver, but this does not mean that the common law would not have reached the same result by itself.

The particular application of the principle with which we are concerned here is the case of covenants made with the owner of the land to which they relate. The law on this subject was fully expounded by Mr. Smith in his note to *Spencer's Case* which has always been regarded as authoritative. Such covenants are clearly intended, and usually expressed, to be for the benefit of whomsoever should be the owner of the land for the time being; and at common law each successive owner has a sufficient interest to sue because he holds the same estate as the original owner. The reason which Lord Coke gave for this rule is the reason which underlies the whole of the principle now under consideration. He said in his work on *Littleton* (p. 385a) that it was "to give damages to the party grieved." If a successor in title were not allowed to sue it would mean that the covenantor could break his contract with impunity, for it is clear that the original owner, after he had parted with the land, could recover no more than nominal damages for any breach that occurred thereafter. It was always held, however, at common law that, in order that a successor in title should be entitled to sue, he must be of the same estate as the original owner. That alone was a sufficient interest to entitle him to enforce the contract. The covenant was supposed to be made for the benefit of the owner and his successors in title, and not for the benefit of anyone else. This limitation, however, was, as is pointed out in *Smith's Leading Cases*, p. 75, capable of being "productive of very serious and disagreeable consequences," and it has been removed by s. 78 of the *Law of Property Act, 1925*, which provides that a covenant relating to any land of the covenantee shall be deemed to be made with the covenantee and his successors in title "and the person deriving title under him or them" and shall have effect as if such successors "and other persons" were expressed. The covenant of the catchment board in the present case clearly relates to the land of the covenantees. It was a covenant to do work on the land for the benefit of the land. By the statute, therefore, it is to be deemed to be made, not only with the original owner, but also with the purchasers of the land and their tenants as if they were expressed. Now, if they were expressed, it would be clear that the covenant was made for their benefit, and they clearly have sufficient interest to entitle them to enforce it because they have suffered the damage. The result is that the plaintiffs come within the principle whereby a person interested can sue on a contract expressly made for his benefit.

[Only that part of Denning L.J.'s decision dealing with third party beneficiaries is reproduced. Tucker and Somerville L.JJ. gave judgments on the contractual aspect but dealt only with the effect of the covenant.]

MIDLAND SILICONES LTD. *v.* SCRUTTONS LTD. [1962] 2 W.L.R. 186 (England. House of Lords). Scruttons Ltd. were stevedores hired to handle a drum of silicone diffusion pump fluid from the ship to a lorry provided by the consignee, Midland Silicones Ltd. The stevedores were just lowering the drum on to the lorry when by their negligence it was dropped and some of the contents were lost. The loss was assessed at £593 12s. By virtue of the bill of lading between the shipper and the carrier, the carrier who moved the drum from New York to London was not to be liable for more than $500 (£179 1s.) in the event of damage. By virtue of the stevedoring contract between the carrier and Scruttons Ltd., Scruttons Ltd. agreed to be liable for damage while they were handling the drum, but they were entitled to "such protection as is afforded by the terms, conditions and exceptions of the bills of lading." By virtue of the sale of goods contract between the shipper and Midland the title in the drum passed from the shipper, or seller, to Midland while it was on board the ship, and thereafter Midland became subject to the same rights in respect of the drum as if the contract in the bill of lading had been made directly with Midland. There was no express contract between Midland and Scruttons Ltd. Diplock J. directed judgment for Midland for £593 12s. 2d. plus interest. The Court of Appeal dismissed an appeal. The House of Lords affirmed the Court of Appeal. On the question whether Scruttons Ltd., who had no contract with Midland, could take advantage of the clause in the bill of lading limiting the carrier's liability to $500, the House, with the exception of Lord Denning, who dissented, denied the protection on the ground that a third party cannot take advantage of a clause in a contract to which he is not a party. VISCOUNT SIMONDS: ". . . But, my Lords, all these contentions were but a prelude to one which, had your Lordships accepted it, would have been the foundation of a dramatic decision of this House. It was argued, if I understood the argument, that if A contracts with B to do something for the benefit of C, then C, though not a party to the contract, can sue A to enforce it. This is independent of whether C is A's undisclosed principal or a beneficiary under a trust of which A is trustee. It is sufficient that C is an 'interested person.' My Lords, if this is the law of England, then, subject always to the question of consideration, no doubt, if the carrier purports to contract for the benefit of the stevedore, the latter can enforce the contract. Whether that premiss is satisfied in this case is another matter, but, since the argument is advanced, it is right that I should deal with it. "Learned counsel for the respondents met it, as they had successfully done in the courts below, by asserting a principle which is, I suppose, as well established as any in our law, a 'fundamental' principle, as Lord Haldane called it in *Dunlop Pneumatic Tyre Co. Ltd.* v. *Selfridge & Co. Ltd.*, [1915] A.C. 847, an 'elementary' principle, as it has been called times without number, that only a person who is a party to a contract can sue upon it. 'Our law,' said Lord Haldane, 'knows nothing of a jus quaesitum tertio arising by way of contract.' Learned counsel for the respondents claimed that this was the orthodox view and asked your Lordships to reject any proposition that impinged upon it. To that invitation I readily respond. For to me heterodoxy, or, as some might say, heresy, is not the more attractive because it is dignified by the name of reform. Nor will I easily be led by an undiscerning zeal for some abstract kind of justice to ignore our first duty, which is to administer justice according to law, the law which is established for us by Act of Parliament or the binding authority of precedent. The law is developed by the application of old principles to new circumstances. Therein lies its genius. Its reform by the abrogation of those principles is the task not of the courts of law but of Parliament. Therefore I reject the argument for the appellants under this head and invite your Lordships to say that certain statements which appear to support it in recent cases such as *Smith & Snipes Hall Farm* v. *River Douglas Catchment Board*, [1949] 2 K.B. 500, and *White* v. *John Warwick & Co. Ltd.*, [1953] 1 W.L.R. 1285, must be rejected. If the principle of jus quaesitum tertio is to be introduced into our law, it must be done by Parliament after a due consideration of its merits and demerits. I should not be prepared to give it my support without a greater knowledge than I at present possess of its operation in other systems of law. . . ." LORD DENNING: ". . . the question is: Did the owners of the goods impliedly authorize the carrier to employ stevedores on the terms that their liability should be limited to $500? I think they did. . . . The carrier simply passed on the self-same limitation as he himself had, and this must have been within his implied authority. It seems to me that when the owner of goods allows the person in possession of them to make a contract in regard to them, then he cannot go back on the terms of the contract, if they are such as he expressly or impliedly authorized to be made, even though he was no party to the contract and could not sue or be sued upon it. It is just the same as if he stood by and watched it being made. And his successor in title is in no better position. . . ." [Lord Reid pointed out that the House had been informed that questions of this kind frequently arise and that this action had been brought as a test case. How will the result affect the revision of the standard forms of the three contracts involved here?]

NOTE ON LEGAL METHOD. Compare Viscount Simonds' attitude toward judicial reform of the common law in the *Midlands Silicone* case with his remarks in *Shaw* v. *Director of Public Prosecutions*, [1962] A.C. 220, where he had to decide whether to invent a new crime at common law, of corrupting public morals. Having said earlier in his judgment, at p. 267, that "I am no advocate of the right of the judges to create new criminal offences," he said, at p. 268, "When Lord Mansfield, speaking long after the Star Chamber had been abolished, said that the Court of King's Bench was the *custos morum* of the people and had the superintendency of offences *contra bonos mores*, he was asserting, as I now assert, that there is in that court a residual power, where no statute has yet intervened to supersede the common law, to superintend those offences which are prejudicial to the public welfare. Such occasions will be rare, for Parliament has not been slow to legislate when attention has been sufficiently aroused. But gaps remain and will always remain since no one can foresee every way in which the wickedness of man may disrupt the order of society. Let me take a single instance to which my noble and learned friend Lord Tucker refers. Let it be supposed that at some future, perhaps, early, date homosexual practices between adult consenting males are no longer a crime. Would it not be an offence if even without obscenity, such practices were publicly advocated and encouraged by pamphlet and advertisement? Or must we wait until Parliament finds time to deal with such conduct? I say, my Lords, that if the common law is powerless in such an event, then we should no longer do her reverence. But I say that her hand is still powerful and that it is for Her Majesty's judges to play the part which Lord Mansfield pointed out to them."

Query. Is the House of Lords better adapted to remould the law of contract or the criminal law in the delicate sphere of public morality? Contrast Lord Reid, in the *Shaw* case at p. 275: "Even if there is still a vestigial power of this kind it ought not, in my view, to be used unless there appears to be general agreement that the offence to which it is applied ought to be criminal if committed by an individual. Notoriously, there are wide differences of opinion today as to how far the law ought to punish immoral acts which are not done in the face of the public. Some think that the law already goes too far, some that it does not go far enough. Parliament is the proper place, and I am firmly of opinion the only proper place, to settle that. When there is sufficient support from public opinion, Parliament does not hesitate to intervene. Where Parliament fears to tread it is not for the courts to rush in."

Lord Reid also said, at p. 276, "I think that the following comments are as valid today as they were in 1824: '. . . I . . . protest . . . against arguing too strongly upon public policy—it is a very unruly horse, and when once you get astride it you never know where it will carry you. It may lead you from the sound law. It is never argued at all but when other points fail' (per Burrough J. in *Richardson* v. *Millish* (1824), 2 Bing. 229, at p. 252)." Do you agree? Is there some rational basis for assigning some reforms to the legislature and some to the courts?

RESTATEMENT OF THE LAW OF CONTRACTS
Washington. American Law Institute. 1932

133. (1) Where performance of a promise in a contract will benefit a person other than the promisee, that person is, except as stated in Subsection (3):

(a) a donee beneficiary if it appears from the terms of the promise in view of the accompanying circumstances that the purpose of the promisee in obtaining the promise of all or part of the performance thereof is to make a gift to the beneficiary or to confer upon him a right against the promisor to some performance neither due nor supposed or asserted to be due from the promisee to the beneficiary;

(b) a creditor beneficiary if no purpose to make a gift appears from the terms of the promise in view of the accompanying circumstances and performance of the promise will satisfy an actual or supposed or asserted duty of the promisee to the beneficiary, or a right of the beneficiary against the promisee which has been barred by the Statute of Limitations or by a discharge in bankruptcy, or which is unenforceable because of the Statute of Frauds;

(c) an incidental beneficiary if neither the facts stated in Clause (a) nor those stated in Clause (b) exist.

(2) Such a promise as is described in Subsection (1a) is a gift promise. Such a promise as is described in Subsection (1b) is a promise to discharge the promisee's duty.

(3) Where it appears from the terms of the promise in view of the accompanying circumstances that the purpose of the promisee is to benefit a beneficiary under a trust and the promise is to render performance to the trustee, the trustee, and not the beneficiary under the trust, is a beneficiary within the meaning of this Section.

Comment:

a. A single contract may consist of a number of promises. One or more of them may require performance to the promisee; others may require performance to persons not parties to the contract. Of these latter promises, some may be of the type stated in Sub-section (1a), others of the type stated in Subsection (1b). In other promises any benefit derived by a third person from their performance may be merely incidental.

b. By performance of a promise is to be understood doing the acts or forbearances undertaken by the promisor—not the discharge of a legal duty though such a discharge may be one of the consequences of doing what the promisor undertakes, whether that is positive action or negative refraining from action.

c. By gift is meant primarily some performance or right which is not paid for by the recipient and which is apparently designed to benefit him. There are also covered by Subsection (1a) cases where, though the promisee receives consideration from the beneficiary, there is manifested an intent that the beneficiary shall acquire a right against the promisor to some performance never due or supposed or asserted to be due to the beneficiary from the promisee (see Illustration 3).

d. A contract for the benefit of a third person usually provides that performance shall be rendered directly to the beneficiary, but this is not necessarily the case. A promise to discharge an indebtedness of one whom the contract is made to benefit, will provide for payment to the creditor of the beneficiary, not to the beneficiary himself who owes the money.

e. Contractual rights of a beneficiary must be distinguished from interests in chattels created by the delivery of the chattels to one person with the expressed intent that another shall have an interest in them. The rights thus acquired are independent of the law of contracts. On the other hand, delivery of chattels to one person with the expressed intent that he shall be merely an agent in their delivery to another creates no right in the latter either under the law of property or of contracts.

Illustrations of Subsection (1a):

1. A owes C $100 for money lent. For sufficient consideration B promises A to pay C $200, both as a discharge of the debt and as an indication of A's gratitude to C for making the loan. C is a donee beneficiary.

2. C is a troublesome person who is annoying A. A dislikes him but believing the best way to obtain freedom from annoyance is to make a

present, secures for sufficient consideration a promise from B to give C a box of cigars. C is a donee beneficiary.

3. A, a corporation, contracts with B, an insurance company, that B shall pay to any future buyer of a motor car from A the loss he may suffer by the burning or theft of the car within one year after sale. Later a car is sold by A to C, who pays a price for which he receives from A the car with A's statement that the insurance has been effected. C is a donee beneficiary.

4. D contracts to build a house for A. A obtains from B a bond in which B promises A that all D's creditors for labour and materials who may acquire a lien on the house shall be paid. C is such a creditor of D's. C is a donee beneficiary.

Illustrations of Subsection (1b):

5. A conveys Blackacre to B in consideration of B's promise to pay $15,000 as follows: $5000 to C, A's wife, on whom A wishes to make a settlement, $5000 to D to whom A is indebted in that amount, and $5000 to E, a life insurance company, to purchase an annuity payable to A during his life. C is a donee beneficiary; D is a creditor beneficiary; E is an incidental beneficiary.

6. A owes C a debt of $100. The debt is barred by the Statute of Limitations, or by a discharge in bankruptcy, or is unenforceable because of the Statute of Frauds. B for sufficient consideration promises A to pay the barred or unenforceable debt. C is a creditor beneficiary.

7. A owes C $100. For sufficient consideration B promises A to pay C $100. B is ignorant of the fact that A owes C any money. C is a creditor beneficiary if on a reasonable interpretation A's words and acts indicate that the payment when made is to be a payment satisfying A's obligation, and a donee beneficiary if A's words and acts indicate that A intends to make a gift of $100, leaving still outstanding the original debt.

8. B promises A for sufficient consideration to furnish support for A's minor child C, whom A is bound by law to support. C is a creditor beneficiary.

9. B promises A for sufficient consideration to pay whatever debts A may incur in a certain undertaking. A incurs in the undertaking debts to C, D and E. If, on a fair interpretation of B's promise, the amount of the debts is to be paid by B to C, D and E, they are creditor beneficiaries; if the money is to be paid to A in order that he may be provided with money to pay C, D and E, they are at most incidental beneficiaries.

10. C asserts that A owes him $100. A does not owe this money, or think that he owes it, but rather than engage in litigation, and in order to obtain peace of mind, A secures, for sufficient consideration, a promise from B to pay C $100. C is a creditor beneficiary.

Illustrations of Subsection (1c):

11. B contracts with A to erect an expensive building on A's land. C's adjoining land would be enhanced in value by the performance of the contract. C is an incidental beneficiary.

12. B contracts with A to buy a new Gordon automobile. The Gordon Company is an incidental beneficiary. Though the contract cannot be performed without the payment of money to the Gordon Company, the payment is not intended as a gift nor is the payment a discharge of a real or supposed obligation of the promisee to the beneficiary.

Illustration of Subsection (3):

13. A, an insurance company, promises B in a policy of insurance to

pay $10,000 on B's death to C, as trustee for B's wife, D, C, and not D, is a donee beneficiary. D's rights must be enforced under the trust.

135. Except as stated in s. 140,

(a) a gift promise in a contract creates a duty of the promisor to the donee beneficiary to perform the promise; and the duty can be enforced by the donee beneficiary for his own benefit;

(b) a gift promise also creates a duty of the promisor to the promisee to render the promised performance to the donee beneficiary.

Comment:

a. No assent by a donee beneficiary to the contract or knowledge on his part of its existence is necessary to give him a right of action on it.

b. The damages recoverable in an action at law by the promisee of a gift promise will generally be nominal; but in Illustration 1 under s. 133, A's damages would be $100. As to the right to specific performance, see s. 138.

136. (1) Except as stated in ss. 140, 143,

(a) a promise to discharge the promisee's duty creates a duty of the promisor to the creditor beneficiary to perform the promise;

(b) a promise to discharge the promisee's duty creates also a duty to the promisee;

(c) whole or partial satisfaction of the promisor's duty to the creditor beneficiary satisfies to that extent the promisor's duty to the promisee;

(d) whole or partial satisfaction of the promisor's duty to the promisee in any other way than by rendering the promised performance in whole or in part does not limit the promisor's duty to the creditor beneficiary.

(2) Whether the extent of the promisor's duty to the creditor beneficiary is measured by the promisee's actual, supposed, or asserted duty to the beneficiary at the time of the making of the contract, or at some other time, depends upon the interpretation of the promise.

Comment on Subsection (1):

a. Though the right of the creditor beneficiary arises immediately on the formation of the contract, his right, unlike that of a donee beneficiary, is not immediately indefeasible. As stated in s. 143, until the creditor brings suit, or otherwise materially changes his position in reliance on the promise, he may lose his right or have it qualified by a new agreement between the promisor and the promisee.

b. A contract to satisfy a duty of the promisee to another is an intangible asset of the promisee, peculiar in this respect, that it cannot generally be made available by any creditor but the beneficiary.

c. If, after breach by the promisor, the beneficiary obtains payment from the promisee, the promisee has an election between a right of action for damages against the promisor and a right to recover the consideration paid. Either right can be made available by general creditors.

d. The value of the promisee's property is increased to the extent that the contract is of value to him. It is an intangible asset. The law allows a direct action by the creditor beneficiary against the promisor without joining the promisee, instead of requiring a procedure like garnishment or a suit to realize on an asset of the debtor not available to seizure by ordinary legal process. Ordinarily the value of the asset is the amount of the debt which the promisor has undertaken to pay; but, . . . this will not always be the case.

e. The promisor who undertakes to pay a debt of the promisee subjects himself to a duty both to the promisee and to the creditor beneficiary. A single performance, however, rendered to the beneficiary will satisfy both obligations. As to the right to specific performance see s. 138.

f. It is immaterial whether the duty of the promisee to the creditor beneficiary arises from a bargain between them or is created by an assumption by the promisee, acting as promisor in a previous contract, of some duty due by another to the creditor beneficiary, or is a non-contractual duty.

Comment on Subsection (2):

g. Where a promisee believes that he is or may be indebted to a third person and contracts with a promisor with a view to his discharge, the promise may take one of four forms: firstly, to pay the third person whatever is due him at the time of the promise; secondly, to pay the third person whatever may be due at the time when performance becomes due him or is claimed by him; thirdly, to pay the third person a fixed sum which the promisee rightly or wrongly assumes to be due, or wishes to have paid whether due or not; or, fourthly, to take whatever measures may be necessary to obtain the promisee's freedom from liability.

h. Promises in the first and second forms present typical cases of creditor beneficiaries. In promises in the third form also the beneficiary is a creditor beneficiary as that term is defined in s. 133 (1,b), even though the claim is not well founded. In promises in the fourth form the creditor is neither a donee beneficiary nor a creditor beneficiary. A promise however that is apparently in the fourth form may in view of accompanying circumstances sometimes be properly interpreted as falling within one of the other classes.

i. Where a promise is to pay a particular claim the proper interpretation of the promise will generally be that no supervening defences to the claim shall excuse the promisor. His undertaking is not discharged by such circumstances as the promisee's subsequent discharge in bankruptcy or the running of the Statute of Limitations in favor of the promisee. Where, however, the promise is to assume the debts of the promisee, as where a new corporation or new partnership makes such a promise to another corporation or partnership, the interpretation will often be proper that the promisor undertakes to pay only creditors who have valid claims when they assert them.

137. A donee beneficiary or a creditor beneficiary who has not previously assented to the promise for his benefit, may, in a reasonable time after learning of its existence and terms, render the duty to himself inoperative from the beginning by disclaimer, unless such action is a fraud on creditors.

138. If specific enforcement of a duty owed to a donee beneficiary or to a creditor beneficiary is possible and in accordance with the rules of equity, a suit for such enforcement can be maintained. The suit may be brought either by the promisee or by the beneficiary.

139. It is not essential to the creation of a right in a donee beneficiary or in a creditor beneficiary that he be identified when a contract containing the promise is made.

140. There can be no donee beneficiary or creditor beneficiary unless a contract has been formed between a promisor and promisee; and if a contract is conditional, voidable, or unenforceable at the time of its formation,

or subsequently ceases to be binding in whole or in part because of impossibility, illegality or the present or prospective failure of the promisee to perform a return promise which was the consideration for the promisor's promise, the right of a donee beneficiary or creditor beneficiary under the contract is subject to the same limitation.

142. Unless the power to do so is reserved, the duty of the promisor to the donee beneficiary cannot be released by the promisee or affected by any agreement between the promisee and the promisor, but if the promisee receives consideration for an attempted release or discharge of the promisor's duty, the donee beneficiary can assert a right to the consideration so received, and on doing so loses his right against the promisor.

143. A discharge of the promisor by the promisee in a contract or a variation thereof by them is effective against a creditor beneficiary if,

(a) the creditor beneficiary does not bring suit upon the promise or otherwise materially change his position in reliance thereon before he knows of the discharge or variation, and

(b) the promisee's action is not a fraud on creditors.

147. An incidental beneficiary acquires by virtue of the promise no right against the promisor or the promisee.

Chapter 5

ASSIGNMENT

By the assignment of a contract is meant merely the substitution of a stranger for one or the other of the original parties to the agreement. If such a substitution is done by mutual agreement the change of parties is called "novation," there being in effect a rescission of the original contract and the creation of a new one. Where one party steps out and substitutes a stranger unilaterally that party is said to "assign the contract." Perhaps the simplest form of substitution is by one party appointing a stranger as his agent to sue in the party's name (giving the stranger a "power of attorney"). From this unobjectionable procedure the common law and equity, over the centuries, assisted by the *Judicature Act, 1873*, developed the current notion of an assignment unilaterally giving the stranger full rights to sue in his own name and to deprive the assignor of his power to grant a release to the debtor.

The commercial importance of the concept of assignment can hardly be overestimated, for upon it rests much of our present day financial and credit system. See, for a short statement, Fuller, *Basic Contract Law*, pp. 580–2. While the common law, assisted by equity and finally by the legislature, slowly recognized the notion of assignment, perhaps the greatest commercial stride was the recognition of the notion of negotiability of certain kinds of contractual obligations. This recognition came first in the law merchant, the legal system of international traders, but was gradually adopted into the common law. For practical purposes the law respecting negotiable instruments is to be found in the *Bills of Exchange Act*, R.S.C., 1952, c. 15. A negotiable instrument differs from an assignment in many ways, the most significant, perhaps, being the right of a "holder in due course" (the "assignee" of a negotiable instrument who takes for value and without notice of any defences available against the assignor by the debtor) to claim against the debtor despite the defences. The assignee, on the other hand, takes subject to these defences, which are sometimes referred to ambiguously as the "equities." Negotiable instruments are limited to bills of exchange which include cheques, and promissory notes.

The cases in the first section present problems concerning the formalities and effects of assignment: must the assignment be in writing, must there be notice, must the assignment be of the whole of the debt, or may a part of the debt be assigned, must it be an absolute assignment or may it merely constitute an "equitable charge" on the fund being assigned? For an understanding of these matters some knowledge of the history of the law is essential. To eke out the rather sketchy statements contained in the cases see Fuller, *Basic Contract Law*, pp. 585–94 for a short account.

1. Formalities and Effects of Assignment

ROW *v.* DAWSON. 1749. 1 Ves. Sr. 331; 27 E.R. 1064 (England. Chancery). Tonson and Cowdery lent money to Gibson, who gave them a draft drawn on Swinburn, the deputy of Horace Walpole, "out of the money due from Horace Walpole out of the Exchequer, and what will be due at Michaelmas, pay to Tonson £400 and to Cowdery £200 value received." Gibson became bankrupt and a question arose whether the money from Walpole should be paid to Gibson's trustees for general distribution to his creditors or to Tonson and Cowdery's executors. The trustees argued that the draft was a bill of exchange and hadn't yet divested Gibson of his right to the money. The court held that it was not a bill of exchange because it was an order to pay out of a specific fund, not to pay generally. LORD HARDWICKE L.C.: ". . . it is a credit on this fund, and must amount to an assignment of so much of the debt; and though the law does not admit an assignment of a chose in action, this Court does; and any words will do; no particular words being necessary thereto. In the case of a bond it may be assigned in equity for valuable consideration, and good although no special form used. . . . This draft, which amounts to an assignment, is deposited with the officer Swinburn, and therefore is attached immediately upon it: so that Swinburn could not have paid this money to Gibson, supposing he had not been bankrupt, without making himself liable to the defendants; because he would have paid it with full notice of this assignment, for valuable consideration."

BILLS OF EXCHANGE ACT
Canada. Revised Statutes. 1952. Chapter 15

127. A bill, of itself, does not operate as an assignment of funds in the hand of the drawee available for the payment thereof, and the drawee of a bill who does not accept as required by this Act is not liable on the instrument.

17. (1) A bill of exchange is an unconditional order in writing, addressed by one person to another, signed by the person giving it, requiring the person to whom it is addressed to pay, on demand or at a fixed or determinable future time, a sum certain in money to or to the order of a specified person, or to bearer.

(3) An order to pay out of a particular fund is not unconditional within the meaning of this section.

WINCH *v.* KEELEY. 1787. 1 T.R. 619; 99 E.R. 1284 (England. King's Bench). Winch was owed money by Keeley for work done which he assigned to one Searle in satisfaction of a valid debt. Winch later became bankrupt. This action by Winch against Keeley was defended by Keeley who contended he had to pay the trustees in bankruptcy. Winch then revealed that he in fact sued in his name but on behalf of Searle. Held, for the plaintiff. ASHURST J.: ". . . It is true that formerly the courts of law did not take notice of an equity or a trust; for trusts are within the original jurisdiction of a court of equity; but of late years, it has been found productive of great expense to send the parties to the other side of the Hall; wherever this Court have seen that the justice of the case has been clearly with the plaintiff, they have not turned him round upon this objection. Then if this Court will take notice of a trust why should they not an equity? It is certainly true that a chose in action cannot strictly be assigned: but this Court will take notice of a trust, and consider who is beneficially interested. . . . if it be once established that this Court will take notice of trusts, it is immaterial whether the person who sues were originally a trustee or afterwards becomes so. Nor is it material at what time they became trustee; for whether he became such by the assignment, or was so originally, it is sufficient to say that he is a trustee now, and as such has a right to maintain this action. If this had been a fraudulent assignment, it would have raised a different question: but on these pleadings it must be taken to have been assigned for valuable consideration."

THE CONVEYANCING AND LAW OF PROPERTY ACT

Ontario. Revised Statutes. 1960. Chapter 66

54. (1) Any absolute assignment, made on or after the 31st day of December, 1897, by writing under the hand of the assignor, not purporting to be any way of charge only, of any debt or other legal chose in action of which express notice in writing has been given to the debtor, trustee or other person from whom the assignor would have been entitled to receive or claim such debt or chose in action is effectual in law, subject to all equities that would have been entitled to priority over the right of the assignee if this section had not been enacted, to pass and transfer the legal right to such debt or chose in action from the date of such notice, and all other remedies for the same, and the power to give a good discharge for the same without the concurrence of the assignor.

[This provision is substantially the same as sec. 25 (6) of the English *Judicature Act* of 1873.]

BRANDT'S SONS & CO. *v.* DUNLOP RUBBER COMPANY LIMITED

England. House of Lords. [1905] A.C. 454

The appellants, Brandt's Sons & Co., are bankers in London. Kamrisch & Co., who are now bankrupt, were rubber merchants in Liverpool. Their business was financed by Brandts. When Kamrisch & Co. made a purchase approved by the bankers, it became the duty of the bankers to provide the necessary funds, and by way of security they took delivery of the goods to themselves. Then when Kamrisch & Co. found a purchaser approved by the bankers they released the goods and gave Kamrisch & Co. a delivery order, relying on a written undertaking in each case that the price should be paid direct to them, and receiving an engagement in writing that in the meantime Kamrisch & Co. would hold the goods and the proceeds in trust on their behalf, and grant them "the sale and absolute lien on said goods and their proceeds" until they obtained full payment of the advance, together with their charges.

In accordance with this arrangement, Kamrisch & Co. bought and sold a parcel of rubber to the respondents, the Dunlop Company, and in connection with this purchase Brandts advanced £3430. When the goods were delivered to the Dunlop plant there was attached to the invoice a note requesting that Dunlop remit the amount to Brandts, but owing to some figures being erroneously inserted in this invoice it was returned to Kamrisch & Co. and a new invoice sent which failed to contain the request of the prior one as to payment.

When the goods were delivered to Dunlops, Kamrisch & Co. sent to Brandts a form letter intended to be signed by or on behalf of Dunlops and to be returned to them direct to Brandts. This letter read as follows: "Herewith we beg to confirm that we shall remit, subject to approval of goods the amount of invoice, £3263 42. 2d. for 75 packages raw rubber received today from Messrs. Kamrisch & Co., when due, direct to your good selves for account of Messrs. Kamrisch & Co."

Brandts sent this letter to Dunlops and confirmed the request for signature. The letter was signed by an employee of Dunlops, who, as the lower courts found and which finding was taken as correct, had no authority to sign, and who did not inform his employers that he had done so. The consequence was that instead of remitting the money to Brandts, Dunlops paid the money over to another bank used by Kamrisch & Co. under a previous standing order to that effect. On Brandts pressing Dunlops for payment, the latter replied that the amount had been paid and that they held Kamrisch & Co.'s receipt for it.

The present action was then brought to recover the amount due.

At the trial Walton J. decided in favour of the plaintiffs. The Court of Appeal reversed this judgment and the plaintiff brings the present appeal.

LORD MACNAGHTEN: . . . Were these documents, sent as they were to the company and received by the company, notice that Brandts were interested in the money, or what was their meaning? Does a business man who merely wants his debtor to pay the amount of the debt into his bank employ such elaborate machinery as this? Did anybody ever hear of such a complicated process, if that was all that was meant? At any rate, the company's secretary, Mr. Bergin, admits that he never heard of such a thing. The strangest part of this case is that nobody seems to have had the slightest doubt as to the meaning of these documents. "That was notice to Dunlops," says Walton J., "and, in fact, was more than notice. It was notice to Dunlops that Messrs. Kamrisch had made over to Brandts the right to receive this sum of money, and had given to Brandts power to give a perfectly good receipt and discharge for it. It is more than notice of course. It is notice plus a request that the bank" (?company) "would acknowldge that notice by undertaking to pay."

The Lord Chief Justice does not seem to have taken a different view on this point. Although he dismissed the action on the ground that the documents did not amount to an absolute assignment, within the section of the Judicature Act on which reliance was placed, and were therefore not a legal or equitable assignment, he thought "the notice would have been a good notice if the assignment had been an absolute assignment," and he thought the documents were "an authority to the Dunlop Company to pay the money over on Kamrisch's behalf to Brandts." Then I would ask your Lordships to turn to the evidence of Mr. Bergin, who was one of the secretaries of the company, and, as the learned counsel for the company said, "a great deal more than secretary," for, as the learned counsel told the Court, "he managed the whole business." Mr. Bergin was asked in cross-examination this question: "(Q.) Supposing that you had received that direction sent on by the Brandts' you would have thought, would you not, that Brandts had a charge or were interested in this money? (A.) I think I would. I would have thought that there was some such arrangement."

That, my Lords, is the whole case. It is difficult to conceive a plainer case of an equitable assignment or a clearer case of notice to the debtor. As between Kamrisch & Co. and Brandts the case was complete, and more than complete, without Brandts' letter of January 7 and its inclosures. There was an undertaking that the money should be paid direct to Brandts. There was besides a declaration of trust. There was an engagement to give Brandts "a sole and absolute lien," that is, sole and absolute control and dominion over the proceeds of the goods. Then the Dunlops receive through Brandts a notice which no man of business could mistake, telling them, on Kamrisch & Co.'s express authority that they are to pay to Brandts the money which they owe their creditors, Kamrisch & Co. What more could be required? Dunlops disregard that notice, and pay the wrong people. They must pay the money over again, and pay it to the right person.

With the utmost deference to the Court of Appeal, I have great difficulty in following their reasoning. The plaintiffs' case was put in two ways. It was presented as a case within subs. 6 of s. 25 of the *Judicature Act*. It was also presented as a simple case of equitable assignment perfected by notice. Unfortunately, the stress of the argument was laid on the *Judicature Act*. The Court of Appeal devoted almost the whole of their attention to it. The substantial question—the only question worth considering—was all but ignored. It was treated as subordinate to the question on the statute and bound up with it. The Lord Chief Justice, with whom the other members of the Court agree, says: "I come to the conclusion that this document"—that is Brandts' letter of January 7 and its inclosures—"does not fulfil that which is necessary in order to entitle the plaintiff to sue, whether suing as equitable or as legal assignee, on the ground that it is not an absolute assignment or an assignment at all within that section."

Why that which would have been a good equitable assignment before the statute should now be invalid and inoperative because it fails to come up to the requirements of the statute, I confess I do not understand. The statute does not forbid or destroy equitable assignments or impair their efficacy in the slightest degree. Where the rules of equity and the rules of the common law conflict, the rules of equity are to prevail. Before the statute there was a conflict as regards assignments of debts and other choses in action. At law it was considered necessary that the debtor should enter into some engagment with the assignee. That was never the rule in equity. . . . In certain cases the *Judicature Act* places the assignee in a better position than he was before. Whether the present case falls within the favoured class may perhaps be doubted. At any rate, it is wholly immaterial for the plaintiffs' success in this action. But, says the Lord Chief Justice "the document does not, on the face of it, purport to be an assignment nor use the language of an assignment." An equitable assignment does not always take that form. It may be addressed to the debtor. It may be couched in the language of command. It may be a courteous request. It may assume the form of mere permission. The language is immaterial if the meaning is plain. All that is necessary is that the debtor should be given to understand that the debt has been made over by the creditor to some third person. If the debtor ignores such a notice, he does so at his peril. If the assignment be for valuable consideration and communicated to the third person, it cannot be revoked by the creditor or safely disregarded by the debtor. I think that the documents which passed between Brandts and the company would of themselves, and apart from Kamrisch & Co.'s undertaking and engagement given to Brandts, have constituted a good equitable assignment. But thc real question is, were they notice to the company that Brandts were interested in the money? As between Kamrisch & Co. and Brandts the assignment was, as I have already said, perfect without them. . . .

Strictly speaking, Kamrisch & Co., or their trustee in bankruptcy, should have been brought before the Court. But no action is now dismissed for want of parties, and the trustee in bankruptcy had really no interest in the matter. At your Lordships' bar the Dunlops disclaimed any wish to have him present, and in both Courts below they claimed to retain for their own use any balance that might remain after satisfying Brandts.

It is quite plain how the error in this case arose. . . . The head office . . . knew nothing about this equitable assignment, and they paid the money to the wrong man because Kamrisch on a former occasion had given them a general direction to pay Kleinwort & Co. The difficulty, as Mr. Bergin admitted, was "owing to the neglect of duty at Birmingham." It would be unreasonable to make Brandts suffer for that.

I think the appeal must be allowed, and the judgment of Walton J. restored with costs here and below.

My noble and learned friend Lord Lindley desires me to say that he has read this judgment and concurs in it.

[The concurring opinions of Lords Halsbury, L.C., and Lord James are omitted.]

PERFORMING RIGHT SOCIETY *v.* LONDON THEATRE. [1924] A.C. 1 (England. House of Lords). LORD SUMNER: "Lord Macnaghten accepts the rule for which the respondents now contend, that the assignor ought to be made a party in order that he might be bound, but points out that Brandts' Case was an exception to it. Plainly the House did not consider itself to be departing from established rules of practice, nor has the case ever been so regarded. . . . If the assignor, Kamrisch, was not made a party, he would not be bound; was it not possible that the debtors, the Dunlop Rubber Company, might be exposed to claims by him or his trustees in bankruptcy? Kamrisch, however, had already been settled with and the Dunlop Company held his receipt. It appears on reference to the arguments in the Courts below that this fact was relied on. Kamrisch was therefore bound already. The respondents admitted that what they wanted was not the presence but the absence of the assignor and that they did not propose to pay the assignor but desired to pay nobody, and this mere non-joinder of parties was not allowed to relieve them."

RULES OF PRACTICE
Ontario. Supreme Court. 1960

89. An assignee of a chose in action may sue in respect thereof without making the assignor a party.

HOLT *v.* HEATHERFIELD TRUST LTD.
England. King's Bench. [1942] 2 K.B. 1

The plaintiff, Richard Henry Holt, claimed against the defendants, Heatherfield Trust, Ltd., and G. & T. Bridgewater, Ltd., a sum of money recovered by Samuel Whitmore Partington, their debtor, under a judgment against the Chloride Electrical Storage Co., Ltd. The judgment was obtained by Partington on June 14, 1940, and on that day Partington assigned the sum due thereunder to Holt, which assignment Holt received on June 15. On June 15, Heatherfield Trust, Ltd., obtained a garnishee order nisi on the same sum, which was served on the Chloride company on June 17. On June 17, the plaintiff sent notice of the assignment to the Chloride company, which was received by the latter on June 18. Hetherfield Trust, Ltd., . . . claimed that on June 17, when the garnishee order became effective, the plaintiff's title was incomplete as being an equitable assignment only until notice was given to the Chloride company on June

18, and also, that the assignment, being made without consideration, was of no avail as against the garnishee order.

ATKINSON J.: . . . The next point is more difficult. It is said that the assignment was ineffective inasmuch as notice of it had not been given before the service of the garnishee order, so that at the date of the service of the garnishee order it was merely an equitable assignment and depended for its efficacy on proof of valuable consideration, and no consideration had been given for it. The mere existence of an antecedent debt is not valuable consideration, but forbearance to sue may be. One or two cases have been referred to in which light has been thrown on the question when the court may draw the inference that the creditor has forgone proceedings in consideration of a promise to assign, or as a result of assignment. There is no evidence in this case of any threat to take proceedings, but I need not determine the difficult question of consideration, because I am satisfied that the validity of the assignment did not depend on its having been given for valuable consideration.

In my view, the authorities establish the following propositions. At common law things in action were not assignable, and an assignee had to go to equity to enforce his claims. If the thing in action was a legal claim, he had to file a bill to compel the assignor to permit him to sue in the name of the assignor, and equity would help him only if he had given valuable consideration for the assignment. . . . now by the Law of Property Act, 1925, s. 136, an absolute assignment of a debt of which express notice in writing has been given to the debtor is effectual in law to transfer the legal right thereto. Absence of notice does not affect the efficacy of the transaction as between the assignor and assignee. Until notice be given the assignment is an equitable assignment, but it is an assignment which requires nothing more from the assignor to become a legal assignment. The assignee may himself give notice at any time before action brought, and further than that, even before notice, he may sue in his own name provided that he makes the assignor a party to the action, as plaintiff if he consents, and as defendant if he does not consent. . . .

Therefore, it seems beyond argument that the absence of notice does not affect the efficacy of the transaction as between assignor and assignee. The Supreme Court of Judicature Act, 1873, relieved the assignee from the necessity of applying to equity for help, and therefore, valuable consideration is no longer necessary. Neither the Act of 1873 nor the Act of 1925 says a word about consideration. It is not suggested that valuable consideration is necessary if there is an absolute assignment and notice is given, but it is contended that, although valuable consideration may be unnecessary if notice be given, it is necessary to give validity to the transaction if notice be not given or until notice be given. If A. holds by way of gift an absolute assignment of an existing debt of which notice has not yet been given, it is said to be unenforceable and invalid. Yet, once A. gives notice, the invalidity is destroyed and the invalid becomes valid. It would, indeed, be strange if mere notice of an invalidity could destroy that invalidity, and, so far from being invalid, the assignment entitles the assignee to sue for the debt assigned even before notice is given so long as he joins the assignor on one side or another.

An assignment can operate as an assignment only with regard to an existing legal chose in action. An assignment purporting to assign a future debt can operate only as a contract to assign. It remains a purely equitable assignment which will be enforced like any other contract only if given for value. The assignment with which I am concerned is absolute in form and purports to assign an existing legal debt. . . .

[It] seems to me perfectly clear that the plaintiff's title is a good one, and I so decide. I hold that his claim to the money is good.

QUESTION. If the debtor pays one garnishee order before he got notice of the assignment has the assignee any remedy against the debtor?

GORDON *v.* GORDON

Saskatchewan. Court of Appeal. 1924. 18 Sask. L.R. 187

LAMONT J.A.: This is a contest for $3,400 insurance moneys, paid into Court by the insurance company, after the destruction by fire of a house which had been insured by the company. The circumstances are as follows: The plaintiff sold [certain land] to his son, the defendant, under an agreement of sale, dated July 22, 1915. That agreement provided that the purchaser would insure and during the continuance of the agreement keep insured "all buildings on the said land," and that he would "assign and deliver over unto the vendor the policy or policies of insurance." At the time of the sale there was a dwelling-house upon the land, which was insured in the sum of $1,200 payable to the Canada Life Assurance Company, as mortgagees. That house was burned down. Both the mortgagees and the plaintiff agreed that the insurance moneys should be paid over to the defendant to assist him in rebuilding. A new house was erected by the defendant, and insured in the sum of $3,400, payable, in case of loss, to the defendant. On November 8, 1922, the new house was likewise destroyed by fire. The policy of insurance had not been assigned to the plaintiff. On November 9, 1922, the defendant gave the following order on the insurance company with whom the house had been insured:

"Please pay to George Markland, of Tantallon, Saskatchewan, the sum of $1,766.00 out of the insurance money which is coming to me under the above policy and for so doing this shall be your full and sufficient authority and discharge."

On November 16, 1922, the defendant gave another order, similar in terms, to Messrs. Grant, Donald & Clements, solicitors, for $655.65 and interest. This was to cover an indebtedness which the defendant owed to one Christie, for whom the solicitors were acting. Two days later, the defendant gave a further order on the insurance moneys to Paynter Bros. for $400, to cover an amount he owed to them. Notice of these orders was given to the insurance company before the company had admitted liability in respect of the insurance. In due time proof of loss was made by the defendant, and the company admitted their liability to pay the whole $3,400.

On April 9, 1923, the plaintiff brought this action against the defendant, and claimed the sum of $3,400 as liquidated damages for the failure of the defendant to assign to him the policy of insurance. Immediately after issuing the writ of summons in the action, the plaintiff garnisheed the insurance moneys in the hands of the company, which had, prior to that, admitted liability. The company paid the moneys into Court, giving notice at the same time of the claims made in respect thereof under the three orders above mentioned. On May 14, 1923, the plaintiff signed judgment against the defendant in default of appearance for the amount of the damages claimed, and on May 17 a summons was taken out before the

Local Master at Moosomin, calling upon the parties claiming the moneys paid into Court under the garnishee summons to establish their claims thereto. Up to the time the plaintiff issued his writ, he had not given notice to the insurance company of any claim he might have to the insurance moneys, nor of his right under the agreement of sale to have the policy assigned to him. The local Master held that the three orders should be paid in priority to the claim of the plaintiff. From that decision the plaintiff apealed to a Judge in Chambers, who affirmed the local Master's order. From the decision of the Judge in Chambers the plaintiff now appeals to this Court.

The contention on behalf of the plaintiff was that, as, under the agreement of sale, the plaintiff was entitled to have the insurance policy assigned to him, he had a valid equitable assignment thereof; that the three orders given by the defendant constituted only equitable assignments of the sums therein specified, and that the plaintiff's equitable assignment, being first in time, took priority.

On behalf of the holders of the three orders two contentions were made: (1) That the orders constituted legal assignments of the sums mentioned respectively in the orders, and were within *The Choses in Action Act*, R.S.S. 1920, ch. 202, and therefore entitled to priority; (2) Even if they amounted only to equitable assignments, they were still entitled to priority, because notice of the assignment was, in each case, given to the insurance company before the plaintiff had been given notice of his equitable right.

In my opinion the agreement of the defendant to insure the buildings on the land and to assign to the plaintiff the insurance policy, gave the plaintiff an equitable right to have the policy assigned to himself, for as said by Jessel M.R., in *Collyer* v. *Isaacs* (1881), 19 Ch. D. 342, at p. 351, 51 L.J. Ch. 14:

"A man can contract to assign property which is to come into existence in the future, and when it has come into existence, equity, treating as done that which ought to be done, fastens upon that property, and the contract to assign thus becomes a complete assignment."

The plaintiff, therefore, stands in the position of equitable assignee, and as between himself and the defendant equity would enforce his claim. The contest, however, is between the plaintiff and the holders of the three orders. These orders, in my opinion, consititute valid assignment of a chose in action arising out of a contract. In England, the weight of authority appears to be that the assignment of part of a debt is not within the statute in force there. *Forster* v. *Baker*, [1910] 2 K.B. 636, *In re Steel Wing Co.*, [1921] 1 Ch. 349, *Conlan* v. *Carlow County Council*, [1912] 2 Ir. R. 535.

Our Act is not limited, as is the English Act, to "debts or legal choses in action," but includes any choses in action, equitable as well as legal, which arise out of a contract. In equity, the assignment of a definite part of a debt was always considered valid if made for good consideration: *Durham Bros.* v. *Robertson*, [1898] 1 Q.B. 765, at p. 769.

In my opinion, the orders in question in this case, although for a portion only of the debt accruing due under the policy of insurance, are valid assignments under the Act on which the assignees could have brought actions in their own names respectively. *In re Miller* (1908), 1 Sask. L.R. 91.

These assignments vested in the assignees the rights of the assignor, and the remedies for their enforcement against the debtor, which, apart from the assignments, would have been the assignor's.

When the insurance company had received notice of these orders, and the fund had come into existence, the company were trustees of that fund for the holders of the orders, and the rights of the holders could not be displaced by any equitable right on the part of the plaintiff to compel an assignment of the policy to himself. *Fraser* v. *Imperial Bank of Canada* (1912), 47 S.C.R. 313.

For the plaintiff it was contended that the orders could not be considered assignments under the Act, because at the time they were given there was no fund in existence to assign, and authorities were cited which showed that, under a policy of insurance, no debt arose until the loss had been established and the company had admitted liability thereunder. In my opinion these authorities do not apply. Our Act includes not only an assignment of a debt, but also the assignment of a chose in action arising under a contract. After the building had been destroyed by fire, the defendant had rights arising under his policy as against the company. These rights arose from his contract of insurance, and, in my opinion, could be made the subject of assignment under the Act.

I am, therefore, of opinion that the orders, being assignments under the Act, took priority over the plaintiff's equitable claim.

But even if the orders were held not to be assignments within the Act, they would, in my opinion, still be entitled to priority. The rule as to priority among equitable assignees—to use the language of Lord Macnaghten in *Ward* v. *Duncombe*, [1893] A.C. 369, at p. 384, is: "An assignee of an equitable interest in personal estate, without notice of an existing prior assignment, may gain priority simply by the act of giving notice to the person who has legal dominion over the fund before notice is given by the earlier assignee." . . .

The evidence in this case establishes that, at the time the holders of the orders received them from the defendant, they had no knowledge whatever of the plaintiff's claim. It also establishes that they gave notice to the company who was under obligation to provide the insurance moneys, before that company had any notice of any claim on the part of the plaintiff.

For the plaintiff it was contended that the notices given to the company were ineffective, because, at the time they were given, although after the fire had taken place, the company had not admitted liability in respect of the insurance. Without inquiring into this question, it is sufficient to say that on February 17, 1923, the company, in a letter to the mortgagees, expressly referred to the claims made in respect of the three orders. At that time the company had no notice of the plaintiff's claim, and prior to that time they had admitted liability. Being at the date of the letter in possession of the insurance moneys, the notice which the company had before it of the claims made under the orders was sufficient notice to them to give the orders priority.

In 4 *Halsbury*, 381, the learned author says: "It is sufficient to show that the debtor has had knowledge of the assignment, regardless of the source or mode of his knowledge."

It was also contended on behalf of the plaintiff that, as equitable assignments, the orders would not take priority, as the only consideration given for each was a pre-existing indebtedness, and that a pre-existing debt was not valuable consideration, which was necessary to support an equitable assignment. . . . It is, I think, established law that every equitable assignment must be supported by valuable consideration, but a past indebtedness coupled with forbearance to sue, as a result of getting the security, is sufficient. . . . The orders are, however, entitled to priority as against the plaintiff only in so far as they are supported by an actual indebtedness. The order taken by Mr. Christie's solicitors was for $655.65, but Mr. Christie in his affidavit shows that on this account the defendant paid $250. on April 1, 1923. That order, therefore, will stand at its face value less $250. The other two orders appear to be sufficiently proved now that Markland's additional affidavit has been filed.

No question was raised before us as to the amounts payable under these orders. I would, therefore, vary the judgment below by reducing the amount of the order given to Mr. Christie's solicitors by $250.

As no question was raised about the correctness of the amounts, this was probably agreed to. The respondents are entitled to their costs of appeal. Appeal dismissed with costs.

[The opinion of Martin J.A. to the same effect is omitted. McKay J.A. concurred with Lamont J.A.]

THE CHOSES IN ACTION ACT
Saskatchewan. Revised Statutes. 1953. Chapter 360

2. Every debt and every chose in action arising out of a contract shall be assignable by any form of writing containing apt words in that behalf, but subject to such conditions and restrictions with respect to the right of transfer as may appertain to the original debt or as may be connected with or be contained in the original contract; and the assignee thereof may bring an action thereon in his own name as the party might to whom the debt was originally owing or to whom the right of action originally accrued, or he may proceed in respect of the same as though this Act had not been passed.

6. If an assignment is made in conformity with this Act and notice thereof is given to the debtor or person liable in respect of the subject of the assignment, the assignee shall have, hold and enjoy the same free of any claims, defences or equities which may arise subsequent to the notice by any act of the assignor or otherwise.

NOTES AND QUESTIONS. Although the English and Ontario sections speak of passing "the legal right" to such chose, does the "legal" right prevail over an equitable assignment (as is indicated in *Gordon* v. *Gordon*) in the absence of notice to the debtor? The priority of competing assignments, whether "legal" or "equitable" would appear to be still based on the doctrine of *Dearle* v. *Hall*, 3 Russ. 1; 38 E.R. 475. For the unsatisfactory reasoning and history behind this rule, see the speech of Lord Macnaghten in *Ward* v. *Duncombe*, [1893] A.C. 369, pp. 383, to which reference is made in *Gordon* v. *Gordon*. How can an assignee of part of debt acquire a "legal" right (as indicated in the principal case) to an indivisible chose?

HUGHES *v.* PUMP HOUSE HOTEL COMPANY, LIMITED
England. Court of Appeal. [1902] 2 K.B. 190

The action was by a builder to recover £2788, being the total of amounts alleged to be due to him from the defendants, an hotel company, as the balance of the contract price of work done under a contract entered into on November 1, 1899, between the plaintiff and the defendants for the completion by the plaintiff of a pump room and the execution of alterations and additions to the defendants' hotel at Llandrindod Wells, and for extra work done in connection with the contract.

The plaintiff on March 7, 1901, signed and gave to Lloyd's Bank, Limited an instrument the material terms of which were: "In consideration of your continuing a banking account with me the undersigned, and by way of continuing security to you for all moneys due or to become due to you from me alone, or jointly with others, either on the said account or otherwise, I hereby asign to you all moneys due, or to become due, to me from the Pump House Hotel Company, Limited, of Llandrindod Wells, under or by virtue of a certain contract dated November 1, 1899, and made between the said company of the one part and myself of the other part. . . . An order had been made for the determination of the preliminary point of law whether the assignment of March 7, 1901, was an absolute assignment within the meaning of the Judicature Act, 1873, s. 25, sub-s. 6, of the subject-matter of the plaintiff's claim, and therefore the plaintiff's claim had passed to the bank.

MATHEW L.J.: In this case the learned judge has decided that the assignment was not absolute . . . and that it purported to be by way of charge only, and, therefore, that the action was properly brought in the name of the assignor. The defendants appeal from his decision, and contend that the instrument in question constituted an absolute assignment within the meaning of the section, and therefore the action in the name of the assignor ought not to be continued. In every case of this kind, all the terms of the instrument must be considered; and, whatever may be the phraseology adopted in some particular part of it, if, on consideration of the whole instrument, it is clear that the intention was to give a charge only, then the action must be in the name of the assignor; while, on the other hand, if it is clear from the instrument as a whole that the intention was to pass all the rights of the assignor in the debt or chose in action to the assignee, then the case will come within s. 25, and the action must be brought in the name of the assignee.

The circumstances under which this litigation arose were as follows. The plaintiff had contracted with the defendants to execute extensive building works. That contract was entered into in November, 1899. On March 7, 1901, the assignment in question was made by the plaintiff to Lloyd's Bank. When the work was completed, a dispute arose between the plaintiff and the defendants as to the balance payable in respect of the price of the work and for extras, and in respect of that balance the action was brought by the plaintiff. The objection was thereupon taken by the defendants that, having regard to the terms of the assignment of March 7, 1901, the action could not be maintained in the name of the assignor. The instrument of March 7, 1901, was in these terms: [Mathew L.J. here read the instrument.] On the same day on which the assignment was executed notice of it was given to the defendants, and an authority was sent to them by the plaintiff requesting them to pay to the bank all sums payable under the contract.

What, then, is the effect of the assignment? It seems to me clear from its terms that the intention was to pass to the assignees complete control of all moneys payable under the building contract, and to put them for all purposes in the position of the assignor with regard to those moneys. That being so, I think, unless there be some difficulty created by the decisions on the subject, this instrument may be properly described as an absolute assignment, because it is one under which all the rights of the assignor in respect of the moneys payable under the building contract were intended to pass to the assignees, and not one which purports to be by way of charge only. The learned judge appears to have been of opinion that the assignment was not absolute, but purported to be by way of charge only, because the object was that it should be a continuing security for such amount as might from time to time be due from the assignor to the assignees. But, if that were the true criterion, it might equally well be argued that a mortgage is not an absolute assignment, because under a mortgage it may become necessary to take an account in order to ascertain how much is due; but, though a mortgage is only a security for the amount which may be due. it is nevertheless an absolute assignment because the whole right of the mortgagor in the estate passes to the mortgagee.

The governing principle with regard to what constitutes an absolute assignment is indicated by the decisions in *Comfort* v. *Betts*, [1891] 1 Q.B. 737 and *Durham Brothers* v. *Robertson*, [1898] 1 Q.B. 765. In the former case an assignment was made of certain debts to a trustee on trust for the benefit of the creditors. It was argued that this did not amount to an absolute assignment of the debts, but it was pointed out in answer that by the terms of the instrument creating the trust the whole interest of the assignors was intended to be conveyed to the assignee, and the subsequent creation of the trust did not derogate from the absolute character of that assignment. The principle laid down in both the cases which I have mentioned appear to be applicable to the present case.

Certain authorities, on the other hand, were relied upon for the plaintiff. It is not necessary, I think, to go through all of them. Those principally relied upon were *Mercantile Bank of London* v. *Evans*, [1899] 2 Q.B. 613 and *Jones* v. *Humphreys*, [1902] 1 K.B. 10. In each of those cases general terms were used in making the assignment, but, when the whole instrument was looked at, it appeared that what was intended was only to assign so much of the debt or chose in action as would provide security for a debt, in the one case of £200 and in the other £22 10s. Upon that becoming apparent, it was held that the true character of the interest given was that of a charge only. It is unnecessary to dwell upon the obvious distinction between those cases and the present. In the course of the argument the question was raised whether an assignment of part of a debt comes within s. 25 of the Judicature Act, 1873. We are not called upon to decide that question in this case, and I will express no opinion upon it further than to say that, as at present advised, I think, when that question arises for decision, much may be said in favour of the view that an assignment of part of a debt could not be an absolute assignment within the section.

[The opinion of Cozens-Hardy L.J. is omitted.]

FORSTER *v*. BAKER
England. High Court. [1910] 2 K.B. 636

BRAY J.: This case raises two questions. The first is, whether the assignment of part of a judgment debt comes within s. 25, sub-s. 6, of the *Judicature Act, 1873* so as to transfer that part of the debt with all its remedies to the assignee. The second question is one of fact, namely, whether there has been a payment of the judgment debt.

With regard to the first question the authorities that have been cited are all referred to in the judgment of Darling J. in *Skipper & Tucker* v. *Holloway*, [1910] 2 K.B. 630. Opinions have been expressed in those authorities on this point, but they are opinions only and not decisions; and it is clear that when the question came before Darling J. there was no binding authority. He has undoubtedly decided the point in a case which came before him at nisi prius. The first question which arises is, am I bound by his decision? I have always understood that one judge is not bound by the decision of another judge on a point of law at nisi prius, and therefore, I think I am bound to consider the case and to decide it according to my own opinion, at the same time, of course, giving great weight to the decision of Darling J.

The question is whether there can be an absolute assignment of part of a debt within s. 25, sub-s. 6, of the *Judicature Act, 1873*. It seems to me that the language of that sub-section prima facie has reference to a whole debt or chose in action. It is said that the language is wide enough to include part of a debt. I will assume for a moment that that may be so. What ought I then to consider? In my opinion I ought to consider what the results would be of holding that there can be a valid legal assignment of part of a debt, and whether those results are such as are contemplated by the section. Now, I do not think it is intended to throw any greater burden on the debtor than had previously existed. The position formerly of a debtor as regards a legal debt which had been assigned was that an action could be brought against him, but the assignor, except in certain exceptional cases, was a necessary party to the action either as plaintiff or defendant, in order that he might be bound, as well as the debtor and the assignee, by the decision of the case. I should certainly assume, although I do not know of any authority to that effect, that if a part of a debt had been assigned to A and another part to B, and A had brought an action to recover his part, he would have been obliged not only to make the assignor a party, but B also, so that there would be one action which would decide the relationship of the debtor to each of the persons who owned part of the debt, and the question would be decided once for all between all the parties. But if an absolute assignment of part of a debt is valid under s. 25, sub-s. 6, the consequence is that the assignee is able to sue the debtor without joining the assignor or the assignee of the other part of the debt, if there have been two assignments; and it might happen that if the debt had been split up into two, three, or four parts, there might be two, three, or four actions with different results. All sorts of difficulties would arise, and a great burden, an unnecessarily great burden, would be placed upon the debtor. In the case of a judgment debt that consideration applies with even greater force, because the remedy on a judgment debt is execution, and the result would be that if a judgment debt was divided into, say, three or four parts, each of which was assigned to a different person, there might be three or four executions, and three or four petitions in bankruptcy, and the debtor might be considerably and unnecessarily harassed. These considerations, in my opinion, point to the fact that I ought not, unless compelled by the language of the section, to construe the words "legal debt or chose in action" as including part of a legal debt or part of chose in action. I think some consideration should also be given to the fact that s. 25, sub-s. 6, deals only with absolute assignments and not with assignments by way of charge. For these reasons I should, apart from authority, come to the conclusion that the assignment of part of a debt or part of a legal chose in action is not within s. 25, sub-s. 6.

I pass to the consideration of the decision of Darling J. in *Skipper & Tucker* v. *Holloway*, and, as I have said, I am bound to give great weight to that decision, because he had all the authorities cited to him and he considered the matter. . . . It seems to me that the reason given by Darling J. for his decision is an insufficient reason, and he does not appear to have considered the great and unnecessary and, as it seems to me, unfair burden which would be thrown on a debtor by holding that there can be an absolute assignment of part of a debt within the section. Certainly Darling J. did not consider the case of a judgment debt, upon which leave to issue execution might, according to the contention of the present plaintiff, be applied for and granted to two or more different persons. I therefore hold that there cannot be an absolute assignment within s. 25, sub-s. 6, of part of a debt or legal chose in action, and inasmuch as a judgment debt is a debt or legal chose in action, it follows that part of a judgment debt cannot be the subject of an assignment within the section.

The other question is a difficult question of fact and as it now becomes unnecessary for me to decide it, I prefer to express no opinion upon it.

In answer to the question in the case I say that Elizabeth Josephine Forster is not entitled to leave to issue execution on the judgment.

[The plaintiff appealed. The appeal was dismissed but some reservation was expressed on the broader question of an assignment of a chose in action. The Court agreed that a judgment creditor who assigned a part of his judgment debt could not give his assignee greater rights than he had himself to issue execution.]

BANK OF LIVERPOOL AND MARTINS, LTD. *v*. HOLLAND, 1926. 43 T.L.R. 29 (England. High Court). Wilkinson had sold his business to Holland and £285 was still owing to him when he assigned that balance by way of security to the Bank with whom he had an overdraft for about £100. The assignment provided in part, "And it is hereby agreed and declared that the amount recoverable under these presents shall not at any time exceed the sum of one hundred and fifty pounds." The Bank sued on the assignment and Holland contended that the effect of the quoted clause was to reduce the assignment to one of part only of the debt and that it was therefore bad. Held, for the Bank. WRIGHT J.: "But . . . even if it was an assignment of only part of the debt it would still be a good equitable assignment. . . . it was not an assignment of part of the debt, but was an absolute assignment to the bank of the whole debt, with a provision that if the bank should recover more than £150 from the debtor they must hold the balance in excess of £150 as trustees for Wilkinson. The fact that a creditor remained trustee of part of the debt did not make the assignment any the less absolute. . . ."

CONLAN *v*. CARLOW. [1912] 2 Ir.R. 535 (Ireland. High Court). GIBSON J.: "A contracts with B to build a house for £1,000; he assigns absolutely £500 thereof to C, and gives D another assignment for £500. If B disputed due performance of the contract, is he to be sold twice over, with perhaps different results according to the view taken in each case by the jury? . . . Is the assignor not to be a party to the action in which the debtor's liability is to be determined?"

BEST *v*. BEATTY. 1919. 61 S.C.R. 576 (Ontario. Supreme Court of Canada). IDINGTON J.: "In my opinion an assignment of anything less than a whole chose in action does not entitle the assignee to sue. . . . The statute enabling an assignee of a chose in action to sue, in my opinion, never was intended to enable the possessor of a valuable chose in action to issue a kind of currency, as it were, by dividing up his right into little bits and distributing them amongst his friends, and giving each of them a chance to worry and annoy the debtor."

FEDERAL DISCOUNT CORPORATION LTD. *v.* ST. PIERRE

Ontario. Court of Appeal. 1962. 32 D.L.R. (2d) 86.

Mrs. St. Pierre agreed to purchase from Fair Isle Knitting (Ontario) Limited, or, as it was sometimes called, Fair Isle Knitting Company, a home knitting machine for $365. She paid a deposit of $35 and promised to pay the balance in twelve monthly instalments of $27.50 each. She signed a conditional sale contract and an indenture collateral to a promissory note "for the protection of [Fair Isle] or its agents or assignees." Both Mrs. St. Pierre and her husband signed the note, which already had been endorsed by Fair Isle to Federal Discount Corporation Ltd. Mrs. St. Pierre also signed a home knitting contract (and paid $2) with Yarncraft Industries Limited, a company having identical shareholders and officers, and occupying the same or adjacent office space with Fair Isle. One clause of the knitting contract provided: "You [Yarncraft] are to supply me on request with sufficient orders I may reasonably be expected to fill in my spare hours at home. . . . My profit for knitting these orders is to be no less than $4.00 per pound of knitted goods." One of the many documents of an "elaborate and confusing nature" presented to Mrs. St. Pierre along with the knitting contract was a "questionnaire" that led her to think she could buy yarn for 35 cents an ounce and sell knitted goods for 60 cents an ounce, and thus pay for the kntting machine in short order.

In fact Mrs. St. Pierre shipped about $150 worth of knitted goods for which she was not paid. On her part, she paid two instalments of $27.50, but having received no further payments for knitted goods from Yarncraft, she made no further payments to Fair Isle or Federal.

From the beginning Federal had been acting as the finance company for Fair Isle and Yarncraft and was familiar with the many and confusing documents used by Fair Isle and Yarncraft in the selling campaign. Shortly after signing the contracts Mrs. St. Pierre received a letter from Federal telling her that the contract had been assigned to their firm. On this letter had been stamped, "Note — Payments must be made when due regardless of amount earned from knitting." Two months later, after Mrs. St. Pierre had fallen in arrears, Federal wrote that $21.50 had been received from Yarncraft on her account and asking for prompt payment of the balance owing, $30. No payment had in fact been made by Yarncraft and this false statement had been made to spur some payment on the purchase contract. Shortly after Yarncraft announced that it was "suspending" operations. In the Division Court Federal claimed $273.30 from Mr. and Mrs. St. Pierre as the amount due on the promissory note of which Federal claimed to be the holder in due course. The trial judge dismissed the claim on the ground that payment could not have been enforced against the defendant by the original payee (Fair Isle) and that Federal was not a holder in due course. Federal appealed.

KELLY J. A.: . . . The rights which accrue to a holder in due course of a bill of exchange are unique and distinguishable from the rights of an assignee of a contract which does not fall within the description of a bill of exchange. The assignee of a contract, unlike the holder in due course of a bill of exchange undertakes subject to all the equities between the original parties, which have arisen prior to the date of notice of the assignment to the party sought to be charged.

The special privileges enjoyed by a holder in due course of a bill of exchange are quite foreign to the common law and have their origin in the law merchant.

There is little difficulty in appreciating how trade between merchants required that he who put into circulation his engagement to pay a specified sum at a designated time and place knowing that it was the custom of merchants to regard such paper much as we do our paper currency, should be held to the letter of his obligation and be prevented from setting up defences which might derogate from the apparently absolute nature of his obligation.

At first the customs prevailing amongst merchants as to bills of exchange extended only to merchant strangers trafficking with English merchants; later they were extended to inland bills between merchants trafficking with one another within England; then to all persons trafficking and finally to all persons trafficking or not.

Thus in time the particular conditions which were recognized as prevailing amongst merchants became engrafted onto the law generally applicable and came to be looked on as arising from the document itself rather than from the character of the parties dealing with the document. It is significant, however, that the transition did not affect the legal position as to one another of immediate parties and that as between any two immediate parties, maker and payee, or endorser and endorsee, none of the extraordinary conditions otherwise attaching to the bill, serve to affect adversely the rights and obligations existing between them as contracting parties. The document itself becomes irreproachable and affords special protection to its holder only, when at some stage of its passage from payee or acceptor to holder, there has been a *bona fide* transaction of trade with respect to it wherein the transferee took for value and without any notice of circumstances which might give rise to a defence on the part of the maker. Unless the ultimate holder or some earlier holder has acquired the instrument in the course of such a transaction the earlier tainting circumstances survive and the holder seeking to enforce payment of it must, on the merits, meet any defence which would have been available to the maker. Thus it appears that the peculiar immunity which the holding of a bill of exchange brings to the holder in due course arises not from the original nature of the document itself but from the quality which had been imparted to it by at least some one transfer of it. It follows that the transfer which is alleged to have given such a special character to the bill of exchange should be subject to more than a casual examination and that the true nature of that transaction be discovered.

There can be no doubt that everyday commercial life demands that the integrity of bills of exchange be recognized and that those acquiring them in good faith should not be required unnecessarily to make inquiries to establish their authenticity. Courts quite properly have refused to recognize that constructive notice has any place in the law of negotiable instruments: *London Joint Stock Bank* v. *Simmonds*, [1892] A.C. 201 at p. 221. Any attempt to weaken the provisions of a valid bill of exchange duly launched into the stream of commercial life, should be avoided. To do so, however, does not require that a prospective purchaser of a bill of exchange who has knowledge of certain circumstances about the seller's business which puts him on inquiry can by avoiding making inquiries or drawing reasonable inferences from the circumstances known to him, improve his position beyond that which it would have been had he made the enquiries he should have made or drawn the inference he should have drawn. This is not charging the holder with constructive notice and does not go beyond the standard of conduct laid down by the House of Lords in *Earl of Sheffield* v. *London Joint Stock Bank* (1888), 13 App. Cas. 333.

It is not necessary for the support of ordinary commercial transactions that the holder of a bill of exchange should under all circumstances be permitted to shield himself behind the guise of a holder in due course and attempt to separate his character as holder in due course from the debilitating effect of facts and circumstances actually known to him at the time he acquired the bill or which were reasonably inferable from facts and circumstances which were brought to his knowledge.

In the examination of any transfer to decide if it constituted the transferee a holder in due course the plaintiff's actual involvement with the transferor will be a major factor; on this account the whole relationship between the plaintiff and its transferor must be examined and considered.

With the growth of the sale of household and personal goods on the extended payment plan, the promissory note, the conditional sales contract and the finance company have become inseparable parts of the procedure whereby the merchant realizes immediately cash from the extended obligation of the purchaser from him. The very existence of the seller's business depends on his ability to convert into cash these obligations and the finance company, standing ready and willing to buy them, has become not only an essential part of retail selling on the time payment plan but is in effect a department of the seller's business, exercising a measure of control over the seller's sales by the requirements laid down with regard to the negotiable paper proposed to be purchased.

In the course of this development an attempt has been made to project into the field of household law the law merchant originally designed for dealings between merchants. The fiction has been permitted to flourish that the finance company is a foreign and independent agency. When it does acquire the contracts which it was incorporated to buy and which it arranged to purchase before the contracts actually came into existence it attempts to shield itself behind the protection of the law merchant which can apply only, if at all, to one of the documents constituting the arrangement between the seller and the buyer; at the same time it takes unto itself all the advantages that can be drawn from the transaction out of which the note arose. It is beyond question that the promissory note is included in the documents required to be signed by the purchaser to the express purpose of enabling the finance company to avoid defences which would otherwise be available to the maker against his vendor and any assignee of his purchase obligation.

The plaintiff was in the business of discounting notes: it was its practice and policy where any note had relationship to a conditional sales contract that the conditional sales contract should also be purchased and assigned to it: when a dealer first approached the plaintiff with a view to having the plaintiff discount notes which were to arise from the dealer's sales, the plaintiff investigated the applicant as to its financial stability, moral responsibility and various other aspects which would qualify the applicant to be a dealer "with the plaintiff"; the plaintiff was interested in knowing the possible volume of the business of the dealer as in the words of the witness McGarry, the plaintiff's Credit and Collection Manager, "It's got to be worthwhile before you can go into business with them". It was also well known to the plaintiff that Fair Isle and Yarncraft were companies having the same principals and officers.

The plaintiff was informed of the manner in which Fair Isle intended to conduct its selling campaign for the distribution of home knitting machines and was told by Turack, an officer of both Fair Isle and Yarncraft, "What we were doing in the other company" (Yarncraft). In fact the form of purchase order, questionnaire, conditional sales contract, and application for home knitting contract which were used in the approach to the female defendant were shown to the plaintiff company at the inception of the dealings between the plaintiff and Fair Isle. The purpose of the incorporation of two distinct companies, Fair Isle Knitting (Ontario) Limited and Yarncraft Industries Limited, was stated by Turack to be that one, Fair Isle, would sell knitting machines in conjunction with the giving of home knitting contract by the other, Yarncraft, and that the operation of Yarncraft and its home knitting contracts was something to facilitate the sale of home knitting machines by Fair Isle.

The plaintiff was fully aware of the general course of operation employed by Fair Isle and Yarncraft in their dealings with the purchasers such as the defendants. The words which were impressed by rubber stamps on exs. 24 and 25, "Note — payments must be made when due, regardless of the amount earned from knitting", proved beyond a shadow of a doubt that the plaintiff knew that the purchasers of home knitting machines would be or at least could have been left with the impression which was in the mind of the female defendant, that is, that the moneys to meet the instalments of purchase-price would be forthcoming from earnings under the home knitting contract.

According to the evidence of Barber, the association of the home knitting contract with the sale of home knitting machine was one of the reasons why the plaintiff dealt with Fair Isle because the plaintiff "felt that if a person could make money, sell their material back to Yarncraft industries, they would be able to pay for the machine".

The course of dealings between the plaintiff and the officers of Fair Isle indicates a relationship much more intimate than that of endorsee or endorser in a normal commercial transaction. The company selling the home knitting machines in conjunction with the awarding by its associate of home knitting contracts and the plaintiff who made possible the operations of the seller by buying the purchaser's instalment obligation were more nearly engaged in one business, each one in the conduct of its particular phase being useless without the association of the other. To pretend that they were so separate that the transfer of each note constituted an independent commercial transaction not affected by the pre-existing arrangements between them would, in my view, be to permit the form to prevail over the substance.

My view of the relationship of the plaintiff and its endorser of the note sued upon is reinforced by the evidence as to the arrangement between the plaintiff and Fair Isle, which resulted in the writing of a letter of March 17, 1959, ex. 13. The conduct of the plaintiff and Fair Isle leading up to the despatch of this letter is of itself of such an extraordinary nature as to require no comment other than to say that it indicates a relationship somewhat beyond what would be expected of a financial institution and a merchant dealing in the ordinary course of business. Even granting that the plaintiff did not have actual notice of facts the knowledge of which would have prevented it from becoming a holder in due course, the transfer of the note to it by Fair Isle fell short of being the type of business transaction between two parties, dealing with respect to the note in complete good faith, which would have imparted to the note the power to endow with the character of holder in due course, one becoming a holder with complete knowledge of its history and the complete facts of the relationship between the maker and the payee.

There appear to be no Canadian cases which have held that the business relationship between a dealer and a finance company is an element to be considered in deciding finance company's claim to be a holder in due course; the question has been dealt with by American Courts in this manner and I would adopt the reasoning of the Judges who decided these cases: *Buffalo Industrial Bank* v. *De Marzio* (1937), 296 N.Y. Supp. 783; *Commercial Credit Co.* v. *T. F. Childs* (1940), 128 A.L.R. 726; *Taylor et ux.* v. *Atlas Security Co.* (1923), 249 S.W. 746.

Under the circumstances of this case I can find no error in the conclusion arrived at by the trial Judge, namely, that the plaintiff was not a holder in due course of the promissory note sued upon in this action.

Counsel for the plaintiff referred to *Commodity Discount Ltd.* v. *Baker*, [1961] O.W.N. 277, as authority for his contention that it could be no defence to an action by a holder in due course of a promissory note, that the note was given to the original payee as part of a conditional sales transaction. I have examined the Appeal Book and read the transcript of evidence in the case cited; in it the point at issue was whether the *mere* fact that the promissory note sued upon was part of a contract which had been entered into between the defendant and the payee of the promissory note, served to disqualify the endorsee of the note as a holder in due course. There was an absence of any evidence as to the relationship between the payee and the finance company and as to knowledge by the plaintiff of the circumstances under which the signature of the promissory note had been procured; the case is distinguishable upon the facts from the case now before this Court.

In view of my conclusion that the plaintiff is not a holder in due course, it falls to be considered whether the learned trial Judge erred in holding that the payee of note sued upon could not have payment from the defendants had it not assigned its rights to the plaintiff.

Those who conceived the scheme which led to Pritchard's activities as a salesman for Fair Isle and Yarncraft intended to achieve a twofold result — to lead prospective purchasers to believe, as actually happened in the case of the defendants, that they were purchasing a revenue-producing machine which could be paid for out of the proceeds of the work to be done on it and marketed by a means of the home knitting contract; and at the same time by the use of documents of an elaborate and confusing nature to secure a document from the purchasers which would accomplish a legal result quite foreign to the impression sought to be created in the purchasers' minds. The method employed displayed sales ability of a high degree and entailed the use of a series of documents which apparently confused even those responsible for their drafting and certainly confused the salesman through whom they were furnished to the defendants. A careful perusal of ex. 7 discloses that it was a blank form of receipt prepared to be given in respect of a full or partial payment on a home knitting contract. Although in the application for home knitting contract, ex. 6, readied by Pritchard for the signature of the female defendant, care was taken to have the application addressed to "Yarncraft Industries Limited", the receipt is headed "Official Receipt Fair Isle Knitting Company". Further the only payment required under the home knitting contract was a nominal one of $2. Pritchard in filling in the blanks in ex. 7 inserted the amount of $35, which was the down payment provided for in the purchase order ex. 5 and the conditional sales contract, ex. 2, both documents tendered in connection with the purchase of the home knitting machine. It is small wonder that the female defendant was unable to appreciate the fine distinction between the allegedly separate legal entities with which she was dealing, when the draftsman of the documents and the salesman who was trained in their use were unable to maintain the necessary separation which at least was essential to maintain that the right hand, Fair Isle, did not know what the left hand, Yarncraft, was doing and *vice versa.*

I find no difficulty in supporting the finding of the learned trial Judge that the female defendant believed what she was intended to believe, namely, that she was engaged in one transaction; the whole course of the conduct of Fair Isle and Yarncraft was to induce that belief, and it did so induce it.

Counsel for the appellant submitted that on two accounts the defendants were not entitled to rescission: first, that there had been no misrepresentation as to any existing fact, but only a statement as to future conduct; second, that the defendants having made payments and having used the machine, their only remedy lay in damages.

The female defendant by her earlier purchase of the machine she disposed of must be assumed to have wished to be the owner of a home knitting machine. She has admitted that the home knitting machine purchased from Fair Isle is still in her possession and that she has made use of it for the purpose of making knit goods for herself and the members of her family, the claim for rescission must be rejected; the defendants' only remedy would then be a counterclaim as to damages: *Kerr on Fraud and Mistake*, 7th. ed., p. 529.

Even if there be accepted as evidence of the measure of damages, the very unsatisfactory testimony of the female defendant concerning the amount due to her for finished knit goods, her estimate would still have to be reduced by the value of the yarn admittedly taken from the premises of Fair Isle and Yarncraft on March 17, 1959. The evidence at trial, though voluminous and dealing at great length with matters of doubtful relevance leaves no sound basis for the assessment of damages. However, I hesitate to prolong further the course of these proceedings. Since the duty and power of the Division Court Judge is to hear and determine in a summary manner all questions of law and fact, and to make such order as appears to him just and agreeable to equity and good conscience, such an order should be made by this Court. I would avoid directing a reference to determine the measure of damages if there be any way in which this can be overcome. There will, therefore, be a reference to the Clerk of the Ninth Division Court of the County of Wentworth to take an account of the amount due the defendant by Fair Isle and Yarncraft for knit goods shipped by the female defendant over and above the value of the yarn obtained by her but only if either party demands it. In default of either party demanding such a reference within 15 days, the amount of the counterclaim is fixed at $140. . . .

[The appeal was allowed, the counterclaim was allowed, and there was no award as to costs.]

2. Personal Contracts and Subcontracting

ROBSON AND SHARPE *v.* DRUMMOND
England. King's Bench. 1831. 2 B. & Ad. 303; 109 E.R. 1156

In February, 1824, Sharpe was a coachmaker carrying on business in South Street, Grosvenor Square. In that month Sharpe agreed to supply Drummond with a new "chariot" for five years, at seventy-five guineas a year, payable in advance. Sharpe was to maintain the chariot in good repair, and it was to become Drummond's property at the end of the five years. Sharpe performed his contract until June, 1826, when he retired from business which he sold to Robson (including the chariot) who offered to continue with the contract with Drummond. Robson had been, from the beginning, a secret partner with Sharpe, but he was unknown to Drummond, who refused to accept him and returned the chariot to Robson in February, 1827, at the end of the then current year of the contract. As late as December 1826 Drummond appealed to Sharpe to continue but Sharpe replied that he was no longer entitled to deal with the chariot. Nevertheless he joined Robson in this action to recover the hire for the last two years. Lord Tenterden held that the action was not maintainable and directed a non-suit, but a rule nisi was obtained to enter a verdict for £157 10s.

Lord Tenterden C.J.: It is unnecessary to decide whether if Sharpe had continued in the partnership till the expiration of the five years during which the contract made by him was to continue in force, the action in the joint names of him and his partner might not have been maintained. Here, after the partnership between Robson and Sharpe had ceased to exist, and after Sharpe had ceased to carry on the business of a coachmaker, the defendant offered to continue the job with Sharpe, but he replied that that was impossible. Now the defendant may have been induced to enter into this contract by reason of the personal confidence which he reposed in Sharpe, and therefore have agreed to pay money in advance. The latter, therefore, having said it was impossible for him to perform the contract, the defendant had a right to object to its being performed by any other person, and to say that he contracted with Sharpe alone, and not with any other person. On that ground I think the nonsuit was right. The rule for setting it aside must therefore be discharged.

Parke J.: . . . It is true that the defendant will have an advantage which he would not have had if the contract had continued for the whole five years; for he will have had the use of the carriage during the first three, and will not be bound to keep it during the last two, when it must be worse for wear; but this arises from the default of one of the plaintiffs in not performing his part of the contract.

The rule was discharged. The judgment of Littledale and Patteson J.J. are omitted.

THE BRITISH WAGGON COMPANY AND THE PARKGATE WAGGON COMPANY *v.* LEA AND COMPANY
England. Queen's Bench. 1880. 5 Q.B.D. 149

Cockburn C.J. delivered the judgment of the Court: This was an action brought by the plaintiffs to recover rent for the hire of certain railway waggons, alleged to be payable by the defendants to the plaintiffs, or one of them, under the following circumstances:

By an agreement in writing of Feb. 10, 1874, the Parkgate Waggon Company let to the defendants, who are coal merchants, fifty railway waggons for a term of seven years, at a yearly rent of £600 a year, payable by equal quarterly payments. By a second agreement of June 13, 1874, the company in like manner let to the defendants fifty other waggons, at a yearly rent of £625, payable quarterly like the former.

Each of these agreements contained the following clause: "The owners, their executors, or administrators, will at all times during the said term, except as herein provided, keep the said waggons in good and substantial repair and working order, and, on receiving notice from the tenant of any want of repairs, and the number or numbers of the waggons requiring to be repaired, and the place or places where it or they then is or are, will, with all reasonable despatch, cause the same to be repaired and put into good working order."

On Oct. 24, 1874, the Parkgate Company passed a resolution, under the 129th section of the Companies Act, 1862, for the voluntary winding up of the company. Liquidators were appointed, and by an order of the Chancery Division of the High Court of Justice, it was ordered that the winding up of the company should be continued under the supervision of the court.

By an indenture of April 1, 1878, the Parkgate Company assigned and transferred, and the liquidators confirmed to the British Company and their assigns, among other things, all sums of money, whether payable by way of rent, hire, interest, penalty, or damage, then due, or thereafter to become due, to the Parkgate Company, by virtue of the two contracts with the defendants, together with the benefit of the two contracts, and all the interest of the Parkgate Company and the said liquidators therein; the British Company, on the other hand, covenanting with the Parkgate Company "to observe and perform such of the stipulations, conditions, provisions, and agreements contained in the said contracts as, according to the terms thereof, were stipulated to be observed and performed by the Parkgate Company." On the execution of this assignment the British Company took over from the Parkgate Company the repairing stations, which had previously been used by the Parkgate Company for the repair of the waggons let to the defendants, and also the staff of workmen employed by the latter company in executing such repairs. It is expressly found that the British Company have ever since been ready and willing to execute, and have, with all due diligence, executed all necessary repairs to the said waggons. This, however, they have done under a special agreement come to between the parties since the present dispute has arisen, without prejudice to their respective rights.

In this state of things the defendants asserted their right to treat the contract as at an end, on the ground that the Parkgate Company had incapacitated themselves from performing the contract, first, by going into voluntary liquidation, secondly, by assigning the contracts, and giving up the repairing stations to the British Company, between whom and the defendants there was no privity of contract, and whose services, in substitution for those to be performed by the Parkgate Company under the contract, they the defendants were not bound to accept. The Parkgate Company not acquiescing in this view, it was agreed that the facts should be stated in a special case for the opinion of this court, the use of the waggons by the defendants being in the meanwhile continued at a rate agreed on between the parties, without prejudice to either, with reference to their respective rights.

The first ground taken by the defendants is in our opinion altogether untenable in the present state of things, whatever it may be when the affairs of the company shall have been wound up, and the company itself shall have been dissolved under the 111th section of the Act. Pending the winding up, the company is by the effect of ss. 95 and 131 kept alive, the liquidator having power to carry on the business, "so far as may be necessary for the beneficial winding up of the company," which the continued letting of these waggons, and the receipt of the rent payable in respect of them, would, we presume, be.

What would be the position of the parties on the dissolution of the company it is unnecessary for the present purpose to consider.

The main contention on the part of the defendants, however, was that, as the Parkgate Company had, by assigning the contracts, and by making over their repairing stations to the British Company, incapacitated themselves to fulfill their obligation to keep the waggons in repair, that company had no right, as between themselves and the defendants, to substitute a third party to do the work they had engaged to perform, nor were the defendants bound to accept the party so substituted as the one to whom they were to look for performance of the contract; the contract was therefore at an end.

The authority principally relied on in support of this contention was the case of *Robson* v. *Drummond* (1831), 109 ER. 1156. . . .

In like manner, where goods are ordered of a particular manufacturer, another, who has succeeded to his business, cannot execute the order, so as to bind the customer, who has not been made aware of the transfer of the business, to accept the goods. The latter is entitled to refuse to deal with any other than the manufacturer whose goods he intended to buy. For this *Boulton* v. *Jones* (1857), 157 E.R. 232, is a sufficient authority. The case of *Robson* v. *Drummond* comes nearer to the present case, but is, we think, distinguishable from it. We entirely concur in the principle on which the decision in *Robson* v. *Drummond* rests . . . Personal performance is in such a case of the essence of the contract, which, consequently, cannot in its absence be enforced against an unwilling party.

But this principle appears to us inapplicable in the present instance, inasmuch as we cannot suppose that in stipulating for the repair of these waggons by the company — a rough description of work which ordinary workmen conversant with the business would be perfectly able to execute — the defendants attached my importance to whether the repairs were done by the company, or by any one with whom the company might enter into a subsidiary contract to do the work. All that the hirers, the defendants, cared for in this stipulation was that the waggons should be kept in repair; it was indifferent to them by whom the repairs should be done. Thus if, without going into liquidation, or assigning those contracts, the company had entered into a contract with any competent party to do the repairs, and so had procured them to be done, we cannot think that this would have been a departure from the terms of the contract to keep the waggons in repair. While fully acquiescing in the general principle just referred to, we must take care not to push it beyond reasonable limits. And we cannot but think that, in applying the principle, the Court of Queen's Bench in *Robson* v. *Drummond* went to the utmost length to which it can be carried, as it is difficult to see how in repairing a carriage when necessary, or painting it once a year, preference would be given to one coachmaker over another. Much work is contracted for, which it is known can only be executed by means of subcontracts; much is contracted for as to which it is indifferent to the party for whom it is to be done, whether it is done by the immediate party to the contract, or by some one on his behalf. In all these cases the maxim *Qui facit per alium facit per se* applies.

In the view we take of the case, therefore, the repair of the waggons, undertaken and done by the British Company under their contract with the Parkgate Company, is a sufficient performance by the latter of their engagement to repair under their contract with the defendants. Consequently, so long as the Parkgate Company continues to exist, and, through the British Company, continues to fulfil its obligation to keep the waggons in repair, the defendants cannot, in our opinion, be heard to say that the former company is not entitled to the performance of the contract by them, on the ground that the company have incapacitated themselves from performing their obligations under it, or that, by transferring the performance thereof to others, they have absolved the defendants from further performance on their part. . . .

We are therefore of opinion that our judgment must be for the plaintiffs for the amount claimed.

KEMP *v.* BAERSELMAN

England. Court of Appeal. [1906] 2 K.B. 604

Kemp was a cake manufacturer at two locations, Annette Road and Martineau Road in London, and with a depot at Cardiff. On March 24, 1904 Kemp and Baerselman agreed that Baerselman would supply Kemp with all the fresh eggs he should need for one year from April 1 (Clause 1) and that Kemp would not purchase eggs from any other merchant (Clause 5). In July, Kemp acquired the business of the National Bakery Company at Brewery Road in London, with which he amalgamated his Cardiff and Annette Road business under the new name of George Kemp, Limited. The Martineau Road business was abandoned. On September 17 Baerselman, having had notice of the amalgamation wrote Kemp that as a trader he, Kemp, was "dead, and consequently the agreement is at an end." Kemp joined with George Kemp, Limited, to bring this action for non delivery of eggs at Brewery Road as well as at Annette Road and Cardiff. Channell J. held that Kemp was entitled to his supply of eggs at Annette Road and Cardiff, but not at Brewery Road. Both parties appealed. Scrutton K.C. and Jacobs, for Baerselman, cited *Tolhurst* v. *Associated Portland Cement Manufacturers*, [1902] 2 K.B. 660, Collins M.R., at p. 672: "The measure of an original contractor's requirements may be very different in a given case from those of a substituted person. In such a case clearly the original contractor could not insist on his contractor furnishing a supply equal to the requirements of the substitute, and could not prove that he required it himself." Counsel then proceeded to distinguish *Tolhurst's* case, which was affirmed in the House of Lords, [1903] A.C. 414, on the ground that there the contract was to supply all requirements of chalk for the company's cement manufacture, and the quantity was determined by the company's plant. Hence that contract was assignable.

Lord Alverstone C.J.: With regard to the subject of the plaintiff's cross appeal I think that Channell J. was clearly right, and that even if the benefit of the contract was assignable so far as it related to the supply of eggs to the business carried on by G. H. Kemp, still the plaintiffs could not in any event claim to have a supply for the Brewery Road business, for Kemp never carried on business there, and consequently never had any requirements for that business. But, with regard to the defendant's appeal, I regret to have to differ from Channell J., and the reasons why I differ from him are these: He seemed to be of opinion that, because this was a contract for the supply of an ordinary marketable commodity like eggs, the benefit of the contract could be assigned, and that it made no difference to the defendant who the persons were to whom the eggs were to be supplied by him. He did not anywhere in his judgment deal with clause 5 — the clause whereby the purchaser bound himself not to buy eggs from any other persons—and did not sufficiently consider the personal element which that clause introduced. I can find nothing in the judgments in *Tollhurst's case* in the House of Lords which can be interpreted as laying down the general principle for which Mr. Hamilton contended, namely, that the benefit of any contract of this kind can be assigned. What the House of Lords did say in that case was that in that particular case the contract for the supply of chalk for fifty years was to be treated as a contract for the supply to a given cement-making place, and not a personal contract. But there is nothing that I can see in the present contract which enables me to say that it is a contract to supply eggs to a particular place. The first clause provides that Baerselman shall supply, and Kemp shall accept, all the fresh eggs that he, Kemp, shall require for manufacturing purposes for one year. Then by clause 5 Kemp undertakes not to purchase eggs from any other merchant. That, as I have said, imposes a personal obligation upon the purchaser which may be very material to the contract. It is not seriously contended that Kemp, Limited, or any other assignee would be bound by that obligation unless there was something amounting to a novation; and here there was no evidence of a novation. I think this contract was not one the benefit of which can be assigned simply by a sale of the business, and that when the facts which were proved had become known to Baerselman he was entitled to refuse to continue the supply. I am not altogether satisfied that there is not also an argument in support of the defendant's contention to be based on the terms of payment, though I do not attach so much importance to it, because it may be that, when the authorities come to be examined, it will be found that the Courts have treated the question of payment as one which does not prevent the benefit of a contract from being assignable. I only mention it so that in the event of the case going further it may not be thought that it has been overlooked. I base my decision on the ground that clause 1 and 5 shew that the contract was a personal one, the measure of the defendant's obligations as to supply being the extent of Kemp's personal requirements, and the undertaking by Kemp not to buy eggs of other merchants being an undertaking which was purely personal to himself. The defendant's appeal, therefore must be allowed.

Judgment for the defendants on appeal and cross appeal.

[The concurring opinions of Sir Gorell Barnes, President, and Farwell L.J. are omitted.]

QUESTIONS. Suppose there had been no clause 5 in the agreement, could it have been assigned? Was it an enforceable contract anyway? Was there mutuality of obligation?

WHITELY, LIMITED *v*. HILT
England. Court of Appeal. [1918] 2 K.B. 808

Whiteley, Limited sold a piano to one Nina Nolan on a hire purchase arrangement for £32 7s., payable £2 13s. 11d. on signing and quarterly thereafter. Miss Nolan specifically agreed that she would not remove the piano without Whiteley, Limited's consent (Clause 3) and Whiteley, Limited agreed that should they retake the piano under the terms of hire, Miss Nolan could reinstate the agreement by paying arrears, securing a guarantor and paying expenses (Clause (c)). A year later Miss Nolan sold the contents of her flat to Mina Hilt for £100, and "solemnly declared" that no one had any claim on the property including the piano. Miss Hilt made all reasonable inquiries and searches respecting the property before she bought it. Shortly after the sale Miss Nolan, by now Mrs. Widlake, paid £2 13s. 11d. to Whiteley, Limited, bringing the amount paid up to £13 9s. 7d. and leaving a balance owing of £18 17s. 5d. When Whiteley, Limited received no further payments they made inquiries and demanded the return of the piano. Miss Hilt refused to give it up but offered to pay the balance of instalments and give a guarantee. Whiteley, Limited rejected this offer and sued for detinue or damages for conversion. Miss Hilt paid £18 7s. 5d. into Court together with a sum for costs. The county court Judge held for the defendant. The Divisional Court held that the defendant had acquired no interest in the piano because Miss Nolan had repudiated her agreement by wrongfully selling the piano and had lost her own interest. She thus had no interest to pass to Miss Hilt. Whiteley, Limited were entitled to recover the piano, or its full value without giving credit for the instalments already received. Miss Hilt appealed.

SWINFEN EADY M.R.: . . . The appellant upon this appeal also contends that the judgment of the Divisional Court was erroneous upon the measure of damages, and that the judgment of the county court judge was right in law. The first question which arises is whether Mrs. Widlake had any interest under the hire-purchase agreement which she could lawfully assign. The plaintiffs insist that the agreement merely amounts to a bailment which was ended by parting with the possession of the chattel bailed, and that the owner thereupon became entitled to its immediate return. It is not disputed that, by virtue of the sale, all the rights, title and interest which Mrs. Widlake could dispose of passed to the defendant. At the date of the sale there had not been any breach of the agreement, and there was not any present right in the plaintiffs to claim the return of the piano. The agreement is not only a letting to hire of a piano, it also confers for a valuable consideration an opinion of purchase. Moreover, clause (c) shows that if default is made in payment of the instalments, or if for any other breach the plaintiffs retake possession of the chattel, the hirer's interest is not thereby terminated, but the hirer has the right to resume the hiring, on paying the arrears of hire up to the date of re-possession, and procuring a satisfactory guarantee. Parting with the possession of the piano would not be a breach of the agreement if the piano remained in the flat and was not removed contrary to clause 3. If Mrs. Widlake had let her flat furnished for three years with the piano, the plaintiffs would not have been entitled on that account to retake the piano. The whole terms of the agreement show that the contract was not merely a bailment for reward, but that it conferred on the bailee an interest in the chattel. It did not amount to a contract for sale, as the hirer was not bound to purchase. But it did confer on the hirer an absolute right to purchase on complying with the provisions of the agreement. The contract was in my opinion assignable by the hirer, but the assignee could only retain possession of the chattel upon the terms of the contract. There was no right to remove the piano from the flat, nor has it been removed. There is no reason whatever for supposing that any personal element entered into the mind of either of the parties to the agreement, or that it would make any difference to the plaintiff by whom the obligations of the contract were fulfilled, or that there were any grounds for taking this contract out of the well-settled general rule that the benefit of a contract is assignable in equity and may be enforced by the assignee. . . .

The defendant therefore acquired all the interest of the vendor, and moreover she had the right in equity to compel the vendor to pay the remaining instalments to the plaintiffs and enforce for the benefit of the defendant all rights conferred by clause (c) of the contract. . . .

Under these circumstances I am of opinion that the appeal should be allowed and the judgment of the county court restored.

[The opinions of Warrington and Duke L.JJ. are omitted.]

DAVIES *v.* COLLINS

England. Court of Appeal. [1945] 1 All E.R. 247

LORD GREENE M.R.: In this case the respondent, an officer in the United States Army, entrusted some uniform to the appellant, Collins, in order to have it cleaned and certain small repairs done upon it. Collins describes himself as a cleaner and dyer, and the respondent had dealt with him on previous occasions. Collins took steps to limit his liability in two ways: first, by exhibiting a notice-board on his premises for the information of customers, and, secondly, by printing certain conditions upon the docket which was handed to customers when goods were accepted for cleaning. The county court judge did not find that the respondent was fixed with notice of the board, but he did find that he must be taken to have seen the printed conditions on the docket which were sufficiently brought to his attention, in spite of the fact that he incautiously did not take the trouble to read them. That finding of the county court judge is not, and could not be, assailed. The conditions printed on the docket are headed with the words, "Please read conditions," and then they are as follows.

"Whilst every care is exercised in cleaning and dyeing garments, all orders are accepted at owner's risk entirely and we are unable to hold ourselves responsible for damage, shrinkage, colour or defects developed in necessary handling. The proprietors' liability for loss is limited to an amount not exceeding 10 times the cost of cleaning."

The uniform was not returned, and must be taken to have been lost for the purposes of this case. It so happened that Collins for some time had not been in the habit of cleaning garments himself, and by "himself" I do not mean himself personally but by his regular employees; his practice at this time was to farm out contracts of this kind to a sub-contractor. He would not, of course, by doing that exclude his duty and his liability under the contract towards his own customer, but that is what he did and it must be taken that the loss took place either when the goods were being sent to the sub-contractor or were being handled by the sub-contractor or were being returned by the sub-contractor, because Collins apparently never had them back. In those circumstances it was said on behalf of the plaintiff that the limitation clause does not apply for the reason that the goods were lost not within the four corners of the contract but while something was being done by or on the instructions of Collins which was outside the terms of the contract altogether. That contention, if it be right, of course would bring into operation the familiar rule, to which I have already alluded in my judgment, just delivered in the laundry case *Alderslade* v. *Hendon Laundry, Ltd.*, [1945] 1 All E.R. 244., that limitation clauses of this kind do not apply where the damage that is suffered or the loss that has occurred is due to or takes place in the course of some operation which was never contemplated by the contract at all. The county court judge held that having regard to the nature of the work to be performed there was no right on the part of Collins to farm it out to a sub-contractor. I am not satisfied that the grounds upon which the judge formed that view are sufficient to support it, but nevertheless the conclusion to which he came was in my opinion the right one.

There is a well-known division of contracts for work and labour into two broad classes. One class is where the work and labour can, on the true construction of the contract, only be performed by the contracting party himself or by some staff that he employs. The other class is where, from all the circumstances of the case, including of course the true construction of the contract, it is to be inferred that it is a matter of indifference whether the work should be performed by the contracting party or by some sub-contractor whom he employs. In many contracts all that is stipulated for is that the work shall be done and the actual hand to do it need not be that of the contracting party himself; the other party will be bound to accept performance carried out by somebody else. The contracting party, of course, is the only party who remains liable. He cannot assign his liability to a sub-contractor, but his liability in those cases is to see that the work is done, and if it is not properly done he is liable. It is quite a mistake to regard that as an assignment of the contract; it is not. Here, again, these principles are well-known. . . .

The question, therefore, in this case is whether the farming out of this work of cleaning was permissible according to the contract or not. If it was not, a loss which occurred by reason of such farming out would not be covered by the limitation clause. In contracts such as we have here, and in a multitude of contracts commonly made, no specific mention at all is made of this question of sub-contracting. Whether or not in any given contract performance can properly be carried out by the employment of a sub-contractor must depend on the proper inference to be drawn from the contract itself, the subject-matter of it, and other material surrounding circumstances. The contract here, as in so many cases, has to be collected partly from the language used and partly from the acts of the parties. The nature of the work to be performed is, of course, always material. The county court judge appears to have thought that the nature of the work by itself was sufficient to exclude the right on the part of the cleaner to have it carried out by a sub-contractor, but as I have said I do not think I should agree that that by itself was sufficient. But there are other matters to which we must look, and although the evidence is not very full and the judge's note is very scanty, what appears to me to be the important consideration to which we have to direct our attention consists of the limitation condition itself and the language there employed. The condition starts off by saying: "Whilst every care is exercised in cleaning and dyeing garments." Now what does that mean? It would obviously be impossible for Collins to exercise care in the cleaning and dyeing of garments when that work is being done by a sub-contractor. He, no doubt, can exercise care in the choice of a sub-contractor, but in the actual work of cleaning and dyeing garments, if that is being carried out by a sub-contractor, there would, as it seems to me, be no room and no opportunity for him to exercise care. There is another phrase in this condition which is as follows: "We are unable to hold ourselves responsible for damage, shrinkage, colour or defects developed in necessary handling." The farming out to a sub-contractor cannot be described as "necessary handling" because there is nothing, so far as the customer knows, to prevent Collins doing the work himself or doing it by his ordinary staff. It seems to me therefore, although the point is perhaps rather a narrow one, that the actual language of this condition is sufficient to exclude any right on the part of the contractor to get the work done by a sub-contractor.

But there is another matter which I think is conclusive, and it is this: it is quite obvious that the risk which a customer runs under a limitation clause of this character is entirely different according as the work is to be carried out by the person with whom he contracts or by a sub-contractor. Let me expand that. If subcontracting is not permissible, the risk that the customer runs in respect of loss is a very limited one because the opportunity of loss is restricted; if, on the other hand, it is permissible to farm out the contract to a sub-contractor, the area within which loss may occur is quite clearly very largely extended; not only does it mean that the negligence of a third party comes into the picture, but all the risks incidental to sending the goods to the sub-contractor and having them returned by the sub-contractor to the head contractor come into the picture too. It seems to me that the mere presence of this limitation clause by itself is sufficient to exclude from the contract any right on the part of the contractor to sub-contract. If it is intended that that customer is to be affected by that extended range of risk to which I have referred, it should be made clear to him that that is the risk which is being imposed upon him.

Now, it is important not to interpret what I have said as going beyond the facts of this case. This is a case where, according to the appellant's argument, the whole contract could be farmed out so that in order that the work might be done the goods could properly be sent to a sub-contractor who might be residing at the other end of England. The fact that the contractual work of cleaning could be farmed out would be a thing which, as I have said, would vastly extend the customer's risk. But it must not be taken from what I have said that the presence of such a clause necessarily precludes every kind of sub-contracting. I am dealing with a case where the sub-contracting which is said to be permissible is the substance of the contract itself. Different considerations may very well apply in the case, let me say, of returning the goods to the customer after they have been dealt with by the contractor. To say that it is illegitimate, or must be taken to be illegitimate, to employ such a sub-contractor for the carrying out of an ancillary service such as sending the goods back to the customer would in the majority of cases be completely unbusinesslike. For instance, goods may have to be returned by post after they have been cleaned; that is nothing more or less than employing a sub-contractor, namely, the Postmaster-General, to effect delivery. The mere handing of the goods to a cartage company such as Carter Paterson for delivery would be the employment of a sub-contractor. It must not be taken from what I have said that the presence of a limitation clause of this kind is sufficient to exclude the right to sub-contract in respect of a purely ancillary matter of that kind. With regard to matters of that sort the presence of a limitation clause would not have, in my judgment, the weight which I attach to it in the present case where the service in respect of which sub-contracting is said to be permissible is not a mere ancillary service of that kind but is the essence of the contract itself, namely, the contract between the customer and the cleaner.

For these reasons I am of the opinion that this appeal must be dismissed. I have the authority of Uthwatt J., for saying that he agrees with the views that I have expressed and with the conclusion at which I have arrived.

[Mackinnon L.J. agreed.]

3. Restrictions on Assignment

QUEBEC BANK *v.* TAGGART

Ontario. Common Pleas. 1895. 27 O.R. 162

One Taggart took out a policy of insurance for $1,000 in September, 1886, which he assigned without reservation to Cloy on October 13, 1891. The insurance company was duly notified. In January, 1892, Cloy assigned the policy to the Quebec Bank in the same terms as Taggart's assignment to him. Taggart died in 1895 and a few weeks later the following letter written in pencil was found in Taggart's desk. The jury found that the signature was Cloy's:

"I, John Cloy, this 13 day of October Do accept and take a Life Policy of 1000 dollars on the life of James L. Taggart of the Town of Thorold to Hold as security for a cirtin amount now due me of $49.50 cts to be Paid from said policy 2598 from the Federal Life Association of Ontario Head Office Hamilton, and further do agree to keep said Policy 2598 in good standing by paying all regular quarter yearly payments notices sent from said Office at Hamilton for renewalls of said Policy 2598 and to receive at the end of James Taggart life to resive all such money paid with 6 per cent. from the time of payment to the end of the said J. L. Taggart Life and all above my Clame to be paid to his wife if alive or to his children Lilly, Jiney, James A. & Wesley Ross Taggart and further does he agree to pay the sum of $900 to the within named in case I do let the said policy 2598 elaps on account of not keeping said Policy 2598 regeruały renewed primions paid up or caused to be paid. All this i fully agree to Do."

The insurance money was paid into Court and the bank contested the right to it as against Mrs. Taggart and the children.

MACMAHON J.: Although the assignment executed by Taggart on the back of the policy is absolute as to all the insured's interest therein, yet, the jury having found that Cloy executed the agreement of defeasance, it was urged that that created an equity between Cloy and Taggart, and that Cloy could only assign to the bank subject to such equity; that is, that Cloy could not assign any greater interest than the agreement between himself and Taggart gave him.

Assent cannot be given to the argument thus advanced. Lord Cairns in *Re Agra and Masterman's Bank* (1867), L.R. 2 Ch. App. at p. 397, thus states the law: "Generally speaking, a chose assignable only in equity must be assigned subject to the equities existing between the original parties to the contract; but this is a rule which must yield when it appears from the nature or terms of the contract that it must have been intended to be assignable free from and unaffected by such equities." And in *Pollock on Contracts*, 5th ed., p. 214, the author, after quoting the above statement of Lord Cairns, says: "Where assignees of a chose in action are enabled by statute to sue at law, similar consequences may be produced by way of estoppel: *Webb* v. *Herne Bay Commissioners* (1870), L.R. 5 Q.B. 642; which really comes to the same thing, the doctrine of estoppel being a more technical and definite expression of the same principle." And the rule of law is thus stated in *Bigelow on Estoppel*, 5th ed., p. 562: "If a man purchase bona fide and for value an unnegotiable chose in action from one upon whom the owner has by assignment or otherwise conferred the apparently absolute ownership, he obtains a valid title against the real owner, supposing the act of purchase to have been induced by such act of the owner."

In *Redfearn* v. *Ferrier* (1813), 1 Dow H. L. 50; 3 E.R. 618 Lord Chancellor Eldon, at p. 72-3, said that if latent equities were allowed to prevail against assignations, the effect would be that nothing could ever be assigned, and he had found no case of authority of any kind to support this position—that an intimated assignation might be defeated by a latent equity, which as being latent *ex necessitate* could not be intimated. And in *Moore* v. *Metropolitan Bank*, 55 N.Y. at p. 47, the point under discussion is thus clearly and concisely dealt with: "Where one, known to be the owner of shares or chattels, delivers to another the script or possession of the chattels, together with an absolute written transfer of all his title thereto, he thereby enables him to hold himself out as owner, and as such, obtain credit upon and make sales of the property; and if, after he had so done, the owner was permitted to come in and assert his title against those dealings upon the faith of these appearances, the dishonest might combine and practise the grossest frauds. . . ."

The terms of the assignment indorsed on the policy and executed by Taggart are such as clearly indicate that the assignment was intended to be unaffected by any equities which may have existed between the parties to it. And the assignment clothed Cloy with authority to deal with the policy and dispose of it absolutely to any one taking it for value without notice of the agreement. And, as it was not pretended that the bank had any notice of the agreement, it has to be seen whether the bank stood in the position of one giving value to Cloy for the assignment to it of the policy. . . .

[The Court found that the assignment by Cloy was for valuable consideration and that the Bank took without notice of the agreement between Cloy and Taggart. Judgment was directed for the plaintiffs.]

NOTE. Insofar as the *Taggart* case proceeds upon the ground that an assignee of a chose in action for value and without notice does not take subject to latent equities, that is, equities of a third person against the assignor, the decision seems contrary to *Cockell* v. *Taylor* (1851), 15 Beav. 103; 51 E.R. 475; where the court indicated that all equities of whatsoever kind ranked in order of their date. Query whether under the statute, a legal assignment now being possible latent equities even in the absence of estoppel may not be cut-off. Query, too, whether all this talk about legal and equitable interests in assignments is not outdated by the growing disregard for the traditional distinction between law and equity.

Where the chose in action has a tangible form, for example, a bond, it has been argued that latent equities do not prevail against a purchaser for value without notice. It may be that this distinction as well as the *Taggart* case depends on some form of estoppel.

Suppose R is the holder of an overdue bill of exchange. He says to his son: "I constitute myself trustee of this bill for you." R then assigns the bill to E who takes for value and without notice. What result? In *Ryckman* v. *Canada Life Assurance Co.* (1870), 17 Gr. Ch. 550 at 557, Strong V.C. said: "... the assignee of a chose in action ... who acquires title by purchase from a trustee, takes subject to all the equities existing between the trustee and those for whom he holds beneficially, and the assignee is not entitled to shelter himself under a defence of purchase for value without notice."

REYNOLDS *v.* NAPIER. 1882. 1 N.Z.L.R. 277 (New Zealand. Court of Appeal). PRENDERGAST C.J., delivering the judgment of the Court: "... the general principle is well settled that such choses in action as are mere nude rights to litigate are not assignable either at law or in equity; and on the other hand that choses in action which are of the nature of property are assignable both at law and in equity. . . . The distinction between the two classes, which may be described at litigious and non-litigious choses-in-action, nearly agrees with that between rights of action for liquidated sums and for unliquidated damages—nearly, but not exactly—because cases may be put which seem to fall within the class of non-litigious rights although the exact amount receivable may have to be ascertained by a jury. The true distinction seems to be between those cases in which the demand is to have a contract performed and those in which the demand is to recover damages either for the non-performance of a contract or for a pure tort. When a money bond is put in suit, or a bill of exchange, or a covenant for the payment of rent, the plaintiff is seeking performance of a contract, and to have handed over to him pursuant to the contract a definite or definable sum of money, which, though not earmarked, is already in an intelligible sense his property. The same may be said of an action for the price of goods, even though the price may not have been exactly fixed, and of actions on policies of assurance, whether of fire or marine assurance, or on life. All those claims are debts, or in the nature of debts. The distinction is obvious between this class of choses-in-action and that in which the demand is not to have the thing done which was agreed to be done, but to have a recompense in damages for its non-performance. There may be cases of which it may be difficult to say on which side of the line they fall, but the criterion suggested will generally be sufficient. . . ."

IWANICKI *v.* LEVIN
Manitoba. Court of Appeal. [1924] 1 D.L.R. 171

Appeal from the decision of Galt J., dismissing the appellant's application made under the Real Property Act, R.S.M. 1913, ch. 171, sec. 139, to vacate a caveat filed by the respondent.

The main facts are as follows:

On October 15, 1921, James Munroe, being the registered owner of two lots in Kildonan, agreed in writing to sell them to Sophia Gramchuk [or Grandchuk] for the sum of $350 payable partly in cash and partly in deferred payments, the said agreement containing, among others, the following clause:

"9. No assignment of this agreement shall be valid unless it shall be for the entire interest of the purchaser and be approved and countersigned by the vendor, his agent or agents, and no agreement or conditions or relations between the purchaser and assignee or any other person acquiring title or interest through the purchaser shall preclude the vendor from the right to convey the premises to the purchaser on the surrender of this agreement and the payment of the unpaid portion of the purchase money which may be due hereunder, unless the assignment hereof be approved and countersigned as follows."

On March 8, 1922, in consideration of one dollar, Sophia Gramchuk assigned to the respondent Levin the agreement for sale that she had from Munroe. The deed of assignment was not at any time approved or countersigned by Munroe. And on the same or the following day, the same parties signed a document which is really a declaration of trust, setting forth that the deed of assignment was given as security for the sum of $584.38 which Sophia Gramchuk owed Levin; that upon Sophia Gramchuk acquitting herself of this debt by a certain date, Levin should assign back to her, and that in case of her defaulting, he be at liberty to sell her interest in the lots and credit her with the proceeds. On April 13, 1922, Levin filed in the Land Titles office the caveat in question, claiming an equitable estate in the lands under the agreement for sale between Munroe and Sophia Gramchuk, and the assignment by the latter to himself (Levin).

On December 1, 1922, in consideration of the sum of $240.41 Munroe, the original vendor, assigned his interest in the agreement for sale to the applicant Iwanicki, and gave him at the same time a transfer of the lands, in consequence of which there issued to the latter on the following day a certificate of title, subject however to Levin's caveat. Galt J. dismissed an application by Iwanicki to vacate the caveat. Iwanicki appealed.

PERDUE C.J.M.. . . . The main question is, it appears to me, whether the clause in the Munroe-Gramchuk agreement requiring the assent of Munroe to an assignment of it is of an assignable nature, or is it a stipulation for his protection which can only be invoked by him and cannot be transferred to another person? . . .

When the purchaser Gramchuk agreed with Munroe that no assignment by her of the agreement of sale should be valid "unless approved and countersigned by the vendor (Munroe) his agent or agents," a confidential relationship was created. She was entitled to expect from him, and no doubt did expect fair and reasonable treatment in giving or withholding assent, if she desired to assign the benefit of the agreement of purchase. But she did not agree that this control over her actions should be handed over by him to be exercised by another person. The words "his agent or agents" I would take to refer only to the countersigning by his agent authorised to express Munroe's approval. The purchaser was entitled to place confidence in Munroe that he would not unreasonably withhold his consent. She might well object to another person being put in his place.

The stipulation in question differs from the provision in a lease that the lessee shall not assign or sublet without leave because the lessor is interested in the protection of his property and in the choice of a tenant. Here the only interest of the vendor is to receive his purchase-money. . . .

I would therefore hold that the stipulation agreed to by Sophia Gramchuk that no assignment of the agreement should be valid unless it be approved and countersigned by Munroe etc., was a purely personal covenant involving a relation of personal confidence in Munroe, in that she relied upon his integrity and fairness in the matter of giving or withholding consent, and did not contemplate that another person in whom she had no such confidence should be put in his place. This, of course, only applies to the above stipulation. As to the rest of the transaction between Munroe and Iwanicki no difficulty arises.

I would dismiss the appeal.

FULLERTON J.A. . . . Iwanicki contends that being the registered owner of the land and the assignee of the agreement for sale he stands precisely in the position of Munroe, and as the latter would have been entitled to remove the caveat so also is he. From a perusal of his reasons for judgment, I gather that the Judge took the view that the clause in question was for the protection of the original vendor alone and that no other, not even an assignee from the vendor, could avail himself of it. He cites and relies on the following statement from the judgment of Idington J., in *McKillop & Benjafield* v. *Alexander* (1912), 1 D.L.R. 586, at p. 590:

"I still adhere to the views I expressed in the unreported case of *Sawyer-Massey Co.* v. *McLeod*, that the clause in agreements of sale denying the right of any purchaser to assign unless with approval of the vendor as between others of no consequence.

They are designed to protect a vendor from annoying entanglements, and that unless and until the vendor sets up for his own protection any of such stipulations in case of a claim made against or through him no one else has a right to do so."

In making the above statement I do not think the question of the rights of an assignee from the vendor were ever in the mind of the Judge. The case involved only a dispute as to title between purchasers.

The Judge appealed from also quotes from the judgment of Anglin J. in *McDougall* v. *MacKay*, 68 D.L.R. 245 at p. 249, where he says:

"The provision of the McClellan-McDougall agreement that no assignment of it should be valid unless approved and countersigned by McClellan is a stipulation for his benefit and can be invoked only by him. It did not prevent MacKay acquiring an equitable interest in the property goods as against McDougall and the subsequent purchaser, Rusconi."

Here again the statement of the Judge should not be taken too literally. The issue was between purchasers and the question of the right of an assignee from the vendor to invoke the benefit of the provision was not in question.

In *Atlantic Realty Co.* v. *Jackson* (1903), 14 D.L.R. 552, it was held by the British Columbia Court of Appeal that an assignee of an agreement for sale of land containing a restriction against assignment without the approval of the registered vendor has no status to file *a lis pendens* or caveat without obtaining such approval.

The same conclusion was arrived at by the Saskatchewan Court of Appeal in *Re Land Titles Act: Re Massey-Harris* (1922), 63 D.L.R. 428.

I think the assignee Iwanicki is entitled to the protection of the provision against assignments to the same extent as his assignor and is therefore entitled to succeed in his application to have the caveat removed.

I would allow the appeal with costs and direct that the caveat be discharged.

DENNISTOUN J.A.: . . . Gramchuk's assignment to Levin, though made without the consent of the registered owner Munroe, was good as between the parties to it. It gave Levin a personal interest against his own vendor which he was entitled to protect and enforce. But he has no interest in the land which he may protect by a caveat, and the moment he attempted to do so, Munroe, as registered owner, might have called upon him to remove it, as in defiance of the terms of the agreement for sale between Munroe and Gramchuk. . . . [After citing cases, Dennistoun J.A. continued:]

In these cases the Judges are dealing with the right of the registered owner only. When they say that third parties cannot claim rights under a covenant which is made for the benefit of the registered owner, they are not dealing with the point before us in this case where Iwanicki has succeeded Munroe as registered owner, and has obtained not only the registered title, but also an assignment of all the rights which Munroe had under the agreement of sale with Sophia Gramchuk. Here Iwanicki is not a third party. He is not a stranger outside the scope of the covenant against assignment. He stands in the very shoes of Munroe, he is assignee of all his rights, under the agreement, he is his attorney to use his name in the enforcement of those rights for the assignment says so, and by transfer from Munroe he has become the registered owner—the person to be protected from embarrassing entanglements, by the very terms of the agreement itself. Keeping the register free from caveats by sub-purchasers is most material to him, and the right to do so has in my humble opinion been assigned and transferred to him by Munroe.

There is no injustice in this. By the terms of Munroe's agreement with Sophia Gramchuk it was stipulated that she should not assign without leave, and that Munroe would convey to her alone.

It was provided that the terms of the original contract should be binding on the executors, administrators and assigns of both parties. Assignment by Munroe was contemplated by this provision, and it was agreed that his assignee should have all his rights.

That the rights in restriction of assignment are of a substantial character and valuable to both vendor and purchaser is demonstrated at length by Duff J., at pp. 591-602 in the *McKillop* case. They are not rights which are merely personal, but are such as affect the whole character of the contract, including the register, and the identity of the purchaser. There is no question in my mind that such rights are assignable by the vendor and that his assignee has full power to assert them. There is here more than the assignment of a covenant not to assign without leave. It is not merely the right to say, "yes," or "no" which is assigned by Munroe to Iwanicki.

There is here an assignment of a chose in action an agreement for sale. This chose in action is founded upon covenants and conditions. One condition of the sale is that conveyance is to be made to Gramchuk alone. That is a substantial condition which goes to the root of the whole agreement. It enables the registered owner to protect the title from clouds which might obscure it, and Gramchuk and Levin acquired their respective rights subject to that condition. . . .

Levin had clearly no right to file a caveat against Munroe, the registered owner, and in my view the giving of a transfer by Munroe to Iwanicki subject to Levin's caveat has in no way improved the position of the latter. The caveat falls by reason of its own weakness. It has no foundation upon which it can be supported.

Iwanicki is therefore entitled to have Levin's caveat removed from the register so that he may be able to make transfer to Gramchuk upon payment of the purchase money. When that transfer is made, it may well appear that Gramchuk is a bare trustee for Levin, but that is a matter with which we are not concerned.

With much respect I would allow the appeal with costs here and in the Court of King's Bench and order that the caveat be vacated.

PRENDERGAST J.A.: . . . Counsel for Iwanicki relies mainly on said clause of the agreement for sale—his contention being that as Sophia Gramchuk's assignment to Levin never received the original owner's approval, it was a nullity and could not be proper ground for Levin's caveat which was thus from the time of its being filed also a nullity.

There seems to be no ground, in my opinion for holding that assignment from Munroe to Iwanicki failed to convey to the latter all the rights which the former had under said clause 9 of the assigned agreement; so that in my views, the matter may be dealt with to all intents and purposes as if the issue were between Munroe, the first owner, and Levin.

The only question to be considered would then seem to be: When an agreement for sale contains such a provision as said clause 9, and the purchaser assigns to a third party without the vendor's approval, is the assignment null and void in such way that the assignee fails to acquire thereunder the equitable interest of his assignor? For if he acquires this interest, he is entitled to protect it by caveat. . . .

I construe the effect of the said clause to be that an unapproved assignment is, not invalid or void, but only voidable, and that, only in the sense that the vendor may disregard it, and thus treat it as void, by refusing to give a transfer to the assignee and giving it instead to his own immediate purchaser.

On a proper reading of this clause, it will be seen that where an unapproved assignment is given, the granting of a transfer by the owner to his purchaser is the only means therein provided by which he can enforce his rights thereunder. It is his only remedy.

And why should he have more? Why should he destroy equities that it is the policy of the law to enforce and protect, when, by giving the transfer direct to the purchaser, he effectually safeguards himself from the entanglement of subsequent assignments,—which, as stated by Idington J., is the object of such provisions.

It will also be seen that his right of approval (although absence of approval justifies the owner in disregarding the assignment) is, considered in itself, very much more apparent than real. For, as between two assignments, he cannot, as held in the two cases above referred to, reverse the order of priority by the fact of his approval; and if his approval is of the one that has priority, the approval adds nothing to its status. So that the exercise of this so-called right of approval of one assignment in preference to others, cannot affect the equitable interests already acquired; and the same thing exactly would be secured in my opinion, if clause 9 simply provided that in the event of the purchaser assigning his interest, the owner reserved the right to give the transfer to him (the purchaser) and not to his assignee. That is the whole effect of the clause.

In fine, the assignment from Sophia Gramchuk to Levin is not void or invalid, and the latter has acquired thereunder an equitable interest which Iwanicki's approval, to whomsoever given if there were several assignees, could neither add to, take from or affect in any way.

Disapproving as he does of the assignment to Levin, all that Iwanicki can do when the balance of the purchase-price is paid to him (be it by Sophia Gramchuk or by Levin), is the one and only thing provided in the clause, —which is, disregarding Levin and voiding the assignment to him to that extent, to give the transfer to Gramchuk.

That will put an end to all his responsibilities, and he need not be concerned if the Land Titles Office, considering Gramchuk as a trustee in the circumstances, issues to her a certificate of title subject to Levin's caveat.

I quite realise that it is also possible in another aspect of the matter, considering that Levin holds the equitable interest that he does only as security for Sophia Gramchuk's indebtedness to him, that Iwanicki's judgment may be a charge on the same. But we need not linger on that phase, and that for two reasons: first, because such a charge would manifestly rank after Levin's own claim by virtue of the order of registrations, and also, because being simply a judgment debt, it has no relation to Iwanicki's status as assignee of the original owner, with which alone we are here concerned.

I would sum up what I have said as follows: The assignment to Levin is not invalid or void; it is voidable only; and the clause provides at the same time the method by which, and in effect the extent to which, the vendor may void it, by allowing him to give the transfer to his immediate purchaser. The assignment stands till voided; the voiding cannot be effected except by something being done by the vendor; and the giving of a transfer to the purchaser is all that the clause contemplates that he can do.

In *McKillop & Benjafield* v. *Alexander*, Duff J.A. said:

"A caveat prevents any disposition of his title by the registered proprietor in derogation of the caveator's claim until that claim has been satisfied or disposed of: but the caveator's claim must stand or fall on its own merits. If the caveator has no right enforceable against the registered owner which entitles him to restrain the alienation of the owner's title, then the caveat itself cannot and does not impose any burden on the registered title."

In the present case, if Iwanicki chose in the present condition of things, to give a transfer to Richard Roe, I am of opinion that Levin has an enforceable right which would entitle him to restrain such an alienation and say: "Clause 9 gives you the privilege of disregarding me to the extent of giving a transfer to Sophia Gramchuk, but not to cut me out arbitrarily by transferring to an outsider.". . .

In my opinion the appeal should be dismissed with costs.

[The Court being equally divided the appeal was dismissed.]

MUS *v*. MATLASHEWSKI. [1944] 4 D.L.R. 522 (Manitoba. Court of Appeal). A crop-sharing lease between Anton Matlashewski, lessor, and Luke Matlashewski, lessee, contained the short form, "And will not assign or sub-let without leave." Toward the end of the lease there had been typewritten the words "the Lessor hereby offers and agrees to sell to the lessee, his heirs and assigns . . . the lands and premises hereinafter described for the sum of $1,550.00 cash; . . . this offer to be irrevocable until the first day of March, 1946." Without consent Luke assigned the lease to Mus, who took up the option. Anton refused to sign the transfer, saying "I will sign a transfer to Luke but not to Joe Mus; Joe Mus has nothing to do with this, all he wants to do is to kick Luke off the farm." The trial Judge granted a decree of specific performance. On appeal, the Court of Appeal divided three to two in favour of the appellant. BERGMAN J.A. speaking for the majority: "I have not found a single case in which the right of a vendor or a lessor to refuse to recognise in any way an unapproved assign of the purchaser or lessee, as the case may be, has been doubted. Different considerations, of course, apply where the contest is purely one between rival assignees both claiming under the same purchaser or lessee. In applying the decided case it is, therefore, necessary to observe this distinction. . . . Three of the four members of the Court [in *Iwanicki* v. *Levin*] expressly uphold the right of the defendant at bar to refuse to recognize the alleged assignment to the plaintiff and to refuse to transfer the land to him, and there is nothing in the reasons for judgment of Perdue C.J.M. dissenting in any way from that view." Trueman and Richards JJ.A., who dissented, found that the typewritten words were repugnant and paramount to the printed form, and accordingly an assignment of the option did not require approval although an assignment of the lease did.

NOTE AND QUESTIONS. Why should there be any doubt about the effect of a clause prohibiting assignment? Is there some ground of "public policy" favouring assignability, such as the alienability of property? If a party to a contract promises not to assign his benefits under the contract and he breaks that promise and assigns, has the assignee any claim against the debtor? Can the debtor safely pay the assignor and take a receipt from him?

If a contract provides that "This contract is non-assignable," or "Any assignment of this contract is invalid," has the assignee any rights whatever? Can he claim against the debtor? If the debtor pays the assignor, can the assignee claim against his assignor? On what ground? Can he claim damages amounting to the value of the assigned debt? Can he claim that the assignor holds the debtor's payment to him as trustee? In *Re Turcan* (1888), 40 Ch. D. 5 a clause saying that an insurance contract should not be assignable was held to mean that the insurance company need not deal with the assignee but the assignee might obtain the benefit of the contract when received by the insured, who had, in that case, already settled it in a marriage settlement.

If a contract provides that an assignment without consent of the debtor, or, as in the most common case, the lessor, gives the debtor or lessor the right to forfeit, and the assignor or lessee assigns without consent, is there any legal relationship between the debtor and assignor to form the subject of the assignment? Would the putative assignor lose all his rights under the contract or lease?

NIAGARA FALLS RAILWAY EMPLOYEES CREDIT UNION *v.* INTERNATIONAL NICKEL CO. OF CANADA LTD. 1959. 23 D.L.R. (2d) 215 (Ontario. Court of Appeal). One Charles Wright in January, 1957, borrowed $1,682 from the plaintiff and gave as security for the loan a promissory note and an assignment of "all the wages, salary, commission and other monies owing to me, or hereafter to become owing to me or earned by me in the employ of C.N. Rlys. or any other person, firm or corporation by whom I may be hereafter employed." Shortly after, Wright left the C.N.R. and worked for a while with the C.P.R. before he joined the defendant Company in October, 1957. In November, 1957, the plaintiff notified the defendant Company of the assignment and asked to have Wright's pay cheques until further advised. (The notice was wrongly addressed but the Court found that it did arrive and held that despite the error it constituted notice under section 53 of *The Conveyancing and Law of Property Act.*) On February 28, 1958, the defendant Company commenced paying Wright's wages to the plaintiff, and this action was commenced to recover the amount of wages paid by the defendant Company to Wright after it received the notice early in November, 1957, and before February 28, 1958. It was objected by the defendant Company that the assignment was contrary to public policy. Held, for the plaintiff. LAIDLAW J.A. delivered the judgment of the court. On the public policy issue he said: "Counsel for the respondent sought to support the opinion of the learned trial Judge that the assignment of wages in this case was contrary to public policy, and endeavoured to invoke the principle that a document or transaction which is in restraint of trade is contrary to public policy. That is not this kind of transaction. In my opinion counsel for the appellant has effectively and successfully met that argument. He referred to and quoted the language of Warrington L.J. in *Horwood* v. *Millar's Timber & Trading Co.*, [1917] 1 K.B. 305 at p. 315. This whole transaction in its real nature and character was a contract between Wright and the plaintiff company whereby Wright assumed contractual obligations for the payment of the indebtedness and as collateral security for that indebtedness made an assignment of the monies to become due and payable to him for wages. I can see nothing contrary to public policy in a private transaction of that kind. The whole dealing and transaction between the parties should be looked at in order to determine the character of it. It is not a covenant in restraint of trade; the rights and liabilities arising under the assignment of wages were part of the whole private transaction for the borrowing and lending of money as between Wright and the plaintiff company.

"Finally, I refer to the case of *Graham* v. *McVeity* (1905), 5. O.W.R. 395; 521. In that case there was a debt owing by the defendant McVeity to the plaintiff and in order to secure the plaintiff McVeity entered into two agreements: One agreement provided for the payment of the debt in instalments; the other agreement was an assignment of the future wages owing to him or to become due and payable to him by the City of Ottawa. There was default on the part of McVeity under his agreement with Graham to pay the instalment and the City of Ottawa, who had notice of the assignment of wages, paid certain monies without regard to the assignment. The Court held that McVeity was liable under the one agreement for the amount owing by him, and also gave judgment against the Corporation for the amount of two instalments that fell due between the service of the notice and the issue of the writ." [In *Horwood's* case Scrutton L.J., although doubtful whether he could express his judgment in language of "sufficiently judicial moderation," described the money-lender's contract in these words (at p. 317): "The document bound the debtor never to change his residence without the consent of the money-lender; it bound him never to change his employment without the consent of the money-lender; it bound him not to consent to a reduction of his salary without the consent of the money-lender; it bound him not to part with any of his property without the consent of the money-lender; it bound him to incur no obligation on credit without the consent of the money-lender, and to incur no obligation, legal or moral, without the consent of the money-lender, and it appears to me that it is not using overstrained or poetical language to say that it made this unfortunate man the slave of the money-lender."]

GRAHAM *v.* McVEITY. 1905. 5. O.W.R. 395 (Ontario. Local Master at Ottawa). McVeity was city solicitor for Ottawa and had assigned his unearned salary to Dr. Graham to secure payment of a debt of $1,715.83. McVeity's salary was $2,500 a year. In an action to enforce the assignment McVeity objected that an assignment of the salary of a public officer was void as against public policy. On this point, THE MASTER: "This is of course clear law, the only question being whether the city solicitor is a public officer within the meaning of the rule . . . it is clear that the city solicitor is not a public officer within the meaning of the rule. . . ."

THE WAGES ACT
Ontario. Revised Statutes. 1960. Chapter 421

7. (1) Seventy percent of any debt due or accruing due to any mechanic, workman, labourer, servant, clerk or employee for or in respect of his wages is exempt from seizure or attachment . . . [a judge may reduce the percentage of exemption in appropriate cases].

(6) Any provision of any contract hereafter made that provides for the assignment by the debtor to the creditor of a greater proportion of the debtor's wages than is liable to seizure or attachment under this section is invalid.

[Subsection (6) was first introduced in 1959.]

NOTE. The Ontario Legislature and the Ontario Court of Appeal in the *Niagara Falls* case seem to take very different views of the public policy of wage assignments. What is wrong with a wage assignment? Who is the Legislature trying to protect? Is there a public interest in preventing the employee from leaving himself penniless? Is it trying to protect the employer? Does the subsection ensure a greater incentive for the employee? Should the employer's consent to the assignment be required if that is the purpose? Is it trying to protect the employee's family? Should the employee's wife have to consent? Could the Court of Appeal have taken any of these factors into account to justify a different result in the *Niagara Falls* case?

PENSION ACT
Canada. Revised Statutes. 1952. Chapter 207

24. (3) No pension shall be assigned, charged, attached, anticipated, commuted or given as security, and the Commission may, in its discretion, refuse to recognise any power of attorney granted by a pensioner with reference to the payment of his pension.

[A "pension" is defined in s. 2(a) to mean a pension on account of the death or disability of a member of the forces.]

CANADIAN STANDARD FORM CONSTRUCTION CONTRACT

Article 39. Assignment.—Neither party to the Contract shall assign the Contract without the written consent of the other.

Article 40. Sub-Contracts.—The Contractor shall, at the time of signing the contract, notify the Architect in writing of the names of sub-contractors proposed for the principal parts of the work and for such others as the Architect may direct and shall not employ any to whom the Architect may reasonably object.

If the change of any name on such list is required by the Architect, and the work has to be awarded to a higher bidder, the contract price shall be increased by the difference between the two bids.

The Architect, shall, on request, furnish to any subcontractor, wherever practicable, evidence of the amounts certified to on his account.

The contractor shall be held as fully responsible to the Owner for the acts and omissions of his subcontractors and of persons directly or indirectly employed by them, as for the acts and omissions of persons directly employed by him.

In view of this responsibility for the acts and omissions of his subcontractors, the Contractor shall not be obliged to employ as a subcontractor any person or firm to whom he reasonably objects.

Nothing contained in the contract documents shall create any contractual relation between any subcontractor and the Owner.

Article 41. Relations of Contractor and Subcontractor.—The Contractor agrees to bind every subcontractor by the terms of the General Conditions, Drawings and Specifications, as far as applicable to his work.

Chapter 6

WRITTEN CONTRACTS AND STANDARD FORMS

This chapter carries on the analysis of mistake in the formation of contracts and brings together a miscellany of problems arising from the fact that a contract happens to be in writing. Whether writing is required or not, a great many contracts are nevertheless reduced to writing for reasons of convenience, but the use of writing has disadvantages as well. Obviously a written record of a transaction is an excellent reference during the administration of the contract, and when it is the result of negotiation and legal assistance in drafting, comparatively little difficulty results. But the modern practice of one party preparing the terms of a contract in advance and offering them on a take-it-or-leave-it basis sometimes results in hardship, perhaps through failure to realize that written terms have been offered, sometimes through the human weakness of not reading the "fine print," and sometimes through the inadequacy of the terms, which reflect the lack of negotiation. These modern problems appeared in the latter half of the 19th century, at a time when our modern business practices could hardly be imagined. The application of principles established then to our contemporary conditions is one of the most difficult tasks in modern contract law.

This ready-made contract, usually called the "standard form" contract, sometimes called by the rather ugly and wholly uncommunicative name "contract of adhesion" (from the French, *contrat d'adhesion*) apparently because one party expects the other to adhere to his terms or not to deal at all, seems to have first appeared in the courts in the so called "ticket cases" where terms were printed on the "receipt" that the traveller got when he deposited his bag with the station attendant. Since the baggage ticket is usually handed over when the baggage has been accepted and the money paid, the traveller might have been excused if he thought the contract had already been entered into and he was getting only a receipt and identification slip. However, the common law seems to have had little sympathy for this notion. Such a belated communication of terms has frequently been held adequate, but the difficulties will become apparent from studying the cases in Section 1. Cases where the aggrieved party is aware of the document as one containing some sort of terms about something, but for some reason assents to it without reading it over, follow in Section 2. You may question whether there is or should be any distinction taken between the two kinds of cases; or indeed, whether there should be said to be two kinds, or two sections.

In 1861, Maine, in his *Ancient Law*, said: "the movement of progressive societies has hitherto been a movement from Status to Contract." If one may construe the present trend as one from Contract to Status, how far ought the law to protect the lazy or indifferent party whose "status" is to be affected, from the more thoughtful and perhaps "predatory" party, who is frequently in a much better bargaining position? (On this problem, see H. B. Sales, "Standard Form Contracts," (1953), 16 *Modern L.R.* 318.)

One rather peculiar aspect of this problem deserves a brief comment. In our time the unit of business organization is becoming more nearly monopolistic. At the same time government enterprise (even more monopolistic) is also increasing; not only in "socialist" Britain, but also in "capitalist" North America. How "free" are such agencies to refuse to deal with the public? Are crown corporations to be classed with common carriers as agencies that have to do business whether they like it or not? If they are not free to refuse to deal, how applicable are the concepts of contract? Should there be a different criterion applied to private and public monopolies? Should we think in terms of the legislative process rather than of private arrangement?

ERIC GNAPP, LTD. *v.* PETROLEUM BOARD. [1949] 1 All E.R. 980 (England. Court of Appeal). A government Petroleum Board refused to deal with the plaintiff, who had alleged that he was getting short measure from the Board, until the allegation was withdrawn. The allegation was withdrawn and the supply restored. (There was a contract in this case although the plaintiff knew but objected to the terms.) TUCKER L.J.: "The Order nowhere in terms requires a supplier to supply to a dealer motor fuel equivalent in quantity to that shown on the coupons surrendered by the dealer. The failure to supply is not made an offence, nor is any such obligation placed on the Board by the Order which gave it the monopoly. This kind of question may some day in a proper case require careful consideration. With the growth of statutory corporations to which monopolies are given by the statutes creating them, it may become of supreme importance to decide, on the construction of the relevant statute, to what extent, if any, a refusal by the statutory body to do business with a particular trader may afford that trader a right of action. In the present case we are dealing with a temporary monopoly given in time of war for the safety of the realm, and I can find nothing in the relevant orders which have been brought to our attention which affords a right of action to a dealer where the Board in the *bona fide* exercise of its discretion has imposed reasonable terms as a condition of doing business with that dealer."

EVANS *v.* ROGERS. [1946] 2 All E.R. 67 (England. King's Bench Division). SINGLETON J.: "I wish to add that it is greatly to be regretted that the Milk Marketing Board cannot adopt a form of contract which will work more satisfactorily. Everyone is anxious that adulteration of milk by farmers or others should be dealt with, and severely dealt with, when it is detected. But this contract, which has been in operation for some years now, is so difficult that a farmer's life is far from easy."

NOTE. Some indication of the severity with which a zealous business man may attempt to protect his interest in a standard form contract without enough thought about the other party can be seen from the following clause, which is in actual use: "I am wholly responsible for the return of the said article or articles and upon failure to return it or them on the due date, it shall be lawful for the lessors, their servants, or agents and with such other assistant or assistants, as they may require, at any time during the day or night to enter in or upon any lands, tenements, houses and premises wheresoever and whatsoever where the said articles or any part thereof may be and for such persons to break and force open doors, locks, bolts, fastenings, hinges, gates, fences, houses, buildings, enclosures and places for the purpose of taking possession of and removing said articles for the purpose of regaining possession of them." Clauses of this sort are not unusual.

1. The "Ticket Cases"

PARKER *v.* THE SOUTH EASTERN RAILWAY COMPANY
England. Court of Appeal. 1877. 2 C.P. D. 416

The plaintiff deposited a bag in a cloak-room at the defendants' railway station, paid the clerk 2d., and received a paper ticket, on one side of which were written a number and a date, and were printed notices as to when the office would be opened and closed, and the words "See Back." On the other side were printed several clauses relating to articles left by passengers, the last of which was, "The company will not be responsible for any package exceeding the value of £10." The plaintiff on the same day presented his ticket and demanded his bag, and the bag could not be found, and has not been since found. Parker claimed £24, 10s. as the value of his bag. The company pleaded that they had accepted the goods on the condition that they would not be responsible for the value if it exceeded £10; and at the trial they relied on the words printed on the back of the ticket, and also on the fact that a notice to the same effect was printed and hung up in the cloak-room. The plaintiff gave evidence and denied that he had seen the notice, or read what was printed on the ticket. He admitted that he had often received such tickets and knew there was printed matter on them, but said that he did not know what it was. He said that he imagined the ticket to be a receipt for the money paid by him. Another case with very similar facts was tried at the same time.

Parker's case was tried at Westminster on the 27th of February, 1876, before Pollock B. The questions left by the judge to the jury were: 1. Did the plaintiff read or was he aware of the special condition upon which the articles were deposited? 2. Was the plaintiff, under the circumstances, under any obligation, in the exercise of reasonable and proper caution, to read or make himself aware of the condition?

The jury answered both questions in the negative, and the judge thereupon directed judgment to be entered for the plaintiff for the amount claimed, reserving leave to the defendants to move to enter judgment for them.

The defendants moved to enter judgment, and also obtained from the Common Pleas Division an order *nisi* for a new trial, on the ground of misdirection. The order was discharged, and the motion was refused by the Common Pleas Division. The Defendants appealed.

Mellish L.J.: In this case we have to consider whether a person who deposits in the cloak-room of a railway company articles which are lost through the carelessness of the company's servants, is prevented from recovering, by a condition on the back of the ticket, that the company would not be liable for the loss of goods exceeding the value of £10. It was argued on behalf of the railway company that the company's servants were only authorized to receive goods on behalf of the company upon the terms contained in the ticket. . . . I am of opinion that this objection cannot prevail. It is clear that the company's servants did not exceed the authority given them by the company. They did the exact thing they were authorized to do. They were authorized to receive articles on deposit as bailees on behalf of the company, charging 2d. for each article, and delivering a ticket properly filled up to the person leaving the article. This is exactly what they did in the present cases, and whatever may be the legal effect of what was done, the company must, in my opinion, be bound by it. The directors may have thought, and no doubt did think, that the delivering the ticket to the person depositing the article would be sufficient to make him bound by the conditions contained in the ticket, and if they were mistaken in that, the company must bear the consequence.

The question then is, whether the plaintiff was bound by the conditions contained in the ticket. In an ordinary case, where an action is brought on a written agreement which is signed by the defendant, the agreement is proved by proving his signature, and, in the absence of fraud, it is wholly immaterial that he has not read the agreement and does not know its contents. The parties may, however, reduce their agreement into writing, so that the writing constitutes the sole evidence of the agreement, without signing it; but in that case there must be evidence independently of the agreement itself to prove that the defendant has assented to it. In that case, also, if it is proved that the defendant has assented to the writing constituting the agreement between the parties, it is, in the absence of fraud, immaterial that the defendant had not read the agreement and did not know its contents. Now if in the course of making a contract one party delivers to another a paper containing writing, and the party receiving the paper knows that the paper contains conditions which the party delivering it intends to constitute the contract, I have no doubt that the party receiving the paper does, by receiving and keeping it, assent to the conditions contained in it, although he does not read them, and does not know what they are. I hold therefore that the case of *Harris* v. *Great Western Ry. Co.* (1876, 1 Q.B.D. 515, was rightly decided, because in that case the plaintiff admitted, on cross-examination, that he believed there were some conditions on the ticket. On the other hand, the case of *Henderson* and *Harris* (1875), L.R. 2 Sc. & Div. 470, is a conclusive authority that if the person receiving the ticket does not know that there is any writing upon the back of the ticket, he is not bound by a condition printed on the back. The facts in the cases before us differ from these in both *Henderson* v. *Stevenson*, because in both the cases which have been argued before us, though the plaintiffs admitted that they knew there was writing on the back of the ticket, they swore not only that they did not read it, but that they did not know or believe that the writing contained conditions, and we are to consider whether, under those circumstances, we can lay down as a matter of law either that the plaintiff is bound or that he is not bound by the conditions contained in the ticket, or whether his being bound depends on some question of fact to be determined by the jury, and if so, whether, in the present case, the right question was left to the jury.

Now, I am of opinion that we cannot lay down, as a matter of law, either that the plaintiff was bound or that he was not bound by the conditions printed on the ticket, from the mere fact that he knew there was writing on the ticket, but did not know that the writing contained conditions. I think there may be cases in which a paper containing writing is delivered by one party to another in the course of a business transaction, where it would be quite reasonable that the party receiving it should assume that the writing contained in it no condition, and should put it in his pocket unread. For instance, if a person driving through a turnpike gate received a ticket upon paying the toll, he might reasonably assume that the object of the ticket was that by producing it he might be free from paying toll at some other turnpike gate, and might put it in his pocket unread. On the other hand, if a person who ships goods to be carried on a voyage by sea receives a bill of lading signed by the master, he would plainly be bound by it, although afterwards in an action against the shipowner for the loss of the goods, he might swear that he had never read the bill of lading, and that he did not know that he had never read the bill of lading, and that he did not know that it contained the terms of the contract of carriage, and that the shipowner was protected by the exceptions contained in it. Now the reason why the person receiving the bill of lading would be bound seems to me to be that in the great majority of cases persons shipping goods do know that the bill of lading contains the terms of the contract of carriage; and the shipowner, or the master delivering the bill of lading, is entitled to assume that the person shipping goods has that knowledge. It is, however, quite possible to suppose that a person who is neither a man of business nor a lawyer might on some particular occasion ship goods without the least knowledge of what a bill of lading was, but in my opinion such person must bear the consequences of his own exceptional ignorance, it being plainly impossible that business could be carried on if every person who delivers a bill of lading had to stop to explain what a bill of lading was.

Now the question we have to consider is whether the railway company were entitled to assume that a person depositing luggage, and receiving a ticket in such a way that he could see that some writing was printed on it, would understand that the writing contained the conditions of contract, and this seems to me to depend upon whether people in general would in fact and naturally, draw that inference. The railway company, as it seems to me, must be entitled to make some assumptions respecting the person who deposits luggage with them: I think they are entitled to assume that he can read, and that he understands the English language, and that he pays such attention to what he is about as may be reasonably expected from a person in such a transaction as that of depositing luggage in a cloak-room. The railway company must, however, take mankind as they find them, and if what they do is sufficient to inform people in general that the ticket contains conditions, I think that a particular plaintiff ought not to be in a better position than other persons on account of his exceptional ignorance or stupidity or carelessness. But if what the railway company do is not sufficient to convey to the minds of people in general that the ticket contains conditions, then they have received goods on deposit without obtaining the consent of the persons depositing them to the conditions limiting their liability. I am of opinion, therefore, that the proper direction to leave to the jury in these cases is, that if the person receiving the ticket did not see or know that there was any writing on the ticket, he is not bound by the conditions; that if he knew there was writing, and knew or believed that the writing contained conditions, then he is bound by the conditions; that if he knew there was writing on the ticket, but did not know or believe that the writing contained conditions, nevertheless he would be bound, if the delivering of the ticket to him in such a manner that he could see there was writing upon it, was, in the opinion of the jury, reasonable notice that the writing contained conditions.

I have lastly to consider whether the direction of the learned judge was correct, namely, "Was the plaintiff, under the circumstances, under any obligation, in the exercise of reasonable and proper caution, to read and to make himself aware of the condition?" I think that this direction was not strictly accurate, and was calculated to mislead the jury. The plaintiff was certainly under no obligation to read the ticket, but was entitled to leave it unread if he pleased, and the question does not appear to me to direct the attention of the jury to the real question, namely, whether the railway company did what was reasonably sufficient to give the plaintiff notice of the condition.

On the whole, I am of opinion that there ought to be a new trial.

BRAMWELL L.J.: . . . Has not the giver of the paper a right to suppose that the receiver is content to deal on the terms in the paper? What more can be done? Must he say, "Read that?" As I have said, he does so in effect when he puts it into the other's hands. The truth is, people are content to take these things on trust. They know that there is a form which is always used—they are satisfied it is not unreasonable, because people do not usually put unreasonable terms into their contracts. If they did, then dealing would soon be stopped. Besides, unreasonable practices would be known. The very fact of not looking at the paper shews that this confidence exists. It is asked: What if there was some unreasonable condition, as for instance to forfeit £1000 if the goods were not removed in forty-eight hours? Would the depositions be bound? I might continue myself by asking: Would he be, if he were told "our conditions are on this ticket," and he did not read them. In my judgment, he would not be bound in either case. I think there is an implied understanding that there is no condition unreasonable to the knowledge of the party tendering the document and not insisting on its being read—no condition not relevant to the matter in hand. I am of opinion, therefore, that the plaintiffs, having notice of the printing, were in the same situation as though the porter had said, "Read that, it concerns the matter in hand"; that if the plaintiffs did not read it, they were as much bound as if they had read it and had not objected.

The difficulty I feel as to what I have written is that it is too demonstrative. But, put in practical language, it is this: The defendants put into the hands of the plaintiff a paper with printed matter on it, which in all good sense and reason must be supposed to relate to the matter in hand. This printed matter the plaintiff sees, and must either read it, and object if he does not agree to it, or if he does read it and not object, or does not read it, he must be held to consent to its terms; therefore, on the facts, the judges should have directed verdicts for the defendants. . . .

[The opinion of Bramwell L.J. has been severely cut and the opinion of Baggallay L.J. omitted altogether. The Court ordered a new trial.]

NOTE ON THE RAILWAY ACT. The *Parker* case must be read, as regards railways, telegraph companies, etc., subject to the provisions of the *Railway Act*, R.S.C. 1952, c. 234. By this Act a commission known as the Board of Transport Commissioners for Canada is constituted (sec. 9) and is invested with jurisdiction to make any orders, give directions, leave, sanction or approval with respect to matters required or sanctioned by the Act. (sec. 33 (1) (b)). The sections pertinent to the problem here considered are as follows:

353. (1) No contract, condition, by-law, regulation, declaration or notice made or given by the company, impairing, restricting or limiting its liability in respect of the carriage of any traffic, shall, except as hereinafter provided, relieve the company from such liability, unless such class of contract, condition, by-law, regulation, declaration or notice has been first authorized or approved by order or regulation of the Board.

(2) The Board may, in any case, or by regulation, determine the extent to which the liability of the company may be so impaired, restricted or limited.

(3) The Board may by regulation prescribe the terms and conditions under which any traffic may be carried by the company.

(4) Railway companies shall print in both the English and French languages the bills of lading that are to be used along their lines within the limits of the province of Quebec.

51. Any rule, regulation, order or decision of the Board, when published by the Board, or by leave of the Board, for three weeks in the *Canada Gazette*, and while the same remains in force, has the like effect as if enacted in this Act, and all courts shall take judicial notice thereof.

Under these sections it would seem that the Board may approve of a form of special contract of carriage limiting liability, in which case the question of assent by the other party still remains to be proved by the railway. But if the Board makes an express order limiting liability in a given case, then section 51 applies and the limitations are not dependent for their efficacy on the assent of the other party. In such a case the question ceases to be one of the contract.

G. N. RAILWAY *v.* L. E. P. 1922. 127 L.T.R. 664 (England. Court of Appeal). SCRUTTON L.J.: "The railway company contended, a contention which in this case would entitle them to recover the sum they had paid, but which in most other cases would put upon them an enormously increased liability, that they were in fact common carriers, and were therefore bound to pay. I personally have been extremely puzzled to know what on earth the railway company are after. There are some people who decline to admit that two and two make four, until they know what use is going to be made of the admission. I have been tempted not to hold that the railway company are common carriers until I know what use they are going to make of it in the future, because, as at present advised, I do not see what use they can make of it in their general business. But after all, my speculation as to what railway companies are after is futile, because their intelligence is far beyond me, and one can only decide the case as one finds it, and wait and see what happens."

HENSON *v.* L.N.E. RAILWAY. [1946] 1 All E.R. 653 (England. Court of Appeal). The plaintiff was given a "walking pass" to show that he was authorized to be on the defendant's premises. He was employed by a third party. On the back of the pass the defendant had denied liability for injury to the holder however caused. In this action to recover damages for injury received by negligence of the defendant's servants, held, for the plaintiff. SCOTT L.J.: "The attempt made by the railway in the pass to put on an ordinary working man employed by others the very burdensome term in question shocks my mind. . . . It is such misuse of contract which makes the legislature tend to substitute status."

McMANUS *v.* LANCASHIRE AND YORKSHIRE RAILWAY. 1859. 4 H. & N. 327; 157 E.R. 865 (England. Exchequer Chamber). ERLE J.: "The notion that customers of railways require protection on account of incapacity to resist oppression, is not more true than the notion that, against a large proportion of customers, railway companies stand in need of every aid the law can afford."

WATKINS *v.* RYMILL

England. Queen's Bench Division. 1883. 10 Q.B.D. 178.

STEPHEN J. delivered the judgment of the court: . . . The facts of the case were as follows: The plaintiff was the owner of a waggonette and the defendant was the keeper of a repository for the sale on commission of horses, carriages, and harness. On the 11th of May, the plaintiff took the waggonette to the repository and left it to be sold, receiving for it a receipt on a printed form which was in these words: "Herbert Rymill's Royal Repository, Barbican, for the sale of horses, carriages, harness, &c. Sales by auction every Tuesday and Friday at 11. Received from . . . *subject to the conditions as exhibited on the premises*" (these words were italicized). "The proceeds paid on Monday between the hours of eleven and four upon the production of the receipt signed by the owner, or forwarded by post if desired."

The conditions exhibited on the premises were printed conditions, exhibited in conspicuous positions in many parts of the premises. The following were the conditions bearing upon the present case:—

"10. Should any horse or other property sent to this repository remain over one month the proprietor shall be at liberty to sell the same by public auction only, with or without notice to the owner, unless all expenses are previously paid. All horses, carriages, carts, &c., sent to this repository for sale remain at the risk of the owner.". . .

The plaintiff swore that he did not read the receipt, but put it in his pocket without noticing it. About one month after leaving the waggonette the plaintiff called and asked for it. He was told (but not so far as it appeared by the manager or by any person authorized to tell him) that the waggonette was sold, and that the settling day was Monday. He returned on Monday and saw the manager, who told him he must bring the receipt. He said he had lost it, but that they must have his name on their books. They refused to go into the matter without the receipt. The receipt was not found until the 25th of October, 1881, and during this time the plaintiff took no steps except calling two or three times to make inquiries. In November, 1881, the plaintiff through his solicitor applied for the waggonette, and found that it had shortly before been sold for £9 19s. 6d., of which the whole except 6s. 10d. was due for charges under the terms stated in the conditions quoted. The defendant sent to the plaintiff a post office order for 16s. 10d., mistaking the amount of his charges, and thus considered himself to have overpaid him.

The defendant's counsel argued that the Common Sarjeant, who sat as judge, ought to direct the jury on these facts to find for the defendant, but the Common Sarjeant held that the question was one "for the jury whether the defendant had or had not given the plaintiff reasonable notice of the conditions." This question the jury answered in the negative, and gave a verdict for the plaintiff for £21. . . . The circumstances of the contract were such that any man of ordinary intelligence must have known that special terms as to its execution must in the nature of things be made, and it appears to us that by handing to the plaintiff the receipt in question the defendants called his attention to the subject as pointedly as if their clerk had said "Read this. It expresses the terms on which we are ready to take your waggonette.". . . A great number of contracts are in the present state of society made by the delivery by one of the contracting parties to the other of a document in a common form, stating the terms by which the person delivering it will enter into the proposed contract. Such a form constitutes the offer of the party who tenders it. If the form is accepted without objection by the person to whom it is tendered this person is as a general rule bound by its contents, and his act amounts to an acceptance of the offer made to him, whether he reads the document or otherwise informs himself of its contents or not. To this general rule however there are a variety of exceptions.

(1) In the first place, the nature of the transaction may be such that the person accepting the document may suppose, not unreasonably, that the document contains no terms at all, but is a mere acknowledgement of an agreement not intended to be varied by special terms. (2) A second exception would be the case of fraud, as, if the conditions were printed in such a manner as to mislead the person accepting the document. (3) A third exception occurs, if, without being fraudulent, the document is misleading and does actually mislead the person who has taken it. (4) An exception has been suggested of conditions unreasonable in themselves or irrelevant to the main purpose of the contract. We now come to apply these principles to the case before us. It is obviously within the general rule. Can it be brought under any of the exceptions? The only one which can apply to it is the one which we have put first. Can it be said that the nature of the transaction was such that the plaintiff might suppose, not unreasonably, that the document contained no terms at all, but was a mere acknowledgement of an agreement not intended to be varied by special terms.

It seems to us impossible to suppose that this can have been the case. The acceptance of a carriage for sale on commission is not a simple contract, the terms of which are established by the common law in the absence of any special agreement by the parties. They must, from the nature of the case, be as special as those of a contract of lease or a bill of lading, and this consideration alone seems to us to establish the conclusion that the receipt and conditions to which it refers constituted the contract between the parties, and that the learned Common Sarjeant misdirected the jury when he told them that the question was whether the defendant had given reasonable notice to the plaintiff of the conditions. We may observe that in no view of the case could this direction be upheld. If any question at all were asked it ought to have been whether the defendant took reasonable means to give notice of the conditions to the plaintiff, which is a very different one from that which was actually put to the jury. . . .

[The verdict was set aside and a new verdict entered for the defendant.]

ALDERSLADE *v.* HENDON LAUNDRY LTD. [1945] 1 All E.R. 244 (England. Court of Appeal). An exculpatory clause offered by the defendant launderer read: "The maximum amount for lost or damaged articles is 20 times the charge made for laundering." Alderslade sent some handkerchiefs to the laundry; they were lost and were not returned to him. Held, for the defendant. LORD GREENE M.R.: "What I may call the hard core of the contract, the real thing to which the contract is directed, is the obligation of the laundry company to launder. That is the primary obligation; it is the contractual obligation which must be performed according to its terms, and no question of taking due care enters into it. . . . But in addition to that, which is the essence of the contract, there are certain ancillary obligations into which the laundry company enters if it accepts goods from a customer to be laundered. The first one relates to the safe custody of the goods while they are in the possession of the laundry. . . . Another relates to the delivery of the goods. . . . It seems to me therefore that the only obligation on the company in the matter of returning the goods is an obligation to take reasonable care and nothing else. . . . If that be right, to construe this clause, so far as it relates to loss, in such a way as to exclude loss occasioned by the lack of proper care would be to leave the clause so far as loss is concerned—I say nothing about damage—without any content at all. The result, in my opinion, is that the clause must be construed as applying to the case of loss through negligence and, accordingly, it has its *prima facie* meaning which is comprehensive and clear."

CONSOLIDATED PLATE GLASS (WESTERN) LTD. *v*. MANITOBA CARTAGE & STORAGE LTD. 1959. 20 D.L.R. (2d) 779 (Manitoba. Court of Appeal). Plaintiff signed an agreement in these terms: "It is understood and agreed that Manitoba Cartage & Storage Ltd. has supplied the undersigned driver, truck and equipment to be used by us for the purpose of hauling plate glass from *CP Freight Shed* to *Cons. Plate Glass* and Manitoba Cartage & Storage in connection with the said work is not acting in any way as carrier, and has no responsibility and is under no liability in connection with the moving of said plate glass, or for any damage to said goods, from any cause whatever and we, the undersigned will hold Manitoba Cartage & Storage harmless in respect of any damage which may occur in the performance of the work." The glass shipment was negligently damaged by the defendant while it was in his care. Held, for the defendant. TRITSCHLER J.A.: "Provided there is no statute limiting his right there is nothing to prevent a carrier insisting upon making his own terms and refusing to carry except on those terms. . . . Plaintiff's agreement that defendant 'is under no liability . . . for any damage to said goods, from any cause whatever' is very broadly expressed and 'by necessary implication' these words must include negligence. As defendant was not acting as common carrier in relation to the goods in question the exclusion of liability must have been referable to negligence."

BROWN *v*. TORONTO AUTO PARKS. [1955] 2 D.L.R. 525 (Ontario. Court of Appeal). Brown left his car on the defendant's parking lot. There was a sign reading "Attendant in Charge" and "Car and contents at owner's risk." He left the keys in the car at the attendant's request. The car was lost. Held, for Brown. LAIDLAW J.A.: "[The appellant (defendant)] has not discharged the onus of proof resting in law on it as a bailee for valuable consideration. But counsel argues that even if it has failed to discharge that onus in law, nevertheless, upon a proper construction of the provisions of the contract as displayed on the signs, it was released from liability for negligence. We cannot agree. We think that the words 'car and contents at owner's risk' do not sufficiently clearly set forth that the appellant would be relieved for responsibility arising through negligence of its employee."

STORY ON BAILMENTS. 1832. "In respect to cases of losses by fraud, there is a salutary principle belonging both to our law and the civil law. It is that the bailee can never protect himself against responsibility for losses occasioned by his own fraud; nay, not even by a contract with the bailor, that he shall not be responsible for such losses. For the law will not tolerate such an indecency and immorality as that a man shall contract to be safely dishonest; and it therefore declares all such contracts utterly void; and holds the bailee liable in the same manner and to the same extent as if no such contract ever existed." [If this statement is true today, would it be equally true if the word "negligence" were substituted for the word "fraud"?]

NOTE. The abuse of exculpatory clauses has engendered some judicial resistance, as the excerpts above suggest. In England there seems to be a fashion to talk about the "doctrine of the fundamental term" or "hard core" or "fundamental breach," by which is apparently meant that no exculpatory clause will be enforced if it is invoked to excuse the defendant from failing to perform one of the basic duties of his contract. Just what are the basic duties is not clear. In the *Alderslade* case, if the defendant had invoked the clause because the laundry was damaged, but not lost, would he have succeeded? Is the core of obligation not to lose (or, to return) the goods "harder" than the obligation not to damage? Or is the hard core the obligation to launder? Two observations may be made. The doctrine as it is developing appears to be nothing more than a stricter application of some traditional ideas about repugnancy, where, if two terms of a contract are inconsistent, one obviously has to go. And if one term doesn't go, the net result may be that the party proferring the exculpatory clause may end up by promising nothing, in which case the contract may fail for want of consideration, and the common law liability of a bailee may reassert itself.

LAMONT *v*. CANADIAN TRANSFER CO. LTD. 1909. 19 O.L.R. 291 (Ontario. Court of Appeal). The plaintiff having arrived in Toronto by steamer handed his baggage checks to his father-in-law in order that his trunks might be sent to his residence. The father-in-law gave the checks to a friend of his, one Horn, a customs officer, and asked him to have the trunks delivered. Horn took the checks and handed them, together with twenty-five cents, to Dunn, an agent of the Canadian Transfer Co., with instructions to send along the trunks. Dunn offered to do it without charge, but Horn refused, saying that he had been given the twenty-five cents. The agent then removed the steamer checks and replaced them by checks of the Can. Transfer Co. Fifteen minutes later Horn came back to Dunn and asked him for a receipt, which, without being read, was later passed on to the plaintiff, and not read by the latter until some ten days afterwards. On the face of the receipt, there was legibly printed a notice that the company should "not be liable for any loss or damage of any trunk for over $50." The trunk was either lost or stolen and the plaintiff sued the company for the value of his trunk, refusing to accept the $50 tendered by the defendants. Held, for the plaintiff. GARROW J.A.: ". . . the real question is, ought knowledge to be imputed to him under the circumstances? This is a pure question of fact, and, in my opinion, the reasonable inference is the other way. He had already made an unconditional contract after having been offered free cartage. He came back, not to get a new or different contract, but a mere receipt. That was what he asked for, and he might under the circumstances fairly and without negligence assume without reading it that he was merely getting what he had asked for and nothing more. If he had not come back no question could have been raised as to the defendants' liability, and the burden is of course upon them to shew that the new contract was substituted, with the plaintiff's consent, for the old, and in this they, in my opinion, fail. . . ."

CHAPELTON *v*. BARRY URBAN DISTRICT COUNCIL. [1940] 1 K.B. 532 (England (Wales). Court of Appeal). The plaintiff was injured when using a deck chair supplied for public use by the defendant Council. When he took the chair from the attendant he was handed a ticket. He glanced at it and slipped it into his pocket. He claimed to have no idea that there were conditions on it. In fact the ticket contained these words:

"Available for 3 hours. Time expires where indicated by cut-off and should be retained and shown on request. The Council will not be made liable for any accident or damage arising from hire of chair." Near the pile of chairs was a notice: "Barry Urban District Council. Cold Knap. Hire of chairs 2d. per session of 3 hours. The public are respectfully requested to obtain tickets properly issued from the automatic punch in their presence from the Chair Attendants." The county court Judge found the damages to be £50 in addition to special damages, but held the plaintiff bound by the notice on the ticket. The Court of Appeal reversed him. SLESSER L.J.: "The very language of that 'respectful request' shows clearly, to my mind, that for the convenience of the local authority the public were asked to obtain from the chair attendants tickets, which were mere vouchers or receipts showing how long a person hiring a chair is entitled to use that chair. It is wrong, I think, to look at the circumstance that the plaintiff obtained his receipt at the same time as he took his chair as being in any way a modification of the contract which I have indicated. This was a general offer to the general public, and I think that it is right to say that one must take into account here that there was no reason why anybody taking one of these chairs should necessarily obtain a receipt at the moment he took his chair—and, indeed, the notice is inconsistent with that, because it 'respectfully requests' the public to obtain receipts for their money. It may be that somebody might sit in one of these chairs for one hour, or two hours, or, if the holiday resort was a very popular one, for a longer time, before the attendant came round for his money, or it may be that the attendant would not come to him at all for payment for the chair, in which case I take it that there would be an obligation upon the person who used the chair to search out the attendant, like a debtor searching for his creditor, in order to pay him the sum of 2d. for the use of the chair and to obtain a receipt for the 2d. paid.

"I think the learned county court judge has misunderstood the nature of this agreement. I do not think that the notice excluding liability was a term of the contract at all. . . . I think the object of the giving and the taking of this ticket was that the person taking it might have evidence at hand by which he could show that the obligation he was under to pay 2d. for the use of the chair for three hours had been duly discharged, and I think it is altogether inconsistent, in the absence of any qualification of liability in the notice put up near the pile of chairs, to attempt to read into it the qualification contended for. In my opinion, this ticket is no more than a receipt, and is quite different from a railway ticket which contains upon it the terms upon which a railway company agrees to carry the passenger."

2. Non Est Factum

FOSTER *v.* MACKINNON

England. Common Pleas. 1869. L.R. 4 C.P. 704

This was an action by an indorsee against an indorser on a bill of exchange for £3000. One Callow, who was called as a witness for the plaintiff, testified that the defendant, an elderly man, signed the note in his presence, he having taken the bill, as drawn and indorsed by one Cooper, to the defendant and asked him to sign it telling him it was a guarantee. The defendant had previously signed a guarantee for £3000 for Callow but no liability had resulted to him. Callow only showed the defendant the back of the paper; it was, however, in the ordinary shape of a bill of exchange, and bore a stamp, the impress of which was visible through the paper. The defendant wrote his signature right after Cooper's. Bovill C.J. at the trial told the jury that, if the indorsement was not the signature of the defendant, or if, being his signature, it was obtained upon a fraudulent representation that it was a guarantee, and the defendant signed it without knowing that it was a bill, and under the belief that it was a guarantee, and if the defendant was not guilty of any negligence in so signing the paper, he was entitled to the verdict. The jury found for the defendant. On a rule nisi for a new trial on grounds of misdirection and that the verdict was against the weight of evidence.

BYLES J. delivered the judgment of the Court: . . . The case presented by the defendant is, that he never made the contract declared on; that he never saw the face of the bill; that the purport of the contract was fraudulently mis-described to him; that, when he signed one thing, he was told and believed that he was signing another and an entirely different thing; and that his mind never went with his act.

It seems plain, on principle and on authority, that, if a blind man, or man who cannot read, or who for some reason (not implying negligence) forgot to read, has a written contract falsely read over to him, the reader misreading to such a degree that the written contract is of a nature altogether different from the contract pretended to be read from the paper which the blind or illiterate man afterwards signs; then, at least if there be no negligence, the signature so obtained is of no force. And it is invalid not merely on the ground of fraud, where fraud exists, but on the ground that the mind of the signer did not accompany the signature; in other words that he never intended to sign, and therefore in contemplation of law never did sign, the contract to which his name is appended.

The authorities appear to us to support this view of the law. In *Thoroughgood's Case* (1582), 2 Co. Rep. 9a; 76 E.R. 408, it was held that, if an illiterate man have a deed falsely read over to him, and he then seals and delivers the parchment, that parchment is nevertheless not his deed. In a note to *Thoroughgood's Case*, in Fraser's edition of *Coke's Reports*, it is suggested that the doctrine is not confined to the condition of an illiterate grantor; and a case in Keilway's *Reports*, 70, pl. 6, is cited in support of this observation. On reference to that case it appears that one of the judges did there observe that it made no difference whether the grantor were lettered or unlettered. That, however, was a case where the grantee himself was the defrauding party. But the position that, if a grantor or covenantor be deceived or misled as to the *actual contents* of the deed, the deed does not bind him, is supported by many authorities. . . . Accordingly, it has recently been decided in the Exchequer Chamber, that, if a deed be delivered, and a blank left therein be afterwards improperly filled up (at least if that be done without the grantor's negligence), it is not the deed of the grantor: *Swan* v. *North British Australasian Land Company* (1863), 2 H. & C. 175; 159 E.R. 73.

These cases apply to deeds; but the principle is equally applicable to other written contracts. Nevertheless, this principle, when applied to negotiable instruments, must be and is limited in its application. These instruments are not only assignable, but they form part of the currency of the country. A qualification of the general rule is necessary to protect innocent transferees for value. If, therefore, a man writes his name across the back of a blank bill-stamp, and part with it, and the paper is afterwards improperly filled up, he is liable as indorser. If he writes it across the face of the bill, he is liable as acceptor, when the instrument has once passed into the hands of an innocent indorsee for the value before maturity, and liable to the extent of any sum which the stamp will cover.

In these cases, however, the party signing knows what he is doing; the indorser intended to indorse, and the acceptor intended to accept, a bill of exchange to be thereafter filled up, leaving the amount, the date, the maturity, and the other parties to the bill undetermined.

But, in the case now under consideration, the defendant, according to the evidence, if believed, and the finding of the jury, never intended to indorse a bill of exchange at all, but intended to sign a contract of an entirely different nature. It was not his design, and, if he were guilty of no negligence, it was not even his fault that the instrument he signed turned out to be a bill of exchange. It was as if he had written his name on a sheet of paper for the purpose of franking a letter, or in a lady's album, or on an order for admission to the Temple Church, or on the fly-leaf of a book, and there had already been, without his knowledge, a bill of exchange or a promissory note payable to order inscribed on the other side of the paper. To make the case clearer, suppose the bill or note on the other side of the paper in each of these cases to be written at a time subsequent to the signature, then the fraudulent misapplication of that genuine signature to a different purpose would have been a counterfeit alteration of a writing with intent to defraud, and would therefore have amounted to a forgery. In that case, the signer would not have been bound by his signature, for two reasons, first, that he never in fact signed the writing declared on, and, secondly, that he never intended to sign any such contract.

In the present case, the first reason does not apply, but the second reason does apply. The defendant never intended to sign that contract, or any such contract. He never intended to put his name to any instrument that then was or thereafter might become negotiable. He was deceived, not merely as to the legal effect, but as to the *actual contents* of the instrument.

We are not aware of any case in which the precise question now before us has arisen on bills of exchange or promissory notes, or been judicially discussed. . . . But, in *Putnam* v. *Sullivan*, an American case, reported in 4 Mass. 45, and cited in *Parsons on Bills*, vol. i, p. 111 n., a distinction is taken by Chief Justice Parsons between a case where an indorser intended to indorse such a note as he actually indorsed, being induced by fraud to indorse it, and a case where he intended to indorse a different note and for a different purpose. And the Court intimated an opinion that, even in such a case as that, a distinction might prevail and protect the indorsee.

The distinction in the case now under consideration is a much plainer one; for, on this branch of the rule, we are to assume that the indorser never intended to indorse at all, but to sign a contract of an entirely different nature.

For these reasons, we think the direction of the Lord Chief Justice was right.

[A new trial was granted because "the case should undergo further investigation."]

HOWATSON *v.* WEBB

England. Chancery Division. [1907] 1 Ch. 537

Webb was the managing clerk of one Hooper, a solicitor, who was engaged in building speculations near Edmonton, north of London, for the purposes of which Hooper had had various leases put in Webb's name as nominee for him. Some time after Webb had left Hooper's service, Hooper called him on the phone and asked him to come over and sign some deeds "transferring the Edmonton property." Webb went the same day and arrived about lunch time. Hooper seemed to be in a great hurry and asked Webb to sign and "Hurry up and come and join me at lunch." Webb asked "What are the deeds?" to which Hooper replied, "They are just deeds transferring that property," presumably meaning the Edmonton property. Hooper then went out and Webb signed a number of deeds left open for signature on a table. One was a mortgage dated that day, June 2, 1899, between Webb and one Whitaker as mortgagee and contained Webb's covenant to pay the mortgagee £1000. During the next seven years Hooper paid the interest and £200 on principal. Webb was not called upon to pay any interest, but on February 2, 1906, the plaintiff, Miss Howatson, asked for payment of the principal. Miss Howatson took a transfer of the mortgage from Whitaker in October, 1902, and paid Whitaker, or possibly Hooper, as solicitor in the transaction, £800. Webb raised the defence of *non est factum*.

WARRINGTON J.: The question in this case is which of two innocent parties is to suffer for the roguery of a third party. . . . [After a careful review of *Foster* v. *Mackinnon* and some other cases, Warrington J. continued:]

What does the evidence in the present case shew? I may go so far in the defendant's favour as to say that Webb, having regard to his knowledge of Hooper, when Hooper said that the deeds were "deeds for transferring the Edmonton property" was justified in believing that they were deeds such as a nominee could be called upon to execute either in favour of a new nominee or for the purpose of putting an end to his own position of nominee, and certainly not a deed creating a mortgage to another person. But in my opinion that is not enough. He was told that they were deeds relating to the property to which they did in fact relate. His mind was therefore applied to the question of dealing with that property. The deeds did deal with that property. The misrepresentation was as to the contents of the deed, and not as to the character and class of the deed. He knew he was dealing with the class of deed with which in fact he was dealing, but did not ascertain its contents. The deed contained a covenant to pay. Under those circumstances I cannot say that the deed is absolutely void. It purported to be a transfer of the property, and it was a transfer of the property. If the plea of *non est factum* is to succeed the deed must be wholly, and not partly, void. If that plea is an answer in this case, I must hold it to be an answer in every case of misrepresentation. In my opinion the law does not go as far as that. The defence therefore fails. There must therefore be judgment for the plaintiff on the claim with costs. . . .

[The judgment of Warrington J., which has been drastically cut, was unanimously affirmed on appeal. [1908] 1 Ch. 1.]

CARLISLE AND CUMBERLAND BANKING CO. *v*. BRAGG
England. Court of Appeal. [1911] 1 K.B. 489

This was an action by the Bank on a written guarantee signed by Bragg in the following circumstances. Bragg and one Rigg had been drinking together. Rigg produced a paper, and asked Bragg to sign it; he didn't read it to Bragg, or tell him that it was a guarantee. Rather he told him that it was a duplicate of a paper Bragg had signed the day before, which had got blurred in the rain. Bragg did not read the paper and testified later that he thought it was an insurance matter which he had previously signed. Rigg later forged the signature of an attesting witness and handed it to the Bank. Rigg owed the Bank the amount claimed from Bragg on the guarantee in this action. The jury were asked and answered: (1) Was the defendant induced to sign the guarantee by the fraud of Rigg? Yes. (2) Did the defendant know that the document which he signed was a guarantee? No. (3) Was the defendant negligent in signing the guarantee? Yes. (4) Was Rigg the agent of the bank? No. Pickford J. on these findings gave judgment for the defendant. The Bank appealed.

VAUGHAN WILLIAMS L.J.: In my opinion the judgment of Pickford J. in this case was quite right. He held that the finding of negligence by the jury was immaterial, and he did so after discussing the case of *Foster* v. *Mackinnon* (1869), L.R. 4 C.P. 704, and coming to the conclusion that the doctrine there laid down as regards negligence really has reference to the particular case of a negotiable instrument, to an action on which the defence that the defendant was included to sign the instrument by fraud and misrepresentation as to its nature is set up as against a bona fide holder for value. As I understand it, that doctrine is limited to negotiable instruments, and that was really the ground of the judgment of Pickford in this case. Now let me deal with the matter apart from any question of negotiable instruments. In this case the finding of the jury is that the signature of the defendant to this document was obtained by fraud. The jury were asked: "Was the defendant induced to sign the guarantee by fraud of Riggs?" They answered that he was. They then were asked: "Did the defendant know that the document which he signed was a guarantee?" They answered in the negative. It seems to me that on those findings alone the defendant would be entitled to say in respect of this guarantee that it was not, in contemplation of law, signed by him. His signature was obtained by fraud, and it is manifest on the evidence and findings of the jury, that he was not intending to sign any such document. What he was intending to sign was some document with reference to insurance. It appears to me that under the circumstances of this case the mere fact that the jury have found that there was negligence on the part of the defendant does not raise such an estoppel as prevents the defendant from setting up the defence that he never signed the guarantee and that his signature to the document was obtained from him by fraud; that he did not know of its nature, or intend to sign a document of that description. If the document in question had been not a guarantee, but a bill of exchange, and the question had arisen what was the position of a holder for value without notice of the fraud, the matter might have been different, because the law merchant, and now the statute law, puts persons who in such circumstances take bills of exchange and such like instruments in the position that they have to prove that they gave value for the bill or other like instrument honestly, but, if they prove that, it does not matter that it was originally procured by fraud.

The only other thing which I wish to say is on the question of negligence. I do not know whether the jury understood that there could be no material negligence unless there was a duty on the defendant towards the plaintiffs. Even if they did understand that, in my opinion, in the case of this instrument, the signature to which was obtained by fraud, and which was not a negotiable instrument, Pickford J. was right in saying that the finding of negligence was immaterial. I wish to add for myself that in my judgment there is no evidence whatsoever to shew that the proximate cause of the plaintiffs' advancing money on this document was the mere signature of it by the defendant. In my opinion, the proximate cause of the plaintiffs' making the advance was that Rigg fraudulently took the document to the bank, having fraudulently altered it by adding the forged signature of an attesting witness, and but for Rigg having done those things the plaintiffs would never have advanced the money at all. Under these circumstances I think that the appeal fails and must be dismissed.

[The concurring opinions of Buckley and Kennedy, L.JJ. are omitted. On the question of estoppel Buckley L.J. said, "On that question I agree that the existence of negligence may be relevant. . . . I do not think that there was in this case proof of any such negligence as would avail the plaintiffs as between themselves and the defendant. The defendant did not owe any duty to the plaintiffs, and the act of the defendant was not the act which involved the plaintiffs in loss. What involved the plaintiffs in loss was the act of Rigg. . . .]

NOTE. If the principle of the "ticket" cases is that a person who manifests acceptance of a writing which he should as a reasonable man understand to be an offer thereby accepts that offer, what is the difference in this situation? Is there any "duty" in the ticket taker to read the ticket?

Dean C. A. Wright, in reviewing the 10th edition of *Pollock on Contracts*, said, (1936), 14 Can. B. Rev. 783 at p. 784: "Under the 'ticket' cases, provided the company has done everything reasonably sufficient to give notice to the purchaser of the ticket, the contract is concluded by accepting a ticket. Does this not mean that the ticket-taker should, as a reasonable man, know the terms of the offer, and would not the jury's finding in *Carlisle* v. *Bragg* mean that the signer should have known of the terms of the offer he was signing? Section 70 of the American Law Institute Restatement reads as follows: 'One who makes a written offer which is accepted or who manifests acceptance of the terms of a writing which he should reasonably understand to be an offer or proposed contract, is bound by the contract though ignorant of the terms of the writing or of its proper interpretation.' It would be interesting to discover to what extent the author believes this statement to represent English law." Sir Frederick did not live to answer his critic but in the current edition, the 13th, by Sir Percy Winfield, there is a note at the end of footnote 56 on p. 42: "A learned reviewer of the 10th edition of this book finds it difficult to reconcile the ticket cases with *Carlisle Banking Co.* v. *Bragg*. . . . But that case is not *in pari materia*."

PRUDENTIAL TRUST CO. LTD. *v.* CUGNET

Saskatchewan. Supreme Court of Canada. 1956. 5 D.L.R. 2d. 1

In January 1951 one Hunter visited Edmund Cugnet at his home in Weyburn where Cugnet was playing cards. He interrupted his game when Hunter told him he wanted to talk about his mineral rights in two quarter sections of land. They went into another room and Hunter then said he wanted an option to take petroleum leases on the expiration of existing leases given by Cugnet to Rio Bravo Oil Co. Ltd. and Bandy Lee in 1949. He offered to pay $32 on each quarter section for the option and $32 yearly rental when the option was exercised. After a short conversation Cugnet signed an "Assignment" which effectively transferred to the Prudential Trust Co. Ltd. an undivided one half interest in the petroleum in his land. He also granted to Prudential an exclusive option to take a petroleum and natural gas lease for 99 years. He also transferred to Prudential an undivided half interest in the mineral rights except coal. Later Prudential sent Cugnet a copy of the assignment and a cheque for $64. Cugnet didn't read either the documents he signed or the copy returned to him. In February Prudential registered a caveat against the land and in September Cugnet's solicitors wrote to Prudential requesting a return of the documents. In April 1952 Cugnet's son Raymond filed a caveat against the lands based on an agreement for sale between Edmund (vendor) and Raymond (purchaser) in 1945. This action was brought by Prudential to establish its rights under its caveat. Hunter had disappeared and was not called as a witness. He had acted as an agent of Amigo Petroleums Ltd., a company incorporated and owned by one Lamarr, who had agreed with Prudential that Prudential would hold its oil agreements in trust. Amigo's interests were later acquired by one Nickle and assigned by him to Canuck Freehold Royalties Ltd. Canuck also had an agreement with Prudential that it would hold Canuck's interests in trust. Prudential was, throughout, a "bare trustee."

The trial Judge held that Cugnet never intended to complete the assignment and transfer and relied on Hunter's misrepresentation that the documents were an option only. He applied the principle of *non est factum*. The Court of Appeal dismissed an appeal but granted special leave to appeal to the Supreme Court of Canada.

LOCKE J.: . . . The question as to whether the respondents are entitled to rely upon the defence [of *non est factum*] is raised by the plea of estoppel by conduct in the reply to the statement of defence. The basis for the contention is that Edmund Cugnet having, by his conduct, enabled Hunter and his principals to sell what appeared on the face of it to be a half interest in the mineral rights to a purchaser for value acting in good faith, he cannot dispute the validity of the instruments as against the latter. The estoppel, it is said, arises by reason of the negligence of Edmund Cugnet. The question is the same as that referred to by Buckley L.J. in *Carlisle & Cumberland Banking Co.* v. *Bragg*, [1911] 1 K.B. 489. . . .

It is my opinion that the result of the authorities was correctly stated in the *Bragg* case. To say that a person may be estopped by careless conduct such as that in the present case, when the instrument is not negotiable, is to assert the existence of some duty on the part of the person owing to the public at large, or to other persons unknown to him who might suffer damage by acting upon the instrument on the footing that it is valid in the hands of the holder. I do not consider that the authorities support the view that there is any such general duty, the breach of which imposes a liability in negligence. . . . it is my opinion that the appeal should fail and be dismissed with costs.

CARTWRIGHT J. (dissenting): . . . Cugnet Senior was induced to sign this document by the fraudulent representation made to him by one Edward Hunter that it contained only the grant of an option. Cugnet Senior is literate, has had experience in buying and selling properties, has been successful, and, in his own words, has "lots of money." He signed the document without reading it. He does not suggest that anything was done to prevent him reading it but appears to have been anxious to return without delay to the game of cards which had been interrupted by Hunter's arrival. He had not met Hunter previously. Hunter took the document away with him but 2 or 3 weeks later Cugnet Senior received a copy of it together with a cheque for $64 the amount of the consideration which he had agreed to accept. He did not read this copy until some months later when his son, the respondent Raymond A. Cugnet, called his attention to its contents. In the meantime the copy had been hanging up on a spike in the kitchen at the home of Cugnet Senior. Prudential in taking the conveyance was acting as bare trustee for Amigo Petroleums Ltd. During February, 1951, the last-mentioned company transferred the one-half interest and the option to one Nickle who, in turn, transferred them for value to the appellant Canuck Freehold Royalties Ltd., hereinafter called "Canuck" for which Prudential holds as bare trustee. Canuck had no notice or knowledge of the fraud practised by Hunter. . . .

It is clear that Cugnet Senior knew that the deed which he was executing was one purporting to deal with the petroleum and natural gas under two correctly specified quarter-sections owned by him. On the assumption that a distinction can validly be drawn between the facts in *Howatson* v. *Webb*, [1907] 1 Ch. 537; [1908] 1 Ch. 1, and those in *Carlisle & Cumberland Banking Co.* v. *Bragg*, it is my view that on its facts the case at bar falls within the class of cases of which the former is an example.

If, however, it be assumed that the Courts below were right in holding that the document of January 26, 1951, was entirely different in nature from what Cugnet Senior believed it to be, it is my opinion that in signing and sealing the document without reading it he was guilty of such negligence that as between himself and Canuck, which gave valuable consideration on the strength of the deed which he had in fact signed and sealed, he must bear the loss.

The general principle was stated as follows by Lord Halsbury sitting in the Court of Appeal in *Henderson & Co.* v. *Williams*, [1895] 1 Q.B. 521 at pp. 528–9: "I think that it is not undesirable to refer to an American authority, which, I observe, was quoted in the case of *Kingsford* v. *Merry*, *Root* v. *French* in which, in the Supreme Court of New York, Savage C.J. makes observations which seem to me to be well worthy of consideration. Speaking of a bona fide purchaser who has purchased property from a fraudulent vendee and given value for it, he says: 'He is protected in doing so upon the principle just stated, that when one of two innocent persons must suffer from the fraud of a third, he shall suffer, who, by his indiscretion, has enabled such third person to commit the fraud. A contrary principle would endanger the security of commercial transactions, and destroy that confidence upon which what is called the usual course of trade materially rests.' "

In *Farquharson Bros. & Co.* v. *C. King & Co.*, [1902] A.C. 325 at pp. 331–2, Lord Halsbury L.C. presiding in the House of Lords reaffirmed the above passage and pointed out that in the case then before the House the Court of Appeal had fallen into error through disregarding the words "who, by his indiscretion."

A branch of the principle so stated is the rule that, generally speaking, a person who executes a document without taking the trouble to read it is liable on it and cannot plead that he mistook its contents, at all events, as against a person who acting in good faith in the ordinary course of business has changed his position in reliance on such document. But it is said that the plea of *non est factum* operates as an exception to this salutary rule. That this is so in the case of a blind or illiterate person may be taken to be established by *Thoroughgood's Case* (1583), 2 Co. Rep. 9a, 76 E.R. 408, but whether the exception extends to an educated person who is not blind is a question which was treated by Sir G. Mellish L.J. in *Hunter* v. *Walters* (1871), L.R. 7 Ch. 75, and by Warrington J. and the Court of Appeal in *Howatson* v. *Webb*, as being still open. . . .

An anxious consideration of all the authorities referred to by counsel and in the Courts below has brought me to the conclusion that, insofar as *Carlisle* v. *Bragg* decides that the rule that negligence excludes a plea of *non est factum* is limited to the case of negotiable instruments and does not extend to a deed such as the one before us, we should refuse to follow it. I do not read the judgment of Sir Lyman P. Duff C.J.C. in *Minchau* v. *Busse*, [1940] 2 D.L.R. 282, and particularly his reference at p. 294 to the judgment of Buckley L.J. as binding us to follow everything that was decided in *Carlisle* v. *Bragg*.

In my view the effect of the decisions prior to *Carlisle* v. *Bragg* is accurately summarized in Cheshire & Fifoot on Contract, 4th ed., pp. 206–7, as follows: "The rule before 1911 was that if A., the victim of the fraud of C., was guilty of negligence in executing a written instrument different in kind from that which he intended to execute, then he was estopped as against innocent transferees from denying the validity of the written contract."

That rule was, I think, laid down by Byles J. delivering the unanimous judgment of the Court in *Foster* v. *Mackinnon* (1869), L.R. 4 C.P. 704, as being applicable to all written contracts. It appears to me that the Court of Appeal in *Carlisle* v. *Bragg* misinterpreted the following passage in the judgment of Byles J. at p. 712:

"Nevertheless, this principle, when applied to negotiable instruments, must be and is limited in its application. These instruments are not only assignable, but they form part of the currency of the country. A qualification of the general rule is necessary to protect innocent transferees for value. If, therefore, a man write his name across the back of a blank bill-stamp, and part with it, and the paper is afterwards improperly filled up, he is liable as endorser. If he write it across the face of the bill, he is liable as acceptor, when the instrument has once passed into the hands of an innocent endorsee for value before maturity, and liable to the extent of any sum which the stamp will cover.

"In these cases, however, the party signing knows what he is doing: the endorser intended to endorse, and the acceptor intended to accept, a bill of exchange to be thereafter filled up, leaving the amount, the date, the maturity, and the other parties to the bill undetermined.

"But, in the case now under consideration, the defendant, according to the evidence, if believed, and the finding of the jury, never intended to endorse a bill of exchange at all, but intended to sign a contract of an entirely different nature. It was not his design, and, if he were guilty of no negligence, it was not even his fault that the instrument he signed turned out to be a bill of exchange."

This does not say that the rule, that the signer if guilty of negligence will be estopped from denying the validity of a document as against a purchaser for value in good faith, is confined to the case of negotiable instruments; but rather that a person who knows he is signing a negotiable instrument cannot deny its validity to a holder in due course although he was guilty of no negligence in affixing his signature.

It may be said that the term negligence is inappropriate because it presupposes a duty owed by Cugnet Senior to Canuck, but in the passages quoted the term is, I think, used as meaning that lack of reasonable care in statement which gives rise to an estoppel. As it was put by Sir William Anson in an article on *Carlisle & Cumberland Banking Co.* v. *Bragg* in 28 L.Q. Rev. 190 at p. 194: "And further, there seems some confusion between the negligence which creates a liability in tort, and the lack of reasonable care in statement which gives rise to an estoppel. Bragg might well have been precluded by carelessness from resisting the effect of his written words, though the Bank might not have been able to sue him for negligence."

On the facts in the case at bar it cannot be doubted that Cugnet Senior failed to exercise reasonable care in signing the document in question. He executed a deed which he knew dealt with the oil and gas under his property without reading it, relying on the statements as to its contents made by Hunter who was a stranger to him. It does not appear that anything was done to prevent his reading the document. He chose to sign it unread rather than to absent himself for a few more minutes from the game of cards. His conduct, in my opinion, precludes him from relying on the plea of *non est factum* as against Canuck which purchased relying on the deed, in good faith, for value, and without notice or knowledge of any circumstances affecting the validity of the deed.

The terms of the deed appear to me to be sufficiently clear and I think that the plea that it is void for uncertainty must be rejected.

In the result I would allow the appeal with costs throughout and direct that judgment be entered for the relief claimed in the amended statement of claim.

[The decision of Locke J. is severely cut. The concurring opinion of Nolan J., with whom Taschereu and Fauteux JJ. concurred, is omitted altogether. The appeal was dismissed.]

QUESTIONS. Should Cartwright J. not have concluded by ordering a new trial? Would evidence have been produced at this trial to show the extent to which Prudential was careless? Should "contributory negligence" (carelessness) be a defence, or should the responsibility be apportioned? Compare *Ingram* v. *Little* above at page 415.

ROSE *v*. MAHONEY. 1915. 34 O.L.R. 238 (Ontario. Appellate Division). The defendants signed an agreement presented to them by their solicitor, with whom they had discussed the proposed sale of their property and the price and terms on which they were willing to sell. No mention was made of paying a commission, or that any real estate agent would be involved. The agreement was signed by the purchaser and it was taken by the solicitor's clerk to the defendants' house, where they signed it without reading it over. Unknown to them, this solicitor had inserted the plaintiff's name as agent to whom the defendants, by signing the agreement promised to pay a commission. They refused and the plaintiff sued. The trial Judge in the county court found in his favour and gave damages for $406.25. On appeal, held, for the defendants; the *Bragg* case and *Foster* v. *Mackinnon* being cited. LATCHFORD J.: "The agreement was presented to the defendants for signature by a clerk of their solicitor. The evidence is conclusive that it was not read or explained to them. They did, however, understand it to be an agreement for the sale of their property for a price which they were willing to accept; and they are bound by it as an agreement of sale. They were not informed that it provided for payment of a commission to the plaintiff, of whose existence even they had no knowledge. They trusted their solicitor; and he, through his agent and associate, the plaintiff, abused their confidence." Kelly J. observed that "the defendants cannot be said to have been negligent, if negligence were here material." [was there any privity of contract between the plaintiff and the defendants?]

OAKBANK OIL CO. LTD. *v*. LOVE & STEWART, LTD. [1918] S.C. 54 (Scotland. House of Lords). A contract for the supply of pit-props was made by an exchange of letters. The lettering offering the contract had printed in red ink at the top of the page on which the whole of the letter appeared: "All offers over a period are subject to stoppages through strikes, lockouts, &c., and the right to cancel is reserved in the event of any of the countries from which our supplies are drawn becoming engaged in war." It was argued that the letter proper which started "Dear Sirs," and ended with "Yours truly" below the clause printed in red ink, did not embody the clause. Held, that it did. FINLAY L.C.: "The case of strikes is, unfortunately, so common that everyone would expect to find a provision made for what was to happen in case an occurrence of that kind took place. The case of war is also provided for by this note. It is said that the pursuers did not, nor did any of the directors or officials, read this clause —that their own attention was not directed to it, and that the attention of none of the higher officers of the Company was called to it. That, to my mind, is utterly immaterial. The question is whether the red ink note was put in such a position in such type that it must be regarded reasonably as forming part of the terms which were offered by those who wrote the letter. It seems to me quite clear that this red ink note did form part of these terms. . . . It appears to me that the cases with regard to tickets on railways, which are merely vouchers for payment of a fare, have no application, and it is impossible to read the contract here apart from the red ink note. . . ."

LONGLEY *v*. BARBRICK

Nova Scotia. Supreme Court. 1962. 36 D.L.R. (2d) 672

COFFIN J.: This is an action for the foreclosure of a mortgage and for deficiency judgment.

The basic documents on which the claim is founded are as follows:

(1) A mortgage dated January 23, 1959, made by Beatrice Barbrick, the defendant herein, as mortgagor, to United Realties Limited, as mortgagee. The consideration set forth in the mortgage is $5,000 and the proviso stipulates that the mortgage shall be void on the payment of this sum with interest at 8% per annum calculated half-yearly not in advance, as well after as before maturity, in 8 years from the date thereof by monthly instalments of $70.40 each including principal and interest on the first day of each and every month commencing on March 1, 1959, to and including January 1, 1966, and the balance of said principal sum and interest on February 1, 1966.

(2) An agreement made January 23, 1959, between the same parties,

reciting the mortgage, and also reciting that the actual sum of money advanced to Beatrice Barbrick by United Realties was $2,500. This agreement followed the above recitals by acknowledging that the difference between the $5,000 and the $2,500 was being given by Beatrice Barbrick to United Realties Ltd. as a bonus in consideration of its granting the loan.

(3) Assignment of mortgage dated April 30, 1959, from United Realties Ltd. to the plaintiff Charles F. Longley. This document recited the mortgage and undertook that the principal sum $4,924.53 together with interest at the rate of 8% on April 1, 1959, was then owing and unpaid.

These then are the main documents to be considered. There are other exhibits to which reference will be made. But the case itself depends on the right of the plaintiff to enforce the original mortgage and the collateral agreement as assigned by the last-mentioned assignment of mortgage.

At this point I am going to refer in some detail to the facts from which the dispute in the case in question arose.

The defendant Beatrice Barbrick described how she originally purchased the property involved in 1946. She had been in the Army from 1942 to November, 1945, retiring as a Lance-Corporal, after which she worked at nursing homes and from 1949 to 1958 or 1959 served in the Polio Clinic.

She had saved some money and this she invested in her house. When questioned as to the background of the mortgage she said that as she needed some money she made inquiries as a result of which she called "Town & Country" at Halifax and talked to "a Mr. John Hickey". He later came out to see her and she informed him that she needed $2,500, to which, according to her evidence, he replied, "I think that can be arranged without any trouble but I'll have to see the Manager". He later called Miss Barbrick and said that the manager agreed to let her have $2,500 at 8% for 96 months.

In two or three days she was instructed to go to a lawyer's office in the Roy Building, which she did, and when she actually entered his office, she was accompanied by a Mrs. Drysdale. Mrs. Drysdale held the existing mortgage on her property and, among other things, the loan which the defendant was seeking was to pay this mortgage.

Miss Barbrick continued in her evidence to say that the lawyer gave Mrs. Drysdale a paper to sign which she supposed was a receipt. Mrs. Drysdale then obtained her cheque and went straight out. He then said to Miss Barbrick " 'Sit down' and 'You sign here for your money,' which was 600 and some dollars. I don't remember the exact amount of the cheque". The defendant then received her cheque, which she understood was the $2,500 less Mrs. Drysdale's account and less certain legal fees.

Miss Barbrick insisted that the mortgage had not been read to her before she signed it. As to the collateral agreement, this, too, she said was not read to her nor explained to her. She did not get a copy of it at the time but it was mailed to her subsequently. . . .

Some evidence as to the actual execution of the mortgage and the agreement was given by the solicitor, in whose office the documents were signed by the defendant. He said that on instructions from United Realties Ltd. he had prepared a mortgage and contacted Miss Barbrick, who came to his office and went through the documents. He also said that there was a mortgage and a collateral agreement. As to whether she asked any questions or he explained anything to her, his answer was, "It's very difficult.

I know what my usual practice was—not only the mortgage but also the collateral agreement to the mortgagors. In my own mind I felt they understood what they were signing in this type of mortgage". On cross-examination he was asked by Mr. Jackson if he remembered explaining the mortgage to Miss Barbrick and he replied—"No. I can't recall this particular transaction. As you will note from the date on the document it took place some time ago and I've done several since then. Q. The same would apply to the collateral agreement, I suppose? A. That is correct." In all fairness to the solicitor I am in agreement with the suggestion of the defendant's counsel that the solicitor understood that all details had been thoroughly discussed with the defendant before she ever reached his office. It was, in fact, to Town & Country Real Estate Limited that she was looking for guidance.

At the time the mortgage was assigned to the plaintiff Mr. Longley, apparently only two payments had been made, and there was a balance owing at that time of $4,924.53. The amount paid by Mr. Longley for this mortgage was $3,170. . . .

The defendant pleaded *non est factum* and something should be said of the authorities on that point. . . .

I accept the evidence of the defendant on the facts leading up to the execution of the relevant documents in this case. I find as a fact that Town & Country Real Estate Ltd. undertook to arrange for her a mortgage of $2,500 at 8% for 96 months and that she understood it was for such a mortgage that she signed the application of January 16, 1959.

I also find that the mortgage and collateral agreement were not fully read and explained to her by the solicitor who drew up the documents, when she was in his office. I have already discussed the reasons for this and it is my view that if Town & Country Real Estate Ltd. had given a detailed explanation of this proposal in advance and instructed the defendant to have independent advice before the documents were signed, the whole unfortunate situation could have have been avoided.

Having found these facts, it is my view that the bonus of $2,500 is . . . void under the plea of *non est factum* because she was so misled as to the contents of the documents that her "mind did not go with her signature". . . .

Mr. Longley's evidence was that he made no inquiries about the security when he took the assignment (and there is no affirmative evidence to contradict him on this point) but he has his remedies against the original mortgagee under the terms of the assignment of mortgage.

The mortgage will be amended and the principal sum reduced from $5,000 to $2,500 with an appropriate reduction in interest charges, resulting in a mortgage bearing the same date as that now under dispute, but securing the principal sum of $2,500 only and interest at 8%. The instalments will be reduced accordingly.

The defendant is entitled to a rectification of the said mortgage and to an accounting showing the correct balance now owing on the basis of the mortgage as so amended.

The defendant will have the costs of this action and as she has succeeded substantially on her counterclaim, the costs of the counterclaim.

[Coffin J. also held that "the bonus of $2,500 is bad as a bonus on the ground that it is unfair and unconscionable within the prohibitions enunciated by *G. & C. Kreglinger* v. *New Patagonia Meat & Cold Storage Co.*, [1914] A.C. 25." This part of the opinion is omitted.]

ROYAL BANK OF CANADA *v.* HALE

British Columbia. Supreme Court. 1961. 30 D.L.R. (2d) 138

In February 1958 the Royal Bank at Kitimat lent ABC Sheet Metal and Plumbing Ltd. $25,000, taking as security five notes for $5,000 each, an assignment of ABC's book debts, and personal guarantees from Hale and his three brothers for the aggregate sum of $25,000. The guarantees signed by the brothers were on the Royal Bank's standard form, which contained the guarantors' promise to guarantee payment, not only of the $25,000 but "of all debts and liabilities, present or future, direct or indirect, absolute or contingent, matured or not, at any time owing by ABC . . . to the bank." The form also stated (Para. 13) that it covered "all agreements between the parties relative to this guarantee . . ." and that "none of the parties shall be bound by any representation . . . which is not embodied herein." At that time the brothers knew that ABC owed nearly $20,000 to companies in which they were interested, and that these debts had been assigned by the companies to the Bank back in 1955. The Bank claimed in this action on the guarantees not only the balance owing on ABC's loan (the direct debt) but on the assignments (the indirect debts) as well. The trial also embraced four other actions arising in almost identical circumstances where the Hale brothers guaranteed a loan by the Bank to the Prince George Heating and Sheet Metal Ltd. In their defence the Hale brothers pleaded that there was mutual mistake or, a unilateral mistake in that they were induced by the Bank to believe that the guarantees applied only to the direct debts. The evidence of the background of the transactions was admitted over the Bank's objection, and showed among other things that in 1957 the Hale brothers had given similar guarantees for $20,000 for ABC and when the loan was repaid the guarantee form was given back, although at that time the indirect debts of 1955 had been assigned to the Bank to the knowledge of its Vancouver officials, but not to the knowledge of the Kitimat manager. In connection with the Prince George guarantees, A. W. Hale had written when returning the guarantee form to the Prince George branch manager, that "it was our understanding that we were personally guaranteeing the loan only." In his reply to this letter the manager did not comment one way or the other on the extent of the personal guarantee.

MUNROE J.: . . . In the circumstances of this case . . . I hold that the evidence tendered by the defendants in support of their pleadings is admissable. How else could the Court determine whether or not any mistake had occurred? . . .

While it is clear beyond any doubt that the defendants and all the representatives of the plaintiff with whom they negotiated did not contemplate, far less intend, that the guarantees were taken and delivered for any purpose beyond the known purpose of securing the bank loans, nevertheless, the intention of the plaintiff corporation, as distinguished from the state of mind of its officials, must be determined from the terms of the document, and not otherwise. Since the guarantee form is not so limited in its terms, I cannot hold that the plaintiff was mistaken as to its legal effect, and the defence of mutual mistake therefore fails.

There remains for consideration the major defence raised on behalf of the defendants, namely, that the guarantees ought not to be enforced *vis-à-vis* the indirect debt because of a unilateral mistake (on the part of the defendants) as to the legal effect of the guarantee, which mistake was induced by the (innocent) misrepresentation of the plaintiff and that it would be inequitable to enforce the guarantees in the manner contended for by the plaintiff.

In my view, the guarantees, in their literal and plain meaning, appear to render the defendants liable to the plaintiffs for the indirect debts herein claimed unless the defence of unilateral mistake should prevail, even though the plaintiff has rarely if ever before sought to enforce such liability. I have no hesitation in finding, upon the evidence, that the defendants when they executed the guarantees, were mistaken in their belief that they were thereby guaranteeing only the bank loans, and not the indirect debt. Then, were the defendants so misled by the words, acts or conduct of the plaintiff's officials? The answer to that question can best be ascertained by a consideration of the evidence and a review of the business dealings between the parties, which dealings began in 1955 when a loan was obtained from the plaintiff for $250,000 for a company in which the defendants were interested and interlocking guarantees given by several companies for $500,000; the 1957 loan to ABC at Kitimat when guarantees of the defendants were given for the same amount as the loans; the return and discharge of that guarantee (which the plaintiff now claims was a vital asset) when the loan was repaid, some 2 years after the assignments of book debts which created the liability which the plaintiff say now exists; the fact that when the current loans were being negotiated, none of the plaintiff's officials nor any of the defendants ever thought about such indirect liability; the fact that all the persons concerned intended that the guarantees were given and accepted in order to provide adequate security only for the loans and not to secure any obligation arising out of the assignment of book debts; the fact that the guarantees contain no specific reference to said pre-existing indirect liability; the significant fact that the guarantees are for amounts identical to the bank loans; the fact that the only consideration received by the defendants for the giving of the guarantees was the loan of the monies to the companies; the covering letter of June 9, 1958, enclosing the guarantee in which the defendant A. W. Hale showed defendants' understanding or misunderstanding when he said, in part: "It was our understanding that we were personally guaranteeing the loan only"; the plaintiff manager's reply of June 10, 1958, wherein no reference is made to that statement; all of these circumstances, when taken together, lead to the irresistible inference and I find that, if the plaintiff's present interpretation of the guarantees is correct, it (the plaintiff) induced the defendants to think otherwise, and thereby misled them, and knew or ought reasonably to have known that that was so.

It is clear from the evidence that all the plaintiff's officials with whom the defendants negotiated, and the defendants, knew and understood that the real purpose of the guarantees was to guarantee only the bank loans, and had the parties been left to their own resources to prepare an appropriate document to set out their common intention, I have no doubt that they would, if properly advised, have prepared a document under which the defendants would have guaranteed the bank loans and nothing more....

In reaching my conclusions, I have not been unmindful of the need of the Courts to restrict the plea of mistake within narrow limits because of the dangerous confusion that would ensue if a man were able to disown his signature merely by proving that he misunderstood the contents or effect of a document. But there is ample authority, founded in good sense, that the Courts will relieve a person of his contract where a misunderstanding as to its true effect was induced, even though innocently, by the other party and where injustice would be done if performance were to be enforced. . . . And once it is shown that the misrepresentation was an inducing cause, it is no answer to suggest or prove that other considerations co-existed and co-operated with the misrepresentation in producing the result. See 23 Hals., 2nd ed., pp. 50–1.

In my view, the defendants, by signing the guarantees in question in these actions, intended to enter into a transaction fundamentally different than that which they actually signed, insofar as the guarantees purport to create liability beyond the bank loans, and that it would be not only inequitable but unconscionable not to relieve them from liability for the indirect obligations sued upon herein, which liability arose by reason of a unilateral mistake on the part of the defendants, induced by the plaintiff, to be inferred from their previous dealings.

The plaintiff submits that para. 13 of the guarantee, above quoted, is conclusive against the defendants and relies upon *Spelchan* v. *Long et al.* (1956), 2 D.L.R. (2d) 707, but in that case it was held that there were no misrepresentations as to the contents of the contract, and it is distinguishable also in several other respects. Paragraph 13 does not purport to say that the guarantor shall be precluded from equitable relief for any inducing misrepresentation, and if it did, it would be ineffective for that purpose. I hold that para. 13 of the guarantee is not a bar to the relief claimed herein by the defendants and in so doing I adopt the views expressed by Denning, L.J., in *Curtis* v. *Chemical Cleaning & Dyeing Co.*, [1951] 1 K.B. at pp. 808 *et seq.* and also in *Neuchatel Asphalte Co.* v. *Barnett*, [1957] 1 All E.R. 362, wherein he stated, in the latter case, at p. 365:

"It is a well settled rule of construction that, if one party puts forward a printed form of words for signature by the other and it is afterwards found that those words are inconsistent with the main object and intention of the transaction as disclosed by the terms specially agreed, then the court will limit or reject the printed words so as to ensure that the main object of the transaction is achieved. . . . We do not allow printed forms to be made a trap for the unwary.". . .

[At the opening of the trial the defendants amended their defence and paid into Court the full balance remaining due upon the loan to ABC and to Prince George, and denied liability on the indirect debts. In the result, there was an order for payment out to the plaintiff's solicitor of the moneys paid into Court and all the actions were dismissed.]

CURTIS *v.* CHEMICAL CLEANING AND DYEING CO., LTD. [1951] 1 All E.R. 631 (England. Court of Appeal). The defendants are cleaners and dryers. The plaintiff took a white satin wedding dress to them for cleaning. When the dress was returned it was found that there was a stain on it which had not been there when it was left for cleaning. The trial judge found that the stain was caused by the defendant's negligence. The defendants relied on a receipt which the plaintiff signed. The receipt set out her name and address and a description of the dress and in the bottom right hand corner under the amount to be charged, was printed: "This or these articles is accepted on condition that the company is not liable for any damage howsoever arising, or delay." The plaintiff was told she had to sign the document because she had to accept responsibility for damage to the beads and sequins on the dress. The trial judge awarded damages at £32 10s. The defendants appealed. The Court of Appeal dismissed the appeal. DENNING L.J.: "If the party affected signs a written document, knowing it to be a contract which governs the relations between him and the other party, his signature is irrefragable evidence of his assent to the whole contract, including the exempting clauses, unless the signature is shown to be obtained by fraud or misrepresentation. . . . What is a sufficient misrepresentation for this purpose? . . . In my opinion, any behaviour by words or conduct is sufficient to be a misrepresentation if it is such as to mislead the other party about the existence or extent of the exemption. If it conveys a false impression, that is enough. If the false impression is created knowingly, it is a fraudulent misrepresentation; if it is created unwittingly, it is an innocent misrepresentation. But either is sufficient to disentitle the creator of it to the benefit of the exemption. . . . In those circumstances, by failing to draw attention to the width of the exemption clause, the assistant created the false impression that the exemption related to the beads and sequins only, and that it did not extend to the material of which the dress was made. It was done perfectly innocently, but, nevertheless, a false impression was created. It was probably not sufficiently precise and unambiguous, to create an estoppel . . . but, nevertheless, it was a sufficient misrepresentation to disentitle the cleaners from relying on the exemption, except in regard to the beads and sequins. . . .

"The second point made by counsel for the defendant was that, even if there was an innocent misrepresentation, the plaintiff cannot, in point of law, avoid the terms of the contract. He said that an innocent misrepresentation gives no right to damages but only to rescission, that rescission was not possible because the contract was executed, and that in any case rescission was of no use to the plaintiff, because, once rescission has taken place, there would be no contract to sue upon. That is an attractive argument, but I do not think it is right. One answer to it is that an executed contract can in proper case be rescinded for innocent misrepresentation; and if the present contract was rescinded, the plaintiff could sue in tort for negligence, because any task undertaken must be done carefully."

QUESTION: If the "receipt" signed in the *Curtis* case had carried the words "None of our agents or employees has any authority to alter, vary or qualify in any way these terms and conditions" would the case have been decided differently?

3. THE PAROL EVIDENCE RULE

GOSS *v.* LORD NUGENT. 1833. 5 B. & Ad. 58; 110 E.R. 713 (England. King's Bench). DENMAN C.J.: "By an agreement in writing, the plaintiff contracted to sell the defendant several lots of land for the sum of £450, and to make a good title to them; and £80 was paid to him as a deposit. It was afterwards discovered that, as to one of the lots, a good title could not be made; and it was then subsequently agreed by the defendant, that he would waive the necessity of a good title being made as to that lot; and the plaintiff afterwards delivered possession of the whole of the lots to the defendant, which he accepted, but now refuses to pay the remainder of the purchase money, and he relies on the objection to the title.

"By the general rules of the common law, if there be a contract which has been reduced into writing, verbal evidence is not allowed to be given of what passed between the parties, either before the written instrument was made, or during the time that it was in a state of preparation, so as to add or subtract from, or in any manner to vary or qualify the written contract; but after the agreement has been reduced into writing, it is competent to the parties, at any time before breach of it, by a new contract not in writing, either altogether to waive, dissolve, or annul the former agreements, or in any manner to add to, or subtract from, or vary or qualify the terms of it, and thus to make a new contract; which is to be proved, partly by the written agreement, and partly by the subsequent verbal terms engrafted upon what will be thus left of the written agreement.

"And if the present contract was not subject to the control of [the *Statute of Frauds*] we think that it would have been competent for the parties, by word of mouth, to dispense with requiring a good title to be made to the lot in question, and that the action might be maintained. . . ."

HENDERSON *v.* ARTHUR. [1907] 1 K.B. 10 (England. Court of Appeal). COLLINS M.R.: "The defence set up by the defendant is that there was an agreement antecedent to the lease in point of time, by which the parties agreed that, instead of payment in advance of each quarter's rent in cash, the lessor should be satisfied by the lessee's giving in respect thereof bills at three months. Assuming that there was in fact such an agreement, the question is whether it is legally available for the purpose of defeating the claim of the lessor upon the covenant. It seems to me that to admit evidence of such an agreement as being so available would be to violate one of the first principles of the law of evidence; because, in my opinion, it would be to substitute the terms of an antecedent parol agreement for the terms of a subsequent formal contract under seal dealing with the same subject-matter."

MORGAN *v.* GRIFFITH
England. Exchequer. 1871. L.R. 6 Ex. 70

The plaintiff became tenant of the defendant on Michaelmas Day, 1867, on oral terms that included the signing of a lease. The plaintiff found the land was overrun with rabbits and when the lease was presented for signature he refused to sign unless the rabbits were destroyed. The defendant later promised to destroy them when the plaintiff threatened to quit. At Michaelmas, 1868, the lease was again tendered. The plaintiff refused to sign it, but the defendant repeated his promise. The plaintiff then asked to have the promise incorporated in the lease, which the defendant refused, although he repeated his promise. The plaintiff signed. The lease contained the plaintiff's promise that he would not hunt or destroy game, but preserve it and allow the defendant and his friends to hunt. The rabbits were not destroyed and the plaintiff quit at Michaelmas, 1870. He then brought this action. The defendant pleaded the parol evidence rule, but the trial judge admitted the oral evidence of his promise, and the plaintiff got a verdict. The defendant appealed this ruling of the judge.

KELLY C.B.: All that is possible has been said on behalf of the defendant, but it has failed to convince me. I think the verbal agreement was entirely collateral to the lease, and was founded on a good consideration. The plaintiff, unless the promise to destroy the rabbits had been given, would not have signed the lease, and a court of equity would not have compelled him to do so, or only on the terms of the defendant performing his undertaking. The decision of the county court judge must therefore be affirmed.

[Pigott B., who was of the same opinion, observed that the "verbal agreement" did not appear to contain any terms which conflicted with the written document.]

ANGELL *v.* DUKE

England. Queen's Bench. 1875. 32 L.T.R. 320

At the trial before Blackburn J., at the London Sittings after Hilary Term, it was proved that the defendant had let the house and furniture to the plaintiff by a written agreement dated the 24th March, 1873, and evidence was tendered of a promise alleged to have been made by the defendant before that date to put more furniture into the house, and to change some of that which was already in it. It was also alleged that there was a promise to the same effect made after the date of the written agreement.

The learned judge rejected evidence of the earlier promise, and ruled that the agreement was conclusive as to all that referred to taking the house and the furniture, and that the plaintiff could not recover upon any prior agreement made during the negotiation and not put into the written record of the agreement, and refused leave to move. He also held, that if the above ruling was right, the plaintiff could not show a fresh consideration, and ruled that there was no subsequent consideration and nonsuited the plaintiff.

COCKBURN C.J.: I am of opinion that there should be no rule. To allow the plaintiff to recover in this action would be to allow a parol agreement to conflict with a written agreement afterwards entered into. I agree with the cases which have been cited to this extent, that there may be instances of collateral parol agreements which would be admissible, but this is not the case here: something passes between the parties during the course of the negotiations but afterwards the plaintiff enters into a written agreement to take the house and the furniture in the house, which is specified. Having once executed that, without making the terms of the alleged parol agreement a part of it, he cannot afterwards set up the parol agreement.

[The opinions of Blackburn, Field and Mellor JJ. are omitted.]

NOTE. The view of Cockburn C.J. in *Angell* v. *Duke* at the trial may be contrasted with his views when, at an earlier stage in the same proceedings, it was argued on a demurrer that the *Statute of Frauds* barred the action as disclosed in the declaration. Cockburn C.J. there said [L.R. 10 Q.B. 174 at p. 127] ". . . We must see what the true history of the transaction is, and, of course, the sequence of events. . . . The agreement for a transfer of the interest in land or the house is posterior. . . . The other is something antecedent and collateral to that contract, that is, a separate agreement entered into in order to induce the intended tenant to accept the tenancy." It is difficult to tell from the reports whether the facts proven at the trial differed materially from the allegations in the declaration, which said, in part, "the plaintiff . . . objected to become tenant . . . upon the ground that the . . . premises were then in imperfect order and repair and insufficiently furnished . . . and the defendant then, in order thereby to induce the [plaintiff] to become . . . tenant . . . verbally promised the plaintiff that he, the defendant, would . . . do such work and repairs and send such additional furniture. . . ."

PYM *v.* CAMPBELL
England. King's Bench. 1856. 6 E. & B. 370; 119 E.R. 903

Campbell proposed to purchase Pym's invention and arranged a meeting at which Pym, Campbell and two engineers, Fergusson and Abernethie were to attend, and the engineers were to inspect and approve the invention. Pym arrived late and after the engineers had left. It was agreed that since the parties were together if the engineers could be found the sale might be arranged. Fergusson was found and approved, but Abernethie could not be found, but Campbell drew up a paper which both he and Pym signed and it was agreed that if later Abernethie approved the invention the paper should be an agreement and if he did not it should not be one. Abernethie did not approve.

The Lord Chief Justice told the jury that, if they were satisfied that, before the paper was signed, it was agreed amongst them all that it should not operate as an agreement until Abernethie approved of the invention, they should find for the defendant on the pleas denying the agreement. Verdict for the defendant.

Thomas Serjt., in the ensuing term obtained a rule nisi for a new trial on the ground of misdirection.

ERLE J.: I think that this rule ought to be discharged. The point made is that this is a written agreement, absolute on the face of it, and that evidence was admitted to shew it was conditional: and if that had been so it would have been wrong. But I am of opinion that the evidence shewed that in fact there was never any agreement at all. The production of a paper purporting to be an agreement by a party, with his signature attached, affords a strong presumption that it is his written agreement; and, if in fact he did sign the paper *animo contrahendi*, the terms contained in it are conclusive, and cannot be varied by parol evidence: but in the present case the defence begins one step earlier: the parties met and expressly stated to each other that, though for convenience they would then sign the memorandum of the terms, yet they were not to sign it as an agreement until Abernethie was consulted. I grant the risk that such a defence may be set up without ground; and I agree that a jury should therefore always look on such a defence with suspicion: but, if it be proved that in fact the paper was signed with the express intention that it should not be an agreement, the other party cannot fix it as an agreement upon those so signing. The distinction in point of law is that evidence to vary the terms of an agreement in writing is not admissible, but evidence to shew that there is not an agreement at all is admissible.

[The opinions of Lord Campbell C.J. and Crompton J. to the like effect, are omitted.]

LONG *v.* SMITH
Ontario. Divisional Court. 1911. 23 O.L.R. 121

Smith agreed on Saturday to buy a piano from Long for $575. The first price quoted was $650, but when Smith returned with his wife for a second look, the price was reduced. Neither Smith nor his wife knew anything about pianos and when Smith wanted to bring an expert on Monday to advise him Long insisted that if he did the price would have to go back to $650. The parties then reached what Smith, who was evidently a foreigner, called a "wordable understanding" that if he afterwards found that he had been overcharged, or that the piano was unsatisfactory,

Smith could return it and get back his $10, or exchange the piano for another. When Smith wanted this oral agreement added to the printed form of the contract of sale, Long said he could not alter it but that his word could be relied on. The printed form provided that it was the whole agreement. Smith had the piano for two or three weeks during which time he had it valued by an expert at $400. The piano was returned but Long would not accept it. Smith then left it on the sidewalk and Long took it in and kept it in "storage." The county court Judge dismissed Long's action for $565. Long appealed.

BOYD C. delivered the judgment of the Court.: . . . The legal objection is that it is not competent to give oral testimony *dehors* the terms of the writing, because it is there printed at the bottom, "This contract contains the whole agreement between myself and William Long" (the plaintiff). This form of expression is referable to the fact that the printed form is intended for the use of local agents, and provides that such persons are "not to make any promises, verbal or otherwise, outside of the agreement, or in any way to alter the same."

The present contract was made direct with Mr. Long, the principal, who, of course, could modify the printed form. The evidence now given goes to shew that the writing does not contain the whole agreement. There was a condition or promise entered into, upon the faith of which the contract was signed, which is not expressed therein. This assertion as to the whole being in writing cannot be used as an instrument of fraud; the plaintiff cannot ignore the means by which he obtained the contract sued upon, falsify his own undertaking, and, by the help of the Court, fasten an unqualified engagement on the defendant. The whole purchase was to be nullified if it turned out as a fact that there had been a gross overcharge. And such appears to be now the actual situation.

Then, apart from this shackle upon the truth, it is argued that it is contrary to the rule of evidence and the decisions of the Courts to allow oral testimony to be given which is inconsistent with or repugnant to the terms of the written instrument. No little difficulty and confusion has arisen in the application of this rule to the varying transactions of business life, which is not lessened by the discordant opinions of the Judges. But, without trying to reconcile differences, there is a well-marked line of cases establishing this doctrine, that evidence may be given of a prior or a contemporaneous oral agreement which constitutes a condition upon which the performance of the written agreement is to depend. The oral evidence may be such as to affect the performance of the written agreement by shewing that it is not to be operative till the condition is complied with. The enforcement of the contract may be suspended or arrested till the stipulation orally agreed on has been satisfied. Here there was to be in substance and in essence no bargain if the piano was not worth the price stated in the writing. At the outset, and before the signing of the contract, the defendant was practically prevented from getting correct information as to the value from a competent person, but it was left for him to satisfy himself on that point forthwith thereafter. Ten dollars he had paid, but there was no intention of paying any more till he was satisfied as to the truth of the representation as to value. . . .

Contract or no contract depended upon this test, whether the piano was or was not overcharged; that was a question of fact and one to be settled as a matter initiatory or precedent. The meaning of the transaction was that, though the writing was signed and $10 paid, yet, if it was found that there had been an overcharge, the $10 was to be returned, the piano taken back, and the contract at an end. This contemplated speedy action; and action was taken forthwith by the purchaser, and the result made known to the seller, and the piano was returned.

The purchaser was inveigled into signing the contract by the representation of the real value of the piano and the accompanying promise. The representation proving untrue, the failure to fulfil the promise introduces the element of deception and fraud on the part of the seller. This suggests another aspect of the case upon which this decision in favour of the defendant may be supported. The evidence here may very well support the finding that there was a deceitful representation as to the fair and reasonable value of the piano—a matter well known to the seller, but not to the purchaser—and the prudence of the purchaser laid asleep by the promise. Though this be not in writing nor mentioned in the written evidence of the contract, it may be relied upon to protect the purchaser when sued for the price. . . . In brief, this contract was induced by material representations which were untrue to the knowledge of the plaintiff, and he has no *locus standi* to enforce a contract so obtained.

Wemple v. *Knopf*, 15 Minn. 440, cited by Mr. Raney, is distinguishable. In that case the parol evidence was offered to shew that, though the obligation in writing was complete and imported an absolute engagement, yet it was subject to be defeated by subsequent revocation on the part of the defendant. That was in defeasance of the obligation already contracted, and so was repugnant to the writing. But here all the circumstances shew that the obligation was not to arise if the piano was not, at the time, of the value represented. The defendant did not agree to purchase a piano only worth in reality $400 for the expressed price of $575.

The judgment should be affirmed with costs.

FARAH *v.* BARKI

Ontario. Supreme Court of Canada. [1955] 2 D.L.R. 657

On March 8, 1951, Barki wrote out and signed a document stating "I hereby declare having sold today to Mr. Bryan Farah 650 shares of Joy Heat and Equipment Company for the price of $6500. payable by Mr. Farah on the 15th of December 1951." Farah read over and signed the document but in an action by Barki on the alleged contract Farah testified that while he read the document he did not appreciate that he was personally becoming the purchaser of the shares. He thought, as Barki had previously proposed to him, that the shares were to be transferred to him and that he should act for Barki in controlling the company and carry out a sale of the shares to one Joy, if that should prove possible. Farah had introduced Barki to Joy, who carried on the furnace business and he and Barki incorporated the company. Joy was given 350 shares at a par value of $10 and continued to manage the business. Barki invested $6,500, for which he got 650 shares. The company did very poorly. Arrangements were proposed, but which fell through, for the sale of Barki's shares to Joy. It was at this stage that Barki made the proposal to Farah on which he relied. The trial judge dismissed the action and remarked that the contract looked to him very much like a "smart trick" by which Barki endeavoured to recompense himself for a bad investment. The Ontario Court of Appeal allowed an appeal and concluded that the trial judge had made no finding of fraud. Farah appealed to the Supreme Court.

KELLOCK J. [after discussing the facts and evidence]: . . . In these circumstances, I think the finding of the learned trial Judge is to be interpreted as a finding of fraudulent misrepresentation on the part of the respondent as to the nature of the document which he asked the appellant to sign, and which he trusted he would sign, as he did, under the influence of the previous discussion without appreciating the real nature of the document, understanding that it was to be followed by a more formal document. The question therefore arises as to whether or not in such circumstances the appellant can successfully resist an action upon the document.

Winfield in his 13th edition of *Pollock on Contracts* at p. 384, quotes the language of Lord Chelmsford in *Wythes* v. *Labouchere* (1858), 3 De G. & J. 593 at p. 601, 44 E.R. 1397, namely: "It may be said generally that a man of business who executes 'an instrument of a short and intelligible description cannot be permitted to allege that he executed it in blind ignorance of its real character'."

Winfield goes on to state that: "Strictly this may be an *inference of fact* rather than a rule of law; but under such conditions the inference is irresistible."

This puts the point too rigidly. As stated by Farwell J. in *May* v *Platt*, [1900] 1 Ch. 616 at p. 623, fraud "unravels everything". The cases, however, such as that presently before the Court, in which a man may escape from a short and clear document, which he admits reading before signing, must be few. But that is not impossible. . . .

In *Blay* v. *Pollard*, [1930] 1 K.B. 628, where fraud was not pleaded, Scrutton L.J., in the course of his judgment, said at p. 633: "As a general rule mistake as to the legal effect of what you are signing, when you have read the document, does not avail. . . . It would be very dangerous to allow a man over the age of legal infancy to escape from the legal effect of a document he has, after reading it, signed, in the absence of an express misrepresentation by the other party of that legal effect."

The learned Lord Justice continued, however, quoting from *Fry on Specific Performance* as follows: " 'It equally follows that the mistake of one party to a contract can never be a ground for compulsory rectification, so as to impose on the second party the erroneous conception of the first. The error of the plaintiff alone may, however, where (but, it is conceived, only where) there has been fraud or conduct equivalent to fraud on the part of the defendant, be a ground for putting the defendant to elect between having the transaction annulled altogether or submitting to the rectification of the deed in accordance with the plaintiff's action.'. . . This rests on unilateral mistake in one party, fraud or conduct equivalent to fraud in the other party." . . .

[The opinions of Kerwin C.J.C. and Rand J. allowing the appeal are omitted. Cartwright and Fauteux JJ. concurred with Kellock J.]

ZELL *v*. AMERICAN SEATING CO.

United States. Circuit Court of Appeals (Second Circuit). 1943. 138 F. 2d. 641

Zell and the American Seating Co. orally agreed that Zell would try to procure defence contracts for American in consideration of $1,000 a month for three months if he was unsuccessful but if he was successful

American would pay him a commission of not less than 3% nor more than 8% of the purchase price of the contracts, the exact amount to be later determined by the parties. Right after this agreement was made the parties executed on October 31, 1941, a written agreement on similar terms, but with no mention of the commission. Instead the instrument provided that the $1,000 a month "will be full compensation, but the company may, if it desires, pay you something in the nature of a bonus." The parties also orally agreed that the previous oral agreement was still their real agreement and that the commissions were deliberately not mentioned because the president of American was concerned about adverse criticism. Just then there was unfavourable talk in Congress about contingent fee arrangments for war contracts. Subsequent written instruments extended the agreement for two periods of three months. Zell, at some considerable expense, procured contracts worth $5,950,000 for American which refused to pay him the 3% commission but paid him $8,950 and offered another $9,000 in full settlement. Zell claimed the commission. The District Court dismissed the action after considering the pleadings and affidavits. Zell appealed.

FRANK J.: . . . It is not surprising that confusion results from a rule called "the parol evidence rule" which is not a rule of evidence, which relates to extrinsic proof whether written or parol, and which has been said to be virtually no rule at all. As Thayer said of it, "Few things are darker than this, or fuller of subtle difficulties." The rule is often loosely and confusingly stated as if, once the evidence establishes that the parties executed a writing containing what appears to be a complete and unambiguous agreement, then no evidence may be received of previous or contemporaneous oral understandings which contradict or vary its terms. But, under the parol evidence rule correctly stated, such a writing does not acquire that dominating position if it has been proved by extrinsic evidence that the parties did not intend it to be an exclusive authoritative memorial of their agreement. If they did intend it to occupy that position, their secret mutual intentions as to the terms of the contract or its meaning are usually irrelevant, so that parties who exchange promises may be bound, at least "at law" as distinguished from "equity," in a way which neither intended, since their so-called "objective" intent governs. When, however, they have previously agreed that their written promises are not to bind them, that agreement controls and no legal obligations flow from the writing. It has been held virtually everywhere, when the question has arisen that (certainly in the absence of any fraudulent or illegal purpose) a purported written agreement, which the parties designed as a mere sham, lacks legal efficacy, and that extrinsic parol or other extrinsic evidence will always be received on that issue. . . . As noted above, the pleadings and affidavits are silent as to the matter of whom the parties here intended to mislead, and we cannot infer a fraudulent or illegal purpose. Even the explanation contained in plaintiff's brief discloses no fraud or illegality: No law existed rendering illegal the commission provision of the oral agreement which the parties here omitted from the sham writing; while it may be undesirable that citizens should prepare documents so contrived as to spoil the scent of legislators bent on proposing new legislation, yet such conduct is surely not unlawful and does not deserve judicial castigation as immoral or fraudulent; the courts should not erect standards of morality so far above the customary. . . .

Candor compels the admission that, were we enthusiastic devotees of that rule, we might so construe the record as to bring this case within the rule's scope; we could dwell on the fact that plaintiff, in his complaint, states that the acceptance of his offer "was partly oral and partly contained" in the October 31 writing, and could then hold that, as that writing unambiguously covers the item of commissions, the plaintiff is trying to use extrinsic evidence to "contradict" the writing. But the plaintiff's affidavit, if accepted as true and liberally construed, makes it plain that the parties deliberately intended the October 31 writing to be a misleading, untrue, statement of their real agreement.

We thus construe the record because we do not share defendant's belief that the rule is so beneficent, so promotive of the administration of justice, and so necessary to business stability, that it should be given the widest possible application. The truth is that the rule does but little to achieve the ends it supposedly serves. Although seldom mentioned in modern decisions, the most important motive for perpetuation of the rule is distrust of juries, fear that they cannot adequately cope with, or will be unfairly prejudiced by, conflicting "parol" testimony. If the rule were frankly recognized as primarily a device to control juries, its shortcomings would become obvious, since it is not true that the execution by the parties of an unambiguous writing, "facially complete," bars extrinsic proof. The courts admit such "parol" testimony (other than the parties' statements of what they meant by the writing) for a variety of purposes: to show "all the operative usages" and "all the surrounding circumstances prior to and contemporaneous with the making" of a writing; to show an agreed oral condition, nowhere referred to in the writing, that the writing was not to be binding until some third person approved; to show that a deed, absolute on its face, is but a mortgage. These and numerous other exceptions have removed most of that insulation of the jury from "oral" testimony which the rule is said to provide.

The rule, then, does relatively little to deserve its much advertised virtue of reducing the dangers of successful fraudulent recoveries and defences brought about through perjury. The rule is too small a hook to catch such a leviathan. Moreover, if at times it does prevent a person from winning, by lying witnesses, a law-suit which he should lose, it also, at times, by shutting out the true facts, unjustly aids other persons to win lawsuits they should and would lose, were the suppressed evidence known to the courts. Exclusionary rules, which frequently result in injustice, have always been defended—as was the rule, now fortunately extinct, excluding testimony of the parties to an action—with the danger-of-perjury argument. Perjury, of course, is pernicious and doubtless much of it is used in our courts daily with unfortunate success. The problem of avoiding its efficacious use should be met head on. Were it consistently met in an indirect manner—in accordance with the viewpoint of the adulators of the parol evidence rule—by wiping out substantive rights provable only through oral testimony, we would have wholesale destruction of familiar causes of action such as, for instance, suits for personal injury and for enforcement of wholly oral agreements.

The parol evidence rule is lauded as an important aid in the judicial quest for "objectivity," a quest which aims to avoid that problem the solution of which was judicially said in the latter part of the fifteenth century to be beyond even the powers of Satan—the discovery of the inner thoughts of man. . . . Today a court generally restricts its attention to the outward behavior of the parties: the meaning of their acts is not what either party or both parties intended but the meaning which a "reasonable man" puts on those acts; the expression of mutual assent, not the assent itself, is usually the essential element. We now speak of "externality," insisting on judicial consideration of only those manifestations of intention which are public ("open to the scrutiny and knowledge of the community") and not private ("secreted in the heart" of a person). . . . Perhaps nine-tenths of legal uncertainty is caused by uncertainty as to what courts will find, on conflicting evidence, to be the facts of cases. Early in the history of our legal institutions, litigants strongly objected to a determination of the facts by mere fallible human beings. A man, they felt, ought to be allowed to demonstrate the facts "by supernatural means, by some such process as the ordeal or the judicial combat: God may be for him, though his neighbours be against him." We have accepted the "rational" method of trial based on evidence but the longing persists for some means of counter-acting the fallibility of the triers of the facts. Mechanical devices, like the parol evidence rule, are symptoms of that longing, a longing particularly strong when juries participate in trials. But a mechanical device like the parol evidence rule cannot satisfy that longing, especially because the injustice of applying the rule rigidly has led to its being riddled with exceptions.

Those exceptions have, too, played havoc with the contention that business stability depends upon that rule, that, as one court put it "the tremendous but closely adjusted machinery of modern business cannot function at all without" the assurance afforded by the rule and that, "if such assurance were removed today from our law, general disaster would result. . . ." We are asked to believe that the rule enables businessmen, advised by their lawyers, to reply with indispensable confidence on written contracts unimpeachable by oral testimony. In fact, seldom can a conscientious lawyer advise his client, about to sign an agreement, that, should the client become involved in litigation relating to that agreement, one of the many exceptions to the rule will not permit the introduction of uncertainty-producing oral testimony. . . . The recognized exceptions to the rule demonstrate strikingly that business can endure even when oral testimony competes with written instruments. If business stability has not been ruined by the deed-mortgage exception, or because juries may hear witnesses narrate oral understandings that written contracts were not to be operative except on the performance of extrinsic conditions, it is unlikely that commercial disaster would follow even if legislatures abolished the rule in its entirety.

In sum, a rule so leaky cannot fairly be described as a stout container of legal certainty. John Chipman Gray, a seasoned practical lawyer, expressed grave doubts concerning the reliance of businessmen on legal precedents generally. If they rely on the parol evidence rule in particular, they will often be duped. It has been seriously questioned whether in fact they do so to any considerable extent. We seen no good reason why we should strain to interpret the record facts here to bring them within such a rule.

[The case was remanded for trial of the facts. The footnotes, which evidence much philosophic inquiry by the court, are omitted. The decision was reversed on appeal to the Supreme Court: 322 U.S. 709. *Per Curiam*: "In this case two members of the Court think that the judgment . . . should be affirmed. Seven are of opinion that the judgment should be reversed and the judgment of the District Court affirmed—four because proof of the contract . . . is precluded by the applicable state parol evidence rule, and three because the contract is contrary to public policy and void. . . ."]

U.S.A. *v.* MOTOR TRUCKS, LIMITED
Ontario. Privy Council. [1924] A.C. 196

By contract dated My 18, 1918, the respondent company contracted to machine high-explosive shells for the appellant Government; the contract provided for cancellation by notice in the event of anticipated termination of the war, and for payments to be made to the respondents thereupon. The payments were to include reimbursement for the cost of buildings, plant, etc., which the respondents had to add to their facilities for the purpose of carrying out the contract. Notice to terminate the contract was given in November 1918, and the parties thereupon negotiated as to the sum to be paid to the respondents. Ultimately a sum of $1,653,115 was agreed, which included $376,496, being the full amount which the respondents claimed in respect of land and buildings. After deducting from the above total a large sum which had been advanced by the appellant Government to the respondents, together with interest thereon, it was agreed that $637,812 was due to the respondents.

The parties accordingly entered into a formal contract dated October 7, 1919, but not actually signed until November 8. The contract provided that it should supersede the original contract of May 18, 1918, which was thereby terminated, and that the appellant Government should pay to the respondents the sum of $637,812 in full settlement for work and goods delivered and expenses incurred under the original contract; it further provided as follows: "(4) Title to all property specified in Schedule A, hereto annexed and made a part hereof, shall vest in the United States immediately upon execution of this agreement."

The land and buildings were not included in the schedule.

The agreed sum was paid on November 10, 1919, but the respondents subsequently denied the right of the appellant Government to possession of the land and buildings.

The appellant Government brought an action against the respondents in the Supreme Court of Ontario, claiming rectification of the schedule by the inclusion of the land and buildings, and specific performance of the contract as so rectified; alternatively they claimed repayment of the sum paid in respect of the land and buildings.

The trial judge (Kelly J.) found that the intention was that the land and buildings should become the property of the appellant Government. He ordered and declared that the respondents were trustees of the land and buildings for such person as the appellant Government might direct, with rectification of the schedule, the respondents to convey the land accordingly.

On appeal to the Appellate Division the judgment of Kelly J. was reversed and the action dismissed, Meredith C.J. dissenting. The judgments of the majority of the Court were based mainly upon conclusions of fact.

THE EARL OF BIRKENHEAD: . . . The question which requires the decision of the Board is whether or not it was the intention of the parties that the land and buildings, which had been paid for as claimed without deduction, should be inserted in schedule A and whether, if so, they were omitted therefrom by mutual mistake, so that rectification of an incomplete schedule should be ordered, or whether on the true interpretation of the intentions of the parties the respondents were entitled to receive all that they had expended upon acquiring the land and erecting the building, and, being so compensated, to retain both as their own.

The answer to these questions can only be found by reference to some legal considerations which their Lordships will hereinafter examine. If the parties intended that the lands and buildings should be included in schedule A, so that the omission in the instrument was accidental, rectification ought undoubtedly to be decreed. The Board, therefore, finds it necessary to examine the actions and the words of the parties at the relevant periods. And in enforcing the conclusions which will hereafter be stated their Lordships think it right to make it plain that they have entirely ignored the memorandum of the minutes of the meeting on October 7, 1919. In the opinion of the Board the terms of this memorandum were not admissible and should not have been admitted as evidence.

Their Lordships have reached the conclusion that both the appellants and the respondents intended that the land and buildings should be included in schedule A. That the appellants so intended has not been seriously disputed; and upon this point the Board entertains no doubt. Their Lordships, after giving careful attention to the matter, are no less confident that the respondents clearly understood that the award contemplated the transfer as owners to the United States of the land and buildings for which under its terms that Government had paid the respondents complete and generous compensation. . . .

It remains, therefore, to consider what view in fact and in law must be taken of the repondents' remaining contention that their agreement to part with the ownership of the lands and buildings (in which is implicit their agreement to insert them in the schedule) was produced by an error as to their legal rights under the original contract. Whether they possessed any such rights as those supposed under that contract it is not necessary to consider, for the trial judge found as a fact that those who represented the company were not at any single relevant moment forgetful of any right whatsoever which they may have possessed under that agreement. And their Lordships, so far from quarrelling with this finding, most expressly accept and approve it. Nothing need be added in parting with this contention, except that in all circumstances it required considerable hardihood to conceive and put it forward.

But even if the company's officials had made a mistake—in the circumstances wholly incredible—such a mistake could not in law have produced any effect upon the rights of the parties. For it is not contended, and could not be, that the mistake was shared by the appellants; and unilateral error, which in such a case as the present would hardly be distinguishable from carelessness, does not afford to the respondents any ground of defence in proceedings such as these.

It was further suggested that the present action involved an attempt to enforce a parol contract inconsistently with the principle of the Statute of Frauds. It is however, well settled by a series of familiar authorities that the Statute of Frauds is not allowed by any Court administering the doctrines of equity to become an instrument for enabling sharp practice to be committed. And indeed the power of the Court to rectify mutual mistake implies that this power may be exercised notwithstanding that the true agreement of the parties has not been expressed in writing. Nor does the rule make any inroad upon another principle, that the plaintiff must show first that there was an actually concluded agreement antecedent to the instrument which is sought to be rectified; and secondly, that such agreement has been inaccurately represented in the instrument. When this is proved either party may claim, in spite of the Statute of Frauds, that the instrument on which the other insists does not represent the real agreement. The statute, in fact, only provides that no agreement not in writing and not duly signed shall be sued on; but when the written instrument is rectified there is a writing which satisfies the statute, the jurisdiction of the Court to rectify being outside the prohibition of the statute.

The respondents, however, advance still a further point of law. They contend that a plaintiff was not allowed to sue in the old Court of Chancery for the specific performance of a contract with a parol variation. There seems no reason on principle why a court of Equity should not at one and the same time reform and enforce a contract; the matter, however, has been much discussed in the Court, and the balance of distinguished authority not unequally maintained. But the difficulty, which was almost entirely technical, has been, in the view of the Board, removed by the provisions of the Judicature Act, 1873, s. 24, which are reproduced in s. 16 of the Judicature Act of the Province of Ontario, ch. 56 of the Revised Statutes of 1914. This section provides that the Court, which is to administer equity as well as law, is to grant, either absolutely or on such reasonable terms and conditions as it shall deem best, all such remedies as any of the parties may appear to be entitled to in respect of any and every legal and equitable claim properly brought forward by them in such cause or matter, so that, as far as possible, all matters so in controversy between the parties may be completely and finally determined, and all multiplicity of legal proceedings discouraged.

The analogous provisions of the English Judicature Act are stated by Sir Edward Fry in his book on *Specific Performance*, 5th ed., para. 816. The learned author holds (and the Board agrees with him) that the controversy between the Chancery judges has now become obsolete, inasmuch as since the Judicature Act the Court can entertain an action in which combined relief will be given simutaneously for the reformation of a contract, and for the specific performance of the reformed contract.

Despite some differences in subsequent decisions, in which the principles of s. 24 of the Judicature Act have not been sufficiently considered, it has been held by P.O. Lawrence J., and by the Court of Appeal in the very recent case of *Craddock Brothers* v. *Hunt*, [1922] 2 Ch. 809, that the principle as laid down by Sir Edward Fry must now pervail.

Their Lordships are of the same opinion, and conclude that under this head no difficulty confronts the appellants in the present case.

The board has thought it proper to consider the matters raised in this appeal with some particularity, partly because of the importance of the case, and partly out of respect for the learned judges who took a different view in the Appellate Division. But on analysis the issue has proved to be extremely simple. Both parties intended the lands and buildings to be included in the schedule. These were inadvertently omitted. Rectification must follow unless some exceptional ground for excluding this remedy is advanced. The respondents have attempted only to show that they agreed to the schedule in its intended form by reason of an error as to their existing legal rights. This contention has been rightly negatived on the facts, and would, in any event, be irrelevant in law.

Their Lordships will, therefore, humbly advise His Majesty that this appeal should be allowed, the judgment of the Appellate Division of the Supreme Court set aside with costs, and the judgment of Kelly J. restored. The respondents will pay the costs of the appeal.

ALLEN *v.* FRITH [1940] 3 W.W.R. 463 (Manitoba. Court of Appeal). A piece of land was mistakenly omitted from an option agreement and the agreement for sale. The court applied *U.S.A.* v. *Motor Trucks, Ltd.*

TRUEMAN J.A.: "In *Barton* v. *Dawes* (1850), 10 C.B. 261; 138 E.R. 106, certain lands were fully described and delineated on a plan. In an action to try the right to a slip of land not included in the description or plan, evidence was offered by the defendant to show that it had always been occupied with certain closes mentioned in said description and shown on said plan, and treated by the owner as part thereof. It was held that as the description was clear the evidence was not admissible. If there is uncertainty in the description, extrinsic evidence is admissible to identify the property conveyed, that is, to connect the language of the deed with the particular property, but not to contradict the description in the deed. . . .

"Because of this rule it follows that the defendant, who asks here for rectification and specific performance, must establish that the omission to include in the writings the acreage in question was due to mutual mistake or contrary to the intention of both parties, a question to be determined on the circumstances, and, as well, it is now settled by recent authority, by parol evidence."

IMPERIAL GLASS LTD. *v.* CONSOLIDATED SUPPLIES LTD. 1960. 22 D.L.R. 2d 759 (British Columbia. Court of Appeal). Consolidated agreed to supply "Twin-Seal" window glass to Imperial, who had been invited to tender for its supply and installation by a sub-contractor on the construction of an elementary school at Kitimat. Imperial had previously phoned for a quotation and had given the specifications to an employee. In calculating the quotation a Consolidated employee mistakenly arrived at a total footage of 202.62 square feet instead of 2026.24 square feet. Consequently a price of $2,000, instead of about $5,000, became the basis of the tender to the sub-contractor on October 11, 1957. The tender was accepted on November 6. On December 11, Consolidated at the request of Imperial, who had had another quotation of $5,400, confirmed its quotation in a letter to Imperial: "We confirm herewith our quotation of $2,000.00 for supplying the following Twin-Seal Units. . . ." On December 13 Imperial asked for the glass and on December 17 Consolidated discovered its mistake and phoned Imperial. On December 23 it confirmed the call by letter and withdrew its offer as of December 17 on the ground of its "obvious error." Imperial claimed on the contract, which was to have been made by its acceptance (request for glass) on December 13 of Consolidated's offer of December 11. The trial Judge found that Imperial knew of Consolidated's error when it accepted on December 13. He dismissed the action. The Court of Appeal reversed him. *Farah* v. *Barki*, [1955] 2 D.L.R. 657 was distinguished as there was no fraud found in this case and the Court regarded *Bell* v. *Lever Brothers*, [1932] A.C. 161 as governing. COADY J.A.: ". . . Whether an inference of fraud, or conduct amounting to fraud, ought to be found in a particular case must depend upon the circumstances. In this case the only evidence from which such inference could be drawn was the failure of the appellant to disclose the mistake of the respondent before entering into the contract. It must be considered on the other hand, however, that the appellant, relying in good faith on the quotation given to him, and which the respondent must have known would be used by the appellant in tendering on some contract, had already committed himself to the subcontractor to supply the glass, basing his tender on the quotation received from the respondent. While it is true no binding contract had been made with the respondent at that time to supply the glass, the appellant relied on and used the quotation as it was expected he would and thus obligated himself to the subcontractor. Had no contract subsequently been made, he would have to bear his own loss for having proceeded as he did. But having done so, I am not convinced that the act on his part in failing to disclose to the respondent the error before entering into the written contract was conduct amounting to fraud. The mistake of the respondent was not induced by any representation, fraudulent or otherwise, of the appellant. . . . I cannot, under the circumstances of this case, hold that the conduct of the appellant, which may be open to question on moral and ethical grounds, amounted to fraud. While the appellant knew of the mistake, it was not a mistake induced by any representation made by the appellant. It was a mistake of the respondent arising from its own negligence or carelessness. The respondent cannot be relieved from the consequence of that mistake, the contract is not voidable and the appellant is entitled to damages. The appeal will therefore be allowed, and the matter referred back to the Court below to assess the damages."

NORTHWESTERN SECURITIES OF VICTORIA LTD. *v.* LEILA WHITE. 1962. 35 D.L.R. (2d) 666 (British Columbia. Court of Appeal). One Smith, a salesman for the plaintiff Company, at the request of a prospective purchaser, drew up an "Agreement of Purchase and Sale" on the Company's form, which the purchaser signed. Smith then took the Agreement to Mrs. White, the owner, and told her that out of the $1,500 down payment there would be a 5% commission to be paid to his firm. Mrs. White replied that she could not afford to pay the commission and that she needed a cash payment of the full $1,500. The agreement provided for a price of $12,900. Mrs. White said she wanted $13,500. Smith then filled in a new Agreement, calling for $13,500 with $1,500 down. Mrs. White signed the document, which contained a clause providing: "And I also agree to pay said agent a commission of 5% of the before mentioned sale price and authorize such agent to deduct the same from the initial payment on the date fixed for completion. . . ." The reference to "such agent" was clearly a reference to Smith, who only signed the document to acknowledge receipt of the deposit. Mrs. White claimed that she supposed the commission would in fact be paid by the purchaser which she thought was the practice in her native province of Alberta. She refused to pay and the Company sued on the written contract between Mrs. White and the purchaser to recover $675. The trial Judge held for the plaintiff. On appeal, the Court of Appeal reversed him on the ground of lack of privity.

DAVEY J.A.: "In the first place, the claim for commission as pleaded is for a sum of money payable under a written contract and not for remuneration for repondent's services as appellant's agent in effecting the sale. No other claim is made and the respondent must stand or fall on that contract. . . . It is to be observed that the only mention of the respondent in the agreement is as agent for the vendor and that the only part of the document respondent signed is the acknowledgement of the money paid to it on behalf of the appellant. In form and in substance, as well, the undertaking to pay the commission appears to be part of the acceptance. It would require the most explicit language to convince me in light of the circumstances in which the agreement was made and is to be construed that it contains an agreement with the respondent to pay it the commission. Since the agreement was not made with the respondent, it cannot sue upon it, and the action must be dismissed. I have no doubt the learned County Court Judge would have reached the same conclusion if this point had been taken before him. . . . Since no amendment is required to enable the appellant to raise this legal defect appearing on the face of the document on which the respondent sues, the fact that the point was not taken in argument below is not sufficient to induce us at this stage to allow an amendment and a new trial to enable the respondent to set up a new and different case. . . ."

BARTLETT *v.* STANCHFIELD

Massachusetts. Supreme Court. 1899. 148 Mass. 394; 19 N.E. 549

HOLMES J.: The only question presented by the exceptions concerns the defendant's liability for extra work and materials furnished in connection with a house which the plaintiff had been building for the defendant under a written contract. The contract contained the following clause: "And it is further agreed that should the owner, during the progress of said construction, request any alteration of, addition to, deviation from, or omissions concerning, the construction of said houses, as set forth herein, and in said plans and specifications, the same shall be made by the said Bartlett, and shall in no way affect this agreement, but shall be added or deducted from the amount thereof, by a fair and reasonable valuation; and that no charge shall be made for extra work or materials, unless the same is ordered in writing, and the price thereof agreed upon." The plaintiff's evidence was that the blind drains—one item in question—were put in during the progress of the work, and that the defendant promised to pay for them; and that the other items—picture moldings, covers for trays, and shelves—were furnished at the defendant's oral request, "after the completion of the house in conformity to the written contract." The evidence was objected to, and the court was asked to rule that, as the work and materials were not ordered in writing, and no price was agreed upon, the plaintiff could not recover. To this it might be enough to answer that, except as to the drains, there was evidence that the work was done after the contract had been performed, and independent of it. But, under the instructions of the court, the jury probably found that the terms of the written contract, if applicable, had been waived, and that the items had been furnished under a substituted oral contract.

The main argument for the defendant is that, if the work fell within the provisions of the contract, there was no evidence of a waiver. We are of opinion that there was evidence for the jury. Attempts of parties to tie up by contract their freedom of dealing with each other are futile. The contract is a fact to be taken into account in interpreting the subsequent conduct of the plaintiff and defendant, no doubt. But it cannot be assumed, as matter of law, that the contract governed all that was done until it was renounced in so many words, because the parties had a right to renounce it in any way, and by any mode of expression, they saw fit. They could substitute a new oral contract by conduct and intimation, as well as by express words.

In deciding whether they had waived the terms of the written contract, the jury had a right to assume that both parties remembered it, and knew its legal meaning. On that assumption, the question of waiver was a question as to what the plaintiff fairly might have understood to be the meaning of the defendant's conduct. If the plaintiff had a right to understand that the defendant expressed a consent to be liable, irrespective of the written contract, and furnished the work and materials on that understanding, the defendant is bound.

As to the drains, the evidence was that the defendant requested the plaintiff to build them, and promised to pay for them. The jury had a right to infer that the request and promise imported a renunciation of any terms in the written contract inconsistent with a duty to pay. As to the other items furnished later, it is stated that there was evidence tending to show that they were furnished at the defendant's own request, but it does not appear what the evidence was, or what were the circumstances or form of the request. So far as appears, certainly, the jury had a right to infer that the request imported a promise to pay, and a like substitution of an oral contract. The furnishing of the items was sufficient consideration for the substitution, as well as for the contract substituted.

Exceptions overruled.

CANADIAN STANDARD FORM CONSTRUCTION CONTRACT

Article 23. Changes in the Work—The owner, or the Architect, without invalidating the contract, may make changes by altering, adding to, or deducting from the work, the contract sum being adjusted accordingly. All such work shall be executed under the conditions of the original contract except that any claim for extension or reduction of time caused thereby shall be adjusted at the time of ordering such change.

Except as provided in Article 18, no change shall be made unless in pursuance of a written order from the Architect, and no claim for an addition to or deduction from the contract sum shall be valid unless so ordered.

Article 18. Emergencies—The Architect has authority to stop the progress of the work whenever in his opinion such stoppage may be necessary to ensure its proper execution. In an emergency affecting or threatening the safety of life, or of the structure, or of adjoining property, he has authority to make such changes and to order such work extra to the contract or otherwise as may in his opinion be necessary.

QUESTIONS. In view of *Bartlett* v. *Stanchfield* what effect should be given to articles 23 and 18? Compare Laidlaw and Young, *Engineering Law* 4th ed. p. 91, "The authority for extras should be established by a written order from the engineer if, under the contract, he has the power to issue such an order. Without the prescribed written order the contractor cannot succeed in a claim." Reference is made to *Toronto* v. *Metallic Roofing Co.* (1906), 37 S.C.R. 692. Do you think that case supports the authors' statement? Can you find an English authority to support the statement? The authors go on to point out, "If the work is not a variation of the work specified, but is independent of, or outside, the contract, the written order required for extras is not then required."

CHAPTER 7

ABSOLUTE AND CONDITIONAL PROMISES

The next chapters deal with problems arising from conditions in contracts. Three aspects of these problems are worth equal attention although only one or two may be apparent from the report of a case.

The most obvious aspect is the familiar one of prediction: If the condition is not expressed by the parties, when will the court imply it? And when will the court find that a condition has been fulfilled?

The second aspect is one of drafting: how could you avoid the difficulty in which the parties find themselves by a more carefully drawn contract? This question, as you may already have discovered, is not an easy one. Frequently the most obvious solution is not acceptable to one or the other of the parties, for reasons not always apparent.

The third aspect is the selection of the most suitable course of action to be followed when a promise is broken or a condition fails. You had an early introduction to this problem in Chapter 1, in the discussion of *Frost* v. *Knight* and *White & Carter (Councils) Ltd.* v. *McGregor.*

No settled nomenclature exists for the terms of a contract. So far in this casebook we have spoken of "promises," and, in a sense, a contract might be defined as a collection of promises. If it were no more than that, the study of remedies pursued in Chapter 1 might be a sufficient account of the problems arising from the breach of a promise. That is, the breach of the promise would give rise to a claim for damages, and in some cases, specific performance, and in some cases, restitution. But the promises in a contract are rarely absolute. There is usually some kind of condition attached, either express, or one that for some reason a court will imply. If a promise is subject to a condition, and the condition fails to happen, then obviously the promisor is relieved of his duty to perform his promise. That is merely the anticipated effect of the agreement. So far there is no problem. The difficulty arises when the existence of the condition, or its failure, is open to dispute. When disputes arise in the administration of the contract, it frequently becomes necessary to "imply" the existence and failure of a condition, in order to bring about what is felt to be justice between the parties.

The most common source from which to imply a condition is the counter promise that is consideration for the absolute promise. When the performance of the counter promise is thus regarded as a condition precedent to the promisor's duty to perform, the counter promise is sometimes called, itself, a condition. Then the failure to perform that counter promise, (i) as a breach of a promise gives rise to damages; (ii) as a failure of the condition excuses the promisor from further performance of his now conditional promise; and (iii) sometimes entitles the innocent party to obtain restitution of money or chattels transferred to the defaulting party, provided he has not enjoyed any benefit under the contract, or, in some circumstances, provided he can make effective restitution of the benefits he has enjoyed. You should have these three consequences clearly in your mind before you attempt any labels for them, because they are called by a variety of names in the cases, and considerable ambiguity attends their use, chiefly because the three consequences themselves are sometimes labelled by the same word.

Consequence two and three have unfortunately frequently been confused by use of a common label of "rescission." One is said to be entitled to "rescind the contract" when one has suffered a failure of condition. One is also said to be entitled to "rescind" when one is entitled to restitution. But the two consequences may be the results of mutually inconsistent legal theory. The "rescission" that takes place on failure of a condition may be in effect an affirmation of the contract, the innocent promisor is merely not performing because his duty to perform does not arise. Because it is an affirmation of the contract, the innocent promisor may also be entitled to damages if the condition is also a promise, as it frequently is. Of course, if the promisor does not carry out his promise that may affect the quantum of damages, but it does not otherwise affect his claim.

On the other hand, the legal theory behind the "rescission" that is accompanied by restitution is a denial or termination of the contract relationship. Upon the failure of the condition, or the inducement that led the promisor to make his promise, he is permitted to set aside the whole contract relationship, with the consequence that what he may have transferred to the promisee when the contract was in effect the promisee is no longer entitled to retain. Clearly, however, if this theory is applied, the promisor cannot claim damages for his expectation interest since there is no contract in respect of which the promisee is in default on a counter promise. The innocent promisor must therefore elect which of these two courses he will adopt—he cannot take both.

The word "rescission" is sometimes used with still another meaning. Sometimes the conduct of a defaulting party is such that the courts may say, to use their own language, that he has "evinced an intention no longer to be bound by his contract." Whether this conduct has to be such that the court would also say there was a failure of a condition is not too clear. The consequence of such conduct, however, is that the aggrieved party may treat it as if the defaulting party had offered to terminate the contractual relations, and in this respect it resembles somewhat the termination of the contractual relationship by mutual agreement, but the innocent party is still able to protect his expectation interest by an action for damages. And he is excused from further performance of his own promise. Read *General Billposting Company* v. *Atkinson* carefully in the light of this paragraph. He may also, instead, ask for restitution in appropriate cases. The sale of land cases, not dealt with in this book (see the course in Real Estate Transactions) suggest somewhat different results, due in part to specially applicable rules of equity.

It follows that clarity would be enhanced if the ambiguous word "rescind" were dropped from the vocabulary of lawyers. Since this is improbable, it is essential that you acquire the habit of thinking in terms of the consequences, and sorting out labels after the picture is clear in your mind. Not only is the word "rescind" ambiguously used, but also a number of expressions such as "repudiation," "breach of contract," "putting an end to the contract," and many others. In each case you must read to see what consequences are contemplated and then see whether the court has been consistent in its use of whatever terms it employs.

One further expression requires comment: In some cases coming within consequence three the innocent party is said to suffer a "total failure of consideration." The expression, of course, is not always used with the same meaning, but it refers, frequently, to a failure of a condition that has resulted in no benefits to the promisor, so that he may get restitution. But do not confuse this with "consideration" in the sense it is used in Chapter 2. There the making of a promise may be consideration. And if the performance of the promise happens to be a condition precedent to the duty to perform another's promise, the failure of that *performance* may be described as a failure of consideration. In one case, reference is to the making of the promise, in the other, it is to performance of the promise. So, there may be "consideration" and "total failure of consideration" in the same contract situation. The failure of consideration may also refer to the non-occurrence of an expected state of things not necessarily promised by either party, but acting as an inducement to one party to make a promise. See the coronation cases in Chapter 8.

Consider this example. If O promises to pay $50,000 to B, and B promises to build O a house according to specifications, there is a mutual exchange of promises, which is good consideration. Now if B fails to build, that is a breach of promise for which O can get damages. And if O fails to pay the $50,000, B can get damages. And if O has advanced $10,000 to B, who nevertheless fails to build, O could recover back his $10,000 on B's failure of consideration. The non-performance of the promise that was the consideration is a failure of consideration. So far, in this example, there is no mention of a condition. But suppose B fails to build the house and O refuses to pay the $50,000, if B sues for the $50,000, can he recover? If there is no implication of a condition precedent to O's duty to pay, he can. And so, also, can O sue B for his breach of promise. Hence there may be two law suits. Now if we *implied* that O's promise was subject to a condition that B first perform his promise, then B would fail in his action, because O would be excused from his duty to perform, or, his duty to perform would not arise. It should be quite clear, therefore, that if a court implies the condition to O's promise, it is changing the bargain struck by O and B. Usually the court denies that it is changing the bargain, and claims that it is giving fuller expression to the undeclared intention of the parties. Sometimes this may be so, sometimes it is not.

In this example, if you ask *why* did the court imply the condition you get at least one sufficient answer, that the implication of the condition made unnecessary one law suit. Sometimes a court will imply a condition where the reason is not so obvious. A student of the law should always ask, *why*? Sometimes the real reason is to do justice in cases where the literal application of previously accepted rules would seem to do injustice. In these cases the implication of conditions is often a less desirable alternative to restating, (or, if you wish, reforming) the law. It is less desirable because no one can be quite sure the next court will "feel" the same way about "justice." In each case care should be taken to see whether a restatement of the law in more direct language is not possible. Such a restatement may help lawyers and judges to keep clearly in mind what it is they are trying to do.

Sometimes the condition is said to be implied from the facts, that is, it is derived from an analysis of the conduct of the parties, and the words they have chosen to express, imperfectly, their intent. Sometimes the condition is said to be implied by law, that is, the court makes no real attempt to justify the condition from the particular facts, but implies it in order to settle a dispute in a just manner. Sometimes it may be literally impossible for the parties to have any intention—they simply do not contemplate the resulting events. In such a case the court may attempt to "imply" a condition that will help the parties reach a fair resolution of their conflict. Notice that Lord Mansfield in *Kingston* v. *Preston* speaks of "the intent of the transaction." Is this the same thing as the "intent of the parties"?

One of the principal problems in the remaining chapters is to decide when to imply a condition and when to limit the parties to their remedies in damages. Do not be misled by the linguistic practices of the court in this situation any more than in their use of words like "rescission." Look to see the realities behind these decisions, because in this way can you gain a real insight into the judicial process and the drafting of contracts.

We may return now to the third aspect of the problem in the remaining chapters, the choices of courses of action to be followed on breach of a promise or a failure of a condition or the inducement to enter into the promise. In reading the cases, ask whether an award of damages is an adequate remedy; whether restitution should be sought; what is the effect of doing nothing; what is the effect of continuing performance despite the failure of the condition (particularly in the cases in Chapter 9); can you demand something less than the promised act (particularly in the cases in Chapter 8); what is the effect of changing the course of action once it has been adopted. These and other courses of action are constantly before the innocent party, and it is the lawyer's task to help him make the best choice.

THE STRUCTURE OF A CONTRACT. At this stage you are turning your attention more frequently to the planning aspect of contracts and you might find it helpful to have some more specific picture of a carefully drafted contract. Needless to say common sense, not to mention the *Statute of Frauds,* demands that the parties be identified. This is usually done in a *recital* at the start of the document, which gives a number of particulars and may read: "This agreement is made this 10th day August, 1962, between John Doe, merchant of the City of Peterborough in the Province of Ontario (hereinafter called Doe) and Richard Roe, wholesaler dealer, of the same City (hereinafter called Roe), and witnesses that: . . .". But from that point on the agreement is peculiar to the circumstances of the case. Although thousands of standard forms are now in use, and any good form book will supply suggestions for clauses to accomplish more or less familiar objectives, the working out of the terms is a matter for individual study of the case. It would be futile to attempt to teach the drafting of contracts as such in a first year law course and only one piece of general advice is offered: Be sure you have found out as much as you possibly can from the party, or parties, about their needs and hopes, before you try to formalize it on paper. Apart from helpful hints to the draftsman, however, there is a matter of nomenclature that can be discussed here. The clauses in a contract, whether oral or written, may consist of promises or conditions. These two ingredients make up the terms of the contract. In addition, apart from the terms, there may have been statements of fact (or misstatements), commonly called representations (or misrepresentations), that may have induced a party to enter into the contract, although the statement is not intended to be a term of the contract. Sometimes such a statement, though not intended to constitute either a promise or a condition, will appear as a recital of fact at the start of the contract, often being introduced by the word "whereas". Sometimes the statements are not recorded in the written document, but are later conjured up by one party, hopefully to his advantage. Sometimes, as you have seen in some of the parol evidence cases, these statements are deliberately excluded from the contract. Needless to say, the Courts reserve unto themselves the final decision on the effect, if any, to be given to these statements, as well as to the terms of the contract.

You will find it useful in discussing the problems raised by the cases to use the suggested terminology consistently. One word of warning, however. The terminology suggested here, of *promises* and *conditions* as terms, and *representations* as non-terms, is by no means universally employed, and you will find that the language used in the cases may be confusing. Sometimes a promise, because its performance is a condition to another promise, is called a condition itself. This confusion of the promise with its performance does not make for clarity of thought. In addition to the word promise, there will be found the words "warranty," "stipulation," "agreement," "independent agreement," sometimes meaning the same thing, sometimes meaning "condition." The representation may be described as "mere," an "assertion," and sometimes it may be construed by the Court to be a "warranty" or a "condition." The case of *Behn* v. *Burness* illustrates this confusion of terms fairly well. The diagram here may be helpful in the adoption of a simple and consistent terminology for the purposes of class discussion.

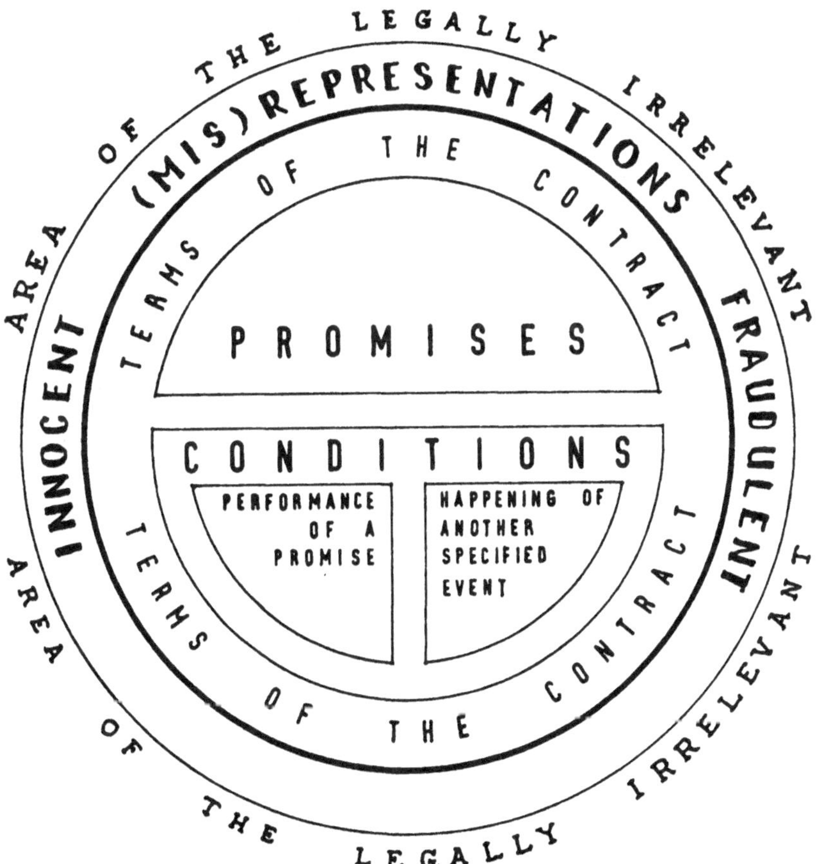

1. Effect of Conditions

BOONE v. EYRE

England. King's Bench 1777. 1 H. Bl. 273, note; 126 E.R. 160, note (a)

Covenant in a deed whereby the plaintiff conveyed to the defendant the equity of redemption of a plantation in the West Indies, together with the stock of negroes upon it, in consideration of £500 and an annuity of £160 per annum for his life; and covenanted that he had a good title to the plantation, and was lawfully possessed of the negroes, and that the defendant should quietly enjoy. The defendant covenanted that, the plaintiff well and truly performing all and everything therein contained on his part to be performed, he the defendant would pay the annuity. The breach assigned was the non-payment of the annuity. Plea: that the plaintiff was not at the time of making the deed legally possessed of the negroes on the plantation, and so had not a good title to convey.

To which there was a general demurrer.

Lord Mansfield: The distinction is very clear, where mutual covenants go to the whole of the consideration of both sides, they are mutual conditions, the one precedent to the other. But where they go only to a part, where a breach may be paid for in damages, there the defendant has a remedy on his covenant, and shall not plead it as a condition precedent. If this plea were to be allowed any one negro not being the property of the plaintiff would bar the action.

Judgment for the plaintiff.

QUESTIONS. As the report of the pleadings is written, is the defendant's covenant subject to an express condition? If so, why does Lord Mansfield set out a test for implying a condition?

DUKE OF ST. ALBAN'S v. SHORE

England. Exchequer Chamber. 1789. 1 H. Bl. 270; 126 E.R. 158

Debt for £500 the penalty of articles of agreement.

The declaration stated the agreement to have been made between the plaintiff and the defendant on the 30th of March, 1787, by which the defendant was to purchase of the plaintiff a certain farm with the appurtenances, together with an acre and half of boggy land, at the price of £2594 which was to be paid at Lady-Day then next.... Plea: "... that after the making of the said agreement, and before Lady-Day then next following, to wit, on the 20th of March A.D. 1788, the said duke cut down divers ... the said trees ... whereby the said duke disabled himself from performing ... for which reason, he the said William declined and refused to carry the said articles into execution on his part, as he lawfully might, &c."

Lord Loughborough delivered the judgment of the Court: It is clear in this case, that unless the plaintiff has done all that was incumbent on him to do, in order to create a performance by the defendant, (if I may use the expression,) he is not entitled to maintain the action. If he has not set forth a sufficient title, judgment must be against him whatever the plea is, and if the plea be a good bar, the same consequence must follow. It was argued on the part of the plaintiff, that the agreement respecting the trees was not a condition precedent, and therefore a breach of that agreement the case of *Boone* v. *Eyre* was cited; but in that case, though the Court of King's Bench held the plea insufficient, yet they laid down a clear and well founded distinction, that where a covenant went to the whole of the consideration on both sides, there it was a condition precedent; but where it did not go to the whole, but only to a part, there it was not a condition precedent, and each party must resort to his separate remedy; and for this plain and obvious reason, because the damages might be unequal. . . . We found our opinion on the present case, on the ground of the distinction in *Boone* v. *Eyre*, which we think a fair and sound one. Then the question is, whether the covenant of the plaintiff goes to the whole consideration of that which was to be done by the defendant? Now the duke clearly covenanted to convey an estate to the defendant, in which all the timber growing on the estate was necessarily included. The timber was not disjoined from the estate by the separate valuation of it. It was expressly agreed that all trees, &c. which then were upon any of the estates should be valued. But it is not to be permitted to a party contracting to convey land which includes the timber, by his own act to change the nature of it between the time of entering into the contract and that of performing it. There may be cases where the timber growing on an estate is the chief inducement to a purchase of that estate. But it is not necessary to inquire whether it be the chief inducement to a purchase or not; for if it may be in any sort of a consideration to the party purchasing to have the timber, the party selling ought not to be permitted to alter the estate by cutting down any of it. This is not an action of covenant where one party has performed his part, but is brought for a penalty on the other party refusing to execute a contract. But to entitle the party bringing the action to a penalty, he ought punctually, exactly, and literally, to complete his part. We are therefore of opinion that the plea is a good bar to the action, and on this we give our judgment . . . [for the defendant].

GRAVES *v*. LEGG

England. Exchequer. 1854. 9 Exch. 709; 156 E.R. 304

The defendants agreed to buy 300 to 350 bales of wool of fair average quality from the plaintiff to be shipped from Odessa with all despatch to Liverpool, Hull or London, "subject to . . . the names of the vessels to be declared as soon as the wool was shipped." Afterwards 333 bales of wool of the prescribed quality were shipped on the "Science" to Liverpool in safe and good condition. The defendants refused to take the wool because the plaintiff had failed to declare the name of the vessel as soon as he had promised, and as a result the defendants lost the market, which had since declined. Demurrer.

PARKE B. delivered the judgment of the Court: The question . . . is, whether the provision, that the names of the vessels should be declared as soon as the wools were shipped, was a condition precedent to the defendants' obligation to accept and pay for the wools according to the contract stated in the declaration, and under the circumstances stated in the plea.

This contract, we think, is to be construed with reference to some of those circumstances. It is stated in the plea, that the wool was bought, with the knowledge of both parties, for the purpose of re-selling it in the course of the defendants' business; that it is an article of fluctuating value, and not saleable until the names of the vessels in which it was shipped should have been declared according to the contract.

The declaration having averred, according to the 57th section of the *Common Law Procedure Act*, the performance of conditions precedent generally, the defendant proceeds in this plea to specify this condition of declaring the names of the vessels, as one on the breach of which he insists. The loss which he avers to have sustained by that breach is immaterial. The only question is whether the performance of the agreement was a condition precedent or not to the defendant's contract to accept and pay for the goods.

In the numerous cases on the subject, in which it has been laid down that the general rule is, to construe covenants and agreements to be dependent or independent according to the intent and meaning of the parties to be collected from the instrument, and of course to the circumstances legally admissible in evidence with reference to which it is to be construed, one particular rule well acknowledged is, that where a covenant or agreement goes to part of the consideration on both sides, and may be compensated in damages, it is an independent covenant or contract. . . . [The] reason . . . besides the inequality of damages, seems to be, that where a person has received part of the consideration for which he entered into the agreement, it would be unjust, that, because he had not the whole, he should therefore be permitted to enjoy that part without either payment or doing anything for it. Therefore the law obliges him to perform the agreement on his part, leaving him to his remedy to recover any damage he may have sustained in not having received the whole consideration. . . . [It] must appear upon the record that the consideration was executed in part. . . . When that appears, it is no longer competent for the defendant to insist upon the non-performance of that which was originally a condition precedent; and this is more correctly expressed, than to say it was not a condition precedent at all.

In this case, if the stipulation, that the names of the vessels should be stated as soon as the wools were shipped, was originally a condition precedent, it is so still. No other benefit was taken under the contract itself, as the consideration for the promise to pay the money, than the shipment and delivery of the goods by the named vessels; nor was any subsequently received by the acceptance of the goods or any part thereof. After such acceptance, the defendants would have been bound to pay the price, or the residue of it, and could not have insisted on the neglect to name in due time, but, if there had been any such neglect, would nevertheless have had their remedy for the damages by cross action on the contract to declare the names. In the state of things on this record, the simple question is, whether this contract was originally a condition precedent or not. Looking at the nature of the contract; and the great importance of it to the object with which the contract was entered into with the knowledge of both parties, we think it was a condition precedent, quite as much, indeed as the shipping of the goods at Odessa with all dispatch after the end of August. And with respect to the shipment itself, Mr. Blackburn [one of the Counsel] did not venture to contend that the performance of the plaintiff's contract in that respect was not a condition precedent.

The defendants, therefore, have a right to object to fulfill the contract on their part, as the plaintiff did not fulfill his, though they could no longer object to the plaintiff's non-performance, had they afterwards taken any benefit under the contract. [Judgment for the defendants.]

KINGSTON *v.* PRESTON

England. King's Bench. 1773. 2 Douglas, 689; 99 E.R. 437
(in argument in *Jones* v. *Barkley*)

This was an action of debt for non-performance of covenants contained in certain articles of agreement between the plaintiff and the defendant. The declaration stated: That, by articles made the 24th of March, 1770, the plaintiff, for the considerations thereinafter mentioned, covenanted with the defendant to serve him for one year and a quarter next ensuing, as a covenant servant, in his trade of a silk-mercer, at £200 a year, and, in consideration of the premises the defendant covenanted that, at the end of the year and a quarter, he would give up his business of a mercer to the plaintiff, and a nephew of the defendant or some other person to be nominated by the defendant, and give up to them his stock in trade, at a fair valuation; and that, between the young traders, deeds of partnership should be executed for fourteen years, and from and immediately after the execution of the said deeds the defendant would permit the said young traders to carry on the said business in the defendant's house.

Then the declaration stated a covenant by the plaintiff, that he would accept the business and stock-in-trade, at a fair valuation, with the defendant's nephew, or such other person, &c., and execute such deeds of partnership, and, further, that the plaintiff should and would, at and before the sealing and delivery of the deeds, cause and procure good and sufficient security to be given to the defendant, to be approved of by the defendant, for the payment of £250 monthly to the defendant, in lieu of a moiety of the monthly produce of the stock in trade, until the value of the stock should be reduced to £4000. Then the plaintiff averred that he had performed and been ready to perform his convenants, and assigned for breach on the part of the defendant, that he had refused to surrender and give up his business at the end of the said year and a quarter.

The defendant pleaded: 1. That the plaintiff did not offer sufficient security; and, 2, that he did not give sufficient security for the payment of the £250, &c.

And the plaintiff demurred generally to both pleas.

Lord Mansfield, in delivering the judgment of the Court, expressed himself to the following effect: There are three kinds of covenants: 1. Such as are called mutual and independent, where either party may recover damages from the other for the injury he may have received by a breach of the covenants in his favor, and where it is no excuse for the defendant to allege a breach of the covenants on the part of the plaintiff. 2. There are covenants which are conditions and dependent, in which the performance of one depends on the prior performance of another, and therefore, till this prior condition is performed, the other party is not liable to an action on his covenant. 3. There is also a third sort of covenants, which are mutual conditions to be performed at the same time; and in these, if one party was ready and offered to perform his part, and the other neglected or refused to perform his, he who was ready and offered has fulfilled his engagement, and may maintain an action for the default of the other though it is not certain that either is obliged to do the first act. His lordship then proceeded to say, that the dependence or independence of covenants was to be collected from the evident sense and meaning of the parties, and that, however transposed they might be in the deed, their precedency must depend on the order of time in which the intent of the transaction requires their performance. That, in the case before the Court, it would be the greatest injustice if the plaintiff should prevail. The essence of the agreement was, that the defendant should not trust to the personal security of the plaintiff, but, before he delivered up his stock and business, should have good security for the payment of the money. The giving such security, therefore, must necessarily be a condition precedent. Judgment was accordingly given for the defendant, because the part to be performed by the plaintiff was clearly a condition precedent.

RULES OF PRACTICE

Ontario. Supreme Court. 1960

148. Any condition precedent, the performance or occurrence of which is intended to be contested, shall be distinctly specified in his pleading by the party relying thereon, and an averment of the performance or occurrence of all conditions precedent necessary for the case by the plaintiff or defendant shall be implied in his pleading.

McDONALD *v.* MURRAY

Ontario. Court of Appeal. 1885. 11 O.A.R. 101

PATTERSON J.A.: This action is brought to recover $40,795, mentioned in an agreement which is in these words:

"Winnipeg, February 23, 1882.

Memorandum of Agreement between John McDonald, of the City of Winnipeg, Gentleman, and Captain James Murray, of St. Catharines, and Robert Cuthbert, of Toronto, Ontario.

The said McDonald sells, and the said Murray and Cuthbert agree to purchase Lots five (5) and six (6), Main Street, of Block three (3), Hudson Bay Reserve, at and for the sum of sixty thousand dollars, payable as follows: $4,000 to be paid at the signing hereof, $40,795 to be paid within sixty (60) days from the date hereof, and the balance, $15,205, to be on mortgage at seven per cent."

The plaintiff, in his statement of claim, sets out the agreement, and avers that he has always been ready and willing to complete the sale and purchase and to execute and deliver to the defendants a proper conveyance of the said lands and premises, and that all conditions were fulfilled, and all things happened, and all times elapsed, necessary to entitle him to a performance of the agreement by the defendants on their part.

He admits payment of the $4,000 at the time of the making of the agreement, and complains of the non-payment of the $40,795, saying nothing as to the $15,205, and giving no reason why he makes no claim in respect of that sum.

The defendants in their pleading deny the alleged agreement; and also allege that the plaintiff has no title to the land, and that he was not owner and cannot give a good title to the defendants; on which account they ask to have the $4,000 paid back to them. . . .

It seems to have been conceded that nothing had been done from the time of the making of the agreement, when the $4,000 had been paid, till the commencement of the action, which was on the 8th May, 1882, two and a half months after the date of the agreement. . . . No title whatever in the plaintiff was shewn.

Upon this state of facts the learned Judge pronounced the following judgment:

"It appearing by the evidence and statement of claim that the action is for the recovery of the purchase money of land, and that the time for completing the transaction on both sides had arrived before the commencement of the action; and it further appearing by the evidence on behalf of the plaintiff that another person is part owner of the land; and no tender of a conveyance to the defendants, or to the defendant Murray, and the assignee of the defendant Cuthbert, having been made, I dismiss the action, with full costs, without prejudice to the plaintiff's right to bring a fresh action, or take any other proceeding that he would have had a right to take if this action had not been brought."

The Divisional Court of the Common Pleas Division having set aside that judgment and ordered a new trial, the defendants have appealed to this Court.

We are not at present required to consider the rights and remedies which would have been recognized and administered by a Court of Equity, on a bill filed by either party for specific performance of the contract. Those rights and remedies may of course be now asserted or pursued in the High Court of Justice; but the present action is not founded upon them. The plaintiff asserts a common law claim for payment of the purchase money of the land, and insists on his right to payment of that money notwithstanding that he has not conveyed, and is not able, as far as the evidence discloses, to convey the land to the defendants.

The question presented is the construction of the contract.

It is a question about which one would scarcely expect to find much difficulty.

When people bargain together, whether it is to barter one piece of property for another, or to exchange property for money, each party ordinarily expects to receive what he bargains for when he parts with what he is to give. If the intention is that either of them is to part with his property, and take his chance of the other afterwards performing his part, or paying damages for his default, it is not the ordinary transaction of sale or exchange, and when it is intended we may reasonably expect to find some express declaration of that intention.

I understand the view of the Court below to be that there was in this case such an intention; that the agreement to pay the large sum of $40,795 was independent of any agreement expressed or implied to convey the land; and that the defendants agreed to pay the money at the named day, not because they were, at or before that day, to receive the land, but because they, without further security than the implied promise of the plaintiff, relied upon his being able at some later time to convey the land, and upon his conveying it to them at that later time.

They would not even have the security of an equitable title to the land; because, as the learned Chief Justice pointed out in delivering the judgment of the Court, it was not essential that the plaintiff should himself have any title to the land until the time arrived for the conveyance to the defendants.

No person, be he lawyer or layman, would, from reading the document without embarrassment from decisions or dicta, gather from it that the defendants were to pay more than the substantial deposit of $4,000, even if that sum was intended to be paid, without receiving something for their money beyond the word of the plaintiff.

The difficulty has arisen from the supposed application to this contract of one or more of the rules laid down by Mr. Serjeant Williams in his notes under *Pordage* v. *Cole* (1668), 1 Wms. Saund. 548, Ed. 1871; 85 E.R. 449, 451–4, for determining when covenants are dependent, and when mutual or independent.

The purpose of rules of construction is to lead us to the real intention of the parties to the instrument. Fixed and technical rules must be cautiously applied; and we may sometimes require to resist a tendency, which is strongest when rules are well defined, to adopt a procrustean method of construction in order to make the contract fit the rules. . . .

From the judgment of Chief Justice Wilson, I gather that the reference in the contract to the mortgage for $15,205 was treated as indicating that the mortgage transaction was to take place *after* the payment of the $40,795, and thus pointing to a later date than the date fixed for that payment for completing the title. . . .

In my opinion we cannot attach to the reference to the mortgage the significance which seems to have been attributed to it in the Court below. I think we may lay it out of sight, and deal with the agreement as one by which the time for the payment of the instalment now demanded is fixed, while no time is named for the making of title or the execution of the conveyance.

When an agreement simply declares that one shall sell and another buy for a stated price, it is undisputed that the conveyance and the payment are to be contemporaneous acts; when we read an agreement in that form we find nothing to indicate that either party meant himself, or expected the other, to give without receiving. Why should there be a difference when the time for payment happens to be postponed to a fixed day, nothing being said in either case about the conveyance?

The passages cited from text books by my Brother Burton are distinctly against the recognition of such a distinction, and I propose to shew that it is not supported by the decisions of the Courts.

The plaintiff alleges that he was always ready and willing to convey, and the defendants traverse that allegation.

The Chief Justice in the Court below treats the allegation as immaterial because, as he holds, the time for conveying had not arrived until after the end of the sixty days, when, if ever, the plaintiff's right of action accrued; and because the contract would be satisfied by his putting himself in a position to give or procure a good title when the time came.

I think the time for conveying had arrived. On that point I cannot take his Lordship's view of the contract.

But he further holds that, if the duty to convey was not postponed, the averment of readiness and willingness was all that was required, and that the issue on that averment had not been tried, wherefore it was proper to grant the new trial.

In connection with this he states the general rule of law as being, in his opinion, clear that the plaintiff was not obliged to tender a conveyance to the defendants, but that it was the defendants' duty to prepare it and to tender it to the plaintiff for execution. . . .

Now, accepting, for the sake of the present argument, the doctrine which may perhaps not be so free from doubt with us as it has come to be, in modern times, in England, that it is the purchaser's duty to prepare the conveyance and tender it for execution, the vendor is nevertheless bound to shew title, before the purchaser can prepare a conveyance he must at least be informed who is to convey. Therefore the plaintiff cannot entitle himself to be paid for land which he has not conveyed, by the fact that no deed has been tendered, unless he shews performance on his own part by deducing title. Until title is shewn the defendants cannot be in default by not tendering a deed, and in the absence of such default, I find nothing in the agreement to justify the conclusion that the plaintiff can insist on payment of this money.

A considerable number of cases have been cited to us. Some of them will require more full examination than the others, the earliest being *Pordage* v. *Cole*, which was decided in 1668, and the latest *Marsden* v. *Moore* (1859), 4 H. & N. 500; 157 E.R.936, nearly two hundred years afterwards.

Marsden v. *Moore*, being the latest case which has any very direct bearing on the question before us, though not the latest that turned on the subject of dependent or independent covenants, it may be useful to discuss it first.

The plaintiff agreed to sell to the defendants one-fourth part of a mining sett for £250 and the defendants agreed to purchase at that price. A company was to be formed and registered, and the defendants agreed that as soon as the company should be registered they would pay to the plaintiff the £250. To an action to recover that sum the defendants pleaded that the plaintiff had not any title to the one-fourth part of the mining sett, nor any right or title to convey the same; and that the plaintiff had never been ready and willing to convey. These pleas were demurred to, raising questions very much like those now in discussion, and the judgments, which are not long, are so apposite that I shall read them in full. Pollock C.B., p. 503, "We are all of opinion that the pleas are good and that the defendants are entitled to judgment. The question is, what did the parties mean by the agreement declared on, whether each party is entitled to insist on performance by the other, without reference to his capacity to perform his own part of the agreement. The plea sets out an agreement by which 'as soon as the company registered, with limited liability,' the defendants agree to pay to the plaintiff the sum of £250 'as hereinbefore stated'; that is as the purchase of a mining sett. I do not think that the reference to the uncertain period depending upon the registration of the company brings the case within the rule laid down in *Pordage* v. *Cole*. It is essential to a contract of buying and selling that one shall pay, the other sell or convey. On that ground this case is distinguishable from *Pordage* v. *Cole*. In such cases each party intends that the other shall perform his part, and not to rely on a right of action. Therefore in the present case the plaintiff is not in a condition to maintain the action."...

Upon the whole I am of the opinion that the views of the law enunciated in *Marsden* v. *Moore*, in place of conflicting with the earlier decisions, are in harmony with the general current of authority, and that they relieve us from any fear of violating settled rules of construction when we give effect to what we cannot avoid feeling to have been the real understanding of the parties to this contract, by holding that the plaintiff is not entitled to demand payment of the money now sued for without performing his part of the contract by making a good conveyance of the land, or at least deducing such title as will enable the defendants to prepare and tender a deed for execution. Until this is done it cannot be truthfully affirmed that the plaintiff is ready and willing to convey. That issue was for him to establish, and it was a material issue. Having failed to establish it, he was properly nonsuited, and therefore this appeal should be allowed, with costs.

[The opinions of Burton J.A. and Rose J.A. to the same effect are omitted. Hagarty C.J.O. dissented, purporting to follow the rule set out in 1668 in *Pordage* v. *Cole*: "if a day be appointed for payment of money or part of it, or for the doing any other act, and the day is to happen or may happen before the thing which is the consideration of the money or other act is to be performed, an action may be brought for the money, or for not doing such other act before performance, for it appears that the party relied upon his remedy and did not intend to make the performance a condition precedent, and so it is when no time is fixed for performance of that which is the consideration of the money or other act."]

NOTE. As to preparation of a conveyance, see now, *The Vendors and Purchasers Act*, R.S.O. 1960, c. 414, section 4 of which provides that unless otherwise stipulated in the agreement, "the conveyance shall be prepared by the vendor and the mortgage, if any, by the purchaser."

PANOUTSOS *v.* RAYMOND HADLEY CORPORATION OF NEW YORK

England. Court of Appeal. [1917] 2 K.B. 473

By a contract in writing made in London and dated September 27, 1915, which was made on the printed form of the "London Flour Trade Association. American Flour Contract," the Raymond Hadley Corporation of New York (herein called the sellers), who had also a place of business in London, sold to Panoutsos (herein called the buyer) 4000 tons of flour to be despatched from the Atlantic seaboard by steamer or steamers to Greece as per bills of lading dated not later than November 7, 1915; "each shipment shall be deemed a separate contract"; and there was this clause written into the contract: "Cash against documents in New York. Payment by confirmed bankers' credit." Any dispute arising out of the contract was to be referred to arbitration according to the printed rules indorsed thereon.

On October 16 the National Bank of Commerce of New York wrote to the sellers in New York stating that they had been requested to open a credit in favour of the sellers for about $270,000 in respect of the shipment of 4,000 tons of flour shipped up to November 7, 1915, and adding: "In advising you that this credit has been opened we are acting merely as agent for our foreign correspondents and cannot assume any responsibility for its continuance." This letter showed that the credit was not irrevocable and therefore was not a "confirmed bankers' credit." The sellers, however, on October 21 and again on October 27, 28, 29, and 30 made shipments of flour in part fulfilment of the contract, for which they were duly paid by the New York bank in pursuance of the credit in exchange for shipping documents. Meanwhile on October 27, the sellers took exception to the credit as not being irrevocable. On November 15 they requested the buyer to extend the time for the shipment of the balance of the flour from November 7 to November 30, and to this the buyer agreed. On November 25 the sellers notified the buyer that the balance of their contract was cancelled on the ground (so far as material) that the buyer had failed to perform the condition as to "payment by confirmed bankers' credit." The buyer refused to accept the cancellation, and the dispute was referred to arbitration. The arbitrators found that the credit was not a confirmed bankers' credit within the meaning of the contract, but that the sellers took no exception to it at the time it was opened.

Before the arbitrators the sellers contended that the buyer had failed to comply with the conditions of the contract, as he had failed to open a credit at New York, which would be irrevocable until November 30; and that the fact that they had made shipments without insisting on this condition did not release the buyer in respect of subsequent shipments, especially having regard to the term of the contract that "each shipment shall be deemed a separate contract." The buyer contended that the sellers had accepted as satisfactory the credit which had been opened, and, having made a shipment under it, had waived any possible objection to it and could not repudiate their obligation to ship the balance of the flour, or could not do so without giving due notice to him so as to enable him to remove any valid objection and furnish such a credit as would satisfy them.

The arbitrators awarded that the sellers were in default in not shipping the balance of the flour in accordance with the contract, and that they should pay a certain sum as damages.

The question for the opinion of the Court was whether or not upon the above facts there was any evidence upon which the arbitrators could properly find that the sellers had waived the term in the contract that payment should be by confirmed bankers' credit.

If the Court should be of opinion that the question should be answered in the affirmative, then the award was to stand; if in the negative, then the award was to be in favour of the sellers.

Bailhache J. held that when the sellers knew that the credit was not in order, and yet proceeded to act upon it as if it was in order, they must be taken to have waived the informality so long as they chose to act upon that credit, but that they were not bound to act upon it to the end merely because they acted upon it at first and waived the informality up to a point. In his opinion the sellers could at any time insist upon the credit being put in order, but if they desired to cancel the contract because the credit upon which they had acted was not in order they must give reasonable notice to the buyer of their intention to do so; which they had not done. He therefore confirmed the award. The sellers appealed.

VISCOUNT READING C.J.: . . . The question put to the Court is "whether or not upon the above findings of fact"—to which must now be added "coupled with our findings of fact"—"there was any evidence upon which the arbitrators could properly find that the sellers had waived the term in the contract that payment should be by confirmed bankers' credit." It was therefore admitted that there was no confirmed bankers' credit, but the buyer contended that there had been a waiver of that condition of the contract. In answer to that the sellers said that there had been no such waiver, and if there had been a waiver that they were entitled at any time to insist upon the condition being performed. The buyer replied that no doubt the sellers were entitled to insist upon the performance of the condition, but that, having waived its performance hitherto, they must give reasonable notice to the buyer of their intention to insist upon its performance in the future so as to give him an opportunity of putting the credit right. Bailhache J. held that the sellers must be taken to have waived the performance of the condition, that the buyer was entitled to reasonable notice, and that such notice had not in fact been given. He therefore answered the question in favour of the buyer.

In my opinion the learned judge was right. It is open to a party to a contract to waive a condition which is inserted for his benefit. If the sellers chose to ship without the safeguard of a confirmed bankers' credit, they were entitled to do so, and the buyer performed his part of the contract by paying for the goods shipped, though there was no confirmed bankers' credit, inasmuch as that condition had been waived. If at a later stage the sellers wished to avail themselves of the condition precedent, in my opinion there was nothing in the facts to prevent them from demanding the performance of the condition if they had given reasonable notice to the buyer that they would not ship unless there was a confirmed bankers' credit. If they had done that and the buyer had failed to comply with the condition, the buyer would have been in default, and the sellers would have been entitled to cancel the contract without being subject to any claim by the buyer for damages.

In *Bentsen* v. *Taylor, Sons & Co.*, [1893] 2 Q. B. 283, Bowen L.J. stated the law as to waiver thus: "Did the defendants by their acts or conduct lead the plaintiff reasonably to suppose that they did not intend to treat the contract for the future as at an end, on account of the failure to perform the condition precedent?" Reading sellers for defendants and buyer for plaintiff in that passage, it applies exactly to the present case. The sellers did lead the buyer to think so, and when they intended to change that position it was incumbent on them to give reasonable notice of that intention to the buyer so as to enable him to comply with the condition which up to that time had been waived.

The case of *In re Tyrer & Co. and Hessler & Co.*, 6 Com. Cas. 143; 7 Com. Cas. 166 was cited as an authority for the proposition that the moment the sellers chose to avail themselves of the failure to perform the condition precedent they could put an end to the contract without giving the buyer an opportunity of remedying the default which had hitherto been waived. That case is not an authority for that proposition. It shows that, where there are stipulated times in a charterparty for payment of the hire of a ship and a power to withdraw the ship if the payment is not made at the stipulated time, the mere fact that there has been default in payment at one or more stipulated times, of which advantage has not been taken, does not entitle the party in default at a subsequent time to a notice so as to enable him to comply with the condition before the right to withdraw arises. That is a totally different case from the present. I cannot find any authority to support the proposition that, when one party has led another to believe that he may continue in a certain course of conduct without any risk of the contract being cancelled, the first-mentioned party can cancel the contract without giving any notice to the other so as to enable the latter to comply with the requirement of the contract. It seems to me to follow from the observations of Bowen L.J. in *Bentsen* v. *Taylor, Sons & Co.* that there must be reasonable notice given to the buyer before the sellers can take advantage of the failure to provide a confirmed bankers' credit. That is the decision of Bailhache J.

The only question which remains is whether reasonable notice has been given. We have more material before us than Bailhache J. had when he came to the conclusion that no reasonable notice had been given. I am not prepared to draw the inference of fact that reasonable notice had been given before the sellers cancelled the contract. If notice had been given on October 27, and on November 25 the sellers had cancelled the contract, I should have thought that that would have been ample notice to enable the buyer to provide the confirmed credit in New York. But I cannot find any such notice on the part of the sellers of their intention to insist upon the performance of the condition. . . .

The result is that the decision of Bailhache J. is right, and the appeal must be dismissed.

[Lord Cozens-Hardy M.R. and Scrutton L.J. agreed.]

TURNEY AND TURNEY *v.* ZHILKA. 1959. 18 D.L.R. (2d) 497 (Ontario. Supreme Court of Canada). A contract for the sale of "all and singular the land and not buildings situate on the East side of the 5th Line west in the township of Toronto and known as 60 acres or more having frontage of about 2046 feet on 5th Line more or less, by a depth of about . . . feet, more or less (lot boundaries about as fenced), being part of west ½ lot 5 Con 5 west" contained a condition, "Providing the property can be annexed to the Village of Streetsville and a plan is approved by the Village Council for subdivision." The vendor only owned 62.37 acres, but he thought he had 65 acres and that he could retain five acres around his buildings. The purchaser claimed 60.87 acres, leaving the vendor 1.5 acres. The Village of Streetsville did not annex the property. An action for specific performance by the purchaser, was dismissed. As to the defence of non-compliance with the *Statute of Frauds*, the Court held that there was not only lack of sufficient certainty of description, "but the evidence makes it quite clear that the parties never reached any agreement, oral or written, on the quantity or description of the land to be retained or the land to be conveyed." The purchaser was willing to waive the annexation condition. On this point, JUDSON J.: "The date for the completion of the sale is fixed with reference to the performance of this condition—'60 days after plans are approved'. Neither party to the contract undertakes to fulfil this condition, and neither party reserves a power of waiver. The purchaser made some enquiries of the village council but the evidence indicates that he made little or no progress and received little encouragement and that the prospects of annexation were very remote. After the trouble arose over the quantity and description of the land, the purchaser purported to waive this condition on the ground that it was solely for his benefit and was severable, and sued immediately for specific performance without reference to the condition and the time for performance fixed by the condition. The learned trial Judge found that the condition was one introduced for the sole benefit of the purchaser and that he could waive it. . . .

"But here there is no right to be waived. The obligations under the contract, on both sides, depend upon a future uncertain event, the happening of which depends entirely on the will of a third party—the village council. This is a true condition precedent—an external condition upon which the existence of the obligation depends. Until the event occurs there is no right to performance on either side. The parties have not promised that it will occur. In the absence of such a promise there can be no breach of contract until the event does occur. The purchaser now seeks to make the vendor liable on his promise to convey in spite of the non-performance of the condition and this to suit his own convenience only. This is not a case of renunciation or relinquishment of a right but rather an attempt by one party, without the consent of the other, to write a new contract. Waiver has often been referred to as a troublesome and uncertain term in the law but it does at least presuppose the existence of a right to be relinquished."

PETER KIEWIT SONS' COMPANY OF CANADA LTD. *v.* EAKINS CONSTRUCTION LTD.

British Columbia. Supreme Court of Canada. 1960. 22 D.L.R. (2d) 465

JUDSON J.: The appellant, on January 9, 1956, entered into a contract with the British Columbia Toll Highways & Bridges Authority, a Government corporation, to build the substructure, approach viaduct and northern approach road to the Second Narrows Bridge across Vancouver Harbour for the sum of $4,314,369.70. The respondent took a sub-contract from the appellant to supply and drive the timber piles for the substructure of pier 1 and piers 7 and 14 at stated unit prices, which amounted to a total of $132,350. The respondent sued the Bridge Authority and the main contractor, the appellant, for damages for breach of contract or, in the alternative, for compensation on a *quantum meruit*. The learned trial Judge dismissed the action against both defendants. On appeal the dismissal against the Bridge Authority was sustained but the appeal was allowed against the main contractor and the case remitted to the trial Court for an assessment of the work done on piers 10 to 14 to be paid for on a *quantum meruit* basis. The main contractor now appeals to this Court and asks for the restoration of the judgment given at the trial. The respondent does not cross-appeal against the judgment of the Court of Appeal affirming the dismissal of the action against the Bridge Authority. The dispute here, therefore, is entirely between the main contractor, as appellant, and the subcontractor, as respondent.

Before making its tender, the sub-contractor, Eakins Construction Ltd., had before it the plans and specifications and the principal contract. The plans required the piles to be driven to a safe bearing capacity of 20 tons. The specifications required them to be driven to a minimum bearing capacity of 20 tons based on a certain formula. The pile driving contract was made on January 10, 1956 but some time in February, the engineer amended the plans by adding a requirement relating to piers 10 to 14 as follows [Note 10]: "Bottom of timber bearing piles to be below bottom of sheet piling." T. K. Eakins, the managing director of the pile driving company, noticed the change at once. Beyond mentioning it to an official of the Kiewit company, he did nothing. This was long before he began to work on the piers affected by the change and probably before any work was done on piers 7, 8, 9, which were not affected by the change. The work on these three piers was abandoned and settled for in March 1956 because the ground was too hard for the driving of wooden piles. Timber piling also proved to be impractical on pier 1. Steel piling was substituted at this pier. Kiewit did this work itself, Eakins having declined to tender for steel piling except on a cost plus basis. This leaves only the work on piers 10 to 14 at issue in this litigation.

Eakins began to work on pier 10, still without having made any protest about the change in the plans. At this pier wooden pile-driving was also unsuccessful. After 22 piles had been driven, the engineer ordered them to be cut off and covered with gravel so that they would not become weight bearing. This work has not been paid for. Eakins submitted an account for this work which Kiewit refused to accept and offered a lesser amount. Eakins is entitled to payment for this work according to the terms of the contract. According to my judgment, this is all that Eakins is entitled to and if the parties cannot agree there will have to be a reference back to ascertain this amount. Clauses 7 and 9 of the contract cover this situation.

Eakins made its first protest that the amended plans provided for pile driving outside the terms of its contract just before it began to work on pier 11. The engineer insisted that the piles had to be driven as he required in accordance with the amended plans and Eakins proceeded with the work. There is no doubt that from this time on Eakins continued to protest that it was being required to do more work than its contract called for and it is equally clear that the engineer insisted that his instructions be followed and that Eakins was entitled to no extra payment for what it chose to call "overdriving". The positions taken by the disputants could not have been more clearly defined, the sub-contractor saying that it was working beyond its sub-contract and the engineer saying that it was not and threatening to put it off the job if it did not follow instructions.

Not until September 1956 did Eakins make any complaint in writing to Kiewit. When this brought no reply, Eakins wrote to the engineers, Messrs. Swan & Wooster, the employers of Stanwick, the resident engineer with whom Eakins had been having its controversy. This firm wrote to Kiewit saying that it realized that driving conditions had been difficult, but not entirely unexpected and that they did not "altogether agree that measures taken to obtain the desired results had been deviations from the contract". There is ample evidence of these difficulties but there is also evidence that not all of them arose from natural conditions. I am in agreement with the learned trial Judge that some of them at least were the result of inefficient operation and inadequate judgment.

On January 29, 1957 a meeting was held at which Eakins, the engineers and Kiewit were represented. Everybody seems to have expressed sympathy for the Eakins company, which was close to being forced to abandon the contract owing to the pressing claims of creditors, but no one made any binding promise to pay anything extra. After this meeting, Eakins made a further complaint to the Bridge Authority on February 6th but did continue with the work which was completed on March 6, 1957.

The learned trial Judge held that the sub-contractor was bound by all the terms of the main contract and that the addendum of which Eakins made so much was not a change in the plans at all but was added by way of clarification and for the information of the men in the field. After a careful analysis of the contract he came to the conclusion that this was within the engineer's defined powers. His conclusion, therefore, was that all the work was within the contract and that the claim for damages or compensation on a *quantum meruit* failed. On the other hand, the Court of Appeal took the directly opposite view that the obligation of the Eakins company was defined by its sub-contract, that the addendum was not a term of the sub-contract and that in any event those clauses of the main contract which were appealed to as authorizing the addendum, did not in fact authorize it. Since Kiewit knew that Eakins expected to be paid for the work done in compliance with the engineer's order and which it claimed to be outside the contract and since Kiewit's officer had told Eakins that it would have to comply with the engineer's orders, the Court of Appeal held that Eakins was entitled to compensation for the whole job, not merely for the extra work, on a *quantum meruit*. The basis for this is that Eakins had not been working to the sub-contract at all but that the parties by their conduct and dealings had substituted for the original sub-contract a new and different contract with more onerous obligations on Eakins.

Had it been necessary to choose between these two views of the legal relations between the parties, I would have preferred the view of the learned trial Judge that the Eakins company was performing no more than its contractual duty. But quite apart from this, it is to me an impossible inference in this case that the parties agreed to substitute a new contract for the original one. From the very beginning, the Eakins company knew of this added term. It began to protest late in the day that the term imposed added obligations. The engineer, who had clearly defined duties under the main contract, denied any such interpretation. Nothing could be clearer. One party says that it is being told to do more than the contract calls for. The engineer insists that the work is according to contract and no more, and that what is asserted to be extra work is not extra work and will not be paid for. The main contractor tells the sub-contractor that it will have to follow the orders of the engineer and makes no promise of additional remuneration. In these circumstances the sub-contractor continues with the work. It must be working under the contract. How can this contract be abrogated and another substituted in its place? Such a procedure must depend upon consent, express or implied, and such consent is entirely lacking in this case. Whatever Eakins recovers in this case is under the terms of the original sub-contract and the provisions of the main contract relating to extras. The engineer expressly refused to order as an extra what has been referred to throughout this case as "over-driving". The work was not done as an extra and there can be no recovery for it on that basis. When this position became clear, and it became clear before any work was done, the remedy of the Eakins company was to refuse further performance except on its own interpretation of the contract and, if this performance was rejected, to elect to treat the contract as repudiated and to sue for damages. In the absence of a clause in the contract enabling it to leave the matter in abeyance for later determination, it cannot go on with performance of the contract according to the other party's interpretation and then impose a liability on a different contract. Having elected to perform in these circumstances, its recovery for this performance must be in accordance with the terms of the contract.

With this view of the relations among the parties, my conclusion is that there was error in the judgment of the Court of Appeal in permitting recovery on a new contract which it found as a fact to exist between the sub-contractor and the main contractor but not between the sub-contractor and the Bridge Authority. The basis of such recovery is obviously purely contractual in character and the principle is simply stated in Winfield on the *Law of Quasi-Contracts*, 1952, p. 52: "Another application of *quantum meruit* is as a mode of redress on a new contract which has replaced an earlier one. The position is that the parties (or one of them) have not observed the terms of the earlier contract, but it can be implied from their conduct that they have substituted another contract for the first. If they do so, and one of the parties does not fulfil his side of the second contract, the other can sue *quantum meruit* upon it for what he has done. The obligation sued upon is genuinely contractual, not quasi-contractual."

Up to this point, there is no suggestion in the reasons of the Court of Appeal that the legal fiction of an implied contract is being applied to enable the plaintiff to recover on a *quasi*-contractual basis. The suggestion of *quasi*-contractual recovery does, however, appear in the reasons of the learned Chief Justice, the doctrine of frustration being invoked to get rid of the original contract: "The evidence is clear that what the appellant (i.e. Eakins Construction Limited) contracted to do and what it actually did while at all times taking the position that the work done was not within the scope of its contract, was so different from that contemplated that in my view the subcontract ceased to be applicable and the work done by the appellant should be paid for as though no contract had been made, on a quantum meruit."

How can it be found that the contract ceased to be applicable? It did not cease to be applicable by consent of the parties and the case is not one where some supervening event or fundamental change in circumstances rendered further performance impossible or radically different from the contractual obligation. How can a dispute over a question whether a certain item of work is an extra bring about frustration of the whole contract when the question of extras is covered in elaborate detail by the contract itself? The principle to be applied is not in doubt. It was examined again as recently as 1956 in *Davis Contractors Ltd.* v. *Fareham Urban Dist. Council*, [1956] A.C. 696, where *Bush* v. *Whitehaven Port & Town Trustees* (1888), Hudson on Building Contracts, 4th ed., vol. 2, p. 122, a case often appealed to in this type of dispute, was finally overruled. I take the statement of the principle from p. 729 of the *Fareham* case: "Frustration occurs whenever the law recognizes that without default of either party a contractual obligation has become incapable of being performed because the circumstances in which performance is called for would render it a thing radically different from that which was undertaken by the contract. Non haec in foedera veni. It was not this that I promised to do. . . . It is not hardship or inconvenience or material loss itself which calls the principle of frustration into play. There must be as well such a change in the significance of the obligation that the thing undertaken would, if performed, be a different thing from that contracted for."

On any view of the facts of this case, there cannot be frustration. The performance of extra work will not justify it, even if such work was done. Extra work of this kind said to have been performed in this case is a contingency covered by the express contract and does not afford a ground for its dissolution. If there was to be extra pile-driving, the character and extent of the obligation to pay were fully covered in the contract. Even on the plaintiff's own view of the case, its performance was not radically different from that called for by the contract. The facts of the case do not justify an inference of frustration.

There is, therefore, no room for the application of any theory of *quasi*-contractual recovery whether by way of the legal fiction of implied contract or the decision of the Court in the particular case to impose an obligation *ex aequo et bono*. The facts upon which such a theory of recovery can be based do not exist in this case, where the parties have made an express contract covering the very facts in litigation and that contract still remains open and unrescinded. Their relations on matters covered by the contract are governed by it and the Court has no power to substitute another form of obligation. This truism is stated in American Law Institute's volume on Restitution, Quasi-Contracts and Constructive Trusts, c. 4, s. 107, in the following terms:

"(1) A person of full capacity who, pursuant to a contract with another, has performed services or transferred property to the other or otherwise has conferred a benefit upon him, is not entitled to compensation therefor other than in accordance with the terms of such bargain, unless the transaction is rescinded for fraud, mistake, duress, undue influence or illegality, or unless the other has failed to perform his part of the bargain."

Since the work done, if not covered by the sub-contract, was an extra which the engineer might have allowed under the terms of the main contract imported into the sub-contract, it was for Eakins to show that the sub-contract had been terminated, either by its repudiation by the contractor and an election to treat the contract as at an end or that it had been abandoned or terminated by agreement between the parties. It is perfectly clear that throughout the performance Kiewit insisted that Eakins was obligated to do the work to the satisfaction of the engineer under the terms of the main contract which, it was contended, were imported into the sub-contract. It is equally clear that Eakins at no time treated the sub-contract as being at an end, simply insisting that it did not cover the additional work.

If Eakins had asked the engineer for a written order for the performance of the work which it claimed to be beyond the sub-contract and that had been refused and Kiewit had persisted in its attitude, Eakins might then have treated the contract as repudiated and sued for damages. Having failed to do this, and with the contract still open and unrescinded, it is my conclusion that any claim based upon any theory of *quasi*-contractual recovery is excluded.

I can find nothing in the terms of the contract under litigation nor in the events that occurred which would lead to the dissolution of this contract at any stage of its performance. I agree with the learned trial Judge and I would allow the appeal with costs. The judgment at trial should be restored subject to a reference to ascertain, in accordance with the contract, the amount to be paid for the 22 piles cut off at pier 10.

CARTWRIGHT J. (dissenting): . . . Counsel for the appellant contends that, throughout the proceedings, the significance of the addition of note 10 to the plans has been greatly exaggerated, as, in his submission, the evidence shows that in the numerous discussions between the engineer and the representatives of the respondent the former reiterated that the piles were to be driven to the depth that satisfied him rather [than] to a depth greater than that to which the sheet piling had been driven. The addition has, however, this importance that without it there was nothing in the principal contract (other than the general powers of the engineer defined in cls. 6 and 7) or in the specifications or in the plans requiring the appellant or the respondent (in so far as the latter had assumed the obligations of the former) to drive the piles to a greater depth than was necessary to achieve the safe bearing capacity of 20 tons in accordance with the specified formula.

It is significant that there was no denial of the testimony of T. K. Eakins and H. G. Eakins that the respondent was compelled to do driving to the extent of three or four times the amount necessary to achieve the specified safe bearing capacity. The only attack made on the accuracy of their evidence on this point is found in the evidence of Stanwick who stated that defects and failures in the driving equipment used by the respondent made it difficult to determine whether any particular pile had been "overdriven".

In my view, on the true construction of the sub-contract interpreted, as it must be, in the light of the circumstances surrounding its execution, the respondent agreed to perform the obligations of the appellant as to the supplying, driving and cutting off of the piles on the piers with which we are concerned as those obligations were defined in the principal contract (including the specifications and plans) as it existed when the sub-contract was made. The evidence shows that the respondent was called upon to do, and did do, work greatly in excess of those obligations. . . .

It can scarcely be denied that the work done by the respondent, under continuing protest, was done under circumstances of practical compulsion. It is clear that Howell [the Project Manager] repeatedly told the officers of the respondent that they must obey the instructions of the engineer as to the depth to which the piles were to be driven regardless of their views as to the meaning of the contract and the specifications. The sort of pressure exerted on the respondent by Howell is testified to by T. K. Eakins and H. G. Eakins and is exemplified in the following passage in the evidence of the latter: "Mr. Howell reported that their project was some months behind in its schedule, that it was of paramount importance to carry this foundation work on to its completion so that they, in turn, could keep up their working schedule, that if we did not continue to the completion of the work he had no alternative but to call in the bonding company to take over, in which case, he pointed out, not only would the company (i.e. the respondent) sacrifice that which remained but would be subject to extraordinary charges which are generally observed when a bonding company takes over." Howell was not called as a witness and there is no denial of this evidence.

Howell, with the fullest knowledge that the respondent was taking the position that it was being called on to do work entirely outside its contract and would expect and demand to be paid for it (a position which, in my opinion, both in fact and in law it was justified in taking) persisted in ordering that work to be done. In these circumstances the law implies an obligation on the part of the appellant to pay for that work of the performance of which it has had the benefit. I find some difficulty in basing the appellant's liability on an implied contract when the evidence shows that the respondent was repeatedly pressing the appellant to agree that it would pay for the work which it was doing and which did not fall within the terms of the sub-contract, and the appellant instead of so agreeing was making only "nebulous statements" to the effect that the respondent ought to be paid or that "there was something coming to" the respondent. I prefer to use the terminology which has the authority of Lord Mansfield and Lord Wright and was adopted by this Court in *Deglman* v. *Guaranty Trust Co. of Canada & Constantineau*, [1954] 3 D.L.R. 785, particularly at pp. 794–5, and to say that the appellant having received the benefits of the performance by the respondent of the work which the latter did at the insistence of the former the law imposes upon the apellant the obligation to pay the fair value of the work performed.

It is said that the respondent (who held what turns out to be the right view as to the meaning of the sub-contract) should have had the courage of its convictions and refused to perform any work beyond that which was required by the sub-contract, and when this resulted in its being put off the job should have sued the appellant for damages. It must, however, be remembered that the sub-contract was so difficult to construe that there has been a difference of judicial opinion as to its true meaning. The appellant (who held what turns out to be a mistaken view as to the meaning of the sub-contract) threatened the respondent with what might well amount to financial ruin unless it did the additional work which the sub-contract did not obligate it to do. To say that because in such circumstances the respondent was not prepared to stop work and so risk the ruinous loss which would have fallen on it if its view of the meaning of the contract turned out to be erroneous the appellant may retain the benefit of all the additional work done by the respondent without paying for it would be to countenance an unjust enrichment of a shocking character, which, in my opinion, can and should be prevented by imposing upon the appellant the obligation to pay to which I have referred above.

The case appears to me to be analogous to those in which a person who has paid money, under protest and under circumstances of practical compulsion, to another who was not in law entitled to the payment can recover it back by action. A number of the leading cases which illustrate the application of that principle are collected and discussed in the judgments delivered in this Court in *Knutson* v. *Bourkes Syndicate*, [1941] 3 D.L.R. 593. . . .

I can discern no difference in principle between compelling a man to pay money which he is not legally bound to pay and compelling him to do work which he is not legally bound to do; in the one case money is improperly obtained, in the other money's worth. The remedy in the former case is to order repayment of the money; the remedy in the latter case should be, in my opinion, to order the person who has compelled the doing and has reaped the benefit of the work to pay its fair value. It would, I think, be a reproach to the administration of justice if we were compelled to hold that the Courts are powerless to grant any relief to a plaintiff in such circumstances.

It is argued for the appellant that if the appeal does not succeed *in toto* the order of the Court of Appeal should be varied to provide that the respondent is entitled to be paid on a *quantum meruit* basis for that work only which was done over and beyond the work called for by the sub-contract. On this point I am in agreement with the Court of Appeal and am content to adopt the reasons of Sheppard J.A. for rejecting this submission.

For the above reasons I have reached the conclusion that the appeal on the substantive claim should be dismissed. . . .

[Locke, Abbott and Martland JJ. concurred with Judson J. in allowing the appeal.]

NOTES. What effect should be given to clauses 3, 4, 6 and 7, in the contract in the *Kiewit* case? Clause 3 provided that "The work shall be . . . prosecuted to completion . . . to the satisfaction of the engineer, but always according to the provisions of this contract. . . ." Clause 4 required the work to be "finished in a workmanlike manner, and in strict conformity with this contract, and to the complete satisfaction of the engineer." Clause 6 authorized the engineer to correct omissions or misstatements in the contract. "The correction of any such error shall not be deemed to be an addition to or deviation from the terms of the contract." Clause 7 authorized the engineer, IN WRITING, to order additional work. "The decision of the engineer as to whether the compliance with such order increases or diminishes the work to be done . . . and as to the amount to be paid or deducted, as the case may be, in respect thereof, shall be final." Note that these clauses are in the principal contract. How do they get into the sub-contract, where no mention is made of extras?

In the course of his testimony Mr. T. Eakins said, when asked why he had not stopped work, "I mean as regards contractually speaking, you quit a job you never work for anybody again. I mean anybody knows that. You just can't walk off a job and say, well, the inspectors or engineers are wrong!" See the Appeal Book at p. 139. And see 19 University of Toronto *Faculty of Law Review* 171 for an excellent critical discussion of the *Kiewit* case by S. R. Ellis.

WOOLF *v.* COLLIS REMOVAL SERVICE
England. Court of Appeal. [1948] 1 K.B. 11

ASQUITH L.J. delivered the judgment of the Court: . . . The plaintiff in the first two paragraphs of his statement of claim alleged that the defendants had contracted to remove certain furniture and other effects from his house in London to the defendants' "Quarry" Store, Marlow, Buckinghamshire, and there safely to keep and take care of the same, and that in breach of the said contract they had removed the goods to a different destination, that is, Hawes Hill Park, Braywood, in Berkshire, where some of them were lost and others damaged. Further or alternatively, he alleges that such goods were lost and damaged owing to the negligence of the defendants in using, when the goods had arrived at Hawes Hill Farm, Braywood, an unsuitable place (a disused piggery) in which to store them and guarding them inefficiently. He claimed damages.

The contract takes the form of a written "estimate," providing for removal of the goods to the Quarry Store, Marlow. Indorsed on its back are a number of conditions, practically all of them limiting the liability of the removers. Number 20 of the indorsed conditions is, however, an arbitration clause, the precise term of which we indicate later.

Before taking any step in the action, the defendants applied under s.4 of the *Arbitration Act* for a stay, which was granted by the master, his decision being upheld by the judge in chambers.

The plaintiff argues that there was in effect no jurisdiction to stay the action and to refer these issues to arbitration, and this, as we understand it, on two broad grounds.

The plaintiff's first broad point is that the second paragraph of the statement of claim alleges a "deviation" or fundamental departure from the contract and that, if such an allegation were proved, the effect would be to deprive the defendants of the benefit of the indorsed conditions, including, as he contends, the arbitration clause; in other words, he argues that the issue raised in these paragraphs is one which, if determined in his favour, would make the arbitration clause inoperative or, put slightly differently, his proposition is that a dispute cannot be referred to arbitration under an arbitration clause the continued existence of which is itself the subject or necessarily involved in the subject of the dispute. The plaintiff's case was, indeed, put higher, it being argued that "deviation" displaced the whole contract, *ab initio*, and for all purposes.

It is a familiar principle of law that, "if you undertake to do a thing in a certain way, or to keep a thing in a certain place, with certain conditions protecting [you] and have broken the contract by not doing the thing contracted for in the way contracted for, or not keeping the article in the place in which you have contracted to keep it, you cannot rely on the conditions which were only intended to protect you if you carried out the contract in the way in which you had contracted to do it." Those are the words of Scrutton L.J. in *Gibaud* v. *Great Eastern Ry. Co.* [1921] 2 K.B. 426. The learned judge cites *Lilley* v. *Doubleday,* 7 Q.B.D. 510,

511, where Grove J. said: "If a bailee elects to deal with the property entrusted to him in a way not authorized by the bailor, he takes upon himself the risks of so doing, except where the risk is independent of his acts and inherent in the property itself."

In *Lilley* v. *Doubleday* the facts were that warehousemen contracted, under a contract which limited their liability to loss by specified causes, to keep the plaintiff's goods in store A., but in fact kept them in store B. When in store B. they were in part lost and in part damaged by fire, without negligence by the warehousemen. It was held that the latter could not rely on the conditions limiting their liability, since these applied only to goods kept in the store authorized by the contract.

The facts alleged in the statement of claim in this case are very similar. The goods, according to the pleading, were carried to and stored in a place and a store unauthorized by the contract. If so, in proceedings taken by the aggrieved party, any "exceptions" clauses (as for brevity we will call clauses limiting the carrier's or warehousemen's liability) would no doubt be unavailable to the party in default.

It is, however, important to observe that the argument which we are considering makes the vital assumption that arbitration clauses are, or at all events this arbitration clause is, on the same footing for the relevant purpose as "exceptions clauses" and in the event of a "deviation" share their fate.

This, we think, is a fallacy. Leaving aside for the moment the special wording of this particular arbitration clause, we are satisfied that "deviation" or its equivalent in contracts not for carriage—we will for brevity call both "deviation"—will not displace an arbitration clause. "Deviation" is a very common phenomenon in contracts of carriage, especially in carriage by sea, and the theme of a vast number of reported cases. In a large proportion at least of these there were (a) an exceptions clause or exceptions clauses, and (b) an arbitration clause. Yet counsel for the appellant was unable to cite any case in which the fact or averment of deviation was held to displace the arbitration clause and to afford a ground for refusing a stay of the action. This, it may be said, is negative and inconclusive.

Affirmatively, however, it appears to us to emerge from two decisions of the House of Lords (a) that deviation does not necessarily displace the whole contract, including any arbitration clause, and (b) that there are radical distinctions for this purpose between exceptions clauses and arbitration clauses.

This last point appears in the following pages in *Heyman* v. *Darwins, Ltd.* [1942] A.C. 356, 375, from the speeches of Lord Macmillan and Lord Porter. Lord Macmillan is speaking of repudiation of a contract, in the sense not of a denial of the existence of the contract, but of conduct evincing an intention no longer to be bound by it. He is speaking of a repudiation in this sense, and no doubt of such a repudiation which has been accepted, for it is well settled that an unaccepted repudiation has no legal consequences whatsoever. So speaking, he says: "The contract is not put out of existence, though all further performance of the obligations undertaken by each party in favour of the other may cease. It survives for the purpose of measuring the claims arising out of the breach, and the arbitration clause survives for determining the mode of their settlement. The purposes of the contract have failed, but the arbitration clause is not one of the purposes of the contract." Lord Porter accepts Lord Macmillan's statement, and for himself, also emphasizes the distinction between exceptions clauses (stipulations inserted for the protection or benefit of one party) and arbitration clauses. "As my noble and learned friend Lord Macmillan has said, the arbitration clause is inserted as a method of settling disputes and is not imposed as a term in favour of one party or the other." Ergo, in the event of a repudiation, the arbitration clause, subject to any exceptional wording, will survive.

Does this apply when the contract is repudiated by deviation? We think that it does. That deviation, whatever else it may be, is repudiation of the contract, and repudiation in an extreme form, appears to us plain both in principle and from the decision of the House of Lords in *Hain Steamship Company, Ltd.* v. *Tate & Lyle, Ltd.*, [1936] W.N. 210; and it is equally plain that it does not of itself abrogate the contract. All the learned Lords were agreed that it was open to the party not in default either to treat the contract as at an end, or to waive the breach and treat it as subsisting. And it is only in the former case that the exceptions clause will cease to apply. But it is quite clear, that whether accepted or not, deviation is a form of repudiation. Indeed it is hardly possible to imagine a clearer way in which a carrier can "evince the intention of not being bound" to perform the transit contracted for than his act in performing a different and inconsistent transit and putting it out of his power to perform the stipulated one. If deviation equals repudiation, then, under the decision in *Heyman* v. *Darwins, Ltd.*, which is binding on this court, even if it is accepted, the arbitration clause survives, although exceptions clause, if the implied repudiation is accepted, becomes a dead letter.

It is argued, however (and this is the last point under this branch of the case), that this particular arbitration clause is, in effect, an exceptions clause, since it is one-sided in its operation and confers advantages or liberties on the defendants which it denies to the plaintiff. The clause reads as follows: "If the customer makes any claims upon or counterclaim to any claim made by the contractors, the same shall in case of difference be referred to the decision of two arbitrators (one to be appointed by each party). All the provisions of the Arbitration Act, 1889, or any modification in force, for the time being shall apply. The arbitration shall, unless otherwise agreed, be held in the town in which the contractor's office at or from which the contract was made is situated, and the making of an award shall be a condition precedent to any right of action or counterclaim."

It is argued for the appellant that, while the clause purports to compel the customer to refer to arbitration claims against the carrier, it leaves the carrier free, as the customer is not, to pursue claims on his part against the customer by action at law. It is, therefore, so the argument runs, in substance a clause protecting the carrier and so far analogous to an exceptions clause.

We think that Mr. Roskill's answer to this contention prevails, namely, that the clause is in essence mere machinery, even if it be one-sided machinery. There is nothing in its unequal operation to divest it, in our view, of the character attributed to arbitration clauses in general in the speeches of Lords Macmillan and Porter in *Heyman* v. *Darwins, Ltd.*, as distinguishing them from exceptions clauses.

The second broad point on which the plaintiff relied was that, although in his statement of claim a claim sounding in contract is given pride of place, yet there is a further or alternative claim for negligence and that such alternative claim cannot be referred to arbitration under the arbitration clause, since it is not made under the contract of which that clause forms part. It is contended that this alternative claim is made either in pure tort or quasi-contract, but at all events not under the contract itself.

The reasoning which led us to our conclusion on the first point is, in our view, equally fatal to this one. While it is true that, without any special contract, the mandatory, when once he has entered upon the execution of the task which he has undertaken, is bound, apart from special contract, to exercise reasonable care and diligence, none the less, where there is a special contract, that contract defines the measures of the obligation.

In the present case there is an obligation of diligence in the contract itself, pleaded in para. 2 of the statement of claim, and apparently co-extensive with the non-contractual obligation of diligence.

The effect of deviation, as we have seen, is not to put an end to the contract for all purposes, but, when accepted, to deprive the mandatory of the benefit of any exceptions in that contract limiting the liability of the mandatory under it.

The deviation in the present case, if it took place as alleged, was accepted as a repudiation by the issue of the writ, but the claim in negligence, like the alternative claim in this action, arose out of acts done before the issue of the writ, that is, before the acceptance of the repudiation. The arbitration clause remains in force to settle all such claims if they fall within its ambit.

The arbitration clause in the present case is, as to the subject matter of claims within its ambit, in the widest possible terms. That clause is not, in terms, limited to claims arising "under" the contract. It speaks simply of "claims." This, of course, does not mean that the term applies to claims of every imaginable kind. Claims which are entirely unrelated to the transaction covered by the contract would no doubt be excluded; but we are of opinion that, even if the claim in negligence is not a claim "under the contract", yet there is a sufficiently close connexion between that claim and that transaction to bring the claim within the arbitration clause, even though framed technically in tort. A claim so framed was treated in *In re Polemis and Furness, Whithy & Co., Ltd.*, [1921] 3 K.B. 560, as falling within an arbitration clause in the contract, which provided that, should any dispute arise between the owners and charterers, the matters in dispute should be referred to three persons in London.

For these reasons, the appeal fails and must be dismissed with costs.

QUESTIONS. Was there a failure of the defendants to perform here? Was the plaintiff's promise to arbitrate subject to that condition? Did the "intent of the transaction" require the defendants' performance of the conditions before the plaintiff's became bound to submit to arbitration? What purpose is served here by the introduction of the idea of "repudiation"? In reading the following passage you might keep in mind that the word "rescission" is as ambiguous as "repudiation."

HEYMAN *v.* DARWINS, LTD. [1942] A.C. 356 (England. House of Lords). LORD WRIGHT: "The word 'repudiation' has also led to difficulties because it is an ambiguous word constantly used without precise definition in contract law. I do not attempt an exhaustive list of the senses in which the word has been used, but I may give some instances. Repudiation of a contract is sometimes used as meaning that the defendant denies that there ever was a contract in the sense of an actual consensus ad idem. If that is the case a submission of disputes under the contract never comes into operative existence any more than the contract to which it was to be ancillary. Short of this, one party, though not denying that there was the appearance of assent, might claim that the consent was vitiated by fraud or duress or mistake or illegality, and in that sense it is often said that he repudiates the contract. There, again, it would be a question of construction whether the collateral arbitration clause could be treated as severable and could be invoked for settling such a dispute. There is, however, a form of repudiation where the party who repudiates does not deny that a contract was intended between the parties, but claims that it is not binding because of the failure of some condition or the infringement of some duty fundamental to the enforceability of the contract, it being expressly provided by the contract that the failure of condition or the breach of duty should invalidate the contract. A dispute on such an issue would generally be within an ordinary submission of disputes under or arising out of the contract of similar words, though the award in a certain event might have the effect of declaring that the contract had ceased to be, or even had never become, binding. Another case to which the word repudiation is applied is when the party, though not disputing the contract, declares unequivocally that he will not perform it and, admitting the breach, leaves the other party to claim damages. There may then be a dispute under the contract, not indeed as to liability but as to damages. Such a dispute would normally fall within the ordinary submission, which should receive effect unless the court exercises its discretion to refuse to stay under s. 4. Except as influencing the exercise of that discretion, I cannot see how defiance or truculence of the party can affect the matter. He is simply breaking his contract. But perhaps the commonest application of the word 'repudiation' is to what is often called the anticipatory breach of a contract where the party by words or conduct evinces an intention no longer to be bound and the other party accepts the repudiation and rescinds the contract. In such a case, if the repudiation is wrongful and the rescission is rightful, the contract is ended by the rescission but only as far as concerns future performance. It remains alive for the awarding of damages either for previous breaches or for the breach which constitutes the repudiation. That is only a particular form of contract-breaking and would generally under an ordinary arbitration clause involve a dispute under the contract like any other breach of contract. There is no difference, for instance, for this purpose between a refusal to take further instalments under a contract for the sale of goods by instalments and a refusal to take the entire contract quantity where the tender is to be a single delivery. I need scarcely add that one party to a contract cannot put an end to it. To produce that effect there must be rescission. An anticipatory breach does not necessarily involve an actual intention to break the contract. Intention is to be judged by the party's conduct. The difference between repudiating a contract and repudiating liability under it must not be overlooked. It is thus necessary in every case in which the word repudiation is used to be clear in what sense it is being used."

WHITE & CARTER (COUNCILS), LTD. *v.* McGREGOR. [1961] 3 All E.R. 1178 (Scotland. House of Lords). LORD KEITH OF AVONHOLM: "Repudiation of a contract is nothing but a breach of contract. Except where it is accepted as an anticipatory breach and as a ground for a claim of damages, a repudiation can never be said to be accepted by the other party except in the sense that he acquiesces in it and does not propose to take any action. Otherwise he founds on it as a cause of action."

GENERAL BILLPOSTING COMPANY *v.* ATKINSON

England. House of Lords. [1909] A.C. 118

The repondent had been manager to a Newcastle billposting company for some years. His contract of employment provided that he should not whilst in the engagement or within two years after its termination carry on a similar business within a certain radius without the company's permission. In 1906 the company dismissed him without notice. In an action against the company for wrongful dismissal he recovered damages, and afterwards began to trade as a billposter on his own account within the radius. The appellants, as assignees of the Newcastle company, brought an action against the respondent for an injunction and for damages for breach of contract. Neville J. held that the appellants were entitled to sue the respondent for damages notwithstanding the wrongful dismissal. This decision was reversed by the Court of Appeal: Hence this appeal.

LORD ROBERTSON: My Lords, if this case be considered for a moment on its own merits and substance (apart in the meantime from authority) it is extremely difficult to be reconciled to the appellants' contention. The respondent's position in entering the contract is a very intelligible one. He says, "I am a bill-poster and I desire occupation either on my own account or in the service of others. If I enter the employment of others I am willing to give up the right to trade on my own account to the extent specified in this agreement. I do not desire to have it both ways." The claim of the appellants, on the other hand, as now put forward, is that, taking him at his word, as expressed in the contract, and getting his services, they are to be entitled both to deprive him (against the contract) of the right to serve them and also of the right to serve himself.

It seems to me that the covenant not to set up business is not only germane to but ancillary to the contract of service, and that once the contract of service is rescinded the other falls with it.

I have only to add that the suggestion that the respondent has already received his *quid pro quo* in that he has had the appellants' wages for a considerable time ignores the equally important fact that they have had his services for the same period.

LORD COLLINS: My Lords, I am of opinion that the unanimous decision of the Court of Appeal in this case should be affirmed. The rule pressed upon us by Mr. Russell [one of counsel] from the notes to *Pordage* v. *Cole* (1668), 85 E.R. 449, "cannot be intended to apply to every case in which a covenant by the plaintiff forms only a part of the consideration and the residue of the consideration has been had by the defendant. That residue must be the substantial part of the contract; and if in the case of *Boone* v. *Eyre* (1777), 126 E.R. 160 two or three negroes had been accepted and the equity of redemption not conveyed we do not apprehend that the plaintiff could have recovered the whole stipulated price and left the defendant to recover damage for the non-conveyance": see per Pollock C.B. delivering the judgment of the Court in *Ellen* v. *Topp* (1851), 6 Ex. 424 155 E.R. 609, at p. 616. Further, in *White* v. *Beeton* (1861), 7 H. & N. 42; 158 E.R. 385, at p. 388, Bramwell B. quotes with approval the remark in Lord Kenyon C.J. in *Campbell* v. *Jones* (1796), 6 T.R. 570; 101 E.R. 708, "Whether these kinds of covenants be or be not independent of each other must certainly depend on the good sense of the case." The reason for the rule itself is said by Serjeant Williams to be that "Where a person has received a part of the consideration for which he entered into the agreement it would be unjust, that because he has not had the whole, he should be permitted to enjoy that part without either paying or doing anything for it." But in this case, as pointed out by Mr. Manisty [one of counsel], the respondent has given an equivalent in service for the remuneration he has received in salary. He stands, therefore, outside the reason of the rule.

But I think this case may be, and in fact has been, decided on broader lines than those laid down in the notes to *Pordage* v. *Cole* as to mutual and independent covenants. I think the true test applicable to the facts of this case is that which was laid down by Lord Coleridge C.J. in *Freeth* v. *Burr* (1874), L.R. 9 C.P. p. 208 and approved in *Mersey Steel Company* v. *Naylor* (1884), 9 App. Cas. 434 in the House of Lords, "That the true question is whether the acts and conduct of the party evince an intention no longer to be bound by the contract." I think the Court of Appeal had ample ground for drawing this inference from the conduct of the appellants here in dismissing the respondent in deliberate disregard of the terms of the contract, and that the latter was thereupon justified in rescinding the contract and treating himself as absolved from the further performance of it on his part.

I think the appeal should be dismissed.

[The Earl of Halsbury concurred.]

KOUSKI *v*. PEET. [1915] 1 Ch. 530 (England. Chancery). NEVILLE J. speaking of the *Billposting* case: "What that case means is this, that where you have an agreement of service for a time long or short, if the employer improperly puts an end to it, that is not a mere breach of the contract, but is in effect saying 'I refuse any longer to employ you under the agreement,' and that involves an abandonment of the agreement and entitles the employee to sue the master for damages."

2. EFFECT OF REPRESENTATIONS

The cases in this section are usually digested under the headings of "mistake," "innocent misrepresentation," or "fraud." If a fact asserted by one party (or both) is not made a term of the contract, the non-occurrence of the fact may give rise to a legal remedy. If a party has been induced to enter into a contract by the assertion of a fact by the other party, and the fact subsequently turns out to be untrue, whether with or without the knowledge of the person asserting it, the situation is practically indistinguishable from the breach of a promise or the failure of performance of a condition so far as the party is concerned. Consequently, the relief afforded the party affected by the innocent misrepresentation or the fraudulent misrepresentation of fact is discussed here with the similar situations where there is non-performance or non-occurrence of a promise or condition contained within the contract. Should the "law" provide less, as much, or greater relief for an innocent or fraudulent misrepresentation of facts "external to the contract" as it does for a breach of promise or a failure of a condition?

BEHN *v*. BURNESS
England. Exchequer Chamber. 1863. 3 B. & S. 751; 122 E.R. 281

WILLIAMS J.: The question in this case is whether the statement in the charter-party, that that ship is "now in the port of Amsterdam," is a "representation" or a "warranty," using the latter word as synonymous with "condition"; in which sense it has been for many years understood with respect to policies of insurance and charter-parties.

It may be expedient to commence the consideration of this question by some examination into the nature of representations. Properly speaking, a representation is a statement, or assertion, made by one party to the other, before or at the time of the contract, of some matter or circumstance relating to it. Though it is sometimes contained in the written instrument, it is not an integral part of the contract; and, consequently, the contract is not broken though the representation proves to be untrue; nor (with the exception of the case of policies of insurance, at all events marine policies, which stand on a peculiar anomalous footing) is such untruth any cause of action, nor has it any efficacy whatever, unless the representation was made fraudulently, either by reason of its being made with knowledge of its untruth, or by reason of its being made dishonestly, with a reckless ignorance whether it was true or untrue. . . .

If this be so, it is difficult to understand the distinction which is to be found in some of the treatises, and is in some degree perhaps sanctioned by judicial authority . . . that a representation, if it differs from the truth to an unreasonable extent, may affect the validity of the contract. Where, indeed, the misrepresentation is so gross as to amount to sufficient evidence of fraud it is obvious that the contract would on that ground be voidable.

The representations are not usually contained in the written instrument of contract, yet they sometimes are. But it is plain that their insertion therein cannot alter their nature. A question, however, may arise, whether a descriptive statement in the written instrument is a mere representation, or whether it is a substantive part of the contract. This is a question of construction which the court, and not the jury must determine. If the court should come to the conclusion that such a statement by one party was intended to be a substantive part of his contract, and not a mere representation, the often-discussed question may, of course, be raised, whether this part of the contract is a condition precedent, or only an independent agreement, a breach of which will not justify a repudiation of the contract, but will only be a cause of action for a compensation in damages. In the construction of charter-parties, this question has often been raised, with reference to stipulations that some future thing shall be done or shall happen, and has given rise to many nice distinctions. Thus a statement that a vessel is to sail, or be ready to receive a cargo, on or before a given day, has been held to be a condition . . . while a stipulation that she shall sail with all convenient speed or within a reasonable time, has been held to be only an agreement. . . . But with respect to statements in a contract descriptive of the subject-matter of it, or of some material incident thereof, the true doctrine, established by a principle as well as authority, appears to be, generally speaking, that if such descriptive statement was intended to be a substantive part of the contract, it is to be regarded as a warranty—that is to say, a condition on the failure or non-performance of which the other party may, if he is so minded, repudiate the contract *in toto*, and so be relieved from performing his part of it, provided it has not been partially executed in his favor. If, indeed, he has received the whole or any substantial part of the consideration for the promise on his part, the warranty loses the character of a condition, or to speak perhaps more properly, ceases to be available as a condition, and becomes a warranty in the narrower sense of the word—viz., a stipulation by way of agreement, for the breach of which a compensation must be sought in damages. . . .

In the present case, as the defendant has not received any benefit or advantage under the contract, but has wholly repudiated it, the question is simply whether, in the true construction of the charter-party, the court ought to infer that the statement as to the ship's being at that date in the port of Amsterdam, was meant to be a substantive part of the contract, or a representation collateral to it. . . .

It is plain that the court must be influenced in the construction, not only by the language of the instrument, but also by the circumstances under which, and the purposes for which, the charter-party was entered into. For instance, if it was made in the time of war, the national character of the vessel is of such importance, that a statement of it in the charter-party might properly be regarded as part of the shipowner's contract, and so amounting to a warranty, whereas, the very same statement in the time of peace, being wholly unimportant, might well be construed to be a mere representation. So if it were shown that the charter-party was made for a purpose such that, unless the vessel began her voyage from the port of loading, with her cargo on board, by a certain time, it was manifest that the object of the charter-party would in all probability be frustrated, the court might properly be led by this circumstance to conclude that a statement as to the locality of the ship, coupled with a stipulation that she should sail with all convenient speed, was a warranty of her then locality.

But we feel a difficulty in acceding to the suggestion which appears to have been, to some extent, sanctioned by high authority that a statement of this kind in a charter-party, which may be regarded as a mere representation if the object of the charter-party be still practicable, may be construed as a warranty if that object turns out to be frustrated; because the instrument, it should seem, ought to be construed with reference to the intention of the parties at the time it was made, irrespective of the events which may afterward occur. It is true that in some of the cases, where the question has been whether a stipulation in a charter-party amounted to a condition, the court decided that question in the negative and in so doing took occasion to suggest that neglect or delay on the part of the shipowner to execute his part of the contract, might be a breach of such an essential stipulation on his part as to justify the charterer in treating the contract as brought to an end thereby, and in refusing on that account to perform his part of it, and further suggested that, in deciding whether the breach on the shipowner's part was of such an essential stipulation as that described, the court might advert to the fact whether such breach had frustrated the whole object which the charterer had in view. . . . But the court did not, we apprehend, mean to intimate that the frustration of the voyage would convert a stipulation into a condition, if it were not originally intended to be one.

The question on the present charter-party is confined to the statement of a definite fact—the place of the ship at the date of the contract. Now the place of the ship at the date of the contract, where the ship is in foreign parts and is chartered to come to England, may be the only datum on which the charterer can found his calculations of the time of the ship's arriving at the port of loading. A statement is more or less important in proportion as the object of the contract more or less depends upon it. For most charters, considering winds, markets, and dependent contracts, the time of a ship's arrival to load is an essential fact, for the interest of the charterer. In the ordinary course of charters in general it would be so; the evidence for the defendant shows it to be actually so in this case. Then, if the statement of the place of the ship is a substantive part of the contract, it seems to us that we ought to hold it to be a condition upon the principles above explained, unless we can find in the contract itself or the circumstances reason for thinking that the parties did not so intend. If it was a condition and not performed, it follows that the obligation of the charterer dependent thereon, ceased at his option, and considerations either of the damage to him or of proximity to performance on the part of the shipowner are irrelevant. . . .

On these grounds we think the judgment of the Queen's Bench should be reversed.

REDGRAVE *v.* HURD

England. Court of Appeal. 1881. 20 Ch.D. 1

The plaintiff, a solicitor, advertised for "a partner an efficient lawyer and advocate about forty, who would not object to purchase advertiser's suburban residence." After two interviews with the defendant in which the plaintiff represented that his business brought in £300 to £400 a year, the plaintiff and defendant met to settle the terms of the partnership and the plaintiff produced three summaries of business done in 1877, 1878 and 1879. The gross receipts amounted to less than £200 a year. When he asked how the difference of income was made up the defendant was shown some papers which represented other business. The defendant did not inspect these papers but Fry J. concluded that they showed business amounting to about £5 a year. The defendant wished the written agreement to set out that the £1600 was for the purchase of both the house and the partnership but the plaintiff refused, and the agreement did not refer to the practice. The agreement was signed on March 2, 1880, and the defendant agreed to pay £1600 for the house. He paid £100 on deposit and on April 17, was let into possession. Finding the law practice was "utterly worthless" he gave up possession and refused to complete the purchase.

The plaintiff brought this action for specific performance. The defendant denied liability because he had been induced into making the agreements by the plaintiff's false representations about the law practice made for that purpose. He counterclaimed for "rescission," the return of his deposit, and damages for his loss in moving his family. Fry J. gave judgment for the plaintiff and dismissed the counterclaim. He said, in part: "If he had intended to rely upon that parol representation . . . having the materials before him he would have made some inquiry into it."

JESSEL M.R.: As regards the defendant's counterclaim, we consider that it fails so far as damages are concerned, because he has not pleaded knowledge on the part of the plaintiff that the allegations made by the plaintiff were untrue, nor has he pleaded the allegations themselves in sufficient detail to found an action for deceit. It only remains to consider the claim of the plaintiff for specific performance, and so much of the counterclaim of the defendant as asks to have the contract rescinded.

Before going into the details of the case I wish to say something about my view of the law applicable to it, because in the text-books, and even in some observations of noble Lords in the House of Lords, there are remarks which I think, according to the course of modern decisions, are not well founded, and do not accurately state the law. As regards the rescission of a contract, there was no doubt a difference between the rules of Courts of Equity and the rules of Courts of Common Law—a difference which of course has now disappeared by the operation of the Judicature Act, which makes the rules of equity prevail. According to the decisions of the Courts of Equity it was not necessary, in order to set aside a contract obtained by material false representation, to prove that the party who obtained it knew at the time when the representation was made that it was false. It was put in two ways, either of which was sufficient. One way of putting the case was, "A man is not to be allowed to get a benefit from a statement which he now admits to be false. He is not to be allowed to say, for the purpose of civil jurisdiction, that when he made it he did not know it to be false; he ought to have found that out before he made it." The other way of putting it was this: "Even assuming that moral fraud must be shewn in order to set aside a contract, you have it where a man, having obtained a beneficial contract by a statement which he now knows to be false, insists upon keeping that contract. To do so is a moral delinquency: no man ought to seek to take advantage of his own false statements." The rule in equity was settled, and it does not matter on which of the two grounds it was rested. As regards the rule of Common Law there is no doubt it was not quite so wide. There were, indeed, cases in which, even at Common Law, a contract could be rescinded for misrepresentation, although it could not be shewn that the person making it knew the representation to be false. They are variously stated, but I think, according to the later decisions, the statement must have been made recklessly and without care, whether it was true or false, and not with the belief that it was true. But, as I have said, the doctrine in equity was settled beyond controversy, and it is enough to refer to the judgment of Lord Cairns in the *Reese River Silver Mining Company* v. *Smith*, Law Rep. 4 H.L. 64, in which he lays it down in the way which I have stated.

There is another proposition of law of very great importance which I think it is necessary for me to state, because, with great deference to the very learned Judge from whom this appeal comes, I think it is not quite accurately stated in his judgment. If a man is induced to enter into a contract by a false representation it is not a sufficient answer to him to say, "If you had used due diligence you would have found out that the statement was untrue. You had the means afforded you of discovering its falsity, and did not choose to avail yourself of them." I take it to be a settled doctrine of equity not only as regards specific performance but also as regards rescission, that this is not an answer unless there is such delay as constitutes a defence under the Statute of Limitations. That, of course, is quite a different thing. Under the statute delay deprives a man of his right to rescind on the ground of fraud, and the only question to be considered is from what time the delay is to be reckoned. It had been decided, and the rule was adopted by the statute, that the delay counts from the time when by due diligence the fraud might have been discovered. Nothing can be plainer, I take it, on the authorities in equity than that the effect of false representation is not got rid of on the ground that the person to whom it was made has been guilty of negligence. . . .

As regards the facts of this case, I agree with conclusions of Mr. Justice Fry on every point but one, and my failure to agree with him in that one is the cause of my concurring in reversing his decision. What he finds in effect is that the defendant Hurd was induced to enter into the contract by a material misrepresentation made to him by the plaintiff Redgrave, but he comes to the conclusion that either he did not finally rely upon that representation, or that if he did rely upon it he made an inquiry which, although ineffectual and made, as he says, carelessly and inefficiently, bound him in a Court of Equity, and prevented him from saying that he relied on the representation. . . .

[The Master of the Rolls then examined the evidence, with particular regard to the fact that the defendant asked for the papers showing the amount of business and was referred to some papers in the plaintiff's office, and continued.]

Then that being so the learned Judge came to the conclusion either that the defendant did not rely on the statement, or that if he did rely upon it he had shewn such negligence as to deprive him of his title to relief from this Court. As I have already said, the latter proposition is in my opinion not founded in law, and the former part is not founded in fact; I think also it is not founded in law, for when a person makes a material representation to another to induce him to enter into a contract, and the other enters into that contract, it is not sufficient to say that the party to whom the representation is made does not prove that he entered into the contract, relying upon the representation. If it is a material representation calculated to induce him to enter into contract, it is an inference of law that he was induced by the representation to enter into it, and in order to take away his title to be relieved from the contract on the ground that the representation was untrue, it must be shewn either that he had knowledge of the facts contrary to the representation, or that he stated in terms, or shewed clearly by his conduct, that he did not rely on the representation. If you tell a man, "You may enter into partnership with me, my business is bringing in between £300 and £400 a year," the man who makes that representation must know that it is a material inducement to the other to enter into the partnership, and you cannot investigate as to whether it was more or less probable that the inducement would operate on the mind of the party to whom the representation was made. Where you have neither evidence that he knew facts to shew that the statement was untrue, or that he said or did anything to shew that he did not actually rely upon the statement, the inference remains that he did so rely, and the statement being a material statement, its being untrue is a sufficient ground for rescinding the contract. . . .

[The opinions of Baggallay and Lush L.JJ. who concurred in allowing the appeal are omitted.]

HEILBUT, SYMONS & CO. *v.* BUCKLETON
England. House of Lords. [1913] A.C. 30

LORD MOULTON: My Lords, in this action the plaintiff sought relief in damages against the defendants in respect of two contracts whereby the defendants undertook to procure for the plaintiff, and the plaintiff undertook to accept, the allotment of 5000 and 1000 shares in a company called the Filisola Rubber and Produce Estates, Limited. The claim for such relief was mainly based on the allegation that the plaintiff had been induced to enter into these contracts by the false and fraudulent representation of the defendants that the said company was a rubber company. This was the sole ground for relief which was put forward by the plaintiff in the proceedings before action and in the indorsement on the writ; but in the statement of claim an alternative claim for damages was included, based on the breach of an alleged warranty given by the defendants that the company was a rubber company.

At the trial the substantial case which was sought to be made on behalf of the plaintiff had reference solely to the alleged false and fraudulent representation. Evidence was given by the plaintiff and not challenged by the defendants as to a conversation which took place over the telephone between the plaintiff and Mr. Johnston, a representative of the defendants, in which undoubtedly Mr. Johnston stated that the company was a rubber company. The making of the alleged representation was therefore not in issue, and the whole of the evidence on both sides was directed to the issue whether such representation was false, and whether, if so, it was fraudulently made. No evidence was given upon the issue of a warranty having been given by the defendants that the company was a rubber company other than so far as the proof of the conversation above referred to may have amounted to such evidence.

In answer to questions put to them by the judge, the jury found (1) that the company could not properly be described as a rubber company; (2) that the defendants did not fraudulently represent, but that (3) they did warrant that it was a rubber company. Against the second of these findings there is no appeal, so that the only questions before us are as to whether the first and third of these findings can stand.

The alleged warranty rested entirely upon the following evidence. The plaintiff got a friend to ring up on the telephone Mr. Johnston (a representative of the defendants, for whose acts they accepted the full responsibility) to tell him that the plaintiff wished to speak to him. The plaintiff's evidence continues thus: "I went to the telephone and I said 'Is that you, Johnston?' He said, 'Yes.' I said 'I understand that you are bringing out a rubber company' and he said 'We are.' "

The material part of the evidence ends here. The further conversation related to the soundness of the company, but no claim for relief is based on what then passed either by way of fraudulent representation or warranty.

The plaintiff then asked if he could have some shares. Mr. Johnston said he thought he could let him have 5000 at a premium of 1s. 3d., which the plaintiff expressed himself ready to take, but no bargain was then concluded. On the next day, however, Mr. Johnston accepted in writing the offer of the plaintiff as to taking 5000 shares. Later on the plaintiff applied to Mr. Johnston for a further 1000 shares and obtained them at a somewhat higher premium. In each case the terms of the contract were reduced to writing by Mr. Johnston, acting for the defendants, and sent to the plaintiff. The contracts were not contracts of sale of the shares of the company (which had not then been issued), but contracts whereby the defendants (who were underwriters of the shares in the forthcoming issue) undertook to procure for the plaintiff the allotment of the shares on his applying for them. There is, of course, no conflict as to the actual terms of these contracts, which appear from the letters. They were acted upon by the plaintiff, who duly applied for and received the allotments of 5000 and 1000 shares of the company, such allotments having been procured by the defendants by the exercise of their rights as underwriters. The plaintiff parted with some of his shares but retained the remainder, and it is in respect of these latter that the damages are claimed in this action. [The trial Judge allowed damages at £406 5s. and the Court of Appeal affirmed the judgment.]

There is no controversy between the parties as to certain points of fact and of law. It is not contested that the only company referred to was the Filisola Rubber and Produce Estates, Limited, or that the reply of Mr. Johnston to the plaintiff's question over the telephone was a representation by the defendants that the company was "a rubber company," whatever may be the meaning of that phrase; nor is there any controversy as to the legal nature of that which the plaintiff must establish. He must shew a warranty, i.e., a contract collateral to the main contract to take the shares, whereby the defendants in consideration of the plaintiff taking the shares promised that the company itself was a rubber company. The question in issue is whether there was any evidence that such a contract was made between the parties.

It is evident, both on principle and on authority, that there may be a contract the consideration for which is the making of some other contract. "If you will make such and such a contract I will give you one hundred pounds." is in every sense of the word a complete legal contract. It is collateral to the main contract, but each has an independent existence, and they do not differ in respect of their possessing to the full the character and status of a contract. But such collateral contracts must from their very nature be rare. The effect of a collateral contract such as that which I have instanced would be to increase the consideration of the main contract by £100, and the more natural and usual way of carrying this out would be by so modifying the main contract and not by executing a concurrent and collateral contract. Such collateral contracts, the sole effect of which is to vary or add to the terms of the principal contract, are therefore viewed with suspicion by the law. They must be proved strictly. Not only the terms of such contracts but the existence of an *animus contrahendi* on the part of all the parties to them must be clearly shewn. Any laxity on these points would enable parties to escape from the full performance of the obligations of contracts unquestionably entered into by them, and more especially would have the effect of lessening the authority of written contracts by making it possible to vary them by suggesting the existence of verbal collateral agreements relating to the same subject-matter.

There is in the present case an entire absence of any evidence to support the existence of such a collateral contract. The statement of Mr. Johnston in answer to plaintiff's question was beyond controversy a mere statement of fact, for it was in reply to a question for information and nothing more. No doubt it was a representation as to fact, and indeed it was the actual representation upon which the main case of the plaintiff rested. It was this representation which he alleged to have been false and fraudulent and which he alleged induced him to enter into the contracts and take the shares. There is no suggestion throughout the whole of his evidence that he regarded it as anything but a representation. Neither the plaintiff nor the defendants were asked any question or gave any evidence tending to shew the existence of any *animus contrahendi* other than as regards the main contracts. The whole case for the existence of a collateral contract therefore rests on the mere fact that the statement was made as to the character of the company, and if this is to be treated as evidence sufficient to establish the existence of a collateral contract of the kind alleged the same result must follow with regard to any other statement relating to the subject-matter of a contract made by a contracting party prior to its execution. This would negative entirely the firmly established rule that an innocent representation gives no right to damages. It would amount to saying that the making of any representation prior to a contract relating to its subject-matter is sufficient to establish the existence of a collateral contract that the statement is true and therefore to give a right to damages if such should not be the case.

In the history of English law we find many attempts to make persons responsible in damages by reason of innocent misrepresentation, and at times it has seemed as though the attempts would succeed. On the Chancery side of the Court the decisions favouring this view usually took the form of extending the scope of the action for deceit. There was a tendency to recognize the existence of what was sometimes called "legal fraud," i.e., that the making of an incorrect statement of fact without reasonable grounds, or of one which was inconsistent with information which the person had received or had the means of obtaining, entailed the same legal consequences as making it fraudulently. Such a doctrine would make a man liable for forgetfulness or mistake or even for honestly interpreting the facts known to him or drawing conclusions from them in a way which the Court did not think to be legally warranted. The high water mark of these decisions is to be found in the judgment by the Court of Appeal in the case of *Peek* v. *Derry* (1887), 37 Ch. D. 541, when they laid down that where a defendant has made a mis-statement of fact and the Court is of opinion that he had no reasonable grounds for believing that it was true he may be made liable in an action of deceit if it has materially tended to induce the plaintiff to do an act by which he has incurred damage. But on appeal to your Lordships' House this decision was unanimously reversed, and it was definitely laid down that, in order to establish a cause of action sounding in damages for misrepresentation, the statement must be fraudulent or, what is equivalent thereto, must be made recklessly, not caring whether it be true or not. The opinions pronounced in your Lordships' House in that case shew that both in substance and in form the decision was, and was intended to be, a reaffirmation of the old common law doctrine that actual fraud was essential to an action for deceit, and it finally settled the law that an innocent misrepresentation gives no right of action sounding in damages.

On the Common Law side of the Court the attempts to make a person liable for an innocent misrepresentation have usually taken the form of attempts to extend the doctrine of warranty beyond its just limits and to find that a warranty existed in cases where there was nothing more than an innocent misrepresentation. The present case is, in my opinion, an instance of this. But in respect of the question of the existence of a warranty the Courts have had the advantage of an admirable enunciation of the true principle of law which was made in very early days by Holt C.J. with respect to the contract of sale. He says [*c.* 1690]: "An affirimation at the time of the sale is a warranty, provided it appears on evidence to be so intended." So far as decisions are concerned, this has, on the whole, been consistently followed in the Courts of Common Law. But from time to time there have been dicta inconsistent with it which have, unfortunately found their way into textbooks and have given rise to confusion and uncertainty in this branch of the law. For example, one often sees quoted the dictum of Bayley J. in *Cave* v. *Coleman* 3 Man. & Ry. 2, where, in respect of a representation made verbally during the sale of a horse, he says that "being made in the course of dealing, and before the bargain was complete, it amounted to a warranty"—a proposition that is far too sweeping and cannot be supported. A still more serious deviation from the correct principle is to be found in a passage in the judgment of the Court of Appeal in *De Lassalle* v. *Guildford*, [1901] 2 K.B. 215, at p. 221, which was cited to us in the argument in the present case. In discussing the question whether a representation amounts to a warranty or not the judgment says: "In determining whether it was so intended, a decisive test is whether the vendor assumes to assert a fact of which the buyer is ignorant, or merely states an opinion or judgment upon a matter of which the vendor has no special knowledge, and on which the buyer may be expected also to have an opinion and to exercise his judgment."

With all deference to the authority of the Court that decided that case, the proposition which it thus formulates cannot be supported. It is clear that the Court did not intend to depart from the law laid down by Holt C. J. and cited above, for in the same judgment that dictum is referred to and accepted as a correct statement of the law. It is, therefore, evident that the use of the phrase "decisive test" cannot be defended. Otherwise it would be the duty of a judge to direct a jury that if a vendor states a fact of which the buyer is ignorant, they must, as a matter of law, find the existence of a warranty, whether or not the totality of the evidence shows that the parties intended the affirmation to form part of the contract; and this would be inconsistent with the law as laid down by Holt C.J. It may well be that the features thus referred to in the judgment of the Court of Appeal in that case may be criteria of value in guiding a jury in coming to a decision whether or not a warranty was intended; but they cannot be said to furnish decisive tests, because it cannot be said as a matter of law that the presence or absence of those features is conclusive of the intention of the parties. The intention of the parties can only be deduced from the totality of the evidence, and no secondary principle of such a kind can be universally true.

It is, my Lords, of the greatest importance, in my opinion, that this House should maintain in its full integrity the principle that a person is not liable in damages for an innocent misrepresentation, no matter in what way or under what form the attack is made. In the present case the statement was made in answer to an inquiry for information. There is nothing which can by any possibility be taken as evidence of an intention on the part of either or both of the parties that there should be a contractual liability in respect of the statement. It is a representation as to a specific thing and nothing more. The judge, therefore, ought not to have left the question of warranty to the jury, and if, as a matter of prudence, he did so in order to obtain their opinion in case of appeal, he ought then to have entered judgment for the defendants notwithstanding the verdict.

It will, of course, be evident that I have been dealing only with warranty or representation relating to a specific thing. This is wholly distinct from the question which arises when goods are sold by description and their answering to that description becomes a condition of the contract. It is, in my opinion, a failure to recognize that in the present case the parties were referring (as is evident by the written contracts) to one specific thing only that led Farwell L.J. to come to a different conclusion from that to which your Lordships ought, in my opinion, to come in this appeal.

[Order of the Court of Appeal reversed and judgment entered for the appellants. Viscount Haldane L.C. and Lord Atkinson also gave reasons for allowing the appeal.]

QUESTIONS. If the defendant had sold his own shares to the plaintiff under the circumstances set out in the principal case, could the plaintiff have claimed "rescission" of the contract? If the representation had been held to be a "term" of the contract, would your answer differ?

DERRY *v.* PEEK

England. House of Lords. 1889. 14 App. Cas. 337

In February, 1883, the appellants as directors of the Plymouth, Devonport and District Tramways Company issued a prospectus containing the following paragraph:

"One great feature of this undertaking, to which considerable importance should be attached, is, that by the special Act of Parliament obtained, the company has the right to use steam or mechanical motive power, instead of horses, and it is fully expected that by means of this a considerable saving will result in the working expenses of the line as compared with other tramways worked by horses."

Soon after the issue of the prospectus the respondent, relying, as he alleged, upon the representations in this paragraph and believing that the company had an absolute right to use steam and other mechanical power, applied for and obtained shares in the company. In fact the Company could use steam or any mechanical power only with the consent of the Board of Trade and subject to the regulations of the Board.

The Company proceeded to make tramways, but the Board of Trade refused to consent to the use of steam or mechanical power except on certain portions of the tramways.

In the result the Company was wound up, and the respondent in 1885 brought an action of deceit against the appellants claiming damages for the fraudulent misrepresentations of the defendants whereby the plaintiff was induced to take shares in the Company.

Stirling J. dismissed the action; but that decision was reversed by the Court of Appeal who held that the defendants were liable to make good to the plaintiff the loss sustained by his taking the shares, and ordered an inquiry. Against this decision the defendants appealed.

LORD HERSCHELL: My Lords, in the statment of claim in this action the respondent, who is the plaintiff, alleges that the appellants made in a prospectus issued by them certain statements which were untrue, that they well knew that the facts were not as stated in the prospectus, and made the representations fraudulently, and with the view to induce the plaintiff to take shares in the company.

"This action is one which is commonly called an action of deceit, a mere common law action." This is the description of it given by Cotton L.J. in delivering judgment. I think it important that it should be borne in mind that such action differs essentially from one brought to obtain recission of a contract on the ground of misrepresentation of a material fact. The principles which govern the two actions differ widely. Where rescission is claimed it is only necessary to prove that there was misrepresentation; then, however honestly it may have been made, however free from blame the person who made it, the contract, having been obtained by misrepresentation, cannot stand. In an action of deceit, on the contrary, it is not enough to establish misrepresentation alone; it is conceded on all hands that something more must be proved to cast liability upon the defendant, though it has been a matter of controversy what additional elements are requisite. I lay stress upon this because observations made by learned judges in actions for rescission have been cited and much relied upon at the bar by counsel for the respondent. Care must obviously be observed in applying the language used in relation to such actions to an action of deceit. Even if the scope of the language used extends beyond the particular action which was being dealt with, it must be remembered that the learned judges were not engaged in determining what is necessary to support an action of deceit, or in discriminating with nicety the elements which enter into it. . . .

One other observation I have to make before proceeding to consider the law which has been laid down by the learned judges in the Court of Appeal in the case before your Lordships. "An action of deceit is a common law action, and must be decided on the same principles, whether it be brought in the Chancery Division or any of the Common Law Divisions, there being, in my opinion, no such thing as an equitable action for deceit." This was the language of Cotton L.J. in *Arkwright* v. *Newbold* (1879), 17 Ch. D. 301, at p. 320. It was adopted by Lord Blackburn in *Smith* v. *Chadwick* (1884), 9 App. Cas. 187, and is not, I think, open to dispute.

In the Court below Cotton L.J. said: "What in my opinion is a correct statement of the law is this, that where a man makes a statement to be acted upon by others which is false, and which is known by him to be false, or is made by him recklessly, or without care whether it is true or false, that is, without any reasonable ground for believing it to be true, he is liable in an action of deceit at the suit of anyone to whom it was addressed or anyone of the class to whom it was addressed and who was materially induced by the misstatement to do an act to his prejudice." About much that is here stated there cannot, I think, be two opinions. But when the learned Lord Justice speaks of a statement made recklessly or without care where it is true or false, that is without any reasonable ground for believing it to be true, I find myself, with all respect, unable to agree that these are convertible expressions. To make a statement careless whether it be true or false, and therefore without any real belief in its truth, appears to me to be an essentially different thing from making, through want of care, a false statement, which is nevertheless honestly believed to be true. And it is surely conceivable that a man may believe that what he states is the fact, though he has been so wanting in care that the Court may think that there were no sufficient grounds to warrant his belief. I shall have to consider hereafter whether the want of reasonable ground for believing the statement made is sufficient to support an action of deceit. I am only concerned for the moment to point out that it does not follow that it is so, because there is authority for saying that a statement made recklessly, without caring whether it be true or false, affords sufficient foundation for such an action.

That the learned Lord Justice thought that if a false statement were made without reasonable ground for believing it to be true an action of deceit would lie, is clear from a subsequent passage in his judgment. He says that when statements are made in a prospectus like the present, to be circulated amongst persons in order to induce them to take shares, "there is a duty cast upon the director or other person who makes those statments to take care that there are no expressions in them which in fact are false; to take care that he has reasonable ground for the material statements which are contained in that document which he prepares and circulates for the very purpose of its being acted upon by others."

The learned judge proceeds to say: "Although in my opinion it is not necessary that there should be what I should call fraud, yet in these actions, according to my view of the law, there must be a departure from duty, that is to say, an untrue statement made without any reasonable ground for believing that statement to be true; and in my opinion when a man makes an untrue statement with an intention that it shall be acted upon without any reasonable ground for believing that statement to be true he makes a default in a duty which was thrown upon him from the position he has taken upon himself, and he violates the right which those to whom he makes the statement have to have true statements only made to them."

Now I have first to remark on these observations that the alleged "right" must surely be here stated too widely, if it is intended to refer to a legal right, the violation of which may give rise to an action for damages. For if there be a right to have true statements only made, this will render liable to an action those who make untrue statements, however innocently. This cannot have been meant. I think it must have been intended to make the statement of the right correspond with that of the alleged duty, the departure from which is said to be making an untrue statement without any reasonable ground for believing it to be true. I have further to observe that the Lord Justice distinctly says that if there be such a departure from duty an action of deceit can be maintained, though there be not what he should call fraud. I shall have by-and-by to consider the discussions which have arisen as to the difference between the popular understanding of the word "fraud" and the interpretation given to it by lawyers, which have led to the use of such expressions as "legal fraud," or "fraud in law"; but I may state at once that in my opinion, without proof of fraud no action of deceit is maintainable. When I examine the cases which have been decided upon this branch of the law, I shall endeavour to shew that there is abundant authority to warrant this proposition.

I return now to the judgments delivered in the Court of Appeal. Sir James Hannen says: "I take the law to be that if a man takes upon himself to assert a thing to be true which he does not know to be true, and has no reasonable ground to believe it to be true, in order to induce another to act upon the assertion, who does so act and is thereby damnified, the person so damnified is entitled to maintain an action for deceit." Again Lopes L.J. states what in his opinion, is the result of the cases. I will not trouble your Lordships with quoting the first three propositions which he lays down, although I do not feel sure that the third is distinct from, and not rather an instance of, the case dealt with by the second proposition. But he says that a person making a false statement, intended to be and in fact relied on by the person to whom it is made, may be sued by the person damaged thereby: "Fourthly if it is untrue in fact, but believed to be true, but without any reasonable grounds for such belief."

It will thus be seen that all the learned judges concurred in thinking that it was sufficient to prove that the representations made were not in accordance with facts, and that the persons making them had no reasonable grounds for believing them. They did not treat the absence of such reasonable ground as evidence merely that the statements were made recklessly, careless whether they were true or false, and without belief that they were true, but they adopted as the test of liability, not the existence of belief in the truth of the assertions made, but whether the belief in them was founded upon any reasonable grounds. It will be seen, further, that the Court did not purport to be establishing any new doctrine. They deemed that they were only following the cases already decided, and that the proposition which they concurred in laying down was established by prior authorities. Indeed, Lopes L.J. expressly states the law in this respect to be well settled. This renders a close and critical examination of the earlier authorities necessary. . . .

I now arrive at the earliest case in which I find the suggestion that an untrue statement made without reasonable ground for believing it will support an action for deceit. In *Western Bank of Scotland* v. *Addie* (1867), Law Rep. 1 H.L., Sc. & Div. 145, 162, the Lord President told the jury "that if a case should occur of directors taking upon themselves to put forth in their report statements of importance in regard to the affairs of the bank false in themselves and which they did not believe, or had no reasonable ground to believe to be true, that would be a misrepresentation and deceit." Exception having been taken to this direction without avail in the Court of Session, Lord Chelmsford in this House said: "I agree in the propriety of this interlocutor. In the argument upon this exception the case was put of an honest belief being entertained by the directors, of the reasonableness of which it was said the jury, upon this direction, would have to judge. But supposing a person makes an untrue statement which he asserts to be the result of a bona fide belief in its truth, how can the bona fides be tested except by considering the grounds of such belief? And if an untrue statement is made founded upon a belief which is destitute of all reasonable grounds, or which the least inquiry would immediately correct, I do not see that it is not fairly and correctly characterised as misrepresentation and deceit."

I think there is here some confusion between that which is evidence of fraud, and that which constitutes it. A consideration of the grounds of belief is no doubt an important aid in ascertaining whether the belief was really entertained. A man's mere assertion that he believed the statement he made to be true is not accepted as conclusive proof that he did so. There may be such an absence of reasonable ground for his belief as, in spite of his assertion, to carry conviction to the mind that he had not really the belief which he alleges. If the learned Lord intended to go further, as apparently he did, and to say that though the belief was really entertained, yet if there were no reasonable grounds for it, the person making the statement was guilty of fraud in the same way as if he had known what he stated to be false, I say, with all respect, that the previous authorities afford no warrant for the view that an action of deceit would lie under such circumstances. A man who forms his belief carelessly, or is unreasonably credulous, may be blameworthy when he makes a representation on which another is to act, but he is not, in my opinion, fraudulent in the sense in which that word was used in all the cases from *Pasley* v. *Freeman*, 2 Smith's L.C. 74, down to that with which I am now dealing. Even when the expression "fraud in law" has been employed, there has always been present, and regarded as an essential element, that the deception was willful either because the untrue statement was known to be untrue, or because belief in it was asserted without such belief existing.

I have made these remarks with the more confidence because they appear to me to have the high sanction of Lord Cranworth. In delivering his opinion in the same case he said: "I confess that my opinion was that in what his Lordship (the Lord President) thus stated, he went beyond what principle warrants. If persons in the situation of directors of a bank make statements as to the condition of its affairs which they bona fide believe to be true, I cannot think they can be guilty of fraud because other persons think, or the Court thinks, or your Lordships think, that there was no sufficient ground to warrant the opinion which they had formed. If a little more care and caution must have led the directors to a conclusion different from that which they put forth, this may afford strong evidence to shew that they did not really believe in the truth of what they stated, and so that they were guilty of fraud. But this would be the consequence not of their having stated as true what they had not reasonable ground to believe to be true, but of their having stated as true what they did not believe to be true."

Sir James Hannen, in his judgment below, seeks to limit the application of what Lord Cranworth says to cases where the statement made is a matter of opinion only. With all deference I do not think it was intended to be or can be so limited. The direction which he was considering, and which he thought went beyond what true principle warranted, had relation to making false statements of importance in regard to the affairs of the bank. When this is borne in mind, and the words which follow those quoted by Sir James Hannen are looked at, it becomes to my mind obvious that Lord Cranworth did not use the words "the opinion which they had formed" as meaning anything different from "the belief which they entertained."...

Having now drawn attention, I believe, to all the cases having a material bearing upon the question under consideration, I proceed to state briefly the conclusions to which I have been led. I think the authorities establish the following propositions: First, in order to sustain an action of deceit, there must be poof of fraud, and nothing short of that will suffice. Secondly, fraud is proved when it is shewn that a false representation has been made (1) knowingly, or (2) without belief in its truth, or (3) recklessly, careless whether it is true or false. Although I have treated the second and third as distinct cases, I think the third is but an instance of the second, for one who makes a statement under such circumstances can have no real belief in the truth of what he states. To prevent a false statement being fraudulent, there must, I think, always be an honest belief in its truth. And this probably covers the whole ground, for one who knowingly alleges that which is false, has obviously no such honest belief.... Thirdly, if fraud be proved, the motive of the person guilty of it is immaterial. It matters not that there was no intention to cheat or injure the person to whom the statement was made.

I think these propositions embrace all that can be supported by decided cases from the time of *Pasley* v. *Freeman*, down to *Western Bank of Scotland* v. *Addie*, in 1867, when the first suggestion is to be found that belief in the truth of what he has stated will not suffice to absolve the defendant if his belief be based on no reasonable grounds. I have shewn that this view was at once dissented from by Lord Cranworth, so that there was at the outset as much authority against it as for it.

In my opinion making a false statement through want of care falls far short of, and is a very different thing from, fraud, and the same may be said of a false representation honestly believed though on insufficient grounds....

At the same time I desire to say distinctly that when a false statement has been made the questions whether there were reasonable grounds for believing it, and what were the means of knowledge in the possession of the person making it, are most weighty matters for consideration. The ground upon which an alleged belief was founded is a most important test of its reality. I can conceive many cases where the fact that an alleged belief was destitute of all reasonable foundation would suffice of itself to convince the Court that it was not really entertained, and that the representation was a fraudulent one. So, too, although means of knowledge are, as was pointed out by Lord Blackburn in *Brownlie* v. *Campbell* (1880), 5 App. Cas. at p. 952, a very different thing from knowledge, if I thought that a person making a false statement had shut his eyes to the facts, or purposely abstained from enquiring into them, I should hold that honest belief was absent, and that he was just as fraudulent as if he had knowingly stated that which was false.

I have arrived with some reluctance at the conclusion to which I have felt myself compelled, for I think those who put before the public a prospectus to induce them to embark their money in a commercial enterprise ought to be vigilant to see that it contains such representations only as are in strict accordance with fact, and I should be very unwilling to give any countenance to the contrary idea. I think there is much to be said for the view that this moral duty ought to some extent to be converted into a legal obligation, and that the want of reasonable care to see that statements, made under such circumstances, are true, should be made an actionable wrong. But this is not a matter fit for discussion on the present occasion. If it is to be done the legislature must intervene and expressly give a right of action in respect of such a departure from duty. It ought not, I think, to be done by straining the law, and holding that to be fraudulent which the tribunal feels cannot properly be so described. I think mischief is likely to result from blurring the distinction between carelessness and fraud, and equally holding a man fraudulent whether his acts can or cannot be justly so designated.

It now remains for me to apply what I believe to be the law of the facts of the present case. . . .

[Lord Herschell then examined the evidence and continued:]

Adopting the language of Jessel M.R. in *Smith* v. *Chadwick*, I conclude by saying that on the whole I have come to the conclusion that the statement, "though in some respects inaccurate and not altogether free imputation of carelessness, was a fair, honest and bona fide statement on the part of the defendants, and by no means exposes them to an action for deceit.". . .

[Order of the Court of Appeal reversed: order of Stirling J. restored. The opinions of Lord Halsbury L.C., and Lords Watson, Bramwell and Fitzgerald are omitted.]

NOTE. Liability of directors and others for false statements made in a prospectus of a company, in the absence of fraud, is now provided for by *The Companies Information Act*, R.S.O. 1960, c. 60, s. 5.

NOCTON *v.* ASHBURTON. [1914] A.C. 932 (England. House of Lords). LORD HALDANE: "It must now be taken to be settled that nothing short of proof of fraudulent intention in the strict sense will suffice for an action of deceit. This is so whether a Court of Law or a Court of Equity, in the exercise of concurrent jurisdiction, is dealing with the claim, and in this strict sense it was quite natural that Lord Bramwell and Lord Herschell should say that there was no such thing as legal as distinguished from moral fraud. But when fraud is referred to in the wider sense in which the books are full of the expression, used in Chancery in describing cases which were within its exclusive jurisdiction, it is a mistake to suppose that an actual intention to cheat must always be proved. A man may misconceive the extent of the obligation which a Court of Equity imposes on him. His fault is that he has violated, however innocently because of his ignorance, an obligation which he must be taken by the Court to have known, and his conduct has in that sense always been called fraudulent. . . . It was thus the expression 'constructive fraud' came into existence. The trustee who purchases the trust estate, the solicitor who makes a bargain with his client that cannot stand, have all for several centuries run the risk of the word fraudulent being applied to them. What it really means in this connection, is not moral fraud, in the ordinary sense, but breach of the sort of obligation which is enforced by a court that from the beginning regarded itself as a court of conscience. If among the great lawyers who decided *Derry* v. *Peek* there had been present some versed in the practice of the Court of Chancery, it may well be that the decision would not have been different, but that more and explicit attention would have been directed to the wide range of the class of cases in which on the ground of a fiduciary duty, Courts of Equity gave a remedy." [The situations in which this type of "fraud" appears are dealt with in courses on Trusts, Companies, Agency, etc.]

NEWBIGGING *v*. ADAM

England. Court of Appeal. 1886. 34 Ch.D. 582

The plaintiff was induced by the misrepresentation of the defendants as to the adequacy of some machinery to contribute £10,024 2s. 7d. to a partnership to which he was admitted. The business proved unsuccessful and this action was brought to dissolve the partnership and for amongst other claims, an order that the defendants repay the plaintiff £9,279 6s. 1d. and indemnify him against all liabilities to which he had or might become liable in the partnership name. It was so ordered and the defendants appealed on the ground that this order amounted to damages for innocent misrepresentation.

BOWEN L.J.: . . . If we turn to the question of misrepresentation, damages cannot be obtained at law for misrepresentation which is not fraudulent, and you cannot, as it seems to me, give in equity any indemnity which corresponds with damages. If the mass of authority there is upon the subject were gone through I think it would be found that there is not so much difference as is generally supposed between the view taken at common law and the view taken in equity as to misrepresentation. At common law it has always been considered that misrepresentations which strike at the root of the contract are sufficient to avoid the contract on the ground explained in *Kennedy* v. *Panama, New Zealand, and Australian Royal Mail Company* (1867), L.R. 2 Q.B. 580; but when you come to consider what is the exact relief to which a person is entitled in a case of misrepresentation it seems to me to be this, and nothing more, that he is entitled to have the contract rescinded, and is entitled accordingly to all the incidents and consequences of such rescission. It is said that the injured party is entitled to be replaced in *statu quo*. It seems to me that when you are dealing with innocent misrepresentation you must understand that proposition that he is to be placed *in statu quo* with this limitation—that he is not to be replaced in exactly the same position in all respects, otherwise he would be entitled to recover damages, but is to be replaced in his position so far as regards the rights and obligations which have been created by the contract into which he has been induced to enter. That seems to me to be the true doctrine, and I think it is put in the neatest way in *Redgrave* v. *Hurd* (1881), 20 Ch. D. 14. [After considering that case and quoting a pasage from Jessel M.R.'s judgment, Bowen L.J. continued.] With great respect for the shadow and memory of that great name I cannot help saying that this is not a perfect exposition of what the common law was, but, so far as the rule of equity goes, I must assume that the Master of the Rolls spoke with full knowledge of the equity authorities, and he treats the relief as being the giving back by the party who made the misrepresentation of the advantages he obtained by the contract.

Now those advantages may be of two kinds. He may get an advantage in the shape of an actual benefit, as when he receives money; he may also get an advantage if the party with whom he contracts assumes some burthen in consideration of the contract. In such a case it seems to me that complete rescission would not be effected unless the misrepresenting party not only hands back the benefits which he has himself received—but also re-assumes the burthen which under the contract the injured person has taken upon himself. Speaking only for myself I should not like to lay down the proposition that a person is to be restored to the position which he held before the misrepresentation was made, nor that the person injured must be indemnified against loss which arises out of the contract, unless you place upon the words "out of the contract" the limited and special meaning which I have endeavoured to shadow forth. Loss arising out of the contract is a term which would be too wide. It would embrace damages at common law, because damages at common law are only given upon the supposition that they are damages which would naturally and reasonably follow from the injury done. I think *Redgrave* v. *Hurd* shews that it would be too wide, because in that case the Court excluded from the relief which was given the damages which had been sustained by the plaintiff in removing his business, and other similar items. There ought, as it appears to me, to be a giving back and a taking back on both sides, including the giving back and taking back of the obligations which the contract has created, as well as the giving back and taking back of the advantages. . . .

I have not found any case which carries the doctrine further, and it is not necessary to carry it further in order to support the order now appealed from. A part of the contract between the Plaintiff and *Adam & Co*. was that the Plaintiff should become and continue for five years partner in a new firm and bring in £10,000. By this very contract he was to pledge his credit with his partners in the new firm for the business transactions of the new firm. It was a burthen or liability imposed on him by the very contract. It seems to me that the £9000 odd, and, indeed, all the moneys brought in by him or expended by him for the new firm up to the £10,000, were part of the actual moneys which he undertook by the true contract with *Adam & Co*. to pay. Of course he ought to be indemnified as regards that. I think, also, applying the same doctrine, he ought to be indemnified against all the liabilities of the firm, because they were liabilities which under the contract he was bound to take upon himself. . . .

[The decisions of Cotton and Fry L.JJ. concurring in dismissing the appeal are omitted.]

REDICAN *v.* NESBITT

Canada. Supreme Court. [1924] S.C.R. 135

The defendants entered into a contract to purchase a leasehold property from the plaintiff represented by one Wing, her agent. In due course an assignment of lease executed by the plaintiff and assented to by the landlord (the City of Toronto) was delivered to the defendants' solicitor with the keys of the property, the cheque of one of the defendants for the purchase money being simultaneously handed to the plaintiff's solicitor. The defendants also took an assignment of insurance and paid some arrears of taxes. On inspecting the property two days later—which is said to have been their first opportunity of doing so—they discovered, as they allege, that it had been misrepresented to them by Wing in several particulars, which they claim are of such importance that, had they known the truth in regard to them, they would not have purchased. On learning of these matters they stopped payment of the cheque given for the purchase money having first notified the vendor's husband that that would be done. An action by the vendor was at once begun for the sum of $2,969.84 being the balance of account owing under an offer to purchase by the defendants from the plaintiff and accepted by her.

The defendants by way of counter-claim asked for rescission. The action was tried by a jury. The questions submitted and the answers returned by the jury are as follows:

1. (a) Did Mrs. Nesbitt's agent, Wing, knowingly, make any untrue statements as to the house or its contents for the purpose of deceiving the defendants in any material way and inducing them to make the offer to purchase? No.

(b) Did they make the offer relying upon such statements? Refer to question 1 (a).

2. If you find there were any such statements, what were they? We find that there is no evidence that such statements were made knowingly.

3. Did Wing make any untrue statement without knowing they were untrue but relying upon which defendants signed, and without having such statements they would not have signed their offer to purchase? Yes.

4. If so, what were such innocent misrepresentations? (a) That the house was lighted electrically. (b) That there were five bedrooms.

Upon these answers the trial judge entered judgment for the plaintiff. This judgment was affirmed by the Appellate Division of the Supreme Court of Ontario. The defendants appealed to the Supreme Court of Canada.

ANGLIN J.: . . . That this is not an action on the cheque referred to in the amendment of the special indorsement allowed at the trial, as the plaintiff now seeks to maintain, is made clear by the facts that the claim and the judgment are not against the maker of the cheque alone, but are against her and her co-purchaser jointly. The amendment made at the trial should not therefore be regarded as having changed the cause of action as originally stated. It merely added an allegation facilitating proof of the amount of the plaintiff's claim as a sum liquidated. The action remained one for money due and owing upon the contract.

It is, however, equally clear that it is in no sense the equitable action for specific performance. The plaintiff asserted a purely common law claim for payment of a sum of money due under a contract, perfectly valid, *Rutherford* v. *Acton-Adams*, [1915] A.C. 866, 868, subject to any defence to which such a claim is open. He did not require the aid of a court of equity to be relieved of the leasehold with its burdens; the defendants by taking the conveyance had assumed them. For the recovery of the purchase money the common law remedy was adequate and there was no ground for the plaintiff invoking the interference of a court of equity. It follows that the defendants will not necessarily succeed by establishing a case which would have disentitled the plaintiff to specific performance in a court of equity. That remedy is so distinctly discretionary that the court may withhold it although a case for rescission has not been made out.

But innocent misrepresentation, such as will support a demand for rescission in equity, though unavailing at common law, will serve as a good equitable defence to a claim for payment under the contract as well as afford ground for a counter-claim for rescission. Rescission is, of course, destructive of the basis of the plaintiff's claim; the right to rescission when established is an effective defence. But whether misrepresentation is set up by way of equitable defence or as the basis of a counter-claim for rescission, the burden on the defendant is the same. If the case made by him would not warrant a decree for rescission it will not avail as a defence to the claim for payment. In preferring this defence a defendant assumes the role of actor and a plea which, if established, would defeat a counter-claim for rescission is equally effective by way of reply to the defence of misrepresentation if set up by the plaintiff. . . .

In the present case the defendants plead misrepresentation as a ground both of defence and of counter-claim. They assert that it was fraudulent and, alternatively, that if innocent it was so material as to afford ground for rescission.

The jury negatived fraud and on this branch of the case, if they are not entitled to have the action dismissed on the other, the defendants ask for a new trial on the ground of misdirection and refusal by the learned trial judge to submit an essential element of it to the jury. I defer dealing with that aspect of the appeal.

The jury found that innocent misrepresentations inducing the contract had been made by the plaintiff's agent, and upon them the defendants maintain they are entitled to rescission. The trial judge rejected this claim on the ground that the contract for sale had been fully executed by the delivery of the deed and the acceptance of the cheque in payment, and that rescission of a contract after execution cannot be had for mere innocent misrepresentation unless it be such as renders the subject of sale different in substance from what was contracted for. . . . The suggestion that the property differed so completely in substance from what the defendants intended to acquire that there was a failure of consideration is not borne out by the facts. Neither is there any foundation for a suggestion of mutual mistake as a basis for rescission. *Debenham* v. *Sawbridge* [1901] 2 Ch. 98, 109. The trial judge regarded the handing over of the cheque as absolute payment and as a completion of the contract by the defendants just as the delivery of the conveyance and possession constituted completion on the part of the plaintiff.

In the Appellate Divisional Court this judgment was sustained, the late Sir W. R. Meredith, C.J.O. giving the judgment of the majority of the court, on the ground that the contract became "executed" upon delivery and acceptance of the conveyance, whether the giving and taking of the cheque should or should not be regarded as payment of the purchase money.

Although Mr. Pollock in his treatise on the *Law of Contracts* (9th ed. p. 593) would seem to imply the existence of some doubt as to the doctrine enunciated in Lord Campbell's dictum in *Wilde* v. *Gibson* (1848), 1 H.L. Cas. 605; 9 E.R. 897 at p. 909, that "where the conveyance has been executed . . . a Court of Equity will set aside the conveyance only on the ground of fraud," pointing out that it has not been uniformly followed (see *Fry on Specific Performance*, 9th ed., p. 312), it is too well established to admit of controversy, assuming that his Lordship meant where the contract had been fully carried out. . . .

But on the question when a contract will, for the purpose of this rule, be deemed to have ceased to be "executory" and to have become "executed" the authorities are not so clear. I have not found any reported case in which it has been determined whether or not after delivery and acceptance of the conveyance and taking of possession a contract of sale remains "executory" until actual payment of the purchase money then due; nor indeed have I found any authority in which the contrary has been categorically determined. In many of the cases it is broadly stated, as it was by Lord Campbell, that after conveyance rescission will not be granted for innocent misrepresentation. But, on examination of the facts in such cases, it is clear either that payment of the purchase money had been made or as in the case of a contract for a lease, that all that the plaintiff seeking rescission was required by the contract to do had been done. . . .

[Anglin J. then quoted from a number of text writers and concluded:]

The foundation of the rule that an executed contract will not be rescinded for innocent misrepresentation appears to be somewhat obscure. In *Angel* v. *Jay*, [1911] 1 K.B. 666, 671, Darling J. states, apparently without disapproval, the contention of counsel that "the foundation of the doctrine" is that "when property has passed the persons concerned cannot be placed in the same position as they were in before the estate became vested." In numerous cases the vesting of the property has been referred to as a serious obstacle to rescission. In other cases the supersession of the contract for sale by the executed conveyance accepted by the purchaser and the resultant restriction of his rights to those assured by the latter instrument appears to be the ground upon which rescission of the contract after acceptance of conveyance is refused. So far does the court go in maintaining this doctrine that, where under a court sale the purchase money was still in court, the purchaser who had accepted the title and taken his conveyance was refused relief in respect of subsequently discovered incumbrances.

In the case now before us it is probably unnecessary to determine the effect on the right of a purchaser to rescission of his acceptance of a conveyance and taking of possession without making payment. What might have been a formidable obstacle to the granting of rescission to the defendants was suggested by the trial judge, namely, the inability of the court to compel the landlord's assent to a re-assignment of the leasehold to the plaintiff. The effect of the acceptance of the conveyance assented to by the lessor and of the taking of possession of the property by the defendants may have been to give to the lessor rights against them as tenants the relinquishment of which the court could not exact.

Although the execution of the contract does not afford an answer to a claim for rescission in cases of fraudulent misrepresentation, inability to effect *restitutio in integrum*, unless that has become impossible owing to action of the wrong-doer, will ordinarily preclude rescission. Kerr on Fraud (5th ed.) 387–90. *A fortiori* is this the case where innocent misrepresentation only is relied upon. . . .

But I strongly incline to the view that while the acceptance of the cheque as payment was in this sense conditional that, if it should be dishonoured, the right to sue for the money due under the contract would revive, the transaction was, nevertheless, intended to be closed and the contract completely executed so far as the purchasers were concerned by their taking of the deed and the keys and handing over the cheque. They had obtained the full consideration for which they contracted and, if the vendor saw fit to accept the cheque they tendered in payment in lieu of cash, they should not be heard to say that the contract had not been fully executed. I cannot think that the vendor's right to have the contract treated as executed and completed can be defeated by the fact that she took a cheque as the equivalent of a cash payment, and still less by the accident that the cheque was not presented for payment during the two days which intervened between the closing of the sale and the stopping of payment. Bearing in mind the well established custom of solicitors with regard to the closing of sales of real estate, when delivery of conveyance and possession was given and accepted and a cheque (then good) for the purchase money was tendered and taken, what was performed was what the parties intended should be done when they contracted.

Without, therefore, necessarily affirming the position taken in the judgment of the majority of the learned judges of the Appellate Divisional Court, I am of the opinion that, under all the circumstances of this case, the contract for sale was executed and that, according to a well settled rule in equity, rescission for innocent misrepresentation is not an available remedy for the defendants.

I am clearly of the opinion, however, that a new trial must be directed because the issue of fraud was not properly presented to the jury. In substance the learned trial judge charged that, in order to establish fraud, the defendants must show that Wing actually knew his representations were false. He did not tell the jury that the representations would be fraudulent if they were false and were made without belief in their truth, or recklessly, careless whether they were true or false. . . . The attention of the trial judge was thus pointedly drawn to the feature of fraudulent misrepresentation which his question did not cover. Counsel expressly asked that it should be covered. The learned judge distinctly stated his view that intention to deceive was essential and impliedly that a false statement made with reckless carelessness as to its truth or falsehood would not be fraudulent. He declined to amend the questions as suggested, stating that he had "covered" the case.

Counsel is not obliged to quarrel with the judge or to press an objection *ad nauseam*. Having stated his position and his request for the submission of a proper question having been refused Mr. Grant had, I think, sufficiently discharged his duty and was not called upon to renew the same objection at the close of the charge. The learned judge had definitely expressed his purpose to adhere to an adverse view of the law. . . .

[Appeal allowed with costs and a new trial granted. Davies C.J. concurred with Anglin J. The opinions of Idington, Duff and Mignault JJ. are omitted. While Idington J. agreed in the result he also went beyond the grounds taken by the rest of the Court in that he appeared willing to grant rescission even though the contract was executed on the apparent ground that the misrepresentation led to an "error *in substantialibus*." "I think a difference of a few acres, is no more important than the four rooms instead of five as misrepresented and electric light in this case to the appellants."]

COLE *v.* POPE. 1898. 29 S.C.R. 291 (British Columbia. Supreme Court of Canada). In June, 1896, the appellant and others had taken up a gold mining claim known as the "Eldorado" in the neighbourhood of Rossland, B.C., of which the appellant represented himself to be the owner of an undivided half. The respondent, believing and relying entirely upon the appellant's representation as to ownership, purchased the undivided half of "Eldorado" for $5,250, which he paid in cash. It shortly appeared that the "Eldorado" claim was almost wholly within a prior claim, the "Mascot," and the balance was in fact included in other claims. The respondent therefore got nothing for his $5,250. Both parties dealt upon the mistaken belief that the "Eldorado" was an actually existing mining right. The respondent brought this action to have the contract rescinded and to obtain repayment of the $5,250. The trial judge dismissed the action. The full court reversed him. The Supreme Court of Canada dismissed the appeal. STRONG C.J.: "The learned trial judge considered the respondent's right to rescission dependent entirely on the misrepresentation, and held that in the present state of the law an executed contract—and especially an executed contract for the sale of an interest in land—will not be rescinded for mere innocent misrepresentation. . . . I conclude therefore in favour of the proposition that mere innocent representation will not warrant the rescission of an executed contract for the sale of an interest in land.

"There is, however, another principle which I think may be invoked in the respondent's favour and which is quite open to him on the pleadings and evidence before us.

"It has been determined by several authorities and is well established law that where by the mutual mistake of the parties to a contract of sale the subject of the sale turns out to be non-existent or is already the property of the purchaser, both parties having fallen into error merely, and there being no fraud or deceit in the case, the purchaser who has paid his purchase money and taken a conveyance will be relieved and the contract rescinded by a Court of Equity. In such a case where there is a complete failure of consideration as in the present case it would be unjust and unconscientious that the vendor should retain money paid to him for a supposed consideration which has utterly failed."

MacKENZIE *v.* ROYAL BANK OF CANADA. [1934] A.C. 468 (Ontario. Privy Council). An action *in forma pauperis* by Mrs. MacKenzie, to set aside a contract of guarantee with a pledge of shares worth about $10,000 on the grounds of undue influence by her husband and innocent misrepresentation by her husband's bank. She lost on the first ground but she established that she had been induced to part with her securities and to guarantee the debts of her husband's business by a misrepresentation. In 1913 she had hypothecated the shares with the Bank to assist the company then just formed by her husband. During the war the company prospered and in 1918 the shares were released to her. By 1920, however, the company was in difficulties, and on December 31, Mrs. MacKenzie again hypothecated her shares, making them "general and continuing collateral security for payment of the present and future indebtedness and liability of MacKenzie Ld." In May of 1921 the company went into bankruptcy and after the Bank realized its security for the company's debt, there ceased to be any "indebtedness and liability of MacKenzie Ld." to which the pledged shares could attach. In November a new company, MacKenzie Manufacturing Company, Ld. was formed. The Bank sold to Mr. MacKenzie the assets of the old company for $125,000, MacKenzie sold them to the new company for the same price, the Bank advanced the price to the company and took the assets as security for the loss, putting the

Bank in much the same relation to the new company as it had been to the old. Mr. MacKenzie and the Bank's manager then asked Mrs. MacKenzie to pledge her shares once again to the Bank and they assured her that her shares were still bound under the hypothecation of December 31, 1920 and that this new guarantee was her only hope of getting them back. After she had signed she was given a form to be taken to a lawyer and signed by him, intimating that he had given her independent advice, and that she fully understood the transaction. Her lawyer signed the document as a matter of form, saying that he had given her no advice for he knew nothing about the new company. LORD ATKIN: "If it had been incumbent upon the bank to prove that the lady had had independent advice, their Lordships would have had the greatest difficulty in coming to the conclusion that the bank had discharged the onus. Independent advice to be of any value must be given before the transaction, for the question is as to the will of the party at the time of entering into the disputed transaction. Advice given after the event when the supposed contracting party is already bound is given under entirely different circumstances, with a different position presented to the minds both of the adviser and his client. It is unnecessary, however, to emphasize this point, for their Lordships are not able to take the view that the transaction was one in respect of which there was an onus upon the bank to prove that the plaintiff had independent advice. . . . But their Lordships have come to the conclusion that the contract cannot be allowed to stand for another reason. A contract of guarantee, like any other contract, is liable to be avoided if induced by material misrepresentation of an existing fact, even if made innocently. In this case it is unnecessary to decide whether contracts of guarantee belong to the special class where, even at common law, such an innocent misrepresentation would afford a defence to an action on the contract. The evidence conclusively establishes a misrepresentation by the bank that the plaintiff's shares were still bound to the bank with the necessary inference, whether expressed or not, and their Lordships accept the plaintiff's evidence that it was expressed, that the shares were already lost, and that the guarantee of the new company offered the only means of salving them. It does not seem to admit of doubt that such a misrepresentation made as to the plaintiff's private rights and depending upon transactions in bankruptcy, of the full nature of which she had not been informed, was a representation of fact. That it was material is beyond discussion. It consequently follows that the plaintiff was at all times, on ascertaining the true position, entitled to avoid the contract and recover her securities. There were subsequent renewals of the guarantee before the plaintiff was advised of the true facts, but counsel for the bank very properly conceded that they would be in the same position as the original guarantee. There is no difficulty as to restitutio in integrum. The mere fact that the party making the representation has treated the contract as binding and has acted on it does not preclude relief. Nor can it be said that the plaintiff received anything under the contract which she is unable to restore."

O'FLAHERTY *v.* McKINLAY

Newfoundland. Court of Appeal. [1953] 2 D.L.R. 514

DUNFIELD J.: The plaintiff in this case, a young lady who had not owned a car before, bought a second-hand Hillman sedan in April, 1950, from the defendant, who is an automobile dealer and garageman. She says she wanted and asked for a 1950 model. He and his staff told her it was a 1950 Hillman, which had gone 4,000 odd miles; that is admitted. She was charged $1325, so far as the defendant was concerned.

The defendant says that the previous owner, who traded the car to him against a Standard "Vanguard" car, for which defendant is agent, told him and his staff it was a 1950 Hillman, and they accepted that statement. It appears that in 1949 Hillman redesigned their car. As often happens in a new design, it had some shortcomings, and these were made good in the 1950 model; but the changes were mostly internal, and the 1949 and 1950 cars were externally very much alike, and would not be readily distinguishable except by their own agents. The previous owner, who was in the witness-box, denies that he represented the car to be a 1950 model; but the plaintiff's counsel accepts the defence position that there was innocent misrepresentation only. The plaintiff asks for rescission of the contract of sale and the return of her money including certain collateral expenditures.

The transaction was not clean-cut. Plaintiff paid down $675. She also signed documents in connection with the finance of the car involving a concern called the Industrial Acceptance Corp. The practical effect of these is as follows: The buyer borrows and the seller gets from the Corporation the balance of the purchase-money, viz., $650. The documents purport to transfer the title to the car and the debt to the Corporation pending payment off by instalments. The Corporation goes on to collect from the buyer by instalments of $47 a month a total sum exceeding $650 by a good deal. The corporation insures the car against collision, theft and fire. There is a provision in the agreement that if the purchaser dies the instalments come to an end. I was struck by the benevolence of this; but I am told by counsel that the Corporation also insures the life of the purchaser for a sufficient period. I note that a blank on the front of the form contains the typewritten statement that the car is a 1950 model, but a clause in small print on the back says that a statement as to year-model is not to affect the situation whether true or not. This appears objectionable, as few read these small type paragraphs; though one can quite see that the finance corporation does not want to take responsibility for any such technical point.

In fact, the plaintiff has paid off the finance corporation since this action began, so it is not necessary to add it as a party, as was suggested when the action first came on; and the action has now been pleaded and fought on the same basis as if it had been a direct sale without the intervention of the finance corporation. We are therefore spared from having to consider the effect of these transactions. It may be that the apparent assignment could be held to be in fact a mortgage to the finance corporation, or a mortgage to the vendor assigned to the corporation.

However, the plaintiff claims a total payment of $1,580.14 with rescission of the contract of sale. The difference, $255.14, between $1,325 and $1,580.14 is made up of [registration, insurance, repairs, taxes and carrying charges].

The defendant counterclaims for $158.53, an unpaid bill for repairs and maintenance done for the plaintiff.

The plaintiff, who was a novice driver, and her two brothers, also novices, drove the car about 7,000 miles during the summer of 1950. In early September 1950 the plaintiff happened to call at Adelaide Motors Ltd., who are agents for the Hillman, and happened to remark that the car was a 1950 model, and was then told that it was a 1949 model. She forthwith saw her solicitors and instructed them to write repudiating the contract of sale. The car was not run after that. It was, however, kept out of doors in the plaintiff's yard, she not having a garage, during the past winter. Defendant says he offered to house the car in his garage for the winter without prejudice to the rights of either party but that this offer was refused. Fortunately it was not a hard winter; but nevertheless a winter in the open is not desirable.

Mr. Furlong, K.C., for the defendant, takes the position that rescission cannot be granted unless the parties can be restored substantially to their original positions, which is not possible, because the car has done 7,000 miles and been subjected to a winter's exposure. But as to this, a dealer in the witness-box remarked that mileage on a second-hand car was not very serious until it began to get up to 15,000 miles. This car has now done about 11,700 miles. Again, it is a known fact that a good many people keep cars in the open during the winter, and most people keep them in unheated garages. There is evidence that plaintiff's brother started the engine now and then to keep the battery alive. I hear nothing about the battery freezing.

It happens that two Courts of Appeal in Canada have dealt with similar cases. In *Addison* v. *Ottawa Auto & Taxi Co.*, (1913), 16 D.L.R. 318, the Ontario Court of Appeal affirming Boyd C., at first instance, dealt with these facts. Plaintiff purchased a car from defendants on the representation that it was a new one. Actually it had been sold, used a few months, involved in an accident, and rebuilt and renovated at a cost of $500. Plaintiff was ignorant of an alleged trade custom to call rebuilt cars "new" cars. What she wanted and thought she was getting was a car that had not been sold to or driven by anybody. She was a complete novice as to cars. She took the car and used it from September until the 3rd of the following May, but repudiated the sale promptly on discovering "the deception which had been practised on her." Defendant put up the same plea as in this case; that it would be unfair for him to have to take it back after the use she had made of it. The Court of Appeal, however, Meredith C.J.O., Maclaren, Magee and Hodgins JJ.A., affirmed the judgment of Boyd C. and dismissed the appeal. Meredith C.J.O. [16 D.L.R. at p. 324] quotes Rigby L.J. in *Lagunas Nitrate Co.* v. *Lagunas Syndicate*, [1899] 2 Ch. 392 at p. 457, where he says: " 'The obligation of the vendors to take back the property in a deteriorated condition is not imposed by way of punishment for wrongdoing, whether fraudulent or not, but because on equitable principles it is thought more fair that they should be compelled to accept compensation than that they should go off with the full of their wrongdoing. Properly speaking it is not now in the discretion of the Court to say whether compensation ought to be taken or not. If substantially compensation can be made, recission with compensation is *ex debito justitiae*.' "

Again Meredith C.J.O. says (p. 325): "The Chancellor allowed as compensation for any deterioration in the car and for the use of it by the respondent the amount of the interest on the purchase-money, to which she would have been entitled, and we cannot see that, under all the circumstances, the allowance is not a reasonable one."

That of course was a case verging on fraud, though Boyd C. suggests that the vendor may have felt justified in treating the car as a new car.

Again in *Gearhart* v. *Kraatz* (1918), 40 D.L.R. 26, 11 S.L.R. 106, the Saskatchewan Appellate Division (Haultain C.J.S., Newlands, Lamont and Elwood JJ.A.) dealt with a case relating to the sale of mules. These animals were sold on a representation that they were of a certain age; they were used for some months; it was discovered that they were very much older than was represented; and the sale was repudiated. Lamont J.A. states the law as to deterioration as follows (pp. 29–30):

"The rule is that where the representee has lost or destroyed the subject matter of the contract, or so dealt with it as to produce an entire alteration in its physical, commercial or legal character, quality or substance, as distinct from mere depreciation, decay or deterioration in the ordinary course of events, the representee is not entitled to his rescission. 20 Hals. 750–51. . . .

"Assuming, therefore, the representation was not fraudulent, it was material; it was false and induced the contract, and the defendant is entitled to have it rescinded."

A well-made car ought to be able to go, with proper maintenance, 50,000 to 100,000 miles; therefore it seems to me that the mere increase of the mileage from 4,700 to 11,700 does not substantially alter the character of the vehicle. It is still a young car.

But I consider also that the representation as to the year-model of a car is very material. A car is not just a car. One make may be better than another, and a car of one year of a certain maker very different in its satisfaction-giving qualities from a car of the same maker of another year. Evidence in this case indicates that the 1950 Hillman is a much better car than the 1949 Hillman in respect of its internal structure, regardless of the similarity in appearance; and it may command a better price on resale. A contract to supply a 1950 model cannot be considered to be satisfied by the supply of a 1949 model. I think there is what is called an *error in substantialibus*. . . .

I think the contract must be avoided, and that the plaintiff must have her money, namely, $1,325, back forthwith; without interest, following the Ontario Court of Appeal in the *Addison* case; and that the car must be immediately returned to the defendant. But as to the subsidiary claims of the plaintiff, for registration, insurance, repairs, tax, and the additional sums paid by her to the finance company, these are not directly connected with the misrepresentation; she would have had to pay such charges as these if it had been a 1950 car and not a 1949 car. And on looking over the bill for repairs and maintenance, after excluding the cost of repairing small damages which she or her brothers did to the car, I cannot see that there is any excessive cost; to my mind she paid or is charged no more than anyone might expect to pay for the maintenance of a second-hand car in good condition running 7,000 miles. Nor has any effort been made to prove the allegation that the defendant's repair or maintenance charges are excessive. The defendant must therefore have judgment for the full amount of his counter-claim on the repair and maintenance bill.

Let judgment be entered accordingly, with costs to plaintiff on the claim and to defendant on the counter-claim, the payment into Court not covering the counter-claim in full.

WINTER J. (dissenting): . . . The action was based upon innocent misrepresentation, the statement of the defendant that the car was a 1950 model. But it is clear that the statement was made in the course of a transaction which resulted in a very simple contract, a contract of sale, and that it was embodied in the contract as a term thereof. . . .

Once the buyer has definitely accepted the goods, he is taken to have elected to rely upon any claim he may have for damages if any condition is afterwards proved to have been broken. (I am assuming what cannot be doubted in both cases, that the representation was a condition and not a mere warranty.) It is too late for him to claim to repudiate the contract and return the goods. At a certain critical time, before he finally accepts the goods or notifies the seller to that effect, he is given an election, a choice between two courses of action. He is supposed to envisage the possibility of the seller failing to carry out all his promises and any loss he may himself suffer as a result. He can, if he wish, rely entirely upon his right in that case to recover the loss. And so he may accept the goods there and then leave it at that. In a pecuniary sense, in theory at least, he will not suffer. Or he may think it preferable to reject the goods altogether if they are not what they should be under the contract. For this purpose he is allowed a reasonable time in which to satisfy himself on that point, and that is usually done by an examination of the goods. What is a reasonable time depends upon the facts and the contract; in the case of unascertained goods it is usually appreciably longer than where the goods are specific. It follows that if the reasonable time passes and he does nothing, he is taken to have accepted the goods. He has made his election. He cannot have it both ways.

Applying all this to the present case and to *Leaf* v. *International Galleries* [1950] 1 A11 E.R. 693, which I purposely include because I can see no essential difference between them, it is abundantly clear that in both instances the buyer kept the goods for a much longer time than could be considered reasonable before seeking any redress. In actual fact, neither buyer made any examination at all. Both clearly elected to follow the former of the two courses of action I have mentioned. Both chose to rely entirely upon what the seller had said and both afterwards complained, it seems to me, most illogically, that the seller was unreliable and that they should be granted the election over again. . . .

I think a distinction must be made between two very different things, though I have never seen it made in any reported case. It is one thing for a buyer to make a genuine inspection of goods, or inquiries about them, with a view to satisfying himself that they are what he wants, and quite another to make up his mind whether he will choose rejection or damages as a remedy if he should need one. It is the latter, as I see it, that the Act contemplates when it speaks of a reasonable time, not the former; or at least, the latter must always be there. The striking feature that I see in both this case and *Leaf* v. *International Galleries* is that they are cases of the latter. Both buyers made up their minds not to examine at all, and both learned the truth quite accidentally. In my view both made the election as to the remedy within a very short time after delivery, if not at that very moment. . . .

I have to add one other observation. It might be argued that, if my view of the case is correct, the plaintiff is without remedy altogether; that, again as in *Leaf* v. *International Galleries*, she chose to limit her claim to rescission. I think that that view would be most unfair and in any case is not the true one. The original statement of claim was confused and it was doubtful whether it claimed rescission or damages. It was later amended to make it clear that rescission was in fact claimed. I think that, if there is any doubt whether damages are claimed in the alternative, the Court has power even now to amend the pleadings to make that clear also. There can be no doubt whatever, on the facts, that the plaintiff is entitled to damages.

[Walsh C.J. also gave reasons for dismissing the appeal.]

LEAF *v.* INTERNATIONAL GALLERIES. [1950] 1 All E.R. 693 (England. Court of Appeal). In an action for rescission of a contract for the sale of a painting in 1944, for £85, it was established that the painting had been innocently misrepresented by the defendant Galleries as a painting by Constable of Salisbury Cathedral. In 1949 the plaintiff tried to sell the painting and learned that it was not a Constable and was really worth very little. Held, for the defendant Galleries. DENNING L.J.: "I agree that on a contract for the sale of goods an innocent material misrepresentation may, in a proper case, be a ground for rescission even after the contract has been executed. . . . Although rescission may in some cases be a proper remedy, it is to be remembered that an innocent misrepresentation is much less potent than a breach of condition; and a claim to rescission for innocent misrepresentation must at any rate be barred when a right to reject for breach of condition is barred. A condition is a term of the contract of a most material character, and if a claim to reject on that account is barred, it seems to me a fortiori that a claim to rescission on the ground of innocent misrepresentation is also barred.

"So, assuming that a contract for the sale of goods may be rescinded in a proper case for innocent misrepresentation, the claim is barred in this case for the self-same reason as a right to reject is barred. The buyer has accepted the picture. He had ample opportunity for examination in the first few days after he had bought it. Then was the time to see if the condition or representation was fulfilled. Yet he has kept it all this time. Five years have elapsed without any notice of rejection. In my judgment he cannot now claim to rescind. His only claim, if any, as the county judge said, was one for damages, which he has not made in this action. In my judgment, therefore, the appeal should be dismissed."

NOTE ON LEGAL METHOD. In the *Leaf* case, above, Evershed M.R. said, after drawing attention to the fact that Joyce J.'s decision in the *Seddon* case was given forty-five years before, "There has been opportunity for Parliament to alter the law if it was thought to be inadequate." Do you consider this fact, if it is a fact, to be a sufficient reason for the Courts not to "reform" the law? How much opportunity has Parliament had? The *Statute of Frauds* was in apparent need of amendment or repeal for a century before political events made it feasible for a busy Parliament to bother with it. What political incentive is there for Parliament to interfere in this area of private law? Compare the attitude of a famous eighteenth century judge, Lord Mansfield, who said (in the argument of *Omychund* v. *Barker* (1744), Atk. 21; 26 E.R. 15 at pp. 22–3) "All occasions do not arise at once . . . a statute very seldom can take in all cases, therefore the common law, *that works itself pure* by rules drawn from the fountain of justice, is for this reason superior to an act of parliament."

SOLLE *v.* BUTCHER. [1950] 1 K.B. 671 (England. Court of Appeal). DENNING L.J.: ". . . the facts are that the plaintiff, the tenant, was a surveyor who was employed by the defendant, the landlord, not only to arrange finance for the purchase of the building and to negotiate with the rating authorities as to the new rateable values, but also to let the flats. He was the agent for letting, and he clearly formed the view that the building was not controlled [by the Rent Restriction Acts]. He told the valuation officer so. He advised the defendant what were the rents which could be charged. He read to the defendant an opinion of counsel relating to the matter, and told him that in his opinion he could charge £250 and that there was no previous control. He said that the flats came outside the Act and that the defendant was 'clear.' The defendant relied on what the plaintiff told him, and authorized the plaintiff to let at the rentals which he had suggested. The plaintiff not only let the four other flats to other people for a long period of years at the new rentals, but also took one himself for seven years at £250 a year. Now he turns round and says, quite unashamedly, that he wants to take advantage of the mistake to get the flat at £140 a year for seven years instead of the £250 a year, which is not only the rent he agreed to pay but also the fair and economic rent; and it is also the rent permitted by the Acts on compliance with the necessary formalities. If the rules of equity have become so rigid that they cannot remedy such an injustice, it is time we had a new equity, to make good the omissions of the old. But, in my view, the established rules are amply sufficient for this case. . . . there was clearly a common mistake, or, as I would prefer to describe it, a common misapprehension, which was fundamental and in no way due to any fault of the defendant; and *Cooper* v. *Phibbs* affords ample authority for saying that, by reason of the common misapprehension, this lease can be set aside on such terms as the court thinks fit.

"The fact that the lease has been executed is no bar to this relief. . . ."

NOTE ON ADVERTISING. Advertising methods common to us today have their origins in the last century, and the cases on misrepresentation are part of the common law background of the subject. Besides these cases you may recall the *Carlill* case, above, p. 361, in which the offeror was conceded a right to "puff" in his offer. The modern problems include a curious distortion of grammar that results in a kind of double talk. The following illustration will suffice.

Under the title "More Canadians are gulled by advertisers than any other brand" Strowan Robertson, in the magazine *Canadian Art* (September/October 1962, p. 347), objects to the advertising slogan, "More Canadians use Colgates' than any other tooth paste." He asks how many Canadians believe that the advertiser has said, "Canadians use Colgates' more than any other tooth paste." Such a claim would, Robertson thinks, "require proof," but he adds that no such claim was made. Let us suppose that the Canadians do believe the advertiser said one thing, and that, grammatically interpreted, he said another. Let us suppose too, that the advertiser knew that he would be taken to mean what "Canadians believe" he meant rather than literally what he said. Should the advertiser's claim then "require proof"? Does it require proof? Who can require it? Is it a misrepresentation?

Professor I. A. Richards points out in his essay "The Future of the Humanities in General Education" in his *Speculative Instruments* (1955) another and greater danger presented by the irresponsible advertiser: the danger of trivialization. He illustrates with a wartime advertisement showing a man drinking beer in comfort surrounded by newspapers with disaster headlines. The caption read, "In a world of strife/There is peace in beer/In these bewildering times, where can a man turn to replenish the wells of his courage . . . to repair the walls of his faith." Would it be cricket to hold the advertiser responsible, not for what he says, grammatically interpreted, but for what he believes his audience believes, in the hope that this responsibility may also counter the trivialization?

WAXMAN *v.* YEANDLE

Ontario. Court of Appeal. [1953] 2 D.L.R. 475

ROACH J.A. delivered the judgment of the Court: . . . The defendants were the owners and operators of the Calcot Hotel in the Township of Sandwich West on the outskirts of the City of Windsor. By an agreement in writing consisting of an offer to purchase signed by the plaintiff and dated July 21, 1950, and an acceptance thereof signed by the defendants and dated August 3, 1950, the plaintiff agreed to purchase and the defendants to sell the said hotel, including the goodwill, land, buildings, chattels and equipment for the sum of $110,000.

The hotel had only 11 bedrooms; its main business was the sale of beer.

The offer to purchase contained the following: "The offer is given on condition that the Vendors represent that their sale of beer for the year ending the 1st day of August, 1950, exceeds Twenty-eight Thousand (28,000) gallons." The actual gallonage sold in that period was only 25,789 gallons.

The trial Judge has exonerated—and I think rightly so—the defendants from any fraud in the making of the representation. It was not made with knowledge of its untruth or recklessly careless as to whether it was true or false.

The plaintiff discovered the discrepancy on or about August 30, 1950, and brought it to the attention of the defendants' solicitors. He claimed to be entitled to an abatement of the purchase-price. The defendants refused to give any abatement and advised the plaintiff that he could either complete the purchase at $110,000 or call the deal off and get back his deposit.

There were protracted negotiations and discussions between the parties thereafter and finally under date September 29, 1950, the defendants wrote the plaintiff as follows:

"We hereby agree with you that provided you proceed with your application for approval of the transfer of licenses of the above hotel to you not later than Thursday, October 5th, 1950 and provided further that in the event that the transfer is approved you close the purchase within one week following the date of such approval, the closing of the transaction will be without prejudice to the rights of all parties arising out of or in any way connected with the conditions contained in the written agreement between the parties as follows:

" 'The offer given on condition that the Vendors represent that their sale of beer for the year 1950 exceeds Twenty-eight Thousand gallons'."

The reference in that letter to the sale of beer for the year 1950 obviously was intended to mean the sale of beer for the year ending August 1, 1950, and the reference to the approval of the transfer of licences refers to approval by the Liquor Control Board of Ontario.

In due course approval was given to the transfer of the licences and the transaction was closed on the basis of the total purchase-price being $110,000. This action followed. [Judson J. dismissed the action.]

The first question which this Court has to decide is whether the statement was a mere representation, a condition or a warranty.

After anxious consideration I have concluded that the statement amounts to no more than a mere representation. The fact that it is contained in the written offer does not make it an integral part of the contract. By embodying that paragraph in the offer the plaintiff, in the event that the defendants should accept the offer, thereby put beyond dispute the fact that the representation was made, but the plaintiff did not thereby put himself in any higher position. He is in no higher legal position than if the paragraph had not been in the written offer and he had proved that the representation had been otherwise made.

The statement was an innocent misrepresentation. . . .

That there was no intended deceit by the vendors is, I think, made abundantly clear by the fact that after the offer had been made and accepted, the vendors authorized the Liquor Control Board to disclose to the plaintiff the total gallonage of beer sold up to August 1, 1950. Monthly returns had to be made by the defendants to the Liquor Control Board and as a result the Board had a record of the monthly sales. I should have thought that a reasonably astute purchaser of such a business would, in any event, have recourse to the records in the possession of the Liquor Control Board as to the volume of sales. In my opinion this plaintiff is an astute purchaser.

In order to succeed in this action the plaintiff would have to prove that the defendants contracted with him that the representation was true and that in the event of its turning out to be untrue they would indemnify him against any loss which might thereby be occasioned to him. I am unable to construe the paragraph in the offer dealing with gallonage as amounting to such a contract. . . .

The plaintiff misconceived his rights. This being an innocent misrepresentation, the plaintiff had the right to rescind and get back his deposit. He did not want to rescind. He wanted to get the hotel, but at a reduced purchase-price.

For the foregoing reasons, in my opinion, the appeal fails and should be dismissed with costs.

[The opinion has been considerably cut.]

BELL *v.* LEVER BROTHERS, LTD.

England. House of Lords. [1932] A.C. 161

Lever Brothers, Ltd., holding practically all the stock of the Niger Company, Limited, entered into an agreement with Bell in 1926 by which the latter was to be employed by Lever Brothers for five years at £8,000 a year, and to act as chairman of the Niger Company. In 1929, in view of the amalgamation of the Niger Company with other companies, Lever Brothers entered into an agreement with Bell on March 19, to pay him £30,000 in satisfaction of all Bell's claims against them. The money was paid and the employment terminated.

Later in the year, Lever Brothers discovered that Bell had been, in 1927, dealing in, and making profits on his own account amounting to perhaps £1,000, in the same materials that the Niger Company dealt in, and had not disclosed these secret profits.

Lever Brothers thereupon brought action claiming the return of the £30,000 paid under the agreement of 1929, alleging fraudulent misrepresentation, and breach of the former employment contracts.

At the trial before Wright J. the jury denied that the agreement of 1929 was induced by fraud, but found that Bell had committed a breach of the employment contract by undertaking the private dealings, and that Lever Brothers were entitled to terminate the employment contract by reason of such breach, and would have terminated such contract had the facts been known. They further found that Lever Brothers did not know of the private dealings in 1929 and would not have entered into the agreement of March 19, 1929 had such facts been known to them.

On these findings Wright J. gave judgment for the plaintiffs, Lever Brothers, stating that the agreement was based on a mutual mistake, which, in the language of *Kennedy* v. *Panama Royal Mail Co.* (1867), L.R. 2 Q.B. 580, went "to the substance . . . or root of the matter." The mistake was the existence of the previous service agreement. Bell appealed.

In the Court of Appeal, Scrutton L.J., said, in part: ". . . In my opinion, on the facts of the present case the defendants were under an obligation, before and at the time of their negotiation of the contracts to terminate their services to disclose their dealings in breach of their contracts, and the contracts to terminate can be avoided by this non-disclosure. Wright J.'s ground of decision, with which I agree, is sufficient to support his judgment, but I think it could also be supported on the ground of failure to disclose material facts.

"I only desire to add that, in my view, the case of *Kennedy* v. *Panama etc. Co.* so far as it decides that an innocent misrepresentation, though material, is not a ground for rescission unless it is also fundamental, is no longer law, in view of the fusion of common law and equity by the Judicature Acts, the rule of equity prevailing. Also I reserve liberty to consider the decision in *Seddon* v. *North Eastern Salt Co.*, [1905] 1 Ch. 326, so far as it decides that executed contracts cannot be rescinded for innocent and material misrepresentation. The appeal must be dismissed with costs." Lawrence and Greer L.JJ. agreed with Scrutton L.J. So Bell appealed again. In the House of Lords, Lords Atkin, Blanesburgh and Thankerton gave reason for allowing the appeal. Viscount Hailsham and Lord Warrington of Clyffe dissented, taking the view that, in the words of Lord Warrington, "the erroneous assumption on the part of both parties to the agreement that the service contracts were undeterminable except by agreement was of such a fundamental character as to constitute an underlying assumption without which the parties would not have made the contract."

Lord Atkin: . . . Two points present themselves for decision. Was the agreement of March 19, 1929, void by reason of a mutual mistake of Mr. D'Arcy Cooper and Mr. Bell?

Could the agreement of March 19, 1929, be avoided by reason of the failure of Mr. Bell to disclose his misconduct in regard to the cocoa dealings?

My Lords, the rules of law dealing with the effect of mistake on contract appear to be established with reasonable clearness. If mistake operates at all it operates so as to negative or in some cases nullify consent. The parties may be mistaken in the identity of the contracting parties, or in the existence of the subject-matter of the contract at the date of the contract, or in the quality of the subject-matter of the contract. These mistakes may be by one party, or by both, and the legal effect may depend upon the class of mistake above mentioned. Thus a mistaken belief by A. that he is contracting with B., whereas in fact he is contracting with C., will negative consent where it is clear that the intention of A. was to contract only with B. So the agreement of A. and B. to purchase a specific article is void if in fact the article had perished before the date of sale. In this case, though the parties in fact were agreed about the subject-matter, yet a consent to transfer or take delivery of something not existent is deemed useless, the consent is nullified. As codified in the Sale of Goods Act the contract is expressed to be void if the seller was in ignorance of the destruction of the specific chattel. I apprehend that if the seller with knowledge that a chattel was destroyed purported to sell it to a purchaser, the latter might sue for damages for non-delivery though the former could not sue for non-acceptance, but I know of no case where a seller has so committed himself. This is a case where mutual mistake certainly and unilateral mistake by the seller of goods will prevent a contract from arising. Corresponding to mistake as to the existence of the subject-matter is mistake as to title in cases where, unknown to the parties, the buyer is already the owner of that which the seller purports to sell to him. The parties intended to effectuate a transfer of ownership: such a transfer is impossible: the stipulation is naturali ratione inutilis. This is the case of *Cooper* v. *Phibbs* (1867), L.R. 2 H.L. 149 where A. agreed to take a lease of a fishery from B., though contrary to the belief of both parties at the time A. was tenant for life of the fishery and B. appears to have had no title at all. To such a case Lord Westbury applied the principle that if parties contract under a mutual mistake and misapprehension as to their relative and respective rights the result is that the agreement is liable to be set aside as having proceeded upon a common mistake. Applied to the context the statement is only subject to the criticism that the agreement would appear to be void rather than voidable. Applied to mistake as to rights generally it would appear to be too wide. Even where the vendor has no title, though both parties think he has, the correct view would appear to be that there is a contract: but that the vendor has either committed a breach of a stipulation as to title, or is not able to perform his contract. The contract is unenforceable by him but is not void.

Mistake as to quality of the thing contracted for raises more difficult questions. In such a case a mistake will not affect assent unless it is the mistake of both parties, and is as to the existence of some quality which makes the thing without the quality essentially different from the thing as it was believed to be. Of course it may appear that the parties contracted that the article should possess the quality which one or other or both mistakenly believed it to possess. But in such a case there is a contract and the inquiry is a different one, being whether the contract as to quality amounts to a condition or a warranty, a different branch of the law. The principles to be applied are to be found in two cases which as far as my knowledge goes, have always been treated as authoritative expositions of the law. The first is *Kennedy* v. *Panama Royal Mail Co.*

In that case the plaintiff had applied for shares in the defendant company on the faith of a prospectus which stated falsely but innocently that the company had a binding contract with the Government of New Zealand for the carriage of mails. On discovering the true facts the plaintiff brought an action for the recovery of the sums he had paid on calls. The defendants brought a cross action for further calls. Blackburn J., in delivering the judgment of the Court (Cockburn C.J., Blackburn, Mellor and Shee JJ.). said: "The only remaining question is one of much greater difficulty. It was contended by Mr. Mellish, on behalf of Lord Gilbert Kennedy, that the effect of the prospectus was to warrant to the intended shareholders that there really was such a contract as is there represented, and not merely to represent that the company *bonâ fide* believed it; and that the difference in substance between shares in a company with such a contract and shares in a company whose supposed contract was not binding, was a difference in substance in the nature of the thing, and that the shareholder was entitled to return the shares as soon as he discovered this, quite independently of fraud, on the ground that he had applied for one thing and got another. And, if the invalidity of the contract really made the shares he obtained different things in substance from those which he applied for, this would, we think, be good law. The case would then resemble *Gompertz* v. *Bartlett* (1853), 2 E. & B. 849; 118 E.R. 985, and *Gurney* v. *Womersley* (1854), 4 E. & B. 133; 119 E.R. 51, where the person who had honestly sold what he thought a bill without recourse to him, was nevertheless held bound to return the price on its turning out that the supposed bill was a forgery in the one case, and void under the stamp laws in the other; in both cases the ground of this decision being that the thing handed over was not the thing paid for. A similar principle was acted on in *Ship's Case* (1865), 2 DeG. J. & S. 544; 46 E.R. 486. There is, however, a very important difference between cases where a contract may be rescinded on account of fraud, and those in which it may be rescinded on the ground that there is a difference in substance between the thing bargained for and that obtained. It is enough to show that there was a fraudulent representation as to any part of that which induced the party to enter into the contract which he seeks to rescind; but where there has been an innocent misrepresentation or misapprehension, it does not authorize a rescission unless it is such as to show that there is a complete difference in substance between what was supposed to be and what was taken, so as to constitute a failure of consideration. For example, where a horse is bought under a belief that it is sound, if the purchaser was induced to buy by a fraudulent representation as to the horse's soundness, the contract may be rescinded. If it was induced by an honest misrepresentation as to its soundness, though it may be clear that both vendor and purchaser thought that they were dealing about a sound horse and were in error, yet the purchaser must pay the whole price unless there was a warranty; and even if there was a warranty, he cannot return the horse and claim back the whole price, unless there was a condition to that effect in the contract."

The Court came to the conclusion in that case that, though there was a misapprehension as to that which was a material part of the motive inducing the applicant to ask for the shares, it did not prevent the shares from being in substance those he applied for.

The next case is *Smith* v. *Hughes* (1871), L.R. 6 Q.B. 597, the well known case as to new and old oats. . . .

In these cases I am inclined to think that the true analysis is that there is a contract, but that the one party is not able to supply the very thing whether goods or services that the other party contracted to take; and therefore the contract is unenforceable by the one if executory, while if executed the other can recover back money paid on the ground of failure of the consideration.

We are now in a position to apply to the facts of this case the law as to mistake so far as it has been stated. It is essential on this part of the discussion to keep in mind the finding of the jury acquitting the defendants of fraudulent misrepresentation or concealment in procuring the agreements in question. Grave injustice may be done to the defendants and confusion introduced into the legal conclusion, unless it is quite clear that in considering mistake in this case no suggestion of fraud is admissible and cannot strictly be regarded by the judge who has to determine the legal issues raised. The agreement which is said to be void is the agreement contained in the letter of March 19, 1929, that Bell would retire from the Board of the Niger Company and its subsidiaries, and that in consideration of his doing so Levers would pay him as compensation for the termination of his agreements and consequent loss of office the sum of £30,000 in full satisfaction and discharge of all claims and demands of any kind against Lever Brothers, the Niger Company or its subsidiaries. The agreement, which as part of the contract was terminated, had been broken so that it could be repudiated. Is an agreement to terminate a broken contract different in kind from an agreement to terminate an unbroken contract, assuming that the breach has given the one party the right to declare the contract at an end? I feel the weight of the plaintiffs' contention that a contract immediately determinable is a different thing from a contract for an unexpired term, and that the difference in kind can be illustrated by the immense price of release from the longer contract as compared with the shorter. And I agree that an agreement to take an assignment of a lease for five years is not the same thing as to take an assignment of a lease for three years, still less a term for a few months. But, on the whole, I have come to the conclusion that it would be wrong to decide that an agreement to terminate a definite specified contract is void if it turns out that the agreement had already been broken and could have been terminated otherwise. The contract released is the identical contract in both cases, and the party paying for release gets exactly what he bargains for. It seems immaterial that he could have got the same result in another way, or that if he had known the true facts he would not have entered into the bargain. A buys B's horse; he thinks the horse is sound and he pays the price of a sound horse; he would certainly not have bought the horse if he had known as the fact is that the horse is unsound. If B has made no representation as to soundness and has not contracted that the horse is sound, A is bound and cannot recover back the price. A buys a picture from B; both A and B believe it to be the work of an old master, and a high price is paid. It turns out to be a modern copy. A has no remedy in the absence of representation or warranty. A agrees to take on lease or to buy from B an unfurnished dwelling-house. The house is in fact uninhabitable. A would never have entered into the bargain if he had known the fact. A has no remedy, and the position is the same whether B knew the facts or not, so long as he made no representation or gave no warranty. A buys a roadside garage business from B abutting on a public thoroughfare; unknown to A, but known to B, it has already been decided to construct a bypass road which will divert substantially the whole of the traffic from passing A's garage. Again A has no remedy. All these cases involve hardship on A and benefit B, as most people would say, unjustly. They can be supported on the ground that it is of paramount importance that contracts should be observed, and that if parties honestly comply with the essentials of the formation of contracts—i.e., agree in the same terms on the same subject-matter—they are bound, and must rely on the stipulations of the contract for protection from the effect of facts unknown to them.

This brings the discussion to the alternative mode of expressing the result of a mutual mistake. It is said that in such a case as the present there is to be implied a stipulation in the contract that a condition of its efficacy is that the facts should be as understood by both parties—namely, that the contract could not be terminated till the end of the current term. The question of the existence of conditions, express or implied, is obviously one that affects not the formation of contract, but the investigation of the terms of the contract when made. A condition derives its efficacy from the consent of the parties, express or implied. They have agreed, but on what terms. One term may be that unless the facts are or are not of a particular nature, or unless an event has or has not happened, the contract is not to take effect. With regard to future facts such a condition is obviously contractual. Till the event occurs the parties are bound. Thus the condition (the exact terms of which need not here be investigated) that is generally accepted as underlying the principle of the frustration cases is contractual, an implied condition. Sir John Simon formulated for the assistance of your Lordships a proposition which should be recorded: "Whenever it is to be inferred from the terms of a contract or its surrounding circumstances that the consensus has been reached upon the basis of a particular contractual assumption, and that assumption is not true, the contract is avoided: i.e., it is void ab initio if the assumption is of present fact and it ceases to bind if the assumption is of future fact."

I think few would demur to this statement but its value depends upon the meaning of "a contractual assumption," and also upon the true meaning to be attached to "basis," a metaphor which may mislead. When used expressly in contracts, for instance, in policies of insurance, which state that the truth of the statements in the proposal is to be the basis of the contract of insurance, the meaning is clear. The truth of the statements is made a condition of the contract, which failing, the contract is void unless the condition is waived. The proposition does not amount to more than this that, if the contract expressly or impliedly contains a term that a particular assumption is a condition of the contract, the contract is avoided if the assumption is not true. But we have not advanced far on the inquiry how to ascertain whether the contract does contain such a condition. Various words are to be found to define the state of things which make a condition. "In the contemplation of both parties fundamental to the continued validity of the contract," "a foundation essential to its existence," "a fundamental reason for making it," are phrases found in the important judgment of Scrutton L.J. in the present case. The first two phrases appear to me to be unexceptionable. They cover the case of a contract to serve in a particular place, the existence of which is fundamental to the service, or to procure the services of a professional vocalist, whose continued health is essential to performance. But "a fundamental reason for making a contract" may, with respect, be misleading. The reason of one party only is presumedly not intended, but in the cases I have suggested above, of the sale of a horse or of a picture, it might be said that the fundamental reason for making the contract was the belief of both parties that the horse was sound or the picture an old master, yet in neither case would the condition as I think exist. Nothing is more dangerous than to allow oneself liberty to construct for the parties contracts which they have not in terms made by importing implications which would appear to make the contract more business-like or more just. The implications to be made are to be no more than are "necessary" for giving business efficacy to the transaction, and it appears to me that, both as to existing facts and future facts, a condition would not be implied unless the new state of facts makes the contract something different in kind from the contract in the original state of facts. Thus, in *Krell* v. *Henry*, [1903] 2 K.B. 740, Vaughan Williams L.J. finds that the subject of the contract was "rooms to view the procession": the postponement, therefore, made the rooms not rooms to view the procession. This also is the test finally chosen by Lord Sumner in *Bank Line* v. *Arthur Capel & Co.*, [1919] A.C. 435, agreeing with Lord Dunedin in *Metropolitan Water Board* v. *Dick Kerr*, [1918] A.C. 119, where, dealing with the criterion for determining the effect of interruption in "frustrating" a contract, he says: "An interruption may be so long as to destroy the identity of the work or service, when resumed, with the work or service when interrupted." We therefore get a common standard for mutual mistake and implied conditions whether as to existing or as to future facts. Does the state of the new facts destroy the identity of the subject-matter as it was in the original state of facts? To apply the principle to the infinite combinations of facts that arise in actual experience will continue to be difficult, but if this case results in establishing order into what has been a somewhat confused and difficult branch of the law it will have served a useful purpose.

I have already stated my reasons for deciding that in the present case the identity of the subject-matter was not destroyed by the mutual mistake, if any, and need not repeat them.

It now becomes necessary to deal with the second point of the plaintiffs—namely, that the contract of March 19, 1929, could be avoided by them in consequence of the non-disclosure by Bell of his misconduct as to the cocoa dealings. Fraudulent concealment has been negatived by the jury; this claim is based upon the contention that Bell owed a duty to Levers to disclose his misconduct, and that in default of disclosure the contract was voidable. Ordinarily the failure to disclose a material fact which might influence the mind of a prudent contractor does not give the right to avoid the contract. The principle of caveat emptor applies outside contracts of sale. There are certain contracts expressed by the law to be contracts of the utmost good faith, where material facts must be disclosed; if not, the contract is voidable. Apart from special fiduciary relationships, contracts for partnership and contracts of insurance are the leading instances. In such cases the duty does not arise out of contract; the duty of a person proposing an insurance arises before a contract is made, so of an intending partner. Unless this contract can be brought within this limited category of contracts *uberrimae fidei* it appears to me that this ground of defence must fail. I see nothing to differentiate this agreement from the ordinary contract of service; and I am aware of no authority which places contracts of service within the limited category I have mentioned. It seems to me clear that master and men negotiating for an agreement of services are as unfettered as in any other negotiation. Nor can I find anything in the relation of master and servant, when established, that places agreements between them within the protected category.

It is said that there is a contractual duty of the servant to disclose his past faults. I agree that the duty in the servant to protect his master's property may involve the duty to report a fellow servant whom he knows to be wrongfully dealing with that property. The servant owes a duty not to steal, but, having stolen, is there superadded a duty to confess that he has stolen? I am satisfied that to imply such a duty would be a departure from the well established usage of mankind and would be to create obligations entirely outside the normal contemplation of the parties concerned. If a man agrees to raise his butler's wages, must the butler disclose that two years ago he received a secret commission from the wine merchant; and if the master discovers it, can he, without dismissal or after the servant has left, avoid the agreement for the increase in salary and recover back the extra wages paid? If he gives his cook a month's wages in lieu of notice can he, on discovering that the cook has been pilfering the tea and sugar, claim the return of the month's wages? I think not. He takes the risk; if he wishes to protect himself he can question his servant, and will then be protected by the truth or otherwise of the answers.

I agree with the view expressed by Avory J. in *Healy* v. *Société Anonyme Française Rubastic*, [1917] 1 K.B. 946, on this point. It will be noticed that Bell was not a director of Levers, and, with respect, I cannot accept the view of Greer L.J. that if he was in fiduciary relationship to the Niger Company he was in a similar fiduciary relationship to the shareholders, or to the particular shareholders (Levers) who held 99 per cent. of the shares. Nor do I think that it is alleged or proved that in making the agreement of March 19, 1929, Levers were acting as agents for the Niger Company. In the matter of the release of the service contract and the payment of £30,000 they were acting quite plainly for themselves as principals. It follows that on this ground also the claim fails.

The result is that in the present case servants unfaithful in some of their work retain large compensation which some will think they do not deserve. Nevertheless it is of greater importance that well established principles of contract should be maintained than that a particular hardship should be redressed; and I see no way of giving relief to the plaintiffs in the present circumstances except by confiding to the Courts loose powers of introducing terms into contracts which would only serve to introduce doubt and confusion where certainty is essential.

I think therefore that this appeal should be allowed; and I agree with the order to be proposed by my noble and learned friend, Lord Blanesburgh.

NOTE. In *Solle* v. *Butcher*, [1950] 1 K.B. 671, at page 694 Denning L.J. said, "*Bell* v. *Lever Brothers, Ltd.* . . . was treated in the House of Lords as a case at law depending on whether the contract was a nullity or not. If it had been considered on equitable grounds, the result might have been different." How might it have been different?

3. Building Contracts

CLARKE *v.* WATSON

England. Common Pleas. 1865. 18 C.B.N.S. 278; 144 E.R. 450

The plaintiffs were builders and agreed with the defendants to do certain works in conformity with certain plans and specifications, for £312 15s., to be paid as follows: £156 7s. 1d. on production by the plaintiffs of the certificate of William Lambert, or other surveyor for the time being of the defendants, certifying that the plaintiff had duly and efficiently completed not less than three quarters of the job, £78 3s. 9d. when the whole job was completed to the surveyor's satisfaction and the balance of £78 3s. 9d. four months after completion during which time the plaintiffs were to keep the works in good repair to the satisfaction of the surveyor. The work was also to be done to the satisfaction of the engineer of the local board of health. £156 7s. 6d. had been paid and the whole of the job completed to the satisfaction of the engineer of the local board of health, but the surveyor "wrongfully and improperly neglected and refused" to give his certificate either for the completion or the satisfactory maintenance for four months.

ERLE C.J.: I am of opinion that the judgment in this case ought to be for the defendants. The contract which they entered into was, to pay to the contractors, the plaintiffs, certain sums on production by them to the defendants, or one of them, of the certificate of William Lambert, or other the surveyor for the time of the defendants. Many contracts are so made. Every man is the master of the contract he may choose to make; and it is of the highest importance that every contract should be construed according to the intention of the contracting parties. And it is important, in a case of this description, that the person for whom the work has been done should not be called upon to pay for it until some competent person shall have certified that the work has been properly done, according to the contract and specification. Here the contract is, that the money shall become payable on production by the plaintiffs to the defendants of the certificate of their (the defendants') surveyor, that the contractors have duly and efficiently performed and completed the work to his satisfaction. No such certificate has been produced. But it is said that the plaintiffs have done all things necessary to entitle them to have the certificate of the surveyor that the works had been duly performed and completed to his satisfaction, and that the said surveyor had "wrongfully and improperly" neglected and refused so to do. That, in my opinion, is not sufficient. If it had been alleged that the defendants wrongfully colluded with the surveyor to cause the certificate to be withheld, they could not have sheltered themselves by their own wrongful act. But the word "wrongfully," as used here, does not intimate any thing of that sort. If the plaintiffs had intended to rely on the withholding of the certificate as a wrongful act on the part of the defendants, they should have stated how it was wrongful. This is in effect an attempt on the part of the plaintiffs to take from the defendants the protection of their surveyor, and to substitute for it the opinion of a jury. That is not the contract which the defendants have entered into. The allegations on the part of the plaintiffs are not in my judgment such as to entitle them to succeed.

[Williams, Willes and Keating JJ. were of the same opinion.]

EAGLESHAM *v.* McMASTER. [1920] 2 K.B. 169 (England. King's Bench). LORD READING: "Reading the two clauses together I am of opinion that their true meaning is that the certificate must be obtained before the plaintiff can sue for payment. It is not the Court which says that the plaintiff shall not come before it except upon production of a certificate; the parties themselves have so agreed. The object of the clauses is to leave these matters to a person, who has expert knowledge of building work and has the confidence of both parties, and the plaintiff was content to enter into the contract upon that footing. . . .

"The plaintiff must fail in the action unless he can show that there was some wrong act done by the defendant entitling him, the plaintiff, to proceed notwithstanding that he has not obtained the architect's certificate. Such a wrong would be fraud or collusion between the defendant and the architect or some moral turpitude amounting to improper conduct which would lead the Court to interfere. . . . If in this case it had been shown that the defendant had given instructions to the architect as to the amount for which he should certify, or as to the decision at which he ought to arrive upon any particular matter, there would be sufficient to override the necessity for obtaining the certificate and the plaintiff would be entitled to proceed without it."

TULLIS *v.* JACKSON. [1892] 3 Ch. 441 (England. Chancery). It was agreed that the certificate of an architect would be final and should not be set aside for any reason, including fraud. The Court held the clause valid, and stated that the stringency of clauses relating to architect's certificates was no bar to their enforcement. CHITTY J.: "It is of course for the contractor when he enters into a contract of this kind to consider whether he will accept it or not."

BRENNAN PAVING CO. LTD. *v.* OSHAWA. [1953] 3 D.L.R. 16 (Ontario. Court of Appeal). A contract for paving King Street in the city of Oshawa provided that "no money shall become due or be payable under this Contract unless and until an Estimate or Certificate therefor shall have been signed by the Engineer . . . the possession of which is hereby made a condition precedent to the Contractor's right to be paid or to maintain any action for such money or for any part thereof." It also provided that "in the event of dispute, the decision of the engineer as to the meaning or intent of the plans and specifications shall be final." In the course of work gravel and asphalt were laid to a greater thickness than the contract appeared to authorize, but the engineer did not interfere at the time and through his inspector, one Courtlee, actually instructed the plaintiff's superintendent to use more materials. Nevertheless the engineer used his interpretation of the contract maximum as to the amount to be considered in certifying payment for the gravel and asphalt used. In an action for the price of the excess, held, affirming McRuer C.J. at the trial, for the contractor despite the refusal of the engineer to certify. ROACH J.A.: "Where, as here, the engineer's certificate is a condition precedent to payment, the engineer occupies two positions: first, one as agent of the owner under the contract; second, a *quasi*-judicial position as certifier between the parties: *Hudson on Building Contracts*, 7th ed., p. 286. The two positions are distinct and separate. Different duties attach to them and different consequences flow from the performance or breach of those duties. Under the law of principal and agent he may within the scope of his duties, bind his principal. As certifier deciding between the parties he must act judicially: *Hickman & Co.* v. *Roberts*, [1913] A.C. 229. To act judicially as certifier requires him, where the question arises, to consider and give effect to any conduct on his part as agent *vis-à-vis* the contractor which has bound the owner as his principal to the advantage of the contractor. In this connection he must act *qua* certifier as independently as if some other person rather than himself has been the agent of the owner under the contract. All that seems crystal-clear to me.

"The issues in and the circumstances of this case require that we inquire into the conduct of the engineer first as agent and second as certifier. If as agent he bound his employer to the advantage of the contractor in relation to this dispute, and if as certifier he has failed to consider and give effect to that conduct, then he has not acted judicially. If he did not act judicially, then the plaintiff was freed from the contractual necessity for having the engineer's certificate as a condition precedent to the right of payment. . . .

"As to the meaning and effect of the plans and specifications, the defendant's case is this: the engineer Meadow's decision as to their meaning is final; he interprets them as calling for no more and no less than 1″ of asphaltic wearing-surface; the inspector Courtlee had no authority to vary them; if the plaintiff laid a thickness in excess of 1″ it did so at its own risk and the defendant is under no obligation to pay for the excess.

"The answer to those contentions is that *during the progress of the work* there was no dispute between the plaintiff and Meadows as to the thickness of the asphaltic wearing-surface called for by the plans and specifications. The plaintiff's interpretation of the plans and specifications as they related to that item differed from the interpretation Meadows now says he intended they should bear, but the parties were not disputing about it. . . .

"It must be conceded that it was the engineer's function under the general conditions to decide the meaning and intent of the plans and specifications. The Court, however, may inquire and determine whether, during the progress of the work, the engineer, by his conduct or otherwise, led the plaintiff to understand, or confirmed the plaintiff in the understanding of its superintendent, that the plans and specifications permitted a thickness of asphaltic top in excess of one inch. If the engineer or those for whom he was responsible, by his or their conduct or otherwise, did either of those things, then he and through him the defendant is estopped from now placing a different interpretation on them. . . .

"Meadows must have known that the plaintiff, laying down a thickness of asphaltic top in excess of 1″, was doing so because its superintendent interpreted the plans and specifications permitting it and requiring it where to do so was necessary for proper drainage. If he felt—and he now says he did—that the plaintiff was thereby exceeding the thickness authorized, he should have interfered at the time. To stand by and do nothing about it was to acquiesce. Even more important that the foregoing is the fact that Courtlee specifically instructed the superintendent to proceed as he did. To my mind it is idle to say that Courtlee thereby exceeded his jurisdiction. He was on the job to see that the work, as it progressed, had that standard of excellence agreed upon between the parties. He gave those instructions not for the purpose of varying the plans and specifications, but for the purpose of requiring the contractor to live up to them.

"In my opinion, this is a clear case of estoppel. . . ." [The Court of Appeal was affirmed with a minor variation by the Supreme Court of Canada: [1955] 1 D.L.R. 321. The minor variation was a deduction of $1,305.02, the value of 160.125 tons of asphalt which is the amount in excess of the estimate of 3000 tons. The plaintiff had claimed for 782.195 tons at $8.15 per ton, or $6,374.89. The Court merely said, "The lack of an order in writing . . . is fatal."

Clause M of the General Conditions provided in part: ". . . The quantities shown are intended to cover all the work embraced under the contract and the contractor is specifically instructed that they may be exceeded only by order from the engineer in writing." Since the excess asphalt was actually supplied and the defendant has been held estopped from denying that the contract required it, should the plaintiff not be entitled to recover on the ground of unjust enrichment?]

NOTE. At the trial of the *Brennan Paving* case McRuer C.J. summed up the law respecting the position of an engineer or architect in a building contract as follows, [1952] 4 D.L.R. 181 at pp. 193–4: "(1) When an engineer (and what I say applies equally to an architect) is placed in a position requiring him to issue certificates under a contract of this nature, he must act judicially notwithstanding that to the knowledge of both parties one of the parties to the contract is his master and paymaster. (2) The engineer must act within the powers conferred on him under the contract. (3) He is not entitled to construe the contract unless the power is expressly conferred on him by its terms. (4) He cannot alter the terms of the contract unless he is given power to do so. (5) If an engineer goes beyond his powers under a contract in granting or refusing a certificate and one of the parties seeks to rely on an unwarranted exercise of his powers, the other party is released from the condition of the contract requiring the certificate to be a condition precedent to payment or, in other words, there is an implied condition in the contract that neither party will rely on the purported exercise by the engineer of a jurisdiction which he does not possess under the contract. (6) Neither party to a contract is permitted to take advantage of his own wrong. All the cases on this subject must be read in the light of the express terms of the respective contracts under consideration. . . ."

KERR *v.* HARRINGTON. [1947] O.W.N. 237 (Ontario. High Court). In a mechanics' lien action, the objection was raised that the defendant owner was bound by the architect's certificate in the absence of fraud or collusion. Fraud was not proven but the facts were nevertheless examined and the plaintiff builder's claim was in part dismissed. MARRIOTT ASS'T. MASTER.: ". . . it is to be noted that in a letter written by the architect long after he had approved the . . . charges . . . he requested the plaintiff to give him particulars of the work for which these charges were made. . . . If he had had before him the particulars . . . and had considered them in relation to the terms of the contract, and had allowed them as proper charges, he could have answered the defendant's objection at once and given his reasons for allowing them. I think it is clear, and I so find, that the architect approved the plaintiff's charges mechanically, and . . . it cannot be said that the architect acted impartially, because in effect he was allowing the plaintiff whatever he charged without considering the rights of the defendant. . . . In a small job of this kind, where there are only three or four men working, the approval of charges for superintending which covered a full day for a period of about seven weeks, without having all particulars before him, convinces me that the architect either was deliberately favouring the plaintiff or shut his eyes to the implication that the charges might possibly be in conflict with the terms of the contract. I do not consider that the facts that the architect knew the plaintiff for some time and that the plaintiff had done work for the architect on earlier jobs and was constructing a building under his supervision when this work was commenced, and that there was delay between the time the defendant requested the architect to allow him to see the invoices and the time the request was granted, would by themselves support a finding of collusion, as suggested by counsel for the defendant, but in view of the other evidence mentioned these facts have some significance in supporting my finding that the architect was not impartial. An architect in this position is considered to be a quasi-arbitrator . . . and in this case his position was a particularly delicate one as he had estimated the cost of the work to be $3,000, whereas it appears it will cost about $6,000."

HUNT *v.* MAGNACCA BUILDING PROJECTS LTD. 1958. 26 W.W.R. 289 (Manitoba. Queen's Bench). Plaintiff claimed damages for defects in the construction of a one storey building over crawl space that the court found not to be properly ventilated, as a result of which the floor rotted and the owner put his foot through it. Chair legs also broke through. The defendant Company denied liability and claimed that the building was constructed according to agreed plans, specifications (drafted by the defendant) and the building code, in a good workmanlike manner. Held, for the plaintiff. MONNIN J.: "Is defendant liable for having failed to provide necessary ventilation? Mr. Magnacca held himself out as able to draw plans and specifications and admits drawing them. . . . Having assumed the responsibility of drafting the plans and preparing the specifications, is defendant liable to the owner if its plans and specifications are defective as I find they were here? One who holds himself out as qualified to draw plans and specifications must use reasonable skill, care and diligence in the preparation of them and where in reliance upon such plans a building is erected in a defective way, the contractor should be held liable for the damages. That principle applies to an architect and I see no reason why it should not apply to a contractor who holds himself out as qualified to draw plans and specifications. Defendant admits that plaintiff was relying on its skill and knowledge as a contractor. . . .

"In the early case of *Duncan* v. *Blundell* (1820) 3 Stark 6, 171 E.R. 749, Bayley, J. said: 'Where a person is employed in a work of skill, the employer buys both his labour and his judgment; he ought not to undertake the work if it cannot succeed, and he should know whether it will or not; of course it is otherwise if the party employing him choose to supersede the workman's judgment by using his own.'. . .

"The estimate of the cost of the repairs is $1,974.15 which includes $123.50 for excavating the sub-floor to an 18-inch depth. I find that defendant was negligent in not levelling the ground and not providing for an 18-inch crawl space. I disallow the costs of the installation of the polythene paper and rigid insulation and there will be judgment for the plaintiff in the sum of $1,843.69 made up as follows: Estimate of cost of repairs, $1,974.15; less polythene paper and labour, $60; less rigid insulation and labour, $70.46; totalling $130.46; balance $1,843. 69.

"Plaintiff will also have judgment against defendant in the amount of $200 for loss of rental during the period of repair, $300 general damages, his costs and a *fiat* for examination for discovery."

ARMSTRONG *v*. ROSLYN PARK LAND CO. AND SIGMORE. 1951. 4 W.W.R. (N.S.) 270 (British Columbia. Supreme Court). The defen-- dant Company agreed to build a house for the plaintiff for $9,000. The house was not started. The plaintiff claimed damages based on the difference between the contract price and what it would cost to build the house at current prices. WHITTAKER J.: "There are many reported cases in which construction was commenced but not completed, but I have not been referred to any case where, as here, there was a complete failure to carry out the terms of the contract. I do not have to decide what the measure of damages would be if the plaintiff did not intend to have the house built through another agency. . . . I think the measure of damages is the difference between the contract price and the cost of building, but not the cost of building at today's prices. It must be the cost of building as of the time when the plaintiff first became aware of the defendant's breach of contract. The plaintiff must proceed diligently." [What difference in damages would there be if the defendant had decided not to build a house at all?]

HULSHAN *v.* NICKLING
Ontario. Court of Appeal. [1957] O.W.N. 587

The defendants and the plaintiff, a builder, agreed in April, 1955, that the plaintiff should build a dwelling with attached garage at Hamilton Beach, "under N.H.A. requirements and built according to plans now on file with the contractor and purchaser" for $14,000. The sum of $3,000 was to be paid on signing, $3,000 when the roof was on and shingled, $3,000 when the first coat of plaster was on, and the "balance of purchase price to be paid to contractor on completion of dwelling to satisfaction of purchaser." By August, 1955, the dwelling was habitable and the defendants moved into it. The first three instalments had been paid and by December the plaintiff claimed the building was finished and demanded payment of the balance of $3,852. The defendants complained in several respects about the work and refused to pay. On January 16, 1956, the plaintiff registered a mechanics' lien against the land for $3,852 and on February 14 commenced this action to enforce it. The trial Judge held that the building was substantially completed but he allowed the defendants $100 for defective workmanship and gave judgment for $3,752. He considered that there was "some justification" for the defendants' dissatisfaction. The defendants appealed on three grounds, only one of which is considered in the following excerpt. The second submission was "that no amount is due to the plaintiff because of the defendants' justifiable dissatisfaction."

Roach J.A. delivered the judgment of the Court.: . . . The second submission also fails. There could be no possible doubt on the authorities that if the words "to satisfaction of purchaser" were not in the instant contract, the plaintiff would be entitled to recover the balance of the contract price less a deduction of an amount sufficient to pay for the minor defects and deficiencies in its performance. *Dakin* v. *Lee* is the leading authority. It has been followed in our own Courts in such cases as *McGregor* v. *Sterling Appraisal*, 57 O.L.R. 485, [1925] 4 D.L.R. 211, and *House Repair and Service Co. Limited* v. *Miller* (1921), 49 O.L.R. 205, 64 D.L.R. 115, and the cases therein referred to, and in England in *Hoenig* v. *Isaacs*, [1952] 2 All E.R. 176, and the cases therein referred to.

Mr. Gibson argued, however, that the addition of the words "to satisfaction of purchaser" distinguishes this case from those governed by *Dakin* v. *Lee*, and the other cases cited above. I do not think it does. The contract provides that the building and garage are "to be erected under N.H.A. requirements and built according to plans now on file with contractor and purchaser." That provision, by reference, sets the standard by which the work, when finished, is to be judged. I do not think those additional words add anything to the contract. It has not been suggested that so far as the defects and/or deficiencies of which complaint was made are concerned, the N.H.A. requirements and the plans are not entire and complete. In other words, in determining whether or not the contract has been completely performed, reference is to be had to the N.H.A. requirements and the plans. The work is to be measured by that standard, and apart from that the satisfaction or dissatisfaction of the purchaser has nothing to do with it. If the contractor complied with all those requirements, the purchaser could not be heard to say that he was not satisfied. If the contractor did not comply with them the purchaser would have a right to say that he was dissatisfied but that right would not arise by virtue of those added words. It would arise by virtue of the builder's contractual obligation to comply with those requirements and his non-compliance therewith.

In *House Repair and Service Co. Limited* v. *Miller, supra,* the contract provided that the contractor should put three old houses in first-class condition and to the entire satisfaction of the owner. There the Court had to determine what was meant by "first-class condition". That was rather a vague expression,—vague certainly in contrast with the condition in the instant contract that the dwelling and garage were "to be erected under N.H.A. requirements and built according to plans now on file with contractor and purchaser." The Court held in that case [at p. 208] that:—

" 'Putting these properties in first class shape' must have reference to their capacity for taking on repairs, which could be only those which their aged condition permitted."

On that question opinions might differ. Then dealing with the requirements in that case that the work should be done to the entire satisfaction of the owner, the Court [at p. 212] said this:—

"Where the work has to be done to the approval of the employer or building owner, in the absence of express and unambiguous provision making such approval a condition precedent, the maximum that 'no man shall be judge in his own cause' (Broom's Legal Maxims) is strong to raise a presumption against the right of the employer or building owner to determine in his own favour and without appeal any dispute as to the character of the workmanship or the amount of the price to be paid; and such approval, therefore, cannot be withheld by him unreasonbly."

As I read that case the Court held that the defendant acted unreasonably both in the interpretation that he placed upon the words "putting the properties in first-class shape" and his refusal to pay the balance claimed, notwithstanding that there had been a substantial compliance by the contractor with what was contemplated under the contract.

In the instant case there is no room for doubt as to what should be done by the contractor under the contract and the manner in which it should be done. Both those matters were covered by the N.H.A. requirements and the plans.

Mr. Gibson cited *Truman* v. *Ford Motor Co. of Canada Ltd.*, 58 O.L.R. 317, [1926] 1 D.L.R. 960, but that case, in my opinion, does not help his argument. That was a case of a sodding contract, which provided, *inter alia*, as follows:—

"*Inspection*: Materials purchased [that is the sod] are subject to first party's risk, and returnable at second party's expense.

"*Cancellation*: The first party (Ford) further reserves the right to cancel this order if material is not in accordance with . . . approved samples or specifications or is defective in workmanship or material or is not satisfactory to first party."

Specifications in that Contract read in part as follows:—

"All sods are to be of a quality satisfactory to the Ford Motor Company of Canada Limited equal to the sample furnished for exhibit.

"All work is to be done in a manner satisfactory to the Ford Motor Company of Canada Limited and as designated by their representative. A first-class job is required."

When the plaintiff started to lay the sods, the defendant was not satisfied with the sods or the work, and cancelled the contract. This action was then brought against the Company for damages. In delivering the judgment of this Court, Ferguson J.A. at page 322, said this:—

"I am of opinion that all the cases turn on the interpretation of the contract, that this appeal also turns on the construction of the contract, and that, according to the true intent and meaning of the parties as expressed in the writing, the condition in this contract is one which makes the view, opinion, or judgment of the promisor final, if honestly arrived at. I think I have said sufficient with respect to the interpretation of the contract in the instant case, to distinguish it from the contract in the *Truman* v. *Ford* case. What the defendants in this case seek to do is to get the benefit of the contract without paying its worth to them. . . .

[The appeal was dismissed with costs.]

DAKIN & CO., LIMITED *v.* LEE

England. King's Bench Division. [1916] 1 K.B. 566

The plaintiffs were builders. The action was brought to recover the sum of £352 4s. 4d., the balance of the price of certain repairs carried out by the plaintiffs at the defendant's house, 37 Wimbledon Park Road, Wandsworth. Part of the claim related to work contained in a specification which by a verbal contract the parties had agreed should be done for £264. The balance of the claim was for extras and additional work. The only question raised on the appeal related to the claim in respect of the contract work.

The defence was that the work referred to in the specification had not been completed, and the official referee found as a fact that the contract had not been fulfilled in the three following instances: (1) A letter from the plaintiffs which accompanied the specification stated that the concrete which was to be placed under a part of one of the side walls of the house, which was to be underpinned, was to be of the depth of 4 feet. Only 2 feet of concrete was placed there. (2) Columns of hollow iron, 5 inches in diameter were to be used for the support of a certain bay window. The columns supplied were of solid iron 4 inches in diameter. (3) The joists over the bay window were to be cleated at the angles and bolted to caps and to each other. This was not done. The defendant had resumed her occupation of the house after the plaintiffs' workmen had left, and after receiving the plaintiffs' account she offered to settle the whole claim by a payment of £250 in addition to a sum of £50 which she had already paid.

The official referee held that the plaintiffs had not performed their contract, in that the defendant had been given something different from, and less strong and secure than, what she was entitled to have under the contract, and that the plaintiffs were therefore not entitled to recover any part of the contract price or any sum in respect of the contract work. The official referee disallowed the claim for extras, but allowed a sum of £70 for the additional work, which was less than the sums paid before action and paid into Court, and the official referee therefore entered judgment for the defendant. The plaintiffs appealed.

SANKEY J.: . . . I do not think that the official referee took the correct view of either the law or the facts. In my opinion the law applicable to cases of this sort is as follows. Where a builder has supplied work and labour for the erection or repair of a house under a lump sum contract, but has departed from the terms of the contract, he is entitled to recover for his services, unless (1) the work that he has done has been of no benefit to the owner; (2) the work he has done is entirely different from the work which he has contracted to do; or (3) he has abandoned the work and left it unfinished.

As to the first case, namely, where the work as done is of no benefit to the owner, the authority is *Farnsworth* v. *Garrard* (1807), 1 Camp. 38; 170 E.R. 867. An illustration of the second case, where the work done is entirely different from the work which the builder contracted to do, may be found, I think, in the case of *Forman & Co. Proprietary* v. *Ship Liddlesdale*, [1900] A.C. 190, 201. The gist of the decision is given where Lord Hobhouse says: "It is also made clear that the substitution of iron for steel not only added to the weight and to the expenses, but altered the structure of the vessel—to her advantage, as the plaintiffs contend, but as the defendant says, causing a rigidity in her framework which is a source of danger to her. That is a matter on which opinions vary; but there is no dispute that the alteration is not consistent with the plaintiffs' obligation to restore the vessel to her original condition prior to the accident."

Another illustration of the same class of case, namely, where the work done is entirely different from the work contracted to be done, may be found in the observations of Day J. in *London School Board* v. *Wall*, Hudson's *Building Contracts*, 3rd ed., vol. 2, p. 165. A similar rule applies in the sale of goods, where the plaintiff cannot recover if he supplies an article entirely different from that which he has contracted to supply.

With regard to the third case, namely, where the builder has abandoned the work or left the house or the repairs unfinished, the authority is *Sumpter* v. *Hedges*, [1898] 1 Q.B. 673. There the plaintiff had abandoned the work and left it incomplete. Mr. Cassels in the course of his argument put by way of illustration the case of a builder who, having contracted to build a 10 foot wall, built a wall of 2 feet only, and he contended that in that case the builder could not recover. In my opinion that would come into the third category of cases which I have mentioned; the builder would be held not to have finished the work and to have abandoned it. . . .

But then it is said that the first contract, not having been performed, has gone, and that there is no evidence of any new contract by the defendant to pay for the work that was actually done. She says that no promise to pay for that work can be implied from the fact that the defendant occupied the house because the work was carried out on the employer's land, and therefore could not be rejected. I think there is a fallacy underlying that argument. I do not think that the contract can be said to have gone where the house has been substantially completed or the repairs have been substantially carried out, though not entirely in the manner provided for by the contract. The true view and the true method of ascertaining the amount due to the plaintiff in such a case is, I think, that given by Parke B. in the case of *Thornton* v. *Place* (1832), 1 Moo. & R. 218; 174 E.R. 74 at p. 75, where he says: "What the plaintiff is entitled to recover is the price agreed upon in the specification, subject to a deduction; and the measure of that deduction is the sum which it would take to alter the work so as to make it correspond with the specification." Where repairs have been substantially completed, or a house has been substantially erected, in accordance with the contract I find no difficulty in holding either that the contract has been performed, or that there is an implied request by the defendant to do the work and an implied promise to pay. I cannot hold that, where a builder has done ninety-nine hundredths of the work according to the contract and the remaining one hundredths in a different way, the building owner is not obliged to pay for any part of the work done. The present case, in my view, is an example of that. Unfortunately, we have not the advantage of hearing exactly what the learned referee said when he gave his judgment, but I am satisfied that there was no finding by him that the work done by the plaintiffs was of no benefit to the defendant, or that it was entirely different from that which the plaintiffs contracted to do, and there is no finding that they either abandoned the work or left the repairs unfinished. I do not think there is any evidence—certainly our attention has not been drawn to it—to show that the contract has not been substantially completed, and I do not think that because there was a slight variation in the depth of the concrete, a very insignificant variation in the columns, and a still more insignificant variation in the beams by their not being cleated, it is possible to say that the repairs have nót been substantially done.

Under these circumstances, I think the judgment of the learned official referee was wrong, and that this appeal ought to be allowed.

[The defendant appealed and the Court of Appeal dismissed the appeal. Ridley J. also gave an opinion in the Divisional Court.]

JACOB & YOUNGS, INC. *v.* KENT

New York. Court of Appeal. 1921. 230 N.Y. 239; 129 N.E. 889

CARDOZO J.: The plaintiff built a country residence for the defendant at a cost of upwards of $77,000, and now sues to recover a balance of $3,483.46, remaining unpaid. The work of construction ceased in June, 1914, and the defendant then began to occupy the dwelling. There was no complaint of defective performance until March, 1915. One of the specifications for the plumbing works provides that "all wrought-iron pipe must be well galvanized, lap welded pipe of the grade known as 'standard pipe' of Reading manufacture."

The defendant learned in March, 1915, that some of the pipe, instead of being made in Reading, was the product of other factories. The plaintiff was accordingly directed by the architect to do the work anew. The plumbing was then encased within the walls except in a few places where it had to be exposed. Obedience to the order meant more than the substitution of other pipe. It meant the demolition at great expense of substantial parts of the completed structure. The plaintiff left the work untouched, and asked for a certificate that the final payment was due. Refusal of the certificate was followed by this suit.

The evidence sustains a finding that the omission of the prescribed brand of pipe was neither fraudulent nor willful. It was the result of the oversight and inattention of the plaintiff's subcontractor. Reading pipe is distinguished from Cohoes pipe and other brands only by the name of the manufacturer stamped upon it at intervals of between six and seven feet. Even the defendant's architect, though he inspected the pipe upon arrival, failed to notice the discrepancy. The plaintiff tried to show that the brands installed, though made by other manufacturers, were the same in quality, in appearance, in market value and in cost as the brand stated in the contract—that they were indeed the same thing, though manufactured in another place. The evidence was excluded, and a verdict directed for the defendant. The Appellate Division reversed, and granted a new trial.

We think the evidence, if admitted, would have supplied some basis for the inference that the defect was insignificant in its relation to the project. The courts never say that one who makes a contract fills the measure of his duty by less than full performance. They do say, however, that an omission, both trivial and innocent, will sometimes be atoned for by allowance of the resulting damage, and will not always be the breach of a condition to be followed by a forfeiture. . . . The distinction is akin to that between dependent and independent promises, or between promises and conditions. . . . Some promises are so plainly independent that they can never by fair construction be conditions of one another. . . . Others are so plainly dependent that they must always be conditions. Others, though dependent and thus conditions when there is departure in point of substance, will be viewed as independent and collateral when the departure is insignificant. . . . Considerations partly of justice and partly of presumable intention are to tell us whether this or that promise shall be placed in one class or in another. The simple and the uniform will call for different remedies from the multifarious and the intricate. The margin of departure within the range of normal expectation upon a sale of common chattels will vary from the margin to be expected upon a contract for the construction of a mansion or a "skyscraper." There will be harshness sometimes and oppression in the implication of a condition when the thing upon which labor has been expended is incapable of surrender because united to the land, and equity and reason in the implication of a like condition when the subject-matter, if defective, is in shape to be returned. From the conclusion that promises may not be treated as dependent to the extent of their uttermost minutiae without a sacrifice of justice, the progress is a short one to the conclusion that they may not be so treated without a perversion of intention. Intention not otherwise revealed may be presumed to hold in contemplation the reasonable and probable. If something else is in view, it must not be left to implication. There will be no assumption of a purpose to visit venial faults with oppressive retribution.

Those who think more of symmetry and logic in the development of legal rules than of practical adaptation to the attainment of a just result will be troubled by a classification where the lines are so wavering and blurred. Something, doubtless, may be said on the score of consistency and certainly in favor of a stricter standard. The courts have balanced such considerations against those of equity and fairness, and found the latter to be the weightier. The decisions in this state commit us to the liberal view, which is making its way, nowadays, in jurisdictions slow to welcome it. *Dakin & Co.* v. *Lee*, [1916] 1 K.B. 566. Where the line is to be drawn between the important and the trivial cannot be settled by a formula. "In the nature of the case precise boundaries are impossible." 2 *Williston on Contracts*, p. 841. The same omission may take on one aspect or another according to its setting. Substitution of equivalents may not have the same significance in fields of art on the one side and in those of mere utility on the other. Nowhere will change be tolerated, however, if it is so dominant or pervasive as in any real or substantial measure to frustrate the purpose of the contract. . . . There is no general license to install whatever, in the builder's judgment, may be regarded as "just as good.". . . The question is one of degree, to be answered, if there is doubt, by the triers of the facts, . . . and, if the inferences are certain, by the judges of the law. . . .

We must weigh the purpose to be served, the desire to be gratified, the excuse for deviation from the letter, the cruelty of enforced adherence. Then only can we tell whether literal fulfillment is to be implied by law as a condition. This is not to say that the parties are not free by apt and certain words to effectuate a purpose that performance of every term shall be a condition of recovery. That question is not here. This is merely to say that the law will be slow to impute the purpose, in the silence of the parties, where the significance of the default is grieviously out of proportion to the oppression of the forfeiture. The willful transgressor must accept the penalty of his transgression. . . . For him there is no occasion to mitigate the rigor of implied conditions. The transgressor whose default is unintentional and trivial may hope for mercy if he will offer atonement for his wrong.

In the circumstances of this case, we think the measure of the allowance is not the cost of replacement, which would be great, but the difference in value, which would be either nominal or nothing. Some of the exposed sections might perhaps have been replaced at moderate expense. The defendant did not limit his demand to them, but treated the plumbing as a unit to be corrected from cellar to roof. In point of fact, the plaintiff never reached the stage at which evidence of the extent of the allowance became necessary. The trial court had excluded evidence that the defect was unsubstantial, and in view of that ruling there was no occasion for the plaintiff to go farther with an offer of proof. We think, however, that the offer, if it had been made, would not of necessity have been defective because directed to difference in value. It is true that in most cases the cost of replacement is the measure. The owner is entitled to the money which will permit him to complete, unless the cost of completion is grossly and unfairly out of proportion to the good to be attained. When that is true, the measure is the difference in value. Specifications call, let us say, for a foundation built of granite quarried in Vermont. On the completion of the building, the owner learns that through the blunder of a subcontractor part of the foundation has been built of the same quality quarried in New Hampshire. The measure of allowance is not the cost of reconstruction. "There may be omissions of that which could not afterwards be supplied exactly as called for by the contract without taking down the building to its foundations, and at the same time the omission may not affect the value of the building for use or otherwise, except so slightly as to be hardly appreciable.". . . The rule that gives a remedy in cases of substantial performance with compensation for defects of trivial or inappreciable importance, has been developed by the courts as an instrument of justice. The measure of the allowance must be shaped to the same end.

The order should be affirmed, and judgment absolute directed in favour of the plaintiff upon the stipulation, with costs in all courts.

McLaughlin J.: I dissent. The plaintiff did not perform its contract. Its failure to do so was either intentional or due to gross neglect which, under the uncontradicted facts, amounted to the same thing, nor did it make any proof of the cost of compliance, where compliance was possible. . . .

No explanation was given why pipe called for by the contract was not used, nor was any effort made to show what it would cost to remove the pipe of other manufacturers and install that of the Reading Manufacturing Company. The defendant had a right to contract for what he wanted. He had a right before making payment to get what the contract called for. It is no answer to say that the pipe put in was just as good as that made by the Reading Manufacturing Company, or that the difference in value between such pipe and the pipe made by the Reading Manufacturing Company would be either "nominal or nothing." Defendant contracted for pipe made by the Reading Manufacturing Company. What his reason was for requiring this kind of pipe is of no importance. He wanted that and was entitled to it. It may have been a mere whim on his part, but even so, he had a right to the kind of pipe, regardless of whether some other kind, according to the opinion of the contractor or experts, would have been "just as good, better, or done just as well." He agreed to pay only upon condition that the pipe installed were made by that company and he ought not to be compelled to pay unless that condition be performed. . . . The rule, therefore, of substantial performance, with damages for unsubstantial omissions, has no application. . . .

NOTE. Dean Havighurst, in his casebook, asks: How do you explain the absence of any issue arising from the refusal of the architect to give a certificate? Why did the owner refuse to make the final payment? Because he did not get Reading pipe? How did the pipe get into the litigation?

FAIRBANKS SOAP CO. LTD. *v*. SHEPPARD

Ontario. Supreme Court of Canada. [1953] 2 D.L.R. 193

CARTWRIGHT J. delivered the judgment of the Court: The appellant is a manufacturer of soap and the respondent is a mechanical engineer. This action arises out of an agreement between the parties for the construction by the respondent in the plant of the appellant of a machine for making and drying soap chips. There is also a claim made by the respondent for $1,000 for the "installation" of the machine in question and of certain pulleys, hangers and shafting to be supplied by the appellant which requires consideration but it will be convenient first to dispose of the questions relating to the contract for the construction of the machine itself. It was a term of the contract that the type of design of the machine and the products produced by it should be "of the standard generally used and produced by all the large soap producers on this continent." It is now common ground that this was an entire contract to construct the machine for a price of $9,800 payable $4,000 in cash on completion and the balance to be secured by promissory notes. For the reasons given by Roach J.A. [1952] 1 D.L.R. 417, I agree with his conclusion, which was also that of the learned trial Judge, that the contract was not one for the sale of goods but for work to be done and materials supplied.

The contract was made in September, 1945. No date for completion was fixed. For reasons with which we are not now concerned there were numerous and lengthy delays in building the machine. By March 1, 1949, according to the evidence of the respondent, the work had progressed to a point where the supplying of a small number of parts and the performance of a few days' work would have resulted in the completion of the machine. At this point the respondent took the position that he would do nothing more unless and until he was paid $3,000, which, added to $1,000 which had been paid to him in November, 1946, would make up the payment of $4,000 which was due on completion. The explanation of this given by the respondent at the trial was that he was afraid that if he completed the machine so that the appellant no longer required his services in connection with it he would not be paid. The appellant offered to deposit the sum mentioned *in escrow* to be paid to the respondent on completion of the machine but the respondent refused to proceed unless payment was made to him. By letter dated March 25, 1949, the appellant required the respondent to complete his contract by April 30, 1949, stating in part that unless he did so "we shall cancel the contract and require you to remove this machine from our premises, and request you to return the $1,000 paid to you, and further reimburse us for the time our employees worked on this machine with your employees, at your request, and for materials supplied at your request."

The letter concluded with the following paragraph: "If for any reason the time limit fixed by us for completion of the machine is unreasonable or insufficient, we would ask you to kindly advise us at once, otherwise we shall presume that we have given you reasonable time for so doing, and will act accordingly."

Counsel for the respondent does not suggest that the date fixed by this letter for completion was unreasonable. His submission is that the contract was already substantially completed. The respondent did nothing further and on May 11, 1949, the appellant commenced this action. The statement of claim recites the contract, alleges that the machine had never been constructed or completed and claims:

"(a) A declaration of this court that the contract between the parties hereto and dated the 21st of September, 1945, has been cancelled.

(b) The sum of $1,000 paid to the defendant.

(c) The sum of $700, value of floor space in the plaintiff's factory, used by the defendant.

(d) The sum of $137.11 the value of materials supplied by the plaintiff to the defendant at his request.

(e) The sum of $355.77 being value of materials purchased by the plaintiff as aforesaid less their salvage values and wasted by reason of the failure of the defendant to complete such machine."

At the opening of the trial the following claim was added by amendment, (e) (1) the sum of $1,191.80 the cost of labour referred to in para. 9 of the statement of claim. The relevant sentence in para. 9 is as follows: "The plaintiff further supplied labour at the request of the defendant in the construction of such machine, such labour costing the plaintiff the sum of $1,191.80."

There was an alternative claim for $15,000 damages, presumably to cover the contingency of its being held that the appellant had to accept and pay for the machine.

Paragraph 5 of the statement of defence reads as follows: "The defendant says and the fact is that he has manufactured upon the premises of the plaintiff a machine as specified in the said agreement referred to in paragraph 3 of the statement of claim and that the plaintiff is now obliged to accept and pay for the same."

The respondent asked that the action be dismissed and counterclaimed (a) $9,584 being the contract price of $9,800 plus $784 sales tax less $1,000 paid on account, (b) $1,000 for "installation" as mentioned above and (c) $500 paid by the respondent for labour which he claimed should have been supplied by the appellant.

The learned trial Judge held that "there was a substantial compliance with the contract" by the respondent, that there was no abandonment of the work by him, and no total failure of consideration, and that the respondent was entitled to be paid the contract price "less the cost of completing the machine, etc. and putting it in working order," which last mentioned cost he fixed at $600. He allowed the respondent's claim on the separate contract at $1,000 and on his claim of $500 he allowed him $200. Judgment was accordingly given for the respondent on his counter-claim for these amounts totalling $10,184, with costs, and the action was dismissed with costs. This judgment was affirmed by the Court of Appeal [1952] 1 D.L.R. 417, and the plaintiff now appeals to this Court. . . .

The judgments in *Dakin* v. *Lee*, [1916] 1 K.B. 566, have been repeatedly approved and followed in Ontario, vide, e.g., *Taylor Hardware Co.* v. *Hunt* (1917), 35 D.L.R. 504 at pp. 506–7, and in my respectful opinion they correctly state the law.

The real question on this appeal is whether the respondent substantially completed his contract to construct the machine. With the greatest respect for the contrary view held by the learned trial Judge and the Court of Appeal, I have reached the conclusion that he did not. . . . In my opinion on the evidence of the respondent himself and of the witnesses called on his behalf there was no substantial completion of the contract. At the time when the respondent definitely refused to proceed further with the construction of the machine it was incomplete in the following respects: the "knife" and "flange" were missing, baffles were required for the canvas apron screening of the dryer, further work was required on the fans and the speed of the machine had to be changed, being about six times as fast as was proper. It is urged on behalf of the respondent that these are comparatively unimportant details and that the allowance of $600 for the completion of the machine made by the learned trial Judge is a generous one. But it appears from the evidence of the respondent and his witnesses that what remained to be done required engineering skill and knowledge. The record is silent as to whether the services of an engineer other than the respondent possessing the necessary skills were available to the appellant. . . .

Counsel for the respondent did not seek to base any claim in regard to this contract on a quantum meruit and I think it clear that, if, as I have held to be the case, there was no substantial completion of the contract, there was no evidence from which any new contract to accept and pay for the work done could be inferred. From the evidence it seems probable that the machine in its present state has become part of the realty which belongs to the appellant. Assuming this to be so it is clear from the reasons in *Sumpter* v. *Hedges*, [1898] 1 Q.B. 673, that the mere fact of the appellant remaining in possession of his land is no evidence upon which an inference of a new contract can be founded. . . .

In the case at bar the appellant has never elected to take any benefit available to him from the unfinished work and Mr. Williston stated that he was willing that, in the event of his appeal succeeding, a term should be inserted in the judgment permitting the respondent to remove the machine within a reasonable time.

For the above reasons I am of opinion that the respondent's claim based on the contract to construct the machine fails and that the appellant is entitled to a declaration that the contract was cancelled and to the return of the $1,000 paid to the respondent in November, 1946.

QUESTION. Is the refusal of quantum meruit here consistent with the decision of the court in the *Deglman* case?

RESTATEMENT OF THE LAW OF CONTRACTS
Washington. American Law Insitute. 1932

275. In determining the materiality of a failure fully to perform a promise the following circumstances are influential:

(a) The extent to which the injured party will obtain the substantial benefit which he could have reasonably anticipated;

(b) The extent to which the injured party may be adequately compensated in damages for lack of complete performance;

(c) The extent to which the party failing to perform has already partly performed or made preparations for performance;

(d) The greater or less hardship on the party failing to perform in terminating the contract;

(e) The wilful, negligent or innocent behaviour of the party failing to perform;

(f) The greater or less uncertainty that the party failing to perform will perform the remainder of the contract.

QUESTIONS. Dean Havighurst invites, in his casebook on Contracts, a comparison of the language of section 275 with the sentence beginning "We must weigh the purpose to be served . . . etc." in Cardozo J.'s judgment in *Jacob and Youngs* v. *Kent*, above. Which do you prefer?

Why did the Institute not simply state rules? Why "influential" or persuasive "circumstances" rather than binding rules?

BIGHAM *v.* BRAKE

Ontario. Divisional Court. 1927. 32 O.W.N. 271

ORDE J.A., in a written judgment, said that the contract in question upon this appeal required the plaintiff to build for the defendant a concrete brick foundation and wall and three piers, the work to be in compliance with a by-law of the City of Toronto, regulating the erection and providing for the safety of buildings, for a lump sum of $400. For work of this character the by-law clearly required the use of cement mortar, which is declared to mean mortar made with Portland cement and clean, sharp sand, in the proportion of one part of cement to not more than three parts of sand, the addition of hydrated lime to the amount of not more than 10 per cent. of the amount of the cement being permitted. The plaintiff did not even attempt to conform to this by-law, but prepared a mortar composed almost wholly of lime and sand with a small quantity of cement, amounting approximately to about three parts of cement to five parts of lime and forty-two parts of sand.

It was contended that but for the damage done by frost, for which the Assistant Master held the defendant and not the plaintiff responsible, the work done by the plaintiff would have been as good as if he had complied with the by-law. This is to some extent mere speculation. The evidence disclosed, and the Assistant Master finds, that the mortar used by the plaintiff was deficient in quality even as lime mortar. It is probable that but for the frost the wall might have stood and perhaps served the purpose for which it was intended, but it could hardly have been as good and safe a wall as if built according to the contract.

The plaintiff relies upon *H. Dakin & Co. Ltd.* v. *Lee*, [1916] 1 K.B. 566, and *House Repair and Service Co. Ltd.* v. *Miller* (1921), 49 O.L.R. 205, and contends that there was here a substantial compliance with the contract entitling him to recover the contract price, or in any case the value of the work done. That contention cannot prevail here. Whether or not a particular case comes within the principle enunciated in the *Dakin* case must be largely a question of fact. Here it is fairly evident that what was done has proved of no value to the defendant, and is so substantially different from what was contracted for as to bring the case within two of the exceptions stated in the head-note to the *Dakin* case.

The appeal should be dismissed.

[Latchford C.J. and Smith J.A. agreed with Middleton J.A., who said, in part: "Contractors and builders should understand that they cannot recover upon a contract unless they comply with its terms, and that the *Dakin* case does not decide that a contractor or builder may substitute something more convenient for him or less expensive and then demand payment, upon the theory that it is 'just as good' or 'almost as good,' and treat the case as one calling for some abatement in the contract price.]

SUMPTER *v.* HEDGES

England. Court of Appeal. [1898] 1 Q.B. 673

The action was for work done and materials provided. The plaintiff, a builder, had contracted with the defendant to build upon the defendant's land two houses and stables for the sum of £565. The plaintiff did part of the work, amounting in value to about £333, and had received payment of part of the price. He then informed the defendant that he had no money, and could not go on with the work. The learned judge found that he had abandoned the contract. The defendant thereupon finished the buildings on his own account, using for that purpose certain building materials which the plaintiff had left on the ground. The judge gave judgment for the plaintiff for the value of the materials so used, but allowed him nothing in respect of the work which he had done upon the buildings.

A. L. SMITH L.J.: . . . In this case the plaintiff, a builder, entered into a contract to build two houses and stables on the defendant's land for a lump sum. When the buildings were still in an unfinished state the plaintiff informed the defendant that he had no money, and was not going on with the work any more. The learned judge has found as a fact that he abandoned the contract. Under such circumstances, what is a building owner to do? He cannot keep the buildings on his land in an unfinished state for ever. The law is that, where there is a contract to do work for a lump sum, until the work is completed the price of it cannot be recovered. Therefore the plaintiff could not recover on the original contract. It is suggested however that the plaintiff was entitled to recover for the work he did on a quantum meruit. But, in order that that may be so, there must be evidence of a fresh contract to pay for the work already done. With regard to that, the case of *Munro* v. *Butt* (1858), 8 E. & B. 738: 120 E.R. 275, appears to be exactly in point. That case decides that, unless the building owner does something from which a new contract can be inferred to pay for the work already done, the plaintiff in such a case as this cannot recover on a quantum meruit. In the case of *Lysaght* v. *Pearson* (not reported except in Times Newspaper of March 3, 1879), to which we have been referred, the case of *Munro* v. *Butt* does not appear to have been referred to. There the plaintiff had contracted to erect on the defendant's land two corrugated iron roofs. When he had completed one of them, he does not seem to have said that he abandoned the contract, but merely that he would not go on unless the defendant paid him for what he had already done. The defendant thereupon proceeded to erect for himself the second roof. The Court of Appeal held that there was in that case something from which a new contract might be inferred to pay for the work done by the plaintiff. That is not this case. In the case of *Whitaker* v. *Dunn* (1887), 3 Times L.R. 602, there was a contract to erect a laundry on defendant's land, and the laundry erected was not in accordance with the contract, but the official referee held that the plaintiff could recover on a quantum meruit. The case came before a Divisional Court, consisting of Lord Coleridge C.J. and myself, and we said that the decision in *Munro* v. *Butt* applied, and there being no circumstances to justify an inference of a fresh contract the plaintiff must fail. My brother Collins thinks that that case went to the Court of Appeal, and that he argued it there, and the Court affirmed the decision of the Queen's Bench Division. I thing the appeal must be dismissed.

COLLINS L. J.: . . . I agree. I think the case is really concluded by the finding of the learned judge to the effect that the plaintiff had abandoned the contract. If the plaintiff had merely broken his contract in some way so as not to give the defendant the right to treat him as having abandoned the contract, and the defendant had then proceeded to finish the work himself, the plaintiff might perhaps have been entitled to sue on a quantum meruit on the ground that the defendant had taken the benefit of the work done. But that is not the present case. There are cases in which, though the plaintiff has abandoned the performance of a contract, it is possible for him to raise the inference of a new contract to pay for the work done on a quantum meruit from the defendant's having taken the benefit of that work, but, in order that that may be done, the circumstances must be such as to give an option to the defendant to take or not to take the benefit of the work done. It is only where the circumstances are such as to give that option that there is any evidence on which to ground the inference of a new contract. Where, as in the case of work done on land, the circumstances are such as to give the defendant no option whether he will take the benefit of the work or not, then one must look to other facts than the mere taking the benefit of the work in order to ground the inference of a new contract. In this case I see no other facts on which such an inference can be founded. The mere fact that a defendant is in possession of what he cannot help keeping, or even has done work upon it, affords no ground for such an inference. He is not bound to keep unfinished a building which in an incomplete state would be a nuisance on his land. I am therefore of opinion that the plaintiff was not entitled to recover for the work which he had done. I feel clear that the case of *Whitaker* v. *Dunn* to which reference has been made, was the case which as counsel I argued in the Court of Appeal, and in which the Court dismissed the appeal on the ground that the case was concluded by *Munro* v. *Butt*.

[The appeal was dismissed. The opinion of Chitty L.J. to the same effect is omitted.]

DELDO *v*. GOUGH SELLERS INVESTMENTS LIMITED
Ontario. Court of Appeal. 1915. 34 O.L.R. 274

HODGINS J. A. delivered the judgment of the Court: . . . On the argument it seemed clear that the lien of the claimants, who are material-men, was filed in time. They were entitled to register it within 30 days from the last delivery of material, and from their account it appears that over 90 per cent. of their material was supplied on the 15th July. This coincides with the evidence as to the duration of the work. The result is that the claimants' lien is established.

The remaining question is, to what amount this lien entitled them as against the owner.

The contract between the owner and the contractor Morris is dated the 22nd June, 1914. It provides for the building of a pair of solid brick houses for $3,850—"the same to be completed in two months from the date of starting." Then follow specifications as to material and quality, winding up with this clause: "All work and material to be first class, the same to be paid for 80 per cent. as work proceeds, and the builder allowed five draws—$300 on completion of stone work, and then $400 when roof is on, $1600 when plastering is all finished, and $700 when complete, and balance within 30 days, upon shewing all receipts paid and work satisfactory.

The owner in his evidence admits that the stone work is completed and that $100 was paid, apparently as an advance to the contractor, on the 27th June, 1914. The claimants now contend that their rights are not limited to the 20 per cent. drawback on the value of the work done, but includes this balance of $200 to which the contractor became entitled under the contract upon the finishing of the stone work.

Under the *Mechanics and Wage-Earners Lien Act,* and apart from the 20 per cent. drawback, the rights of lien-holders are measured by the amount "justly owing" by the owner to the contractor, and the owner is not liable for a greater sum than is payable to the contractor.

The contract here does not make entire completion a condition precedent to payment, but expressly divides the $3,850, the consideration, into five sums, one of which has become "payable" under the terms of the contract.

In *Terry* v. *Duntze* (1795), 2 H Bl. 389; 126 E.R. 611, Buller J., said: "It is a rule long established in the construction of covenants, that if any money is to be paid before the thing is done, the covenants are mutual and independent. . . . The plaintiffs covenant to finish and complete the buildings on or before the 20th of September then next: in consideration of which the defendant covenants to pay £3,800 by instalments, viz., a certain sum when the second floor should be laid, a further sum etc. . . . By the terms of the contract then two several sums of money were to be paid, before the thing to be done was done. The plaintiffs, therefore, were clearly entitled to their action for the money without averring performance, and the defendant to his remedy on the covenants."

In that case the action was not for the instalments, as stated in Hudson on Building Contracts, but for the whole price, and the defence was non-completion within the stipulated time, but the rule of construction laid down is applicable to this case. It was adopted in *Government of Newfoundland* v. *Newfoundland R. W. Co.* (1888), 13 App. Cas. 199, and acted on in *Workman Clark & Co. Limited* v. *Lloyd Brazileno*, [1908] 1 K.B. 968.

The amount payable or justly due is, *prima facie*, $200, and this is, of course, subject to any deduction which the owner can establish by reason of the non-completion of the whole contract, for it contemplates entire performance, although providing for payment in advance of that time.

The head-note in the case of *Sherlock* v. *Powell* (1899), 26 A.R. 407 cited on the argument, is somewhat misleading. That case does not deal at all with the right to recover instalments of the price. The instalments of 80 per cent. provided for in the contract had all been paid, and Lister J.A., states the point of the case thus: "The question is, whether the plaintiff is entitled under the circumstances" (i.e., not having completed the work), "to recover the balance of the contract price or any portion of it." He then adds: "Manifestly, performance is a condition precedent to the right of the plaintiff to enforce payment of the balance of the contract price."

This statement is based upon the fact that the balance was payable only after completion and upon acceptance of the work.

The judgment of the Official Referee should be reversed, and the appellants declared entitled to a lien. The amount payable will be the $200, subject to the owner's right to shew that, by reason of non-completion or otherwise, it is not justly due and owing, or to reduce it. Other lien-holders will be entitled to share if their rights are affected by this judgment. The Referee must ascertain the value of the work done so as to calculate the 20 per cent. drawback. The appellants may add their costs to their lien, subject to the provisions of the Mechanics' and Wage-Earners Lien Act as to the percentage of costs recoverable.

Appeal allowed.

[*The Mechanics' and Wage-Earners' Lien Act* is now *The Mechanics' Lien Act.*]

NOTE ON MECHANICS' LIENS. At least since 1873, Ontario has had legislation providing for a "lien" for the workman who puts his labour into another person's real property, or for the seller who supplies materials (a material man) to be used in construction on another person's real property. The common law itself invented the possessory lien, whereby a workman, or mechanic, could retain in his possession goods upon which he had worked, until he was paid for his labour. It was obviously difficult to apply (or extend) this idea to a builder, because he didn't have possession of the real property on which he built and the common law supposed that each board, and each nail, as it was fastened into place, became fixed to the realty, and became the property of the owner.

The Ontario Act is *The Mechanics' Lien Act*, R.S.O. 1960, c. 233. Sections 5 (1) and (2) are the basic sections, and they are set out in full as illustrations of a past age of drafting.

CREATION OF LIEN

5. (1) Unless he signs an express agreement to the contrary and in that case subject to section 4, any person who performs any work or service upon or in respect of, or places or furnishes any materials to be used in the making, constructing, erecting, fitting, altering, improving or repairing of any erection, building, railway, land, wharf, pier, bulkhead, bridge, trestlework, vault, mine, well, excavation, fence, sidewalk, pavement, fountain, fishpond, drain, sewer, aqueduct, roadbed, way, fruit or ornamental trees, or the appurtenances to any of them for any owner, contractor, or subcontractor, by virtue thereof has a lien for the price of the work, service or materials upon the estate or interest of the owner in the erection, building, railway, land, wharf, pier, bulkhead, bridge, trestlework, vault, mine, well, excavation, fence, sidewalk, paving, fountain, fishpond, drain, sewer, aqueduct, roadbed, way, fruit or ornamental trees, and appurtenances and the land occupied thereby or enjoyed therewith, or upon or in respect of which the work or service is performed, or upon which the materials are placed or furnished to be used, limited, however, in amount to the sum justly due to the person entitled to the lien and to the sum justly owing, except as herein provided, by the owner, and the placing or furnishing of the materials to be used upon the land or such other place in the immediate vicinity of the land designated by the owner or his agent is good and sufficient delivery for the purpose of this Act,

but delivery on the designated land does not make such land subject to a lien.

(2) The lien given by subsection 1 attaches to the land as therein set out where the materials delivered to be used are incorporated into the buildings, erections or structures on the land, notwithstanding that the materials may not have been delivered in strict accordance with subsection 1.

What is the necessity for such particularizing of the real property to which the Act applies? Even in subsection (2), the reference to "buildings, erections or structures" seems a bit verbose, since "buildings" alone is probably clear enough, and certainly "buildings and structures" would cover the same things. The 1873 Act (c. 27) referred to "building, erection or mine."

Section 4 of the Act makes every agreement whereby a workman (mechanic) waives the Act "null and void," but the section does not protect a manager, officer or foreman, or any person whose wages are more than $15 a day. The dollar limitation is rather anachronistic.

Section 11 provides for a "holdback" of 20% of the contract price (15% where the price exceeds $25,000) so that funds are available to pay subcontractors to whom the contractor may be in default. The holdback is to be retained thirty-seven days. Originally it was thirty days, and workmen, knowing this, put off until the thirtieth day, the imposing of the lien. It was thought that by quietly extending the time another week, those who put it off until a tomorrow thirty-one days later, would still be protected. Now the thirty-seven day period is so well known that many liens are registered on the thirty-eighth day!

QUESTIONS: Suppose in *Deldo* v. *Gough* the facts had been that when the stone-work was completed the owner announced on Saturday that he could not pay the $300. Should the builder (*a*) send his men to work on Monday as if nothing untoward had happened? (*b*) Put his men to work but sue for damages for breach of the promise to pay? (*c*) Refuse to go on? (*d*) Refuse to go on until he had been paid? (*e*) Refuse to go on until some security had been offered? (*f*) Take another job until the owner finds the $300? (*g*) Insist upon new terms being agreed upon? What terms? Reread the *Kiewit* case above.

CANADIAN STANDARD FORM CONSTRUCTION CONTRACT

Article 36. *Contractor's Right to Stop Work or Terminate Contract.* If the work should be stopped under an order of any court, or other public authority, through no act or fault of the Contractor or of any one employed by him, or if the Owner should fail to pay to the Contractor, within seven days of its maturing and presentation, any sum certified by the Architect or awarded by arbitrators, then the Contractor may, upon three days' written notice to the Owner and the Architect, stop work or terminate this contract and recover from the Owner payment for all work executed and any loss sustained upon any plant or material with reasonable profit and damages.

BRAZEAU *v.* WILSON

Ontario. Court of Appeal. 1916. 36 O.L.R. 396

An appeal by the plaintiff from the judgment of the Judge of the District Court of the District of Temiskaming dismissing an action to enforce a mechanic's lien for $396.33 and awarding the defendant Wilson $200 on his counterclaim for moneys paid on account of the contract price.

The plaintiff's contract with the defendant Wilson, the owner in equity of certain lots, was to install a heating system in a house built upon these lots.

The District Court Judge found that the system was defective, and based his judgment upon that finding.

MEREDITH C.J.C.P.: The evidence on each side is unsatisfactory; no reasonable effort seems to have been made fairly to try out the matters in question in this action; and, if the case had been tried before me, I should have declined to deal with it on such efforts, and would have availed myself of the right, afforded by the practice, to appoint some competent person to make the necessary examination of the work in question and give an impartial report, and, if necessary, give evidence, upon the matters in question: see Rule 268. But the case must now be dealt with upon the evidence which the parties chose to adduce, and upon that evidence it is plain—indeed it is admitted by the plaintiff—that he was to put into the defendant's house a heating system that would properly heat it, and there is evidence upon which it might be found, as the trial Judge has found, that that has not been done.

The plaintiff's attempt to put the blame on the defendant for not building a better chimney was not given effect to at the trial, and cannot be here; the plaintiff knew the condition of the chimney, and should not have contracted as he did except upon the condition that better draught should be supplied by the defendant, if he then really thought the flue insufficient.

The result is, that the plaintiff has not furnished that which he contracted to supply; he has not substantially fulfilled his contract, and so is not entitled to the price that was to be paid to him on fulfilment of the contract; and to that extent the judgment is right. But the defendant is not entitled to retain the boiler, radiators, pipes, etc., put in by the plaintiff. The defendant recovers, according to his defence on which the judgment in appeal is based, on the ground that the whole work is useless, and must be, as he terms it, scrapped, which means necessarily taking out and discarding these articles. When so taken out, they must be the property of the plaintiff, not of the defendant, and the plaintiff is then entitled to them. The principle applied in such a case as *Oldershaw* v. *Garner* (1876), 38 U.C.Q.B.R. 37, adopting and following the ruling in *Munro* v. *Butt* (1858), 8 E. & B. 738; 120 E.R. 275, is obviously not applicable to such a case as this, to fixtures which are to be unfixed and taken out, or, as I really think was intended by the defendant, not to be taken out, but to be utilised for his benefit under a new contract for the heating of his house.

The judgment in appeal should be varied so as to give to the plaintiff the right to remove the boiler, radiators, pipes, etc., doing no unnecessary damage, during the month of June next, upon paying to the defendant the amount of his judgment and costs.

The result is, that the plaintiff recovers his goods, and the defendant his money. In addition to that, the defendant has had two seasons' use of the heating system, such as it was, which is sufficient to compensate him for the plaintiff's breach of the contract.

There should be no order as to the costs of this appeal. This applies to all parties to the appeal.

RIDDELL J. I would dismiss the appeal without costs.

By consent the plaintiff is to be allowed to remove his materials. This logically would imply his doing no unnecessary damage, and would be without prejudice to the defendant's right of action for breach of contract &c.; but, to put an end to this litigation, I agree with the disposition made by my Lord.

Appeal allowed in part.

[The opinion of Riddell J. is drastically curtailed. Lennox and Masten JJ. concurred.]

QUESTIONS. Would Riddell J. have allowed both "expectation damages" and "restitution" in this case? What does Meredith C.J.C.P. mean by the words, "sufficient to compensate him for the plaintiff's breach of the contract"?

4. TIME STIPULATIONS AND INSTALMENT CONTRACTS

The cases in the preceding section hinted at difficulties that could arise on the failure of a promisor to pay or perform on time, especially if payment or performance is not made an express condition to the counter promise to continue, or if there is not some such provision as that used in the standard form construction contract. The most common clause simply says, "Time is of the essence of this agreement." But business men frequently make fairly generous concessions in the actual working out of their contracts and the difficulties are often increased by this generosity.

CHARLES RICKARDS, LTD. *v.* OPPENHEIM
England. Court of Appeal. [1950] 1 All E.R. 420

DENNING L.J.: Early in 1947 the defendant, Mr. Oppenheim, wanted a new Rolls Royce car, and he placed an order in two parts with the plaintiffs, Charles Rickards, Ltd., who are motor car traders. He first ordered the chassis, a Rolls Royce Silver Wraith chassis, for estimated delivery in June, 1947, but he also wanted a body built on the chassis, and he particularly wanted to know the time within which that body could be made. The plaintiffs made inquiries of various firms for an estimated time for buiding a body on to the chassis. In July, 1947, Rolls Royce themselves estimated twenty-one months, and Park Ward at about the same time estimated fifteen months. Those times were too long for the defendant's satisfaction, so the plaintiffs obtained an estimate from Jones Brothers (Coachbuilders), Ltd., who said that they could do it within "six months or, at the most, seven months." Thereupon, the plaintiffs gave the same time to the defendant and he gave them the order for the body on that footing. The order was placed in July. The plaintiffs sub-contracted it and put out the work with Jones Brothers (Coachbuilders), Ltd. The actual time from which the six or seven months started is not precisely ascertained. The chassis was actually delivered to the sub-contractors on July 30, 1947, and, if that is taken as the date from which the time ran, the seven months would be up at the end of February, 1948, but the specification for the body was not finally agreed until Aug. 20, 1947. If that date is taken, the latest time for delivery would be Mar. 20, 1948. Whichever date is taken, though, is immaterial, for the time was plainly exceeded. The body was not built on to the chassis by Mar. 20, nor, indeed, until many months later—not until Oct. 18, 1948, was the car completed.

Meanwhile, however, as from Mar. 20, 1948, at least, onwards, the defendant had been pressing for delivery. During the winter of 1947/8 he went to America, and in the autumn of 1947, before he left, he told the plaintiffs that he hoped the car would be ready by the time he came back. He came back in March, and the car was not ready by Mar. 20, 1948. He could have cancelled the contract there and then, but he did not do so. By pressing for delivery he waived the stipulation as to time. He asked for delivery in time for Ascot, but he did not get it. He asked for delivery in time to take the car on his holiday abroad at the beginning of August, 1948. He did not get it. He was given promises from time to time for early delivery—not definite guarantees, but promises which were not fulfilled. These promises were made not so much by the plaintiffs as by the sub-contractors, but the defendant was well justified in dealing direct with the sub-contractors, as, not only were they actually doing the work, but, on Aug. 7, 1947, the plaintiffs had written to them telling them that it was in order for them to accept any instructions with regard to the body that were given by the defendant, and asking them to keep the plaintiffs *au fait* with the situation. It was, therefore, quite natural for the defendant to deal direct with the sub-contractors, to talk to them about the work, and to press them for delivery. He also pressed the plaintiffs for delivery, but they did not go further than to say that the car would be delivered as early as possible.

Eventually, not having got the car for Ascot and wanting it in time to take it abroad at the beginning of August, on June 28, 1948, the defendant saw Mr. Musk, the sub-contractors' manager, who told him that it would be ready in two weeks' time. On the next day the defendant wrote to the sub-contractors a letter on which much of this case turns. He sent it "For the attention of the managing director." It says:

"Further to my conversation with Mr. Musk today, I regret that I shall be unable, unless my plans change, to accept delivery of the Rolls you are making for me after July 25. For six months I have had a reservation to take a car abroad on Aug. 3 for my holiday and it would appear to me to be impossible for me to alter this date. I shall therefore have to buy another car."

He also asked in the letter whether there was any definite likelihood of receiving the car before July 25. A week later, about July 7, Mr. Musk intimated that the car would not even be ready for him to take abroad by Aug. 3. Thereupon the defendant bought elsewhere another car, a Rolls Bentley, and asked the plaintiffs to return the money which he had paid for the chassis—he was ready to let them keep the chassis and have the advantage of the work that had been done on the body. This request was followed by an interview on July 10 at which, according to the evidence of the plaintiffs, the defendant in effect waived his notice of cancellation and agreed that the plaintiffs should go on with the work and he would take the car later. The judge has negatived any such waiver on the facts, and I do not see any reason to differ from his finding. After that interview the plaintiffs, through the sub-contractors, completed the car. On Oct. 18, 1948, it was finished, but delivery was refused by the defendant. This action is now brought by the plaintiffs for the price of the body, and a counter-claim is made by the defendant claiming the return of the chassis or its value.

It is clear on the findings of the judge that there was an initial stipulation making time of the essence of the contract between the plaintiffs and the defendant, namely, that it was to be completed "in six, or, at the most, seven months." Counsel for the plaintiffs did not seek to disturb that finding—indeed, he could not successfully have done so—but he said that that stipulation was waived. His argument was that, the stipulated time having been waived, the time became at large, and that thereupon the plaintiffs' only obligation was to deliver within a reasonable time. He said that, in accordance with well-known authorities, "a reasonable time" meant a reasonable time in the circumstances as they actually existed, i.e., that the plaintiffs would not exceed a reasonable time if they were prevented from delivering by causes outside their control, such as strikes or the impossibility of getting parts, and so forth, and that, on the evidence in this case, it could not be said that a reasonable time was in that sense exceeded. . . .

If this had been originally a contract without any stipulation in regard to time, and, therefore, with only the implication of reasonable time, it may be that the plaintiffs could have said that they had fulfilled the contract, but, in my opinion, the case is very different when there was an initial contract, making time of the essence, of "six, or, at the most, seven months." I agree that that initial time was waived by reason of the requests for delivery which the defendant made after March, 1948, and that, if delivery had been tendered in compliance with those requests, the defendant could not have refused to accept. Supposing, for instance, delivery had been tendered in April, May, or June, 1948, the defendant would have had no answer. It would be true that the plaintiffs could not aver and prove that they were ready and willing to deliver in accordance with the original contract. They would have had, in effect, to rely on the waiver almost as a cause of action. At one time there would have been theoretical difficulties about their doing that. It would be said that there was no consideration, or, if the contract was for the sale of goods, that there was nothing in writing to support the variation. *Plevins* v. *Downing* (1876), 1 C.P.D. 220, coupled with what was said in *Besseler, Waechter Glover & Co.* v. *South Derwent Coal Co., Ltd.*, [1938] 1 K.B. 408, gave rise to a good deal of difficulty on that score, but all those difficulties are swept away now. If the defendant, as he did, led the plaintiffs to believe that he would not insist on the stipulation as to time, and that, if they carried out the work, he would accept it, and they did it, he could not afterwards set up the stipulation in regard to time against them. Whether it be called waiver or forbearance on his part, or an agreed variation or substituted performance, does not matter. It is a kind of estoppel. By his conduct he made a promise not to insist on his strict legal rights. That promise was intended to be binding, intended to be acted on, and was, in fact, acted on. He cannot afterwards go back on it. That, I think, follows from *Panoutsos* v. *Raymond Hadley Corpn. of New York* [1917] 2 K.B. 473, a decision of this court. . . . It is a particular application of the principle which I endeavoured to state in *Central London Property Trust, Ltd.* v. *High Trees House, Ltd.*, [1947] 1 K.B. 130.

Therefore, if the matter stopped there, the plaintiffs could have said that, notwithstanding that more than seven months had elapsed, the defendant was bound to accept, but the matter does not stop here, because delivery was not given in compliance with the requests of the defendant. Time and time again the defendant pressed for delivery, time and time again he was assured that he would have early delivery, but he never got satisfaction, and eventually at the end of June he gave notice saying that, unless the car was delivered by July 25, he would not accept it. The question thus arises whether he was entitled to give such a notice, making time of the essence, and that is the question which counsel for the plaintiffs has argued before us. He agrees that, if this is a contract for the sale of goods, the defendant could give such a notice. He accepted the statement of McCardie J. in *Hartley* v. *Hymans*, [1920] 3 K.B. 405, as accurately stating the law in regard to the sale of goods, but he said that that statement did not apply to contracts for work and labour. He said that no notice making time of the essence could be given in regard to contracts for work and labour. The judge thought that the contract was one for the sale of goods, but, in my view, it is unnecessary to determine whether it was a contract for the sale of goods or a contract for work and labour, because, whichever it was, the defendant was entitled to give a notice bringing the matter to a head. It would be most unreasonable if, having been lenient and having waived the initial expressed time, he should thereby have prevented himself from ever thereafter insisting on reasonably quick delivery. In my judgment, he was entitled to give a reasonable notice making time of the essence of the matter. Adequate protection to the suppliers is given by the requirement that the notice should be reasonable.

The next question, therefore, is: Was this a reasonable notice? Counsel for the plaintiffs argued that it was not. He said that a reasonable notice must give sufficient time for the work then outstanding to be completed, and that, on the evidence in this case, four weeks was not a reasonable time because it would, and did, in fact, require three and a half months to complete it. In my opinion, however, the words of Lord Parker of Waddington in *Stickney* v. *Keeble* [1915] A.C. 419, apply to such a case as the present, just as much as they do to a contract for the sale of land. Lord Parker said:

"In considering whether the time so limited is a reasonable time the court will consider all the circumstances of the case. No doubt what remains to be done at the date of the notice is of importance, but it is by no means the only relevant fact. The fact that the purchaser has continually been pressing for completion, or has before given similar notices which he has waived, or that it is specially important to him to obtain early completion, are equally relevant facts. . . ."

To that statement I would add, in the present case, the fact that the original contract made time of the essence. In this case, not only did the defendant press continually for delivery, not only was he given promises of speedy delivery, but, on the very day before he gave the notice, he was told by the sub-contractors' manager, who was in charge of the work, that it would be ready within two weeks. He then gave a four weeks' notice. The judge found that it was a reasonable notice and, in my judgment, there is no ground on which this court could in any way differ from that finding. The reasonableness of the notice must, of course, be judged at the time at which it is given. It cannot be held to be a bad notice because, after it is given, the suppliers find themselves in unanticipated difficulties in making delivery.

The notice of June 29, 1948, was, therefore, a perfectly good notice so as to make time of the essence of the contract, subject, however, to another point that counsel for the plaintiffs made. He said it was bad because it was given, not to the plaintiffs direct, but to the sub-contractors, and it would appear that the sub-contractors did not send it on to the plaintiffs for another eight or nine days. The answer to that argument is that the notice was given to the people who were actually doing the work, and the plaintiffs had, from the beginning, authorised the defendant to give instructions direct to the sub-contractors. This notice was, no doubt, important, and it would have been better for the defendant to have given it both to the plaintiffs and to the sub-contractors, but it seems to me that, in view of the authorisation in August, 1947, the fact that it was not given to the plaintiffs direct cannot make it a bad notice. In any event, the plaintiffs received it within eight or nine days, and, even if it was only received then, there was still more than a fortnight to go before July 25, and it would still be a reasonable notice. That point also, therefore, does not hold good. . . .

The case, therefore, comes down to this. There was a contract by the plaintiffs to supply and fix a body on the chassis within six or seven months. They did not do it. The defendant waived that stipulation. For three months after the time had expired he pressed them for delivery, asking for it first for Ascot and then for his holiday abroad. But still they did not deliver it. Eventually at the end of June, being tired of waiting any longer, he gave a four weeks' notice and said: "At all events, if you do not supply it at the end of four weeks I must cancel," and he did cancel. I see no injustice to the plaintiffs in saying that that was a reasonable notice. Having originally stipulated for six to seven months, having waited eleven months, and still not getting delivery, the defendant was entitled to cancel the contract.

On the counter-claim the judge has held that the chassis should be returned or its value paid. I assume that the plaintiffs will exercise their option of paying for the chassis. They will then own the whole car, which they can sell for whatever they can realise. I cannot help sharing the regret of the judge that this car was not sold before and the proceeds used to meet the cost of the work, but we have only to deal with the strict legal rights of the parties. They are that the plaintiffs made a contract which they have not fulfilled and which the defendant justifiably cancelled. I think that the learned judge was right and that this appeal should be dismissed.

[Bucknill L.J. agreed that the appeal should be dismissed. The opinion of Singleton L.J. to the same effect is omitted.]

RESTATEMENT OF THE LAW OF CONTRACTS
Washington, American Law Institute, 1932

276. In determining the materiality of delay in performance, the following rules are applicable:

(a) Unless the nature of a contract is such as to make performance on the exact day agreed upon of vital importance, or the contract in terms provides that it shall be so, failure by a promisor to perform his promise on the day stated in the promise does not discharge the duty of the other party.

(b) In mercantile contracts performance at the time agreed upon is important, and if the delay of one party is considerable having reference to the nature of the transaction and the seriousness of the consequences, and is not justified by the conduct of the other party, the duty of the latter is discharged.

(c) If delay of one party in rendering a promised performance occurs before any part of his promise has been rendered, less delay discharges the duty of the other party than where there has been part performance of that promise.

(d) In contracts for the sale or purchase of land delay of one party must be greater in order to discharge the duty of the other party than in mercantile contracts.

(e) In a suit for specific performance of a contract for the sale or purchase of land, considerable delay in tendering performance does not preclude enforcement of the contract where the delay can be compensated for by interest on the purchase money or otherwise, unless

(i) The contract expressly states that performance at or within a given time is essential, or

(ii) The nature of the contract, in view of the accompanying circumstances, is such that enforcement will work injustice.

QUESTION. Why in clause 276 of the Restatement are *rules* "applicable" and in clause 275, above, are *circumstances* "influential"?

THE MERCANTILE LAW AMENDMENT ACT

Ontario. Revised Statutes. 1960. Chapter 238

15. Stipulations in contracts as to time or otherwise that would not, before the coming into force of *The Ontario Judicature Act, 1881*, have been deemed to be or to have become of the essence of such contracts in a court of equity shall receive in all courts the same construction and effect as they would prior to the coming into force of that Act have received in equity.

SALE OF GOODS ACT

Ontario. Revised Statutes. 1960. Chapter 358

11. Unless a different intention appears from the terms of the contract, stipulations as to time of payment are not deemed to be of the essence of a contract of sale, and whether any other stipulation as to time is of the essence of the contract or not depends on the terms of the contract.

NOTE. The difficulties mentioned at the beginning of this section are more acute where the element of time is mixed with the complication that the failure to perform on time is only a failure to perform one instalment. Is the failure to pay or to perform a single instalment to be regarded as a failure of a condition? If not, what courses of action are open if a party defaults on an early instalment out of, say, five instalments? The cases below show how the Courts have dealt with the problem in a series of cases on the sale of goods. These cases illustrate the groping in the judicial process that resulted in a relatively functional proposition in *Maple Flock Co. Ltd.* v. *Universal Furniture Products (Wembly) Ltd.* in 1933. Do you think that case provides a working rule? How far is the thinking about sales cases applicable to building or employment cases? Little is said here about the sale of land cases, for which, through the intervention of the courts of equity, rather special rules were developed, to which some reference was made by Denning L.J. in the *Oppenheim* case above.

WITHERS *v.* REYNOLDS

England. King's Bench. 1831, 2 B. & Ad. 882; 109 E.R. 1370

Assumpsit for not delivering straw to the plaintiff pursuant to agreement.

At the trial before Lord Tenterden, C.J., at the Sittings in Middlesex after last Hilary Term, the agreement proved was as follows:

John Reynolds undertakes and agrees to supply Joseph Withers with wheat straw of good quality sufficient for his use as a stablekeeper, and delivered on his premises as above (i.e., at Long Acre, London), till the 24th of June, 1830, at the sum of thirty-three shillings per load of thirty-six trusses, to be delivered at the rate of three loads in a fortnight, in a dry state and without damage. And the said J.W. hereby agrees to pay to the said J.R. or his order the sum of thirty-three shillings per load for each load of straw so delivered on his premises from this day till the 24th of June, 1830, according to the terms of this agreement. (signed) Joseph Withers, John Reynolds.

The straw was regularly sent in from the 20th of October, 1829, when this agreement was made, till the end of January, 1830. At that time, the plaintiff being in arrears for several loads of straw, the defendant called upon him for the amount, and he thereupon tendered to the defendant £11 11s., being the price of all the straw delivered, except the last load, saying that he should always keep one load in hand. The defendant objected to this, but was at length obliged to take the sum offered; and he then told the plaintiff that he would send no more straw unless it was paid for on delivery; and accordingly no more was sent. On the part of the defendant it was submitted that there must be a nonsuit, inasmuch as the plaintiff, on his own showing, had not performed his own part of the contract, which was, in effect, to pay for each load on delivery. Lord Tenterden C.J., was of this opinion, but directed a verdict for the plaintiff, reserving the point. A rule nisi was afterwards obtained for entering a nonsuit.

LORD TENTERDEN C.J.: I am of opinion that the plaintiff is not entitled to recover. There is, I think, no doubt that by the terms of this agreement the plaintiff was to pay for the loads of straw as they were delivered. If that were not so, the defendant would have been liable to the inconvenience of giving credit for an indefinite length of time, and, in case of non-payment, bringing an action for a very large sum of money, which does not appear to have been intended by the contract. Then the only question is, whether, upon the plaintiff saying "I will not pay for the goods on delivery" (for that was the effect of his communication to the defendant), it was incumbent on the defendant to go on supplying straw; and he clearly was not obliged to do so.

PATTERSON J.: If the plaintiff had merely failed to pay for any particular load, that of itself might not have been an excuse to the defendant for delivering no more straw; but the plaintiff here expressly refuses to pay for the loads as delivered; the defendant, therefore, is not liable for ceasing to perform his part of the contract.

[The opinions of Parke and Taunton JJ. are omitted. The rule was made absolute.]

HOARE *v.* RENNIE

England. Exchequer. 1859. 5 H. & N. 19; 157 E.R. 1083

POLLOCK C.B.: We are all agreed that the defendants are entitled to judgments upon the pleas. The foundation of my opinion is shortly this, that a man has no right to say that which is a breach of an agreement is a performance of it. On that ground, this case is distinguishable from almost every other which has been cited. It does not turn upon any question of condition precedent. The only question is whether, if a man who is bound to perform his part of a contract does not do so, he can enforce the contract against another party. The plaintiffs contracted with the defendants to ship a large quantity of iron in June, July, August, and September, about one-fourth part in each month; but instead of shipping about 160 tons, as they should have done, they shipped little more than twenty tons, as a performance of the contract. The first count states that the plaintiffs performed all things necessary on their part to be performed, that they were ready and willing to do all things which according to agreement it was necessary they should be willing to do, and that all things happened to entitle the plaintiffs to a performance of the agreement on the part of the defendants. This is denied by the plea. The second count states that the plaintiffs, in part performance of the contract, shipped a certain portion of the iron, and in further performance of the agreement tendered and offered to deliver the said portion so shipped, yet defendants refused to accept the same. The pleas raise the question whether the defendants were bound to accept and pay for what was sent and tendered; the plaintiffs having, in June, shipped from Sweden a quantity much less than they were bound to have shipped, and the defendants having insisted that this was a breach of the contract, and given notice that they refused to accept the residue. The pleas expressly state that the plaintiffs were not ready to deliver such a quantity of iron shipped from Sweden in June as is specified in the contract, and were not ready and willing to deliver the small quantities shipped until after the month of June had elapsed, and until after the defendants had notice that the plaintiffs were not ready and willing to perform their part of the agreement. The only question we have to deal with is whether, on a contract like this, if the sellers at the outset send a less quantity than they are bound to send, so as to begin with a breach, they can compel the purchasers to accept and pay for that the sending of which was a breach and not a performance of the agreement. The argument on the part of the plaintiffs is that this was not a condition precedent. I do not think that is the test. It was said that if the plaintiffs had sent the one-hundredth part, instead of one-fourth part, in June, the defendants' remedy would have been by a cross-action. The case was put of the plaintiffs sending a short quantity after one shipment had been accepted. Possibly that might have made a difference. Where a person has derived a benefit from a contract he cannot rescind it, because the parties cannot be put in *statu quo*. Probably, therefore, in such case the defendants could not have repudiated the contract, and must have been left to their cross-action. Here, however, the defendants refused to accept the first shipment, because, as they say, it was not a performance, but a breach of the contract. Where parties have made an agreement for themselves, the courts ought not to make another for them. Here they say that in the events that have happened one-fourth shall be shipped in each month, and we cannot say that they meant to accept any other quantity. At the outset, the plaintiffs failed to tender the quantity according to the contract: they tendered a much less quantity. The defendants had a right to say that this was no performance of the contract, and they were no more bound to accept the short quantity than if a single delivery had been contracted for. Therefore the pleas are an answer to the action.

[The concurring opinions of Watson and Channell BB., are omitted.]

QUESTIONS. What difference can it make whether one shipment has been received or not? Is there any analogy between an instalment contract and such a case as *Boone* v. *Eyre*? Is *Hoare* v. *Rennie* consistent with viewing an instalment contract as a number of separate contracts?

If the contract called for 150 tons a month in *Hoare* v. *Rennie* suppose:

(*a*) In the first month 150 were sent and received. In the second month 50 were sent. Could the defendant refuse them? See *Jackson* v. *Rotax Motor & Cycle Co.*, [1910] 2 K.B. 937. Could he refuse to go on with the balance of the contract?

(*b*) In the first month 75 were sent and received. In the second month 75 more were tendered. Could the defendant refuse them? Would it make any difference if the first 75 were received in the middle of the month and the defendant expected the balance before the month expired?

SIMPSON *v.* CRIPPIN

England. Queen's Bench. 1872. L.R. 8 Q.B. 14

At the trial before Lush J., at the Liverpool Spring Assizes, 1872, it appeared that the defendants were coal proprietors, and the plaintiffs were coal merchants. On the 10th of June, 1871, the plaintiffs wrote to the defendants the following letter: "We agree to take from you about 6,000 to 8,000 tons of your best Wigan four-feet coal, at 5s. 6d. per ton of 21 cwt. to the ton, put into our wagons at the colliery. Delivery to commence from the 1st of July next, and to be taken in about equal monthly quantities over the next twelve months. It is understood that you are not bound to supply in case of accidents or strikes. Terms, cash monthly, less 2½% discount."

The defendants, by letter also dated the 10th of June, replied as follows: "We agree to supply you from 6,000 to 8,000 tons of our best four-feet Wigan coal, properly screened, and free from slack, to be delivered into your wagons at our collieries, in equal monthly quantities during the period of twelve months from the 1st of July next—strikes of our workmen, accidents, and other circumstances beyond our control excepted—at 5s. 6d. per ton of 21 cwt. Terms, cash monthly, less 2½% discount."

On the 8th of July the defendants wrote, complaining that the first week for the fulfilment of the contract had terminated without the plaintiffs sending wagons or orders for coals. The correspondence continued, the defendants requesting that wagons might be sent, and the plaintiffs promising to comply. During the month of July the plaintiffs took from the defendants only 158 tons of coal. On the 1st of August the defendants wrote to the plaintiffs, that inasmuch as the latter had only taken 158 tons during the month of July, and as the sole inducement for the defendants to entertain the contract was the regular and punctual withdrawal by the plaintiffs of the stipulated quantity during the summer months, which they had failed to perform, the defendants gave notice that the contract was cancelled. On the 2nd of August the plaintiffs replied, stating that they would not allow the contract to be cancelled.

On these facts the learned judge told the jury, that as the plaintiffs did not intend to break the contract month by month, and only broke it for the first month's delivery, that did not justify the defendants, in point of law, in cancelling the contract, and left the question of damages to them.

The jury found a verdict for the plaintiffs for £475, leave being reserved to move to enter a verdict for the defendants.

A rule was afterwards obtained upon the ground that under the circumstances the plaintiffs had disentitled themselves to sue for the breach of the contract, and that the defendants were entitled to cancel the contract, and refuse to deliver the residue of the coal.

BLACKBURN J.: I think that the rule ought to be discharged. It cannot be denied that the plaintiffs were bound in every month to send wagons capable of carrying at least 500 tons, and that by failing to perform this term they have committed a breach of the contract, and the question is, whether by this breach the contract was determined. The defendants contend that the sending of a sufficient number of wagons by the plaintiffs to receive the coal was a condition precedent to the continuance of the contract, and they rely upon the terms of the letter of the 1st of August. No sufficient reason has been urged why damages would not be a compensation for the breach by the plaintiffs, and why the defendants should be at liberty to annul the contract; but it is said that *Hoare* v. *Rennie* (1859), 157 E.R. 1083, is in point, and that we ought not to go counter to the decision of a court of co-ordinate jurisdiction. It is, however, difficult to understand upon what principle *Hoare* v. *Rennie* was decided. If the principle on which that case was decided is that, wherever a plaintiff has broken his contract first he cannot sue for any subsequent breach committed by the defendant, the decision would be opposed to the authority of many other cases. I prefer to follow *Pordage* v. *Cole*, 1 Wms. Saund. 310. No reason has been pointed out why the defendants should not have delivered the stipulated quantity of coal during each of the months after July, although the plaintiffs in that month failed to accept the number of tons contracted for.

FREETH *v.* BURR

England. Common Pleas. 1874. L.R. 9 C.P. 208

LORD COLERIDGE C.J.: The question in this case arises upon a contract for the sale of iron entered into between the plaintiffs and the defendant on the 28th of November, 1871, in the following terms: "bought of Messrs. D. M. Burr & Co., 250 tons of pig-iron, at 56s. per ton alongside our wharf, Millwell. Half to be delivered in two weeks, remainder in four weeks. Payment net cash fourteen days after delivery of each parcel." The material facts were these: There was no delivery in the terms of the contract of either parcel of the iron. In point of fact, the delivery of the first 125 tons was by mutual arrangement delayed, and the last delivery of that parcel did not take place until the 12th of May, 1872. There was a correspondence between the parties, pressure by the purchasers for delivery, and excuses by the vendor for the non-delivery. That the former were anxious for the completion of the contract appears to be clear, as well from the tenor of the correspondence as from the fact that the market was rising. A few days after the full delivery of the first parcel, viz., on the 29th of May, 1872, the defendant demanded payment for the 125 tons, which the plaintiffs refused, claiming to set off damages for the defendant's breach of contract. The plaintiffs afterwards demanded delivery of the remaining 125 tons; and upon the defendant's refusal to comply with that demand this action was brought. The question is whether the fact of the plaintiffs' refusal to pay for the 125 tons delivered was such a refusal on the part of the purchasers to comply with their part of the contract as to set the seller free and to justify his refusal to continue to perform it. This certainly appears, viz., that there was an extension by mutual consent of the time for the delivery of the iron from December, 1871, to May, 1872, with constant pressure on the one side and excuses and resistance on the other. I mention that because it is important to express my view that, in cases of this sort, where the question is whether the one party is set free by the action of the other, the real matter for consideration is whether the acts of conduct of the one do or do not amount to an intimation of an intention to abandon and altogether to refuse performance of the contract. I say this in order to explain the ground upon which I think the decisions in these cases must rest. There has been some conflict amongst them. But I think it may be taken that the fair result of them is as I have stated, viz., that the true question is whether the acts and conduct of the party evince an intention no longer to be bound by the contract. Now, non-payment on the one hand, or non-delivery on the other, may amount to such an act, or may be evidence for a jury of an intention wholly to abandon the contract and set the other party free. That is the true principle on which *Hoare* v. *Rennie* was decided, whether rightly or not upon the facts, I will not presume to say. Where, by the non-delivery of part of the thing contracted for, the whole object of the contract is frustrated, the party making default renounces on his part all the obligations of the contract. The principle to be applied in these cases is, whether the non-delivery or the non-payment amounts to an abandonment of the contract or a refusal to perform it on the part of the person so making default. That being so, and my brother Brett having ruled that the mere non-payment for the first portion of the iron contracted for, unattached by any other act on the part of the purchasers, did not put an end to the contract so as to disentitle the purchasers to maintain an action for the non-delivery of the second portion, but only gave the seller a remedy by cross-action (of which he has availed himself), I am of opinion that his ruling was correct, and that the rule should be discharged.

[The opinions of Keating and Denman JJ. to the same effect are omitted. Keating J. said, in part: "Non-payment is an element. But, looking at all the circumstances of this case—a rising market; a failure on the part of the defendant to deliver the iron according to the terms of the contract; a series of deliveries in small quantities long after the times for delivery provided for by the contract; and a refusal on the part of the plaintiffs to pay for the iron delivered, not only accompanied by remonstrances, but with a requisition to the seller to fix a day for the delivery of a certain quantity; I do not think they show an intention on the part of the plaintiffs to abandon the contract."]

HONCK *v.* MULLER

England. Court of Appeal. 1881. 7 Q.B.D. 92

The defendant in October, 1879, sold to the plaintiff, and the plaintiff bought of the defendant, 2000 tons of pig-iron at 42s. a ton, to be delivered to the plaintiff free on board at maker's wharf, at Middlesborough, "in November, 1879, or equally over November, December, and January next, at 6d. per ton extra." The plaintiff failed to take delivery of any of the iron in November, but claimed to have delivery of one-third of the iron in December and one-third in January. The defendant refused to deliver these two-thirds, and gave notice that he considered that the contract was cancelled by the plaintiff's breach to take any iron in November.

The present action was then brought, in which the plaintiff claimed the difference between the contract price and the market price of 666⅔ tons at the end of December, and of 666⅔ tons at the end of January.

At the trial judgment was given for the plaintiff for £933 6s. 8d., less £66 13s. which the defendant had paid into court. The defendant obtained from the Queen's Bench Division a rule nisi for a new trial, which was subsequently discharged. Thereupon the defendant appealed to the Court of Appeal, asking for judgment in his favour.

BRAMWELL L.J.: I think it unnecessary to determine which of the several meanings put on the agreement in this case is right. For whichever is adopted I think the result should be the same. . . .

The case for the plaintiff is, that by the contract, or what was done under it, he was to take and was entitled to have 666⅔ tons in each of the months of November, December, and January. That though he (the plaintiff) broke his contract in not taking the 666⅔ in November, and though the defendant at once gave notice that he would not go on with the contract he (the plaintiff) has a right to insist on the December and January deliveries. In other words, the plaintiff says that having agreed to take 2000 tons he has a right or power to demand and take 1333⅓ and no more. I cannot think so. I think that contention is contrary to law and justice alike. I think where no part of a contract has been performed, and one party to it refuses to perform the entirety to be performed by him, the other party has a right to refuse to perform any part to be performed by him. I think if a man sells 2000 tons of iron he ought not to be bound to deliver 1333⅓ only, if it can be avoided. I can see no difference in principle between where the deliveries are at different dates and where they are to be all at once. I think the plaintiff no more entitled to the delivery of these 1333⅓ tons than he would be if he was to take 2000 tons in November, and send shipping for 1333⅓ tons only in that month at such a time that no more could be delivered, and he said that he would take no more.

Suppose it was a purchase of 100 yards of silk at so much a yard, and the buyer came for fifty only, could he insist on it? Would it make any difference that fifty yards were to be taken and paid for on Monday and fifty on Tuesday, and the Monday's delivery was not taken but refused, and then the Tuesday's was demanded? If there was a charter for an out-and-home voyage, and the charterer refused to load for the out voyage, could he insist on the ship taking his cargo for the home voyage? Suppose 10,000 tons of coal bought to be delivered at Gibraltar, Aden, and Bombay, in equal quantities—at Bombay in January, at Aden in February, and at Gibraltar in March, and no delivery at Bombay, could the buyer be made to take the other deliveries? Suppose a contract to supply bread to a workhouse for a year from the 1st of January, and the contractor says he will supply and does supply none in January, can he insist on supplying in the other eleven months? Suppose he does not supply for eleven months, can he insist on supplying in December? Would it make any difference if he was paid monthly? I hope not—I think not. Suppose a man orders a suit of clothes, the price being £7—£4 for the coat, £2 for the trousers and £1 for the waiscoat, can he be made to take the coat only, whether they were all to be delivered together, or the trousers and waistcoat first?

The party to a contract so broken has a right not to rescind the contract, for rescission is the act of both parties, but a right to declare he will not perform a part only of his contract, viz., what would remain to be performed if the other party had performed his part, and so enabled the performance of the whole. If, indeed, the contract has been part performed and cannot be undone then it must be proceeded with without such power of declaring off. If in this case the plaintiff had taken the November delivery, but had refused the December, the defendant would have been bound to make the January delivery. See what the consequence is of a different conclusion. The defendant would sell 2000 tons of iron and have so many pounds sterling. He is made to sell two-thirds only of the iron and have two-thirds only of the pounds sterling and a right of action. Suppose the November delivery would have been a profit to the defendant, and the December and January deliveries a loss, why is he to bear the loss and have no security that he will get the profit? This reasoning would no doubt apply where there is part performance, but then there is no help for it.

It is asked whether every trifling breach of contract is attended with this consequence. I know not; but 666⅔ tons out of 2000 are not a trifle. If it must be something which goes to the "root" of the contract, as was said, surely one-third of the subject-matter does. The case of *Hoare* v. *Rennie* (1859), 157 E.R. 108, is in point. The same thing was decided a few days ago in *Englehart* v. *Bosanquet* (not reported). It was there held that on a sale of 2000 tons of sugar to come in two ships when the first ship was not equal to contract, the buyer was not bound to take the other. But it is said that *Hoare* v. *Rennie* has been overruled by *Simpson* v. *Crippen* (1872), L.R. 8 Q.B. 14. That is not so. That decision was quite right. The case was distinguishable from *Hoare* v. *Rennie*, for the contract had been part performed and could not therefore be undone. One may express a respectful agreement with what the learned judges said in *Simpson* v. *Crippen*, viz., that they did not understand *Hoare* v. *Rennie*. The other cases cited are distinguishable on the same ground. It has never yet been held that a man may break his contract, render the performance of the whole impossible, and though nothing has been done under it, insist on the performance of the remainder. *Pordage* v. *Cole* (1668), 1 Wm. Saund. 319, has absolutely nothing to do with the case. That was an action on a specialty. This is not. As to the argument that in a case like the present there are really three contracts for three parcels that is wholly erroneous. In parol contracts, the whole of what is to be done on one side is the consideration for the whole of what is to be done on the other. The seller does not sell, the buyer does not buy, any parcel of 666⅔ tons any more than when the suit of clothes is sold there is a separate sale of coat, waistcoat, and trousers.

I am of opinion that the judgment should be reversed.

[Baggallay L.J. gave reasons for reaching the same conclusion. Brett L.J. dissented, stating that a breach as to one instalment did not entitle the other party to refuse to go on. In other words, that as the parties split up performance, they impliedly state that an action of damages would be sufficient compensation.]

QUESTIONS. What is the purpose of dividing a performance up into instalments? Would the view taken by Brett L.J. defeat that purpose? If the parties agreed that each instalment is to be regarded as a separate contract, would that agreement indicate a different purpose?

MERSEY STEEL AND IRON CO. *v.* NAYLOR, BENZON & CO.
England. House of Lords. 1884. 9 App. Cas. 434

The respondents bought from the appellant company 5000 tons of steel blooms of the company's make, to be delivered 1000 tons monthly, commencing January, 1881, payment within three days after receipt of shipping documents. In January the company delivered part only of the month's instalment, and in the beginning of February made a further delivery. On the 2nd of February, shortly after payment for these deliveries became due, a petition was presented to wind up the company. The respondents bona fide, under the erroneous advice of their solicitor that they could not without leave of the Court safely pay pending the petition, objected to make the payments then due unless the company obtained the sanction of the Court, which they asked the company to obtain. On the 10th of February the company informed the respondents that they should consider the refusal to pay as a breach of contract, releasing the company from any further obligations. On the 15th of February an order was made to wind up the company by the Court. A correspondence ensued between the respondents and the liquidator, in which the respondents claimed damages for failure to deliver the January instalment, and a right to deduct these damages from any payment then due; and said that they had been and still were ready to accept such deliveries and make such payments as ought to be accepted and made under the contract, subject to the right of set-off. The liquidator made no further deliveries, and brought an action in the name of the company for the price of the steel delivered. The respondents counterclaimed for damages for breaches of contract for non-delivery.

Lord Coleridge C.J. held that the respondents had been guilty of such a breach of the contract as entitled the company to treat it as at an end, and had therefore no claim for damages against the company. Judgment was accordingly given for the company.

The respondents appealed to the Court of Appeal which made an order to the following effect: "Discharge the judgment. Declare that the defendants are entitled to set off against the £1713 admitted to be due to the plaintiffs, such damages as they, the defendants, may have sustained by reason of the failure or refusal of the plaintiffs to deliver to the defendants the remainder of the blooms deliverable under the contract. Reference to ascertain the amount of such damages. Order the plaintiffs to pay the defendants' cost of the appeal. Reserve further consideration, and the costs of the action to follow the event." 9 Q.B.D. 648.

LORD BLACKBURN: . . . As to the first point, I myself have no doubt that *Withers* v. *Reynolds* (1831), 109 E.R. 1370, correctly lays down the law to this extent, that where there is a contract which is to be performed in future, if one of the parties has said to the other in effect, "If you go on and perform your side of the contract I will not perform mine" (in *Withers* v. *Reynolds* it was, "You may bring your straw but I will not pay you upon delivery as under the contract I ought to do. I will always keep one bundle of straw in hand so as to have a check upon you."), that in effect amounts to saying, "I will not perform the contract." In that case the other party may say, "You have given me distinct notice that you will not perform the contract. I will not wait until you have broken it, but I will treat you as having put an end to the contract, and if necessary I will sue you for damages, but at all events I will not go on with the contract." That was settled in *Hochester* v. *De La Tour* (1853), in the Queen's Bench and has never been doubted since; because there is a breach of the contract although the time indicated in the contract has not arrived.

That is the law as laid down in *Withers* v. *Reynolds*. That is, I will not say the only ground of defence, but a sufficient ground of defence. In *Freeth* v. *Burr* (1874), L.R. 9 C.P. 208, there it was also so laid down; and Lord Coleridge here thinks the facts were such as to bring the case within that principle. I will not at this time of the day go through them, but when the facts are looked at it is clear to me that that is not so. So far from the respondents saying that when the iron was brought in future they would not pay for it, they were always anxious to get it, and for a very good reason, that the price had risen high above the contract price. There was a statement that for reasons which they thought sufficient they were not willing to pay for the iron at present; and if that statement had been an absolute refusal to pay, saying "Because we have power to do wrong we will refuse to pay the money that we ought to pay," I will not say that it might not have been evidence to go to the jury for them to say whether it would not amount to a refusal to go on with the contract in future, for a man might reasonably so consider it. But there is nothing of that kind here; it was a bona fide statement, and a very plausible statement. I will not say more. I refrain from weighing its value at this moment; but, as I said before, it prevents the case from coming within the authority of *Withers* v. *Reynolds* and *Freeth* v. *Burr*, and consequently, as I understand it, Lord Coleridge made a mistake in the ground on which he went. The rule of law, as I always understood it, is that where there is a contract in which there are two parties, each side having to do something (it is laid down in the notes to *Pordage* v. *Cole*) if you see that the failure to perform one part of it goes to the root of the contract, goes to the foundation of the whole, it is a good defence to say, "I am not going on to perform my part of it when that which is the root of the whole and the substantial consideration for my performance is defeated by your misconduct."

But Mr. Cohen contended that whenever there was a breach of the contract at all (I think he hardly continued to contend that after a little while, but he said whenever there was a breach of a material part of the contract) it necessarily went to the root of the matter. I cannot agree with that at all. I quite agree that when there were a certain number of tons of the article delivered, it was a material part of the contract that the man was to pay, but it was not a part of the contract that went to the root of the consideration in the matter. There was a delay in fulfilling the obligation to pay the money. It may have been with or without good reason (if that would have made any difference), but it did not go to the root or essence of the contract, nor do I think that there is any sound principle upon which it could do so. I repeatedly asked Mr. Cohen whether or not he could find any authority which justified him in saying that every breach of a contract, or even a breach which involved in it the non-payment of money which there was an obligation to pay, must be considered to the root of the contract, and he produced no such authority. There are many cases in which the breach may do so; it depends upon the construction of the contract. With regard to the case of *Hoare* v. *Rennie* (1859), 5 H. & N. 19; 157 E.R. 1083, it has been said that the Chief Baron there went so far as to say that it was the essence and substance of the contract that the whole of the 166 tons of iron, and no less, should be delivered. If it was so, it would follow that when in the present case the January shipment had not been made, and the company could only deliver part of the quantity, it went to the essence of the contract. The question depends upon whether the whole and no less is the essence of it.

And again in *Honck* v. *Muller* (1881), 7 Q.B.D. 92, which has been referred to, it is expressly and pointedly shown that that is the ground taken, and the noble and learned Lord opposite (Lord Bramwell) stated that in his opinion the contract of the one party was to deliver and of the other to take 2000 tons of iron, and that inasmuch as it was to be by three instalments and the first one was gone and there never could be more than two-thirds of the quantity, the thing bargained for being the whole quantity of iron and no less, the defendant was not bound to deliver two-thirds when the plaintiffs required the two-thirds only. Supposing that that was the true construction of the contract, I think that that would would be the right conclusion. The present Master of the Rolls [Brett M.R. (afterwards Lord Esher) who had succeeded Jessel M.R. in 1883] seems, if I understand him rightly, to have thought that that was not the true construction of the contract—whether it was or not I do not express any opinion, except to point out that whatever be the construction of other contracts, there is not in my mind the slightest pretext for saying that such is the construction of this contract; and that being so, these cases have really no bearing upon the matter.

The circumstances being as I have said, the contract not being such as to make this payment a condition precedent, or to make punctual payment for one lot of iron which has been delivered a matter causing the contract to deliver other iron afterwards to be a dependent contract, being of opinion that that is not the meaning of the contract, I think that the decision of the Court of Appeal was right.

LORD BRAMWELL: My Lords, I am of the same opinion, and shall say but very few words. My Lord Coleridge says that the defendants, the now respondents, positively refused to pay for the iron already delivered, and for all which might be subsequently delivered. Now whether, if they had positively refused to pay for that already delivered, it would have given any justification to the company or the liquidator for refusing to go on with the contract, it is not necessary for me to say at the present moment. I do not say that it would not; but if they had positively refused to pay for all which might be subsequently delivered, it would undoubtedly be an answer upon the authority of *Withers* v. *Reynolds*, and the reasoning which you have heard. But I really cannot, with great submission to the noble Lord, find any evidence of that, and Mr. Cohen certainly did not attempt to prove it; but he set up a new ground, which was that the payment of the debt due was a condition precedent to the further performance of the agreement, with which I cannot at all agree.

I have just one other word to say. I cannot tell why *Honck* v. *Muller* and *Hoare* v. *Rennie* should be brought forward upon this occasion. I do not think that I said in *Honck v. Muller*, what Sir George Jessel (9 Q.B.D. 658) supposed me to have said, namely, that "In no case where the contract has been part performed could one party rely on the refusal of the other to go on." If I did say so I recall it, because I do not think so; it depends on the nature of the contract and the circumstances of the case. What I was busy upon in that case was in showing that there had been no performance at all there, and that in truth what the plaintiff was seeking to do was to make the defendant accept the performance of something entirely different from what had been agreed upon, and I think in that opinion I was right. But what has that to do with this case? Suppose I was wrong, what then? Suppose *Honck v. Muller* was wrongly decided, how does it bear upon this case? Not in the least. Nor indeed does the case of *Hoare* v. *Rennie*, which, in my opinion, was decided upon the considerations which I have mentioned, and which I think should be supported.

Orders appealed from affirmed and appeal dismissed.

[The opinions of the Earl of Selbourne L.C. and Lord Watson are omitted. Lord Fitzgerald concurred.]

THE SALE OF GOODS ACT

Ontario. Revised Statutes. 1960. Chapter 358

30. (2) Where there is a contract for the sale of goods to be delivered by stated instalments that are to be separately paid for and the seller makes defective deliveries in respect of one or more instalments or the buyer neglects or refuses to take delivery of or pay for one or more instalments, it is a question in each case depending on the terms of the contract and the circumstances of the case whether the breach of contract is a repudiation of the whole contract or whether it is a severable breach giving rise to a claim for compensation but not to a right to treat the whole contract as repudiated.

MAPLE FLOCK COMPANY, LTD. *v.* UNIVERSAL FURNITURE PRODUCTS (WEMBLEY), LTD.

England. Court of Appeal. [1934] 1 K.B. 148

Lord Hewart C.J. The judgment which I am about to read is the judgment of the whole Court.

The appellant company are manufacturers of rag flock, and the respondents are manufacturers of furniture and bedding for which they use such flock. The action was brought by the appellants for breach by the respondents of a contract in writing, dated March 14, 1932, for the sale by the appellants to the respondents of 100 tons of black lindsey flock at £15 2s. 6d. per ton, to be delivered in three loads per week as required. It was further stipulated that there should be a written guarantee that all flock supplied under the contract should conform to the Government standard. The load was 1½ tons or 60 bags. The Government standard was that required under the *Rag Flock Act, 1911*, which had been fixed by regulation under the Act at not more than 30 parts of chlorine in 100,000 parts of flock. The Act made it a penal offence punishable by fine for any person (inter alia) to sell or have in his possession for sale or use or to use flock not conforming to that standard. A person charged under the Act might, however, if he could prove that he bought it from some one resident in the United Kingdom under a warranty that it complied with the Government standard, and that he had taken reasonable steps to ascertain and did in fact believe in the accuracy of the warranty, bring the seller before the Court by information and transfer the burden of the offence to him.

The appellant company duly gave a written guarantee as required by the contract and deliveries were at once commenced and continued of 1½ tons each. The sixteenth of these deliveries was made on April 28, 1932, and, according to the respondent's evidence, was duly accepted and the stuff put into use; a further delivery was made on April 29, 1932, and another on May 2, 1932. On that latter date the respondents notified the appellants that a sample drawn from the delivery of April 28, 1932, had been analysed and showed a contamination of 250 parts of chlorine, instead of the maximum allowed by law of 30 parts. The respondents thereupon claimed to rescind the contract; the appellants protested, and some negotiations took place, during which two more deliveries were tendered and taken, each of 1½ tons. Eventually the respondents adhered to their claim that they were entitled to rescind, and the writ was issued by the appellants claiming damages on the ground that the refusal of the respondents to take further deliveries was wrongful.

No complaint is made in respect of the 15 deliveries made before April 28, 1932, or in respect of the four deliveries made after that date. The respondents made no claim for damages in respect of the delivery said to be defective, because it had all been used before the report was received on the sample. The learned Judge finds that the sample was taken in the usual way—namely, one handful drawn from one bag of the 60 bags which constituted the delivery, and he held that the respondents were entitled, applying the ordinary rules of probability, to say that such must be the condition of the whole or substantially the whole of that delivery of 1½ tons. On the other hand the appellants produced analyses of the flock they had in store from time to time, including an analysis dated April 29, 1932, all of which showed percentages of chlorine well below the Government maximum, though they could not identify any sample as drawn from the flock actually delivered to the respondents. In their evidence they described the process of manufacture by washing which they used. The learned Judge finds that it would be quite wrong to make any general criticism at all of the way in which the appellants conducted their business; he was very favourably impressed, he said, by the evidence of Mr. Jebb, who gave evidence for them; he seemed to the Judge a careful, scrupulous and honourable man. Mr. Jebb could give no explanation of so gross a degree of contamination and was disposed to think some mistake had been made as to the sample. The learned Judge, however, finding that the sample must be taken as a fair test of the delivery, held that the defendants, as prudent traders, could properly say to themselves, in regard to the defective delivery, "it might happen again." He nowhere finds that it was a reasonable inference that it would happen again. His conclusion appears to us to be that there was a mere possibility, not a reasonable probability, that it would happen again. On the contrary, he finds that the occurrence was a very extraordinary thing. We think that on the evidence, and the findings of the learned judge, the true inference of fact is that there was no reasonable probability of any such improper delivery being repeated under the contract.

The decision of this case depends on the true construction and application of s. 31, sub-s. 2, of the *Sale of Goods Act, 1893*, which is in [substantially the language of the Ontario Act reproduced above]. That subsection was based on decisions before the Act, and has been the subject of decisions since the Act. A contract for the sale of goods by instalments is a single contract, not a complex of as many contracts as there are instalments under it. The law might have been determined in the sense that any breach of condition in respect of any one or more instalments would entitle the party aggrieved to claim that the contract has been repudiated as a whole; or on the other hand the law as established might have been that any breach, however serious, in respect of one or more instalments should not have consequences extending beyond the particular instalment or instalments or affecting the contract as a whole. The sub-section, however, which deals equally with breaches either by the buyer or the seller, requires the Court to decide on the merits of the particular case what effect, if any, the breach or breaches should have on the contract as a whole.

The language of the Act is substantially based on the language used by Lord Selborne L.C. in *Mersey Steel and Iron Co.* v. *Naylor, Benzon & Co.* (1884), 9 App. Cas. 434, where he said: "I am content to take the rule as stated by Lord Coleridge in *Freeth* v. *Burr* (1874), L.R. 9 C.P. 208, which is in substance, as I understand it, that you must look at the actual circumstances of the case in order to see whether the one party to the contract is relieved from its future performance by the conduct of the other; you must examine what the conduct is, so as to see whether it amounts to a renunciation, to an absolute refusal to perform the contract, such as would amount to a rescission if he had the power to rescind, and whether the other party may accept it as a reason for not performing his part." In *Freeth* v. *Burr*, Lord Coleridge C.J. stated the true question to be: "Whether the acts and conduct of the party evince an intention no longer to be bound by the contract." These were both cases of breach by the buyer in not making punctual payment, and in each case it was clear that the buyer had some justification for the course he took. The case of breach by the seller in making defective deliveries may raise different questions. Lord Selborne in the passage above quoted did not refer to any question of intention, but said that what is to be examined is the conduct of the party. Lord Coleridge in *Freeth* v. *Burr*, citing *Hoare* v. *Rennie* (1859), 5 H. & N. 19; 157 E.R. 1083, on the question of a seller's breach, states thus one aspect of the rule: "Where by the non-delivery of part of the thing contracted for the whole object of the contract is frustrated, the party making default renounces on his part all the obligations of the contract." In other words, the true test will generally be, not the subjective mental state of the defaulting party, but the objective test of the relation in fact of the default to the whole purpose of the contract.

Since the Act, the sub-section has been discussed by a Divisional Court in *Millars' Karri and Jarrah Company (1902)* v. *Weddel, Turner & Co.* (1909), 14 Com. Cas. 25, where the contract being for 1100 pieces of timber, the first instalment of 750 pieces was rejected by the buyers; an arbitrator awarded "that the said shipment was, and is, so far from complying with the requirements of the said contract as to entitle the buyers to repudiate and to rescind the whole contract and to refuse to accept the said shipment and all further shipments under the said contract." The Court upheld the award. Bigham J. thus stated what in his opinion was the true test, "Thus, if the breach is of such a kind, or takes place in such circumstances as reasonably to lead to the inference that similar breaches will be committed in relation to subsequent deliveries, the whole contract may there and then be regarded as repudiated and may be rescinded. If, for instance, a buyer fails to pay for one delivery in such circumstances as to lead to the inference that he will not be able to pay for subsequent deliveries; or if a seller delivers goods differing from the requirements of the contract, and does so in such circumstances as to lead to the inference that he cannot, or will not, deliver any other kind of goods in the future, the other contracting party will be under no obligation to wait to see what may happen; he can at once cancel the contract and rid himself of the difficulty." Walton J. concurred.

This ruling was more recently applied in *Robert A. Munroe & Co.* v. *Meyer*, [1930] 2 K. B. 312, where under a contract for the sale of 1500 tons of bone meal, 611 tons were delivered which were seriously adulterated. The sellers were middlemen, who relied on their suppliers, the manufacturers, for correct delivery; when the buyers discovered that the deliveries did not conform to the contract they claimed that they were entitled to treat the whole contract as repudiated by the sellers. It was held that they were right in so claiming, on the ground that "in such a case as this, where there is a persistent breach, deliberate so far as the manufacturers are concerned, continuing for nearly one-half of the total contract quantity, the buyer, if he ascertains in time what the position is, ought to be entitled to say that he will not take the risk of having put upon him further deliveries of this character." [1930] 2 K. B. 331, per Wright J. On the other hand in *Taylor* v. *Oakes Roncoroni & Co.* (1922), 27 Com. Cas. 261, Greer J., as he then was, and the Court of Appeal, declined to hold that the buyers were entitled to refuse to go on with the contract, but held that the breach was a severable breach, as it was a case "where the instalment delivered failed in a slight but appreciable degree to come up to the standard required by the contract description."

With the help of these authorities we deduce that the main tests to be considered in applying the sub-section to the present case are, first, the ratio quantitatively which the breach bears to the contract as a whole, and secondly the degree of probability or improbability that such a breach will be repeated. On the first point, the delivery complained of amounts to no more than 1½ tons out of a contract for 100 tons. On the second point, our conclusion is that the chance of the breach being repeated is practically negligible. We assume that the sample found defective fairly represents the bulk; but bearing in mind the judge's finding that the breach was extraordinary and that the appellant's business was carefully conducted, bearing in mind also that the appellants were warned, and bearing in mind that the delivery complained of was an isolated instance out of 20 satisfactory deliveries actually made both before and after the instalment objected to, we hold that it cannot reasonably be inferred that similar breaches would occur in regard to subsequent deliveries. Indeed, we do not understand that the learned judge came to any different conclusion. He seems, however, to have decided against the appellants on a third and separate ground, that is, that a delivery not satisfying the Government requirements would or might lead to the respondents being prosecuted under the Act. Though we think he exaggerates the likelihood of the respondents in such a case being held responsible, we do not wish to under-rate the gravity to the respondents of their being even prosecuted. But we cannot follow the judge's reasoning that the bare possibility, however remote, of this happening would justify the respondents in rescinding in this case. There may indeed be such cases, as also cases where the consequences of a single breach of contract may be so serious as to involve a frustration of the contract and justify rescission, or furthermore, the contract might contain an express condition that a breach would justify rescission, in which case effect would be given to such a condition by the Court. But none of these circumstances can be predicated of this case. We think the deciding factor here is the extreme improbability of the breach being repeated, and on that ground, and on the isolated and limited character of the breach complained of, there was, in our judgment, no sufficient justification to entitle the respondents to refuse further deliveries as they did.

The appeal must accordingly be allowed and judgment entered for the appellants, with costs here and below, for damages for their breach of contract in refusing further deliveries.

5. Employment Contracts

BARDAL *v.* THE GLOBE & MAIL LTD.
Ontario. High Court. 1960. 24 D.L.R. (2d) 140

McRuer C.J.H.C.: . . . In the year 1942 the plaintiff, who at that time was manager of the Canadian Street Car Advertising Co. and had been previously assistant advertising manager of the Winnipeg Tribune, a paper published in the City of Winnipeg, was approached by the Globe Printing Co. Ltd. with a view to interesting him in becoming the assistant advertising manager of that company. It was explained to him that when the advertising manager retired he would likely succeed him.

During the discussions the plaintiff says that he impressed on Mr. Butler, who was interviewing him on behalf of the Globe company, that it was important at his age that his employment should be permanent. In due course the plaintiff was interviewed by Mr. McCullagh, the publisher, to whom he repeated what he had previously said with reference to the importance of a decision to change his employment at his age. After full consideration the plaintiff decided to accept the office as offered with an initial salary of $6,500 a year, his employment commencing on October 1, 1942.

In 1955 the assets of the Globe Printing Co. were sold to the Globe & Mail Ltd. and the plaintiff, together with other employees, transferred their employment to the purchaser without any new agreement as to terms of employment. In 1954 the plaintiff was appointed advertising manager and in 1955 he was appointed director of advertising and a member of the Board of Directors of the defendant.

Throughout his employment with the defendant the plaintiff's salary was increased periodically until on the termination of his employment he was receiving $1,479.16 per month, together with one week's salary by way of a Christmas bonus. In addition to the salary received the plaintiff was a beneficiary of three distributions made to selected employees pursuant to a profit-sharing plan which was administered under the sole direction of the principal shareholders of the defendant. The receipts from this source were as follows:

April 1956 — $6,538
April 1957 — $6,467
December 1958 — $3,095

In addition to salary and bonuses received the plaintiff participated in a pension plan for employees.

On April 23, 1959, the plaintiff was called to the office of Mr. Dalgleish, the president, publisher and editor of the defendant, who with a few preliminary remarks asked him for his resignation. Mr. Dalgleish told the plaintiff that if he resigned he would be given 6 months' salary and allowed 1 month to look around for new employment. According to the plaintiff's evidence, the reason given to him for requesting his resignation was that the defendant had been losing money and Mr. Dalgleish wanted to get someone who could improve business in the advertising department.

The plaintiff told Mr. Dalgleish that he couldn't agree to accept accusations of incompetency and he would consider what course he should take. In an interview the next day the plaintiff refused to resign either as an employee or as a director and he was thereupon given a letter signed by Mr. Dalgleish which reads as follows:

"Dear Mr. Bardal:

"This is to confirm the notice given to you today of the termination of your employment with the Globe and Mail Limited as of this date."

The plaintiff was given a cheque for the balance of his salary owing to the date of his dismissal. Immediately after his dismissal the plaintiff made efforts to secure other employment and finally made arrangements with another employer in the advertising business for employment at a salary of $15,000 a year for 2 years, with provision for certain stock option rights.

At the time of his dismissal under the provisions of the defendant's pension plan the plaintiff had earned a right to receive a refund of his contributions with interest which would amount to approximately $5,000, or an alternative right to accept a pension of approximately $1,350 per annum, commencing on February 1, 1970. The plaintiff accepted the latter alternative.

In the statement of defence filed the defendant denied that the plaintiff was wrongfully dismissed and pleaded that he voluntarily withdrew from the employment of the defendant. In the alternative it was pleaded that if the defendant did terminate the plaintiff's employment it was justified in doing so by reason of the fact that the advertising department did not, during the period the plaintiff was advertising manager, obtain the results which the defendant was reasonably entitled to expect. During the trial it was admitted both by Mr. Dalgleish and counsel for the defendant that it could not be contended that the defendant was justified in dismissing the plaintiff without notice. No improper conduct on the part of the plaintiff was proved or suggested and I think the evidence of Mr. Dalgleish can be summed up by saying that he had come to the conclusion that he thought he could get an advertising manager who would produce better results than the plaintiff. In view of this it is quite unnecessary for me to discuss the evidence of the plaintiff with reference to the results he produced and the circumstances that gave rise to some decline in revenue from the advertising department preceding his dismissal. It remains only for me to consider what damages the plaintiff is entitled to recover.

In every case of wrongful dismissal the measure of damages must be considered in the light of the terms of employment and the character of the services to be rendered. In this case there was no stipulated term during which the employment was to last. Both parties undoubtedly considered that the employment was to be of a permanent character. All the evidence goes to show that the office of advertising manager is one of the most important offices in the service of the defendant. In fact, it is by means of the revenue derived under the supervision of the advertising manager that the publication of a newspaper becomes a profitable enterprise. The fact that the plaintiff was appointed to the Board of Directors of the defendant goes to demonstrate the permanent character of his employment and the importance of the office.

It is not argued that there was a definite agreement that the plaintiff was employed for life but the case is put on the basis of an indefinite hiring of a permanent character which could be terminated by reasonable notice.

In *Carter* v. *Bell & Sons*, [1936], 2 D.L.R. 438 at p. 439, O.R. 290 at p. 297, Mr. Justice Middleton concisely and with great clarity stated the law applicable to this case in this way: "In the case of master and servant there is implied in the contract of hiring an obligation to give reasonable notice of an intention to terminate the arrangement."

On this branch of the case the only remaining matter to be considered is what should be implied as reasonable notice in the circumstances of the contract in question. In *Carter* v. *Bell* Middleton J.A. went on at p. 439 D.L.R., p. 297 O.R. to say: "This notice in a case of an indefinite hiring is generally 6 months, but the length of notice is always a matter for inquiry and determination, and in special circumstances may be less."

The contractual obligation is to give reasonable notice and to continue the servant in his employment. If the servant is dismissed without reasonable notice he is entitled to the damages that flow from the failure to observe this contractual obligation, which damages the servant is bound in law to mitigate to the best of his ability.

In 13 C.E.D. (Ont. 2nd), p. 227, it is stated: "In Ontario damages in cases of indefinite hiring are limited to wages for six months." I am convinced this is not a correct statement of the law. The authority for this statement is *Norman* v. *Nat'l Life Ass'ce Co. of Canada*, [1938] O.W.N. 509. In this case the plaintiff was employed at a yearly salary as a medical referee. At the time of his employment he was told that the defendant would require a medical referee and that he had no cause to worry about the duration of employment. During his employment he carried on a medical practice in addition to the services he rendered to the defendant. On the termination of his employment he was paid approximately 6 months' salary in lieu of notice. Godfrey J. stated [p. 511]:

"In this Province, however, it seems to be well established that six months is the maximum notice required to terminate a contract of indefinite hiring."

He referred to *Harnwell* v. *Parry Sound Lumber Co.* (1897), 24 O.A.R. 110; *Normandin* v. *Solloway Mills* (1931), 40 O.W.N. 429; *Messer* v. *Barrett Co.* (1926), 59 O.L.R. 566, and *Carter* v. *Bell, supra.* With great respect I do not think any of these cases warrant a statement as a proposition of law that a Court in Ontario cannot decide that the reasonable notice required as implied in the contract of hiring should not in any case be greater than 6 months.

In *Abbot* v. *G. M. Gest Ltd.*, [1944] O.W.N. 524, Hogg J. made reference to the *Norman* case, but cannot be said to have passed on it as the learned Judge found on the facts of the case he was considering that the plaintiff was only entitled to 4 months' notice.

In *Campbell* v. *Business Fleets Ltd.*, [1953], 4 D.L.R. 223, O.W.N. 707, and in appeal [1954], 2 D.L.R. 263, O.R. 87, the contract in question was an oral one of somewhat indefinite terms. The trial Judge held that it came within the *Statute of Frauds* and the action was dismissed. The only evidence of the contract was the evidence of the plaintiff who, as the learned trial Judge put it, referred to it as a contract "for life" or "as long as there was no wrongdoing on my part I would be there." The Court of Appeal held that the *Statute of Frauds* did not apply and at p. 268 D.L.R., p. 95 O.R., Mackay J.A., writing the judgment of the Court, said: "The Court is of opinion that the contract in the case at bar was one that could be terminated only on reasonable notice and reasonable notice in all the circumstances of this case, in the considered opinion of this Court is one year." . . .

In *Grundy* v. *Sun Printing & Publishing Ass'n* (1916), 33 T.L.R. 77, the plaintiff was an editor of a newspaper earning a salary of £20 a week. The jury awarded the plaintiff damages based on the failure to give 12 months' notice of termination of the contract. On appeal to the Court of Appeal this award was sustained. In delivering the judgment of the Court Lord Justice Swinfen Eady said at p. 78: "In cases which had come before this Court a custom has been proved that an editor was entitled to 12 months' notice, and a sub-editor to six months' notice. In the absence of evidence of custom it could not be said that the view of the jury in this case was unreasonable."

There is no evidence of custom in the case before me and I think I must determine what would be reasonable notice in all the circumstances and proper compensation for the loss the plaintiff has suffered by reason of the breach of the implied term in the contract to give him reasonable notice of its termination.

There can be no catalogue laid down as to what is reasonable notice in particular classes of cases. The reasonableness of the notice must be decided with reference to each particular case, having regard to the character of the employment, the length of service of the servant, the age of the servant and the availability of similar employment, having regard to the experience, training and qualifications of the servant.

Applying this principle to this case, we have a servant who, through a lifetime of training, was qualified to manage the advertising department of a large metropolitan newspaper. With the exception of a short period of employment as manager of a street car advertising agency, his whole training has been in the advertising department of two large daily newspapers. There are few comparable offices available in Canada and the plaintiff has in mitigation of his damages taken employment with an advertising agency, in which employment he will no doubt find useful his advertising experience, but the employment must necessarily be of a different character.

I have come to the conclusion, as the jury did in the *Sun Printing & Publishing Ass'n* case and as the Court of Appeal agreed, that 1 year's notice would have been reasonable, having regard to all the circumstances of this case.

That being true, the next question to decide is what damages have flowed from the failure of the defendant to give a year's notice and how far have those damages been mitigated by the receipt by the plaintiff of a salary from another employer

The plaintiff's salary with the defendant was $17,750 per year. In his new employment he has been receiving $15,000 per year since July 1, 1959. He is therefore entitled to recover $3,254.15 for loss of salary from April 25th to July 1st and $2,245.20, being the difference between the salary which would have been received from July 1, 1959 to April 24, 1960, and the salary actually received in his new employment during that time. . . .

[There was a reference to ascertain the true value of the pension rights. Damages claimed for loss of a Christmas bonus participation in a profit-sharing plan and director's fees were denied on the ground that these matters did not arise out of the contract but were voluntary and at the will of the defendant.]

EMLER *v.* DISPLAY FIXTURES LTD.

Manitoba. Court of Appeal. [1953] 2 D.L.R. 450

BEAUBIEN J.A. delivered the judgment of the Court: . . . This is an appeal by special leave from the judgment of Keith, Co. Ct. J., allowing an appeal from the decision of D. G. Potter, Police Magistrate, who awarded the appellant the sum of $48.80 in lieu of a week's notice terminating his employment with the respondent.

In May, 1950, the appellant was hired by the respondent as a spray painter. The contract of hiring was an oral one. He says:

"Q. Were you advised about conditions of employment with respect to termination of your services, the question of notice? A. Nothing said at any time regarding it. Q. Any notice in respect to termination of employment with or without notice posted in the shop? A. No there was not. Q. Any meeting of employees at which that question was brought to their attention in any form by their employer? A. No. Q. Prior to your dismissal? A. No."

He was hired ("put on") at 90c per hour, and if he "proved up" on the job he was to get a dollar an hour at the end of two weeks. That was the only arrangement made between the parties.

The appellant worked for the respondent steadily . . . except for short periods of time during his wife's illness and during his holidays . . . until October 4, 1951, when he was discharged. He was told at 4 p.m. on that day that he would be "through" at 5.15 p.m. and was paid his wages at an hourly rate until that time. Nine other workmen were "let out" on the day the appellant's employment was terminated. Two days before (October 2nd) the appellant was paid the amount he had earned during the week ending the previous Friday.

The County Court Judge says in his reasons for judgment that "all their men were hired by the hour but were paid once a week for convenience."

One Hill, assistant manager of the respondent, claims he told the appellant when discharging him that his employment would be temporarily terminated due to lack of business for the immediate future. Hill says he asked the appellant to return if there should be work to do and that the appellant said he would. This the latter denies. The respondent's manager said it was the practice of the company to lay off employees without notice and that he knew of no instance where an employee was laid off with notice.

The County Court Judge held that it was the practice of the respondent to dismiss or lay off employees on an hour's notice and that the appellant knew this.

The point for decision is in respect of the nature of the hiring. The appellant contends that it was a weekly hiring, terminable on a week's notice.

It was held in *Fiddes* v. *Famous Players Corp.*, [1924] 4 D.L.R. 1260, 34 Man. R. 476 that: "A contract of hiring at weekly wages will be deemed to be a weekly hiring and terminable on a week's notice in the absence of any circumstances from which a different duration of the contract can be inferred."

In Batt's *Law of Master and Servant*, 4th ed., the learned author says, at p. 54: "Except where the hiring is for a definite period, the contract must be terminated by notice, and where the parties are silent at the time of making the contract as to notice, the courts will not construe this as meaning that no notice on either side is required to terminate the contract."

In support of that statement he relies on the case of *Payzu Ltd.* v. *Hannaford*, [1918] 2 K.B. 348. In that case Darling J. (with whom the other members of the Court concurred) says, at pp. 349–350: "The magistrate has held that in the case of a weekly hiring, where nothing is said as to the giving of notice to terminate the employment, it is not an implied term of the contract that notice shall be given. In other words, that the workman may leave, or the employer may dismiss him, without giving any notice. That is, in my opinion, contrary to the general rule, which is that a reasonable notice must be given." That case was remitted to the Magistrate for him to consider whether it was a weekly or a daily hiring; that if it were the latter the respondent would only be bound to give a day's notice.

In Batt's *Law of Master and Servant*, 4th ed., at p. 51 it is said: "It is a question of fact for the court to determine what length of notice the parties contemplated at the time of the creation of the engagement in order to terminate it, and this intention, if the terms of the contract, written or oral, are silent, must be gathered from the circumstances of the case, the nature of the employment, the periods at which wages or salaries are paid, and the length of notice customary to such engagements in the locality or trade in which the agreement is made."

And again, at p. 55: "It must be remembered that in many trades and occupations the hiring or service is expressly or by custom of the trade limited to a daily or even to an hourly hiring, or merely for the particular job for which the employee is engaged."

In the case of the *Hebrew Nat'l Ass'n.* v. *Kramer*, [1943] 1 D.L.R. 414, O.R. 49, decided by the Ontario Court of Appeal, Robertson C.J.O. who delivered the judgment of the Court, says at p. 419 D.L.R. p. 57 O.R.:

"In the absence of some custom or of some provision, express or implied, in the contract governing the matter, the notice that an employee is entitled to receive of termination of the hiring is reasonable notice, and what is reasonable notice is a question of fact: *Payzu Ltd.* v. *Hannaford*, [1918] 2 K.B. 348; *Carter* v. *Bell*, [1936] 2 D.L.R. 438, O.R. 290 and see 22 Hals., (2nd ed.), p. 150, and 7 C.E.D. (Ont.) pp. 162–164."

Dealing with the question of notice of termination of employment, the following statements are to be found in 22 Hals., 2nd ed., pp. 145 and 150:

Para. 237: "The circumstance that the remuneration is paid at intervals of less than a year, as monthly or weekly, does not of itself destroy the presumption of a hiring for a year, for it may simply indicate the mode of payment. On the other hand, it does not follow that a servant is a weekly or monthly rather than a daily servant simply because he has agreed to work from week to week or month to month and to be paid for his work at weekly or longer intervals . . ."

Para. 249. "If no usage or stipulation as to notice exists, and if the contract of service is not one which can be regarded as a yearly hiring, the service is terminable by reasonable notice."

In his reasons for judgment the County Court Judge says:

"The evidence of the appellant [respondent here] which was not contradicted was that all their men were hired by the hour but were paid once a week for convenience. That the men could quit any time they wished and that they could be discharged by the company on an hour's notice. It is admitted that in the case of the respondent nothing was said to him of this system except that he was to get so much money per hour. When discharged he was notified at 4 p.m. that he was to be laid off and was paid up to 5.15 of that day.

I hold that the respondent knew about the system followed by the company. He was in their employ for sixteen months, was off work on at least two occasions and was active in organizing a union among the employees and would have particular knowledge of the system followed by the company."

The appellant bases his appeal on two grounds. He relies on his common law right which he claims gives him the right to reasonable notice, and says that in any event he is, under the provisions of the *Hours and Conditions of Work Act, 1949* (Man.) c. 28 entitled to a week's notice of termination of his employment. That Act was amended by 1951 c. 26, s. 6, by adding s. 6B, the pertinent provisions of which are as follows:

"6B (1) Subject as in this section otherwise provided,

(a) no person having control or direction of, or responsible directly or indirectly for, the employment, or termination of the employment of any person in any industry carried on or operating anywhere in the province shall terminate the employment of a person so employed; and

(b) no person employed in an industry to which paragraph (a) applies shall terminate his employment: unless notice is given as in this section provided to the person so employed, in a case to which paragraph (a) applies, or to the person who provides the employment, in a case to which paragraph (b) applies.

(2) Subsection (1) does not apply where

(a) there exists in an establishment a custom or practice respecting the termination of employment that is contrary in whole or in part to subsection (1) . . .

(3) Where the period of the employment is not fixed and the wages are, or the salary is, paid once a month or more often, the person desiring to terminate the employment shall give to the person employed, or to the person who provides employment, as the case may be, notice of the date on which the employment is to terminate."

Subsection (2) says that "Subsection (1) does not apply where (a) there exists in an establishment a custom or practice respecting the termination of employment that is contrary in whole or in part to subsection (1)." The County Court Judge evidently interprets that subsection as not being applicable to the case because, in his reasons for judgment, he says:

"I hold, (a) That the custom and practice of the company was to dismiss or lay off employees on an hour's notice, that the respondent knew this was the custom and practice of the company. . . .

(c) That the employees could quit without notice and that the company could lay off the men or dismiss them on an hour's notice.

(d) That the notice was reasonable considering the operations of the company and the custom or practice respecting the termination of employment existing at the time of the layoff or dismissal."

On the evidence the County Court Judge was justified in holding that there existed at the time of the termination of the appellant's employment a custom or practice established by the respondent in its business contrary to the provisions of s-s. (1). However, in my view the fact that the subsection does not apply does not deprive the appellant of his common law rights. See judgment of Riddell J.A., speaking for the Court, in *McKittrick* v. *Byers*, [1926] 1 D.L.R. 342 at p. 344, 58 O.L.R. 158 at p. 162, where he adopts the following dictum of McCardie J. in *Henshall* v. *Porter*, [1923] 2 K.B. 193 at p. 197: "But there is 'a settled, recognized and beneficent rule of law that existing rights are not to be deemed to be destroyed by a statute unless there be express words or the plainest implication to that effect.' "

I can find nothing in the Act that would in any way deprive the appellant of his common law rights. This leaves his case to be disposed of in accordance with those rights. The finding of the County Court Judge that the appellant was employed by the hour, and that in the circumstances the notice given him was reasonable, in my opinion should not be disturbed.

I would dismiss the appeal with costs and a factum fee of $15.

QUESTIONS: Is an "hourly paid" employee, whether he receives it weekly or fortnightly, working under a "contract" of employment? What are the terms? What does the employer promise? Is it correct to say that each hour's work is a requested act in acceptance of an offer of a unilateral contract? How would a union approach this problem? Is it necessary for management to be able to lay off staff at an hour's notice? A day's notice?

NOTE: During the Second World War the law required seven days' notice for the layoff of workmen. Why?

THE MASTER AND SERVANT ACT

Ontario. Revised Statutes. 1960. Chapter 230

2. No voluntary contract of service or indenture shall be binding for longer than a term of nine years from the date thereof.

[Section 4 and the succeeding sections provide the machinery to enable a workman to collect unpaid wages by a form of prosecution before a magistrate.]

12. (1) Every agreement or bargain, verbal or written, expressed or implied, on the part of any workman, servant, labourer, mechanic, or other person employed in any kind of manual labour intended to be dealt with in this Act whereby it is agreed that this Act shall not apply, or that the remedies hereby provided shall not be available for the benefit of any person entering into such agreement, is hereby declared to be null and void and of no effect as against any such workman, servant, labourer, mechanic, or other person.

(2) This section shall not apply to any manager, officer or foreman or to any other person whose wages are more than $5 a day.

NOTE. Section 2 of Chapter 15 of the Nova Scotia statutes for 1945, *An Act Respecting the Closing of Industry or Industrial Enterprises in the Province* provides that where an employer is about to close down, discontinue or abandon the whole of his industry or any portion thereof which may effect (*sic*) fifty or more employees he must before closing give three months' notice to the Minister of Industry and Publicity for Nova Scotia. If an industry is wrongly closed down in breach of the Act the Minister may cause the industry to be reopened at the expense of the employer for a time not exceeding three months. For the history of this Act see the *Report of the Commissioner on Trenton Steel Works* (Halifax), King's Printer, 1944.

REGINA *v.* CANADIAN PACIFIC RAILWAY CO. 1961. 31 D.L.R. (2d) 209 (Ontario. High Court). During the course of a strike called by the accused's employees at the Royal York Hotel in Toronto in compliance with the *Labour Relations Act*, R.S.O. 1960, c. 202, the accused on June 26, 1961, informed the strikers that having withdrawn from service on April 24, they must either return to work or resign by July 15. If they elected to return to work, jobs would be offered as they became available. If neither option was exercised by July 15, they would be dismissed as of July 16. On July 18 the accused notified the strikers that as they had failed to exercise either option, they were dismissed effective July 16. In due course two charges were laid against the accused, that it had unlawfully threatened dismissal to compel its employees to stop the strike, and that it had unlawfully dismissed its employees because they were engaged in a lawful strike. The Magistrate acquitted the accused apparently because, having gone on strike, the strikers must be taken to have resigned, this being a prerequisite to a strike at common law. An appeal by stated case was allowed and the Magistrate was directed to deal with the matter according to the law as it was found to be by the Court. On the question of the common law right to strike, MCRUER C.J.H.C.: "Mr. Jackett argues that all strikes are unlawful at common law as the concerted act of employees failing to report for work without just cause is an unlawful agreement to commit a breach of contract. Counsel principally relies on a dictum of Lord Loreburn in *Denaby & Cadeby Main Collieries Ltd.* v. *Yorkshire Miners' Ass'n*, [1906] A.C. 384 at p. 387, where the learned Lord Chancellor said:

'Inasmuch as the men were all working under contracts which could not be terminated except after fourteen days' notice, it is manifest that the abrupt cessation of work on June 29 involved a breach of contract and was unlawful.'

This excerpt from the judgment cannot be taken as an authority for the broad statement of law put forward by Mr. Jackett. The dictum is part of a judgment in which it was held that the employer had no right of action against a labour union. It is a simple statement of law that an employee who is required to give 14 days' notice is guilty of breach of contract if he stops work without giving such notice.

"The whole course of jurisprudence in the last century establishes that a strike is not an unlawful conspiracy unless it involves something more than the motive or purpose of advancing the interests of the employees. . . .

"All the leading authorities were discussed in the House of Lords in *Crofter Hand Woven Harris Tweed Co.* v. *Veitch*, [1942] A.C. 435. Lord Wright said at p. 463:

'Where the rights of labour are concerned, the rights of the employer are conditioned by the rights of the men to give or withhold their services. The right of workmen to strike is an essential element in the principle of collective bargaining.'. . .

"On the authority of the cases that I have discussed and many others, I am forbidden to accept the argument put forward by Mr. Jackett that on the facts as found by the learned Magistrate the strike is unlawful at common law. I am not called upon to decide whether or not in the absence of any statutory provision an employer is entitled to refuse to reemploy an employee because he has participated in a strike. At common law an employer may terminate an employee's employment either at will or with reasonable notice depending on the nature of the employment and the contract. Failure to report for work without reasonable excuse would be good cause for terminating the employment of an employee. Whether or not failure to report for work on account of a strike is reasonable excuse does not come before me for decision. It was this condition of the common law that gave rise to the whole development of labour legislation in Ontario and throughout Canada. The legislation had its birth in Ontario in the *Ontario Trade Disputes Conciliation and Arbitration Act,* 1894, c. 42, or, as it was otherwise known, *the Trades Disputes Act, 1894*. The preamble to this statute indicates that as one of its purposes it was designed to prevent strikes and lock-outs. The first Dominion statute was the *Industrial Disputes Investigation Act,* 1907 (Can.), c. 20 (held unconsitutional in *Toronto Electric Com'rs* v. *Snider,* [1925] 2 D.L.R. 2, A.C. 396).

"The proper interpretation of s. 1(2) is the crux of this case. The relevant parts read as follows:

'1(2) For the purposes of this Act, no person shall be deemed to have ceased to be an employee by reason only of his ceasing to work for his employer as the result of a . . . strike or by reason only of his being dismissed by his employer contrary to this act.'

This subsection preserves the relationship of employer and employee for the purposes of the statute notwithstanding a strike and even though the true relationship of employer and employee may have been terminated at common law on account of the strike. . . .

"Although the Act does not purport to create a statutory right to strike, as I have indicated it recognizes the common law right to strike and so doing, limits it. There must be no strike while a collective agreement is in force nor while conciliation procedure is in progress. When the conciliation procedure has been exhausted if a strike is proposed the strike vote shall be by secret ballot: s. 54 (3). Section 57 expressly refers to lawful strikes and s. 67 gives the Labour Relations Board power to determine whether a strike is or is not lawful. I think the irresistible conclusion is that in Ontario there is statutory recognition of a right to strike within the limits of the provisions of the statute law. I can find no basis in law for the theory that in order that employees may engage in a lawful strike they must first resign from their employment. If an employee resigns he is no longer an employee. It is clear to me that the statute contemplates a strike that is a cessation of work 1 (1) (*i*) defines a strike as a cessation of work by 'employees' not a refusal by ex-employees to go back to work. In fact, s."

"There remains to be discussed one other argument put forward by Mr. Jackett. Counsel asks the question, 'If the law is as I have stated it to be, what is the legal position where a strike is never concluded by a settlement?' This is a question that it may not be necessary for me to answer. However, I think the answer is quite simple. In such a case the employees have either gone back to work, taken employment with other employers, died or become unemployable. Such employees could not any longer, adapting the language of s. 1(2), be deemed to have ceased to be employees by reason only of their ceasing to work for their employer as the result of a strike."

[On this question McRuer C.J.H.C. was affirmed by the Court of appeal, 33 D.L.R. (2d) 30. Roach J.A. for the Court, dismissed the appeal with an amendment to the order so that it directed the Magistrate to record convictions. He said, in part: " . . . in the circumstances and facts of this case, it would be lawful under the common law for the employees here concerned to go on strike. . . ."]

AGREEMENT between Canadian Westinghouse Company, Ltd. and United Electrical, Radio & Machine Workers of America Local 504. Hamilton, Ontario. March 9, 1959. Article 13, headed SENIORITY, provides in part:

"13.02 (a) An employee's seniority date (departmental, intraplant, or inter-plant) shall be his last hiring date, except that upon returning to work following a lay-off, his seniority date shall be adjusted in accordance with his length of service pursuant to the provisions of Section 13.09 (a) hereof. An employee shall acquire departmental, intra-plant, and inter-plant seniority on the following basis:

(i) On completion of sixty worked days with the Company an employee shall acquire departmental seniority.

(ii) On completion of ten months' service with the Company, an employee shall acquire intra-plant seniority.

(iii) On completion of sixty months' service with the Company, an employee shall acquire inter-plant seniority.

(b) For purposes of lay-off (meaning here and elsewhere in this Article lay-off from employment) or transfers due to lack of work, an employee shall exercise his seniority as follows:

(i) An employee with not more than 10 months' seniority shall be limited to exercising his departmental seniority.

(ii) An employee with more than 10 months' seniority but not more than 60 months' seniority will first exercise his departmental seniority and then shall be limited to exercising his intra-plant seniority.

(iii) An employee with seniority in excess of 60 months will first exercise his departmental seniority and then shall exercise his inter-plant seniority.

(c) In the event an employee with seniority, as defined in this Section, is laid off, he will be included in the inter-plant recall list.

"13.03 The exercising of intra-plant seniority as herein provided shall take place within one of the following plants:

Plant #1 — East Plant
Plant #2 — West Plant
Plant #3 — Beach Road Plant.

"13.07 Lay-offs or transfer due to lack of work will be governed by the following provisions:

(a) Seniority as defined in Sections 13.02 and 13.03 hereof.

(b) Seniority will be the major factor governing lay-offs or transfers due to lack of work, in accordance with Section 13.07 (g) (i) hereof, subject to the retained employees being able to meet the normal requirements of the work.

(c) The Company will give seven calendar days' notice to an employee of a lay-off, the duration of which is expected to exceed fifteen calendar days. Such notice will indicate, whenever reasonably possible, whether the lay-off is expected to be of short or indefinite duration. This provision will not, however, apply with respect to the following:

(i) probationary employees;

(ii) lay-offs under Section 13.05 although the employee will be informed when the lay-off takes place thereunder;

(iii) lay-offs resulting from lack of work owing to any slowdown, strike, or other work stoppage or interference with work by employees covered by this Agreement;

(iv) lay-offs resulting from such matters as fire, lightning, flood, tempest or power failure.

(d) Employees who are laid off shall be recalled in the reverse order to which they are laid off (with due regard to length of service at the time of lay-off). The Company will confirm an employee's recall by registered letter sent to the employee's last address on record with the Company as furnished by the employee. An employee must return to work within ten calendar days from the day such registered letter is mailed, except in case of verified illness.

(e) An employee who has been transferred within his department, as a result of the provisions of this Article, shall be given an opportunity of returning to his original job or a comparable one, when the vacancy occurs.

(f) An employee who has been transferred to another department as a result of the provisions of this Article, shall be given an opportunity, if and when production conditions improve, and before additional employees are hired in the department, of returning to his original or a comparable job in the department from which he was transferred.

(i) The provisions of (e) and (f) will be limited to a period of two years from the date of original transfer. An employee who declines the opportunity of returning to his original or a comparable job in the original department, shall forfeit the right to return thereafter.

(g) (i) The Company and the Union recognize that it is desirable to keep displacement of one employee by another (bumping) to a minimum, consistent with employees maintaining their seniority rights. Therefore, in locating a comparable job, one held by an employee with less seniority or an open job, the procedure will be to commence from the bottom of the appropriate seniority list and work upwards.

(ii) The Company shall include as criteria in locating a comparable job, as provided for in Section 13.07 (g) (i) and elsewhere in this article, the following:

(a) Skill and ability required to perform the job as possessed by the employee and verified by the Company's records.

(b) Similarity of earning opportunity based upon earning experience of other employees on the jobs.

(c) Similarity of job working conditions, and

(d) Whether jobs under comparison are normally performed by male or female employees.

The criteria set forth in (a), (b), (c) and (d) will be given equal consideration after the condition of (a) above has been met.

(iii) Following the application of the procedure under Section 13.07 (g) (i), an employee, who is about to be laid off (without prejudice to his right of grievance under such Section 13.07 (g) (i), will be transferred to a job held by an employee with less seniority or an open job, on a trial basis, where the company has reasonable evidence either that the employee has transferable skills which would enable him to meet the normal requirements of the work of such job within a maximum period of five working days (which may be extended by agreement), or that having previously worked on such job (or on a job requiring similar skills) he could so perform it within such period. The employee so transferred will be acquainted, through demonstration and information, with the normal duties of the work. Should the employee upon being so transferred be unable to meet such requirements during the maximum period of five working days (or as extended by agreement), or should it become so apparent in a lesser time than the five day period, he will be eligible for one further transfer to a lesser skilled job held by an employee with less seniority or an open job, which he can perform without trial as otherwise provided in this clause. In laying off an employee because such a lesser skilled job is not available, the provisions of Section 13.07 (c) with respect to notice of lay-off will not apply.

"13.08 An employee shall accumulate seniority under the following conditions:

(a) During absence due to illness not to exceed fifty-two consecutive weeks.

(b) During leave of absence granted by the Company in writing.

"13.09 An employee shall maintain seniority under the following conditions:

(a) During a period of lay-off not in excess of thirty-six months.

(b) During absence due to illness for a period in excess of fifty-two consecutive weeks.

"13.10 An employee shall lose his seniority standing under the following conditions:

(a) If the employee leaves the employ of the Company.

(b) If continuously laid off for more than thirty-six months.

(c) If discharged for just cause and such discharge is not reversed through the grievance procedure provided herein.

(d) If the employee fails after a lay-off to return to work within ten calendar days from the date the registered letter is mailed, in accordance with Section 13.07 (d) above.

(e) If an employee overstays a leave of absence for a period of seven working days without the written permission of the Company.

"13.11 An employee of the Company shall, upon being transfered to a job within the bargaining unit, have seniority computed from the last date of hiring, if he has previously been employed in the bargaining unit.

"13.12 A department steward who has five or more years' seniority shall have preferential seniority, exercisable within his department in respect of a lay-off or transfer out of the department resulting from lack of work, and he shall be given a comparable job provided he can meet the normal requirements of the work available. Chief Stewards shall have preferential seniority on the same basis in their respective Zones.

"13.13 An employee claiming that he has been laid off or transferred contrary to the provisions of this Article, or that he has not been recalled in conformity therewith, may lodge a grievance in writing with the Company. . . ."

DIGGLE *v.* OGSTON MOTOR CO.

England. King's Bench Division. 1915. 84 L.J.K.B. 2165

The contract was contained in the correspondence between the parties. On December 13, 1913, the defendants wrote to the plaintiff a letter which, so far as material, was as follows: "With reference to our conversation, we have pleasure in informing you that we have decided to engage your services for the position of shop superintendent which we have vacant in our Acton works. The terms of the engagement are as follows: Salary £182 per year, payable by equal monthly payments due on the 1st of each month. . . . The engagement will be for one year, subject, of course, to your carrying out your duties to the satisfaction of the directors and to economical costs of production. After one year to have the option of renewing the agreement for a further period of six years."

On December 15, 1913, the plaintiff wrote to the defendants accepting their offer of the position of works superintendent, and on January 1, 1914, he entered on his duties in the defendants' service.

On April 30, 1914, the defendants' works manager wrote to the plaintiff a letter which, so far as material, was as follows: "I much regret to have to inform you that it has been found necessary to dispense with your services from to-day. I feel certain that you will have anticipated this for some little time, although I have been unwilling to take this step, having in mind the energies you put into your duties during the first few weeks of your engagement. Your intention no doubt in this respect was good, but, viewing your attitude and manner of conduct of your duties during the last few months in the light of recent events, I am afraid that you will agree with me that you have not carried out satisfactorily, in a manner calculated to inspire me and my directors with the confidence we should have in you for the future success of the company. Your attention has repeatedly been called, as you know, to the exorbitant producing costs in your department, and the general manner in which the work has been coming through the machine shops . . . has been by no means satisfactory. . . . If I may say so, I think that the trouble is due to the fact that your abilities for getting work through the shops systematically, economically, methodically and to anything like a reasonable standard of workmanship, are somewhat limited." The plaintiff brought the action for damages for wrongful dismissal.

The County Court Judge left the following questions to the jury: (1) Were the defendants in fact really and genuinely dissatisfied with the plaintiff's discharge of his duties? Yes. (2) If so, had they good reasons for such dissatisfaction? No. Upon these findings judgment was entered for the defendants. The plaintiff appealed.

Ridley J.: In this case I think that the decision of the County Court Judge was right. The matter arises upon an agreement between the plaintiff and the defendants under which he was engaged by them for a year, subject to a clause in a letter from the defendants of December 13, 1913, in which they said "The engagement will be for one year, subject, of course, to your carrying out your duties to the satisfaction of the directors and to economical costs of production."

The plaintiff entered on his service under that agreement, but before the year terminated he was dismissed by the defendants, and the question is whether they were within their rights in dismissing him. . . .

[T]he learned County Court Judge entered judgment for the defendants, thinking the answer to the first question to be the one which really determined the issue in the case—namely, that the defendants had been really and genuinely dissatisfied with the plaintiff's discharge of his duties, and that therefore they had the right to dismiss the plaintiff within the meaning of the agreement. We think that that is the right view of the case. Counsel for the plaintiff has, however, put before us this contention—that the jury having found that there were no good reasons for dissatisfaction on the part of the defendants, they had no right to dismiss the plaintiff. The case therefore raises the question as to what is the position where a person is really and genuinely dissatisfied, when he ought, in someone else's opinion, to have arrived at another conclusion. The defendants were genuinely dissatisfied, but while they have arrived at that conclusion the jury have arrived at another. It is a strong thing to say that in such a case the genuine opinion of a party to a contract is to be set aside and that of the jury substituted. There is no case which goes that length, and I should be sorry to come to such a conclusion.

In the text-books a distinction is drawn between what is honest and genuine dissatisfaction and what is not. Thus in Leake's *Law of Contracts* (6th ed.) p. 457, it is said, "Contracts may be made to pay for work upon condition of the work being done to the satisfaction or approval of the promisor." It goes on, "In such a case the right of approval on which the contract is dependent must in general be exercised in a reasonable and not arbitrary or capricious manner." I think that is a correct statement as far as it goes; but if you are not going to rely on the distinction between what is genuine satisfaction and what is not, but are going to substitute for it the opinion of a jury, then it is not a sufficient statement of the principle. Take *Dallman* v. *King* (1837), 7 L.J.C.P. 6, which was a question of repairs to be done by a lessee to a house, the agreement being that if they were done with the approval of the lessor the lessee should retain the expense out of the first year's rent. Chief Justice Tindal said: "It never could have been intended that he should be allowed capriciously to withhold his approval; that would have been a condition which would go to the destruction of the thing granted, and if so, according to the well known rule, the thing granted would pass discharged of the condition." I think there is no reason to question that decision, and it has met with subsequent approval, but it has no application to the present case. This was not a capricious withholding of approval because, upon the finding of the jury, the defendants were really and genuinely dissatisfied. There is here no question of capriciously withholding approval. The next case cited was *Braunstein* v. *Accidental Death Insurance Co.* (1861), 31 L.J.Q.B. 17. The gist of the decision is to be found—and it is the key of all the judgments—in the judgment of Mr. Justice Blackburn. Speaking of the proof of the accident or death required by the insurance company from the policy-holder, he says, "I think for reasons which need not be repeated, that it must be understood to mean such proof as reasonably would be satisfactory, and not such matters as the directors might capriciously require. Taking the plea and the replication together, we must take it as a fact that the directors required information which they thought proper to require, but which, in point of fact, was capriciously and unreasonably required." I think that case cannot be carried beyond what those words necessarily convey. It falls within the same category as the earlier one. In *Stadhard* v. *Lee* (1863), 32 L.J.Q.B. 75, *Braunstein* v. *Accidental Death Insurance Co.* was cited, and Chief Justice Cockburn stated the rule, as applied in that case, to be that "An insurance Company cannot be allowed to frustrate the object of a policy by refusing to be satisfied with reasonable evidence of the death" of the insured. If that is the meaning of *Braunstein's* case, it is far from justifying the argument of counsel for the appellant in this case. In *Stadhard* v. *Lee* what the Lord Chief Justice said was that the clause in the contract gave the whole control of the contract to the defendants, and the question was whether their dissatisfaction was conclusive or not. Chief Justice Cockburn said, "on carefully considering the contract between these parties, we are satisfied that the intention was that the defendants, if dissatisfied, whether with or without sufficient reason, with the progress of the work, should have the absolute and unqualified power to put on additional hands and get the work done, and deduct the cost from the contract price payable to the plaintiff, and therefore, if these terms had been ever so unreasonable, we should have felt bound to give effect to them, and to hold that, so long as the defendants were acting *bona fide* under an honest sense of dissatisfaction, although that dissatisfaction might be ill-founded and unreasonable, they were entitled to insist on the condition, and consequently that the replication, which only alleges that their dissatisfaction was unreasonable and capricious, but which stops short of alleging *mala fides* in the defendants in acting as it stated in the plea, is insufficient." If there had been *mala fides* on the part of the defendants, I doubt if the decision would have been the same. The result is that there is a clear distinction to be drawn between a case where there is an honest or *bona fide* dissatisfaction and a case where there is not. Where there is such a dissatisfaction, that is all the contract requires.

Other cases have been cited where the decisions turned on questions relating to chattels. As to those cases, the extent of the option left to the purchaser depends on the circumstances of each case, but there are several cases where the dissatisfaction of the party, if honestly arrived at, has been allowed to prevail. One of them is *Repetto* v. *Friary Steamship Co.* (1901), 17 Times L.R. 265. There Mr. Justice Mathew found as a fact that the rejection of the vessel by the plaintiff was in the circumstances reasonable —that is, he found the opposite to what the jury have found here. He said that a capricious objection on the part of the buyer would not do; but provided that he acted in good faith, the fact that he magnified defects would disentitle him to reject the article.

Having regard to these cases, and the distinction drawn between honest and *bona fide* dissatisfaction on the one hand and deceitful and *mala fide* dissatisfaction on the other, I think that the learned County Court Judge was right. The answer of the jury to the first question shews that the defendants' dissatisfaction with the services of the plaintiff was honest and *bona fide*, and their answer to the second was not material. Judgment was therefore properly entered for the defendants.

LAWRENCE J.: I agree. In this contract the engagement was to be for a year "subject, of course, to your carrying out your duties to the satisfaction of the directors and to economical costs of production." The action was brought because the plaintiff was dismissed within the year. I think it was a conditional engagement for a year, and that it lies upon the plaintiff to prove that the directors were in fact satisfied with his services, or dishonestly professed to be dissatisfied, or at least were capriciously dissatisfied. I do not agree that the contract must have the word "reasonably" introduced into it. The only question of reasonableness in the matter is this: if it can be said that a reasonable man could not honestly have come to the conclusion, then a ground is made out for saying that the defendants came to the conclusion dishonestly. But if you admit that a reasonable man could have come to the conclusion, then the only question is, Did they in fact do so? and the decision is for them and not for the jury. The argument that there is a distinction between contracts respecting chattels and contracts as to other subject-matter is not supported by any authority. It is a difficult matter to explain with complete accuracy, but I think it depends on this—that the words of the contract must be read in connection with the subject-matter. In regards to chattels there may be a slightly different construction, but I think it is perfectly true also where you are speaking of performing duties to the satisfaction of directors. This involves also that they must honestly exercise their discretion, and does not mean that they must afterwards satisfy a jury that their decision was reasonable. I do not think that any of the cases cited shew that it is right to introduce the word "reasonable." The plaintiff has not made out his case, because he has not proved either that the directors were in fact satisfied or that they could not, as reasonable men, have been dissatisfied. As the jury have found that the defendants were genuinely dissatisfied, their second finding is merely equivalent to saying that the plaintiff was not an incompetent person. The findings do not imply caprice or dishonest intention on the part of the directors, and without that the cases cited on behalf of the plaintiff shew that he was not entitled to succeed. None of the cases establish the proposition contended for by counsel for the plaintiff, and I think the County Court Judge was right in entering judgment for the defendants.

NOTE. Is the *Diggle* case an instance of an illusory promise? The objection to "illusory" promises is shortly stated by Vaughan Williams L.J. in *Loftus* v. *Roberts* (1902), 18 T.L.R. 532 (agreement of employment at a salary "to be mutually arranged") as follows: "Wherever words which by themselves constituted a promise were accompanied by words which showed that the promisor was to have a discretion or option as to whether he would carry out that which purported to be the promise, the result was that there was no contract on which an action could be brought at all."

What is the return consideration for the employee's promise to work in the *Diggle* case? Could the defendant have sued the plaintiff for failing to serve to their satisfaction?

ANDREWS *v.* BELFIELD. (1857). 2 C.B.N.S. 779; 140 E.R. 622. A agreed to supply, and B agreed to buy, a carriage to be manufactured by A. In the agreement, B stated that he was buying "on the assumption that you undertake to execute it in a manner which shall meet my approval, not only on the score of workmanship, but also that of convenience and taste." B having refused the carriage when tendered, it was argued by A that the defendant was bound to accept it, if it was "such as in the judgment of the jury no reasonable man ought to have objected to." B argued that he could reject unqualifiedly, no matter how capriciously, provided it was done *bona fide*. The Court upheld B's contention. [Suppose the defendant had refused to examine the promisor's performance?]

DALLMAN *v.* KING. 1837. 7 L.J.C.P. 6. A distinction was taken between promises to pay subject to a third person's approval and promises subject to the approval of the party himself. It was suggested that while a third person may act capriciously, a party may not. Why the distinction?

McINTYRE *v.* HOCKIN
Ontario. Court of Appeal. 1889. 16 A.R. 498

The action was one for wrongful dismissal. The plaintiff was employed as a clerk by the defendants, who were country store-keepers, the engagement being in writing and being for one year from the 4th of April, 1887. The plaintiff agreed to serve the defendants as a skillful and diligent clerk ought to do, and to give and devote to their interests his whole time and labour, except on lawful holidays. He was to be paid $550.00 for the year's service in equal one-twelfth payments on the 7th day of each month. The defendants dismissed him on the 7th of December, having paid his salary up to that time, the reason assigned for dismissal being that he had been in the habit of absenting himself to play croquet. At the time of his dismissal the defendants offered the plaintiff other employment at lower wages.

The grounds of dismissal set up in their defence and particulars were, that on two occasions, without the defendants' knowledge or consent, he absented himself from his duties to visit fairs at Rodney and London; that he absented himself two days to attend a foot race at St. Thomas; that he spent a great deal of time during business hours in the months of June, July, August and September, in playing croquet, and that on one occasion he was absent running a foot race, and hurt his foot so as to be incapable of attending to business for six weeks.

The case was tried before the Judge of the County Court of Elgin with a jury, and after a great deal of evidence had been taken, the case was submitted to the jury, the Judge leaving it to them to say whether there was good cause for the dismissal, and whether there had been condonation. Upon the answers returned by the jury judgment was subsequently delivered in favour of the plaintiff, the Judge, however, stating that in his opinion he had not acted properly in leaving the matter as he did to the jury, and intimating that he would be willing to grant a new trial if applied for by the defendants; and upon a subsequent motion by the defendants a new trial was ordered. The plaintiff appealed,

MACLENNAN J.A. delivered the judgment of the Court: I am clearly of opinion that the learned Judge was right in directing a new trial, and that the appeal must be dismissed.

Notwithstanding some earlier cases to the contrary, I think it is now settled that it is for the Judge to say whether the facts are sufficient in law to warrant a dismissal, and for the jury to say whether the alleged facts are proved to their satisfaction. The Judge should, as a matter of law, direct them whether the facts proved are sufficient cause: Macdonell's *Law of Master and Servant*, p. 217. and cases there cited. In the present case, the learned Judge virtually left the question both of fact and law to the jury when he asked them to find whether there existed a cause for dismissal at the time it was done. I think what was proved, if believed by the jury, was ample cause in law to warrant the dismissal. It is now settled law that if a good cause of dismissal really existed, it is immaterial that at the time of dismissal the master did not act or rely upon it, or even did not know of its existence, or that he acted upon some other cause in itself insufficient. The main question always is, were there at the time of dismissal facts sufficient in law to warrant it, and, as I have said, while it is for the jury to say whether the alleged fact or facts are proved to their satisfaction, it is the province of the Judge, as a matter of law, to direct them whether the facts are sufficient.

The causes which are sufficient to justify dismissal must vary with the nature of the employment and the circumstances of each case. Dismissal is an extreme measure, and not to be resorted to for trifling causes. The fault must be something which a reasonable man could not be expected to overlook, regard being had to the nature and circumstances of the employment, and it cannot be said that an occasional absence from his business, even for the purpose of amusement, is so serious a matter in the case of a store in a small country village, as it would be in the case of a shop in a large city with a great trade and numerous customers. So, also, while it is not necessary that any actual pecuniary loss or damage should be shewn, yet the absence of such damage or the contrary is not immaterial to be considered.

The learned Judge in his judgment refers to and relies upon the case of *Pearce* v. *Foster* (1886), 17 Q.B.D. 536; but there is a still later case, also a judgment of the Court of Appeal in England, *Boston Deep Sea Fishing Co.* v. *Ansell* (1888), 39 Ch.D. 339, in which the subject is very fully discussed, and which makes it unnecessary to say more upon the question of sufficient cause.

It may be proper, however, to add a few words on the subject of condonation. When an employer becomes aware of misconduct on the part of his servant, sufficiently to justify dismissal, he may adopt either of two courses. He may dismiss, or he may overlook the fault. But he cannot retain the servant in his employment, and afterwards at any distance of time turn him away. It would be most unjust if he could do that, for one of the consequences of dismissal for good cause is, that the servant can recover nothing for his services beyond the last pay day, whether his engagement be by the year or otherwise: Smith's *Law of Master and Servant*, 4th ed., p. 220; *Boston Deep Sea Fishing Co.* v. *Ansell*. If he retains the servant in his employment for any considerable time after discovering his fault, that is condonation, and he cannot afterwards dismiss for that fault without anything new. No doubt the employer ought to have a reasonable time to determine what to do to consider whether he will dismiss or not, or to look for another servant. So, also, he must have full knowledge of the nature and extent of the fault, for he cannot forgive or condone matters of which he is not fully informed. Further, condonation is subject to an implied condition of future good conduct, and whenever any new misconduct occurs, the old offences may be invoked and may be put in the scale against the offender as cause for dismissal.

It does not seem to be necessary to say anything further than that condonation is a question of fact for the jury, if in the opinion of the Judge there is any evidence of it to be laid before them, and we cannot say there was a total absence of such evidence here.

TOZER *v.* HUTCHISON. 1869. 12 N.B.R. (1 Hannay) 548 (New Brunswick. Court of Appeal). "The plaintiff's absence from the store was one of the grounds of complaint made against him by the defendant when he discharged him and if another ground of dismissal existed, the defendant has a right to avail himself of it at the trial, though he was not aware of the existence of it at the time, because if good ground of dismissal existed the plaintiff suffered no wrong from not having been accused of it." [Allen J.]

COOKE *v.* SCHOOL COMMISSIONERS, HALIFAX. 1902. 35 N.S.R. 405 (Nova Scotia. Supreme Court *en banc*). In spite of irregularities which might have justified the dismissal of a servant, the employer may elect to go on with the contract or to "condone" such conduct. Such previous acts may, however, be looked at together with later breaches, and the combined effect may justify dismissal.

NOTE ON DISMISSAL. It is commonly thought that an employee can only be dismissed for "cause," but it is important to remember that a general hiring may usually be terminated by giving notice, either the agreed notice, or notice implied from the situation. Accordingly, unless the employer has some reason for not wanting an employee around, he may be able to "dismiss" him by giving him a month's notice, or longer, without stating any reasons, or cause. In fact he may be able to terminate the employment immediately by giving the employee the amount of wages or salary he would have earned during the period of the notice. In this connection, reread *Addis* v. *Gramophone Company Ltd.* and *Clayton* v. *Oliver.* Has the employee a right to work?

If the employer does not want to have to pay wages or salary in lieu of notice, he must find cause to terminate the employment at once. His promise to employ is subject to a condition, sometimes express, but most often implied, that the employee will not give cause for his dismissal. Cause, then, may be nothing more than an implied condition that the employee conduct himself consistently with his promise to work. Misconduct, such as immorality, or drunkenness, insubordination or disobedience to lawful orders, incompetence or negligence, and absenteeism have been held to be cause. There always arises a question of fact: are the facts alleged as constituting cause sufficiently important to justify the extreme remedy of dismissal, since the employer seeks to say that he is excused from further performance of his promise to keep the employee in his employ?

NOTE ON DISMISSAL AND DISCIPLINE. The problem of *dismissal* for "just cause," or "proper cause," or just for "cause" without any adjective before it, now more frequently arises in labour arbitration awards than in the courts. An increasing number of Canadian workmen are governed by a collective agreement, which must, under the Canadian Labour Acts generally, provide for settlement of all disputes arising under the agreement without stoppage of work. In almost all cases this requirement has resulted in the collective agreement providing for arbitration. Management, in the same agreement, usually reserves the right to discharge an employee for cause. In this context, the following misconduct has been considered as cause: A refusal, without reasonable excuse, to work overtime where the collective agreement is silent on the subject; wildcat strikes; insubordination: an employee threatened his foreman with "bodily harm"; an employee accused by his foreman of malingering retorted impolitely. (In the last example, coupling this impolite conduct with past offences the employer discharged the employee. The arbitration board held the vulgar term did not justify dismissal. Mr. Justice Roach of the Ontario Court of Appeal, sitting as chairman of the board said: "We think we should be realistic and give effect to the plain fact that workmen in industry, some more than others, are not sufficiently careful in the language they use. That criticism applies equally to foremen and supervisors in the plant as well as workmen below that level.") Absenteeism, alone, or coupled with illness. (Since collective agreements usually have provisions for sick leave, the cases have sometimes turned on the necessity for notifying the employer and obtaining a medical certificate. Discharge was held to be justified where an employee did not return to work for another two weeks after his doctor had certified his fitness for work.) Altogether the arbitrators do not seem to have analysed the problem any more clearly than the judges have.

The problem of *discipline* in a modern industrial plant (factory) raises more interesting questions when examined from a common lawyer's point of view. Arbitration boards are frequently asked to uphold, modify or correct, not only dismissal for cause, but disciplinary action falling short of dismissal taken against an employee thought to be guilty of some misconduct. The disciplinary action usually involves suspension for a day or so, or perhaps transfer to a less desirable job. If this action is taken in a case where the misconduct would have justified dismissal, no difficulty arises. The employer in effect is saying to the employee, "You have your choice, accept this suspension or transfer or go." But if the misconduct would not have justified dismissal without notice, no such option can be offered; and since the employer may not even have the right to lay off the employee with notice, because of his seniority, the justification must be found in the express or implied terms of the contract of employment or in the collective agreement. If the collective agreement is silent on the question, it must be supposed that the right to discipline is included in that mysterious expression "management prerogatives" which are almost always retained by management in at least the undefined state. If management is to have such rights it could get them only if they are interpreted as coming within the expression agreed to by the Union, or are expressed or implied in the individual contract of employment. Since they are not usually talked about at the time an employee is taken on strength they must be implied by someone, probably the arbitrator.

When written rules setting standards of conduct and penalties are announced from time to time, as they often are, another problem arises in addition to the question of consent, which may be implied fairly easily. Since the requested promise to comply with such rules is unilateral, what is the consideration? Review *Roscorla* v. *Thomas* above. It is usual to announce new regulations with the added clause: "Continuation in the employ of this Company will be taken as acceptance of these regulations." Is this an effective way of securing consent? What is the consideration? Is this a "practical" problem or only one suitable for law school examinations?

In fact most collective agreements spell out, in some detail, management's right to discipline and make regulations. The following clause is typical: "The exercise of such rights [management] shall include but not be limited to . . . the making and enforcement of rules and regulations not inconsistent with this agreement, relating to discipline, safety, and general conduct of the employees, and to suspend or discharge or otherwise discipline employees for just cause."

[On this subject see Levinson, *A Digest of Arbitration Board Decisions Involving Discharge and Discipline in Ontario* (1959), and Phelps, *Discipline and Discharge in the Unionized Firm* (1959).]

NOTE ON ABSENTEEISM AND ILLNESS. One of the comon "causes" of dismissal is absenteeism. If the parties have not agreed to length of absence which will amount to cause the courts may have to imply some maximum length of time beyond which absence will justify dismissal. Clearly if an employee does not appear for work, he cannot be said to be performing his promise, and he may also be breaking a condition precedent to his employer's obligation to employ. The following cases raise the complex question of absenteeism coupled with illness. The cases may perhaps be better understood if they are regarded first as mere cases of absenteeism and then as cases of illness. The distinction between "temporary" illness and "permanent" illness, which is ambiguously taken throughout the cases may be rendered more intelligible this way. The crucial question is, at what point does an absence due to illness become "cause" for dismissal without notice?

BETTINI *v.* GYE

England. Queen's Bench Division. 1876. 1 Q.B.D. 183

The defendant was the director of the Royal Italian Opera in Covent Garden, London and the plaintiff was a professional singer who agreed with the defendant as follows (in an English translation from the French):

1. Mr. Bettini undertakes to fill the part of prime tenor assoluto in the theatres, halls, and drawing-rooms, both public and private, in Great Britain and in Ireland, during the period of his engagement with Mr. Gye.
2. This engagement shall begin on the 30th of March, 1875, and shall terminate on the 13th of July, 1875.
3. The salary of Mr. Bettini shall be £150 per month, to be paid monthly.
4. Mr. Bettini shall sing in concerts as well as in operas, but he shall not sing anywhere out of the theatre in the United Kingdom of Great Britain and Ireland, from the 1st of January to the 31st of December, 1875, without the written permission of Mr. Gye, except at a distance of more than fifty miles from London, and out of the season of the theatre.
5. Mr. Gye shall furnish the costumes to Mr. Bettini for his characters, according to the ordinary usage of theatres.
6. Mr. Bettini will conform to the ordinary rules of the theatre in case of sickness, fire, rehearsals, &c.
7. Mr. Bettini agrees to be in London without fail at least six days before the commencement of his engagement, for the purpose of rehearsals.
8. In case Mr. Gye shall require the services of Mr. Bettini at a distance of more than ten miles from London, he shall pay his travelling expenses.
9. Mr. Bettini shall not be obliged to sing more than four times a week in opera. Mr. Bettini, in order to assist the direction of Mr. Gye, will sing, upon the request of Mr. Gye, in the same characters in which he has already sung, and in other characters of equal position. In case of the sickness of other artists, Mr. Bettini agrees to replace them in their characters of first tenor assoluto.
10. Mr. Gye shall have the right to prolong the period limited above upon the same conditions, provided that the period does not go beyond the end of the month of August.

The plaintiff was prevented by temporary illness from being in London before March 28, although the agreement required him to be there "without fail" by March 24. The defendant terminated the agreement on the ground that the plaintiff was late in arrival and had given no notice of his inability to be in London for the purpose of rehearsals. The case was argued on a demurrer to the plea of the plaintiff's late arrival.

BLACKBURN J. delivered the judgment of the Court: In this case the parties have entered into an agreement in writing, which is set out on the record.

The Court must ascertain the intention of the parties, as is said by Parke, B., in delivering the judgment of the Court in *Graves* v. *Legg* (1854), 156 E.R. 304, "To be collected from the instrument and the circumstances legally admissible in evidence with reference to which it is to be construed." He adds: "One particular rule well acknowledged is, that where a covenant or agreement goes to part of the consideration on both sides, and may be compensated in damages, it is an independent covenant or contract." There was no averment of any special circumstances existing in this case, with reference to which the agreement was made, but the Court must look at the general nature of such an agreement. By the 7th paragraph of the agreement, "Mr. Bettini agrees to be in London, without fail at least six days before the commencement of his engagement, for the purpose of rehearsals," the engagement was to begin on the 30th of March, 1875. It is admitted on the record that the plaintiff did not arrive in London till the 28th of March, which is less than six days before the 30th, and therefore it is clear that he has not fulfilled his part of the contract.

The question raised by the demurrer is, not whether the plaintiff has any excuse for failing to fulfil this part of his contract, which may prevent his being liable in damages for not doing so, but whether his failure to do so justified the defendant in refusing to proceed with the engagement, and fulfil his, the defendant's part. And the answer to that question depends on whether this part of the contract is a condition precedent to the defendant's liability or only an independent agreement, a breach of which will not justify a repudiation of the contract, but will only be a cause of action for a compensation in damages. . . .

We think the answer to this question depends on the true construction of the contract taken as a whole.

Parties may think some matter, apparently of very little importance, essential; and if they sufficiently express an intention to make the literal fulfilment of such a thing a condition precedent, it will be one; or they may think that the performance of some matter, apparently of essential importance and prima facie a condition precedent, is not really vital, and may be compensated for in damages, and if they sufficiently expressed such an intention, it will not be a condition precedent.

In this case, if to the 7th paragraph of the agreement there had been added words to this effect: "And if Mr. Bettini is not there at the stipulated time, Mr. Gye may refuse to proceed further with the agreement"; or if, on the other hand, it had been said, "And if not there, Mr. Gye may postpone the commencement of Mr. Bettini's engagement for as many days as Mr. Bettini makes default, and he shall forfeit twice his salary for that time," there could have been no question raised in the case. But there is no such declaration of the intention of the parties either way. And in the absence of such an express declaration, we think that we are to look to the whole contract, and applying the rule stated by Parke B. to be acknowledged, see whether the particular stipulation goes to the root of the matter, so that a failure to perform it would render the performance of the rest of the contract by the plaintiff a thing different in substance from what the defendant has stipulated for; or whether it merely partially affects it and may be compensated for in damages. Accordingly as it is one or the other, we think it must be taken to be or not to be intended to be a condition precedent.

If the plaintiff's engagement had been only to sing in operas at the theatre, it might very well be that previous attendance at rehearsals with the actors in company with whom he was to perform was essential. And if the engagement had been only for a few performances, or for a short time, it would afford a strong argument that attendance for the purpose of rehearsals during the six days immediately before the commencement of the engagement was a vital part of the agreement. But we find, on looking to the agreement, that the plaintiff was to sing in theatres, halls, and drawing rooms, both public and private, from the 30th of March to the 13th of July, 1875, and that he was to sing in concerts as well as in operas, and was not to sing anywhere out of the theatre in Great Britain or Ireland from the 1st of January to the 31st of December, 1875, without the written permission of the defendant, except at a distance of more than fifty miles from London.

The plaintiff, therefore, has, in consequence of this agreement, been deprived of the power of earning anything in London from the 1st of January to the 30th of March; and though the defendant has, perhaps, not received any benefit from this, so as to preclude him from any longer treating as a condition precedent what had originally been one, we think this at least affords a strong argument saying that subsequent stipulations are not intended to be conditions precedent, unless the nature of the thing strongly shows they must be so.

And, as far as we can see, the failure to attend at rehearsals during the six days immediately before the 30th of March could only affect the theatrical performances and, perhaps, the singing in duets or concerted pieces during the first week or fortnight of this engagement, which is to sing in theatres, halls, and drawing-rooms, and concerts, for fifteen weeks.

We think, therefore, that it does not go to the root of the matter so as to require us to consider it a condition precedent.

The defendant must, therefore, we think, seek redress by a cross-claim for damages.

Judgment must be given for the plaintiff.

QUESTIONS. Is this decision consistent with *Kingston* v. *Preston*, above? If the defendant cross-claimed for damages, as suggested, would the plaintiff have any defence in the fact that his absence was caused by illness? See *Poussard* v. *Spiers and Pond*. If the plaintiff's absence had been caused by some capricious delay on his part, would it have affected the decision in the case?

POUSSARD *v.* SPIERS and POND
England. Queen's Bench Division. 1876. 1 Q.B.D. 410

BLACKBURN J.: This was an action for the dismissal of the plaintiff's wife from a theatrical engagement. On the trial before my brother Field it appeared that the defendants, Messrs. Spiers & Pond, had taken the Criterion Theatre, and were about to bring a French opera, which was to be produced simultaneously in London and Paris. Their manager, Mr. Hingston, by their authority, made a contract with the plaintiff's wife, which was reduced to writing in the following letter:

Criterion Theatre, Oct. 16th, 1874.

To Madame Poussard.

On behalf of Messrs. Spiers & Pond I engage you to sing and play at the Criterion Theatre on the following terms:

You to play the part of Friquette in Lecocq's opera Les Pres Saint Gervais, commencing on or about the 14th of November next, at a weekly salary of eleven pounds (£11) and to continue on at that sum for a period of three months, providing the opera shall run for that period. Then, at the expiration of the said three months, I shall be at liberty to re-engage you at my option, on terms then to be arranged, and not to exceed fourteen pounds per week for another period of three months. Dresses and tights requisite for the part to be provided by the management, and the engagement to be subject to the ordinary rules and regulations of the theatre.

E. P. Hingston, Manager.

Ratified:

Spiers & Pond.

Madame Poussard, 46 Gunter Grove, Chelsea.

The first performance of the piece was announced for Saturday, the 28th of November. No objection was raised on either side as to this delay, and Madame Poussard attended rehearsals, and such attendance, though not expressed in the written engagement, was an implied part of it. Owing to delays on the part of the composer, the music of the latter part of the piece was not in the hands of the defendants till a few days before that announced for the production of the piece, and the latter and final rehearsals did not take place till the week on the Saturday of which the performance was announced. Madame Poussard was unfortunately taken ill, and though she struggled to attend the rehearsals, she was obliged on Monday, the 23rd of November, to leave the rehearsal, go home and go to bed, and call in medical attendance. In the course of the next day or two an interview took place between the plaintiff and Mr. Leonard (Madame Poussard's medical attendant) and Mrs. Liston, who was the defendant's stage manager, in reference to Madame Poussard's ability to attend and undertake her part, and there was a conflict of testimony as to what took place. According to the defendant's version, Mrs. Liston requested to know as soon as possible what was the prospect of Madame Poussard's recovery, as it would be very difficult on such short notice to obtain a substitute; and that in the result the plaintiff wrote stating that his wife's health was such that she could not play on the Saturday night, and that Mrs. Liston had better, therefore engage a young lady to play the part; and this, if believed to be accurate, amounted to a rescission of the contract. According to the evidence of the plaintiff and the doctor, Mrs. Liston told them that Madame Poussard was to take care of herself and not come out till quite well, as she, Mrs. Liston, had procured, or would procure, a temporary substitute; and Madame Poussard could resume her place as soon as she was well. This, it was contended by the plaintiff, amounted to a waiver by the defendants of a breach of the condition precedent, if there was one.

The jury found that the plaintiff did not rescind the contract, and that Mrs. Liston, if she did waive the condition precedent (as to which they were not agreed), had no authority from the defendants so to do.

These findings, if they stand, dispose of those two questions.

There was no substantial conflict as to what was in fact done by Mrs. Liston. Upon learning, on the Wednesday (the 25th of November), the possibility that Madame Poussard might be prevented by illness from fulfilling her engagement, she sent to a theatrical agent to inquire what artistes of position were disengaged, and learning that Miss Lewis had no engagement till the 25th of December, she made a provisional arrangement with her, by which Miss Lewis undertook to study the part and be ready on Saturday to take the part, in case Madame Poussard was not then recovered so far as to be ready to perform. If it should turn out that this labor was thrown away, Miss Lewis was to have a douceur for her trouble. If Miss Lewis was called on to perform, she was to be engaged at £15 a week up to the 25th of December, if the piece ran so long. Madame Poussard continued in bed and ill, and unable to attend either the subsequent rehearsals or the first night of the performance on the Saturday, and Miss Lewis's engagement became absolute, and she performed the part on Saturday, Monday, Tuesday, Wednesday, and up to the close of her engagement, the 25th of December. The piece proved a success, and in fact ran for more than three months.

On Thursday, the 4th of December, Madame Poussard, having recovered, offered to take her place, but was refused, and for this refusal the action was brought.

On the 21st of January Madame Poussard left England.

My brother Field, at the trial, expressed his opinion that the failure of Madame Poussard to be ready to perform, under the circumstances, went so much to the root of the consideration as to discharge the defendants, and that he should therefore enter judgment for the defendants; but he asked the jury five questions.

The first three related to the supposed rescission and waiver. The other questions were in writing and were: 4. Whether the non-attendance on the night of the opening was of such material consequence to the defendants as to entitle them to rescind the contract? To which the jury said, "No." And, 5. Was it of such consequence as to render reasonable for the defendants to employ another artiste, and whether the engagement of Miss Lewis, as made, was reasonable? To which the jury said, "Yes." Lastly, he left the question of damages, which the jury assessed at £83.

On these answers he reserved leave to the plaintiff to move to enter judgment for £83.

A cross rule was obtained on the ground that the verdict was against evidence and that the damages were excessive.

We think that, from the nature of the engagement to take a leading, and, indeed, the principal, female part (for the prima donna sang her part in male costume as the Prince de Conti) in a new opera which (as appears from the terms of the engagement) it was known might run for a longer or shorter time, and so be a profitable or losing concern to the defendants, we can, without the aid of the jury, see that it must have been of great importance to the defendants that the piece should start well, and consequently that the failure of the plaintiff's wife to be able to perform on the opening and early performances was a very serious detriment to them.

This inability having been occasioned by sickness was not any breach of contract by the plaintiff, and no action can lie against him for the failure thus occasioned. But the damage to the defendants and the consequent failure of consideration is just as great as if it had been occasioned by the plaintiff's fault, instead of by his wife's misfortune. The analogy is complete between this case and that of a charter-party in the ordinary terms, where the ship is to proceed in ballast (the act of God, &c., excepted) to a port, and there load a cargo. If the delay is occasioned by excepted perils, the ship owner is excused. But if it is so great as to go to the root of the matter, it frees the charterer from his obligation to furnish a cargo: see per Bramwell B., delivering the judgment of the majority of the Court of Exchequer Chamber in *Jackson* v. *Union Marine Insurance Co.* (1874), L.R. 10 C.P. 125 at p. 141.

And we think that the question, whether the failure of a skilled and capable artiste to perform in a new piece through serious illness is so important as to go to the root of the consideration, must to some extent depend on the evidence; and is a mixed question of law and fact. Theoretically, the facts should be left to and found separately by the jury, it being for the judge or the Court to say whether they, being so found, show a breach of a condition precedent or not. But this course is often (if not generally) impracticable; and if we can see that the proper facts have been found, we should act on these without regard to the form of the questions.

Now, in the present case, we must consider what were the courses open to the defendants under the circumstances. They might, it was said on the argument before us (though not on the trial), have postponed the bringing out of the piece till the recovery of Madame Poussard, and if her illness had been a temporary hoarseness incapacitating her from singing on the Saturday, but sure to be removed by the Monday, that might have been a proper course to pursue. But the illness here was a serious one, of uncertain duration, and if the plaintiff had at the trial suggested that this was the proper course, it would, no doubt, have been shown that it would have been a ruinous course; and that it would have been much better to have abandoned the piece altogether than to have postponed it from day to day for an uncertain time, during which the theatre would have been a heavy loss.

The remaining alternatives were to employ a temporary substitute until such time as the plaintiff's wife should recover; and if a temporary substitute capable of performing the part adequately could have been obtained upon such a precarious engagement on any reasonable terms, that would have been a right course to pursue; but if no substitute capable of performing the part adequately could be obtained, except on the terms that she should be permanently engaged at higher pay than the plaintiff's wife, in our opinion it follows, as a matter of law, that the failure on the plaintiff's part went to the root of the matter and discharged the defendants.

We think, therefore, that the fifth question put to the jury, and answered by them in favour of the defendants, does find all the facts necessary to enable us to decide as a matter of law that the defendants are discharged.

The fourth question is, no doubt, found by the jury for the plaintiff; but we think in finding it they must have made a mistake in law as to what was a sufficient failure of consideration to set the defendants at liberty, which was not a question for them.

This view taken by us renders it unnecessary to decide anything on the cross-rule for a new trial.

The motion must be refused with costs.

QUESTIONS. Was illness a material factor in this case? Why can no action lie against M. Poussard for the failure occasioned by Madame Poussard's illness? Is there not a breach of the promise to sing? What terms must the court imply in this contract in order that Madame Poussard be excused? What reason in policy is there for such implied terms?

ROBINSON *v.* DAVISON

England. Exchequer. 1871. 40 L.J. Exch. 172

In December, 1869, the plaintiff, a professor of music, agreed with the defendant's wife (a pianist of great renown in her profession under the name of Arabella Goddard), that for a certain fee she should provide a vocalist and a pianoforte, and herself play on the pianoforte, at a concert to be given by the plaintiff at Brigg on the evening of the 14th of January, 1870. In pursuance of this agreement the plaintiff incurred expenses in preparing for the concert. About 9 a.m. on the 14th of Jan., the plaintiff received at Brigg a letter from the defendant's wife, posted in London on the afternoon of the 13th, in which she told him that a sudden attack of illness would prevent her from fulfilling her engagement on the 14th, and enclosed her doctor's certificate to that effect. The plaintiff therefore incurred further expenses in despatching mounted messengers to warn people not to come, and taking other steps to put off the concert. It was proved that the illness was such as to make it dangerous to life for the defendant's wife to go to Brigg or attempt to play, and that she knew this about midday on the 13th. The plaintiff's counsel admitted, both at nisi prius and on this argument, that if any illness could excuse non-performance of the contract, the illness of the defendant's wife was sufficient to do so, but denied that anything short of death could do so. . . .

At the trial Brett J. ruled that it was an implied term of the contract that if the defendant's wife was so ill as to make it unreasonable to expect her to go to Brigg and play, she would be excused, and the defendant would not be liable.

Plaintiff's counsel obtained a rule nisi for a new trial.

KELLY C.B.: This is a contract not merely for personal service, but for a service which can be performed by one person only, and the question is whether illness, which prevents that person from performing the contract, is a lawful and sufficient excuse? I think it is. In *Hall* v. *Wright* (1859), 120 E.R. 695 Pollock C.B. laid down the law very clearly, and though he was in the minority there, yet very correctly as I think. "Now it must be conceded on all hands that there are contracts to which the law implies exceptions and conditions which are not expressed. All the contracts for personal services which can be performed only during the lifetime of the party contracting are subject to the implied condition that he shall be alive to perform them; and should he die, his executor is not liable to an action for the breach of contract occasioned by his death. So, a contract by an author to write a book within a reasonable time, or by a painter to paint a picture within a reasonable time, would, in my judgment, be deemed subject to the condition that, if the author became insane or the painter paralytic, and so incapable of performing the contract by the act of God, he would not be liable personally in damages, any more than his executors would be if he had been prevented by death."

If so, that law is applicable to this case. This is a contract—not indeed by an artist to paint—but by an artist of another description, to play the piano at a certain time and place. Now, the principle laid down in *Taylor* v. *Caldwell* (1863), 122 E.R. 309, *Boast* v. *Firth* (1868), L.R. 4 C.P. 1, and the other cases referred to is the same, namely, that where the service is of this kind—personal to the contracting party—paralysis or blindness or any disability or incapacity, whatever be its nature, which arises from the act of God and falls on the contracting party, excuses him from the performance of his contract. . . .

[Kelly C.B. then discussed *Taylor* v. *Caldwell* which he was prepared to regard as a direct authority.]

BRAMWELL B.: . . . The main question is this: It being admitted that the lady was not fit to perform her contract, and that it was dangerous for her either to go down to the place or to play, and that if there she was not well enough to play efficiently—is it not—I do not say an implied condition—but is it not a part of the bargain between the parties, as much so as if stated in black and white, that under these circumstances she shall be excused? Nay, further, that she shall not be at liberty to play? Because this tells both ways. If she had gone down, being unable to play efficiently, and had insisted on playing and receiving the fee, the plaintiff would have had a right to say and with reason, "No, you shan't play, and I shan't pay you."

But it is said that this is engrafting a condition on an express contract. That was the fallacy in some Judges among the majority in *Hall* v. *Wright* first to suppose the contract and then say "You must not imply a condition that is not properly in it," the whole question being what was the contract? I retain the opinion I expressed there in unabated strength, and I think the reasons of that opinion are applicable here. That opinion is that where the contract is for personal services, which you cannot do by deputy, and which your executors cannot do for you if you die, and you are without intentional default incapacitated either in body or mind from performance, then you are excused by virtue of the original terms of the bargain.

Of course if any one chooses to say in black and white, "I agree to play absolutely, on such a day, and not to die in the meantime, or if I die or fall ill, to pay damages," that is a possible contract, and if so drawn out would be—play or pay. But what is the contract? Perhaps only one hundredth part of the things in the mind of the parties is expressed. But are we not to suppose there were many other things left unexpressed, which they would have a right to insist on? To suppose that the parties made such a contract as that the lady was to play in any event, and whether able to do so with safety or not, is utterly irrational, and unless there were much more cogent evidence of it, I think they did not make such a contract. . . .

CLEASBY B.: . . . This is a contract to perform as a pianist, and one which requires the exercise of the highest faculties of the art, the greatest skill and the most exquisite taste, and if not well done it is not done at all. It is, moreover, to be done by one person only. The contract is based on the assumption which both parties make of the continuance of life, and sufficient health to perform the contract. Both parties make the assumption; both are equally guilty of the imprudence and folly, if there be any, of making such a contract; and not one more than the other. This is the foundation of the contract; if the foundation fails, everything fails. As soon as the act of God has caused an incapacity to do the thing contracted for, the whole falls to the ground.

This is very well expressed in *Boast* v. *Firth,* which was a case of service as an apprentice, and therefore most like this. Brett J. there said: "It has been argued with much force that the covenant is absolute and unconditional, and therefore that, though the apprentice was prevented by the act of God from performing the stipulated services, still the defendant is bound to pay damages. If the first proposition could be sustained, the second, I apprehend, would follow. But the first is denied on the part of the defendant. It is said that where the contract is for personal services, and both parties must have known and contemplated, at the time of entering into it, that the performance of the services was dependent on the servant's continuing in a condition of health to make it possible for him to render them, and a disability arises from the act of God, the non-performance of the contract is excused; and that this is a contract of that nature. I agree with both these propositions." The contract here is of that nature.

Rule discharged.

NOTE. The death of an employer is usually held to terminate the liability to employ on the same grounds, *Farrow* v. *Wilson* (1869), L.R. 4 C.P. 744, but this is not necessarily so, if the contract did not call for the personal co-operation of the deceased. *Phillips* v. *Alhambra Palace Co.*, [1901] 1 K.B. 59.

CUTTER *v.* POWELL

England. King's Bench. 1795. 6 T.R. 320; 101 E.R. 573

To assumpsit for work and labour done by the intestate Cutter, the defendant pleaded the general issue. And at the trial at Lancaster the jury found a verdict for the plaintiff for £31 10s. subject to the opinion of this court on the following case.

The defendant being at Jamaica subscribed and delivered to T. Cutter the intestate a note, whereof the following is a copy: "Ten days after the ship Governor Parry, myself master, arrives at Liverpool, I promise to pay to Mr. T. Cutter the sum of thirty guineas, provided he proceeds, continues and does his duty as second mate in the said ship from hence to the port of Liverpool. Kingston, July 31st, 1793." The ship Governor Parry sailed from Kingston on the 2nd of August, 1793, and arrived in the port of Liverpool on the 9th of October following. T. Cutter went on board the ship on the 31st of July, 1793, and sailed in her on the 2nd day of August, and proceeded, continued and did his duty as second mate in her from Kingston until his death, which happened on the 20th of September following, and before the ship's arrival in the port of Liverpool. The usual wages of a second mate of a ship on such a voyage, when shipped by the month out and home is four pounds per month; but when seamen are shipped by the run from Jamaica to England, a gross sum is usually given. The usual length of a voyage from Jamaica to Liverpool is about eight weeks.

ASHURST J.: We cannot collect that there is any custom prevailing among merchants on these contracts; and therefore we have nothing to guide us but the terms of the contract itself. This is a written contract, and it speaks for itself. And as it is entire, and as the defendant's promise depends on a condition precedent to be performed by the other party, the condition must be performed before the other party is entitled to receive anything under it. It has been argued however that the plaintiff may now recover on a quantum meruit: but she has no right to desert the agreement; for wherever there is an express contract the parties must be guided by it; and one party cannot relinquish or abide by it as it may suit his advantage. Here the intestate was by the terms of his contract to perform a given duty before he could call upon the defendant to pay him anything; it was a condition precedent, without performing which the defendant is not liable. And that seems to me to conclude the question: the intestate did not perform the contract on his part; he was not indeed to blame for not doing it; but still as this was a condition precedent, and as he did not perform it, his representative is not entitled to recover.

Postea to the defendant: Unless some other information relative to the usage in cases of this kind should be laid before the Court before the end of this term: but the case was not mentioned again.

[The opinions of Lord Kenyon C.J. and Grose and Lawrence JJ. are omitted.]

NOTE. The rights of seamen in circumstances like those in *Cutter* v.

Powell are now governed by the *Canada Shipping Act,* R.S.C., 1952, c. 29. See especially ss.200–209.

STUBBS *v.* HOLYWELL RAILWAY COMPANY. 1867. L.R. 2 Ex. 311 (England. Exchequer). Stubbs was appointed consulting engineer to the defendants, to complete the construction of certain works. The work was to be completed in fifteen months from Dec. 5th, and Stubbs was to be paid £500 as his salary, in five equal quarterly instalments. Stubbs worked one quarter and was paid in March £100. He worked for two more quarters, and part of the fourth quarter when he died. His administrator sued for £200. MARTIN B.: "Suppose a man enters into a contract to do a certain piece of work for a certain sum, then if he die before he completes it, he can recover nothing, not even if before his death he had done nine-tenths of it. For the contract was for the whole work, and not for nine-tenths of it. But suppose that the contract is for performance of a certain piece of work for a certain sum, to be paid at the rate, say of £50 a month, then the person employed earns £50 at the end of each successive month. It is true that if, after doing a portion of the work, he refused to do the rest, he might not be able to recover, because he could not prove that he was ready and willing to perform his part of the contract. But such a case as the present has no analogy with that of a refusal by the person employed to continue performance. The contract, no doubt, is ended by the death of Stubbs, but only in this sense, that the act of God has made further performance impossible. . . . No vested right of action is taken away by death. The contract is at an end, but it is not rescinded, for rescission is the act of two parties, not of one."

THE APPORTIONMENT ACT

Ontario. Revised Statutes. 1960. Chapter 16

3. All rents, annuities, dividends, and other periodical payments in the nature of income, whether reserved or made payable under an instrument in writing or otherwise, shall, like interest on money lent, be considered as accruing from day to day, and are apportionable in respect of time accordingly.

NOTES AND QUESTIONS. In his article, "Conditions in Contract," (1905), 14 *Yale L.J.* 424, Professor Clarence D. Ashley poses the following problem. An author promises to write an article between October 1 and May 1 and the publisher promises to pay $1,000 on January 5.

"Here it is evident that no conditions can be implied because the terms of the contract show a contrary intent. The result is that the promises are independent, and if the $1,000 is not paid on January 5, an action will lie at once therefor, and it is, of course, unnecessary to allege writing of the article, since this cannot constitute a condition precedent. This seems clear enough. But suppose the proposed author dies prior to January 5, without having written the article. His estate is not liable, of course, because death is an excuse in such a case. Can his legal representatives successfully maintain an action for the $1,000, if not paid on January 5? Logically it would seem that there would be no defence, because the promise is independent. . . .

"The same question in another form would arise in the event that the $1,000 should be paid on January 5, and the author should die before May 1 without having written the article. How can this money be recovered by the publisher? There is no failure of consideration because the author's promise was valid, and was just what the publisher asked for. There are no principles of conditions either implied in law or found in the language of contract, which can be invoked to work out a satisfactory solution, and one seems forced to the logical conclusion that as the promises must be found to be independent the results of such independence must follow."

Can you suggest other acceptable solutions? Do you agree that "no conditions can be implied"? Do you agree that there has been no failure of consideration?

THE DARTMOUTH FERRY COMMISSION *v.* JANET MARKS

Nova Scotia. Supreme Court of Canada. 1903. 34 S.C.R. 366

This action was brought by the plaintiff, a widow, as executrix of the last will and testament of her husband, the late John H. Marks, deceased. The defendant is a body corporate and maintains and operates a line of ferry steamers across the harbour of Halifax, between the Town of Dartmouth and the City of Halifax. John H. Marks in his lifetime was in the employ of the defendant as captain of one of the defendant's ferry steamers. The agreement under which he was employed was in writing and is as follows.

"No. 7 Memorandum of Agreement between the Dartmouth Ferry Commission of the one part and John H. Marks of Dartmouth in the County of Halifax of the other part.

"The said John H. Marks agrees to serve the Dartmouth Ferry Commission in the capacity of captain at the monthly wages of sixty dollars per month. Such service to commence on the first day of March, A.D. 1899, the wages for each calendar month to be paid on the 10th day of the following month, and such service to be terminated by one calendar month's notice on either side, to be given at any time. Should either party wish to terminate the service without such notice the Commission to be entitled to do so by paying one month's pay, and the said John H. Marks by forfeiting to the Commission one month's pay. Any period of service prior to the commencement of a calendar month to be paid pro rata on the 10th day of such calendar month. Nothing in these presents to effect the right of either party to terminate the relation hereby created for lawful causes.

"In witness whereof, the party of the first part has hereunto subscribed his name, and the parties of the second part have hereto affixed their corporate seal.

Witness		John H. Marks
H. Watt		A. C. Johnson, Chairman
	[Seal]	Walter Creighton, Act. Sect'y."

Under this agreement Marks began serving the defendant as captain on the first day of March, 1899. A resolution was passed at the meeting of the Commission held on 8th January, 1900, as follows, namely "Resolved. That after this date no employee will be paid for any time he or she be absent from duty." There is no evidence of any formal notice to Marks of the contents of this resolution but he submitted to a deduction of wages under it and admitted knowledge of it to other employees. Marks became ill on the 15th December, 1900, and from that time until the date of his death was not able to perform his duties as captain of the defendant's steamer. He was confined to the house for three or four months. In May, June, and July, he was able to be out of doors and apparently was recovering. Dr. Cunningham, who attended him thought that he might be able to get back to work in the summer and told him so. Dr. Stewart, a consulting physician who was called in consultation with Dr. Cunningham, also considered the illness a temporary one. However, early in July, 1901, Marks became much worse and called Dr. Smith in attendance upon him, who diagnosed the case as cancer of the stomach in an advanced stage. He died on 16th July, 1901.

The plaintiff, as executrix, brought this action to recover $416.00 wages from 15th December, until 16th July, 1901, at $60.00 per month under said agreement.

The action came on for trial before the Chief Justice of Nova Scotia with a jury, at Halifax. Questions were submitted to the jury whose answers were as follows:

"1. Was the resolution of January 8th, 1900, communicated to John H. Marks shortly after its adoption by the defendant Commission? A. No."

"2. Did the said John H. Marks continue in the employ of the defendant Commission after notice of this resolution and acquiesce in said employment under the terms of said resolution? A. No."

"3. Did the said John H. Marks remain in the active discharge of his duties in the employment of the defendant Commission until his death. A. In the employ but not active."

"4. Was the illness of the said John H. Marks and of which he died of temporary or permanent character. A. Temporary."

"5. Was John H. Marks after the 16th day of December, 1900, prevented by a permanent illness from performing any service under his contract with the defendant? A. No."

On these findings the learned Judge directed judgment to be entered for the plaintiff for $416.00, the amount of her claim.

From that judgment the defendant appealed to the Supreme Court of Nova Scotia *in banco* and moved to set aside the findings of the jury and for judgment in favour of the defendant.

The said appeal and motion came on for argument before four judges of the Supreme Court of Nova Scotia *in banco*. The court were evenly divided in opinion, Mr. Justice Weatherbe and Mr. Justice Graham being of opinion that the appeal and application for a new trial should be dismissed and that the plaintiff should have judgment, while Mr. Justice Townshend and Mr. Justice Meagher were of the opinion that judgment should be entered for the defendant. In accordance with the practice of the Supreme Court of Nova Scotia an order was granted dismissing the appeal and application without costs. From this judgment the present appeal has been asserted by the defendants.

DAVIES J.: . . . In the view I take of the law, it is not necessary for me to say anything on that branch of the appeal which relates to the "no work no pay" resolution, so-called.

I agree with Mr. Justice Townshend on the substantial question of the liability of the defendants to pay Captain Marks wages for the seven months during which he never worked or was able to work. From the day when he first gave up his work, 15th December, until the day of his death, Captain Marks was a sick man, utterly unable to discharge his duties and made no pretense of being able to do so. He was from that date, beyond any doubt, permanently disabled by sickness from attending to his work. Some argument was attempted to be advanced that when he was first taken ill, he himself hoped and his medical adviser also hoped and believed his illness was only temporary. But in the face of the facts which subsequently developed that he was suffering from an incurable malady, which soon afterwards caused his death, it does not appear to me possible seriously to argue that the deceased's illness was only temporary. The findings of the jury on this point are clearly contrary to the evidence and the facts and must be set aside.

It is quite true that the deceased and his medical adviser both hoped and believed, at first, that his illness was only temporary, but their belief or hope cannot alter the truth subsequently disclosed. That truth is now admitted and is beyond controversy that on and after the 15th of December, when Captain Marks ceased working, he was permanently disabled from doing his work he had contracted to do. In law, this disablement is termed the act of God. It not only, in my opinion, justified the Commission in formally determining the contract, if they had chosen to take that course, but by rendering it impossible that he could ever afterwards discharge his duties under his contract, the permanent disablement determined and ended the contract. The consideration which moved the Commission to promise wages was gone. The mutuality necessary for longer continuance of the contract ceased. Captain Marks could not be sued by the Commission for non-performance by him of his promise to serve them in the capacity of captain of one of their steamers. He could plead to any such action, disablement or incapacity by the act of God. The same result would have followed if he had become insane or had lost the physical use of his limbs.

The fact of the disablement arising from occult internal troubles cannot make any difference. There is no analogy between such permanent disablement and temporary sickness. The law permits the latter on the ground of common humanity to be offered as an excuse for not discharging duty temporarily and suffers the disabled party to recover wages for the time he is temporarily away from his work. But while releasing the permanently disabled workman from damages for the non-performance of this contract, it does not permit him to recover wages without doing work. No case can be found so deciding. We are asked to create a precedent. This permanent disability goes to the very root of the consideration for the promise on the part of the Commission to pay wages. The covenant on the part of the employee to serve as master was not one independent of the employer's covenant to pay wages. They were interdependent and the promise to pay was dependent upon the performance of the work covenanted to be done. The belief of the employee or his medical adviser that the former's disability was only temporary cannot affect the question in the light of the subsequent knowledge which revealed its permanency. The excuse for not working for a short time which a temporary illness would justify, cannot apply to absence from work caused by permanent disability. . . .

The action, therefore, must fail, but while setting aside the findings of the jury on the fourth and fifth questions, as being contrary to the evidence, we are not able, under the Judicature Rules of Nova Scotia . . . to direct judgment to be entered for the defendant as such a judgment would be inconsistent with the findings of the jury.

The appeal should be allowed with costs in this court and in the court appealed from and a new trial ordered, the costs of the trial to abide the event.

KILLAM J.: . . . There is a singular dearth of clear authority respecting the effect of the disability of an employee arising from illness upon the right to wages and in determining or giving the right to determine the contract of service. . . .

The case usually cited as the leading authority is *Cuckson* v. *Stones* (1858), 1 E. & E. 248; 120 E.R. 902. In reality, however, the decision was founded upon the special nature of the contract in question, as Lord Campbell C.J. distinctly indicated.

The plaintiff was employed as an expert brewer for ten years. The defendants were to pay him a lump sum in advance and weekly wages and to furnish him with a house and with coals for the whole term. About a year from the end of the term, the plaintiff became ill and continued so for about seven months, during which time he was unable to personally attend to the business, but gave advice to the defendants who consulted him from time to time. The defendants paid the wages for some months of the period of illness and, upon the plaintiff's recovery, he went on with his work and was paid as before. It was admitted that the contract continued. As declared and as proved, the promise to pay was clearly an independent promise, the consideration for which was the plaintiff's executory promise to serve; and the agreement to pay wages was only a part of the consideration for the plaintiff's promise. There was but one entire contract. Upon general principles, the performance of the service was not a condition precedent to the obligation to pay. Disability arising from natural illness was an absolute excuse for non-performance. There was no default on the part of the plaintiff. The decision affords very little assistance in determining whether, under a contract such as that now in question, actual service is an absolute condition precedent to the right of payment. It is important, however, for an expression of opinion by Lord Campbell regarding the effect of illness upon the relation of the parties. He said: "We concur in the observation of Willes J. in *Harmer* v. *Cornelius* (1858), 5 C.B.N.S. 236; 141 E.R. 94, and if the plaintiff from unskilfulness had been wholly incompetent to brew, or by the visitation of God he had become, from paralysis or any other bodily illness, permanently incompetent to act in the capacity of brewer for the defendant, we think the defendant might have determined the contract. He could not be considered incompetent by illness of a temporary nature; but if he had been struck with disease so that he could never be expected to return to his work, we think the defendant ought to have dismised him and employed another in his stead. Instead of being dismissed, he returned to the service of the defendant when his health was restored and the defendant employed him and paid him as before. At the trial the defendant's counsel admitted that the contract was not rescinded. The contract being in force, we think that there was no suspension of the weekly payments by reason of the plaintiff's illness and inability to work. It is allowed that under this contract, there could be no deduction from the weekly sum in respect of his having been disabled by illness from working for one day of the week; and while the contract remained in force, we see no difference between his being so disabled for a day or for a week or for a month."

These views were pronounced as indicating the considered opinion of the court. They do not seem to have been since questioned by any court. They should, I think, be accepted as governing the rights of the parties under contracts of a similar nature.

In *K* v. *Raschen* (1878), 38 L.T. 38, the plaintiff had been employed at a yearly salary subject to dismissal on one month's notice. The service began on the 2nd of July, and continued until the 30th of July, when the plaintiff was given leave of absence until the 6th of August, on account of illness. He remained unable to work until the 2nd of September, when he returned and tendered his services, which were refused. On the 20th of August he was given notice that he was dismissed. He was held entitled to recover his wages for the whole period of illness. So far as the report shows the only serious position raised was upon the defendant's contention that there was no liability because, it was claimed, the illness was due to the plaintiff's own misconduct. It appeared, however, that the misconduct occurred before the engagement, and there was nothing to indicate that the plaintiff knew, when he contracted, that he was afflicted with an infirmity likely to disable him. The court considered that illness was to be taken as prima facie due to the act of God, and that the plaintiff should not be deemed to have warranted his permanent capacity for work. . . .

It seems clearly settled that under a contract to furnish the personal services of a particular person, there is an implied qualification that it is subject to such person being in health to perform the services when the time for their performance comes, and that the party so contracting is excused by the disability, without his fault, of the person who is to render the services. . . .

In *Poussard* v. *Spiers* (1876), 1 Q.B.D. 410, the employer was held excused for refusing to accept the services where the performer was disabled when the time came for entering upon them and the time was deemed so material as to be of the essence of the contract.

The contract in question in the present case was in writing and was set out and admitted in the pleadings . . .

If, upon a proper construction of this contract, the actual performance of service during each month was an absolute condition precedent to the right to payment of the wages for the month, the action should have been dismissed.

In *Lampleigh* v. *Brathwaite* (1615), 80 E.R. 255, it is said: "But if it be executory, as in consideration that you will serve me a year I will give you ten pounds, here you cannot bring your action till the service is performed. But if it were a promise, on either side, executory, it needs not to aver performance; for it is the counter-promise and not the performance that makes the consideration." . . .

The modern principle is to endeavour to ascertain from an examination of the whole contract what was the real intention of the parties; but if it appears that it was the performance and not the promise that was to constitute the consideration for the counter-promise, this still gives rise to the presumption that performance was intended to be a condition precedent.

Here the only specific promise is that of Marks to serve in a certain capacity at certain wages. The counter-promise to pay must be inferred from the words "to be paid." The monthly wages were to be paid after the month's service was to be rendered. Upon these circumstances alone, the natural presumption would appear to be that the performance of each month's service was to be a condition precedent to the right to the month's wages. But, if so, complete performance would be necessary. Failure of performance for one day would, unless some qualification is to be implied from the nature and subject matter of the contract, involve the same result as a failure for all but one day. It is a well established principle that, under such a contract, failure to serve for a portion of a month, when attributable to the fault of the employee, disentitles him to the wages for the whole month. For each month the contract is entire. I do not think that, in the absence of an express stipulation, an intention would be implied that, upon partial failure of performance due to illness, the monthly wages were to be apportioned. In the case of a domestic servant this would certainly not be done. I see no greater reason for implying it in the case of a clerk employed in an office or shop, or of one in the occupation of the deceased. . . .

The real qualification to be implied is, I think, the one recognized in the cases to which I have referred. As the employee does not warrant the continuance of his physical ability to work, he does not contract absolutely and at all events to do so. Disability due to illness excuses him. And since his promise is so qualified, strict and full performance of service is not a condition precedent to the right to wages. The wages are payable for such service as he can reasonably be called upon to give and for such only. These appear to be the principles justifying the decision in *K* v. *Raschen*, and the judicial opinions expressed in *Beale* v. *Thompson* (1803), 3 B. & P. 405; 127 E.R. 221. And there seems to be no ground for distinguishing between different periods of illness, so long as the contract subsists. Disability due to this cause and lasting for months would not seem to have a different effect from such disability lasting for nine-tenths of a month or for one day only. There is no precise point at which a line can be drawn. I cannot concur in the opinion which I understand to be held by the other members of this Court, that the illness of Marks *ipso facto*, put an end to the contract. Both the question as to whether the illness of which Marks died was of a temporary or permanent character and the answer appear, at first sight, anomalous. But they were evidently dictated by the peculiar nature of the case. Apparently, Marks' illness was not considered to be permanent until a few days before his death. He appeared to be recovering, but he then had a relapse which resulted fatally. And it was fully open to the jury to find, upon the medical evidence, that the malady which incapacitated him for nearly the whole of the seven months was independent of that which brought about the death and that the existence of the latter was unsuspected until the relapse occurred.

The jury have found that Marks remained in the employ of the commission until his death, that is, they found that the contract remained undetermined. The evidence appears to me to have justified the finding. There was no date, prior to the end of June, when the parties deemed the contract as determined. Month by month, as I interpret the original contract, the wages would accrue. And once accrued, the right to them could not be taken away by what subsequently occurred or became apparent.

In the words of Lord Alvanley in *Beale* v. *Thompson*, "as long as that contract subsists there can be no such thing as an interruption; it is either entirely at an end or entirely subsists."

Lord Campbell, in *Cuckson* v. *Stones*, put incapacity arising from illness on the basis of incompetency, as giving a right to determine the contract. But it would be clearly in the power of the master to waive a right to discharge for the incompetency of the servant; and so, I think, the right to discharge for incapacity arising from illness would be waived and lost by conduct shewing a continuance of the employment.

Appeal allowed with costs.

[Killam J. agreed to allow the appeal on the ground that the answer to the second question as to acquiescence in the Company's "no work, no pay" resolution was against the weight of evidence. Taschereau C.J. and Sedgewick and Nesbitt JJ. concurred in the opinion of Davies J.]

NOTE. Graham J. in the lower court, 36 N.S.R. 158 at 172, said: "Permanent illness is a good ground for discharging an employee. And if an employee is sued by the employer for not performing the contract—that is for the breach of it—permanent illness is a good defence. . . . But I think an employer, in the case of illness of a servant, must elect. He may discharge the employee, and, if an action is brought for the dismissal, permanent illness will be a defence. While death *ipso facto* terminates the contract, I think permanent illness does not. At what stage would it be terminated? Here, by retaining him in their employ, and not requiring him to work—and that often happens—they treated the illness as temporary illness."

Compare the language used by Lord Campbell in *Cuckson* v. *Stones,* and quoted by Killam J.: "If the plaintiff . . . had become . . . permanently incompetent . . . we think the defendant *might have* determined the contract . . . if he had been struck with disease . . . we think the defendant *ought to have dismissed* him. . . . Instead of being dismissed he returned to the service of the defendant. . . . The contract being in force, we think that here there was no suspension of the weekly payments."

MARRISON *v.* BELL

England. Court of Appeal. [1939] 2 K.B. 187

Appeal by the plaintiff from a decision of the County Court. The plaintiff was employed by the defendant as a salesman at a weekly wage. On Saturday, Dec. 4, 1937, the plaintiff became ill, and the defendant was informed of the fact on Monday, Dec. 6. When the plaintiff returned to work on Saturday, Mar. 26, 1938, the defendant paid the plaintiff one week's wages in lieu of notice to terminate the contract of service. During the period of his sickness, the plaintiff did not receive any wages from the defendant, but he did receive certain benefits under the National Health Insurance Act. The plaintiff sued the defendant for arrears of wages accruing during the period that the plaintiff was ill; and the County Court judge dismissed the action, on the ground that as the Act gave the workman rights to benefits under that Act during his incapacity, there was a term implied in the contract of service that, whilst in receipt of benefit, the workman's contract under which he had the right to receive wages was modified by an implied term that the right to wages was wholly suspended.

SCOTT L.J.: . . . The learned county court judge decided the case not on the ground that the contract was wholly terminated, but on the ground that, although it was not terminated, the right to wages under it was brought to an end. The reason that he did not decide that the contract was brought to an end was, I think, because on the correspondence that passed between the parties it was quite impossible for him to take that view. It is clear from a letter dated April 8, written by the plaintiff's solicitors to the defendant, that the plaintiff was taking the view that he had received a proper notice to terminate his employment on that date. That view was assented to by the defendant himself, because, in answer to that letter, he wrote on April 11: "In accordance with the terms of

Mr. Marrison's engagement as a shop assistant he was given a correct and proper notice to terminate his employment with me. For your information, Mr. Marrison was duly paid £3 10s. on the 26th ultimo, in lieu of him working the week's notice."

On those facts it is clear that the parties treated the contract of service as continuing until the expiration of that notice and, therefore, it was impossible for the learned county court judge to uphold the defence, the terms of which I have stated.

We have been furnished by counsel for the appellant, the workman, with a copy of a note of the learned judge's judgment, and from that note, which is accepted as approximately accurate by counsel for the respondent, we find what were the views expressed by the learned judge. It says: "I find as a fact that Mr. Marrison never received any wages when off sick." It then says: "When off sick in the absence of any express contract no wages due." That is a statement or proposition of law that, unless the right to wages is expressly preserved by an express term of the contract, wages are not due during sickness. It then appears that the learned county court judge said that the employment was still in existence, but there was no contract for any specific period and the case must be "decided on its own particular facts. It is a question if a man is not working by reason of sickness, he is entitled to wages. We have no authority at all in regard to position of a man under National Health Insurance Act." He then expressed the view that it would be inequitable for a man to be entitled to his wages at a time during which he was receiving benefit under the National Health Insurance Act and held that that was a sufficient reason to support his general view that there is no such right to wages during sickness as had been alleged on behalf of the plaintiff.

The learned county court judge supported his view by reference to two cases, to which I will refer in due course. A long series of decisions has been given in our Courts making it quite clear that the common law of this country does not recognize any such rule in contracts of service as is suggested by the learned county court judge. On the contrary, those cases say, in my opinion quite clearly, that under a contract of service, irrespective of the question of the length of notice provided by that contract, wages continue through sickness and incapacity from sickness to do the work contracted for until the contract is terminated by a notice by the employer in accordance with the terms of the contract.

An argument was addressed to us by the respondent's counsel based upon the doctrine of frustration. I say nothing more about it for the moment; but I will deal with that presently. Apart from that, the law I think is quite clear to the effect that I have stated.

The first and leading case on the subject is *Cuckson* v. *Stones* (1858), 28 L.J.Q.B. 25. That was the first of the decided cases on this particular topic. It is a case very different in its facts from this case. That was the case of an employee who was employed under an agreement in writing for a period of ten years to act in the capacity of a professional brewer to the defendant. He fell sick and was unable to work for a considerable time, but during the time that he could not do the work attaching to his office of a brewer he gave some assistance to his employer in teaching him how to do the work himself. The question in the case was primarily whether the plea was or was not demurrable. The plea in question averred that "the plaintiff was not, during any part of the time for and in respect of which such wages are by that count claimed, ready and willing or able to render, and did not in fact during any part of such time render, the agreed or any service." On a rule as to entering the verdict on that plea, the Court held that a verdict in favour of the plaintiff given by a jury ought not to be disturbed and that the rule granted for the purpose ought to be discharged. Lord Campbell, delivering the judgment of the Court, said, "The contract being in force, we think that here there was no suspension of the weekly payments by reason of the plaintiff's illness and inability to work. It is allowed that, under this contract, there could be no deduction from the weekly sum in respect of his having been disabled by illness from working for one day of the week: and, while the contract remained in force, we see no difference between his being so disabled for a day, or a week, or a month." That then was the decision in the case of a contract for ten years of definite service.

Next in order of date comes the case of *Warren* v. *Whittingham* (1902), 18 Times L.R. 508, where the plaintiff was engaged by the defendant "for a period of five years at a yearly salary, the plaintiff undertaking to devote the whole of his time to the defendant's business. During the period the plaintiff became temporarily ill, and was in consequence prevented from performing his work. Held, that the plaintiff was entitled to salary during the time of his illness." Bruce J., who regarded the case as covered by *Cuckson* v. *Stones* to which he referred, added that he "could not find that that decision had ever been questioned. In the present case the plaintiff was ready and willing to perform his work, and was only prevented by temporary illness." Judgment was given for him accordingly.

After that came a case of *Niblett* v. *Midland Ry. Co.* (1907), 96 L.T. 462; before a divisional court consisting of Darling J. and Phillimore J. The plaintiff was a railway employee who, upon entering the company's service, signed an undertaking to abide by the rules of the company. One of these rules required him to join the railway company's friendly society, which was independent of the company, but to the funds of which the company contributed. By the rules of the society a member was entitled to sick pay during illness, but not if he was receiving wages from the company. The plaintiff became ill in February, 1905, and received sick pay until September, when he received notice terminating his employment. It was held that he was not entitled to his wages during the period of his illness on the ground that, having regard to the rules which had to be signed by an employee as a term of his contract of service, the rules must be read into the contract of service, and, when so read in, necessarily involved the implication of a term of the contract of service to the correlative effect of the rules of the society—namely, that, whilst entitled to sick benefit, his right to wages should be suspended. That again, was a case in which the principle laid down in *Cuckson* v. *Stones* was recognized by the Court; but the decision was that, by reason of the special terms of that contract, the ordinary principle of law was excluded. Both the learned judges expressed their decision in those terms.

The next case in order of date is *Storey* v. *Fulham Steel Works Co.* (1907), 24 Times L.R. 89. It is a decision of the Court of Appeal, consisting of Lord Alverstone C.J., Buckley and Kennedy L.JJ. In that case there was an agreement for five years and the same sort of question arose. There was a passing reference to the doctrine of frustration, but the decision of the case was that *Cuckson* v. *Stones* had expressed the ruling principle in such cases.

The next case is *Elliott* v. *Liggens* [1902] 2 K.B. 84., in which a different question was raised for the first time, namely, whether accepting the rule laid down in *Cuckson's* case that there was no implied term suspending the right to wages during incapacity by illness, none the less, if a workman so employed under such a contract claimed compensation under the then *Workmen's Compensation Act, 1897*, and was in receipt of compensation during partial incapacity for work (compensation being based, as is well known, upon a comparison with his weekly earnings), the Act must be treated as introducing a modification of the contract of service which had the effect of depriving the workman, whilst claiming from his employer compensation, which roughly may be described as half the weekly wages, from recovering from his employer at the same time his whole weekly wages. Lord Alverstone there said, "It seems plain from the sections to which I have referred, and from the fact of the plaintiff having given notice and received this weekly payment, that his conduct was inconsistent with the view that he was still entitled to the whole of his original wages." In the next sentence but one he says: "I think that a workman who takes the benefit of the Act on the ground of his incapacity to earn wages, and obtains compensation based on the footing of those wages, cannot turn round and say he is entitled to the balance of his wages during the time in which he has been disabled from work and receiving compensation." It is to be observed that Lord Alverstone does not in express terms say that the Act in question shall be interpreted as modifying the contract of employment and does not give a specific legal reason for his conclusion. Darling J., however, came nearer to the reason, because he said: "The compensation is, therefore, payable in lieu of the wages which he has lost." Channell J. said: "I think the best way of putting it is that the plaintiff, by claiming and accepting something which is absolutely inconsistent with his right to claim his wages, is estopped from saying that he is entitled to recover those wages."

The last case to which I need refer is a case which was heard first before a Divisional Court and then in the Court of Appeal, the name of the case being *Warburton and Another* v. *Co-operative Wholesale Society, Ltd.* [1917] 1 K.B. 663. The headnote is: "The fact that a workman stays away from work and receives compensation from his employers during temporary incapacity for work resulting from injury received by him during the course of his employment does not of itself terminate the employment, even though the contract of employment is merely at will." This is one of the cases mentioned by the learned judge in his judgment, and no doubt he had that decision in mind when he held that the contract of employment was not terminated by the plaintiff's illness. In that case, where the workman was suing for wages, Lord Cozens Hardy M.R. said, p. 665: "It has been long settled that a contract of service is not terminated by incapacity to work by reason of temporary illness, and that on return to work the man can recover his wages during the period of his absence." He then refers to *Cuckson* v. *Stones* as the authority. It is to be observed that that sentence is absolutely unlimited and unqualified in its terms and it is a direct negative to the view of the learned county court judge in this case and to the argument of the respondent that the wages ceased to be payable at common law as a result of incapacity to work by reason of temporary illness. Lord Cozens-Hardy goes on to say: "I think this principle must apply to a case where a workman is receiving compensation under the *Workmen's Compensation Act*. It was held in a Divisional Court in the case of *Elliott* v. *Liggens* [1902] 2 K.B. 84, that the service was not ended, although the man could not, while in receipt of compensation, receive wages, and apparently not even wages less the compensation. I feel some difficulty in understanding the ground upon which the latter point was decided, and I desire to keep an open mind if it should hereafter be necessary for this Court to consider it." Warrington L.J. said, p. 667: "It is clear that mere absence from work owing to illness or accident does not determine the contract of service: *Cuckson* v. *Stones*; and I am unable to see how a claim to and receipt of compensation under the Act"—that is the *Workmen's Compensation Act*—"could have that effect." Scrutton L.J. said, p. 668: "Under decided cases a servant incapacitated by illness and in the absence of notice under the contract does not cease to be employed unless the illness is such as seriously to interfere with or frustrate the business purpose of the contract." He refers to *Cuckson* v. *Stones*, and *Storey* v. *Fulham Steel Works Co.* He then says: "But, though still in employment, he is not entitled to full or any wages while receiving sick pay under the rules," which were made part of the contract as in *Niblett*'s case, "or compensation under the statute," as in *Elliott*'s case. Scrutton L.J. said: "The reason for this latter proposition is based either on an implied contract that a man who is receiving money because he is not able to work should not also claim the full money he would receive were he able to work, or, as in *Elliott* v. *Liggens*, on some kind of estoppel, which I do not clearly understand." Those are the whole of the cases which have been decided in our Courts bearing on this question, though there was a decision the other way in the Manx Court, to which I do not think I need refer.

As in the contract of employment by reason of the incorporation of rules, as in *Niblett* v. *Midland Ry. Co.* one may imply a term of the contract suspending wages during the receipt of the benefit which those rules contemplate shall take the place of wages, so, in my view, it also results from the cases that, where under the *Workmen's Compensation Act* a man is getting half his wages in the form of compensation, it is right to interpret that Act as suspending the right at common law to the receipt of full wages during incapacity from accident or from a disease within that Act. I think that is the true ground upon which to base the suspension of wages where a man is receiving by reason of incapacity compensation under the *Workmen's Compensation Act*.

It is sought to say that the same principle that applies in the case of the *Workmen's Compensation Act* ought also to be applied where a servant is in receipt of benefit under the *National Health Insurance Acts*, the Act in question being the Act of 1936, which is the last of the series of statutes which began with the Act of 1911.

The first comment on that argument is that the benefits conferred by that last Act of 1936 and by its predecessors are in their nature additional benefits conferred on the classes in the country who come within the scope of those Acts, being mostly persons engaged as workmen. Those benefits are intended to be an addition to such financial emoluments as the workman may have during his life; improving their position by giving them medical assistance, disablement benefit and others of a long list of additional benefits which will better the lot of the working man. Those benefits are in their nature irrespective of the amount of wages as determined by the workman's individual contract of service. Under these Acts rights are given as a general principle independently of any relation between the rights and the wages, and there is absent, at any rate from most of the earlier Acts and certainly from the Act of 1936, any such ground as there is in the *Workmen's Compensation Act* for supposing that Parliament intended by the Act which conferred the benefits of Health Insurance to take away from the workman any rights to wages that he might have. I suppose that the great majority of employed persons in this country are employed on terms of a week's or, at any rate, a month's notice—mostly a week's notice; and consequently there is no social need for protecting the employer from the liability of having to go on paying wages which he is always able to terminate after a short time.

Putting it quite shortly, I can see no ground in that Act, the provisions of which we have considered, for saying that in it is to be implied a term modifying all contracts of service of persons who come within the scope of these benefits, and I think it is enough for the decision of this case to express the decision of the Court in that negative form. I do not propose therefore to examine the particular provisions of that Act to which we have been referred.

On those grounds I think that the learned judge was wrong in his decision, that the plaintiff succeeds in his action and is entitled to recover the past payments and the week's wages in lieu of notice, in view of the fact that he treated the payment of £3 10s. which was given to him as the payment of one week's wages, his action being for the balance. The appeal will be allowed with costs here and below.

[Finlay and DuParcq L.JJ. agreed that the appeal be allowed.]

PETRIE *v.* MAC FISHERIES, LTD.
England. Court of Appeal. [1940] 1 K.B. 258

SLESSER L.J.: . . . In this case the plaintiff sued the defendant company [and recovered in the Mayor's and City of London Court] for the sum of £82 17s. 10d. for twenty-eight weeks' wages and a week's wages in lieu of notice. The basis on which those wages are claimed is that they are due to the plaintiff in respect of a period when he was temporarily sick, but still in the employment of Mac Fisheries, Ltd.

In such a case it is necessary at the outset to determine what are the terms of the contract between this man and his employers. It has been argued that there is a general principle of law that where a man is employed on a weekly service and is not paid in respect of specific work done he is entitled to receive wages during a period of incapacity through illness because of the faithful service which either he has performed or which he would have performed but for his illness. In support of this contention reliance is placed on the recent decision in *Marrison* v. *Bell*, [1939] 2 K.B. 187, citing Lord Cozens-Hardy in *Warburton* v. *Co-operative Wholesale Society, Ltd.*, [1917] 1 K.B. 669. In *Marrison's* case it is stated, in the headnote, that "illness of a servant, which, while it lasts, incapacitates him for the performance of his duties, but is not so long-continued or so serious as to terminate the contract of service, does not at common law suspend his right to wages under the contract." The headnote takes that form because in *Marrison* v. *Bell* there was no question of any specific or implied arrangement concerning sickness. The contract in that case was silent on the point. Nor did the question whether the contract was of that order where the right to wages may depend on the specific work done as affecting rights during sickness arise. As I read *Marrison* v. *Bell*, it was assumed that it was a case of a contract of service without more.

The real contention in *Marrison* v. *Bell* was whether, if during illness the servant receives benefit under the *National Health Insurance Act*, it does or does not deprive him of his right to wages under the contract of service while sick, assuming that he is entitled to them during that period. The error has crept into some people's minds that, apart from this important question of the effect of the *National Health Insurance Act*, *Marrison* v. *Bell* purported to lay down a new principle of law. In my opinion, it does nothing of the kind. Scott L.J., who gave the judgment of the Court, cited *Cuckson* v. *Stones* (1858), 28 L.J.Q.B. 25, and *Warburton*'s case, which deal with unqualified service, but I find nothing in that judgment, which is directed primarily to the question of the effect of the *National Health Insurance Act*, to suggest that it purports to, or does in fact, lay down any new principle of law.

In the present case it is said that the plaintiff's service was of the type contemplated in *Marrison* v. *Bell*—that is an agreement without any special provision as to sickness and that therefore the plaintiff was entitled to wages during temporary incapacity. The case here is not quite so simple. The plaintiff entered into the defendants' employment in 1930, at the wage of £2 15s. a week. Before his employment a notice had been put up by the employers in the place where he worked, and, I suppose, in other places, to this effect: "Camden Town Staff. Allowance during absence due to sickness or accident. Commencing April 24, 1926, the undermentioned allowances will be made when men are absent: 1. During sickness: Half-pay commencing from the first day's absence, up to a total of 21 days per annum. No allowance after." Then follows this rider: "These allowances are purely an 'Act of Grace' on the Company's part, and cannot be claimed as a 'right'. The above applies to men with over six months' service with the Company." Had the evidence been that the plaintiff when he entered into the employment in 1930, knew and acquiesced in these terms, I think there could have been but little doubt that, whatever rights he may have had when no question of any term as to what was to happen when he was ill had been raised, he would have disentitled himself to rely on any such implication, because the notice seems to be inconsistent with a right to receive pay during sickness. True it is that it is stated that the allowances are an act of grace, and cannot be claimed as a right. If the plaintiff had accepted the allowances on that basis, it would be difficult to reconcile that with his having agreed by implication—of course, if there had been an express agreement, it would be quite different—to receive wages during sickness as a right. One asks oneself whether this payment, made under an act of grace, would be set off against the wages, or whether when he was ill, he would be in the fortunate position that he would get his wages and half his wages again in the form of this *ex gratia* payment, or whether he would be only entitled to receive half his wages. I think the implication which one would be entitled to draw would be that the *ex gratia* payment would be in substitution for any right which he might otherwise have. However that may be, Mr. Weitzman is perfectly right in saying that the evidence proves conclusively, or at any rate it satisfied the judge, that the plaintiff never had his attention drawn to the notice at all. He behaved at all times as if he knew of the notice, but it was never brought to his attention, and possibly was not even in existence at the time when he went into the works in 1930 . . .

In my opinion the evidence on this matter being all one way, the plaintiff has, by his own evidence, stated that all he could get, in his opinion, in 1933, in 1936, and in 1938, was half-pay *ex gratia* when he was ill. If he had made an arrangement that when he was ill he was to take half-pay, it seems to me to negative any presumption that he was working on the terms that he was to get wages while he was temporarily sick. By the terms of his contract he disentitled himself to any such right to wages during sickness as he might otherwise possess.

I pass to consider the judgment of the judge. He says this: "Well, if it had been established that the position was that the defendants intended to contract with their employees in this particular part of their premises on those terms"—that is, that they should receive the *ex gratia* payment —"and that that should be a binding contract, I think it might be possible to find that the plaintiff had accepted those terms, and I should have been very glad to have been able to find so . . . But it has not been proved that it was intended by the defendants even to be a term of the contract." But that is to misconceive the position. The plaintiff argues: "I am entitled to these wages by reason of an implied term in my contract that I should be paid during sickness." His evidence is that he got all that he could get, and that gratuitously. He never asked for more. He never thought to ask for more, for all he could hope to get in 1933, in 1936, and in 1938, was an *ex gratia* payment his employers had given him. The fact of its gratuitous nature negatives any legal obligation.

I have come to the conclusion, therefore, that there was no evidence on which the judge could find that a contract had been made between the plaintiff and the defendants to remunerate him so as to entitle him to the wages during sickness.

Consequently this appeal succeeds.

Du Parcq L.J.: I have come to the same conclusion. I have no doubt, now that we have heard the matter fully argued, that the judge's error was a mistake of law. I think he formed a wrong opinion of the result of the decision in *Marrison* v. *Bell*. There is a passage in the judge's judgment where he says this: "What is the position so far? There was a contract of service and it had not been terminated. The result of the decision in *Marrison* v. *Bell* is that unless the defendants can raise something else the plaintiff is entitled to his wages, subject to deduction of what he has already received." The judge appears to have thought that when once a contract of service is proved one must assume, without more, that the workman is entitled to his wages during temporary illness. It is interesting to see that the judge says "subject to deduction of what he has already received," which means, I take it, subject to deduction of certain *ex gratia* payments. I say this parenthetically, because it shows that the judge did not think it possible to say that the plaintiff was entitled to his full wages in addition to the gift, which on one view he has received, of a sum equivalent to half his wages. I thought at one time that Mr. Weitzman plaintiff's counsel was suggesting that the view put forward by his client, or on behalf of his client, and possibly adopted by the judge, was that the plaintiff should get his full wages in addition to those ex gratia payments. The words of the judge which I have quoted enable one to dismiss that from one's mind.

I quite see, looking again at *Marrison* v. *Bell*, and at the case which was there cited of *Warburton* v. *Co-operative Wholesale Society, Ltd.*, that if a reader of the report of *Marrison* v. *Bell* confines his attention to one sentence and reads it divorced from its context, and without relation to the subject-matter, he may come to a wrong conclusion as to what the case decided. It is true that *Marrison* v. *Bell* adopted and approved the observations of Lord Cozens-Hardy in the *Warburton* case, which, when they were spoken by Lord Cozens-Hardy, were, I think, merely dicta and not binding on the Court. It is true, if you look at the single sentence which was cited by Scott L.J.: "It has been long settled that a contract of service is not terminated by incapacity to work by reason of temporary illness, and that on return to work the man can recover his wages during the period of his absence," that in citing it he pointed out, as was perfectly correct, that the words were unlimited and unqualified. It was right to point out in *Marrison* v. *Bell* that no qualification was introduced by Lord Cozens-Hardy, because so far as *Marrison* v. *Bell* was concerned it was material to notice that no such qualification was introduced or suggested as would have prevented those words from applying to the particular facts of that case, and I venture to say with great respect that Lord Cozens-Hardy said nothing inaccurate in that statement if it is read by somebody who does not expect to find in a short sentence a complete statement of the whole law. Lord Cozens-Hardy was stating a general proposition, which I believe to be accurate, and I think it is clearly this: If you have a weekly hiring of a servant without more, and with nothing in the terms of it, whether they are expressed or implied, to suggest that during temporary absence through illness he is not to be paid, then you may assume that he is to be paid, and that it was the intention of the parties that he should be paid. . . .

The first thing to remember is that one must find out what the contract is. It is plain that Lord Cozens-Hardy did not mean that every contract of service, whatever terms were contained in it, must result in a liability to pay a workman during the time that he is ill. The terms in the contract may be express, or they may be implied. You may have a custom. It appears in one of the cases that there is a custom that agricultural labourers are not paid during the time they are off work through illness. It would be idle in such a case to assert that Lord Cozens-Hardy said that under a contract of service the servant must always be paid wages during his absence through illness. Apart from express terms, or terms imported through some well known custom, the terms may obviously be implied in other ways. I do not dwell on that, because in this case, when the whole of the facts are looked at, it seems to me plain—and I think that if the judge had not attached undue importance, as I think he must have done, to the isolated passage from *Marrison* v. *Bell* to which I have referred, he could have come to no other conclusion—that there was here, at the material time in 1938, a contract, one of the terms of which was that during absence through illness the workman was to have no right to any remuneration whatever. It is, in my view, impossible to draw any other conclusion from the facts.

Suppose that in 1938 the plaintiff had not known of the defendants' intention to pay him nothing except an *ex gratia* payment for a portion of his absence through illness, and suppose that, let us say on a Monday, the defendants, being under an obligation to employ him until the end of the week and thereafter unless they give him a week's notice and the week's notice came to an end, had said to him: "We shall not pay you anything if you are away ill." Suppose that at that stage he had said: "I do not agree to that at all and I will not work for you on those terms." If on Tuesday he had fallen ill and had been away for two days I do not think that the defendants would have been entitled to say: "We are going to deduct something from your wages in respect of those two days." They would have been entitled to say: "If you are not prepared to work for us in the future on these terms, we will give you a week's notice," and if the plaintiff had said: "Very well, I agree. I quite understand that if I am ill I shall have no right to remuneration at all," and had gone on working for them, nobody could suggest that because originally, when his employment began, no such term was agreed that term had not become a part of the agreement.

In effect, when one looks at the substance of the matter, that is what happened in this case. If you assume that the plaintiff is a reasonable man—and if I do not assume that I am quite unable to put any construction at all on the conduct of the parties—he knew, as he admits he knew, long before 1938, that if he was away ill he would not be paid a penny as of right. It is not suggested that he thought, when he was paid *ex gratia*, that he was still entitled to wages over and above the *ex gratia* payment. He knew that it was the intention of the firm to pay him nothing whatever as of right if he was ill, and he knew that it was on that footing that the defendants understood that they contracted with him. If one finds that, knowing that, he makes no objection and makes no claim for wages, but goes back to work, and accepts, as he later did, an increase in his wages, it appears to be quite impossible for him to say that he did not agree to work for the defendants on the footing that that was a term of the contract.

It is impossible for us, as it seems to me it would have been impossible for the judge had he correctly applied the law, to come to any other conclusion that that at the material time in 1938 it was as much a term of the contract between the plaintiff and the defendants that he should have no right to remuneration during illness as if that term had been embodied in a written contract, executed in solemn form by both parties.

I want to make it quite clear, in case any words of mine are misunderstood, that I do not rest that in any way upon the doctrine of estoppel. For reasons which I do not think it necessary to go into, I see many reasons against making any use here of the doctrine of estoppel against the plaintiff. I simply say that the facts, proved or admitted, prove beyond doubt that at the material time it was a term of the contract that the plaintiff should not be entitled to any payment during his absence through temporary illness. That does not mean that the employment terminated. It means no more than what I have said, and that is quite enough for the decision of this case. I agree that this appeal should be allowed.

[Atkinson J. also delivered reasons for allowing the appeal.]

O'GRADY *v*. M. SAPER, LTD.

England. Court of Appeal. [1940] 2 K.B. 469

MACKINNON L.J.: . . . In this case the plaintiff was a commissionaire who had been employed by the defendants to attend to a gate at their works. He was engaged in December, 1936, first at a wage of £2 15s a week and then it was raised to £3 a week. He continued in their employment for more than three years. During the time when he was working for them he was away ill for four weeks in 1938, and during his absence he did not receive any wages. Again in 1938, later on, he was away ill for nine weeks and again he was not paid any wages during his absence. In 1939 he was away through illness for two weeks and again he did not receive any wages. He said in his evidence that at these times he never expected to be paid and it never occurred to him that he had any claim for wages whilst he was not working. Then he went on to say: "Till I saw the piece in the paper I neither asked for payment during illness nor expected it." Now the piece in the paper was, one may gather, some journalistic summary of a recent decision in the Court of Appeal in the case of *Marrison* v. *Bell*. [1939] 2 K.B. 187. Unhappily that is one of the cases which, as I think, was unnecessarily reported and, more unhappily, the headnote of the case —which I cannot think can be justified by anything which was decided by the Court—reads thus: "Illness of a servant, which, while it lasts, incapacitates him for the performance of his duties, but is not so long-continued or so serious as to terminate the contract of service, does not at common law suspend his right to wages under the contract." That, in terms, appears to be a statement of a principle of common law, but it is not and cannot be any statement of any principle of the common law. The whole question in such a case as this is: What were the terms of the contract between the employer and the servant and what did those terms provide in regard to payment of wages to him during his absence from the service by reason of illness? It was rightly said in a later case by Atkinson J. *Petrie* v. *Mac Fisheries, Ltd.*, [1940] 1 K.B. 258, "The question must depend, as is indicated in the notes to *Cutter* v. *Powell* (1795), on the terms of the contract. 'The right to wages depends upon whether the consideration therefor has been performed.' It is submitted in the notes to that case, as I think rightly, that it must be ascertained from the contract whether the consideration for the payment of wages is the actual performance of the work, or whether the mere readiness and willingness, if of ability to do so, is the consideration."

Now the sort of contract which is involved is usually concluded orally by people who rarely think out, and still more rarely, express any terms. The whole difficulty in such a case is to ascertain what in truth were the terms of the contract. Where the thing is not expressed it may be that you have to ascertain the terms as a matter of implication, but, in any case, it is a question upon the evidence in the case: What were the terms of the employment? Were they an agreement that the man should be paid when ready and willing to work, or only that he should only be paid when he was actually working? It depends upon the evidence what the terms were. In this case, as it seems to me, there was abundant evidence that the terms, not expressed but no doubt implied, upon which this man was employed were that he should not be paid wages whilst he was sick. The conclusive evidence of that is that on at least three occasions, during the time he had been employed, when he was away sick he was not paid wages, and he acquiesced in that position and, as he said: "Till I saw the piece in the paper I neither asked for payment during illness nor expected it." As was rightly pointed out by Tucker J. during the discussion, if you are to ascertain what the implied terms are you have got to ask yourself: If somebody had raised the question when they were originally making the bargain what would they both have said about it? What in this case they would both have said about it is best proved, and I think is conclusively proved, by what the parties did when the event arose. When the event arose, and he was away ill, and he was not paid, he acquiesced in it, and, as he said, he did not think he ought to have it; he did not expect to get it. I come without hesitation to the conclusion that the terms of the contract between these parties were that he should be paid not during the period when he was ready and willing to work but only during such period as he did work, and I regard it as most unfortunate that the headnote in *Marrison* v. *Bell* should have purported to state as a principle of common law that a man who is incapacitated through illness is entitled to his wages during that illness. What the results may be I do not know, but this case is not at all a bad example of the effect of that unhappy report filtering down through the ordinary newspapers. It may be that county courts are now being deluged with stale claims by workmen for wages during the periods when in the past six years they were away from work through sickness. The result of that it is easy to imagine; subject to the Statute of Limitations an unhealthy workman might now, if there was any such principle of common law, claim for frequent periods of absence through illness during six years, and if that was the rule of common law the employer would have no answer to the claim. Whereas, obviously, if any such claim had been made on the first occasion when he was ill at the beginning of the six years and the man had said: "I ought to be paid although I was away sick," the employer would have said: "Good gracious, if that is your idea of the terms of your engagement it is not mine, and you will take a week's notice to end our contract." The learned judge, misled, as I think, and perhaps very reasonably misled, by the headnote in *Marrison* v. *Bell,* said: "In the absence of evidence as to what were the terms agreed when the man was engaged in 1936 in my view there was no express and no implied term to prevent the normal rule applying." I understand that to mean that he accepted as the normal rule of common law that which is stated in that misleading case. It is nothing of the sort; it is a pure question of fact in every case. In this one I am quite satisfied that the agreement was that he should not be paid during illness and that therefore the claim ought to have been dismissed.

As a result I think the appeal should be allowed and judgment entered for the defendants with costs here and below.

[Luxmoore and Tucker L.JJ., agreed that the appeal be allowed. For a comment on the three preceding cases, see 56 L.Q.R. 161 and 57 L.Q.R. 10.]

RE ALBERTA WHEAT POOL AND LOCAL 333 OF THE INTERNATIONAL UNION OF UNITED BREWERY, FLOUR, CEREAL, SOFT DRINK AND DISTILLERY WORKERS OF AMERICA

British Columbia. Supreme Court. 1962. 35 D.L.R. (2d) 433

LORD J.: This is an application by way of originating notice for an order setting aside a majority award of a Board of Arbitrators. The dispute arose out of the refusal of the employer to pay wages to a monthly rated employee for a period of approximately two months during which time he was absent from work due to temporary illness. He made a claim under the grievance provisions of the collective agreement between his union and the employer company, which claim eventually came before the Board of Arbitrators.

There is no provision in the agreement for paying wages under such circumstances. The Board found that the company had in the past paid certain hourly rated employees a full day's wages although they had not worked a full day. None was for illness. The company had also paid three monthly rated employees for varying terms of absence in 1957 and 1958. One of these was for illness. The company took the position that such payments were made *ex gratia* and in any event the supervisory staff were warned in December, 1960, that no such payments were to be made in the future. It is to be noted that out of all the instances cited, only one was for illness. The Board then described the issue to be determined as follows:

"At this stage the issue may be resolved into the question whether it must be taken to have been the intent of the parties bound by the collective agreement that monthly rated employees be paid during periods of absence for reason of illness so long as the employment relationship prevails."

It is difficult to see how an intent to pay wages during periods of illness can be inferred from only one isolated instance in 1957.

After reciting extracts from such cases as *Orman* v. *Saville Sportswear Ltd.* [1960] 3 All E.R. 105; *Petrie* v. *MacFisheries, Ltd.*, [1939] 4 All E.R. 281, and *Dartmouth Ferry Com'n* v. *Marks* (1903), 34 SC.R 366, and finding that the principles of law stated therein were applicable to the collective agreement, the Board went on to say:

"It now becomes necessary to determine whether there is an express or implied term of the collective agreement that monthly rated employees are not to be paid during periods of absence through illness. The only express provision of the collective agreement dealing with the subject of illness is to be found in Article 4.01, which states in so many words that an employee who is absent during the standard work week because of illness is entitled to premium pay for work performed on the following Saturday."

This statement completely ignores Article 8.05 of the collective agreement which reads as follows:

"8.05 The Company shall make available to each employee who qualifies thereunder a sickness indemnity plan to provide weekly benefits of not less than forty dollars, thirteen weeks duration, commencing on the first day of an accident and on the eighth day of sickness. The Company will bear one-half of the cost of such plan and the remaining one-half will be paid by the employees."

Furthermore, Article 8.04 makes provision for the cost of the M.S.A. plan being borne equally by employer and employee. In my opinion, Article 8.05 is an agreement for payment by the employer of limited benefits during illness. The parties bargained in this manner and I do not see how the cases cited by the Board can be applicable. In *Orman* v. *Saville Sportswear Ltd.*, *supra*, the Board quoted this passage from the judgment of Pilcher J., at p. 113:

". . . when the written contract (of employment) is silent as to payment during absence through sickness, the employer must continue to pay his employee unless he, the employer, can satisfy the court that it is a case in which a term negativing the employee's right to remuneration can properly be implied."

The quotations from the other cases are to the same effect. Here the collective agreement is not silent as to the payment during absence through sickness, but is directly dealt with. It would be inconsistent to find that there is an implied term to pay full wages during absence as well. The implication would be the other way, namely, that absence from illness having been dealt with there would be an implication that no wages were to be paid except as provided for. In the cases relied on by the Board there was no such clause as Article 8.05 and those cases become inapplicable. The headnote in *Lyle* v. *Baynes Manning Ltd.* (1956), 21 W.W.R. 42 reads:

"The court will not hold that a contract contains an implied term unless the implication is clearly necessary to give effect to the intention of the parties as shown by the express terms."

The circumstances of this case, in my opinion, negative any suggestion of an intention of the parties that wages would be paid as found by the Board.

In *Niblett* v. *Midland Ry. Co.* (1907), 96 L.T. 462, there is a passage in the judgment of Phillimore J., at p. 464, which is very much in point in this case:

"Under this provision the man is suspended from his work and from his usual pay, and is given instead sick pay, which is provided partly by the funds contributed by himself and his fellow servants and party by funds contributed by the company. He receives it from the officers of the company, and it might be called sick pay or wages, or partly one and partly the other .... I am of opinion that he is not entitled to recover the sum claimed, and that the decision of the County Court judge was right." ...

In *Absalom, Ltd.* v. *Gt. Western (London) Garden Village Soc.* (1933), 102 L.J.K.B. 648, the authorities are extensively reviewed and Lord Russell of Killowen, at p. 654, refers to the following passage in *A–G. Man.* v. *Kelly*, 62 D.L.R. 370 at p. 386, [1922] 1 A.C. 268 at p. 283:

"Where a question of law has not specifically been referred to an umpire, but is material in the decision of matters which have been referred to him, and he makes a mistake, apparent on the face of the award, an award can be set aside on the ground that it contains an error of law apparent on the face of the award."

In my opinion, the Board has misconstrued the collective agreement, which must be considered as part of the award, by holding that there was no provision other than Article 4.01 relating to illness. This wrongful construction led to a second mistake when they applied certain decisions which were inapplicable. This mistake and misconstruction amount to an error in law on the face of the award, and it must be set aside.

CHAPTER 8

UNEXPECTED CHANGES IN CIRCUMSTANCES

The title for this chapter is intended to encourage an imaginative and creative attitude toward a subject that has been developed rather restrictively and absolutely by English and Canadian courts. The cases in this chapter are usually classified under the label of Impossibility of Performance or Frustration or both. Since it is quite clear that a man may promise the impossible and a court may award damages on his inevitable breach of his promise, impossibility is not always a defence. Moreover, what is legally "impossible" is sometimes capable of performance if, say, the performer goes to inordinate expense. During the Second World War it was commonly said that "the impossible only takes a little longer." The label is therefore a bit misleading. Nor is Frustration an entirely satisfactory single label. On the other hand a study of the House of Lords' decision in the *British Movietonews* case shows the perhaps unduly optimistic use of a more suggestive title.

The cases in the first section are intended to raise the first problem: when ought changed or unforseen circumstances to provide some defence?

The cases in the second section are of course equally useful in discussing this problem, but they are separated in order to stress a rather neglected problem in English and Canadian cases: should the defence operate as an excuse for failure to perform in all circumstances, or should the defaulting party remain liable for some lesser performance if the innocent or aggrieved party should desire it?

The cases in the third section raise the question of compensation for partial benefits conferred and relief for partial losses sustained.

1. RELAXATION OF THE RULE OF ABSOLUTE PROMISES

TAYLOR *v.* CALDWELL
England. Queen's Bench. 1863. 3 B. & S. 826; 122 E.R. 309

BLACKBURN J. delivered the judgment of the Court: In this case the plaintiffs and the defendants had, on the 27th May, 1861, entered into a contract by which the defendants agreed to let the plaintiffs have the use of The Surrey Gardens and Music Hall on four days then to come viz., the 17th June, 15th July, 5th August, and 19th August, for the purpose of giving a series of four grand concerts, and day and night fetes at the Gardens and Hall on those days respectively; and the plaintiffs agreed to take the Gardens and Hall on those days, and pay £100 for each day.

The parties inaccurately called this a "letting" and the money to be paid a "rent"; but the whole agreement is such as to shew that the defendants were to retain the possession of the Hall and Gardens so that there was to be no demise of them, and that the contract was merely to give the plaintiffs the use of them on those days. Nothing however, in our opinion, depends on this. The agreement then proceeds to set out various stipulations between the parties as to what each was to supply for these concerts and entertainments, and as to the manner in which they should be carried on.

The effect of the whole is to shew that the existence of the Music Hall in the Surrey Garden in a state fit for a concert was essential for the fulfilment of the contract,—such entertainments as the parties contemplated in their agreements could not be given without it.

After the making of the agreement, and before the first day on which a concert was to be given, the Hall was destroyed by fire. This destruction, we must take it on the evidence, was without the fault of either party, and was so complete that in consequence the concerts could not be given as intended. And the question we have to decide is whether, under these circumstances, the loss which the plaintiffs have sustained is to fall upon the defendants. The parties when framing their agreement evidently had not present to their minds the possibility of such a disaster, and have made no express stipulation with reference to it, so that the answer to the question must depend upon the general rules of law applicable to such a contract.

There seems no doubt that where there is a positive contract to do a thing, not in itself unlawful, the contractor must perform it or pay damages for not doing it, although in consequence of unforseen accidents the performance of his contract has become unexpectedly burthensome or even impossible. The law is so laid down in 1 Roll. Abr. 450, Condition (G), and in the note (2) to *Walton* (1673), 2 Wms. Saund. 421 a. 6th ed.; 85 E.R. 1234, and is recognised as the general rule by all the judges in the much discussed case of *Hall* v. *Wright* (1859), 120 E.R. 695. But this rule is only applicable when the contract is positive and absolute, and not subject to any condition either express or implied; and there are authorities which, as we think, establish the principle that where, from the nature of the contract, it appears that the parties must from the beginning have known that it could not be fulfilled unless when the time for the fulfilment of the contract arrived some particular specified thing continued to exist, so that, when entering into the contract, they must have contemplated such continuing existence as the foundation of what was to be done; there, in the absence of any express or implied warranty that the thing shall exist, the contract is not to be construed as a positive contract, but as subject to an implied condition that the parties shall be excused in case, before breach, performance becomes impossible from the perishing of the thing without default of the contractor.

There seems little doubt that this implication tends to further the great object of making the legal construction such as to fulfil the intention of those who entered into the contract. For in the course of affairs men in making such contracts in general would, if it were brought to their minds, say that there should be such a condition.

Accordingly, in the Civil law, such an exception is implied [in some obligations]. . . .

Although the Civil law is not of itself authority in an English Court, it affords great assistance in investigating the principles on which the law is grounded. And it seems to us that the common law authorities established that in such a contract the same condition of the continued existence of the thing is implied by English law.

There is a class of contracts in which a person binds himself to do something which requires to be performed by him in person; and such promises, e.g. promises to marry, or promises to serve for a certain time, are never in practice qualified by an express exception of the death of the party; and therefore in such cases the contract is in terms broken if the promisor dies before fulfilment. Yet it was very early determined that, if the performance is personal, the executors are not liable; *Hyde* v. *The Dean of Windsor* (1597), Cro. Eliz. 552; 78 E.R. 798. See 2 *Wms. Exors.* 1560, 5th ed. where a very apt illustration is given. "Thus," says the learned author, "if an author undertakes to compose a work, and dies before completing it, his executors are discharged from this contract: for the undertaking is merely personal in its nature, and, by the intervention of the contractor's death, has become impossible to be performed." For this he cites a dictum of Lord Lyndhurst in *Marshall* v. *Broadhurst* 1 Tyr. 348, 349, and a case mentioned by Patteson J. in *Wenworth* v. *Cock* (1839), 10 A. & E. 42; 113 E.R. 17 at p. 18. In *Hall* v. *Wright*, Crompton J., in his judgment, puts another case. "Where a contract depends upon personal skill, and the act of God renders it impossible, as, for instance, in the case of a painter employed to paint a picture who is struck blind, it may be that the performance might be excused."

It seems that in those cases the only ground on which the parties or their executors can be excused from the consequences of the breach of the contract is, that from the nature of the contract there is an implied condition of the continued existence of the life of the contractor, and, perhaps, in the case of the painter of his eyesight. In the instances just given, the person, the continued existence of whose life is necessary to the fulfilment of the contract, is himself the contractor, but that does not seem in itself to be necessary to the application of the principle; as is illustrated by the following example. In the ordinary form of an apprentice deed the apprentice binds himself in unqualified terms to "serve until the full end and term of seven years to be fully complete and ended," during which term it is covenanted that the apprentice his master "faithfully shall serve," and the father of the apprentice in equally unqualified terms binds himself for the performance by the apprentice of all and every covenant on his part. (See the form, 2 Chitty on Pleading, 370, 7th ed. by Greening.) It is undeniable that if the apprentice dies within the seven years, the covenant of the father that he shall perform his covenant to serve for seven years is not fulfilled, yet surely it cannot be that an action would lie against the father? Yet the only reason why it would not is that he is excused because of the apprentice's death.

These are instances where the implied condition is of the life of a human being, but there are others in which the same implication is made as to the continued existence of a thing. For example, where a contract of sale is made amounting to a bargain and sale, transferring presently the property in specific chattels, which are to be delivered by the vendor at a future day; there, if the chattels, without the fault of the vendor, perish in the interval, the purchaser must pay the price and the vendor is excused from performing his contract to deliver, which has thus become impossible.

That this is the rule of the English law is established by the case of *Rugg* v. *Minett* (1809), 11 East, 210; 103 E.R. 985, where the article that perished before delivery was turpentine, and it was decided that the vendor was bound to refund the price of all those lots in which the property had not passed; but was entitled to retain without deduction the price of those lots in which the property had passed, though they were not delivered, and though in the conditions of sale, which are set out in the report, there was no express qualification of the promise to deliver on payment. It seems in that case rather to have been taken for granted than decided that the destruction of the thing sold before delivery excused the vendor from fulfilling his contract to deliver on payment.

This also is the rule in the Civil law, and it is worth noticing that Pothier, in his celebrated *Traite du Contrat de Vente* (see Part 4, 307, &c; and Part 2, Ch. 1, sect. 1, art. 4, 1), treats this as merely an example of the more general rule that every obligation *de certo corpore* is extinguished when the thing ceases to exist. See *Blackburn on the Contract of Sale*, 173.

The same principle seems to be involved in the decision of *Sparrow* v. *Sowgate* (1625), W. Jones, 29; 82 E.R. 16, where, to an action of debt on an obligation by bail, conditioned for the payment of the debt or the render of the debtor, it was held a good plea that before any default in rendering him the principal debtor died. It is true that was the case of a bond with a condition, and a distinction is sometimes made in this respect between a condition and a contract. But this observation does not apply to *Williams* v. *Lloyd* (1629), W. Jones, 179, 82 E.R. 95. In that case the count, which was in assumpsit, alleged that the plaintiff had delivered a horse to the defendant, who promised to redeliver it on request. Breach, that though requested to redeliver the horse he refused. Plea, that the horse was sick and died, and the plaintiff made the request after its death; and on demurrer it was held a good plea, as the bailee was discharged from his promise by the death of the horse without default or negligence on the part of the defendant. "Let it be admitted," say the Court, "that he promised to deliver it on request, if the horse die before, that is become impossible by the act of God, so the party shall be discharged, as much as if an obligation were made conditioned to deliver the horse on request, and he died before it." And Jones, adds the report, cited 22 Ass. 41, in which it was held that a ferryman who had promised to carry a horse safe across the ferry was held chargeable for the drowning of the animal, only because he had overloaded the boat, and it was agreed that notwithstanding the promise no action would have lain had there been no neglect or default on his part.

It may, we think, be safely asserted to be now English law, that in all contracts of loan of chattels or bailments, if the performance of the promise of the borrower or bailee to return the things lent or bailed becomes impossible because it has perished, this impossibility (if not arising from the fault of the borrower or bailee from some risk which he has taken upon himself) excuses the borrower or bailee from the performance of his promise to redeliver the chattel.

The great case of *Coggs* v. *Bernard* (1703), 1 Smith's L.C. 171, 5th ed., 2 L. Raym. 909; 92 E.R. 107, is now the leading case on the law of bailments, and Lord Holt, in that case, referred so much to the Civil law that it might perhaps be thought that this principle was there derived direct from the civilians, and was not generally applicable in English law except in the case of bailments; but the case of *Williams* v. *Lloyd*, above cited, shews that the same law had been already adopted by the English law as early as *The Book of Assizes*. The principle seems to us to be that, in contract in which the performance depends on the continued existence of a given person or thing, a condition is implied that the impossibility of performance arising from the perishing of the person or thing shall excuse the performance.

In none of these cases is the promise in words other than positive, nor is there any express stipulation that the destruction of the person or thing shall excuse the performance; but that excuse is by law implied, because from the nature of the contract it is apparent that the parties contracted on the basis of the continued existence of the particular person or chattel. In the present case, looking at the whole contract, we find that the parties contracted on the basis of the continued existence of the Music Hall at the time when the concerts were to be given; that being essential to their performance.

We think, therefore, that the Music Hall having ceased to exist, without fault of either party, both parties are excused, the plaintiffs from taking the Gardens and paying the money, the defendants from performing their promise to give the use of the Hall and Gardens and other things. Consequently the rule must be absolute to enter the verdict for the defendants.

QUESTIONS. Why is it necessary to imply a condition to excuse the plaintiff? Is that part of the decision an *obiter dictum*? Has the plaintiff not suffered a "total failure of consideration"?

NOTE. Is the condition one implied from the facts or one implied by law? From the vantage point of having read the cases in Chapter 7, do you think it is possible to draw any sharp distinction between a condition implied in fact and one implied in law? Do you think any useful purpose is served by drawing the distinction anyway? If the condition must be implied from the facts, how would you deal with a judge who adopted an attitude like that of Lord Wright in *Vandepitte's* case?

Perhaps the greatest insight into the problem may be had from a study of Fuller, *Basic Contract Law*, pp. 666–70. Professor Fuller develops the notion of "tacit assumptions." He says, in part:

"In *Taylor* v. *Caldwell* the court says that when framing their agreement the parties 'had not present to their minds the possibility' of a disaster affecting the Music Hall, and concludes that the parties 'must have contemplated' the 'continuing existence' of the Hall 'as the foundation' of their agreement.

"Is there a contradiction here? The court seems to say that the parties did not think of the possibility of the Hall's burning and therefore assumed it would not burn. But how can the parties assume that no fire will occur, when the possibility of a fire was never present to their minds? If this possibility was not present to their minds, would it not be more accurate to say that they assumed nothing about a fire, either that it would or would not occur?

"The difficulty here does not lie in any dispute about psychological fact, but in the inappropriateness of the language ordinarily used to describe certain elementary psychological truths. Words like 'intention,' 'assumption,' 'expectation' and 'understanding' all seem to imply a *conscious* state involving an awareness of alternatives and a deliberate choice among them. It is, however, plain that there is a psychological state which can be described as 'tacit assumption' that does not involve a consciousness of alternatives. The absent-minded professor stepping from his office into the hall as he reads a book 'assumes' that the floor of the hall will be there to receive him. His conduct is conditioned and directed by this assumption, even though the possibility that the floor has been removed does not 'occur' to him, that is, is not present in his conscious mental processes.

". . . Underlying questions of this sort, and indeed, underlying much of contract law generally, are certain basic problems of psychology that have never been satisfactorily solved. We speak constantly of things that were 'intended' or 'assumed' without having a clear conception of the psychological processes involved in 'intending' and 'assuming.' The lawyer or judge who turns to psychology for help in dealing with these problems is likely to be disappointed.

". . . In spite of hopeful beginnings promising a more comprehensive psychological treatment of human behaviour, for the time being the only methods available for dealing with problems like that raised by *Taylor* v. *Caldwell* are essentially those resting on intuition and introspection. We 'just know' that the burning of a music hall violates a tacit assumption of the parties who executed a contract for hiring it; we 'just know' that a two per cent increase in the price of beans does not violate a tacit assumption underlying a contract to deliver a ton of beans for a fixed price. . . ."

PARADINE *v.* JANE

England. King's Bench. 1647. Aleyn 26; 82 E.R. 897

In debt the plaintiff declares upon a lease for years rendering rent at the four usual feasts; and for rent behind for three years, ending at the Feast of the Annunciation, 21 Car. brings his action; the defendant pleads, that a certain German prince, by name Prince Rupert, an alien born, enemy to the King and kingdom, had invaded the realm with an hostile army of men; and with the same force did enter upon the defendant's possession, and him expelled, and held out of possession from the 19th of July 18 Car. till the Feast of Annunciation, 21 Car. whereby he could not take the profits; whereupon the plaintiff demurred, and the plea was resolved insufficient. . . .

It was resolved, that the matter of the plea was insufficient; for though the whole army had been alien enemies, yet he ought to pay his rent. And this difference was taken, that where the law creates a duty or charge, and the party is disabled to perform it without any default in him, and hath no remedy over, then the law will excuse him. As in the case of waste, if a house be destroyed by tempest, or by enemies, the lessee is excused. Dyer, 33.a. Inst. 53. d. 283 c. 12 H.4.6. so of an escape. Co. 4.84.b. 33 H. 6.1. So in 9 E.3.16, a *supersedeas* was awarded to the justices, that they should not proceed in a *cessavit* upon a cesser during the war, but when the party by his own contract creates a duty or charge upon himself, he is bound to make it good, if he may, notwithstanding any accident by inevitable necessity, because he might have provided against it by his contract. And therefore if the lessee covenant to repair a house, though it be burnt by lightning, or thrown down by enemies, yet he ought to repair it. Dyer 33.3; 40 E. III.6.h. Now the rent is a duty created by the parties upon the reservation, and had there been a covenant to pay it, there had been no question but the lessee must have made it good, notwithstanding the interruption by enemies, for the law would not protect him beyond his own agreement, no more than in the case of reparations; this reservation then being a covenant in law, and whereupon an action of covenant hath been maintained (as Roll said) it is all one as if there had been an actual covenant. Another reason was added, that as the lessee is to have the advantage of casual profits so he must run the hazard of casual losses, and not lay the whole burthen of them upon his lessor; and Dyer 56.6. was cited for this purpose, that though the land be surrounded, or gained by the sea, or made barren by wildfire, yet the lessor shall have his whole rent: and judgment was given for the plaintiff.

CRICKLEWOOD PROPERTY AND INVESTMENT TRUST, LTD. *v.* LEIGHTON'S INVESTMENT TRUST, LTD.

England. House of Lords. [1945] A.C. 221

The facts, stated by Viscount Simon L.C. and Lord Wright, were as follows: By a lease dated May 12, 1936, the predecessors in title of the respondents demised certain land at Potters Bar to the appellant company for a term of ninety-nine years from March 25, 1936, and the other two appellants joined in the lease as guarantors for the payment of the rent and performance of the covenants. The lessors were developing a building estate for residential purposes and the lease in question was a building lease under which the appellants were to build a number of shops to form what is commonly called a shopping centre for the residents on the estate. The subject of the demise was two parcels of land adjoining the residential area, one coloured red and the other blue on the plan attached to the lease. A question had previously arisen between the lessors and the local authority under a town planning scheme for the area and there had been an appeal to the Minister. This appeal was compromised on terms which were scheduled to the lease and which in effect provided that not more than twenty-four shops in all should be built on these two parcels of land; that eight might be built at once, and, in addition, that not less than four shops to each two hundred houses occupied should be permitted to be built in the future till the total of twenty-four was reached.

The rent reserved by clause 1 was the aggregate of the following rents, (a) as to each of the ten shop sites on the red land a peppercorn for the first year and thereafter a yearly rent of £35 for each site, and (b) as to each of the fourteen shop sites on the blue land a peppercorn till the expiration of one year from notification by the landlords that erection of a shop thereon might proceed and thereafter a yearly rent of £35 for each site in respect of which such notification had been given. This notification that building might proceed was rendered necessary because of the compromise referred to above.

Clause 2 of the lease contained covenants by the appellant company to pay the rent and outgoings and to build twenty-four shops on the demised land, ten on the red and fourteen on the blue, the first eight were to be built on the red land, not later than March 25, 1937; the remainder were to be built within one year from the notification by the landlords that building might proceed, but in certain circumstances, which need not be set out in detail, an "abeyance period," as it was called, might arise which would have the effect of postponing the obligation to build beyond the year. It was, however, expressly provided that nothing in the clause which provided for this abeyance period should "in any way affect the rent or rents payable in respect of the demised property or any part thereof or the time or manner of such payment."

The lease, by clause 3, gave the appellant company the option to purchase the freehold of the demised property, both the red and blue sites. (This option was exercised as regarded the red sites and accordingly no question arose in connection with them or with the shops built on them.)

By clause 4, a right of re-entry for non-payment of rent or breach of covenant was reserved, but it was provided by clause 5, that after any of the shops had been assigned or underlet this right should only be exercisable upon the particular shop in respect of which the breach had occurred, the intention being that each should be held separately and independently of the others. There was also a provision in clause 6 of the lease enabling the appellant company, at the expiration of seven years from the date of the agreement, to give notice to determine the lease as to any of the sites in respect of which notice that building might proceed had not been given.

As regarded the blue land, no shops had been erected when notice that building might proceed was given as to two sites on September 24, 1937. Further notices were given on May 30, 1938, and August 25, 1939, in each case as to four sites. No building was begun on any of these ten sites. On May 17, 1938, the original lessors conveyed the land subject to and with the benefit of the lease to the respondents, and as the appellant company paid no rent after the outbreak of war, the respondents issued a writ dated April 8, 1942, against the appellant company as tenants and against the other two appellants as guarantors, claiming arrears of rent since September, 1939, this being the only claim in the action. The shop sites in respect of which rent was claimed were six in the earlier period till September 30, 1940, and ten in the later period till March 25, 1942, all of them forming part of the fourteen sites included in the land marked blue on the plan. If the appellants were liable for any rent, there was no dispute that the amount due in the action was £419 14s. 3d. The writ was specially endorsed under Or. 14, and the respondents applied for summary judgment. The appellants filed an affidavit by way of defence, para. 6 of which was in the following terms: "No obligation on the part of the [appellant] company to erect shops upon any of these fourteen sites arose until after the outbreak of the present war. By reason of the outbreak of the war the demand for these shops ceased, finance for their erection became unobtainable, and the restrictions placed by the Government upon building and materials therefore made it impossible to erect shops upon any of these sites or to continue the development of the same." The appellants in para. 7 of their affidavit went on to submit that in consequence of the facts so alleged the agreements as to the fourteen sites were frustrated and the appellents were under no liability thereunder. On this affidavit the master gave leave to defend and on appeal to the judge in chambers the respondents declared that they did not dispute the allegations in para. 6. Thereupon the judge gave the appellants liberty to defend on these allegations of fact and no others, the admission being embodied in his order. He made the usual order for trial in the short cause list; the affidavit was treated as a pleading and no further defence was ordered. Asquith J., who tried the case, rejected the appellants' defence and gave judgment for the respondents. He said that the sole issue before him was whether the doctrine of frustration applied to a building lease such as that involved in the case. He held that it did not, though if it did he would have held that the contract had been discharged. However, he thought, there was clear authority that the doctrine of frustration cannot be applied to a demise of real property. The Court of Appeal affirmed his judgment on the ground that the doctrine of frustration could not be applied to a lease of real estate. The appellants appealed to the House of Lords.

VISCOUNT SIMON L.C.: My Lords, before this House, and apparently in both courts below, the appellants did not attempt to rely on the fact that the demand for shops had ceased, or on their inability to procure finance, as establishing a defence. They relied entirely on the impossibility of building created by the restrictions imposed on work of this character and on the acquisition of materials. Though these restrictions were not particularized it must be taken that they were imposed by valid orders or prohibitions under the Defence Regulations, and while it would have been more satisfactory if the documents relied on had been set out or referred to, the case has proceeded (as must this appeal) on the footing that the performance of the covenant to build was impossible, and continues to be so while the orders or prohibitions are in force. Asquith J., who tried the case, held on the authorities that the doctrine of frustration did not apply to a lease at all, and that for this purpose there was no distinction between a building lease and any other lease, though he said that had the doctrine applied he would have decided that the contract had been discharged. The Court of Appeal, in a judgment delivered by MacKinnon L.J., said [1943] K.B. 493, 496, that the doctrine had never been applied to a demise of real property and that there was clear authority that it cannot be. "It is impossible for the defendants to rely on the doctrine of frustration to relieve them from their obligations as tenants under a demise of land for ninety-nine years." Against that judgment the tenants appeal to this House. Two questions are raised by the appeal: first, can the doctrine of frustration apply to determine a lease? and, secondly, even if it can, are the circumstances in the present case such as to produce the result that the lease has been determined by frustration? If, my Lords, we all agree (as I understand we do) that the answer to the second question is in the negative, it is not essential in the present case to reach a conclusion on the first question (as to which I gather that our opinions are divided). Nevertheless, I propose to express my opinion with regard to both questions, since the more general issue has been much discussed and was pronounced on in the courts below, where it was regarded as concluded by authority, including the authority of this House, in *Matthey* v. *Curling* [1922] 2 A.C. 180.

The broad issue must first be considered as though it were *res integra*: then I propose to consider the effect of previous decisions. Frustration may be defined as the premature determination of an agreement between parties, lawfully entered into and in course of operation at the time of its premature determination, owing to the occurrence of an intervening event or change of circumstances so fundamental as to be regarded by the law both as striking at the root of the agreement, and as entirely beyond what was contemplated by the parties when they entered into the agreement. If, therefore, the intervening circumstance is one which the law would not regard as so fundamental as to destroy the basis of the agreement, there is no frustration. Equally, if the terms of the agreement show that the parties contemplated the possibility of such an intervening circumstance arising, frustration does not occur. Neither, of course, does it arise where one of the parties had deliberately brought about the supervening event by his own choice. (See the cases collected in *Joseph Constantine Steamship Line, Ltd.* v. *Imperial Smelting Corporation, Ltd.*, [1942] A.C. 154). But where it does arise, frustration operates to bring the agreement to an end as regards both parties forthwith and quite apart from their volition. Is there any good reason why this conception of frustration should not ever apply to a lease of land and result in its premature determination? I do not feel able to assert any a priori or absolute impossibility, though the instances in which the doctrine might apply to such a lease are undoubtedly very rare.

A lease of land creates in the lessee an estate, which is a chattel interest. (*Law of Property Act, 1925*, s. 1, sub-s. 1(b).) Such an estate, by the nature of the case, lasts at most for the term stipulated and may come to an end sooner. In normal circumstances, the estate continues to exist for the period of the agreed term—in the present instance, for ninety-nine years from March 25, 1936—but it is liable to be determined by the landlord's re-entry for non-payment of rent or for breach of covenant. This is expressly provided for by clause 4 of the present lease. The question therefore is whether, in addition to pre-determination under such express provisions it is possible that a lease for years should pre-determine from a supervening cause which amounts to frustration. If so, the term ends, no further rent is payable, and the lessor recovers the property with all permanent structures erected upon it, at once.

It is said that this cannot be so, because a lease is more than a contract and amounts to an estate: but this reasoning seems to me to be dangerously near to arguing in a circle; if we assume that frustration can only arise in cases where there is a contract and nothing else, the conclusion of course follows that frustration cannot arise in the case of a lease. Where the lease is a simple lease for years at a rent, and the tenant, on condition that the rent is paid, is free during the term to use the land as he likes, it is very difficult to imagine an event which could prematurely determine the lease by frustration—though I am not prepared to deny the possibility, if, for example, some vast convulsion of nature swallowed up the property altogether, or buried it in the depths of the sea. The lease, it is true, is of the "site," but it seems to be not inconceivable that, within the meaning of the document the "site" might cease to exist. If, however, the lease is expressed to be for the purpose of building, or the like, and if the lessee is bound to the lessor to use the land for such purpose with the result that at the end of the term the lessor would acquire the benefit of this development, I find it less difficult to imagine how frustration might arise. Suppose, for example, that legislation were subsequently passed which permanently prohibited private building in the area or dedicated it as an open space for ever, why should this not bring to an end the currency of a building lease, the object of which is to provide for the erection on the area, for the combined advantage of the lessee and lessor, of buildings which it would not be unlawful to construct? It is no answer to say that it may be presumed that the legislature would make express provision, by compensation clauses or otherwise, to deal with such a case: we are entitled to test the applicability of the doctrine by assuming supervening illegality, without any qualification.

Neither, I think, is the theoretic possibility of frustration got rid of by stressing the complications that might in some cases arise between the parties if the relation of lessor and lessee is prematurely terminated for all purposes by such a cause. In the case of pure contract also, the situation resulting from frustration has raised questions of difficulty which, after forty years of doubt, were only settled by the decision of this House in *Fibrosa Spolka Akcyjna* v. *Fairbairn Lawson Combe Barbour, Ltd.* [1943] A.C. 32, and even then it was considered just and necessary to modify the common law consequences by a subsequent Act of Parliament, the *Law Reform (Frustrated Contracts) Act, 1943*, 6 & 7 Geo. 6, c. 40.

I now turn to the cases. A careful examination of the decided cases to which the Court of Appeal refers satisfies me that it is erroneous to suppose that there is authority binding on this House to the effect that a lease cannot in any circumstances be ended by frustration. In *Matthey* v. *Curling*, the House did not say so: the decision there was that requisitioning by the Government was no answer to a claim on the covenant for rent, any more than ouster by a trespasser would be: the remedy of the tenant was against the Government for compensation. Equally, destruction by fire, after the Government had requisitioned the place, left the tenant still liable on his covenant to deliver up in proper condition, for the tenant could have covered the risk by insurance. Thus, on the true construction of the document, the two covenants still bound the tenant. It seems clear that, if the actual decision in *Matthey* v. *Curling* is as above set out, the Court of Appeal was mistaken in treating it as "clear authority" that the doctrine of frustration "cannot" be applied to a demise of real property. It is noteworthy that when *Matthey* v. *Curling* was before the Court of Appeal, Atkin L.J., in his dissenting judgment, observed: "It does not appear to me conclusive against the application to a lease of the doctrine of frustration that the lease, in addition to containing contractual terms, grants a term of years. Seeing that the instrument as a rule expressly provides for the lease being determined, at the option of the lessor, upon the happening of certain specified events, I see no logical absurdity in implying a term that it shall be determined absolutely on the happening of other events—namely, those which in an ordinary contract work a frustration." This passage exactly expresses my view. I may further point out that in *Taylor* v. *Caldwell* [1863], 122 E.R. 309, when the question was raised whether the hall which was burnt down was demised to the defendant or not, Blackburn J. said: "Nothing however, in our opinion, depends on this. . . ."

So much for the abstract and theoretical question. But there remains the practical issue whether what is proved to have happened in the present case could be enough to constitute frustration of such a lease. I do not agree with Asquith J. that the orders requiring a suspension of building are sufficient to strike at the root of the arrangement. The lease at the time had more than ninety years to run, and though we do not know how long the present war, and the emergency regulations which have been made necessary by it, are going to last, the length of the interruption so caused is presumably a small fraction of the whole term. Frustration, where it exists, does not work suspension but brings the whole arrangement to an inevitable end forthwith. Here, the lease itself contemplates that rent may be payable although no building is going on, and I cannot regard the interruption which has arisen as such as to destroy the identity of the arrangement or make it unreasonable to carry out the lease according to its terms as soon as the interruption in building is over: this is the nature of the test for frustration suggested in the well-known case of *Metropolitan Water Board* v. *Dick Kerr & Co. Ltd.*, [1918] A.C. 119. I therefore conclude, on the facts, that the liability for rent under the covenant continued uninterrupted, and I move your Lordships to dismiss the appeal with costs.

LORD RUSSELL OF KILLOWEN: . . . My Lords, I share the opinion, which all your Lordships entertain, that no question as to what is called frustration can arise on the facts of the present case. . . .

On the broader question I confess that I am unable to grasp how the doctrine of frustration can ever apply so as to put an end to a lease and the respective liabilities of landlord and tenant thereunder. A lease is much more than a contract. It creates and vests in the lessee an estate or interest in the land, a chattel interest, it is true, but a vested estate or interest none the less. As was said by Lush J. in *London & Northern Estates Co.* v.

Schlesinger [1916] 1 K.B. 20, 24., "It is not correct to speak of this tenancy agreement as a contract and nothing more. A term of years was created by it and vested in the appellant, and I can see no reason for saying that because this order disqualified him from personally residing in the flat, it affected the chattel interest which was vested in him by virtue of the agreement. In my opinion it continues vested in him still." That dictum of Lush J. was approved in *Whitehall Court, Ltd.* v. *Ettlinger* [1920] 1 K.B. 680, 686, 687, a case which itself was approved by Lord Atkinson in your Lordships' House without any dissent from his colleagues in the case of *Matthey* v. *Curling*. When a contract is frustrated it is because what is called the "venture" or "undertaking" in which the parties have contracted to engage can no longer be carried out. The court in such circumstances declares the contract to be, or treats it as being, no longer binding on the parties. That is an end of the matter. But when a lease is in question, and has been granted by one another, it is the lease which is the "venture" or "undertaking" upon which the parties have embarked. The contractual obligations thereunder of each party are merely obligations which are incidental to the relationship of landlord and tenant created by the demise, and which necessarily vary with the character and duration of the particular lease. It may well be that circumstances may arise during the currency of the term which render it difficult, or even impossible, for one party or the other to carry out some of its obligations as landlord or tenant, circumstances which might afford a defence to a claim for damages for their breach, but the lease would remain. The estate in the land would still be vested in the tenant. I know of no power in the court to declare a lease to be at an end except upon findings that some event has occurred on the happening of which the lease terminates by reason of some express provision contained in the document. In such a case the term ends not because the court exercises a power to terminate it, but because in the events which have happened the lease operated only as a demise for the shorter period. Nor do I know of any power in the court to order a tenant (who, be it observed, might have sublet part by way of mortgage or otherwise) to surrender his term to the landlord. The lease must of necessity continue. Some of the obligations thereunder may from time to time, from various circumstances, become difficult or impossible of performance by one or other of the parties; but, in my opinion, it cannot have applied to it the doctrine of frustration. The rent will continue to be payable in accordance with the terms of the document.

Since preparing my opinion in this case I have had an opportunity of perusing a print of the remarks which my noble and learned friend Lord Wright proposes to address to your Lordships and of considering the numerous references therein to a series of authorities cited by him. I wish to guard against it being said that your Lordships are in agreement with all my noble friend's statements. For myself I disagree with many of them: in particular I disagree with the view in relation to a lease of land, which is expressed in the following terms: "If the contract is avoided or dissolved, as it may be by either party, under the express terms of the lease, the estate in land falls with it." If by these words my noble friend only wishes to record the proposition that the exercise of a power to determine a lease will put an end to the lessee's estate in the land, well and good; but if he means that the estate in land necessarily comes to an end with cesser of contractual liability, I disagree. A lease may come to an end, and with it the estate in the land and all contractual liability by virtue of some provision in the lease, or by reason of some defect in the title of the person who purported to grant it. But, in my opinion, the cesser or suspension of some contractual liability under the lease will not destroy the estate in land which is vested in the lessee, unless the lease provides that in that event the term of years shall cease. Further I disagree with the view that there is anything in Lord Buckmaster's judgment in the case of *Matthey* v. *Curling* or in the cases of *Brewster* v. *Kitchell* (1698), 1 Salk. 198, or *Bailey* v. *de Crespigny* (1869), L.R. 4 Q.B. 180, inconsistent with the view that the doctrine of frustration cannot apply to a lease of land, or favouring the view that it may so apply. I concur in the motion proposed.

[On the question of the application of the frustration doctrine to a lease, Lord Wright, whose opinion is omitted, agreed with Viscount Simon L.C. Lord Goddard delivered a judgment (also omitted) agreeing on this question with Lord Russell of Killowen. Lord Porter reserved the point in his decision.]

MERKUR *v.* H. SHOOM & CO. LTD.

Ontario. Court of Appeal [1954] 1 D.L.R. 85

PICKUP C.J.O. orally delivered the judgment of the Court: . . . The action was to recover the sum of $900, being the balance alleged to be owing on a cheque given by the defendant to the plaintiff, payment of which was stopped. The cheque was given in payment of rental under a lease, or what is said to be a lease. The document is in writing and dated April 20, 1951, and by it the defendant purports to rent from the plaintiff from about the first week in May to about the first week in October, 1952, "summer market space; same stall occupied in previous seasons on Esplanade St. East of Scott St., at a rental consideration for the entire period paid in advance . . . prior to occupancy."

The defence raised by the pleadings was that the lease was made upon the express condition and waranty that the building owned by the plaintiff, of which the premises leased to the defendant formed a part, would be occupied for the season in question by dealers in fruit and produce as a summer market. There is nothing to that effect stated in the lease. The defendant also pleads that the plaintiff represented and warranted to the defendant that the remainder of the stalls in the summer market had been leased to certain specific fruit and produce merchants, from whom the plaintiff had received payment of rent, and the defendant claims to have relied, in giving the cheque in question, upon such representation and warranty.

The learned trial Judge found against the defendant on the issue of misrepresentation. He found that although the plaintiff did indicate to the defendant that seven wholesalers would move in, and they did move in, the plaintiff at no time represented that they would remain there for the duration of the summer market.

After the defendant went into possession there was a fire in adjoining premises—not the premises of the plaintiff. As a result of that fire the plaintiff's tenants moved out from the plaintiff's premises which had been used as a summer market for years.

The learned judge permitted an amendment at the trial so that the defendant might raise a plea of frustration and after permitting that defence to be raised the learned trial Judge held that in the circumstances of this case the doctrine of frustration applied. He found that it was in the contemplation of both parties that the particular stall leased by the defendant was to be part of a summer market and that if anything occurred which defeated the object of the lease the doctrine of frustration came into play. In our opinion the doctrine of frustration does not apply in this case. It is not enough that the parties should have had in contemplation that the defendant and the plaintiff's other tenants would use the premises as a summer market. So far as the plaintiff was concerned there was nothing to prevent the tenants using their several stalls which they had rented from the plaintiff as a summer market. The subject-matter of the contract never ceased to exist. The learned trial Judge found against any warranty or agreement as to the existence of a summer market or the continuance of one. If the defendant company intended the contract to be dependent upon other tenants or producers being there or in the vicinity, so as to create a summer market, it should have so provided in the contract.

Many cases were cited to us, but we do not think we need discuss them. The weight of judicial authority is that the doctrine of frustration does not apply to leases, particularly where the subject-matter of the lease was in existence at the time the lease was entered into, and the tenant entered into possession thereof.

Counsel for the respondent argues, however, that this was not a lease at all but merely a license for a particular purpose, which failed. We think it was a lease, not only in form, but in fact, and in any event the subject-matter of the contract continued, the subject-matter being the right of occupancy of certain premises during certain periods.

The result is that the appeal must be allowed and judgment will be entered in favour of the plaintiff for the sum of $900 as claimed, with interest at 5% per annum from May 14, 1952, and costs of the action and of the appeal.

BRECKNOCK AND ABERGAVENNY CANAL NAVIGATION *v.* PRITCHARD

England (Wales). King's Bench. 1796. 6 T.R. 750; 101 E.R. 807

This was an action of covenant on articles of agreement, dated the 6th of August, 1793, in which the defendants covenanted to erect and finish in a substantial and workmanlike manner a bridge across the river Usk in the county of Brecknock on or before the 10th of December then next, and to uphold and keep it in complete repair for seven years; the declaration stated that though the defendants did build and finish the bridge they had not upheld and kept it in complete repair, &c., for that on the 10th of February, 1795, it was washed broken and fell down, and that the defendants had not upheld and rebuild it, &c.

To this the defendants pleaded that until and at the time when the same was so washed broken and fell down as mentioned in the declaration, the bridge was well built and in complete repair, and capable of resisting any usual or ordinary flood, &c.; and that then the said bridge by the act of God by a great unusual and extraordinary flood of water, such as such bridge so well built and in complete repair could not reasonably be expected to resist, by means of the waters of the said flood rushing and pressing against the same was without the default of the defendants, or its being in their power to prevent, washed broken and fell down, &c. The plaintiffs demurred to this plea.

Wood in support of the demurrer. . . . And here a loss by a flood must have been the very loss in the contemplation of the parties.

Praed contrà. Although a loss by a common flood was probably in the contemplation of the parties, they did not look forward to the extraordinary flood which is alleged in the plea as the occasion of this loss, nor was it in their contemplation to become insurers. They covenanted to build a bridge in a substantial manner and to keep it in repair for a certain term. Now it is admitted on the record that the bridge was built in a substantial manner, and was in complete repair and capable of resisting any ordinary flood at the time when the accident happened; but under this covenant the defendants are not answerable for losses occasioned by extraordinary floods. Even in cases of covenant, as well as in cases of legal obligation on the parties, impossibility will discharge the party from the performance of his contract. . . .

Lord Kenyon C.J.: It has been usual for many years past to insert covenants of this kind in contracts for building bridges; and though accidents like the present have frequently happened, this defence is now for the first time made. A similar accident happened some years ago to a bridge in Northumberland, but it did not occur either to the parties, or their counsel in law or equity, for the cause was in both Courts, to set up this defence. This sort of loss must have been in the contemplation of all the parties in this case; the bridge was to be built in such a manner as to resist any body of water. The principle stated by the counsel for the plaintiffs is the true one: if the defendants had chosen to except any loss of any kind, it should have been introduced into the contract by way of exception. It is sufficient to say here that the contract of the defendants extends to this case, that they have not fulfilled it, and therefore that they are answerable.

QUESTIONS. Does *Taylor* v. *Caldwell* overrule this case? Is a bridge builder to be taken to guarantee his bridge against a flood no bridge builder could have met in the existing state of engineering knowledge and at whatever cost?

SMITH *v.* DAWSON. 1923. 53 O.L.R. 615 (Ontario. Court of Appeal). Middleton J.: "The plaintiffs undertook to build the house for the contract price and to hand it over complete to the defendant. In the absence of any provision to the contrary in the contract, the destruction of the building by fire would not afford any excuse for non-performance of the contract.

"When the work was going on, the material and labour which went into the building became the defendant's property subject to any lien in the plaintiff's favour; so she had an insurable interest in the property, and she effected an insurance for her own protection.

"The builders had an insurable interest, not only because of their lien, but also because the destruction of the property by fire would injure them, as under the building contract they would be bound to replace. They did not insure, preferring to carry the risk themselves. There was no obligation on the part of the owner to insure for the benefit of the contractors, and the contractors have no equitable or other claim upon the money received by the owner as the result of her prudence and expenditure.

"As I understand the evidence, there was no more than a demand by the owner upon the contractor to complete his contract. If there was more, it did not amount to a new contract, as there was no consideration.

"In its essence the defence is an attempt to shift the loss resulting from the fire—legally a loss falling upon the contractors—to the shoulders of the owner, who, fortunately for her, is not liable." [This case is also reproduced in part on page 148.]

HOWELL *v.* COUPLAND

England. Queen's Bench Division, 1876. 1 Q.B.D. 258

The plaintiff is a potato merchant at Holbeach, Lincolnshire, and the defendant a farmer at Whaplode in the same county.

In 1872 the defendant, at the proper season, and in the due course of husbandry, appropriated between eighty and ninety acres of land for the growth of potatoes,—sixty-eight acres at Whaplode, and about twenty at Holbeach.

In March of the same year the plaintiff and the defendant entered into the following contract: "A memorandum of agreement, made this . . . day of . . . , 1872, between Robert Coupland, of Whaplode, and John Howell, of Holbeach, whereby Robert Coupland agrees to sell, and the said John Howell agrees to purchase, 200 tons of regent potatoes grown on land belonging to the said Robert Coupland in Whaplode, at and after the rate of £3 10s. 6d. per ton, to be riddled on 1 5/8 in. riddle, and delivered at Holbeach railway station, good and marketable ware, during the months of September or October, as the said John Howell may direct, and, under his direction, the purchaser to find riddles. It is further agreed between the said Robert Coupland and the said John Howell that the said potatoes shall be paid for when and as they are taken away."

At the time of making the contract, out of the sixty-eight acres in Whaplode twenty-five were actually sown with potatoes, and the remaining forty-three acres were ready for sowing. The forty-three acres were afterwards sown in due course, and the whole sixty-eight acres together were amply sufficient, in an ordinary season and in the ordinary course of cultivation, to produce a much larger quantity than two hundred tons, the land producing, on an average, seven tons to the acre.

In July and August, without any fault on the part of the defendant, a disease, which no skill or care on the part of the defendant could have prevented attacked the crop and caused it to fail; and when the time for taking it up arrived, the whole marketable produce of the crop of the lands of the defendant, both in Whaplode and Holbeach together, amounted to no more than 79 tons 8 cwt., and this quantity the defendant delivered to the plaintiff. The rest of the crop had perished from the disease.

If the defendant had had other land to plant with potatoes at the time when the disease was discovered, which in fact he had not, it would have been too late to sow it.

The present action was brought to recover damages for the non-delivery of the residue of the two hundred tons. The verdict at the trial was entered for £432 5s., but a rule was obtained to enter the verdict for the defendant, on the ground that he was not liable to deliver the ungrown potatoes. It was made absolute by the Court of Queen's Bench. The plaintiff appealed.

LORD COLERIDGE C.J.: I am of opinion that the judgment ought to be affirmed. [The Lord Chief Justice read the contract and facts.] The Court of Queen's Bench held that, under these circumstances, the principle of

Taylor v. *Caldwell* (1863), 122 E.R. 309, and *Appleby* v. *Myers* (1867), L.R. 2 C.P. 651, applied, and the defendant was excused from the performance of his contract. The true ground, as it seems to me, on which the contract should be interpreted, and which is the ground on which, I believe, the Court of Queen's Bench proceeded, is that by the simple and obvious construction of the agreement, both parties understood and agreed that there should be a condition implied that before the time for the performance of the contract the potatoes should be, or should have been in existence, and should still be existing when the time came for the performance. They had been in existence, and had been destroyed by causes over which the defendant, the contractor, had no control, and it became impossible for him to perform his contract; and, according to the condition which the parties had understood should be in the contract, he was excused from the performance. It was not an absolute contract of delivery under all circumstances, but a contract to deliver so many potatoes, of a particular kind, grown on a specific place, if deliverable from that place. On the facts the condition did arise and the performance was excused. I am, therefore, of opinion that the judgment of the Queen's Bench should be affirmed.

MELLISH L.J.: I am of the same opinion. The words of the contract are clear the defendant "agrees to sell two hundred tons of regent potatoes grown on land belonging to him in Whaplode." That is, potatoes which shall be grown in Whaplode. They are to be grown there, and delivered to the plaintiff provided they are grown there. Is not that a condition,—so that, according to the cases on which the Court of Queen's Bench acted, if the thing perishes before the time for performance, the vendor is excused from performance by the delivery of the thing contracted for? No doubt there is a distinction in the present case, that the potatoes, the things contracted for, were not in existence at the time the contract was entered into. But can that make any real difference in principle? Suppose the potatoes had been full grown at the time of the contract, and afterwards the disease had come and destroyed them; according to the authorities it is clear that the performance would have been excused; and I cannot think it makes any difference that the potatoes were not then in existence. This is not like the case of a contract to deliver so many goods of a particular kind, where no specific goods are to be sold. Here there was an agreement to sell and buy two hundred tons out of a crop to be grown on specific land, so that it is an agreement to sell what will be and may be called specific things; therefore neither party is liable if the performance becomes impossible. The language of this contract is much easier to imply a condition from than in most former cases where it has been held to be implied.

CLEASBY B.: I am of the same opinion. I put my decision, not so much on the ground that the defendant was excused by the act of God rendering the performance impossible, as upon the terms of the contract itself. This is not like a contract where the parties have agreed to deliver a cargo of grain at Odessa or any other port by a given time, in which case the parties are bound by the contract, although its performance has become impossible by *vis major*. Here there was not an absolute contract to deliver two hundred tons of potatoes in September and October, but two hundred tons of potatoes grown on particular land. Not two hundred tons of potatoes simply, but two hundred tons off particular land. The crop on this particular land has failed, and there is nothing to which the promise can apply. If the crop had existed at the time of the contract, and had afterwards failed, there can be no doubt that the principle of the decided cases would apply and the defendant would be excused; and I cannot see any difference in principle from the fact that the crop had not been sown at the date of the contract.

[James and Baggallay L.JJ. also delivered judgments agreeing that the appeal be dismissed]

QUESTION. If the defendant had refused to deliver the 79 tons 8 cwt. of potatoes to the plaintiff in the *Howell* case, could the plaintiff have recovered damages to that extent?

SNIPES MOUNTAIN CO. *v*. BENZ BROS. & CO.
Washington. Supreme Court. 1931. 298 P. 714

PARKER J.: The plaintiff, Snipes Mountain Company, seeks reformation of a written contract for the sale of one hundred tons of potatoes by it to the defendant, Benz Bros. & Co., and recovery of an unpaid balance claimed to be due upon the agreed purchase price of sixty-four tons of the potatoes delivered under the contract. The reformation sought is to have the written contract show that the potatoes contracted to be sold were only potatoes growing upon certain specified land, to the end that the plaintiff will be entitled to recovery for the potatoes grown upon that land, all of them having been delivered under the sale contract, though amounting only to sixty-four tons. The defendant resists the plaintiff's claims of reformation and recovery, and by cross-complaint claims damages from the plaintiff for its failure to deliver thirty-six tons of the potatoes. The cause, being of equitable cognizance, proceeded to trial in the superior court for Yakima county, sitting without a jury, and resulted in a decree awarding to the plaintiff reformation of the contract and recovery as prayed for, and, in effect, denying the defendant's claim of damages. From this disposition of the case in the superior court, the defendant has appealed to this court.

The contract, as partly printed and partly written, in so far as need be here noticed, reads as follows: . . .

"We hereby confirm purchase from you of One Hundred tons Yakima Netted Gem Potatoes, graded 75% U. S. No. 1 Grade and 25% U. S. No. 2 grade, packed in new branded bags, even weight 100 lbs. each, and screened at car door, at $25.00 per ton, sacked, f. o. b. Nass or Granger, Wash. For Delivery not before Oct. 10th, 1929, when mature and for delivery not later than Nov. 1st, 1929. Receipt is hereby acknowledged of cash payment of Five Hundred and no/100 Dollars ($500.00). Balance to be paid on delivery. . . ."

During the negotiations leading up to the signing of the written contract, two members of the defendant's firm visited the growing crop of potatoes on the plaintiff's land, knowing that was all the potatoes being grown by the plaintiff during the season of 1929. The potatoes were then found to be in promising condition, having matured to the extent that they were then from about the size of a walnut to about the size of a hen's egg. Those participating in the negotiations were then well convinced that the crop would yield considerably more than one hundred tons, and then so expressed themselves. The evidence shows practically conclusively that all who conducted the negotiations and participated in the execution of the contract contemplated that it was a contract for the sale and purchase of one hundred tons of those particular potatoes, and no others; and that, in so far as the written contract failed to expressly so provide, there occurred a mutual mistake of the parties in its preparation. The contract was by the decree reformed by inserting therein between the words "potatoes" and "graded" the words "grown during the year 1929 on the following described premises: [Here follows a description of the land, being the land on which the members of the defendant's firm saw and examined the growing potatoes.]" We are of the opinion that the evidence well supports the reformation portion of the decree.

Was the plaintiff absolved from liability for its failure to deliver to the defendant the whole of the one hundred tons of potatoes as contracted for? The evidence renders it plain that the failure of the crop to yield one hundred tons or more was not in the least the fault of the plaintiff. The small yield, less than half the normal yield, was wholly the result of a partial crop failure from natural causes. The plaintiff harvested and delivered to the defendant the whole of the crop, constituting sixty-four tons of potatoes. To that extent the contract was strictly performed by the plaintiff. The applicable law, we think, is well stated in general terms in a note in 12 A. L. R. 1288 by the editors, as follows: "Whether or not a contract for the sale of produce to be delivered at a certain future date contemplates that it shall be grown on a particular tract of land, so that a failure of the crop on that land will excuse nondelivery, is often a close question of construction of the particular contract. The rule appears to be that if the parties contemplate a sale of the crop, or of a certain part of the crop, of a particular tract of land, and by reason of a drought or other fortuitous event, without the fault of the promisor, the crop of that land fails or is destroyed, non-performance is to that extent excused; the contract, in the absence of an express provision controlling the matter, being considered as subject to an implied condition in this regard. . . ." Our decision in Robinson Co. v. McClaine, 98 Wash. 322, 167 P. 912, and authorities therein noticed, are in harmony with this view of the law. We are of the opinion that the failure of the crop to produce more than sixty-four tons of potatoes absolved the plaintiff from liability for its failure to deliver to the defendant any additional potatoes, and that therefore the plaintiff is entitled to recover from the defendant the unpaid portion of the purchase price of the sixty-four tons of potatoes delivered; and that the defendant is not entitled to damages as claimed by it.

The judgment is affirmed.

[Tolman, C.J., and Holcomb, Mitchell, and Main, JJ., concur.]

BAILY *v.* DE CRESPIGNY

England. Queen's Bench. 1869. L.R. 4 Q.B. 180

HANNEN J. delivered the judgment of the Court: This was an action on a covenant contained in a lease of certain premises granted by the defendant to the plaintiff in 1840, for a term of eighty-nine years, whereby the defendant covenanted that "neither he nor his assigns should or would, during the term, permit to be built any messuage, etc., on a paddock fronting the demised premises." The breaches alleged are: (1) That the defendant during the term permitted a railway station to be built on the paddock. (2) That the defendant assigned the paddock to the London and Brighton Railway Company, who erected the railway station on the paddock.

To this declaration the defendant pleaded that, after the making of the deed, the railway company required to take the paddock under powers given them by Act of Parliament, 1862, for purposes for which they were by the act empowered to take the same; that the paddock was land which the company were empowered to take compulsorily for the purpose of the undertaking authorized by the act, and that the company under the powers so conferred, did compulsorily purchase and take the paddock, and that the assignment by defendant to the company was the assignment in completion of such compulsory purchase; that the company afterwards built on the paddock the erections complained of, which were erections reasonably required for the purposes of the undertaking authorized by the act, and that, except as aforesaid, the defendant did not permit the said erections to be built. The plaintiff demurred to this plea; and also replied that the erections, though reasonable, were not necessary or compulsory for the company to build. To this replication there was a demurrer.

It must be taken on these pleadings that the assignment by the defendants to the railway company was altogether made under the requirements of the act of Parliament, and without any stipulation introduced into the conveyance of the vendor or the purchaser, which would alter its character as an act done by the defendant in obedience to the command of the legislature. The 75th section of the *Lands Clauses Consolidation Act, 1845*, is imperative that the owner of lands shall, on the performance of the conditions imposed on the company, when required so to do, duly convey the lands to the promoters, or as they shall direct, and in default thereof it shall be lawful for the promoters to execute a deed poll declaring the fact of such default having been made, and thereupon all the estate and interest in such lands, capable of being sold and conveyed by such owner shall vest absolutely in the promoters of the undertaking.

We think that no distinction can be drawn between the case of an owner of lands who does that which it is his duty to do—namely, conveys to the company—and one who by refusing to convey obliges the company to obtain a title to the lands by the execution of a deed poll. In the one case, as in the other, the transfer of the title is compelled by the legislature, and it cannot be supposed that it was intended that the landowner who acts solely in obedience to the law should be in a worse position than one who refuses compliance. In either case the railway company must be regarded as the assignee of the land, not by the voluntary act of the former owner, but by compulsion of law.

The substantial question, therefore, raised on this record is whether the defendant is discharged from his covenant by the subsequent act of Parliament, which put it out of his power to perform it.

We are of opinion that he is so discharged on the principle expressed in the maxim *Lex non cogit ad impossibilia*.

We have first to consider what is the meaning of the covenant which the parties have entered into. There can be no doubt that a man may by an absolute contract bind himself to perform things which subsequently become impossible, or to pay damages for the non-performance and this construction is to be put upon an unqualified undertaking, where the event which causes the impossibility was or might have been anticipated and guarded against in the contract, or where the impossibility arises from the act or default of the promisor.

But where the event is of such a character that it cannot reasonably be supposed to have been in the contemplation of the contracting parties when the contract was made, they will not be held bound by general words which, though large enough to include, were not used with reference to the possibility of the particular contingency which afterwards happens. It is on this principle that the act of God is in some cases said to excuse the breach of a contract. This is in fact an inaccurate expression, because, where it is an answer to a complaint of an alleged breach of contract that the thing done or left undone was so by the act of God, what is meant is that it was not within the contract; for, as is observed by Maule J., in *Canham* v. *Barry,* (1855), 15 C.B. 596; 159 E.R. 558, at p. 567, a man might by apt words bind himself that it shall rain tomorrow or that he will pay damages. This is the explanation of the case put by Lord Coke in *Shelley's case* (1579), 1 Rep, 936; 76 E.R. 206, at p. 219: "If a lessee covenants to leave a wood in as good a plight as the wood was at the time of the lease, and afterwards the trees were blown down by tempest, he is discharged of his covenant," because it was thought that the covenant was intended to relate only to the tenant's own acts, and not to an event beyond his control, producing effects not in his power to remedy. (See Shep. Touch. 173). It is on this principle that it has been held that an impossibility, arising from an act of the legislature subsequent to the contract, discharges the contractor from liability. Again, to quote an observation of Maule J. in *Mayor of Berwick* v. *Oswald* (1854), 3 E. & B. 633; 118 E.R. 1286, at p. 1291, there is nothing "to prevent parties if they choose by apt words to express an intention so to do, from binding themselves by a contract as to any future state of the law . . . but people in general must always be considered as contracting with reference to the law as existing at the time of the contract. . . . And the words showing a contrary intention ought to be pretty clear to rebut that presumption." To hold a man liable by words, in a sense affixed to them by legislation subsequent to the contract, is to impose on him a contract he never made. This is the principle of that which was laid down in *Brewster* v. *Kitchell* (1698), 1 Salk. 198; 91 E.R. 177, that "where H. covenants not to do an act or thing which was lawful to do, and an act of Parliament comes after and compels him to do it, the statute repeals the covenant. So if H. covenants to do a thing which is lawful, and an act of Parliament comes in and hinders him from doing it, the covenant is repealed."

To apply the foregoing observations to the present case: The defendant has covenanted that his "assigns" shall not build. The word "assigns" is a term of well-known signification, comprehending all those who take either immediate or remotely from or under the assignor, whether by conveyance, devise, descent, or act of law. *Spencer's* case (1583), 5 Rep. 16; 77 E.R. 72. The defendant when he contracted used the general word "assigns," knowing that it had a definite meaning, and he was able to foresee and guard against the liabilities which might arise from his contract so interpreted. The legislature, by compelling him to part with his land to a railway company, whom he could not bind by any stipulation, as he could an assignee chosen by himself, has created a new kind of assign, such as was not in the contemplation of the parties when the contract was entered into. To hold the defendant responsible for the acts of such an assign, is to make an entirely new contract for the parties. On the other hand, to confine the word "assigns" to those who take by the voluntary act of the assignor would not, as was suggested in argument, limit the operation of the covenant to his immediate grantee; because all those who take from the first assignee do so in consequence of the original voluntary act of the assignor, and it was his own fault that he assigned at all, or that he did not in the original conveyance guard against the acts of subsequent assignees. To exempt him from liability for such acts would be contrary to the intention of the parties, to be collected from their words, interpreted according to their known ordinary significance.

It was, indeed, conceded on the argument by the plaintiff's counsel, that the defendant would not be liable for all acts of the railway company as he would have been for the acts of any other assignee; but it was contended that the defendant was relieved from liability on his covenant as to those acts only which the company was required by the act of Parliament to do, and not as to those which the company was merely empowered to do.

We do not think that this distinction is well founded. The rule laid down in *Brewster* v. *Kitchell* rests upon this ground, that it is not reasonable to suppose that the legislature, while altering the condition of things with reference to which the covenantor contracted, intended that he should remain liable on a covenant which the legislature itself prevented his fulfilling; but the covenantor in this case is equally disabled from preventing the railway company from doing those things which it is *empowered* to do, as those which it is *required* to do, why, then, should there be a difference in the liability of the covenantor with respect to the one and the other?

But, assuming that the imposing on the defendant by the legislature of assigns whom he could not control would, without more, free him from the engagements which he entered into with reference to assigns whom he could control, it remains necessary to deal with the argument that, though the company was empowered to take the lands free from the restrictions upon building, this was only on condition of paying full compensation for what they got, and that it must be supposed that the defendant obtained from the company not only the value of the land as he held it, encumbered with a covenant not to build, but also what was deemed a fair consideration for the right to build.

It appears to be assumed in this argument that the difference between the price of the land encumbered with the covenant not to build and the price of it freed from that covenant, would be the amount of damages to be paid by the defendant to the plaintiff in the present action. But that is not so; the plaintiff, if entitled to recover at all in this action, would be entitled to the damage he had sustained by the breach of the covenant, even if these damages should exceed the whole value of the land taken. No doubt, if the legislature had in express terms, or by necessary implication from its language, given to persons in the defendant's situation a remedy over against the railway company in respect of acts done by the company, this would have indicated that the legislature did not intend that the defendant should be freed from liability on his covenant, although he was disabled from performing it. But we cannot find in the railway acts any express or implied enactment to this effect. It has been already pointed out that there is no relation between the compensation which the defendant would be entitled to for his land and the damages for which he would be liable to the plaintiff. How could it be possible for the defendant to lay before the compensation jury evidence of the extent of his liability on such a covenant as that under consideration? How could he, in an inquiry to which the plaintiff was no party, offer evidence of the injury which the plaintiff might by any possibility sustain in the uncertain event of the company erecting a station or other building on the land taken?

Further, if the covenant of the defendant is to be considered as broken by the act of the railway company so as to entitle the plaintiff to damages, it must be deemed to carry with it the other consequences of a breach of contract. Thus, if the situation of the plaintiff and the defendant in this case had been reversed, and the covenant not to build on land adjoining the demised premises had been entered into by a lessee, with the usual proviso for re-entry in the event of breach of any covenant, the lessee would have been liable to forfeiture of his whole interest by reason of an act over which he had no control; and the railway company would be liable, if the plaintiff's contention be correct, to pay, by way of compensation for a piece of land taken, the whole value of the interests of the lessee in the adjoining estate.

The solution of the case appears to be that the plaintiff is one of a numerous class of persons injured by the construction of a railway, for whom the legislature has not provided compensation. This may be illustrated by reference to the special damage claimed in the declaration. It is there alleged that the amenity and comfort of the land demised have been diminished by reason of the prospect therefrom being interfered with, and by being overlooked by the windows of the station with the appurtenances, including water-closets and urinals. These are heads of damage for which railway companies are not in ordinary circumstances bound to give compensation, but for which the defendant would be liable in an action on his covenant.

We do not think that it was the intention of the legislature to make a railway company liable for such damages in the exceptional case of a person, in the position of the plaintiff, having taken a covenant from his lessor on the terms of that under consideration, or that, if such had been the intention of the legislature, so peculiar a head of compensation as that now suggested, namely, for liability to damages for breach of collateral covenants resulting from the taking of lands, would have been left to be conjectured from the vague language of the *Lands Clauses Consolidation Act*.

For these reasons we are of opinion that our judgment ought to be for the defendant.

SHIPTON *v*. HARRISON. [1915] 3 K.B. 676 (England. King's Bench Division). A contract to deliver specific wheat. Before delivery and before the property passed the government requisitioned the wheat under an act of Parliament in existence at the date of the contract. The seller was held to be excused from performance.

WALTON HARVEY, LTD. *v*. WALKER AND HOMFRAYS, LTD.
England. Court of Appeal. [1931] 1 Ch. 274

The facts were agreed. The plaintiffs were advertising agents and the defendants were brewers trading in and near Manchester who held a lease of the St. Peter's Hotel in that city. The lease had some fourteen years to run on December 31, 1924, when the defendants entered into two contracts with the plaintiffs for the purpose of enabling the plaintiffs to exhibit for a term of seven years, renewable for a further five, an illuminated advertising sign on the roof of the Hotel. The plaintiffs erected their sign in October, 1925. At the time the contract was entered into the Manchester Corporation was authorized by the *Manchester Corporation Act, 1920*, to acquire compulsorily (to expropriate) certain lands including the St. Peter's Hotel. The powers were exercisable until December 31,

1925. When the plaintiffs commenced the erection of their sign, they obtained, on May 6, 1925, a license from the Manchester Corporation authorizing them to erect or set up the sign for a term of two years and afterwards until the expiration of three months after notice requiring its demolition and removal had been given by the Corporation. This license was granted under the authority of the *Manchester Corporation Act, 1891.*

On December 18, 1925, the Manchester Corporation served notice on the defendants to treat for the purchase of their interest in the Hotel. No notice was served on the plaintiffs. In January 1928 an arbitrator was appointed to assess the compensation. On April 19, the defendants and the Corporation agreed on the sum of £3,850 and it was admitted that this sum included a sum for the value of the defendants' right to receive the rent payable by the plaintiffs under the contracts of December 31, 1921.

On March 7, 1929 the Manchester Corporation notified the plaintiffs to remove their sign at the expiration of three months. On September 25 the Corporation closed the Hotel and began to demolish it. In January, 1930, the plaintiffs' sign was removed by the Corporation with their consent. No rent was paid by the plaintiffs after December 25, 1929, nor has any been claimed. The plaintiffs commenced this action for damages for breach of the contracts. The trial Judge held for the plaintiffs and the defendants appealed.

LORD HANWORTH M.R.: . . . Now comes the question whether or not we should treat this case as one in which the parties had contracted on the implication on both sides that there should be a continued existence of the St. Peter's Hotel whereon this sky sign was to be. . . .

As I have said, and the learned judge has found, it would appear that the defendants were aware of the fact that their premises might be taken under the statutory powers in the Act of 1920, s. 11. The plaintiffs had no such knowledge, nor can knowledge be imputed to them. But there seems to be a difficulty in saying that the parties impliedly agreed that there should be a continued existence of the St. Peter's Hotel as the basis of their contract, for the defendants must have known that while they had a sure and certain continuance of their rights until October 31, 1925 (that is for at least some ten months beyond the date when the agreement was made), there was some risk after that date. They could have provided against that risk, but they did not. The Court is not very ready to imply subsidiary additions to an agreement made between parties and, in the absence of such implication, the law as stated in *Paradine* v. *Jane* (1647), 82 E.R. 897, still applies. The parties must, if they desire to be safeguarded against subsequent contingencies, provide for them in their agreement. If they do not do so, but have entered into a contract in terms which are absolute, those terms must be carried out unless in the somewhat rare cases where it can be found that there was an implied understanding on both sides that the basis of the contract was the continued existence of an essential matter to the contract. Having regard to the knowledge on the part of the defendants, the terms of the contract and the fact that the defendants were sure of their possessory rights for a certain time only, it does not seem to the Court to be possible to apply the principles illustrated in *Baily* v. *De Crespigny* (1869), L.R. 4 Q.B. 180, and the subsequent cases which have been referred to which arose during the war. . . .

[The appeal was dismissed but the trial Judge had proceeded on a different ground. The opinions of Romer L.J. and Eve J. have been omitted and Lord Hanworth's opinion has been cut considerably.]

ZIGER *v.* SHIFFER & HILLMAN CO., LTD.

Ontario. Court of Appeal. [1933] O.R. 407

In 1931 the defendant company entered into an agreement with the plaintiffs and others by which the defendant promised to employ the plaintiffs and others for one year, if there was work to be done, in consideration of the plaintiffs and others withdrawing from their union, The Amalgamated Clothing Workers of America. The plaintiffs brought action against the defendant company for breach of the contract to employ.

At the trial Logie J. gave judgment for the plaintiffs. The defendant company appealed.

MIDDLETON J.A. delivered the judgment of the Court: An appeal by the defendants from the judgment of Logie J., dated November 4, 1932, finding that the plaintiffs were each employed by the defendants for a period of one year from July 2, 1931, if there was work to do, and are each entitled to recover damages from the defendants for being wrongfully dismissed on October 5, 1931, and referring it to the Master to ascertain and report what damages each of the plaintiffs is entitled to recover, and directing payment of that which was found due by the Master forthwith, after the confirmation of his report, and further giving to the plaintiffs their costs of this action. . . .

Apparently, before the making of the agreement, the defendants' shop was a union shop. The defendants themselves were members of the Manufacturers' Association. The employees were all members of the Amalgamated Clothing Workers of America, an international body. This meant co-operation between the shop and the workers' union. No one could be employed in the shop unless he was a member of the union. The union controlled the employment. Business being very dull, the defendants apparently conceived the plan of establishing an independent shop and themselves resigning from the Manufacturers' Association. It was expected that this would enable goods to be manufactured at a lower price, and consequently steadier work would be secured for the employees and greater profit for the shop. With this in view, the agreements were drawn up and executed, the defendants withdrew from the Manufacturers' Association and the employees from their local union. As might have been foreseen, this provoked keen antagonism on the part of the Amalgamated Clothing Workers of America. The shop was besieged, the workers were intimidated and beaten, the police force failed to give any adequate protection and, in the end, the defendants found themselves unable to carry on and capitulated, making an agreement with the workers' union to operate in future under it. About half the workers who had resigned from the union had repented and, yielding to persuasion and violence, had rejoined the union before this decision was arrived at by the defendants. Some of the remaining workers were received back into the union; others, including the plaintiffs, who had resigned from the union and had not been reinstated found themselves unemployed, hence this action. . . .

I think the parties here must be held to have made their bargain on the footing that it would be possible to operate and maintain an independent shop, that the police force would be able to protect both parties from mob violence and permit them to enjoy the freedom of contract which is rightly deemed to be an essential privilege in civilized countries, and that, therefore, a term is to be implied, although not expressed, in the contract, that it is founded on the continued existence of an independent shop, the destruction of which by *vis major* would free either party from liability if the terms of the contract should be frustrated by acts of violence and misconduct over which neither contracting party had control and which the police force of the community did not keep in hand. . . .

It is needless to quote other authorities. The independent shop here ceased to exist without default of either of the contracting parties and solely because those responsible for maintaining order in the community proved unequal to this task.

If, as counsel said, this result was brought about by the action of hired thugs imported from the United States by the union the situation is so much the worse. . . .

The appeal must be allowed and the action dismissed with costs, if asked.

NOTE. There is a criticism of this decision in (1933), 11 Can. Bar Rev. 567, on the ground that the trouble that occurred might reasonably have been foreseen or was actually in the minds of the defendants. If the writer means that the defendant foresaw or could have foreseen, but the plaintiffs did not, nor could have reasonably foreseen, the criticism seems well founded. Where both foresaw the difficulty, must not the contract be read in the light of circumstances known to both? If so, how should the contract be read, as if it contained absolute promises, or promises subject to an agreed and understood but unexpressed condition?

McKENNA *v.* McNAMEE

British Columbia. Supreme Court of Canada. 1887. 15 S.C.R. 311

The defendants had been engaged by the Government of British Columbia to construct the Esquimalt Graving Docks but had failed to carry out the work to the Government's satisfaction and the work had been taken out of their hands. The defendants believed, however, that they could get the contract reinstated, and entered into an agreement with the plaintiffs by which the plaintiffs were to complete the work and receive 90 per cent of the profits. The agreement recited that the defendants had agreed to take the plaintiffs into their service for the purpose of completing the contract. This course was adopted because the contract with the Government contained a clause which prohibited them from sub-letting.

The plaintiffs at the time of making this agreement were aware of the fact that the defendants had lost the contract, and had examined its various provisions, but reliance was placed on the political influence of the plaintiff, Mitchell, for its restoration. After the execution of the agreement Mitchell went to British Columbia and used every endeavour to induce the Government to restore the contract to the defendants but was finally obliged to return without accomplishing his object. The plaintiffs then brought their action claiming $100,000 as damages for breach of contract to take them into defendants' service, and $25,000 for moneys expended on the work.

The defendants claimed that the condition of their contract with the Government was known to the plaintiffs when the agreement was made; that it was made on the express understanding that it was not to take effect unless the contract was restored; and that it was not intended to create the relation of master and servant between the parties the agreement being made in the form it was on account of the clause against sub-letting.

RITCHIE C.J.: . . . It is clear that unless the contract was restored by British Columbia there could be no performance on either side. We cannot shut our eyes to the state of facts thus existing and known to both parties, and with reference to which the plaintiff and defendant were negotiating with a view to arriving at a right construction of the agreement into which the parties finally entered. It is our duty to construe the contract with the aid of the surrounding circumstance influenced in the construction not only by the instrument but also by the circumstances under which, and the objects for which, it was entered into and with reference to the intention of the parties at the time it was made. Reading the contract in the light of the surrounding circumstances I think what both parties contemplated was, an agreement based on the restoration of the contract to McNamee, which both parties thought would be obtained through their united efforts and influence; failing in this the contract necessarily fell through, because, without the fault of either party, it could be fulfilled by neither, it not, in my opinion, being contemplated that any liability should arise on either side until the restoration should be obtained through their joint endeavours. If the contract was restored then the agreement became capable of fulfilment but not before; in other words, conditional on the restoration of the contract. The government having refused without the fault of either party, the non-fulfilment of the agreement happened without fault on either side. This was not a contract the performance of which was dependent on the continued existence of a given state of things, but the opposite, the performance was dependent on the action of the Government of British Columbia over which neither party had any control.

In the absence, then, of any express or implied contract or warranty on either side that the consent of the Government of British Columbia would or could be obtained, a matter in which both parties were equally interested and which, from the evidence, it is obvious both parties were to use their endeavours to obtain and which the plaintiff Mitchell thought they had sufficient political influence to accomplish, can this contract be construed into a positive contract on the part of the defendant to procure such consent? On the contrary, looking at the surrounding circumstances, must it not be construed as subject to an implied condition on both sides that it was not to take effect, as it could not, in the event of the refusal of British Columbia to give back the contract to the defendant? Though it may appear on its face to be presently operative both parties must have known that it was not intended to operate, because it could not operate until the happening of a given event. The agreement being silent on the subject there was nothing, in my opinion, to prevent the defendant from showing by parol testimony that it was not intended to, because it could not, take effect until the happening of something else. To hold that the agreement was not to have effect if the Government of British Columbia refused to restore, neither varied nor contradicted the writing. . . .

BELL *v.* LEVER BROTHERS. [1932] A.C. 161 (England. House of Lords). LORD ATKIN: "The condition . . . that is generally accepted as underlying the principle of the frustration cases is contractual, an implied condition. Sir John Simon formulated for the assistance of your Lordships a proposition which should be recorded: 'Whenever it is to be inferred from the terms of the contract or its surrounding circumstances that the consensus has been reached upon the basis of a particular contractual assumption, and that assumption is not true, the contract is voided: i.e., it is void *ab initio* if the assumption is of present fact and it ceases to bind if the assumption is of future fact.' "

NICKOLL & KNIGHT *v.* ASHTON, EDRIDGE & CO.
England. Court of Appeal. [1901] 2 K.B. 126

By a contract dated October 24, 1899, the defendants sold to the plaintiffs a cargo of Egyptian cotton-seed, to consist of from 1600 to 1900 tons, to be shipped per steamship Orlando, at Alexandria and/or Port Said and/or Ismailia, during the month of January, 1900, at £6 3s. 9d. per ton, and to be delivered in the United Kingdom. In drawing up the contract the words "ship or ships" in print had been obliterated, and the words "per steamship Orlando" substituted for them in writing. Clause 5 of the contract provided that, "in case of prohibition of export, blockade, or hostilities preventing shipment, this contract or any unfulfilled part thereof is to be cancelled."

The Orlando had been chartered for the carriage of the cargo in question, not by the defendants, but by persons from whom they had bought the cargo. In December, 1899, the Orlando stranded in the Sound through perils of the sea, and was so badly damaged as to make it impossible for her to arrive at the ports of loading under contract in time to load during the month of January; and notice of the fact was given by the charterers to the plaintiffs on December 20. . . . On December 28 the defendants wrote to the plaintiffs to the effect that, as performance of the contract was rendered impossible, they considered the transaction as cancelled. The plaintiffs subsequently brought the action against the defendants for failure to ship a cargo of cotton-seed under the contract.

Mathew J. held that the contract must be read as subject to an implied condition that, in the event of the Orlando's being through perils of the sea rendered unfit to ship the cargo in January at the port of loading, the contract should be treated as at an end, and therefore gave judgment for the defendants. The plaintiffs appealed.

A. L. SMITH M.R.: This is an action for damages by the buyers of a cargo of Egyptian cotton-seed against the sellers for not shipping the same pursuant to a contract dated October 24, 1899, and the question is whether upon its true construction the contract is a positive and absolute contract to ship the seed, or a contract subject to any, and what, implied condition.

The contract upon which the question arises, so far as material, is as follows: "Sold this day to Messrs. Nickoll & Knight the following Egyptian cotton seed—namely, a cargo to consist of from 1600 tons to 1900 tons to be shipped by the steamship Orlando at Alexandria . . . during the month of January, 1900. (Signed) Ashton & Co." Clause 5 is as follows: "In case of prohibition of export, blockade, or hostilities preventing the shipment the contract or any unfulfilled part thereof is to be cancelled." It is perfectly plain upon the fact of the signed contract that the parties deliberately agreed that the shipment of the seed should not be in any ship or ships, but in one particular named ship, for the words in print "ship or ships" are obliterated, and the words "per steamship Orlando" are inserted in writing in their place, and it is equally plain that the contract could only be performed by the defendants shipping the seed contracted for in the steamship Orlando during the month of January, 1900, and in no other ship.

Now, is a contract such as this a positive and absolute contract by the shipper to ship on board the named ship the contracted cargo, or is it a contract subject to any, and what, implied condition? [After citing *Taylor* v. *Caldwell* (1863), 122 E.R. 309, and quoting from the case the Master of the Rolls continued:]

In my judgment the contract in the present case falls directly within this rule, for, from the beginning, the parties must have known that the performance of the contract would become impossible unless the particular thing specified that is, the steamship Orlando, continued to exist as a cargo-carrying ship down to and during the month of January, 1900; and I have no doubt that the true construction of the contract is that it is not a positive and absolute contract as contended for by the plaintiffs, but is a contract subject to the condition that the parties shall be excused if, before breach, performance becomes impossible by reason of the particular specified thing, that is, the steamship Orlando ceasing to exist as a cargo-carrying ship without the defendants' default.

But it is argued that, although there may be this implied condition, it only applies if the particular thing actually perishes; for instance, it is suggested that, if the roof of the music-hall in *Taylor* v. *Caldwell*, had alone been destroyed and the hall itself not burnt to the ground, the judgment in that case would not have been given, even although with the roof off the hall could not have been used for the purpose for which it was let, and it is said that, as the steamship Orlando did not actually perish, this case is not within the implied condition. I do not agree. In my judgment, if the ship ceased to exist as a cargo-carrying ship when the time for the performance of the contract arrived, so that it could not be used to ship the cargo in, the implied condition would attach. If the steamship had gone to the bottom before the month of January, 1900, and remained there during that month, so as to be wholly unable to take in a cargo, would not the ship have ceased to exist, whereby the performance of the contract became impossible, the ship being then at the bottom of the sea? Quoad the performance of the contract, it would have perished; and what is the difference in principle between the ship being at the bottom of the sea and being stranded upon a rock in the Baltic, as the Orlando was, and thereby wholly unable to take in a cargo pursuant to the contract? In either case, in my opinion, the performance of the contract became impossible by reason of the particular specified thing, i.e., the ship, ceasing to exist as a cargo-carrying ship, or, in other words, as regards that purpose having perished. This is not a case in which the thing contracted for is possible in itself, and the contracting party is unable to perform it only through causes beyond his own control, such as an unexpected sudden frost: *Kearon* v. *Pearson* (1861), 7 H. & N. 386; 158 E.R. 523. In such a case it is the party's own fault for undertaking unconditionally to fulfil a promise. In the present case, as before pointed out, he has not done so, for the promise he has made is conditional. It also seems to me that the suggested point of the detention of a ship by adverse winds clearly would not fall within the above rule, for in such a case the ship has not ceased to exist at all. It exists as a cargo-carrying ship, but is merely behind time on its voyage.

The next point taken by the plaintiffs was that by reason of clause 5 of the contract the implied condition of the continued existence of the ship was negatived, and that it was only the matters mentioned in that clause which excused the performance of the contract. In my opinion the matters mentioned in clause 5 in no way negative the true construction of the contract, which is that the contract is not positive and absolute, and that clause 5 affords an excuse for the not shipping of the cargo, over and above the perishing of the ship, which is the implied condition. In my judgment it is not true to say that there is a warranty in this contract that the ship shall be in existence in January, 1900. I think that the judgment of Mathew J. is correct, and that this appeal must be dismissed.

[The opinion of Romer L.J. to the same effect is omitted. Vaughan Williams L.J. delivered a dissenting opinion.]

LORD CLIFFORD *v.* WATTS
England. Common Pleas. 1870. L.R. 5 C.P. 577

WILLES J.: This was an action upon a demise of grant by Lord Clifford to Watts of certain mines, pits, etc., of clay, by which demise the rent was made payable at a certain rate per ton upon the clay raised; and the indenture contained, amongst others, a covenant that Watts shall work and make trials for clay under the lands in question. The first breach is founded upon that covenant, and in respect of that the defendant has paid 40s. into court. The indenture also contains a covenant that Watts shall dig and raise from the land an aggregate amount of not less than 1,000 tons, or more than 2,000 tons, of pipe or potter's clay in each year of the term. The term granted was twelve years; and for the pipe or potter's clay the defendant was to pay a royalty of 2s. 6d. per ton. The breach assigned on that covenant is that with which we have to deal on this occasion; it is, that the defendant has not dug an aggregate amount of not less than 1,000 tons of pipe or potter's clay in each year of the demise. The plea, the validity of which is now in question, is, that the defendant could not dig 1,000 tons of clay each year according to his covenant, because there was not at the time of the demise, nor since existing under the lands, 1,000 tons of such clay; that the performance of the covenant had always been impossible, and that such impossibility was unknown to the defendant at the time, and he had no reasonable means of knowing or ascertaining the same. To that plea there is a demurrer.

It is obvious that this plea may be considered from two points of view: First, with reference to the abstract question whether a covenant to perform an impossibility is or is not valid in point of law; whether the covenantor can set up such impossibility from the beginning as an answer to a breach, or must pay damages, which, according to Mr. Preston [one of the counsel] may only be nominal. The second, and with reference to this case the most important, consideration appears to me to arise from the question whether the defendant has by this covenant contracted to perform an impossibility, or whether the true meaning of the covenant, construing it by the rest of the deed, is, not that the defendant undertakes to get the stipulated quantity of clay whether it be there or not, or to pay the stipulated tonnage as if the clay had been raised, but rather, dealing with it as subsidiary to the main object of the demise, that he will raise such pipe or potter's clay as may be found under the land, at the rate and price specified. If the latter be the true construction of the covenant, it is not an independent covenant to do the thing contracted for, whether possible or not, but only a stipulation as to the rate at which that is to be done which both parties at the time contemplated. According to that construction of the covenant, the plea is a good defence to the second breach. And this is the view to which, after the best consideration I am able to bring to the case, and after having heard the very learned arguments on both sides, my opinion inclines.

The deed, without any recital, witnesses that Lord Clifford, in consideration of the rent, payments, covenants, etc., demised to Watts the mines, pits, etc., of clay under certain lands particularly described. It then proceeds to grant Watts a license to enter upon the land to dig and search for clay and to make pits, etc., with rights of way for carrying it away, etc., subject to compensation for damage. Then comes the habendum.—to have, hold, etc., the said mines, etc., of pipe and potter's or other clay, with the powers thereby granted, for twelve years; and to have and to hold all and every the said beds or veins of clay that shall be found and raised within the term out of any part of the land so authorized to be worked, unto Watts, his executors, etc., unto his and their own use. So far we are dealing with the demising part of the instrument, which refers to specific lands and to specific clay which is believed by both parties to be under the lands described at the time. The whole scope of the contract is that the defendant shall take that clay. Whether the speculation would turn out to be a profitable one to the tenant or not was uncertain. So far it was natural that he should take the risk. But the question is whether we are justified in importing another element into a bargain like this, namely, a warranty by the tenant that clay shall be found, or an undertaking to pay for the quantity stipulated for, whether found or not . . . The bare statement of the provisions of the deed leads me to the conclusion that the tenant never intended to warrant that there was clay upon the land, and that neither party contemplated that he should, in the event of no clay being found there, at all events pay a minimum fixed rent during the term. It is a bare stipulation as to the rate of payment for the clay which should be raised. That appears to me to be the natural and ordinary construction of the covenant when read by the light of the context. It turned out that there was no clay of the descriptions mentioned on the land. The covenant therefore becomes inapplicable, and has not been broken. . . .

Cases may be conceived in which a man may undertake to do that which turns out to be impossible, and yet he may still be bound by his agreement. I am not prepared to say that there may not be cases in which a man may have contracted to do something which in the present state of scientific knowledge may be utterly impossible, and yet he may have so contracted as to warrant the possibility of its performance by means of some new discovery, or be liable in damages for the non-performance, and cannot set up by way of defence that the thing was impossible. But before we arrive at such a conclusion we must be satisfied, if no other reasonable construction suggests itself, that the party really did intend to warrant that to be possible which was impossible. The authorities relied on for the plaintiff appear to me to be cases where a man either undertook to do a thing which was possible at the time, but which, without any fault of his adversary, became afterwards impossible, or where he, notwithstanding the thing was impossible of performance, took upon himself to warrant that it should be possible.

Barker v. *Hodgson* (1814), 3 M. & S. 267; 105 E.R. 612, was a case where the charterer of a ship had covenanted to send a cargo alongside at a foreign port, but in consequence of the prevalence of an infectious disorder at the port, all public intercourse was prohibited by the authorities of the place, and yet he was held to be responsible in damages for the non-performance of his covenant. If the intercourse with the foreign port had been prohibited by the law of this country the act would have been illegal, and the defendant would have been excused, not because he could not, but because he ought not to do it. But where the performance of the thing covenanted to be done is not made impossible by the law of this country, the case falls within the principle laid down in the leading case of *Paradine* v. *Jane*. . . . Where a thing becomes impossible of performance by the act of a third person, or even by the act of God, its impossibility affords no excuse for its non-performance; it is the defendant's own folly that has led him to make such a bargain without providing against the possible contingency. In the present case, if the allegations in the plea be true, there was nothing upon which the covenant could attach at the time it was entered into.

Hills v. *Sughrue* (1846), 15 M. & W. 253; 153 E.R. 844, has not application, for another reason. There the charterer by his contract warranted that, the ship being ready to take a cargo of guano at Ochaboe, he would there provide her with a full cargo. The impossibility of obtaining a cargo there was no excuse for the non-performance of his contract. That case therefore falls within the second category of cases, where the defendant had warranted the possibility of doing the thing contracted for. . . .

There is only a covenant to work out all the clay under the land, and this covenant was not broken by the defendant's failure to work clay if none was to be found there. I therefore think the defendant is entitled to judgment.

QUESTIONS. What is the difference between existing impossibility of which the contracting parties are ignorant, and supervening impossibility? Do not parties contract only with reference to what they know in both cases?

THE SALE OF GOODS ACT

Ontario. Revised Statutes. 1960. Chapter 358

6. Where there is a contract for the sale of specific goods, and the goods without the knowledge of the seller have perished at the time when the contract is made, the contract is void.

ISABELLA HALL *v.* GEORGE WRIGHT

England. Exchequer Chamber. 1859. E.B. & E. 765; 120 E.R. 695

Action for breach of promise to marry. The defendant pleaded that after the agreement and before any breach thereof, the defendant "became and was, and thenceforth hitherto has been and still is, afflicted with dangerous bodily disease, which has occasioned frequent and severe bleeding from his lungs, and by reason of which disease defendant then became and was, and from thenceforth hitherto has been, and still is, incapable of marriage without great danger of his life, and therefore unfit for the marriage state: whereof the plaintiff had notice before the commencement of this action."

At the trial the jury found for the defendant on this plea and judgment was entered in his favour.

On appeal to the Queen's Bench, E.B. & E. 746; 120 E.R. 6, Lord Campbell C.J. and Crompton J. held the defence insufficient. Wightman and Erle JJ. held the defence good.

The difference of opinion is indicated by the following extracts from the judgments of Lord Campbell C.J. and Wightman J.

LORD CAMPBELL C.J.: . . . The only English authority bearing directly on the question, how far a contract to marry is dissolved by supervening disease, is the dictum of Lord Kenyon in *Atchinson* v. *Baker* (1796), 170 E.R. 209: "If the condition of the parties was changed after the time of making the contract, it was a good cause for either party to break off the connection." But this was said merely obiter in a case in which the refusal to marry was on the part of the lady, who, subsequently to her promise, discovered that the gentleman had an abscess in his breast, which he had concealed from her: and the dictum in its latitude is not supported by any decision to be found in our books. As yet there has been no decision that for anything supervening after the contract to marry, unfitting either party fully to perform the duties of the married state, the party so unfitted may treat the contract as dissolved, the other still desiring that the marriage ceremony should be performed. . . .

The counsel for the defendant argued that, in his dangerous state of health, as described in the plea, he is in the same situation as if by disease, or accident, or violence, he had suffered mutilation. In that case he certainly could not have maintained an action against the lady for refusing on that account to marry him. But I am by no means prepared to say that, if she had desired to be married by him and he had refused to marry her, he would not have been liable to an action. By such a marriage she could not have become the mother of children; but she might nevertheless have been affectionately attached to him, and might have innocently desired to enjoy the *consortium vitae* with him; she might have obtained rank and station in society as his wife; and, as his widow, she might have been dowable of his lands. The defendant suggests the impossibility of entering into the married state under such circumstances; but he may well pay damages for refusing to do so.

WIGHTMAN J.: . . . The question is, Whether this plea, proved as it is to the satisfaction of the jury, shews a sufficient excuse for the non-performance of the promise to marry as alleged in the declaration. Is a man bound by law to fulfil a promise to marry, which, by reason of circumstances occurring since the promise, and by no default of his, cannot be fulfilled without great danger to his life? If the performance of the promise had become impossible by the act of God, it would have been an excuse for non-performance: but, in the present case, the performance of the promise is not alleged to be, nor is it, impossible, but only highly dangerous to the life of the person promising.

The nature of the contract to marry is such that it seems only reasonable that, if, from disease subsequently intervening, it cannot be fulfilled without great danger to the life of one of the parties, its performance should on that ground be excused. Such a disease, as long as it exists, would, I think, be a "just impediment" to the marriage.

The plea does not amount to a rescinding of the contract by the defendant: nor is it an attempt to rescind it; as he may recover, and be able to perform it: but it shews a state of circumstances existing down to the time of plea pleaded, which, he says, justifies the refusal to marry as stated in the declaration. The want of notice does not appear to me to be material.

The plaintiff appealed to the Exchequer Chamber.

BRAMWELL B.: . . . At present, the question is, Does the plea justify the particular breach alleged? Now the plea alleges that, before and at the time of the breach, the defendant was afflicted by the bodily disease which made him incapable of marriage without great danger of his life, and unfit for the married state. The question was at first argued as though this meant an unfitness for sexual intercourse: But Mr. James said it meant, and it appears from the judgment of Erle J. to mean, not only that, but also an incapacity to bear the fatigue and excitement of the marriage ceremony. It was proved to be true in both its meanings. I think either matter a justification for not marrying.

But it is necessary to examine both; as some seem to consider the plea merely to mean unfitness for the ceremony of marriage, others the other unfitness I have mentioned. As neither fraud nor illegality is alleged, the excuse for not performing the contract must be found in the terms of the contract itself. The plea therefore assumes that it is a term of the contract declared on, that, in the event named in the plea, the defendant should be excused from marrying; and, as there is no reason why such terms should be in this particular contract unless it is in all such contracts, the question is reduced to this: Is it a term in an ordinary agreement to marry that, if the man from bodily disease cannot marry without danger to his life, and is unfit for marriage from the cause mentioned at the time appointed, he shall be excused marrying then? The plea assumes it is. I think it is. Of course I admit that parties might stipulate otherwise; but, if they do not, I think they are implied terms of the ordinary contract.

I quite agree that, where parties can make their own terms, the law ought not lightly to imply any. But there are instances in which it is done from the necessity, or almost necessity, of the case; and, if ever it is reasonable to do it, it is in the contract to marry. . . . The contract is a contract to marry and perform the duties of marriage. I think it better to recognise what we all know exists, and to assume it exists for a good purpose, than to affect to ignore it. Besides, there is abundant warranty for so doing. The marriage of an impotent man is null; and two of the three reasons for matrimony given in the marriage service involve the capacity for sexual intercourse. Can it be doubted, then, if death were the certain result of the fatigue and excitement of the ceremony, that the defendant would be excused, or that impotency supervening on the promise would excuse him? Could he be bound, in performance of his promise, to commit suicide, or go through a ceremony which would be a nullity? But, if the certainty of a fatal result would excuse, so would great danger of it; if death from the exercise of capacity, more so. I desire to speak with all reserve: but to possess the lawful means of gratifying a powerful passion with the alternative of abstaining or perilling life is indeed to incur a risk of "intense misery instead of mutual comfort": and it does seem to me, with great respect a great mistake to lose sight of these considerations, and suppose happiness can be found in such a marriage by the gratification of an innocent desire to enjoy the *consortium vitae* with the man, obtain rank and station as his wife, and be dowable of his lands. Moreover, this is to think only of the woman and not of the man, who might object that her wishes, however innocent, were very unreasonable towards him in wishing him to put himself in the temptation of perilling his life; and he might even doubt the innocence of such a desire, certainly of wishing him to go through a ceremony which might be fatal to him.

This suggests the following. If the man is not excused, but bound, is the woman bound in such a case? Impossible, one would think. But, if not, it must be on account of some implied condition in the contract. It is not as though the man was in default. She could not refuse to marry, in such a case, on the ground that he had broken his contract by not continuing fit for marrying, for, if so, she might not only refuse to marry him, but maintain an action against him for becoming unfit. That cannot be: he does not thereby break his contract; yet she is excused. If so, so must he be; for, if without default of one party to a contract the other has a right to refuse to perform on the happening of a certain event, it must be assumed, till the contrary appears, that right is common to both. If in such case she could rely on an implied condition to excuse her marrying him, why may not he on one to excuse his marrying her? . . .

No doubt, if a contract made by the parties is unconditional, death or disease is no excuse: but the question in this case is, Whether the contract is not conditional on the continuance of life and health. Why, if the defendant died before breach, could not his executors be liable? The answer is, because he has not undertaken to live. Neither has he to continue competent in health. And the one is as much a condition of matrimony as the other. . . .

If I am to say whether I think the contract ended by such an event, I say I do; and on this ground: that it is so vitally for the benefit of both parties that that should be the agreement between them, that common sense requires it to be so implied. The disability of the defendant, if not incurable, was one of indefinite duration, and of a lasting character. Had it been that he broke a leg, or was afflicted with a fever which disabled him for marriage at the time appointed, I should have thought him not liable to an action for not marrying then, but bound to marry on his recovering. This last consideration seems to me to suggest an argument in favour of the contract being conditional as suggested. For in ordinary contracts, if not liable at the day appointed, a person would not be at another time; but in this contract it is absurd to suppose that if a day was named for a marriage and the man broke his leg, was ill of a fever, lost a parent, or from some other consideration of health or decency could not marry on the day in question, he would either be liable to an action, or wholly discharged from his promise to marry. But the same good sense and convenience which would reject such a conclusion, in my judgment, requires that the contract should be construed with the conditions I attach.

For these reasons, as well as those of Mr. Justice Wightman and Lord Chief Justice Erle, I think the judgment should be affirmed.

WILLES J.: . . . The contract in this case is stated by the plaintiff in the declaration, and admitted by the defendant in his plea, to have been in terms an unconditional one: and it is guesswork, not construction, to read it as conditional. Its performance is not impossible; and it is not enough to shew, in answer to an action upon a contract, that its performance is inconvenient or may be dangerous. The delicacy of health, alleged as an excuse, is the man's misfortune, not to be visited, beyond what is inevitable, upon the woman. If either party is to have the option of breaking off the match, it ought to be the woman. The Court have no right to say what is best for her. If the man were rich or distinguished, and the woman mercenary or ambitious, she might still desire to marry him for advancement in life. I do not sympathize with such a woman, if any there be: but this is not a question of sentiment. If it were, I might put the case of a real attachment, where such an illness as that stated in the plea supervening might make the woman even more anxious to marry, in order to be the companion and the nurse, if she could not be the mistress, of her sweetheart.

The judgment for the defendant ought therefore to be reversed, and judgment given for the plaintiff, with costs.

[Williams J., Martin B., and Crowder J. gave judgment to the same effect as Willes J., supporting the view of Lord Campbell in the lower court. Judgment was therefore given for the plaintiff. In the main the majority proceed on the ground that, having created a duty or charge by contract, he must make it good. Martin B. said: "I think it very much better to adhere to the rule than to create an arbitrary exception. . . . To admit exceptions of this kind utterly destroys the certainty of the law, and in my opinion is inconvenient." Pollock C.B. and Watson B. gave reasons to the same effect as Bramwell B.]

JEFFERSON *v.* PASKELL. [1916] 1 K.B. 57 (England. Court of Appeal). PHILLIMORE L.J.: "On principle it would seem that there must be some cases of mental or physical infirmity (as it has been decided that there are cases of moral infirmity) which supervening after the promise, or I would add, first coming to the knowledge of the party after the promise, will justify him or her in refusing to marry." In this case the defendant pleaded that the female plaintiff had contracted tuberculosis, but the defence failed. The jury, having seen the plaintiff, remained unconvinced of her unfitness for marriage and set the damages at £500.

KRELL *v.* HENRY

England. Court of Appeal. [1903] 2 K.B. 740

The plaintiff, Paul Krell, sued the defendant, C. S. Henry, for £50, being the balance of a sum of £75 for which the defendant had agreed to hire a flat at 56A Pall Mall on the days of June 26 and 27, for the purpose of viewing the processions to be held in connection with the coronation of His Majesty. The defendant denied his liability, and counterclaimed for the return of the sum of £25, which had been paid as a deposit, on the ground that, the procession not having taken place owing to the serious illness of the King, there had been a total failure of consideration for the contract entered into by him.

Darling J. held that there was an implied condition in the contract that the procession should take place, and gave judgment for the defendant on the claim and counter-claim. The plaintiff appealed. The defendant on the appeal abandoned his counter-claim for £25.

VAUGHAN WILLIAMS L.J.: The real question in this case is the extent of the application in English law of the principle of the Roman law which has been adopted and acted on in many English decisions, and notably in the case of *Taylor* v. *Caldwell* (1863), 122 E.R. 309. That case at least makes it clear that "where, from the nature of the contract, it appears that the parties must from the beginning have known that it could not be fulfilled unless, when the time for the fulfilment of the contract arrived, some particular specified thing continued to exist, so that when entering into the contract they must have contemplated such continued existence as the foundation of what was to be done; there, in the absence of any express or implied warranty that the thing shall exist, the contract is not to be considered a positive contract, but as subject to an implied condition that the parties shall be excused in case, before breach, performance becomes impossible from the perishing of the thing without default of the contractor."

Thus far it is clear that the principle of the Roman law has been introduced into the English law. The doubt in the present case arises as to how far this principle extends. The Roman law dealt with obligations *de certo corpore*. Whatever may have been the limits of the Roman law, the case of *Nickoll* v. *Ashton,* [1901] 2 K.B. 126, makes it plain that the English law applies the principle not only to cases where the performance of the contract becomes impossible by the cessation of existence of the thing which is the subject-matter of the contract, but also to cases where the event which renders the contract incapable of performance is the cessation or non-existence of an express condition or state of things, going to the root of the contract, and essential to its performance. It is said, on the one side, that the specified thing, state of things, or condition the continued existence of which is necessary for the fulfilment of the contract, so that the parties entering into the contract must have contemplated the continued existence of that thing, condition, or state of things as the foundation of what was to be done under the contract, is limited to things which are either the subject-matter of the contract or a condition or state of things, present or anticipated, which is expressly mentioned in the contract.

But, on the other side, it is said that the condition or state of things need not be expressly specified, but that it is sufficient if that condition or state of things clearly appears by extrinsic evidence to have been assumed by the parties to be the foundation or basis of the contract, and the event which causes the impossibility is of such a character that it cannot reasonably be supposed to have been in the contemplation of the contracting parties when the contract was made. In such a case the contracting parties will not be held bound by the general words which, though large enough to include, were not used with reference to a possibility of a particular event rendering performance of the contract impossible.

I do not think that the principle of the civil law as introduced into the English law is limited to cases in which the event causing the impossibility of performance is the destruction or non-existence of some thing which is the subject-matter of the contract or of some condition or state of things expressly specified as a condition of it. I think that you first have to ascertain, not necessarily from the terms of the contract, but, if required, from necessary inferences, drawn from surrounding circumstances recognised by both contracting parties, what is the substance of the contract, and then to ask the question whether that substantial contract needs for its foundation the assumption of the existence of a particular state of things. If it does, this will limit the operation of the general words, and in such case, if the contract becomes impossible of performance by reason of the non-existence of the state of things assumed by both contracting parties as the foundation of the contract, there will be no breach of the contract thus limited.

Now what are the facts of the present case? The contract is contained in two letters of June 20 which passed between the defendant and the plaintiff's agent, Mr. Cecil Bisgood. These letters do not mention the coronation, but speak merely of the taking of Mr. Krell's chambers, or, rather, of the use of them, in the daytime of June 26 and 27, for the sum of £75,

£25 then paid, balance £50 to be paid on the 24th. But the affidavits, which by agreement between the parties are to be taken as stating the facts of the case, shew that the plaintiff exhibited on his premises, third floor, 56A Pall Mall, an announcement to the effect that windows to view the Royal coronation procession were to be let, and that the defendant was induced by that announcement to apply to the housekeeper on the premises, who said that the owner was willing to let the suite of rooms for the purpose of seeing the Royal procession for both days, but not nights, of June 26 and 27. In my judgment the use of the rooms was let and taken for the purpose of seeing the Royal procession. It was not a demise of the rooms, or even an agreement to let and take the rooms. It is a licence to use rooms for a particular purpose and none other. And in my judgment the taking place of these processions on the days proclaimed along the proclaimed route which passed 56A Pall Mall, was regarded by both contracting parties as the foundation of the contract; and I think that it cannot reasonably be supposed to have been in the contemplation of the contracting parties, when the contract was made, that the coronation would not be held on the proclaimed days, or the processions not take place on those days along the proclaimed route; and I think that the words imposing on the defendant the obligation to accept and pay for the use of the rooms for the named days, although general and unconditional, were not used with reference to the possibility of the particular contingency which afterwards occurred.

It was suggested in the course of the argument that if the occurrence, on the proclaimed days, of the coronation and the procession in this case were the foundation of the contract, and if the general words are thereby limited or qualified, so that in the event of the non-occurrence of the coronation and procession along the proclaimed route they would discharge both parties from further performance of the contract, it would follow that if a cabman was engaged to take some one to Epsom on Derby Day at a suitable enhanced price for such a journey, say £10, both parties to the contract would be discharged in the contingency of the race at Epsom for some reason becoming impossible; but I do not think this follows, for I do not think that in the cab case the happening of the race would be the foundation of the contract. No doubt the purpose of the engager would be to go to see the Derby, and the price would be proportionately high; but the cab had no special qualifications for the purpose which led to the selection of the cab for this particular occasion. Any other cab would have done as well. Moreover, I think that, under the cab contract, the hirer even if the race went off, could have said, "Drive me to Epsom; I will pay you the agreed sum; you have nothing to do with the purpose for which I hired the cab," and that if the cabman refused he would have been guilty of a breach of contract, there being nothing to qualify his promise to drive the hirer to Epsom on a particular day.

Whereas in the case of the coronation, there is not merely the purpose of the hirer to see the coronation procession, but it is the coronation procession and the relative position of the rooms which is the basis of the contract as much for the lessor as the hirer; and I think that if the King, before the coronation day and after the contract, had died, the hirer could not have insisted on having the rooms on the days named. It could not in the cab case be reasonably said that seeing the Derby race was the foundation of the contract, as it was of the licence in this case. Whereas in the present case, where the rooms were offered and taken, by reason of their peculiar suitability from the position of the rooms for a view of the coronation procession, surely the view of the coronation procession was the foundation of the contract, which is a very different thing from the purpose of the man who engaged the cab—namely, to see the race—being held to be the foundation of the contract.

Each must be judged by its own circumstances. In each case one must ask oneself, first, what, having regard to all the circumstances, was the foundation of the contract? Secondly, was the performance of the contract prevented? Thirdly, was the event which prevented the performance of the contract of such a character that it cannot reasonably be said to have been in the contemplation of the parties at the date of the contract? If all these questions are answered in the affirmative (as I think they should be in this case), I think both parties are discharged from further performance of the contract. I think that the coronation procession was the foundation of this contract, and that the non-happening of it prevented the performance of the contract; and, secondly, I think that the non-happening of the procession, to use the words of Sir James Hannen in *Baily* v. *De Crespigny* (1869), L.R. 4 Q.B. 180, was an event "of such a character that it cannot reasonably be supposed to have been in the contemplation of the contracting parties when the contract was made, and that they are not to be held bound by general words which, though large enough to include, were not used with reference to the possibility of the particular contingency which afterwards happened."

The test seems to be whether the event which causes the impossibility was or might have been anticipated and guarded against. It seems difficult to say, in a case where both parties anticipate the happening of an event, which anticipation is the foundation of the contract, that either party must be taken to have anticipated, and ought to have guarded against, the event which prevented the performance of the contract. In both *Jackson* v. *Union Marine Insurance Co.*, (1873), L.R. 8 C.P. 572; 10 C.P. 125, and *Nickoll* v. *Ashton* the parties might have anticipated as a possibility that perils of the sea might delay the ship and frustrate the commercial venture; in the former case the carriage of the goods to effect which the charter-party was entered into; in the latter case the sale of the goods which were to be shipped on the steamship which was delayed. But the Court held in the former case that the basis of the contract was that the ship would arrive in time to carry out the contemplated commercial venture, and in the latter that the steamship would arrive in time for the loading of the goods the subject of the sale.

I wish to observe that cases of this sort are very different from cases where a contract or warranty or representation is implied, such as was implied in *The Moorcock*, (1889), 14 P.D. 64, and refused to be implied in *Hamblyn* v. *Wood*, [1891] 2 Q.B. 488. But *The Moorcock* is of importance in the present case as shewing that whatever is the suggested implication—be it condition, as in this case, or warranty or representation —one must, in judging whether the implication ought to be made, look not only at the words of the contract, but also at the surrounding facts and the knowledge of the parties of those facts. There seems to me to be ample authority for this proposition. Thus in *Jackson* v. *Union Marine Insurance Co.*, in the Common Pleas, the question whether the object of the voyage had been frustrated by the delay of the ship was left as a question of fact to the jury, although there was nothing in the charter-party defining the time within which the charterers were to supply the cargo of iron rails for San Francisco, and nothing on the face of the charter-party to indicate the importance of time in the venture; and that was a case in which, as Bramwell B. points out in his judgment at p. 148 in 10 C.P., *Taylor* v. *Caldwell* was a strong authority to support the conclusion arrived at in the judgment—that the ship not arriving in time for the voyage contemplated, but at such time as to frustrate the commercial venture, was not only a breach of the contract but discharged the charter, though he had such an excuse that no action would lie.

And, again, in *Harris* v. *Dreesman* (1854), 23 L.J. (Ex.) 210, the vessel had to be loaded, as no particular time was mentioned, within a reasonable time; and, in judging of a reasonable time, the Court approved of evidence being given that the defendants, the charterers, to the knowledge of the plaintiff, had no control over the colliery from which both parties knew that the coal was to come; and that, although all that was said in the charter-party was that the vessel should proceed to Spital Tongue's Spout (the spout of the Spital Tongue's Colliery), and there take on board from the freighters a full and complete cargo of coals, and five tons of coke, and although there was no evidence to prove any custom in the port as to loading vessels in turn.

Again it was held in *Mumford* v. *Gething* (1859), 7 C.B. (N.S.) 305; 141 E.R. 834, that, in construing a written contract of service under which A was to enter the employ of B, oral evidence is admissible to shew in what capacity A was to serve B. . . . The rule seems to be that which is laid down in *Taylor on Evidence*, vol. ii, s. 1028: "It may be laid down as a broad and distinct rule of law that extrinsic evidence of every material fact which will enable the Court to ascertain the nature and qualities of the subject-matter of the instrument, or, in other words, to identify the persons and things to which the instrument refers, must of necessity be received." And Lord Campbell in his judgment says: "I am of opinion that, when there is a contract for the sale of a specific subject-matter, oral evidence may be received, for the purpose of shewing what the subject-matter was, of every fact within the knowledge of the parties before and at the time of the contract." See per Campbell C.J., *Macdonald* v. *Longbottom* (1859), 1 E. & E. 977; 120 E.R. 1177 at p. 1179. It seems to me that the language of Willes J. in *Lloyd* v. *Guibert* (1865), 35 L.J. (Q.B.) 74, 75, points in the same direction.

I myself am clearly of opinion that in this case, where we have to ask ourselves whether the object of the contract was frustrated by the non-happening of the coronation and its procession on the days proclaimed, parol evidence is admissible to shew that the subject of the contract was rooms to view the coronation procession, and was so to the knowledge of both parties. When once this is established, I see no difficulty whatever in the case. It is not essential to the application of the principle of *Taylor* v. *Caldwell* that the direct subject of the contract should perish or fail to be in existence at the date of the performance of the contract. It is sufficient if a state of things or condition expressed in the contract and essential to its performance perishes or fails to be in existence at that time. In the present case the condition which fails and prevents the achievement of that which was, in the contemplation of both parties, the foundation of the contract, is not expressly mentioned either as a condition of the contract or the purpose of it; but I think for the reasons which I have given that the principle of *Taylor* v. *Caldwell* ought to be applied.

This disposes of the plaintiff's claim for £50 unpaid balance of the price agreed to be paid for the use of the rooms. The defendant at one time set up a cross-claim for the return of the £25 he paid at the date of contract. As that claim is now withdrawn it is unnecessary to say anything about it. I have only to add that the facts of this case do not bring it within the principle laid down in *Stubbs* v. *Holywell Ry. Co.* (1867), L.R. Ex. 311; that in the case of contracts falling directly within the rule of *Taylor* v. *Caldwell* the subsequent impossibility does not affect rights already acquired, because the defendant had the whole of June 24 to pay the balance, and the public announcement that the coronation and processions would not take place on the proclaimed days was made early on the morning of the 24th, and no cause of action could accrue till the end of that day. I think this appeal ought to be dismissed.

[The concurring opinions of Romer L.J. and Stirling L.J. are omitted.]

HERNE BAY STEAM BOAT CO. *v*. HALTON. [1903] 2 K.B. 683 (England. Court of Appeal). The defendant who had agreed to charter a boat in order to take passengers to see the royal naval review at Spithead, was held not excused by the King's illness which caused the review to be cancelled. While it might have been the defendant's purpose so to use the boat, such purpose was not contemplated by both parties as the foundation of the contract. ROMER L. J.: . . . "the object was a matter with which the defendant, as hirer of the ship, was alone concerned."

VANCOUVER BREWERIES, LTD. *v*. DANA
British Columbia. Supreme Court of Canada. 1915. 52 S.C.R. 134

FITZPATRICK C.J.: This is an action by the respondents (plaintiffs) to recover the rent of certain hotel property. The defence was that by certain covenants in the lease the plaintiffs or their assigns undertook to enlarge the premises so as to comply with the by-laws and regulations of the city governing places for which liquor licenses were granted. Their defence alleges that by those regulations an enlargement of the premises and certain structural changes with respect to heating, lighting, etc., were required. The plaintiffs refused to make the necessary improvements and as a result the appellants lost their licence. They thereupon gave up possession and refused to pay rent and counterclaimed for damages. The trial judge gave judgment for the plaintiffs (respondents) and dismissed the counterclaim. The appellants (defendants) thereupon appealed to the full court and their appeal was dismissed.

I am of opinion that the judgment below should be confirmed on the very short ground that the land and house, and not the licence, were the subject matter of the lease and the right of the tenant to occupy the house for any other purpose continued after the cancellation of the licence.

The appeal should be dismissed with costs.

LONDON & NORTHERN ESTATES CO. *v*. SCHLESINGER. [1916] 1 K.B. 20. England. King's Bench Division). The plaintiff had rented a house to the defendant, an Austrian. Under war legislation the defendant was forbidden to live in the area in which the house was located. The defendant denied liability on the lease, but the court held that personal occupancy was not "the foundation of the contract."

BLACKBURN BOBBIN CO. LTD. *v.* T. W. ALLEN & SONS, LTD.
England. King's Bench. [1918] 1 K.B. 540

The claim is for damages for breach of contract. The plaintiffs are manufacturers of bobbins for spinning. Their office is at Blackburn. The defendants are timber merchants at Hull. In the early part of 1914 the defendants sold to the plaintiffs seventy standards of Finland birch timber at the price of £10 15s. per standard free on rail at Hull. Deliveries were to commence about June or July, 1914, and to continue during the season which would expire about November in that year. The contracts were not formal; they were created by correspondence. They contained no war or force majeure or suspension provisions. They were simple bargains of sale and purchase. Finland produces birch timber of a clean and pliable character. It is particularly useful for the purpose (inter alia) of manufacturing bobbins. The contract required that the timber to be supplied to the plaintiffs should come from Finland. Prior to the war the unvarying practice was to load the timber into vessels at ports in Finland for direct sea carriage to English ports. No timber was railed across Scandinavia for shipment from a Scandinavian port to England.

Up to August, 1914, the defendants had made no deliveries to the plaintiffs. Then war broke out. Imports of timber from Finland stopped at once. German war vessels traversed the Baltic. Transport was paralysed. No vessels left Finland for Sweden. Swedish vessels ceased to sail for Finland. The vast disorganizing effect of the war on trade and transport need not be further indicated. It undoubtedly effected a revolution of circumstances, and rendered it impossible for the defendants to deliver the timber in accordance with their bargain. The English timber merchants who deal in Finnish timber do not hold stocks. Their timber as it arrived before the outbreak of war had gone to the customers to whom it had been already sold.

Following upon the outbreak of war the defendants did not supply the plaintiffs with any portion of the timber to which the plaintiffs were entitled during the season of 1914. Correspondence took place between the parties up to November, 1914. Thenceforward no letter or communication passed between them until July, 1916. In that month the plaintiffs asked for delivery. The defendants then asserted for the first time that the contracts had been dissolved by the outbreak of war in 1914. The plaintiffs disputed this assertion; hence their claim to damages. The defence contained no plea that the contract was mutually abandoned, nor was any such point raised in argument.

McCardie J.: . . . It is obvious that the principle raised by the case is one of vital and general importance. The question at issue is this: When will a change of circumstances (not due to the default of either party) cause a dissolution of contract? The law upon the matter is undoubtedly in process of evolution: see per Atkin J. in *Lloyd Royal Belge Societe Anonyme* v. *Strathatos* (1917), 33 Times L.R. 390, and per Pickford L.J. in *Hulton & Co.* v. *Chadwick & Taylor*, (1918), 34 Times L.R. 230. The point must presumably be solved upon broad existing principles of contract law. Those principles, I conceive, should be the same whether the case be one of charterparty, building contract, or sale of goods: see per Lord Loreburn in the *Tamplin Case* [1916] 2 A.C. 397, 404. But the application of the principles may vary with the terms and subject-matter of the contract. Is there a conflict at the present time between the rules which are relevant to the present case? The original rule of English law was clear in its insistence that where a party by his own contract creates a duty or charge upon himself he is bound to make it good notwithstanding any accident by inevitable necessity, because he might have provided against it by his contract: see per Curiam, *Paradine* v. *Jane* (1647), 82 E.R. 897. That principle was applied with full severity during the eighteenth century. I need not discuss the decisions in detail; many are referred to in *Leake on Contracts*, 6th ed., pp. 494–498. In some of those cases there was clearly a grave change of circumstances not within the contemplation of the parties at the time of the contract, yet it was held that no dissolution of contractual obligation took place. I mention the decisions referred to in Leake because it is, I think, essential to remember them if the pending evolution of principle proceeds. The original rule has again and again been restated. . . . To what extent has the original rule been modified by later decision? . . . The first true modification of the original rule was created, I think, by the doctrine of commercial frustration. I need not review the decisions on this doctrine; they are fully and historically considered in the judgments, both in the Common Pleas and the Exchequer Chamber, in *Jackson* v. *Union Marine Insurance Co.* (1873), L.R. 8 C.P. 572; (1874), L.R. 10 C.P. 125. The effect of that decision is best stated by Brett J., L.R. 8 C.P. 581 as follows: "Where a contract is made with reference to certain anticipated circumstances, and where, without any default of either party, it becomes wholly inapplicable to or impossible of application to any such circumstances, it ceases to have any application; it cannot be applied to other circumstances which could not have been in the contemplation of the parties when the contract was made." If these words of Brett J. are to be applied to their widest extent they may well effect a revolution of contract law. It has been pointed out by Lord Loreburn that the rule stated in *Jackson* v. *Union Marine Insurance Co.* is a mere application to commercial adventures of a broad contractual principle: see the *Tamplin Case*. The next true modification of the original rule was finally effected by the decision in *Taylor* v. *Caldwell* (1863), 122 E.R. 309. There the contract was held dissolved by the destruction of its subject-matter. The doctrine of *Taylor* v. *Caldwell* was extended by *Nickoll & Knight* v. *Ashton, Edridge & Co.*, [1901] 2 K.B. 126, and still more strikingly enlarged by the Coronation cases, of which *Krell* v. *Henry*, [1903] 2 K.B. 740, is the most vivid example, for in *Krell* v. *Henry* the Court held that a collateral, though important, circumstance was the basis of the contract between the parties, and that when the basis ceased it followed that the contract was dissolved. *Krell* v. *Henry* has been frequently cited and adopted in the highest tribunal.

So stood the decisions at the outbreak of the present war. Since that event judgments have been delivered as to the true effect of the decisions I have stated. On the one hand the original rule has been stated to exist in its integrity, whilst on the other hand the modification of the rule is deemed to be clearly settled: see per Lord Wrenbury in *Horlock* v. *Beal*, [1916] 1 A.C. 486, 525. The explanation of the lines of cases represented (a) by *Jackson* v. *Marine Union Insurance Co.* and (b) by *Krell* v. *Henry* has been finally and authoritatively stated. It was put with clearness by

Lord Shaw in *Horlock* v. *Beal*, where he said: "The underlying ratio is the failure of something which was at the basis of the contract in the mind and intention of the contracting parties." It was stated with equal clearness by Lord Haldane in the *Tamplin* Case, where he said: "The occurrence itself may . . . be of a character and extent so sweeping that the foundation of what the parties are deemed to have had in contemplation has disappeared, and the contract itself has vanished with that foundation." In every case it is now necessary "to examine the contract and the circumstances in which it was made, not of course to vary, but only to explain it, in order to see whether or not from the nature of it the parties must have made their bargain on the footing that a particular thing or state of things would continue to exist.And if they must have done so, then a term to that effect will be implied, though it be not expressed in the contract": per Lord Loreburn in the *Tamplin* Case. It is obvious that what I will call the *Krell* v. *Henry* rule as now formulated is theoretically capable of application to all contracts, whether as between shipowner and seaman, as in *Horlock* v. *Beal*, or to building contracts, as in *Metropolitan Water Board* v. *Dick, Kerr & Co*., [1918] A.C. 119.

But by what tests and subject to what limitation is the *Krell* v. *Henry* rule to be applied? No indication has yet been given as to the extent of its operation. At the outbreak of war a vast body of commercial contracts existed which contained no clauses whatever providing for that event. No one can doubt that such contracts had been made upon the assumption that peace would continue. Neither side contemplated the occurrence of war. But it cannot be that all such contracts were dissolved by the events of August, 1914. The mere continuance of peace was not a condition of the contract: see per Lord Loreburn in the *Tamplin* Case. The destruction of a state of peace is not of itself a destruction of any specific set of facts within the *Krell* v. *Henry* rule. Nor can it be that grave difficulty on the part of a vendor in procuring the contract articles will excuse him from the performance of his bargain. If such were the case, then the decision of the House of Lords in *Tenants (Lancashire)* v. *Wilson & Co*., [1917] A.C. 495, with respect to the force majeure clause there in question would have been unnecessary, for the contract would have been dissolved by a basic change of circumstances and the principle of *Metropolitan Water Board* v. *Dick, Kerr & Co.* would have applied.

What, then, are the limits of the *Krell* v. *Henry* rule as most recently exemplified by the last-named case, *Metropolitan Water Board* v. *Dick, Kerr & Co*.? At the same time I deem it well to ask this further question: Have the recent decisions in the House of Lords impliedly overruled the judgment of the Court of Appeal in *Jacobs, Marcus & Co*. v. *Credit Lyonnais*? (1884), 12 Q.B.D. 589. There the defendants, a London firm, sold to the plaintiffs, London merchants, 20,000 tons of Algerian esparto to be shipped by a French company at an Algerian port on vessels to be provided by the plaintiffs. The defendants pleaded that performance of their contract had become impossible by reason of an insurrection in Algeria, and a consequent prohibition by the territorial Government of the collection and transport of esparto. It was held by the Court of Appeal (Brett M.R. and Bowen L.J.), affirming Manisty and Denman JJ., that such plea afforded no answer to the plaintiff's claim for damages. The pith of the case was put by Bowen L.J.:

"Now, one of the incidents which the English law attaches to a contract is that (except in certain excepted cases as that of common carriers and bailees, of which this is not one), a person who expressly contracts absolutely to do a thing not naturally impossible, is not excused for non-performance because of being prevented by vis major. 'The rule laid down in the case of *Paradine* v. *Jane* has,' says Lord Ellenborough, 'been often recognized in Courts of law as a sound one; i.e. that "when the party by his own contract creates a duty or charge upon himself, he is bound to make it good, if he may, notwithstanding any accident by inevitable necessity, because he might have provided against it by his contract." *Atkinson* v. *Ritchie* (1809), 10 East, 530, 533. See also *Spence* v. *Chodwick*, 10 Q.B. 517, 530; *Lloyd* v. *Guibert* (1865), L.R. 1 Q.B. 115, 121. If inevitable necessity occurring in this country would not excuse non-performance, why should non-performance be excused on account of the inevitable necessity arising abroad? So to hold would be to alter the liability which English law attaches to contracts, and would, in the absence of an expressed or implied intention to that effect, be contrary to authority as well as principle, see *Barker* v. *Hodgson* (1814), 3 M. & S. 267; *Sjoerds* v. *Luscombe* (1812), 16 East, 201."

The change of circumstances in *Jacob's Case* was serious and clearly was not forseen by the parties. . . .

To supply an answer to the above question is a task of great difficulty in the absence of any authoritative guidance, for it calls not only for a reconciliation of apparently conflicting lines of cases, but it calls also for the ever-embarassing duty of deciding whether an implied term shall be read into a given contract to the effect that dissolution shall take place if an uncontemplated and serious change of circumstances occurs. The decisions with respect to personal service throw, I feel, but little light on the matter, for it seems just and reasonable to imply a condition in such agreements that the contract shall be dissolved upon the death or physical incapacity of the person who has agreed to give his personal services. . . . Death and illness are unceasing features of human society. I think, however, that assistance is derived from considering broadly the nature of the cases in which the *Krell* v. *Henry* rule has been applied, whether before or after that decision in 1903. It will be observed that they apparently fall into several classes: First, where British legislation or Government intervention has removed the specific subject-matter of the construction from the scope of private obligation (*Bailey* v. *De Crespigny* (1869), L.R. 4 Q.B. 180, is a good example of this class; see also *In re Shipton, Anderson & Co.* and *Harrison Brothers & Co.*, [1915] 3 K.B. 676, the case of specific goods. I myself venture to think that this is an independent class of case, though, for the purpose of clearness, I classify it as falling within *Krell* v. *Henry*); secondly, where the actual and specific subject-matter of the contract has ceased to exist, apart from British legislation or administrative intervention (*Taylor* v. *Caldwell* is the best example of this class; *Horlock* v. *Beal* is really, I think, a further example of this class); thirdly, where a specific set of facts directly affecting a specific subject-matter has ceased to exist (see *Jackson* v. *Union Marine Insurance Co.*, the case of a ship, and *Scottish Navigation Co.* v. *Souter & Co.*, [1917] 1 K.B. 222, also the case of a ship); fourthly, where a specific set of facts collaterally only affecting a specific subject-matter, but yet constituting the basis of contract, has ceased to exist (see *Nickoll & Knight* v. *Ashton, Edridge & Co.* the case of a ship, and *Krell* v. *Henry*, the letting of specific premises); and, fifthly, where British administrative intervention has so directly operated upon the fulfilment of a contract for a specific work as to transform the contemplated conditions of performance (*Metropolitan Water Board* v. *Dick, Kerr & Co.*). I need not, of course, classify or illustrate the cases in which British legislation has directly prohibited the performance of a contract. In such cases the doctrine of illegality dissolves the bargains: see *Brewster* v. *Kitchell*, (1697), 1 Salk. 198. In none of the cases in the above classes has it been stated or substantially suggested that the principle of *Krell* v. *Henry* applies to the case of a bare sale of unascertained goods. The illuminating judgment of Scrutton L.J. in *Metropolitan Water Board* v. *Dick, Kerr & Co.* seems throughout to be dealing with specific subject-matters.

But the above classification, imperfect as I fear it is, does not exhaust the decisions which call for consideration, and here I must point out that in not a few of the decisions since the outbreak of the war the question of trading with the enemy has crept directly or indirectly into the determination of the matters in dispute. The doctrine of prohibition against any intercourse whether commercial or otherwise, with an enemy subject, is severe and far-reaching. . . . It is important to remember this point in approaching the cases which I next mention. Such cases apparently deal with a sale of unascertained goods. They are as follows: (a) *Jager* v. *Tolme & Runge*, [1916] 1 K.B. 939 (Court of Appeal). The facts of this case were complicated, but the substance of the matter was that the vendors had agreed to deliver sugar f.o.b. Hamburg in August, 1914. The parties were British. The Courts held that the contract was dissolved by the outbreak of war. In my opinion, however, it is clear that the ratio of the decision was that performance of the contract would be illegal inasmuch as it would involve commercial intercourse with the enemy. The Court of Appeal ignored the expressly-raised contention that the contracts had been dissolved on the principle of *Krell* v. *Henry*. The case of *Grey & Co.* v. *Tolme* (1915), 31 Times L.R. 551 was decided by Bailhache J. on the same ratio. (b) *Smith, Coney & Barrett* v. *Becker, Gray & Co.*, [1916] 2 Ch. 86. Here, again, the facts were complicated. The parties were British firms. The vendors had agreed on August 1, 1914, to sell sugar f.o.b. or into warehouse Hamburg. In view of the special provisions in the contract the Court held that the contract was not dissolved. Had it held otherwise, I venture to think that the true ratio would again have been that performance would have involved trading with the enemy. But it is right to say that although the majority of the Court (Lord Cozens-Hardy M.R. and Swinfen Eady L.J.) did not apparently favour the application of the *Krell* v. *Henry* rule, yet Phillimore L.J. seems to have thought that it might apply under certain circumstances—for instance, if the sugar had been wholly destroyed by fire. The point does not seem to have been fully argued, and such cases as *Jacobs, Marcus & Co.* v. *Credit Lyonnais*, were not brought to the attention of the Court. (c) *Hulton & Co.* v. *Chadwick & Taylor*. The facts in this decision more closely approach the facts of the present case. It was recognized by Pickford L.J. that the principle of dissolution of contract by change of circumstances had been largely extended in operation. But I respectfully suggest that the true ratio of the decision of the Court of Appeal is to be found not so much in the change of circumstance, though serious in extent, as in the fact that an administrative intervention of the British Government had in substance prevented the fulfilment of the contract by the vendor in accordance with his obligations. *Hulton & Co.* v. *Chadwick & Taylor*, represents, in my view, an extension of the principle of *Brewster* v. *Kitchell* or *Baily* v. *De Crespigny*, rather than a true extension of the broader principle of *Krell* v. *Henry*. The former principle is one which admits of many applications in these days of administrative intervention, and in some cases the facts may be covered as much by *Krell* v. *Henry* as by *Baily* v. *De Crespigny*. The principles may overlap. The rule contended for by Mr. MacKinnon must have applied, if at all, as much to that case as to the present, for there had been in *Hulton*'s Case a revolution of circumstance, yet it is clear that Pickford L.J. rested his judgment on administrative intervention, that is to say, on *Baily* v. *De Crespigny*, rather than on the application of the *Krell* v. *Henry* rule.

My conclusion upon the matter is that in the absence of any question as to trading with the enemy, and in the absence also of any administrative intervention by the British Government authorities, a bare and unqualified contract for the sale of unascertained goods will not (unless most special facts compel an opposite implication) be dissolved by the operation of the principle of *Krell* v. *Henry*, even though there has been so grave and unforeseen a change of circumstance as to render it impossible for the vendor to fulfil his bargain. If I were to hold otherwise, I should create a rule the results of which no man can foresee, and to the operation of which no judge can satisfactorily fix the limits.

By stating the above conclusion I maintain the original rule of English law whereby a man is bound by his contract whilst I leave a field as yet undefined for the operation and extension of the *Krell* v. *Henry* principle. I am fortified in the view I express by the fact that *Jacobs, Marcus & Co.* v. *Credit Lyonnaise*, has remained unchallenged amidst the testing breadth of recent decisions. I can see no sound distinction between impossibility of foreign law and impossibility created by an outbreak of war involving a complete cessation of transport facilities. Just as it seems clear that a vendor is not absolved from the duty to deliver unascertained goods by reason of the destruction of his factory or warehouse, so a vendor is not relieved from his obligation in such a case as the present. An ordinary and bare contract for the sale of unascertained goods gives no scope for the operation of *Krell* v. *Henry* rule, unless the special facts show that the parties have clearly (though impliedly) agreed upon a set of circumstances as constituting the contractual basis. Here no such agreement exists. In the present case, I ask the question put by Denman J. in *Jacobs, Marcus & Co.* v. *Credit Lyonnais*: "Looking at the nature of this contract, what is there to show that the intention of the parties was that the defendants should be relieved from the performance of their contract by reason of difficulties arising out of circumstances which were unforseen?" My answer in the present case is that there is nothing to show such an intention. There is here no question of illegality or public policy, or actual prohibition or of intervention by the Government. There is merely an unforseen event which has rendered it practically impossible for the vendor to deliver. That event the defendants could easily have provided for in their contracts. If I approved the defendants' contention, I should be holding in substance that a contract which did not contain a war clause was as beneficial to the vendor as a contract which contained such a provision.

In my view the rule in *Jacobs, Marcus & Co.* v. *Credit Lyonnais* holds good today, and I think that it covers the present case. I desire respectfully to add that in my opinion the *Krell* v. *Henry* rule should not be unduly extended. It is only in exceptional cases that it can be safely applied. The difficulties of its application are amply indicated by the judgment of the

Court of Appeal in *Herne Bay Steam Boat Co.* v. *Hutton* [1903] 2 K.B. 683 and by the actual decision of the majority of the Law Lords in the *Tamplin* Case. The perils of the rule may appear in later years. If it be extended too far, it may tend to sap the foundations of contract law as they now exist. It is, I venture to say, of the utmost importance to a commercial nation that vendors should be held to their business contracts. When a change of circumstances is to absolve from liability, provision to that effect should be inserted in the margin. If I pronounce in favour of the defendants I should be giving a decision of a legislative rather than judicial character, and I might well be rendering superfluous in many cases the provisions contained in the *Courts (Emergency Powers) Act, 1917* (7 & 8 Geo. 5, c. 25).

I may mention that in the present case I am satisfied that the plaintiffs were unaware at the time of the contract of the circumstances that the timber from Finland was shipped direct from a Finnish port to Hull. They did not know whether the transport was or was not partly by rail across Scandinavia, nor did they know that the timber merchants in this country did not hold stocks of Finnish larch.

I decide against the first contention of the defendants. . . .

I therefore give judgment for the plaintiffs for £1,067 10s. with costs.

[Part of the judgment is omitted. The judgment of McCardie J. was affirmed by the Court of Appeal, [1918] 2 K.B. 467. Pickford L.J. said at p. 469: "I accept the finding that in fact the method of dispatching this timber was not known to the plaintiffs. But there remains the question, must they be deemed to have contracted on the basis of the continuance of that method although they did not in fact know of it? I see no reason for saying so. Why should a purchaser of goods, not specific goods, be deemed to concern himself with the way in which the other is going to fulfil his contract by providing the goods he has agreed to sell? The sellers in this case agreed to deliver the timber free on rail at Hull, and it was no concern of the buyers as to how the sellers intended to get the timber there. I can see no reason for saying—and to free the defendants from liability this would this would have to be said—that the continuance of the normal mode of shipping the timber from Finland was a matter which both parties contemplated as necessary for the fulfilment of the contract. To dissolve the contract the matter relied on must be something which both parties had in their minds when they entered into the contract, such for instance as the existence of the music-hall in *Taylor* v. *Caldwell* or the continuance of the vessel in readiness to perform the contract as in *Jackson* v. *Union Marine Insurance Co.* Here there is nothing to show that the plaintiffs contemplated, and there is no reason why they should be deemed to have contemplated, that the sellers should continue to have the ordinary facilities for dispatching the timber from Finland. As I have said, that was a matter which to the plaintiffs was wholly immaterial. It was not a matter forming the basis of the contract they entered into."]

VANCOUVER MILLING & GRAIN CO. *v.* C. C. RANCH CO. [1924] S.C.R. 671 (British Columbia. Supreme Court of Canada). ANGLIN C.J.C.: "By a contract made through a broker the defendants (respondents) sold to the plaintiffs (appellants) 30,000 bushels of wheat to be delivered during the months of September and October, 1922, f.o.b. cars Cayley, Alberta, 80 per cent of the price to be advanced against bills of lading. Although the broker's note is silent on the point, both parties treated the contract which it evidences as providing for shipment to Vancouver—and that should, we think, be deemed one of its terms.

"It is common ground that the Canadian Pacific Railway is the only railway at Cayley and was the carrier contemplated by the contract. The evidence abundantly establishes that the defendants had wheat ready for delivery to meet the obligation of their contract, which they were anxious to fulfil, that they made every effort to obtain cars but could procure only four during the period fixed for shipment and those cars were duly loaded and forwarded; that, but for the shortage of cars, in no wise attributable to any fault of the defendants, and the absolute refusal of the railway company to accept grain for shipment to Vancouver during a considerable period in the month of October, owing to congestion at that port, the defendants would have carried out their contract and that their failure to do so is ascribable solely to the inability or unwillingness of the railway company to supply cars to make their wheat available for shipment to the plaintiffs.

"Under these circumstances is the defendants' obligation to deliver the wheat so absolute that, although not at all at fault, they must pay damages for failure to implement it? Or, having regard to the fact known to both parties that the only available carrier was the Canadian Pacific Railway Co. and to the further fact that the defendants exhausted every reasonable means to obtain cars from it, should that obligation be so qualified that, to the extent to which it was prevented by the railway company's inability or refusal to supply the necessary cars, delivery within the stipulated period was excused? The Appellate Division has taken the latter view (Hyndman J. dissenting) and we are, with respect, of the opinion that its judgment was right and should be affirmed."

ONTARIO ELECTRIC LIGHT AND POWER CO. *v*. THE BAXTER & GALLOWAY COMPANY, LTD. 1903. 5 O.L.R. 419 (Ontario. Divisional Court). Ontario Power agreed to supply Baxter for five years with "electric current, to the extent of fifty horsepower" for $1,250 a year, payable monthly. The power was to be supplied to Baxter "in the premises" of the Company for the purpose of operating Baxter's machinery and for its general purposes as a miller, but for no other purpose. At the time of the agreement Baxter had a mill on its premises. Later the mill was destroyed by fire and Baxter claimed to be excused from its obligation to take the current. MEREDITH C.J.: "The object of this provision, as it appears to me, was to guard against the current being used by the customers for any other than power purposes for use in their own business as millers, and there is nothing in the provision, as I read it, to prevent the customers using the current for those purposes in any place to which they might choose after it was delivered to them, to transmit it, and certainly, nothing to confine the use of it by the customers to any existing mill on the premises to which it was to be brought by [Ontario Power]."

TSAKIROGLOU & CO. LTD. *v*. NOBLEE THORL G.M.B.H.
England. House of Lords. [1962] A.C. 93

The respondents agreed on October 4, 1956, to buy 300 tons of Sudanese groundnuts from the appellants for shipment from Port Sudan to Hamburg during November or December. On October 29 the British and French forces began military operations against Egypt to protect the Suez Canal. The Canal was blocked to navigation from November 2 until April 9,

1957. The usual route for such a shipment was via the Canal and the respondents refused to ship the nuts, although it was feasible to have shipped them via the Cape of Good Hope during November and December. The Cape route is 11,137 miles. The Canal route is 4,386 miles. Freight surcharges were imposed, first of 25%, as from November 10, and then of 100% as from December 13. The rate was £7 10s. per ton. The market price of Sudanese nuts in Hamburg was about £68 15s. per ton between January 1 and 13, 1957.

The case was heard by an umpire under arbitration proceedings who awarded £5,625 as damages, to the respondents. The board of appeal of the Incorporated Oil Seed Association upheld the award and Diplock J. on a stated case upheld the award. His decision was affirmed by the Court of Appeal. Clause 6 of the I.O.S.A. standard form contract provided that "in case of . . . war . . . and in all cases of force majeure preventing the shipment within the time fixed . . . the period allowed . . . shall be extended by not exceeding two months. After that, if the case of force majeure be still operating, the contract shall be cancelled." It was unanimously agreed that clause 6 did not relieve the defendants: there was no "war" and the "shipment" was not prevented via the Cape.

VISCOUNT SIMONDS: . . . I come then to the main issue and, as usual, I find two questions interlocked: (1) What does the contract mean? In other words, is there an implied term that the goods shall be carried by a particular route? (2) Is the contract frustrated?

It is convenient to examine the first question first, though the answer may be inconclusive. For it appears to me that it does not automatically follow that, because one term of a contract, for example, that the goods shall be carried by a particular route, becomes impossible of performance, the whole contract is thereby abrogated. Nor does it follow, because as a matter of construction a term cannot be implied, that the contract may not be frustrated by events. In the instant case, for example, the impossibility of the route via Suez, if that were assumed to be the implied contractual obligation, would not necessarily spell the frustration of the contract.

It is put in the forefront of the appellants' case that the contract was a contract for the shipment of goods via Suez. This contention can only prevail if a term is implied, for the contract does not say so. To say that that is nevertheless its meaning is to say in other words that the term must be implied. For this I see no ground. It has been rejected by the learned trial judge and each of the members of the Court of Appeal. . . .

I turn now to what was the main argument for the appellants: that the contract was frustrated by the closure of the Canal from November 2, 1956, till April 1957. Were it not for the decision of McNair J. in *Green's* case, [1959] 1 Q.B. 131, I should not have thought this contention arguable and I must say with the greatest respect to that learned judge that I cannot think he has given full weight to the decisions old and new of this House upon the doctrine of frustration. He correctly held upon the authority of *Reardon Smith Line Ltd.* v. *Black Sea and Baltic General Insurance Co. Ltd.*, [1939] A.C. 562, that "where a contract, expressly or by necessary implication, provides that performance, or a particular part of the performance, is to be carried out in a customary manner, the performance must be carried out in a manner which is customary at the time when the performance is called for." But he concluded that the continued availability of the Suez route was a fundamental assumption at the time when the contract was made and that to impose upon the sellers the obligation to ship by an emergency route via the Cape would be to impose upon them a fundamentally different obligation which neither party could at the time when the contract was performed have dreamed that the sellers would be required to perform. Your Lordships will observe how similar this line of argument is to that which supports the implication of a term that the route should be via Suez and no other. I can see no justification for it. We are concerned with a c.i.f. contract for the sale of goods, not a contract of affreightment, though part of the sellers' obligation will be to procure a contract of affreightment. There is no evidence that the buyers attached any importance to the route. They were content that the nuts should be shipped at any date in November or December. There was no evidence, and I suppose could not be, that the nuts would deteriorate as the result of a longer voyage and a double crossing of the Equator, nor any evidence that the market was seasonable. In a word, there was no evidence that the buyers cared by what route or, within reasonable limits, when the nuts arrived. What, then, of the sellers? I recall the well-known passage in the speech of Lord Atkinson in *Johnson* v. *Taylor Bros. & Co. Ltd.*, [1920] A.C. 144, where he states the obligations of the vendor of goods under a c.i.f. contract, and ask which of these obligations is (to use McNair J.'s word) "fundamentally" altered by a change of route. Clearly the contract of affreightment will be different and so may be the terms of insurance. In both these respects the sellers may be put to greater cost: their profit may be reduced or even disappear. But it hardly needs reasserting that an increase of expense is not a ground of frustration: see *Larrinaga & Co. Ltd.* v. *Société Franco-Américaine des Phosphates de Medulla, Paris* (1922), 38 T.L.R. 739.

Nothing else remains to justify the view that the nature of the contract was "fundamentally" altered. That is the word used by Viscount Simon in *British Movietonews Ltd.* v. *London and District Cinemas Ltd.*, [1952] A.C. 166, at p. 185, and by my noble and learned friend Lord Reid in *Davis Contractors Ltd.* v. *Fareham Urban District Council*, [1956] A.C. 696, at p. 723. In the latter case my noble and learned friend Lord Radcliffe used the expression "radically different" and I think that the two expressions mean the same thing, as perhaps do other adverbs which have been used in this context. Whatever expression is used, I venture to say what I have said myself before and others more authoritatively have said before me: that the doctrine of frustration must be applied within very narrow limits. In my opinion this case falls far short of satisfying the necessary conditions. Reluctant as I am to differ from a judge so experienced in commercial law as McNair J., I am glad to find that my view is shared by Ashworth J. and all the members of the Court of Appeal.

Upon this part of the case I have not thought it necessary to deal with Pearson J.'s decision in *Société Franco Tunisienne D'Armement,* v. *Sidermar S.P.A.*, [1961] 2 Q.B. 278. There the question was whether a charterparty was frustrated by the blocking of the Suez Canal. The learned judge held that it was, but was at pains to point out that the position was very different in a contract for the sale of goods. Upon that point I agree with him and need not discuss the matter further.

I come finally to a question which has given me some trouble. I refer to the sixth finding in the special case which I have already fully set out. It will be remembered that the vital words were "not commercially or fundamentally different." Diplock J., regarding this as a finding of fact, thought that the case was thereby concluded. I cannot regard this as a correct decision. It is a question of law whether a contract has been frustrated and it is commonly said that frustration occurs when conditions arise which are fundamentally different from those contemplated by the parties. But it does not follow from the use by the arbitrator of the word "fundamentally" in describing the difference between the actual and the contemplated conditions that the court is precluded from forming its own judgment whether or not a contract has been frustrated. It is of great value to the court to know that lay arbitrators with special knowledge do or do not regard the new circumstances as so different from those contemplated that they think "fundamental" an appropriate word to use. But the value is evidential only. It has not the sanctity of a finding of fact. I do not say that an arbitrator should be debarred from the use of the word "fundamental" or "radical" or any other word which he thinks apt to give emphasis to his view. But if he does so he must not be taken indirectly to determine the question of law which the court must decide.

In my opinion, the appeal should be dismissed with costs.

LORD RADCLIFFE: . . . This contract was a sale of goods, which involved dispatching the goods from Port Sudan to Hamburg; but, of course, the transport was not the whole but only one of the incidents of the contract, in which particular incident neither vendors nor buyers were directly implicated. There was nothing to prevent the vendors from dispatching the goods as contracted, unless they were impliedly bound as a term of the contract to use no other route than that of the Suez Canal. I do not see why that term should be implied and, if it is not implied, the true question seems to me to be, since shipment was due to be made by some route during November/December, whether it was a reasonable action for a mercantile man to perform his contract by putting the goods on board a ship going round the Cape of Good Hope and obtaining a bill of lading on this basis. A man may habitually leave his house by the front door to keep his appointments; but, if the front door is stuck, he would hardly be excused for not leaving by the back. The question, therefore, is what is the reasonable mercantile method of performing the contract at a time when the Suez Canal is closed, not at a time when it is open. To such a question the test of "the usual and customary route" is ex hypothesi inapplicable.

On the facts found by the special case I think that the answer is inevitable. The voyage would be a much longer one in terms of miles; but length reflects itself in such matters as time of arrival, condition of goods, increase of freight rates. A change of route may, moreover, augment the sheer hazard of the transport. There is nothing in the circumstances of the commercial adventure represented by the appellants' contract which suggests that these changes would have been material. Time was plainly elastic. Not only did the vendors have the option of choosing any date within a two-month period for shipment, but also there was a wide margin within which there might be variations of the speed capacity of the carrying vessel or vessels selected. There was no stipulated date for arrival at Hamburg. Nothing appears to suggest that the Cape voyage would be prejudicial to the condition of the goods or would involve special packing or stowing, nor does there seem to have been any seasonal market to be considered. With all these facts before them, as well as the measure of freight surcharge that would fall to the vendors' account, the board of appeal made their finding that performance by shipping on the Cape route was not "commercially or fundamentally different" from shipping via the Suez Canal. We have no material which would make it possible for us to differ from that conclusion.

It has been a matter of debate whether this finding ought to be treated as a finding of fact, by which a court would be bound, or as a holding of law, which as such, would be open to review. It was treated as the first by the learned trial judge: it was treated more as the second by the Court of Appeal whose view of it was, I think, that, while of the utmost relevance for the determination of the final issue of the case, it did not bind the court so as to dictate what it should decide. So far as the distinction can be made between law and fact, I agree with the Court of Appeal. I regard it as a mixed question of fact and law whether transport via the Cape of Good Hope was so materially different from transport via the Suez Canal that it was not within the range of the c.i.f. contract or, alternatively, was so radically different that it left that contract frustrated. The ultimate conclusion is a conclusion of law, but in a case of this sort that conclusion is almost completely determined by what is ascertained as to mercantile usage and the understanding of mercantile men.

I do not believe that in this, as in many other branches of commercial law, it is possible to analyse very precisely where law begins and facts ends. That is because in this field legal obligations and legal rights are largely founded upon usage and practice, which themselves are established as matters of fact. Many things which are now regarded as settled principles of law originated in nothing more than common mercantile practice, and the existence and terms of this practice have been vouched sometimes by questions put to and answered by special juries, sometimes by the findings and views of commercial arbitrators and sometimes by the bare statements of the judges, founded upon their experience at the Bar or on the Bench. It would be difficult, for instance, to separate the judgments on commercial law delivered by three such masters as Lord Esher, Scrutton L.J. and Lord Sumner from their personal acquaintance with mercantile usages and their translation of the one into the terms of the other.

I do not think, therefore, that it is right to be very analytical in distinguishing between questions of law and questions of fact in matters of this kind. Since Lord Mansfield's day commercial law has been ascertained by a co-operative exchange between judge and jury, and now that arbitrators have taken the place of juries I do not think that we can start all over again with an absolute distinction between the respective spheres of judge and arbitrator. Generally speaking, I do not think that a finding in the form which we have here can ever be conclusive on the legal issue. When all necessary facts have been found it remains a question of law for the court what on the true construction of the contract are the obligations imposed or whether, having regard to the terms of the contract and the surrounding circumstances, any particular term is to be implied. But, when the implication of terms depends essentially upon what is customary or usual or accepted practice, it is inevitable that the findings of fact, whatever they may be, go virtually the whole way towards determining the legal result.

The finding in this case is perhaps unusual in that it does not speak for any usage or practice of trade—ex hypothesi, there was no established usage once the Suez Canal was blocked—but rather for the view of mercantile men as to the significance of adopting the alternative route. It is a summary way of stating that a voyage by that route would not involve any elements of difference that would be regarded as material by persons familiar with the trade. It would be contrary to common sense that a court, which cannot uninstructed assess the commercial significance of, say, a surcharge of £7 10s. per ton for freight in a c.i.f. contract of this kind, should not pay careful attention to such a view from such a source; just as it would be, I think, contrary to principle that a court should regard a view so expressed as finally conclusive of the legal issue.

I must add that I do not think that such a finding is altogether satisfactory for the purposes of a special case. It is in essence a summary of the commercial significance of several separate aspects of the Cape route as contrasted with the Suez Canal route, and it is embarrassing for a court which has to answer the question raised by the case to have before it only the summary and not the arbitrator's findings upon the individual aspects which make up the conclusion. I can see that, if this form came into general use, a court might feel obliged to send back the case containing it for further and more explicit findings. It would have been better if the special case had identified the several aspects of difference, length, time, cost, risk, etc., which, as it is, the court is left to infer, and had made with regard to them, both separately and together, the finding that was clearly intended, that they were not significant from the mercantile point of view.

I agree with the opinions already expressed by my noble and learned friends who have preceded me, that the exception clause, clause 6 of the contract, does not apply.

I would dismiss the appeal.

[The opinions of Lords Reid, Hodson and Guest dismissing the appeal are omitted.]

JOSEPH CONSTANTINE STEAMSHIP LINE, LTD. *v.* IMPERIAL SMELTING CORPORATION, LTD.

England. House of Lords. [1942] A.C. 154

Lord Wright. My Lords, this appeal has to deal with an award of an arbitrator in which he states for the decision of the court the question whether on the facts as found and on the true construction of the charterparty the respondents in this appeal are entitled to damages from the appellants for non-performance of the charterparty.

The dispute arose out of an explosion which occurred in the auxiliary boiler of the appellants' steamship Kingswood while she was anchored in the roads of Port Pirie. She had arrived there in pursuance of a charterparty of August 5, 1936, made between appellants as owners and the respondents as charterers. Under it she was to be ready to load a full ore cargo at Port Pirie at any customary wharf or wharves as ordered for carriage to a port or ports in England or the continent. She was expected to arrive at Port Pirie about the end of December, 1936, or early January, 1937. On December 26, 1936, she anchored in the roads of Port Pirie, having sailed in ballast from Lourenço Marques. It was agreed between the parties that the Kingswood should remain at her anchorage until January 4, 1937, and then proceed to her loading berth, on arrival at which time should count. While she lay at the anchorage and before she became an arrived ship the explosion occurred in the auxiliary boiler. It was of unprecedented character (in the words of the arbitrator) and took place within the boiler. The arbitrator found that it was due to the fact that there was a sudden opening of communication between the water and steam space and one or both of the combustion chambers. The energy released was such that the main boilers situated aft of the auxiliary boiler were set aft by the concussion of the explosion four feet and five feet six inches respectively, at which point their movement was arrested, whereas the auxiliary boiler itself was projected forward through two watertight bulkheads, finally piercing the collision bulkhead and breaking the shell plates at the starboard bow. The damage to the steamer was so serious that the appellants gave notice that they could not perform the charterparty. The respondents then claimed damages in the arbitration.

It was admitted in the arbitration that the delay caused by the damage to the steamer was such as to frustrate the commercial object of the adventure. The appellants resisted the claim on the ground that the frustration released them from liability for further performance. The respondents contested this defence on the ground that such a defence was only maintainable if the frustration took place without fault on the part of the appellants, and that it was for the appellants to show absence of fault. There had, in fact been a Board of Trade inquiry, but the arbitrator observed that neither those who were responsible for conducting the Board of Trade inquiry nor any of the witnesses who gave evidence before him claimed to be able to state with any certainty the causes of the disaster or the sequence of events that led up to it, and that no sequence of events which was other than improbable was suggested as capable of having given rise to it. The arbitrator stated three principal theories of the disaster which had been put forward, but the most he could say was that, though each theory might be possibly correct, he was not satisfied by it. He summed up the final result in the words: "I am not satisfied that the true cause of the disaster has as yet been suggested." Subject to the case stated, he awarded in favour of the respondents.

Thus the question has come before the court whether in the case of an admitted frustration of the adventure, without default of either party being proved, the promisors, in this case the appellants, are liable in damages as for breach of the contract. Atkinson J., before whom the special case came in the King's Bench Division, decided in favour of the appellants, on the ground that no default was established, but the casualty was unexplained, and, accordingly, he set aside the arbitrator's award. His decision was overruled by the Court of Appeal and the arbitrator's award was restored. In the Court of Appeal Scott L.J., in giving the leading judgment said: "A party prima facie guilty of a failure to perform his contract cannot escape under the plea of frustration unless he proves that the frustration occurred without his default. There is no frustration in the legal sense *unless he proves affirmatively* that the cause was not brought into operation by his default." The gist of the whole judgment, which is very brief, is contained in the words which I have italicised. No authority is cited.

The statement of the principle by Scott L.J. is manifestly different from the statement of Blackburn J. in *Taylor* v. *Caldwell* (1863), 122 E.R. 309.

But Blackburn J., though he qualified the rule he stated by excepting the fault or default of the contractor or of either party, did not add that the defendant relying on impossibility of performance must prove affirmatively that the impossibility was not due to his own default. The Court of Appeal in so stating the rule, have made a vital change in the rule. I must consider what justification there is for that change. To do so I must briefly explain my conception of what is meant in this context by impossibility of performance, which is the phrase used by Blackburn J. . . .

It is thus seen that the court is not claiming to exercise a dispensing power, or to modify or alter contracts. The parties did not express the qualification because they did not think of the possibility of the occurrence, but as Lord Watson said in *Dahl* v. *Nelson, Donkin & Co.* (1881), 6 App. Cas. 38, 59, "When one or other of these possibilities becomes a fact, the meaning of the contract must be taken to be not what the parties did intend (for they had neither thought nor intention regarding it) but that which the parties, as fair and reasonable men, would presumably have agreed upon, if having such possibility in view they had made express provision as to their several rights and liabilities in the event of its occurrence." In short, in ascertaining the meaning of the contract and its application to the actual occurrences, the court has to decide, not what the parties actually intended, but what as reasonable men they should have intended. The court personifies for this purpose the reasonable man. In Lord Sumner's words in *Hirji's* case [1926] A.C. 497, 507: "An event occurs, not contemplated by the parties and therefore not expressly dealt with in their contract, which when it happens frustrates their object. Evidently it is their common object that has to be frustrated not merely the individual advantage which one party or the other might have gained from the contract. If so, what the law provides must be a common relief from this common disappointment and an immediate termination of the obligation as regards future performance. This is necessary, because otherwise the parties would be bound to a contract, which is one that they did not really make. If it were not so, a doctrine designed to avert unintended burdens would operate to enable one party to profit by the event and to hold the other, if he so chose, to a new obligation." Lord Sumner added that "rights and wrongs which have already come into existence, remain, and the contract remains, too, for the purpose of giving effect to them."

I have quoted these statements of law to emphasize that the court is exercising its powers, when it decides that a contract is frustrated, in order to achieve a result which is just and reasonable. It would indeed be strange if it clogged its decision with the qualification which the Court of Appeal would impose, but which seems to me, as I shall seek to explain, inconvenient and unreasonable.

It does not seem to be here necessary to embark on the inquiry whether the doctrine of impossibility or frustration should be explained as based on an implied term or exception or on common mistake or some other principle. . . .

Whatever explanation is adopted, cannot affect the decision of this, or, so far as I can see, of any case. If the question is still open in English law, I should prefer to rest the principle simply on the true meaning of the contract as it appears to the court. The essential feature of the rule is that the court construes the contract, having regard both to its language, its nature and the circumstances, as meaning that it depended for its operation on the existence or occurrence of a particular object or state of things, as its basis or foundation. If that is gone, the life of the contract in law goes with it, at least as regards future performance. The contract remains only to enforce accrued rights. The explanation that the ground of the rule is an implied term or exception may, however, seem to bring the rule into line with the general jurisdiction of the court to imply in a contract terms which the parties have not expressed. . . . It was, however, agreed in argument that the decision of this appeal cannot depend on what is the true explanation of the rule. . . .

Scott L.J. seems, however, to be leading up to the proposition that frustration is the only possible defence, and then excluding it, not on the ground that the appellants cannot rely on their own fault if that had been proved, but on the ground that, though no fault was proved, they had not affirmatively proved absence of fault. I think that the Lord Justice is basing his decision on the view that affirmative proof of absence of fault is an essential part of the case of the party relying on frustration, so that, if he fails to establish it, there is no case to go to the jury even though in all other respects impossibility or frustration is established, as, in the present case, it is, indeed, admitted.

I have tried to find authority for the rule enunciated by the Court of Appeal, but have found none either in English or American cases or in the writings of eminent legal authors. Cases in which the courts have refused to give relief on the ground of frustration because the frustration was due to the fault of the promisor or of either party, or have considered the question, are very rare in the English reports. In the vast majority of cases, questions of responsibility do not arise. There is Lord Sumner's observation in the *Bank Line* case, [1919] A.C. 452, where the facts did not raise the question. "I think it is now well settled that the principle of frustration of an adventure assumes that the frustration arises without blame or fault on either side. Reliance cannot be placed on a self-induced frustration; indeed, such conduct might give the other party the option to treat the contract as repudiated." In *Mertens* v. *Home Freeholds Co.* [1921] 2 K.B. 526, a builder was sued for damages for failing to complete a building which he had agreed to erect. He pleaded by way of defence that he was discharged from further performance by a refusal of the Minister of Munitions to give a licence to proceed under the Defence of the Realm Regulations existing in 1916. The defendant had applied for a licence, but it was refused because he had intentionally (as it was found), in order to get out of a losing contract, delayed in the work. It was held by the Court of Appeal, reversing the decision of the Divisional Court, that the defence failed. Lord Sterndale M.R., without any precise examination of the doctrine of frustration, proceeded on the broad common sense view that a man could not take advantage, by way of defence to an action for breach of contract, of circumstances as excusing him from further performance of the contract, if he had brought those circumstances about himself. Lord Sterndale observed that in *Taylor* v. *Caldwell*, if the defendant had burned down the music hall himself, he would not have been entitled to say that the subject-matter was gone and the contract frustrated. But it might be added that no one until now had gone so far as to decide or suggest that the defendant could not have relied on the destruction of the music hall unless he had affirmatively proved that he was not responsible for it and was not in fault. Lord Sternsdale's conclusion followed from the facts proved, which showed actual fault on the part of the defendant.

In *Maritime National Fish, Ltd.* v. *Ocean Trawlers, Ltd.* [1935] A.C. 524, a similar conclusion was reached. The case was somewhat peculiar. The defendants chartered the plaintiffs' trawler, but, it was held, on the basis that it could be used for trawling with the use of otter or similar trawling gear. That could not be done without a licence. A licence was refused because the defendants were not permitted to obtain licences for more than three trawlers, and had applied for and obtained licences for three trawlers of their own, thus making it impossible to obtain a licence for the plaintiffs' trawler. The Privy Council held that the defendants were liable. The result is shortly stated: "... it was the appellants' own default which frustrated the adventure; the appellants cannot rely on their own default to excuse them from liability under the contract." That was all that was necessary for the decision of the case. No question of onus of proof was raised because all the facts were before the court. Earlier in the judgment I had said that "the essence of 'frustration' is that it should not be due to the act or election of the party," and had gone on to observe that Lord Sumner in *Hirji's* case had quoted from *Dahl* v. *Nelson, Donkin & Co.* Lord Blackburn's reference to frustration as a matter "caused by something for which neither party was responsible," and again had quoted Brett J.'s words which postulate that one of the conditions of frustration is that it should be "without any default of either party."

But for such expressions of opinion, it would be tempting to say that the more logical view might be that there are two elements to be considered: (1) impossibility or frustration under the contract and the facts, and (2) the causation of that impossibility or frustration, whether or not it is imputable to the fault of either party. The question has generally been approached from the point of view of a party relying on frustration as an excuse for failure to perform his contract, and obviously if frustration means not only that performance has become impossible but that neither party is responsible, there can be no frustration in that sense unless both conditions are fulfilled. It is that definition which English law seems to have accepted, and I think the Court of Appeal must have proceeded on it. But I can conceive a case in which the injured party, instead of electing to rescind on the ground of the other party's breach and claiming damages for a repudiation, might wish to rely on frustration as involving automatically the destruction of the contract and at the same time claim damages for the breach of contract which has frustrated and destroyed the contract, except so far as it remains alive to enforce rights accrued under it. So far as I know, such a case has never arisen, but logically it might be open, if the authorities have not excluded it. This way of looking at the matter might explain the reference to the fault of either party instead of the fault of the party relying upon the doctrine, though "either party" may simply mean "one party or the other, if either is responsible." This view of the matter would obviously be fatal to the conclusion of the Court of Appeal, because there would then be two separate issues to be separately proved by the parties who severally raised the one or the other.

But I do not desire to decide the question in this appeal on that debatable or untenable ground. The appeal can, I think, be decided according to the generally accepted view that frustration involved as one of its elements absence of fault, by applying the ordinary rules as to onus of proof. If frustration is viewed (as I think it can be) as analogous to an exception, since it is generally relied on as a defence to a claim for failure to perform a contract, the same rule will properly be applied to it as to the ordinary type of exceptions. The defence may be rebutted by proof of fault, but the onus of proving fault will rest on the plaintiff. This is merely to apply the familiar rule which is applied, for instance, where a carrier by sea relies on the exception of perils of the seas. If the goods owner then desires to rebut that prima facie defence on the ground of negligence or other fault on the part of the shipowner, it rests on the goods owner to establish the negligence or fault.

Thus, on the view most favorable to the conclusion of the Court of Appeal I still reject it. In addition, the ordinary rule is that a man is not held guilty of fault unless fault is established and found by the court. This rule, which is sometimes described as the presumption of innocence, is no doubt peculiarly important in criminal cases or matters, but it is also true in civil disputes. . . .

It is clear that the rule which the Court of Appeal laid down would in many cases work serious injustice and nullify the beneficial operation of the doctrine of frustration which has been somewhat empirically evolved with the object of doing what is reasonable and fair, as I have already explained. That the rule adopted by the Court of Appeal is inconvenient seems to me to be obvious. It is true that in many cases of frustration there is little or no room for human activity. As instances, I might mention earthquakes and unusual floods. In other cases there is little room for intervention by the parties, such as in case of governmental requisition or the refusal of a licence. But it cannot be that in any of these cases the party claiming that the contract is frustrated has to prove affirmatively that he has not caused or induced the frustration. Where natural forces have operated there may still be room for inquiry, but, if a ship is lost with all hands in a cyclone, must the shipowners establish affirmatively that the master did not receive and ignore warnings of the danger area? There may be many maritime losses in which evidence how they happened is impossible. If a ship is torpedoed with all hands, must the shipowner prove affirmatively absence of fault, such as that a light was not shown on the ship or that the ship obeyed the convoy regulations? In any case of unexplained sinking it may be impossible to exclude the possibility of fault on the part of the owner, as in the case of *Ajum Goolam* [1901] A.C. 362. But, indeed, the present is a sufficiently good illustration of an unprecedented and unexplained casualty where the real cause cannot be ascertained even after prolonged and exhaustive inquiry.

On the ruling of the Court of Appeal the shipowners have placed on them the unusual task of proving a negative. It is sought to say that the rule is not anomalous because of some other cases in which a party is required to prove a negative, but what are cited as parallels are so different and are so few in number as to emphasize the general rule. . . .

The Court of Appeal do not define what in this context is the meaning of "fault" or "default.". . . On the other hand, mere negligence seems never to have been suggested as sufficient to constitute "fault" in this connection. In *Taylor* v. *Caldwell*, where the fire was described as accidental, no one suggested an inquiry whether any servant of the defendant had negligently caused the fire, and in the cases of personal incapacity defeating a contract for personal service, like *Poussard* v. *Spiers & Pond* (1876), 1 Q.B.D. 410, no investigation seems to have been suggested whether the party claiming to be excused was careful of his or her health. But even there a case of gross delinquency might perhaps be construed as amounting to a repudiation of the obligations of the contract. I do not here think it necessary to attempt the definition. This difficulty or absence of definition makes the rule enunciated by the Court of Appeal even more open to objection.

In my opinion, this is a case in which it is found that there has been an unexplained casualty frustrating the contract. The real cause cannot be ascertained. No fault is shown against the appellants. I think that they are entitled to rely on the frustration as a defence to the claim. The judgment of the Court of Appeal should, in my opinion, be set aside, and that of Atkinson J. restored.

[Concurring opinions of Viscount Simon L.C., Viscount Maugham, Lord Russell of Killowen and Lord Porter are omitted.]

BRITISH MOVIETONEWS LTD. *v.* LONDON AND DISTRICT CINEMAS

England. Court of Appeal. [1951] 1 K.B. 190
House of Lords [1952] A.C. 166

On July 25, 1941, the plaintiffs, film distributors, agreed to supply their newsreels to the defendants, film exhibitors, for showing at the Pavilion Theatre, Aylesbury, at ten guineas a week for a minimum period of twenty-six weeks, and thereafter determinable by four weeks' notice. It was agreed, however, that notwithstanding the minimum period of twenty-six weeks the exhibitors might terminate the agreement by one month's notice at any time after the first month. Newsreels were still being distributed under this agreement when by the *Cinematograph Film (Control) Order, 1943*, dated March 19, 1943, and made under *Defence Regulation 55* which had been made under the *Emergency Powers (Defence) Act, 1939*, no person in the film industry was to acquire or supply any film except under the authority of a licence granted by the Board of Trade. At that time there was a great demand for raw film for military purposes and the Board of Trade only granted the distributors of newsreels two-thirds of what they had previously used. At that time the newsreels were practically all war films supplied by film service units, and they played a considerable part in the war effort.

In consequence of the order, the distributors and the exhibitors made a supplemental agreement dated May 3, 1943. It recited the principal agreement of July 25, 1941, and continued: "Whereas by the *Cinematograph Film (Control) Order, 1943*, it has become necessary to restrict the consumption of raw film stock, now it is hereby agreed as follows: I. That during the continuance of the *Cinematograph Film (Control) Order, 1943*, the following special conditions shall apply to the principal agreement: (a) The principal agreement shall remain in full force and effect until such time as the said order is cancelled and thereafter for any unexpired period stipulated in the principal agreement. (b) One copy of a newsreel will if necessary be used to serve two exhibitors during the same period, and this shall, if necessary, be deemed to include newsreels supplied by other distributors not parties hereto. . . . (d) The stipulated rental payable under the principal agreement shall continue to be paid irrespective of ownership of the film which is supplied to the exhibitor and notwithstanding that the same may not be that stipulated for in the principal agreement or not actually supplied by the distributor party hereto. . . . 3. All the conditions of the principal agreement shall remain in full force and effect in so far as the same are not excluded, modified or varied hereby."

Paragraph 1 (b) referred to a "cross-over" system under which one newsreel was made to serve two cinemas in one town by being sent from one cinema to the other during the performance and thus being shown at both. The newsreels of the various distributors—there were five of them—were made interchangeable. There was no difficulty about that, at the time, since the newsreels were nearly all war films. The exhibitors bound themselves to take the films, since that was in the national interest. The arrangements were made under the aegis of the Board of Trade. The order had been made under reg. 55 because it appeared by the terms of the regulation to be necessary in the interests of the defence of the realm, or the efficient prosecution of the war, or for maintaining supplies and services essential to the life of the community.

The *Emergency Powers (Defence) Act, 1939*, expired on February 24, 1946, and was replaced by the *Supplies and Services (Transitional Powers) Act, 1945. The Cinematograph Film (Control) Order, 1943*, was continued in force. It was no longer continued for the same purposes but "for the purpose of so maintaining, controlling and regulating supplies and services as (a) to secure a sufficiency of those essential to the well-being of the community or their equitable distribution or their availability at fair prices . . .": see s. 1 sub.-s. 1 of the Act of 1945.

On July 15, 1946, the Board of Trade took off all restrictions on cinematograph films "except the acquisition of newsreel prints by a distributor for distribution in the United Kingdom." In 1947 the *Supplies and Services (Extended Purposes) Act, 1947*, was passed which enabled regulations and orders to be continued in force inter alia "for reducing imports . . . from all or any countries and for redressing the balance of trade."

After the war, newsreels ceased to consist largely of war films. On May 24, 1948, the exhibitors gave four weeks' notice to terminate the agreements with the distributors and at the end of that period stopped taking the newsreels. At that time the *Film (Control) Order, 1943*, was still in force. The distributors brought this suit claiming that the exhibitors, whether they took the newsreels or not, by virtue of the supplemental agreement of May 3, 1943, must continue to pay £10 10s. a week until the order of 1943 was cancelled. Slade J. upheld this contention, and the defendants, the exhibitors, appealed.

DENNING L.J.: The question in this case is whether an agreement, which was made during the war for the exhibition of newsreels, is still in force. That agreement was expressed to remain in full force and effect "during the continuance of the *Cinematograph Film (Control) Order, 1943*," and that control order does still continue. So the film distributors insist that the agreement still remains in force. But the exhibitors say that the circumstances have changed so much that it has come to an end. [His Lordship stated the facts and continued:] The first point taken by the defendants, the exhibitors, is that they were entitled by the terms of the two agreements taken together to give four weeks' notice to determine them. They say that in the principal agreement there was a special condition enabling them, notwithstanding the minimum period of twenty-six weeks, to determine the agreement on four weeks' notice. They say that this special condition still remains in full force and effect notwithstanding that the supplemental agreement introduced a new minimum period, namely, "during the continuance of the *Cinematograph Film (Control) Order, 1943*." This is an attractive argument, but I doubt whether it is correct. The supplemental agreement says distinctly that the principal agreement shall remain in full force and effect "until such time as the said order is cancelled." That seems to be inconsistent with any power to terminate beforehand. Any special condition enabling the distributors to terminate by four weeks' notice is clearly gone. So also the special condition providing for prior determination by the exhibitors also goes.

The second point taken by the exhibitors is that the supplemental agreement must be regarded as having come to an end on February 24, 1946, when the *Emergency Powers (Defence) Act, 1939*, expired, or at any rate before they gave notice in May, 1948. They say that the change of circumstances justifies this conclusion. It cannot be doubted that there was a great change of circumstances. In 1943 the war was still on. The *Cinematograph Film (Control) Order, 1943*, was made under *Defence Regulation 55*, which in turn was made under the *Emergency Powers (Defence) Act, 1939*. It was only made because it appeared to be necessary or expedient "for securing the public safety, the defence of the realm, the maintenance of public order and the efficient prosecution of any war in which His Majesty may be engaged, and for maintaining supplies and services essential to the life of the community." No doubt it was expedient in 1943 to make the order in order to maintain the supplies of raw film which were essential for the life of the community.

But after February 24, 1946, the order could not be justified on that ground. The war was over. The life of the community was no longer in jeopardy. The military forces no longer required raw film with which to take photographs of the enemy positions. They were being demobilized. The service film units were being disbanded. The newsreels were no longer all of one pattern, filled with war films supplied by the Services' departments. They were supplied by the producers who had to go out to find their own subjects and make their own photographs. So the newsreels of one distributor might be of a very different pattern from those of another.

This change of circumstances was reflected by a change in the statutes. The *Emergency Powers (Defence) Act, 1939*, expired on February 24, 1946, and was replaced by the *Supplies and Services (Transitional Powers) Act, 1945*. The *Cinematograph Film (Control) Order, 1943*, was continued in force, but it was no longer continued for the same purposes. It was only continued because it appeared to be necessary or expedient "for the purpose of so maintaining controlling and regulating supplies and services as (a) to secure a sufficiency of those essential to the well-being of the community or their equitable distribution or their availability at fair prices." No doubt supplies of raw film were essential to the well-being of the community, and no doubt in February, 1946, they were in short supply and it was expedient to continue the order so as to secure their equitable distribution. But this is a very different justification for the order from that which held during the war. Then supplies of film were essential to the "life of the community." Now they were only essential to its "well-being."

In the course of 1946 it evidently became easier to obtain supplies of films, because on July 15, 1946, the Board of Trade took off all restrictions on cinematograph films "except the acquisition of newsreel prints by a distributor for distribution in the United Kingdom." This meant that films were free of any control for all purposes and for all persons—big film companies and small home photographers alike—except for newsreels. It may be that newsreels used up so much raw film that there was not at that time enough available to free them too. But, as more supplies became available, this particular restriction might not be justified on the ground of shortage alone. It might have to be justified by additional grounds such as conserving dollars. If we imported less raw film, we spent less dollars; and one way of keeping down the imports of raw film was by keeping the restriction on newsreels. So long as the restriction existed, it was an inducement for the trade to keep the "crossover" arrangements which meant, of course, that less film would be used and less dollars expended. This change of circumstances was reflected by another change in the statutes. The *Supplies and Services (Extended Purposes) Act, 1947*, was passed which enabled the regulations and orders to be continued in force, amongst other things, "for reducing imports . . . from all or any countries and for redressing the balance of trade."

To sum up these changes, therefore, the *Cinematograph Film (Control) Order, 1943*, was made in 1943, in order to maintain supplies of raw film which was essential to the life of the community in time of war. It was continued after February 24, 1946, in order to ensure the equitable distribution of raw film which was essential to the well-being of the community in time of peace, but which then was in short supply owing to the difficulties of transition from war to peace. It was continued after July, 1946, for newsreels alone, probably in order to maintain the cross-over arrangements, and thus import less raw film and save dollars. Alongside these changes in the legal position, there were the great changes in the general situation. In 1943, when the supplemental agreement was made, the war was on, the newsreels of all five distributors were all of one pattern, being nearly all war films supplied by the service units, the exhibitors were expected, if not required, to show them in the national interest, and there was a shortage of raw film owing to military need. In 1948, when the exhibitors gave notice to terminate, the war was over, the newsreels of the five distributors were of different patterns, being made by the various producers on their own lines, and there was no national interest which required them to be shown. There was still a restriction on raw film for newsreels but this was not owing to military needs, but to conserve dollars. In this new situation, rival views may be entertained as to what is the best policy. Why, it may be asked, should not an exhibitor be able to give up taking the newsreels if he wants to? That would appear to save raw film, not expend it. But, it may be answered, the cross-over arrangement is the best way of saving film. It is dependent on all exhibitors being parties to it; and if any one can fall out if he likes, the whole arrangement is imperilled. These arguments of policy are, however, not for us. We must consider the legal position without regard to them.

The contest is a familiar one. On the one hand, the distributors point to the letter of the contract and say that it governs the case. The words "during the continuance of the *Cinematograph Film (Control) Order, 1943*," are plain enough. So apply them. The order still continues. On the other hand, the exhibitors say that, as events have turned out, we must disregard the letter of the contract and look to what the parties really had in mind. The order was made in war to cover war conditions. The parties did not contemplate that it would be continued in peace, and they should not be held bound to it now.

Sir Roland Burrows, who appeared for the exhibitors, put his argument on three grounds: (1) On the true construction of the supplemental agreement; (2) on an implied term in it; and (3) on the change of circumstances, since it was made, which was, he said, analogous to a frustration. But he said that these three grounds shaded into one another, because they were all really concerned in finding out whether the contract applied in the new situation. I agree with him. Let me explain why. (1) When we construe a contract, we see whether the parties have actually expressed in words an intention which covers the situation, and we apply the principles stated by Lord Wright in *Inland Revenue Commissioners* v. *Raphael*,

[1935] A.C. 96, 142. (2) When we imply a term, we recognize that the parties have not expressed themselves in words which cover the situation, but we impute to them an intention which, we say, they would have expressed if they had put their minds to it, and we apply the principles stated by Bowen L. J., in *The Moorcock* (1889), 14 P.D. 64, 68–70, and by MacKinnon L.J., in *Shirlaw* v. *Southern Foundries*, [1939] 2 K.B. 206, 227. (3) When we say that a contract does not apply in a new situation because it is frustrated, we recognise that the words are wide enough to cover the situation, but we hold that they do not apply because the parties did not contemplate such a surprising turn of events, and we apply the principles stated by Lord Wright in *Joseph Constantine Steamship Line Ltd.* v. *Imperial Smelting Corporation Ltd.*, [1942] A.C. 154, and *Denny Mott & Dickson Ltd.* v. *James B. Fraser & Co. Ltd.*, [1944] A.C. 265.

In these frustration cases, as Lord Wright said, the court really exercises a qualifying power—a power to qualify the absolute, literal or wide terms of the contract—in order to do what is just and reasonable in the new situation; and it can now by statute make ancillary orders to that end. Until recently the court only exercised this power when there was a frustrating event, that is a supervening event which struck away the foundations of the contract. But in the important decision of *Parkinson & Co. Ltd.* v. *Commissioners of Works*, [1949] 2 K.B. 632, this court exercised a like power when there was no frustrating event, but only an uncontemplated turn of events. The facts were that under a building contract the employer stipulated, in addition to the contract work, for power to order extra work without any stated limit, and it was expressly provided that the sum to be paid to the contractor "should not be greater than the actual cost plus a net profit remuneration of £300,000." The parties had contemplated that the work would cost about £5,000,000, but there was no provision in the contract to that effect. Extras were ordered, bringing the total cost up to £6,683,056. The employers paid that sum, plus the profit of £300,000. The contractors then claimed extra profit because of the extra work, and, despite the absolute terms of the contract, this court held that they were entitled to reasonable extra remuneration on this account.

The judgments, if I may say so, are so valuable that they should be read in full, and I will not venture to read extracts from them. They are based on *Bush* v. *Whitehaven Trustees*, which in turn was based on the leading frustration case of *Jackson* v. *Union Marine Insurance Co. Ltd.* (1874), 10 C.P. 125. The judgments show that, no matter that a contract is framed in words which taken literally or absolutely, cover what has happened, nevertheless, if the ensuing turn of events was so completely outside the contemplation of the parties that the court is satisfied that the parties, as reasonable people, cannot have intended that the contract should apply to the new situation, then the court will read the words of the contract in a qualified sense; it will restrict them to the circumstances contemplated by the parties; it will not apply them to the uncontemplated turn of events, but will do therein what is just and reasonable.

This principle, as Devlin J., has since pointed out, is the same principle as that which underlies the ejusdem generis rule and the suspension clauses in frustration cases: see *Chandris* v. *Isbrandtsen-Moller Co. Inc.*, [1950] 1 All E.R. 768, 772. It is, as he says, a recognition of the fact that parties with their minds concerned with the particular objects about which they are contracting are apt to use words, phrases or clauses which, taken literally, are wider than they intend, or, I may add, cover situations which they never contemplated. Recognizing this fact, the court refuses to apply them literally to an uncontemplated turn of events.

This does not mean that the courts no longer insist on the binding force of contracts deliberately made. It only means that they will not allow the words, in which they happen to be phrased, to become tyrannical masters. The court qualifies the literal meaning of the words so as to bring them into accord with the true scope of the contract. Even if the contract is absolute in its terms, nevertheless if it is not absolute in intent, it will not be held absolute in effect. The day is done when we can excuse an unforseen injustice by saying to the sufferer "It is your own folly. You ought not to have passed that form of words. You ought to have put in a clause to protect yourself." We no longer credit a party with the foresight of a prophet or his lawyer with the draftsmanship of a Chalmers. We realize that they have their limitations and make allowances accordingly. It is better thus. The old maxim reminds us that *Qui haeret in litera, haeret in cortice*, which, being interpreted, means: He who clings to the letter, clings to the dry and barren shell, and misses the truth and substance of the matter. We have of late in this court paid heed to this warning, not only in *Parkinson's* case [1949] 2 K.B. 632, but also in *John Lee & Son (Grantham) Ltd.* v. *Railway Executive* (1949), 65 T.L.R. 604, *Dennis Reed Ltd.* v. *Goody*, [1950] 2 K.B. 277, and *Bennett Walden & Co.* v. *Wood*, [1950] 2 All E.R. 134., and we must pay like heed now.

Applying these principles, the supplemental agreement says that it is to apply, "during the continuance of the *Cinematograph Film (Control) Order, 1943*." Those words, taken literally, mean that the supplemental agreement is in full force and effect today, for the order still continues and may for aught one knows, continue for a long time yet. But the parties cannot have contemplated that the order would ever last so long. It was an order made in wartime to deal with war conditions, and they must have contemplated that it would be cancelled at or shortly after the end of the war. They cannot have contemplated that it would be continued in peacetime to deal with dollar shortages—certainly not that it would still be continuing five years after the war had ended. That being so, the court should not apply the agreement in this uncontemplated turn of events.

Mr. Paull says (and he puts it in the forefront of his argument) that the court can only do this by virtue of an implied term; and he challenged Sir Roland Burrows to formulate the term which should be implied. That is, I think, a fallacy, because the principle to be applied is not based on a term implied by the parties; it is a qualifying power exercised by the courts. But, if it is necessary to formulate the term, I think that Sir Roland gave the right answer when he said that it was to be implied that the supplemental agreement continued for the duration of the emergency contemplated by the *Emergency Powers (Defence) Act, 1939*, under which and for the purposes of which alone the order was made in 1943 and, therefore, came to an end when that Act came to an end on February 24, 1946, and with it the purposes for which the order was made.

In my opinion the supplemental agreement ceased to apply before May, 1948, and the defendants, the exhibitors, were entitled to give, as they then did, four weeks' notice to terminate the principal agreement. The appeal should therefore be allowed and the action dismissed with costs.

[Bucknill and Roxburgh L.JJ. agreed. The distributors then appealed to the House of Lords.]

VISCOUNT SIMON: My Lords, the question involved in this appeal is not difficult to state, but in answering the question there has emerged a difference of opinion between Slade J., who tried the action and decided in favour of the appellant company, and the Court of Appeal which in a judgment prepared by Denning L.J. allowed the appeal of the respondent company. It now becomes necessary to decide which party in the litigation is right. Moreover, the judgment delivered in the Court of Appeal included an expression of some general views as to the nature and extent of the judicial function in deciding the rights and obligations of parties under an executory contract which will require careful and candid consideration from the House. . . . [His Lordship stated the facts and continued:]

The respondent company advance two arguments. They first contend that the modification in the principal agreement effected by the supplemental agreement does not touch their original right to end the whole arrangement by four weeks' notice at any time. This contention has not prevailed in either of the courts below, and I cannot accept it. Clause 1(a) provides in effect that the principal agreement is to remain in full force and effect till the *Cinematograph Film (Control) Order, 1943*, is cancelled and "thereafter" until four weeks' notice is given to terminate it, and this appears to me to rule out the exhibitor's previous right of determination at any time and to substitute a new minimum period for both parties alike. So long as the Order of 1943 continues, neither side can give notice to terminate.

The respondent company next contend—and this raises the real difficulty—that "the *Cinematograph Film (Control) Order, 1943*," in the sense in which that expresion is used in the supplemental agreement, was no longer "continuing" when they gave their notice to terminate, but that it had already been "cancelled" within the meaning of clause 1(a) of that agreement on February 24, 1946. In order to appreciate this contention, and to decide whether it should prevail, it is necessary to set out the history of the Order and of the authority which from time to time has given to it statutory force. . . .

The effect of this Order was, therefore, to control the supply of film to renters such as the appellant company and, as the recital of the supplemental agreement recognized, to restrict the consumption of raw film stock. One result of this scarcity would be to make it more difficult for renters to supply newsreels for the exclusive use of one exhibitor, and another result would be likely to be that the price charged to exhibitors in future contracts would rise. It was therefore in the interests of both parties to arrange for a more economical use of newsreels and, at the same time, to secure that existing prices charged to exhibitors should not be increased unreasonably. Both these purposes were secured by the supplemental agreement, the terms of which were settled by the organizations representing the two parties in a common form.

After the Supplemental Agreement was made, the *Cinematograph Film (Control) Order, 1943*, continued under the authority of *Defence Regulation 55* without material change until it was revoked by the *Cinematograph Film (Control) (Revocation) Order, 1950*, made on September 4 of that year, which came into force on October 1, 1950. This, of course, is after the date of the writ in this action, or, indeed, of the judgment in the court of Appeal which is now before the House. But, whereas *Defence Regulation 55* derived its force originally from the *Emergency Powers (Defence) Act, 1939*, after February 24, 1946, its authority rested upon the *Supplies and Services (Transitional Powers) Act, 1945*. The question is whether, in these circumstances, the supplemental agreement, when referring to "the continuance" of the Order and to "such time as the said Order is cancelled," ought to be construed as referring to a period which ends when the statutory basis upon which *Defence Regulation 55* rests is thus altered.

This is, primarily at any rate, a question of construction. The respondent company contend that the expression "during the continuance of the *Cinematograph Film (Control) Order, 1943*," means so long as the Order is and remains in force by virtue of the *Emergency Powers (Defence) Act, 1939*, or any statutory amendment of the enactment thereto, and that the expression "until such time as the said Order is cancelled," means until the date when the Order ceases to be in force by virtue of the aforesaid authority, or until the date when the same is revoked, whichever shall be the earlier. This restricted construction is quite legitimate if that is, in the circumstances, the correct interpretation of the language used. But it is not the natural meaning of the words used and I can find no sufficient ground for construing them in this narrow sense. The economic considerations which must have influenced the parties in making the supplemental agreement did not change on February 24, 1946. The restriction in the consumption of raw film stock, which is referred to in the recital, continued after that date, and though a general licence was issued under the Order of July 15, 1946, for the acquisition of film used for other purposes, the restriction on film for newsreels continued until the cancellation of the Order late in 1950. The parties to the supplemental agreement chose to define the minimum period of its operation by reference to the continuance of the Order. What the length of that continuance might be was necessarily uncertain. It might have come to an end while the war was going on, if *Defence Regulation 55* was revoked or if Parliament had not adopted addresses to continue in force the *Emergency Powers (Defence) Act, 1939*. In fact, the Order continued for five years after the fighting ceased, but all that time there was in operation a restriction on the consumption of raw film stock. And it was throughout the original order, not a new order in the same terms. I agree with Slade J. that the restricted meaning sought to be put on the language of the supplemental agreement by the respondent company is not the correct interpretation of the words used.

It is urged, in the alternative, that the supplemental agreement should be regarded as having terminated in February, 1946, owing to the operation of a doctrine "analogous to a frustration." But what is the change of circumstances in 1946 which would cause Mackinnon L.J.'s "officious bystander" (see *Shirlaw v. Southern Foundries (1926) Ltd.*, [1939] 2 K.B. 206 to get instant acceptance from both sides if he suggested that of course the supplemental agreement would come to an end, although restriction on the consumption of raw film stock continued, if the *Cinematograph Film (Control) Order, 1943*, and *Defence Regulation 55* are no longer authorized by the *Emergency Powers (Defence) Act, 1939*, but gain their validity from a later Act of Parliament? It is by no means clear to me that the parties would have assented. Hannen J., in *Baily* v. *De Crespigny* (1869), L.R. 4 Q.B. 180, observed that "to hold a man liable by words, in a sense affixed to them by legislation subsequent to the contract, is to impose on him a contract he never made." But here, though the legislative authority behind the words of the Order altered, the words themselves mean the same thing throughout. This is not a case in which there has been "a vital change of the law . . . operating on the circumstances" (to use Lord Wright's phrase in *Joseph Constantine Steamship Line Ltd.* v. *Imperial Smelting Corporation Ltd.*, [1942] A.C. 154); here the restriction on the consumption of raw film stock continued and the Order creating the restriction was not changed, vitally or at all.

I should have been glad to conclude at this point by expressing agreement with the careful judgment of Slade J., but my colleagues who heard this appeal concur with me in the view that it is desirable, in order to remove the possibility of misunderstanding hereafter, to refer to certain passages in the judgment delivered by Denning L.J. where phrases occur which give us some concern. I will quote from the revision of his written judgment. . . .

With all respect to the learning and acumen of the learned Lord Justice, I do not agree that there has been a recent change as the result of which the courts now exercise a wider power in this regard than they previously used. Apart from the adjustment effected by the *Law Reform (Frustrated Contracts) Act, 1943*, which is quite irrelevant to the present point, there has been no recent change; the possibility that a fundamental alteration in circumstances may sometimes bring a contract to a premature end has long been recognized. The general principle upon which the court acts is well settled; so Lord Finlay L.C. stated in *Bank Line Ltd.* v. *Arthur Capel & Co.*, [1919] A.C. 452. It can be found, for example, as Lord Porter observed in *Denny, Mott & Dickson Ltd.* v. *James B. Fraser & Co. Ltd.*, [1944] A.C. 265, in Earl Loreburn's judgment in *F. A. Tamplin Steamship Co. Ltd.* v. *Anglo-Mexican Petroleum Products Co. Ltd.*, [1916] 2 A.C. 397, where it is thus expressed: "But a court can and ought to examine the contract and the circumstances in which it was made, not of course to vary, but only to explain it, in order to see whether or not from the nature of it the parties must have made their bargain on the footing that a particular thing or state of things would continue to exist. And if they must have done so, then a term to that effect will be implied, though it be not expressed in the contract. . . . No court has an absolving power, but it can infer from the nature of the contract and the surrounding circumstances that a condition which is not expressed was a foundation on which the parties contracted." While the principle remains the same, particular applications of it may greatly vary, and theoretical lawyers may debate whether the rule should be regarded as arising from an implied term, or because the basis of the contract no longer exists. In any view, it is a question of construction, as Lord Wright pointed out in *Constantine's* case, and as has been repeatedly asserted by other masters of the law.

When the authorities referred to by Denning L.J. as justifying the proposition that judges now exercise a wider power in these matters than they did some years ago are examined it will be found that they do not support any such notion. The decision of the Court of Appeal in *Parkinson's* case does not mark a new departure at all. No extracts from the judgments in that case were quoted by the Lord Justice on the ground that they were "so valuable that they should be read in full." When they are read in full, however, it seems to me indisputable that what was there decided was merely that, having regard to the terms of the variation deed and to the circumstances which led up to its execution, the deed could not, on its true construction, be interpreted as authorizing the Commissioners of Works at their pleasure to order an infinite quantity of extra work, to be executed over an unlimited time, on which the plaintiffs could never make any profit beyond the figure named. Asquith L.J.'s judgment makes it clear that the only question was this question of construction. He says: "Where the language of the contract is capable of a literal and wide, but also of a less literal and a more restricted, meaning, all relevant circumstances can be taken into account in deciding whether the literal or a more limited meaning should be ascribed to it." Cohen L.J. reached the same conclusion as a matter of construction, and incidentally expounded *Bush* v. *Whitehaven Trustees*—to which Denning L.J. also referred as though it embodied some new doctrine—in a way which shows that no novel principle was involved. Singleton L.J. was of the same opinion. In substance, the decision in *Parkinson's* case was that the work that had been executed by the contractors included more than was covered, on its true construction, by the variation deed, and that the cost of the uncovenanted addition had therefore to be paid for by a quantum meruit.

The three other cases referred to in the Court of Appeal's judgment as further illustrations of the expanded doctrine are equally mere applications of established rules of construction. In *John Lee & Sons (Grantham) Ltd.* v. *Railway Executive*, Denning L.J. himself so explained the decision, preferring "a limited construction" of which the words were capable to the wider interpretation suggested. *Dennis Reed Ltd.* v. *Goody* was again merely a case of interpreting the language of a contract; Denning L.J. was again a party to the decision and said so. *Bennett, Walden & Co.* v. *Wood* is also a pure case of construction; the Court of Appeal held that the words "in the event of our securing for you an offer" referred to a firm offer, which by acceptance would give rise to a contractual relationship. None of these three decisions illustrate the exercise of any recent extension of judicial practice or power.

It is of the utmost importance that the action of a court, when it decides that in view of a supervening situation the rights and obligations under a contract have automatically ceased, should not be misunderstood. The suggestion that an "uncontemplated turn of events" is enough to enable a court to substitute its notion of what is "just and reasonable" for the contract as it stands, even though there is no "frustrating event," appears to be likely to lead to some misunderstanding. The parties to an executory contract are often faced, in the course of carrying it out, with a turn of events which they did not all anticipate—a wholly abnormal rise or fall in prices, a sudden depreciation of currency, an unexpected obstacle to execution, or the like. Yet this does not in itself affect the bargain they have made. If, on the other hand, a consideration of the terms of the contract, in the light of the circumstances existing when it was made, shows that they never agreed to be bound in a fundamentally different situation which has now unexpectedly emerged, the contract ceases to bind at that point—not because the court in its discretion thinks it just and reasonable to qualify the terms of the contract, but because on its true construction it does not apply in that situation. When it is said that in such circumstances the court reaches a conclusion which is "just and reasonable" (Lord Wright in *Constantine's* case) or one "which justice demands" (Lord Sumner in *Hirji Mulji* v. *Cheong Yue Steamship Co. Ltd.*, [1926] A.C. 497), this result is arrived at by putting a just construction upon the contract in accordance with an "implication . . . from the presumed common intention of the parties" (Lord Sumner in *Bank Line Ltd.* v. *Arthur Capel & Co.*).

If the decisions in "frustration" cases are regarded as illustrations of the power and duty of a court to put the proper construction on the agreement made between the parties, having regard to the terms in which that agreement is expressed, and to the circumstances in which it was made, including any necessary implication, such decisions are seen to be examples of the general judicial function of interpreting a contract when there is disagreement as to its effect. What distinguishes "frustration" cases is that the interpretation involves the consequence that, in view of what has happened, further performance is automatically ended. This is because the frustrating event (such, for example, as war or prolonged delay) must be regarded as introducing a new situation to which no limit can be put. But there are, of course, many other examples where the court has to put an interpretation on the agreement made, not with the result that the contract is brought to an end by frustration, but with the result that the contract goes on and continues to bind the parties according to its true construction. *Bennett, Walden & Co.* v. *Wood*, quoted by Denning L.J., is an obvious example. The advantage of approaching the topic in this way seems to me to be that it makes plain that in all cases alike the question is really at bottom a question of construction.

In my opinion the appeal succeeds, and I move that it be allowed with costs here and below.

[Lord Simonds, Lord Morton of Henryton, and Lord Tucker agreed with Viscount Simon and gave very short judgments. On the notion of a broader basis for the frustration rule, Lord Simonds said:

"I hesitate to make any brief comment upon the judgment of Denning L.J. lest by taking a passage out of its context I should do injustice to the whole. But I must at least dissent from the suggestion of the learned Lord Justice that the court, whether it is exercising its function in construing a document or in applying the law of frustration to particular circumstances, 'really exercises a qualifying power . . . in order to do what is just and reasonable in the new situation.' Nor can I accept the theory, which appears to underlie his judgment, that in recent cases and in *Parkinson's* case in particular there has been some development of this branch of the law, which would justify such a proposition as that just cited. It is no doubt essential to the life of the common law that its principles should be adapted to meet fresh circumstances and needs. But I respectfully demur to the suggestion that there has been recently been, or need be, any change in the well known principles of construction or (except so far as the recent Act of 1943 provides) in the application of the law of frustration to commercial agreements, and, if indeed, as Denning L.J. appears to suggest, such cases as *John Lee & Son (Grantham) Ltd.* v. *Railway Executive*, *Dennis Reed Ltd.* v. *Goody* and *Bennett, Walden & Co.* v. *Wood*, illustrate such a change they would have to be regarded as of doubtful authority. They can, however, be justified on more orthodox grounds."]

CAHAN *v.* FRASER

British Columbia. Court of Appeal. [1951] 4 D.L.R. 112

ROBERTSON J.A.: The plaintiff appeals from the dismissal of his action to recover $1,000 paid to the defendants under the following circumstances: On March 29, 1948, the defendants in consideration of the sum of $500 then paid to them, gave an option, irrevocable within the time for acceptance, to purchase, up to and inclusive of April 30, 1948, certain property near Agassiz, B.C., for $21,000, payable in instalments.

The option provided that the said sum of $500 was paid by the plaintiff to the defendants "as part consideration of the giving of the option," and any further sum that might thereafter be paid by the plaintiff for an extension of the option should upon the acceptance of the option by the plaintiff be allowed as part payment of the sum of $6,500, the instalment payable on the exercise of the option. The plaintiff obtained an extension of time for acceptance up to May 31, 1948. On the property was an "imposing fifteen-room Tudor Manor house." As stated by the learned Chief Justice of the Supreme Court the week-end of May 24, 1948, marked the beginning of the famous floods of that year in British Columbia.

By letter of May 27, 1948, the plaintiff pointed out to the defendants that these floods had prevented the consummation of negotiation under way by him for the sale of the property in question and the exercise by him of his option to purchase the same until an examination of estimates of damage of said property could be made. The defendants made no reply to this letter. It is admitted by the defendants that when the plaintiff wrote the said letter of May 27, 1948, he did not know the extent of the inundated lands or the damage or the consequences thereof. It is clear on admissions of the defendants that "during a few days previous to the 31st May and a few days subsequent thereto the lands and premises in question were flooded; that the basement of the Manor House was filled with water that the said Manor House was inaccessible except by boat; that the heating equipment and electric lights in the Manor House were not in working condition; and the said Manor House was not fit, available or suitable for habitation."

The defendants having refused to return the $1,000 the plaintiff brought this action, claiming that the contract was no longer enforceable by reason of frustration; there was a complete failure of consideration, and he was entitled to the return of the monies paid by him. The defendants submit that the option constituted consideration for the payments and therefore there was no failure of consideration. Alternatively, there was no frustration because, as subsequently determined, repairs to the house, garage, barn and otherwise would have cost about $700, and this amount could have been allowed on the purchase-price. The cost of these repairs, of course, could not be ascertained until after the floods had subsided.

The learned Chief Justice found that the option was the consideration for the $1,000. There was no failure of consideration up to April 30, 1948, as at that time the property was intact and as represented; and he applied the language of Middleton J.A. in *Goulding* v. *Rabinovitch*, [1927] 3 D.L.R. 820 at p. 821, 60 O.L.R. 607, wherein it was stated that although frustration had taken place in that case the plaintiff could not recover money paid for an option as there had been no failure of consideration. The legal effect of the frustration of a contract does not depend on the intention of the parties or their opinions or even knowledge as to the event which brought about frustration, but upon its occurrence in such circumstances as show it to be inconsistent with the further prosecution of the adventure: *Hirji Mulji* v. *Cheong Yue SS. Co.*, [1926] A.C. 497 at p. 509.

The plaintiff, had he wished to exercise his option on May 31, 1948, could not have taken possession of the property in the manner contemplated by the option, in view of the admissions, *supra*. On that date he would have had no means of knowing the extent of the damage, nor how long the condition of affairs would continue. The parties could never have contemplated the extraordinary events which happened . . . [After quoting Denning L.J. in the *British Movietonews* case, Robertson J.A. continued:]

I think therefore there was frustration, but even if there were not, the principles laid down in *British Movietonews* would apply, and the Court will do what is just and reasonable. . . .

[After discussing *Fibrosa's* case, Robertson J.A. concluded:]

With regard to the first $500 paid by the appellant, I think there was no partial failure of consideration. At any time he could have exercised his option up to April 30 and there would have been no question of frustration. He therefore enjoyed his option for the full period and to that extent received consideration. As to the money paid for the extension of the option, I think there was a complete failure of consideration.

The appeal should be allowed with costs both here and below; the appellant to have judgment for $500.

Appeal allowed in part.

DAVIS CONTRACTORS LTD. *v*. FAREHAM URBAN DISTRICT COUNCIL

England. House of Lords. [1956] A.C. 696

Davis tendered for the construction of seventy-eight houses within a period of eight months, at Gudgeheath Lane, Fareham, for £92,425. In a letter dated March 18, 1946 (ref. RL/JEM) accompanying the tender, Davis said, "Our tender is subject to adequate supplies of material and labour being available as and when required to carry out the work within the time specified." The agreement which was later signed by Davis contained only one reference to the letter. Appendix I to the agreement was headed "Materials and goods to be purchased directly by the contractor in respect of which variation of the contract sum is desired in accordance with clause 68B of the conditions of the contract." Under this heading Davis wrote, "As terms of letter attached dated March 18, 1946, reference RL/JEM." In later negotiations Davis actually supplied a detailed schedule of prices which was intended to constitute the appendix I schedule. The tender was made a part of the agreement. The contract took twenty-two months to complete, the delay being caused chiefly by the lack of skilled labour. With extras, the payments by Fareham amounted to £94,424. Davis claimed in this action that the contract price was inapplicable owing to the delay, and asked to be paid a total of £115,233 on a quantum meruit basis. The arbitrator awarded damages amounting to £17,258, but the Court of Appeal held that the letter was not incorporated into the contract and the contract was not frustrated. Davis then appealed to the House of Lords. The appeal was dismissed. Only the question of frustration is dealt with in the following excerpt.

LORD RADCLIFFE: . . . But, in my opinion, full weight ought to be given to the requirement that the parties "must have made" their bargains on the particular footing. Frustration is not to be lightly invoked as the dissolvent of a contract.

Lord Loreburn ascribes the dissolution to an implied term of the contract that was actually made. This approach is in line with the tendency of English courts to refer all the consequences of a contract to the will of those who made it. But there is something of a logical difficulty in seeing how the parties could even impliedly have provided for something which ex hypothesi they neither expected nor foresaw; and the ascription of frustration to an implied term of the contract has been criticized as obscuring the true action of the court which consists in applying an objective rule of the law of contract to the contractual obligations that the parties have imposed upon themselves. So long as each theory produces the same result as the other, as normally it does, it matters little which theory is avowed (see *British Movietonews Ltd.* v. *London and District Cinemas Ltd.*, [1952] A.C. 166, at p. 184, *per* Viscount Simon). But it may still be of some importance to recall that, if the matter is to be approached by way of implied term, the solution of any particular case is not to be found by inquiring what the parties themselves would have agreed on had they been, as they were not, forewarned. It is not merely that no one can answer that hypothetical question: it is also that the decision must be given "irrespective of the individuals concerned, their temperaments and failings, their interest and circumstances" (*Hirji Mulji* v. *Cheong Yue Steamship Co. Ltd.*, [1926] A.C. 497, at p. 510). The legal effect of frustration "does not depend on their intention or their opinions, or even knowledge, as to the event." On the contrary, it seems that when the event occurs "the meaning of the contract must be taken to be, not what the parties did intend (for they had neither thought nor intention regarding it), but that which the parties, as fair and reasonable men, would presumably have agreed upon if, having such possibility in view, they had made express provision as to their several rights and liabilities in the event of its occurrence" (*Dahl* v. *Nelson* (1881), 6 App. Cas. 38, *per* Lord Watson).

By this time it might seem that the parties themselves have become so far disembodied spirits that their actual persons should be allowed to rest in peace. In their place there rises the figure of the fair and reasonable man. And the spokesman of the fair and reasonable man, who represents after all no more than the anthropomorphic conception of justice, is and must be the court itself. So perhaps it would be simpler to say at the outset that frustration occurs whenever the law recognizes that without default of either party a contractual obligation has become incapable of being performed because the circumstances in which performance is called for would render it a thing radically different from that which was undertaken by the contract. Non haec in foedera veni. It was not this that I promised to do.

There is, however, no uncertainty as to the materials upon which the court must proceed. "The data for decision are, on the one hand, the terms and construction of the contract, read in the light of the then existing circumstances, and on the other hand the events which have occurred" (*Denny, Mott & Dickson Ltd.* v. *James B. Fraser & Co. Ltd.*, [1944] A.C. 265, at p. 274, *per* Lord Wright). In the nature of things there is often no room for any elaborate inquiry. The court must act upon a general impression of what its rule requires. It is for that reason that special importance is necessarily attached to the occurrence of any unexpected event that, as it were, changes the face of things. But, even so, it is not hardship or inconvenience or material loss itself which calls the principle of frustration into play. There must be as well such a change in the significance of the obligation that the thing undertaken would, if performed, be a different thing from that contracted for.

I am bound to say that, if this is the law, the appellants' case seems to me a long way from a case of frustration. Here is a building contract entered into by a housing authority and a big firm of contractors in all the uncertainties of the post-war world. Work was begun shortly before the formal contract was executed and continued, with impediments and minor stoppages but without actual interruption, until the 78 houses contracted for had all been built. After the work had been in progress for a time the appellants raised the claim, which they repeated more than once, that they ought to be paid a larger sum for their work than the contract allowed; but the respondents refused to admit the claim and, so far as appears, no conclusive action was taken by either side which would make the conduct of one or the other a determining element in the case.

That is not in any obvious sense a frustrated contract. But the appellants' argument, which certainly found favour with the arbitrator, is that at some stage before completion the original contract was dissolved because it became incapable of being performed according to its true significance and its place was taken by a new arrangement under which they were entitled to be paid, not the contract sum, but a fair price on quantum meruit for the work that they carried out during the 22 months that elapsed between commencement and completion. The contract, it is said, was an eight months' contract, as indeed it was. Through no fault of the parties it turned out that it took 22 months to do the work contracted for. The main reason for this was that, whereas both parties had expected that adequate supplies of labour and material would be available to allow for completion in eight months, the supplies that were in fact available were much less than adequate for the purpose. Hence, it is said, the basis or the footing of the contract was removed before the work was completed; or, slightly altering the metaphor, the footing of the contract was so changed by the circumstances that the expected supplies were not available that the contract built upon that footing became void. These are the findings which the arbitrator has recorded in his supplemental award.

In my view, these are in substance conclusions of law, and I do not think that they are good law. All that anyone, arbitrator or court, can do is to study the contract in the light of the circumstances that prevailed at the time when it was made and, having done so, to relate it to the circumstances that are said to have brought about its frustration. It may be a finding of fact that at the time of making the contract both parties anticipated that adequate supplies of labour and material would be available to enable the contract to be completed in the stipulated time. I doubt whether it is, but, even if it is, it is no more than to say that when one party stipulated for completion in eight months, and the other party undertook it, each assumed that what was promised could be satisfactorily performed. That is a statement of the obvious that could be made with regard to most contracts. I think that a good deal more than that is needed to form a "basis" for the principle of frustration.

The justice of the arbitrator's conclusion depends upon the weight to be given to the fact that this was a contract for specified work to be completed in a fixed time at a price determined by those conditions. I think that his view was that, if without default on either side the contract period was substantially extended, that circumstance itself rendered the fixed price so unfair to the contractor that he ought not to be held to his original price. I have much sympathy with the contractor, but, in my opinion, if that sort of consideration were to be sufficient to establish a case of frustration, there would be an untold range of contractual obligations rendered uncertain and, possibly, unenforceable.

Two things seem to me to prevent the application of the principle of frustration to this case. One is that the cause of the delay was not any new state of things which the parties could not reasonably be thought to have foreseen. On the contrary, the possibility of enough labour and materials not being available was before their eyes and could have been the subject of special contractual stipulation. It was not made so. The other thing is that, though timely completion was no doubt important to both sides, it is not right to treat the possibility of delay as having the same significance for each. The owner draws up his conditions in detail, specifies the time within which he requires completion, protects himself both by a penalty clause for time exceeded and by calling for the deposit of a guarantee bond and offers a certain measure of security to a contractor by his escalator clause with regard to wages and prices. In the light of these conditions the contractor makes his tender, and the tender must necessarily take into account the margin of profit that he hopes to obtain upon his adventure and in that any appropriate allowance for the obvious risks of delay. To my mind, it is useless to pretend that the contractor is not at risk if delay does occur, even serious delay. And I think it a misuse of legal terms to call in frustration to get him out of his unfortunate predicament. . . .

[The decisions of Viscount Simonds and Lords Morton of Henryton, Reid, and Somervell of Harrow, dismissing the appeal, are omitted.]

2. Does Frustration "put an end to" the Contract?

PAINE *v*. MELLER
England. Chancery. 1801. 6 Ves. Jr. 349; 31 E.R. 1088

Upon the 1st of September, 1796, the plaintiffs sold to the defendant by auction some houses in Ratcliffe Highway, upon the usual terms, a deposit of 25 per cent, and a proper conveyance to be executed upon payment of the remainder of the purchase money at Michaelmas next. An abstract was delivered to the defendant at the end of September. On the 4th or 5th of November the defendant's solicitor sent a draft for a conveyance. The draft was returned to the defendant's solicitor; the deeds were engrossed; and upon the 16th or 17th of December he declared himself satisfied with the title; and the said deeds would be ready in two or three days. Upon the 18th of December the houses were burnt; the insurance having been suffered to expire at Michaelmas, 1796.

The bill was then filed; praying a specific performance of the contract.

Lord Eldon L.C.: First, it is said, the title was never accepted in fact: secondly, if not, under these circumstances a court of equity will not compel a specific performance. As to the second point the objection is grounded upon two circumstances: First, the simple fact of the fire; secondly, that the premises had been insured prior to the contract; that that fact and the fact that the insurance expired at Michaelmas, 1796, were not disclosed; and that the premises afterwards remained uncovered by any insurance. The authority of Sir Joseph Jekyll has been mentioned: but no case has been cited in support of that dictum; and it is in a degree suggested, not admitted at the bar, that it may be considered overruled by subsequent cases. As to the mere fact of the accident itself no solid objection can be founded upon that simply; for if the party by the contract has become in equity the owner of the premises, they are his to all intents and purposes. They are vendible as his, chargeable as his, capable of being incumbered as his; they may be devised as his; they may be assets; and they would descend to his heir. If a man had signed a contract for a house upon that land, which is now appropriated to the London Docks, and that house was burnt, it would be impossible to say to the purchaser, willing to take the land without the house, because much more valuable on account of this project, that he should not have it. As to the annuity cases and all the others, the true answer has been given; that the party has the thing he bought; though no payment may have been made; for he bought subject to contingency. If it is a real estate, he of course has it. Then as to the non-communication, I cannot say that in my judgment forms an objection; for I do not see how I can allow it, unless I say, this court warrants to every buyer of a house that the house is insured, and not only insured, but to the full extent of the value. The house is bought, not for the benefit of any existing policy. However general the practice of insuring from fire is, it is not universal; and it is yet less general that houses are insured to their full value, or near it. The question, whether insured or no, is with the vendor solely, not with the vendee; unless he proposes something upon that; and makes it matter of contract with the vendor, that the vendee shall buy according to that fact, that the house is insured. I am therefore of opinion, that if the agent on behalf of this purchaser did accept this title previously to the destruction of the premises, the vendors are in the situation, in which they would have been if the title and the conveyance were ready at Michaelmas, 1796, but by the default of the vendee were not executed, but the title was accepted and the premises were burnt down on the quarter day.

[The statement of Sir Joseph Jekyll M.R. referred to is found in *Stent* v. *Bailis* (1724), 2 P. Wms. 217; 24 E.R. 705 at p. 706: "If I should buy an house, and, before such time as by the articles I am to pay for the same, the house be burnt down by casualty of fire, I shall not, in equity, be bound to pay for the house."]

LEISTON GAS COMPANY *v*. LEISTON-CUM-SIZEWELL URBAN DISTRICT COUNCIL
England. Court of Appeal. [1916] 2 K.B. 428

SCRUTTON J.: An action was brought by the Leiston Gas Company, Limited, whom I call "the gas company" against the Leiston Urban District Council, whom I call "the council," to recover £157 15s., being three quarterly payments due from the council under an agreement dated June 2, 1911. The defendants alleged that the agreement was for the supply of lighted gas lamps, and that, under orders from a competent military authority acting under the *Defence of the Realm Act* and *Regulations*, such lamps could not be lighted for more than half the first quarter, and for the whole of the second and third quarters sued for. Low J. held that this was no defence and gave judgment for the plaintiffs, the gas company. The defendants, the council, appeal to this court. The case raises questions of general importance and some difficulty. It is necessary first to appreciate exactly what the agreement sued under provides. It is a contract to last for five years from August 1, 1911, and thereafter till determined by six months' notice terminating on July 31 of any year after and including 1916. The gas company are to provide 105 gas standards and burners with automatic lighters, which remain their property, and to connect them with their mains, and to supply gas and incandescent mantles and chimneys for and light, extinguish, clean, repair, paint, and maintain the said lamps. The lamps are to be lit every night between certain hours varying with sunset and sunrise except on bright moonlight nights. The council is not to pay in proportion to gas supplied, but pays an annual rate for each of the lamps contracted for, reduced on a scale if the gas company reduce their charge for gas. The annual sum is payable quarterly. The quarterly payment therefore, does not immediately depend on gas supplied; it is the same in the winter and summer quarters, and the same whether the quarter contains many or few bright moonlight nights. It includes an unapportioned sum for supply and maintenance of plant. The gas company are liable for damages or penalty (both words are used) for each lamp they fail to light on any night when it ought to be lit unless the failure is due to circumstances beyond their control; and the parties provide that if there is delay in starting the lamps on August 1, 1911, the penalty shall not apply, but the quarterly payment shall be reduced pro rata. They make no express provision for any reduction from the quarterly payment in case of failure to light from causes beyond the gas company's control; nor do they say whether the company are to suffer a reduction of payment as well as damages in the case of failure to light from causes within their control.

At first sight it is very tempting to say "This is a contract to provide illumination, and the person who does not provide illumination cannot ask to be paid for it." But when the consequences come to be more closely looked into it is not so easy to follow them. The gas company supplies lighted gas for half the first quarter; is then prevented by causes beyond its control from supplying lights till the middle of the second quarter, when the impediment is removed and the supply of light recommences. What is the consequence? Can the council refuse payment for the first quarter and for the second quarter because a full quarter's gas is not supplied in either case; but does the contract remain in existence, the company being bound to go on as soon as the impediment is removed? Or is there to be an apportionment of the quarter's payments according to the time which lighted gas is supplied, the time of darkness being written out of the contract? Does the contract come to an end when the supply of lighted gas has ceased for so long a time as to go to the root of the contract, to adopt the language of Blackburn J. in *Bettini* v. *Gye* (1876), 1 Q.B.D. 183, citing with approval Parke B. in *Graves* v. *Legg* (1854), 156 E.R. 304, or to defeat the commercial purpose of the adventure, in the language of Bramwell B. in *Jackson* v. *Union Marine Insurance Co.* (1874), 10 C.P. 125? The attempt to answer these questions suggests that the Court may really be being asked to make an agreement for the parties in a matter which they have not thought of or expressly dealt with. Since the time of *Paradine* v. *Jane* (1647), 82 E.R. 897 . . . when the question was discussed whether a loyal Englishman need pay rent to his landlord when the house he rented had been destroyed by the King's enemies, the "wild Scots"—the distinction has been taken between duties or charges imposed by the law, where the party cannot perform it by events occurring without any default in him, in which case he is excused by the impossibility, and duties created by the agreement of the party, when he is "bound to make good, notwithstanding any accident by inevitable necessity, because he might have provided against it by his contract." Since then the Courts have steadily refused to make contracts for parties, which they might have, and have not, made for themselves, unless the term is so obvious and necessary that it must be implied as a matter of business in such contract: *The Moorcock* (1889), 14 P.D. 64, 68. It is said that the supply of lighted gas has become illegal. This is true for an uncertain time; at any moment the illegality may be removed by peace or changed conditions of war. But the payment of the quarterly sum has not become illegal, and part of it is not for light supplied, but for plant which has been supplied and of which the council has had the benefit. To excuse themselves from breaking the contract to pay, not being an illegal contract, the council must, I think, satisfy the Court of one of two things. Either they must establish that the performance of the contract to supply lighted gas is a condition precedent of the necessity to observe the contract to make a quarterly payment, so that the two contracts are "dependent" and not "independent" to use the language of . . . Lord Mansfield in *Kingston* v. *Preston,* cited in *Jones* v. *Barkley* (1773), 99 E.R. 437, in which case the company, not having supplied lighted gas for the whole of three quarters respectively, cannot sue for payment; or the council must satisfy the Court that, though a mere failure to supply lighted gas for a short time will not relieve them from payment, there is in this case such an extensive and permanent failure to supply as "goes to the root of the matter, so that the performance of the rest of the contract by the plaintiffs is rendered a different thing in substance from what the defendant has stipulated for": Blackburn J. in *Bettini* v. *Gye*. First, can it be said that any failure to supply lighted gas, beyond these trifling failures to which the maxim "De minimus" might apply, prevents the company from recovering payment in respect of the quarter in which the failure occurs? Counsel for the defendants, I think argued that it was so; and though I think they argued that a subsequent acceptance by the council of lighted gas after the failure might waive the breach, they, as I understood them, contended that a fortnight's or a month's failure not waived in this way annulled the whole contract. I cannot take the view that such a failure by itself annuls the contract, or that the contract might be treated as twenty quarterly separate contracts, one of which might be cancelled or blotted out while the rest remained. The payment is a flat rate payment, not a payment by meter for gas supplied; and it includes something for plant supplied and still available. For certain kinds of failure to supply light the parties have provided a remedy in damages, and in other cases a deduction from the quarterly payment. They have not expressly provided for the case of a failure to supply light owing to causes beyond the company's control, and I do not think the Court ought to make such a contract for them, when the consideration for the payment claimed has not wholly failed.

There remains the question whether, though a mere failure to supply will not by itself be sufficient to relieve from payment, a failure of such a lengthy and permanent character as substantially to alter the mode of performance of the contract will have this effect and terminate the contract. I think this must be so, even if the contract is one for a fixed time. I put to the counsel concerned the case of an Act of Parliament being passed, after the agreement had been in operation for a quarter, prohibiting lighting the gas for four years, and asked whether the agreement would remain alive or would be in force for the last nine months only when the operation of the Act had ceased. I think the agreement would be anulled for the reason that a supply of gas for a year in two broken periods would be a totally different thing from the five years' supply which the council bargained for, and that the obligation to supply gas for three months, and again four years later for nine months, for four quarterly payments would be a totally different contract from that which the company entered into. If this principle is granted the question is then one of fact. Is the period from the first total failure to supply on January 26 to the issue of the writ on November 10, that is nine and a half months, sufficient to annul a contract which is to last for at least five years, perhaps more, and of which the council has already had the benefit for three and a half years? These questions of degree are always difficult, but, treating it as a question of fact, I should hold that there had not at the issue of the writ, been sufficient change of character in performance to destroy the contract. For these reasons I arrive at the same result as Low J., and think that the appeal should be dismissed with costs.

[The opinions of Lord Reading C.J. and Warrington J. giving reasons for dismissing the appeal are omitted.]

TAMPLIN STEAMSHIP CO. *v.* ANGLO-MEXICAN PETROLEUM PRODUCTS CO. [1916] 2 A.C. 397 (England. House of Lords). Anglo-Mexican chartered a tankship from Tamplin for five years from 1912 until 1917. The vessel was used to carry petroleum and petroleum products. The charterparty provided that Anglo-Mexican could sub-let on Admiralty service without prejudice to the charterparty, but Anglo-Mexican would remain wholly responsible. The charterparty was to continue during "restraint of princes" and the freight remained payable. In 1914 the British Government requisitioned the ship and used it to carry water. No question was raised. In 1915 it was again requisitioned and converted to a troop ship. The hire of the ship at that time was £1700 a month. Tamplin claimed the charterparty was determined or suspended by the requisitioning and alterations. Anglo-Mexican were willing to continue payment and contested the claim. Atkin J. and the Court of Appeal held that the requisitioning and alterations did not end or suspend the charterparty. The House of Lords affirmed the Court of Appeal by a three to two decision. At the time of the hearing in the House of Lords the ship had been restored as an oil ship. EARL LOREBURN: "Ought we to imply a condition in the contract that an interruption such as this shall excuse the parties from further performance of it? I think not. I think they took their chance of lesser interruptions, and the condition I should imply goes no further than that they should be excused if substantially the whole contract became impossible of performance, or, in other words impracticable, by some cause for which neither was responsible." The House did not take into account the fact that Anglo-Mexican, as Bankes L.J. described it in the Court of Appeal, "appear to receive from the Government a substantially increased hire over and beyond what they pay to the appellants, and they not unnaturally claim to be entitled to receive this and retain it." The dissenting views of Lords Haldane and Atkinson are more frequently referred to in later cases than are the majority opinions.

METROPOLITAN WATER BOARD *v.* DICK, KERR & CO.
England. Court of Appeal. [1917] 2 K.B. 1

By a contract dated July 24, 1914, as amended by a supplemental contract dated May 10, 1915, the defendants agreed to construct for the plaintiffs a large reservoir at Littleton in the county of Middlesex for a price of £675,000. By the terms of the contract the reservoir was to be completed within six years from the date of commencement of the work, and time was to be considered "as of the essence of the contract on the part of the contractor," provided (clause 32) that if by "reason of any difficulties or impediments . . . whatsoever or howsoever occasioned the contractor shall in the opinion of the engineer (whose decision shall be final) have been unduly delayed or impeded in the completion of this contract" it should be lawful for the engineer to extend the time, "and every such extension of time shall be deemed to be in full compensation" for any damage caused to the contractor by such delay. The contract further provided by clause 6 that the contractors were to provide all plant and labour necessary for contract; and by clause 10 that "The plant tools and material provided by the contractor shall from the time at which they respectively may be brought upon the site of the said works or the lands of the Board, and during the construction and until the completion of the said works, become and continue the property of the Board, and the contractor shall not remove the same or any part thereof without the consent in writing of the engineer." By clause 28 the contractors were to make good any loss or damage arising to the works or plant by any accident; and by clause 42 they were to be advanced 50 per cent of the value of the plant, such advances to be repaid at the rate of 5 per cent per month by deduction from monthly certificates. The works were commenced on August 16, 1914. By the beginning of 1916 the defendants had made insufficient progress with the works owing to the difficulty of getting enough labour, and it had become impracticable for them to finish the work within the contract time.

By reg. 8A of the *Defence of the Realm Regulations Consolidated,* "It shall be lawful for . . . the Minister of Munitions . . . (b) to regulate or restrict the carrying on of any work in any factory workshop or other premises . . . or to remove the plant therefrom, with a view to maintaining or increasing the production of munitions in other factories." Acting under the powers thereby vested in him the Minister of Munitions on February 21, 1916, ordered the defendants to cease work upon the reservoir and to hold their plant and labour at the disposal of the Minister. By his directions the defendants removed a considerable portion of the plant and sold it to owners of munition factories, and received the proceeds to the amount of £46,000 on behalf of the Minister. The defendants claimed that by reason of the stoppage of the works by the order of the Minister their contract with the plaintiffs had terminated, and that the property in the plant which was still on the site had revested in them. The plaintiffs then brought this action, claiming (1) a declaration that the contract was still binding; (2) a declaration that they were entitled to all the plant still on the site of the works, and to the proceeds of such as was sold; (3) or alternatively, as to the plant removed and sold, damages for conversion; and (4) an injunction against the removal of further plant.

At the trial before Bray J. judgment was given for the plaintiffs and the contract was declared to be still in existence. The defendants appealed.

Lord Cozens-Hardy M.R.: It has not been argued before us that anything done or any order given, by the munition authorities was illegal or in excess of their powers. This being so, I do not deem it necessary to discuss these powers. Questions soon arose between the Board and the contractors as to their respective rights under the contract, and on May 19, 1916 the writ in this action was issued, seeking a declaration that the contract was still in existence as a binding contract and had not been determined. Bray J. has held that the contract was not abrogated or determined, and granted an injunction to restrain the contractors from removing any of the plant still remaining on the site. The contractors appeal from this judgment. The principles of law which have to be applied to the facts of the present case have, I think, been settled within the last few years. I do not propose to go through the authorities beginning with *Taylor* v. *Caldwell* (1863), 122 E.R. 309, and ending with *Tamplin Steamship Co.* v. *Anglo-Mexican Petroleum*

Products Co., [1916] 2 A.C. 397. I propose to read a few lines of the speeches of some of the noble Lords who took part in the last case. Those noble Lords all agreed with the general principles, but differed as to their application to the particular facts. Lord Loreburn says:

"When a lawful contract has been made and there is no default, a Court of law has no power to discharge either party from the performance of it unless either the rights of some one else or some Act of Parliament give the necessary jurisdiction. But a Court can and ought to examine the contract and the circumstances in which it was made, not of course to vary, but only to explain it, in order to see whether or not from the nature of it the parties must have made their bargain on the footing that a particular thing or state of things would continue to exist. And if they must have done so, then a term to that effect will be implied though it be not expressed in the contract." And: "The condition I should imply goes no further than that they should be excused if substantially the whole contract became impossible of performance, or in other words impracticable, by some cause for which neither was responsible."

Lord Haldane says: "Where the interruption is simply one of an interim character and likely to cease so soon as to leave the rest of the period stipulated free for the revival of the rights and duties of the parties after what amounts to no more than a temporary cessation of the power of performance, then, not only where there is an express stipulation covering the case which has occurred, but possibly even where there is no such stipulation, the contract may be regarded as not becoming destroyed but only suspended. The question must always turn mainly on the facts. But if the facts be such that it appears that the power of performance has been wholly swept away to such an extent that there is no longer in view a definite prospect of this power being restored, then the contract must be looked upon as being wholly dissolved, and the Courts cannot take any course which would in reality impose new and different terms on the parties."

Lord Atkinson says: "In my view there is here involved such a substantial invasion of that freedom of both parties to exercise the rights and discharge the obligations secured to and imposed upon them by the charter-party, the continued existence of which must, I think, have necessarily been in their contemplation as to the foundation of their contract when they entered into it, that, in the events which have happened, each of them is now entitled to treat it as at an end."

Applying these principles to the facts which I have shortly stated, I find that the contract could not be performed after the receipt of the notice of February 21, 1916, by reason of the lawful act of the Minister of Munitions making it illegal and a criminal offence to continue work under the contract. This was not in form a temporary prohibition. The continuance of a state of war has in many cases been held to be too uncertain to be regarded as temporary. The contractors treated it as of such a nature as to terminate their liabilities under the contract, and the fact that the restraint which had been in force for six months at the date of the trial, has now been in existence for twelve months is a matter which we are entitled to have regard to: see *Attorney-General* v. *Birmingham Tame, and Rae District Drainage Board*, [1912] A.C. 788. On this ground alone I think the appeal ought to succeed. Even if, which is not proved, the parties may have contemplated the possibility of the outbreak of war, they cannot have contemplated the existence of statutes the like of which have never been known, or the exercise of extraordinary powers justified by those statutes. It might be sufficient to decide the case on the ground of illegality alone, but, out of respect for the arguments addressed to us and for the judgment of the learned judge, I think it right to add a few observations. The contract was one for the execution of very extensive works, the cost of which would not fall short of three-quarters of a million pounds, and involved the employment of several thousand men. It was to be performed within six years, subject, no doubt, to a power in the engineer of the Board to enlarge the time in certain conditions. It gave the Board a limited property in all the plant provided by the contractors for the work. Speaking roughly, £100,000 worth of plant was provided. All this plant has been claimed by the Minister of Munitions and the greater part of it has been removed and either sold or used elsewhere. There is no provision in the contract enabling the contractors to recover a penny from the Board towards the cost of restoring, or replacing, the necessary plant. It is in my view impossible to consider this otherwise than as an event not in contemplation by either party at the time. It is quite true that there is in clause 32 provision for delays due to certain specified causes, such as strikes, which are not to be any excuse for the contractors, but in my opinion these events do not extend to the case of illegality; and, further, I do not think that those events can prevent the Court from considering whether interference due to a subsequent Act of Parliament has been of such a nature as to render the contract substantially a new contract. Lastly, I do not base my judgment on the view that there is no physical possibility of the performance of the contract at the end of the war, and after the removal of the restraint imposed by the Minister of Munitions. Nothing is impossible to an engineer provided sufficient time and money can be secured. Nor do I base my judgment on commercial impossibility or impracticability. The mere circumstance that the contractors might lose money would not suffice to terminate the contract. I base my judgment on the view that it was the manifest intention of the parties that there should be freedom of action on the part of both parties and that there should be read into the contract an implied term or condition that the liability of performance should cease in the event of the Executive Government acting lawfully and within their powers, making performance of the contract illegal and impossible. With great respect to Bray J. I think he took a wrong view, and the appeal must be allowed. This will involve the discharge of the injunction as to the plant and the substitution of a new declaration, and the Board must pay the costs of the action here and below. I think it right that we should add a declaration that this judgment is without prejudice to any question as to the rights of either party to the proceeds of sale of plant which has been sold, or as to any retention moneys under the contract. We have not listened to any arguments on these points, which must be dealt with in a separate action.

[The opinions of Warrington L.J. and Scrutton L.J. to the same effect are omitted. The decision of the Court of Appeal was affirmed on appeal to the House of Lords, [1918] A.C. 119.]

OCEAN TRAWLERS *v.* MARITIME NATIONAL FISH CO. [1934] 1 D.L.R. 621 (Nova Scotia. Supreme Court). The facts of this case are set out briefly by Lord Wright in his speech in the *Constantine* case above. The Supreme Court *en banc* reversed the trial Judge and the Privy Council affirmed the full Court in [1935] 3 D.L.R. 12. DOULL J.: "In the opinion of Lord Dunedin we have some illuminating remarks in reference to *Tamp-*

lin Steamship Co. v. *Anglo-Mexican Petroleum Products Co.*, [1916] 2 A.C. 397, where it was held that a requisition of a ship did not cancel the charter:—'I return to *Tamplin's Case* to show that the views of the majority (for obviously I need not deal with those of the minority) were based upon circumstances which find no proper analogy in the circumstances here. In the first place the person who wanted the contract declared at an end was the owner. The charterer, notwithstanding what had happened, was content to go on paying the hire, and to refrain, during the period while the Government were in possession of the ship, from demanding any services from the owners. Under the contract, as Lord Parker put it, "The owners are not concerned in the charterers doing any specific thing beyond the payment of freight as it becomes due." That payment the charterers, as I have already said, were ready to make. The reason, no doubt, was that they had already got, or thought they would get, from the Government a larger sum of money than they had to pay to the owners. So that one view that I think ran through the opinions of the majority was this: No one was hurt by the continuance of the charter, and if the Government relinquished the ship there was no reason why the charter should not be effective for the remaining period of its duration, which might be considerable. But suppose the facts had been slightly different. *Suppose the Government had taken the ship, and had said they would pay nothing*—a proceeding within their powers—*and then suppose that the owner had sued the charterer* for the hire during the period while the Government kept the ship. What then? I may be wrong, but it seems to me it would have fallen within the lines of *Horlock* v. *Beal*, [1916] 1 A.C. 486.'

"It is apparent that the party who seeks to set aside must be the party who is damaged (hurt as Lord Dunedin puts it). No doubt the man who hired the window to look at the coronation procession could still have insisted on paying his money and using the space. It is the fact that the circumstances which were the vital basis of the contract have changed which enables him to treat the contract as at an end. . . .

"It is possible to obtain from the cases a set of principles which we can apply in the case before the Court?

"These principles seem to be: . . .

"(3) The contract is avoided only on the complaint of the party who is damaged and if in spite of the changed condition one party is uninjured, he can not complain if the other party wishes to continue: Lord Dunedin in the *Metropolitan Water Board* case explaining the *Tamplin* case."

[Doull J. is quoting Lord Dunedin's speech in the House of Lords in the *Metropolitan Water Board* case. In *Horlock* v. *Beal* a British ship, the *Coralie Horlock*, was detained in a German port at the outbreak of the First World War. The crew was later imprisoned. An action by the wife of the first mate for wages during the detention was dismissed. Judicial opinion was sharply divided. Should the "impossibility" date from the detention of the ship or the imprisonment of the crew?]

CLAUDE NEON GENERAL ADVERTISING LTD. *v.* SING

Nova Scotia. Supreme Court. [1942] 1 D.L.R. 26

DOULL J.: This action is brought by the plaintiff for rentals alleged to be due by the defendant in respect of an advertising sign of the kind usually known as a Neon Sign, that is an electrical sign equipped with fixtures for lighting the same with a type of electric lights.

The parties entered into an agreement in writing on June 23, 1939, under which the plaintiff agreed to construct, and when constructed to lease to the defendant, a sign to be erected on the building No. 258 Quinpool Road, Halifax, N.S., which building was occupied by the defendant as "Oriental Cafe Parlor." The defendant was to pay a rental of $13 per month to the plaintiff for a term of 60 months. The plaintiff was to install the sign and keep it in repair but the defendant was to pay for the electric power. There was nothing in the agreement to release the defendant from payment of the rentals on the happening of any contingency.

Canada entered the present war on September 10, 1939 and on September 18, 1939 certain lighting restrictions were imposed by competent authority in the district in which the defendant's cafe is situate. It is agreed that these lighting restrictions are as follows:

"The use of lighted outdoor electric signs of every kind is prohibited between sunset and sunrise.

"No light source shall be so operated that it is directly visible from the sky at any time between sunset and sunrise.

"There shall be no light showing from unattended premises at any time between sunset and sunrise.

"When an air raid warning is given all lights of every kind except those behind adequate shades must be extinguished, and shall be kept extinguished until the 'all clear' signal is given.

"Such further orders as may appear necessary or expedient to enable the Air Raid Precautions Committee to function effectively will be issued by me from time to time."

The defendant admits that, if there were no such restrictions, the amount claimed in the statement of claim, viz. $234, would be due. He tenders $27.73 as the amount due to September 18, 1939 and says that the carrying out of the contract has become impossible by a change of the law and in effect that he is relieved from further payment on the principles established by the cases which are referred to as cases of frustration.

The matter is not without difficulty and it will be necessary to consider some of the cases in which the principles of the doctrine of frustration have been developed. . . .

The common law rule was said to be that if a man makes a contract absolute and possible on its face, subsequently arising impossibility does not excuse from performance. . . .

This doctrine, in some cases apparently rather harsh, was explained by Lord Ellenborough on the ground that the law will not imply a term in a contract which the parties might have expressed: *Atkinson* v. *Ritchie* (1809), 10 East 530; 103 E.R. 877. There was, however, a class of cases in which impossibility had been held to be a defence. In the law of the contract of bailments, if the chattel bailed or loaned perishes without fault of the bailee before the time for the return to the bailor and the return thereby becomes impossible, this impossibility excuses the borrower or bailee from performance of his promise to redeliver the chattel.

So, when the case arose of the proprietor of a music hall, who had agreed to let the hall for a concert and before the day of the concert the hall was destroyed by fire, through no fault of the proprietor, the Court imported into the case the law applicable to bailment and held that the proprietor was excused from providing the concert hall. It was said that there was an implied condition "that the parties shall be excused in case, before breach, performance becomes impossible from the perishing of the thing without default of the contractor"; *Taylor* v. *Caldwell* (1863), 122 E.R. 309.

The principle that the perishing of "the thing" without fault of the contractor runs through many of the following cases. Before the last war, the cases in which a party to a contract was relieved under this principle by reason of a subsequent happening might be divided into three classes:

1. Where the contract is for the providing of a specific article and the contract becomes impossible by the perishing of that thing or by the destruction of some particular thing essential to the performance: *Taylor* v. *Caldwell*; *Appleby* v. *Myers* (1867), L.R. 2 C.P. 651; *Nickoll* v. *Ashton, Edridge & Co.*, [1901] 2 K.B. 126; *Howell* v. *Coupland* (1876), 1 Q.B.D. 258. A statutory provision under this heading is found in the *Sale of Goods Act*, R.S.N.S., 1923, c. 206, s. 9. This principle also applies where a specific article contracted for is requisitioned by the Government: *Re Shipton, Anderson & Co. and Harrison Bros. & Co.*, [1915] 3 K.B. 679.

2. Contracts for personal services are avoided if rendered impossible by death or incapactitating illness.

This class of cases does not concern us in the present case.

3. Where performance becomes impossible through a change in the law: *Baily* v. *De Crespigny* (1869), L.R. 4 Q.B. 180.

Since the beginning of the present century, these rules have been considerably extended and the doctrine which has been applied has been called frustration. There are two classes of these cases: (1) The "Coronation Cases," in which the contract could be carried out but the circumstances which formed its basis had wholly changed; (2) Cases in which a change in the law or the advent of war involved such a fundamental change in the contract that it might be said that any contract that could be carried out would essentially differ from what the parties had in contemplation. . . .

The Judicial Committee in *Maritime National Fish Ltd.* v. *Ocean Trawlers Ltd.*, [1935] A.C. 524, said: "This case is more analogous to such a case as *Krell* v. *Henry*, [1903] 2 K.B. 740, where the contract was for the hire of a window for a particular day: it was not expressed but it was mutually understood that the hirers wanted the window in order to view the Coronation procession: when the procession was postponed by reason of the unexpected illness of King Edward, it was held that the contract was avoided by that event: the person who was letting the window was ready and willing to place it at the hirer's disposal on the agreed date; the hirer, however, could not use it for the purpose which he desired. It was held that the contract was dissolved because the basis of the contract was that the procession should take place as contemplated. The correctness of this decision has been questioned, for instance, by Lord Finlay, L.C. in *Larrinaga & Co.* v. *Société Franco-Americaine des Phosphates (1923)*, 39 T.L.R. 316 at p. 318. Lord Finlay observes:

"It may be that the parties contracted in the expectation that a particular event would happen, each taking his chance, but that the actual happening of the event was not made the basis of the contract."

The authority is certainly not one to be extended: it is particularly difficult to apply where . . . the possibility of the event . . . was known to both parties when the contract was made, but the contract entered into was absolute in terms so far as concerned that known possibility. It may be asked whether in such cases there is any reason to throw the loss on those who have undertaken to place the thing or service . . . at the other parties' disposal and are able and willing to do so.

It is worth while noting that in the same volume of reports one of the "Coronation Cases" was decided differently from *Krell* v. *Henry* by the same Court. *Herne Bay Steam Boat Co.* v. *Hutton*, [1903] 2 K.B. 683, where the defendant had chartered a ship to take a party of persons to see the Naval Review and for a day's cruise around the fleet following the King's Coronation. The Naval Review did not take place and the defendant repudiated the contract. It was held that the venture was at the defendant's risk and that there was not total failure of consideration or subject-matter. The defendant could have had the cruise around the fleet although he would not have seen any Naval Review. The plaintiff therefore recovered.

During and after the late war, the number of reported cases in which the principle of frustration was involved was greatly increased. These arose out of changes in the law or the advent of war or some consequent regulation by which either the carrying out of the contract became impossible or the changes in circumstances were so great that the contract, if carried out, would be an essentially different contract from the original undertaking. . . .

It seems therefore that the doctrine of frustration has been based upon two theories: (1) that there is an implied term that entitled one or other of the parties to have the contract dissolved if certain events make it impossible of performance; (2) that the basis or foundation of the contract has disappeared and that the contract is to be regarded as dissolved.

It is not necessary to return to the cases, but it will be seen that one or other theory is more applicable to different cases. It may be that the two theories are different ways of giving effect to what the Courts have considered substantial justice under the facts.

The cases which we have considered have been cases where the law has rendered the further performance of the contract impossible, as in *Metropolitan Water Board* v. *Dick, Kerr & Co.*, or where the very thing which is the substance of the contract has disappeared, as in *Taylor* v. *Caldwell* or in the chartering cases and in addition the Coronation Cases, of which *Krell* v. *Henry* is the outstanding example of a frustration where the actual contract could have been carried out on both sides but where it would have been of no benefit to the party who asked that it be discharged. We now go back to another case arising in the time of the late war, *Leiston Gas Co.* v. *Leiston-Cum-Sizewell, Urban Council*, [1916] 2 K.B. 428. . . . The part which was impossible was the supplying of gas for lighting; the part which was possible was the supplying, erecting and maintaining the standards, lamps and other plant. In the present case the plaintiff is not required to supply the power for light but has performed services which were not unlike those which were held in the *Leiston* case to be not "a trivial part."

A recent case, *Williams* v. *Mercer*, [1940] 3 All E.R. 292, bears superficial resemblance to the present case as the subject-matter was a neon sign but it depended upon conditions in the lease of the wall of a building. It perhaps illustrates the principle that a lessee or licensee is not released from paying rent because the benefit which they expected is lost by reason of government action.

In the case which we are considering, the neon sign was constructed for the purposes of the defendant, it was erected on the defendant's premises and was operated for some time. The monthly rental was for the purpose of paying the cost of construction and erection as well as maintenance over a period of 60 months. No part of the contract between the parties became impossible. The defendant certainly gets very much less benefit from the sign, but it is not entirely useless as a daylight sign. The lighting of it, even when legal, is a matter for the defendant. It is true that the defendant does not get an illuminated sign and in that respect the case approaches *Krell* v. *Henry*; but having regard to the remarks concerning *Krell* v. *Henry* in the *Trawlers* case, I do not think that I should say that the contract is for an illuminated sign. The *Herne Bay* case was not so very different from *Krell* v. *Henry*, but it was there held that the charterers took the risk. I think that the principles upon which the *Leiston* case was decided apply to the present case.

The plaintiff will therefore have judgment for the amount of its claim and costs.

DENNY, MOTT & DICKSON, LTD. *v*. JAMES B. FRASER & CO. LTD.
Scotland. House of Lords. [1944] A.C. 265

The appellants were timber merchants and importers. The respondents were timber merchants and saw millers. In 1929 they entered into a contract under which the respondents agreed to buy all their supplies of red and white pine from the appellants and to let to the appellants the Drumalbyn Timber Yard "which let shall continue during the period of the . . . trading agreement." The appellants agreed to supply the respondents with the pine "so far as their stocks will permit." An elaborate pricing system was provided. Clause 5 provided that the agreement should commence as at May 28, 1929 and the appellants could terminate it with one year's notice, the respondents with three years' notice. Clause 8 provided that in the event of termination, by either party, the appellants could purchase the ground and all buildings for £4,000. Alternatively, the appellants could take the ground and buildings on lease for £500 per annum. Clause 9 provided that the lease should be for a term of five years, renewable at the option of the appellants for further terms of five years from time to time to a total of 99 years from May 28, 1929.

At the outbreak of war emergency legislation severely regulated the sale of pine. The appellants' stocks were exhausted about the end of September, 1939, and from that date it was impossible for them to supply any further timber. The appellants admitted that the regulations wholly prevented the current operation of the agreement. On July 17, 1941, the appellants purported to terminate the agreement by giving a year's notice, and to exercise the option to purchase for £4,000. The respondents brought this action to determine the rights of the parties.

The Lord Ordinary, Lord Robertson held that the agreement had two distinct parts and that the "trading agreement" had been terminated by frustration, but that the "purchase" agreement remained operative and that the option was validly exercised. The Court of Session held that the agreement was a single contract and that it had been terminated by frustration. The appellants appealed to the House of Lords.

VISCOUNT SIMON L.C.: . . . The option of purchase conferred by clause 8 on the appellants only arises "in the event of the foregoing trading agreement being terminated by either party as aforesaid" (i.e., by notice under clause 5). If, therefore, the agreement had already been terminated by intervening events such as the war regulations above referred to, and its further performance had been frustrated by supervening illegality, the basis on which the option might have been exercised by the appellants had ceased to exist. The termination by either party to which clause 8 refers is the termination of the agreement when it is alive and operative, but the notice of termination in the respondents' letter of July 17 refers to an agreement which has already been brought to an end by supervening events.

This view of the case really concludes the matter, but I should mention two arguments which have been urged by the appellants against the inevitable result. The first is that the contract is, as the Lord Ordinary described it, "of a composite character," with the result that the the part dealing with the sale and purchase of timber might be terminated by frustration without the part dealing with the option to buy the land being brought to an end. This contention breaks down on an examination of the terms of the agreement. It is one agreement, and, as already pointed out, the exercise of the option as to the land depends on the termination of the purchase agreement arising by notice from either party. The other contention was that the substantial purpose of the whole agreement was to provide the option, and that the trading clauses were quite subsidiary, so that the contract survived as a whole and advantage could still be taken of the option clause. It is undoubtedly true that the principles on which frustration depends require the contract to be examined as a whole, and it may be that the supervening impossibility of fulfilling some minute provision may not be regarded as going to the length of preventing substantial performance of the contract as a whole. If *Leiston Gas Co.* v. *Leiston-cum-Sizewell Urban District Council*, [1916] 2 K.B. 428, was rightly decided, that case would furnish an instance, but, on the facts of the present case, there is no room for the application of such an argument. The preamble of the contract indicates, and the language of most of its clauses shows, that the trading in timber was the main object of the contract. This trading was frustrated and the opportunity for exercising the option thereupon lapsed. I move that the decision of the Court of Session be affirmed and that the appeal be dismissed with costs.

LORD MACMILLAN: My Lords, the principle of contract law which has come to be known as the doctrine of frustration and which has recently in England been accorded statutory recognition, is common to the jurisprudence alike of Scotland and of England, although the leading cases are to be found in the English law reports. It is a principle so inherently just as inevitably to find a place in any civilized system of law. The manner in whch it has developed in order to meet the problems arising from the disturbances of business due to world wars is a tribute to the progresssive adaptability of the common law. In the works of the Scottish institutional writers the matter receives only rudimentary treatment. In Bell's Principles of the Law of Scotland it is not until after the death of the original author that, in the editions which we owe to Sheriff Guthrie, the doctrine begins to assume its modern shape, and is well stated as follows: "When by the nature of the contract its performance depends on the existence of a particular thing or state of things, the failure or destruction of that thing or state of things, without default on either side, liberates both parties." The earlier cases both in England and in Scotland are mostly concerned with the consequences of the perishing of the thing on whose continued existence the contract depended for its fulfilment, but many of the recent cases have arisen from the supervention of emergency legislation rendering the implement of the contract illegal. It is plain that a contract to do what it has become illegal to do cannot be legally enforceable. There cannot be default in not doing what the law forbids to be done.

The present case belongs to the latter category. It seems to me a very clear one for the application of the principle I have just enunciated. Here is an agreement between two parties for carrying on dealings in imported timber. By emergency legislation the importation of timber has been rendered illegal. Neither party can be said to be in default. The further fulfilment of their mutual obligations has been brought to an abrupt stop by an irresistible extraneous cause for which neither party is responsible. But it has been suggested, and the Lord Ordinary and Lord Jamieson have taken the view, that one of the stipulations of the contract is severable from the rest and remains enforceable, inasmuch as its fulfilment would involve no illegality. This contention is, in my opinion, untenable. It is true that the respondents could, without infringing the emergency legislation sell or let their Grangemouth timber yard to the appellants on the terms stated in agreement, but the right to require such a sale or lease is conferred on the appellants only as a consequence of one or other of the parties having voluntarily taken advantage of the right to terminate the agreement on notice. The operation of the agreement having been compulsorily terminated, neither party can thereafter terminate it voluntarily. You cannot slay the slain.

I would only add that, in judging whether a contract has been frustrated, the contract must be looked at as a whole. The question is whether its purpose as gathered from its terms has been defeated. A contract whose purpose has been defeated may contain subsidiary stipulations which it would still be possible and lawful to fulfil, but to segregate and enforce such a stipulation would be to do something which the parties never intended. It cannot be suggested with any reason in the present case that the respondents would have conferred on the appellants an option to purchase or take on lease the respondents' timber yard independently of the trading arrangements into which they had agreed to enter. The consideration for the option was the fulfilment of those arrangements and there was no severable consideration. The House is not concerned in this appeal with any question as to the reliefs consequent on frustration as to which the law of Scotland may differ from the law of England. I agree with your Lordships that the appeal should be dismissed and the interlocutor of the Second Division affirmed.

LORD WRIGHT: . . . It is now I think well settled that where there is frustration a dissolution of a contract occurs automatically. It does not depend, as does rescission of a contract on the ground of repudiation or breach, on the choice or election of either party. It depends on what actually has happened on its effect on the possibility of performing the contract. Where, as generally happens, and actually happened in the present case, one party claims that there has been frustration and the other party contests it, the court decides the issue and decides it *ex post facto* on the actual circumstances of the case. The data for decision are, on the one hand, the terms and construction of the contract, read in the light of the then existing circumstances, and on the other hand the events which have occurred. It is the court which has to decide what is the true position between the parties. The decision is as Lord Sumner said in *Hirji Mulji* v. *Cheong Yue Steamship Co., Ltd.*, [1926] A.C. 497, 510, irrespective of the individuals concerned, their temperaments and failings, their interest and circumstances. The court has formulated the doctrine by virtue of its inherent jurisdiction, just as it has developed the rules of liability for negligence, or for the restitution or repayment of money where otherwise there would be unjust enrichment. I find the theory of the basis of the rule in Lord Sumner's pregnant statement (loc. cit.) that the doctrine of frustration is really a device by which the rules as to absolute contracts are reconciled with the special exceptions which justice demands. Though it has been constantly said by high authority, including Lord Sumner, that the explanation of the rule is to be found in the theory that it depends on an implied condition of the contract, that is really no explanation. It only pushes back the problem a single stage. It leaves the question what is the reason for implying a term. Nor can I reconcile that theory with the view that the result does not depend on what the parties might, or would as hard bargainers, have agreed. The doctrine is invented by the court in order to supplement the defects of the actual contract. The parties did not anticipate fully and completely, if at all, or provide for what actually happened. It is not possible, to my mind, to say that, if they had thought of it they would have said: "Well, if that happens, all is over between us." On the contrary, they would almost certainly on the one side or the other have sought to introduce reservations or qualifications or compensations. As to that the court cannot guess. What it can say is that the contract either binds or does not bind. It is a separate matter whether some ancillary relief should be given, as for a failure of consideration consequent on the frustration, as was held to be proper in *Fibrosa Spolka Akcyjna* v. *Fairbairn Lawson Combe Barbour Ltd.*, [1943] A.C. 32. To my mind, the theory of the implied condition is not really consistent with the true theory of frustration. It has never been acted on by the court as a ground of decision, but is merely stated as a theoretical explanation. I only refer to the point here because it seems to me that the conclusions of both Lord Robertson and Lord Jamieson were affected to some extent by reflecting on what the parties as individuals might or would have decided if they had thought of the possible frustrating cause. I must admit that the view I have stated is somewhat heretical, but the general nature of the doctrine of frustration has given rise to many irreconcilable explanations. . . .

Looking at this contract and to the frustrating event, I think it would be unreasonable not to regard the trading agreement as the substantial matter, so that when that is frustrated so is the contract as a whole. It would not be possible, in my opinion, to regard the whole contract as surviving when the trading agreement became frustrated. I need not consider another possible view, namely, that clauses 8 and 9 survived as a separate agreement, in the way that the arbitration clause in *Heyman* v. *Darwins, Ltd.*, [1942] A.C. 356, was, in the opinion of the Lord Chancellor, capable of surviving as an independent clause. That would not help the appellants here, because clause 8, for whatever reason, is quite plain and specific, as I have already said, in the limited and grudging terms in which it grants the option to purchase. The option does not derive from the general character of the contract, but from the specific words of clause 8. When the trading ceased the free use of the yard would revert to its owners in the absence of a new and special grant. The stringent and limited character of the express condition of the option under clause 8 must receive effect from the court. The condition was not, and in the events could not be, complied with by the appellant. The question whether Scots law would give any or what restitution to the appellants for alterations and improvements effected upon the yard during the period of their occupation is not before the House. I would dismiss the appeal.

[The opinions of Lord Thankerton and Lord Porter are omitted. Lord Wright's opinion is considerably curtailed.]

3. Restitution: Quantum Meruit, Quasi-Contract and Unjust Enrichment

APPLEBY *v.* MYERS
England. Exchequer Chamber. 1867. L.R. 2 C.P. 651

This was an action brought to recover £419 for work done and materials provided by the plaintiffs, engineers, for the defendant, under the circumstances hereinafter mentioned. The following case was stated, by consent, without pleadings, for the opinion of the Court:

On the 30th of March, 1865, the plaintiffs entered into an agreement with the defendant, which was headed, "Specification and estimate of engine, boiler, lifts, etc., for B. Meyers, Esq., Southwark Street. Messrs. Tillott & Chamberlain, architects, 30th March, 1865." This contract contained ten distinct parts or divisions, viz. 1. boiler; 2. engine; 3. shafting; 4. lifts; 5. shafting; 6. drying-room; 7. copper pans; 8. tanks; 9. pump; 10. steam-boxes; under each of which headings were particular descriptions of the work to be done in connection with each respectively, and the prices to be charged for the same; and the document concluded with these words:

"We offer to make and erect the whole of the machinery of the best materials and workmanship of their respective kinds, and to put it to work, for the sum above named respectively, and to keep the whole in order, under fair wear and tear, for two years from the date of completion. All brickwork, carpenters' and masons' work, and materials, are to be provided for us; but the drawings and general instructions required for them to work to will be provided by us, subject to the architects' approval.

(signed) Appleby Brothers."

The total cost of the above works, if they had been completed under the contract, would have amounted to £459.

On the 4th of July, 1865, a fire accidentally broke out on the premises of the defendant in Southwark Street, which entirely destroyed the premises and the works which then had been erected by the plaintiffs in part performance of the contract. At the time of the fire the works contracted for had not been completed.

At the time of the fire, portions of the items Nos. 1 to 8 were erected and fixed, and some of the materials for the others were on the premises. The defendant had not completed the carpenters' and masons' work. The tank had been erected by the plaintiffs, and was used by the defendant by taking water therefrom for the purpose of his business; but the other apparatus connected with it, as specified in No. 8 was not complete. The plaintiff's workmen were still engaged in continuing the erection and completion of the same at the time of the fire.

The premises were the property of the defendant, in his occupation, and under his entire control. The plaintiffs had access to them only for the purpose of performing their contract.

The question for the opinion of the Court was, whether, under the above circumstances, the plaintiffs were entitled to recover the whole or any portion of the contract price.

The Court of Common Pleas gave judgment for the plaintiffs for an amount equal to the value of the work and materials actually done and provided by them under the agreement. The defendants appealed to the Court of Exchequer Chamber.

BLACKBURN J. delivered the judgment of the Court: This case was partly argued before us at the last sittings; and the argument was resumed and completed at the present sittings.

Having had the advantage of hearing the very able arguments of Mr. Holl and Mr. Hannen, and having during the interval had the opportunity of considering the judgment of the Court below, there is no reason that we should further delay expressing the opinion at which we have all arrived, which is, that the judgment of the Court below is wrong and ought to be reversed.

The whole question depends upon the true construction of the contract between the parties. We agree with the Court below in thinking that it sufficiently appears that the work which the plaintiffs agreed to perform could not be performed unless the defendant's premises continued in a fit state to enable the plaintiffs to perform the work on them; and we agree with them in thinking that, if by any default on the part of the defendant, his premises were rendered unfit to receive the work, the plaintiffs would have had the option to sue the defendant for this default, or to treat the contract as rescinded, and sue on a quantum meruit. But we do not agree with them in thinking that there was an absolute promise or warranty by the defendant that the premises should at all events continue so fit. We think that where, as in the present case the premises are destroyed without fault on either side, it is a misfortune equally affecting both parties; excusing both from further performance of the contract, but giving a cause of action to neither.

Then it was argued before us, that, inasmuch as this was a contract of that nature which would in pleading be described as a contract for work, labour, and materials, and not as one of bargain and sale, the labour and materials necessarily became the property of the defendant as soon as they were worked into his premises and became part of them, and therefore were at his risk. We think that, as to a great part at least of the work done in this case, the materials had not become the property of the defendant; for, we think that the plaintiffs, who were to complete the whole for a fixed sum, and keep it in repair two years, would have had a perfect right, if they thought that a portion of the engine which they had put up was too slight, to change it and substitute another in their opinion better calculated to keep in good repair during the two years, and without consulting or asking the leave of the defendant. But, even on the supposition that the materials had become unalterably fixed to the defendant's premises, we do not think that, under such a contract as this, the plaintiffs could recover anything unless the whole work was completed. It is quite true that materials worked by one into the property of another become part of that property. This is equally true, whether it be fixed or movable property. Bricks built into a wall become part of the house; thread stitched into a coat which is under repair, or planks and nails and pitch worked into a ship under repair, become part of the coat or the ship; and therefore, generally, and in the absence of something to shew a contrary intention, the bricklayer, or tailor, or shipwright, is to be paid for the work and materials he has done and provided, although the whole work is not complete. It is not material whether in such a case the non-completion is because the shipwright did not choose to go on with the work, as was the case in *Roberts* v. *Havelock* (1832), 3 B. & Ad. 404; 110 E.R. 145, or because in consequence of a fire he could not go on with it, as in *Menetone* v. *Athawes* (1764), 3 Burr. 1592; 97 E.R. 998. But, this is the prima facie contract between those who enter into contracts for doing work and supplying materials, there is nothing to render it either illegal or absurd in the workman to agree to complete the whole, and be paid when the whole is complete, and not till then: and we think that the plaintiffs in the present case had entered into such a contract. Had the accidental fire left the defendant's premises untouched, and only injured a part of the work which the plaintiffs had already done, we apprehend that it is clear the plaintiffs under such a contract as the present must have done that part over again, in order to fulfil their contract to complete the whole and "put it to work for the sums above named respectively." As it is, they are, according to the principle laid down in *Taylor* v. *Caldwell* (1863), 122 E.R. 309, excused from completing the work; but they are not therefore entitled to any compensation for what they have done, but which has, without any fault of the defendant, perished. The case is in principle like that of a shipowner who has been excused from the performance of his contract to carry goods to their destination, because his ship has been disabled by one of the excepted perils, but who is not therefore entitled to any payment on account of the part-performance of the voyage, unless there is something to justify the conclusion that there has been a fresh contract to pay freight pro rata.

On the argument, much reference was made to the Civil Law. The opinions of the great lawyers collected in the Digest afford us very great assistance in tracing out any question of doubtful principle; but they do not bind us: and we think that, on the principles of English law laid down . . . the plaintiffs, having contracted to do an entire work for a specific sum, can recover nothing unless the work be done, or it can be shewn that it was the defendant's fault that the work was incomplete, or that there is something to justify the conclusion that the parties have entered into a fresh contract. . . .

KING *v.* LOW. 1901. 3 O.L.R. 234 (Ontario. Court of Appeal). The defendants agreed to build a house on an island in the St. Lawrence for one George F. Benson at a price of $4,450. The plaintiffs were plumbing sub-contractors who agreed with the defendants to install the plumbing for $500. When $488 worth of plumbing work had been completed the house was destroyed by fire and the defendants refused to pay the plaintiffs anything on account of their work. Boyd C. at a jury trial, said, "The evidence shews substantial completion (to within $12), and the omission to do the greater part of the work arose from delays to be charged against the contractors rather than the plaintiffs." He was reversed on appeal. ARMOUR C.J.O.: "The plaintiffs did not bring this action for the contract price, alleging that they had substantially completed their contract; but admitted that they had not completed their contract, and brought it for the value of the work done by them." *Appleby* v. *Myers* was cited.

GOULDING *v.* RABINOVITCH. 1927. 60 O.L.R. 607 (Ontario. Court of Appeal). On February 25, 1926, Rabinovitch gave Goulding a 60-day option to purchase land for $68,000. Goulding paid $1,000 for the option.

On March 12 the C.N.R. commenced proceedings to expropriate the land. Goulding claimed the return of the $1,000. Lennox J. held that the contract was frustrated and Goulding could recover on a total failure of consideration. Rabinovitch appealed. MIDDLETON J.A.: "I agree with the findings of the learned trial Judge, but not with his legal conclusion. . . . Without the fault of either party, by the action of the railway company, the completion of the contract became impossible. But there was by no means a total failure of consideration. The plaintiff had the benefit of the option for the period between the making of the option-contract and the registration of the plan, and during the same period the defendant's hands were tied—he could not sell the land. In the end he had to accept from the railway company a sum considerably below the price named in the contract. Each will lose money; each must bear his own misfortune."

FONG *v*. KERWIN. [1929] 3 D.L.R. (Ontario. Court of Appeal). Kerwin agreed to lease his premises to Fong to be used as a laundry and to make the necessary changes (at a cost of some $800), but only if Fong would give him four months' rent in advance. Fong advanced the money, went into possession and put his name on the door. Kerwin got a building permit and commenced the renovations. Kerwin and Fong together applied for a laundry licence, but were told it could not be issued until the tubs were in and "everything installed." All was proceeding well until a petition presented by the neighbours against a laundry at that place was heeded and the licence refused. RIDDELL J.A.: "No doubt, the intention was that the premises should be used as a laundry; and the question whether the defendant can insist upon the lease does not arise here—the whole question being whether when the money was paid as a term of the lease being entered into at all, it can be recovered back. To ask that question is to answer it—the money was paid as a consideration for the defendant making the necessary changes and entering into the lease, for whatever it was worth; I can find no semblance of foundation for the proposition that it was paid for a consideration that has failed, and in my view it would be grossly unjust to compel the defendant to pay back the money received as a condition precedent to his making the expenditures he was required to make, and leave him out the money so expended by him."

FIBROSA SPOLKA AKCYJNA *v*. FAIRBAIRN LAWSON COMBE BARBOUR LTD.
England. House of Lords. [1943] A.C. 32

The respondents were a limited company carrying on at Leeds the business of manufacturing textile machinery, and by a contract in writing dated July 12, 1939, the respondents agreed to supply the appellants, a Polish company, of Vilna, with certain flax-hackling machines as therein specified and described, at a lump sum price of £4,800. The machines were of a special kind. The place of erection of the machinery was not mentioned in the contract, but it was agreed that it was the intention of the parties that it was to be erected at Vilna. By the terms of the contract, delivery was to be in three to four months from the settlement of final details. The machines were to be packed and delivered by the respondents c.i.f. Gydnia, the services of a skilled monteur to superintend erection were to be provided by the respondents and included in the price, and payment was to be made by cheque on London, one-third of the price (£1600) with the order and the balance (£3200) against shipping documents. By clause

7 of the conditions of sale attached to the contract:". . . Should dispatch be hindered or delayed by your instructions, or lack of instructions, or by any cause whatsoever beyond our reasonable control including strikes, lock-outs, war, fire, accidents . . . a reasonable extension of time shall be granted. . . ." By clause 10 provisions were made for dispatch and possible storage pending dispatch.

On July 18, 1939, the appellants paid to the respondents £1000 on account of the initial payment of £1600 due under the contract. On September 1, 1939, Germany invaded Poland and on September 3, Great Britain declared war on Germany. On September 7, the appellants' agents in England wrote to the respondents: "Owing to the outbreak of hostilities, it is now quite evident that the delivery of the hackling machines on order for Poland cannot take place. Under the circumstances we shall be obliged if you will kindly arrange to return our initial payment of £1000 at your early convenience." To this request, the respondents replied on the next day refusing to return the sum and stating that "considerable work had been done upon these machines and we cannot consent to the return of this payment. After the war the matter can be reconsidered." There was further correspondence between the parties or their agents which failed to produce agreement, and on May 1, 1940, the appellants issued a writ and by their statement of claim alleged that the respondents had broken the contract by refusing to deliver the machines, while the appellants "are and have at all material times been ready and willing to take delivery of the said machinery and pay for the same." The prayer of the claim was (a) for damages for breach of contract, (b) for specific performance or, alternatively, return of the £1000 with interest, and (c) for further or other relief. The substantial defence of the respondents was that the contract had been frustrated by the German occupation of Gdynia in September, 1939, and that in these circumstances the appellants had no right to the return of the £1000. Tucker J. dismissed the action on March 7, 1941, and the Court of Appeal affirmed his decision on May 15, 1941. The appellants appealed to the House of Lords.

VISCOUNT SIMON L.C.: My Lords, this is the appeal of a Polish company who were plaintiffs in the action against the decision of the Court of Appeal composed of Mackinnon and Luxmoore L.JJ. and Stable J., affirming the judgment of Tucker J. at the trial in favour of the respondents. After the Court of Appeal's judgment and before the appeal came to be argued at your Lordships' bar, the town of Vilna, where the appellants had carried on its business, and indeed the whole of Poland, under the laws of which state the appellants were incorporated, were occupied by our enemy, Germany. The question might, therefore, arise whether the appellants should now be debarred from prosecuting its appeal. . . . To obviate any difficulty on this head, the appellants, at the suggestion of the House, applied to the Board of Trade, and the department gave to the appellants' solicitors a licence to proceed with the appeal, notwithstanding that their clients might be in the position of an alien enemy. The House was content to let the case proceed on this basis. . . . If, as the result of the decision of the House, any payment becomes due to the appellants, and if they were in the position of alien enemies within the meaning of the *Trading with the Enemy Act, 1939*, the payment would be regulated by that Act.

Before passing to the main question involved in the appeal, I must mention another contention of the appellants which was based on clause 7 of the conditions of sale attached to the contract. This clause contained the provision that "should dispatch be hindered or delayed by . . . any cause beyond our reasonable control including . . . war . . . a reasonable extension of time shall be granted." The appellants argued that there could be no frustration by reason of the war which broke out during the currency of the contract because this contingency was expressly provided for in clause 7, and, therefore, there was no room for an implied term such as has often been regarded as a suitable way in which to express and apply the doctrine of frustration. I entirely agree with the Court of Appeal that in the circumstances of the present case this is a bad point. The ambit of the express condition is limited to delay in respect of which "a reasonable extension of time" might be granted. That might mean a minor delay as distinguished from a prolonged and indefinite interruption of prompt contractual performance which the present war manifestly brings about. A similar argument was unsuccessfully urged in *Bank Line, Ltd.* v. *Arthur Capel & Co.*, [1919] A.C. 435, and in other cases, a recent instance of which is *W. . Tatem, Ltd.* v. *Gamboa*, [1939] 1 K.B. 132. The principle is that where supervening events, not due to the default of either party, render the performance of a contract indefinitely impossible, and there is no undertaking to be bound in any event, frustration ensues, even though the parties may have expressly provided for the case of a limited interruption. As MacKinnon L.J. points out, the unsoundness of the contrary view is implicit in *Jackson* v. *Union Marine Insurance Co., Ltd.* (1874), L.R. 10 C.P. 125, for the charterparty in that case contained an exception of perils of the sea, but none the less the contract was held to have been terminated and the adventure to have been frustrated by the long delay due to the stranding of the ship. The situation arsing from the outbreak of the present war, so far as this country, Germany and Poland are concerned, makes applicable Lush J.'s well-known observation in *Geipel* v. *Smith* (1872), L.R. 7 Q.B. 404, 414: "A state of war" (in that case the Franco-German war of 1870) "must be presumed to be likely to continue so long and so to disturb the commerce of merchants as to defeat and destroy the object of a commercial adventure like this." There is a further reason for saying that this contention of the appellants must fail, namely, that, while this country is at war with Germany and Germany is occupying Gdynia, a British subject such as the respondents could not lawfully make arrangements to deliver c.i.f. Gdynia, and, therefore, the contract could not be further performed because of supervening illegality. A provision providing for a reasonable extension of time if dispatch is delayed by war cannot have any application when the circumstances of the war make dispatch illegal. . . .

Mr. Linton Thorp, in conducting the argument for the appellants before us, admitted that, if the point with which I have already dealt was decided against him, the only other issue to be determined was whether, when this contract became frustrated, the appellants could, in the circumstances of the present case, claim back from the respondents the £1000 which they had paid when placing the order. As to this, MacKinnon L.J., in delivering the judment of the Court of Appeal said: "Tucker J. held that having regard to the principle laid down in *Chandler* v. *Webster* [1904] 1 K.B. 493, and other like cases, this claim must fail. We think he was right, and, further, that that principle must equally bind this court to reject the claim. Whether the principle can be overruled is a matter that can only concern the House of Lords." This alleged principle is to the effect that where a contract has been frustrated by such a supervening event as releases from further performance, "the loss lies where it falls," with the result that sums paid or rights accrued before that event are not to be surrendered, but all obligations falling due for performance after that event are discharged. This proposition, whether right or wrong, first appears, not in *Chandler* v. *Webster* but in *Blakely v. Muller & Co.* [1903] 2 K.B. 670n., decided in January, 1903, by a Divisional Court, which was also a case arising out of the abandonment of the coronation procession owing to King Edward VII.'s sudden illness. In that case, Channell J. said: "If the money was payable on some day subsequent to the abandonment of the procession, I do not think it could have been sued for. If, however, it was payable prior to the abandonment of the procession, the position would be the same as if it had been actually paid and could not be recovered back, and could be sued for. . . . It is impossible to import a condition into a contract which the parties could have imported and have not done so. All that can be said is that, when the procession was abandoned, the contract was off, not that anything done under the contract was void. The loss must remain where it was at the time of the abandonment. It is true like the case of a charterparty where the freight is payable in advance, and the voyage is not completed, and the freight, therefore, not earned. Where the non-completion arose through impossibility of performance, the freight could not be recovered back." In *Civil Service Co-operative Society Ltd.*, v. *General Steam Navigation Co.* [1903] 2 K.B. 756., which was decided in the Court of Appeal in October, 1903, Lord Halsbury L.C. expressed entire concurrence with this passage in the judgment of Channell J. Lord Alverston C.J., who was a party to both these decision, took the same view.

If we are to approach this problem anew, it must be premised that the first matter to be considered is always the terms of the particular contract. If, for example, the contract is "divisible" in the sense that a sum is to be paid over in respect of completion of a defined portion of the work, it may well be that the sum is not returnable if completion of the whole work is frustrated. If the contract itself on its true construction stipulates for a particular result which is to follow in regard to money already paid, should frustration afterwards occur, this governs the matter. The ancient and firmly established rule that freight paid in advance is not returned if the completion of the voyage is frustrated . . . should, I think, be regarded as a stipulation introduced into such contracts by custom, and not as the result of applying some abstract principle.

And so, a fortiori, if there is a stipulation that the prepayment is "out and out." To take an example, not from commerce, but from sport, the cricket spectator who pays for admission to see a match cannot recover the entrance money on the ground that rain has prevented play if, expressly or by proper implication, the bargain with him is that no money will be returned. Inasmuch as the effect of frustration may be explained as arising from an implied term: see *Joseph Constantine Steamship Line, Ltd.*, v. *Imperial Smelting Corporation, Ltd.* [1942] A.C. 154, it is tempting to speculate whether a further term could be implied as to what was to happen, in the event of frustration, to money already paid, but, if the parties were assumed to have discussed the point when entering into the contract, they could not be supposed to have agreed on a simple formula which would be fair in all circumstances, and all that could be said is that, in the absence of such agreement, the law must decide. The question now to be determined is whether, in the absence of a term in the contract dealing with the matter, the rule which is commonly called the rule in *Chandler* v. *Webster* should be affirmed.

This supposed rule has been constantly applied in a great variety of cases which have since arisen—and necessarily so, because the rule had been laid down in plain terms by the Court of Appeal in England in 1904, and the present appeal provides the first occasion on which it can be effectively challenged. A very different rule prevails in Scotland, as was made plain by the decision of this House in *Cantiare San Rocco S.A.* v. *Clyde Shipbuilding and Engineering Co., Ltd.* [1924] A.C. 226. In that case the Earl of Birkenhead was careful to reserve the question whether *Chandler* v. *Webster* and the other English cases on the ponit were rightly decided, saying: "The question is as to the law of Scotland, and I desire to say nothing which may in any way fetter opinion if those authorities hereafter come to be reviewed by this House, for none of them is binding upon your Lordships." Similarly in the same case, Viscount Finlay observed that it would be out of place on that occasion to enter into the question dealt with in *Chandler* v. *Webster*, adding: "The principle of English law was re-stated with great clearness by Lord Parmoor in the case of *French Marine* v. *Compagnie Napolitaine d'Eclairage et de Chauffage par le Gaz* [1921] 2 A.C. 494, 523. This statement forms no part of the judgment of the House of Lords in that case, but there is no doubt that the principle has been repeatedly acted on in the Court of Appeal." Lord Dunedin in the *Cantiare San Rocco* case referred to the different angle of approach from which an English or a Scottish judge would look at the question, and thought that the cause was to be found in the reluctance of the English law to order the repayment of money once paid. But he added: "I do not enlarge on the topic, for I am not at all concerned to criticize English law. . . . For the purpose of this case, it is sufficient to say, as I unhesitatingly do, that *Chandler* v. *Webster*, if it had been tried in Scotland, would have been decided the other way." Lord Dunedin's restraint was not imitated by Lord Shaw whose pronouncement included a vigorous denunciation of the proposition that the loss lies where it falls as amounting to a maxim which "works well enough among tricksters, gamblers and thieves." The learned Lord asserted that this was part of the law of England (presumably meaning that it had been so laid down by the English Court of Appeal), but patriotically rejoiced that had never been part of the law of Scotland.

Mr. Valentine Holmes, in his able argument for the respondents, asked us to consider whether this House would be justified in disturbing a view of the law which has prevailed for nearly forty years, which has been so frequently affirmed, which has been constantly aplied in working out the rights of the parties to commercial contracts, and which, moreover at any rate furnishes a simple rule against the effect of which the parties to a contract can, if they so desire, expressly provide. These are weighty considerations, but I do think they ought to prevail in the circumstances of this case over our primary duty of doing our utmost to secure that the law on this important matter is correctly expounded and applied. If the view which has hitherto prevailed in this matter is found to be based on a misapprehension of legal principles, it is of great importance that these principles should be correctly defined, for, if not, there is a danger that the error may spread in other directions, and a portion of our law be erected on a false foundation. Moreover, though the so-called rule in *Chandler* v. *Webster* is nearly forty years old, it has not escaped much unfavourable criticism. My noble and learned friend Lord Atkin when sitting in the Court of Appeal as Atkin L.J., in *Russkoe Obschestvo d'lia Izgstovlenia Snariadov I' voennick Pripassov* v. *John Stirk & Sons, Ltd.* (1922), 10 Ll. L. Rep. 214, doubted whether any two business people in the world would ever make a contract which embodied such a doctrine as *Chandler* v. *Webster* laid down, and in the present case the Court of Appeal, while bound by previous authority, hinted a hope that this House might be able to substitute a "more civilized rule". I think, therefore, that we ought to regard ourselves as at liberty to examine the challenged proposition freely, and to lay down what we regard as the true doctrine in English law without being hampered by a course of practice based on previous decisions in the Court of Appeal.

The locus classicus for the view which has hitherto prevailed is to be found in the judgment of Collins M.R. in *Chandler* v. *Webster*. It was not a considered judgment, but it is hardly necessary to say that I approach this pronouncement of the then Master of the Rolls with all the respect due to so distinguished a common lawyer. When his judgment is studied, however, one cannot but be impressed by the circumstance that he regarded the proposition that money in such cases could not be recovered back as flowing from the decision in *Taylor* v. *Caldwell* (1863), 122 E.R. 309. *Taylor* v. *Caldwell*, however, was not a case in which any question arose whether money could be recovered back, for there had been no payment in advance, and there is nothing in the judgment of Blackburn J., which, at any rate in terms, affirms the general proposition that "the loss lies where it falls." The application by Collins M.R. of *Taylor* v. *Caldwell* to the actual problem with which he had to deal in *Chandler* v. *Webster* deserves close examination. He said: "The plaintiff contends that he is entitled to recover the money which he has paid on the ground that there has been a total failure of consideration. He says that the condition on which he paid the money was that the procession should take place, and that, as it did not take place, and that, as it did not take place, there has been a total failure of consideration. That contention does no doubt raise a question of some difficulty, and one which has perplexed the courts to a considerable extent in several cases. The principle on which it has been dealt with is that which was applied in *Taylor* v. *Caldwell*—namely, that where from causes outside the volition of the parties, something which was the basis of, or essential to the fulfilment of, the contract has become impossible, so that, from the time when the fact of that impossibility has been ascertained, the contract can no further be performed by either party, it remains a perfectly good contract up to that point, and everything previously done in pursuance of it must be treated as rightly done, but the parties are both discharged from further performance of it. If the effect were that the contract were wiped out altogether, no doubt the result would be that money paid under it would have to be repaid as on a failure of consideration. But that is not the effect of the doctrine; it only releases the parties from further performance of the contract. Therefore the doctrine of failure of consideration does not apply."

It appears to me that the reasoning in this crucial passage is open to two criticisms:

(a) The claim of a party, who has paid money under a contract, to get the money back, on the ground that the consideration for which he paid it has totally failed, is not based on any provision contained in the contract, but arises because, in the circumstances that have happened, the law gives a remedy in quasi-contract to the party who has not got that for which he bargained. It is a claim to recover money to which the defendant has no further right because in the circumstances that have developed the money must be regarded as received to the plaintiff's use. It is true that the effect of frustration is that, while the contract can no further be performed, "it remains a perfectly good contract up to that point, and everything previously done in pursuance of it must be treated as rightly done," but it by no means follows that the situation existing at the moment of frustration is one which leaves the party that has paid money and has not received the stipulated consideration without any remedy. To claim the return of money paid on the ground of total failure of consideration is not to vary the terms of the contract in any way. The claim arises not because the right to be repaid is one of the stipulated conditions of the contract, but because, in the circumstances that have happened, the law gives the remedy. It is the failure to distinguish between (1) the action of assumpsit for money had and received in a case where the consideration has wholly failed, and (2) an action on the contract itself, which explains the mistake which I think has been made in applying English law to this subject-matter. Thus, in *Blakely* v. *Muller & Co.*, [1903] 2 K.B. 760, Lord Alverstone C.J. said "I agree that *Taylor* v. *Caldwell* applies, but the consequence of that decision is that neither party here could have sued on the contract in respect of anything which was to be done under it after the procession had been abandoned." That is true enough, but it does not follow that because the plaintiff cannot sue "on the contract" he cannot sue the contract for the recovery of a payment in respect of which consideration has failed. In the same case, Wills J. relied on *Appleby* v. *Myers* (1867), L.R. 2 C.P. 651, where a contract was made for the erection by A. of machinery on the premises of B., to be paid for on completion. There was no prepayment and in the course of the work the premises were destroyed by fire. It was held that both parties were excused from further performance, and that no liability accrued on either side, but the liability referred to was liability under the contract, and the learned judge seems to have thought that no action to recover money in such circumstances as the present could be conceived of unless there was a term of the contract, express or implied, which so provided. Once it is realized that the action to recover money for a consideration that has wholly failed rests, not on a contractual bargain between the parties, but as Lord Sumner said in *Sinclair* v. *Brougham*, [1914] A.C. 398, 452., "upon a notional or imputed promise to repay," or (if it is preferred to omit reference to a fictitious promise) upon an obligation to repay arising from the circumstances, the difficulty in the way of holding that a prepayment made under a contract which has been frustrated can be recovered back appears to me to disappear.

(b) There is, no doubt, a distinction between cases in which a contract is "wiped out altogther," e.g., because it is void as being illegal from the start or as being due to fraud which the innocent party has elected to treat as avoiding the contract, and cases in which intervening impossibility "only releases the parties from further performance of the contract." But does the distinction between these two classes of case justify the deduction of Collins M.R. that "the doctrine of failure of consideration does not apply" where the contract remains a perfectly good contract up to the date of frustration? This conclusion seems to be derived from the view that, if the contract remains good and valid up to the moment of frustration, money which has already been paid under it cannot be regarded as having been paid for a consideration which has wholly failed. The party that has paid the money has had the advantage, whatever it may be worth, of the promise of the other party. That is true, but it is necessary to draw a distinction. In English law, an enforceable contract may be formed by an exchange of a promise for a promise, or by the exchange of a promise for an act—I am excluding contracts under seal—and thus, in the law relating to the formation of contract, the promise to do a thing may often be the consideration, but when one is considering the law of failure of consideration and of the quasi-contractual right to recover money on that ground, it is, generally speaking, not the promise which is referred to as the consideration, but the performance of the promise. The money was paid to secure performance and, if performance fails the inducement which brought about the payment is not fulfilled.

If this were not so, there could never be any recovery of money, for failure of consideration, by the payer of the money in return for a promise of future performance, yet there are endless examples which show that money can be recovered, as for a complete failure of consideration, in cases where the promise was given but could not be fulfilled: see the notes in Bullen and Leake's *Precedents of Pleading*, 9th ed., p. 263. In this connexion the decision in *Rugg* v. *Minett* (1809), 11 East, 210; 103 E.R. 985, is instructive. There the plaintiff had bought at auction a number of casks of oil. The contents of each cask were to be made up after the auction by the seller to the prescribed quantity so that the property in a cask did not pass to the plaintiff until this had been done. The plaintiff paid in advance a sum of money on account on his purchases generally, but a fire occurred after some of the casks had been filled up, while the others had not. The plaintiff's action was to recover the money he had paid as money received by the defendants to the use of the plaintiffs. The Court of King's Bench ruled that this cause of action succeeded in respect of the casks which at the time of the fire had not been filled up to the prescribed quantity. A simple illustration of the same result is an agreement to buy a horse, the price to be paid down, but the horse not to be delivered and the property not to pass until the horse had been shod. If the horse dies before the shoeing, the price can unquestionably be recovered as for a total failure of consideration, notwithstanding that the promise to deliver was given. This is the case of a contract de certo corpore where the certum corpus perishes after the contract is made, but, as Vaughan Williams L.J.'s judgment in *Krell* v. *Henry*, [1903] 2 K.B. 740, explained, the same doctrine applies "to cases where the event which renders the contract incapable of performance is the cessation or non-existence of an express condition or state of things, going to the root of the contract, and essential to its performance." I can see no valid reason why the right to recover prepaid money should not equally arise on frustration arising from supervening circumstances as it arises on frustration from destruction of a particular subject-matter. The conclusion is that the rule in *Chandler* v. *Webster* is wrong, and that the appellants can recover their £1000.

While this result obviates the harshness with which the previous view in some instances treated the party who had made a prepayment, it cannot be regarded as dealing fairly between the parties in all cases, and must sometimes have the result of leaving the recipient who has to return the money at a given disadvantage. He may have incurred expenses in connexion with the partial carrying out of the contract which are equivalent, or more than equivalent, to the money which he prudently stipulated should be prepaid, but which he now has to return for reasons which are no fault of his. He may have to repay the money, though he has executed almost the whole of the contractual work, which will be left on his hands. These results follow from the fact that the English common law does not undertake to apportion a prepaid sum in such circumstances—contrast the provision, now contained in s. 40 of the *Partnership Act, 1890*, for apportioning a premium if a partnership is prematurely dissolved. It must be for the legislature to decide whether provisions should be made for an equitable apportionment of prepaid moneys which have to be returned by the recipient in view of the frustration of the contract in respect of which they were paid. I move that the appeal be allowed, and that judgment be entered for the appellants.

[The opinions (allowing the appeal) of Lords Atkin, Russell of Killowen, Macmillan, Wright, Roche and Porter are omitted.]

NOTE. The facts of *Chandler* v. *Webster* are stated briefly by Lord Atkin as follows:

"In that case the plaintiff had hired a room to view the coronation procession on Thursday, June 26, 1902. On June 10 he wrote to the defendant: 'I beg to confirm my purchase of the first floor room of the Electric Lighting Board at 7 Pall Mall to view the procession on Thursday, June 26, for the sum of £141 15s., which amount is now due. I shall be obliged if you will take the room on sale, and I authorize you to sell separate seats in the room, for which I will erect a stand.' It became the subject of controversy whether, in view of certain other terms arranged between the parties the whole sum became due before the procession became impossible, but the courts decided, as was clearly the case, that it did so become due. It may be noted that the defendant had nothing to do under the contract but allow the plaintiff the use of the room. On June 19 the plaintiff paid the defendant £100 on account of the price of the room, but had not paid the balance at the time of the procession was abandoned. The plaintiff claimed the return of the £100 on a total failure of consideration, the defendant counter-claimed for the balance of £41 15s."

NOTE ON RESTITUTION. On the general theory of the English law of restitution, or unjust enrichment, or quasi-contract, Lord Wright said in the *Fibrosa* case:

"It is clear that any civilized system of law is bound to provide remedies for cases of what has been called unjust enrichment or unjust benefit, that is to prevent a man from retaining the money of or some benefit derived from another which it is against conscience that he should keep. Such remedies in English law are generally different from remedies in contract or in tort, and are now recognized to fall within a third category of the common law which has been called quasi-contract or restitution. The root idea was stated by three Lords of Appeal, Lord Shaw, Lord Sumner and Lord Carson, in *R. E. Jones, Ltd.* v. *Waring & Gillow, Ltd.* [1926] A.C. 670, 696, which dealt with a particular species of the category, namely, money paid under a mistake of fact. . . ."

After quoting from *Moses* v. *Macferlan* Lord Wright continued:

"Lord Mansfield does not say that the law implies a promise. The law implies a debt or obligation which is a different thing. In fact, he denies that there is a contract; the obligation is as efficacious as if it were upon a contract. The obligation is a creation of the law, just as much as an obligation in tort. The obligation belongs to a third class, distinct from either contract or tort, though it resembles contract rather than tort. This statement of Lord Mansfield has been the basis of the modern law of quasi-contract, notwithstanding the criticisms which have been launched against it. Like all large generalizations, it has needed and received qualification in practice. There is, for instance, the qualification that an action for money had and received does not lie for money paid under an erroneous judgment or for moneys paid under an illegal or excessive distress. The law has provided other remedies as being more convenient. The standard of what is against conscience in this text has become more or less canalized or defined, but in substance the juristic concept remains as Lord Mansfield left it.

"The gist of the action is a debt or obligation implied, or, more accurately, imposed, by law in much the same way as the law enforces as a debt the obligation to pay a statutory or customary impost. This is important because some confusion seems to have arisen though perhaps only in recent times when the true nature of the forms of action have become obscured by want of user. . . .

"Lord Atkin in the *United Australia* case [1941] A.C. 1, 29, after instancing the case of the blackmailer, says: 'The man has my money which I have not delivered to him with any real intention of passing to him the property. I sue him because he has the actual property taken.' He adds: 'These fantastic resemblances of contracts invented in order to meet requirements of the law as to forms of action which have now disappeared should not in these days be allowed to affect actual rights.' Yet the ghosts of the forms of action have been allowed at times to intrude in the ways of the living and impede vital functions of the law. Thus in *Sinclair* v. *Brougham* [1914] A.C. 398, 452, Lord Sumner stated that 'all these causes of action [sc. for money had and received] are common species of the genus assumpsit. All now rest, and long have rested, upon a notional or imputed promise to repay.' This observation, which was not necessary for the decision of the case, obviously does not mean that there is an actual promise of the party. The phrase 'notional or implied promise' is only a way of describing a debt or obligation arising by construction of law. The claim for money had and received always rested on a debt or obligation which the law implied or more accurately imposed, whether the procedure actually in vogue at any time was debt or account or indebitatus assumpsit. Even the fictitious assumpsit disappeared after the Act of 1852. I prefer Lord Sumner's explanation of the cause of action in *Jones's* case. This agrees with the words of Lord Atkin which I have just quoted, yet serious legal writers have seemed to say that these words of the great judge in *Sinclair* v. *Brougham* closed the door to any theory of unjust enrichment in English law. I do not understand why or how. It would indeed be a reductio ad absurdum of the doctrine of precedents. In fact, the common law still employs the action for money had and received as a practical and useful, if not complete or ideally perfect, instrument to prevent unjust enrichment, aided by the various methods of technical equity which are also available, as they were found to be in *Sinclair* v. *Brougham*."

Compare Denning J. in *Nelson* v. *Larholt* [1948] 1 K.B. 339, at p. 343:

"The rightful owner can recover the amount from anyone who takes the money with notice, subject, of course, to the limitation that he cannot recover twice over. This principle has been evolved by the courts of law and equity side by side. In equity it took the form of an action to follow moneys impressed with an express trust, or with a constructive trust owing to a fiduciary relationship. In law it took the form of an action for money had and received or damages for conversion of a cheque. It is no longer appropriate, however, to draw a distinction between law and equity. Principles have now to be stated in the light of their combined effect. Nor is it necessary to canvass the niceties of the old forms of action. Remedies now depend on the substance of the right, not on whether they can be fitted into a particular framework. The right here is not peculiar to equity or contract or tort, but falls naturally within the important category of cases where the court orders restitution, if the justice of the case so requires."

And contrast Lord Porter in *Reading* v. *Attorney-General* in the House of Lords [1951] A.C. 507, at p. 513–4, reproduced above at page 278, where the Canadian position is also noted.

THE FRUSTRATED CONTRACTS ACT
Ontario. Revised Statutes. 1960. Chapter 157

1. In this Act,

(a) "contract" includes a contract to which the Crown is a party;

(b) "court" means the court or arbitrator by or before whom a matter falls to be determined;

(c) "discharged" means relieved from further performance of the contract.

2. (1) This Act applies to any contract that is governed by the law of Ontario whether it was made before or after the 1st day of June, 1949, that after the 1st day of June, 1949, has become impossible of performance or been otherwise frustrated and the parties to which for that reason have been discharged.

(2) This Act does not apply,

(a) to a charterparty or a contract for the carriage of goods by sea, except a time charterparty or a charterparty by way of demise;

(b) to a contract of insurance; or

(c) to a contract for the sale of specific goods where the goods, without the knowledge of the seller, have perished at the time the contract was made, or where the goods, without any fault on the part of the seller or buyer, perished before the risk passed to the buyer.

3. (1) The sums paid or payable to a party in pursuance of a contract before the parties were discharged,

(a) in the case of sums paid, are recoverable from him as money received by him for the use of the party by whom the sums were paid; and

(b) in the case of sums payable, cease to be payable.

(2) If, before the parties were discharged, the party to whom the sums were paid or payable incurred expenses in connection with the performance of the contract, the court, if it considers it just to do so having regard to all the circmstances, may allow him to retain or to recover, as the case may be, the whole or any part of the sums paid or payable not exceeding the amount of the expenses, and, without restricting the generality of the foregoing, the court, in estimating the amount of the expenses, may include such sum as appears to be reasonable in respect of overhead expenses and in respect of any work or services performed personally by the party incurring the expenses.

(3) If, before the parties were discharged, any of them has, by reason of anything done by any other party in connection with the performance of the contract, obtained a valuable benefit other than a payment

of money, the court, if it considers it just to do so having regard to all the circumstances, may allow the other party to recover from the party benefitted the whole or any part of the value of the benefit.

(4) Where a party has assumed an obligation under the contract in consideration of the conferring of a benefit by any other party to the contract upon any other person, whether a party to the contract or not, the court, if it considers it just to do so having to all the circumstances, may, for the purposes of subsection 3, treat any benefits so conferred as a benefit obtained by the party who has assumed the obligation.

(5) In considering whether any sum ought to be recovered or retained under this section by a party to the contract, the court shall not take into account any sum that, by reason of the circumstances giving rise to the frustration of the contract, has become payable to that party under any contract of insurance unless there was an obligation to insure imposed by an express term of the frustrated contract or by or under any enactment.

(6) Where the contract contains a provision that upon the true construction of the contract is intended to have effect in the event of circumstances that operate, or but for the provision would operate, to frustrate the contract, or is intended to have effect whether such circumstances arise or not, the court shall give effect to the provision and shall give effect to this section only to such extent, if any, as appears to the court to be consistent with the provisions.

(7) Where it appears to the court that a part of the contract can be severed properly from the remainder of the contract, being a part wholly performed before the parties were discharged, or so performed except for the payment in respect of that part of the contract of sums that are or can be ascertained under the contract, the court shall treat that part of the contract as if it were a separate contract that had not been frustrated and shall treat this section as applicable only to the remainder of the contract.

[This Act is modelled on that prepared by the Conference of Commissioners on Uniformity of Legislation in Canada (see their 1948 Proceedings) and that in turn is based on *The Law Reform (Frustrated Contracts) Act, 1943* of the United Kingdom. Williams, *Law Reform (Frustrated Contracts) Act, 1943* is a valuable monograph on the history of the Act and the changes it introduced.]

CHAPTER 9

ANTICIPATORY REPUDIATION

HOCHSTER *v*. DE LA TOUR
England. Queen's Bench. 1852. 2 E. & B.; 118 E.R. 922

On the trial, before Erle J., at the London sittings in last Easter Term, it appeared the plaintiff was a courier, who, in April, 1853, was engaged by defendant to accompany him on a tour to commence on June 1st, 1852, on the terms mentioned in the declaration. On May 11th, 1852, defendant wrote to the plaintiff that he had changed his mind, and declined his services. He refused to make him any compensation. The action was commenced on May 22nd. The plaintiff, between the commencement of the action and June 1st, obtained an engagement with Lord Ashburton on equally good terms, but not commencing till July 4th. The defendant's counsel objected that there could be no breach of the contract before the 1st of June. The learned judge was of a contrary opinion, but reserved leave to enter a nonsuit on this objection. The other questions were left to the jury, who found for plaintiff.

Hugh Hill, in the same term, obtained a rule nisi to enter a nonsuit or arrest the judgment. In last Trinity Term,

Hannen showed cause.... If one party to an executory contract gave the other notice that he refused to go on with the bargain, in order that the other side might act upon the refusal in such a manner as to incapacitate himself from fulfilling it, and he did so act, the refusal could never be retracted; and, accordingly, in *Cort* v. *Ambergate &c. Ry. Co.* (1851) 117 E.R. 1229, this court after considering the cases decided that in such a case the plaintiff might recover, though he was no longer in a position to fulfil his contract. . . It is true, however, that in the case the writ was issued after the time when the chairs ought to have been received. In the present case, if the writ had been issued on the 2nd of June, *Cort* v. *Ambergate &c. Ry. Co.* would have been expressly in point. The question, therefore, comes to be: Does it make any difference that the writ was issued before the 1st of June? If the dicta of Parke B., in *Phillpotts* v. *Evans* (1839), 5 M. & W. 475; 151 E.R. 200, are to be taken as universally applicable it does make a difference; but they cannot be so taken. In a contract to marry at a future day, a marriage of the man before that a day is a breach. *Short* v. *Stone* (1846), 115 E.R. 911. The reason of this is, that the marriage is a final refusal to go on with the contract. It is not on the ground that the defendant has rendered it impossible to fulfil the contract; for, as was urged in vain in *Short* v. *Stone*, the first wife might be dead before the day came. So also, on a contract to assign a term of years on a day future, a previous assignment to a stranger is a breach. *Lovelock* v. *Franklyn* (1846), 8 Q.B. 371; 115 E.R. 916 [Lord Campbell C.J. It probably will not be disputed that an act on the part of the defendant incapacitating himself from going on with the contract would be a breach. But how does the defendant's refusal in May incapacitate him from travelling in June? It was possible that he might do so.] It was; but the plaintiff, who, so long as the engagement subsisted, was bound to keep himself disengaged and make preparations so as to be ready and willing to travel with the defendant on the 1st of June, was informed by the defendant that he would not go on with the contract, in order that the plaintiff might act upon that information; and the plaintiff then was entitled to engage himself to another, as he did. In *Planche* v. *Colburn* (1831), 8 Bing. 14; 131 E.R. 305, the plaintiff had contracted with defendants to write a work for "The Juvenile Library"; and he was held to be entitled to recover on their discontinuing the publication; yet the time for the completion of the contract, that is for the work being published in "The Juvenile Library," had not arrived, for that would not be till a reasonable time after the author had completed the work. Now in that case the author never did complete the work. [Lord Campbell C.J. It certainly would have been cruelly hard if the author had been obliged, as a condition precedent to redress, to compose a work which he knew could never be published. Crompton J. When a party announces his intention not to fulfil the contract, the other side may take him at his word and rescind the contract. That word "rescind" implies that both parties have agreed that the contract shall be at an end as if it had never been. But I am inclined to think that the party may also say: "Since you have announced that you will not go on with the contract, I will consent that it shall be at end from this time; but I will hold you liable for the damage I have sustained; and I will proceed to make that damage as little as possible by making the best use I can of my liberty." This is the principle of those cases in which there has been a discussion as to the measure of damages to which a servant is entitled on a wrongful dismissal. They were all considered in *Elderton* v. *Emmens* (1848), 6 C.B. 160; 136 E.R. 1213, Lord Campbell, C.J. The counsel in support of the rule have to answer a very able argument.]

Hugh Hill and Deighton, contra. In *Cort* v. *Ambergate &c. Ry. Co.* the writ was taken out after the time for completing the contract. That case is consistent with the defendant's position, which is, that an act incapacitating the defendant, in law, from completing the contract is a breach, because it is implied that the parties to a contract shall keep themselves legally capable of performing it; but that an announcement of an intention to break the contract when the time comes is no more than an offer to rescind. It is evidence, till retracted, of a dispensation with the necessity of readiness and willingness on the other side; and, if not retracted, it is, when the time performance comes, evidence of a continued refusal; but till then it may be retracted. Such is the doctrine of *Phillpotts* v. *Evans* and *Ripley* v. *McClure* (1849) 4 Exch. 345; 154 E.R. 1245. [Crompton J. May not the plaintiff, on notice that the defendant will not employ him, look out for other employment, so as to diminish the loss?] If he adopts the defendant's notice, which is in legal effect an offer to rescind, he must adopt it altogther. [Lord Campbell, C.J. So that you say the plaintiff, to preserve any remedy at all, was bound to remain idle. Erle J. Do you go one step further? Suppose the defendant, after the plaintiff's engagement with Lord Ashburton, had retracted his refusal and required the plaintiff to travel with him on the 1st of June, and the plaintiff had refused to do so, and gone with Lord Ashburton instead. Do you say that the now defendant could in that case have sued the now plaintiff for a breach of contract?] It would be, in such a case, a question of fact for a jury, whether there had not been an exoneration. . . . *Cur. adv. vult.*

LORD CAMPBELL C.J. delivered the judgment of the Court: On this motion in arrest of judgement, the question arises, whether, if there be an agreement between A and B, whereby B engages to employ A on and from a future day for a given period of time, to travel with him into a foreign country as a courier, and to start with him in that capacity on that day, A being to receive a monthly salary during the continuance of such service, B may, before the day, refuse to perform the agreement and break and renounce it, so as to entitle A before the day to commence an action against B to recover damages for breach of the agreement; A having been ready and willing to perform it, till it was broken and renounced by B. The defendant's counsel very powerfully contended that, if the plaintiff was not contented to dissolve the contract and to abandon all remedy upon it, he was bound to remain ready and willing to perform it till the day when the actual employment as courier in the service of the defendant was to begin; and that there could be no breach of the agreement before that day to give a right of action. But it cannnot be laid down as a universal rule that, where by agreement an act is to be done on a future day, no action can be brought for a breach of the agreement till the day for doing the act has arrived. If a man promises to marry a woman on a future day, and before that day marries another woman, he is instantly liable to an action for breach of promise of marriage. *Short* v. *Stone*. If a man contracts to execute a lease on and from a future day for a certain term, and before that day executes a lease to another for the same term, he may be immediately sued for breaking the contract. *Ford* v. *Tiley* (1827), 6 B. & C. 325; 108 E.R. 472. So, if a man contracts to sell and deliver specific goods on a future day, and before the day he sells and delivers them to another, he is immediately liable to an action at the suit of the person with whom he first contracted to sell and deliver them. *Bowdell* v. *Parsons* (1808), 10 East 359; 103 E.R. 811. One reason alleged in support of such an action is, that the defendant has, before the day, rendered it impossible for him to perform the contract at the day, but this does not necessarily follow; for prior to the day fixed for doing the act, the first wife may have died, a surrender of the lease executed might be obtained, and the defendant might have repurchased the goods so as to sell and deliver them to the plaintiff. Another reason may be that, where there is a contract to do an act on a future day, there is a relation constituted between the parties in the meantime by the contract, and that they impliedly promise that in the meantime neither will do anything to the prejudice of the other inconsistent with that relation. As an example, a man and woman engaged to marry are affianced to one another during the period between the time of the engagement and the celebration of the marriage.

In this very case of traveller and courier, from the day of the hiring till the day when the employement was to begin, they were engaged to each other; and it seems to be a breach of an implied contract if either of them renounces the engagement. This reasoning seems in accordance with the unanimous decision of the Exchequer Chamber in *Elderton* v. *Emmens*, which we have followed in subsequent cases in this court. The declaration in the present case, in alleging a breach, states a great deal more than a passing intention on the part of the defendant which he may repent of, and could only be proved by evidence that he had utterly renounced the contract, or done some act which rendered it impossible for him to perform it.

If the plaintiff has no remedy for breach of the contract unless he treats the contract as in force, and acts upon it down to the 1st of June, 1852, it follows that, till then, he must enter into no employment which will interfere with his promise "to start with the defendant on such travels on the day and year," and that he must then be properly equipped in all respects as a courier for a three months' tour on the continent of Europe. But it is surely much more rational, and more for the benefit of both parties, that, after the renuciation of the agreement by the defendant, the plaintiff should be at liberty to consider himself absolved from any future performance of it, retaining his right to sue for any damage he has suffered from the breach of it. Thus, instead of remaining idle and laying out money in preparations which must be useless, he is at liberty to seek service under another employer, which would go in mitigation of the damages to which he would otherwise be entitled for a breach of the contract. It seems strange that the defendant, after renouncing the contract, and absolutely declaring that he will never act under it, should be permitted to object that faith is given to his assertion, and that an opportunity is not left to him of changing his mind. If the plaintiff is barred of any remedy by entering into an agreement inconsistent with starting as a courier with the defendant on the 1st of June, he is prejudiced by putting faith in the defendant's assertion, and it would be more consonant with principle, if the defendant were precluded from saying that he had not broken the contract when he declared that he entirely renounced it.

Suppose that the defendant, at the time of his renunciation, had embarked on a voyage for Australia, so as to render it physically impossible for him to employ the plaintiff as a courier on the continent of Europe in the months of June, July, and August, 1852, according to decided cases, the action might have been brought before the 1st of June; but the renunciation may have been founded on other facts, to be given in evidence, which would equally have rendered the defendant's performance of the contract impossible. The man who wrongfully renounces a contract into which he has deliberately entered cannot justly complain if he is immediately sued for a compensation in damages by the man whom he has injured; and it seems reasonable to allow an option to the injured party, either to sue immediately, or to wait till the time when the act was to be done, still holding it as prospectively binding for the exercise of this option, which may be advantageous to the innocent party, and cannot be prejudicial to the wrongdoer. An argument against the action before the 1st of June is urged from the difficulty of calculating the damages, but this argument is equally strong against an action before the 1st of September, when the three months would expire. In either case, the jury in assessing the damages would be justified in looking to all that had happened, or was likely to happen, to increase or mitigate the loss of the plaintiff down to the day of the trial. We do not find any decision contrary to the view we are taking of this case. *Leigh* v. *Patterson* (1818), 8 Taunt. 540; 129 E.R. 493, only shews that, upon a sale of goods to be delivered at a certain time, if the vendor before the time gives information to the vendee that he cannot deliver them, having sold them the vendee may calculate the damages according to the state of the market when they ought to have been delivered. If this was a sale of specific goods, the action, according to *Bowdell* v. *Parsons*, might have been brought before that time, as soon as the vendor had sold and delivered them to another. *Phillpotts* v. *Evans* was a similar case, and the only question there was as to the mode of calculating the damages on a breach of contract for the sale and delivery of wheat; the Court very properly holding that the plaintiff was entitled to damages according to the state of the market when the wheat was to be delivered; the Court professing to proceed upon the rule laid down in *Startup* v. *Cortazzi* (1835), 2 C.M. & R. 165; 150 E.R. 71, where no question arose as to the right to bring an action before the stipulated day of delivery on a remuneration of the contract.

Parke B. whose dicta are entitled to a very great weight, certainly does say in *Phillpotts* v. *Evans*, with reference to the notice by the defendants that they would not accept the corn: "I think no action would then have lain for the breach of the contract but that the plaintiffs were bound to wait until the time arrived for delivery of the wheat, to see whether the defendant would then receive it." But the learned judge might suppose that the notice did not amount to a renunciation of the contract; and, if he thought that, after such a renunciation, the plaintiffs were bound to proceed with the performance of the contract on their part, and to incur expense and loss in tendering the wheat before they could have any remedy on the contract, we cannot agree with him. In *Ripley* v. *McClure*, it is said that, under a contract for the sale and delivery of goods, a refusal to receive them at any time before they ought to be delivered was not necessarily a breach of the contract; but the court intimated no opinion upon the question whether, there being a contract to do an act at a future day, if one party the day renounces the contract, the other thereupon has a remedy for a breach of the contract. And they held that a refusal by one party before the day when the act is to be done, if unretracted, would be evidence of a continual refusal down to, and inclusive of, the time when the act was to be done.

The only other case cited in the argument which we think it necessary to notice is *Planche* v. *Colburn*, which appears to be an authority for the plaintiff. There the defendants had engaged the plaintiff to write a treatise for a periodical publication. The plaintiff commenced the composition of the treatise; but, before he had completed it, and before the time when in the course of conducting the publication it would have appeared in print, the publication was abandoned. The plaintiff thereupon, without completing the treatise, brought an action for breach of contract. Objection was made that the plaintiff could not recover on the special contract for want of having completed, tendered, and delivered the treatise, according to the contract. Tindal C.J. said: "The fact was, that the defendants not only suspended, but actually put an end to, 'The Juvenile Library'; they had broken their contracts with the plaintiff." The declaration contained counts for work and labour: but the plaintiff appears to have retained his verdict on the count framed on the special contract, thus showing that, in the opinion of the court, the plaintiff might treat the renunciation of the contract by the defendants as a breach and maintain an action for that breach, without considering that it remained in force so as to bind him to perform his part of it before bringing an action for the breach of it. If it should be held that, upon a contract to do an act on a future day, a renunciation of the contract by one party dispenses with a condition to be performed in the meantime by the other, there seems no reason for requiring that other to wait till the day arrives before seeking his remedy by action, and the only ground on which the condition can be dispensed with seems to be that the renunciation may be treated as a breach of the contract.

Upon the whole, we think that the declaration in this case is sufficient. It gives us great satisfaction to reflect that, the question being on the record, our opinion may be reviewed in a court of error. In the meantime we must give judgment for the plaintiff.

MARY SHORT *v.* STONE

England. Queen's Bench. 1846. 8 Q.B. 358; 115 E.R. 911

Assumpsit. The declaration stated that heretofore, to wit, on, &c., "in consideration that the plaintiff, being then unmarried, at the request of the defendant, had then promised the defendant to marry him the defendant, he the defendant then promised the plaintiff to marry her within a reasonable time next after he should be thereunto requested by the plaintiff so to do; and the plaintiff avers that she, confiding in the said promise of the defendant, hath always hitheto remained and continued, and still is, sole and unmarried, and was always, from the time of the making of her said promise until the marriage of the said defendant as hereinafter mentioned, ready and willing to marry the defendant, whereof the defendant hath always had notice: yet the defendant, disregarding his said promise, after the making thereof and before the commencement of this suit, to wit on" &c., "wrongfully and injuriously married a certain other person, to wit one Edith Collins, contrary to his said promise: to the damage" &c. . . .

Plea 2. (a) "Defendant says that he was not at any time before the commencement of this suit requested by the plaintiff to marry her according to his said promise in that behalf." Verification.

Demurrer, assigning for causes, among others that the plea confesses, but does not sufficiently avoid, and defendant has therein alleged a fact wholly immaterial to the merits: "for, inasmuch as it appears by the declaration the defendant, before the commencement of this suit, had married another person, the plaintiff need not nor ought not to have requested the defendant to marry her." Also, that the plea "tenders too large and an insufficient issue, to wit whether a request were made before the commencement of this suit; whereas, if the request be material at all, it should have been alleged not to have been made before the marriage of the defendant: for, if the plaintiff were to traverse the allegation as it now stands in the said plea, and the same should be found for her, still it would not shew conclusively that she was and is entitled to maintain her action, as it would be consistent with the said issue, the verdict thereon, that the request found to have been made by the plaintiff was after the said marriage, and between it and the commencement of the suit." Also that the plea should have concluded to the country.

Joinder in demurrer.

LORD DENMAN C.J.: We must look at this case with a view to the feelings and intentions of the parties at the time of entering into such a contract: and the intention clearly is, to marry in the state in which the parties respectively are at the time. If neither party puts himself out of that state, he must be taken to dispense with the contract so far that the other may have an action against him without a request to marry. It is unnecessary to inquire what cases, among those which have been mentioned, are analogous to this, because here the intent must be considered: and, looking to that, the fact stated on the record is a necessary dispensation. According to this, which appears to me the true construction of the contract, the plaintiff shews a good right of action, and is entitled to judgment.

PATTESON J.: The only difficulty I had was on the averment of a promise to marry within a reasonable time after request. If the allegation had been of a promise, generally, to marry, or a promise to marry on request, or in a reasonable time, the application of the case in Lord Raymond would have been clearer. But, on the consideration, I do not see any rational distinction between the averments of a promise to marry on request and a promise to marry in reasonable time after request. We must look to the intention; and, if a party puts himself out of the condition in which a request could properly be made, he dispenses with the request. Here it is alleged that the defendant married another person. It was not necessary to shew that that person was living when the action was commenced: there was a breach of contract at once when the defendant married.

COLERIDGE J.: The declaration is good, and the plea bad, for the same reasons. The promise to marry within a reasonable time after request must mean after request within a time when it might reasonably be made. If the defendant disables himself from fulfilling such a request, then, in the first place, he dispenses with the request, because it has become impossible to make the request effectually, and, secondly, he has broken his own contract, because he is no longer able to fulfil that. It is no matter how long the person whom the defendant has married lives, the contract having been once broken; and the averment of a request to fulfil it is immaterial.

WIGHTMAN J.: I am of the same opinion. The facts stated in the count shew a dispensation with the request to marry.

Judgment for the plaintiff.

FROST *v.* KNIGHT

England. Exchequer Chamber. 1872. L.R. 7 Exch. 111

[This case is reproduced on page 82.]

CORT AND GEE *v.* AMBERGATE RY. COMPANY

England. Queen's Bench. 1851. 17 Q.B. 127; 117 E.R. 1229

Action for damages for breach of contract by the defendants to take and pay for chairs to be manufactured by the plaintiff. After the plaintiff made and delivered some chairs the defendant company notified the plaintiff that they would take no more. The chairs were to be made and delivered by May, 1848. The plaintiff on receipt of such notice made no more chairs and made no further tender. At the trial a verdict was found for the plaintiff. A rule nisi was obtained for a new trial.

[A "chair" in this context is an iron or steel socket spike to be embedded in a wooden tie and onto which a steel rail may be fitted.]

LORD CAMPBELL C.J. delivered the judgment of the Court: We are of opinion that the verdict found for the plaintiffs ought not to be disturbed. As to the supposed misdirection: the learned Judge at the trial did not direct the jury that in point of law the engineer had authority to bind the company, but only left it to the jury to consider whether,in point of fact, the Company by their mode of dealing had authorized and sanctioned his acts. His Lordship intimated that he thought the evidence was strong to show that they had done so, but that it was for the jury to give the evidence its due weight. The objection of misdirection therefore fails.

Next we have to consider whether the plaintiffs were entitled to a verdict on the issue whether they were ready and willing to execute and perform the said contract according to the said conditions and stipulations, in manner and form, &c.; and on the issue whether the defendants did refuse to accept or receive the residue of the chairs, or prevent or discharge the plaintiffs from supplying the said residue, and from the further execution and performance of the said contract. It is not denied that, if the defendants would have regularly accepted and paid for the chairs, the plaintiffs would have gone on regularly making and delivering them according to the contract: the objection is that, although the plaintiffs were desirous that the contract should be fully performed, yet, after receiving the notice that the Company did not wish to have any more chairs, and would not accept any more, they ceased to make any more, insomuch that the residue which the Company are alleged to have to accept never were made. The defendants contend that, as the plaintiffs did not make and tender the residue of the chairs, they cannot be said to have been ready and willing to perform the contract; that the defendants cannot be charged with a breach of it; that, after the notice from the defendants, which in truth amounted to declaration that they had broken and thenceforward renounced the contract, the plaintiffs, if they wished to have any redress, were bound to buy the requisite quantity of the peculiar sort of iron suited for these railway chairs, to make the whole of them according to the pattern, with the name of the Company upon them, and to bring them to the appointed places of delivery and tender them to the defendants, who, from insolvency, had abandoned the completion of the line for which the chairs were intended, desiring that no more chairs might be made, and declaring, in effect, that no more should be accepted or paid for. We are of opinion, however, that the jury were fully justified upon the evidence in finding that the plaintiffs were ready and willing to perform the contract, although they never made and tendered the residue of the chairs. In common sense the meaning of such an averment of readiness and willingness must be that the non-completion of the contract was not the fault of the plaintiffs, and that they were disposed and able to complete it if it had not been renounced by the defendants. What more can reasonably be required by the parties for whom the goods are to be manufactured? If, having accepted a part, they are unable to pay the residue, and have resolved to accept them, no benefit can accrue to them from a useless waste of materials and labour, which might possibly enhance the amount of damages to be awarded against them.

Upon the last issue, was there not evidence that the defendants refused to accept the residue of the chairs? If they had said, "Make no more for us, we will have nothing to do with them," was not that refusing to accept or receive them acording to the contract? But the learned counsel for the defendants laid peculiar stress upon the words "nor did they prevent or discharge the plaintiffs from supplying the said residue" of the chairs "and from the further execution and performance of the said contract." We consider the material part of the allegation which the last plea traverses to be, that the defendants refused to receive the residue of the chairs. But, assuming that the whole must be proved, we think there is evidence to show that the defendants did prevent and discharge the plaintiffs from supplying the residue of the chairs, and from the further execution of the contract. It is contended that "prevent" here must mean an obstruction by physical force; and, in answer to a question from the Court, we told it would not be a preventing of the delivery of goods if the purchaser were to write, in a letter to the person who ought to supply them, "Should you come to my house to deliver them, I will blow your brains out." But may

I not reasonably say that I was prevented from completing a contract by being desired not to complete it? Are there no means of preventing an act from being done, except physical force or brute violence? Again, we are told there can be no "discharge" by a corporation unless by deed under the corporate seal. Of a discharge in one sense of the word this is true. A discharge is sometimes used as equivalent to a release, which must be under seal; *Brymer* v. *Thames Haven Dock & Railway Company* (1848), 2 Exch. 549; 154 E.R. 609. But we conceive that, in the allegation traversed by the last plea, discharge only means, like prevent, that the act of the defendants was the cause of the residue of the chairs not being delivered, and of the contract not being further executed or performed. Taking the language employed in its natural and reasonable sense, there was abundant evidence to support the finding of the last issue for the plaintiffs.

It is averred, however, that there are express authorities to shew that there could be no readiness and willingness to perform the contract unless all the chairs were finished and tendered; that to prevent must be by positive physical obstruction, and that there can be no discharging unless by instrument under seal. . . .

The most recent case cited by the defendants' counsel was *Ripley* v. *M'Clure* (1849), 4 Exch. 345; 154 E.R. 1245. This case is very complicated in its circumstances; but the second point decided in it is the only one applicable to the question which we have to consider. There being an executory contract, whereby the plaintiff agreed to sell and the defendant to buy, on arrival, certain goods, to be delivered at Belfast at a certain price, payable on delivery, it was held that a refusal by the defendant before the arrival of the cargo to perform the contract was not of itself necessarily a breach of it, but that such refusal, unretracted down to and inclusive of the time when the defendant was bound to receive the cargo, was evidence of a continuing refusal and a waiver of the condition precedent of delivery, so as to render the defendant liable for the breach of contract. But, in the case at bar, the refusal never was retracted; and therefore there was a continuing breach down to the time when this action was commenced.

Upon the whole, we think we are justified, on principle and without trenching on any former decision, in holding that, when there is an executory contract for the manufacturing and supply of goods from time to time, to be paid for after delivery, if the purchaser, having accepted and paid for a portion of the goods contracted for, gives notice to the vendor not to manufacture any more as he has no occasion for them, the vendor having been desirous and able to complete the contract, he may, without manufacturing and tendering the rest of the goods, maintain an action against the purchaser for breach of contract; and that he is entitled to a verdict on pleas traversing allegations that he was ready and willing to perform the contract, that the defendant refused to accept the residue of the goods, and that he prevented and discharged the plaintiff from manufacturing and delivering them.

We are likewise of opinion that, in this case, the damages are not excessive as the jury were justified in taking into their calculation all the chairs which remained to be delivered, and which the defendants refused to accept. They were all included in the declaration and in the issues joined: the time mentioned in the proposal for the delivery of some of them had arrived before the notice was given, but the time of delivery was not of the essence of the contract; and the obligation was still incumbent upon the defendants to accept the whole of the residue.

The rule must therefore be discharged.

RIPLEY *v.* McCLURE. 1849. 4 Ex. 345; 154 E.R. 1245 (England. Exchequer Chamber). PARKE B.: "We think that if the jury had been told that a refusal before the arrival of the cargo was a breach, that would have been incorrect. . . . But we cannot collect that the learned judge ever told the jury that a refusal at any time was a breach. He left the question in writing, whether there was a refusal at any time, and whether that refusal had been subsequently retracted; and the jury having found . . . that it had not, there was certainly evidence of a continued refusal down to and inclusive of the time when the defendant was bound to receive, which would render the defendant liable, if all the conditions precedent had been performed or waived."

MACNAUGHTON *v.* STONE

Ontario. High Court. [1950] 1 D.L.R. 330

MCRUER C.J.H.C.: The plaintiff's claim is for specific performance of an alleged contract for the purchase and sale of No. 23 Park Rd., in the City of Toronto, or, in the alternative, for damages.

It is alleged that the defendant and her husband, the late Professor Stone, contracted to sell the property in question to the plaintiff for the sum of $10,500 payable $300 as a deposit on the date of the signing of the agreement, $3,200, subject to adjustments, on the date of closing and the balance to be secured by a first mortgage payable $50 monthly together with interest at 5% per annum, the balance of the principal sum to be payable in 5 years with the right of renewal for a further period of 5 years. The agreement, which is in writing, is dated August 27, 1948. The day fixed for the completion of the contract was October 1, 1948.

The property was owned by the defendant and the late Professor Stone (to whom I shall hereafter refer as the vendors) as joint tenants. They had listed it for sale with one Blamire, a real estate agent, at the price of $11,500. In the month of August, 1948, the plaintiff placed an advertisement in the newspapers indicating that he was in the market to buy a house. Blamire communicated with him and introduced him to the vendors. At first the vendors asked $12,000 for the property. The plaintiff refused to pay this amount but expressed a willingness to pay the sum of $10,500, which the vendors refused to accept. Negotiations were reopened a few days later at the instance of Blamire when some further bargaining took place. During the discussions and before the agreement was signed, the plaintiff stated to the vendors that he would act as their solicitor, without charge, in carrying out the transaction. To this the vendors agreed, subject to the plaintiff paying all the registration fees.

Following this the written contract was signed. It makes no reference to the fact that the plaintiff was to act for the vendors free of charge and pay the registration fees, but it contains the following term, which is part of the printed form used: "It is agreed that there is no representation, warranty, collateral agreement or condition affecting this agreement or the real property supported hereby other than as expressed herein in writing." Notwithstanding this term the written contract does not in fact express the whole agreement between the parties. The plaintiff gave his evidence in a very frank and straightforward manner and from his evidence and that of the defendant there can be no doubt that the plaintiff agreed to act for the vendors without charge and pay the costs of registration in completing the transaction and this was undoubtedly taken into account when the agreement was signed. The following endorsement appears on the back of the agreement: "Vendors' solicitor: Alex MacNaughton, El. 8307 19 Melinda St."

Following the signing of the contract, Professor Stone attended on the plaintiff and delivered the title-deeds of the property to him, for the purpose of having the necessary conveyances drawn. Early in September the defendant telephoned the plaintiff and told him that she and her husband had decided that they would not carry out the contract. The defendant says that she did this because of medical advice that Professor Stone was not in such good health as would permit him to travel to British Columbia where they had planned to go to live. The plaintiff says that when the defendant told him she would not complete the transaction he asked her to return the deposit and she said he would have to get it from Mr. Blamire, the agent. The plaintiff says that he telephoned Mr. Blamire and asked him to return the deposit but Mr. Blamire stated that he did not know of any legal or moral reason why he should and refused to do so. The plaintiff said in evidence that if the deposit had been returned he would have treated the matter as closed.

Notwithstanding this, on September 8th the plaintiff wrote a letter to the vendors insisting that the contract should be carried out and stating: "It will be impossible for us to act for you any further in this connection and we must therefore advise you to consult another solicitor." The letter concludes:

"Should you unfortunately persist in refusing to complete the sale of the above property, the undersigned will attend at your home on Friday, October 1, 1948 and formally tender you, as required by law, the balance owing to you for the purchase of your property, together with Mortgage duly executed pursuant to the terms of the agreement. If you do not accept this money and the Mortgages as tendered and in exchange give the undersigned a properly executed deed to your property and vacant possession of the ground floor and basement, he will *immediately* bring an action against you in the courts of the Province for an Order directing you to grant the property to him or, in the alternative, directing the Registry Office to enter the undersigned as the owner. All Court costs will, of course, by court order be deducted from the balance owing to you.

"Needless to say, we shall be most pleased to hear from you to the effect that you have reconsidered your decision."

Following the receipt of this letter the vendors consulted a solicitor, Mr. R. T. Hunter, who had some negotiations with the plaintiff but these were "without prejudice" and cannot affect the outcome of the case. The defendant persisted in her refusal to complete the contract and on September 21st Professor Stone suffered a stroke and was admitted to the hospital. From the stroke he died on October 8th. On the death of Professor Stone the legal estate in the property passed to the defendant.

On October 1st the plaintiff attended at the defendant's home with legal tender to the amount of the purchase price but did not have with him a proper conveyance. He found no one at home and no further effort was made to make formal tender. It is not argued that sufficient tender was made, but it is argued that notwithstanding what was said in the plaintiff's letter of September 8th, tender was excused as it would have been useless. . . .

[After discussing the effect on the plaintiff's case of his being the vendor's solicitor, and concluding that "if the plaintiff should be permitted to succeed in this action he would in effect be in the position of a solicitor getting a judgment against his clients for specific performance which might have been avoided if the clients had been properly advised by him to return the deposit when that course would have closed the matter," his Lordship continued:]

A further difficulty, however, stands in the way of the plaintiff's success. When the defendant told him that they would not carry out the contract there was an anticipatory breach of the contract. The effect of a declaration made by one party to a contract in advance of the date fixed for performance that he will not carry it out is not to rescind it; it takes two parties to bring a contract to an end. But when one party assumes to renounce a contract of this sort before the date fixed for its performance, the other party has three courses open to him:

(1) he may elect to treat the contract then and there as at an end and demand the return of his deposit; or

(2) he may treat the contract as broken as of the date on which the other party has renounced it and sue for damages sustained by the breach; or

(3) he may treat the contract as valid and subsisting and bring an action for specific performance if it is not performed according to the terms

In the last case the party who renounces the contract may, at any time before the time fixed for completion, elect to carry it out and the other party will then be bound by its terms. *Frost* v. *Knight* (1872), L.R. 7 Ex. 111, and *Johnstone* v. *Milling* (1886), 16 Q.B.D. 460, are the two leading cases in which these principles are propounded. In the latter case Lord Esher M.R. at p. 467 said: "The other party may adopt such renunciation of the contract by so acting upon it as in effect to declare that he too treats the contract as at an end, except for the purpose of bringing an action upon it for the damages sustained by him in consequence of such renunciation. He cannot, however, himself proceed with the contract on the footing that it still exists for other purposes, and also treat such renunciation as an immediate breach. If he adopts the renunciation, the contract is at an end except for the purposes of the action for such wrongful renunciation; if he does not wish to do so, he must wait for the arrival of the time when in the ordinary course a cause of action on the contract would arise. He must elect which course he will pursue."

The course followed by the plaintiff when the defendant told him that she and her husband would not carry out the contract cannot be rationalized wth any other view than that he regarded that as a termination of the contractual relationship. The request for the return of the deposit is not consistent with an intention to treat the contract as valid and subsisting and to bring an action for specific performance if the contract was not performed according to the terms thereof. The plaintiff, having elected to treat the contract as at an end by demanding the return of the deposit, could not by himself revive it when the deposit was not returned. It is just as true that it takes two to revive a contract as it is that it takes two to rescind one.

The plaintiff's position may be tested in another way. If nothing more had happened after the agent had refused to return the deposit and the vendors had brought action after October 1st to enforce the contract, could it be said that the plaintiff would not have had a perfect defence by saying "You repudiated the contract and I asked for a return of the deposit which was refused"? How could he say that "I was keeping the contract alive for your benefit"? If in those circumstances there would be no contractual relationship on October 1st, the letter of September 8th could not create one.

Having come to the conclusion that the plaintiff cannot succeed for the reasons stated, it is unnecessary for me to discuss what bearing the plaintiff's statement in his letter of September 8th that he would make formal tender and the failure to do so might have on his right to succeed.

I wish to make it quite clear that nothing I have said is to be taken as any reflection on the personal integrity of the plaintiff. I think he misconceived his legal position and duties and that only. But where solicitors mix their professional services with their private transactions they must expect to have strictly applied the law which throws around their clients great protection. This is in the public interest and is particularly important when the clients are of the great age and in the otherwise helpless condition to protect themselves that the vendors were in this case.

The action fails with respect to the claims for specific performance and damages. I think, however, that the plaintiff is entitled under the general prayer to judgment for $300, being the amount of the deposit paid on account of the contract. There will be no order as to costs.

McBRIDE *v.* JOHNSON (or McBRIDE)

Alberta. Supreme Court of Canada. 1962. 31 D.L.R. (2d) 763

RITCHIE J. delivered the judgment of the Court: This is an appeal from a judgment of the Appellate Division of the Supreme Court of Alberta insofar as it affirmed those portions of a judgment of Mr. Justice Cairns which ordered that the respondent recover $10,000 from the appellants for breach of promise of marriage and that all the furniture and furnishings in a house at 4750 55th St., Red Deer, Alberta, belonged to the respondent with the exception of one chesterfield, two chairs and one bed. The respondent also appeals from the orders as to costs in the Courts below.

The appellants are the executors of the will of Alfred Edward McBride who was killed in an automobile accident on February 28, 1959, and who, at the time of his death, was living at Red Deer aforesaid in the same house with the respondent and holding her out as his wife to at least some other members of the community although they were not married.

The story of the relationship between the respondent and McBride between September 18, 1952 when he obtained a decree absolute dissolving his first marriage and the time of his death discloses a consistent and continuing belief in, and assertion of, an existing contract of marriage between them on the part of the respondent and a consistent attitude of procrastination on the part of McBride. The respondent's evidence which is uncontradicted is that the couple became engaged to be married in 1953 at which time she was 51 years of age and her finance 54. Pursuant to this engagement, she says that they went together on a trip to Idaho in July, 1954 for the purpose of getting married, but unfortunately the day which they selected for the ceremony was July 4th, and as this was a public holiday they were unable to get blood tests, and so decided that they "would go on to Coulee Dam and come back and get married another day". At this stage there was apparently a quarrel, as a result of which McBride refused to go through with the wedding, and they returned to Red Deer. Shortly after returning home, a contract was prepared by the respondent, signed by both her and McBride and duly witnessed which read as follows:

"I, Alfred Edward McBride & I Dorothy Barbara Johnson the undersigned do solemnly promise that on the 15th day of July, 1954 shall marry each other.

"Both of us being of sound mind do declare this covenant. No bills or debts of the other are either of our responsibility. Fat shall do his own business & I shall obey & mind my own."

When July 15th came, the respondent says that McBride "wanted a little more time, and he thought that we would wait until he had time that we could go away again". In preparation for the marriage, the couple went to a clinic and had their blood tests taken on August 19th, and the necessary form in this regard, pursuant to the *Solemnization of Marriage Act* was duly completed by a physician. This initial step having been completed, the respondent says that they "started making preparations to have a honeymoon and go away and get married", and finally in September McBride "booked off" some time from his work and they proceeded to the Court House at Red Deer for the purpose of getting a marriage licence, but when they got there it appeared that McBride did not have "a certificate of no appeal" from the Clerk of the Court in Edmonton where he had obtained his divorce without which certificate a marriage licence could not be obtained. McBride was "quite angry" and seemed to think that "he had paid enough already for a divorce without having to pay any more" and he refused to get the required certificate, but as he was all packed and he had his time "booked off" the couple decided to go for "a honeymoon" anyway; they proceeded on a trip to the States and on their return the respondent moved in to the house where McBride was living and where she had been keeping house for him, although she had been living elsewhere. She says of this move:

"We were going to get married as soon as we had the furniture and things moved in, and were preparing to get the certificate from Edmonton, he said that when he went up he would go to the Court House and get it."

And again:

"A. Yes, he refused to marry me on the 15th of July when he wouldn't get his certificate, when he postponed the marriage until later on. Q. But whatever happened then, you moved in with him later, didn't you? A. I had no alternative but to move in with the promise I would be married when we got our house straightened up."

The furniture which was moved was found by the learned trial Judge to be the property of the respondent, but in ordering that "all of the furniture and furnishings in the house . . . belong to the Plaintiff with the exception of 1 chesterfield, 2 chairs and 1 bed", he included a stove, a television set and a refrigerator which had been purchased by McBride and which the appellants now claim to have been his property.

From the time of the move in September, 1954 until McBride's death he and the respondent appear to have lived happily with each other and to have gone on holidays together. The respondent produced some valentine cards, letters and a photograph indicating that McBride's affection for her continued over the years and in 1957 she adopted her own granddaughter, a child of 2 years, of whom she says: "I took this child to raise because we loved her and she brought a great deal of comfort and happiness into the home of the deceased and myself." There is evidence that except when

McBride was not sober he treated her well, and she says, "He led me to believe that he was going to marry me at all times". The following exchange occurred on the cross-examination of the respondent:

"Q. And he never repudiated his agreement, did he? A. He never repudiated his agreement, no. Q. And he never said anything to you to lead you to believe that he was misleading you in any way? A. No. Q. And he continued his promise right up to the time of his death, didn't he? A. That's right, Mr. Mayson."

In support of the argument that McBride did not intend to marry the respondent after September, 1954, counsel laid great stress on the fact that he made no provisions for her in the will which he made in 1956, but in my view this falls into the same category as the evidence to the effect that the respondent would have lost her widow's pension of $90 a month if she had married. Both are circumstances from which inferences could be drawn but neither is of sufficient weight to support a conclusion as to the intention of the parties.

It is contended on behalf of the appellants that on February 28, 1959, the marriage was still in contemplation and that there was then an existing contract outstanding between the parties which was brought to an end by McBride's death on that date. The respondent, on the other hand, contends that there was a breach of the contract during McBride's lifetime, giving rise to a cause of action against his executors.

If there had been a breach of the contract during McBride's lifetime, it is not disputed that in accordance with the decision of this Court in *Smallman* v. *Moore*, [1948] 3 D.L.R. 657, [1948] S.C.R. 295, an action could be maintained against his executors. . . .

In the present case, however, it is contended on behalf of the appellants that there had been no breach of McBride's promise, that the respondent never recognized any repudiation by him being at all times ready, willing and anxious to carry out her part of the bargain, and that the obligations incidental to such a promise must, in the nature of things, be brought to an end by the death of the promisor.

The following paragraph in the reasons for judgment of the learned trial Judge contains the essence of his finding on this branch of the case, and as the Appellate Division gave no reasons for dismissing the appeal these observations must be taken to have been adopted by that Court.

"The plaintiff was very frank to say that he intended to marry her as far as she knew to the date of his death and there is no doubt that he indicated this to her, but I am completely convinced from all of the evidence, excluding certain hearsay evidence at the trial, on which point I have considerable doubt, that he never had the slightest intention of marrying her after September, 1954, even though he did indicate his good intentions to her to such an extent that he convinced her of his sincerity. In my view, a breach of the contract occurred in 1954 when he refused to marry her and that breach continued until his death in spite of his protestations of love for her and his good intentions. Even though he did heal the breach as far as she was concerned, to some extent, by promises of marriage later, to the extent that he deceived her completely, his continued delay of four and a half years, in my view, also amounts to a breach of his contract, and that prior to his death he had completely repudiated his contract, if not expressly, at least by his conduct although this had not been communicated to the plaintiff. McBride had a scheme to maintain the status quo without incurring the obligations incident to marriage. There is no doubt that where the breach occurred prior to the death, a cause of action for breach of promise of marriage will lie against the representatives: *Smallman* v. *Moore*."

This statement is a long way from the clear-cut findings of fact made by the jury in *Smallman* v. *Moore* and the analysis of what was passing through McBride's mind over the years must be based almost entirely on inference. There are nevertheless included in this forceful expression of the learned trial Judge's deductions certain findings of fact which are directly supported by the respondent's evidence, namely, that McBride renewed his promise of marriage after September, 1954, that he indicated his intention of carrying it out, and that up to the date of his death no repudiation of this promise was ever communicated to the respondent by him.

These findings of fact standing alone support the contention that McBride at no time repudiated the promise of marriage which he made after September, 1954. Repudiation of a contract is not to be readily inferred in the case of a promisor who reiterates his intention to carry out his promise and whose conduct, however inconsistent with this intention it may appear to be, has at no time had the effect of communicating such repudiation to the promissee. The nature of the conduct which would justify an inference of repudiation is discussed by the Earl of Selborne, L.C., in the case of *Mersey Steel & Iron Co.* v. *Naylor, Benzon & Co.* (1884), 9 App. Cas. 434, where he says at pp. 438–9:

". . . You must look at the actual circumstances of the case in order to see whether the one party to the contract is relieved from its future performance by the conduct of the other; you must examine what that conduct is, so as to see whether it amounts to a renunciation, to an absolute refusal to perform the contract . . . and whether the other party may accept it as a reason for not performing his part."

Even if it is accepted, however, that McBride's behaviour was such as to make it entirely apparent that he never had the slightest intention of marrying her, it is nevertheless equally clear from the evidence that the respondent never accepted his conduct as meaning any such thing, and that notwithstanding his repeated delays she insisted on the continued existence of the contract and was at all times ready to carry out her part of it.

In delivering his well-known decision in *Frost* v. *Knight* (1872), L.R. 7 Ex. 111, Cockburn, C.J., was concerned with the repudiation of a promise to marry before the date due for fulfilment had arrived. . . .

The present case, however, is not one in which performance was conditional on the happening of some future event nor is it one of repudiation prior to the time fixed for performance. The effect of the failure to marry on the day named in the written contract had been erased by the subsequent renewal and by the conduct of the parties, and the promise was one of which performance was currently due from day to day. . . .

In the present case there was ample evidence that the respondent was insisting on holding McBride to his bargain and that she was continuing until the day of his death to tender due performance of her part of the contract.

Whether or not McBride's conduct amounted to an absolute refusal to perform his contract so as to give the respondent the right to sue for damages, the respondent's conduct in my opinion had the effect of keeping the contract alive, and the only remaining question is whether McBride's death was a supervening event not due to his own fault which brought it to an end. In my opinion it undoubtedly was. . . .

It seems to me to be obvious that McBride's continued existence was an implied condition of the contract in the present case and that the contract ended with his death.

There is included in the statement of claim the following alternative plea: "In the alternative the Plaintiff states that the said Alfred Edward McBride, deceased, fraudulently misrepresented to her that he intended at all times to marry her from the date that he entered into the said Agreement until the date of his death, and that as a result of the said misrepresentation and the fraud which he perpetrated on her, she took up residence in the said premises and kept house for the said Alfred Edward McBride and accepted the responsibilities which she would not otherwise have undertaken and was entirely misled by the representations made by the said Alfred Edward McBride, deceased."

I do not find it necessary to deal with the arguments presented concerning this plea because, with all respect to the learned trial Judge, I do not think that it is supported by the evidence. The respondent was the mother of six grown-up children by her first husband and had been a nurse at a provincial training centre, she had known McBride for 15 years, been engaged to him for 6 years and had lived with him for the last 5 years of his life, and I am, with respect, unable to accept as probable the inference that such an experienced woman could be completely deceived from day to day as to the meaning of the words and actions of a man with whom she had been so intimate for so long a time concerning a subject of such vital importance to them both. In my view, McBride's conduct as disclosed by the evidence is at least as consistent with honest procrastination as it is with fraudulent misrepresentation and that of the respondent suggests that although she was apparently ready to put up with the loose arrangement of cohabitation without marriage on a temporary basis, she was in constant expectation of the relationship being regularized by McBride carrying out his continuing promise of marriage which remains unfulfilled and unreleased at his death.

As has been indicated, the appellants appeal also from that part of the order of the learned trial Judge which awarded a stove, television set and a refrigerator to the respondent. The respondent says that she bought the stove with the house, and as there is no appeal from the finding that she had no interest in the house, I am, with respect, unable to see any ground for declaring that the stove is her property. The television set and refrigerator were purchased by McBride, and although the respondent states that they were both given to her, there is no corroboration of this evidence as required by s. 13 of the *Alberta Evidence Act*, R.S.A. 1955, c. 102, and as there is no presumption of a gift under the circumstances here disclosed I do not think there is sufficient evidence to justify the award of these items to the respondent.

On the evidence I am not satisfied that the learned trial Judge was wrong in failing to award damages to the appellants in respect of the respondent's refusal to deliver up the house to them nor do I find any evidence of the appellants having suffered damage by reason of the respondent retaining and using the stove, television set and refrigerator.

Save as aforesaid, I would allow this appeal and set aside the order appealed from insofar as it awards $10,000 in damages to the respondent and insofar as it adjudges that the three last-mentioned items to be property belonging to the respondent and accords her the right to remove them. The appellants should have their costs of the claim and counterclaim on the trial and their costs of the appeal to the Appellate Division of the Supreme Court of Alberta and to this Court.

WHITE & CARTER (COUNCILS), LTD. *v.* McGREGOR. [1961] 3 All E.R. 1178 (reproduced above at page 85) (Scotland. House of Lords). LORD KEITH OF AVONHOLM: "The other case is *White & Carter (Councils), Ltd.* v. *A. R. Harding* (May 21, 1958, unreported) in which MORRIS, L.J., gave the judgment of the court with which LORD EVERSHED, M.R., and ORMEROD, L.J., agreed. Copies were provided during the hearing of this appeal. The form of contract there was identical with that in the present case. The contractors were the present appellants. But the circumstances in which the claim arose were different. The advertiser, the defendant, entered into the contract on Nov. 13, 1956. Nothing was done under the contract until May 8, 1957, when the advertising plates were first displayed by the contractors. The defendant was then asked for payment under the contract and as he refused to pay he was sued in Westminster County Court for the full 156 weeks under condition 8 of the contract (32) and judgment issued against him. On two separate occasions, one in November, 1956, and the other in April, 1957, before the plates had been exhibited, he asked to be released from his contract, but the plaintiffs did not agree to do so. MORRIS, L.J., held that there had been no termination or repudiation of the contract by the defendant prior to the exhibition of the plates, only requests to be released. Some two months after the display of the plates the defendant wrote to the plaintiffs with a cheque for £81 which he asked to be accepted in payment for the first year's advertising. He also asked to be allowed to withdraw from the remainder of the contract. The plaintiffs refused to accede to this and returned the cheque for £81. The learned lord justice in these circumstances held that the claim was a claim for debt, under the contract, and upheld the judgment of the county court judge."

TREDEGAR IRON AND COAL COMPANY LIMITED *v.* HAWTHORN BROTHERS AND CO.
England. Court of Appeal. 1902. 18 T.L.R. 716

This was an appeal from the judgment of Mr. Justice Phillimore at the trial of the action without a jury. The action was brought to recover damages for breach of contract in non-acceptance of goods. By a contract dated January 29, 1901 the plaintiffs agreed to sell and the defendants agreed to buy from 1,500 to 1,700 tons of Tredegar large steam coal at 16s. a ton, for delivery f.o.b. Cardiff, Penarth, Barry, or Newport, during the month of February. The contract contained a condition that the quantity of coal therein named was for bona fide exportation by the purchasers to Messina or Palermo, and not for sale to any other export merchants or any other person in Great Britain or Ireland. The defendants, having discovered that, in consequence of delay on the part of the steamer by which they had intended to send the coal to Sicily, by reason of the steamer having broken down, the coal would be useless to them, wrote to the plaintiffs on February 16, informing them of their inability to take delivery; and they procured and communicated to the plaintiffs a written offer from other purchasers, Messrs. Pyman, Watson, and Co., of Cardiff, for the coal at 16s. 3d. a ton. The plaintiffs declined to accept this offer, and insisted upon the performance of the contract, and subsequently, early in March, sold the coal against the defendants, the market price then being

15s. a ton. The plaintiffs brought this action claiming £85 as damages, 1s. per ton on 1700 tons. The defendants' case was that, in the circumstances, the plaintiffs had suffered no damage by the defendants' breach of contract, and they paid into Court the sum of £1 by way of nominal damages. Mr. Justice Phillimore found as a fact that there was a repudiation of the contract by the defendants notified to the plaintiffs on or before February 23; that it was a repudiation which amounted to a statement of a fact, future but none the less certain; that it would not be possible to carry out the contract, as it was obvious that a ship could not as a matter of business be procured during the few days that remained of the month; and he held that, as soon as the plaintiffs knew that the contract would not be carried out, it became their duty at once to minimize the loss by reselling the coals, and that, as the market price at that date exceeded 16s. a ton, they might have sold the coal for a higher price than the contract price, and they were therefore only entitled to nominal damages. From this judgment the plaintiffs appealed.

THE MASTER OF THE ROLLS said that this was a contract for the sale by the plaintiffs to the defendants of 1,500 to 1,700 tons of Tredegar large steam coal at 16s. a ton for delivery f.o.b. Cardiff, Penarth, Barry or Newport, during February, 1901, for exportation to Sicily. Before the month of February had expired the defendants found that, by reason of circumstances over which they had no control, there was a practical difficulty, if not an impossibility, of shipping the coal to Sicily. They tried to free themselves from the contract. At that time there was a rising market for coal. The plaintiffs refused to make terms. They told the defendants that they insisted upon the performance of the contract. Some days before the end of February the defendants repudiated the contract and notified the repudiation to the plaintiffs; and the question really came to this, whether, upon an act which amounted to a repudiation of the contract and which entitled the plaintiffs to treat the repudiation as a final breach of the contract by the defendants, the defendants were entitled to say to the plaintiffs that the latter must against their will accept the repudiation as putting an end to the contract for this purpose, that the plaintiffs were debarred of their rights under the contract, and were bound to accept the contract as broken on a day before the date named in it for performance so as to be bound by the measure of damages on the day of repudiation and no other. That was a strong proposition, and was directly in the teeth of the authorities. The plaintiffs could not maintain an action for damages except upon the footing that the contract had been broken. It was clear law that the repudiation was a nullity unless it was accepted by the other party to the contract. If the other party chose to treat the repudiation as a breach, then matters proceeded on the footing that there had been a breach and the damages must be assessed as for a breach on that date and he would be bound to act reasonably in the circumstances, that was to say, to take advantage of any mitigating circumstances there might be. All the discussions as to how the damages were to be mitigated rested on the foundation that there had been a breach of the contract. The argument came to this, that the plaintiffs ought to have treated the repudiation as a breach, and that it was unreasonable in them not to have so treated it, seeing that the market was then a rising one. There was no foundation in the authorities for that proposition. . . . In his Lordship's opinion the decision of Mr. Justice Phillimore was wrong. There was no breach of the contract until the expiration of the time for the delivery of the goods, and the plaintiffs retained the right to claim that the defendant should take delivery of the coal at the time fixed in the contract. The appeal must therefore be allowed, and judgment must be entered for the plaintiffs.

LORD JUSTICE MATTHEW concurred: The law was perfectly clear. Repudiation was of no effect unless it was acted upon by the other party. If acted upon by the other party there was what was called an anticipatory breach of contract, and the damages were to be calculated as on the date of the acceptance of the repudiation—as if the contract had then run out. The argument came to this, that the Court ought to hold that in every executory contract for the sale of goods a term should be implied that either party should be at liberty to terminate the contract when he chose and to estimate the damages as on that date. If that were so the business of the country could not be carried on. A party was entitled to rely upon his contract, and to expect the other party to carry it out at the time fixed for its performance. The plaintiffs here, for business purposes, sold coal to the defendants for exportation to Sicily, and yet it was contended that the defendants could compel them to sell the coal elsewhere. Such a contention could not be supported.

LORD JUSTICE COZENS-HARDY agreed.

QUESTION. Is this decision consistent with the well-accepted doctrine of mitigating damages? Review *Payzu* v. *Saunders* and *White & Carter (Councils) Ltd.* v. *McGregor.*

AVERY *v.* BOWDEN

England. Queen's Bench. 1855. 5 El. & Bl. 714; 119 E.R. 647

It was agreed between the plaintiff and the defendant that the plaintiff's ship, called the "Lebanon," then in London, should proceed in ballast to Constantinople, and thence to Odessa, or so near thereto as she might safely get, and there load from the factors of the defendant a full and complete cargo of tallow, wheat, seed, or other stowage goods or grain, and should therewith proceed to Hull: the act of God, the Queen's enemies, fire, and all and every other dangers and accidents of the seas, rivers and navigation, of what nature or kind soever, during the said voyage, always excepted: forty-five running days to be allowed the defendant (if the ship should not be sooner dispatched) for loading; to commence at her port of loading on her being ready to load; detention by frost or quarantine not to be reckoned as lay days. And, in case of war having commenced before the ship's arrival in Constantinople, and continuing, the defendant was bound to load the ship at that port at 10s. per ton tallow less than from Odessa.

The "Lebanon" proceeded in ballast to Constantinople, and thence to Odessa and remained in Odessa a large part of the forty-five running days, calculated as mentioned, and was ready to stay there the residue of the days, but the defendant dispensed with the ship remaining at Odessa for any part of the residue and requested the ship to depart from Odessa without the agreed cargo. The defendant defaulted in loading the agreed cargo.

The Lord Chief Justice left the issues as to The "Lebanon" to the jury, who found for the plaintiff. His Lordship then directed a verdict for the plaintiff on all the issues on both counts, subject to leave for the defendant to move to enter a verdict on the . . . two last issues to the second count, if the Court should be of opinion that there was no evidence of a dispensation by the defendant, nor of a breach of contract before the declaration of war was known at Odessa.

Watson, in the ensuing term, obtained a rule nisi pursuant to the leave reserved.

LORD CAMPBELL C.J. delivered the judgment of the Court: . . . We have next to consider the rule as it concerns the second count of the declaration, on the ship "Lebanon": the breach here being for not loading the ship at Odessa. The plaintiff alleges that the ship lay there a certain number of her running days, and was ready to stay the remainder of her running days and days of demurrage, but that the defendant dispensed with her doing so, and requested the ship to depart from Odessa. Yet that he provided no cargo for her; and she was obliged to return to England in ballast.

Among other pleas, the defendant pleaded to the second count that after the ship arrived at Odessa, and before the defendant dispensed with the ship remaining at Odessa, and before the accruing of the causes of action in the second count mentioned, war was declared between our Lady the Queen and the Emperor of Russia, whereby he was prevented from loading the ship with a cargo at Odessa. Issue was joined upon this plea. At the trial, it was proved or admitted that the ship "Lebanon" arrived at Odessa on the 11th of March, 1854. That the war between England and Russia had broken out, and was known at Odessa, on the 1st of April following. And that the ship sailed away from Odessa, in ballast, on the 17th of April, before her running days had expired. But the plaintiff attempted to prove that, before the 1st of April, the defendant had broken the charterparty by absolutely refusing to provide any cargo for the ship, and intimating that none would be provided. The question arose, whether he had adduced any evidence to go to the jury in support of these allegations. The verdict was entered for the plaintiff on this issue: but leave was reserved to enter a verdict upon it for the defendants, if the Court should be of opinion that there was no such evidence.

And, upon consideration, we are of opinion that there was no such evidence. The war having dissolved the contract on the 1st of April, when the defendant was prevented from loading the ship without trading with the Queen's enemies, it was incumbent upon the plaintiff to prove that the cause of action on which he sues had previously accrued to him. But we think that, giving credit to what his witnesses swore, no previous cause of action is proved.

The plaintiff, as to this part of the case, relied upon three witnesses, Robert Parsons, John Crutwell, Allan Gough. Parsons, the master of another ship, stated that, four or five days after the "Lebanon" arrived at Odessa, he heard Grimmer, her captain, ask the defendant's agent if he had a cargo for him. The agent said he had none. And, upon another day, he heard similar words pass between them. Crutwell, master of another ship, stated that, about a week after the "Lebanon" arrived at Odessa, he heard her captain ask the defendant's agent for a cargo; and the agent said he had no cargo for him. Next day he heard the captain ask the same question; when the same answer was given. He had frequently heard the captain ask the agent for cargo; and this continued three or four weeks. Gough, master of another ship, said that, a few days after the arrival of the "Lebanon" at Odessa, he heard her captain ask the defendant's agent for cargo. The agent said he had no cargo for him. The same thing happened again, the day before the "Lebanon" sailed away from Odessa. On this occasion the captain of the "Lebanon" again asked the agent for cargo; when the agent said, "I have no cargo for you; you had better go away."

It thus appears that the captain of the "Lebanon," who represented the plaintiff down to the 16th day of April, and long after the declaration of war was known at Odessa, continuously insisted on the performance of the charterparty by the defendant, and remained at Odessa demanding a cargo. Was there any evidence that, on or before the 1st of April, a cause of action had accrued to the plaintiff for breach of the charterparty? We think not. According to our decision in *Hochster* v. *De La Tour* (1852), 118 E.R. 922, to which we adhere, if the defendant, within the running days and before the declaration of war, had positively informed the captain of the "Lebanon" that no cargo had been provided or would be provided for him at Odessa, and that there was no use in his remaining there any longer, the captain might have treated this as a breach and renunciation of the contract; and thereupon, sailing away from Odessa, he might have loaded a cargo at a friendly port from another person; whereupon the plaintiff would have had a right to maintain an action on the charterparty to recover damages equal to the loss he had sustained from the breach of contract on the part of the defendant. The language used by the defendant's agent before the declaration of war can hardly be considered as amounting to a renunciation of the contract: but, if it had been much stronger, we conceive that it could not be considered as constituting a cause of action after the captain still continued to insist upon having a cargo in fulfilment of the charterparty.

[Judgment for defendant. The decision was affirmed in the Exchequer Chamber (1856), 6 El. & Bl. 953; 119 E.R. 1119.]

DALRYMPLE *v.* SCOTT

Ontario. Court of Appeal. 1891. 19 A.R. 477

The action was brought to recover damages for the breach of a contract for the sale of flour. The plaintiffs were dealers in flour and grain, carrying on business in the village of Lakeside; and the defendants were dealers in flour at the village of Caledonia.

The following was the correspondence between the plaintiffs and defendants in respect of which the action arose:

The plaintiffs telegraphed to the defendants as follows:

"Quote for May shipment ninety per cent patent straights and low grade flours stating quantity can offer. Reply quick."

The defendants replied by letter as follows: "Dear Sirs: Your telegram received and noted. Our Mr. Scott being away at the time, hence the delay. We will ship you 500 bbls. 90 per cent patent at $4.25 per bbl. f.o.b. here, May shipment. We have no straight grade to offer at present. We can supply you with 300 bags low grade at $1.25 per 98 lbs., sacks included, May delivery. If these figures meet with your approval we would be pleased to open up business with you."

The plaintiffs telegraphed to the defendants as follows: "Letter received offer accepted; writing."

The defendants wrote to the plaintiffs as follows: "Dear Sir: We received a telegram from you some days ago enquiring prices for patent straight and low grade flours, to which we replied offering you 500 bbls. 90 per cent at $4.25, and one car low grade at $1.25 per sack, f.o.b. here, which you accepted by wire, stating at the time you were writing. As yet we have received no letter from you with instructions. We desire you to make a deposit on the purchase of $200. An early reply from you with instructions will oblige."

The plaintiffs wrote the following letter to the defendants: "Dear Sirs: If you are wanting any flour will sell you the lot we purchased from you, but prices must be right, as we fully expect to see wheat here $1.20 before ten days, but you can make us an offer."

The defendants telegraphed to the plaintiffs as follows: "Your order is cancelled. You did not put up two hundred dollars, as requested nor write as agreed."

The plaintiffs stated in evidence that they would have been willing to have accepted and paid for the flour in May, had it been offered to them then; and the defendants stated that they had set apart the flour they had sold to the plaintiffs, but that they had not notified the plaintiffs that they had done so.

There was no further correspondence or communication between the plaintiffs and the defendants.

It was shewn that ninety per cent patent flour was worth from $4.65 to $5.00 a barrel in May, and low grade about $1.00 less per barrel.

Robertson J. dismissed the action on the ground that there was no completed contract. This judgment was reversed by the Queen's Bench Division. The defendants appealed.

OSLER J.A.: I see no reason to differ from the opinion of the learned Judges of the Divisional Court that there was a completed contract between the parties.

The plaintiffs asked the defendants to make them an offer; they made it, and they accepted it. The addition to their telegram accepting it, of the word "writing," cannot, I at present think, be construed as an intimation that the acceptance was subject to terms not disclosed in the telegram. Therefore, I am unable to agree with the finding upon which judgment was given for the defendants at the trial.

In the Divisional Court the plaintiffs have been held entitled to recover on the ground that the defendants' telegram of the 15th April, informing them that their order was cancelled because they had failed to make a deposit of $200 on account of the price of the flour, "was a distinct and unequivocal and absolute refusal on the defendant' part to perform their contract, and the plaintiffs were entitled to treat it as such, and act upon it as they did, taking no further action with respect to the contract."

The authority cited in the judgment is the *Danube and Black Sea Co.* v. *Xenos* (1861), 13 C.B.N.S. 825; 142 E.R. 753. The declaration in that case set forth the alleged contract, averred the plaintiffs' willingness to perform it; and then averred that before the time fixed for the performance the defendant refused to perform it, and gave the plaintiffs notice to that effect, whereby the plaintiffs were discharged from the performance of the agreement, and were obliged to charter another vessel to carry the goods which the defendant had agreed to carry for them, etc. It was thus shewn in the pleadings, and was also proved at the trial, that the plaintiffs had treated the renunciation as a breach of the contract without waiting for the arrival of the day fixed for its performance. The Court approved and acted upon the case of *Hochster* v. *De La Tour* (1852), 118 E.R. 922. . . .

In the case at bar, the plaintiffs declare upon the contract and aver the performance of it on their part according to its original terms; that is to say, they aver that they duly demanded the delivery of the flour, and that they were always ready and willing to accept and pay for the same. They say nothing about the renunciation or repudiation of the contract by the defendants, or of their having adopted or acted upon such repudiation. The Divisional Court appears to have regarded their "taking no further action in respect of the contract" as a sufficient acting upon the refusal of the defendants to perform it to bring the case within the rule, but with all deference, I think that cannot be so. All that can be said is, that the plaintiffs had taken no notice of the defendants' attempted rescission of the contract. They had done nothing to interfere with the performance of it on their part according to its original terms. They might, notwithstanding the defendants' notice have demanded its performance at the proper time, and they did nothing to shew that they did not intend to do so. Their statement of claim on the contrary, shews that they are proceeding as upon a breach of the contract at the time fixed for the performance; and they allege, as they were in that view bound to allege and prove, a performance of conditions precedent on their part, one of which at least was a demand for the delivery of the flour. But they proved no demand, and seem to have relied upon the fact of their not having made one as evidence that they had adopted the defendants' notice as a breach of their contract, or else that not having retracted their notice, it was evidence of a continued refusal on their part to perform it, so as to dispense with the performance of conditions precedent on their part.

The case of *Frost* v. *Knight* (1872), L.R. 7 Exch. 111, is entirely opposed to this. Cockburn C.J., delivering the judgment of the Court, there says, in a passage which has often been quoted: " . . . The promisee, if he pleases, may treat the notice of intention as inoperative, and await the time when the contract is to be executed, and then hold the other party responsible for the consequences of non-performance; but in that case, he keeps the contract alive for the benefit of the other party as well as his own. . . ."

This statement of the law was again affirmed and approved by the Court of Appeal in the recent case of *Johnstone* v. *Milling* (1886), 16 Q.B.D. 460. Clearly what the plaintiffs have done here is to adopt the first of the two alternatives shewn to be open to them. They have treated the defendants' notice of intention to break their contract as inoperative, and have chosen to await the time when the contract was to be executed, and then in an action for the breach of the contract at that time to attempt to hold the defendants responsible without proof of performance of the conditions precedent on their part.

In the case of *Ripley* v. *McClure* (1849), 4 Exch. 345; 154 E.R. 1245, it was held that the anticipatory refusal to perform a contract was not a breach of it, but that such refusal unretracted down to and inclusive of the time when the defendant was bound to perform it was evidence of a continuing refusal, and a waiver of a condition precedent to be performed by the plaintiff.

This case was much discussed in *Hochster* v. *De La Tour* (1852), 118 E.R. 922, and the law laid down in that and the subsequent cases as before stated is as follows: "The only ground upon which the condition can be dispensed with appears to be that the renunciation may be treated as a breach of the contract." But if the plaintiffs have not shewn before the arrival of the time for the performance of the contract that they mean to treat it as such, they cannot do so merely by then treating it as a waiver of or dispensation with the performance of the condition precedent, which they ought to perform at that time. *Byrne* v. *Van Tienhoven* (1880), 5 C.P.D. 344, where *Ripley* v. *McClure*, is also cited, is not the case of an anticipatory breach or refusal, but one in which the refusal was reiterated and continued down to the time when the contract should be performed and hence was held to operate as a waiver of the condition to be performed on the plaintiff's part.

For those reasons, I am of opinion that the appeal should be allowed, and the judgment at the trial restored. . . .

MACLENNAN J.A. (dissenting): . . . Before the time for performance arrived, the defendants renounced the contract. They said: "Your order is cancelled; you did not put up $200, as requested, nor write as agreed."

In *Ripley* v. *McClure,* which was an action by a vendor against a purchaser, it was held, as stated in the head note, that "a refusal by the defendant before the arrival of the cargo, to perform the contract, was not a breach of it; but that such refusal unretracted down to and inclusive of the time when the defendant was bound to receive the cargo, was evidence of a continuing refusal and a waiver of the condition precedent of delivery, and consequently the defendant was liable for breach of the contract." That case was cited with approval and followed in *Cort* v. *Ambergate etc. R.W. Co.* (1851), 117 E.R. 1229, by Lord Campbell, who delivered the judgment of the Court. That was the case of a contract for the manufacture and supply of a large quantity of railway chairs. After a quantity had been supplied, the purchaser gave notice to the vendor not to manufacture any more as the purchaser had no occasion for them. It was held that the vendor could maintain an action without manufacturing or tendering the rest of the goods, and was entitled to a verdict on the issue of readiness and willingess to perform his part; and also on the issue that the defendant refused to accept the residue of the goods; and also that as the refusal never was retracted, there was a continuing breach down to the time when the action was commenced.

There is no suggestion anywhere that I have found that this law is doubted or has been overruled.

In the case last cited Lord Campbell said, in the course of the argument, that if after such a refusal it was necessary to manufacture or tender the goods, or in case of a refusal beforehand to load a ship, to send the ship, "if it were law, it could not be sense."

In the last edition of *Benjamin on Sales,* p. 548, it is said: "A positive, absolute refusal by one party to carry out the contract, is in itself a complete breach of the contract on his part, and dispenses the other party from the useless formality of tendering performance of the condition precedent," and *Cort* v. *Ambergate etc. R.W. Co.,* is cited as authority for the proposition.

But it is said that *Hochster v. De La Tour* and the cases which have followed it, have qualified the law as understood by Parke B., and Campbell L.C., in the cases cited. With great respect, I do not understand, and am unable to see, that this is so. As I understand these cases they merely decide that, when one party to a contract renounces performance, the other may assent to the renunciation and at once bring an action, and he need not wait until the time for performance. They do not decide that he must assent at once or bring his action at once, or that he must do so within any limited time; nor do they deny the proposition that a refusal or renunciation continues until retracted. What was decided in *Ripley* v. *McClure,* and *Cort* v. *Ambergate etc. R.W. Co.,* was the effect of the antecedent refusal or renunciation as evidence. They held that, unretracted, it was evidence of a continuing refusal up to the day and time fixed for performance. The other cases do not touch that point, as I understand them. They merely decide that the innocent party may accept the refusal at once, and that, if he do, it puts an end to the contract and enables him to bring an action, But they also decide that he need not do so, and that if not the contract remains open, and the other party may retract his refusal. They do not decide that the unretracted refusal is to be regarded as if it had never been made and is to go for nothing.

In *Hochster* v. *De La Tour*, the judgment of the Court was delivered by Lord Campbell, and I do not think he intended to qualify anything he had said in *Cort* v. *Ambergate etc., R.W. Co.* At p. 691, he says: "The man who wrongfully renounces a contract into which he has deliberately entered cannot justly complain if he is immediately sued for a compensation or damages by the man whom he has injured and it seems reasonable to allow an option to the injured party, either to sue immediately or to wait till the time when the act was to be done, still holding it as prospectively binding for the exercise of this option, which may be advantageous to the innocent party, and cannot be prejudicial to the wrong-doer."

As I understand it, it was conceded and not doubted that in such a case, the innocent party could wait until the time of performance, and then bring his action if the renunciation was not in the meantime retracted; and the question in *Hochster* v. *De La Tour*, and the cases which have followed it, was, whether he was obliged to wait, and whether he could not sue at once; and these cases have decided that he could. As Lord Campbell expresses it, he has an option; he can either sue at once or wait until the time when the thing is to be done. And if he do wait, what is the effect? Why, the renunciation is speaking all the time unless it is revoked, as it is conceded it may be at any time before it is accepted by the other party.

In *Johnstone* v. *Milling*, Lord Esher says, at p. 467, that a renunciation before the time for performance, does not of itself amount to a breach of contract, but may be so acted upon and adopted by the other party as a rescission as to give an immediate right of action. But he does not say what the effect is if not retracted before the time arrives for performance, except that if the other party does not wish to accept it, he must wait for the arrival of the time when in the ordinary course a cause of action on the contract would arrive. He nowhere says that in that case the renunciation, if unretracted, is to go for nothing. Cotton L.J., says the same thing at p. 470. His language is, that where there is a refusal to perform or be bound by a contract, the other party, if he chooses, may treat it as a breach and bring his action; and to the same effect is Bowen L.J. Neither is there anything, as I humbly think, in *Mersey Steel Co.* v. *Naylor* (1884), 9 App. Cas. 434, or in any of the other cases which have followed *Hochster* v. *De La Tour*, conflicting with *Ripley* v. *McClure*, and *Cort* v. *Ambergate etc. R.W. Co.*, in deciding that a refusal unrevoked until the time for performance dispenses with conditions precedent by the other party, and the latter may then sue as for a breach, not at the time of refusal, but at the time for performance.

With great respect, I do not see how it can be otherwise. What is the meaning of a renunciation of a contract or a refusal to perform it? Is it not this: I notify you that when the time arrives for doing what I have agreed to do, I shall not do it. If that is its meaning, why should the other party be obliged to go to trouble or expense which he has been distinctly told will be useless? Can he not wait to see whether the other will change his mind and do what is right after all? He may do so. The other is doing no wrong in waiting. In my judgment in such a case the contract continues up to the time of performance, and is binding on both parties to the last moment; and the sole effect of the renunciation, if unretracted, is, as was decided in the two cases referred to, to dispense with the performance of conditions precedent by the other party.

It is said if the innocent party do not act upon or accept the refusal or renunciation, he must, in order to recover as for a breach at the time fixed for performance, do whatever would otherwise be necessary to be done on his part; or, in other words, let the previous refusal go for nothing, or treat it as revoked. I think, with great respect, there is no authority for that proposition, and that the cases I have referred to are distinct authorities against it.

To put the matter to a practical test, suppose that in the present case the refusal had been received just as the plaintiffs were on the point of ordering cars for the loading of the flour, would it be sense or reason that they must still send the cars or demand the flour? And if not, can it make any difference that the refusal was a week or a month before the time for performance? I do not see how it can. How can the persons who have refused to complain, if they are treated as having meant what they said, namely, that when the time arrived they would not do what they had agreed to do, even though the plaintiffs did everything to be done on their part?

But it is also said, that, at all events, the damages to be recovered should not be based on prices or values at the time of performance, but at the time of refusal, for the party could then have supplied himself with other goods. But why should he do that? He has fixed the time at which he wants them by the contract. Must he go into the market and buy before he requires them, because the other party has done wrong, and to save the wrongdoer from loss? I do not think so. I think both upon principle and upon the authorities, that he may wait till the time for performance without accepting the renunciation; and if it is persisted in, and not revoked, he may then sue as for a breach at that time and recover his damages with reference to the state of the market at that time, and he may use the refusal as an excuse for the performance of conditions precedent on his part, such as, in the present case, the providing of cars on which to load the flour which was the subject of the contract.

Some reliance was placed on the form of the plaintiffs' statement of claim, but I think that argument is completely met by Lord Campbell's judgment in *Cort* v. *Ambergate etc. R.W. Co.* The averment in the statement of claim, is, that the plaintiffs duly demanded the delivery of the said flour, and were always ready and willing to accept and pay for the same. I think that the plaintiffs should not, under the present system of pleading and practice, be tripped up and denied justice upon any such objection, and that they should have liberty to amend their pleading so as to make it conform to the undisputed facts of the case—it not appearing that the defendants were or could be prejudiced or misled by the pleading as it stands on the record.

I think the judgment of the Divisional Court is right, and should be affirmed.

Appeal allowed with costs.

[The judgment of Burton J.A. to the same effect as that of Osler J.A. is omitted. Hagarty C.J.O. concurred without reasons.]

BRAITHWAITE *v.* FOREIGN HARDWOOD COMPANY
England. Court of Appeal [1905] 2 K.B. 543

Collins M.R.: In this appeal the amount at stake is small, but the principles of law involved are of some nicety and importance. The question arises thus. The plaintiff, who was the owner of a quantity of rosewood growing in British Honduras, made a contract with the defendants for the sale to them of 100 tons of rosewood answering to a particular description in the contract. The defendants were in the first instance desirous that the rosewood should be sent to them in small instalments of about twenty-five tons each; they did not, in fact, want quite so much as 100 tons, but the vendor would not sell less than that quantity, and wanted to sell it in one block; in the end, however, it was arranged that it should be sent in instalments, the size of which was not definitely ascertained or fixed, to be spread over the year 1903. About or shortly before the time when the first consignment was sent, the plaintiff sold, and sent a consignment of rosewood to a competitor of the defendants in their trade: at this the defendants were annoyed, considering it to be a breach of a fundamental stipulation, to which they asserted that the plaintiff had agreed, not to deliver rosewood during 1903 to any one but themselves; they therefore wrote to the plaintiff or his agent repudiating all obligation on their part to take any rosewood under their contract with the plaintiff. The terms of the letter of repudiation written by the defendants were unquestionably absolute, and extended to their entire quantity of rosewood comprised in the contract. When that letter was received the first consignment of rosewood was actually upon the seas, and the bill of lading had been sent to the plaintiff's agents in England, who informed the defendants that they were ready to hand it over to them in exchange for cash as provided by the contract. In their reply the defendants adhered to their general repudiation, which involved the refusal to accept the particular consignment, and refused to pay. The consignment, amounting to about sixty-three tons, came forward, and in view of the refusal of the defendants to accept it or pay for it, it was consigned to brokers in London for sale on the best terms possible. Of that consignment of sixty-three tons which had arrived by the Spheroid about seventeen tons was not in accordance with the contract in respect of quality. Later on the plaintiff shipped the balance of the rosewood, and as to that consignment no question now arises; it is admitted that it was in conformity with the contract, and there is no defence to the plaintiff's claim in respect of it. At the trial Kennedy J. found as a fact that the alleged fundamental stipulation as to not selling rosewood to other customers than the defendants had not been made; therefore the ground upon which the defendants claimed the right to repudiate the whole contract failed, and they were liable to the plaintiff for breach of the contract. There is therefore no answer to the plaintiff's claim in respect of the second consignment.

I now come to the point as regards the first consignment which has been the subject of such keen discussion. The defendants contend that the true measure of damages is not the difference in market price of the whole of the rosewood comprised in the contract upon the footing that it was all of marketable quality, inasmuch as it was admitted that in some respects the quality of a portion of the first consignment was inferior to that stipulated for in the contract; at the trial Kennedy J., in assessing the damages, gave effect to this contention based on inferiority of quality, but the defendants contend that the allowance made by him was insufficient. They say that upon the repudiation of the contract the plaintiff had two courses open to him. In the first place, he might have accepted the repudiation as absolving him as well as the defendants from the performance of the contract, and as giving him a right once for all to damages for a breach of the entire contract; or, in the second place, the plaintiff might have adhered to the contract, and from time to time have gone into the market when the instalments of rosewood arrived and the defendants refused to accept them, thus keeping open the obligation on the plaintiff's part to be ready and willing to perform the conditions of the contract to be performed by him. The defendants, the buyers, say that the plaintiff took the second course—in other words, that instead of accepting the defendants' repudiation of the contract he took it upon himself to keep the contract alive, and that he must therefore shew that he was ready and willing to carry out his part of the contract when the time came to tender each instalment. They further say that the first instalment was not such as they were bound to accept, because a considerable percentage of it did not conform to the standard of quality prescribed by the contract, and they pray in aid the observation of Kennedy J. that, if it had been necessary to tender that consignment formally, the buyers, that is the defendants, would have been entitled to reject the whole of it. The defendants further contend that, if the learned judge was right in his view, the buyers would have been entitled to refuse to accept the instalment on the ground of difference in quality, that instalment must, for the purpose of assessing the damages, be wholly wiped out, because the plaintiff, not being able to shew that he was himself able and ready and willing to fulfil his part of the contract according to its terms, could be entitled to no damages in respect of that instalment; and that the question of damages was thus narrowed down to the damages in respect of the second instalment.

At first sight this contention of the defendants seems to be a formidable one, but upon a more careful analysis I think it is untenable. We must for this purpose deal with the contract upon the footing that it was kept alive. The obligation upon the plaintiff was to deliver the rosewood by instalments. Where such an obligation exists, as each instalment is tendered under the contract, the buyer must be ready and willing to perform the contract as well as the seller, and if he is not willing to perform it he may by his conduct or by express words absolve the seller from his obligation. In the present case, after there had been a general repudiation of the contract by the defendants, the plaintiff's agent informed them that he had received the bill of lading for the first instalment; but the defendants again wrote refusing to take the bill of lading on the ground that they had previously repudiated the whole contract and refused to be bound by it. In my opinion that act of the defendants amounted in fact to a waiver by them of the performance by the plaintiff of the conditions precedent which would otherwise have been necessary to the enforcement by him of the contract which I am assuming he had elected to keep alive against the defendants notwithstanding their repudiation, and it is not competent for the defendants now to hark back and say that the plaintiff was not ready and willing to perform the conditions precedent devolving upon him, and that if they had known the facts they might have rejected the instalment when tendered to them. One answer to such a contention on the part of the defendants is that, tested by the old form of pleadings, it would have been a good replication by the plaintiff to aver that the defendants had waived performance by him of the conditions precedent by adhering to their original repudiation of the whole contract, and would not accept any instalment if tendered to them. The defendants are not in a position now, by reason of their after-acquired knowledge, to set up a defence which they previously elected not to make. We must in such a case look to see whether, at the time of each alleged breach, each side was ready and willing to perform the conditions of the contract which it lay upon them to perform, and there was clearly a breach by the defendants, for they had by their own act absolved the plaintiff from the performance of the conditions of the contract. In such a case the ordinary rule as to the measure of damages is the proper rule to apply. In the present case it has, I think, been applied, if anything, somewhat too favourably for the defendants. Logically, the damages should, I think, have been assessed upon the footing that the wood which the plaintiff was excused from delivering was up to the standard stipulated for in the contract, though it turns out that it in fact fell slightly short of the monetary value of wood quite up to that standard; but the learned judge has assessed the damages from the point of view of common sense rather than of strict law, and has made an allowance, of which the defendants cannot complain. This really decides the whole case, for there is no dispute as to the second consignment.

The ground on which our judgment proceeds relieves us from considering whether the fact that a portion of the first consignment did not correspond in all respects with the standard stipulated for in the contract would, had it stood alone, have given the defendants the right to reject the whole consignment. The learned judge thought they would have had the right, and, though there was evidence both ways, I should have been loth to differ from a judge of so great experience in this class of case had it been necessary to decide it. The appeal must, therefore, be dismissed.

[Cozens-Hardy L.J. agreed with the reasons of Collins M.R. Mathew L.J. gave reasons for dismissing the appeal, saying in part: "But they repudiated the whole contract, and by so doing clearly absolved the plaintiff from the performance of conditions precedent which in the ordinary course he would have been obliged to perform, The plaintiff took the only course open to him in selling the wood against the defendants, and that terminated the first part of the contract, which, by reason of the provision for delivering the goods in different shipments, was a severable one. Then the second consignment of wood arrived, and again the defendants refused to accept the bill of lading. Under these circumstances it is to me an astonishing suggestion that the plaintiff is in a difficulty as to the first consignment because he was not in a condition to perform the conditions precedent under the contract, although the performance of those conditions had been waived by the defendant."]

QUESTIONS. Is the principal case consistent with the doctrine of election enunciated in *Frost* v. *Knight*? With *Dalrymple* v. *Scott*? If A is under contract to deliver goods of a certain quality to B before the end of June, suppose that on June 1, A tenders goods not up to quality, B refuses them. On June 15, A tenders proper goods. May B refuse them? See *Borrowman* v. *Free* (1878), 4 Q.B.D. 500.

BRITISH AND BENNINGTONS, LIMITED *v.* NORTH WESTERN CACHAR TEA COMPANY, LIMITED

England. House of Lords [1923] A.C. 48

The respondents were tea growers in India. They contracted to ship and sell tea to the appellants, delivery to be made in bonded warehouses in London. No particular date was set for time of delivery. The sellers consigned shipments to London, but owing to congestion at that port, the ships were diverted by the Shipping Controller to various ports in England and Scotland, where a further delay occurred due to congestion. Abortive attempts to secure the buyers to take delivery at these ports failed, and the buyer finally repudiated liability to take the tea at all, on the ground that a reasonable time for delivery had expired.

Under provisions of the contract, the sellers asked for arbitration. The arbitrator found that a reasonable time had not elapsed at the time of the repudiation and that the sellers by taking arbitration proceedings had accepted the repudiation and were entitled to recover damages.

On appeal to McCardie J. it was decided in favour of the buyer. The Court of Appeal reversed this decision and upheld the arbitrator's decision. Appeal was then taken by the buyer to the House of Lords.

LORD ATKINSON: . . . "[If] the buyers had not repudiated . . . and had been suing for some breach . . . I did not understand it to be contended that at the time of the alleged breach they were ready and willing to deliver the goods. Lord Abinger in *De Medina* v. *Norman* (1842), 9 M. & W. 820; 152 E.R. 347 at p. 350, laid down that the words, "readiness and willingness," used in such a connection, imply not only the disposition but the capacity to perform the contract. But the point has been urged by the respondents, and was much relied upon by the Court of Appeal that when a buyer, before breach of a contract for the sale of goods, repudiates it, as was held by the arbitrator the appellants did in this case, and that repudiation is accepted and acted upon by the seller, as it evidently was in this case, the seller is relieved from the performance of all conditions precedent, including the condition of being ready and willing at the date of repudiation to deliver the goods. In *Jones* v. *Barkley*, (1781) 2 Doug. 684; 99 E.R. 434, at p. 440, Lord Mansfield says: "Take it on the reason of the thing. The party must shew he was ready; but, if the other stops him on the ground of an intention not to perform his part, it is not necessary for the first to go farther, and do a nugatory act. Here, the draft was shewn to the defendant for his approbation of the form, but he would not read it, and, upon a different ground, namely, that the means not to pay the money, discharges the plaintiffs." In the case of *Hotham* v. *East India Co.* (1787), 1 T.R. 638; 99 E.R. 1295, where there was a covenant that the allowance for short tonnage should not be made unless the shipowner procured a certificate from the freighter's agent at the commencement of the voyage, the Court held that a demand and refusal of this certificate was sufficient. [Lord Atkinson referred to *Cort* v. *Ambergate, &c., Ry Co.*, and *Braithwaite* v. *Foreign Hardwood Company.*]

LORD SUMNER: . . . It is perfectly clear that the buyers did refuse to be bound by the contracts, and that, by demanding arbitration on the point and making no further attempt to deliver the tea in dispute, the sellers accepted that as a final repudiation. This being so, after the opinions above expressed, I am bound to think, and do think, that the buyers must justify the position which they so took up or must fail.

Their answer, as I understand it, is that the sellers cannot claim damages for this anticipatory repudiation unless they were in such a position, when they accepted it, as to be able to prove that they were then for their part able and willing to perform their obligations under the contracts in accordance with their terms, and that in such proof they must fail, because, as regards the tea lying at Scotch ports, they manifestly could not satisfy an agreed condition precedent—namely, to ship all the tea direct to London and there deliver it ex bonded warehouse. The sellers successfully contested this below on the authority of *Braithwaite* v. *Foreign Hardwood Co.*, [1905] 2 K.B. 543, a decision which bound the Court of Appeal.

My Lords, as reported, that decision is not quite easy to understand. It was presented to your Lordships by the respondents, fortified by the opinion of Scrutton L.J. as a decision that, when there has been a repudiation by one party on a given ground, and an acceptance of that repudiation by the other party, the former can no longer rely on any other ground for refusing to perform his obligations, and particularly cannot require the latter to prove his readiness and willingness to perform any of his obligations under the contract, thus repudiated. I have no recollection of that case to carry me beyond the language of the report, as I do not doubt Scrutton L.J. had, but, in my opinion, the case as reported either does not lay down this proposition or, if it does so, is wrong. The majority in the Court of Appeal in that case expressly refused to decide the question whether the deficiency in the quality of the first consignment would have justified the rejection of the whole of that consignment, had it stood alone, while Mathew L.J., differing from the findings of Kennedy J. (as I think under some misapprehension as to the percentage of the cargo which was inferior to the contract quality), expressly says that it would not. The case was dealt with as one in which the buyers had explicitly waived all conditions precedent, while retaining a right to rely on them as terms, the breach of which would sound in damages that could be given in evidence in reduction of the claim, and the judgment of Kennedy J., who had thus reduced the plaintiff's damages, was consequently affirmed. In effect it was said that, even after the seller had, as it was called, kept the contract alive and proposed to tender the cargo, he had been told a second time, in terms of the first refusal, "you need not tender any cargo to us at all; *a fortiori* you need not tender a cargo which is in conformity with the contract. You have a cargo of some sort, which we refuse to take; and you may prove your damages for that, if we fail to prove you wrong." Furthermore it does not anywhere appear that, even if the first cargo might rightly have been rejected, the seller could not have found another exactly conforming with the contract, which he might have duly tendered and so have put himself right.

So far the case does not affect the present argument, except that it is ground for saying that this point only went to damages, unless and until it was shown, that the Spheroid's cargo and that alone was available for delivery by the plaintiff. I do not think that the case, as reported, lays it down that a buyer, who has repudiated a contract for a given reason which fails him, has, therefore, no other opportunity of defence, either as to the whole or as to part but must fail utterly. If he had repudiated, giving no reason at all, I suppose all reasons and all defences in the action, partial or complete, would be open to him. His motives certainly are immaterial, and I do not see why his reason should be crucial. What he says is of course very material upon the question whether he means to repudiate at all, and, if so, how far, and how much, and on the question in what respects he waives the performance of conditions still performable *in futuro* or dispenses the opposite party from performing his own obligations any further; but I do not see how the fact, that the buyers have wrongly said "we treat this contract as being at an end, owing to your unreasonable delay in the performance of it" obliges them, when that reason fails, to pay in full, if, at the very time of this repudiation, the sellers had become wholly and finally disabled from performing essential terms of the contract altogether. Braithwaite's case says nothing, which affects the regular consequences, when it appears that at the time of breach the plaintiff is already completely disabled from doing his part at all.

I am not, however, satisfied in this case that the position of the sellers was one of this kind. It is not found that they could not have forwarded the tea to London, or that the tea, when so forwarded, would not have been still such as the contract provided for. All that can be said is that the tea had not been brought to London direct from India. . . .

My Lords, I am of opinion that in all three cases the appeals fail.

My Lords, I am requested to say that my noble and learned friend Lord Buckmaster concurs in the opinion which I have just read.

[The order of the Court of Appeal was affirmed. Lord Wrenbury and Lord Carson agreed in the result without written reasons. The facts have been greatly condensed and only those parts of the facts and opinions dealing with the effect of repudiation are given.]

QUESTIONS. Suppose that A promises to sell goods of a certain kind to B, and to make delivery to B on August 15th. A is in England, B in Canada. On August 1, B says "I repudiate my contract. I will not take the goods." A immediately sues. It turns out that A has just that day (August 1) shipped the goods to Canada. Moreover they could not and did not in fact reach Canada by August 15. Has A a cause of action against B? On Lord Atkinson's theory? On Lord Sumner's?

Suppose A, on December 1, agrees to sell and B to buy A's horse, delivery to be made January 15. On December 15 B repudiates the contract. If A's horse is dead at that date has A a cause of action? If A's horse dies two days after the repudiation, has A a cause of action? Suppose A has commenced suit?

Y. P. BARLEY PRODUCERS LTD. *v*. E. C. ROBERTSON PTY. LTD.
Victoria. Supreme Court. [1927] V.L.R. 194

Action by sellers against buyers for breach of contract. Question arose at the trial as to the nature of the contract, but for purposes of the doctrine of repudiation the court assumed it to be a c.i.f. contract, i.e. one of which the seller, having shipped the goods, is entitled to payment on tender of shipping documents including policy of insurance. The Court further found that the seller had until March 1 to tender the documents. On February 25 the buyer absolutely refused to perform the contract.

McArthur J.: . . . Assuming, then, that the contract was a c.i.f. contract, and that by the 25th February the time for its performance had not yet arrived, the defendant's absolute refusal on that date to perform the contract amounted to a repudiation by the defendant of the c.i.f. contract. The plaintiff did not at once elect to accept and act upon that repudiation, but he did nothing in the direction of himself proceeding with the contract, and thus keeping the contract alive. He merely endeavoured, between the 25th February and the 1st of March, to persuade the defendant to withdraw his repudiation; but failing to persuade him to do so, the plaintiff on the 2nd March elected to accept and act upon the repudiation and so informed the defendant. But the date which must be taken as the date of the repudiation is the 25th February. It was a repudiation on the 25th February which was continuously persisted in from that date onwards. Mr. Lowe's contention is that, notwithstanding this repudiation, the plaintiff was bound to prove that at the time of the repudiation he was ready and willing to perform the contract—that is to say (as I understand the contention), that he could have performed it at its due date, and would have done so if he had not been excused from doing so by the defendant's repudiation. The argument was really confined to the policy of insurance, and narrowed itself down to this, that, assuming that by reason of the defendant's repudiation, the plaintiff was excused from actually tendering the policy of insurance, he was bound to prove that he was ready and willing to tender it, and, but for the repudiation, would have tendered it within contract time.

If the time has arrived for the performance of the ordinary c.i.f. contract, cash (or as the case may be) against documents, the seller is bound to tender the usual documents, unless excused by the buyer from doing so, and upon such tender the buyer is bound to pay the contract price. If, upon such tender, the buyer refuses to accept the documents and to pay in accordance with the contract, such refusal is an actual breach of contract on his part. If the refusal were before actual tender, the circumstances of the refusal might be such as to amount to a waiver of the requirement of actual tender. In such a case, the refusal would still be an actual breach —as distinguished from an anticipatory breach—but the seller, not being able to prove actual performance, would have to prove that the buyer had dispensed with performance, and that involves proving that he was ready and willing to perform, and would have performed but for the dispensation. And the question is whether the same considerations apply where before the time for the performance of the contract has arrived, the buyer repudiates the contract and the repudiation is accepted and acted on by the seller. This must depend upon the exact nature of the cause of action, and the precise proofs which the plaintiff must adduce in order to establish a cause of action. There has been a considerable amount of judicial discussion on this subject. The judgments most frequently quoted on the subject are those of Lord Campbell C.J., in *Hochster* v. *De La Tour* (1852), 118 E.R. 922, of Cockburn C.J. in *Frost* v. *Knight* (1872), L.R. 7 Exch. 111 and of Lord Esher M.R., Cotton L.J. in *Johnstone* v. *Milling* (1886), 16 Q.B.D. 460.

These learned judges all agree that the repudiation of the contract by one party entitles the other party to accept the repudiation as putting an end to the contract for all purposes, except for the purpose of bringing an action for damages, and entitles such other party to bring an action for damages, but they do not all agree as to what the precise nature of the action is. They all agree, with perhaps the exception of Lord Campbell, that the repudiation itself is not a breach of contract. Lord Campbell suggested that one ground upon which it might be put was that a contract to do an act on a future day constituted a relationship between the parties in the meantime, and that there was an implied promise that, in the meantime, neither would do anything to the prejudice of the other inconsistent with that relationship. Cockburn C.J. puts it that the other party "may treat the repudiation as a wrongful putting an end to the contract, and may at once bring his action *as on a breach of it*." Lord Esher, M.R. refers to the repudiation as "wrongful," even before the other party elects to treat it as putting an end to the contract, but I think he there means wrongful in the sense that there was no just cause for the repudiation. He expressly says that the repudiation does not in itself amount to a breach of contract, but he says that it "may be so acted upon and adopted by the other party as a rescission of the contract as to give an immediate right of action"—he does not say for breach of contract. Cotton L.J. at page 470 says—"The other party, if he chooses, may elect to act upon such statements as a renunciation of the entire contract, and may thereupon *treat the same as a breach* of the contract and bring his action.

Bowen L.J. makes it clear that, in his opinion, the repudiation is neither a breach of contract nor a wrongful act (by which I presume he means an act giving rise to a cause of action) until acted on by the other party. He sums it up at page 473 by saying—"but such declaration (that is to say, the repudiation) only becomes a wrongful act if the promisee elects to treat it as such. If he does so elect, it becomes a breach of contract, and he can recover upon it as such." They are all, except Bowen L.J., careful not to say that the action is for "breach of contract," but they use expressions such as it may be "treated as a breach of contract" or that the action may be brought "as upon a breach of contract." And in *Bradley* v. *Newsom Sons & Co.*, [1919] A.C. 16, Viscount Haldane makes use of a similar expression. He says, at page 33, "The repudiation in advance, therefore, *entitled the plaintiff to say* that there had been a breach of contract."

It is difficult to understand how an act which is not itself a breach of contract or otherwise wrongful, can be converted into a breach of contract by the election of the other party to the contract. In *Wilkinson* v. *Verity* (1871), L.R. 6 C.P. 206, Willes J. says, at page 209, "in cases where a man undertakes to do an act upon a future day, and before the day arrives, disables himself from performing the act, or positively and absolutely refuses to be bound by or perform the contract, and, so to speak, declares off the bargain himself, and absolves the other party, it is in the option of such party at his election to treat that conduct as of itself a violation and breach of the contract, or to insist upon holding the repudiating party liable, and sue him for non-performance when the day arrives." So far, it would appear as if His Lordship was in agreement with the opinions of the other judges that there was no actionable wrong until the other party elected to treat it as such, but His Lordship continues—"the misconduct of the party who acts in fraud of the bargain in such cases gives the other party thereto the election of suing either for the first violation or for non-performance at the day." This looks as if His Lordship had intended to convey that the "first violation" constituted in itself a cause of action. And this view is rather strengthened by the fact that he thereupon proceeds to give instances of cases in which there is a similar right of election, and, in those cases, there existed, quite independently of any election, two separate and distinct causes of action, either one of which was open to the plaintiff to pursue. His Lordship gave no instance in which a party may elect to treat as a good cause of action something which, but for such election, would not have been a cause of action.

In *Bradley* v. *Newson Sons & Co.*, Lord Wrenbury, at page 52, puts it as an example of "consensus." The person repudiating, he says, "offers" to cancel the contract and accept the consequences, knowing that those consequences are that he may be sued for damages for his refusal to perform the contract. If this be so, the action should not be an action for damages for breach of the original contract, but an action on the new contract to pay such damages as the other party has suffered by the repudiation of the original contract. At page 54 His Lordship criticizes the expression "anticipatory breach" which had been used by Lord Esher in *Johnstone* v. *Milling*, and he says "he is repudiating his promise which binds him in the present." "He is recalling or repudiating his promise, and that is wrongful. His breach is a breach of a presently binding promise." One may ask, what does His Lordship mean by "wrongful?" And what is the "presently binding promise," which he has broken? And if it is a breach of a presently binding promise, how is it also an offer to rescind the contract and pay damages for the repudiation? His Lordship continues —"To take Bowen L.J.'s words in *Johnstone* v. *Milling*, it is a wrongful renunciation of the contractual relation into which he has entered." A reference to the passage in Bowen L.J.'s judgment from which these words are taken will show that what Lord Justice Bowen actually did say was that if the promisee *chose* to accept the repudiation and act upon it, he could then "treat it as a wrongful renunciation of the contractual relation into which he has entered." In the sentence immediately preceding the one from which the words quoted by Lord Wrenbury are taken, Bowen L.J. makes it quite clear that the renunciation is not in itself a breach of contract or a wrongful act. He says (p. 472, bottom, and 473, top)—"It would seem on principle that the declaration of such intention by the promisor is not in itself, and unless acted on by the promisee, a breach of the contract; and that it only becomes a breach when it is converted by force of what follows it into a wrongful renunciation of the contract."

These authorities show, in my opinion, that the action is not based on any of the general principles of the law of contract. It is an artificial cause of action in the nature of an action for breach of contract, though not actually an action for breach of contract. The repudiation accepted and acted upon by the other party gives such party the right to at once bring an action for damages as for a breach of contract.

The plaintiff has a complete cause of action if he proves—

(1) The contract;

(2) The repudiation of the contract by the defendant;

(3) That he (the plaintiff) accepted and acted upon the repudiation.

It being in the nature of an action for breach of contract, and the plaintiff being entitled to treat the repudiation as a breach of contract, he has not to prove as part of the cause of action that he has suffered any actual damage, but, as in an ordinary action for damages for breach of contract, he is entitled to nominal damages if he fails to prove substantial damages.

By accepting and acting upon the repudiation, the contract is rescinded —is put an end to for all purposes except for the purpose of bringing an action for damages. The promisee is entirely exonerated and discharged from performance of the contract, and is therefore, in my opinion, entirely relieved from the necessity of proving that at the time of the repudiation he was ready and willing to perform the contract, meaning by the expression "readiness and willingness" that he was "disposed and able to complete the contract if it had not been renounced by the defendant" (to use the words of Lord Campbell, in *Cort* v. *Ambergate etc. Ry. Co.*); that he had "not only the disposition but the capacity to perform the contract" (to use the words of Lord Abinger in *De Medina* v. *Norman* (1842), 152 E.R. 347.

In an ordinary action for breach of contract (as I have already pointed out) the time having arrived for the performance of the contract, the plaintiff has, prima facie, to prove that he has performed all conditions precedent; he must prove either performance or that he was excused from performance, and the latter involves proof of readiness and willingness to perform. But, in an action for repudiation before the time for performance has arrived, the plaintiff has not, either prima facie, or at all, to prove performance of conditions precedent, and is therefore not required to prove any excuse for non-performance, and so the question of readiness and willingness to perform does not arise.

There has not been, so far as I am aware, any actual decision on this point, unless it can be said that that very unsatisfactory case, *Braithwaite* v. *Foreign Hardwood Co.*, [1905] 2 K.B. 543, decided it, but there are a number of conflicting judicial opinions on the subject.

The judgment of the trial judge, Kennedy J., in *Braithwaite*'s case is reported in 92 L.T., page 637. At page 639, 2nd column, His Lordship says—"Nobody doubts, I think could doubt, as a general statement of law that, if, before the time of its performance, one of the two parties to a contract says unmistakably 'in consequence of your conduct, or for any other reason good or bad, I am not going to perform the contract,' that that relieves the other party to the contract from the necessity otherwise laid upon him, in order to maintain successfully the action, of showing he was willing on his part to perform the contract. You have absolved him from doing that by telling him 'I will not perform it on my part.' There is exoneration and discharge on the part of the defendant of the plaintiff's obligation."

In *British & Benningtons Ltd.* v. *N. W. Cachar Tea Co. Ltd. and Others*, [1923] A.C. 48, Lord Sumner, at page 70, expresses the opinion that if *Braithwaite*'s case decided that the defendant could not require the plaintiff to prove "his readiness and willingness to perform any of his obligations under the contract thus repudiated," it is wrong. But reading this with the rest of His Lordship's observations on this subject at pages 71 and 72, I am inclined to think that His Lordship meant that the damages would not be assessed on the assumption that the plaintiff was ready and willing to perform the contract, but in order to prove his damages, the plaintiff would have to prove readiness and willingness to perform the contract.

In the same case, Lord Atkinson was, apparently, of opinion that it was not necessary for the plaintiff to prove readiness and willingness. . . .

In *Bowes* v. *Chaleyer*, [1923] 32 C.L.R. 159, Higgins J., though not in express words stating his opinion on the subject, at page 192 quotes with approval a passage from the judgment of Scrutton L.J., in *Taylor and Others* v. *Oakes, Roncoroni & Co.*, [1922] 27 Com. Cases, 261, at 267, where His Lordship said—"Once they had repudiated the contract and the repudiation had been accepted, the vendor was relieved from the necessity of proving his readiness and willingness." The opinion of Isaacs J., and Rich J., appearing at page 184, does not, I think, go beyond this, that the plaintiff is not entitled to recover damages on the assumption that he would have been able to carry out his contract to the letter. At page 198, Starke J., in the passage already quoted, states quite definitely his opinion that the promisee is "relieved from proving readiness and willingness on his part to perform the contract." . . .

In *Taylor and Others* v. *Oakes, Roncoroni & Co.*, in the Court of Appeal, all the learned Lord Justices (Bankes, L.J., Scrutton, L.J., and

Atkin, L.J.) were of opinion that it was unnecessary to prove readiness and willingness. Bankes L.J., at page 271, puts it quite shortly and definitely thus—"Where there has been a repudiation by way of anticipatory breach, the contract is at an end if the repudiation is accepted, and it is immaterial afterwards to consider what would have happened if there had been no repudiation and the contract had continued and the plaintiff had been obliged to perform it." Scrutton L.J. expressed a similar opinion in the passage quoted by Higgins J., to which I have referred, and Atkin L.J., agreed with them on the point. Both Bankes L.J. and Scrutton L.J. rely on *Braithwaite*'s case, and Atkin L.J. relies not only on that case, but also on *Ripley* v. *McClure* (1849), 154 E.R. 1245. In the *British & Benningtons'* case, which was decided in the same year but later than *Taylor* v. *Oakes,* Lord Sumner, at page 70, says of *Braithwaite*'s case that, as reported, the decision is "not quite easy to understand." And with regard to the particular point under discussion, he made the observation which I have already referred to. It may therefore be said that Lord Sumner, at all events. would not agree with the opinions of the learned Lord Justice in *Taylor* v. *Oakes* which are based on *Braithwaite's* case, and for that reason it may be said that those opinions are somewhat weakened as authoritative opinions. But having regard to the exact nature of this cause of action, I am of opinion that the question whether the plaintiff at the time of the repudiation was ready and willing to perform the contract, is immaterial to the cause of action. In these cases of repudiation, it may be said that proof of readiness and willingness can mean nothing more than proof that, up to the time of the repudiation, nothing had happened to disable the plaintiff from performing the contract, and that up to that time he fully intended to perform it. But whether the expression be given this limited meaning or its ordinary meaning, I am of opinion, for the reasons already given, that the question of readiness and willingness is immaterial to the cause of action.

It may, however, be most material, in my opinion, on the question of damages. The true measure of damages in most, if not all, cases would be either the difference between contract price and market value at date of repudiation; or the difference between contract price and cost to the seller of fulfilling the contract. In those cases there must always necessarily be taken into consideration on the one side, as the fundamental basis, the contract price. If, therefore, it appears that—quite apart from the repudiation—the seller could never have performed the contract, and therefore could never have earned the contract price, it is clear that he cannot have suffered substantial damage by the repudiation. I think this is what Lord Sumner is referring to in *British & Benningtons'* case when he says at page 72 "but I do not see how the fact that the buyers have wrongly said 'we treat this contract as being at an end, owing to your unreasonable delay in the performance of it' obliges them, when that reason fails, to pay in full, at the very time of this repudiation, the sellers have become wholly and finally disabled from performing essential terms of the contract altogether. *Braithwaite's* case says nothing which affects the regular consequences when it appears that at the time of breach the plaintiff is already completely disabled from doing his part at all." And I think this is what Isaacs J. and Rich J. are referring to in *Chaleyer's* case when, at page 184, they express their entire dissent from the view presented by counsel for the respondent that "the latter may sue and recover damages as if he has been fully prepared to carry out his contract to the letter." As in ordinary cases, the onus would be upon the plaintiff to prove his substantial damages, and he would therefore have to satisfy the jury that, but for the repudiation, he would have earned the contract price.

He might, of course, not be able to prove that he could have earned the whole of the contract price, but, that in accordance with the terms of the particular contract, he could have earned part of it, in which case the damages would be reduced accordingly. It was on this principle (though I do not admit that the facts justified the conclusion arrived at) that Kennedy J., reduced the damages claimed by the plaintiff in *Braithwaite's* case. The way it was put by His Lordship was this:

Seventeen tons out of the sixty-three tons of timber shipped in the Spheroid were of inferior quality to that prescribed by the contract, and therefore the plaintiff would not, when the time for performance arrived, have been able to claim from the defendant the contract price for the whole of the cargo, but only for forty-six tons of it, and therefore the true measure of damages was not the difference between the contract price of the whole sixty-three tons, and the amount realized on the sale thereof (which was what the plaintiff claimed), but the difference between the contract price of forty-six tons plus the value of the seventeen tons, and the price realized on the sale.

It is clear that Kennedy J. found as a fact that the plaintiff could not, when the time for the performance of the contract arrived, have delivered timber in accordance with the contract, and he expressly found as a fact that the quantity of inferior timber was so great that the defendant could have rejected the whole shipment (see page 639, first column, bottom of page). That being so, it seems to me to follow that the damages in relation to that shipment should have been reduced to 1s., because the plaintiff could not in any event have obtained the contract price from the defendant, and therefore he suffered no substantial damage from the defendant's repudiation.

If it be assumed, as from his judgment in *British & Benningtons'* case Lord Sumner appears to think it can be assumed, that there was no evidence, or, at all events, no proof, that that plaintiff could not have supplied timber of the contractual quality, then I agree that the damages should have been reduced substantially to the same extent as that to which Kennedy J. reduced them, but on a different basis. On this assumption the plaintiff would, if the contract had been carried out, have been entitled to receive from the defendant the contract price. He was therefore entitled to recover as damages the difference between the contract price and the market price at the time of breach of timber of the contractual quality. But the plaintiff claimed the difference between the contract price and the amount actually realized on the sale of the timber. But part of the timber sold was of inferior quality and, therefore, the amount realised on sale of timber was less than would have been realised if all the timber had been of proper quality—which is, in effect, the same as saying that it realised less than the market price of timber of the contractual quality. Therefore, the plaintiff was claiming too much by the difference between the amount actually realised for the seventeen tons of inferior timber and the amount such seventeen tons would have realised if they had been of contractual quality.

In the result this is exactly the amount—so I would gather, though the figures are not set out in the report—which Kennedy J., allowed in reduction of damages, though he approached it from a totally different standpoint.

According to my view, therefore, the question whether in these cases the plaintiff has to prove that he was ready and willing to perform the contract, becomes little more than academic—my opinion being (as I have indicated) that he need not prove it is an essential element of his cause of action, but that he must (at all events, in most cases) prove it in order to recover substantial damages. . . .

QUESTIONS. Was there an "election" in this case to treat the repudiation as a breach? If the action was brought as appears, after the due date, is the case consistent with *Dalrymple* v. *Scott*? Suppose the defendant on March 1 has said, "I withdraw my repudiation. Please tender your documents." What results? If a repudiation is an offer to rescind, when does it become an agreement to rescind? When made or when accepted?

JOHNSTONE *v.* MILLING
England. Court of Appeal. 1886. 16 Q.B.D. 460

In June, 1881, premises, of which the plaintiff was owner subject to certain mortgages, were demised to the defendant by the plaintiff and his mortgagees for the term of twenty-one years from May 12th, 1880, subject to a proviso for sooner determination of the same, the rent being by the terms of the lease made payable to the plaintiff, until the mortgagees gave notice to the lessee in writing to pay it to them, and, upon such notice being given to the mortgagees. The lease contained a covenant by the plaintiff that after the expiration of the first four years of the term the plaintiff would, on receipt from the lessee of six calendar months' notice in writing requiring him so to do, forthwith proceed to rebuild the premises within the period and in the manner specified by the covenant. It was provided that the lessee might at the end of the first four, seven, or fourteen years of the lease determine the same by giving to the person or persons for the time being in the receipt of the rent six calendar months' notice in writing of his intention so to do.

The defendant gave the requisite notice to determine the lease at the end of the first four years. He stated in evidence at the trial that during his tenancy he spoke to the plaintiff constantly about getting the money to rebuild the premises; that the plaintiff said he was unable to do so, but that he expected a loan society who had a second mortgage on the premises might advance money; that the plaintiff's declaration of inability to get the money for rebuilding extended over the last two years and a half of the defendant's tenancy, that he made it constantly in answer to the defendant's direct question, and at other times in conversation both before and after the expiration of the four years; and that it was on consequence of such declaration that he (the defendant) gave notice to determine the lease. The defendant further stated that he continued to occupy the premises for about three months after the determination of the lease paying rent to the mortgagees; that after the lapse of the lease the plaintiff came to him and voluntarily told him that he was utterly unable to find the money, but that he (the defendant) continued the tenancy on the chance of the plaintiff's getting the money. This report relates only to the defendant's counterclaims for damages for breach of the promise to rebuild. The plaintiff replied that he had received the required notice to rebuild from the defendant.

LORD ESHER M.R.: The question before us arises entirely on the counterclaim. The claim therein set up is for damages for breach of a covenant in a lease whereby the landlord undertook to rebuild the premises upon notice. It is quite clear that there was no breach of the covenant in the ordinary sense of the term, because no notice to rebuild had been given, and the tenant had exercised the right given him by the lease of putting an end to the term at the expiration of the first four years, and consequently the lease was determined before the time at which the obligation to rebuild under the covenant would have accrued.

The lease being so put an end to, it is quite clear that the lessee could not sue the lessor for breach of the covenant in not rebuilding after the expiration of the four years. That being so, the cause of action is thus shaped on behalf of the defendant. It is alleged that a breach of the contract was committed by the plaintiff before the end of the four years, inasmuch as he had declared that he was unable and would be unable to find the money for rebuilding when the time came. It is insisted that such declaration amounted to a declaration of his intention not to perform the contract, and was intended as a repudiation of it, or that, if it was not so intended, the expressions used by the plaintiff were such that the defendant was entitled to treat them as equivalent to a repudiation of the contract; and it is accordingly contended that there was a breach of the contract by anticipation before the time for its performance arrived, for which the defendant was entitled to damages, and that the fact that the defendant afterward exercised his option of determining the lease is immaterial, for in so doing the defendant only acted for the benefit of the landlord in order to minimize the damages arising from his repudiation of the contract. The evidence shows, and the county court judge has found as a fact, that the lessor did a considerable time before the expiration of the four years, in answer to the questions of the lessee, repeatedly say that he was unable and would be unable to find the money for rebuilding, and the judge finds that in consequence the defendant surrendered the lease. It appears, however, from the evidence that he did not at once throw up the lease and give the premises into the hands of the plaintiff, but that he waited till the last six months of the four years and then gave the requisite notice to determine the term in accordance with the provisions of the lease. Upon these findings the county court judge decided that the defendant could not maintain his counterclaim. The case then went to the Divisional Court, which held that, either upon those findings, or on the inferences that ought to be drawn from them, the defendant had a right of action on the covenant, and therefore that the county court judge was wrong.

Now on what principle can it be that the defendant had a right of action on the covenant? As I have said, it cannot be on the ground that there was a breach of the covenant in the ordinary sense of the term, because the defendant never gave any notice to rebuild, and he put an end to the term, so that the time when the covenant was to be performed never arrived. Accordingly the defendant has recourse to the doctrine laid down in several cases cited, the best known of which is perhaps the case of *Hochster* v. *De La Tour* (1852), 118 E.R. 922. In those cases the doctrine relied on has been expressed in various terms more or less accurately; but I think that in all of them the effect of the language used with regard to the doctrine of anticipatory breach of contract is that a renunciation of a contract, or, in other words, a total refusal to perform it by one party before the time for performance arrives, does not, by itself, amount to a breach of contract, but may be so acted upon and adopted by the other party as a rescission of the contract as to give an immediate right of action. When one party assumes to renounce the contract—that is, by anticipation refuses to perform it, he thereby, so far as he is concerned, declares his intention then and there to rescind the contract. Such a renunciation does not of course amount to a rescission of the contract, because one party to a contract cannot by himself rescind it, but by wrongfully making such a renunciation of the contract he entitles the other party, if he pleases, to agree to the contract being put an end to, subject to the retention by him of his right to bring an action in respect of such wrongful rescission. The other party may adopt such renunciation of the contract by so acting upon it as in effect to declare that he too treats the contract as at an end, except for the purpose of bringing an action upon it for the damages sustained by him in consequence of such renunciation. He cannot, however, himself proceed with the contract on the footing that it still exists for other purposes, and also treat such renunciation as an immediate breach. If he adopts the renunciation, the contract is at an end except for the purposes of the action for such wrongful renunciation; if he does not wish to do so, he must wait for the arrival of the time when in the ordinary course a cause of action on the contract would arise. He must elect which course he will pursue. Such appears to me to be the only doctrine recognized by the law with regard to anticipatory breach of contract. We are asked, as it seems to me, by the counsel for the defendant to lay down a new principle, but I do not think we can do so consistently with the established doctrines of law on the subject. We have therefore to consider whether the defendant can bring his case within the doctrine as to anticipatory breach of contract as already laid down.

The first question is whether the plaintiff intended to repudiate the contract when he made the statements relied upon with regard to his inability to find the money for rebuilding. Did he mean to say that, whatever happened, whether he came into money or not, his intention was not to rebuild the premises? It does not seem to me that what he said naturally leads to the inference that such was his intention, and I think, having regard to the terms of his finding, that the county court judge declined to draw that inference. If he declined to do so, I think we ought not to do so, unless it is a necessary inference from what the plaintiff said. It does not appear to me that it is. If we ought not to draw that inference from what the plaintiff said, it seems to me to follow as a matter of course that the defendant was not entitled to draw it; and the result is that the defendant fails in the very first point which it is necessary for him to establish—viz., that the plaintiff at the time when he made these declarations of his inability to find the money for rebuilding intended to repudiate his liability on the contract, or that he made use of expressions entitling the defendant to suppose that he did so. That being so, his case is gone.

But, assuming the contrary, then comes the question whether the defendant elected to treat the plaintiff's statement as a wrongful repudiation of the contract. That involves first of all, the question whether he could so treat it. The contract made between the plaintiff and the defendant was the whole lease. The covenant in question is a particular covenant in the lease not going to the whole consideration. If there were an actual breach of such a covenant at the time fixed for performance, such breach would not, according to the authorities, entitle the tenant to throw up his lease. That being so, I do not hesitate to say, though it is not necessary in this case to decide the point, that an anticipatory breach could not entitle him to do so, and that it does not appear to me that he could elect to rescind part of the contract.

Therefore it seems to me that the defendant could not elect to put an end to the contract in consequence of what the plaintiff stated. But whether he could do so or not, it seems to me that in fact he did not. He did not renounce the lease or give up the premises. He did not do any act which affected the existence of the contract. He made no declaration of intention to treat it as rescinded except for the purpose of bringing his action upon it. On the contrary, at the time fixed by the contract he gave the requisite notice to determine the lease.

I think, therefore, that on every point necessary to establish his counterclaim the defendant fails. For these reasons, with great deference to the Divisional Court, before whom these points do not appear to have been developed so clearly as they have been before us, I think their decision cannot be supported, and that the judgment of the county court judge was correct.

[The concurring opinions of Bowen and Cotton L.JJ. are omitted.]

SYNGE *v.* SYNGE
England. Court of Appeal. [1894] 1 Q.B. 466

The claim in this action was on an ante-nuptial promise, made by the defendant in consideration of marriage, to leave by will to the plaintiff a certain house and land for her lifetime. It was alleged that the defendant had conveyed his whole estate and interest in the property to third persons, and thereby incapacitated himself from keeping his promise; and the plaintiff claimed a declaration that she was entitled to a life estate in the premises commencing on the death of her husband, and that the conveyance thereof was subject to her life estate, and in the alternative, the plaintiff claimed damages for breach of agreement. Mathew J. gave judgment for the defendant and plaintiff appealed.

KAY L.J. delivered the judgment of the Court: . . . We are of opinion . . . that accordingly there was a binding contract on the defendant's part to leave to his wife the house and land at Ardfield for her life. Counsel elect to ask for damages only. Sir R. Synge had all his lifetime to perform this contract; but, in order to perform it, he must in his lifetime make a disposition in favour of Lady Synge. If he died without having done so, he would have broken his contract. The breach would be omitting in his lifetime to make such a disposition. True, it would only take effect at his death; but the breach must take place in his lifetime, and as by the conveyance to his daughters he put it absolutely out of his power to perform this contract, Lady Synge, according to two well-known decisions (*Hochster* v. *De La Tour* (1852), 118 E.R. 922, and *Frost* v. *Knight* (1872), 7 Exch. 111), had a right to treat that conveyance as an absolute breach of contract, and to sue at once for damages; and as this court has both legal and equitable jurisdiction, we are of opinion that such relief should be granted.

We have not before us the materials for assessing such damages. The amount must depend on the value of the possible life estate which Lady Synge would be entitled to if she survived her husband. Their comparative ages, would, of course, be a chief factor in such a calculation. There must be an inquiry as to the proper amount of damages.

Sir R. Synge must pay the costs of the action here and in the court below.

[The appeal was allowed. Part of the opinion has been omitted.]

QUESTIONS. What is the effect of repudiation of a unilaterial contract? Can you speak of "election" in such cases? For example, if A, for value received, makes a promissory note payable to B in six years time, and A repudiates his liability the day after making the note, will an action lie at once? For what? *Ex hypothesi* in such cases the promise is independent. Was it not so in *Synge* v. *Synge*?

ROTH & CO. *v.* TAYSEN, TOWNSEND & CO.

England. Court of Appeal. 1896. 1 Comm. Cas. 306

This was an action for damages for the non-acceptance by the defendants, Grant and Grahame, of a cargo of maize. The alleged contract was contained in telegrams which passed between the parties on May 23, 1895, and the trial judge and the Court of Appeal found it to be a contract to ship the cargo by a named boat, the ship to be ready to load on July 15, and the buyers to have the power of cancelling on Aug. 15 if the ship was not ready to load by that day. On May 29 defendants repudiated. The plaintiff did not sue until July 24 and did not resell the cargo until September 5, the last day in which a delivery might have been made under the contract. The resale on September 5 was at a loss of £3807 3s. 8d. The trial court (Mathew J.) fixed the damages at £1557 which would have been the amount of the loss if the cargo had been sold on July 24, when the plaintiffs issued the writ.

Against this judgment the defendants, Grant & Grahame, appealed on the ground that there was no binding contract between the parties, and that the damages were excessive. The damages, they contended, if payable, were £688 only, the amount of the loss if the cargo had been sold on May 29, when they repudiated the contract. The plaintiffs entered a cross-appeal, claiming by way of damages £3807 3s. 8d., the amount of the loss sustained by the sale of the cargo on September 5.

LORD ESHER M.R.: . . . Then comes the question of damages. When there is a repudiation which the other party chooses to treat as a breach, the primary rule is that the damages are the difference between the contract price and the market price of the goods at the date of the breach. If the repudiation takes place before the day of delivery, the other party has the right to bring an action immediately, and it follows that he has the right to have his damages assessed at the time he brings his action. In such a case the damages are not the difference between the contract and market price on the day the action is brought. It is the duty of the jury to assess them, having regard to, and making allowance for, the fact that the party plaintiff is receiving damages before the date of delivery has arrived. There is this further rule. The party who has treated a repudiation as a breach is bound to do what is reasonable to prevent the damages from being inflamed or increased. Now, did the plaintiffs do what was unreasonable in declining to sell till September 5? . . .

The evidence before the judge was that the market was falling steadily from day to day and from week to week, and was still falling when the writ was issued. Any one acquainted with the market must have seen the strong probability that the market would continue to fall. The plaintiffs had no right to suppose that the market would begin to rise, and no ordinary business man who was not a speculator would have thought that it was likely to do so. Buyers were refusing to come forward, being of opinion that they would have to sell at a still lower price. The judge had the right to come to the conclusion, as a jury, that ordinary business men (such as the plaintiffs), who were desirous of diminishing the loss, would have sold the maize at an earlier date, and I cannot undertake to say that his finding was wrong. The appeal and the cross-appeal therefore fail.

LOPES L.J.: . . . What are the plaintiffs' rights? Ever since the case of *Hochster* v. *De La Tour* (1852), 118 E.R. 922, it has been the rule that if a payor repudiates a contract and the payee accepts his repudiation, the payee may bring an action. If no time has been fixed for the fulfilment of the contract, the plaintiff is entitled to such damage as he has sustained calculated at the date of the breach; if a time has been fixed for fulfilment, the damages are the loss of the plaintiff calculated as at the date of fulfilment. Here the breach was on July 24. The plaintiffs were bound to take reasonable steps to mitigate the damages; and, if they could have sold the cargo at any time previous to the date of fulfilment of the contract, or about the time of the breach, they ought to have done so. The learned judge held that they might have sold, and that they ought to have done so, about July 24. It is said for the plaintiffs that, though there is that rule of law, there was no evidence upon which a judge or jury could hold that it would have been prudent for the plaintiffs to sell. Of course, it is true that if the plaintiffs had sold and the market had then risen, they might have been told that they were wrong to sell; but I think that they were indiscreet in holding on when the market was falling, and that they would have been well advised if they had sold at an earlier date. The learned judge has held that they did not act reasonably, and I am not prepared to say that he was wrong. I think the amount of damages which he awarded was right.

RIGBY L.J.: ... The only question, then, is as to the measure of damages. Now, taking in its full effect in favour of the plaintiffs the rule laid down in *Roper* v. *Johnson* (1873), L.R. 8 C.P. 167, it may be that prima facie, this being the breach of a contract to deliver goods, the damages are to be assessed as at the agreed date of delivery. But here the plaintiffs put an end to the contract at an earlier date. Judges have always held that a person availing himself of his right to accept repudiation of a contract must take measures to mitigate the damages which he has sustained by the breach. It is true that by so doing he may take some risk upon himself, but the tribunal will take that fact into consideration. In the present case there seems to be sufficient evidence though it is not conclusive, to justify the learned judge in holding that the plaintiffs ought to have sold the cargo when they put an end to the contract by accepting the defendants' repudiation. I gather that there was evidence that the market was falling, and that the state of things did not render a recovery of prices probable within a reasonable time. I cannot accept the argument of Mr. Bigham [of counsel for the plaintiffs] that it is sufficient to show that the plaintiffs acted to the best of their judgment. The standard which one must use in these cases is the conduct of an ordinary prudent man under similar circumstances. The result is that both appeals must be dismissed.

Appeal and cross-appeal dismissed.

[Only that part of the case dealing with the question of damages is reproduced.]

MELACHRINO *v.* NICKOLL and KNIGHT

England. King's Bench Division. [1920] 1 K.B. 693

Melachrino and Kaniskeri, as sellers, made two contracts with Nickoll and Knight, each dated November 24, 1916, and precisely similar in terms except as to price.

The form of the contracts used was the printed form of contract issued by the Incorporated Oil Seed Association for adoption by persons engaged in the oil-seed trade in sales of cargoes of Egyptian cotton seed with slight variations adopted by the parties. Each contract was for the sale of half a cargo of Egyptian cotton seed per steamship Asaos, to be shipped by the above steamship from Alexandria expected ready to load during December, 1916. Payment to be made in London fourteen days from the seed being ready for delivery in exchange for shipping documents and for delivery order. By clause 11 of the contracts it was provided that in default of fulfilment of contracts by either party the other party should after giving notice in writing, have the right of resale or repurchase as the case might be and the defaulters should make good the loss if any on demand and that in the event of the right of resale or repurchase not being exercised the damages if any for which the party in default might be liable should be settled by arbitration. On December 14, 1916, the sellers repudiated the contracts and wrongfully refused to deliver the cotton seed. On the same day the buyers accepted the repudiation and there was thus an anticipatory breach.

The arbitrators found that an average voyage from Alexandria to the United Kingdom was at the time about three or four weeks; that the seed might have been expected to be delivered at any time between January 10 and February 10, 1917; that the market price was above the contract price on December 14, 1916; that it began to fall on December 18, and was below the contract price during the whole of the period between January 10 and February 10, 1917. The buyers did not give notice in writing under clause 11 to repurchase and did not buy against the sellers but in accepting repudiation on December 14, 1916, claimed arbitration.

The sellers contended before the arbitrators that inasmuch as the buyers did not buy against the contracts, the proper time for assessing the measure of damages was the time at which the cotton seed ought to have been delivered.

The buyers contended that the measure of damages should be assessed at the time the sellers wrongfully refused to deliver the cotton seed, namely, on December 14, 1916.

BAILHACHE J.: . . . Upon these facts the question arises: Are the buyers' damages to be fixed with reference to the market prices on December 14, 1916, or with reference to the prices ruling at the time when the goods might be expected to be delivered? If the former the damages are substantial, if the latter nominal. The arbitrators have assessed the damages as at the date of the anticipatory breach.

There was a market for the goods and in that case the prima facie rules for the measurement of damages as laid down in s. 51 of the *Sale of Goods Act, 1893,* vary according to whether there is a fixed time for delivery or not. If there is no fixed time the measure is the difference between the contract price and the market price at the time of refusal to deliver. The first point to determine therefore is whether this was a contract of that kind. In my opinion it was not. The time was not certain but it was fixed by reference to the happening of an event—namely, the arrival of the Asoas in the United Kingdom. I take it that when s. 51 speaks of no time being fixed for delivery it refers to those contracts in which no mention of time is made and which therefore are to be performed within the indefinite period known as a reasonable time under the circumstances.

In regard to other cases of which this is one the prima facie measure of damages is said to be the difference between the contract price and the market price at the time the goods ought to have been delivered—in this case the period between January 10 and February 10, 1917. In a constantly fluctuating market and if the prices during that period had ruled higher than the contract prices there might have been some difficulty in determining the proper price to be taken, but in this case that point does not arise, as at all times between those dates the market prices were below the contract prices.

Sect. 51 does not in terms deal with an anticipatory breach, and in the case of a breach by effluxion of time it is clear that it makes no difference to the measure of damages whether a buyer goes into the market or is content to take the difference in price without troubling to buy against the defaulting seller. The question to be decided is whether the same rule applies in the case of an anticipatory breach.

An anticipatory breach occurs when the seller refuses to deliver before the contractual time for delivery has arrived and the buyer accepts his refusal as a breach of contract.

In that case the following rules are well established, subject of course to any express provisions to the contrary in any particular contract.

Immediately upon the anticipatory breach the buyer may bring his action whether he buys against the seller or not.

It is the duty of the buyer to go into the market and buy against the defaulting seller if a reasonable opportunity offers. This is expressed by the phrase "It is the buyer's duty to mitigate damages." In that event the damages are assessed with reference to the market price on the date of the repurchase. If the buyer does not perform his duty in this respect the seller is none the less entitled to have damages assessed as at the date when a fresh contract might and ought to have been made.

As a corollary to this rule the buyer may if he pleases go into the market and buy against the seller; as he is bound to do so to mitigate damages, so he is entitled to do so to cover himself against his commitments or to secure the goods. In that case again the damages are assessed with reference to the market price at the date of the repurchase.

It is also settled law that when default is made by the seller by refusal to deliver within the contract time the buyer is under no duty to accept the repudiation and buy against him but may claim the difference between the contract price and the market price at the date when under the contract the goods should have been delivered.

Further, in the case of an anticipatory breach the contract is at an end and the defaulting seller cannot take advantage of any subsequent circumstances which would have afforded him a justification for non-performance of his contract had his repudiation not been accepted.

In logical strictness it would appear to follow that equally the defaulting seller cannot take advantage of a fall in the market before the due date for delivery to escape liability for damages.

It looks therefore at first sight as though the date at which the difference between the contract price and the market price ought to be taken for the assessment of damages when the buyer does not buy against the seller should follow by analogy the rule adopted where the buyer goes into the market and buys, or where the breach is failure to deliver at the due date and should be at or about the date when the buyer intimates his acceptance of the repudiation though he does not actually go into the market against the seller. If so, in this case the date would be about Dec. 14, when the buyer claimed arbitration and so the arbitrators have found.

As against this line of reasoning it must be remembered that the object of damages is to place a person whose contract is broken in as nearly as possible the same position as if it had been performed. This result is secured by measuring damages either at the date of the repurchase, in the case of repurchase on an anticipatory breach, or at the date when the goods ought to have been delivered when there is no anticipatory breach whether there is a repurchase or not. In these cases the buyer gets a new contract as nearly as may be like the broken contract and the defaulting seller pays the extra expenses incurred by the buyer in restoring his position.

Where however there is an anticipatory breach but no buying against the defaulting seller, and the price falls below the contract price between the date of the anticipatory breach and the date when the goods ought to have been delivered, the adoption of the date of the anticipatory breach as the date at which the market price ought to be taken would put the buyer in a better position than if his contract had been duly performed. He would if that date were adopted be given a profit and retain his money wherewith to buy the goods . . . if so minded on the fall of the market. It would be in effect, to use a homely phrase, to allow him to eat his cake and have it. Perhaps it is better to avoid figures of speech however picturesque and to say, to make a profit from the anticipatory breach while the contract if duly performed would have shown a loss—a position which is, I think, irreconcilable with the principles upon which damages are awarded as between buyer and seller.

In my opinion the true rule is that where there is an anticipatory breach by a seller to deliver goods for which there is a market at a fixed date the buyer without buying against the seller may bring his action at once, but that if he does so his damages must be assessed with reference to the market price of the goods at the time phen they ought to have been delivered under the contract. If the action comes to trial before the contractual date for delivery has arrived the Court must arrive at that price as best it can.

To this rule there is one exception for the benefit of the defaulting seller—namely, that if he can show that the buyer acted unreasonably in not buying against him the date to be taken is the date at which the buyer ought to have gone into the market to mitigate damages.

I have discussed the position on principle apart from authority because, in my limited experience, I do not remember a case precisely like this.

I might perhaps have contented myself with basing my judgment upon the authority of *Roper* v. *Johnson* (1873), L.R. 8 C.P. 167, and I should have done so but for the fact that I am not sure that when that case was decided one year after *Brown* v. *Muller* (1872), L.R. 7 Ex. 319, the distinction between an accepted and unaccepted repudiation was as well established as it has since become. There are some observations in the judgment in that case which would not, I venture to think, now be supported, and the case turned largely on where the burden of proof lay. Subject however to these criticisms *Roper* v. *Johnson* seems to me to support the conclusion at which I have arrived. The result in this case is that damages are nominal.

TURNER *v*. BLADIN. 1951. 82 C.L.R. 463 (Victoria, High Court of Australia). An oral contract made in October, 1945, provided for the sale to the defendant of the plant and goodwill of a quarry business carried on by the plaintiffs at Ferntree Gully. The full price was £7,500, of which £2,100 was paid as a deposit, and £500 was to be paid in October,

1946, and £500 every six months thereafter for five years from the date of the deposit, when the balance would become due. The defendant entered into and remained in possession until he sold the business in September, 1948 to F. C. Kerr Pty. Ltd. The defendant defaulted in his payments and the plaintiffs brought this action for specific performance. At the date of the writ six instalments had become payable. Since then three further instalments had become payable, leaving only the instalments payable in October, 1951, and April, 1952, still outstanding. Held, for the plaintiffs. The defendant was ordered to pay to the plaintiffs within twenty-eight days nine instalments of £500 with interest at three per cent on £5,400 from October 1, 1945 to the date of judgment, and the plaintiffs were given liberty to apply to the Supreme Court in respect of the instalments and interest to become payable in the future. The *Instruments Act* (which embodied the *Statute of Frauds*) was no defence. THE COURT: "We are of opinion that the contract was specifically enforceable. We reject the contention that a contract, some part of which is not immediately performable, is not capable of specific performance. In our opinion proceedings for the specific performance of a contract which is of such a kind that it can be specifically enforced can be commenced as soon as one party threatens to refuse to perform the contract or any part thereof or actually refuses to perform any promise for which the time of performance has arrived. The court can then make a decree that the contract ought to be specifically performed and carried into execution, and can so mould its decree and order such inquiries, accounts and other proceedings under the decree as may be necessary to carry into effect all the promises of both parties whether they are presently performable or are only performable in the future.

"The statement of Dixon J. in *J. C. Williamson Ltd.* v. *Lukey* (1931), 45 C.L.R. 282, at p. 297, that 'the remedy (of specific performance) is not available unless complete relief can be given, and the contract carried into full and final execution so that the parties are put in the relation contemplated by their agreement' relied upon by counsel for the appellant lends no support to his submission. His Honour was discussing the kind of contract that is capable of specific performance and not the time at which a suit for the specific performance of such a contract may be instituted. In the present case the only terms of the agreement not presently performable at the date of the writ were the terms for the payment of the instalments which had not then become payable and *Nives* v. *Nives* (1880), 15 Ch.D. 649, is a direct authority that a vendor whose purchase money is payable by instalments, some of which are not yet payable, can obtain a decree for specific performance and an order for payment of the instalments that are overdue, the plaintiff to have liberty to apply in respect of future instalments as they become payable.

"We are of opinion that where the contract is of such a kind that the purchaser can sue for specific performance, the vendor can also sue for specific performance, although the claim is merely to recover a sum of money and that he can do so although at the date of the writ the contract has been fully performed except for the payment of the purchase money or some part thereof. The law is, we think, correctly stated by Nicholas J. (as he then was) in *Eastwood-Epping Ice & Fuel Co. Ltd.* v. *Pittock* (1938), 38 S.R. (N.S.W.) 671, at p. 677: 'The right of a vendor to sue for a decree in equity that payment should be made according to a contract, although it is a claim for a money payment only, appears to be an additional right recognized in every case in which the other party to the contract might have sued for specific performance had he been the party complaining of the breach (see *Fry on Specific Performance*, 6th ed. (1921) p. 33; *Maitland on Equity*, 1st ed. (1936), p. 239). In *Clifford* v. *Turrell*, 62 E.R. 826, it was said by Knight-Bruce V.C.—"A case is stated in which, setting the Statute of Frauds out of the question, a bill might have been maintained by the defendant against the plaintiff, to compel him to execute the assignment. That, therefore, is a reason to compel the performance of the terms upon which the plaintiff agreed to execute the assignment." This decision was confirmed by Lord Lyndhurst (1845), 9 Jur. 633, on this aspect upon the ground that damages would have proved an inadequate remedy. But in *Walker* v. *Eastern Counties Railway Co.*, 67 E.R. 1300 at p. 1303., Wigram V.C. used similar reasoning to that of Knight-Bruce V.C., saying that the jurisdiction cannot be denied in a converse case in which the vendor is plaintiff.' The case of *Cogent v. Gibson* 55 E.R. 485, is directly in point. There Lord Romilly held that a contract for the sale of a patent was specifically enforceable at the suit of the vendor, although all he required was the payment of the purchase money. The case of *Brough* v. *Oddy*, 39 E.R. 22, was relied on by counsel for the appellant. But the contract there in question was simply a contract under which one party upon the happening of an event agreed to pay periodical sums of money to the other party. It was not a contract of the class which would have attracted the equitable remedy of specific performance at the suit of either party."

KLOEPFER WHOLESALE HARDWARE & AUTOMOTIVE CO. *v.* ROY

Ontario. Supreme Court of Canada. [1952] 3 D.L.R. 705

[This case is reproduced on page 92.]

CHAPTER 10

INFANTS' CONTRACTS

The law does not recognize that everyone is equally able to bind himself or liable to be held bound by a contract. As you have already seen in *Holt* v. *Ward Clarencieux* and in *Rex* v. *Rash* an infant is not always bound by his promises, and this chapter carries on with an exploration of the problems of infants' contracts generally. It should be clearly understood, however, that this chapter makes no attempt to deal with the whole problem of capacity to contract. Time does not permit a proper study of this problem in a first year course.

Apart from contracts by persons of unsound mind or by persons under the influence of alcohol, or some other drug and by married women (see Married Women's Property legislation and the courses in real property) the modern problems arise from two classes of case: contracts by corporations, which are usually dealt with in second years courses in company law, and contracts by governments, including municipal corporations, which are usually not dealt with in any course, unless they come in incidentally, in Constitutional Law, Administrative Law or Municipal Law, if such courses are offered.

THE STATUTE OF FRAUDS
Ontario. Revised Statutes. 1960. Chapter 381

7. No action shall be maintained whereby to charge a person upon promise made after full age to pay a debt contracted during infancy or upon a ratification after full age of a promise or simple contract made during infancy, unless the promise or ratification is made by a writing signed by the party to be charged therewith or by his agent duly authorized to make the promise or ratification.

SALE OF GOODS ACT
Ontario. Revised Statutes. 1960. Chapter 358

3. (1) Capacity to buy and sell is regulated by the general law concerning capacity to contract, and to transfer and acquire property; provided that where necessaries are sold and delivered to an infant or minor or to a person who by reason of mental incapacity or drunkenness is incompetent to contract, he must pay a reasonable price therefor.

(2) Necessaries in this section mean goods suitable to the conditions in life of such infant or minor or other person, and to his actual requirements at the time of the sale and delivery.

INFANTS ACT
British Columbia. Revised Statutes. 1960. Chapter 193

2. All contracts, whether by specialty or by simple contract, entered into by infants for the repayment of money lent or to be lent, or for goods supplied or to be supplied (other than contracts for necessaries), and all accounts stated with infants, shall be absolutely void: Provided always

that this enactment shall not invalidate any contract into which an infant may, by any existing or future Statute, or by the rules of the common law or equity, enter, except such as now by law are voidable. [37 & 38 Vict., c. 62, s. 1.]

3. No action shall be brought whereby to charge any person upon any promise made after full age to pay any debt contracted during infancy, or upon any ratification made after full age of any promise or contract made during infancy, whether there shall or shall not be any new consideration for such promise or ratification after full age. [37 & 38 Vict., c. 62, s. 2.]

4. Where a minor over the age of sixteen years, who has no parent or legal guardian, or who does not reside with his parent or guardian, enters into an engagement, written or verbal, to perform any service or work, he shall be liable upon the same, and shall have the benefit thereof, as if he had been of legal age, and the provisions of the last two preceding sections shall not apply to such engagement.

THE LOUDEN MANUFACTURING COMPANY *v.* MILMINE

Ontario. High Court. 1907. 14 O.L.R. 552
Ontario. Divisional Court. 1907. 15 O.L.R. 53

RIDDELL J.: This action is for the price of certain articles of merchandise sold to the son on the son's sole credit and charged to him in the books of the plaintiff. It was sought to make the father liable either as an actual partner of his son or from his holding himself out as such partner. At the trial, I held that the father was not liable, and the action must be dismissed against him with costs.

As regards the son the plea of infancy was set up, to which was answered ratification after full age. The document relied upon is a letter written in answer to one by the solicitor for the plaintiffs, as follows:

"Messrs William S. Milmine and Alex. Milmine,
Grassey Corners, Ont.

Dear Sirs,

We have been instructed to demand prompt payment from you of $287.68 owing to the Louden Manfg. Co. We have to ask that you will give this your immediate attention, as our instructions are peremptory. Remittance will be made to our office.

Yours truly,
McKinnon & Howitt."

The answer of the son is as follows:

"Grassie, Jan. 26, 1907.

McKinnon & Howitt,
Guelph, Ont.

Dear Sirs:

Your letter of the 23rd inst. received and contents noted, and in reply I would say that the company have apparently misinformed you relative to my [the word has originally been written 'this'] account. As to your reason for putting Alex. Milmine's name in my letter, I do not know, but I would kindly ask for an explanation from you, and it will be to the best interest of company if they gave you the right explanation of this case, and not try such high-handed tricks as apparently they are trying to work.

Yours truly,
Wm. S. Milmine."

Does this letter—silly, bumptious and ill-mannered as it is—constitute a ratification within the statute?

I adopt as the test what is said by Rolfe B., giving the judgment of the court in *Harris* v. *Wall* (1847), 1 Ex. 122; 154 E.R. 51, at p. 55: "Any act or declaration which recognizes the existence of the promise as binding as a ratification of it, as, in the case of agency, anything which recognizes as binding an act done by an agent, or by a party who has acted as agent, is an adoption of it. Any written instrument, signed by the party, which in the case of adults would have amounted to the adoption of the act of a party acting as agent, will in the case of an infant who has attained his majority amount to a ratification." . . .

Rowe v. *Hopwood* (1868), L.R. 4 Q.B. 1, is the case nearest to this which I have found. There goods had been supplied to the defendant while an infant; when he came of age an account with items and prices was submitted to him, at the foot of which he signed the following: "Particulars of account to the end of 1867, amounting to £162 11s. 6d., I certify to be correct and satisfactory."

It was held that this did not amount to a recognition of the debt as an existing liability so as to be a ratification of the contract within the statute; and Cockburn C.J. says, p. 3: "There ought to be at least on the part of the debtor an admission of an existing liability, and we ought not to strain the meaning of the words in the document signed by the debtor, so as to defeat the operation of the statute passed for his protection."

Lush, Hannanand Hayes, JJ., concurred.

I think the present case is much weaker for the plaintiff than that just cited. No doubt there is a recognition that an account exists and that it has been charged against the defendant, but there cannot be imputed into the writing "a recognition of an existing liability"—"an enforceable promise," without a "straining of the meaning of the document signed by the debtor."

But it was argued after the defendant came of age he retained and sold certain of the goods, and this gives the plaintiffs a cause of action for at least so much of the goods as he had in hand at majority.

I cannot follow this argument. If the acts of the defendant be claimed as a ratification, it was not in writing as required by the statute. The plaintiffs do not and did not claim to rescind the contract of sale, but affirm the contract and insist that the defendant pay the price of the goods. That right can exist in a case like the present only if the defendant owns the goods, i.e., if the property has passed. There is no pretence of fraud, and I cannot see that any action in the nature of trespass trover or assumpsit for goods bargained and sold or for money had and received can lie. The action should be dismissed.

The action will be dismissed with costs on the High Court scale to both the defendants.

[The plaintiffs appealed.]

MEREDITH C.J. delivered the judgment of the Court: We agree with the conclusion to which the learned Judge came, that the letter which is relied upon as a ratification of the contract for the purchase of the goods sued for was not sufficient to satisfy the provisions of the statute.

Upon the other question, which is not raised upon the pleadings, as the pleadings stood we would entirely agree with the learned Judge. The claim which is made is one quite inconsistent with the claim presented in the pleadings, which treat the contract as a subsisting one. The alternative claim now set up is one which treats the contract as repudiated and claims that the goods which remained in the possession of the respondent at the time he became of age revested in the appellants.

Upon principle, and the authorities cited by Mr. McKinnon make it also abundantly clear, it must be that if an infant avails himself of the right he has to avoid a contract which he has entered into and upon the faith of which he has obtained goods, he is bound to restore the goods which he has in possession at the time he so repudiates. If that were not so, a man might buy a farm for a large sum of money, give a mortgage upon it shortly before coming of age, then repudiate the contract, and insist upon holding the property. The authorities are all the other way, and establish that the effect of repudiating the contract is to revest the property in the vendor.

No application was made to the trial Judge to amend by setting up the alternative claim, but it would be a misfortune, the whole of the evidence being in now, if this matter of trifling amount should have to be investigated again, with all the attendant expense; and, therefore, although it is very late, we think it is not improper that the appellants should have leave, upon proper terms, to set up the alternative claim upon which they now rely.

There is some difficulty in determining the quantity of goods which the respondent had on hand when he attained his majority, but we think that $75, upon his own testimony, fairly represents the value of them, and we therefore think that there should be judgment for the plaintiffs for that sum.

There should be no costs to either party. There should be none to the appellants, because they have persisted in their action upon the contract, which was taken down to trial and was pressed there and here. The respondent should not get his costs because he is liable ultimately for the $75.

We think, therefore that the proper judgment will be to give leave to amend in the way indicated, and direct judgment to be entered upon the alternative claim for $75, without costs of the action, and that there should be no costs of the appeal to either party.

STEINBERG *v.* SCALA (LEEDS), LTD.
England. Court of Appeal. [1923] 2 Ch. 452

On February 5, 1920, the plaintiff, Miss Tulip Steinberg, who was then of the age of eighteen years, applied for an allotment of 500 ordinary shares of £1 each in the defendant company on the terms of a prospectus dated January 21, 1920, issued by the defendant company. Under the terms of the prospectus the sum of 2s. per share was payable on application, the sum of 4s. per share on February 24, 1920, and the sum of 4s. per share on April 24, 1920. The defendant company accepted the application and on February 18, 1920, allotted to the plaintiff 500 ordinary shares of £1 each in the capital of the defendant company. The plaintiff paid the defendant company the sum of £50 on making the application and two further sums of £100 each on February 24 and April 24, 1920, as provided by the terms of the prospectus. Her name was duly entered on the register as the holder of the shares. She did not attend any meeting of the defendant company and did not receive any dividend on the shares.

On December 13, 1921, the plaintiff by her solicitors wrote a letter to the solicitors of the defendant company repudiating the allotment of the shares and claiming the return of the £250 paid by her to the defendant company. The defendant company refused to take steps for the cancellation of the allotment of the 500 shares or the removal of the name of the plaintiff from the register or to repay the £250.

On August 1, 1922, the plaintiff by her next friend issued the writ in this action in the Leeds District Registry, claiming (1) a declaration that the allotment to her of the 500 shares standing in her name in the register of shareholders of the defendant company was not binding on her and ought to be cancelled; (2) that the register of the defendant company might be ordered to be rectified by striking out the name of the plaintiff as a shareholder in respect of the said 500 ordinary shares; (3) that the defendant company might be ordered to repay to the plaintiff the sum of £250 paid by her to the defendant company in respect of the shares together with interest at the rate of 5 per cent per annum from the several dates of payment thereof till the date of repayment; and (4) that the defendant company might be restrained by injunction from enforcing any calls made, or to be made, on the plaintiff in respect of the shares.

The action was tried by Roche J. for Astbury J. at the Leeds Assizes on March 21, 1923. It appeared from the evidence at the trial that fully paid shares of the defendant company had been dealt with at prices ranging from £1 down to 9s. or 10s. a share.

ROCHE J.: . . . The case must therefore be decided upon the basis that a minor has become a shareholder; that she has been entered upon the register of the defendant company and has remained so entered for at least eighteen months, or more, without protest on her part.

The question is whether, under these circumstances, she is entitled to the relief claimed, which resolves itself ultimately into a declaration that she is entitled to avoid the contract, giving her a right to have her name removed from the register, and whether she is further entitled to recover the £250 which she claims. On the authority of Stirling J. in *Hamilton* v. *Vaughan-Sherrin Electrical Engineering Co.*, [1894] 3 Ch. 589, I am compelled to decide that the plaintiff is so entitled. I need not say that I should not venture to question the decision of that very learned judge without great hesitation and I do not question it. I only say that if there were not that direct authority it would seem to be a very arguable point whether the holding of the shares, and the remaining on the register of a company without protest and with all the opportunities of taking part in voting and receiving payment of a dividend, are not an enjoyment of a consideration, and whether such employment is not sufficient to preclude a plaintiff, though an infant, from recovering moneys paid on the ground that no consideration has been enjoyed at the time when the application for the return of the money or rescission of the contract is made: whether, in short, the infant under such circumstances can say that no consideration had been enjoyed and that the consideration for the contract has wholly failed. It is unnecessary and wholly impossible for me to consider that matter because I can see no distinction between *Hamilton* v. *Vaughan-Sherrin Electrical Engineering Co.* and the present case. It is true, as Mr. Perks has pointed out in his very helpful argument, that in *Hamilton* v. *Vaughan-Sherrin Electrical Engineering Co.* the liquidator had, before the application to the Court, removed the name of the infant shareholder from the register, but that in my judgment makes no difference. The liquidator and the Court had merely done in two successive stages what I am, in effect, doing in one. The cases cited by Mr. Perks of *Holmes* v. *Blogg* (1818), 8 Taunt, 508; 129 E.R. 481; *Ex parte Taylor* (1856), 8 D.M. & G. 254; 44 E.R. 388; *Corpe* v. *Overton* (1833), 10 Bing. 252; 131 E.R.

901, are all cases which quite rightly received attention in argument, but in my judgment they do not require further discussion by me because the whole matter is, in my opinion, summed up and decided by *Hamilton* v. *Vaughan-Sherrin Electrical Engineering Co.*

I therefore give judgment for the plaintiff for the return of £250 and a declaration that she has a right to rescind the contract to take shares.

[The defendant company appealed.]

LORD STERNDALE M.R.: I think in this case the appeal must be allowed and judgment must be entered for the defendant company. In saying that I think I am agreeing with what would have been Roche J.'s own opinion if he had not felt himself bound, as indeed I think he was bound, by the decision of Stirling J. in *Hamilton* v. *Vaughan-Sherrin Electrical Engineering Co.* I think I see a possible—I will not say more than that—distinction between this case and that before Stirling J. If that be not a valid distinction I am afraid I should have to say that I do not agree with that decision, although of course I differ from any judgment of Stirling J. with great hesitation and trepidation.

The action is brought for two objects: first, for rectification of the register of the defendant company by the removal therefrom of the plaintiff's name, as to which no question now arises because it is not opposed, and, secondly, for judgment for the recovery of money which the plaintiff has paid in order to become a shareholder in the company.

The plaintiff is a young lady still an infant, and when still more an infant some year or two ago she paid £50 as a payment on application for shares in the defendant company and subsequently paid a further sum of £200 for calls after the shares had been allotted to her, so that she paid altogether £250 for shares in the defendant company. There was a question as to certain further calls being made and the plaintiff, who had found the £250 out of money given to her. I think by an uncle, for the purpose of providing her with a dowry, could not find any more money, and then, awaking to the position that she had shares in a company on which there would be calls made and that she had not the money to meet them, she also awoke to the position that she was an infant and could rescind the contract, and she did so. There is no doubt that she was entitled to do so and to have the register rectified by the removal of her name therefrom. But then there came another question. She also wanted the £250 back, and, to a certain extent, I think the argument for the respondent has rather proceeded upon the assumption that the question whether she can rescind and the question whether she can recover her money back are the same. They are two quite different questions, as is pointed out by Turner L.J. in his judgment in *Ex parte Taylor*. He there says: "It is clear that an infant cannot be absolutely bound by a contract entered into during his minority. He must have a right upon his attaining his majority to elect whether he will adopt the contract or not." Then he proceeds: "It is, however, a different question whether, if an infant pays money on the footing of a contract, he can afterwards recover it back. If an infant buys an article which is not a necessary, he cannot be compelled to pay for it, but if he does pay for it during his minority he cannot on attaining his majority recover the money back." That seems to me to be only stating in other words the principle which is laid down in a number of other cases that, although the contract may be rescinded the money paid cannot be recovered back unless there has been an entire failure of the consideration for which the money has been paid. Therefore it seems to me that the question to which we have to address ourselves is: Has there been a total failure of the consideration for which the money was paid?

Now the plaintiff has had the shares; I do not mean to say she had the certificates; she could have had them at any time if she had applied for them; she has had the shares allotted to her and there is evidence that they were of some value, that they had been dealt in at from 9s. to 10s. a share. Of course her shares were only half paid up and, therefore, if she had attempted to sell them she would only have obtained half of that amount, but that is quite a tangible and substantial sum.

In those circumstances it is impossible to say that there was a total failure of consideration. If the plaintiff were a person of full age suing to recover the money back on the ground, and the sole ground, that there had been a failure of consideration it seems to me it would have been impossible for her to succeed, because she would have got the very thing for which the money was paid and would have got a thing of tangible value.

The argument for the respondent is I think to this effect: That it is necessary, in order to show that the consideration has not entirely failed, to prove that the plaintiff has not only had something which was worth value in the market and for which she could have obtained value, but that she has in fact received that value. It was admitted that if she had in this case sold the shares and received the £125 which would have been receivable according to one of the prices mentioned in evidence she could not have recovered the money back, but it is said that as she did not in fact do that and had only an opportunity of receiving that benefit, there has been a total failure of consideration. I cannot see that. If she has obtained something which has money's worth then she has received some consideration, that is, she has received the very thing for which she paid her money, and the fact that, although it was money's worth, she has not turned that money's worth into money does not seem to me to prevent it being some valuable consideration for the money which she has paid. I cannot see any difference when you come to consider whether there has been consideration or not between the position of a person of full age and an infant. The question whether there has been consideration or not must, I think, be the same in the two cases. That is, on the face of it, an opinion opposed to the decision of Stirling J. in *Hamilton* v. *Vaughan-Sherrin Electrical Engineering Co.* unless this is a distinction, that in that case there was no evidence at all that the shares had any marketable value. I do not mean to say they had none, but there is no evidence one way or the other, and the learned judge does not seem to have addressed himself to the question whether that would make any difference. He seems, as far as I can make out, rather to put as a test, whether the company was a prosperous one out of which money could be made or whether it was not. I cannot think that that is the true test and I am not quite sure that he applied it, but it looks to me rather as if he did. If the fact that these shares had a marketable value, whereas there was no such evidence in the case before Stirling J., is a valid distinction between the two cases, then that is not an authority. If that be not a valid distinction then, although I say it with great trepidation, I am afraid I do not agree with the decision of Stirling J. in *Hamilton* v. *Vaughan-Sherrin Electrical Engineering Co.*

There is only one other thing I wish to say. It was argued for the respondent that my decision is contrary to the judgment of the Court of Common Pleas in *Corpe* v. *Overton.* I do not think it is so. The £100 that was sought to be recovered in that case was in quite a different position from the money which the plaintiff sues to recover in this case. In that case there was an agreement that the infant and another person would enter into partnership, and there was also beyond that—the consideration for that agreement being, as it seems to me, the mutual promises of the parties —a further agreement that to secure the proper fulfilment of the contract when it was made because it was for a future contract, the infant should deposit £100 as a sort of security for the performance by him of the contract. That £100 seems to me to be in a totally different position from the money which was paid in this case. It is quite true that in that case, in addition to the fact of it being a deposit in the way I have mentioned, the Court did say that it was recoverable as on a total failure of consideration. I think that is quite right. The promise of the partnership was not obtained by the payment of the £100. The £100 was paid down as a deposit for the due performance of the contract by the plaintiff, and when that contract was once rescinded, of course there was no consideration for that £100 having been paid and it had to be paid back.

I do not think that my judgment in any way conflicts with *Corpe* v. *Overton*. It does or may conflict with *Hamilton* v. *Vaughan-Sherrin Electrical Engineering Co.* If it does, I regret to say that I do not agree with that case, and I think, for the reasons I have stated, that this appeal should be allowed and judgment should be entered for the defendant company with costs here and below.

[The concurring opinions of Warrington and Younger L.JJ. are omitted.]

PEARCE *v*. BRAIN

England. Divisional Court. [1929] 2 K.B. 310

The plaintiff, an infant suing by his next friend, brought this action in the county court for the recovery of a motor-cycle and side-car or in the alternative for their value on the ground that the contract under which he delivered the motor-cycle to the defendant was void under the *Infants Relief Act, 1874*, or in the alternative was voidable and had been avoided by him.

The contract in question was made on February 10, 1928, when the plaintiff exchanged his motor-cycle and side-car for a second-hand motor-car belonging to the defendant. For the purpose of the transaction it was agreed that each vehicle was of the value of £30.

The plaintiff took possession of the car and drove it away, handing over his motor-cycle to the defendant.

On February 14, 1928, after being driven by the plaintiff for about 70 miles in all, the car broke down owing to a defect in the back axle. On February 16, 1928, the plaintiff wrote repudiating the contract on the ground that he was an infant when he entered into the contract.

He claimed the return of the motor-cycle and offered to return the damaged car to the defendant. The defendant refused, and the plaintiff then brought this action in the county court, which was tried at Clerkenwell by a judge and jury. The jury found that the car was not a "necessary" for the plaintiff, that the defendant gave no warranty as to the car and that it was worth £15 only, but that the motor-cycle and side-car was worth £30. It was admitted by the plaintiff that the defendant had acted in good faith.

The county court judge held that the contract was one of exchange and not, as the plaintiff alleged, a sale of the motor-cycle for £30 with a sale of the car by the defendant for £30; that it was void under the *Infants Relief Act, 1847*, s. 1, but that as the plaintiff had enjoyed the benefit of the contract he was not entitled to recover the consideration which he had given: *Valentini* v. *Canali* (1889), 24 Q.B.D. 166.

The plaintiff appealed from this decision, the material grounds of appeal being that the county court judge was wrong in law in holding (1) that notwithstanding the proved inadequacy of the consideration the contract was for the benefit of the infant so as to disentitle him to the protection of the *Infants Relief Act, 1874*; (2) that notwithstanding the defect in the rear axle of the car at the time of the contract, the plaintiff by using the car on five days without knowledge of the defect took benefit under the contract so as to deprive him of the protection of the Act; (3) that the inability of the plaintiff to return the car in the same condition as at the contract disentitled him to the protection of the Act, although the defect causing the inability was in existence at the time of the contract.

SWIFT J.: The only point left is the contention of the plaintiff that, as he was an infant at the time the contract was entered into, the contract was rendered void by s. 1 of the *Infants Relief Act, 1874*. It was said that the property in the motor bicycle never passed from the plaintiff to the defendant and that the plaintiff was entitled to have it back by virtue of s. 1 of the Act, which provided: "All contracts, whether by specialty or by simple contract, henceforth entered into by infants for the repayment of money lent or to be lent, or for goods supplied to to be supplied (other than contracts for necessaries), and all accounts stated with infants, shall be absolutely void: Provided always, that this enactment shall not invalidate any contract into which an infant may, by any existing or future statute, or by the rules of common law or equity, enter, except such as now by law are voidable."

In his able argument counsel for the plaintiff contended that the transaction was one which was void under that section, and that therefore the plaintiff had never ceased to be the owner of the motor bicycle and was entitled to have it back. I am quite clear that the transaction was, as the county court judge has found, a contract of exchange of goods. But it comes within the words "goods supplied or to be supplied," which are as much applicable to exchange as to sale.

If I were at liberty to decide this case without authority, I should be inclined to accept the argument for the plaintiff and decide that the contract being by way of exchange it was void under the Act and that no property passed. [See contra *Stocks* v. *Wilson* [1913] 2 K.B. 235.—F.P. Editor of the Law Reports.] But I cannot see any difference in principle between the recovery of a chattel given in exchange and the recovery of money paid as the purchase price of goods. If the contract were void by statute I should have thought, apart from authority, that money paid could have been recovered as money had and received to the use of an infant plaintiff. Money paid under a merely voidable contract is in a very different position. But there is direct authority that money paid under a void contract cannot be recovered unless there is a total failure of consideration. In *Valentini* v. *Canali*, which was decided by Lord Coleridge C.J. and Bowen L.J. sitting as a Divisional Court, Lord Coleridge said: "The construction which has been contended for on behalf of the plaintiff would involve a violation of natural justice. When an infant has paid for something and has consumed or used it, it is contrary to natural justice that he should recover back the money which he has paid. Here the infant plaintiff who claimed to recover back the money which he had paid to the defendant had had the use of a quantity of furniture for some months. He could not give back this benefit or replace the defendant in the position in which he was before the contract. The object of the statute would seem to have been to restore the law for the protection of infants upon which judicial decisions were considered to have imposed qualifications. The legislature never intended in making provisions for this purpose to sanction a cruel injustice."

That case the county court judge treated as binding on him and adopted as the basis of his decision. He came to the conclusion that the plaintiff had had the benefit of the contract and that, although he had not had everything which he expected to get, there was not a total failure of consideration.

In view of *Valentini* v. *Canali* I think his decision was right. I cannot distinguish between the recovery of a specific chattel under a void contract and the recovery of money. If the latter cannot be recovered, neither can the former. In order to succeed here it was incumbent on the plaintiff to show complete failure of consideration; this he has failed to do, and in my view the decision of the county court judge was right and the appeal must be dismissed.

ACTON J.: I agree.

NOTE. On the reasoning of these cases suppose an infant exchanges certain real property which he owns for some of another person. The infant then uses this land, destroys trees, or it may be the land is taken from him by expropriation or other proceedings. On attaining 21, can the former infant demand a reconveyance? See *Whalls* v. *Learn* (1888), 15 O.R. 481; *Murray* v. *Dean* (1926), 30 O.W.N. 271, in both of which a recovery was ordered subject to paying the defendant the value of the land received by the infant where reconveyance was impossible, and when possible, on reconveying and paying an amount equal to loss of rental value and damages for waste.

In accordance with the real estate cases if the plaintiff in *Pearce* v. *Brain* had tendered £15, why could he not have recovered the car?

Some cases speak as though the "receipt of a benefit" by the infant, and and, "inability to restore the other party to his former position" were the same thing. See *Sturgeon* v. *Starr* (1911). 17 W.L.R. 402 (Man.) and compare *McDonald* v. *Baxter* (1911), 46 N.S.R. 149 (Nova Scotia).

Was there inability to restore the *status quo* in *Pearce* v. *Brain*? In *Steinberg* v. *Scala*? Was there a benefit received in the land cases?

NASH *v.* INMAN

England. Court of Appeal. [1908] 2 K.B. 1

The action was brought by specially indorsed writ by a tailor carrying on business in Saville Row, London, for £145 10s. 3d. for clothes supplied to the defendant while an undergraduate at Cambridge University between October 29, 1902, and June 16, 1903. The defendant was an infant at the time of the sale and delivery of the goods. He had been at school at Uppingham, and in October, 1902, he went up as a freshman to Trinity College, Cambridge. He was the son of an architect of good position, who had a town house at Hampstead, and a country establishment, called Wade Court, near Havant. The clothes supplied to the defendant included, among other things, eleven fancy waistcoats at two guineas each, or £1 15s. for cash. Upon an application for judgment under Order xiv., the defendant set up the plea of infancy, and the action was adjourned into Court and was tried before Ridley J. and a special jury. At the trial the plaintiff claimed only £122 19s. 6d., the cash price of the goods, in lieu of £145 10s. 3d., the credit price. The only witness called on behalf of the plaintiff was a traveller in his employ, who stated that he went to Cambridge and other places to solicit orders for the plaintiff, and that, hearing that the defendant was spending money freely and was likely to be a good customer, he called upon him personally at his lodgings in Cambridge and obtained the first order for clothes; and he gave evidence as to the goods supplied, and stated that they were charged for at the usual prices.

Counsel for the defendant thereupon submitted that, subject to his formally proving infancy, which was not admitted, there was no evidence to go to the jury, and he called the defendant's father, who proved the date of the defendant's birth, and then went on to state that he was satisfied that his son on going to the university was amply supplied wih proper clothes according to his position; and he gave particulars of his outfit. The learned judge then held that there was no evidence to go to the jury that the goods were necessaries, and directed judgment to be entered for the defendant.

The plaintiff applied for judgment or a new trial, on the ground that the judge himself had decided the issues of fact instead of leaving them to the jury.

COZENS-HARDY M.R.: This case is undoubtedly one of difficulty and also, I think, one of importance. It is an action by a tailor against Mr. Inman, who was at the date of the transactions in question an infant. There were no pleadings in the action. There was merely a writ and an application under Order xiv., and the action was adjourned into Court, and came on for trial before Ridley J. and a special jury. In substance the position is this: The plaintiff sues the defendant for goods sold and delivered. The defendant pleads infancy at the date of the sale, and his plea is proved. What is the consequence of that? The consequence of that is that the *Infants' Relief Act, 1874*, becomes applicable. Under that Act all contracts for goods supplied are absolutely void, the only exception being contracts for necessaries. Then s. 2 of the *Sale of Goods Act, 1893*, provides as follows: "Capacity to buy and sell is regulated by the general law concerning capacity to contract, and to transfer and acquire property." That, of course, includes the Act of 1874. Then follows this proviso: "Provided that where necessaries are sold and delivered to an infant, or minor, or to a person who by reason of mental incapacity or drunkenness is incompetent to contract, he must pay a reasonable price therefor." The section then defines necessaries as follows: "Necessaries in this section mean goods suitable to the condition in life of such infant or minor or other person, and to his actual requirements at the time of the sale and delivery." What is the effect of that? The plaintiff sues for goods sold and delivered. The defendant pleads infancy. The plaintiff must then reply, "The goods sold were necessaries within the meaning of the definition in s. 2 of the *Sale of Goods Act, 1893*." It is not sufficient, in my view, for him to say, "I have discharged the onus which rests upon me if I simply shew that the goods supplied were suitable to the condition in life of the infant at the time."

There is another branch of the definition which cannot be disregarded. Having shewn that the goods were suitable to the condition in life of the infant, he must then go on to shew that they were suitable to his actual requirement at the time of the sale and delivery. Unless he establishes that fact, either by evidence adduced by himself or by cross-examination of the defendant's witnesses, as the case may be, in my opinion he has not discharged the burden which the law imposes upon him. Our attention has been called by Mr. McCardie, in his very able and learned argument, to a number of authorities going back for a very long period, which he said established that the burden on a plaintiff who supplied goods to an infant was simply to shew that the goods were of a class which might be necessaries, having regard to the position in life of the defendant and his family, and that, unless the judge withdrew the case from the jury on the ground that the articles in question could not be necessaries, it was for the jury to find as a matter of fact, Aye or No, were these articles necessaries? It had never, he said, been the law that the plaintiff was required to go into the question, which might present great difficulties, of whether or not the goods were actually required by the defendant at the date of the sale, or, in other words, to say what was the state of the defendant's wardrobe at the time when the goods were ordered.

I think there is very great force up to a certain point in that argument. But it must be remembered that the law on this subject has been developed and altered in the course of the last century. It was until quite recently doubted whether it was even admissible to prove that the infant was supplied with goods of the class—being goods which might properly be necessary—at the date when the contract was made, so that he really did not want any more. It was not until the decision of the Divisional Court in *Barnes* v. *Toye*, 13 Q.B.D. 410, in 1884, overruling the direction given by A.L. Smith J., that it could be said to be at all established that that was even admissible evidence unless you went further and proved that the plaintiff knew he was sufficiently supplied. The point arose again in *Johnstone* v. *Marks* (1887), 19 Q.B.D. 509, before what was no doubt a Divisional Court, but it was composed of three members of the Court of Appeal, Lord Esher M.R., Lindley L.J., and Lopes L.J. In that case the county court judge had rejected evidence to prove that the defendant was sufficiently supplied with clothes at the time of the sale. Lord Esher said: "I am of opinion that the evidence was improperly rejected. It lies upon the plaintiff to prove, not that the goods supplied belong to the class of necessaries as distinguished from that of luxuries, but that the goods supplied when supplied were necessaries to the infant. The circumstance that the infant was sufficiently supplied at the time of the additional supply is obviously material to this issue, as well as fatal to the contention of the plaintiff with respect to it." Lindley L.J. said: "If an infant can be made liable for articles which may be necessaries without proof that they are necessaries, there is an end to the protection which the law gives him. If he has enough of such articles, more cannot possibly be necessary to him." Although it may be true that the language which I have just read from the judgments of Lord Esher and Lindley L.J. goes further than was absolutely necessary for the decision of the case, that language is perfectly clear and unambiguous, and seems to me to be logically involved in the definition of necessaries.

After those two decisions there was passed in the year 1893 an Act of Parliament which defines, in a manner that admits of no doubt, what are those necessaries for which, and for which alone, an infant can be made liable on assumpsit, and that definition in terms includes the second element which Lord Esher and Lindley L.J. said was involved in the term "necessaries," and the burden of proving which, they said, rested on the plaintiff. That being so, how does the matter stand? The plaintiff called evidence to prove the delivery of the goods. It is not of course contended, and it could not be contended, that the infant would be liable for the credit price or for the cash price of the goods, because by the terms of the statute he is only liable for a reasonable price, but that is a subsidiary point. There being no pleadings, the infancy of the defendant was not admitted, and the father was called to prove the date of his son's birth. There was no cross-examination as to that, and the infancy is not disputed. Then he went on to give evidence, which was quite clear and explicit and was not shaken in cross-examination, that the infant, who was an undergraduate at Cambridge, and had just gone up to the university when these goods were supplied, was in fact supplied with clothes suitable and necessary and proper for his condition in life, and for his position as an undergraduate of Trinity College, Cambridge.

The learned judge ruled as a matter of law that there was no evidence fit to be submitted to the jury that these articles, or any of them, were necessaries within the meaning of the statutory definition, and, thinking as I do that there was no evidence in support of that which was a necessary issue, I cannot say that the learned judge was wrong in the view which he took. We have scarcely heard any suggestion that there was even a scintilla of evidence to support that which is an affirmative issue, that the goods were suitable to the requirements of the infant. Nay more, I think, if the matter had been left to the jury, and the jury had found that they were suitable to the requirements of the infant at that time, and application had been made for a new trial, it would have been the duty of this Court to grant a new trial on the ground that there was no evidence to support the verdict, and that it was perverse. Under these circumstances it seems to me that this appeal fails, and that there is no ground for interfering with the judgment which was entered for the defendant.

FLETCHER MOULTON L.J.: I am of the same opinion. I think that the difficulty and at the same time the suggestion of hardship to the plaintiff in such a case as this disappear when one considers what is the true basis of an action against an infant for necessaries. It is usually spoken of as a case of enforcing a contract against the infant, but I agree with the view expressed by the Court in *Rhodes* v. *Rhodes* (1890), 44 Ch. D. 94, in the parallel case of a claim for necessaries against a lunatic, that this language is somewhat unfortunate. An infant, like a lunatic, is incapable of making a contract of purchase in the strict sense of the words; but if a man satisfied the needs of the infant or lunatic by supplying to him necessaries, the law will imply an obligation to repay him for the services rendered, and will enforce that obligation against the estate of the infant or lunatic. The consequence is that the basis of the action is hardly contract. Its real foundation is an obligation which the law imposes on the infant to make a fair payment in respect of needs satisfied. In other words the obligation arises *re* and not *consensu*. I do not mean that this nicety of legal phraseology has been adhered to. The common and convenient phrase is that an infant is liable for goods sold and delivered provided that they are necessaries, and there is no objection to that phraseology so long as its true meaning is understood. But the treatment of such actions by the Courts of Common Law has been in accordance with that principle I have referred to. That the articles were necessaries had to be alleged and proved by the plaintiff as part of his case, and the sum he recovered was based on a *quantum meruit*. If he claimed anything beyond this he failed, and it did not help him that he could prove that the prices were agreed prices. All this is very ancient law, and is confirmed by the provisions of s. 2 of the *Sale of Goods Act, 1893*—an Act which was intended to codify the existing law. That section expressly provides that the consequence of necessaries sold and delivered to an infant is that he must pay a reasonable price therefor.

The Sale of Goods Act, 1893, gives a statutory definition of what are necessaries in a legal sense, which entirely removes any doubt, if any doubt previously existed, as to what that word in legal phraseology means.... Hence, if an action is brought by one who claims to enforce against an infant such an obligation, it is obvious that the plaintiff in order to prove his case must shew that the goods supplied come within this definition. That a plaintiff has to make out his case is, I should have thought, the first lesson that any one studying English law would learn; and the elaborate argument of Mr. McCardie that if you look at the authorities in the past, going back nearly a hundred years, you will find cases in which particular defendants might have taken a higher standpoint and insisted upon a right which they did not insist on does not appear to me to touch the plain and obvious conclusion that in order to succeed in the action the plaintiff must shew that he has supplied necessaries. That is to say, the plaintiff has to shew, first, that the goods were suitable to the condition in life of the infant; and secondly, that they were suitable to his actual requirements at the time—or, in other words, that the infant had not at the time an adequate supply from other sources. There is authority to show that this was the case even before the Act of 1893. In *Johnstone* v. *Marks* this doctrine is laid down with the greatest clearness, and the *ratio decidendi* of that case applies equally to cases since that Act. Therefore there is no doubt whatever that in order to succeed in an action for goods sold and delivered to an infant the plaintiff must shew that they satisfy both the conditions I have mentioned. Everything which is necessary to bring them within s. 2 it is for him to prove.

Passing on from general principles, let me take the facts of the present case. In my opinion they raise no point whatever as to the duty of the judge as contrasted with the duty of the jury arising from the peculiar character of the action. We have only to follow the lines of the law consistently administered by this Court for many more years than I can think of, an example of which as applied to the case of the supply of necessaries to an infant is given by the decision of the Court of Exchequer Chamber in the case of *Ryder* v. *Wombwell* (1868), L.R. 4 Ex. 32. Questions of law are for the judge; questions of fact are for the jury, but, as the Court there laid down, the particular question of fact in issue in such a case, like all other questions of fact, ought not to be left to the jury by the judge unless there is evidence upon which they could reasonably find in the affirmative. The issue in that case was whether certain articles were suitable to the condition in life of the defendant, the infant, and the Court of Exchequer Chamber thought that no jury could reasonably find that those articles were suitable to the condition of that defendant, and therefore they said that the judge—not by reason of any peculiar rule applicable to actions of this kind, but in the discharge of his regular duties in all cases of trial by a jury—ought not to have left the question to the jury because there was no evidence on which they could reasonably find for the plaintiff. We have before us a similar case, in which the issue is not only whether the articles in question were suitable to the defendant's condition in life, but whether they were suitable to his actual requirements at the time of the sale and delivery; and how does the evidence stand? The evidence for the plaintiff shewed that one of his travellers, hearing that a freshman at Trinity College was spending money pretty liberally, called on him to get an order for clothes, and sold him within nine months goods which at cash prices came to over £120, including an extravagant number of waistcoats and other articles of clothing, and that is all that the plaintiff proved. The defendant's father proved the infancy, and then proved that the defendant had an adequate supply of clothes, and stated what they were. That evidence was uncontradicted. Not only was it not contradicted by any other evidence, but there was no cross-examination tending to shake the credit of the witness, against whose character and means of knowledge nothing could be said. On that uncontradicted evidence the judge came to the conclusion, to use the language of the Court in *Ryder* v. *Wombwell*, that there was no evidence on which the jury might properly find that these goods were necessary to the actual requirements of the infant at the time of sale and delivery, and therefore, in accordance with the duty of the judge in all cases of trial by jury, he withdrew the case from the jury and directed judgment to be entered for the defendant. In my opinion he was justified by the practice of the Court in so doing, and this appeal must be dismissed.

[The concurring opinion of Buckley L.J. is omitted.]

ROBERTS *v.* GRAY

England. Court of Appeal. [1913] 1 K.B. 520

This was an action in which the plaintiff claimed from the defendant, an infant, born March 28, 1891, £6000 damages for a breach of a contract to join him in a billiard-playing tour.

On May 12, 1910, an agreement was entered into between John Roberts of the first part, Joseph George Gray of the second part, and Harry William Gray (all described as billiardists) of the third part, whereby it was agreed:

"1. The said John Roberts shall take the said Joseph George Gray in company with his father the said Harry William Gray and the said Joseph George Gray shall go with the said John Roberts so accompanied on a tour of the world as professional billiardists on the terms and conditions hereinafter contained.

(A) The term of the said tour shall be for a period of eighteen months from the 2nd day of April, 1911.

(B) The said John Roberts shall pay all hotel and travelling expenses both by sea and land of himself and the said Joseph George Gray and the like hotel and travelling expenses of his father the said Harry William Gray.

Travelling to be first class; accounts to be rendered.

(C) [provided for keeping accounts and furnishing weekly statements.]

(D) [provided for equal division of all receipts and emoluments.]

(E) [Roberts to be entitled to deduct disbursements in account.]

(F) It is hereby agreed and understood between the parties hereto that the total hotel and travelling expenses of the said John Roberts and Joseph George Gray shall be paid and borne by each of them equally but that the said John Roberts shall defray the whole of same in the first place and also that of the said Harry William Gray and reimburse himself from the said Joseph George Gray's share of profits all such sums so incurred and expended by him as aforesaid but that in the event of such receipts earnings emoluments and gifts being insufficient to satisfy such expenditure neither of them the said Joseph George Gray or Harry William Gray shall be personally liable or responsible therefor.

(G) The tour to be under the sole control and management of the said John Roberts.

"2. Nothing herein contained shall create or be deemed to create a partnership between the parties hereto and the said John Roberts shall save as aforesaid be solely liable for all payments and shall be solely responsible for all losses (if any) from the date hereof until the 1st day of October, 1912.

"3. The parties hereto shall where same are available play exclusively on billiard tables the manufacture of Alcock & Company Proprietary Limited."

The plaintiff alleged that under the contract he expended much time and trouble and incurred liabilities in making arrangements for billiard matches and had suffered damage in consequence of the defendant's breach of the agreement. The plaintiff returned to England in March, 1911, and in April made various payments to the Grays for their expenses. Disputes arose about the kind of billiard balls to be used, and on April 20, 1911, the defendant J. G. Gray repudiated the contract. The plaintiff brought this action in May, 1911, and J. G. Gray counterclaimed rescission of the contract.

The action was tried in February, 1912, before the Lord Chief Justice and a special jury, when the jury found a verdict for the plaintiff on the questions left to them, namely, whether there was a false representation by the plaintiff; whether the defendant was thus induced to enter into the contract; and whether the plaintiff was ready and willing to carry out the contract. They assessed the damages at £1500. The question whether the contract was beneficial to the infant was left to the Lord Chief Justice, who decided in favour of the plaintiff. J. G. Gray appealed.

COZENS-HARDY M.R.: This appeal has been very ably argued by Mr. Matthews, but, having listened to everything he has urged upon us, I see no reason to differ from the view taken by the Lord Chief Justice. We have had our attention called to a great number of cases dealing with the circumstances under which and the extent to which an infant may be bound by, and be incapable of repudiating, a contract made by him during infancy. Far be it from me to say there has not been some development of this law since the age when the earliest cases which have been cited were decided, but it is important to remember that as early as Lord Coke—Co. Litt. 172A—it has been held that infant's contract for necessaries is binding, and it was laid down by him that that doctrine also applied not merely to bread and cheese and clothes, but to education and instruction. That has been construed by this Court in the case of *Walter* v. *Everard* [1891] 2 Q.B. 369 in a very wide sense. Fry L.J. in that case pointed out that education must not be taken in its narrow technical sense as merely meaning education to enable a man by the work of his hands to hereafter maintain himself as an artisan, but has a much wider meaning than that; it applies to education and instruction in the social state in which the infant is, and in which he may expect to find himself when he becomes an adult.

Now, what is the effect of a contract which is entered into by an infant with reference to necessaries, including instruction and education? We have heard an argument forcibly put before us that such a contract may be good so far as the consideration has been executed, but that it cannot be enforced so far as it is executory. For that proposition I think there is no authority, and I certainly think that it is not open to this Court to say that there is any such rule. We are bound by *Clements* v. *London and North Western Ry. Co.* [1894] 2 Q.B. 482. There the contract was a contract of service by an infant. A term of the service was that he should become a member of a society for the employees of the London and North Western Railway Company, and, in consideration of certain benefits, he was not to bring any action against the company in case of accidents whether due to the company's negligence or not. The Court considered the contract as a whole. It is quite idle to say "look at the contract and see if there is one clause which is adverse to the infant." The Court cannot consider whether that is for the infant's benefit and, if it is not, say that the whole contract is therefore void; it must look at the contract as a whole and see whether, looking at it as a whole, it is a contract for the infant's benefit, not merely a contract for necessaries, but if it is a contract which is on the whole for the infant's benefit. If so, what is the result? Lord Esher says if upon consideration of the whole of the contract there is a manifest advantage to the infant he cannot avoid it (p. 490). Then Kay L.J. says (p. 492): "I agree with the Divisional Court that, on examination of the whole contract, it is for the benefit of the infant, although it contains terms that standing alone, would not be for his advantage. There is, therefore, no right on the part of the infant to repudiate the contract." A. L. Smith, L.J., quoting with approval the passage in the judgment of Fry L.J., sitting, not in the Court of Appeal, but as a judge of the Chancery Division, in *De Francesco* v. *Barnum* (1890), 45 Ch.D. 430, says (p. 495): "There is another exception which is based on the desirableness of infants employing themselves in labour, therefore, when you get a contract for labour, and you have a remuneration of wages, that contract, I think, must be taken to be prima facie binding upon an infant. I take this to be good law. Prima facie, therefore, this contract is binding on the infant." If, therefore, this is a contract falling within a class to which the doctrine of necessaries applies, and if, taken as a whole, it is for the infant's benefit, I see no foundation whatever for the argument that the infant is not liable for damages in the event of his repudiating or declining to perform the contract entered into. The Court has acted upon that in *Gadd* v. *Thompson* [1900] 1 K.B. 304 to the extent of granting an injunction to restrain an infant from being guilty of a breach of a clause in a contract of service after he has left the employment. Here only damages are claimed and have been given.

It only remains, therefore, to consider that which I think is not really a very difficult problem. What is the nature of this contract? What was the station of the parties and what is the meaning of the agreement?

[His Lordship went through the contract, and was clearly of opinion that playing billiards in company with a noted player like John Roberts must be instruction of the most valuable kind for an infant who desired to make playing billiards the occupation of his life; and agreed with the Lord Chief Justice that the agreement was in effect for teaching, instruction and employment, and was reasonable and for the benefit of the infant.]

That being so, the Lord Chief Justice gave judgment for the plaintiff against the infant, and in my opinion the judgment which he gave was perfectly right and cannot be interfered with.

This appeal must be dismissed with costs.

FARWELL L.J.: I am of the same opinion. The chief point in Mr. Matthew's argument does not, in my opinion, really arise. He has sought to convince us that assuming this contract was not a contract for necessaries it would be voidable by the infant. It is unnecessary to express any opinion on the point which Kay L.J. dealt with in the case of *Clements* v. *London and North Western Ry. Co.* The question to what extent that rule applies does not arise. This is clearly a contract for necessaries within the meaning which that phrase has had attached to it in the course of many centuries since Lord Coke wrote. It is in effect for board, lodging, travelling and employment all found at the plaintiff's expense for the infant and involved in the employment, and the education which a billiard player of receptive capacity could not fail to obtain from playing continually month after month with a great billiard player like John Roberts. Every item which goes to make up necessaries in the sense of a labour and education contract, except the express term to give the education, which would be necessary if it were an apprenticeship deed, is in this particular contract as much as though, instead of finding the board and lodging on board ship and in various hotels, Roberts had found it in a house of his own where he gave exhibitions. I cannot doubt that this a contract for necessaries.

Then the next thing is, is it for the benefit of the infant, because, although a contract for necessaries is prima facie binding, it may be shewn to contain terms so harsh as not to be binding on the infant. In my opinion, it is clearly for the benefit of the infant, and I see nothing to suggest that it is in the least harsh upon him.

Then the only point which remains is, is it not, notwithstanding that, voidable by the infant? It appears to me that is answered in an *obiter dictum* of Lord Abinger's in *Wood* v. *Fenwick* (1842), 10 M. & W. 195; 152 E.R. 439, at p. 443. Lord Abinger says: "There can be no doubt that, generally speaking, a contract by an infant to receive wages for his labour is binding upon him." To which counsel interjects: "At all events, he may determine it at any time by notice." Then Lord Abinger says: "That would be a contradiction in terms: because, to say that he may contract, is to say that he may bind himself by the contract; how then can it be determined at his election the next day?" That is adopted by the decision of Lord Esher and the other Lords Justices in *Clements* v. *London and North Western Ry. Co.*, and it would render the rule futile if we were to say that although the contract is for necessaries and although it is for his benefit he can yet repudiate it if he thinks fit. In my opinion he cannot do so; the judgment was quite right; and this appeal fails.

HAMILTON L.J.: I entirely agree. The first question is whether this was a contract for necessaries, or, in the words of Lord Coke, whether it was a contract for the infant's "good teaching or instruction whereby he may profit himself afterwards." I think it is quite clear, as a matter of law, that this contract as framed was capable of being, and was rightly held to be, such a contract for necessaries. The circumstances that it is not expressed as a contract for employment; that the consideration for that which has to be done by the infant does not take the form of wages; and that he is not placed in such a relation to the plaintiff as would make him a servant, appear to me to be far from conclusive of the matter. Whether the contract is one for necessaries in this sense must depend upon its substance and not upon its form, and there was abundance of evidence here upon which it could be found by the learned Lord Chief Justice, who was, by agreement, the tribunal of fact, so far as the facts were involved, as well as of the law on this point, that a part and a most important part of this contract was the instruction that would be received by the defendant from playing constantly with the plaintiff, and also from playing under the conditions of a world-wide tour, a thing which a distinguished billiard player apparently contemplates as part of his career. It seems to me to be clear, therefore, upon the first question, that this contract is one for necessaries, and, in so far as the antitheses framed in *Cowern* v. *Nield*, [1912] 2 K.B. 419 by the Divisional Court is presented to us. I entertain no doubt that this is not such a contract as could be called a trading contract and is amply within the other side of the antithesis as stated by Phillimore J., namely, contracts relating to infant persons such as contracts for necessaries, of which he there mentions various kinds.

If this is a contract for necessaries, is there anything about it to prevent it being binding upon the infant? For this purpose it is necessary to consider whether it contains unusual and harsh and burdensome terms such as would prevent it from being a contract enforceable against the infant. The Lord Chief Justice being again a tribunal both of fact and law, decided that there were no terms in this contract that would have that effect, and no reason has been suggested to us for differing from him upon this point.

There remains only one further argument, and that goes not to the nature of the contract, but to the form of the action. This contract was repudiated by the infant, the defendant, at an early stage, though not before some portion of the services contemplated by the plaintiff had been rendered by him, and was to a large extent an executory contract so that the remedy takes the form of a claim for damages. It is therefore suggested that the contract is not enforceable against the infant, although had he taken the benefit of the plaintiff's instruction he might then have been compellable to pay a quantum meruit for services received. I am unable to appreciate why a contract which is in itself binding, because it is a contract for necessaries not qualified by unreasonable terms, can cease to be binding merely because it is still executory. To my mind, it is the character of the contract, namely, a contract for necessaries in the wide sense of the term, and not the form of the remedy for its breach which the particular accidents of the case may give rise to, that must determine whether it is a contract that is binding on the infant or is only voidable at his option. If the contract is binding at all, it must be binding for all such remedies as are appropriate to the breach of it. Although no doubt the exception is introduced, not for the benefit of the tradesman, but for the benefit of the infant himself, when the circumstances of the contract are such as to bind the infant, he must in common justice be liable to a judgment for any form of remedy which his breach of contract has made it necessary for the plaintiff to seek.

I agree this appeal must be dismissed with costs.

COKE ON LITTLETON: "An infant may bind himself to pay for his necessary meat, drink, apparel, necessary physicke, and such other necessaries, and likewise for his good teaching or instruction whereby he may profit himself afterwards" [p. 172A].

NOTE. Roberts v. *Gray* in many respects seems to illustrate a nebulous "third" class of contracts, commonly stated as "contracts for the infant's benefit." See Salmond & Winfield, *Contracts*, pp. 450 et seq. for a discussion of this problem. If however the decision is to be taken as a holding on "necessaries" it gives rise to serious doubts as to the nature of recovery in such cases; i.e. whether it be quasi-contractual or truly contractual. This becomes of extreme importance in regard to executory contracts for the sale of "necessaries," as to which see an article by Sir John C. Miles in (1927), 43 Law Q. Rev. 389.

IN RE SOLTYKOFF, EX PARTE MARGRETT

England. Court of Appeal. [1891] 1 Q.B. 413

The petitioner was the indorsee of some bills of exchange which had been accepted by the Prince when he was an infant. There was evidence that the bills had been given in payment for goods supplied to the Prince by the drawer. It was assumed for the purpose of the argument that the goods were necessaries.

The registrar held that an infant could not make himself liable by accepting a bill of exchange, even though he accepted the bill in order to pay for necessaries supplied to him by the drawer. The petitioner appealed:

LORD ESHER M.R.: The claim of the petitioning creditor is founded upon a debt alleged to be due to him as the indorsee of some bills of exchange accepted by the respondent, who at the time of the acceptance was an infant. The petitioner is not a person who supplied necessaries to the respondent when he was an infant. He supplied no necessaries to the infant; he is only the indorsee of some bills of exchange accepted by him. As regards an indorsee of a bill of exchange it is immaterial whether there was any consideration for the bills as between the drawer and the acceptor, he can sue the acceptor as the indorsee of the bills, and nothing else. The question, therefore, whether necessaries were supplied to the infant by the drawer of the bill, is immaterial.

It has been held in a long series of cases that an infant cannot make himself liable by the custom of merchants either by a bill of exchange or by a promissory note. It is said that those decisions are not binding on this Court. That may be so. But, in my opinion, it would be absolutely wrong at the present day to overrule those cases, which have been so long accepted as law. But I do not wish to rest my decision solely upon case law. The principle long established by English law is this—that an infant cannot make himself liable upon any contract whatever, except a contract for the supply of necessaries. I will go further and say this, that the principle of the cases goes to this extent, that, if an infant accepted a bill of exchange or gave a promissory note for the price of necessaries supplied to him, and he were sued upon the bill or the note by the man who had supplied the necessaries, and the plaintiff relied only on the bill or note, and gave no evidence of the supply of necessaries, the infant would not be liable. He is not liable upon a bill of exchange or a promissory note under any circumstances. It is not necessary for the protection of persons dealing with an infant that he should be liable on such a contract. The person who has supplied an infant with necessaries can always sue on that contract for the price of what he has supplied. Whether such a debt would support a bankruptcy petition I will not decide at present. The cases cited are against the appellant, and so is the established principle of English law. I think the *Infants' Relief Act* is also against him; it seems to me to assume that an infant is not liable upon a bill of exchange or a promissory note. I think this is a necessary implication from that Act, and also from the *Bills of Exchange Act*. In my opinion, the decision of the registrar was quite right.

[The concurring opinions of Bowen and Lopes L.JJ. are omitted.]

BILLS OF EXCHANGE ACT
Canada. Revised Statutes. 1952. Chapter 15

47. (1) Capacity to incur liability as a party to a bill is co-extensive with capacity to contract.
48. Where a bill is drawn or endorsed by an infant, minor, or corporation having no capacity or power to incur liability on a bill, the drawing or endorsement entitles the holder to receive payment of the bill, and to enforce it against any other party thereto.

JENKINS *v.* WAY
Nova Scotia. Supreme Court. 14 N.S.R. 394

This was an action for goods sold and delivered, to which the defendant pleaded infancy, and the plaintiff replied that the goods were necessaries. Plaintiff admitted on the trial that the goods had been furnished to the defendant in the way of trade, the defendant being a storekeeper at Torbay. Defendant swore that he traded off the goods so supplied and used none of them as his living, but he stated that he had paid his board out of the proceeds of his trade. Under this evidence and other evidence referred to in the judgment, the learned judge of the County Court held that the plaintiff could recover for part of the goods. The following was the judgment of the County Court.

JOHNSTONE J.: It is well settled that an infant is not liable for goods purchased for the purpose of carrying on his trade by which he earns his livelihood, but he would be liable for such portion of the goods so purchased as were actually consumed by him, as necessaries. The plaintiff swore that the defendant told him that he frequently got goods from him to give to his boarding-house keeper. The defendant stated that his boarding-house keeper, if he purchased goods from him, paid him for them,—they did not go against his board. This last statement I receive *cum grano salis*, for it is hardly credible that in a country place cash would be paid to a boarder for provisions taken from his store while his board bill was running. I can see no difference in principle between an infant sending groceries, etc., from his shop to be consumed in his own family, (in which case he would be liable for their price as necessaries,) and giving them to his boarding-house keeper to be used by him. The difficulty I had was the vagueness of the testimony as to the amount so consumed, but the evidence in *Turberville* v. *Whitehouse* (1823), reported in 1 C. & P., 94; 171 E.R. 1116, and more at large in 12 Price 692; 147 E.R. 848, was not more precise. There it came out on cross-examination that the defendant was constantly in the habit of supplying the wants of the house with the articles in which he dealt from the shop. On that evidence the judge left it to the jury to say whether any and what part of the goods supplied by the plaintiff had been used by the defendant's family. The jury found for plaintiff. Upon argument, the direction to the jury and the verdict were sustained. One of the Judges remarked that he was forcibly struck with the barefaced unconscientiousness of the defendant, and I do not know that I should go far astray in applying language nearly as strong to the defence set up in this case. However, as a jury, I think I shall probably be within the mark if I find that one-third of the plaintiff's claim was for provisions consumed by the defendant supplied from his shop to his boarding-house keeper. I give the plaintiff judgment for $57.30.

The defendant appealed.

RITCHIE E.J. delivered the judgment of the Court: The defendant, it appears from the evidence, was an infant when the goods sued for were supplied to him by the plaintiff. The defendant was then engaged in trade at Torbay, in Guysboro', and the goods were furnished him for his business there in the way of his trade, as the plaintiff himself alleges. He attempts, however, to extract from the defendant that some of them were necessaries for which he is entitled to recover, and this view the Judge of the County Court has adopted. The amount sued for was $175.91, and judgment was given for one-third of that amount.

I should be glad if I could come to the same conclusion, as the defence set up is by no means a creditable one, especially so as the defendant was very nearly twenty-one years of age and no doubt was supposed to be of age by the plaintiff when the sale was made.The ground on which the judgment was given was that some of the merchandise was supplied to the keeper of the boarding-house at which the defendant lodged and were credited to his board; and the case of *Turberville* v. *Whitehouse*, was relied on as the authority for the decision.

It is evident from the testimony that the goods were supplied to the defendant for the purpose of trade and went to his shop at Torbay; he boarded at the time with a man named Webber, who occasionally obtained goods from the shop as every other purchaser might, to what amount does not appear, which were either paid for or charged in the usual way. None of the goods went in any other way to Webber except some articles which defendant purchased expressly for him at Halifax to the value of $8.00, which amount was credited against his board. *Turberville* v. *Whitehouse* was the case of goods supplied to the infant to trade with, and it was held that the plaintiff could recover for such as were consumed as necessaries in his own family. There is a wide distinction between that case and this. The goods there, though not in the first instance supplied as necessaries, were used as such by the defendant. Here they were not, they were merely sold as merchandise to the lodging-house keeper, in the way of his trade, by the defendant, and were used by the lodging-house keeper for his family and for his boarders it may be, including the defendant. I cannot view this otherwise than as a disposal of the goods by the defendant in the way of his trade, as much as if they had been sold to any other customer.

I am reluctantly compelled to say that the plaintiff cannot recover, and that the appeal must be allowed and judgment entered for defendant.

NOTE. Early English decisions held that money lent for the express purpose of enabling an infant to purchase necessaries was not recoverable, even though such money was actually spent in for this purpose, "as the plaintiff thereby put it in the defendant's power to misapply the money."—Buller J. in *Probart* v. *Knouth* (1783), 2 Esp. 472 note; 170 E.R. 423. See also *Darby* v. *Boucher* (1694), 1 Salk. 279; 91 E.R. 244: "One lends an infant money who employs it in paying for necessaries, whether in that case the infant be liable, and it was held clearly by the Chief Justice that the infant is not liable, for it is upon the lending that the contract must arise, and after that time there could be no contract raised to bind the infant, because after that he might waste the money, and the infant's applying it afterward for necessaries will not by matter *ex post facto* entitle the plaintiff to an action." See the early cases collected in *Williston on Contracts*, sec. 243. It has however been held in equity that in such case the infant is liable and since the Judicature Acts, this must now be taken as the ordinary rule. See *Marlow* v. *Pitfield* (1719), 1 P. Wms. 558; 24 E.R. 516: "Though the law be, that if one actually lend money to an infant, even to pay for necessaries, yet as the infant in such case may waste and misapply it, he is therefore not liable, according to the resolution in Salk. 279. It is however otherwise in equity; for if one lends money to an infant to pay a debt for *necessaries*, and in consequence thereof the infant does pay the debt, here although he may not be liable at law, he must nevertheless be so in equity; because in this case the lender of the money stands in the place of the person paid *viz*., the creditor for necessaries, and shall recover in equity as the other should have done at law."

MARTIN *v*. GALE. 1876. 4 Ch. 428 (England. Chancery). A loan to an infant for necessaries was secured by an assignment of a real property interest. The deed was held not binding but there was liability to account for money advanced.

JENNINGS *v*. RUNDALL

England. King's Bench. 1799. 8 T.R. 335; 101 E.R. 1419

LORD KENYON C.J.: The law of England has very wisely protected infants against their liability in cases of contract; and the present case is a strong instance to shew the wisdom of that law. The defendant, a lad, wished to ride the plaintiff's mare a short journey; the plaintiff let him the mare to hire; and in the course of the journey an accident happened, the mare being strained; and the question is whether this action can be maintained? I am clearly of opinion that it cannot; it is founded on a contract. If it were in the power of a plaintiff to convert that, which arises out of a contract into a tort, there would be an end of that protection which the law affords to infants. Lord Mansfield indeed frequently said that this protection was to be used as a shield, and not as a sword; therefore if an infant commit an assault, or utter slander, God forbid that he should not be answerable for it in a court of justice. But where an infant has made an improvident contract with a person who has been wicked enough to contract with him, such person cannot resort to a court of law to enforce such contract. And the words "wrongfully, injuriously, and maliciously," introduced into this declaration cannot vary this case.

GROSE J.: I am of the same opinion. In the case of *Manby* v. *Scott* (1659), 1 Sid. 109; 82 E.R. 1000, this distinction was taken, that if the action against an infant be grounded on a contract the plaintiff shall not convert it into a tort; "If one deliver goods to an infant on a contract knowing him to be an infant, the infant shall not be charged for them in trover and conversion; for by that means all infants in England would be ruined." A very few years after the decision of that case the case of *Johnson* v. *Pie* 1 Keb. 905; 83 E.R. 1312, arose, according to one report of which Lord Ch. J. Keeling expressed great indignation at the attempt to charge an infant in tort for that which was the foundation of an action of assumpsit; he said "The judgment will stay for ever, else the whole foundation of the common law will be shaken, for this was but a slip, and he might have pleaded his minority here."

LAWRENCE J.: The true distinction is that mentioned by my Brother Grose, and not that stated at the bar between negligence and an act done by the infant. It is argued that if no act be done by the infant he may plead his infancy, but that infancy is not a defence where an act has been done: if that were so, an infant would not be liable in many instances of trover, where the conversion consists merely in a non-delivery; and yet in trover an infant is always liable. According to the same rule, if an action were brought against an infant for negligently keeping the plaintiff's cattle by which they died, infancy might be pleaded in bar; but if the declaration charged the defendant with having given the cattle bad food, by which they died, it could not. But this certainly is not the true distinction.

LE BLANC J.: The plea of infancy is a good bar to this action, on the ground that the act done in this case is the foundation of an action of assumpsit. And the reason of the distinction taken in the case in Siderfin is, that the plaintiff shall not by changing the form of the action vary the liability of the infant. Now if the plaintiff could not have maintained an action of assumpsit against the infant, neither can he maintain the action in its present form. On this short ground, therefore, I think that the plea of infancy is a good defence to this action.

Judgment for the defendant.

BURNARD *v.* HAGGIS

England. Common Pleas. 1863. 14 C.B.N.S. 451; 143 E.R. 360

Upon the trial the following facts, interalia, appeared in evidence. The plaintiff was a livery-stable keeper residing in Cambridge, and the defendant was an undergraduate of Trinity College, Cambridge, whose father was formerly a surgeon, but for some years past ceased to practice his profession, and was thereupon appointed a magistrate for the county of Somerset. The defendant was born on the 23rd of May, 1842.

On the 11th of March, 1862 the defendant, accompanied by a friend named Bonner, who was also an undergraduate of Trinity College, went into the yard of the plaintiff, to whom both of them were strangers, and the defendant stated to the plaintiff's servant, and afterwards to the plaintiff, that he, the defendant, wanted a horse for a ride. A mare was shewn to him, and he asked if she would jump. The plaintiff said he had no doubt she would, but he did not let her out for jumping or larking, and that if he, the defendant, wanted a horse for jumping plaintiff could shew him a horse for that purpose. The defendant replied that he did not want a horse for jumping, but merely for a ride, and he said he would have the mare, and he directed it to be sent for him. The plaintiff stated, at the trial, that the usual charge for a ride was 7s. 6d., and that he had charged that sum against the defendant, who, however, had not paid it; and that the usual charge for a horse for jumping or larking was a guinea.

It appeared that, after the mare had been taken by the plaintiff's servant to the place to which it had been directed to be taken by the defendant, it was mounted by Mr. Bonner.

The defendant stated, at the trial, that he hired the mare, and that he did not tell the plaintiff or his servant, that he wanted the mare for Mr. Bonner. The defendant also stated that, on the same day, he hired a horse of another livery-stable keeper, and that he rode that horse and directed Bonner to ride the plaintiff's mare. The defendant and Bonner rode together from Cambridge, and the defendant stated that between Cambridge and the adjoining village of Grantchester they left the highway, and rode together across the fields to the adjoining village of Barton, being a distance of about three miles, and in doing so they jumped their horses over several hedges and ditches, and that on Mr. Bonner endeavouring to jump the plaintiff's mare over a fence it fell, and a stake entered its body. The mare was afterwards brought back to the plaintiff's yard, where it was put under the care of a veterinary surgeon, but it died on the 23rd of March, 1862; and the jury found that it died from the wound received whilst ridden by Bonner. The jury also found, *inter alia*, that the defendant was an infant under the age of twenty-one at the time of the contract with the plaintiff; that the plaintiff did not know that the mare was ridden by Bonner; that the hiring of the mare was a contract for a necessary suitable to the defendant's station in life, and that the amount of damage which the plaintiff had sustained was £30.

The learned Judge having, upon the finding of the jury, directed a verdict to be entered for the plaintiff for £30 damages, and having given judgment accordingly, the defendant appealed thereform, and the question for the opinion of this Court was, whether, under the circumstances, the plaintiff or the defendant was entitled to judgment.

ERLE C.J.: . . . I am of opinion that our judgment ought to be for the plaintiff. It appears that the defendant went to the stables of the plaintiff and contracted with the plaintiff for the hire of a horse for a ride on the road and not to be taken across the fields and used for jumping. The defendant having so got the horse, lent it to his friend, who took it across the fields, and in endeavouring to jump the animal over a fence, transfixed it on a stake. Now it is clear to me that on these facts there has been an actionable wrong committed, for which the defendant is liable independently of the finding of the jury that the hiring of the horse was a necessary suitable to the degree and station in life of this young man. Putting aside all question as to there being evidence or not sufficient to satisfy such finding, I am of opinion that the defendant is legally liable for, and can be made to pay the damage claimed in this action.

WILLES J.: I am of the same opinion. The act of riding this horse at the fence where it met its death is just as much a trespass as if the defendant without any hiring, and without the plaintiff's leave, had mounted the plaintiff's horse and gone with it into the fields and had there used it as this horse was in fact used. What was done by the defendant was not an abuse of a contract, but was the doing of an act which he was expressly forbidden by the owner to do with the animal.

BYLES J.: I am of the same opinion. I agree that one cannot make an infant liable for the breach of a contract by changing the form of action to one *ex delicto*. This, however, is the case of a horse hired for one purpose and used for another; and more than that, it was let out to be used by one person and was used by another person; it was let for riding on the road, and was used for jumping over fences in the fields. There was therefore an independant tort, for which the infant was liable, and it is wholly unnecessary to consider any question about what are necessaries.

KEATING J.: I am of the same opinion. The defendant was liable for a tort wholly independent of any contract.

BALLETT *v.* MINGAY

England. Court of Appeal. [1943] 1 All E.R. 143

LORD GREENE M.R.: The appellant is an infant who obtained on loan from the respondent an amplifier and a microphone. In dealing with this case, there arises a difficulty of a type that often occurs in appeals from county courts. The note is quite short. It is made rather more difficult to follow because it embodies a note of evidence in a previous action where questions of the same character were raised. The county court judge gives no reasons for his judgment, and there are no findings of fact stated. He, in fact, gave judgment for the plaintiff for the sum of £38 8s., the value of the goods which the defendant had failed to return on demand. I think it is a right rule in dealing with judgments of county court judges in these cases to assume, unless the contrary is proved, that the judge has found all relevant facts necessary to support his decision in law. I think that that is in general the proper assumption to make, and one which is fair to the county court judge himself. In the present case the contrary is now shown and, therefore, I approach this matter on the footing that the county court judge did find all the facts sufficient to enable his judgment to be supported. It is said that, if his judgment stands, the appellant, who was an infant, will have been held liable for breach of contract which was not one that bound him. It was said that the attempt to make him liable in tort was a breach of the principle which is laid down in *Jennings* v. *Rundall* (1799), E.R. 1419 where an infant, having hired a mare, rode it carelessly with the result that she was injured. As Byles J., pointed out in the argument in a subsequent case (to which I shall refer in a moment), that was a case where the act of the defendant was not an act distinct from the contract of hire, but was an act which was within the four corners of the contract itself. In my opinion, the present case does not fall under that principle at all, because here the respondent parted with possession of the articles to Chapman and Chapman failed to produce them, various stories being told by him, or apparently at his instigation, as to what had happened to them. On looking at the evidence, it seems to me that, when properly construed, the terms of the bailment of these articles to the infant appellant did not permit him to part with their possession at all. If it was the bargain that he might part with them, it was for the infant to establish that fact, and it seems to me that he has failed to do so. On that basis, the action of the appellant in parting with the goods was one which fell outside the contract altogether and that fact brings the case within the subsequent case, to which I have referred, of *Burnard* v. *Haggis* (1863), 143 E.R. 360. There Byles J., drew the distinction between that case and *Jennings* v. *Rundall*. He said that in *Burnard* v. *Haggis*, the action of the defendant was an act of tort just as distinct from the contract as if the defendant had run a knife into the mare and killed her. What had happened was that the undergraduate who had hired the mare, having been told that he must not jump her, lent her to a friend who jumped her, as a result of which the mare was injured and killed. . . .

In the present case it seems to me, therefore, that the infant was properly sued in detinue in that, on receiving a demand for the return of the goods, he refused or neglected to return them, and failed to prove that in parting with the goods he had not stepped outside the bailment altogether. On that basis, there is a remedy against the infant in tort because the circumstances in which the goods passed from his possession and untimately disappeared were circumstances outside the purview of the contract of bailment altogether or, at any rate, were not shown by him to be within it. In all the circumstances, and dealing as best I can with the rather scanty evidence and the fact that there is no note of the county court judge's reasons or his findings of fact, I am of opinion that the appellant has failed to establish his case and that the appeal must be dismissed with costs.

[Scott and Mackinnon L.JJ. agreed.]

R. LESLIE, LIMITED *v*. SHIELL
England. Court of Appeal. [1914] 3 K.B. 607

The plaintiffs were a firm of registered money-lenders, and they sued the defendant, to whom they had made two advances of £200 each, to recover £475, being the amount of the advances with interest, on the ground that the defendant had obtained the advances by fraudulently representing that he was of full age at the time; in the alternative, they claimed £475 as money had and received by the defendant to the use of the plaintiffs; the defendant was still a minor at the date of the issue of the writ, though he attained full age before the trial. The learned judge left the following question to the jury: "Were the plaintiffs induced to make the two advances of £200 each, or either of them, by the fraudulent misrepresentation of the defendant that he was twenty-one?"; to which the jury answered "Yes—both." Upon further consideration, Horridge J. ordered judgment to be entered for the plaintiffs for £400.

The defendant appealed.

LORD SUMNER.: At the time of the transaction in question the appellant was an infant. He succeeded in deceiving some money-lenders by telling them a lie about his age, and so got them to lend him £400 on the faith of his being an adult. Perhaps they were simpler than money-lenders usually are; perhaps the infant looked unusually mature. At any rate when they awoke to the fact that they could not enforce their bargain and sought to recover the £400 paid, charging him with fraud, the jury found that the appellant had been guilty of fraud, and he does not now complain of the verdict. On further consideration Horridge J. gave judgment against him for the full amount that he had received.

It is not a pretty story to begin life with, and one might have expected that the appellant's chief anxiety would have been to live down, but money is money, and I suppose £400 is more than he cares to pay, or rather to repay, if he can manage to avoid it. Accordingly he appeals, alleging that there is no process of law by which the money-lenders can get their money back from him, and, if this is so, he must succeed on this appeal.

The claim first pleaded is for the amount of principal and interest, as damages sustained because by his fraud the plaintiffs have been induced to make and act upon an unenforceable contract. So long ago as *Johnson* v. *Pye* 1 Sid. 258; 82 E.R. 1091, it was decided that, although an infant may be liable in tort generally, he is not answerable for a tort directly connected with a contract which, as an infant, he would be entitled to avoid. "One cannot make an infant liable for the breach of a contract by changing the form of action to one *ex delicto*": per Byles J. in *Burnard* v. *Haggis* (1863), 143 E.R. 360. "A married woman," says Pollock C.B. in *Liverpool Adelphi Loan Association* v. *Fairhurst*, (1854), 23 L.J. (Ex.) 163, speaking before the common law had been altered by *Married Women's Property Acts*, "is liable for frauds committed by her on any person as for any other personal wrong. But when the fraud is directly connected with the contract with the wife and is the means of effecting it and parcel of the same transaction, the wife cannot be responsible or the husband be sued for it together with the wife. If this were allowed, it is obvious that the wife would lose the protection which the law gives her against contracts made by her during coverture, for there is not a contract of any kind, which a *feme covert* could make whilst she knew her husband to be alive, that could not be treated as a fraud, for every such contract would involve in itself a fraudulent representation of her capacity to contract.... In the case of an infant it was held for a similar reason that he could not be made liable for a fraudulent representation that he was of full age, whereby the plaintiff was induced to contract with him.... If the action should be maintainable 'all the pleas of infancy would be taken away, for such affirmations are in every contract.' " The Chief Baron's quotation is from *Johnson* v. *Pye.* As Lord Kenyon says in *Jennings* v. *Rundall* (1799), alluding to *Zouch* v. *Parsons,* (1765), 3 Burr. 1804; "this protection was to be used as a shield and not as a sword; therefore if an infant commit an assault or utter slander God forbid that he should not be answerable for it in a Court of Justice. But where an infant has made an improvident contract with a person who has been wicked enough to contract with him, such person cannot resort to a Court of law to enforce such contract." It is perhaps a pity that no exception was made where, as here, the infant's wickedness was at least equal to that of the person who innocently contracted with him, but so it is. It was thought necessary to safeguard the weakness of infants at large, even though here and there a juvenile knave slipped through. The rule is well settled. No action of deceit lay against the present appellant and this claim was abandoned, but for the purpose of this case it is important to observe the principles on which an infant's immunity is established in this regard.

Nor does the other cause of action pleaded fare any better. To the claim for return of the principal moneys paid to the infant under the contract that failed, as money had and received to the plaintiff's use, there are at least two answers: the infancy itself was an answer before 1874 at common law, and the *Infants' Relief Act, 1874,* is an answer now. An action for money had and received against an infant has been sustained, where in substance the cause of action was *ex delicto*: *Bristow* v. *Eastman* (1794), 1 Esp 172; 170 E.R. 317, approved before 1874 in *In re Seager,* 60 L.T. 665, and cited without disapproval in *Cowern* v. *Nield,* [1912] 2 K.B. 419. Even this has been doubted, but where the substance of the cause of action is contractual, it is certainly otherwise. To money had and received and other indebitatus courts infancy was a defense just as to any other action in contract.... Further, under the statute the principle, which at common law relieved an infant from liability for a tort directly connected with a voidable contract, namely, that it was impossible to enforce in a roundabout way an unenforceable contract, equally forbids courts of law to allow, under the name of an implied contract or in the form of an action *quasi ex contractu,* a proceeding to enforce part of a contract, which the statute declares to be wholly void. This has been recently illustrated in the closely analogous case of a claim on the footing of money had and received for moneys paid but irrecoverable under what in law was a lending and borrowing ultra vires: *Sinclair* v. *Brougham,* [1914] A.C. 398.

The ground on which Horridge J. held the appellant liable was that by reason of his fraud he was compellable in equity to repay the money, actually received and professedly borrowed, and compellable too by a judgment *in personam* for the amount, not by any more proprietary remedy. The rule in equity has been so stated at times by text-writers, both remote and recent . . . but of authority for it there is very little. *Evroy* v. *Nicholas* (1720), 2 Eq. Cas. Abr. 488; 22 E.R. 415, a decision of Lord King's, was much relied upon. He is reported to have said "infants have no privilege to cheat men," a wholesome truth indeed, but I should hardly call it a principle. The case was examined by Knight Bruce V.C. in *Stikeman* v. *Dawson* (1847), 1 DeG. & Sm. 90; 63 E.R. 984, who concluded that the facts as reported do not support the decree as made. . . .

For a very long time and in many forms equity has interfered to give relief against frauds committed by infants, or has refused it to infants guilty of fraud; but the practice and even the principles applicable to such cases were long ill-defined. "An infant," says Knight Bruce V.C. in *Stikeman* v. *Dawson* "however generally for his own sake protected by an incapacity to bind himself by contracts, may be *doli capax* in a civil sense and for civil purposes in the view of a Court of Equity, though perhaps only when *pubertati proximus* or older . . . and may therefore commit a fraud for which or the consequences of which he may after his majority be made civilly liable in equity. . . . I agree . . . that in what cases in particular a Court of Equity will thus exert itself it is not easy to determine." Though many cases have been decided on this subject, none has been cited to us till one last year in which the decision has directly been that the defendant must pay back under a judgment purely *in personam* a sum equal to that which he obtained during infancy under a purported contract of lending and borrowing, which was entered into by the lender on the faith of the borrower's fraudulent assertion that he was of full age.

There are, however, some dicta of importance and some decisions which are alleged to bear indirectly on the point. . . .

As to the cases, *Clarke* v. *Cobley*, (1789), 2 Cox, 173; 30 E.R. 80, is one in which the Court restored the status quo affected by an infant's fraud by ordering him to return promissory notes, the surrender of which he had procured by falsely stating that he was of age, and by putting him under terms not to plead the *Statute of Limitations* if sued upon them, but a decree against him to pay the amount of the notes, hough he was now of age, was expressly refused. In *Cory* v. *Gertken*, (1816), 2 Madd. 40; 56 E.R. 250, where Sir T. Plumer says "though in general a payment to an infant may be bad, yet if the infant practises a fraud he is liable for the consequences," he only decided that a person could not make his trustee pay over again a sum that he had got from him by fraudulently representing himself, while still an infant, to be already of full age, and in *Chubb* v. *Griffiths* (1865), 35 Beav. 127; 55 E.R. 843, Lord Romilly M.R., when saddling an infant defendant with costs who had been passing off his safes as Chubb's safes, says that he does so "on the principle laid down in *Cory* v. *Gertcken*." What he conceived this principle to be I can hardly tell, but at any rate it is not a general liability in equity for fraud. Jessel M.R. in *In re Jones* (1881), 18 Ch.D. at p. 118 regards *Cory* v. *Gertcken* as a pure action of tort. The grounds of an infant defendant's liability for costs were again discussed in *Woolff* v. *Woolff*, [1899] 1 Ch. 343, another case of similar dishonesty, and the liability was rested on the above principle and authority, also without any hint of a wider one that in equity an infant is generally liable for fraud. I think that the whole current of decisions down to 1913, apart from dicta which are inconclusive, went to shew that, when an infant obtained an advantage by falsely stating himself to be of full age, equity required him to restore his ill-gotten gains, or to release the party deceived from obligations or acts in law induced by the fraud, but scrupulously stopped short of enforcing against him a contractual obligation, entered into while he was an infant, even by means of a fraud. This applies even to *In re King, Ex parte Unity Joint Stock Mutual Banking Association* (1858), 3 De G. & J. 63; 44 E.R. 1192. Restitution stopped where repayment began; as Kindersley V.C. puts it in *Vaughan* v.

Vanderstegen, (1854), 2 Drew. 363; 61 E.R. 759, an analogous case, "you take the property to pay the debt."

Last year, in *Stocks* v. *Wilson*, [1913] 2 K.B. 235, an infant, who had obtained furniture from the plaintiff by falsely stating that he was of age and had sold part of it for £30, was personally adjudged by Lush J. to pay this £30 as part of the relief granted to the plaintiff. This is the case which more than any other influenced Horridge J. in the Court below. I think it is plain that Lush J. conceived himself to be merely applying the equitable principle of restitution. The form of the claim was that, by way of equitable relief, the infant should be ordered to pay the reasonable value of the goods, which he could not restore because he had sold them. The argument was that equity would not allow him to keep the goods and not pay for them, that if he kept the property he must discharge the burthen, and that he could not better his position by having put it out of his power to give up the property. Lush J. expressly says [1913] 2 K.B. at p. 247, "it is a jurisdiction to compel the infant to make satisfaction," and, at p. 246, "the remedy is not on the contract." At pp. 242–243 he says "what the Court of Equity has done in cases of this kind is to prevent the infant from retaining the benefit of what he has obtained by reason of his fraud. It has done no more than this and this is a very different thing from making him liable to pay damages and compensation for the loss of the other party's bargain. If the infant has obtained property by fraud he can be compelled to restore it"; but now comes the proposition, which applies to the present case and is open to challenge, "if he has obtained money he can be compelled to refund it.". . . In the present case . . . there is no fiduciary relation: the money was paid over in order to be used as the defendant's own and he has so used it and, I suppose, spent it. There is no question of tracing it, no possibility of restoring the very thing got by the fraud, nothing but compulsion through a personal judgment to pay an equivalent sum out of his present or future resources, in a word nothing but a judgment in debt to repay the loan. I think this would be nothing but enforcing a void contract. So far as I can find, the Court of Chancery never would have enforced any liability under circumstances like the present, any more than a Court of law would have done so, and I think that no ground can be found for the present judgment, which would be an answer to the *Infants' Relief Act*.

Accordingly the appeal succeeds; the judgment must be set aside and entered for the defendant.

KENNEDY L.J.: . . . It appears to me that Horridge J. intended to dismiss the plaintiffs' claim not only so far as it rested upon the claim for damages for fraudulent misrepresentation, but also so far as it rested upon the claim on an implied contract for money had and received to the use of the plaintiffs. I think that is so although he gave judgment for the plaintiffs in an action in which those were the only claims pleaded, and in which so far as the report informs us, no amendment of the plaintiffs' pleadings was asked for or granted. Reading the concluding portion of the judgment commencing with the words "There remains, however, the question whether or not a Court of Equity would order restitution to be made by an infant who had obtained property by fraud" (1913), 29 Times L.R. 555, I think that the learned judge held that, having all the facts and the findings of the jury before him, the just and proper course was, without requiring any formal amendment, to treat the plaintiffs as basing their claim upon an assertion such as was pleaded by the plaintiff in the recent case of *Stocks* v.

Wilson, before Lush J., to which Horridge J. expressly refers in an earlier passage in his judgment. Such a course was, in my opinion not only unobjectionable, but right.

We have, therefore, to consider in this Court whether or not the defendant lay under such an equitable liability to the plaintiffs as entitled them to the judgment for £400 which the learned judge has entered in their favour. Now, beyond all question, there are cases in which a Court of Equity will interfere to prevent the fraud of an infant, such as an express misrepresentation of full age, from working an injustice. There is, at the same time, excellent authority for declining to define in positive terms the range of such interference. . . .

In the first place, it appears to me that whilst Courts of Equity have interfered to make an infant restore property found in his possession which he had obtained by fraudulent misrepresentation, as e.g., the promissory note in the old case of *Clarke* v. *Cobley*; to compel the recognition, in regard to property in his possession, of rights and interests of persons whom he has misled into entering into transactions in regard to it (cf. *Watts* v. *Cresswell* (1714), 22 E.R. 435); and to prevent the payment over again to the infant of moneys of which he has procured the payment already by a representation of full age, as in *Cory* v. *Gertcken*; there is no case in which I can find that a Court of Equity has given judgment against an infant in circumstances like the present, that is to say, in which it has interfered on the ground of the fraud of the infant, whereby he induced the making of the contract of loan, to order the infant to pay the plaintiff a sum equal to the sum borrowed under the void contract, and so, in effect, to the amount of the principal lent, to give validity as against the infant to a void contract.

A. T. Lawrence J.: . . . It has been the policy of the law to protect infants; they have been held incapable of binding themselves by their contracts—with certain exceptions not material to this case. That this is the law was admitted. But it was argued for the plaintiffs that these considerations do not affect the claim for "money had and received." Horridge J. was induced to take the view (following a decision of Lush J. in *Stocks* v. *Wilson*) that there was in equity a right to relief to the extent of the money actually received. It was said for the plaintiffs that the action for money had and received was not founded upon a promise implied by law, but rested upon what was called by counsel a "doctrine of equity." I do not think this argument is well founded. There are no doubt many cases in which equity will give relief against frauds perpetrated by infants. Wherever the infant requires as a plaintiff the assistance of any Court, it will be refused until he has made good his fraudulent representation. Wherever the infant is still in possession of any property which he has obtained by his fraud he will be made to restore it to its former owner. But I think that it is incorrect to say that he can be made to repay money which he has spent, merely because he received it under a contract induced by his fraud.

The contracts of an infant, which were formerly voidable only, are now by the *Infants' Relief Act, 1874*, made absolutely void. He is further protected in respect of loans by 55 and 56 Vict. c. 4, ss. 3, 4, 5. These statutes are as binding upon the equitable, as they are upon the common law, jurisdiction of the Court. I do not think that it is correct to say that the action for money had and received is wholly independent of contract. It arises wherever money has been received which *ex aequo et bono* belongs to the plaintiff. In such case the law implies a promise to pay it to the plaintiff, but where the express promise to repay the money is by statute "absolutely void" it is impossible to imply a promise to repay the same money: see observations of Jessel M.R. in *Ex parte Jones*, 18 Ch.D. at p. 118. To do so would be to (in large part) defeat the policy of the statute, and would violate the well-established principle that where there is an express promise no other like promise can be implied.

Lord Mansfield in *Moses* v. *Macferlan* (1760), 97 E.R. 676 excepted debts "contracted during infancy" from the operation of the action for money had and received, shewing that he regarded it as an action depending upon an implied promise.

None of the authorities cited to us in my opinion extend to establish the plaintiffs' claim in this case.

The judgment in *Stocks* v. *Wilson* seems to treat the subsequent sale of the property by the infant as wrongful, and as affording a foundation for treating the money obtained thereby as received to the plaintiff's use. If this had been so, if it had been a wrong independent of contract, it would no doubt have made a case in which the plaintiff could by waiving the tort, have afforded a consideration for the implied promise to pay over the proceeds, and he could have recovered on the common count for "money had and received." But this is rendered impossible by the judge finding that the property in the goods had passed to the infant before he disposed of them (and as to the major portion thereof that he did so with the concurrence of the plaintiff in the action). The really wrongful act was the obtaining the goods under the contract of purchase by the pretence that he was of full age; as to that, it was admitted that he could not be sued in tort for the fraud. There was therefore no actionable tort independent of contract which could be waived to form a consideration for the implied promise.

If the cause of action for money had and received existed, I should expect to find ample authority for it, as, whenever an honest money-lender lends to an infant, he has probably been deceived as to the age of the borrower.

I think that this appeal should be allowed and judgment entered for the defendant.

Appeal allowed.

NOTE. Attempts have been made to distinguish the decision of *Stocks* v. *Wilson* on the ground of the existence of a fiduciary relationship between the parties. See *Salmond & Winfield on Contracts*, p. 466. It would appear to be the better opinion however that insofar as that decision proceeded on the grounds of a personal judgment against the defendant regardless of whether the defendant had any property remaining in his hands, it is overruled by *Leslie* v. *Shiell*. If and only insofar as it proceeded on the principle of following the property, i.e. restitution of property in the defendant's hands, is it consistent with the later case. As to the need for an implied promise in "money had and received" cases, see the *Deglman* case. If there is justification for denying recovery apart from the difficulty of implying a promise, should the new and as yet undeveloped doctrine of unjust enrichment be blindly applied?

SLADE *v*. METRODENT LTD.
England. Queen's Bench. [1953] 2 Q.B. 113

This was an appeal from the Master's refusal to stay proceedings commenced by writ under an apprenticeship agreement between the plaintiffs, the infant apprentice and his father, and the defendant, who undertook to instruct the infant plaintiff in the art of dental mechanics over a five year period. The plaintiffs claimed that the defendant failed to teach the infant plaintiff anything, and had repudiated the contract. Before taking further steps in the action the defendant applied for a stay of proceedings under section 4 of the *Arbitration Act, 1950*. Clause 6 of the apprenticeship agreement provided for the settlement by arbitration of "all questions or differences whatsoever" arising out of the agreement. Counsel for the plaintiffs relied on ancient and modern texts for the proposition that an infant "is not bound by an agreement to refer a dispute to arbitration" (*Chitty on Contracts*, 20th ed., p. 598; and see 1 *Halsbury* 625). The defendant appealed.

McNair J.: . . . In my judgment the question before me falls to be determined on two well-established principles, (1) that an infant, even during infancy, is bound by any contract which the court considers, after examining all its terms, is for the benefit of the infant, and (2) that if the contract as a whole is beneficial, the infant cannot pick and choose and adopt those terms which are clearly beneficial while rejecting those terms which are not beneficial or not clearly beneficial: see *Clements* v. *London and North Western Railway*, [1894] 2 Q.B. 482. The judgment in that case of Kay L.J. sets out a quotation from *Coke upon Littleton*, 172a, to the effect that there are some exceptions to the infant's liability to bind himself by contract, as "an infant may bind himself to pay for his "necessary meat, drink, apparel, necessary physicke, and such other necessaries, and likewise for his good teaching or instruction, whereby he may profit himself."

The question for the court in any particular case of an apprenticeship deed is whether the agreement as a whole is for the benefit of the infant. In *Wood* v. *Fenwick* (1842), 10 M. & W. 195; 152 E.R. 439, the interlocutory observations of Alderson B. and Abinger C.B. clearly indicate that an apprenticeship deed containing an arbitration clause might in their view be beneficial to an infant. Having examined the apprenticeship deed here in question, I am clearly of the opinion that the deed as a whole is beneficial as it provides for the instruction of the infant in the art of dental mechanics by an active practitioner at a wage and under conditions approved by certain professional and trade bodies of high standing. The deed itself requires registration with the National Joint Council of the Craft of Dental Technicians, a body upon which, as I am informed, both employees and craftsment are represented, and it is improbable that such a body would accept for registration any deed which was not beneficial to the apprentice.

Even assuming, but not accepting, that the clause providing for the reference of disputes arising thereunder to the arbitrament of the Joint Council would, standing by itself, be considered not beneficial to the infant, he would, in my judgment, nevertheless be bound by it if the agreement as a whole was for his benefit, as I have found.

An attempt was made to meet this conclusion by the submission that the arbitration clause is to be treated as an independent agreement separate from the deed itself. The argument in support was based on the decisions which have established that the arbitration clause may be effective even though the main contractual obligations have been discharged by breach or by frustration or by illegality. In my judgment, this argument is unsound and is not supported by the decision in *Heyman* v. *Darwins Ld.*, [1942]

A.C. 356: see in particular the speech of Lord Macmillan. Furthermore, in the present case, seeing that the infant is adopting the apprentice deed by suing upon it, it is not open to him to reject the arbitration clause which forms part of it.

As regards the question of discretion, I feel no hesitation at all in holding that, in my judgment, the arbitration clause should be given effect to. The nature of the dispute as shown by the statement of claim is essentially one fit to be adjudicated upon, at any rate so far as concerns matters of fact and the practice of the art of dental mechanics, by a body such as the Joint Council. Adjudication before such a body would avoid the necessity of calling a body of expert evidence. Furthermore, the clause in no way involves an ouster of the jurisdiction of the court or in any way interferes with the jealous regard which the court observes for the interests of infants. In my judgment, the action should be stayed under section 4 of the *Arbitration Act, 1950*, and the appeal allowed with costs.

INDEX

www.ingramcontent.com/pod-product-compliance
Lightning Source LLC
LaVergne TN
LVHW010445080826
844660LV00027B/1219

* 9 7 8 1 4 8 7 5 7 8 9 7 8 *